Microsoft Office 2003

COM 130

Patrick Carey
Carey Associates, Inc.

June Jamrich Parsons

Dan Oja

Roy Ageloff
University of Rhode Island

Joseph J. Adamski
Grand Valley State University

Ann Shaffer

THOMSON
COURSE TECHNOLOGY™

Australia • Canada • Mexico • Singapore • Spain • United Kingdom • United States

THOMSON

COURSE TECHNOLOGY

Microsoft Office 2003

Patrick Carey / June Jamrich Parsons / Dan Oja / Roy Ageloff / Joseph J. Adamski / Ann Shaffer

Custom Editor:
Kenna Roots

Custom Consultant:
Clinton Kernen

Marketing Coordinator:
Sara Mercurio

Production/Manufacturing Supervisor:
Donna M. Brown

Senior Project Coordinator:
Jennifer Flinchpaugh

Pre-Media Services Supervisor:
Dan Plofchan

Senior Prepress Specialist:
Phil Beran

Cover Design:
Krista Pierson

Printer:
Globus Printing & Packaging

Printed in the
United States of America
1 2 3 4 5 6 7 8 9 07 06 05

For more information, please contact Thomson Custom Solutions, 5191 Natorp Boulevard, Mason, OH 45040.
Or you can visit our Internet site at www.thomsoncustom.com

The Adaptable Courseware Program consists of products and additions to existing Course Technology products that are produced from camera-ready copy.

Peer review, class testing, and accuracy are primarily the responsibility of the author(s).

For permission to use material from this text or product, contact us by:
Tel (800) 730-2214
Fax (800) 730 2215
www.thomsonrights.com

ISBN 1-418-84837-9

Brief Contents

Table of Contents

Tutorial 2 155

Tutorial 3 203

Tutorial 6 299

Internet

Creating Web Pages with Microsoft Office 2003 347

Excel

Integration

PowerPoint

New Perspectives on

Essential Computer Concepts

Essential Computer Concepts

Photo Credits

Figure 1: © PhotoDisc/Getty Images

Figure 3: Courtesy of Acer America Inc.; Courtesy of Gateway Inc.; Courtesy of ViewSonic Corporation

Figure 4: Courtesy of palmOne, Inc. palmOne, Zire, and Tungsten are among the trademarks owned by or exclusively licensed to palmOne, Inc.

Figure 5: Courtesy of IBM Corporation

Figure 6: Courtesy of NASA

Figure 7: Courtesy of Microsoft Corporation

Figure 8: Courtesy of Microsoft Corporation

Figure 10: Courtesy of ViewSonic Corporation

Figure 11: Courtesy of Lexmark International Inc.

Figure 20: Courtesy of Seagate Technology

Figure 22: Courtesy of Acer America Inc.

Objectives

In this tutorial, you will:

- Describe the components of a computer system
- Compare the types of computers
- Define a personal computer's hardware in terms of its functions: input, output, processing, and storage
- Examine data representation and the ASCII code
- Describe how peripheral devices are connected to a personal computer
- Identify the hardware and software that are used to establish a network connection
- Explain how Internet access, e-mail, and the World Wide Web affect the use of computers
- Discuss the types of system software and their functions
- Identify popular application software
- Describe how data is shared among different types of application software

Essential Computer Concepts

Case

Paik's Oriental Rug Gallery

Paik's Oriental Rug Gallery, located in the university town of Lake Thompson, specializes in the sale of new and used Oriental carpets. Paik's also performs beautiful renovations of damaged or old Oriental rugs. Thanks to his excellent customer service and professional reputation, owner Sang Kee Paik has broadened his customer base over the course of the last two years and is finding it hard to keep up with the paperwork. He recently hired you, a college graduate of the school of business, to assist him.

After several days on the job, you suggest to Mr. Paik that he would find it much easier to manage his inventory and payroll if he purchased several computers. He tells you he's considered that before, but hasn't had time to shop around. He asks you to research the features and prices of today's computers and recommend what he should purchase.

You go to the library to review computer trade magazines and examine the features of current models. Computers and their prices are constantly changing, but most of today's computers are well-suited to running a small business. You are sure you will be able to find computers that will meet Mr. Paik's needs. Figure 1 (on the next page) shows an advertisement for a computer you think might be appropriate for Mr. Paik's business.

Labs

Student Data Files

There are no student Data Files needed for this tutorial.

Figure 1 Computer ad

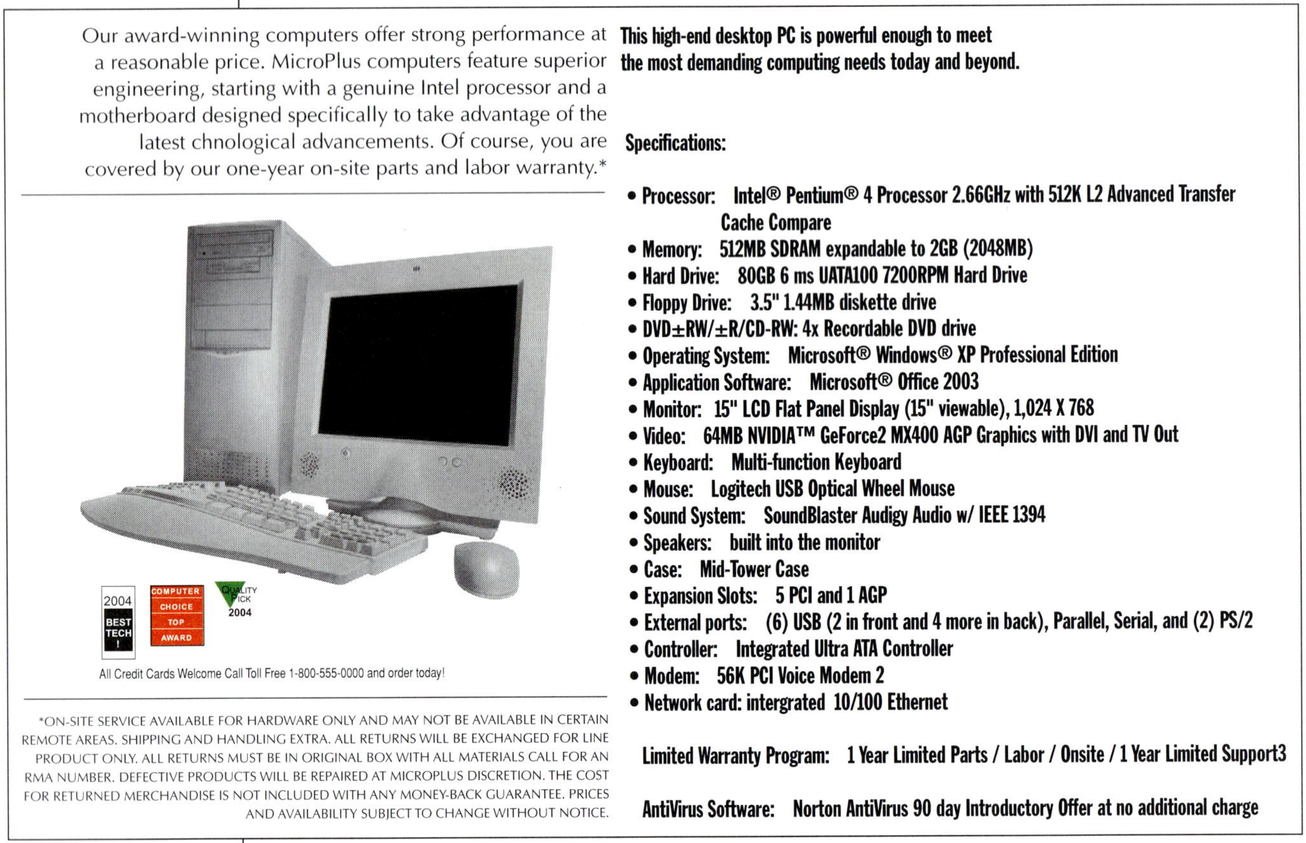

What Is a Computer?

Computers have become essential tools in almost every type of activity in virtually every type of business. A **computer** is defined as an electronic device that accepts input, processes data, stores data, and produces output. It is a versatile tool with the potential to perform many different tasks.

A **computer system** includes a computer, peripheral devices, and software. The physical components of a computer are referred to as **hardware**. The design and construction of a particular computer is referred to as its **architecture**, or **configuration**. The technical details about each component are called **specifications**. For example, a computer system might be *configured* to include a printer; a *specification* for that printer might be a print speed of eight pages per minute or the capacity to print in color. The computer itself takes care of the processing function, but it needs additional components, called **peripheral devices**, to accomplish its input, output, and storage functions. In this tutorial, you will learn more about the hardware that performs these basic computer functions.

Software refers to the intangible components of a computer system, particularly the **programs**, or lists of instructions, that the computer needs to perform a specific task. Software is the key to a computer's versatility. When your computer is using word processing software—for example, the Microsoft Word program—you can type memos, letters, and reports. When your computer is using accounting software, you can maintain information about what your customers owe you or display a graph showing the timing of customer payments.

The hardware and the software of a computer system work together to process data—the words, figures, sounds, and graphics that describe people, events, things, and ideas. Figure 2 illustrates how you and the computer system interact to complete a task. Suppose you want to use the computer to write a report. First you instruct the computer to use the word processing program. After activating the word processing program, you begin typing the text of your report. The data you type into the computer is called **input**. You use an **input device**, such as a keyboard or a mouse, to input data and issue commands. **Commands** are another type of input that instruct the computer on how to process the data. For example, in your report, you might want to center the title and double-space the text of the report. You issue the appropriate commands in the word processing program that will instruct the computer to modify the data you have input so the text is double-spaced and the title of the report is centered. Modifying data in this way is referred to as **processing**. In a computer, processing tasks occur on the **motherboard**, which is the main circuit board of the computer. The motherboard contains the **processing hardware**, the computer's major electronic components.

Figure 2 How a computer works

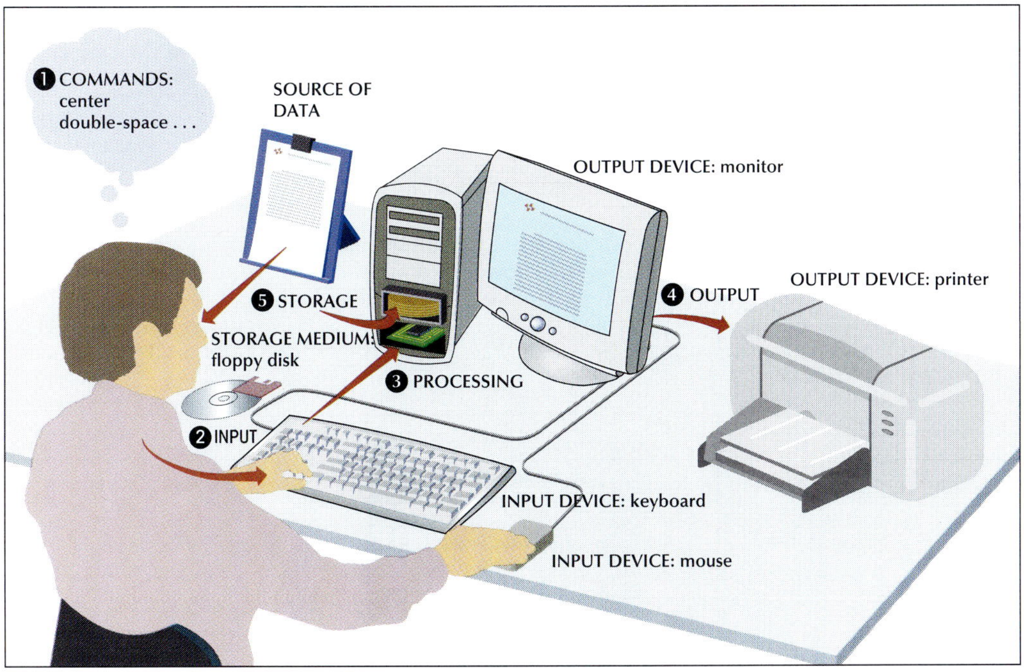

The result of the computer processing your input is referred to as **output**. Output can be in many different forms, for example reports, documents, graphs, sounds, and pictures. Computers produce output using **output devices**, such as a computer monitor or a printer. The output you create using a computer can be stored either inside the computer itself, or on an external storage device, such as a floppy disk. You will learn more about storage devices later in this tutorial.

Using a computer has several advantages. The first is the speed at which you can perform tasks. Second, the capability of storing the output and using it over and over again, in so many different ways, makes using a computer the most effective way to perform many personal and business tasks. Finally, an important advantage is sharing data and output with others. You make a note to find out whether Paik employees will need to share their data.

Types of Computers

There are many types of computers, which are classified by their size, speed, capabilities, and cost. Computers are categorized as personal computers, hand-held computers, mainframes, and supercomputers.

Personal computers, originally called **microcomputers**, are the computers typically used by a single user, for use in the home or office. Examples of personal computers are shown in Figure 3.

Figure 3 Examples of personal computers

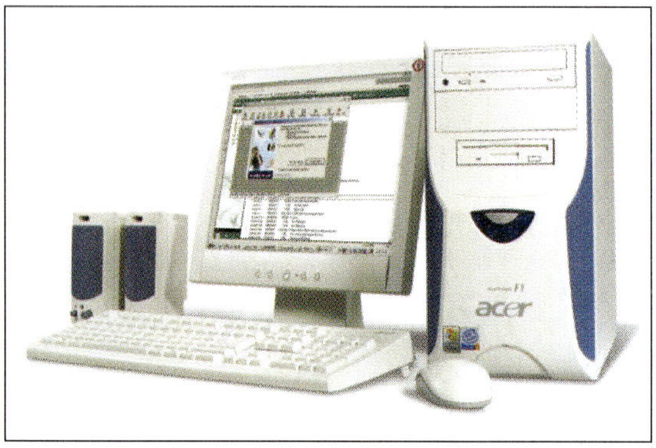

A desktop computer fits on a desk and runs on power from an electrical wall outlet. The monitor can be a flat panel monitor (like the one shown) or a CRT monitor, which takes up more space on the desk, but is less expensive.

A notebook computer is small and lightweight, giving it the advantage of portability. It can run on power supplied by an electrical outlet, or it can run on battery power.

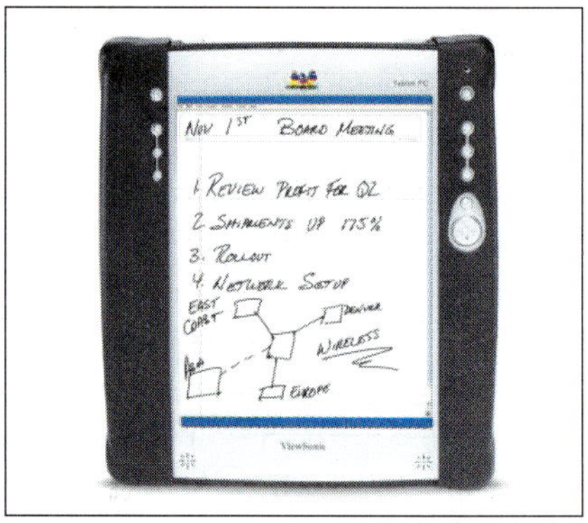

A Tablet PC is a portable computer that has a screen on which the user can execute commands and write with a stylus. The computer recognizes the handwriting and integrates it into the program being used. On some models, the screen can be moved out of the way so that the user can access an attached keyboard; on other models, you can attach a keyboard if you wish.

A personal computer is used for general computing tasks such as word processing, working with photographs or graphics, e-mail, and Internet access. A personal computer is available as a **desktop computer**, which is designed to sit compactly on a desk; as a **notebook computer** (also referred to as a **laptop computer**), which is designed for portability; or as a **Tablet PC**, which is also designed for portability, but includes the capability of recognizing ordinary handwriting on the screen. Tablet PCs also include speech recognition software. Personal computers cost between $500 and $3000, but the average computer user spends $800 to $1300 when purchasing a personal computer. A notebook computer with similar capability is usually more expensive than a desktop computer, and Tablet PCs are more expensive than notebook computers.

Hand-held computers, also known as **PDAs** (Personal Digital Assistants), are small computers designed to fit in the palm of your hand, as shown in Figure 4. Hand-held computers are compact enough to fit in your pocket, and they run on batteries. Hand-held computers have more limited capabilities than personal computers, and are generally used to maintain an electronic appointment book, address book, calculator, and notepad, although high-end PDAs are all-in-one devices that can be used to send and receive e-mails and make phone calls. Hand-held computers cost between $100 and $700.

Figure 4 Example of a hand-held computer

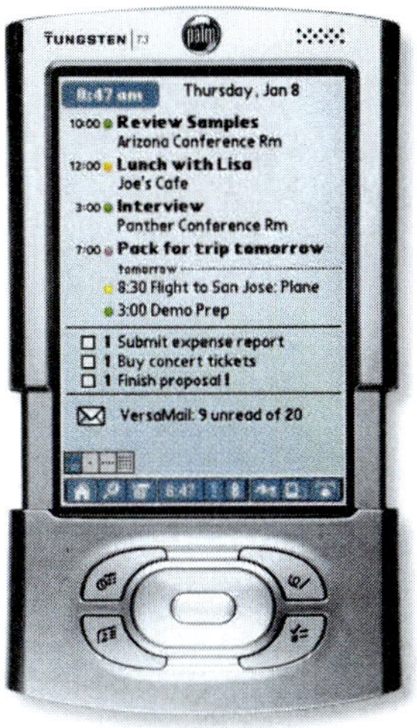

You assume that your recommendation to Mr. Paik will include personal computers because most daily tasks can be performed very efficiently using them. However, you wonder whether some employees might need the portability of notebook computers or Tablet PCs, and whether others might need a PDA. You add these notes to your list of questions to ask Mr. Paik.

Many small and large businesses use personal computers extensively. But some businesses, government agencies, and other institutions also use larger and faster types of computers such as mainframes and supercomputers. Usually, a company decides to purchase a mainframe computer when it must carry out the processing tasks for many users, especially when the users share large amounts of data. Each user inputs processing requests and views output through a terminal. A **terminal** has a keyboard for input and a monitor for output, but is not capable of processing data on its own.

Mainframe computers, like the one shown in Figure 5, are typically used to provide centralized storage, processing, and management for large amounts of data. The price of a mainframe computer varies widely, from several hundred thousand dollars to several million dollars.

Figure 5 **The system unit for the IBM S/390 G5 mainframe computer**

The largest and fastest computers, called **supercomputers**, were first developed for high-volume computing tasks such as weather prediction. Supercomputers, like the one shown in Figure 6, are also being used by large corporations and government agencies when the tremendous volume of data would seriously delay processing on a mainframe computer. Although its cost can be tens of millions of dollars, a supercomputer's processing speed is so much faster than that of personal computers and mainframes that the investment can be worthwhile.

Figure 6 **A supercomputer**

How would you classify the computer in the advertisement shown in Figure 1 at the beginning of the tutorial? If your answer is a desktop personal computer, you are correct. The computer in that ad fits on a desk and is not portable.

Based on what you have learned about the computing process and types of computers, you decide to recommend that Mr. Paik purchase some personal computers. When you look at the ad, however, you realize that there are several specifications that Mr. Paik may not understand. Your recommendation will have to explain what each listed component does, and why it is important. The remainder of this tutorial will focus on personal computer hardware and software in more detail, so you can learn what you need to know to make a better recommendation.

Computer Hardware

As you've already learned, computer hardware can be defined as the physical components of a computer. Now look at the hardware you might use in a typical personal computer system.

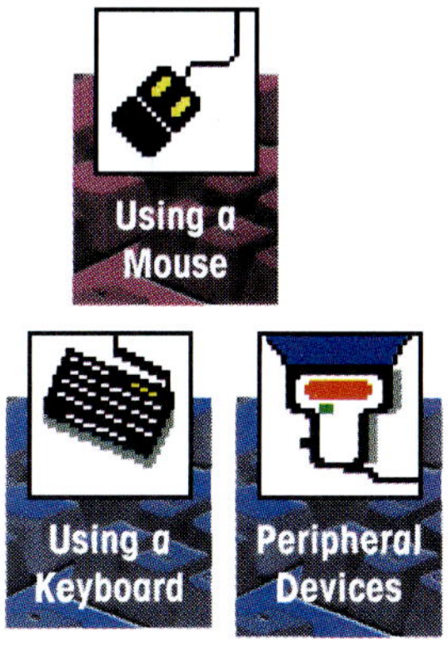

Input Devices

You input data and commands by using an input device such as a keyboard or a mouse. The computer can also receive input from a storage device. This section takes a closer look at the input devices you might use. Output and storage devices are covered in later sections.

The most frequently used input device is a **keyboard**. The top keyboard in Figure 7 is a standard 101-key keyboard. Newer keyboards, such as the bottom keyboard in Figure 7, are **ergonomic**, which means that they have been designed to fit the natural placement of your hands and should reduce the risk of repetitive-motion injuries. All keyboards consist of three major parts: the main keyboard, the keypads, and the function keys.

Figure 7 Keyboards

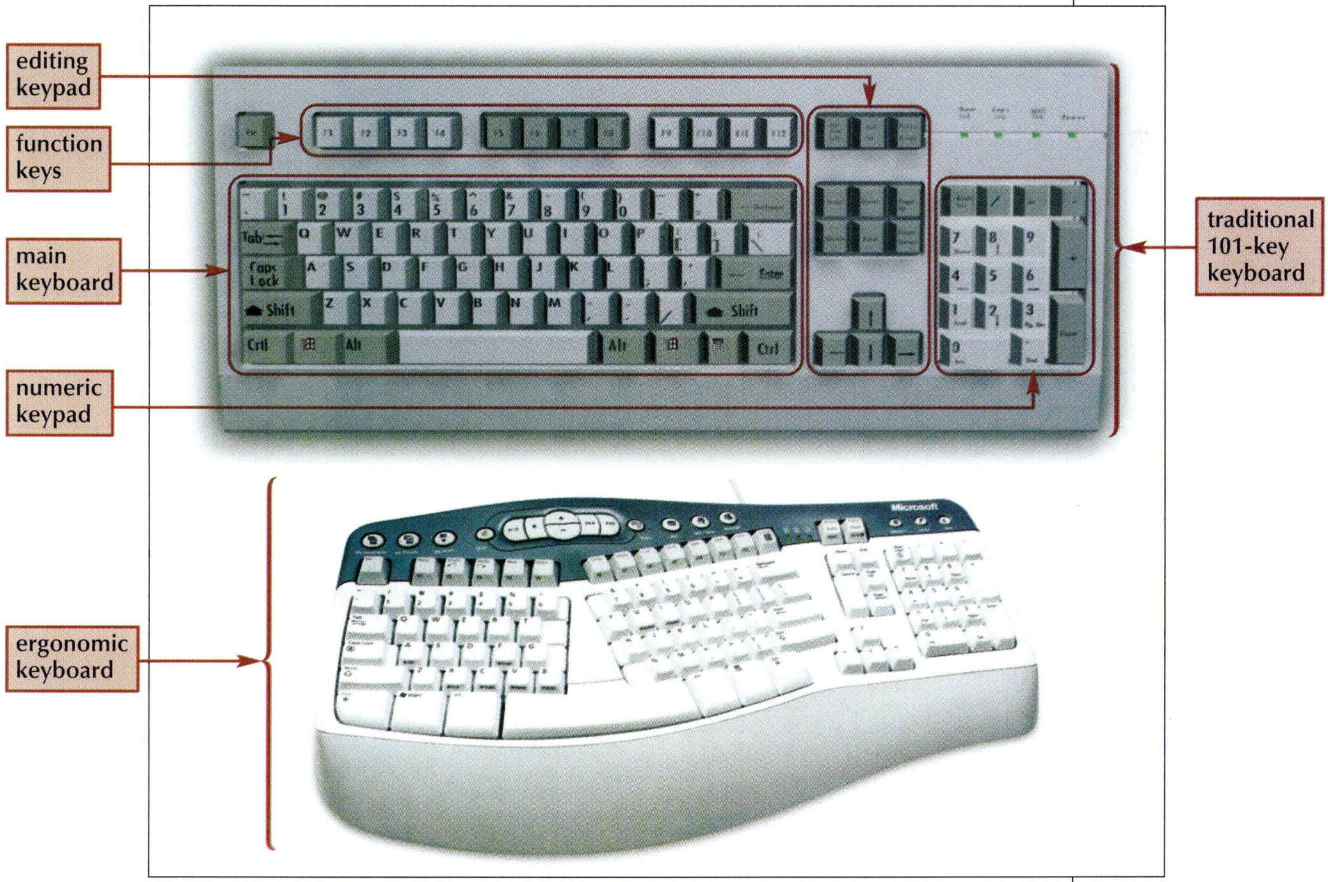

All personal computers are equipped with a pointing device. The most popular is a **mouse**, such as the ones shown in Figure 8; notebook computers are usually equipped with one of the other options pictured in Figure 9.

Figure 8 Personal computer pointing devices

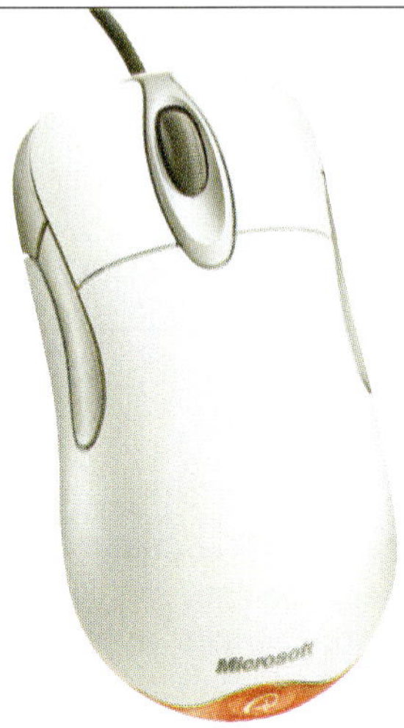

Mouse with a cord

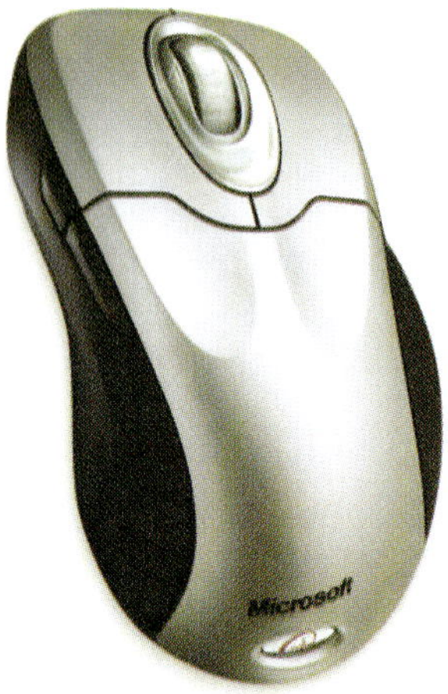

Cordless mouse

Figure 9 Notebook pointing devices

A **track point** is a small eraser-like device embedded among the typing keys. To control the on-screen pointer, you push the track point up, left, right, or down. Buttons for clicking and double-clicking are located in front of the spacebar.

A **touch pad** is a touch-sensitive device. By dragging your finger over the surface, you control the on-screen pointer. Two buttons equivalent to mouse buttons are located in front of the touch pad.

The **pointing device** controls a **pointer**, a small arrow or other symbol, on the display screen. Using a pointing device is an important skill because most personal computers depend on such devices to select commands and manipulate text or graphics on the screen. People with physical impairments or disabilities can also use pointing devices because of recent advances in making computers accessible to everyone. For example, people who do not have the use of their arms can use adaptive pointing devices to control the pointer with foot, head, or eye movements.

Computers used for presentations often feature remote input devices, sometimes called **wireless pointers**, that work like the remote control used for a TV, VCR, or DVD. The remote input device allows you to control the pointer from the back of the auditorium.

Now that you have read about input devices, refer back to the computer advertisement shown in Figure 1 at the beginning of the tutorial. Can you list the input devices included with the advertised system? A mouse and a keyboard are considered essential peripheral devices, so advertisements do not always list them. Unless the ad specifies some other input device, such as a track ball, you can safely assume the computer comes equipped with a traditional keyboard and mouse.

Output Devices

As stated earlier, output is the result of processing data; output devices show you those results. The most commonly used output devices are monitors and printers. A **monitor** is the device that displays the output from a computer, as shown in Figure 10. The monitor on the left is a **CRT** (**cathode ray tube**) **monitor**, which uses gun-like devices that direct beams of electrons toward the screen to activate dots of color to form the image you see on the screen. The monitor on the right is a **flat panel monitor**. Most flat panel monitors use **LCD (liquid crystal display)** technology, which creates the image you see on the screen by manipulating light within a layer of liquid crystal. This is the same technology used in digital watches or the time display on a microwave oven. Flat panel display monitors take up very little room on the desktop, are lightweight, and are very easy to read, but are much more expensive than CRT monitors. However, many graphic artists prefer CRT technology because it displays uniform color from any viewing angle.

Monitor types **Figure 10**

CRT monitor — Flat panel display monitor

Factors that influence the quality of a monitor are screen size, resolution, and dot pitch. **Screen size** is the diagonal measurement in inches from one corner of the screen to the other. Measurements for today's desktop monitors range from 15" to 23". The monitors on notebook computers range from 12" to 17". The first personal computer monitors and many terminals still in use today are character-based. A **character-based display** divides the screen into a grid of rectangles, one for each typed character. A monitor that is capable of displaying graphics, called a **graphics display**, divides the screen into a matrix of small dots called **pixels**. **Resolution** is the maximum number of pixels the monitor can display. Standard resolutions are 640 × 480, 800 × 600, 1,024 × 768, 1,280 × 1,024, and 1,600 × 1,200. The resolution you use depends on your monitor size. If your screen is small, 1,600 × 1,200 resolution will make the objects on the screen too small to see clearly. Resolution is easy to adjust on most monitors. **Dot pitch** measures the distance between pixels, so a smaller dot pitch means a sharper image. A .28 or .26 dot pitch (dp) is typical for today's monitors.

A computer display system consists of a monitor and a **graphics card**, also called a **video display adapter** or **video card**. A **card** is a rigid piece of insulating material with circuits on it. The circuits control the functions of the card. The graphics card is installed inside the computer on the motherboard, and controls the signals the computer sends to the monitor. If you plan to display a lot of images on the monitor, you may also need a **graphics accelerator card** to speed up the computer's ability to display them. When purchasing a monitor, you must be sure that it comes with a video card that is compatible with your computer.

Refer back to the computer ad in Figure 1. Does this personal computer include a monitor and video card? The correct answer is yes, both are included. What is the type, size, and resolution of the monitor? The monitor is a 15" 1,024 × 768 flat panel monitor.

A **printer** produces a paper copy of the text or graphics processed by the computer. A printed copy of computer output is called **hard copy**, because it is more tangible than the electronic or magnetic copies found on a disk, in the computer memory, or on the monitor. There are three popular categories of printers, and each has special capabilities.

The most popular printers for business use are **laser printers**, like the one shown on the left in Figure 11, because they use the same technology as a photocopier. A temporary laser image is transferred onto paper with a powdery substance called **toner**. This produces high-quality output quickly and efficiently. The speed of laser printers is measured in **pages per minute (ppm)**. Color laser printers use several toner cartridges to apply color to the page. Non-color laser printers are less expensive than color laser printers.

A less expensive alternative to the laser printer is to use a color **inkjet printer** such as the one shown on the right in Figure 11. These printers spray ink onto paper. The quality of the inkjet output is almost comparable to a laser printer's output. Inkjet printers, with and without color capabilities, are very popular printers for home use. The speed of inkjet printers is also measured in pages per minute.

Figure 11 **Types of printers**

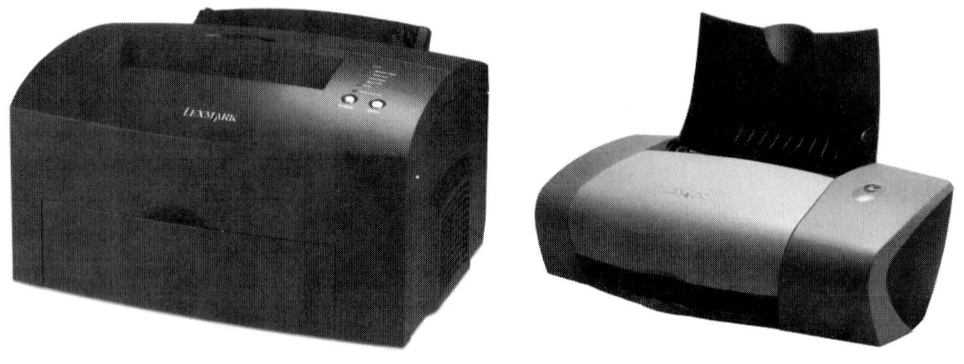

Laser Printer | Inkjet Printer

Another type of printer is the dot matrix printer, the oldest printing technology currently found on the computer market. Dot matrix printers transfer ink to the paper by striking a ribbon with pins. Using more pins controls the quality of the print, so a 24-pin dot matrix printer produces better quality print than a 9-pin. Dot matrix printers are most often used when a large number of pages need to be printed fairly quickly or when a business needs to print on multi-page continuous forms. The speed of dot matrix printers is measured in characters per second (cps). Some examples of their usefulness are the printing of grade reports, bank statements, or payroll checks.

You notice that the computer ad in Figure 1 does not include a printer, so you make a note to ask Mr. Paik if your recommendation should include one. If so, you decide to recommend a color laser printer to print correspondence, advertisements, and brochures.

Multimedia devices are another category of peripheral devices. **Multimedia** refers to an integrated collection of computer-based media including text, graphics, sound, animation, and video. Most personal computers come equipped with a sound card and speakers that can play digital sounds. The sound card converts sounds so that they can be broadcast through speakers.

The computer advertised in Figure 1 includes a sound card and speakers that are built into the monitor. These are also output devices that you need to mention in your recommendation. Mr. Paik will need these output devices for a variety of activities, such as participating in teleconferences on product availability attended by suppliers in widespread locations, or recording announcements that employees can play back at their convenience. Later in this tutorial, you will learn how business users are sharing a variety of data resources, including digital sound.

Processing Hardware

The most important computer function is processing data. Before you can understand this function and the hardware that executes it, you first need to learn how the computer represents and stores data.

Data Representation

The characters used in human language are meaningless to a computer because it is an electronic device. Like a light bulb, the computer must interpret every signal as either "on" or "off." To do so, a computer represents data as distinct or separate numbers. Specifically, it represents "on" with a 1 and "off" with a 0. These numbers are referred to as **binary digits**, or **bits**.

A series of eight bits is called a **byte**. As Figure 12 shows, the byte that represents the integer value 0 is 00000000, with all eight bits "off" or set to 0. The byte that represents the integer value 1 is 00000001, and the byte that represents 255 is 11111111.

Binary representation of numbers — **Figure 12**

Number	Binary Representation
0	00000000
1	00000001
2	00000010
3	00000011
4	00000100
5	00000101
6	00000110
7	00000111
8	00001000
⋮	⋮
253	11111101
254	11111110
255	11111111

Personal computers commonly use the **ASCII** code to represent character data. ASCII (pronounced "ASK-ee") stands for **American Standard Code for Information Interchange**. The ASCII system translates the decimal numbers 0 through 255 into binary data. Each ASCII code represents a letter or character on the keyboard; for example, the ASCII code 65 represents the character *A*, and the ASCII code 97 represents *a*. Computers translate ASCII code into binary data so that they can process it. Figure 13 shows sample ASCII code.

Figure 13 **Sample ASCII code representing letters and symbols**

Character	ASCII code	Binary Number
(space)	32	00100000
$	36	00100100
A	65	01000001
B	66	01000010
a	97	01100001
b	98	01100010

As a computer user, you don't have to know the binary representations of numbers, characters, and instructions, because the computer handles all the necessary conversions internally. However, because the amount of memory in a computer and its storage capacity are expressed in bytes, you should be aware of how data is represented. **Storage**, or **memory capacity**, is the amount of data, or number of characters, that the device can handle at any given time. A **kilobyte** (KB or simply K) is 1,024 bytes, or approximately one thousand bytes. A **megabyte** (MB) is 1,048,576 bytes, or about one million bytes. A **gigabyte** (GB) is 1,073,741,824 bytes, or about one billion bytes. You will see the symbols KB, MB, and GB refer to both processing and storage capacity.

The Microprocessor

The two most important components of personal computer hardware are the **microprocessor**, a silicon chip designed to manipulate data, and the **memory**, which stores instructions and data. The type of microprocessor and the memory capacity are two factors that directly affect the price and performance of a computer.

The microprocessor, such as the one shown in Figure 14, is an integrated circuit (an electronic component called a **chip**) which is located on the motherboard inside the computer. The terms **processor** and **central processing unit** (CPU) also refer to this device, which is responsible for executing instructions to process data.

Figure 14 **An Intel Pentium 4 microprocessor**

The speed of a microprocessor is determined by its clock speed, word size, and cache size. Think of the **clock speed** as the pulse of the processor. It is measured in millions of cycles per second, or **megahertz** (MHz), or **gigahertz** (GHz), a billion cycles per second. **Word size** refers to the number of bits that are processed at one time. A computer with a large word size can process faster than a computer with a small word size. The earliest personal computers had an 8-bit word size, but now a 64-bit word size is common. **Cache**, sometimes called **RAM cache** or **cache memory**, is special high-speed memory reserved for the microprocessor's use. It speeds up the processing function by accessing data the computer anticipates you will request soon, while you are still working on something else.

Take another look at the computer advertised in Figure 1. What is the type and speed of its microprocessor? Your answer should be that it has a Pentium 4 microprocessor that can operate at 2.66 GHz and has 512 K cache.

Memory

Computer **memory** is a set of storage locations on the motherboard. Your computer has four types of memory: random access memory, virtual memory, read-only memory, and complementary metal oxide semiconductor (CMOS) memory.

Random access memory (RAM) is active during the processing function. It consists of electronic circuits on the motherboard that temporarily hold programs and data while the computer is on. RAM is **volatile**, which means that it is constantly changing as long as the computer is on and is cleared when the computer is turned off. The microprocessor uses RAM to store and retrieve instructions and data as they are needed. For example, if you are writing a paper, the word processing program that you are using is temporarily copied into RAM so the microprocessor can quickly access the instructions that you will need as you type and format your paper. As you type, the characters are also stored in RAM, along with the many fonts, special characters, graphics, and other objects that you might use to enhance the paper. How much you can include in your paper depends on the RAM capacity of the computer you are using. Most personal computers on the market today use **SDRAM** (synchronous dynamic RAM) or **RDRAM** (Rambus dynamic RAM). SDRAM is plenty fast for the average computer user and inexpensive. RDRAM was originally designed for use in computer game systems and is more expensive than SDRAM. When paired with a microprocessor of 1 GHz or faster, RDRAM can improve a computer system's overall performance.

Look at the computer ad in Figure 1. Notice that this computer has 512 MB of SDRAM. In other words, it has the capacity to temporarily store over 512 million characters at any one time. Although your paper might not be that long, the computer uses a lot of that available memory for programs and other data it needs to process your paper. The notation "expandable to 2 GB (2048 MB)" tells you that you can add more RAM to this computer. Expandability is an important feature of any computer; you need to be able to change your computer's capability as your needs change.

When the programs running on a computer use all the available RAM, the software uses space on the computer's storage devices to simulate RAM. This extra memory is called **virtual memory**. Figure 15 explains how it works. The disadvantage of using virtual memory is that it is much slower than RAM, so expanding the RAM capacity of a computer will improve its performance.

Figure 15 How virtual memory works

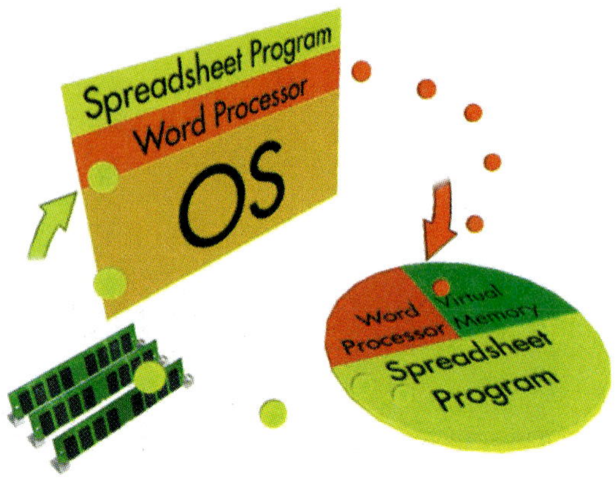

1. Your computer is running a word processing program that takes up most of the program area in RAM, but you want to run a spreadsheet program at the same time.

2. The operating system moves the least-used segment of the word processing program into virtual memory on disk.

3. The spreadsheet program can now be loaded into the RAM vacated by the least-used segment of the word processing program.

4. If the least-used segment of the word processing program is later needed, it is copied from virtual memory back into RAM. To make room, some other infrequently used segment of a program will need to be transferred into virtual memory.

Read-only memory (ROM) is another set of electronic circuits on the motherboard inside the computer. Although you can expand your RAM capacity, you cannot add to ROM capacity. In fact, the manufacturer of the computer permanently installs ROM. It is the permanent storage location for a set of instructions that the computer uses when you turn it on. Because ROM never changes and it remains intact when the computer is turned off, it is called **nonvolatile**.

The events that occur between the moment you turn on the computer and the moment you can actually begin to use the computer are called the **boot process**, as shown in Figure 16, and the act of turning on the computer is sometimes called **booting up**. When the computer is off, RAM is empty. When the computer is turned on, the set of instructions in ROM checks all the computer system's components to make sure they are working, and activates the essential software that controls the processing function.

ROM boot program activated — **Figure 16**

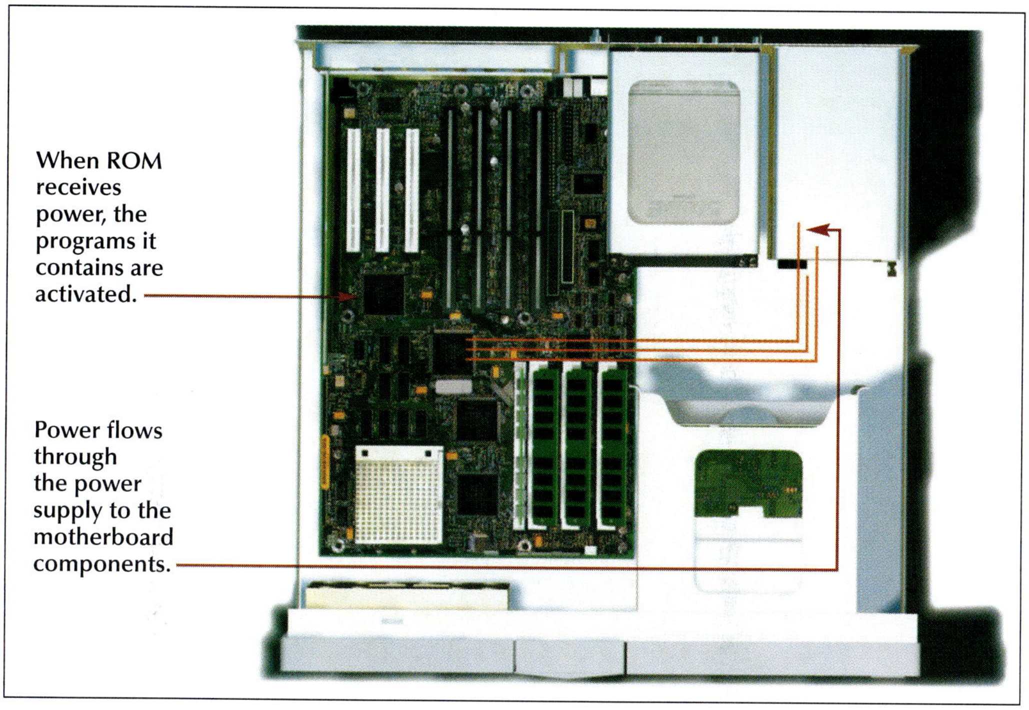

Complementary metal oxide semiconductor (CMOS) memory (pronounced "SEE-Moss") is another chip that is installed on the motherboard. It is also activated during the boot process and contains information about where the essential software is stored. A small rechargeable battery powers CMOS so its contents will be saved between computer uses. Unlike ROM, which cannot be changed, CMOS must be changed every time you add or remove hardware to your computer system. Thus, CMOS is often referred to as semipermanent memory, ROM as permanent memory, and RAM as temporary memory.

Storage Devices and Media

Because RAM retains data only while the power is on, your computer must have a more permanent storage option. As Figure 17 shows, a storage device receives data from RAM and writes it on a storage medium, such as a disk. Later the data can be read and sent back to RAM to use again.

Figure 17 **Storage devices and RAM**

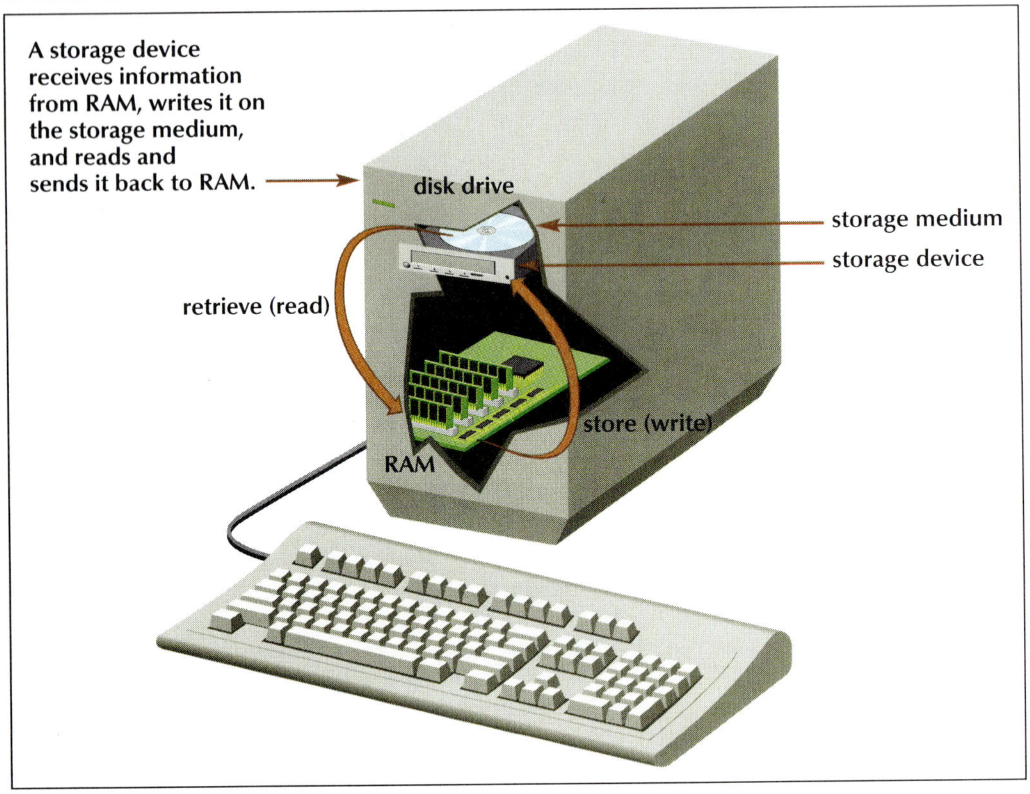

Before you can understand the hardware that stores data, you need to know how data is stored. All data and programs are stored as files. A computer **file** is a named collection of related bits that exists on a storage medium. There are two categories of files: executable files and data files. An **executable file** contains the instructions that tell a computer how to perform a specific task. The files that are used during the boot process, for instance, are executable. Users create **data files**, usually with software. For instance, a paper that you write with a word processing program is data, and must be saved as a data file if you want to use it again.

The storage devices where computer files are kept can be categorized by the method they use to store files. **Magnetic storage devices** use oxide-coated plastic storage media called **mylar**. Figure 18 illustrates the process of storing data on magnetic media.

Storing data on magnetic media **Figure 18**

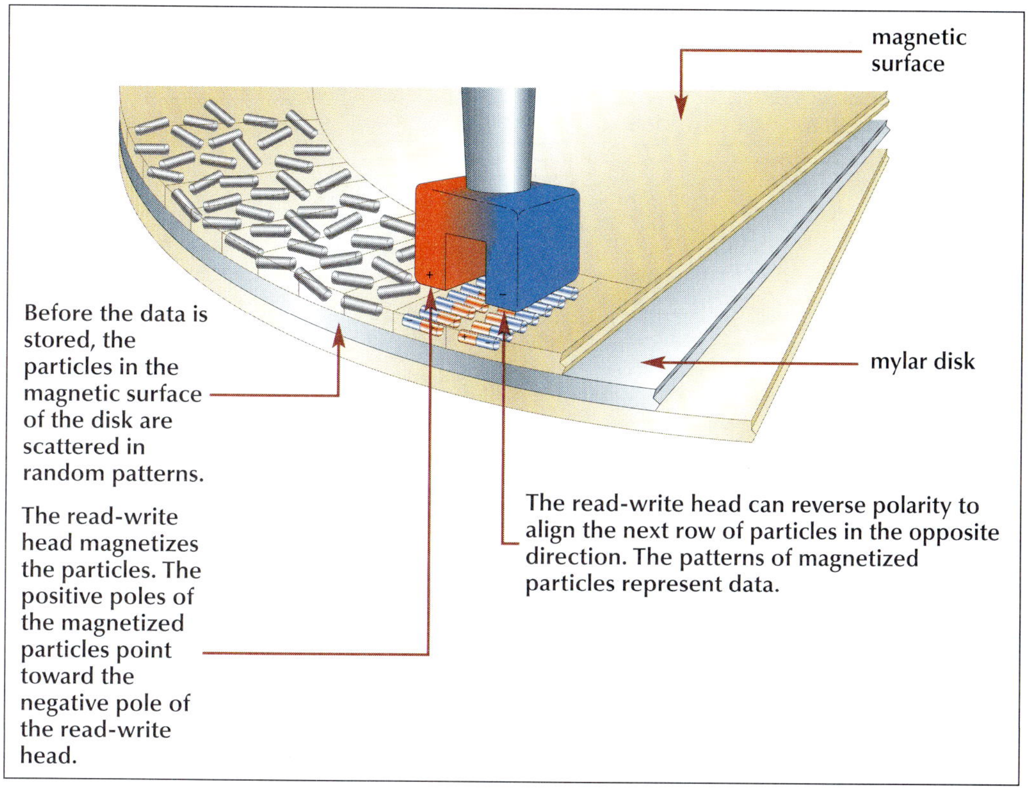

The most common magnetic storage devices are floppy disk drives, hard disk drives, and tape drives. **Floppy disks**, sometimes called **diskettes**, are flat circles of iron oxide-coated plastic enclosed in a hard plastic case (see Figure 19). Floppy disks are sometimes called 3½" disks because of the size of the hard plastic case. Floppy disks have the capacity to store 1.44 MB, or 1,440,000 bytes, of data. Although some computers are now manufactured without a floppy disk drive, floppy disks are still very common. The computer shown in the advertisement in Figure 1 has a floppy disk drive that accepts 3½" floppy disks with 1.44 MB capacity.

3½" disk **Figure 19**

Write protection prevents additional files from being stored on the disk and any file from being erased from the disk. To write protect a 3½" floppy disk, you open the write-protect window, as shown in Figure 19.

The other most common magnetic storage device is a **hard disk drive**, such as the one shown in Figure 20. This drive contains several iron oxide-covered metal platters that are usually sealed in a case inside the computer. Hard disk storage has two advantages over floppy disk storage: speed and capacity.

Figure 20 **Internal components of a hard disk drive**

The speed of a disk drive is measured by its **access time**, the time required to read or write one record of data. Access time is measured in **milliseconds** (ms), one-thousandths of a second. The hard disk drive included in Figure 1, for instance, has 6 ms access time. Its capacity is 80 GB. Although this seems like a very high number, a Windows-based computer fully loaded with typical software can use up to 1 GB, and the addition of data and multimedia files can add up quickly.

Another magnetic storage device is a **tape drive**, which provides inexpensive archival storage for large quantities of data. Tape storage is much too slow to be used for day-to-day computer tasks; therefore, tapes are used to make backup copies of data stored on hard disks. If a hard disk fails, data from the backup tape can be reloaded on a new hard disk with minimal interruption of operations. Large corporations use tape drives for backup, but smaller companies and home computer systems rely on other storage methods.

Optical storage devices use laser technology to read and write data on silver platters. The first standard optical storage device on personal computers was the **CD-ROM** drive, which stands for **Compact Disk Read Only Memory**. One CD-ROM can store up to 700 MB, equivalent to more than 450 floppy disks. Today's personal computers are also equipped with **DVD**, or **Digital Video Disk**, drives. DVDs, though the same size as CD-ROMs, can store up to 4.7 GB of data, depending on whether data is stored on one or two sides of the disk, and how many layers of data each side contains. This is a little less than seven times the capacity of a CD. A DVD has more than enough storage capacity for an entire feature-length film—up to 9 hours of video or 30 hours of CD-ROM-quality audio.

Optical storage technology records data as a trail of tiny pits in the disk surface. The data that these pits represent can then be "read" with a beam of laser light. Figure 21 shows how data is stored on optical media.

Storing data on an optical disk **Figure 21**

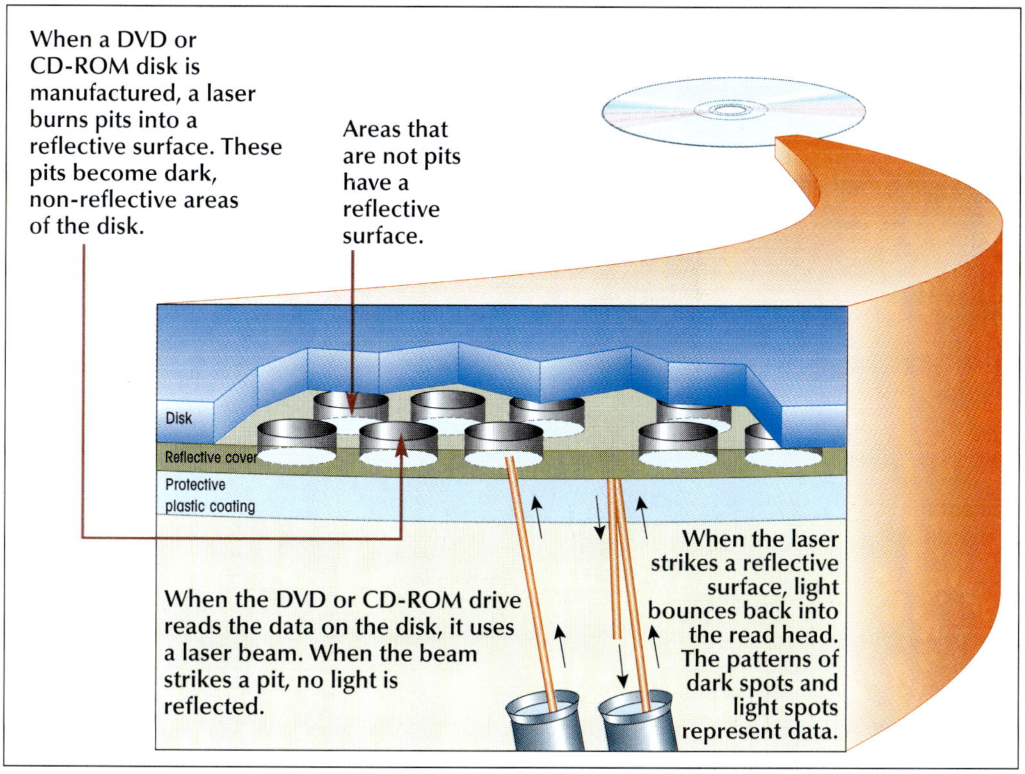

The most common uses of CD-ROMs or DVDs are for software distribution and storing large files that typically include graphics, animation, and video. Optical storage media are very durable. Unlike magnetic media, such as floppy and hard disks, CD and DVD platters are not susceptible to humidity, dust, fingerprints, or magnets. They are not indestructable, however. Take care not to scratch the disk surface or expose the disk to high temperatures.

CD-ROMs are for "read-only" access, meaning you can read data stored on them, but you cannot use them to record or store your own data. In order to record data on a CD, you need a **CD-R** (compact disc recordable) drive and a CD-R disk. Instead of storing data in pits made on the surface of the disk, as with a CD-ROM drive, the drive is designed so that a laser changes the reflectivity of a dye layer on a blank CD-R disk, creating dark spots on the disk's surface that represent the data. Once the data is recorded, you cannot erase or modify it, but you can append new data to the data currently stored on the CD-R disk. A **CD-RW** (compact disk rewritable) drive is designed so that you can write data on a special CD-RW disk and continually access and modify that data. CD-R disks can be read by a standard CD-ROM drive or a DVD drive; CD-RW disks can be read only by CD-RW drives or CD-ROM drives labeled "multi-read."

Both CD-Rs and CD-RWs are useful for storing large amounts of data, or for transferring large files from one computer to another. The original CD-ROM drive had a relatively slow access time: 600 ms. As the technology has improved, that access time has decreased to less than 200 ms. A lower number means faster access. Also consider the drive's data transfer rate, measured in kilobits per second (**Kbps**), to classify it as 1X (the original), 2X (twice the original), 3X, and so on.

Recordable DVD drives are becoming more common. As with CDs, you can buy a DVD to which you can record only once, or a rewritable DVD to which you can record and then re-record data. Recordable and rewriteable DVDs come in several formats; for example, recordable DVDs are available as DVD-R and DVD+R. Make sure you know which type of DVD your DVD drive uses. The computer shown in Figure 1 includes a 4x recordable/rewritable DVD drive. It supports both the -RW and +RW formats, and it can read and record CDs as well.

Figure 22 shows the typical storage configuration of a personal computer. It includes a DVD±RW drive, a floppy disk drive, and a hard drive.

Figure 22 Typical personal computer storage configuration

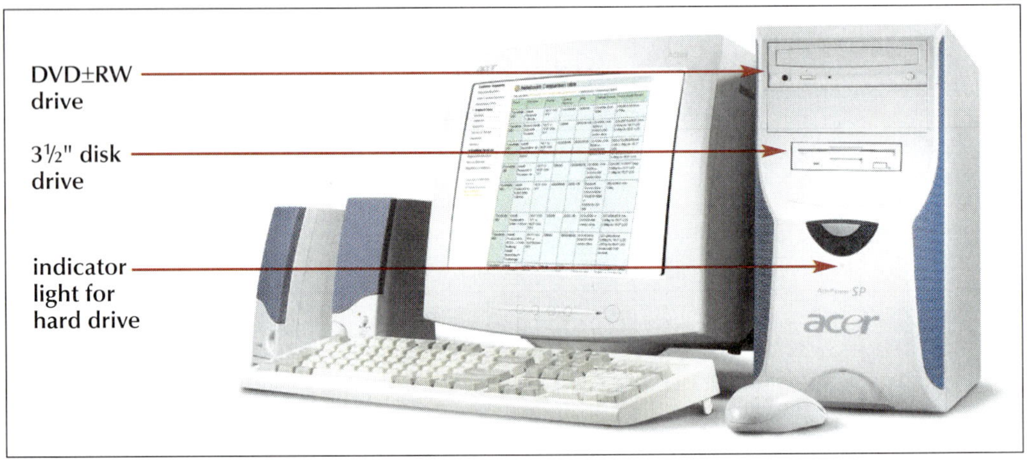

You decide that your recommendation to Mr. Paik should include computers with at least CD-RW drives, and some computers with DVD±RW drives. As computers are used, the storage devices fill up quickly with software and data, so it's a good idea to purchase as much storage capacity as your budget allows. Even though floppy disks are becoming less popular as recordable CD and DVD drives drop in price, they are still frequently used, so you will include them, too. You also decide to recommend at least 80 GB hard drives and perhaps 120 GB hard drives for some of the machines. You will also recommend at least 512 MB of RAM for each machine.

Data Communications

The transmission of text, numeric, voice, or video data from one computer to another is called **data communications**. This broad-based definition encompasses many critical business activities, from sending a letter to the printer upstairs to sending an **e-mail** (**electronic mail**) message to the company offices around the globe.

The four essential components of data communications are a sender, a receiver, a channel, and a protocol. The computer that originates the message is the **sender**. The message is sent over some type of **channel**, such as telephone or coaxial cable, a microwave signal, or optical fibers. The computer at the message's destination is called the **receiver**. The rules that establish an orderly transfer of data between the sender and the receiver are called **protocols**. Communication software and hardware establish these protocols at the beginning of the transmission, and both computers follow them strictly to guarantee an accurate transfer of data.

Data Bus

As noted earlier, peripherals are devices that can be added to a computer system to enhance its usefulness. Starting at the microprocessor, and passing through a continuous channel, the data travels out to the appropriate device. From an input device back to the microprocessor, the path is reversed. This communication between the microprocessor, RAM, and the peripherals is called the **data bus**.

An external peripheral device must have a corresponding **port** and **cable** that connect it to the back of the computer. Inside the computer, each port connects to a **controller card**, sometimes called an **expansion** or **interface card**. These cards, which provide an electrical connection to a variety of peripheral devices, plug into electrical connectors on the motherboard called **slots** or **expansion slots**. Figure 23 shows the data path that connects a printer to a computer. An internal peripheral device such as a hard disk drive may plug directly into the motherboard, or it may have an attached controller card. The transmission protocol is handled by a **device driver**, or simply **driver**, which is a computer program that can establish communication because it contains information about the characteristics of your computer and of the device.

Components for connecting a printer to a computer **Figure 23**

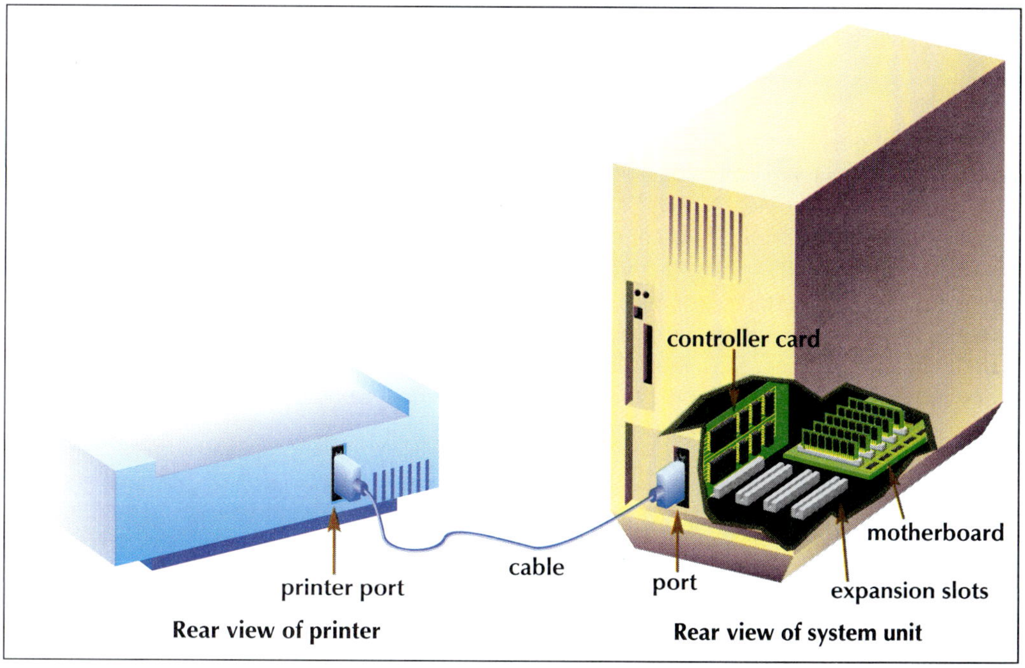

Personal computers can have several types of ports, including USB, parallel, serial, SCSI, and MIDI. Figure 24 diagrams how the ports on a desktop personal computer might appear.

Figure 24 Computer expansion ports

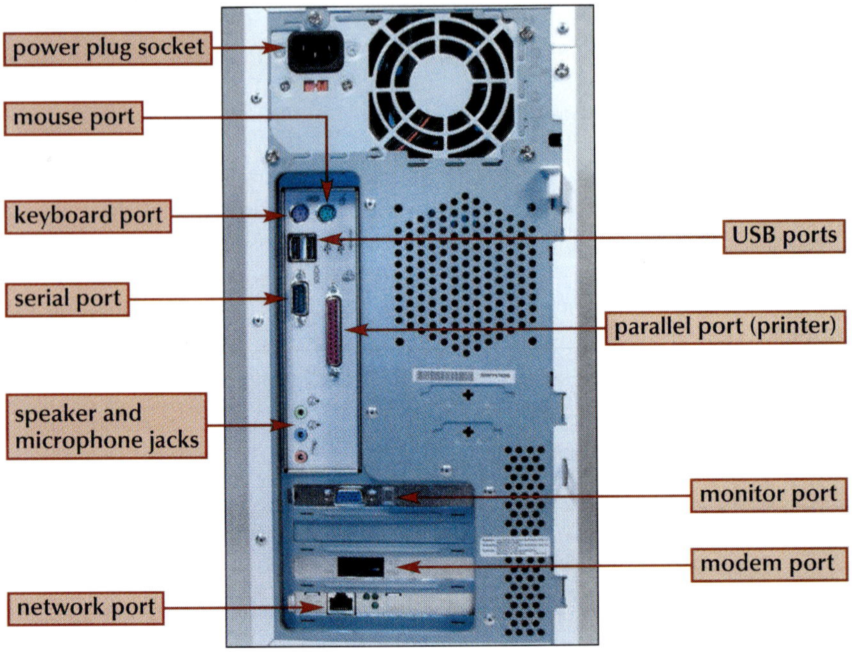

A **parallel port** transmits data eight bits at a time. Parallel transmissions are relatively fast, but increase the risk for interference, so they are typically used to connect a printer that is near the computer. A **serial port** transmits data one bit at a time. Typically, a mouse, keyboard, and modem are connected with serial interfaces.

SCSI (pronounced "scuzzy") stands for **small computer system interface**. One SCSI port provides an interface for one or more peripheral devices. The first is connected directly to the computer through the port, and the second device is plugged into a similar port on the first device. SCSI connections can allow many devices to use the same port. They are particularly popular on Macintosh computers and notebook computers.

Figure 24 shows some other ports for telephone cables to connect a modem, a video port to connect a monitor, and a network port. The interface to a sound card usually includes jacks for speakers and a microphone, which are designed to work with a **MIDI (musical instrument digital interface) card**, which is pronounced "middy." MIDI cards are used to record and play back musical data.

Notebook computers may also include a **Personal Computer Memory Card International Association (PCMCIA) device**. PCMCIA devices are credit-card-sized cards that plug directly into the PCMCIA slot and can contain additional memory, a modem, or a hard disk drive.

Another type of port found in computers is a **USB (Universal Serial Bus) port**. USB is a high-speed technology that facilitates the connection of external devices, such as joysticks, scanners, keyboards, video conferencing cameras, speakers, modems, and printers, to a computer. The device you install must have a **USB connector**, a small rectangular plug. You simply plug the USB connector into the USB port, and the computer recognizes the device and allows you to use it immediately. USB-compatible computers work more like stereo systems, in that you don't have to completely disassemble the unit to add a component. Any USB device can use any USB port, interchangeably and in any order. You can "daisy chain" up to 127 devices, plugging one device into another, or you can connect multiple devices to a single inexpensive hub. Data is transferred through a USB port 10 times faster than through a serial port, for example. For many USB devices, power is supplied via the port, so there is no need for extra power cables. Older computers can have numerous connectors—a keyboard connector, a mouse port, a parallel port, a joystick port, two audio ports, and two serial ports. USB computers replace this proliferation of ports with one standardized plug and port combination.

Look at the computer advertised in Figure 1. Does this computer include any of the ports illustrated in Figure 24? It mentions PS/2, USB, and parallel ports. Ports for a monitor, mouse, and keyboard are also included, because the advertisement lists those devices.

Networks

One of the most important types of data communications in the business world is a network connection. A **network** connects one computer to other computers and peripheral devices, enabling you to share data and resources with your coworkers. There are a variety of network configurations, too many to discuss thoroughly here. However, any type of network has some basic characteristics and requirements that you should know.

In a **local area network** (LAN), computers and peripheral devices are located relatively close to each other, generally in the same building. If you are using such a network, it is useful to know three things: the location of the data, the type of network card in your computer, and the communications software that manages protocols and network functions.

Some networks have one or more computers, called **servers**, that act as the central storage location for programs and provide mass storage for most of the data used on the network. A network with a server and computers dependent on the server is called a **client/server network**. The dependent computers are the **clients**. These networks are dependent on the server because it contains most of the data and software. When a network does not have a server, all the computers essentially are equal, and programs and data are distributed among them. This is called a **peer-to-peer network**.

Each computer that is part of the network must have a **network interface card (NIC)** installed. This card creates a communications channel between the computer and the network. A cable is used to connect the NIC port to the network. **Wi-Fi** (short for wireless fidelity) refers to a high-frequency **wireless local area network (WLAN)**. Wi-Fi is used to connect computers in a network by transmitting data through the air from an alternative to a wired LAN. Wi-Fi can be especially useful in buildings with older wiring. **Network software** is also essential, establishing the communications protocols that will be observed on the network and controlling the "traffic flow" as data travels throughout the network.

A personal computer that is not connected to a network is called a **standalone computer**. When it is connected to the network, it becomes a **workstation**. You have already learned that a terminal has a keyboard and monitor used for input and output, but it is not capable of processing on its own. A terminal is connected to a network that uses mainframes as servers. Any device connected to the network is called a **node**. Figure 25 illustrates a typical network configuration.

Figure 25 Network nodes include workstations, printers, and servers

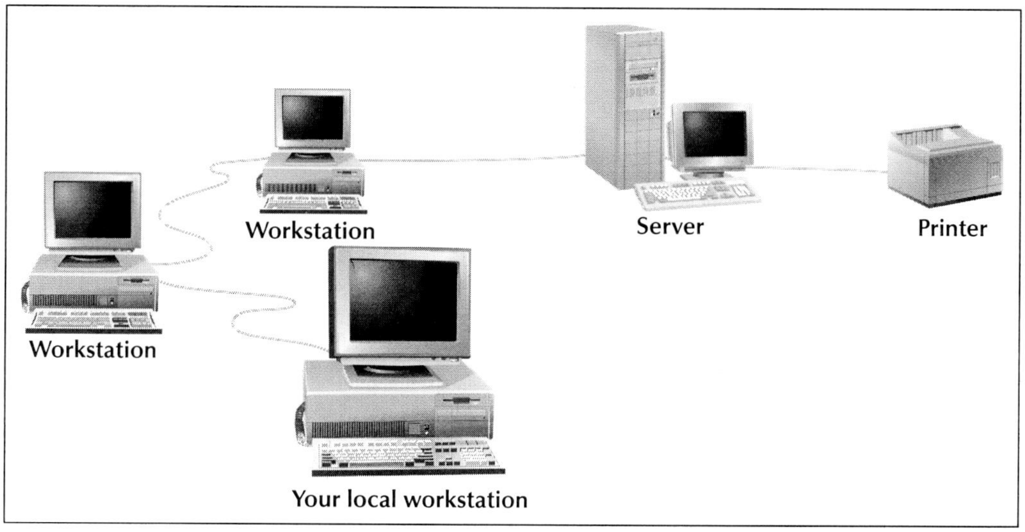

Look at the computer ad in Figure 1. Is this computer networked? Can it be networked? Why or why not? Your answer should be that the computer is not currently part of a network but does include an integrated network adapter card. With the appropriate network software, this computer can be connected to a network.

Telecommunications

Telecommunications means communicating over a comparatively long distance using a phone line. When it is not possible to connect users on one network, then telecommunications allows you to send and receive data over the telephone lines. To make this connection, you must use a communications device called a **modem**. A modem, which stands for *mo*dulator-*dem*odulator, is a device that connects your computer to a standard telephone jack. The modem converts the **digital**, or stop-start, **signals** your computer outputs into **analog**, or continuous wave, **signals** (sound waves) that can traverse ordinary phone lines. Figure 26 shows the telecommunications process, in which a modem converts digital signals to analog signals at the sending site (modulates) and a second modem converts the analog signals back into digital signals at the receiving site (demodulates).

Figure 26 Using modems to send and receive a memo

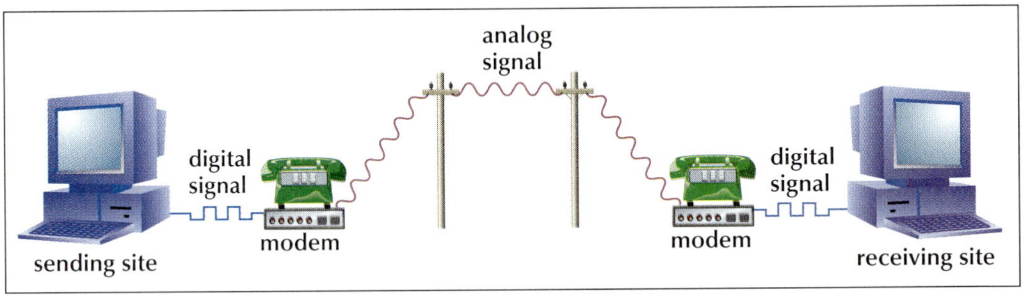

Most computers today come with a built-in 56K modem. The number 56 represents the modem's capability to send and receive about 56,000 **bits per second (bps)**. Actual speed may be reduced by factors such as distance, technical interference, and other issues. This speed is adequate for Paik employees to connect to suppliers at other locations around the world.

The Internet

The Internet was originally developed for the government to connect researchers around the world who needed to share data. Today, the **Internet** is the largest network in the world, connecting millions of people. It has become an invaluable communications channel for individuals, businesses, and governments around the world.

The first Internet experience most people have is to use **electronic mail**, more commonly called **e-mail**. This is the capability to send a message from one user's computer to another user's computer where it is stored until the receiver opens it. The vast network of networks that make up the Internet pass the message along through electronic links called **gateways**. E-mail has become such an integral part of business that you know you must recommend it to Mr. Paik. Your recommendation will list its advantages: speed and ease of communication with vendors and customers, lower postage costs, lower long-distance charges, and increased worker productivity.

Another benefit of using the Internet is the emergence of the **World Wide Web**, sometimes referred to simply as the **Web**. The Web is a huge database of information that is stored on network servers in places that allow public access. The information is stored as text files called **Web pages**, which can include text, graphics, sound, animation, and video. A collection of Web pages is called a **Web site**. Figure 27 shows a sample Web page.

Figure 27 A Web page on the World Wide Web

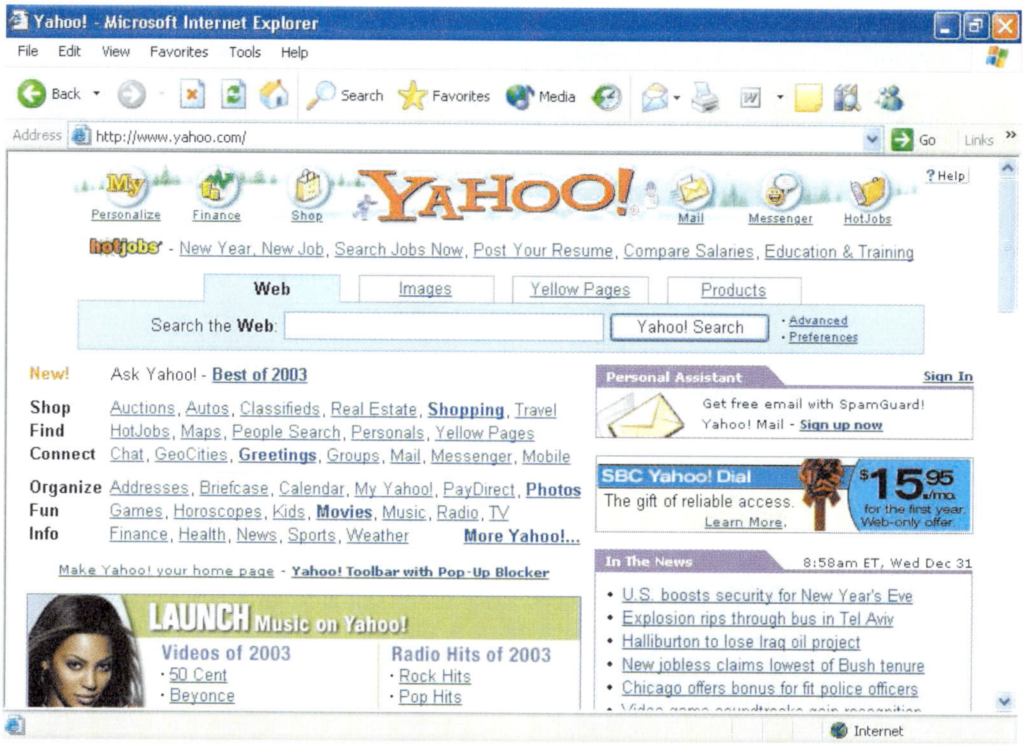

The evolution of multimedia and Internet technologies has made the World Wide Web the perfect communications tool for marketing business services and products. Hyperlinks are the primary resource for making the Web possible. A **hyperlink**, or **link**, is a place on a Web page that is programmed to connect to a particular file on the same network server, or even on a network server on the other side of the globe. The communications software that helps you navigate the World Wide Web is called **Web browsing software**, or a **Web browser**. You decide to include the benefits of Internet and World Wide Web access in your recommendation to Mr. Paik. Specifically, you plan to convince him that he could sell carpets and advertise his carpet renovation services through the Web.

Computer Software

Just as a tape player or DVD player is worthless without tapes or DVDs, computer hardware is useless without software. **Software** is defined as the instructions and associated data that direct the computer to accomplish a task. Sometimes the term *software* refers to a single program, but often the term refers to a collection of programs and data that are packaged together. A **software package** contains disks or a CD-ROM and reference manual. The CD-ROM contains one or more programs and possibly some data. For example, the Microsoft Office 2003 software includes programs that help you draw graphics, create documents, and make calculations. The software includes some data, such as a thesaurus of words and their synonyms.

Software can be divided into two major categories: system software and application software. **System software** helps the computer carry out its basic operating tasks. **Application software** helps the user carry out a variety of tasks.

System Software

System software manages the fundamental operations of your computer, such as loading programs and data into memory, executing programs, saving data to disks, displaying information on the monitor, and transmitting data through a port to a peripheral device. There are four types of system software: operating systems, utilities, device drivers, and programming languages.

An **operating system** controls basic input and output, allocates system resources, manages storage space, maintains security, and detects equipment failure. You have already learned the importance of data communications, both from a standalone computer and from a workstation to other users on a network. The flow of data from the microprocessor to memory to peripherals and back again is called basic **I/O**, or **i**nput/**o**utput. The operating system controls this flow of data just as an air-traffic controller manages airport traffic.

A system resource is any part of the computer system, including memory, storage devices, and the microprocessor, that can be used by a computer program. The operating system allocates system resources so programs run properly. Most of today's computers are capable of **multitasking**—opening and running more than one program at a time—because the operating system is allocating memory and processing time to make multitasking possible. An example of multitasking is producing a document in your word processing program while you check a resource on the Internet. Both the word processing program and the Web browsing program are allowed to use parts of the computer's resources, so you can look at the resource periodically while you are writing about it in your paper. The operating system is also responsible for managing the files on your storage devices. Not only does it open and save files, but it also keeps track of every part of every file for you and lets you know if any part is missing. This activity is like a filing clerk who puts files away when they are not being used, and gets them for you when you need them again.

While you are working on the computer, the operating system is constantly guarding against equipment failure. Each electronic circuit is checked periodically, and the moment a problem is detected, the user is notified with a warning message on the screen.

The operating system's responsibility to maintain security may include requiring a username and password or checking the computer for virus infection. Unscrupulous programmers deliberately construct harmful programs, called **viruses**, which instruct your computer to perform destructive activities, such as erasing a disk drive. Some viruses are more annoying than destructive, but some can be harmful, erasing data or causing your hard disk to require reformatting. Computer users should protect themselves from viruses by using virus protection software. **Virus protection software** searches executable files for the sequences of characters that may cause harm and disinfects the files by erasing or disabling those commands. The computer advertised in Figure 1 comes with virus protection software preinstalled, and with the operating system Windows XP Professional.

Microsoft Windows, used on many personal computers, and the MAC OS, used exclusively on Macintosh computers, are referred to as **operating environments** because they provide a **graphical user interface** (**GUI**, pronounced "goo-ey") that acts as a liaison between the user and all of the computer's hardware and software. In addition to the operating system, Windows and the Mac OS also include utilities, device drivers, and some application programs that perform common tasks.

Utilities are another category of system software that augment the operating system by taking over some of its responsibility for allocating hardware resources. There are many utilities that come with the operating system, but some independent software developers offer utilities for sale separately. For example, Norton Utilities is a very popular collection of utility software.

Each peripheral device requires a **device driver**, or simply **driver**, which is system software that helps the computer communicate with that particular device. When you add a device to an existing computer, part of its installation includes adding its device driver to the computer's configuration.

The last type of system software is computer **programming languages**, which a programmer uses to write computer instructions. The instructions are translated into electrical signals that the computer can manipulate and process. Some examples of popular programming languages are BASIC, Visual Basic, C, C++, Ada, Java, JavaScript, CGI, and Perl.

As you get ready to make your recommendations to Mr. Paik, you realize that the primary factor in deciding the computer specifications you choose to purchase is the software his employees will be using.

Application Software

Application software enables you to perform specific computer tasks. In the business world, some examples of tasks that are accomplished with application software are document production, spreadsheet calculations, and database management. In addition, businesses sometimes use graphics and presentation software, including multimedia applications.

Document production software includes word processing software, desktop publishing software, e-mail editors, and Web authoring software. All of these production tools have a variety of features that assist you in writing and formatting documents. Most offer **spell checking** to help you avoid typographical and spelling errors, as shown in Figure 28.

Spell checking a document — **Figure 28**

Many also assist you with grammar checking and thesaurus tools to improve your writing by offering suggestions and alternatives. Most document production software allows you to perform **copy-and-paste** and **cut-and-paste operations**; these operations allow you to copy or move words around. Document production software may also include **search** or **replace** features that allow you to look for a sequence of characters and substitute new text.

A **document template** is a preformatted document into which you type your text. A template might include format settings such as margins, line spacing, **font** (the style of type), and font size. Templates make it easier to produce consistent documents, such as letterhead or business cards. Figure 29 shows some of the document templates available with Microsoft Word, a popular word processing software package.

Figure 29 Document templates

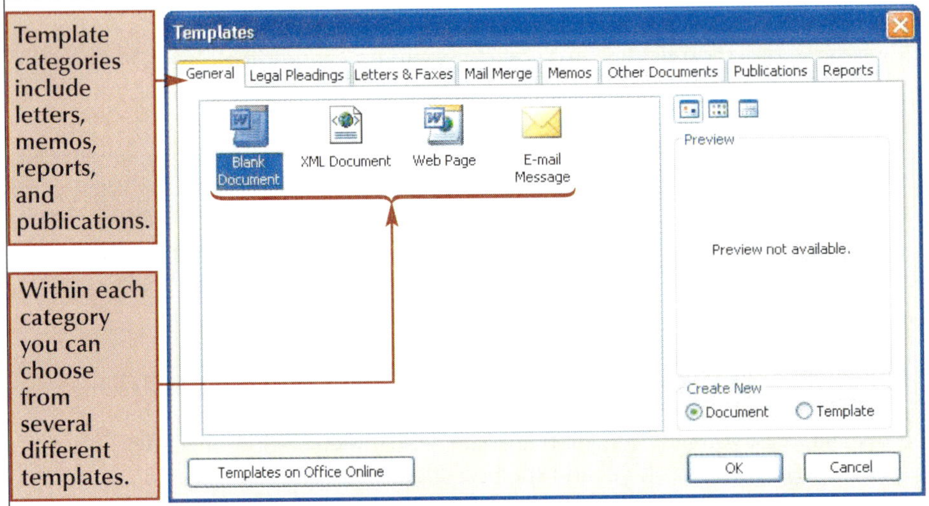

Desktop publishing software is a variation of word processing software that focuses on the format or printed appearance of documents. It is particularly useful for the design of brochures, posters, newsletters, and other documents that are printed in special sizes and formats. Desktop publishing features, such as automatic page numbering and the use of styles, facilitate the development of multiple-page documents. A **style** is a collection of formatting options that are given a name and used repeatedly throughout a document to maintain consistency. Most word processing software includes desktop publishing features such as the automatic generation of a table of contents or index and the ability to insert graphics.

Data communications makes possible the production of documents referred to as **electronic publishing**. Instead of printing and distributing documents on paper, many businesses and individuals are transmitting them electronically by including them in e-mail messages, posting them to the World Wide Web, or participating in electronic conferences where participants can view documents simultaneously. **Web authoring software** allows you to easily create Web pages. With Web authoring software, you can add text, images, links, animation, and sound to a Web page for a Web site. You can also transform word processing documents into Web pages.

Spreadsheet software is a numerical analysis tool that both businesses and individuals use extensively. You can use spreadsheet software, for example, to maintain your checkbook register. Most people use a calculator to keep track of their bank accounts, but using a spreadsheet has several advantages. Spreadsheet software creates a **worksheet**, composed of a grid of columns and rows. Each column is lettered, and each row is numbered. The intersection of a column and row is a **cell**, and each cell has a unique address, called its **cell reference**. Figure 30 shows a typical worksheet that includes a simple calculation.

Figure 30 A typical worksheet

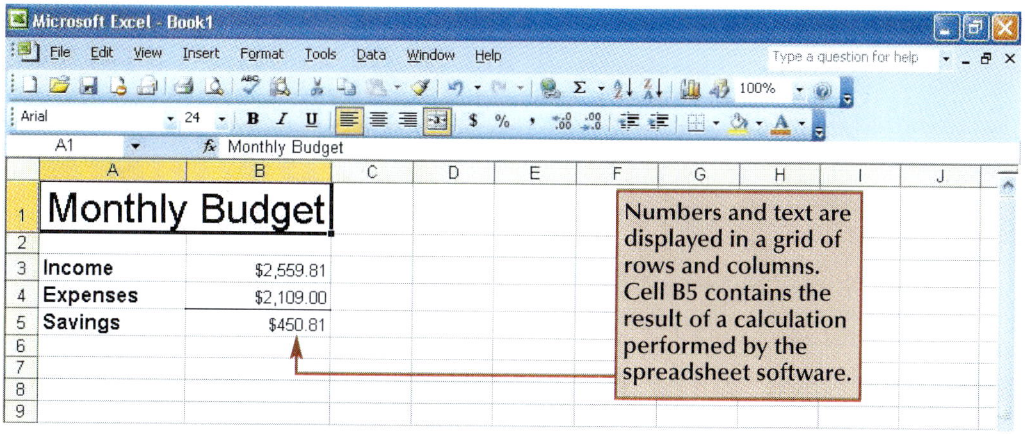

You type numbers into the grid, then create formulas that perform calculations using these numbers. In many ways, a spreadsheet is the ultimate calculator. Once your numbers are on the screen, you don't have to reenter them when you want to redo a calculation with revised or corrected numbers.

With the appropriate data and formulas, you can use an electronic spreadsheet to prepare financial reports, analyze investment portfolios, calculate amortization tables, examine alternative bid proposals, and project income, as well as perform many other tasks involved in making informed business decisions. As an additional benefit, spreadsheet software allows you to produce graphs and reports based upon the data. Figure 31 shows the data in the spreadsheet in Figure 30 represented as a simple graph.

Figure 31 **Worksheet data displayed as a graph**

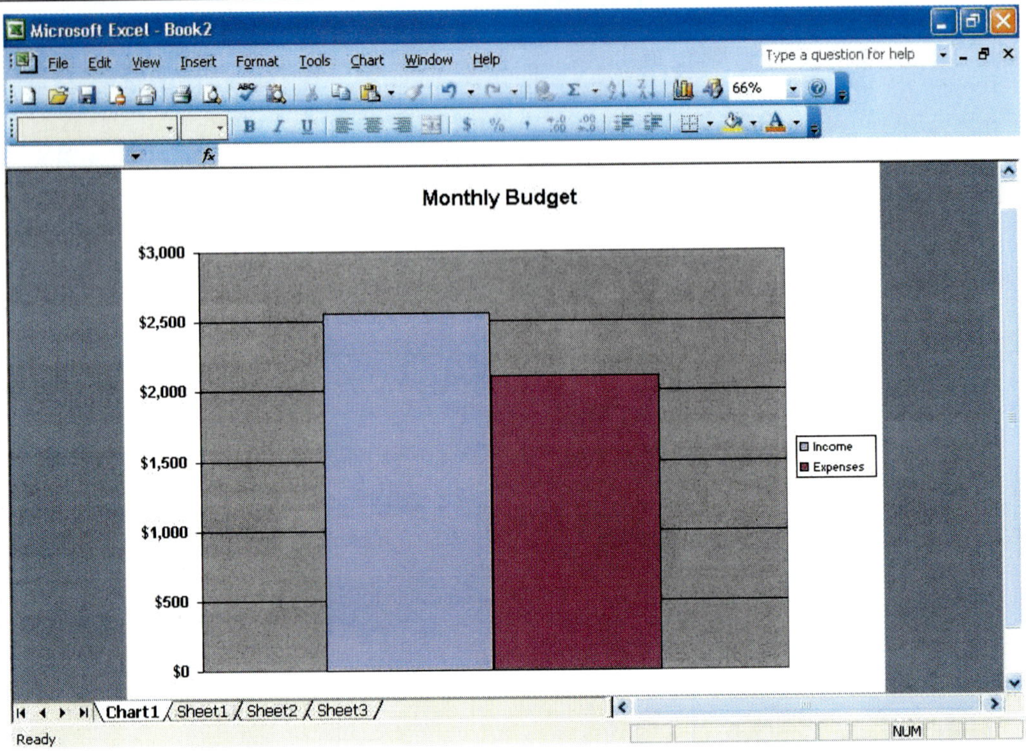

One of the most common types of application software is database management software, which lets you collect and manage data. A database is a collection of information stored on one or more computers. The explosion of information in our society is primarily organized and managed in databases. A structured database is organized in a uniform format of records and fields. A record is a collection of data items in a database. A **field** is one piece of information in the record. Data is the actual information in a field. A familiar example of a structured database is the online catalog of books at a library. This database contains one record for each book in the library, and within each record, several fields that identify the title, the author, and the subjects that the book can be classified under. The information in each field is the data for that record.

Structured databases typically store data that describes a collection of similar entities. Some other examples are student academic records, medical records, a warehouse inventory, or an address book.

A **free-form database** is a loosely structured collection of information, usually stored as documents rather than as records. The collection of word processing documents you have created and stored on your computer is an example of a free-form database. Another example is an encyclopedia stored on a CD-ROM containing documents, photographs, and even video clips. The most familiar example of a free-form database in our society is the World Wide Web with its millions of documents stored worldwide.

Graphics and **presentation software** allow you to create illustrations, diagrams, graphs, and charts that can be projected before a group, printed out for quick reference, or transmitted to remote computers. Most application software allows you to include graphics that you can create yourself using graphics software, such as Microsoft Paint or Adobe PhotoShop. You can also use **clip art**, simple drawings that are included as collections with many software packages. Figure 32 shows a slide from a presentation created in Microsoft PowerPoint—a popular presentation software program that allows you to create colorful presentations and transparencies.

Figure 32 Presentation software

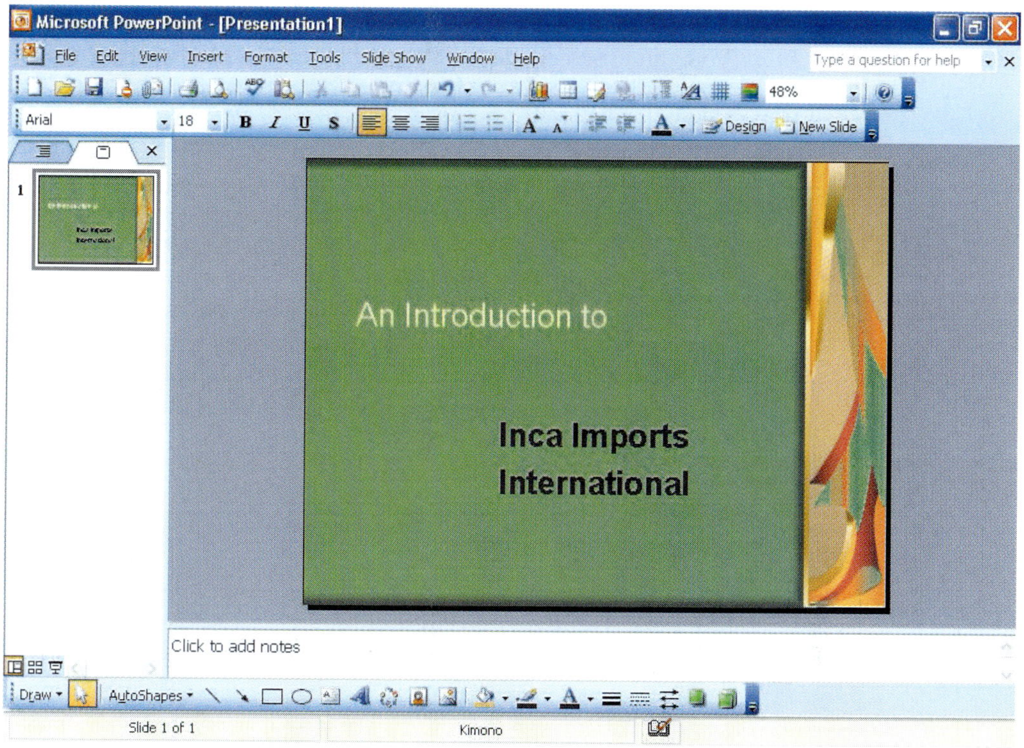

Many programs allow users to use data created in one application in a document created by another application. In fact, it is so easy to add a graphic to your word processing document that you may forget the graphic was created and saved using graphics software. **Object linking and embedding** (**OLE**) refers to the ability to use data from another file, called the **source**. **Embedding** occurs when you copy and paste the source data in the new file. Think of embedding as taking a snapshot of the original. No matter what happens to the original, you still have the copy, as it appeared when you first copied it. **Linking** allows you to create a connection between the source data and the copy in the new file. The link updates the copy every time a change is made to the source data. The seamless nature of OLE among some applications is referred to as **integration**, and the ability to integrate data from all of your applications has become an important skill in business.

Photo editing software allows you to manipulate digital photos. You can make the images brighter, add special effects to the photo, add additional images to a photo, or crop the photo to include only relevant parts of the image. Examples of photo editing software are Adobe Photoshop and Microsoft Picture It!

Multimedia authoring software allows you to record digital sound files, video files, and animations that can be included in presentations and other documents. Macromedia Director and MicroMedium Digital Trainer Professional are two examples of software that you can use to create files that include multimedia. You can sequence and format the screens into tutorials or presentations. Like Web authoring software, multimedia authoring software also uses hypertext to link documents so that the reader can easily navigate from one document to another. Most application software allows users to integrate these multimedia elements into other types of files.

Finally, you must also consider **information management** software. Business people benefit greatly from using this type of software, which keeps track of their schedules, appointments, contacts, and "to-do" lists. Most e-mail software allows users to add all the information about contacts to the list of e-mail addresses. In addition, some software, such as Microsoft Outlook, combines a contact list with information management components, such as a calendar and to-do list. Some information software allows you to synchronize information between a PDA and a desktop or notebook computer. The main screen of Microsoft Outlook is shown in Figure 33.

Figure 33 **Information management software**

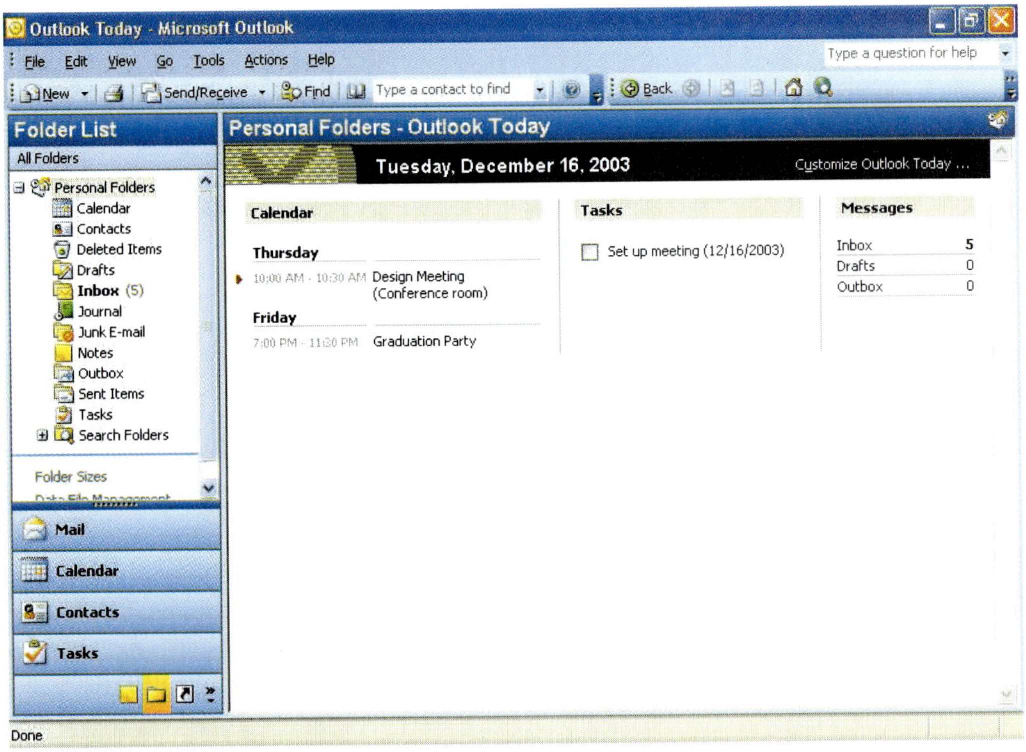

You are now ready to approach Mr. Paik with your recommendations for personal computer hardware, network access, and software. Look back at Figure 1 to be sure that you understand each specification listed. Also consider the software options you should recommend. What will you include? The computer ad already lists Microsoft Windows, so your recommendation should include document production, spreadsheet, and database management software that is compatible with Microsoft Windows. Current versions of Windows include e-mail and network communication software, including Web browsing and Web authoring software. Here's hoping that Mr. Paik approves your recommendations. Good luck!

Review

Tutorial Summary

In this tutorial, you learned about computers and their components. You learned about the different types of computers and their uses. You also learned about peripheral devices and how they are connected to the computer. You learned to distinguish between input and output, and you learned how a computer processes data. You then learned about the motherboard and its components, how a computer stores information, and how information is transmitted. You learned that computers can be connected to form networks and that networks can communicate with each other. Finally, you learned about software and how to distinguish between system and application software.

Key Terms

access time
analog signals
application software
architecture
ASCII (American Standard Code for Information Interchange)
binary digits (bits).
boot process
booting up
bps
byte
cable
cache
cache memory
card
CD-R
CD-ROM (Compact Disk Read Only Memory)
CD-RW
cell
cell reference
central processing unit (CPU)
channel
character-based display
cps
chip
client
client/server network
clip art
clock speed
commands
complementary metal oxide semiconductor (CMOS)
computer
computer system
configuration
controller card
copy-and-paste operation
CRT (cathode ray tube) monitor
cut-and-paste operation
data
data bus
data communications
data files
database
database management software
desktop computer
desktop publishing software
device driver
digital signals
diskette
document production software
document template
dot matrix printer
dot pitch
driver
DVD (Digital Video Disk)
e-mail (electronic mail)
electronic publishing
embed
ergonomic
executable file
expansion card
expansion slot
field
file
flat panel monitor
floppy disk
font
free-form database
gateway
gigabyte (GB)
gigahertz (GHz)
graphics software
graphical user interface (GUI)
graphics accelerator card
graphics card
graphics display
hand-held computer
hard copy
hard disk drive
hardware
hyperlink (link)
I/O
information management software
ink-jet printer
input
input device
integration
interface card
Internet
Kbps
keyboard

kilobyte (KB)
laptop computer
laser printers
link
liquid crystal display (LCD)
local area network (LAN)
mainframe
magnetic storage devices
megabyte (MB)
megahertz (MHz)
memory
memory capacity
microcomputer
microprocessor
MIDI (musical instrument digital interface) card
milliseconds (ms)
modem
monitor
motherboard
mouse
multimedia
multimedia authoring software
multitasking
mylar
network
network interface card (NIC)
network software
node
nonvolatile
notebook computer
object linking and embedding (OLE)
operating environment
operating system
optical storage device
output
output device
pages per minute (ppm)
parallel port
PDA (Personal Digital Assistant)
peer-to-peer network
peripheral devices
Personal Computer Memory Card International Association (PCMCIA) device
personal computer
photo editing software
pixel
pointing device
pointer
port
presentation software
processing
processing hardware
processor
programming language
protocols
printer
RAM cache
random access memory (RAM)
RDRAM
read-only memory (ROM)
receiver
record
replace
resolution
screen size
SCSI (small computer system interface)
SDRAM
search
sender
serial port
server
slot
software
software package
source
specifications
spell checking
spreadsheet software
standalone computer
storage
structured database
style
supercomputers
system software
Tablet PC
tape drive
telecommunications
template
terminal
toner
USB
USB connector
USB port
utilities
video display adapter
video card
virus
virus protection software
virtual memory
volatile
Web authoring software
Web browsing software (Web browser)
Web page
Web site
Wi-Fi
wireless local area network (WLAN)
wireless pointer
word size
worksheet
workstation
World Wide Web (Web)
write protection

Review

Review Questions

1. What is the key to a computer's versatility?
   a. software
   b. hardware
   c. price
   d. peripherals
2. Which one of the following would not be considered a personal computer?
   a. desktop
   b. notebook
   c. mainframe
   d. personal digital assistant
3. Keyboards, monitors, hard disk drives, printers, and motherboards are all examples of which of the following?
   a. input devices
   b. output devices
   c. peripherals
   d. hardware
4. The selection of components that make up a particular computer system is referred to as the ______________________.
   a. configuration
   b. specification
   c. protocol
   d. device driver
5. Moving text, sorting lists, and performing calculations are examples of which of the following?
   a. input
   b. output
   c. processing
   d. storage
6. What do you call each 1 or 0 used in the representation of computer data?
   a. a bit
   b. a byte
   c. an ASCII
   d. a pixel
7. What usually represents one character of data?
   a. a bit
   b. a byte
   c. an integer
   d. a pixel
8. What is a megabyte?
   a. 10 kilobytes
   b. about a million bytes
   c. one-half a gigabyte
   d. about a million bits
9. Which one of the following microprocessors is fastest?
   a. 200 MHz
   b. 2.66 GHz
   c. 2.4 GHz
   d. 233 MHz
10. Which of the following temporarily stores data and programs while you are using them?
    a. ROM
    b. a floppy disk
    c. RAM
    d. a hard disk
11. What do you call a collection of data stored on a disk under a name that you assign it?
    a. a file
    b. the operating system
    c. a protocol
    d. a pixel

12. Which of the following storage media does not allow you to recycle by writing over old data?
    a. hard disk
    b. floppy disk
    c. CD-ROM
    d. tape
13. A computer display system consists of a monitor and a ______________.
    a. parallel port
    b. network card
    c. graphics card
    d. sound card
14. A personal computer that is connected to a network is called a ______________.
    a. desktop
    b. workstation
    c. terminal
    d. PDA
15. What telecommunications hardware is needed to convert digital signals to analog signals?
    a. mouse
    b. device driver
    c. modem
    d. slot
16. Which one of the following is system software?
    a. Microsoft Excel
    b. Microsoft Windows
    c. Microsoft Paint
    d. Microsoft Word
17. Which of the following is not a function of an operating system?
    a. controls basic input and output
    b. allocates system resources
    c. manages storage space
    d. carries out a specific task for the user
18. Random access memory (RAM) is measured in ______________.
19. Disk access time is measured in ______________.
20. The clock speed of a microprocessor is measured in ______________.
21. ______________ is the maximum number of pixels a monitor can display.
22. The transmission of text, numeric, voice, or video data from one computer to another is called ______________.
23. A(n) ______________ includes a computer, peripheral devices, and software.
24. The capability to send a text message from one user to another user's account where it is stored until the receiver opens it is called ______________.
25. The ______________ is a huge database of information that is stored on network servers around the world, and which users access by using browser software.
26. For each of the following data items, indicate how many bytes of storage would be required:

Data Item	Number of Bytes
North	
U.S.A.	
General Ledger	

27. Read the following requirements for using Microsoft Office 2003 Professional (taken from the documentation that accompanies the software). Then turn back to the computer advertisement shown in Figure 1 at the beginning of the tutorial and determine if the computer specifications listed in the ad are sufficient to run Office 2003.
    To use Microsoft Office 2003 Professional, you need:
    - PC with a Pentium III or equivalent, 233 MHz or higher processor; Pentium 4 or equivalent recommended
    - 128 MB of RAM plus an additional 8 MB of RAM for each Office application running simultaneously; 256 MB recommended
    - 400 MB of available hard disk space minimum; 880 MB recommended

28. Using the system requirements listed in Question 27, look through a recent computer magazine and find the least expensive computer that will run the Microsoft Office 2003 Professional software. Make a photocopy of the ad showing the specifications, price, and vendor. Write the name of the magazine and the issue date at the top of the photocopied ad. Write a short paper that supports your selection.
29. You have learned that the use of multimedia requires special hardware and software. Look for current prices and specifications of multimedia hardware in advertisements in magazines or in your local newspaper. What are the highest priced devices, and why are they so expensive? In the following chart, add the specifications and price for the most expensive examples of these devices that you can find. Look at the computer advertisement shown in Figure 1 and determine if the computer specifications listed in the ad are sufficient to run multimedia. If not, write a statement that justifies adding the cost of the higher-quality device you listed here.

Multimedia Device	Specifications	Price
DVD-ROM drive		
Speakers		
Headphones		
Large, high-resolution monitor		

Reinforce

Lab Assignments

The New Perspectives Labs are designed to help you master some of the key concepts and skills presented in this text. The steps for completing the Labs are located on the Course Technology Web site. Log on to the Internet and use your Web browser to go to the Student Online Companion for New Perspectives Office 2003 at **www.course.com/np/office2003**. Click the Lab Assignments link, and then navigate to the assignments for this tutorial.

Objectives

Session 1
- Start Windows XP and tour the desktop
- Explore the Start menu
- Run software programs, switch between them, and close them
- Manipulate windows
- Identify and use the controls in menus, toolbars, and dialog boxes

Session 2
- Navigate your computer with Windows Explorer and My Computer
- Change the view of the items in your computer
- Get help when you need it
- Shut down Windows

Labs

Student Data Files

There are no student Data Files needed for this tutorial.

Exploring the Basics of Microsoft Windows XP

Investigating the Windows XP Operating System

Case

Your Computer Training

Your Computer Training is a small business in Tampa, Florida, that provides lessons and instruction on how to use a computer, offering courses for beginning, intermediate, and advanced computer users. The instruction includes detailed explanations, definitions, and descriptions as well as hands-on practice of computer skills. First-time and novice users learn a full range of basic tasks—from starting the computer and opening and closing programs to shutting down the computer. Steve Laslow teaches an introductory course on the fundamentals of using the Microsoft Windows XP operating system.

In this tutorial you will start Windows XP and practice some basic computer skills. Then you'll learn how to navigate with My Computer and Windows Explorer. Finally, you'll use the Windows XP Help system.

Session 1

Starting Windows XP

Steve Laslow begins the course by discussing the operating system. The **operating system** is software that helps the computer perform essential tasks such as displaying information on the computer screen and saving data on disks. (Software refers to the **programs**, or **applications**, that a computer uses to complete tasks.) Your computer uses the **Microsoft Windows XP** operating system—**Windows XP** for short. Windows is the name of the operating system, and XP indicates the version you are using. Microsoft has released many versions of Windows since 1985, and is currently developing new versions.

Much of the software created for Windows XP shares the same look and works the same way. This similarity in design means that once you learn how to use one Windows XP program, such as Microsoft Word (a word-processing program), you are well on your way to understanding how to use other Windows XP programs. Windows XP allows you to use more than one program at a time, so you can easily switch between your word-processing program and your appointment book program, for example. Windows XP also makes it easy to access the **Internet**, a worldwide collection of computers connected to one another to enable communication. All in all, Windows XP makes your computer an effective and easy-to-use productivity tool.

Windows XP starts automatically when you turn on your computer. After completing some necessary startup tasks, Windows XP displays a Welcome screen. Depending on the way your computer is set up, the Welcome screen might simply welcome you to Windows XP or it might list all the users for the computer. If a list of users appears, you must click your user name and perhaps type a password to start using Windows XP. A **user name** is a unique name that identifies you to Windows XP, and a **password** is text—often a confidential combination of letters and numbers—that you must enter before you can work with Windows XP. The Welcome screen might reappear if there's been no activity on the computer for a while.

To start Windows XP:

1. Turn on your computer. After a moment, Windows XP starts and the Welcome screen appears.

   Trouble? If you are asked to select an operating system, do not take action. Windows XP should start automatically after a designated number of seconds. If it does not, ask your instructor or technical support person for help.

   Trouble? If this is the first time you have started your computer with Windows XP, messages might appear on your screen informing you that Windows is setting up components of your computer.

2. On the Welcome screen, click your user name, if necessary. The Windows XP screen appears, as shown in Figure 1.

   Trouble? If your user name does not appear in the list of users on the Welcome screen, ask your instructor or technical support person which name you should click.

   Trouble? If you need to enter a user name and a password, type your assigned user name, press the Tab key, type your password, and then click the Continue button or press the Enter key to continue.

Figure 1 Windows XP desktop

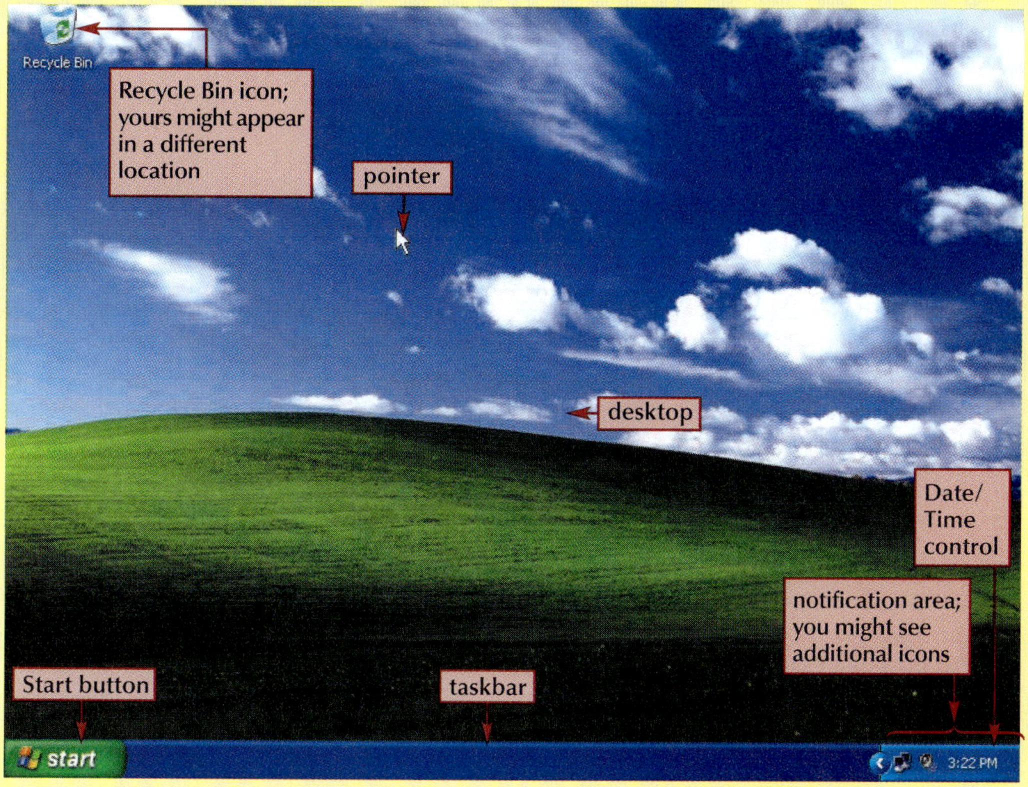

3. Look at your screen and locate the objects labeled in Figure 1. The objects on your screen might appear larger or smaller than those in Figure 1, depending on your monitor's settings. Figure 2 describes the function of each of these objects.

Figure 2 Elements of the Windows XP desktop

Element	Description
Icon	A small picture that represents an object available to your computer
Pointer	A small object, such as an arrow, that moves on the screen when you move the mouse
Desktop	Your workplace on the screen
Date/Time control	Shows the current date and time and lets you set the clock
Taskbar	Contains buttons that give you quick access to common tools and the programs currently running
Start button	Provides access to Windows XP programs, documents, and information on the Internet
Notification area	Displays icons corresponding to services running in the background, such as an Internet connection

Trouble? If a blank screen or animated design replaces the Windows XP desktop, your computer might be set to use a screen saver, a program that causes a monitor to go blank or to display an animated design after a specified amount of idle time. Press any key to restore the Windows XP desktop.

The Windows XP screen uses a **graphical user interface** (**GUI**, pronounced "gooey"), which displays icons that represent items stored on your computer, such as programs and files. **Icons** are pictures of familiar objects, such as file folders and documents. Windows XP gets its name from the rectangular work areas, called "windows," that appear on your screen as you work (although no other windows should be open right now). You will learn more about windows later in this tutorial.

Touring the Windows XP Desktop

In Windows terminology, the area displayed on your screen when Windows XP starts represents a **desktop**—a workspace for projects and the tools that you need to manipulate your projects. When you first start a computer, it uses **default** settings, those preset by the operating system. The default desktop you see after you first install Windows XP, for example, displays an image of green hills and clouds in a blue sky. However, Microsoft designed Windows XP so that you can easily change the appearance of the desktop. You can, for example, change images or add patterns and text to the desktop background.

Interacting with the Desktop

To interact with the objects on your desktop, you use a **pointing device**. Pointing devices come in many shapes and sizes. The most common one is called a **mouse**, so this book uses that term. If you are using a different pointing device, such as a trackball, substitute that device whenever you see the term "mouse." Some pointing devices are designed to ensure that your hand won't suffer fatigue while using them. Some are attached directly to your computer via a cable, whereas others work like a TV remote control and allow you to access your computer without being right next to it.

You use a pointing device to move the mouse pointer over objects on the desktop, or to **point** to them. The pointer is usually shaped like an arrow, although it changes shape depending on the pointer's location on the screen and what tasks you are performing. As you move the mouse on a surface, such as a mouse pad, the pointer on the screen moves in a corresponding direction.

When you point to certain objects, such as the objects on the taskbar, a "tip" appears in a yellow box. These tips are called **ScreenTips**, and they tell you the purpose or function of the object to which you are pointing.

To view ScreenTips:

1. Use the mouse to point to the **Start** button on the taskbar. After a few seconds, you see the ScreenTip "Click here to begin," as shown in Figure 3.

Figure 3 Viewing ScreenTips

2. Point to the time displayed at the right end of the taskbar. A ScreenTip for today's date (or the date to which your computer's time clock is set) appears.

Clicking refers to pressing a mouse button and immediately releasing it. Clicking sends a signal to your computer that you want to perform an action on the object you click. In Windows XP you perform most actions with the left mouse button. If you are told to click an object, position the mouse pointer on that object and click the left mouse button, unless instructed otherwise.

When you click the Start button, the Start menu opens. A **menu** is a group or list of commands, and a **menu command** is a word that you can click to complete tasks. If a right-pointing arrow follows a menu command, then you can point to the command to open a **submenu**, which is a list of additional choices related to the command. The **Start menu** provides you with access to programs, documents, and much more. You can click the Start button to open the Start menu.

To open the Start menu:

1. Point to the **Start** button on the taskbar.
2. Click the left mouse button. The Start menu opens. An arrow ▶ follows the All Programs command on the Start menu, indicating that you can view additional choices by navigating to a submenu. See Figure 4; your Start menu might show different commands.

Figure 4 **Start menu**

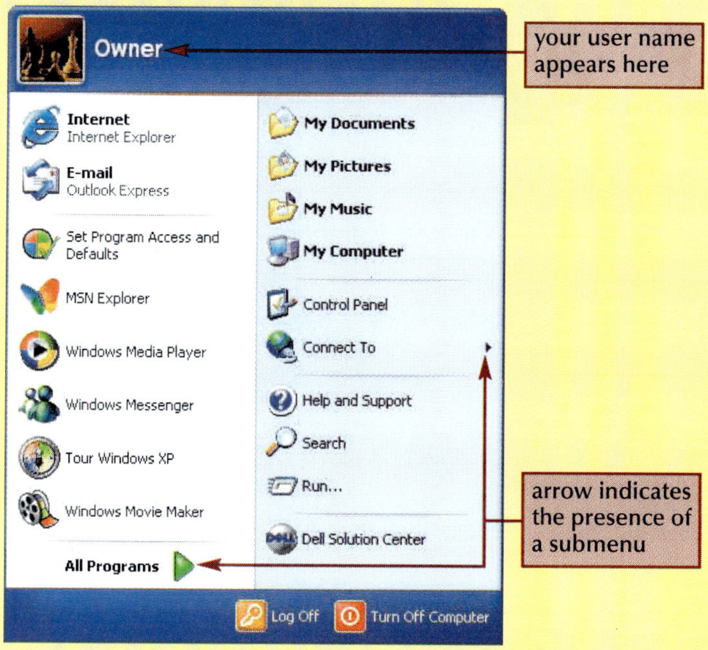

3. Click the **Start** button on the taskbar to close the Start menu.

You need to select an object to work with it. To **select** an object in Windows XP, you point to and then click that object. Windows XP shows you which object is selected by highlighting it, usually by changing the object's color, putting a box around it, or making the object appear to be pushed in.

In Windows XP, depending on your computer's settings, you can select certain objects by pointing to them and others by clicking them. You'll point to the All Programs command on the Start menu to open the All Programs submenu.

To select a menu command:

1. Click the **Start** button on the taskbar. The button appears to be pushed in, indicating that it is selected.
2. Point to (but don't click) **All Programs** on the Start menu. When you first point to the All Programs command, it is highlighted to indicate it is selected. After a short pause, the All Programs submenu opens. See Figure 5.

Figure 5 All Programs submenu

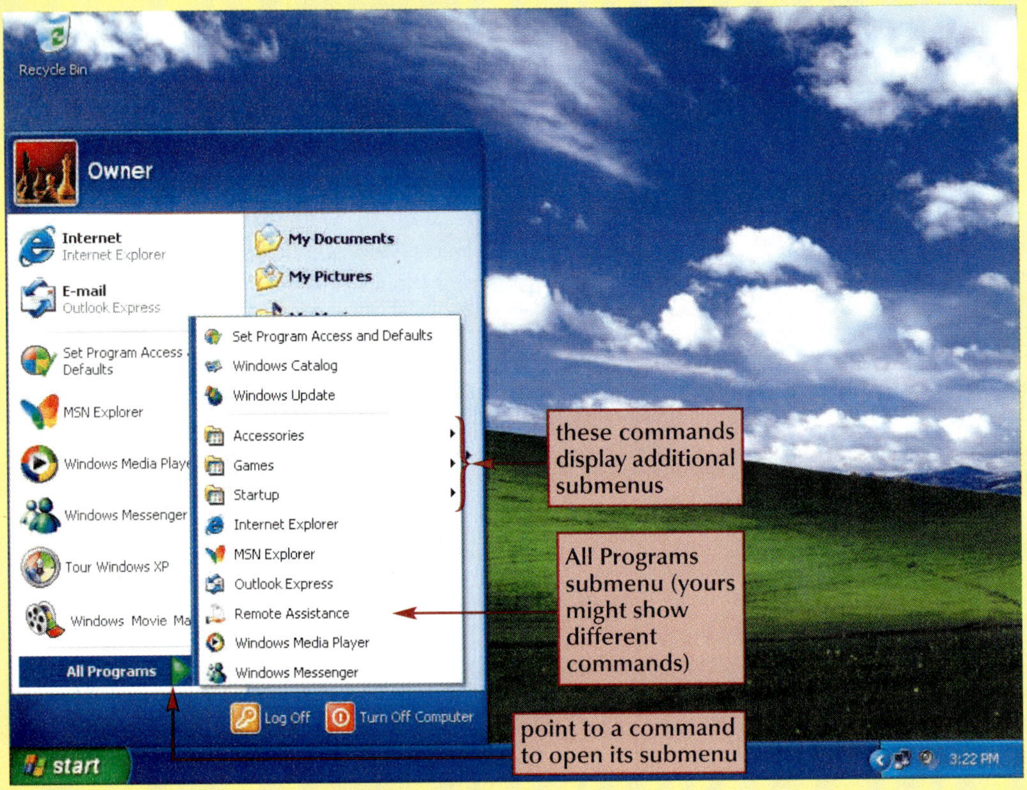

Trouble? If a submenu other than the All Programs menu opens, you pointed to the wrong command. Move the mouse so that the pointer points to All Programs.

3. Click the **Start** button on the taskbar to close the Start menu. You return to the desktop.

In addition to clicking an object to select it, you can double-click an object to open or start the item associated with it. For example, you can double-click a folder icon to open the folder and see its contents. Or you can double-click a program icon to start the program. **Double-clicking** means to click the left mouse button twice in quick succession.

You can practice double-clicking now by opening the Recycle Bin. The Recycle Bin holds deleted items such as folders until you remove them permanently.

To view the contents of the Recycle Bin:

1. Click the desktop, and then point to the **Recycle Bin** icon on the desktop. After a few moments, a ScreenTip appears that describes the Recycle Bin.
2. Click the left mouse button twice quickly to double-click the **Recycle Bin** icon. The Recycle Bin window opens, as shown in Figure 6.

Figure 6 Contents of the Recycle Bin

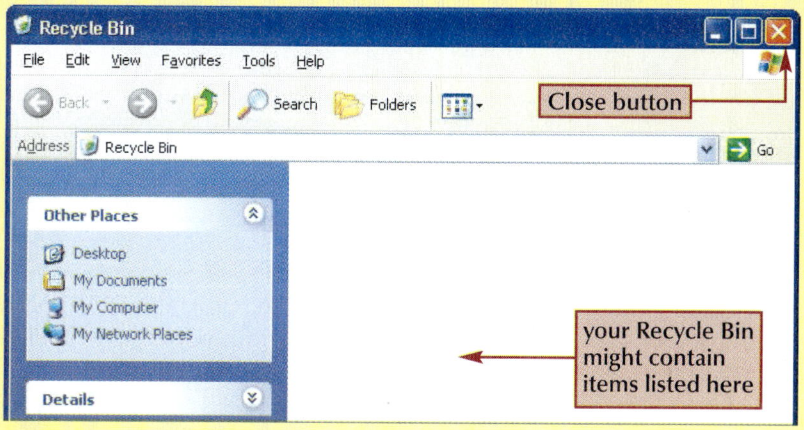

Trouble? If the Recycle Bin window does not open, and you see only the Recycle Bin name highlighted below the icon, you double-clicked too slowly. Double-click the icon again more quickly.

Now you can close the Recycle Bin window.

3. Click the **Close** button in the upper-right corner of the Recycle Bin window.

   You'll learn more about opening and closing windows later in this session.

Your mouse has more than one button—in addition to the left button, the mouse has a right button that you can use for performing certain actions in Windows XP. However, the term "clicking" continues to refer to the left button; clicking an object with the *right* button is called **right-clicking**.

In Windows XP, right-clicking selects an object and opens its **shortcut menu**, which is a list of commands directly related to the object that you right-clicked. You can right-click practically any object—the Start button, a desktop icon, the taskbar, and even the desktop itself—to view commands associated with that object. Recall that you clicked the Start button with the left mouse button to open the Start menu. Now you can right-click the Start button to open the shortcut menu for the Start button.

To right-click an object:

1. Position the pointer over the **Start** button on the taskbar.
2. Right-click the **Start** button on the taskbar to open its shortcut menu. This menu offers a list of commands related to the Start button. See Figure 7.

Figure 7 Start button shortcut menu

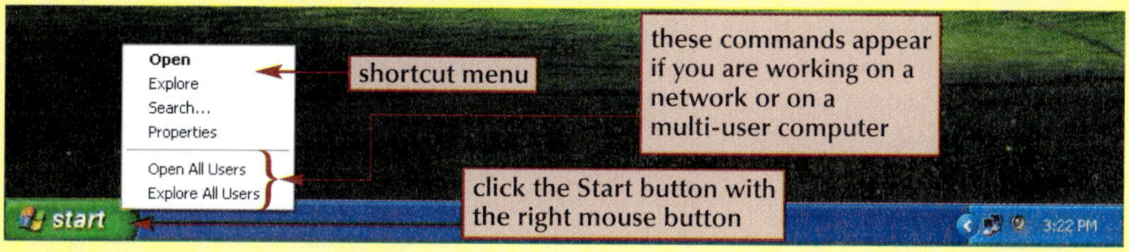

Trouble? If the shortcut menu does not open and you are using a trackball or a mouse with three buttons or a wheel, make sure you click the button on the far right, not the one in the middle.

Trouble? If your menu looks slightly different from the one in Figure 7, don't worry; different computers often have different commands.

3. Press the **Esc** key to close the shortcut menu. You return to the desktop.

Now that you've opened the Start menu and its shortcut menu, you're ready to explore the contents of the Start menu.

Exploring the Start Menu

Recall that the Start menu is the central point for accessing programs, documents, and other resources on your computer. The Start menu is organized into two panels, as shown in Figure 8, and each panel lists items you can point to or click.

Figure 8 Start menu

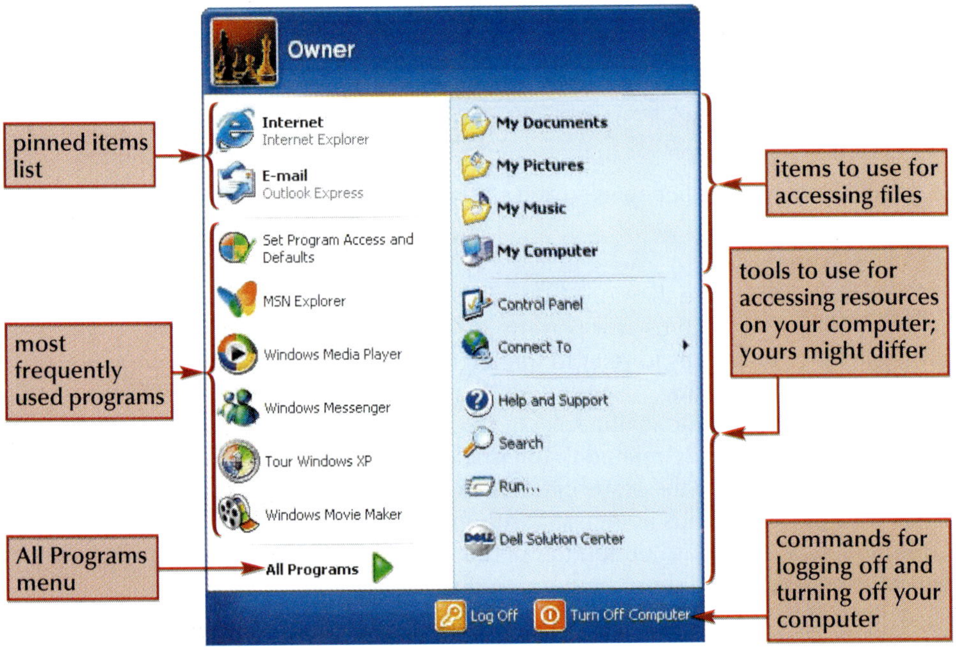

The left panel organizes programs for easy access. The area at the top of the left panel is called the **pinned items list**. Pinned items stay on the Start menu unless you remove them. By default, Windows XP lists the Web browser and e-mail program on your computer in the pinned items list. You can pin other items to this list if you like. When you use a program, Windows XP adds it to the **most frequently used programs list**, which appears below the pinned items list. Windows XP can list only a certain number of frequently used programs—after that, the programs you have not opened recently are replaced by the programs you used last.

The last item in the left panel is the All Programs menu, which you have already used to display a list of programs currently installed on your computer. You'll use the All Programs menu shortly to start a program.

From the right panel, you can access common locations and tools on your computer. For example, **My Documents** is your personal folder, a convenient place to store documents, graphics, and other work. **My Computer** is a tool that you use to view, organize, and access the programs, files, and drives on your computer.

From the lower section of the right panel, you can open windows that help you work effectively with Windows XP, including the **Control Panel**, which contains specialized tools that you can use to change the way Windows XP looks and behaves, and the **Help and Support Center**, which provides tutorials, demonstrations, and steps for performing tasks in Windows XP. (You'll explore the Help and Support Center later in this tutorial.) Finally, you also log off and turn off your computer from the Start menu. When you **log off**, you end your session with Windows XP but leave the computer turned on.

Now that you've explored the Start menu, you're ready to use it to start a program.

Starting a Program

Reference Window

- Click the Start button on the taskbar, and then point to All Programs.
- If necessary, point to the submenu that contains the program you want to start.
- Click the name of the program you want to start.

or

- Click the name or icon of the program you want to start in the pinned items list or the most frequently used programs list on the Start menu.

Windows XP includes an easy-to-use word-processing program called WordPad. Suppose you want to start the WordPad program and use it to write a letter or report. You open Windows XP programs from the Start menu. Programs are usually located on the All Programs submenu or on one of its submenus. To start WordPad, for example, you navigate to the All Programs and Accessories submenus.

To start the WordPad program from the Start menu:

1. Click the **Start** button on the taskbar to open the Start menu.
2. Point to **All Programs** to open the All Programs submenu.
3. Point to **Accessories**. The Accessories submenu opens. Figure 9 shows the open menus.

Start menu and related submenus | **Figure 9**

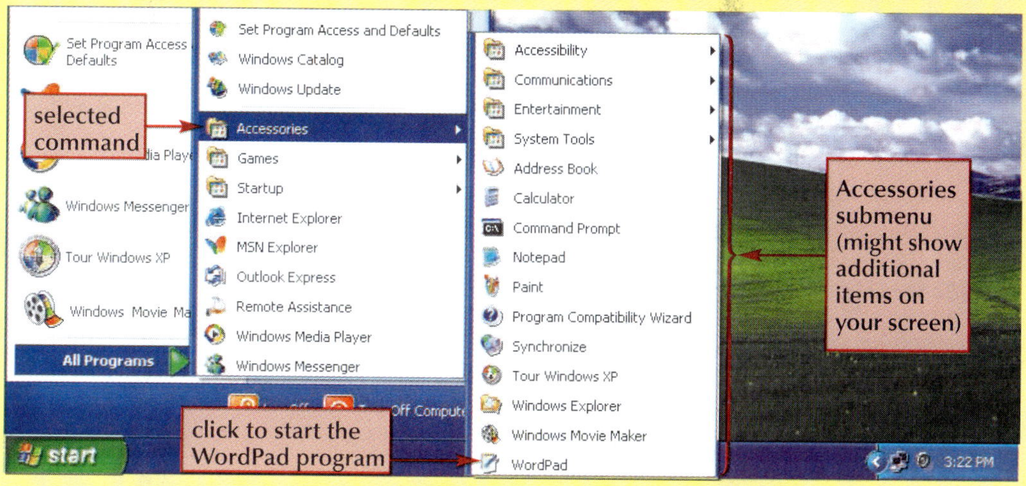

Trouble? If a different menu opens, you might have paused the pointer over a different menu command, which opened its submenu. Move the pointer back to All Programs, and then move the pointer up or down to point to Accessories.

4. Click **WordPad** on the Accessories submenu. The WordPad program window opens, as shown in Figure 10.

Figure 10 WordPad program window

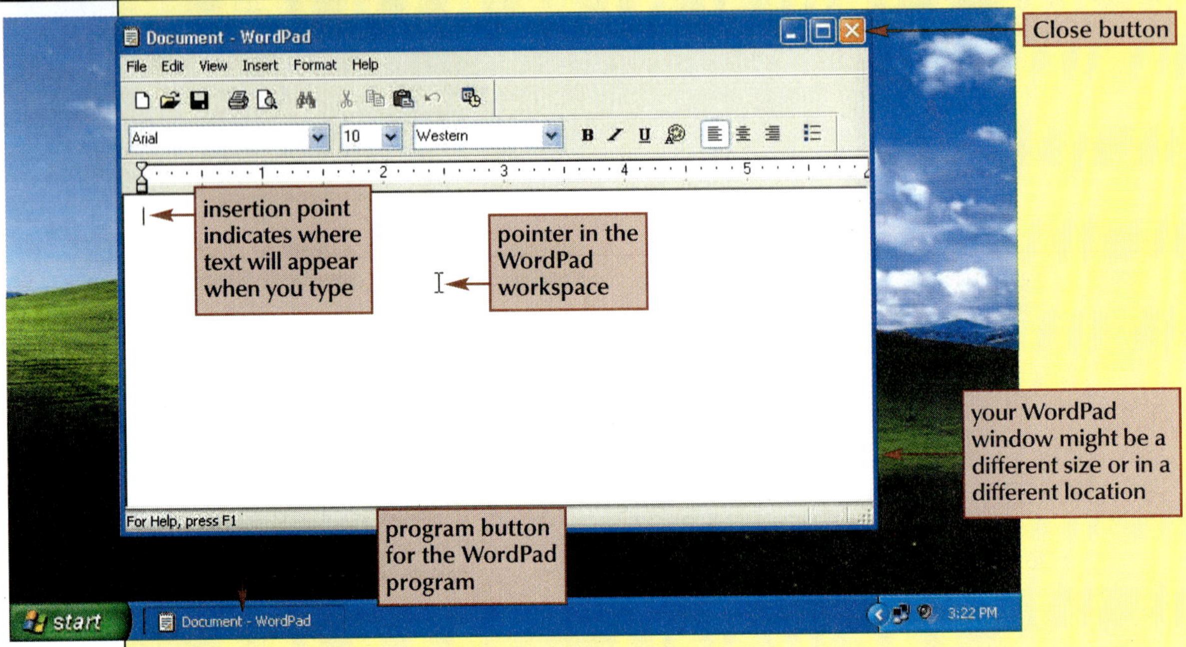

Trouble? If the WordPad program window fills the entire screen, don't worry. You will learn how to manipulate windows shortly.

When a program is started, it is said to be open or running. A **program button** appears on the taskbar for each open program. You click a program button to switch between open programs. When you are finished using a program, you can click the Close button located in the upper-right corner of the program window to **exit**, or close, that program.

To exit the WordPad program:

1. Click the **Close** button on the WordPad title bar. The WordPad program closes and you return to the Windows XP desktop.

Running Multiple Programs

One of the most useful features of Windows XP is its ability to run multiple programs at the same time. This feature, known as **multitasking**, allows you to work on more than one task at a time and to switch quickly between projects. For example, you can start WordPad and leave it running while you start the Paint program.

To run WordPad and Paint at the same time:

1. Start WordPad again.
2. Click the **Start** button on the taskbar.
3. Point to **All Programs**, and then point to **Accessories**.
4. Click **Paint**. The Paint program window opens, as shown in Figure 11. Now two programs are running at the same time.

Figure 11 **Two programs open**

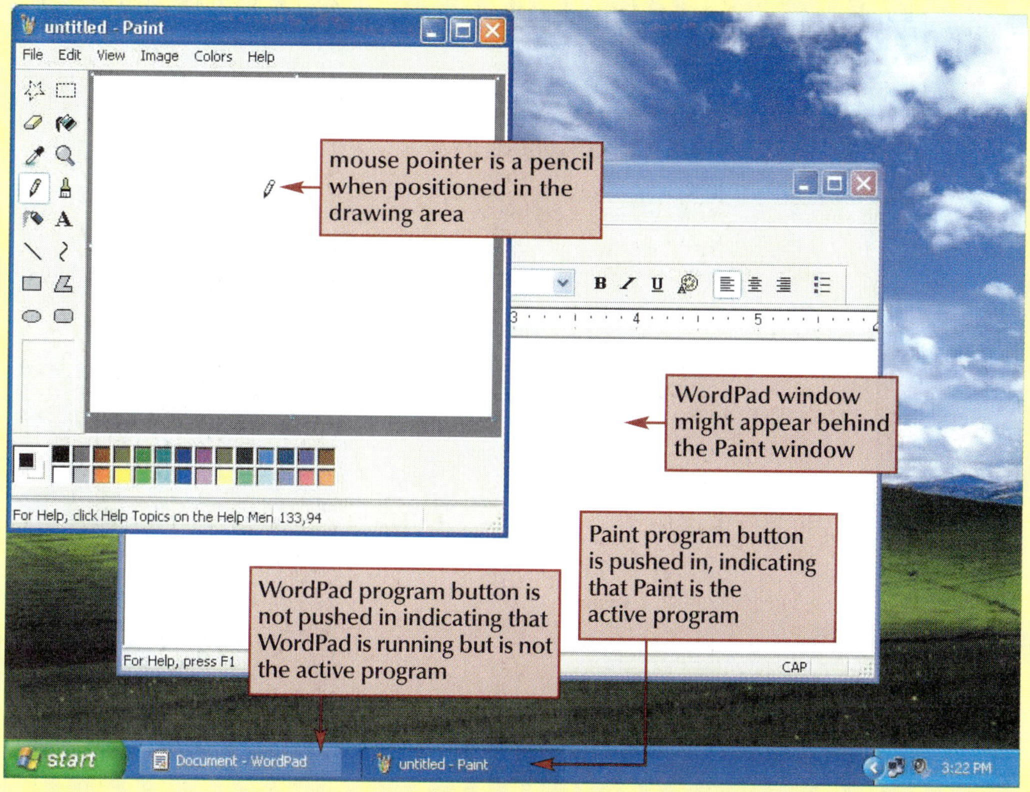

Trouble? If the Paint program fills the entire screen, continue with the next set of steps. You will learn how to manipulate windows shortly.

The **active program** is the one you are currently using—Windows XP applies your next keystroke or command to the active program. Paint is the active program because it is the one in which you are currently working. The WordPad program button is still on the taskbar, indicating that WordPad is still running even if you can't see its program window. Imagine that the WordPad program window is stacked behind the Paint program window.

Switching Between Programs

Because only one program is active at a time, you'll need to switch between programs if you want to work in one or the other. The easiest way to switch between programs is to use the program buttons on the taskbar.

To switch between WordPad and Paint:

1. Click the program button labeled **Document - WordPad** on the taskbar. The WordPad program window moves to the front, and now the Document - WordPad button looks pushed in, indicating that WordPad is the active program.
2. Click the program button labeled **untitled - Paint** on the taskbar to switch to the Paint program. The Paint program is again the active program.

In addition to using the taskbar to switch between open programs, you can also close programs from the taskbar.

Closing Programs from the Taskbar

You should always close a program when you are finished using it. Each program uses computer resources, such as memory, so Windows XP works more efficiently when only the programs you need are open. You've already seen how to close an open program using the Close button on the title bar of the program window. You can also close a program, whether active or inactive, by using the shortcut menu associated with the program button on the taskbar.

To close WordPad and Paint using the program button shortcut menus:

1. Right-click the **untitled - Paint** button on the taskbar. The shortcut menu for the Paint program button opens. See Figure 12.

Figure 12 Program button shortcut menu

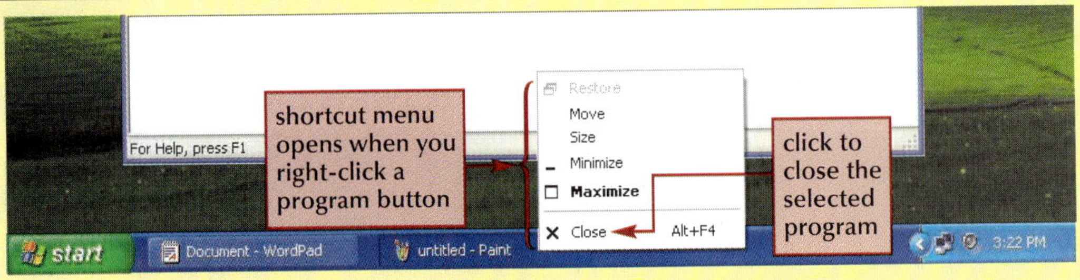

2. Click **Close** on the shortcut menu. The Paint program closes and the program button labeled "untitled - Paint" disappears from the taskbar.
3. Right-click the **Document - WordPad** button on the taskbar, and then click **Close** on the shortcut menu. The WordPad program closes and its program button no longer appears on the taskbar.

Now that you've learned the basics of using the Windows XP desktop, you're ready to explore other Windows XP features, including windows and dialog boxes.

Using Windows and Dialog Boxes

Recall that when you run a program in Windows XP, the program appears in a window. A **window** is a rectangular area of the screen that contains a program, text, graphics, or data. Windows, spelled with an uppercase "W," is the name of the Microsoft operating system. The word "window" with a lowercase "w" refers to one of the rectangular areas on the screen. A window also contains **controls**, which are graphical or textual objects used for manipulating the window and for using the program. Figure 13 describes the controls you are likely to see in most windows.

Window controls **Figure 13**

Control	Description
Menu bar	Contains the titles of menus, such as File, Edit, and Help
Sizing buttons	Let you enlarge, shrink, or close a window
Status bar	Provides you with messages relevant to the task you are performing
Title bar	Contains the window title and basic window control buttons
Toolbar	Contains buttons that provide you with shortcuts to common menu commands
Window title	Identifies the program and document contained in the window
Workspace	Part of the window you use to enter your work—to enter text, draw pictures, set up calculations, and so on

The WordPad program is a good example of a typical window. You'll start WordPad and identify its window controls.

To look at the window controls in WordPad:

1. Make sure that Windows XP is running and the Windows XP desktop is displayed.
2. Start WordPad.
3. On your screen, identify the controls that are labeled in Figure 14.

WordPad window controls **Figure 14**

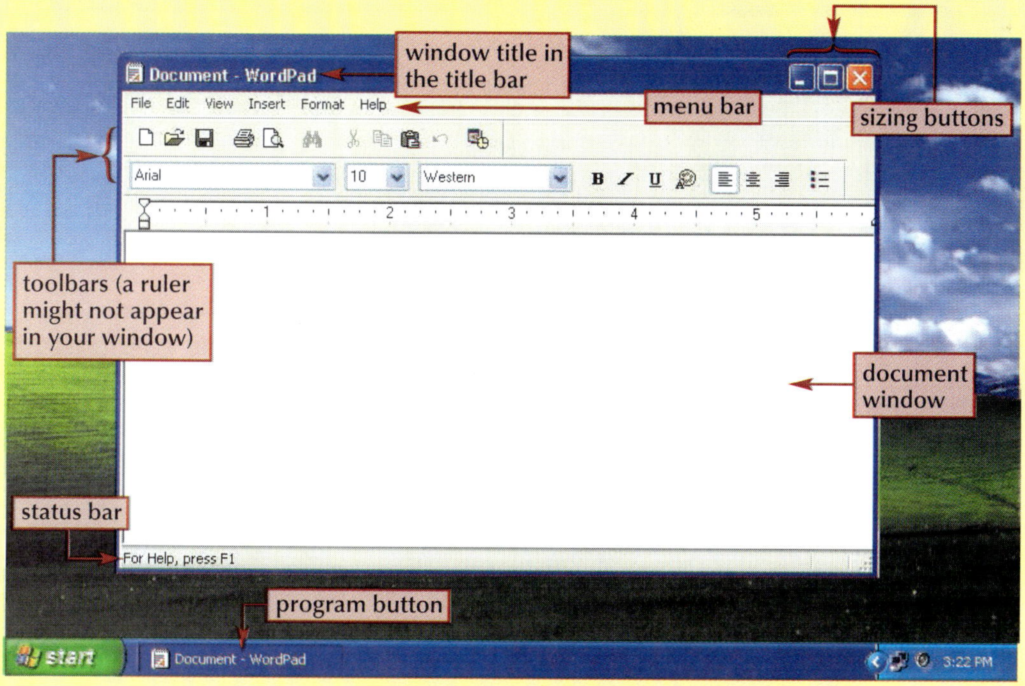

Trouble? If your WordPad program window fills the entire screen or differs in size, you can still identify all the controls.

After you open a window, you can manipulate it by changing its size and position.

Manipulating Windows

On the right side of the title bar are three buttons. The Minimize button, which is the first of the three buttons, hides a window so that only its program button is visible on the taskbar. The other button changes name and function depending on the status of the window (it either maximizes the window or restores it to a predefined size). You are already familiar with the last button—the Close button. Figure 15 shows how these buttons work.

Figure 15 Window buttons

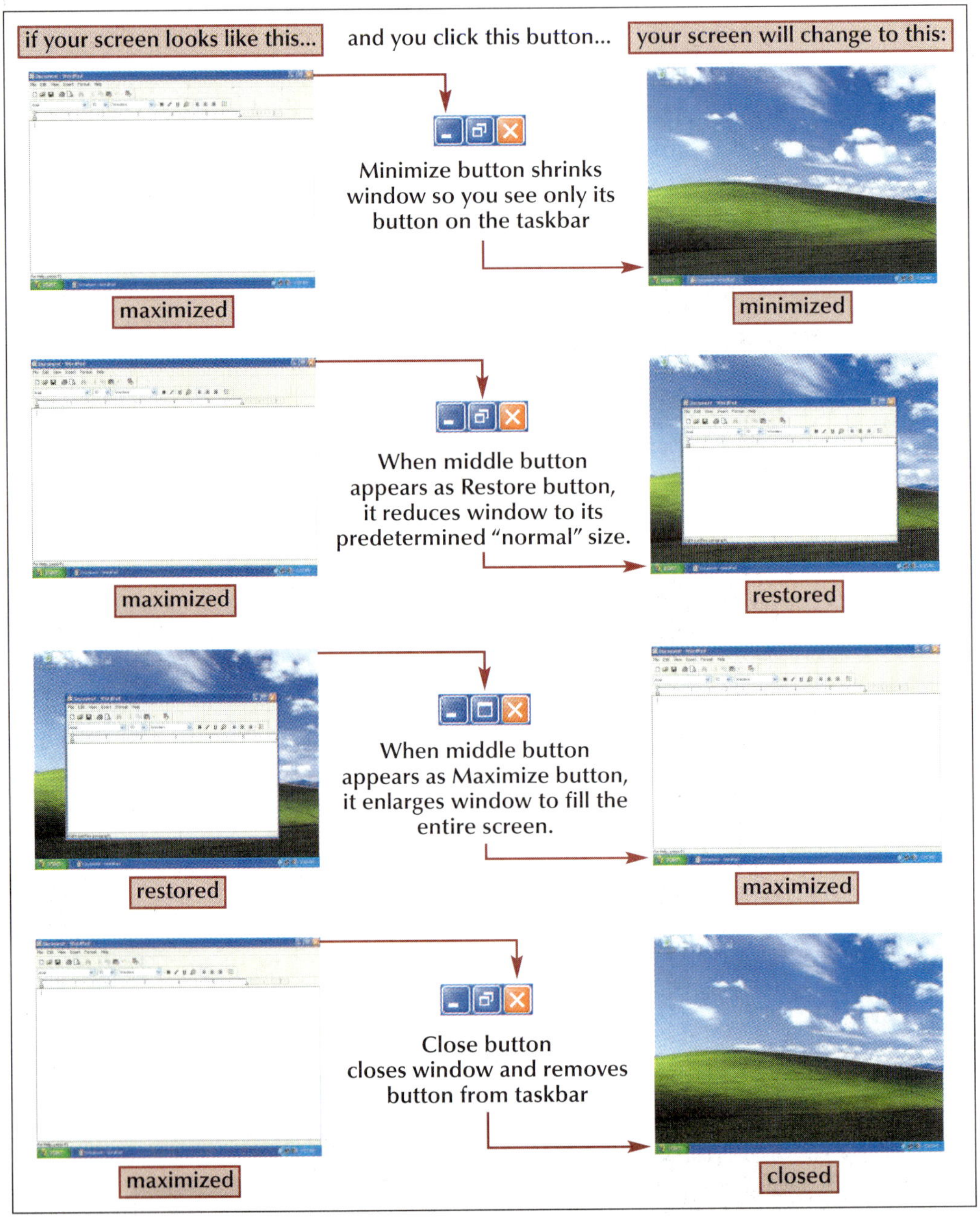

You can use the Minimize button when you want to temporarily hide a window but keep the program running.

To minimize the WordPad window:

1. Click the **Minimize** button on the WordPad title bar. The WordPad window shrinks so that only the Document - WordPad button on the taskbar is visible.

   Trouble? If the WordPad program window closed, you accidentally clicked the Close button. Use the Start button to start WordPad again, and then repeat Step 1. If you accidentally clicked the Maximize or Restore button, repeat Step 1.

You can redisplay a minimized window by clicking the program's button on the taskbar. When you redisplay a window, it becomes the active window.

To redisplay the WordPad window:

1. Click the **Document - WordPad** button on the taskbar. The WordPad window is restored to its previous size.

   The taskbar button provides another way to switch a window between its minimized and active states.

2. Click the **Document - WordPad** button on the taskbar again to minimize the window.
3. Click the **Document - WordPad** button once more to redisplay the window.

The Maximize button enlarges a window so that it fills the entire screen. You will probably do most of your work using maximized windows because they allow you to see more of the program and your data.

To maximize the WordPad window:

1. Click the **Maximize** button on the WordPad title bar.

   Trouble? If the window is already maximized, it will fill the entire screen, and the Maximize button won't appear. Instead, you'll see the Restore button. Skip Step 1.

The Restore button reduces the window so that it is smaller than the entire screen. This feature is useful if you want to see more than one window at a time. Also, because the window is smaller, you can move the window to another location on the screen or change the dimensions of the window.

To restore a window:

1. Click the **Restore** button on the WordPad title bar. Once a window is restored, the Restore button changes to the Maximize button.

You can use the mouse to move a window to a new position on the screen. When you click an object and then press and hold down the mouse button while moving the mouse, you are said to be **dragging** the object. You can move objects on the screen by dragging them to a new location. If you want to move a window, you drag the window by its title bar. You cannot move a maximized window.

To drag the restored WordPad window to a new location:

1. Position the mouse pointer on the WordPad title bar.
2. Press and hold down the left mouse button, and then move the mouse up or down a little to drag the window. The window moves as you move the mouse.
3. Position the window anywhere on the desktop, and then release the left mouse button. The WordPad window appears in the new location.
4. Drag the WordPad window to the upper-left corner of the desktop.

You can also use the mouse to change the size of a window. Notice the sizing handle at the lower-right corner of the window. The **sizing handle** provides a visible control for changing the size of a window.

To change the size of the WordPad window:

1. Position the pointer over the sizing handle in the lower-right corner of the WordPad window. The pointer changes to ↖↘. See Figure 16.

Figure 16 Preparing to resize a window

2. Press and hold down the mouse button, and then drag the sizing handle down and to the right.
3. Release the mouse button. Now the window is larger.
4. Practice using the sizing handle to make the WordPad window larger or smaller, and then maximize the WordPad window.

You can also use the resize pointer to drag the left, right, top, or bottom window borders left, right, up, or down to change a window's size in any one direction.

Selecting Options from a Menu

Most Windows XP programs use menus to organize the program's features and available functions. The menu bar is typically located at the top of the program window and shows the names of the menus, such as File, Edit, and Help. Windows XP menus are relatively standardized—most programs designed for Windows XP include similar menus. This makes it easier to learn new programs because you can make a pretty good guess about which menu contains the task you want to perform.

When you click any menu name, the choices for that menu appear below the menu bar. Like choices on the Start menu, these choices are referred to as menu commands. To select a menu command, you click it. For example, the File menu is a standard feature in most Windows XP programs and contains the commands typically related to working with a file: creating, opening, saving, and printing. Menu commands that are followed by an ellipsis open a dialog box. A **dialog box** is a special kind of window where you enter or choose settings for how you want to perform a task. For example, you use the Page Setup dialog box to set margins and some printing options. If you open a menu, and then decide not to select a command, you can close the menu by clicking its name again or pressing the Esc key.

To select the Page Setup menu command from the File menu:

1. Click **File** on the WordPad menu bar to open the File menu. See Figure 17.

Figure 17 File menu

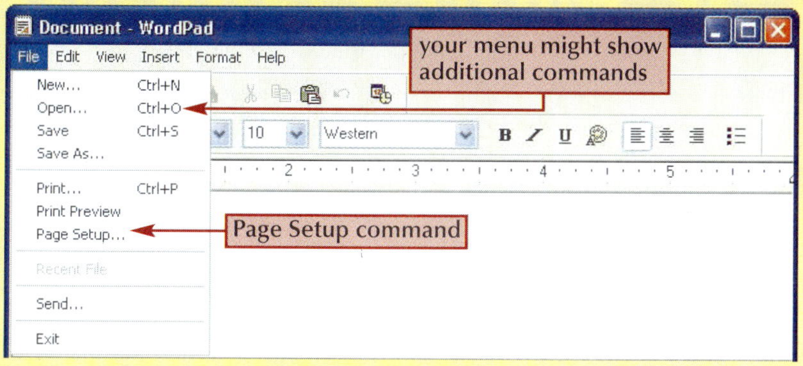

2. Click **Page Setup** to open the Page Setup dialog box.
3. After examining the dialog box, click the **Cancel** button to close the Page Setup dialog box.

   If you had selected options in the Page Setup dialog box that you wanted to retain, you would click the OK button instead of the Cancel button.

Not all menu items and commands immediately carry out an action—some show submenus or ask you for more information about what you want to do. The menu gives you visual hints about what to expect when you select an item. These hints are sometimes referred to as **menu conventions**. Figure 18 shows examples of these menu conventions.

Figure 18 Examples of menu conventions

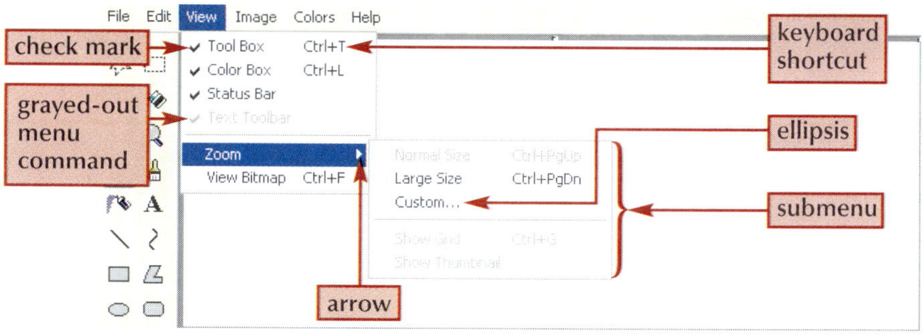

Figure 19 describes the Windows XP menu conventions.

Figure 19 Menu conventions

Convention	Description
Check mark	Indicates a toggle, or "on-off" switch (like a light switch) that is either checked (turned on) or not checked (turned off).
Ellipsis	Three dots that indicate you must make additional selections after you select that command. Commands without dots do not require additional choices—they take effect as soon as you click them. If a command is followed by an ellipsis, a dialog box opens that allows you to enter specifications for how you want a task carried out.
Triangular arrow	Indicates the presence of a submenu. When you point to a menu option that has a triangular arrow, a submenu automatically appears.
Grayed-out command	Command that is not currently available. For example, a graphics program might display the Text Toolbar command in gray if there is no text in the graphic to work with.
Keyboard shortcut	A key or combination of keys that you can press to select the menu command without actually opening the menu.

Using Toolbars

Although you can usually perform all program commands by using menus, you also have one-click access to frequently used commands on the toolbars in the program window. Using the buttons on the toolbars, you can quickly access common commands. Just as menu commands are grouped on menus according to task, the buttons on a toolbar are also grouped and organized by task.

Recall that Windows XP programs often display ScreenTips, which indicate the purpose and function of a window component such as a button. You'll explore the WordPad toolbar buttons by looking at their ScreenTips.

To determine the names and descriptions of the buttons on the WordPad toolbar:

1. Position the pointer over the **Print Preview** button on the WordPad toolbar. After a short pause, the ScreenTip for the button appears below the button, and a description of the button appears in the status bar just above the Start button.

   Trouble? If you closed WordPad after the previous set of steps, restart the program.

2. Move the pointer to each button on the toolbar to display its name and purpose.

You select a toolbar button by clicking it, which performs the button's command. One of the buttons you pointed to on the WordPad toolbar is called the Undo button. Clicking the Undo button reverses the effects of your last action.

To use the Undo button on the WordPad toolbar:

1. Type your name in the WordPad window.
2. Click the **Undo** button on the WordPad toolbar. WordPad reverses your last action by removing your name from the WordPad window.

Besides menus and toolbars, windows can contain list boxes and scroll bars, which you'll learn about next.

Using List Boxes and Scroll Bars

As you might guess from the name, a **list box** displays a list of available choices from which you can select one item. In WordPad, you can choose a date and time format from the Available formats list box in the Date/Time dialog box. List box controls usually include arrow buttons, a scroll bar, and a scroll box. A scroll bar appears when the list of available options is too long or wide to fit in the list box. The arrows and scroll box enable you to move through the complete list.

To use the Date/Time list box:

1. Click the **Date/Time** button on the WordPad toolbar to open the Date and Time dialog box, which lists the current date in many formats. See Figure 20.

List box — **Figure 20**

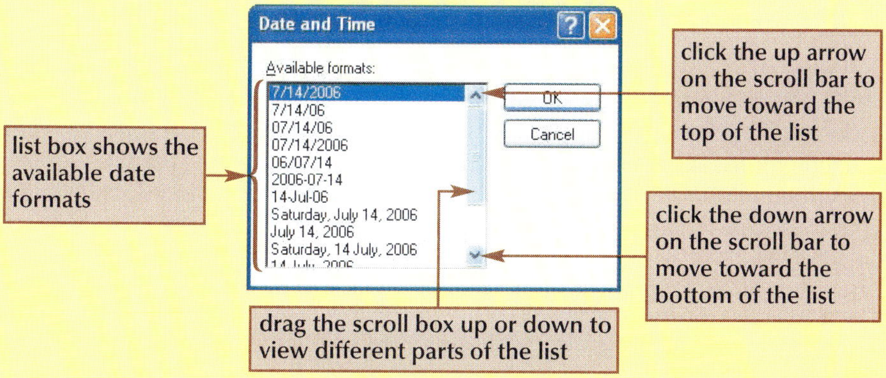

2. To scroll down the list, click the **down arrow** button on the scroll bar three times.
3. Drag the **scroll box** to the top of the scroll bar by pointing to the scroll box, pressing and holding down the left mouse button, dragging the scroll box up, and then releasing the left mouse button. The list scrolls back to the beginning.
4. Find a date format similar to "July 14, 2006" in the Available formats list box, and then click that date format to select it.
5. Click the **OK** button to close the Date and Time dialog box. The current date is inserted into your document.

A list box is helpful because it only includes options that are appropriate for your current task. For example, you can select only dates and times in the available formats from the list box in the Date and Time dialog box—no matter which format you choose, WordPad will recognize it. Sometimes a list might not include every possible option, so you can type the option you want to select. In this case, the list box includes a **list arrow** on its right side. You can click the list arrow to view options and then select one, or you can type appropriate text.

Buttons can also have list arrows. The list arrow indicates that there is more than one option for that button. Rather than crowding the window with a lot of buttons, one for each possible option, including a list arrow on a button organizes its options logically and compactly into a list. Toolbars often include list boxes and buttons with list arrows. For example, the Font Size button list box on the WordPad toolbar includes a list arrow. To select an option other than the one shown in the list box or on the button, you click the list arrow, and then click the option that you want to use.

To select a new font size from the Font Size button list box:

1. Click the **Font Size** button list arrow 10 on the WordPad toolbar.
2. Click **18**. The Font Size list closes, and the font size you selected appears in the list box.
3. Type a few characters to test the new font size.
4. Click the **Font Size** button list arrow 10 on the WordPad toolbar again.
5. Click **12**.
6. Type a few characters to test this type size. The text appears in the smaller font size.

Dialog boxes also contain scroll bars and list boxes. You'll examine a typical dialog box next.

Working with Dialog Boxes

Recall that when you select a menu command or item followed by an ellipsis, a dialog box opens that allows you to provide more information about how a program should carry out a task. Some dialog boxes organize different kinds of information into bordered rectangular areas called groups. Within these groups, you will usually find tabs, option buttons, check boxes, and other controls that the program uses to collect information about how you want it to perform a task. Figure 21 displays examples of common dialog box controls.

Figure 21 **Examples of dialog box controls**

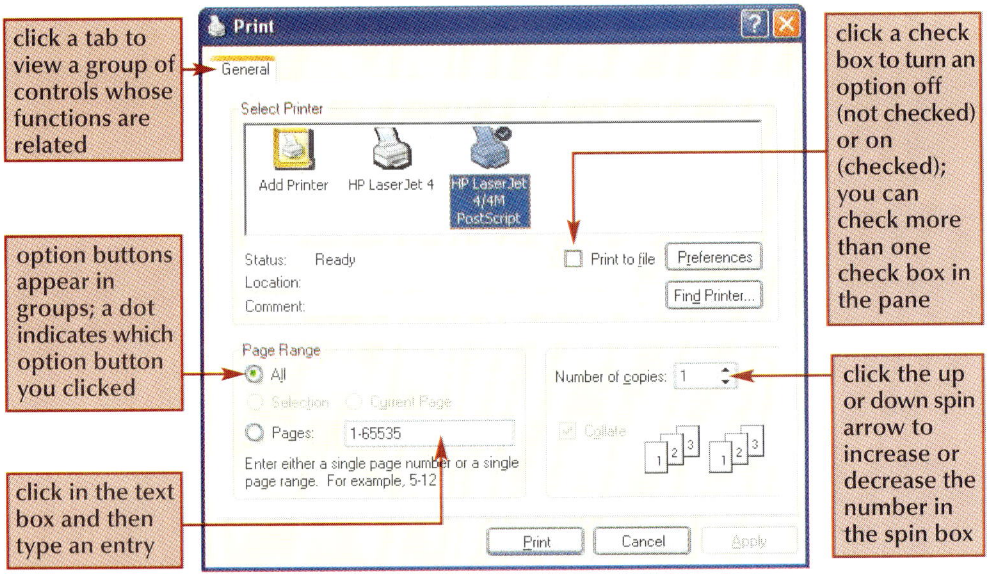

Now you can open a typical Windows XP dialog box in WordPad. To learn how dialog box controls work, you'll open the Options dialog box, which you use to determine how text fits in the WordPad window and which toolbars appear. You'll remove the check mark from a check box and select an option button, and then see how these settings affect the WordPad window. Note that by default the status bar appears at the bottom of the WordPad window and that the ruler uses inches.

To work with a typical Windows XP dialog box:

1. Click **View** on the WordPad menu bar, and then click **Options**. The Options dialog box opens, by default, to the Rich Text tab.

   Trouble? If the Options dialog box does not display the Rich Text options, click the Rich Text tab.
2. Click the **Status bar** check box to remove the check mark.
3. Click the **Options** tab to select the measurement units that the WordPad ruler uses.
4. Click the **Centimeters** option button.
5. Click the **OK** button. WordPad accepts your changes and closes the Options dialog box.

Examine the WordPad window and note that the ruler now uses centimeters instead of inches and the status bar no longer appears at the bottom of the window. You can use the Options dialog box again to restore the WordPad window to its original condition.

To restore the WordPad window:

1. Click **View** on the WordPad menu bar, and then click **Options**. The Options dialog box opens.
2. On the Rich Text tab, click the **Status bar** check box to insert a check mark.
3. Click the **Options** tab, and then click the **Inches** option button.
4. Click the **OK** button. The WordPad window now includes a status bar and a ruler that uses inches as its measurement unit.
5. Click the **Close** button on the WordPad title bar to close WordPad.
6. When you see the message "Save changes to Document?" click the **No** button.

In this session, you started Windows XP and toured the desktop, learning how to interact with the items on the desktop and on the Start menu. You also started two Windows programs, manipulated windows, and learned how to select options from a menu, toolbar, and dialog box.

Session 1 Quick Check

Review

1. What is the purpose of the taskbar?
2. What is a ScreenTip?
3. The ______________ is a list of options that provides you with access to programs, documents, submenus, and more.
4. Which feature of Windows XP allows you to run more than one program at a time?
5. Even if you can't see an open program on your desktop, the program might be running. How can you tell if a program is running?
6. Why should you close each program when you are finished using it?
7. A(n) ______________ consists of a group of buttons, each of which provides one-click access to important program functions.
8. A(n) ______________ is helpful because it only includes options that are appropriate for your current task.

Session 2

Exploring Your Computer

To discover the contents and resources on your computer, you explore, or navigate, it. **Navigating**, in this context, means to move from one location to another on your computer, such as from one window to another. Windows XP provides two different ways to navigate, view, and work with the contents and resources on your computer—My Computer and Windows Explorer.

Navigating with My Computer

The My Computer icon on the Start menu represents your computer, its storage devices, printers, and other objects. The My Computer icon opens the My Computer window, which contains an icon for each of the storage devices on your computer, as shown in Figure 22. These icons appear in the right pane of the My Computer window. By default, the My Computer window also has a left pane, which shows icons and links to other resources. You'll learn more about the left pane shortly.

Figure 22 Relationship between computer and My Computer window

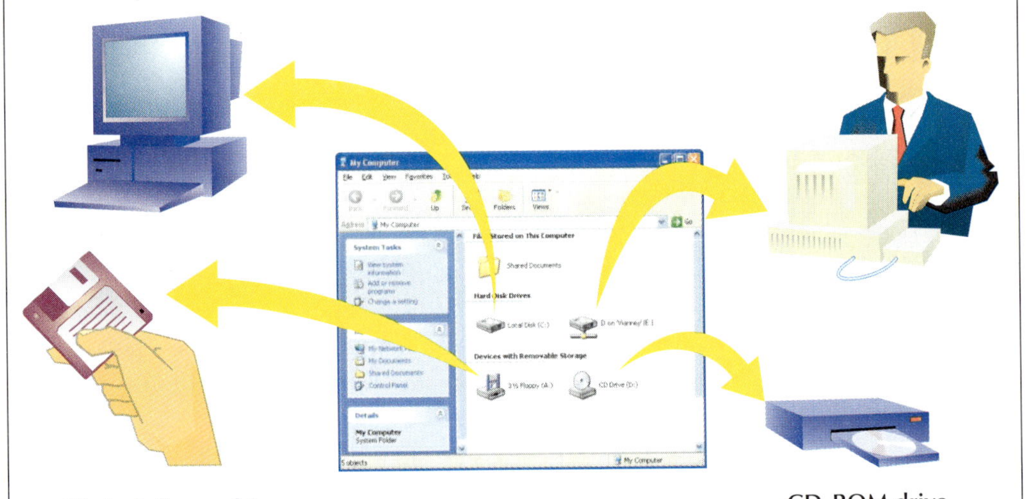

Each storage device you have access to on your computer has a letter associated with it. The first floppy drive on a computer is usually designated as drive A (if you add a second drive, it is usually designated as drive B), and the first hard drive is usually designated as drive C (if you add additional hard drives, they are usually designated D, E, and so on). If you have a CD or DVD drive, it usually has the next letter in the alphabetic sequence. If you have access to hard drives located on other computers in a network, those drives will sometimes (although not always) have letters associated with them as well. Naming conventions for network drives vary. In the example shown in Figure 22, the network drive has the drive letter E.

You can use the My Computer window to keep track of where your files are stored and to organize your files. In this session, you will explore the contents of your hard disk, which is assumed to be located in drive C. If you use a different drive on your computer, such as drive E, substitute its letter for "C" throughout this session.

Now you'll open the My Computer window and explore the contents of your computer.

To explore the contents of your computer using the My Computer window:

1. If you took a break after the previous session, make sure that your computer is on and Windows XP is running.
2. Click the **Start** button on the taskbar, and then click **My Computer**. The My Computer window opens. See Figure 23. Your window might look different. For example, in addition to the Shared Documents folder, your window probably lists folders with names for each user on your computer, such as "Andrea's Documents."

My Computer window | **Figure 23**

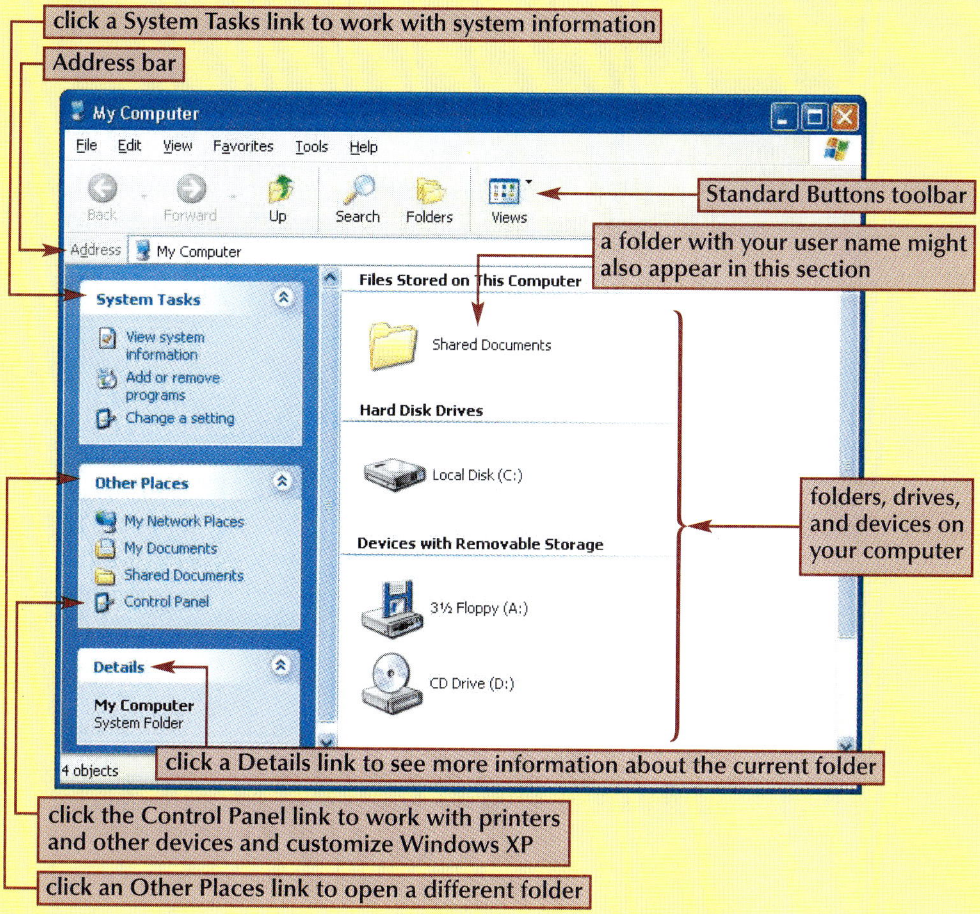

3. In the Files Stored on This Computer section, double-click the folder with your user name. A window opens showing the contents of that folder. See Figure 24.

Figure 24 Contents of the folder with your user name

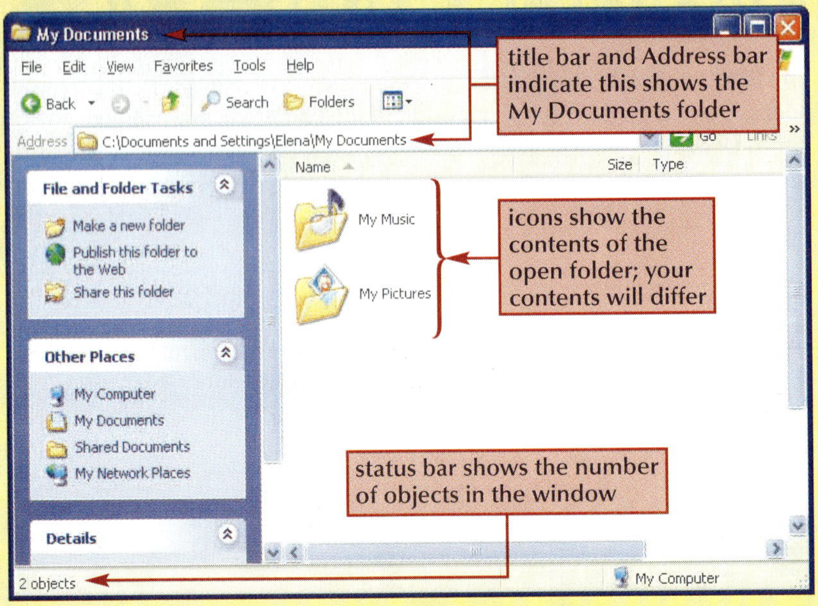

Trouble? If your window looks different from Figure 24, you can still perform the rest of the steps. For example, your window might contain additional folders and files.

Trouble? If you see a list of folder names or filenames instead of icons, click View on the menu bar, and then click Tiles.

Trouble? If the status bar does not appear in your window, click View on the menu bar, and then click Status Bar.

4. Double-click each folder in the My Documents window until you find one that contains files. Record the name of the folder you opened. Your window will be similar to the one shown in Figure 25, which shows the contents of the My Music folder.

Figure 25 Viewing files in a folder

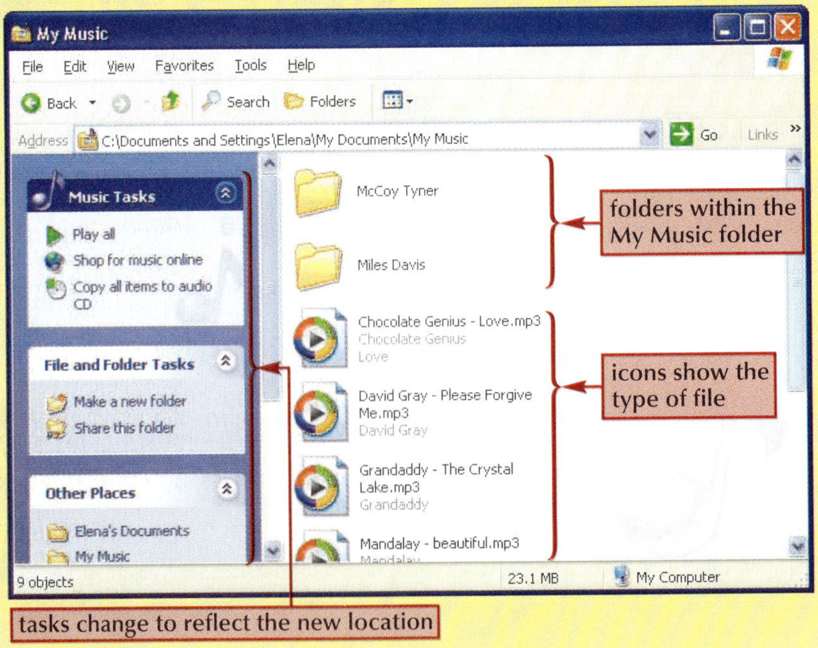

The tasks in the left pane change so that they are appropriate for the new location—in Figure 25, the left pane lists music tasks and other folders you might want to open. The right pane shows the contents of the folder you double-clicked. The file icon indicates its type. In Figure 25, the icon indicates that these are music files.

You can change the appearance of most windows to suit your preferences. You'll change the view of the My Computer window next.

Changing the View

Windows XP offers several options that control how toolbars, icons, and buttons appear in the My Computer window. The My Computer window, in addition to featuring a Standard Buttons toolbar, allows you to display the same toolbars that can appear on the Windows XP taskbar, such as the Address bar or the Links toolbar. You can use these toolbars to access the Web from the My Computer window. In this tutorial, however, you need to see only the Address bar and Standard Buttons toolbar.

To display only the Address bar and Standard Buttons toolbar:

1. Click **View** on the menu bar, and then point to **Toolbars**. The Standard Buttons and Address Bar commands on the Toolbars submenu should be checked, indicating that they are displayed in the My Computer window. The Links option should not be checked.
2. If the Standard Buttons or Address Bar commands *are not checked*, click the command to select it. Or if the Links command *is checked*, click it to deselect it. You must display the Toolbars submenu to select or deselect each command.
3. If necessary, click **View** on the menu bar, and then point to **Toolbars**. Make sure that only Standard Buttons, Address Bar, and Lock the Toolbars are checked.
4. Press the **Esc** key twice to close the menus.

Windows XP also provides five ways to view the contents of a disk—Thumbnails, Tiles, Icons, List, and Details. The default view, Tiles view, displays a large icon, title, file type, and file size for each file. The icon provides a visual cue to the type of file. You can also find this same information with the smaller icons displayed in the Icons and List views, but in less screen space. In Icons and List views, you can see more files and folders at one time, which is helpful when you have many files in one location.

All of the three icon views (Tiles, Icons, and List) help you quickly identify a file and its type, but what if you want more information about a set of files? Details view shows more information than the other three views. Details view shows the file icon, filename, file size, program used to create the file, and the date and time the file was created or last modified.

If you have graphic files, you can use Thumbnails view, which displays a small preview image of the graphic. In Thumbnails view, you can quickly see not only the filename, but also which picture or drawing the file contains. Thumbnails view is great for browsing a large collection of graphic files, but switching to this view can be time-consuming because Windows XP must first create all the preview images.

To practice switching from one view to another, you'll start by displaying the contents of the folder you opened earlier in Details view. So far, you've used the View menu to change the window view. Now you can use the Views button, which displays the same commands for changing views as the View menu.

To view a detailed list of files:

1. Click the **Views** button on the Standard Buttons toolbar, and then click **Details** to display details for the files on your disk. See Figure 26. Your files might differ or be listed in a different order.

Figure 26 Details view

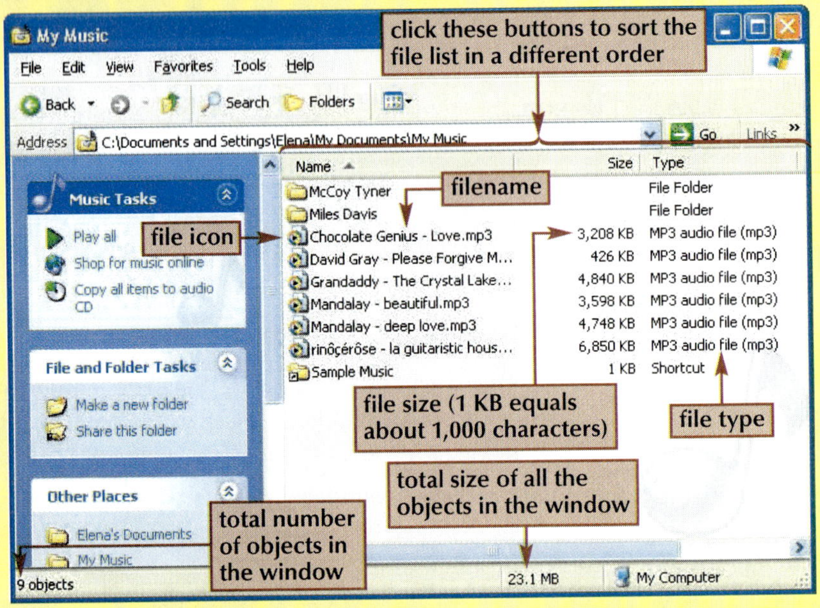

2. Look at the file sizes. Which files are the largest?
3. Look at the Type column. Which file is a shortcut?

Note that in Figure 26, the Sample Music item is a **shortcut**, a special type of file that serves as a direct link to another location that your computer can access, such as a folder, a document in a file, a program, a Windows tool, or a Web site.

One of the advantages of Details view is that you can sort the file list by filename, size, type, or date. This helps if you're looking for a particular file in a long file listing. For example, suppose you know that you created a file recently, but can't remember its name. You could sort the file list by date so that the most recent files appear at the top of the list.

To sort the file list by date:

1. Click **View** on the menu bar, click **Choose Details**, click the **Date Modified** check box if it is not checked, and then click the **OK** button.
2. Click the **Date Modified** button at the top of the list of files. The files are now sorted in descending order by date, starting with the most recent files.
3. Click the **Date Modified** button again. The sort order is reversed, with the oldest files now at the top of the list.
4. Click the **Name** button at the top of the file list. The files are now sorted in alphabetical order by filename.

Now that you have looked at the file details, you can switch back to Tiles view.

To switch to Tiles view:

1. Click the **Views** button on the Standard Buttons toolbar, and then click **Tiles** to return to Tiles view.
2. Click the **Close** button to close the window.

Now you can compare My Computer to Windows Explorer, another navigation tool.

Navigating with Windows Explorer

Like My Computer, Windows Explorer also lets you easily navigate the resources on your computer. Many of the techniques you use with the My Computer window apply to Windows Explorer—and vice versa. Both let you display and work with files and folders. By default, however, Windows Explorer also lets you see the hierarchy of all the folders on your computer. Viewing this hierarchy makes it easier to navigate your computer, especially if it contains many files and folders.

You will use Windows Explorer to open the same folders you opened in My Computer. As with other Windows XP programs, you start Windows Explorer using the Start menu.

To start Windows Explorer:

1. Click the **Start** button on the taskbar, point to **All Programs**, point to **Accessories**, and then click **Windows Explorer**. The Windows Explorer window opens, as shown in Figure 27. By default, this window shows the contents of your My Documents folder when you first open it.

Windows Explorer window | Figure 27

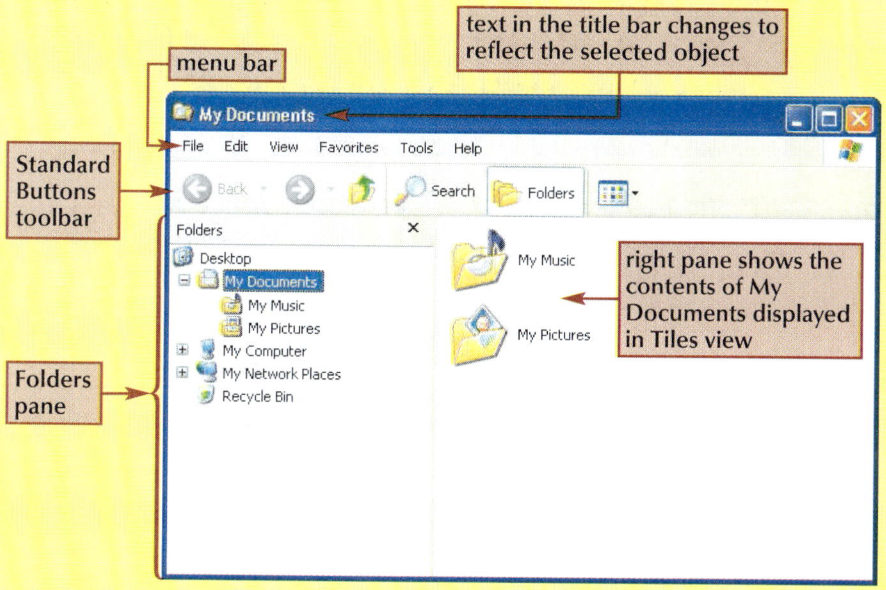

Trouble? If your Windows Explorer window looks slightly different from the one displayed in Figure 27, the configuration of your computer probably differs from the computer used to take this figure. Continue with Step 2.

2. If the Windows Explorer window is not maximized, click the **Maximize** button on the Windows Explorer title bar.

Windows Explorer is divided into two sections called **panes**. The left pane, also called the **Explorer bar**, shows different ways of locating specific files or folders on your computer. The right pane lists the contents of these files and folders, similar to the view of files and folders in My Computer.

The Explorer bar can be displayed in one of five ways: as a Search, Favorites, Media, History, or Folders pane. The Search pane includes tools to help you search for a particular file or folder on your computer. The Favorites pane lists your favorite files and folders on your computer and sites on the World Wide Web. The Media pane lists multimedia files, such as videos and music. The History pane organizes the files and folders on your computer by the date you last worked with them. The Folders pane organizes your files and folders based on their location in the hierarchy of objects on your computer. To move between these different panes, you click the appropriate command on the View menu. You can also quickly open the Search and Folders panes by clicking either the Search button or the Folders button on the Standard Buttons toolbar. Note that the Explorer bar is available in any Windows XP window that displays files and folders. You can, for example, use the Explorer bar in the My Computer window.

You'll start working with Windows Explorer using the Folders pane.

To view the Folders pane:

1. Click **View** on the menu bar, and then point to **Explorer Bar**.
2. If necessary, click **Folders** to check that option; otherwise, click a blank area of the screen to close the View menu. Your Windows Explorer window should now resemble Figure 28.

Figure 28 **Folders pane in the Windows Explorer window**

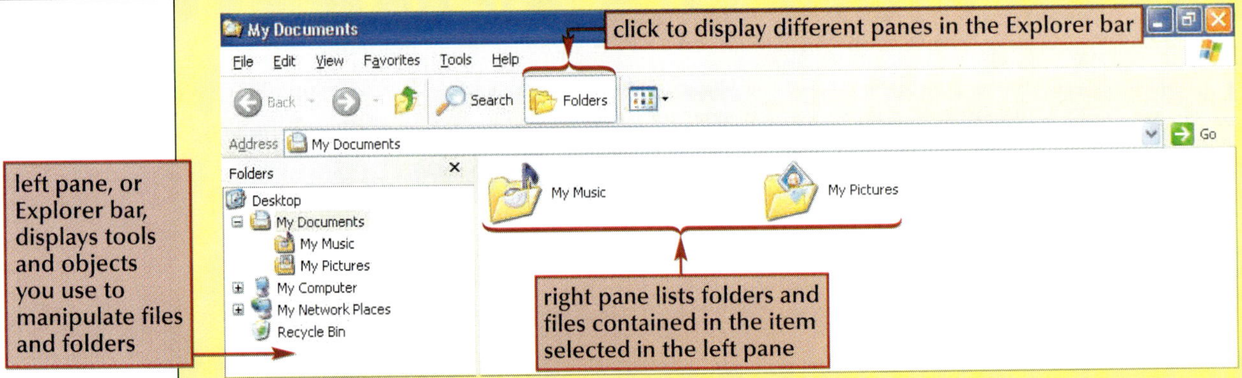

Trouble? If your Windows Explorer window looks slightly different from the one displayed in Figure 28, the configuration of your computer probably differs from the computer used to take this figure. For example, you might have different folders listed in the left and right panes of the window.

The Folders pane initially displays a list of the objects on your desktop: the My Documents folder, the My Computer window, the My Network Places window, and the Recycle Bin. If your desktop contains other folders or objects, those are displayed as well. The right pane of the Windows Explorer window displays the contents of the object selected in the Folders pane. In this case, the My Documents folder is the selected object, and it contains two items—the My Music and My Pictures folders. Icons for these objects are therefore displayed in the right pane.

Now you can open the same folder you opened before in the My Computer window.

To open a folder:

1. Double-click the folder you double-clicked earlier in the My Computer window, such as the My Music folder. The contents of that folder appear in the right pane of the Windows Explorer window, and the folder you opened is selected in the left pane.
2. Click the **Close** button on the title bar to close the window.

Getting Help

Windows XP **Help** provides on-screen information about the program you are using. Help for the Windows XP operating system is available by clicking the Start button on the taskbar and then clicking Help and Support on the Start menu. If you want Help for a particular program, such as WordPad, you must first start the program, and then click Help on the program's menu bar.

When you start Help for Windows XP, a Windows Help and Support Center window opens, which gives you access to Help files stored on your computer as well as Help information stored on Microsoft's Web site. If you are not connected to the Web, you only have access to the Help files stored on your computer.

To start Windows XP Help:

1. Click the **Start** button on the taskbar.
2. Click **Help and Support**. The Help and Support Center window opens. See Figure 29.

Figure 29 Windows XP Help and Support Center window

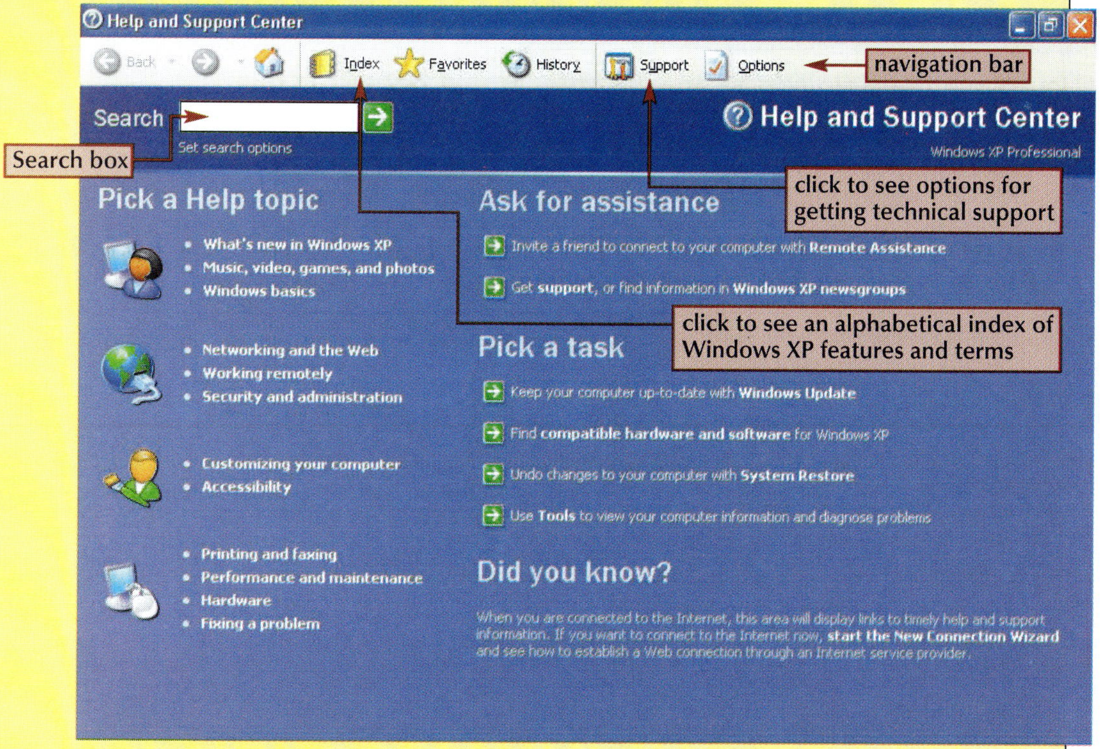

Trouble? If the Help and Support window does not display the information you see in Figure 29, click the Home icon on the navigation bar at the top of the window to view Help contents.

The Windows XP Help and Support Center window organizes the vast amount of help and support information into pages. These six pages—the Home, Index, Favorites, History, Support, and Options page—are designed to aid users in locating information on a particular topic quickly. To open one of these pages, click its button on the navigation bar. The Home page lists common tasks under the heading "Pick a Help topic" in the left pane on the page. Click a task to see detailed information or instructions about that task in the right pane of the page. The right pane of the Home page lists common tasks, tips, and ways you can ask for assistance. For example, you can contact a support professional or download the latest version of Windows XP.

The Index page displays an alphabetical list of all the Help topics from which you can choose. The Favorites page shows Help topics you've added to your Favorites list. To add a topic to the Favorites list, open the topic, and then click the Favorites button on the Help window. The History page lists links you've recently selected in Help. The Support page includes links that you can click to connect to the Microsoft Web site, if possible, for additional assistance. The Options page provides ways you can customize Help. For example, you can change the appearance of the navigation bar.

If you can't find the topic you want listed on any of the six Help and Support Center pages, the word that you are using for a feature or topic might be different from the word that Windows XP uses. You can use the Search box to search for all keywords contained in the Help pages, not just the topic titles. In the Search box, you can type any word or phrase, click the Search button, and Windows XP lists all the Help topics that contain that word or phrase.

Viewing Topics on the Windows XP Help and Support Center Home Page

Windows XP Help includes instructions on using Help itself. You can learn how to find a Help topic by using the Help and Support Center Home page.

To use the Help and Support Center Home page:

1. Click **Windows basics**. A list of topics related to using Windows XP appears in the left pane of the Help and Support Center window.
2. Click **Tips for using Help**. A list of Help topics appears in the right pane of the Help window.
3. Click **Change fonts in Help and Support Center**. The instructions appear in the right pane of the Help and Support Center window.

   Besides listing the pages in the Help and Support Center window, the navigation bar contains two buttons—the Back button and the Forward button. You use these buttons to navigate the pages you've already opened. You'll use the Back button next to return to the previous page you viewed. Once you do, you activate the Forward button, which you can click to go to the next page of those you've opened.

4. Click the **Back** button on the navigation bar. You return to the Tips for using Help page. The Forward button is now active.

Selecting a Topic from the Index

The Index page allows you to jump to a Help topic by selecting a topic from an alphabetical list. For example, you can use the Index page to learn how to arrange open windows on your desktop.

To find a Help topic using the Index page:

1. Click **Index** on the navigation bar. A long list of indexed Help topics appears in the left pane.
2. Drag the **scroll box** down to view additional topics in the list box.

   You can quickly jump to any part of the list by typing the first few characters of a word or phrase in the box that appears above the Index list.
3. If necessary, click in the Type in the keyword to find text box above the Index list, and then type **windows**. As you type each character in the word, the list of Index topics scrolls and eventually displays topics that relate to windows.
4. Under the "windows and panes on your computer screen" topic, click the topic **reducing windows to taskbar buttons**, and then click the **Display** button. When there is just one topic, it appears immediately in the right pane; otherwise, the Topics Found window opens, listing all topics indexed under the selected entry.

   The information you requested appears in the right pane. This topic has two underlined phrases, "taskbar" and "Related Topics," which you can click to view definitions or additional information.
5. Click the underlined phrase **taskbar**. A ScreenTip shows the definition of "taskbar."
6. Click a blank area of the Help and Support Center window to close the ScreenTip.

If you have an Internet connection, you can use another Help page, Support, to contact Microsoft support or get in touch with other users of Windows XP. The Support page works like the Home page. To get support on a particular feature, you click a support option and then click the topic for which you need help. Continue clicking topics, if necessary, until you get help from a Microsoft support person or an experienced Windows XP user.

Searching the Help Pages

If you can't find the topic you need by using the Home or Index pages, or if you want to quickly find Help pages related to a particular topic, you can use the Search box. Suppose you want to know how to exit Windows XP, but you don't know if Windows refers to this as exiting, quitting, closing, or shutting down. You can search the Help pages to find just the right topic.

To search the Help pages for information on exiting Windows XP:

1. Click in the Search box. A blinking insertion point appears.
2. Type **shutdown** and then click the **Start Searching** button. A list of Help pages containing the word "shutdown" appears in the left pane of the Help and Support Center window. The ones listed under Suggested Topics are topics where "shutdown" has been assigned as a keyword—meaning the topics have to do with shutting something down.
3. Click the **Full-text Search Matches** button. In these topics, "shutdown" is included in the text of the Help topic.
4. Click the **Suggested Topics** button, and then click **Turn off the computer**. A Help topic appears in the right pane of the Help and Support Center window, as shown in Figure 30.

Figure 30 Using search to find a Help page

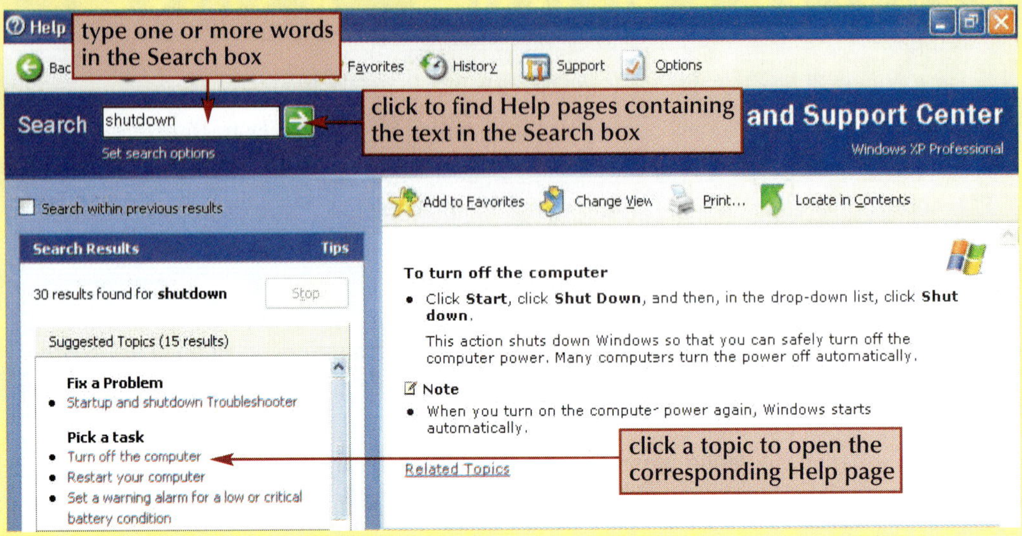

If this topic were longer than the Help and Support Center window, you could use the scroll bar to read the entire topic.

5. Click the **Close** button on the title bar to close the Help and Support Center window.

Now that you know how Windows XP Help works, don't forget to use it. Use Help when you need to perform a new task or when you forget how to complete a procedure.

Shutting Down Windows XP

You should always shut down Windows XP before you turn off your computer. If you turn off your computer without shutting it down correctly, you might lose data and damage your files.

Typically you will use the Turn Off Computer command on the Start menu when you want to turn off your computer. However, your school might prefer that you select the Log Off command on the Start menu. This command logs you out of Windows XP but leaves the computer turned on, allowing another user to log on without restarting the computer. Check with your instructor or technical support person for the preferred method at your lab.

When you select the Turn Off Computer command on the Start menu, the Turn Off Computer dialog box opens with four buttons: Standby, Turn Off, Restart, and Cancel. You choose Standby when you want to put your computer into an idle state in which it consumes less power, but is still available for immediate use. Choose Turn Off to shut down Windows and turn off the power, and choose Restart to shut down Windows and then immediately start it again. Choose Cancel if you do not want to end your Windows session, but want to return to your previous task.

To shut down Windows XP:

1. Click the **Start** button on the taskbar.
2. Click the **Turn Off Computer** command at the bottom of the Start menu. The Turn Off Computer dialog box opens. See Figure 31.

Figure 31

Shutting down the computer

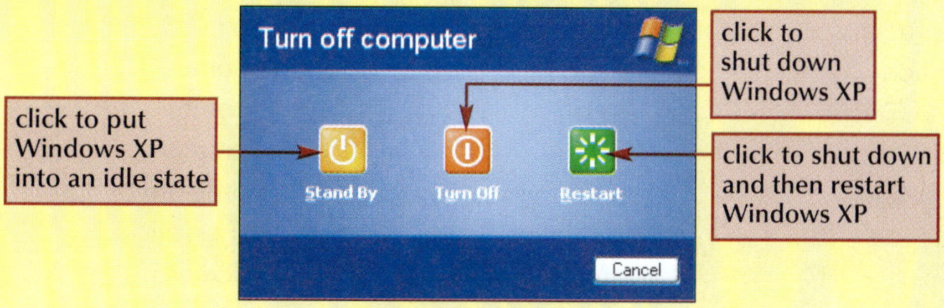

Trouble? If you are supposed to log off rather than shut down, click Log Off instead and follow your school's logoff procedure.

3. Click the **Turn Off** button.
4. Wait until you see a message indicating that it is safe to turn off your computer. If your lab procedure includes switching off your computer after shutting it down, do so now; otherwise, leave the computer running. Some computers turn themselves off automatically.

In this session you learned how to start and close programs and how to use multiple programs at the same time. You learned how to work with windows and the controls they employ. Finally, you learned how to get help when you need it and shut down Windows XP. After completing Steve's introductory course, you are well on your way to mastering the fundamentals of using the Windows XP operating system.

Session 2 Quick Check

Review

1. The ______________ icon on the Start menu represents your computer, its storage devices, printers, and other objects.
2. Explain the difference between the left pane in My Computer (the Tasks pane) and the Folders pane in Windows Explorer.
3. What information does Details view supply about a list of folders and files?
4. True or false: A shortcut is a special type of file that serves as a direct link to another location that your computer can access, such as a folder or a document in a file.
5. Name the five ways that you can display the Explorer bar in Windows Explorer.
6. In the Help and Support Center window, the ______________ page displays an alphabetical list of all the Help topics from which you can choose.
7. To learn how to perform new tasks, you can use ______________.
8. You should always ______________ Windows XP before you turn off your computer.

Tutorial Summary

Review

In this tutorial, you learned the basics of Windows XP. You toured the desktop and learned how to open objects on the desktop. You explored the Start menu and opened its submenus. You started programs from the Start menu, and then switched between multiple programs. You worked with windows by manipulating them. You selected options from a menu and buttons on a toolbar. You also examined typical dialog boxes and their controls. Then you explored your computer with My Computer and Windows Explorer, learned how to get help when you need it, and finally shut down Windows XP.

Key Terms

active program
application
click
control
Control Panel
default
desktop
dialog box
double-click
drag
exit
Explorer bar
graphical user interface (GUI)
Help
Help and Support Center
icon
Internet
list arrow
list box
log off
menu
menu command
menu convention
Microsoft Windows XP
most frequently used programs list
mouse
multitask
My Computer
My Documents
navigate
operating system
pane
password
pinned items list
point
pointing device
program
program button
right-click
ScreenTip
select
shortcut
shortcut menu
sizing handle
Start menu
submenu
user name
window
Windows XP

Practice

Practice the skills you learned in the tutorial.

Review Assignments

There are no Data Files needed for the Review Assignments.

Steve Laslow offers a practice session as a follow-up to his basic Windows XP course. You'll start working on the Windows XP desktop, with no windows opened or minimized. Complete the following steps, recording your answers to any questions according to your instructor's preferences:

1. Start Windows XP and log on, if necessary.
2. Use the mouse to point to each object on your desktop. Record the names of each object as they appear in the ScreenTips.
3. Click the Start button. How many menu items or commands are on the Start menu?
4. Run the WordPad program located on the Accessories menu. How many program buttons are now on the taskbar (don't count toolbar buttons or items in the notification area)?
5. Run the Paint program and maximize the Paint window. How many programs are running now?
6. Switch to WordPad. What are two visual clues that tell you that WordPad is the active program?
7. Close WordPad, and then restore the Paint window.
8. Open the Recycle Bin window. Record the number of items it contains.
9. Drag the Recycle Bin window so that you can see it and the Paint window.
10. Close the Paint window from the taskbar.
11. Open the File menu in the Recycle Bin window. Write down the commands on the menu. Press the Esc key to close the menu.
12. Use any menu in the Recycle Bin window to open a dialog box. What steps did you perform? What dialog box did you open? For what do you think you use this dialog box? Click Cancel to close the dialog box.
13. Close the Recycle Bin window.

14. Open the My Computer window, and then open the My Documents folder that is designed to contain your documents.
15. Open a folder in the My Documents window that you did not open in the tutorial. List the name and contents of that folder.
16. Close the My Documents window.
17. Start Windows Explorer. Use the Folders pane to navigate to the same folder you opened in Step 14. What steps did you perform?
18. Change the view of the icons in the right pane of the Windows Explorer window. What view did you select? Describe the icons in the Windows Explorer window.
19. Close the Windows Explorer window.
20. Open the Help and Support Center window.
21. Use the Help and Support Center window to learn something new about Windows Explorer. What did you learn? How did you find this topic?
22. Use the Index page to find information about the topic of speech recognition, a feature new to Windows XP. How many topics are listed? What is their primary subject matter?
23. Use the Search box to find information about the topic of speech recognition. How many topics are listed?
24. Open the Home page in the Help and Support Center window, click What's new in Windows XP, and then click Windows XP Articles: Walkthrough ways to use your PC.
25. Click Walkthrough: Making Music.
26. Read the Get Started page. (*Hint:* The contents of the article are listed in a box in the upper-left corner of the window. Each topic is a link you can click to go to another page in the article.)
27. Click the links in the contents box, and then answer the following questions using the information you find:
    a. How can you listen to music using Windows XP?
    b. What is a playlist? What is the first step you take to create one?
    c. What is the advantage of listening to Internet radio?
28. Close Help, and then close WordPad.
29. Shut down or log off Windows.

Apply

Use the skills you learned in the tutorial to explore the contents of other folders on your computer for JL Productions.

Case Problem 1

There are no Data Files needed for this Case Problem.

JL Productions JL Productions is a company in Fort Wayne, Indiana, that produces videos and hosts advertising events for businesses in the Midwest. You have recently been hired by Julian Letice, the owner of JL Productions, to help him with office management. Your first task is to explore Julian's new Windows XP computer. Because he is visually oriented, he is particularly interested in features that improve the appearance of his desktop or that would enhance the materials he sends to his clients. Complete the following steps:

1. Start Windows XP and log on, if necessary.
2. From the desktop or the Start menu, open My Computer, and then maximize the window.
3. **Explore** If necessary, change the My Computer window to Tiles view, arrange icons by type, and organize icons by group. (*Hint:* Click View on the menu bar, point to Arrange Icons by, and then click Show in Groups.) List the names of the drives on your computer.
4. Click the Shared Documents link in the Other Places area of the Tasks pane. What are the names of the Shared folders within this folder?
5. Display the Folders pane in the My Computer window. (*Hint:* Click the Folders button on the Standard Buttons toolbar.) Where is the Shared Documents folder located in the folder structure of your computer? Describe its relation to the My Documents folder.

6. Close the Folders pane, open the My Pictures folder, click the View as a slide show link in the Picture Tasks dynamic menu, and enjoy the slide show. When you are ready to exit the slide show, press the Esc key.
7. Navigate to a folder that contains graphics, music, or other media files, such as My Pictures or My Music. Switch to Details view. What types of files are contained in this folder?
8. Double-click the icon for one of the files in this folder. What happens? Close any windows that open.
9. Close the My Computer window, if necessary, and then start Windows Explorer. Open the Search pane in the Windows Explorer window. (*Hint:* Click the Search button on the Standard Buttons toolbar.)
10. Open the Help and Support Center window and then find and read topics that explain how to use the Search pane to find types of files.

Explore

11. Use the Search pane to find .bmp files, a common type of graphics file, on your computer. (*Hint:* Use *.bmp as the search text.) Name at least two locations where your computer stores .bmp files.
12. Close all open windows.

Apply

Apply what you learned in the tutorial to work with Windows XP installed on a computer for a landscaping business.

Case Problem 2

There are no Data Files needed for this Case Problem.

Rolling Hills Landscaping After working for a number of gardening and landscaping firms in Towson, Maryland, Elaine Rodriguez founded her own company, named Rolling Hills Landscaping. She works with property owners and businesses to create garden and landscaping designs, and contracts with local professional gardeners to plant and maintain the landscapes. She hired you to help her perform office tasks, and asks you to start by teaching her the basics of using her computer, which runs Windows XP. She especially wants to know which programs are installed on her computer and what they do. Complete the following:

1. Open the Start menu and write down the programs on the pinned items list.
2. Start one of the programs on the pinned items list and then describe what it does. Close the program.
3. Open the Start menu and write down the programs on the most frequently used programs list.
4. Start one of the programs on the most frequently used programs list and then describe what it does. Close the program.
5. Open the All Programs menu, point to the Accessories folder, and then open a program in the Accessories folder. What program did you start?
6. Use the Help and Support Center to research the program you started in Step 5. Find out how to perform a task using that program.
7. Perform the steps you researched in Step 6. What task did you complete? Write down the steps you performed and the results.
8. Close all open windows.
9. Start another program using the Start menu. Make sure the program includes a Help menu on its menu bar. Describe the steps you performed.
10. Click Help on the menu bar and then click each command on the menu until you open a window listing Help topics for this program. Describe the typical tasks users perform when they use this program.

Explore

11. If possible, perform one set of steps you researched in Step 10. Describe the task you performed and the results. Then close the program.

Challenge

Extend what you've learned to customize the My Computer window for a consumer research organization.

Case Problem 3

There are no Data Files needed for this Case Problem.

Yamamoto Research Ken Yamamoto runs a small business called Yamamoto Research, which researches and tests consumer products, focusing on those used in the home health care industry. Ken has created many files and folders on his new Windows XP computer, and asks you to catalog his options for working in the My Computer window. Complete the following steps:

1. Open the My Computer window. Open each menu in the My Computer window, and write down any items that seem related to changing the appearance of the window.
2. **Explore** Display the My Computer window so that no toolbars appear. Then restore the window to its original condition.
3. Navigate to a folder containing graphic files. Display the icons using Thumbnail view.
4. Change the view to Icons view. Describe the differences among Icons, Thumbnail, and Tiles view.
5. **Explore** In Icons view, arrange the icons by type. Then arrange them by name.
6. Switch to Details view. On the View menu, open a dialog box that lets you choose the details displayed in Details view. Note which items are currently checked.
7. **Explore** Use the Choose Details dialog box to show only the name, type, and size of the items in Details view. Close the Choose Details dialog box and then sort the contents of the My Computer window by size.
8. Use the Choose Details dialog box to restore your original settings. Then sort the contents of the My Computer window by name.
9. **Explore** On the Tools menu, click Folder Options to open the Folder Options dialog box. Select the option that uses Windows Classic folders, and then click the OK button. Describe the changes in the My Computer window.
10. Open the Folder Options dialog box again and click the Restore Defaults button.
11. Open the Help and Support Center window from the My Computer window and search for information about folder options. Find a definition of hidden files, and how to hide and show hidden files in the My Computer window. Record your findings.
12. Close all open windows.

Research

Work with the skills you've learned, and use the Internet, to provide information to a translation company.

Case Problem 4

There are no Data Files needed for this Case Problem.

Janus Translation Several years ago, Doug Janus and Mohammed Amos started a company that translates software programs so that they can be used in Europe, Asia, and South America. Doug often works from home, and recently set up a computer running Windows XP. He asks you to help him get connected to the Internet. You suggest using the Help and Support Center to find information. Doug also needs to know more about the Help and Support Center itself. Complete the following steps:

1. In the Help and Support Center, find information about the hardware and software Doug needs to connect to the Internet.
2. Use the Help and Support Center to find two ways that Doug can connect to the Internet. Describe these two methods.
3. **Explore** Choose a topic you'd like to research using the Windows XP online Help system. Look for information on your topic using the Help and Support Center Home page, Index page, Search box, and Support page. (*Hint*: Click the Support button on the navigation bar to open the Support page.) From the Support page, go to a Windows Web site forum to research your topic. (You must be connected to the Internet to complete this step.)

4. Once you've found all the information you can, compare the four methods (Home page, Index page, Search box, and Support page) of looking for information. Write a paragraph that discusses which method proved the most useful. Did you reach the same information topics using all four methods? In a second paragraph, summarize what you learned about your topic. Finally, in a third paragraph, indicate under what circumstances you'd use which method.

Assess

SAM Assessment and Training

If you have a SAM user profile, you may have access to hands-on instruction, practice, and assessment of the skills covered in this tutorial. Log in to your SAM account and go to your assignments page to see what your instructor has assigned.

Reinforce

Using a Mouse

Using a Keyboard

Lab Assignments

The New Perspectives Labs are designed to help you master some of the key concepts and skills presented in this text. The steps for completing this Lab are located on the Course Technology Web site. Log on to the Internet and use your Web browser to go to the Student Online Companion for New Perspectives Office 2003 at **www.course.com/np/office2003**. Click the Lab Assignments link, and then navigate to the assignments for this tutorial.

Review

Quick Check Answers

Session 1

1. to provide access to common tools and programs currently running
2. text that displays the purpose and function of a window component, such as a button
3. Start menu
4. multitasking
5. its button appears on the taskbar
6. to conserve computer resources such as memory
7. toolbar
8. list box

Session 2

1. My Computer
2. The Tasks pane (the left pane) of My Computer lists tasks that change so that they are appropriate for the new location. When the left pane in Windows Explorer shows the Folders pane, it shows different ways of locating specific files or folders on your computer.
3. filename, file size, file type, and date modified
4. true
5. Search, Favorites, Media, History, and Folders panes
6. Index
7. online Help or Help and Support Center
8. shut down

Browser and E-mail Basics

Introduction to Microsoft Internet Explorer and Microsoft Outlook Express

Objectives

Session 1

- Learn the relationship between the Internet and the World Wide Web
- Learn about Web pages and Web browsers
- Learn about Web addresses
- Navigate links on Web pages
- Return to Web sites using the History list
- Create and organize favorites
- Print a Web page
- Save a Web page and a graphic from a Web page

Session 2

- Learn about e-mail and e-mail software
- Send, receive, reply to, and print an e-mail message
- Gain an understanding of e-mail etiquette
- Add and delete contacts in the Address Book
- Add an attachment to a message

Lab

Case

McKiernan's Irish B&B

Susan McKiernan and her husband, Preston, moved to Lewistown, Pennsylvania, from Ballyconnell, Ireland, several years ago because Preston's company relocated its manufacturing division. In Ireland Susan's family ran a bed-and-breakfast (B&B) for many years, and eager to begin her own business, Susan decided to open a B&B in Lewistown.

The house that she and Preston bought was perfect for a B&B, having once provided lodging during the late 1800s and early 1900s for travelers. The house has three floors, a large kitchen, a large living room, and a dining room in the front of the house, separated by a large foyer. There are three bedrooms on the second floor, each with its own bathroom, and two bedrooms that share a bath on the third floor. There is also an attached barn, which has been converted into a master suite.

The business has grown steadily to the point that Preston now manages the front desk while Susan attends to the daily running of the inn. Most of their business comes by word of mouth, and they have decided to expand using more formal marketing channels. Susan and Preston have recently hired an advertising firm, Capital Ads Online, to develop a marketing campaign that will utilize the Internet as an advertising medium. Next week, Susan, who will be responsible for implementing and managing the inn's Web site, will meet with Martha Kent, the account executive at Capital Ads assigned to the McKiernans' account. In preparation for the meeting, Martha suggested that Susan view the design and layout of Web sites for other B&Bs to give her some ideas for her own advertisements on the Internet. Martha also gave Susan her e-mail address so they can communicate electronically.

You work for Susan and Preston as an intern, getting hands-on experience in the hotel management industry. They want you to help Susan prepare for her meeting with Martha by researching other B&Bs that advertise using the Internet. You explain to them that, although you are familiar with computers, you haven't spent much time

Student Data Files

▼**BEB folder**

▽ Tutorial folder
B&B Ideas.doc

▽ Review folder
(no starting Data Files)

▽ Cases folder
(no starting Data Files)

"surfing" the Internet. Susan is familiar with computers and the Internet. She will help you get up to speed and familiarize you with the kind of information she wants you to research. Your goal is to learn as much as you can about using the Internet and the World Wide Web for finding information and about communicating using electronic mail.

Session 1

The Internet: World Wide Web

The Internet and the World Wide Web

The **Internet**, in the simplest of terms, is a worldwide collection of networks. A **network** is composed of two or more computers that are linked together and that share and exchange information. The Internet is the world's largest network, made up of computers located all over the world. The computers and networks that make up the Internet are connected by fiber-optic cables, satellites, phone lines, and other forms of electronic communication media, as shown in Figure 1.

Figure 1 **How computers are connected to the Internet and World Wide Web**

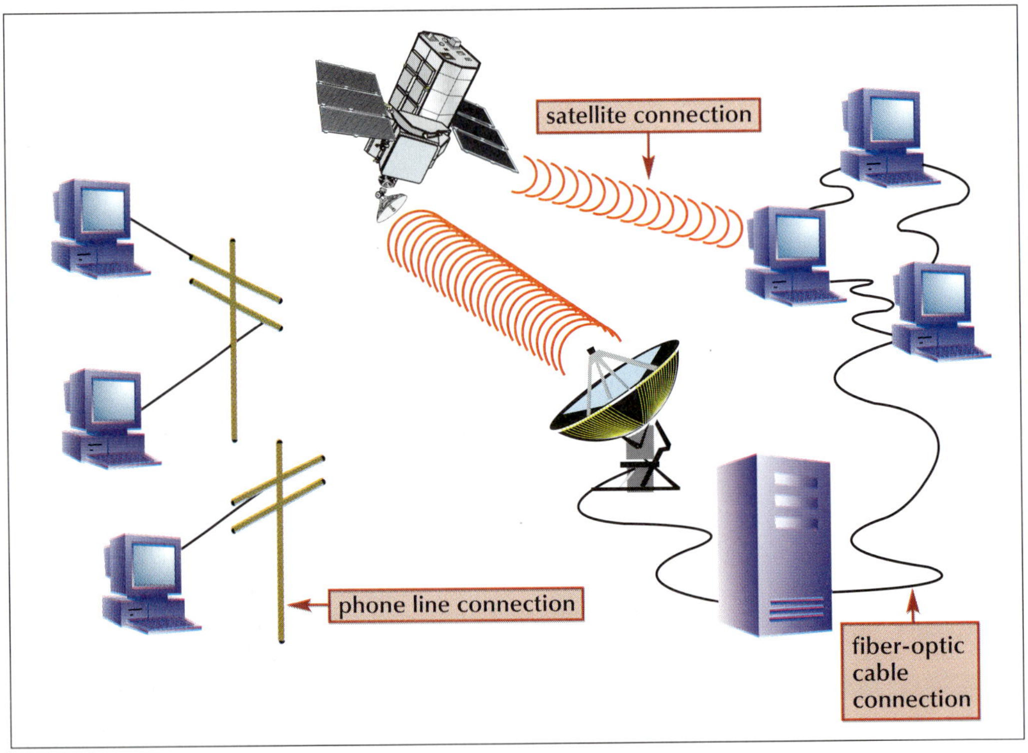

The Internet and the services it provides allow people all over the world to communicate and share information quickly and easily. The **World Wide Web (WWW)**, or simply the **Web**, is a service the Internet offers that enables individuals and businesses to test and market products and services to a global audience. The Web is a system of electronic documents, called **Web pages**, that are linked together by **hyperlinks** (or just **links**), which are words, phrases, or graphics in a Web page that target another place in the document or another document altogether. When a user clicks a hyperlink, the information at the target location is displayed, as shown in Figure 2.

Using hyperlinks to go to related information **Figure 2**

Web pages are ordinary text files, much like the files created by word-processing software. However, the text must be formatted according to a generally accepted standard, and the standard format used on the Web is the **Hypertext Markup Language (HTML)**. HTML provides a variety of text-formatting tags that you can use to indicate headings, paragraphs, bulleted lists, numbered lists, and other useful text formats in an HTML document. The real power of HTML, however, lies in its ability to enable you to access multiple HTML documents through hyperlinks.

The computers on the Internet that store Web pages are called **Web servers**. A **Web site** is a collection of hyperlinked Web pages that have a common theme or focus and are stored on a Web server belonging to an organization or individual. Web sites can be used to provide information about an organization or an individual. They can also be used by businesses to sell or advertise their products and to communicate information to their customers or employees. The McKiernans want to create a Web site to advertise their inn.

To help locate and navigate the large number of Web sites and Web pages, you can use a Web directory or a search engine. A **Web directory** is a special type of Web page that contains a list of Web sites organized by topical categories, such as education or recreation. The hyperlinks on a Web directory page lead either to other pages containing lists of subcategories or to Web pages that relate to the category topics. **Web search engines** are Web pages that conduct searches of the Web to find the words or expressions that you enter as search criteria. The result of such a search is a Web page that contains hyperlinks to Web pages that contain matching text or expressions. There are general search engines, such as Google, that you can use to find a wide variety of information. There are also business search engines, such as Business.com, that you can use to find news, finance, technology, and industry-specific information. Figure 3 provides a list of common search engines.

Figure 3 **Examples of search engines**

Search Engine	Description
AltaVista	One of the first full-text Internet search engines
AskJeeves	A real-language search engine that lets users ask questions without knowledge of specialized search techniques
Business.com	Features a database of companies, with profiles, news, and stock quotes; also includes industry-specific updates, research-based data, and resources
Google	Returns keyword search results based on relevance of content and the number of links to other sites

Home Pages and Web Browsers

The main page that all of the pages in a particular Web site are organized around and link back to is called the site's **home page**. The term "home page" is used in at least three different ways on the Web, and it is sometimes difficult to tell which meaning people intend when they use the term. The first definition of home page indicates the main page for a particular site; this use of "home page" refers to the first page that opens when you visit a Web site. The second definition of home page is the first page that opens when you start your Web browser. A **Web browser** is a software program used to retrieve and display Web pages and to navigate them. You will learn more about Web browsers in the next section. This type of home page might be an HTML document on your own computer. Some people create such home pages and include hyperlinks to Web sites that they frequently visit. The third definition of home page is the Web page that a particular Web browser loads the first time you use it. This page usually is stored at the Web site of the firm or organization that created the Web browser software. Home pages that fall within the second or third definitions are sometimes called **start pages**.

To use your computer to gather information from the Internet and have access to the HTML documents stored on the Web, your computer needs to have a Web browser installed on it. As stated earlier, Web browser software is designed to access, retrieve, and display Web pages on your computer. Although the Internet connects many different types of computers running different operating system software, Web browser software lets your computer communicate with all of these different types of computers easily and effectively. Two popular browsers are Microsoft Internet Explorer, or simply Internet Explorer, and Netscape Navigator, or simply Navigator.

In addition to Web browser software, you also need a means of connecting to the Internet. If you are a student at a university, you might be connected to the Internet through the university's computer network. If you use a computer from your home, you might have a connection to the Internet through your phone line and a modem. This is called a **dial-up connection**. Another connection option for home-based Internet users is a **DSL (Digital Subscriber Line) connection**, which uses your phone line to establish a high-speed connection. Home connections require an account with an **Internet service provider (ISP)**, a company that sells Internet access. This company guides you in configuring your computer to connect to one of its servers via a telephone or cable modem. When you are logged on to your ISP account, meaning you are connected to your ISP's server, you can use the browser software on your computer to access files and other resources located anywhere on the Internet.

Starting Microsoft Internet Explorer

Microsoft Internet Explorer is the Web browser that installs with Windows 9x, Windows 2000, and Windows XP. It provides all the tools you need to communicate, access, and share information on the Web. Your first step in helping Susan find information about other B&Bs is to start Internet Explorer.

To start Internet Explorer:

1. Click the **Start** button on the taskbar, point to **All Programs**, and then click **Internet Explorer**. The Internet Explorer program window opens.

   Trouble? This tutorial assumes that you have Internet Explorer 6 or later installed on your computer. If you are using another Web browser, ask your instructor or technical support person for assistance or program-specific instructions.

   Trouble? If you cannot find Internet Explorer on the All Programs menu, check to see if an Internet Explorer shortcut icon appears on the desktop, and then double-click it. If you do not see the shortcut icon, ask your instructor or technical support person for help. The program might be installed in a different folder on your computer.

   Trouble? If a Dial-up Connection dialog box opens, enter your user name and password into the appropriate text boxes, and then click the Connect button. If you do not know your user name or password, ask your instructor or technical support person for assistance; you must have an Internet connection to complete the steps in this tutorial. After a connection is made, continue with Step 2.

2. If the program window does not fill the screen entirely, click the **Maximize** button on the Internet Explorer title bar. Your screen should look similar to the one shown in Figure 4.

MSN home page displayed in Internet Explorer

Figure 4

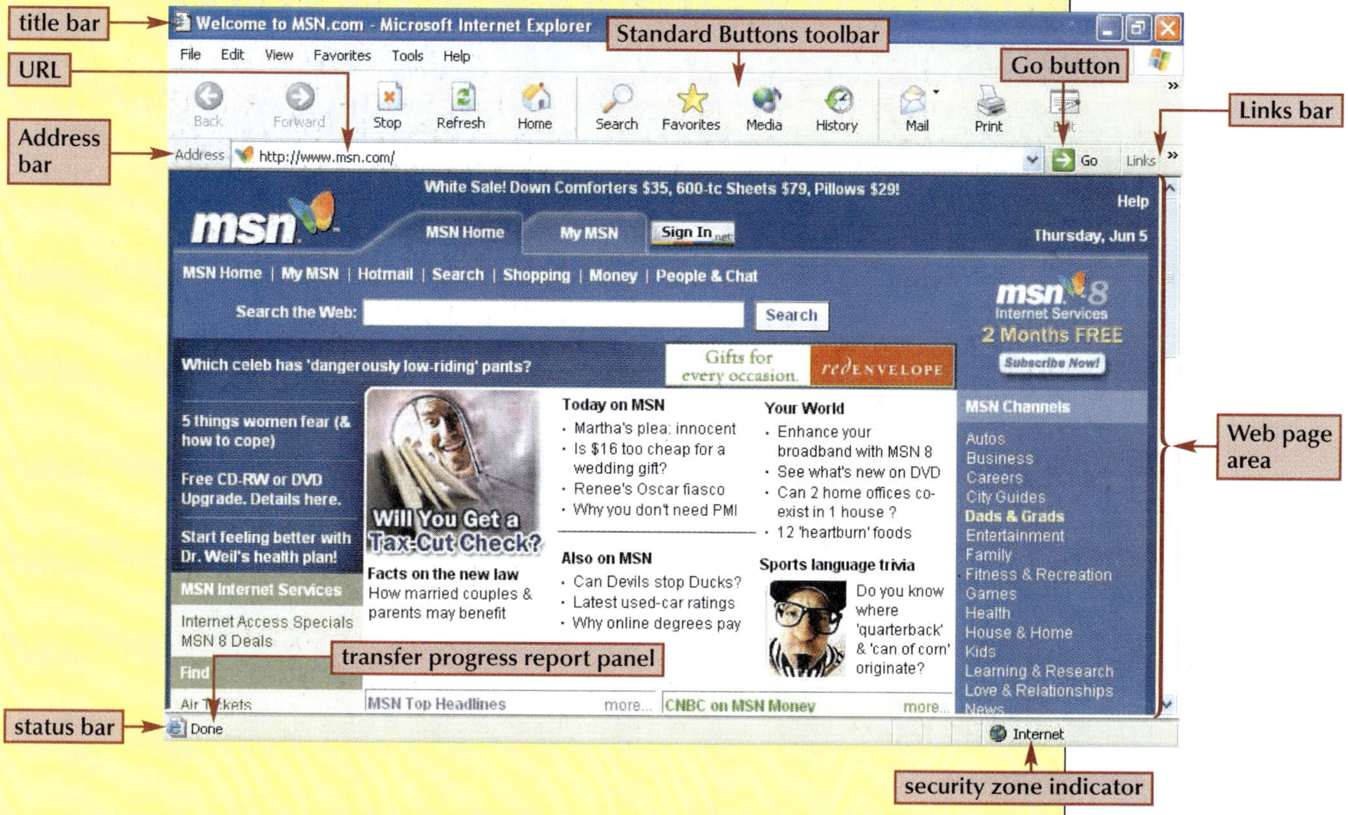

Trouble? Your computer might be configured to open to a different Web page or to no page at all. Figure 4 shows the MSN home page, which is the home page that Internet Explorer opens the first time it starts.

Trouble? If the Standard Buttons toolbar does not look like the one shown in Figure 4, you need to change its appearance. Click View on the menu bar, point to Toolbars, and then click Customize. In the Customize dialog box, click the Text options list arrow, and then click Show text labels; click the Icon options list arrow, and then click Large icons. Click the Close button. The Standard Buttons toolbar should now look like the one in the figure.

The design of Internet Explorer is similar to other Office 2003 programs. Most Windows programs use a standard graphical user interface (GUI) design that includes a number of common Windows components. These common elements include a title bar at the top of the window, a scroll bar on the right side of the window, and a status bar at the bottom of the window. Some of the other components in Internet Explorer, such as the Address bar and Links bar, are program-specific. Figure 5 describes the elements of the Internet Explorer window.

Figure 5 **Elements of the Internet Explorer window**

Element	Description
Title bar	Shows the name of the open Web page and includes the sizing buttons
Standard Buttons toolbar	Contains buttons you can click to perform commonly used tasks, such as moving to the next or previous page and printing a Web page
Address bar	Shows the address of the current Web page or the address you have entered for the Web page you want to go to
Web page area	Shows the contents of the current Web page
Status bar	Shows information about the browser's actions, for example, indicates a page is loading or is done loading
Scroll bars	Enable you to display the contents of a Web page that is wider or longer than the browser window by scrolling up and down or left and right
Home button	Returns you to the Web page that you have set as the home or start page
Go button	Displays the Web page for the address you have entered in the Address bar
Links bar	Contains links to Web pages you visit often
URL	Uniform Resource Locator, which is the address of the Web page you want to visit

Uniform Resource Locators

When you use a Web browser to access a Web page stored on a Web server, the browser software locates and retrieves the Web page content and downloads it to your computer. For this to occur, you need to provide the browser with a **Uniform Resource Locator (URL)**. A URL is a Web page's address and identifies where the Web page is stored on the Internet. The URL is a four-part addressing scheme that provides the Web browser the following information:

- Protocol to use when transporting the Web page
- Server address of the computer on which the Web page resides
- Pathname of the folder or directory on the computer on which the Web page resides
- Filename of the Web page

Figure 6 identifies the parts of a URL.

Figure 6 **Structure of a URL**

Web pages transmitted over the Internet use a communication protocol for transferring information. A **protocol** is a standardized procedure that computers use to exchange data. The most common protocol used on the Internet is the **Hypertext Transfer Protocol (HTTP)**. A Web page whose URL begins with "http://" indicates that the Web browser should use HTTP when retrieving the page.

The server address portion of a URL may consist of numbers or letters. Every computer on the Internet has an **IP (Internet Protocol) address**. An IP address is a unique number consisting of four sets of three-digit numbers from 000 to 255 separated by periods (such as 216.035.148.254) and identifies the specific server or computer connected to the Internet. Because IP addresses can be difficult for people to remember, domain names were created as another means of identifying computers and servers connected to the Internet. **Domain names** are IP addresses consisting of letters (such as www.course.com) instead of numbers. Domain names are most commonly used in the server address portion of a URL because they more clearly identify a Web site and are easier for users to remember. The URL shown in Figure 6 has a domain name of www.centralpenn.edu. In this domain name, *www* indicates that the server is a Web server; *centralpenn* is the identifying name chosen by the organization to which the Web site belongs, in this case Central Pennsylvania College; and *.edu* indicates that the server is operated by an educational entity. Other common types of Web servers in the United States are .com (commercial business), .org (not-for-profit organization), and .gov (government). A more complete list is given in Figure 7.

Figure 7 **Types of Web servers**

Web Server Types	Description
.com	Businesses and other commercial enterprises
.edu	Educational institutions
.gov	U.S. government agencies, bureaus, or departments
.int	International organizations
.mil	U.S. military units or agencies
.net	Network service providers or resources
.org	Other organizations, usually charitable or not-for-profit

In addition, all Web pages stored on Web servers have unique pathnames, just like files stored on a disk. The pathname in a URL includes the folder name(s) where the Web page is stored and its filename and file extension. The file extension for most Web pages is either .htm or .html. In the sample URL shown in Figure 6, the pathname that follows the server address www.centralpenn.edu specifies a file named *index.html*, which is stored in a folder named *library*.

Not all URLs include a filename. If a URL does not include a filename, most Web browsers will load the file named index.htm. The **index.htm** filename is the default name for a Web site's home page.

As stated earlier, you need to know a Web page's URL in order to open it in Internet Explorer. You can find URLs in many places; for example, newspapers and magazines often publish URLs of Web sites that might interest their readers. Friends who know about the subject area in which you are interested are also good sources. Once you have the URL of the Web page you want to view, you can enter it in the Address bar.

Entering a URL in the Address Bar

As discussed, you navigate from one Web page to another by clicking hyperlinks. Another way to display a specific Web page in Internet Explorer is to enter its URL in the Address bar. In most cases, URLs are not case-sensitive; however, in situations where the computer storing the Web page uses the UNIX operating system, URLs *are* case-sensitive. Therefore, if you are entering a URL that includes mixed cases and you do not know the type of computer on which the file resides, it is safer to retain the mixed-case format of the URL.

Reference Window

Entering a URL in the Address Bar

- Select the current URL in the Address bar.
- Type the URL of the Web page you want to retrieve.
- Press the Enter key to display the Web page in the browser window.

For this exercise, you will enter the URL for the New Perspectives Student Union Web page. In this tutorial, you will go to this Course Technology page and then click hyperlinks to go to other Web pages.

To enter the URL for the New Perspectives Student Union Web page:

1. Click the **Address bar** to select the current URL.

   Trouble? If you double-click in the Address bar, you switch to edit mode. If this occurs, click a blank space in the browser window to deactivate edit mode, and then repeat Step 1.

2. Type **www.course.com/NewPerspectives/studentunion/** in the Address bar. This is the URL for the New Perspectives Student Union Web page on the Course Technology Web site.

   Trouble? If a list box appears on the Address bar while you are typing the URL, just finish typing the URL. When the AutoComplete feature is enabled on your computer, Internet Explorer opens the Address bar list box as you begin typing a URL so that if you have gone to this location previously you can select the URL from a list, instead of typing it again.

3. Press the **Enter** key. As soon as you press the Enter key, Internet Explorer adds the http:// protocol to the URL for you, and then it transfers and displays the New Perspectives Student Union Web page in the browser window. Sometimes when a Web page contains a large amount of text and graphics, it takes a short amount of time to transfer to your computer and display fully in the browser window. The transfer time depends on the speed of your Internet connection, the amount of traffic on the Internet, and the complexity of the Web page being transferred. When the entire page has been transferred, the graphical transfer progress indicator in the status bar will stop moving, and the transfer progress report panel will display the text "Done."

   Trouble? If a Dial-up Connection dialog box opens after you press the Enter key, click the Connect button. You must have an Internet connection to complete the steps in this tutorial.

4. Scroll down the list of Student Online Companion links, and then click the **Microsoft Office 2003** link to open the Microsoft Office 2003 Student Online Companion page.
5. Click the **Office First Course** link, click the **Browser and E-Mail Basics** link, and then click the appropriate **click here** link to open the page that contains the links for this tutorial.

Martha Kent has suggested that Susan locate some Web sites advertising B&Bs to give her an idea of designs and layouts that appeal to her. This will help her in planning and designing the Web site for McKiernan's Irish B&B. Susan asks you to work with her to find some appropriate sites.

To go to the Web site for a B&B:

1. Scroll down to the Browser and E-mail Basics page to the Session 1 heading for this text.
2. Click one of the links listed under this heading to open the home page for a bed-and-breakfast. The home page for the B&B opens and may look similar to the sample shown in Figure 8.

Figure 8 Centre Mills Bed and Breakfast home page

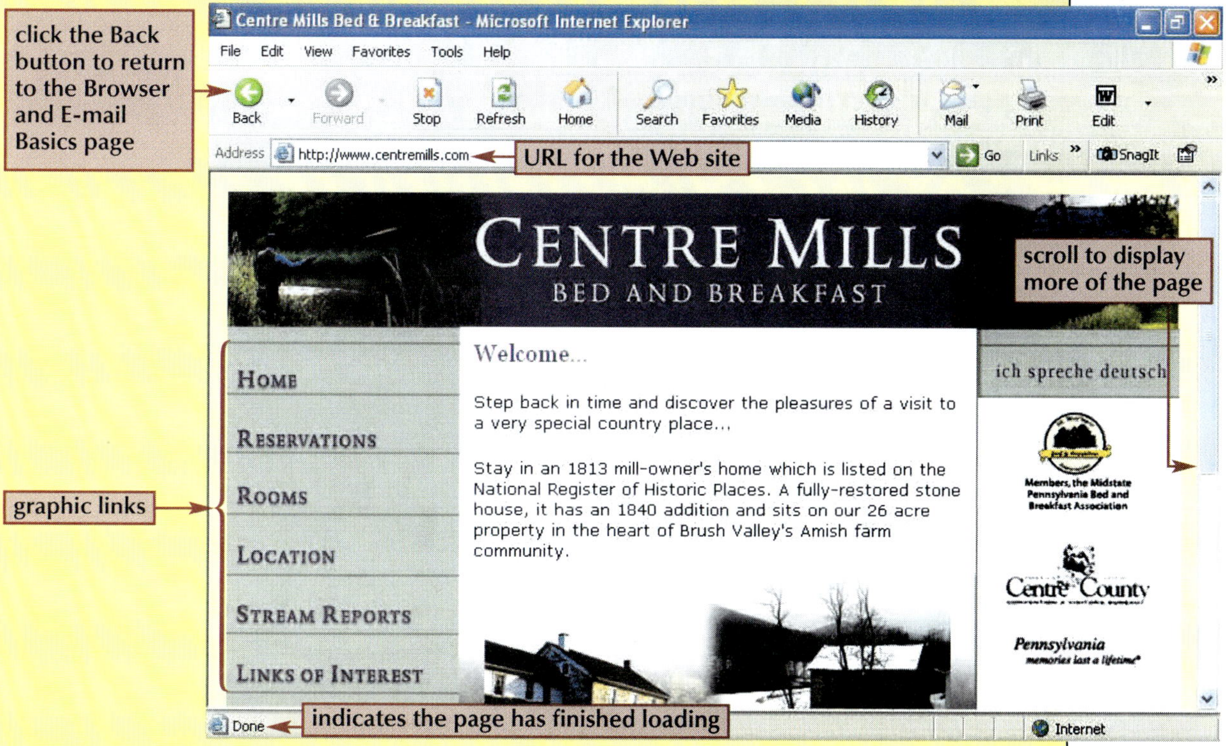

3. Read the Web page using the scroll bar on the right, if necessary, but do not click any area on the page.
4. Scroll back to the top of the page.

Once you arrive at the Web site in which you are interested, you can begin moving around the site by clicking the different links that are available. To help you navigate a Web site, you can also use the Back and Forward buttons on the Standard Buttons toolbar.

Navigating Links on a Web Page

The easiest way to move from one Web page to another is to use the hyperlinks that the authors of Web pages embed in their HTML documents. Web page authors use a word, phrase, or graphic image as a hyperlink. Sometimes, it is difficult to identify which objects and text are hyperlinks just by looking at a Web page. Fortunately, when you move the mouse pointer over a hyperlink in a Web browser, the pointer changes to and the URL of the Web page is displayed in the status bar. Sometimes, depending on the design of the page, a ScreenTip will also appear, indicating the purpose of the link or its target destination.

Susan likes the layout of the Web site shown in Figure 8, so you will check out some of the links provided on the left side of the page.

To navigate Web pages on the bed-and-breakfast Web site:

1. Move your pointer over the link for **Rooms** until the pointer changes to , and then click that link. The address for this Web page appears in the Address bar, and the Back button is active. Figure 9 shows the Rooms page for the Centre Mills Bed and Breakfast.

Figure 9 Rooms Web page

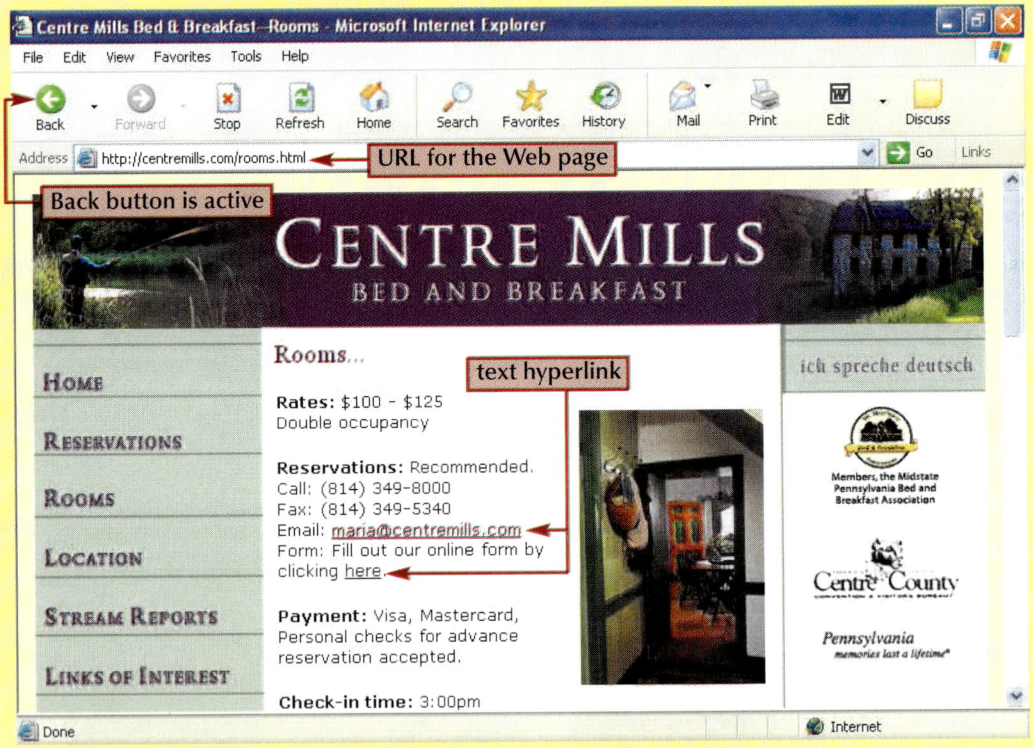

Trouble? If the Web site you chose in the previous set of steps does not have a Rooms link, then select another link of interest on the page, such as Rates or Reservations.

2. Click the **Back** button on the Standard Buttons toolbar to return to the home page for the bed-and-breakfast. The Back and Forward buttons are now active.
3. Position the pointer on the **Forward** button on the Standard Buttons toolbar to display information about the Rooms page. Clicking the Forward button now would return you to that page.
4. Locate another link on the page, and then click it. The target Web page for the link appears in the browser window.

Trouble? If the Web page appears in its own window, the Back button will not be available. Click the Close button to close the window and then skip Step 5. The home page for the bed-and-breakfast will be redisplayed.

5. Click the **Back** button on the Standard Buttons toolbar to return to the home page for the bed-and-breakfast.

The Back and Forward buttons also have list arrows that, when clicked, display a list of the Web pages you have recently visited. You can also click the Address bar list arrow to display a list of Web sites that you have visited.

To return to the Browser and E-mail Basics page using the Back button list arrow:

1. Click the **Back** button list arrow to view the list of Web pages you have just navigated.
2. Click **New Perspectives on Microsoft Office 2003** in the list to return to the Browser and E-mail Basics page.

   Trouble? If the New Perspectives Student Union or Student Online Companion page appears, you clicked its URL in the list. Navigate to the Browser and E-mail Basics link by clicking the Forward button.
3. If necessary, scroll down the Browser and E-mail Basics page to display the Session 1 heading for this text.

Returning to the Home Page

As you browse different Web sites, you can always return to your home or start page for your browser by clicking the **Home button** on the Standard Buttons toolbar. Once you return to the home page, you can begin browsing again by clicking a link on the home page or by using any of the other available tools provided there.

Reloading a Web Page

When you visit a Web site, your browser loads the Web page from a remote Web server and stores a copy of the Web page in a folder on the hard drive of your computer. Storing copies of the Web pages you have visited increases the speed at which the browser can redisplay these pages as you navigate back and forward between them. When you click the **Refresh button** on the Standard Buttons toolbar, the browser contacts the remote Web server to see if the Web page has changed since it was stored on your computer. If the Web page has changed, the browser gets the new page from the Web server; otherwise, it loads the copy that is already stored on your computer.

Stopping a Web Page Transfer

If a Web page seems to be taking a long time to load, you can stop the page from loading altogether. If you accidentally click a hyperlink that you do not want to follow, you can stop the transfer of the Web page. To stop the transfer of a Web page from its server, click the **Stop button** on the Standard Buttons toolbar. In the case of the Web page taking too long to transfer, you might want to try reloading the page again by clicking the Refresh button.

Unavailable Sites

The Internet and WWW are dynamic—they are always changing, and inherent in that change is the fact that some Web sites may no longer exist or their addresses might change. Web sites are consistently being updated as well. If you click a link, you might encounter an error message. Two common messages that appear in dialog boxes are "server busy" and "DNS entry not found." Either of these messages means that your browser was unable to communicate successfully with the Web server that stores the page you requested. The cause of this inability might be temporary—in which case, you will be able to use the hyperlink later—or the cause might be permanent, and the Web site or Web page no longer exists. The browser has no way of determining the cause of the connection failure, so it provides the same error messages in both cases. Another error message that you might receive is displayed as a Web page and includes the text "File not Found." This error message usually means that the Web page's location has changed permanently or that the Web page no longer exists.

As you continue to research information for Susan, you may not be able to remember all the URLs of the sites you visit. The Back and Forward buttons only store URLs for a current session, but what if you want to return to sites you visited two days ago? Internet Explorer has a feature, the History list, that tracks sites visited for a specified period of time, and you can access this information using the History Explorer bar.

Using the History List

You have used the Back and Forward buttons as a means for navigating through Web pages viewed in your current browser session. Once you close the browser, the trail of visited sites is lost. However, Internet Explorer provides another feature, the History list, which tracks the Web sites that you have visited over a time period, not just during a browsing session. The **History list** contains the URLs for the Web sites and pages that you have visited. You click the History button on the Standard Buttons toolbar to open the History Explorer bar, which displays the History list. To return to a particular page, click that page's entry in the list. You can see the full URL of any item in the History Explorer bar by moving the mouse pointer over the History list item. The entries in the History Explorer bar are listed in alphabetical order and not in the order in which you visited the sites. You change the way in which the sites are listed by clicking View in the History Explorer bar, and choosing to view By Date, By Site, By Most Visited, and By Order Visited Today. You can also search the History list by clicking Search in the History Explorer bar.

The History list displays not only sites visited today, but also sites visited yesterday, the day before that, even last week, depending on the number of days specified in the Internet Options dialog box. You open the Internet Options dialog box from the Tools menu. (Changing Internet Explorer settings goes beyond the scope of this tutorial.)

To view the History list for this session:

1. Click the **History** button on the Standard Buttons toolbar to open the History Explorer bar in the left pane of the Internet Explorer window. The History list stores each URL you have visited today and for other specified time periods (for example, 2 Weeks Ago, 3 Weeks Ago, and Last Week) in folders. It also maintains the hierarchy of each Web site; that is, pages you visit at a particular Web site are stored in a separate folder for that site. You can right-click any entry in the History list and copy the URL or delete it from the list. Internet Explorer stores each entry in the History list as a shortcut in the History folder, which is in the Windows folder.

As you become more and more familiar with Web sites on the Internet, you will probably want to return to certain sites because they provide information that you need on a regular basis. When you find a site that you know you will return to more than once, you can save it as a "favorite."

Using the Favorites Feature

Web addresses can be very long and, as a result, difficult to remember. Using the History list to locate important pages will be a terrific asset as you collect the information you need. In Internet Explorer, you can also save the URL of a Web site as a favorite in the Favorites list. The **Favorites list** is a feature that you can use to store and organize a list of Web pages you want to revisit. You click the Favorites button on the Standard Buttons toolbar to open the Favorites Explorer bar, which displays your list of favorites.

Susan wants you to save as a favorite any Web site that you think is well designed and easy to navigate. Then, when she has time, she will choose a few to show Martha Kent at their planning meeting next week.

To open the Favorites Explorer bar and then save a Web page as a favorite:

1. Display the Web page you want to save as a favorite.
2. Click the **Favorites** button on the Standard Buttons toolbar. The Favorites Explorer bar opens in the left pane of the Internet Explorer window.
3. Click the **Add** button in the Favorites Explorer bar. The Add Favorite dialog box opens. See Figure 10. The text in the Name text box is the name of the currently displayed Web page as it appears in the Internet Explorer title bar. You can change the name of the favorite, but make sure you give it a meaningful name.

Figure 10 Add Favorite dialog box

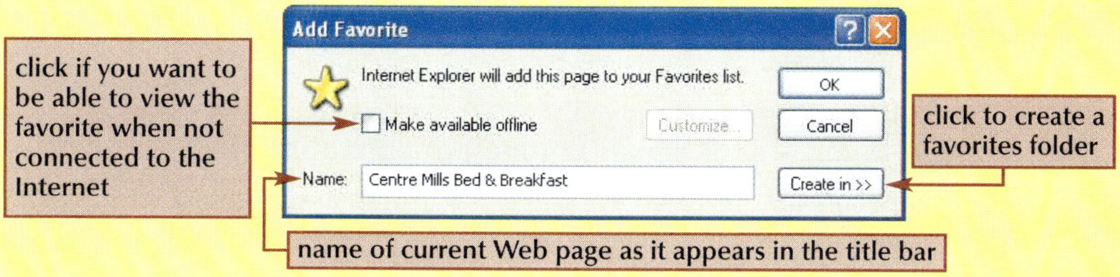

Trouble? If your Add Favorite dialog box is expanded and displays the Create in list box, click the Create in << button to reduce the size of the dialog box so it matches the one shown in the figure.

4. Select the text in the Name text box, and then type an appropriate name. For example, if you were to create a favorite for the Centre Mills Bed and Breakfast site, you might enter "Centre Mills" in the Name text box.
5. Click the **OK** button to close the Add Favorite dialog box. The favorite you just created appears in the Favorites list in the Favorites Explorer bar.

If you select the Make available offline option in the Add Favorite dialog box, Internet Explorer saves a copy of the Web page in a special folder on your hard drive. This means that you can display the Web page without connecting to the Internet. For example, if you are using a laptop in a place where there is no Internet access available, you can still display the Web page.

Saving Web sites as favorites is easy and will come in handy as you gather more information. However, having a long list of favorites may not be as helpful as you want. If the list is too long, you will waste time scrolling through the list, which defeats the purpose of the Favorites list—having ready access to a frequently visited Web page. To address this potential pitfall, you can create folders to organize and store multiple favorites.

Organizing Favorites

Internet Explorer offers an easy way to organize your favorite sites. You can use the Organize Favorites dialog box to create folders for storing your favorites. This dialog box provides options for creating folders, moving favorites into different folders, renaming favorites and folders, and deleting favorites and folders.

Reference Window

Organizing the Favorites List

- Click the Favorites button on the Standard Buttons toolbar, and then click the Organize button in the Favorites Explorer bar to open the Organize Favorites dialog box.
- To create a new folder, click the Create Folder button, and then type the name for the new folder.
- To move a favorite into a folder, select the item, click the Move to Folder button, select the folder for the item in the Browse for Folder dialog box, and then click the OK button.
- To remove an item from the Favorites list, select the item from the list in the Organize Favorites dialog box, and then click the Delete button.

Because Susan likes the Centre Mills Bed and Breakfast Web site and Preston hasn't seen it yet, you will save it as a favorite. Susan suggests that you create a folder to be used to store other appropriate Web sites that you find.

To create a new favorites folder and move a favorite into it:

1. Click the **Organize** button in the Favorites Explorer bar to open the Organize Favorites dialog box. See Figure 11.

Organize Favorites dialog box **Figure 11**

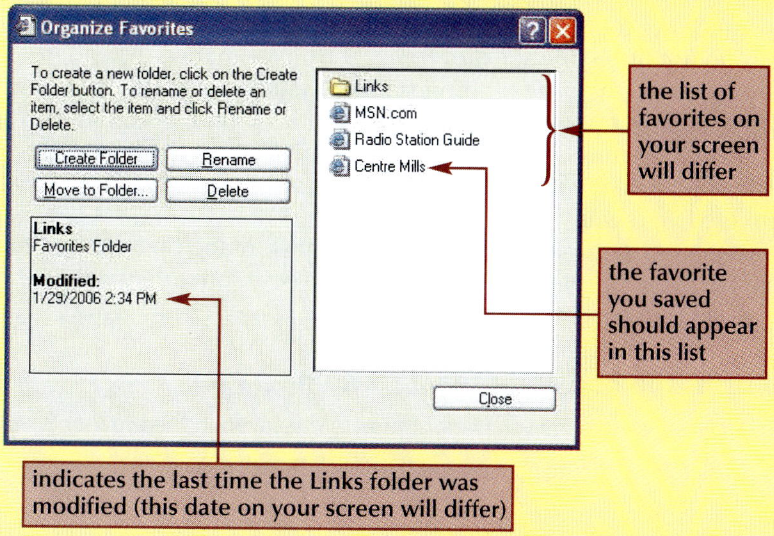

2. Click the **Create Folder** button, type **B&B Sites** for the new folder name, and then press the **Enter** key. Now you can move the favorite you created in the previous steps into this new folder.
3. Click the name of the favorite you created earlier, and then click the **Move to Folder** button. The Browse for Folder dialog box opens. You can use this dialog box to locate the folder in which you want to store the selected favorite.
4. Click the **B&B Sites** folder, and then click the **OK** button.
5. Click the **Close** button to close the Organize Favorites dialog box. Now the favorite you created is saved as a favorite in the B&B Sites folder, which appears in the Favorites list in the Favorites Explorer bar.
6. Click the **B&B Sites** folder in the Favorites Explorer bar. The contents of the folder appear, displaying the name of the favorite you created.

As you use the Web to find information about bed-and-breakfasts and other items, you might find yourself creating many favorites so you can return to sites of interest. Sometimes you will find you no longer need a favorite or a folder of favorites. You can remove the folder and any favorites contained within it using the Delete button in the Organize Favorites dialog box. You also can delete an item from the Favorites list by right-clicking the item in the Favorites Explorer bar, and clicking Delete on the shortcut menu. Because you may be working in a computer lab and sharing this computer with other users, you need to delete the folder you just created.

To delete the item from the Favorites list:

1. Right-click the **B&B Sites** folder in the Favorites list in the Favorites Explorer bar. A shortcut menu displays commands for working with favorites.
2. Click **Delete** on the shortcut menu, and then click the **Yes** button in the Confirm Folder Delete dialog box. The B&B Sites folder and the favorite you created are removed from the Favorites list.
3. Click the **Close** button ☒ in the Favorites Explorer bar to close it.

Printing a Web Page

You can make a printed copy of most Web pages. Web pages can be any size and often do not fit on one sheet of 8 ½ × 11 (letter) paper. Instead, the browser automatically reformats the page to fit on standard letter-size paper, so one Web page may take several sheets of paper to print. If you want to print a Web page using your computer's default print settings, you can click the Print button on the Standard Buttons toolbar. If you want to change the settings, you must open the Print dialog box, which you access from the File menu.

Susan likes the simple, straightforward layout of the Centre Mills home page, and she wants to show Preston the design. She asks you to print this page.

To print the bed-and-breakfast home page:

1. Make sure the page you want to print is displayed in the browser window.
2. Click **File** on the menu bar, and then click **Print** to open the Print dialog box.
3. Make sure the printer you need to use is selected, the **All** option button is selected in the Page Range section, and the Number of copies box shows you want to print one copy.
4. Click the **Print** button to print the Web page and close the Print dialog box.

Saving a Web Page

You have learned how to use most of the Internet Explorer tools for loading Web pages and saving favorites. Now, you'll learn how to save a Web page.

You need to display the Web page that you want to save and then open the Save Web Page dialog box from the File menu. There are several options for saving a Web page, depending on what portion of the Web page you want. The "Web Page, complete" option (the default) saves the entire Web page, including its graphics and other elements that make up the page. When you save the complete Web page, Internet Explorer saves an HTML file and a folder with all of the site's related files, including page elements such as images and sounds. If you select the "Web Archive, single file" option, you will save a "picture" of the current Web page. You might use this option if you want to send a copy of the Web page to someone in an e-mail message.

The two other options—"Web Page, HTML only" and "Text File"—let you save just the HTML code or the text from the Web page, respectively, without saving the graphics, frames, or styles on the Web page.

Susan and Preston like the design layout of the Centre Mills Bed and Breakfast home page, and they want you to save the home page so they can show it to Martha at Capital Ads.

To save the bed-and-breakfast home page:

1. Make sure the B&B home page you want to save is displayed in the browser window. (Note that this can be a B&B Web page of your choice; it doesn't have to be the home page for Centre Mills.)

   Trouble? If you cannot display a B&B home page, display the Browser and E-mail Basics page.
2. Click **File** on the menu bar, and then click **Save As** to open the Save Web Page dialog box.
3. Navigate to the BEB\Tutorial folder included with your Data Files.

4. Change the default filename to **B&B Page**.
5. Click the **Save as type** list arrow, and then click **Web Page, HTML only (*.htm or *.html)**, if necessary, as shown in Figure 12.

Figure 12 Save Web Page dialog box

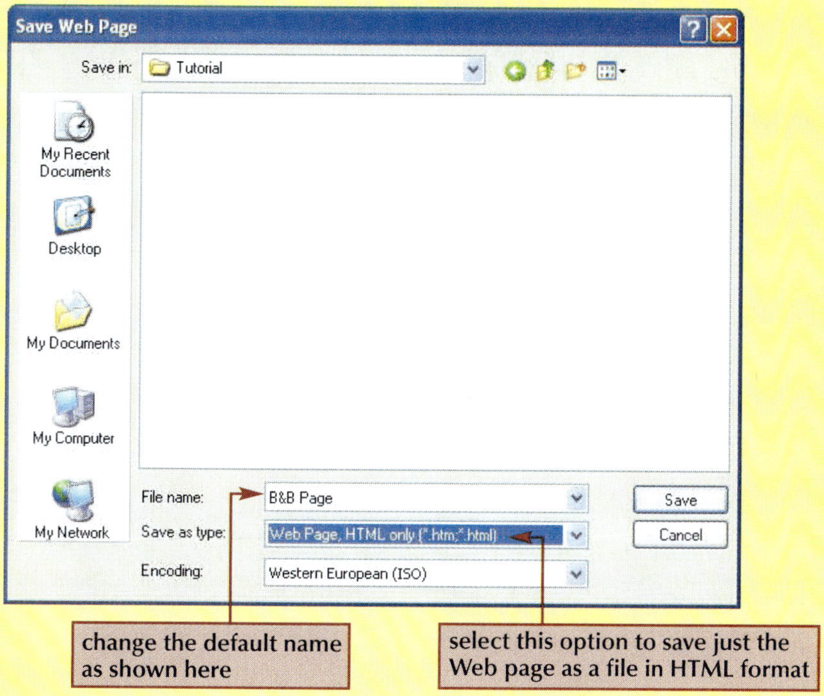

6. Click the **Save** button. The Save Web Page dialog box closes. Internet Explorer saves the Web page as an HTML file and automatically adds the .html file extension.

Saving a Web Page Graphic

You can also save images that you find. In this case, Susan wants you to save an image of one of the rooms on the Centre Mills Bed and Breakfast site.

Saving an Image from a Web Page to a Disk

Reference Window

- Open the Web page in Internet Explorer.
- Position the pointer over the graphic and then click the Save as Picture button on the shortcut toolbar (or right-click the image you want to save, and then click Save Picture As on the shortcut menu).
- Navigate to where you want to save the image, and then change the default filename if you want.
- Click the Save button.

To save the image from the Web page:

1. Go to the Web page that displays images of the B&B or rooms offered.
2. Right-click an image on the page to display the shortcut menu. See Figure 13. A toolbar of graphic commands may also display; you can use either one of these elements to save the graphic. Note that the shortcut menu provides more options. The toolbar provides quick and easy access to the four most frequently performed graphics-related tasks: saving an image, printing an image, sending an image in an e-mail message, and opening the My Pictures folder.

Figure 13 Options for saving a Web page graphic

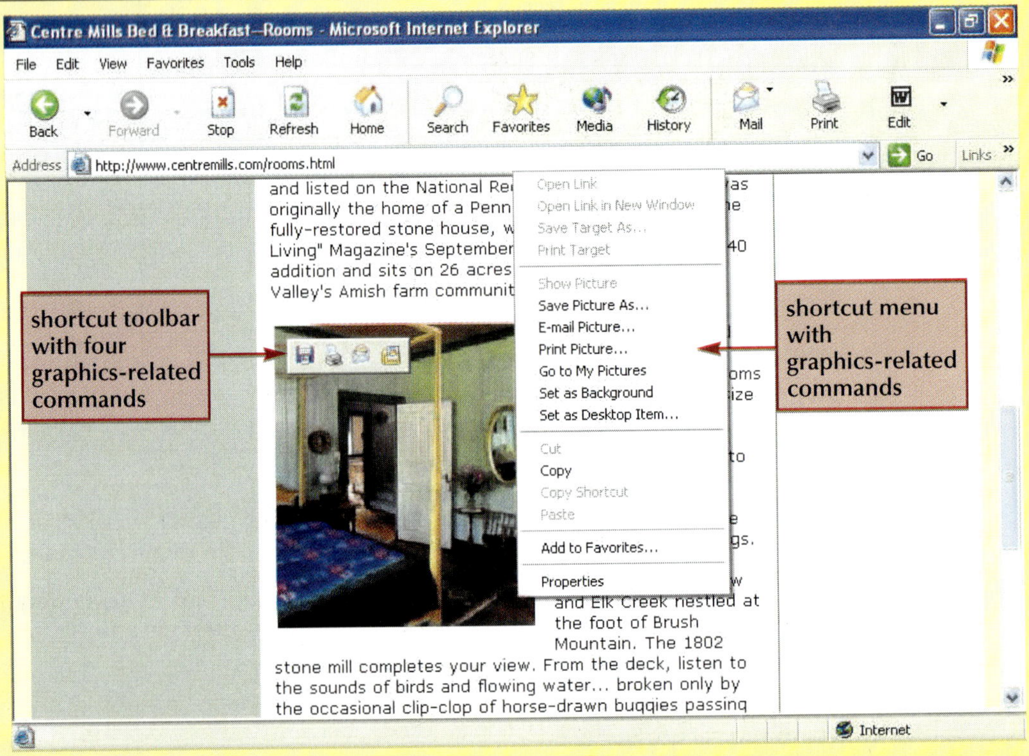

3. Click **Save Picture As** on the shortcut menu to open the Save Picture dialog box, and then navigate to the BEB\Tutorial folder.
4. Change the default filename to **Web Page Graphic**, and make sure **JPEG (*.jpeg)** appears in the Save as type list box. A JPEG file is a common file type for an image or picture.
5. Click the **Save** button.
6. Close your Web browser.

There are many graphics used on Web pages that you can save for use in your own materials. Some graphics, however, are copyrighted, and you need permission to copy and use them.

Copyright Law for the Internet

The term **copyright** applies to the exclusive legal right to reproduce, publish, or sell a product (in its literary, musical, or artistic form) by its originator. Copyright laws have served to protect the use of original and creative products of individuals and groups for many years. You have probably seen the copyright symbol © on the inside cover of almost every book you have ever read and have been made aware of the repercussions of copying someone else's work without giving that person credit—in other words, **plagiarism**.

Now, with the availability of and accessibility to a seemingly infinite amount of products and information, the scope of copyright law has taken a new direction and given rise to the term **cyberlaw**. Whether you refer to copyright law or cyberlaw, you need to be aware of the legal issues that revolve around the use and reproduction of the information that is readily available on the World Wide Web.

Before you download or copy the graphics, maps, images, sounds, or information on Web sites that you visit, you need to find out if and how you can use the materials. If you want to use materials that you have found on a Web site, you need to get permission from the owner of the site. Often, Web sites include their copyright and permission-request information on their home pages. Some Web sites indicate that the material is "free," but almost everything on the Internet is copyrighted. Even if you think that information or material you have found on a Web site does not fall within the scope of copyright protection, you should always request permission to use it. For example, you might be able to copy a picture to your computer, but you do not have a right to reproduce it in your own work.

You may also encounter the term **fair use**. This term applies to material that can be used for educational or nonprofit purposes, as opposed to commercial profit. Information that is considered factual or materials that are so old that copyright protection no longer exists fall under the category of fair use. You should still give credit to any Web site that you used in your research.

You have learned about the Internet and the World Wide Web, and how to use Internet Explorer to browse Web pages. You have saved a Web page and a graphic that Susan wants to send to the ad agency. In the next session, you will learn about e-mail.

Session 1 Quick Check

Review

1. Describe the relationship between the Internet and the World Wide Web.
2. What is the purpose of a Web browser?
3. Identify and define each part of the following URL: *http://www.savethetrees.org/main.html.*
4. Not all URLs include a filename, so most Web browsers load the file ______________ as the default name for a Web site's home page.
5. Briefly define the term "home page."
6. What are some of the ways you can return to a Web site you have previously visited?
7. What are search engines and why are they important to people using the Internet?
8. To save an entire Web page, including graphics, frames, and styles, you select the ______________ option in the Save Web Page dialog box.

Session 2

Exploring E-mail

Electronic mail, or better known simply as **e-mail**, enables you to communicate with other users on a network such as the Internet. Sending and receiving e-mail messages is more efficient than using ground or air mail services. Instead of composing a message on a piece of paper, inserting it into an envelope, attaching the correct postage and address to the envelope, and then depositing it in a mailbox, you compose, address, and send a message directly from your computer to someone's electronic mailbox. You can avoid making many phone calls or printing memos by sending one message to many people. You can also attach files, such as word-processing documents, graphics, or spreadsheets, to an e-mail message.

Examining How E-mail Works

When you exchange e-mail, you send and receive messages with another person on your network, such as a LAN (local area network) or the Internet. An **e-mail message** is a simple text document that you can compose and send using an **e-mail program**, also called **e-mail client software,** such as Microsoft Outlook Express. When you send a message, it travels from your computer, through the network, and arrives at a computer that has been designated and set up as an **e-mail server**. Typically, the system administrator of your network or ISP manages the e-mail server.

The e-mail server stores the e-mail messages until the recipients request them. Then the server forwards the messages to the appropriate computers. Because e-mail uses this **store-and-forward technology**, you can send messages to anyone on the network, even if they do not have their computers turned on. When it's convenient, your recipients log on to the network and use their e-mail programs to receive and read their messages. The process of sending and receiving e-mail messages is illustrated in Figure 14.

Figure 14 **Sending and receiving e-mail**

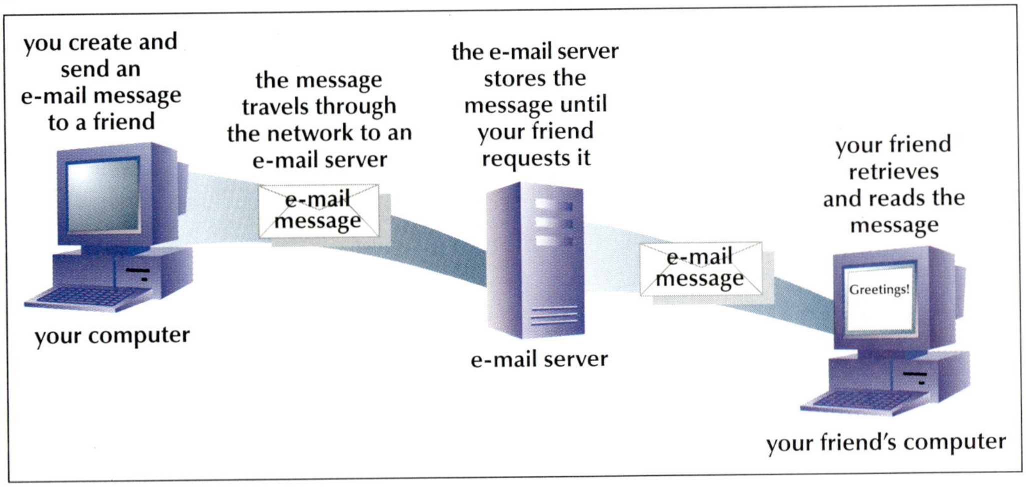

As shown in the figure, to send and receive e-mail, you must be able to access an e-mail server on a network. If your computer is part of a network at a college or university, for example, you log on to the network to access its services. An e-mail server provides mail services to faculty, staff, and students who have access to the network. When someone sends you a message, it is stored on your e-mail server until you log on to the network and use an e-mail program to check your mail. The e-mail server then transfers new messages to your electronic mailbox. You use an e-mail program to open, read, print, delete, reply to, forward, and save the mail.

If your computer is not part of a network, you can access an e-mail server on the Internet. To do so, you open an **e-mail account** with a service that provides Internet access. For example, e-mail accounts are included as part of the subscription fee for America Online (AOL) and most ISPs. E-mail accounts are also provided free of charge by advertiser-supported Web sites, such as Yahoo! and Hotmail. After you establish an e-mail account, you can connect to the Internet, most likely by using a phone line and your computer's modem, to send and receive your e-mail messages.

Reference Window

Signing Up for a Hotmail Account

- Start Internet Explorer (or any Web browser).
- Type *www.hotmail.com* in the Address Bar to go to the Hotmail Web site, and then click the New Account Sign Up tab to open the Registration page.
- Complete the Profile Information and the Account Information sections.
- Complete the .NET Passport Profile, and indicate how much information you want shared with other .NET Passport sites.
- Read the Hotmail Terms of Use and the .NET Passport Terms of Use, and then click the button to accept the terms to the agreement.

Addressing E-mail

You address an e-mail message just as you would an ordinary piece of mail. The e-mail address you enter directs the message to its destination. Your e-mail address is included in the message as a return address, so your recipients can easily respond to your message. Anyone who has an e-mail address can send and receive electronic mail. If you work for a company or attend a school that provides e-mail, there is probably a system administrator of your e-mail server who will assign you an e-mail address. Other times, such as when you sign up for a Hotmail account, you create your own e-mail address, though it must follow a particular format. Figure 15 illustrates a typical format of an e-mail address.

Figure 15 Typical format of an e-mail address

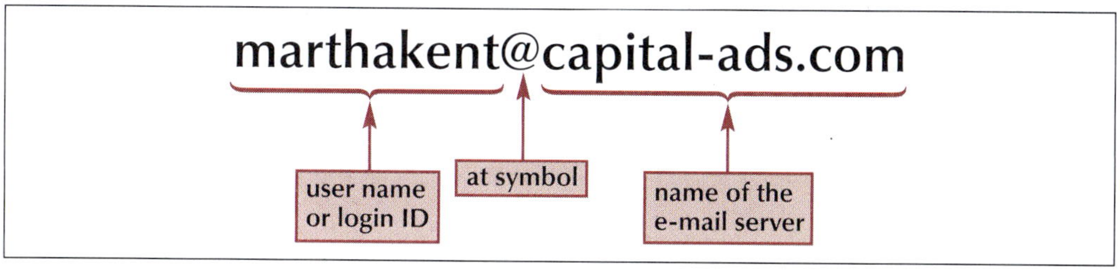

The **user name**, or login ID, is the name that you enter or are assigned when your e-mail account is being set up. The @ symbol signifies that the e-mail server name will be provided next. In the figure, *marthakent* is the user name and *capital-ads.com* is the e-mail server.

The easiest way to find an e-mail address is to ask someone. You can also look up an e-mail address in a LAN or Internet directory. Most businesses and schools publish a directory listing e-mail addresses of those who have e-mail accounts on their network. Many Web sites also provide e-mail directories for people with e-mail accounts on the Internet, such as *www.worldemail.com* and *www.people.yahoo.com*.

When you sign up for an e-mail account, you can send your new e-mail address to friends, colleagues, and clients. If your e-mail address changes—for example, if you use a different network or e-mail service—you can subscribe to an e-mail forwarding service so you don't miss any mail sent to your old address.

Before you begin sending e-mail, Susan wants you to understand some of the basic rules for appropriate e-mail communication.

Observing E-mail Etiquette

With the emergence of e-mail as a widespread form of communication, there are guidelines that will serve you well to follow. Many of these guidelines are common-sense practices, such as using appropriate language. One guiding principal that you may not realize, but should be aware of, is that e-mail is not private. When you correspond with others using e-mail, the information you send can be read by other users, especially if you work for a corporation or private institution. Your correspondents can easily forward your message to others, deliberately or inadvertently revealing information you consider confidential. Therefore, it's a good idea to be professional and careful about what you say to and about others.

Another guideline is providing meaningful information in the subject line. Most e-mail programs show the subject line, date, and sender address for incoming mail. Let your correspondents know what your message concerns by including information in the subject line that concisely and accurately describes the message contents. For example, a subject such as "Staff meeting rescheduled" is more informative than "Meeting." Even after people read your message, the subject helps them quickly locate information they might need later.

If you attach a large file to an e-mail message, it can take a long time for your recipient to download your message. Most e-mail servers have a limit to the size of the files you can attach; some allow files no larger than 1 MB. Check with your correspondents before sending large file attachments to find out about size restrictions and set up a convenient time to send the attachment.

Sending and Receiving E-mail Using Outlook Express

The Outlook Express e-mail program installs as part of Internet Explorer. You can use this program to send, receive, and manage e-mail.

Susan knows that e-mail will be the primary source of communication with Martha and the staff at Capital Ads as they develop the Web site for the McKiernans. She suggests that you practice creating and sending a few messages. First, you will start Outlook Express and review its components and layout.

Note: This tutorial assumes your installation of Outlook Express is already configured to send and receive e-mail. See your instructor or technical support person if this is not the case.

To start Outlook Express:

1. Click the **Start** button on the taskbar, point to **All Programs**, and then click **Outlook Express**. After a moment, Outlook Express opens, as shown in Figure 16. The default name that appears in this window is "Main Identity." Outlook Express can be configured to manage mail for more than one user on a computer, and for each account, there is an "identity." One of the accounts is considered the default account, or main identity. The other accounts are identified by the user name. The account shown in the figures in this tutorial belongs to the fictitious character Susan McKiernan. The account you are using will be the main identity or another identity that has been added to the account you are using.

Figure 16 Outlook Express window

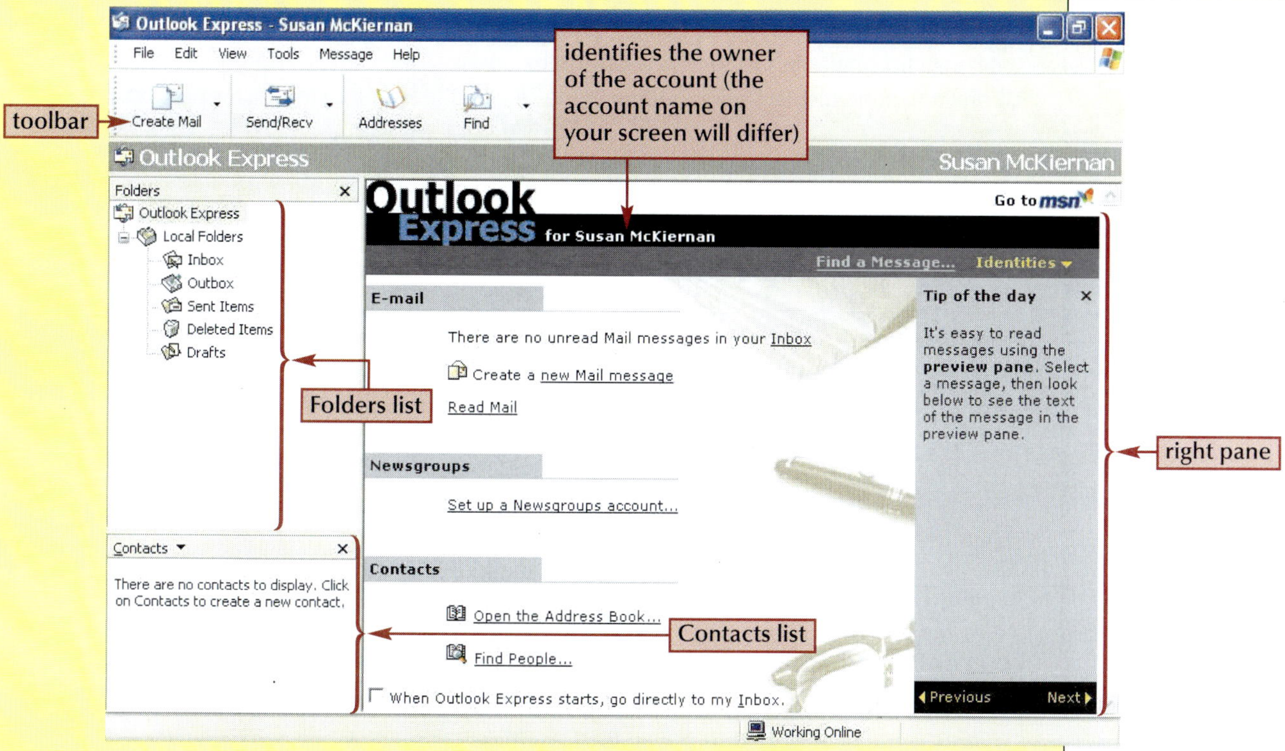

Trouble? If you cannot find Outlook Express on the All Programs menu, check to see if an Outlook Express shortcut icon appears on the desktop or on the taskbar, and then double-click it. If you do not see the shortcut icon, ask your instructor or technical support person for help. The program might be installed in a different folder on your computer.

Trouble? If you see a dialog box with the message "Outlook Express is not currently your default mail client. Would you like to make it your default mail client?" click the No button and then continue with the tutorial.

Trouble? If the title bar on the open window says "Microsoft Outlook" instead of "Microsoft Outlook Express," click the Close button to exit the program, and then repeat Step 1.

Trouble? If a Dial-up Connection dialog box opens, enter your user name and password into the appropriate text boxes, and then click the Connect button. If you do not know your user name or password, ask your instructor or technical support person for assistance. After you make a connection, continue with the tutorial.

In addition to the standard Windows components, such as the title bar, menu bar, scroll bars, Close button, and status bar, the Outlook Express window includes the following elements:

- **Toolbar**: Provides the buttons for frequently performed commands, such as composing a new message, sending or receiving mail, or replying to a message you receive.
- **Folders list**: Displays the default Outlook Express folders, which include the Inbox, Outbox, Sent Items, Deleted Items, and Draft folders. Your mail is organized in these folders automatically. You can create additional folders for the messages you create and receive.
- **Contacts list**: Displays the list of the people, companies, and organizations to which you send mail. The Contacts list appears below the Folders list.

- **Right pane**: Displays information in the large viewing area on the right side of the Outlook Express window. The information displayed depends on the folder you select in the Folders list. For example, when you click the Inbox folder, the right pane displays two sections: a message list of all the messages in your Inbox appears in the upper portion of the pane, and a preview pane displays the contents of the selected message in the lower portion.

Now that you have identified the components of the Outlook Express window, you are ready to create and send a message. To practice creating and sending messages, Susan suggests that you send yourself a test e-mail message.

Reference Window

Creating and Sending an E-mail Message

- Click the Create Mail button on the toolbar to open the New Message window.
- In the To and/or Cc text boxes, type the e-mail address of each recipient, separating names with a comma or semicolon.
- In the Subject text box, type a subject or title for the message.
- Click in the message area, and then type your message.
- Click the Send button on the Standard Buttons toolbar.

To create and send an e-mail message:

1. Click the **Create Mail** button on the toolbar to open the New Message window, and then click the **Maximize** button on the New Message window title bar to maximize this window, as shown in Figure 17.

Figure 17 New Message window

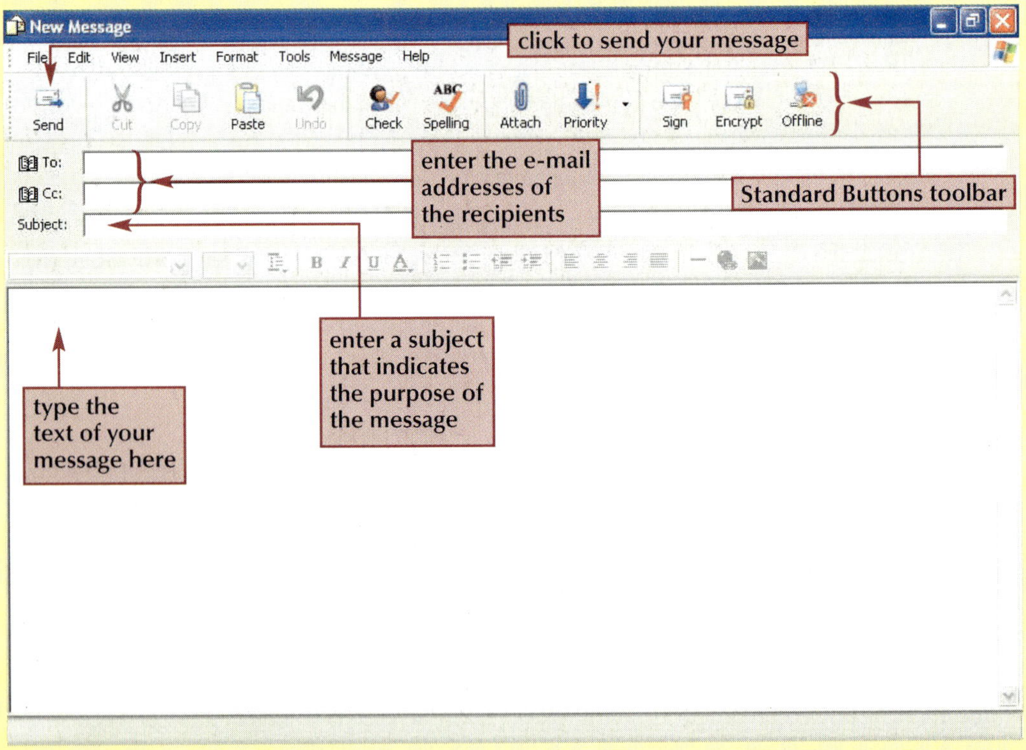

Trouble? If you do not see the toolbar, click View on the menu bar, point to Toolbars, and then click Standard Buttons.

2. Type your e-mail address in the To text box. For example, type *yourname@hotmail.com*.

   Trouble? Check with your instructor or technical support person if you are not sure what e-mail address you should enter.

3. Click the **Subject** text box, and then type **Test**.
4. Click in the message area, type **This is just a practice test message**, press the **Enter** key twice, and then type *your name*.
5. Click the **Send** button on the Standard Buttons toolbar. Outlook Express sends the message to the Outbox, and then to your e-mail address. You may see a number enclosed in parentheses appear briefly to the right of the Outbox folder in the Folders list. The number indicates that Outlook Express has moved the message to the Outbox, which in turn will send the message to the e-mail server for delivery.

If you wanted to send this message to many people, you could have typed more than one e-mail address in the To or Cc text box. You must separate each address with a comma or semicolon. You can also add the e-mail addresses of people (your contacts) to your Address Book, which you will do shortly.

Viewing Sent Messages

When you click the Send button, Outlook Express moves your message to the Outbox folder, and from there the mail server sends the message out. Usually the message remains in the Outbox folder for a brief moment. Sometimes the transmission happens so quickly, you might not notice the number that appears beside the Outbox folder because it just flashes. To make sure your message has been sent, you can open the Sent Items folder to see all the messages you have sent or replied to.

To view the message you sent:

1. Click the **Sent Items** folder in the Folders list. Your message appears in the pane on the right, as shown in Figure 18.

Figure 18 Sent Items folder

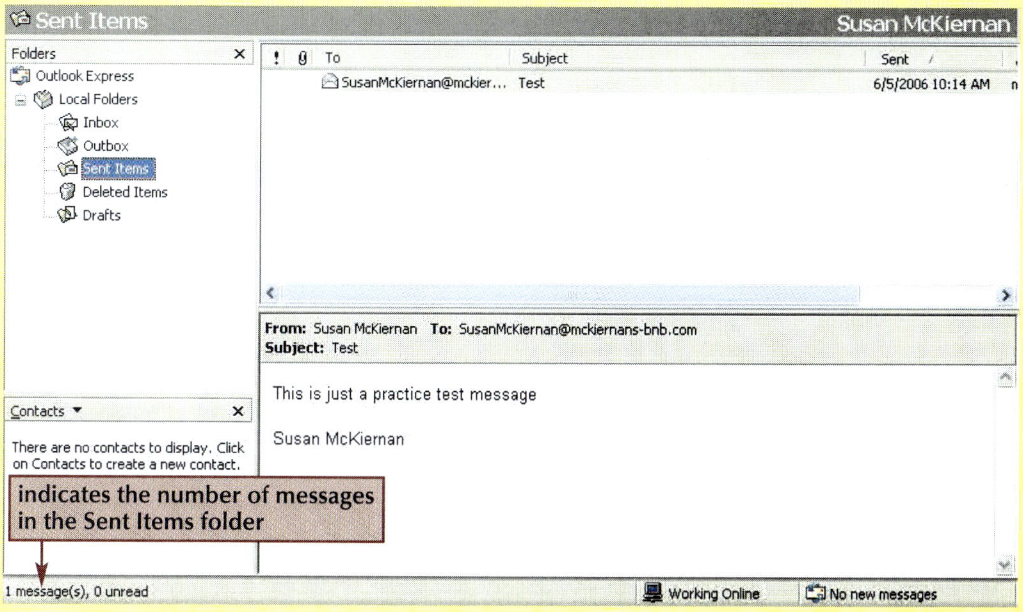

Trouble? If you do not see the Folders list in the Outlook Express window, click View on the menu bar, click Layout, click the Folder List check box in the Window Layout Properties dialog box to select this option, and then click the OK button. Repeat Step 1.

Working with E-mail Messages

Outlook Express transfers, or downloads, messages addressed to you from your e-mail server to your Inbox. Once your messages have been downloaded, they appear in a list with the name of the sender and the subject displayed. To preview a message, you click the message in the list to display its contents in the preview pane, or you can double-click the message to open it in a separate window. You can also print the messages that you receive.

To receive, read, and print the Test e-mail message:

1. Click the **Send/Recv** button on the toolbar. Outlook Express contacts your e-mail server and downloads your e-mail messages. When messages are retrieved from the e-mail server, the number of messages retrieved appears to the right of the Inbox folder. This list of messages appears in the upper portion of the right pane.

   Trouble? If a dialog box opens, asking for your user name and password, enter the information and continue with Step 2. See your instructor or technical support person if you need help entering the correct user name or password.

2. Click the **Inbox** folder in the Folders list. The number of new, unread messages in the Inbox appears to the right of the Inbox folder in the Folders list. A list of e-mail messages you have received appears in the message list, and the content of the selected message in the list appears in the preview pane. The status bar indicates how many messages there are and if any have been read. See Figure 19.

Figure 19 Inbox folder

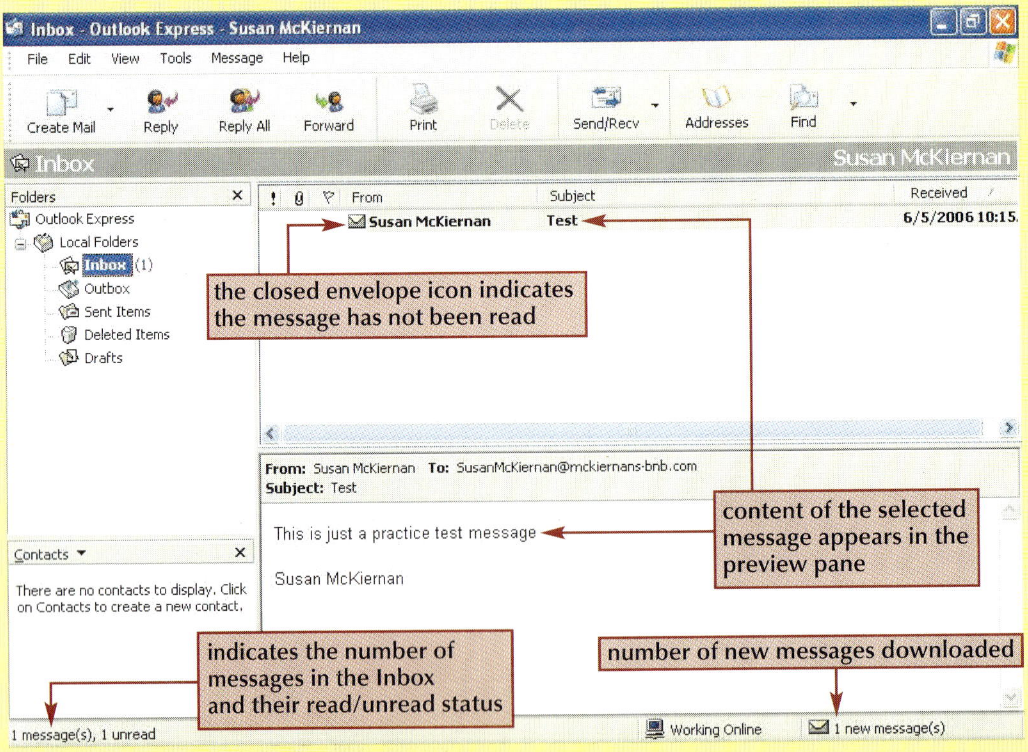

Trouble? Your message list might differ. Just make sure that the Test message you sent to yourself is listed.

3. Click **Test** in the message list. The message is displayed in the preview pane.
4. Double-click **Test** in the message list to open the test message in its own window, and then click the **Maximize** button in the Test message window to maximize it. (Note: You do not need to open a message in its own window to work with the message.)
5. Click the **Print** button on the toolbar. The Print dialog box opens.
6. Click the **Print** button to print the message, and then click the **Close** button on the title bar of the Test message window.

Next you'll perform another common e-mail task: replying to the messages you receive.

Replying to E-mail Messages

Some of the e-mail you receive asks you to provide information, answer questions, or confirm decisions. Instead of creating a new e-mail message, you can reply directly to the message. As part of the reply, Outlook Express fills in the To and Subject text boxes and includes the text of the original message.

Susan suggests that you practice replying to your own e-mail message.

To reply to the Test e-mail message:

1. Make sure the Test message is selected in the message list, and then click the **Reply** button on the toolbar. The Re: Test window, shown in Figure 20, opens. Click the **Maximize** button in the Re: Test window to maximize it. The sender's e-mail address is automatically entered in the To text box, and the subject appears as "Re: Test." If copies of the message have been sent to more than one person, you can send a reply to everyone by clicking the Reply All button.

Figure 20 Replying to a message

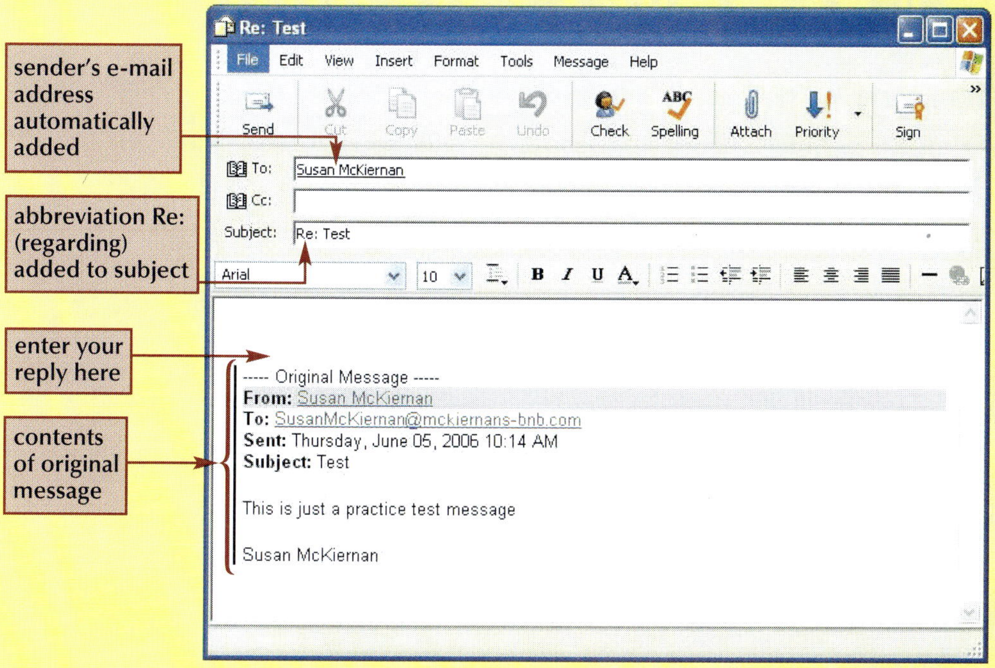

2. In the message area, type **This test was successful!**
3. Click the **Send** button on the toolbar. Note that Susan's name (or your name) now appears in the Contacts list. The name was automatically added to the Address Book. You will learn more about the Address Book later in this session.

   Trouble? If the Contacts list is not displayed in your Outlook Express window, click Tools on the menu bar, click Layout to open the Window Layout Properties dialog box, click the Contacts check box to select it, and then click the OK button. The Contacts list should appear in the lower-left corner of the window under the Folders list.

Deleting E-mail Messages

After you read and respond to your messages, you should delete any message that you no longer need. To delete a message, simply click the message in the message list, and then click the Delete button on the toolbar. When you delete a message, it moves to the Deleted Items folder. This folder might be set up to "empty" its contents automatically when you exit the program; if not, you should empty it periodically. Emptying the contents of the Deleted Items folder permanently removes those items from your computer. To empty the Deleted Items folder, right-click the Deleted Items folder in the Folders list, click Empty 'Deleted Items' Folder on the shortcut menu, and then click the Yes button to confirm the deletion. You can move a deleted message from the Deleted Items folder to another folder if you don't want the message permanently deleted; however, once the Deleted Items folder is emptied, the message no longer exists.

You are done practicing sending and replying to messages, so you can delete the test message you sent to yourself.

To delete the Test e-mail message:

1. Click **Test** in the message list, and then click the **Delete** button on the toolbar.

   The message list no longer displays the Test message.

Adding Contacts to the Address Book

You can use the **Address Book** to keep track of all the people and organizations with which you correspond electronically. In addition to storing e-mail addresses, you can keep all related information about your **contacts** in the Address Book. You can enter home addresses, home phone numbers, business addresses, business phone numbers, and personal information, such as anniversaries and birthdays.

To retrieve a contact's information quickly and easily, you can give the contact a **nickname**, a shortened version of the individual's name. You enter the nickname as the recipient and the correct e-mail address is automatically entered. You can also select the "Automatically put people I reply to in my Address Book" option on the Send tab in the Options dialog box so contacts are automatically added when you reply to a message.

Adding a Contact to the Address Book

Reference Window

- Click the Addresses button on the toolbar (or click Tools on the menu bar, and then click Address Book) to open the Address Book window, click the New button, and then click New Contact.
- In the Properties dialog box, enter the first and last names (the middle name, title, and nickname are optional). Modify the display name if necessary.
- Enter the e-mail address and then click the Add button.
- Enter additional information on the remaining tabs (optional).
- Click the OK button, and then close the Address Book.

or

- Display a message from the sender you want to add as a contact.
- Right-click the sender's name in the From text box, and then click Add to Address Book on the shortcut menu.

Martha at Capital Ads wants to set up an initial meeting with Susan at her earliest convenience. Susan asks you to send Martha an e-mail message with the times she could meet with Martha. Susan also wants you to attach a list of the ideas and questions she has regarding the design of the Web site. But first she wants you to add Martha Kent to the Address Book.

To add a contact to the Address Book:

1. Click the **Addresses** button on the toolbar to open the Address Book window, and then, if necessary, click the **Maximize** button on the Address Book window title bar to maximize the window.
2. Click the **New** button on the toolbar, and then click **New Contact**. The Properties dialog box opens with the Name tab displayed. You enter the basic e-mail address information here.
3. Type **Martha** in the First text box, press the **Tab** key twice, and then type **Kent** in the Last text box. As you enter the information in this top row of text boxes, the information appears in the Display list box. The display name is the name that appears when the message is displayed in the message list. The first and last names also appear in the title bar, changing the "Properties" dialog box to "Martha Kent Properties."
4. Click the **Nickname** text box, and then type **Martha**. When creating a message, you can easily and quickly retrieve an e-mail address saved in the Address Book by typing the nickname of the contact.
5. Click the **E-Mail Addresses** text box, type **marthakent@capital-ads.com**, and then click the **Add** button. See Figure 21.

Figure 21 Properties dialog box for contact Martha Kent

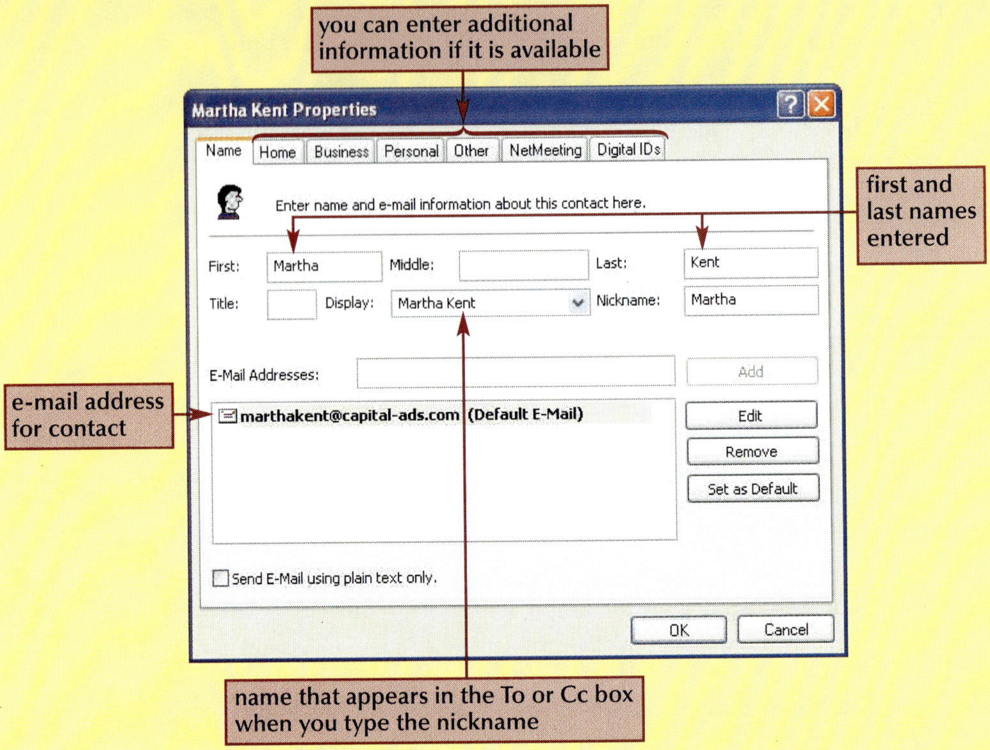

6. Click the **Business** tab in the Martha Kent Properties dialog box, and then enter **Capital Ads Online** in the Company text box. You can enter as much or as little additional information as you have available and deem important. For now, this is all you have on Martha, so you can close the Address Book.
7. Click the **OK** button to save the contact information to the Address Book, and then click the **Close** button to close the Address Book. Martha's name now appears in the Contacts list.

You can make changes to the contact entries in the Address Book or delete a contact when you no longer need to communicate with that individual. To edit contact information or to delete a contact, open the Address Book, select the contact, and then click the Properties button to make changes, or click the Delete button on the toolbar and then click the Yes button to confirm the deletion. The Properties and Delete commands are available on the shortcut menu that appears when you right-click a contact in the Contacts list.

Although you can easily open the Address Book from the toolbar, you also may want to have the Contacts list displayed on a regular basis. You can double-click a name in the Contacts list to create a new message addressed to the contact.

Attaching a File to a Message

Recall that Susan wants to send Martha a list of ideas as an attachment to an e-mail message. Before you send the message with the attachment, Susan suggests you try sending it to yourself first.

To create a message with an attachment:

1. Click the **Create Mail** button on the toolbar to open the New Message window, and then click the **Maximize** button on the New Message window title bar to maximize this window.
2. Type your e-mail address in the To text box. Your display name automatically appears.
3. Type **First Meeting** in the Subject text box.
4. Click in the message area, and then, using Figure 22 as a guide, enter the message text, pressing the **Enter** key between paragraphs and substituting your name for Susan McKiernan's.

Figure 22 First Meeting message to Martha Kent

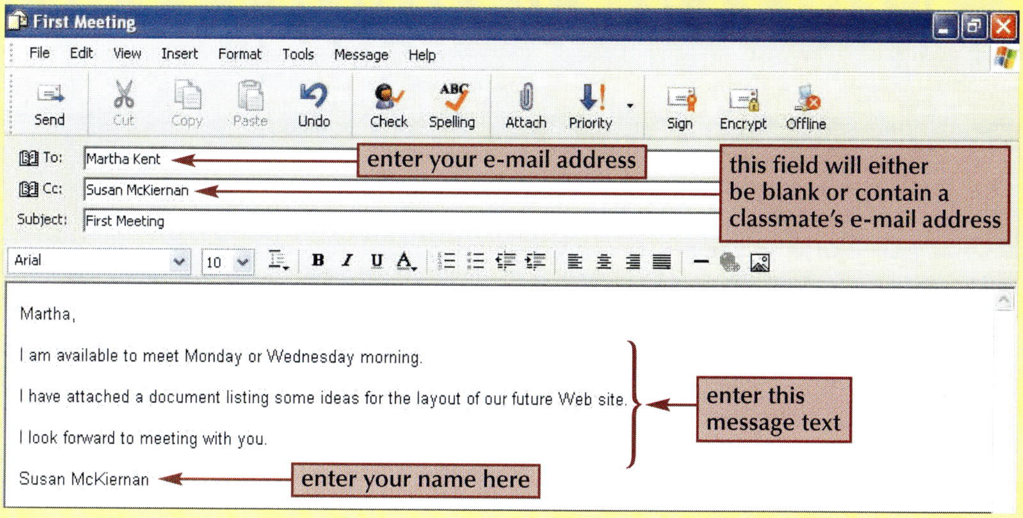

5. Click the **Attach** button on the toolbar to open the Insert Attachment dialog box, navigate to the BEB\Tutorial folder included with your Data Files, click **B&B Ideas** in the file list, and then click the **Attach** button. The file attachment information appears in the Attach text box, as shown in Figure 23.

Figure 23 First Meeting message with file attached

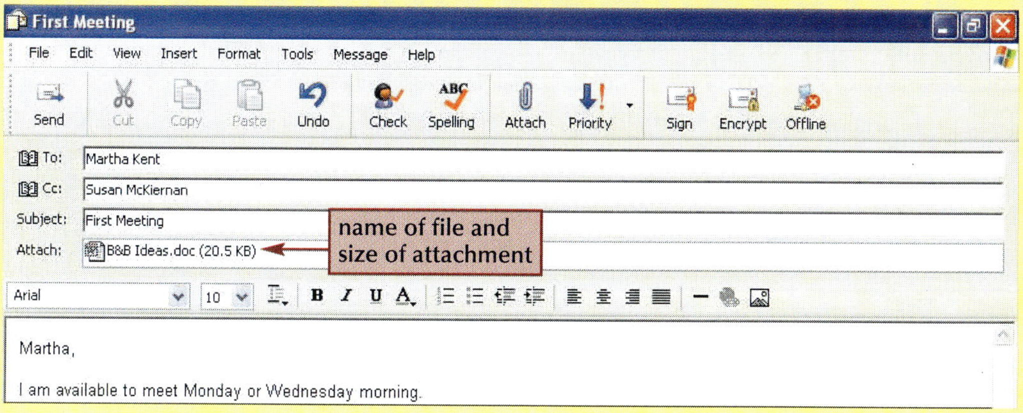

6. Click the **Send** button on the toolbar. Outlook Express moves your message to the Outbox folder before sending it to the e-mail server. You might see a "1" appear briefly next to the Outbox folder.

If you receive a message that contains an attachment, you can choose to save or open the attachment. To open the attachment, you need to make sure the program used to create the attachment is installed on your computer. If the program is not installed, sometimes you can use a text editor, such as WordPad or Notepad, to open and read the attached file. The file attached to the First Meeting message will open in Microsoft Word.

To open the message containing the attachment:

1. Click the **Send/Recv** button on the toolbar.
2. Click the **First Meeting** message in the message list so the contents appear in the preview pane. See Figure 24. The paperclip icon in the upper-right corner of the preview pane indicates that the message contains an attachment.

Figure 24 Message with attachment

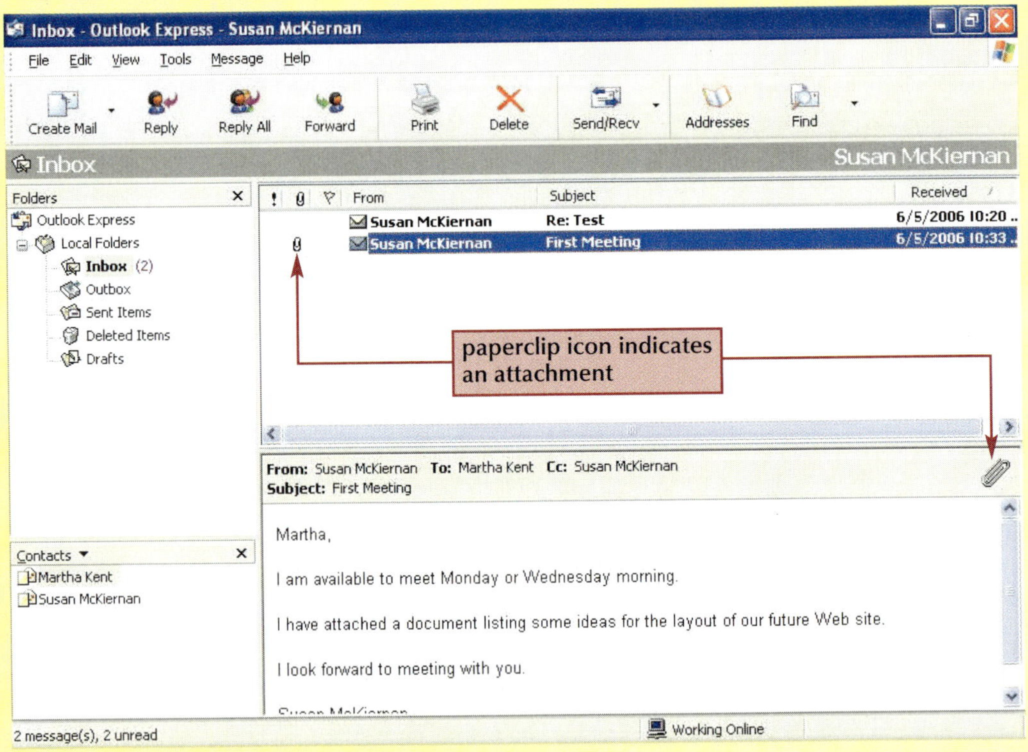

3. Click the **paperclip** icon to display a list of attachments and the Save Attachments option.
4. Click the **B&B Ideas** file. The Open Attachment Warning dialog box opens. Outlook Express displays this dialog box not only to provide options for saving or opening the attachments, but also to warn you that attachments can contain **viruses**, which are programs that can harm your computer. Only open or save a file from known sources to ensure that the files you download to your computer are safe and virus-free.

   You could save the file, but try opening the file instead.
5. Click the **Open it** option button. The file opens in the program in which it was created (in this case, Word). Opening the file before saving it can save time in the end. You can read the file and then decide if you want to save it. You can save it from within the program with the same name or a new name.

6. Click the **Close** button on the Word title bar to close the document and exit the program.
7. Close Outlook Express.

Susan congratulates you for completing the basic tasks in Outlook Express and for sending Martha the message with the attached file. She is sure that you will be able to research the information that she wants and to send and receive messages easily.

Session 2 Quick Check

Review

1. What is the role of an e-mail server?
2. What are the default folders in Outlook Express?
3. Which toolbar button do you click to compose a message?
4. List three guidelines that you should follow when composing e-mail messages.
5. What are two ways that you can enter an e-mail address in the To text box?
6. Multiple e-mail addresses in the To text box must be separated by a(n) ______________ or ______________.
7. Describe two ways to enter contacts in the Address Book.
8. When attaching a file to an e-mail message, why must you consider the size of the file before sending the message with the attachment?

Tutorial Summary

Review

In this tutorial you were introduced to the basics of Web browsers, specifically Internet Explorer. You learned about the major components of the Internet Explorer window. You also learned how to navigate to Web sites and between Web pages on a Web site. You learned how to return to visited sites and pages using the Back and Forward buttons and the History Explorer bar. You also learned how to save a Web site as a favorite so you can return to the site with one click.

The tutorial presented some basic information on e-mail using Outlook Express. You learned the components and features of Outlook Express. You learned how to create and send an e-mail message, receive and reply to a message, and attach a file to a message. You also learned about the Address Book and how to add contacts to it.

Key Terms

Address Book
contact
copyright
cyberlaw
dial-up connection
domain name
DSL (Digital Subscriber Line) connection
electronic mail
e-mail
e-mail account
e-mail client software
e-mail message
e-mail program
e-mail server
fair use
Favorites list
History list
home page
hyperlink
Hypertext Markup Language (HTML)
Hypertext Transfer Protocol (HTTP)
index.htm
Internet
Internet Protocol (IP) address
Internet service provider (ISP)
link
network

nickname
plagiarism
protocol
Refresh button
start page
Stop button
store-and-forward technology
Uniform Resource Locator (URL)
user name
virus
Web browser
Web directory
Web page
Web search engine
Web server
Web site
World Wide Web (WWW)

Practice

Practice the skills you learned in the tutorial using the same case scenario.

Review Assignments

There are no Data Files needed for the Review Assignments.

In preparation for her meeting with Martha Kent, Susan wants you to compile some additional information about the Web sites that specialize in Irish food, which she and Preston want to feature at their B&B.

Complete the following:

1. Start your Web browser, go to the New Perspectives Student Union Web page (*http://www.course.com/NewPerspectives/studentunion*), click the **Microsoft Office 2003** link, click the **Office First Course** link, click the **Browser and E-Mail Basics** link, click the appropriate **click here** link, and then click the **Review Assignments** link.
2. Click the hyperlinks listed under the category heading Irish Foods to explore the Web pages for each entry.
3. Using the History Explorer bar, return to three sites that have the most interesting home pages, and then print the home page of each.
4. Create a favorites folder named "Irish Foods," and save as favorites the three sites whose home pages you printed in the preceding step.
5. Using the Favorites Explorer bar, return to each site and answer the following questions:
   a. Which sites include graphic links?
   b. Which sites include links to other Web sites? (*Hint*: If the Back button is not available when the Web page is displayed, the link has taken you to a new Web site. Click the Close button to return to the previous site.)
   c. Which sites include download links?
6. Choose your favorite image from any one of the sites, and save it in the BEB\Review folder provided with your Data Files.
7. Start your e-mail program and create a message addressed to your instructor and copied to yourself. Write the answers to Assignment 5 as the message text, attach the image you saved in Assignment 6, send the message, and then close Outlook Express.
8. In Internet Explorer, delete the Irish Foods favorites folder (and all its contents) that you created in Assignment 4, and then close Internet Explorer.

Apply

Use the skills that you learned about Internet Explorer to research several business Web sites.

Case Problem 1

There are no Data Files needed for this Case Problem.

Businesses on the Web Business Web sites range from very simple informational sites to comprehensive sites that offer information about a firm's products or services, history, current employment openings, and finances. An increasing number of businesses offer products or services for sale on their Web sites. You just started a position on the public relations staff of Value City Central, a large retail chain of television and appliance stores. Your first assignment is to research and report on the types of information that other large firms offer on their Web sites.

Complete the following:

1. Start your Web browser, go to the New Perspectives Student Union Web page (*http://www.course.com/NewPerspectives/studentunion*), click the **Microsoft Office 2003** link, click the **Office First Course** link, click the **Browser and E-Mail Basics** link, click the appropriate **click here** link, and then click the **Case Problems** link.
2. Use the Case Problem 1 hyperlinks to open the business sites on that page.
3. Choose three business sites that you believe would be most relevant to your assignment.
4. Print the home page for each Web site that you have chosen.
5. Select one site that you feel does the best job in each of the following five categories: overall presentation of the corporate image, description of featured products or services, presentation of the history or background of the firm, description of employment opportunities, and presentation of financial statements or other financial information about the company.
6. Prepare a report that includes one paragraph describing why you believe each of the sites you identified in the preceding step did the best job.
7. Close your Web browser and your Internet connection, if necessary.

Apply

Use the skills you learned about Internet Explorer to investigate how charitable or not-for-profit organizations use the Internet to present themselves.

Case Problem 2

There are no Data Files needed for this Case Problem.

Columbus Suburban Area Council The Columbus Suburban Area Council is a charitable organization devoted to maintaining and improving the general welfare of people living in the suburbs of Columbus, Ohio. As the director of the council, you are interested in encouraging donations and other support from local citizens and would like to stay informed of grant opportunities that might benefit the council. You are especially interested in developing an informative and attractive presence on the Web.

Complete the following:

1. Start your Web browser, go to the New Perspectives Student Union Web page (*http://www.course.com/NewPerspectives/studentunion*), click the **Microsoft Office 2003** link, click the **Office First Course** link, click the **Browser and E-Mail Basics** link, click the appropriate **click here** link, and then click the **Case Problems** link.
2. Follow the Case Problem 2 hyperlinks to charitable organizations to find out more about what other organizations are doing with their Web sites.

3. Select three of the Web sites you visited and, for each, prepare a list of the site's contents. Note whether each site includes financial information and whether the site discloses how much the organization spends on administrative, or nonprogram, activities. Also note whether the site lets visitors communicate with the organization via e-mail.
4. Identify which site you believe would be a good model for the Columbus Suburban Area Council's new Web site. Explain why you think your chosen site would be the best example to follow.
5. Close your Web browser and your Internet connection, if necessary.

Research

Use the skills you learned about Internet Explorer to research two of today's most popular advertising vehicles on the Internet.

Case Problem 3

There are no Data Files needed for this Case Problem.

Pretzel Piazza You are working for the Pretzel Piazza during your summer break. This shop offers a large variety of coffees and teas, but its specialty is gourmet pretzels. The pretzels come in a wide variety of flavors, from the standard salted pretzel to the most decadent Belgium chocolate-covered pretzels. There are pretzels covered with a variety of chocolate, caramel, nuts, and candies. The owners of Pretzel Piazza have a Web site, but they are wondering if using a pop-up ad and junk mail campaign for a short period of time might be a better way to advertise their products to a wider customer base. One of your assignments is to research information and articles dealing with pop-up ads, which are independent windows that appear when you are online, and junk mail, also known as spam. After researching these topics, you will report back to the owners with your recommendation.

Complete the following:

1. Start your Web browser, go to the New Perspectives Student Union Web page (*http://www.course.com/NewPerspectives/studentunion*), click the **Microsoft Office 2003** link, and then click the **Office First Course** link.
2. Click the **Browser and E-Mail Basics** link, click the appropriate **click here** link, and then click the **Case Problems** link.
3. Use the hyperlinks under the Case Problem 3 heading to learn more about pop-up advertising.
4. Send an e-mail message to your instructor listing the pros and cons of pop-up ads on the Internet. Give your opinion on whether pop-ups are effective advertising tools.
5. Return to the Case Problem 3 links, and use the hyperlinks to learn more about spam.
6. Send an e-mail message to your instructor listing the pros and cons of spam on the Internet. Provide the names of the Web sites that you feel were the most helpful, and explain what kind of information they provided. Indicate whether you feel spam is an effective advertising tool.

Challenge

Learn more about the features and tools of Outlook Express.

Case Problem 4

There are no Data Files needed for this Case Problem.

Learning More About Outlook Express Outlook Express is a convenient way to handle e-mail. Although not considered a full-featured or robust e-mail program, Outlook Express does offer many useful tools and features. To learn more about this application, you will use Microsoft Outlook Express Help.

Complete the following:

1. Start Outlook Express.
2. **Explore** Use Outlook Express Help to learn about stationery. (*Hint*: Click Help on the menu bar, click Contents and Index, click the Index tab, type "stationery" in the text box, click the Search button to display a list of related topics, and then click the "Use stationery with outgoing messages" topic.)
3. **Explore** Compose a message to your instructor using stationery. The content of the message should include the steps you used to add the stationery to the message. Also include how to set stationery as the default background for all new messages that you create. Send a copy of the message to yourself.
4. **Explore** Use Outlook Express Help to learn how to set up Outlook Express to receive e-mail from a Hotmail account. (*Hint*: Click Help on the menu bar, point to Microsoft on the Web, click Search the Web to open the Search Companion pane, type "How do I set up Outlook Express to receive Hotmail" in the text box, and then click the Search button to go to the Microsoft Support Web page for information on Outlook Express and Hotmail.)
5. Compose a message to your instructor, with a copy to yourself, explaining the steps for the setup procedure. If you have a Hotmail account, *do not* set up Outlook Express to receive your e-mail unless your instructor or technical support person instructs you to do so.

Assess

SAM Assessment and Training

If you have a SAM user profile, you may have access to hands-on instruction, practice, and assessment of the skills covered in this tutorial. Log in to your SAM account and go to your assignments page to see what your instructor has assigned.

Reinforce

The Internet: World Wide Web

Lab Assignments

The New Perspectives Labs are designed to help you master some of the key concepts and skills presented in this text. The steps for completing this Lab are located on the Course Technology Web site. Log on to the Internet and use your Web browser to go to the Student Online Companion for New Perspectives Office 2003 at **www.course.com/np/office2003**. Click the Lab Assignments link, and then navigate to the assignments for this tutorial.

Review

Quick Check Answers

Session 1

1. The Internet is a collection of networked computers, and located on these computers is a system of electronic documents that are linked together and referred to as the World Wide Web. You need to be connected to the Internet to have access to the World Wide Web.
2. A Web browser is the software that runs on your computer so it can communicate with all different types of computers connected to the Internet and access the HTML documents that reside on those computers.
3. The *http* stands for Hypertext Transfer Protocol (HTTP), used to transport the file; the *www.savethetrees* indicates the domain name of the computer on which the file resides; the *.org* identifies the Web server type; and *main.html* is the name of the file.
4. index.htm
5. A home page is the main page that all of the pages on a particular Web site are organized around and link back to.
6. You can click the Back or Forward button, use the History list, or save a site as a favorite.
7. Search engines are Web pages that conduct searches of the Web to find the words or expressions that you enter. The result of a search is a Web page that contains hyperlinks to Web pages with matching text or expressions. These pages can give users an easy way to find information on the Web.
8. Web Page, complete

Session 2

1. An e-mail server uses store-and-forward technology to store e-mail messages until recipients request them and to forward the messages to the requesting computers.
2. Inbox, Outbox, Sent Items, Drafts, and Deleted Items
3. Create Mail
4. Remember e-mail is not private; provide meaningful information in the subject line; check with recipients before sending large file attachments to find out about size restrictions and set up a convenient time to send the attachment.
5. Type the e-mail address in the To text box; select a contact from the Address Book; double-click the contact in the Contacts list.
6. comma or semicolon
7. Enter the information manually in the Address Book; or reply to an e-mail address or right-click the name of the sender in the From column, then click Add Sender to Address Book on the shortcut menu.
8. Messages with large attachments can take a long time for the recipient to download. Most e-mail servers have a limit to the size of the files you can attach; some allow files no larger than 1 MB. You need to check with your recipients before sending large file attachments to find out about size restrictions.

Objectives

Session 1.1
- Plan a document
- Identify the components of the Word window
- Choose commands using toolbars and menus
- Create a new document

Session 1.2
- Scroll a document and move the insertion point
- Correct errors and undo and redo changes
- Save, preview, and print a document
- Enter the date with AutoComplete
- Remove Smart Tags
- Create an envelope

Lab

Student Data Files

There are no student Data Files needed for this tutorial.

Creating a Document

Writing a Business Letter

Case

Art4U, Inc.

Megan Grahs is the owner and manager of Art4U, Inc., a graphics design firm in Tucson, Arizona. When Megan founded Art4U in the early 1980s, the company drew most of its revenue from design projects for local magazines, newspapers, advertising circulars, and other print publications. The artists at Art4U laboriously created logos, diagrams, and other illustrations by hand, using watercolors, ink, pastels, and a variety of other media. Since the advent of the Internet, however, Art4U has become one of the Southwest's leading creators of electronic artwork. The firm's artists now work exclusively on computers, saving each piece of art as an electronic file that they can e-mail to a client in a matter of minutes.

Thanks to e-mail, Art4U is no longer limited to the local Tucson market. As a result, Art4U has nearly doubled in size over the past ten years. Most of the increase in business has come from Web page designers, who continually need fresh and innovative graphics to use in their Web pages. In fact, Megan has just signed a contract with Web Time Productions agreeing to create a series of logos for a high-profile Web site. She needs to return the signed contract to Web Time Productions' office in Chicago.

In this tutorial, you will create the cover letter that will accompany the contract. You will create the letter using **Microsoft Office Word 2003** (or simply **Word**), a popular word-processing program. Before you begin typing the letter, you will learn how to start the Word program, identify and use the elements of the Word screen, and adjust some Word settings. Next, you will create a new Word document, type the text of the cover letter, save the letter, and then print the letter for Megan. In the process of entering the text, you'll learn several ways to correct typing errors.

Session 1.1

Four Steps to a Professional Document

Word helps you produce quality work in minimal time. Not only can you type a document in Word, but you can also quickly make revisions and corrections, adjust margins and spacing, create columns and tables, and add graphics to your documents. The most efficient way to produce a document is to follow these four steps: (1) planning, (2) creating and editing, (3) formatting, and (4) printing.

In the long run, planning saves time and effort. First, you should determine what you want to say. State your purpose clearly and include enough information to achieve that purpose without overwhelming or boring your reader. Be sure to organize your ideas logically. Decide how you want your document to look as well. In this case, your letter to Web Time Productions will take the form of a standard business letter. It should be addressed to Web Time's president, Nicholas Brower. Megan has given you a handwritten note indicating what she would like you to say in the letter. This note is shown in Figure 1-1.

Figure 1-1 **Megan's notes for the contract letter**

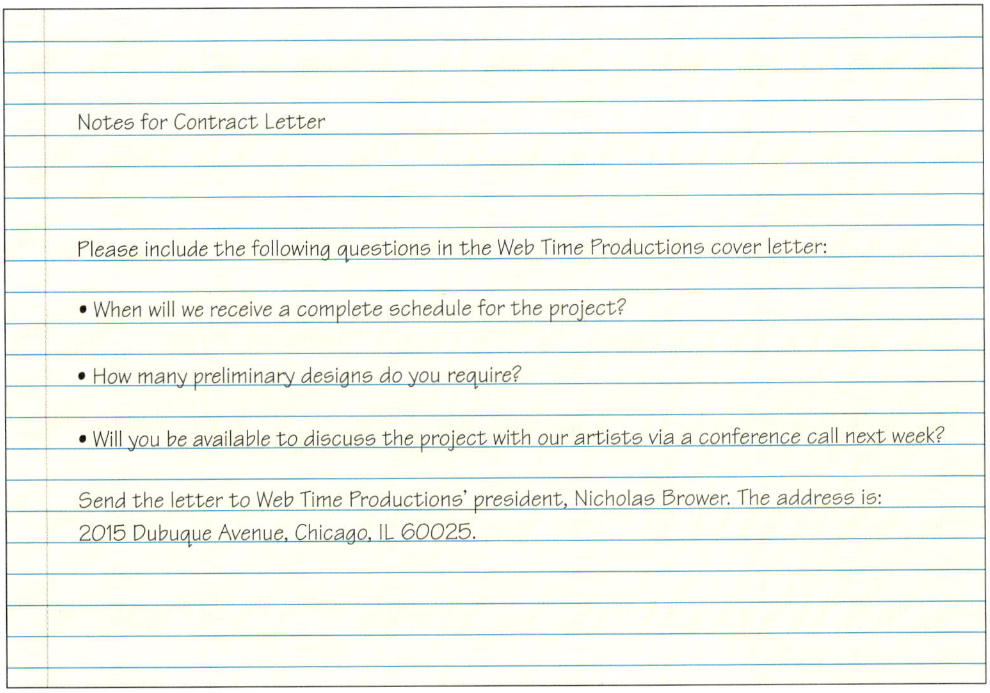

Notes for Contract Letter

Please include the following questions in the Web Time Productions cover letter:

- When will we receive a complete schedule for the project?
- How many preliminary designs do you require?
- Will you be available to discuss the project with our artists via a conference call next week?

Send the letter to Web Time Productions' president, Nicholas Brower. The address is:
2015 Dubuque Avenue, Chicago, IL 60025.

After you plan your document, you can go ahead and create and edit it using Word. Creating the document generally means typing the text of your document. Editing consists of reading the document you've created, correcting your errors, and, finally, adding or deleting text to make the document easy to read.

Once your document is error-free, you can format it to make it visually appealing. Formatting features, such as adjusting margins to create white space (blank areas of a page), setting line spacing, and using bold and italic, can help make your document easier to read.

Printing is the final phase in creating an effective document. In this tutorial, you will preview your document before you spend time and resources to print it.

Exploring the Word Window

Before you can apply these four steps to produce a letter in Word, you need to start Word and learn about the general organization of the Word window. You'll do that now.

To start Microsoft Word:

1. Click the **Start** button on the taskbar, point to **All Programs**, point to **Microsoft Office**, and then click **Microsoft Office Word 2003**. The Word window opens. See Figure 1-2.

   Trouble? If you don't see the Microsoft Office Word 2003 option on the Microsoft Office submenu, look for it in a different submenu or as an option on the All Programs menu. If you still can't find the Microsoft Office Word 2003 option, ask your instructor or technical support person for help.

Maximized Word window — **Figure 1-2**

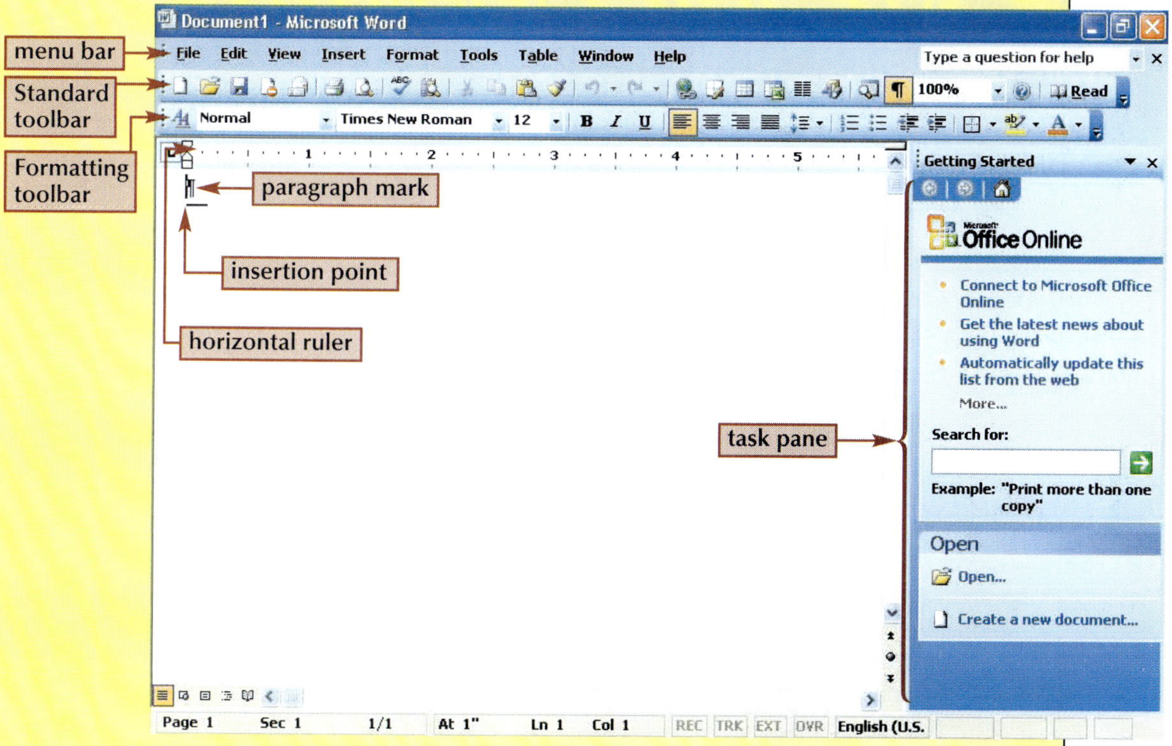

2. If the Word window does not fill the entire screen, click the **Maximize** button in the upper-right corner of the Word window. Your screen should now resemble Figure 1-2.

   Trouble? If your screen looks slightly different from Figure 1-2, just continue with the steps. You will learn how to change the appearance of the Word window shortly.

   Word is now running and ready to use. Don't be concerned if you don't see everything shown in Figure 1-2. You'll learn how to adjust the appearance of the Word window soon.

The Word window is made up of a number of elements, which are described in Figure 1-3. You are already familiar with some of these elements, such as the menu bar and toolbars, because they are common to all Windows programs.

Figure 1-3 Parts of the Word window

Screen Element	Description
Formatting toolbar	Contains buttons that affect how the document looks.
horizontal ruler	Shows page margins, tabs, and column widths.
insertion point	Shows where characters will appear when you start typing.
menu bar	Contains lists, or menus, of all the Word commands. When you first display a menu, you see a short list of the most frequently used commands. To see the full list of commands in the menu, you can click the menu and then wait a few seconds for the remaining commands to appear, double-click the menu, or click the menu and then click or point to the downward-facing double-arrow at the bottom of the menu.
paragraph mark	Marks the end of a paragraph.
Standard toolbar	Contains buttons for activating frequently used commands.
task pane	Provides links and buttons that you can use to perform common tasks.

If at any time you would like to check the name of a Word toolbar button, position the mouse pointer over the button without clicking. A ScreenTip, a small box with the name of the button, will appear. (If you don't see ScreenTips on your computer, click Tools on the Word menu bar, click Options, click the View tab, click the ScreenTips check box to insert a check, and then click OK.)

Keep in mind that the menus initially display the commands that are used most frequently on your particular computer. When you leave a menu open for a few seconds or point to the double-arrow, a complete list of commands appears. Throughout these tutorials, you should point to the double-arrow on a menu if you do not see the command you need.

Setting Up the Window Before You Begin Each Tutorial

Word provides a set of standard settings, called **default settings**, which control how the screen is set up and how a document looks when you first start typing. These settings are appropriate for most situations. However, these settings are easily changed, and most people begin a work session by adjusting Word to make sure it is set up the way they want it.

As you gain experience, you will learn how to customize Word to suit your needs. But to make it easier to follow the steps in these tutorials, you should take care to arrange your window to match the tutorial figures. The rest of this section explains what your window should look like and how to make it match those in the tutorials. Depending on how many people use your computer (and how much they adjust Word's appearance), you might have to set up the window to match the figures each time you start Word.

Setting the Document View to Normal

The View buttons in the lower-left corner of the Word window change the way your document is displayed. You will learn how to select the appropriate view for a document in a later tutorial. For now, you want the document displayed in Normal view.

To make sure the document is displayed in Normal view:

1. Click the **Normal View** button to the left of the horizontal scroll bar. See Figure 1-4. If your Document window was not in Normal view, it changes to Normal view now. The Normal View button is now highlighted, indicating that it is selected.

Figure 1-4 Changing to Normal view

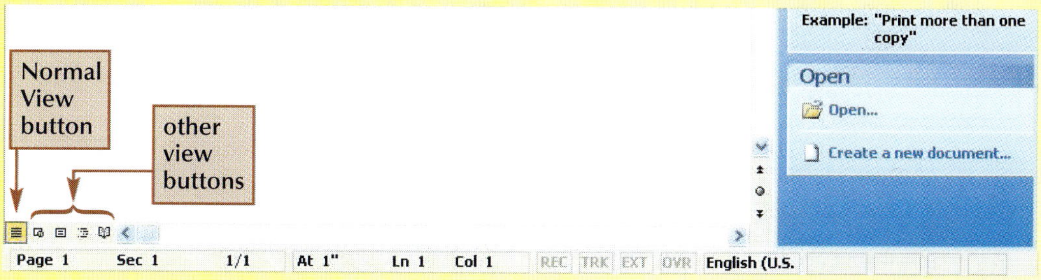

Displaying the Toolbars, Task Pane, and Ruler

The Word toolbars allow you to perform common tasks quickly by clicking a button. To eliminate on-screen clutter while you work through these tutorials, you should check to make sure that only the Formatting and Standard toolbars appear on your screen. The Standard toolbar should be positioned on top of the Formatting toolbar, as shown previously in Figure 1-2.

Depending on the choices made by the last person to use your computer, you may not see both toolbars or you may see both toolbars on one row. You also may see additional toolbars. In the following steps, you will make sure that your Word window shows only the Standard and Formatting toolbars. At the same time, you will verify that the task pane is displayed as it is in Figure 1-2.

To verify that your Word window shows the correct toolbars and the task pane:

1. Position the pointer over any toolbar and click the right mouse button. A shortcut menu appears. The menu lists all available toolbars with a check mark next to those currently displayed. If the Standard and Formatting toolbars are currently displayed on your computer, you should see check marks next to their names. You should also see a check mark next to "Task Pane," indicating that the task pane is displayed on the right side of the screen. (You saw the task pane earlier in Figure 1-2.)
2. Verify that you see a check mark next to the word "Standard" in the shortcut menu. If you do not see a check mark, click **Standard** now. (Clicking any item on the shortcut menu closes the menu, so you will need to re-open it in the next step.)
3. Redisplay the shortcut menu, and click **Formatting** if you don't see a check mark next to it.
4. If you don't see the task pane, click View on the menu bar and then click **Task Pane**.
5. Redisplay the shortcut menu. If any toolbar besides the Formatting and Standard toolbars is open, click the toolbar name to remove the check mark and hide the toolbar.

   Trouble? If you see a task pane other than the Getting Started task pane, click the down pointing arrow at the top of the task pane, and then click Getting Started.

If the toolbars appear on one row, perform the next steps to arrange them in two rows.

To arrange the Standard and Formatting toolbars on two rows:

1. Click **Tools** on the menu bar, and then click **Customize**. The Customize dialog box opens.
2. Click the **Options** tab if it is not already selected, and then click the **Show Standard and Formatting toolbars on two rows** check box to select it (that is, to insert a check).
3. Click **Close**. The Customize dialog box closes. The toolbars and task pane on your screen should now match those shown earlier in Figure 1-2.

Setting Up Other Screen Elements

Next, you'll take care of a few other parts of the screen, including:

- The horizontal ruler, which appears below the Formatting toolbar and is used to adjust margins and align parts of a document
- The Zoom setting, which controls the document's on-screen magnification; a setting of 100% displays the text in the same size as it will appear when printed
- The default font setting, which controls the size and shape of the characters that appear when you start typing

You'll learn more about these topics later. For now, you simply need to make your screen match the figures in this book by displaying the horizontal ruler, setting the Zoom setting to 100%, and verifying that 12-point Times New Roman is the default font.

To display the ruler, check your Zoom setting, and select the correct default font:

1. Click **View** on the menu bar, and then point to the double-arrow at the bottom of the menu to display the hidden menu commands.
2. If "Ruler" does not have a check mark next to it, click **Ruler**. The horizontal ruler should now be displayed, as shown earlier in Figure 1-2.
3. Click the **Zoom** list arrow 100% on the Standard toolbar. A list of screen magnification settings appears. In Figure 1-5, the currently selected setting is 100%.

Figure 1-5 Zoom settings

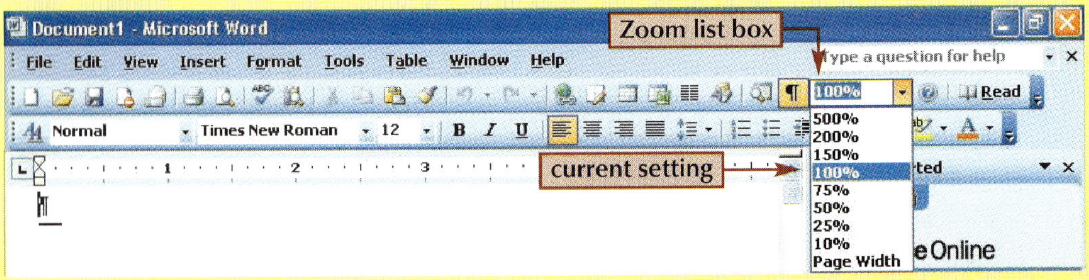

4. If 100% is not selected on your computer, click **100%** to select it. If you don't need to change your Zoom setting, press the **Esc** key to close the Zoom list. Next, you will check the default font setting.
5. Click **Format** on the menu bar, and then click **Font**. The Font dialog box opens. Click the **Font** tab if it is not already selected. See Figure 1-6.

Font dialog box — **Figure 1-6**

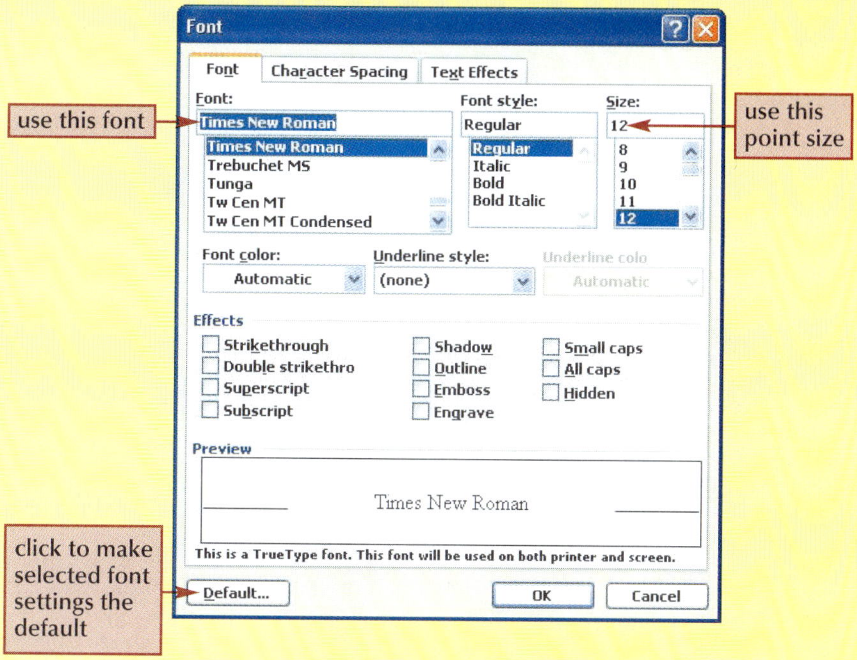

6. In the Font list box, click **Times New Roman**.
7. In the Size list box, click **12** if it is not already selected.
8. Click the **Default** button to make Times New Roman and 12 point the default settings. Word displays a message asking you to verify that you want to make 12-point Times New Roman the default font.
9. Click the **Yes** button.

Displaying Nonprinting Characters

Nonprinting characters are symbols that can appear on the screen but are not visible on the printed page. For example, one nonprinting character marks the end of a paragraph (¶) and another marks the space between words (•). It's helpful to display nonprinting characters so you can see whether you've typed an extra space, ended a paragraph, and so on.

Depending on how your computer is set up, nonprinting characters might have appeared automatically when you started Word. In Figure 1-7, you can see the paragraph symbol (¶) in the blank Document window. Also, the Show/Hide ¶ button is highlighted in the Standard toolbar. Both of these indicate that nonprinting characters are displayed. If they are not displayed on your screen, you need to perform the following step.

Figure 1-7 Nonprinting characters displayed

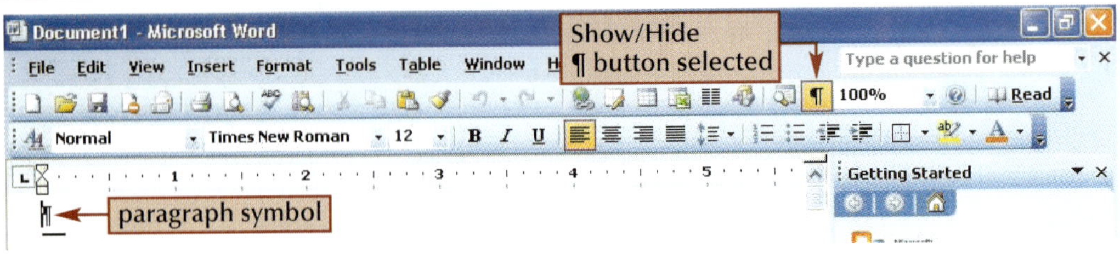

To display nonprinting characters:

1. Click the **Show/Hide** ¶ button ¶ on the Standard toolbar. A paragraph mark (¶) appears at the top of the Document window. Your screen should now match Figure 1-7.

   Trouble? If the Show/Hide ¶ button was already highlighted before you clicked it, you have now deactivated it. Click the Show/Hide ¶ button a second time to select it.

To make sure your window always matches the figures in these tutorials, remember to complete the checklist in Figure 1-8 each time you sit down at the computer.

Figure 1-8 Word window checklist

Screen Element	Setting
Default font	Times New Roman
Default font size	12 point
Document view	Normal view
Formatting toolbar	Displayed below Standard toolbar
Horizontal ruler	Displayed
Nonprinting characters	Displayed
Other toolbars	Hidden
Standard toolbar	Displayed below menu bar
Task pane	Displayed
Word window	Maximized
Zoom box	Setting identical to setting shown in figures

Now that you have planned your letter, opened Word, identified screen elements, and adjusted settings, you are ready to begin typing a letter.

Beginning a Letter

Word Processing

You're ready to begin typing Megan's letter to Nicholas Brower at Web Time Productions. Figure 1-9 shows the completed letter printed on company letterhead. You will create this letter by completing the steps in this tutorial.

Completed letter **Figure 1-9**

Art4U, Inc.
5725 Mesa Avenue
Tucson, AZ 85703
Art4U@Earth-World-Art.com

February 15, 2006

Nicholas Brower
Web Time Productions
2015 Dubuque Avenue
Chicago, IL 60025

Dear Nicholas:

Enclosed you will find the signed contract. As you can see, I am returning all three pages, with my signature on each.

Now that we have finalized the contract, I have a few questions: When will we receive a complete schedule for the project? Also, how many preliminary designs do you require? Finally, will you be available to discuss the project with our artists via a conference call some afternoon next week? Thursday or Friday afternoon would be ideal, if either of those options work for you.

Thanks again for choosing Art4U. We look forward to working with you.

Sincerely yours,

Megan L. Grahs

You'll begin by opening a new blank document (in case you accidentally typed something in the current page). Whenever you need to perform a common task such as opening a document, you can usually start with the task pane. In this case, you can use a special task pane that is devoted to creating new documents.

To open a new document:

1. Click the **Create a new document** button in the Open section at the bottom of the Getting Started task pane. Instead of the Getting Started task pane, you now see the New Document task pane. See Figure 1-10.

Figure 1-10 New Document task pane

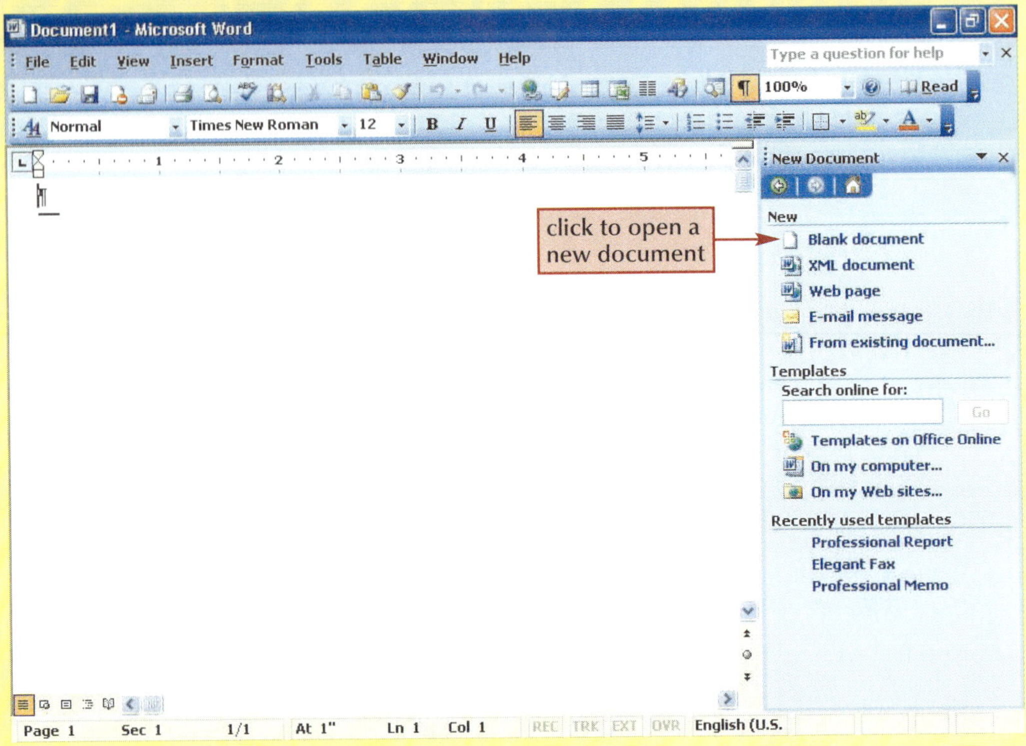

2. Click the **Blank document** button in the New Document task pane. A new document named Document2 opens and the task pane closes.

Now that you have opened a new document, you need to insert some blank lines in the document to ensure that you leave enough room for the company letterhead.

To insert blank lines in the document:

1. Press the **Enter** key eight times. Each time you press the Enter key, a nonprinting paragraph mark appears. In the status bar (at the bottom of the Document window), you should see the setting "At 2.5"," indicating that the insertion point is approximately 2.5 inches from the top of the page. Another setting in the status bar should read "Ln 9," indicating that the insertion point is in line 9 of the document. See Figure 1-11. (Your settings may be slightly different.)

Figure 1-11 Document window after inserting blank lines

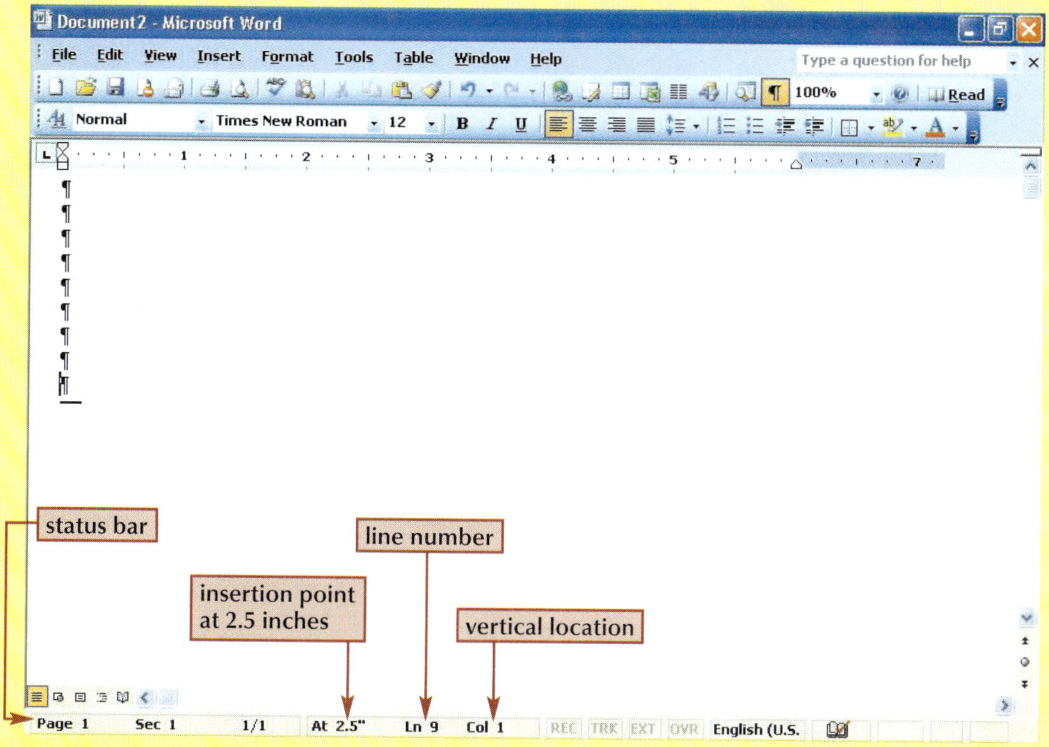

Trouble? If the paragraph mark doesn't appear each time you press the Enter key, the non-printing characters might be hidden. Click the Show/Hide ¶ button on the Standard toolbar.

Trouble? If you pressed the Enter key too many times, press the Backspace key to delete each extra line and paragraph mark. If you're on line 9 but the "At" number is not 2.5", don't worry. Different monitors produce slightly different measurements when you press the Enter key.

Pressing Enter is a simple, fast way to insert space in a document. When you are a more experienced Word user, you'll learn how to insert space without using the Enter key.

Entering Text

Normally, you begin typing a letter by entering the date. However, Megan tells you that she's not sure whether the contract will be ready to send today or tomorrow. So she asks you to skip the date for now and begin with the inside address. Making changes to documents is easy in Word, so you can easily add the date later.

In the following steps, you'll type the inside address (shown on Megan's note, in Figure 1-1). If you type a wrong character, press the Backspace key to delete the mistake and then retype the correct character.

To type the inside address:

1. Type **Nicholas Brower**, and then press the **Enter** key. As you type, a nonprinting character (•) appears between words to indicate a space. See Figure 1-12.

Figure 1-12 **First line of inside address**

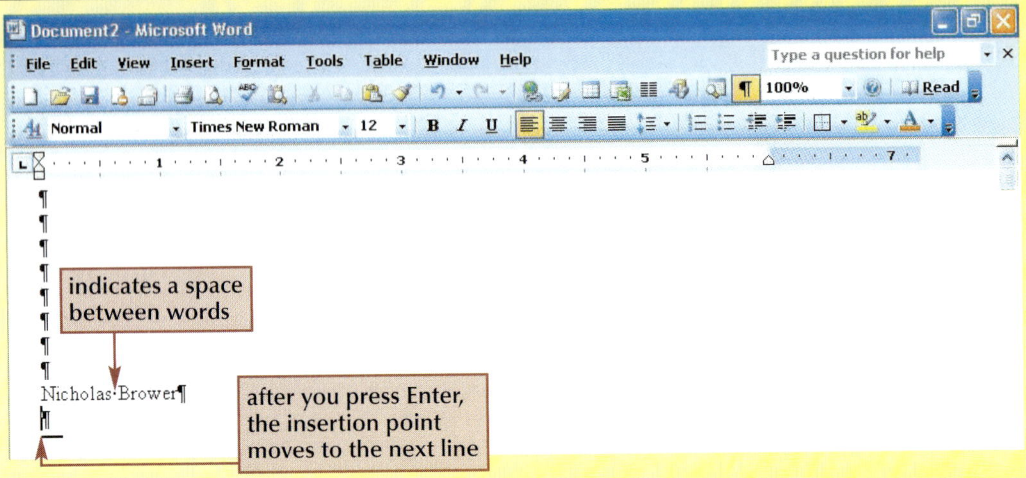

Trouble? If a wavy line appears beneath a word, check to make sure you typed the text correctly. If you did not, use the Backspace key to remove the error, and then retype the text correctly.

2. Type the following text, pressing the **Enter** key after each line to complete the inside address:

   Web Time Productions
   2015 Dubuque Avenue
   Chicago, IL 60025

   Be sure to press the Enter key after you type the ZIP code. Ignore the dotted underline below the street address. You'll learn the meaning of this underline later in this tutorial.

3. Press the **Enter** key again to add a blank line after the inside address. (You should see a total of two paragraph marks below the inside address.) Now you can type the salutation.

4. Type **Dear Nicholas:** and then press the **Enter** key twice to double space between the salutation and the body of the letter. See Figure 1-13.

Figure 1-13 **Letter with inside address and salutation**

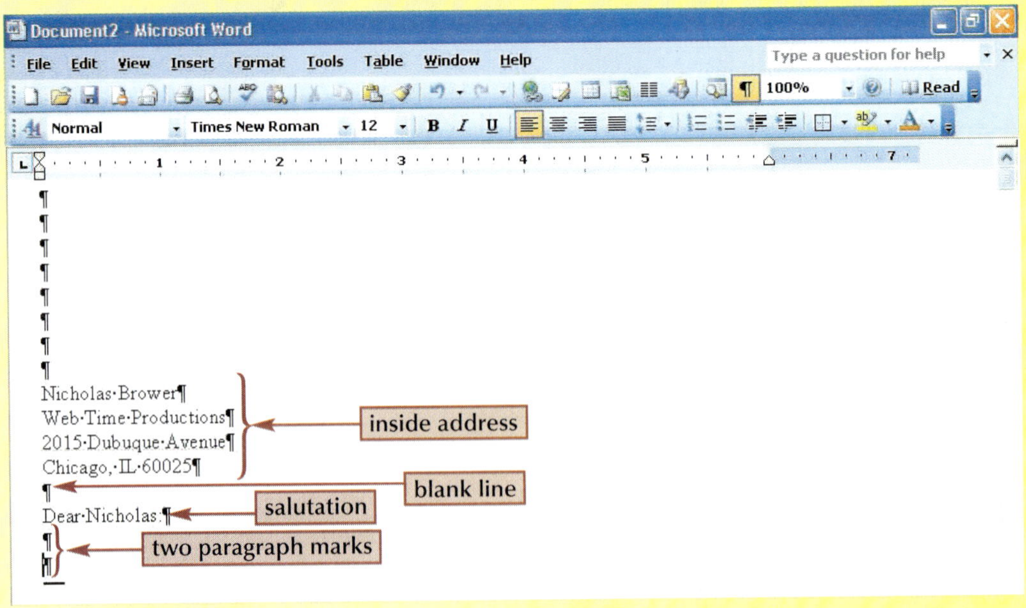

Before you continue with the rest of the letter, you should save what you have typed so far.

To save the document:

1. Click the **Save** button on the Standard toolbar. The Save As dialog box opens. Note that Word suggests using the first few words of the letter ("Nicholas Brower") as the filename. You will replace the suggested filename with something more descriptive.
2. Type **Web Time Contract Letter** in the File name text box. Next, you need to tell Word where you want to save the document. In this case, you want to use the Tutorial subfolder in the Tutorial.01 folder.
3. Click the **Save in** list arrow, click the drive containing your Data Files, double-click the **Tutorial.01** folder, and then double-click the **Tutorial** folder. The word "Tutorial" is now displayed in the Save in box, indicating that the Tutorial folder is open and ready for you to save the document. See Figure 1-14.

   Trouble? The Tutorial.01 folder is included with the Data Files for this text. If you don't have the Word Data Files, you need to get them before you can proceed. Your instructor will either give you the Data Files or ask you to obtain them from a specified location (such as a network drive). In either case, be sure that you make a backup copy of your Data Files before you start using them, so that the original files will be available on your copied disk in case you need to start over because of an error or problem. If you have any questions about the Data Files, see your instructor or technical support person for assistance.

Figure 1-14 Save As dialog box

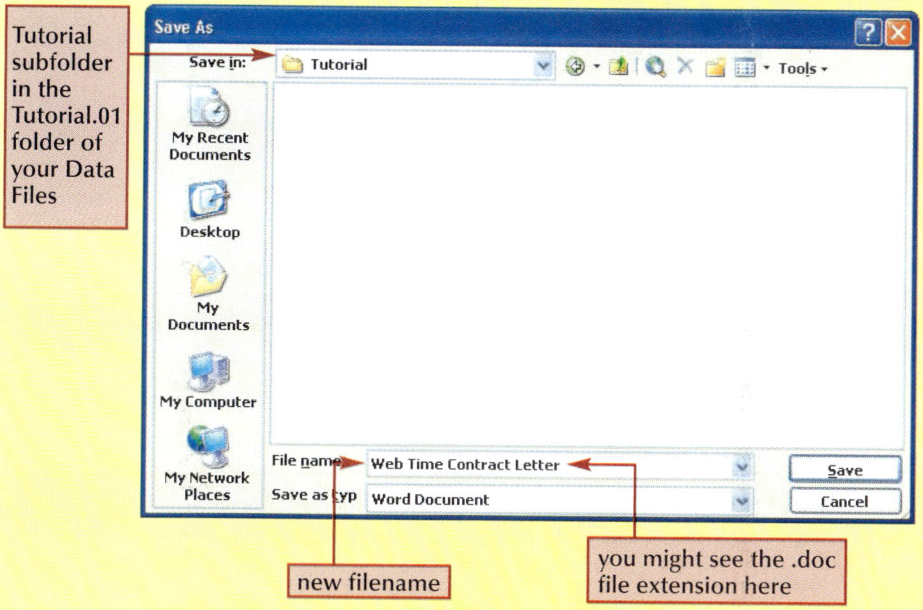

   Trouble? If Windows XP is configured for Web style, you can single-click, rather than double-click, folders to open them in the Save As dialog box.

   Trouble? If Word automatically adds the .doc extension to your filename, your computer is configured to show file extensions. Just continue with the tutorial.

4. Click the **Save** button in the Save As dialog box. The dialog box closes, and you return to the Document window. The new document name (Web Time Contract Letter) appears in the title bar.

Note that Word automatically appends the .doc extension to document filenames to identify them as Microsoft Word documents. However, unless your computer is set up to display file extensions, you won't see the .doc extension in any of the Word dialog boxes or in the title bar. These tutorials assume that file extensions are hidden.

You've made a good start on the letter, and you've saved your work so far. In the next session, you'll finish typing the letter and then you'll print it.

Review

Session 1.1 Quick Check

1. In your own words, list the steps in creating a document.
2. Define each of the following in your own words:
   a. nonprinting characters
   b. Zoom setting
   c. font settings
   d. default settings
3. Explain how to change the document view to Normal view.
4. Explain how to display or hide the Standard toolbar.
5. True or False: To display the Formatting toolbar, you need to use a button on the Standard toolbar.
6. True or False: Each time you press the Enter key, a nonprinting paragraph character (¶) appears in the status bar.
7. Word automatically appends the ______________ extension to all document file names, even if you can't see the file extensions on the screen.

Session 1.2

Continuing Work on the Letter

Now that you have saved your document, you're ready to continue working on Megan's letter. As you type the body of the letter, you do not have to press the Enter key at the end of each line. Instead, when you type a word that extends into the right margin, both the insertion point and the word move automatically to the next line. This automatic line breaking is called **word wrap**. You'll see how word wrap works as you type the body of the letter.

To continue typing the letter:

1. If you took a break after the previous session, make sure that Word is running. Also, review the check list in Figure 1-8 and verify that your screen is set up to match the figures in this tutorial.
2. Make sure the insertion point is at Ln 16 (according to the setting in the status bar). If it's not, move it to line 16 by pressing the arrow keys.
3. Type the following sentence: **Enclosed you will find the signed contract.**
4. Press the **spacebar**.
5. Type the following sentence: **As you can see, I am returning all three pages, with my signature on each.** Notice how Word moves the last few words to a new line when the preceding line is full.
6. Press the **Enter** key to end the first paragraph, and then press the **Enter** key again to create a double space between the two paragraphs.

7. Type the following text:

Now that we have finalized the contract, I have a few questions: When will we receive a complete schedule for the project? Also, how many preliminary designs do you require?

When you are finished, your screen should look similar to Figure 1-15, although the line breaks on your screen might be slightly different.

Figure 1-15 **Beginning of second main paragraph**

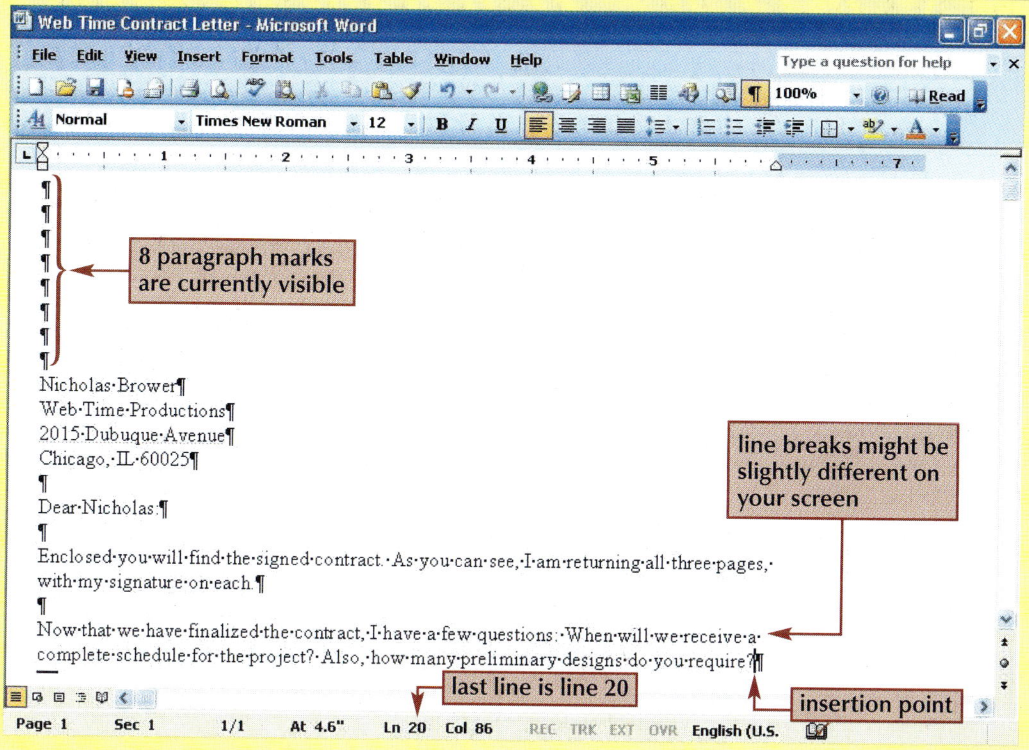

Trouble? If your screen does not match Figure 1-15 exactly, don't be concerned. The letter widths of the Times New Roman font can vary, which produces slightly different measurements on different monitors. As a result, the word or letter where the line wraps in your document might be different from the one shown in Figure 1-15.

Scrolling a Document

After you finish the last set of steps, the insertion point should be near the bottom of the Document window. Unless you are working on a large monitor, your screen probably looks like there's not enough room to type the rest of Megan's letter. However, as you continue to add text at the end of your document, the text that you typed earlier will **scroll** (or shift up) and disappear from the top of the Document window. You'll see how scrolling works as you enter the rest of the second paragraph.

To observe scrolling while you're entering text:

1. Make sure the insertion point is positioned to the right of the question mark after the word "require." The insertion point should be positioned at the end of line 20. See Figure 1-15.
2. Press the **spacebar**, and then type the following text:

   Finally, will you be available to discuss the project with our artists via a conference call some afternoon next week? Thursday or Friday afternoon would be ideal, if either of those options works for you.
3. Press the **Enter** key twice. The document scrolls up.

   At some point (either as you type the text in Step 2 or when you press the Enter key in Step 3), one or more paragraph marks at the top of the letter scroll off the top of the Document window. (Exactly when this happens depends on the size of your monitor.) When you are finished typing, your document should look like Figure 1-16. (Don't worry if you make a mistake in your typing. You'll learn a number of ways to correct errors in the next section.)

Figure 1-16 Part of document scrolled off the screen

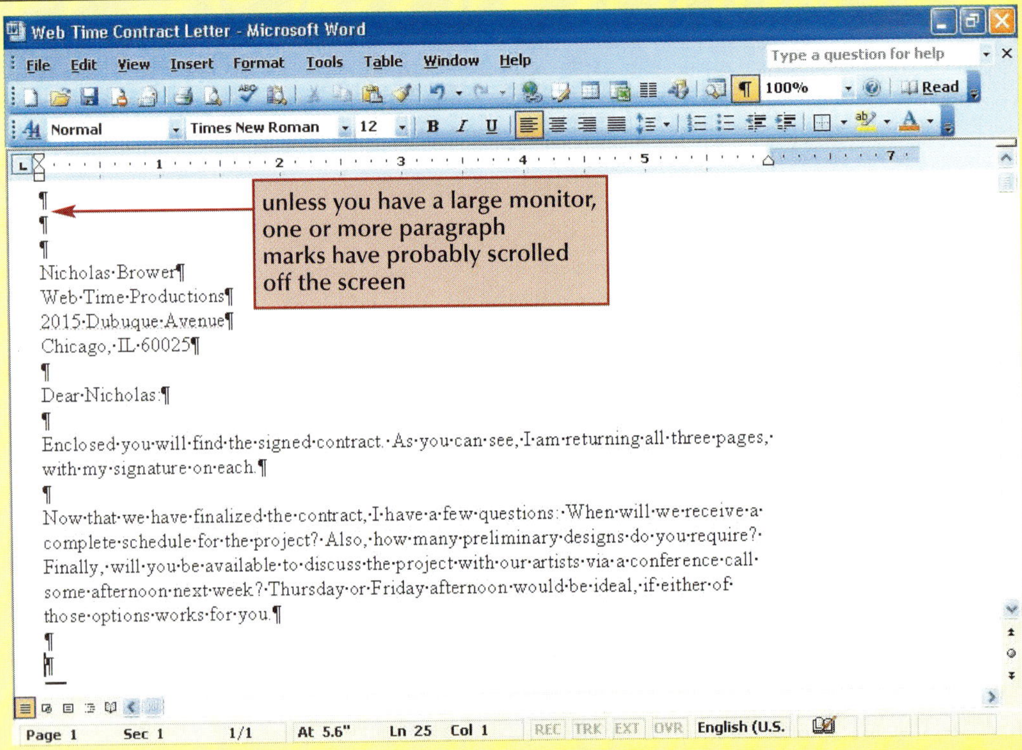

4. Type the following text:

   Thanks again for choosing Art4U. We look forward to working with you.
5. Press the **Enter** key twice.
6. Type **Sincerely yours,** (including the comma) to enter the complimentary closing.
7. Press the **Enter** key five times to allow space for a signature. Unless you have a very large monitor, part or even all of the inside address scrolls off the top of the Document window.
8. Type **Megan Grahs**, and then press the **Enter** key. A wavy red line appears below "Grahs." In Word, such lines indicate possible spelling errors. Because Megan's last name is not in the Word dictionary, Word suggests that it might be spelled incorrectly. You'll learn more about Word's error checking features in the next section. For now, you can ignore the wavy red line.

You've completed the letter, so you should save your work.

9. Click the **Save** button on the Standard toolbar. Word saves your letter with the same name and in the same location you specified earlier. Don't be concerned about any typing errors. You'll learn how to correct them in the next section.

In the last set of steps, you watched the text at the top of your document move off your screen. You can scroll this hidden text back into view so you can read the beginning of the letter. When you do, the text at the bottom of the screen will scroll out of view. To scroll the Document window, you can click the up or down arrows in the vertical scroll bar, click anywhere in the vertical scroll bar, or drag the scroll box. See Figure 1-17.

Note: If you are using a very large monitor, your insertion point may still be some distance from the bottom of the screen. In that case, you may not be able to perform the scrolling steps that follow. Read the steps to familiarize yourself with the process of scrolling. You'll have a chance to scroll longer documents later.

Figure 1-17 Parts of the scroll bar

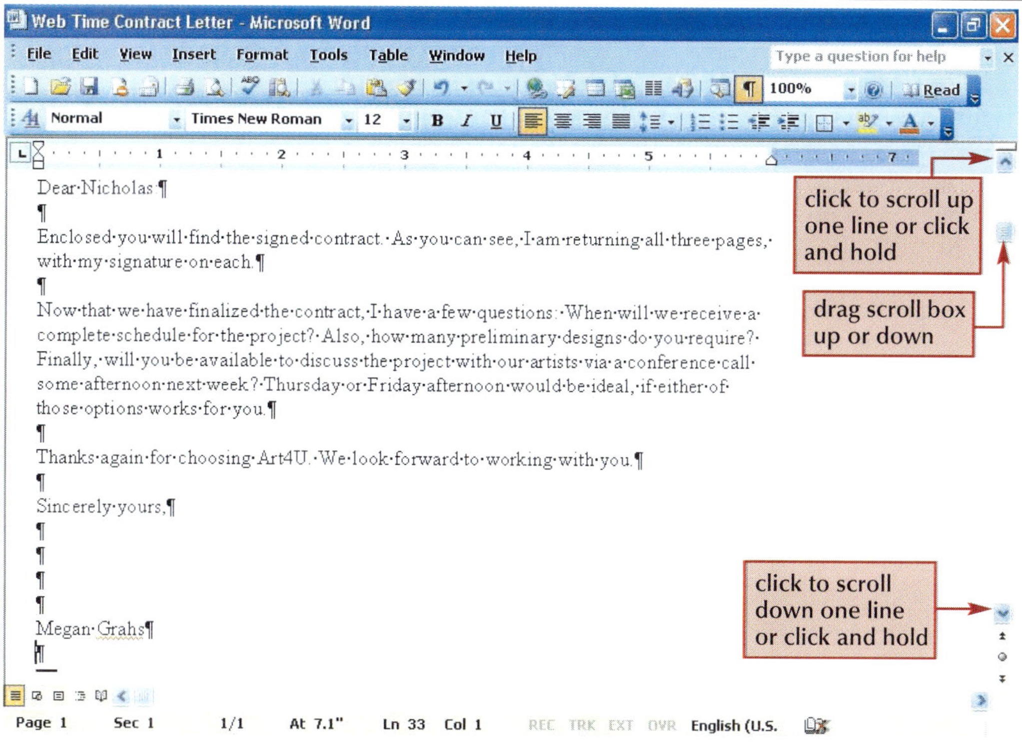

In the next set of steps, you will practice using the vertical scroll bar.

To scroll the document using the vertical scroll bar:

1. Position the mouse pointer on the up arrow at the top of the vertical scroll bar. Press and hold the mouse button to scroll the text. When the text stops scrolling, you have reached the top of the document and can see the beginning of the letter. Note that scrolling does not change the location of the insertion point in the document.
2. Click the down arrow on the vertical scroll bar several times. The document scrolls down one line at a time.

3. Click anywhere in the vertical scroll bar, below the scroll box. The document scrolls down one full screen.
4. Drag the scroll box up until the first line of the inside address ("Nicholas Brower") is positioned at the top of the Document window.
5. Scroll down to show the last line of the letter.

Correcting Errors

If you notice a typing error as soon as you make it, you can press the Backspace key, which deletes the characters and spaces to the left of the insertion point one at a time. Backspacing erases both printing and nonprinting characters. After you erase the error, you can type the correct character(s). You can also press the Delete key, which deletes characters to the right of the insertion point one at a time.

In many cases, however, Word's **AutoCorrect** feature will do the work for you. Among other things, AutoCorrect automatically corrects common typing errors, such as typing "adn" for "and." For example, you might have noticed AutoCorrect at work if you forgot to capitalize the first letter in a sentence as you typed the letter. AutoCorrect can automatically correct this error as you type the rest of the sentence. You'll learn more about using AutoCorrect as you become a more experienced Word user. For now, just keep in mind that AutoCorrect corrects certain spelling errors automatically. Depending on how your computer is set up, some or all AutoCorrect features might be turned off. You'll learn how to turn AutoCorrect on in the following steps.

Whether or not AutoCorrect is turned on, you can always rely on Word's **Spelling and Grammar checker**. This feature continually checks your document against Word's built-in dictionary and a set of grammar rules. If you type a word that doesn't match the correct spelling in Word's dictionary or if a word isn't in the dictionary at all (as is the case with Megan's last name, Grahs), a wavy red line appears beneath the word. A wavy red line also appears if you type duplicate words (such as "the the"). If you accidentally type an extra space between words or make a grammatical error (such as typing "He walk to the store." instead of "He walks to the store."), a wavy green line appears beneath the error.

The easiest way to see how these features work is to make some intentional typing errors.

To correct intentional typing errors:

1. Click to the left of the last paragraph mark to position the insertion point there (if it is not already there), and then press the **Enter** key to create a double space after Megan's last name, which is in the signature line. Before you start typing, you'll check to make sure AutoCorrect is turned on.
2. Click **Tools** on the menu bar, and then click **AutoCorrect Options**. The AutoCorrect: English (U.S.) dialog box opens.
3. Click the **Capitalize first letter of sentences** check box and the **Replace text as you type** check box to insert checks if these options are not already checked, and then click **OK**. (It is okay if other check boxes have checks.)
4. Carefully and slowly type the following sentence exactly as it is shown, including the spelling errors and the extra space between the last two words: **microsoft Word corects teh commen typing misTakes you make**. Press the **Enter** key when you are finished typing.

   Notice that as you press the spacebar after the word "commen," a wavy red line appears beneath it, indicating that the word might be misspelled. Notice also that Word automatically capitalized the word "Microsoft" because it's the first word in the sentence. And, when you pressed the spacebar after the words "corects," "teh," and "misTakes," Word automatically corrected the spelling. After you pressed the Enter key, a wavy green line appeared under the last two words, alerting you to the extra space. See Figure 1-18.

Figure 1-18 **Document with intentional typing errors**

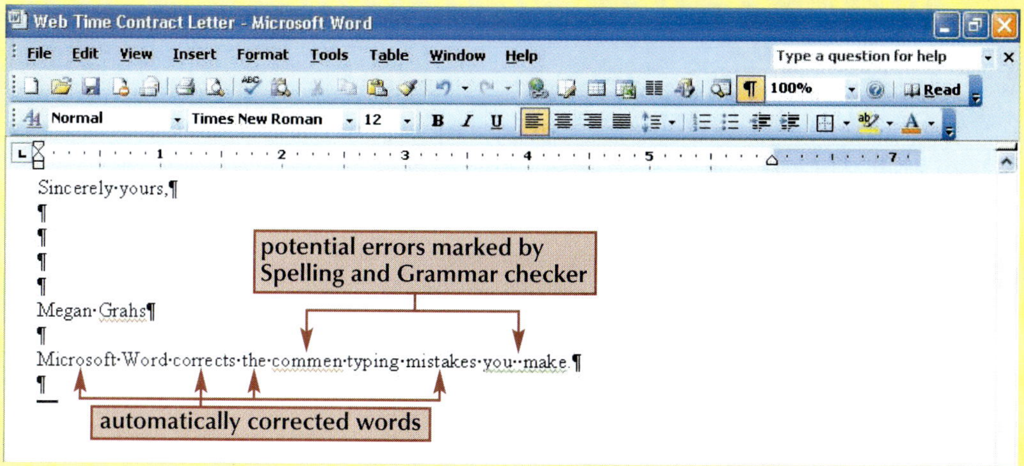

Trouble? If red and green wavy lines do not appear beneath mistakes, Word is probably not set to check spelling and grammar automatically as you type. Click Tools on the menu bar, and then click Options to open the Options dialog box. Click the Spelling & Grammar tab. If necessary, insert check marks in the "Check spelling as you type" and the "Check grammar as you type" check boxes, and then click OK.

Working with AutoCorrect

Whenever AutoCorrect makes a change, Word inserts an **AutoCorrect Options button** in the document. You can use this button to undo a change, or to prevent AutoCorrect from making the same change in the future. To see an AutoCorrect Options button, you position the mouse pointer over a word that has been changed by AutoCorrect.

To display an AutoCorrect Options button:

1. Position the mouse pointer over the word "corrects." A small blue rectangle appears below the first few letters of the word, as shown in Figure 1-19.

Figure 1-19 **Word changed by AutoCorrect**

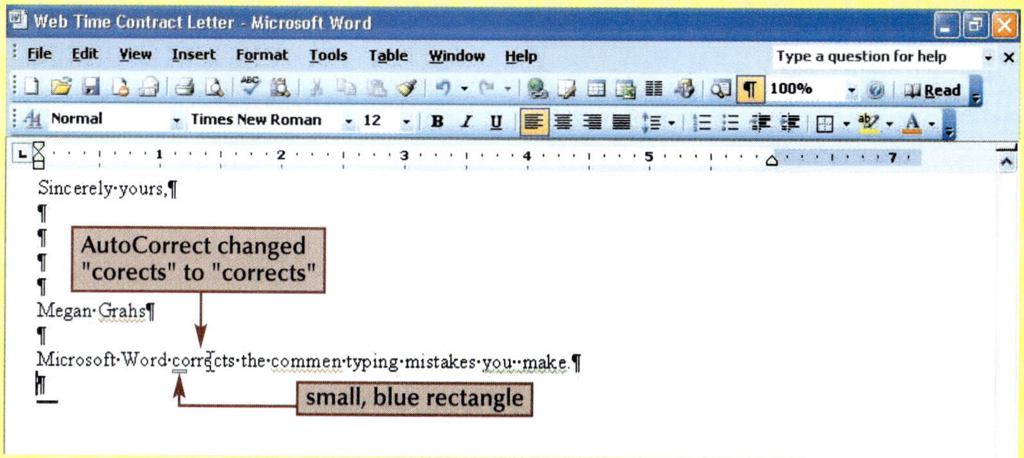

Trouble? If you see a blue button with a lightning bolt, move the pointer slightly to the right so that only the rectangle is visible, and then continue with the next step.

2. Point to the blue rectangle below "corrects." The blue rectangle is replaced by the AutoCorrect Options button and the entire word "corrects" is highlighted.
3. Click the **AutoCorrect Options** button. A menu with commands related to AutoCorrect appears. You could choose to change "corrects" back to "corects." You could also tell AutoCorrect to stop automatically correcting "corects." This second option might be useful if you found that AutoCorrect continually edited a word, such as a brand name or technical term, which was in fact spelled correctly. In the "corects" example, the change made by AutoCorrect is acceptable, so you can simply close the AutoCorrect menu.
4. Click anywhere in the document. The AutoCorrect menu closes.

Correcting Spelling and Grammar Errors

After you verify that AutoCorrect made changes you want, you should review your document for wavy underlines. Again, the red underlines indicate potential spelling errors, while the green underlines indicate potential grammar or punctuation problems. In the following steps, you will learn a quick way to correct such errors.

To correct spelling and grammar errors:

1. Position the I-Beam pointer over the word "commen," and then click the right mouse button. A shortcut menu appears with suggested spellings. See Figure 1-20.

Figure 1-20 Shortcut menu with suggested spellings

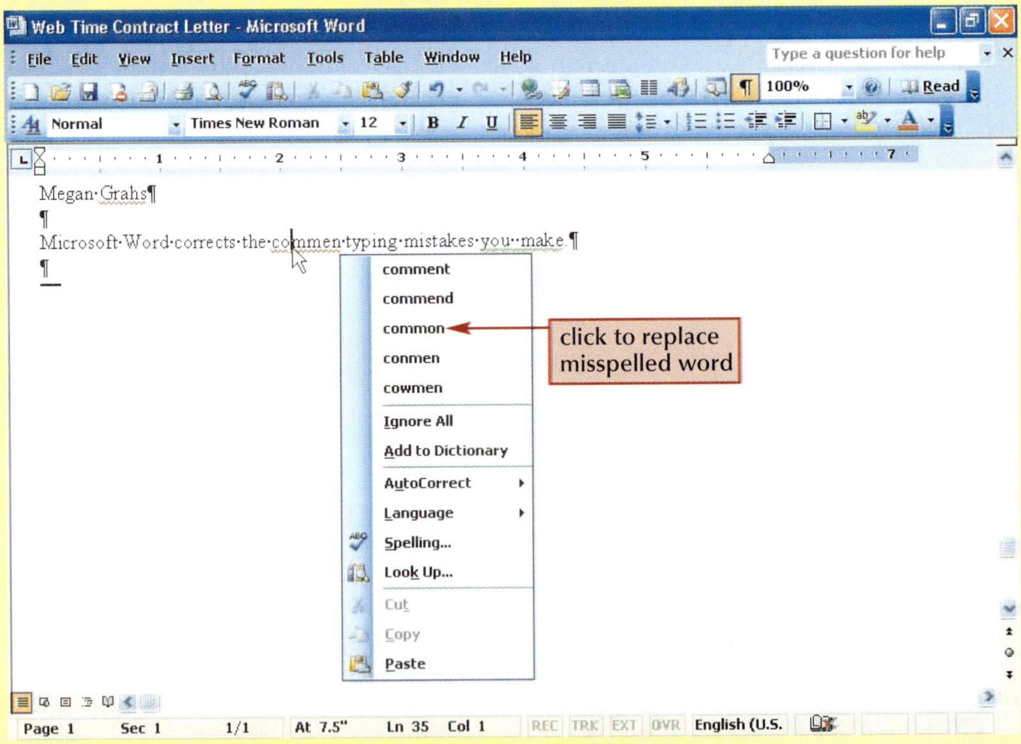

Trouble? If the shortcut menu doesn't appear, repeat Step 1, making sure you click the right mouse button, not the left one. If you see a different menu from the one shown in Figure 1-20, you didn't right-click exactly on the word "commen." Press the Esc key to close the menu, and then repeat Step 1.

2. Click **common** in the shortcut menu. The menu disappears, and the correct spelling appears in your document. Notice that the wavy red line disappears after you correct the error.
3. Click to the right of the letter "u" in the word "you." Press the **Delete** key to delete the extra space.

You can see how quick and easy it is to correct common typing errors with AutoCorrect and the Spelling and Grammar checker. Remember, however, to proofread each document you create thoroughly. AutoCorrect will not catch words that are spelled correctly, but used improperly (such as "your" for "you're").

Proofreading the Letter

Before you can proofread your letter, you need to delete the practice sentence.

To delete the practice sentence:

1. Confirm that the insertion point is to the right of "you" in the sentence you just typed, and then press the **Delete** key repeatedly to delete any spaces and characters to the right of the insertion point, including one paragraph mark.
2. Press the **Backspace** key repeatedly until the insertion point is to the left of the paragraph mark below Megan's name. There should only be one paragraph mark below her name. If you accidentally delete part of the letter, retype it, using Figure 1-17 as a guide.

Now you can proofread the letter for any typos. You can also get rid of the wavy red underline below Megan's last name.

To respond to possible spelling errors:

1. Be sure the signature line is visible. Because Word doesn't recognize "Grahs" as a word, it is marked as a potential error. You need to tell Word to ignore this name wherever it occurs in the letter.
2. Right-click **Grahs**. A shortcut menu opens.
3. Click **Ignore All**. The wavy red underline disappears from below "Grahs."
4. Scroll up to the beginning of the letter, and proofread it for typos. If a word has a wavy red or green underline, right-click it and choose an option in the shortcut menu. To correct other errors, click to the right or left of the error, use the Backspace or Delete key to remove it, and then type a correction.
5. Click the **Save** button on the Standard toolbar. Word saves your letter with the same name and to the same location you specified earlier.

Inserting a Date with AutoComplete

The beauty of using a word-processing program such as Microsoft Word is that you can easily make changes to text you have already typed. In this case, you need to insert the current date at the beginning of the letter. Megan tells you that she wants to send the contract to Web Time Productions on February 15, so you need to insert that date into the letter now.

Before you can enter the date, you need to move the insertion point to the right location. In a standard business letter, the date belongs approximately 2.5 inches from the top. (As you recall, this is where you started the inside address earlier.) You also need to insert some blank lines to allow enough space between the date and the inside address.

To move the insertion point and add some blank lines:

1. Scroll up to display the top of the document.
2. Click to the left of the "N" in "Nicholas Brower" in the inside address. The status bar indicates that the insertion point is on line 9, 2.5 inches from the top. (Your status bar might show slightly different measurements.)
3. Press the **Enter** key four times, and then press the ↑ key four times. Now the insertion point is positioned at line 9, with three blank lines between the inside address and the line where you will insert the date. See Figure 1-21.

Figure 1-21 Position of insertion point

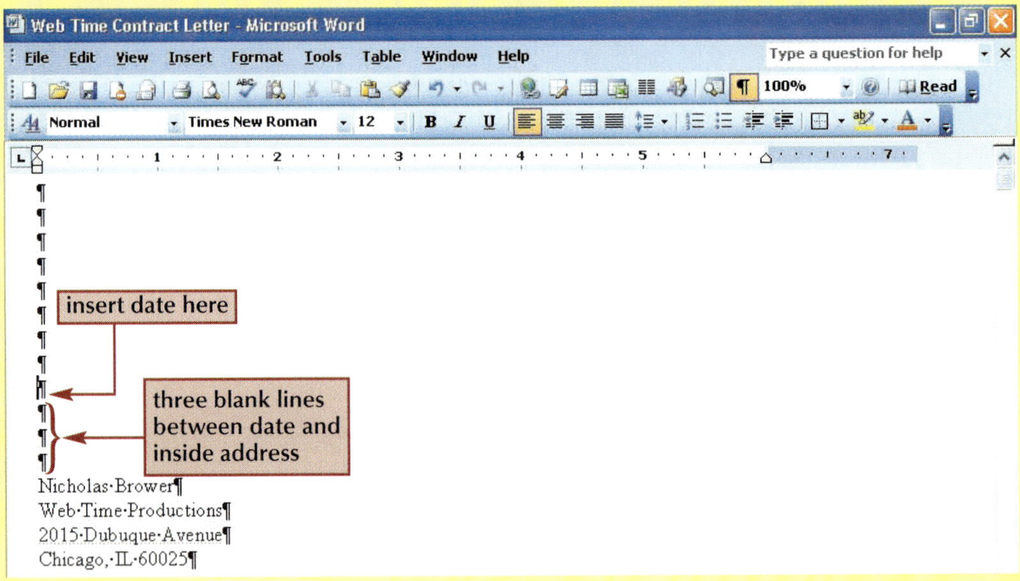

You're ready to insert the date. To do this you can take advantage of Word's **AutoComplete** feature, which automatically inserts dates and other regularly used items for you. In this case, you can type the first few characters of the month, and let Word insert the rest. (This only works for long month names like February.)

To insert the date:

1. Type **Febr** (the first four letters of February). A rectangular box appears above the line, as shown in Figure 1-22. If you wanted to type something other than February, you could continue typing to complete the word. In this case, though, you want to accept the AutoComplete suggestion, which you will do in the next step.

AutoComplete suggestion **Figure 1-22**

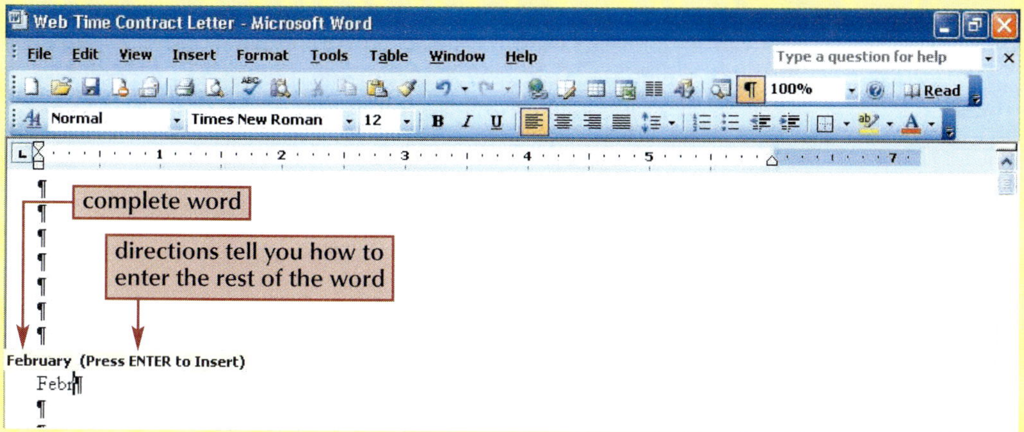

Trouble? If the AutoComplete suggestion doesn't appear, this feature may not be active. Click Tools on the menu bar, click AutoCorrect Options, click the AutoText tab, click the Show AutoComplete suggestions check box to insert a check, and then click OK. Delete the characters "Febr" and begin again with Step 1.

2. Press the **Enter** key. The rest of the word "February" is inserted in the document.
3. Press the **spacebar**, and then type **15, 2006**.

Trouble? If February happens to be the current month, you will see a second AutoComplete suggestion displaying the current date after you press the spacebar. To ignore that AutoComplete suggestion, continue typing the rest of the date as instructed in Step 3.

4. Click one of the blank lines below the date. Depending on how your computer is set up, you may see a dotted underline below the date. (You will learn the meaning of this underline later in this tutorial.) You have finished entering the date. See Figure 1-23.

Date entered in the document **Figure 1-23**

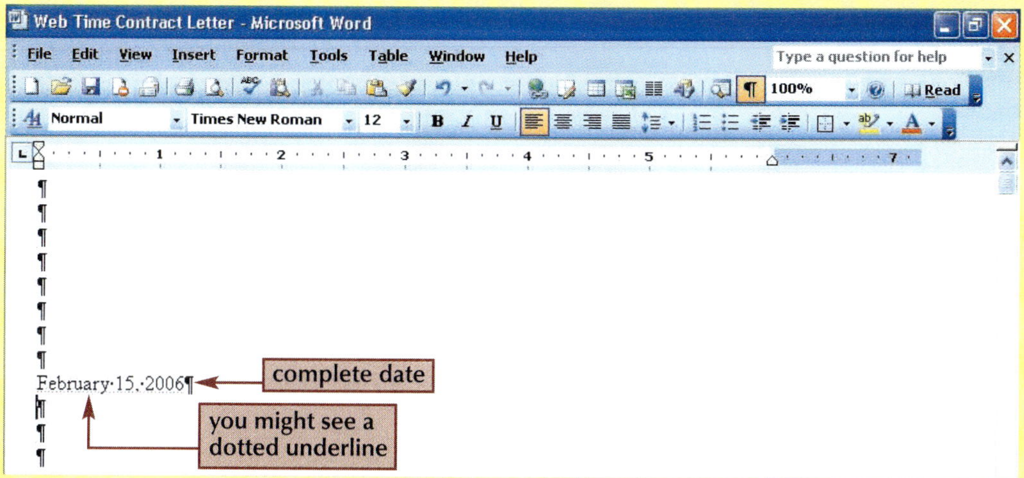

Moving the Insertion Point Around a Document

When you scroll a document, you change the part of the document that is displayed on the screen. But to change the location in the document where new text will appear when you type, you need to move the insertion point. In the last section, you moved the insertion point by scrolling up and then clicking where you wanted to insert new lines and text. You can also use the arrow keys on your keyboard, ←, →, ↑, and ↓, to move the insertion point one character at a time to the left or right, or one line at a time up or down. In addition, you can press a combination of keys to move the insertion point. As you become more experienced with Word, you'll decide which method you prefer.

Megan asks you to add her middle initial to the signature line. Before you can do that, you need to make sure you're comfortable moving the insertion point around the document. To see how quickly you can move through the document, you'll use keystrokes to move the insertion point to the beginning and end of the document.

To move the insertion point with keystrokes:

1. Press the **Ctrl** key and hold it down while you press the **Home** key. The insertion point moves to the beginning of the document.
2. Press the **Page Down** key to move the insertion point down to the top of the next screen.
3. Press the ↓ key several times to move the insertion point down one line at a time, and then press the → key several times to move the insertion point to the right one character at a time.
4. Press the **Ctrl+End** keys. The insertion point moves to the end of the document.
5. Use the arrow keys to position the insertion point to the right of the "n" in "Megan."
6. Press the **spacebar**, and then type the letter **L** followed by a period.

Figure 1-24 summarizes the keystrokes you can use to move the insertion point around the document. When you simply need to display a part of a document, you'll probably want to use the vertical scroll bar. But when you actually need to move the insertion point to a specific spot, it's helpful to use these special keystrokes.

Figure 1-24 Keystrokes for moving the insertion point

Press	To move the insertion point
← or →	Left or right one character at a time
↑ or ↓	Up or down one line at a time
Ctrl+← or Ctrl+→	Left or right one word at a time
Ctrl+↑ or Ctrl+↓	Up or down one paragraph at a time
Home or End	To the beginning or to the end of the current line
Ctrl+Home or Ctrl+End	To the beginning or to the end of the document
Page Up or Page Down	To the previous screen or to the next screen
Alt+Ctrl+Page Up or Alt+Ctrl+Page Down	To the top or to the bottom of the document window

Using the Undo and Redo Commands

To undo (or reverse) the very last thing you did, click the **Undo button** on the Standard toolbar. If you want to restore your original change, the **Redo button** reverses the action of the Undo button (or redoes the undo). To undo more than your last action, you can click the Undo list arrow on the Standard toolbar. This list shows your most recent actions. Undo reverses the action only at its original location. You can't delete a word or phrase, move the surrounding text, and then undo the deletion at a different location.

Megan asks you to undo the addition of her middle initial, to see how the signature line looks without it.

To undo the addition of the letter "L":

1. Place the mouse pointer over the **Undo** button on the Standard toolbar. The label "Undo Typing" appears in a ScreenTip, indicating that your most recent action involved typing. See Figure 1-25.

Figure 1-25 Using the Undo button

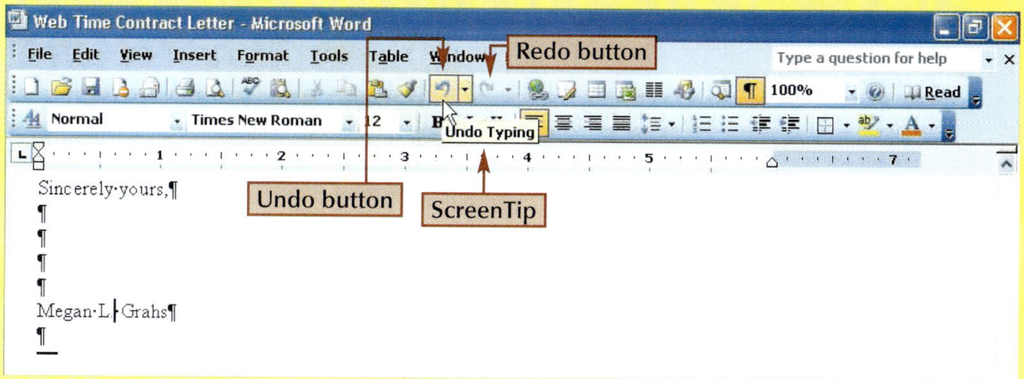

2. Click the **Undo** button. The letter "L," the period, and the space you typed earlier are deleted.

   Trouble? If something else changes, you probably made another edit or change to the document between the addition of Megan's middle initial and the undo. Click the Undo button on the Standard toolbar until the letter "L," the period, and the space following it are deleted. If a list of possible changes appears under the Undo button, you clicked the list arrow next to the Undo button rather than the Undo button itself. Press the Esc key to close the list.

   As she reviews the signature line, Megan decides that she does want to include her middle initial after all. Instead of retyping it, you'll redo the undo.

3. Place the mouse pointer over the **Redo** button on the Standard toolbar and observe the "Redo Typing" ScreenTip.
4. Click the **Redo** button. Megan's middle initial (along with the period and an additional space) are reinserted into the signature line.
5. Click the **Save** button on the Standard toolbar to save your changes to the document.

Your letter is nearly finished. All that remains is to remove the straight dotted underlines and then print the letter.

Removing Smart Tags

A straight dotted underline below a date or address indicates that Word has inserted a Smart Tag in the document. A **Smart Tag** is a feature that allows you to perform actions (such as sending e-mail or scheduling a meeting) that would normally require a completely different program. When you point to Smart Tag text, a Smart Tag Actions button appears, which you can click to open a menu with commands related to that item. (For example, you might click a Smart Tag on an address to add that address to your e-mail address book.) You don't really need Smart Tags in this document, though, so you will delete them. (Your computer may not be set up to show Smart Tags at all, or it might show them on dates but not addresses. If you do not see any Smart Tags in your document, simply read the following steps.)

To remove the Smart Tags from the document:

1. Scroll up so you can see the inside address. If you see a straight dotted underline below the street address (2015 Dubuque Avenue), position the mouse pointer over that line. A Smart Tag icon appears over the street address.
2. Move the mouse pointer over the **Smart Tag** icon. The icon is transformed into the Smart Tag Actions button, as shown in Figure 1-26.

Figure 1-26 Displaying the Smart Tag Actions button

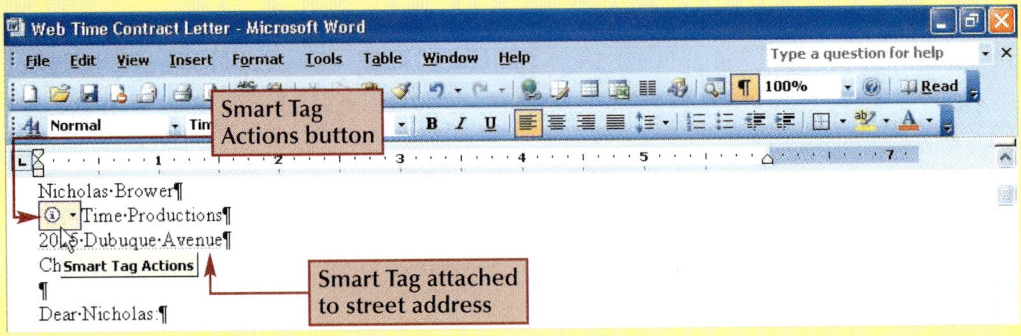

3. Click the **Smart Tag Actions** button. A menu of commands related to addresses appears.
4. Click **Remove this Smart Tag**. The Smart Tag menu closes. The address is no longer underlined, indicating that the Smart Tag has been removed. Depending on how your computer is set up, the Smart Tag on the street address may have been the only one in your document. But it's possible you see others.
5. Remove any other Smart Tags in the document, including any on the date or elsewhere in the inside address.
6. Click the **Save** button on the Standard toolbar.

Previewing and Printing a Document

Do you think the letter is ready to print? You could find out by clicking the Print button on the Standard toolbar and then reviewing the printed page. With that approach, however, you risk wasting paper and printer time. For example, if you failed to insert enough space for the company letterhead, you would have to add more space, and then print the letter all over again. To avoid wasting paper and time, you should first display the document in the **Print Preview window**. By default, the Print Preview window shows you the full page; there's no need to scroll through the document.

To preview the document:

1. Proof the document one last time and correct any new errors. Always remember to proof your document immediately before printing it.
2. Replace "Megan L. Grahs" with your first and last name, at the end of the letter. This will ensure that you will be able to identify your copy of the letter.
3. Click the **Print Preview** button on the Standard toolbar. The Print Preview window opens and displays a full-page version of your letter, as shown in Figure 1-27. This shows how the letter will fit on the printed page. The Print Preview toolbar includes a number of buttons that are useful for making changes that affect the way the printed page will look.

Figure 1-27 Full page displayed in Print Preview window

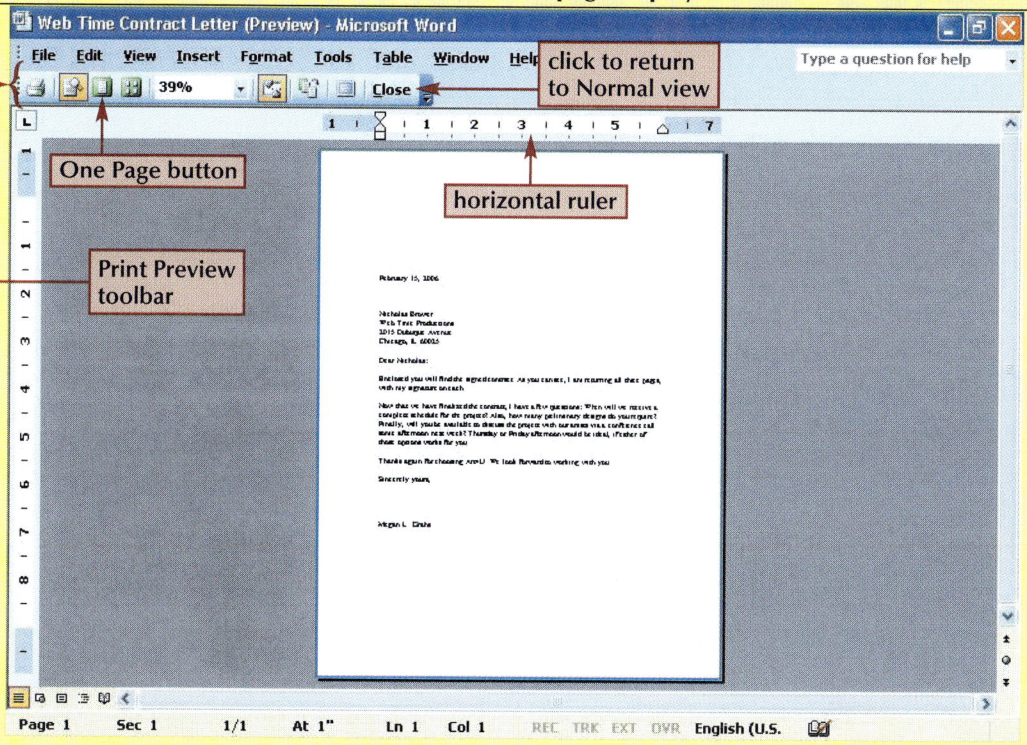

Trouble? If your letter in the Print Preview window is smaller and off to the left rather than centered in the window, click the One Page button on the Print Preview toolbar.

Trouble? If you don't see a ruler above the document, your ruler is not displayed. To show the ruler in the Print Preview window, click View on the menu bar and then click Ruler.

4. Click the **Close** button on the Print Preview toolbar to return to Normal view.
5. Click the **Save** button on the Standard toolbar.

Note that it is especially important to preview documents if your computer is connected to a network so that you don't keep a shared printer tied up with unnecessary printing. In this case, the text looks well spaced and the letterhead will fit at the top of the page. You're ready to print the letter.

When printing a document, you have two choices. You can use the Print command on the File menu, which opens the Print dialog box in which you can adjust some printer settings. Or, if you prefer, you can use the Print button on the Standard toolbar, which prints the document using default settings, without opening a dialog box. In these tutorials, the first time you print from a shared computer, you should check the settings in the Print dialog box and make sure the number of copies is set to 1. After that, you can use the Print button.

To print the letter document:

1. Make sure your printer is turned on and contains paper.
2. Click **File** on the menu bar, and then click **Print**. The Print dialog box opens.
3. Make sure the Printer section of the dialog box shows the correct printer. If you're not sure what the correct printer is, check with your instructor or technical support person. Also, make sure the number of copies is set to 1.

   Trouble? If the Print dialog box shows the wrong printer, click the Name list arrow, and then select the correct printer from the list of available printers.
4. Click the **OK** button. Assuming your computer is attached to a printer, the letter prints.

Your printed letter should look similar to Figure 1-9, but without the Art4U letterhead. The word wraps, or line breaks, might not appear in the same places on your letter because the size and spacing of characters vary slightly from one printer to the next.

Creating an Envelope

After you print the letter, Megan asks you to print an envelope in which to mail the contracts. Creating an envelope is a simple process because Word automatically uses the inside address from the letter as the address on the envelope.

Reference Window

Printing an Envelope

- Click Tools on the menu bar, point to Letters and Mailings, and then click Envelopes and Labels.
- In the Envelopes and Labels dialog box, verify that the Delivery address box contains the correct address. If necessary, you can type a new address or edit the existing one.
- If necessary, type a return address. If you are using preprinted stationery that already includes a return address, click the Omit check box to insert a check.
- To print the envelope immediately, insert an envelope in your printer, and then click Print.
- To store the envelope along with the rest of the document, click Add to Document.
- To print the envelope after you have added it to the document, open the Print dialog box and print the page containing the envelope.

Megan tells you that your printer is not currently stocked with envelopes. She asks you to create the envelope and add it to the document. Then she will print the envelope later, when she is ready to mail the contracts to Web Time Productions.

To create an envelope:

1. Click **Tools** on the menu bar, point to **Letters and Mailings**, and then click **Envelopes and Labels**. The Envelopes and Labels dialog box opens, as shown in Figure 1-28. By default, Word uses the inside address from the letter as the delivery address. Depending on how your computer is set up, you might see an address in the Return address box. Because Megan will be using Art4U's printed envelopes, you don't need to include a return address on this envelope.

Figure 1-28 Envelopes and Labels dialog box

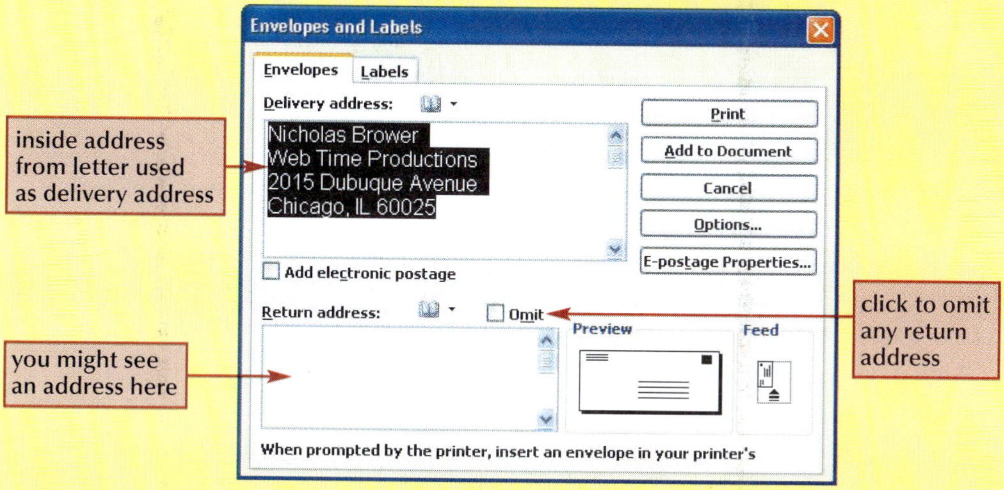

2. Click the **Omit** check box to insert a check, if necessary.
3. Click the **Add to Document** button. The dialog box closes, and you return to the Document window. The envelope is inserted at the top of the document, above a double line with the words "Section Break (Next Page)." The double line indicates that the envelope and the letter are two separate parts of the document. The envelope will print in the standard business envelope format. The letter will still print on standard 8.5 x 11-inch paper. (You'll have a chance to print an envelope in the exercises at the end of this tutorial.)
4. Click the **Save** button on the Standard toolbar.

You are finished with the letter and the envelope, so you can close the document.

To close the document:

1. Click the **Close Window** button on the menu bar. The Web Time Contract Letter document closes.

   Trouble? If you see a dialog box with the message "Do you want to save the changes to 'Web Time Contract Letter?'," click the Yes button.

2. Close any other open documents without saving them.

Congratulations on creating your first letter in Microsoft Word. You'll be able to use the skills you learned in this tutorial to create a variety of professional documents.

Review

Session 1.2 Quick Check

1. True or False: The term "word wrap" refers to automatic line breaking.
2. Explain how to enter the name of a month using AutoComplete.
3. What button can you use to reverse your most recent edit immediately?
4. List the steps required to print an envelope.
5. In your own words, define each of the following:
   a. scrolling
   b. AutoComplete
   c. Redo button
   d. Smart Tag
   e. Print Preview

Review

Tutorial Summary

In this tutorial you learned how to set up your Word window to match the figures in this book, create a new document from scratch, and type a professional-looking cover letter. You practiced correcting errors, and moving the insertion point. You learned how to undo and redo changes, how to insert a date with AutoComplete and how to remove Smart Tags from a document. Finally, you previewed and printed a document, and created an envelope.

Key Terms

AutoComplete
AutoCorrect
AutoCorrect Options button
default settings
nonprinting characters
Print Preview window
Redo button
scroll
Smart Tag
Spelling and Grammar checker
Undo button
word wrap

Practice

Practice the skills you learned in the tutorial using the same case scenario.

Review Assignments

There are no Data Files needed for the Review Assignments.

Megan received an e-mail from Nicholas Brower at Web Time Productions, confirming their plans for a conference call. Megan has e-mailed the graphic artists at Art4U, informing them about the call. To make sure everyone remembers, she would like you to post a memo on the bulletin board in the break room. She also asks you to create an envelope so the memo can be mailed to freelance artists who work outside the Art4U offices. Create the memo shown in Figure 1-29 by completing the following steps. The steps show quotation marks around text you type; do not include the quotation marks in your letter.

Figure 1-29

Art4U, Inc.
5725 Mesa Avenue
Tucson, AZ 85703
Art4U@Earth-World-Art.com

TO: Art4U Staff Artists

FROM: Megan L. Grahs

DATE: February 20, 2006

SUBJECT: Conference Call

Please plan to join us for a conference call at 3 p.m. on Friday, March 1. Nicholas Brower, president of Web Time Productions, will be taking part, as will five of his company's most experienced Web page designers. This will be your chance to ask the designers some important questions.

You will be able to join the call from your desk by dialing an 800 number and a special access code. You'll receive both of these numbers via e-mail the day of the call.

1. Make sure a new blank document is open.
2. Compare your screen to the checklist in Figure 1-8 and change any settings if necessary. In particular, make sure that nonprinting characters are displayed and the Getting Started task pane is open.
3. Press the Enter key eight times to insert enough space for the company letterhead.
4. Type "TO:" in capital letters, and then press the spacebar.
5. Turn off capitalization if you turned it on in Step 4, and then type "Art4U Staff Artists". Throughout the rest of this exercise, turn capitalization on and off as needed.
6. Press the Enter key twice, type "FROM:", press the spacebar, turn off capitalization, and then type your name.

7. Press the Enter key twice, type "DATE:", and then press the spacebar.
8. Enter the date February 20, 2006 using AutoComplete when possible to reduce the amount of typing required.
9. Press the Enter key twice, type "SUBJECT:", press the spacebar, type "Conference Call", and then press the Enter key three times.
10. Continue typing the rest of the memo as shown in Figure 1-29. (You will have a chance to correct any typing errors later.) Ignore any AutoCorrect suggestions that are not relevant to the text you are typing.
11. Save your work as **Call Memo** in the Tutorial.01\Review folder provided with your Data Files.
12. Practice using the keyboard to move the insertion point around the document. Use the arrow keys so the insertion point is positioned immediately to the left of the "A" in "Art4U" in the "TO" line.
13. Type "All" and a space, so the TO line reads "TO: All Art4U Staff Artists".
14. Undo the change and then redo it.
15. Scroll to the beginning of the document and proofread your work.
16. Correct any misspelled words marked by wavy red lines. If the correct spelling of a word does not appear in the shortcut menu, close the list, and then make the correction yourself. Remove any red wavy lines below words that are actually spelled correctly. Then correct any grammatical or other errors indicated by wavy green lines. Delete any extra words or spaces.
17. Remove any Smart Tags.
18. Save your most recent changes.
19. Preview and print the memo.
20. Add an envelope to the document. Use your own address as the delivery address. Do not include a return address.
21. Save your changes and close the Call Memo document. If any other documents are open, close them without saving any changes.

Apply

Apply the skills you learned to create a letter about a school field trip.

Case Problem 1

There are no Data Files needed for this Case Problem.

Luis Sotelo Elementary School You are a teacher at Luis Sotelo Elementary School. Your students have been raising money all year for a trip to Roaring Rapids Water Park. Before you can finalize plans for the outing, you need to write for some information. Create the letter by completing the following steps. The steps show quotation marks around text you type; do not include the quotation marks.

1. Open a new blank document if one is not already open, and then check your screen to make sure your settings match those in Figure 1-8.
2. Type your name, press Enter, and then type the following address:
   Luis Sotelo Elementary School
   1521 First Avenue
   Raleigh, North Carolina 21101

Explore

3. Press the Enter key four times, and then type the name of the current month. (If an AutoComplete suggestion appears, accept it to complete the name of the month.) Press the spacebar. After you press the spacebar, an AutoComplete suggestion appears with the current date. Accept the suggestion.

4. Press the Enter key three times, and, using the proper business letter format, type the inside address: "Scott Shimanski, Roaring Rapids Water Park, 2344 West Prairie Street, Durham, North Carolina 27704".
5. Double space after the inside address (that is, press the Enter key twice), type the salutation "Dear Mr. Shimanski:", and then insert a blank line.
6. Type the paragraph as follows: "I'd like some information about a class field trip to Roaring Rapids Water Park. Please answer the following questions:"
7. Save your work as **Field Trip Information Letter** in the Tutorial.01\Cases folder provided with your Data Files.
8. Insert one blank line, and then type these questions on separate lines with one blank line between each:
   "How much is a day pass for a 10-year-old child?"
   "How much is a day pass for an adult?"
   "Are lockers available for storing clothes and other belongings?"
9. Move the insertion point up to the beginning of the third question (which begins "Are lockers available…"). Insert a new line, and add the following as the new third question in the list: "Can you offer a discount for a group of 25 children and 5 adults?"
10. Correct any spelling or grammar errors indicated by red or green wavy lines. Because "Sotelo" is spelled correctly, use the shortcut menu to remove the wavy red line under the word "Sotelo" and prevent Word from marking the word as a misspelling. Repeat to ignore "Shimanski."
11. Insert another blank line at the end of the letter, and type the complimentary closing "Sincerely," (include the comma).
12. Use the Enter key to leave room for the signature, and type your full name. Then press the Enter key and type "Luis Sotelo Elementary School". Notice that "Sotelo" is not marked as a spelling error this time.
13. Scroll up to the beginning of the document, and then remove any Smart Tags in the letter.
14. Save your changes to the letter, and then preview it using the Print Preview button.
15. Print the letter, and then close the document.

Apply

Apply the skills you learned to create a letter confirming the catering needs for a client's annual convention.

Case Problem 2

There are no Data Files needed for this Case Problem.

Rocky Mountain Convention Center As catering director for the Rocky Mountain Convention Center, you are responsible for managing food service at the city's convention center. The American Rock Climbers Association has scheduled a daily breakfast buffet during its annual convention (which runs July 6–10, 2006). You need to write a letter confirming plans for the daily buffet.

Complete the following steps to create the letter using the skills you learned in the tutorial. The steps show quotation marks around text you type; do not include the quotation marks in your letter.

1. Open a new, blank document if one is not already open, and then check your screen to make sure your settings match those in Figure 1-8.
2. Press the Enter key until the insertion point is positioned about two inches from the top of the page. (Remember that you can see the exact position of the insertion point, in inches, in the status bar.)

3. Enter "June 6, 2006" as the date.
4. Press the Enter key four times after the date, and, using the proper business letter format, type the inside address: "Neil Skinner, American Rock Climbers Association, 222 Sydney Street, Whitewater, CO 77332".
5. Double space after the inside address (that is, press the Enter key twice), type the salutation "Dear Mr. Skinner:", and then double space again.
6. Write one paragraph confirming the daily breakfast buffets for July 6–10, 2006.
7. Insert a blank line and type the complimentary closing "Sincerely,".
8. Use the Enter key to leave room for the signature, and then type your name and title.
9. Save the letter as **Buffet Confirmation Letter** in the Tutorial.01\Cases folder provided with your Data Files.
10. Remove any Smart Tags. Reread your letter carefully, and correct any errors. Use the arrow keys to move the insertion point, as necessary.
11. Save any new changes, and then preview and print the letter.

Explore

12. Create an envelope for the letter, and add it to the document. Click the Omit check box if necessary to deselect it, and then, for the return address, type your own address. Add the envelope to the document. If you are asked if you want to save the return address as the new default return address, click No. If your computer is connected to a printer that is stocked with envelopes, click File on the menu bar, click Print, click the Pages option button, type 1 in the Pages text box, and then click OK.
13. Save your work, and then close the document.

Create

Use your skills to create the congratulatory letter shown in Figure 1-30.

Case Problem 3

There are no Data Files needed for this Case Problem.

Boundary Waters Technical College Liza Morgan, professor of e-commerce at Boundary Waters Technical College in northern Minnesota, was recently honored by the Northern Business Council for her series of free public seminars on developing Web sites for nonprofit agencies. She also was recently named Teacher of the Year by a national organization called Women in Technology. As one of her former students, you decide to write a letter congratulating her on these honors. To create the letter, complete the following steps:

1. Open a new blank document if one is not already open, and then check your screen to make sure your settings match those in Figure 1-8.
2. Create the letter shown in Figure 1-30. Replace "Your Name" with your first and last name.

Figure 1-30

August 13, 2006

Professor Liza Morgan
Department of Business Administration
Boundary Waters Technical College
1010 Sturgeon Drive
Blue Pines, Minnesota 50601

Dear Professor Morgan:

I was happy to hear about your recent honors. You certainly deserve to be recognized for your Web site development seminars. As a grateful former student, I heartily endorse your Teacher of the Year award. Congratulations!

Sincerely,

Your Name

3. Save the document as **Congratulations Letter** in the Tutorial.01\Cases folder provided with your Data Files.
4. Correct any typing errors, remove any Smart Tags, and then preview and print the letter.
5. Create an envelope, using your address as the return address, and then add the envelope to the document. (*Hint*: Click the Omit check box to deselect it if it is selected before attempting to type the return address.) Do not save the return address as the default.
6. Save the document and close it.

Challenge

Go beyond what you've learned to write a memo for a small e-business company.

Case Problem 4

There are no Data Files needed for this Case Problem.

Head for the Hills You are the office manager for Head for the Hills, a small company that sells hiking equipment over the Internet. The company has just moved to a new building, which requires a special security key card after hours. Some employees have had trouble getting the key cards to work properly. You decide to hold a meeting to explain the security policies for the new building and to demonstrate the key cards. But first you need to post a memo announcing the meeting. The recently ordered letterhead (with the company's new address) has not yet arrived, so you will use a Word template to create the memo. Word provides templates—that is, models with predefined formatting—to help you create complete documents (including a professional-looking letterhead) quickly. To create the memo, do the following steps. The steps show quotation marks around text you type; do not include the quotation marks in your letter.

1. Open a new blank document if one is not already open, and then check your screen to make sure your settings match those in Figure 1-8.
2. Open the New Document task pane. You see a number of options related to creating new documents.
3. **Explore** In the "Templates" section, click On my computer. The Templates dialog box opens.
4. **Explore** Click the Memos tab, click Professional Memo, and then click the OK button. A memo template opens containing generic, placeholder text that you can replace with your own information.
5. Display the template in Normal view, if it is not already. Click immediately to the right of the last "e" in the text "Company Name Here" (at the top of the document), press the Backspace key repeatedly to delete the text, and type "Head for the Hills".
6. Click the text "Click here and type name" in the To: line, and type "All Employees". Click the text after "From:", and replace it with your name.
7. Click the text after "CC:", press Delete to delete the placeholder text, and then delete the entire "CC:" line. Note that Word inserts the current date automatically after the heading "Date."
8. Click the text after "Re:", and then type "Using key cards".
9. Delete the placeholder text that begins "How to Use..." but do not delete the paragraph mark (¶) at the end of the line, and then type "Meeting Tomorrow".
10. **Explore** Delete the text in the body of the letter but do not delete the paragraph mark (¶) at the end of the paragraph, and then type a paragraph announcing the meeting, which is scheduled for tomorrow at 2 p.m. in the Central Conference Room.
11. Save the letter as **Key Card Meeting Memo** in the Tutorial.01\Cases folder provided with your Data Files.
12. **Explore** To make it easier to review your work, you can change the Zoom setting in Normal view. Click the Zoom box in the Standard toolbar, type 110%, and then press the Enter key. Continue to type values in the Zoom text box until the document fills the window.
13. Review the memo. Correct any typos and delete any Smart Tags. Save the memo again, preview it, and then print it.
14. Close the document.

Research

Go to the Web to find information you can use to create documents.

Internet Assignments

The purpose of the Internet Assignments is to challenge you to find information on the Internet that you can use to work effectively with this software. The actual assignments are updated and maintained on the Course Technology Web site. Log on to the Internet and use your Web browser to go to the Student Online Companion for New Perspectives Office 2003 at **www.course.com/np/office2003**. Click the Internet Assignments link, and then navigate to the assignments for this tutorial.

Assess

SAM Assessment and Training

If you have a SAM user profile, you may have access to hands-on instruction, practice, and assessment of the skills covered in this tutorial. Log in to your SAM account and go to your assignments page to see what your instructor has assigned.

Reinforce

Lab Assignments

The New Perspectives Labs are designed to help you master some of the key concepts and skills presented in this text. The steps for completing this Lab are located on the Course Technology Web site. Log on to the Internet and use your Web browser to go to the Student Online Companion for New Perspectives Office 2003 at **www.course.com/np/office2003**. Click the Lab Assignments link, and then navigate to the assignments for this tutorial.

Review

Quick Check Answers

Session 1.1

1. (1) Plan the content, purpose, organization, and look of your document. (2) Create and then edit the document. (3) Format the document to make it visually appealing. (4) Preview and then print the document.
2. a. symbols you can display on-screen but that don't print
   b. controls the document's on-screen magnification
   c. settings that control the size and shape of the characters that appear when you start typing
   d. standard settings
3. Click the Normal View button.
4. Right-click a toolbar or the menu bar, and then click Standard.
5. False
6. False
7. .doc

Session 1.2

1. True
2. Type the first few characters of the month. When an AutoComplete suggestion appears, press the Enter key.
3. Undo
4. Click Tools on the menu bar, point to Letters and Mailings, and then click Envelopes and Labels. In the Envelopes and Labels dialog box, verify that the Delivery address contains the correct address. If necessary, you can type a new address or edit the existing one. If necessary, type a return address. If you are using preprinted stationery that already includes a return address, click the Omit check box to insert a check. To print the envelope immediately, insert an envelope in your printer, and then click Print. To store the envelope along with the rest of the document, click Add to Document. To print the envelope after you have added it to the document, open the Print dialog box, and then print the page containing the envelope.
5. a. the means by which text at the bottom of the document shifts out of view when you display the top of the document, and text at the top shifts out of view when you display the bottom of a document
   b. a feature that automatically enters dates and other regularly used items
   c. a button that redoes changes
   d. a window in which you can see how the document will look when printed
   e. a feature that that allows you to perform actions (such as sending e-mail or scheduling a meeting) that would normally require a completely different program.

Objectives

Session 2.1
- Check spelling and grammar
- Select and delete text
- Move text within the document
- Find and replace text

Session 2.2
- Change margins, line spacing, alignment, and paragraph indents
- Copy formatting with the Format Painter
- Change fonts and adjust font sizes
- Emphasize points with bullets, numbering, bold, underlining, and italic
- Preview formatted text
- Add a comment to a document
- Use the Research task pane

Editing and Formatting a Document

Preparing an FAQ Document

Case

Long Meadow Gardens

Marilee Brigham is the owner of Long Meadow Gardens, a landscape and gardening supply company. The firm's large nursery provides shrubs and trees to professional landscape contractors throughout the Minneapolis/St. Paul area. At the same time, Long Meadow Gardens' retail store caters to home gardeners, who often call the store with questions about planting and caring for their purchases.

Marilee has noticed that retail customers tend to ask the same set of questions. To save time, she would like to create a series of handouts designed to answer these common questions. (Such a document is sometimes known as an FAQ—which is short for "frequently asked questions.") The company's chief horticulturist, Peter Chi, has just finished creating an FAQ containing information on planting trees. Now that Marilee has commented on and corrected the draft, Peter asks you to make the necessary changes and print the document.

In this tutorial, you will edit the FAQ document according to Marilee's comments. You will open a draft of the document, resave it, and edit it. You will check the document's grammar and spelling, and then move text using two different methods. You will also find and replace one version of the company name with another.

Next, you will change the overall look of the document by changing margins and line spacing, indenting and justifying paragraphs, and copying formatting from one paragraph to another. You'll create a bulleted list to emphasize the species of water-tolerant trees and a numbered list for the steps involved in removing the burlap from around the base of a tree. Then you'll make the title more prominent by centering it, changing its font, and enlarging it. You'll add bold to the questions to set them off from the rest of the text and underline an added note about how to get further

Student Data Files

▼**Tutorial.02**

▽ Tutorial folder
- FAQ.doc

▽ Review folder
- Statmnt.doc

▽ Cases folder
- Form.doc
- Product.doc
- Training.doc
- Tribune.doc

information. Finally, before you print the FAQ document, you will add a comment, and look up information using the Research task pane.

Session 2.1

Reviewing the Document

Marilee's editing marks and notes on the first draft are shown in Figure 2-1. You'll begin by opening the first draft of the document, which has the filename FAQ.

Figure 2-1 Draft of FAQ with Marilee's edits (page 1)

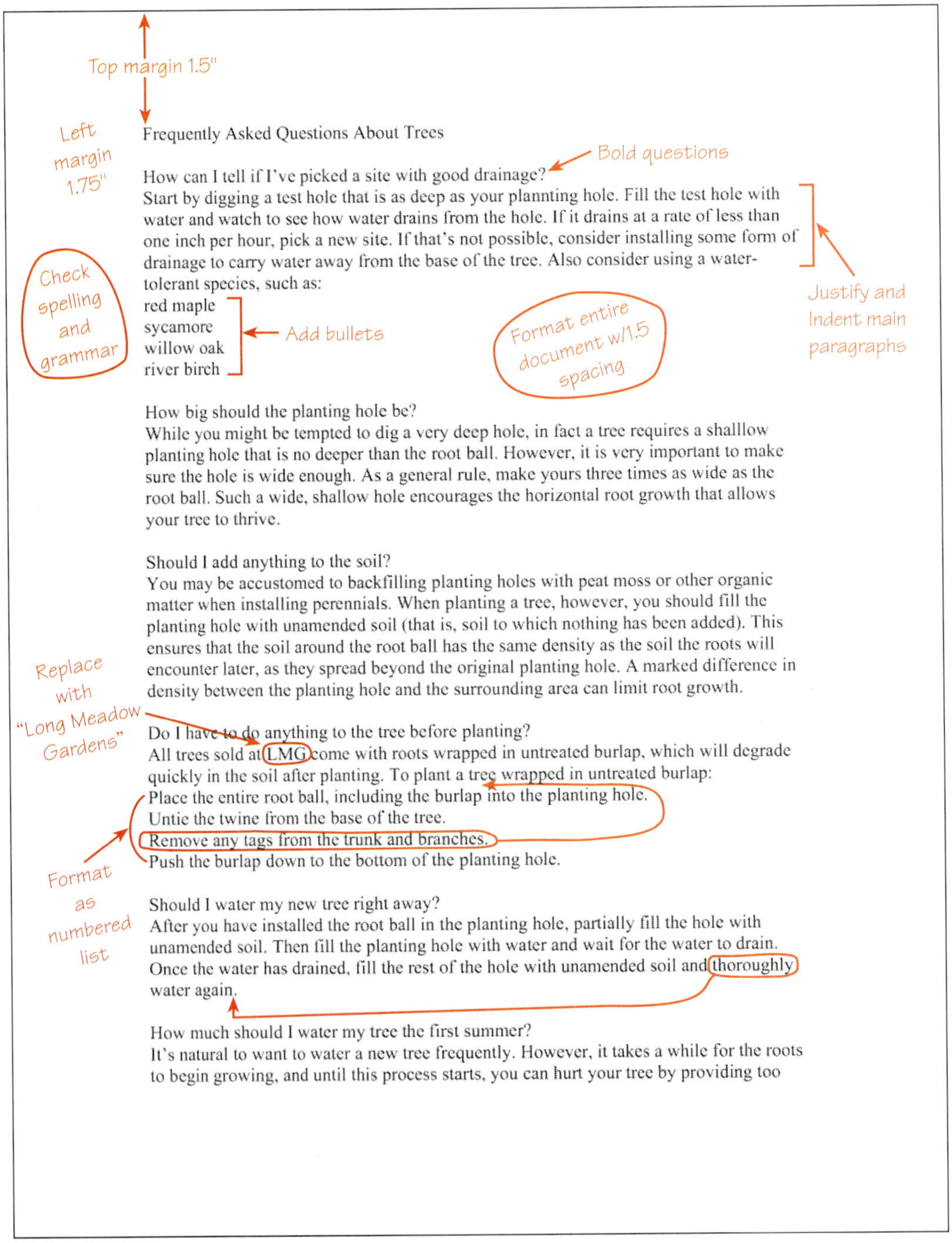

Frequently Asked Questions About Trees

How can I tell if I've picked a site with good drainage?
Start by digging a test hole that is as deep as your plannting hole. Fill the test hole with water and watch to see how water drains from the hole. If it drains at a rate of less than one inch per hour, pick a new site. If that's not possible, consider installing some form of drainage to carry water away from the base of the tree. Also consider using a water-tolerant species, such as:
red maple
sycamore
willow oak
river birch

How big should the planting hole be?
While you might be tempted to dig a very deep hole, in fact a tree requires a shalllow planting hole that is no deeper than the root ball. However, it is very important to make sure the hole is wide enough. As a general rule, make yours three times as wide as the root ball. Such a wide, shallow hole encourages the horizontal root growth that allows your tree to thrive.

Should I add anything to the soil?
You may be accustomed to backfilling planting holes with peat moss or other organic matter when installing perennials. When planting a tree, however, you should fill the planting hole with unamended soil (that is, soil to which nothing has been added). This ensures that the soil around the root ball has the same density as the soil the roots will encounter later, as they spread beyond the original planting hole. A marked difference in density between the planting hole and the surrounding area can limit root growth.

Do I have to do anything to the tree before planting?
All trees sold at LMG come with roots wrapped in untreated burlap, which will degrade quickly in the soil after planting. To plant a tree wrapped in untreated burlap:
Place the entire root ball, including the burlap into the planting hole.
Untie the twine from the base of the tree.
Remove any tags from the trunk and branches.
Push the burlap down to the bottom of the planting hole.

Should I water my new tree right away?
After you have installed the root ball in the planting hole, partially fill the hole with unamended soil. Then fill the planting hole with water and wait for the water to drain. Once the water has drained, fill the rest of the hole with unamended soil and thoroughly water again.

How much should I water my tree the first summer?
It's natural to want to water a new tree frequently. However, it takes a while for the roots to begin growing, and until this process starts, you can hurt your tree by providing too

Figure 2-1 (cont.) Draft of FAQ with Marilee's edits (page 2)

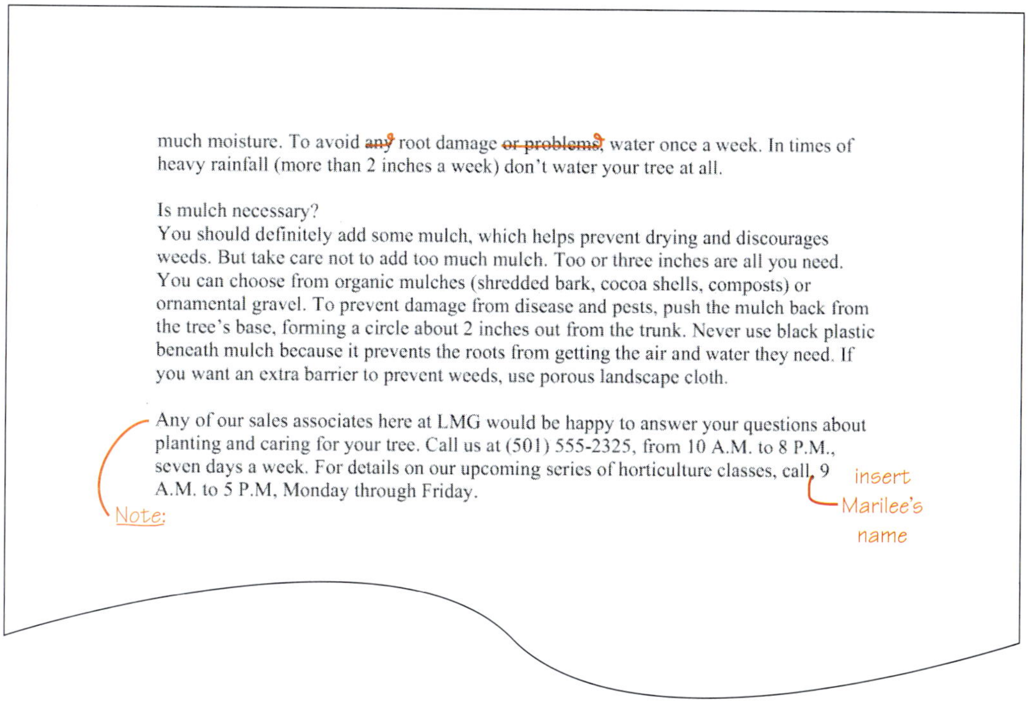

much moisture. To avoid ~~any~~ root damage ~~or problems,~~ water once a week. In times of heavy rainfall (more than 2 inches a week) don't water your tree at all.

Is mulch necessary?
You should definitely add some mulch, which helps prevent drying and discourages weeds. But take care not to add too much mulch. Too or three inches are all you need. You can choose from organic mulches (shredded bark, cocoa shells, composts) or ornamental gravel. To prevent damage from disease and pests, push the mulch back from the tree's base, forming a circle about 2 inches out from the trunk. Never use black plastic beneath mulch because it prevents the roots from getting the air and water they need. If you want an extra barrier to prevent weeds, use porous landscape cloth.

Any of our sales associates here at LMG would be happy to answer your questions about planting and caring for your tree. Call us at (501) 555-2325, from 10 A.M. to 8 P.M., seven days a week. For details on our upcoming series of horticulture classes, call, 9 A.M. to 5 P.M, Monday through Friday.

To open the document:

1. Start Word, and then verify that the Getting Started task pane is displayed.
2. In the Open section of the Getting Started task pane, click the **Open** button. You may have to point to the down arrow at the bottom of the task pane to scroll down in order to display the Open button. (Depending on how your computer is set up, the label next to this button might read "More" or "Open.") The Open dialog box opens, as shown in Figure 2-2. (Note that you could also use the Open button on the Standard toolbar to open this dialog box.)

Figure 2-2 Open dialog box

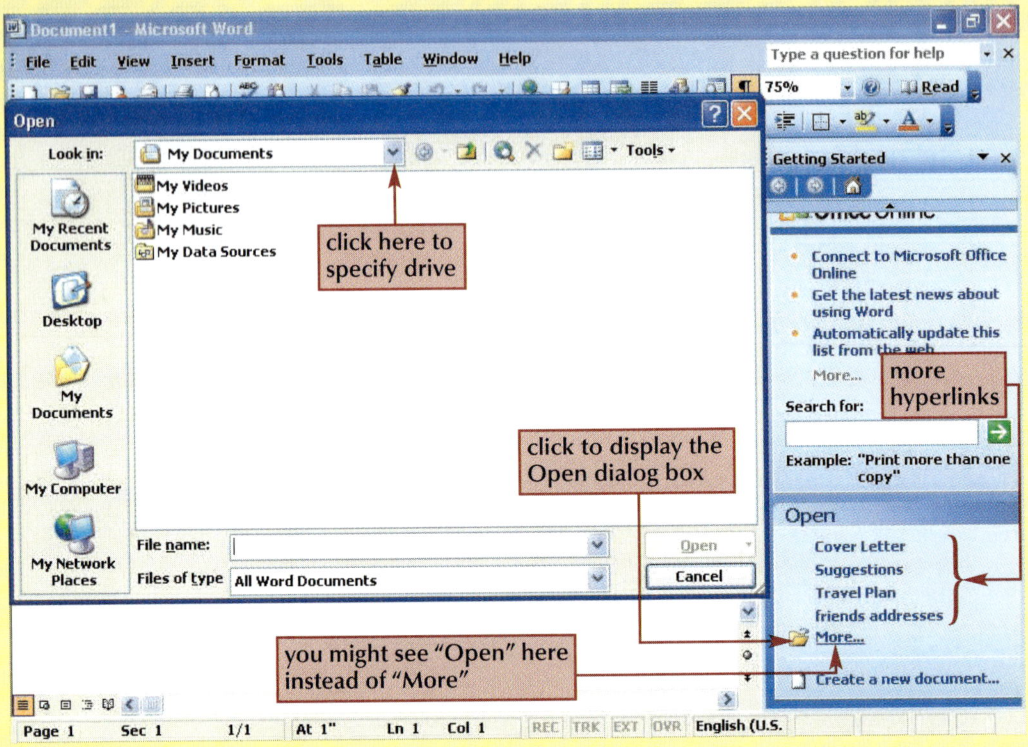

3. Click the **Look in** list arrow, and then navigate to the Tutorial.02 folder included with your Data Files.
4. Double-click the **Tutorial.02** folder, and then double-click the **Tutorial** folder.
5. Click **FAQ** to select the file, if necessary.

   Trouble? If you see "FAQ.doc" in the folder, Windows is configured to display file extensions. Click FAQ.doc and continue with Step 6. If you can't find the file with or without the file extension, make sure you're looking in the Tutorial subfolder within the Tutorial.02 folder included with your Data Files, and check to make sure the Files of type text box displays All Word Documents or All Files. If you still can't locate the file, ask your instructor or technical support person for help.
6. Click the **Open** button. The document opens with the insertion point at the beginning of the document. Notice that the document consists of a series of questions and answers.
7. Verify that the document is displayed in Normal view, and then scroll down until you can see the question "Is mulch necessary?" Notice the dotted line in the middle of the preceding paragraph. This line shows where Word has inserted a page break, dividing the document into two pages. See Figure 2-3. Word automatically inserts a page break (called an **automatic page break**) whenever your text fills up all the available lines on a page. In Normal view, a page break is represented by the dotted line shown in Figure 2-3. In some views, page breaks are not visible at all.

Document with automatic page break

Figure 2-3

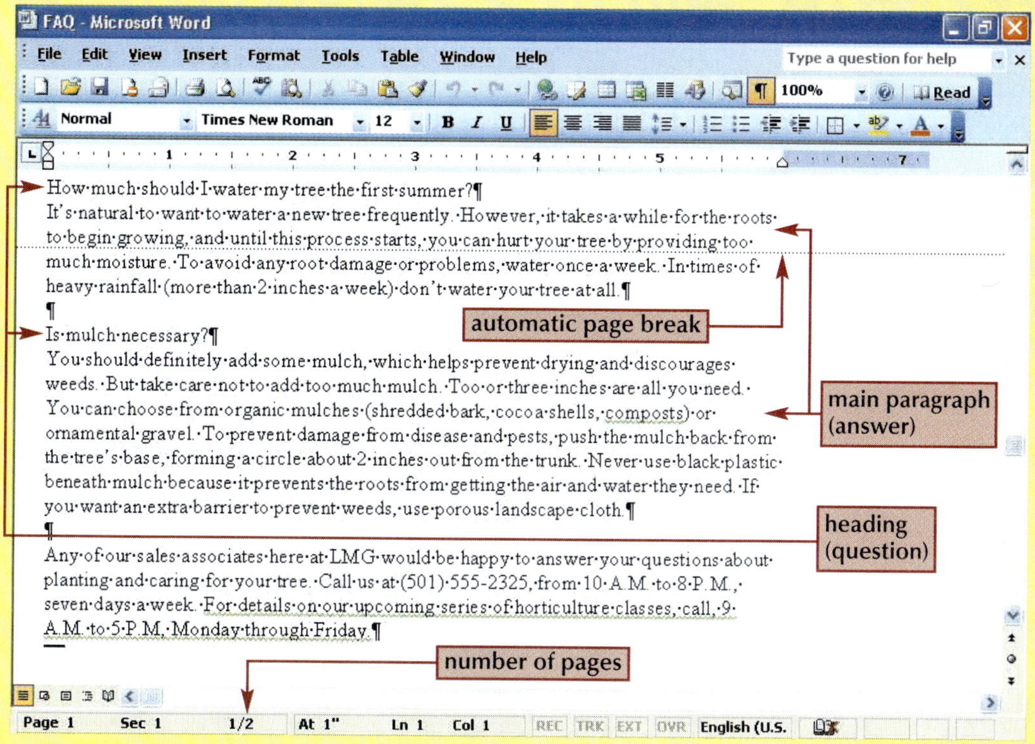

8. Check that your screen matches Figure 2-3. If necessary, click the **Show/Hide ¶** button ¶ to display nonprinting characters. This will make formatting elements (paragraph marks, spaces, and so forth) visible and easier to change.

Now that you've opened the document, you can save it with a new name. To avoid altering the original file, FAQ, you will save the document using the filename Tree FAQ. Saving the document with another filename creates a copy of the file and leaves the original file unchanged in case you want to work through the tutorial again.

To save the document with a new name:

1. Click **File** on the menu bar, and then click **Save As**. The Save As dialog box opens with the current filename highlighted in the File name text box. You could type an entirely new filename, or you could edit the current one.
2. Click to the left of "FAQ" in the File name text box, type **Tree**, and then press the **spacebar**.
3. Verify that the Tutorial.02\Tutorial folder is selected in the Save in box.
4. Click the **Save** button. The document is saved with the new filename "Tree FAQ".

Now you're ready to begin working with the document. First, you will check it for spelling and grammatical errors.

Using the Spelling and Grammar Checker

When typing a document, Word highlights possible spelling and grammatical errors. You can quickly recognize these possible errors by looking for words underlined in red (for possible spelling errors) or green (for possible grammatical errors). When you're working on a document that someone else typed, it's a good idea to start by using the Spelling and Grammar checker. This feature automatically checks a document word by word for a variety of errors. Among other things, the Spelling and Grammar checker can sometimes find words that, though spelled correctly, are not used properly.

Reference Window

Checking a Document for Spelling and Grammatical Errors

- Move the insertion point to the beginning of the document, and then click the Spelling and Grammar button on the Standard toolbar.
- In the Spelling and Grammar dialog box, review any errors highlighted in color. Possible grammatical errors appear in green; possible spelling errors appear in red. Review the suggested corrections in the Suggestions list box.
- To accept a suggested correction, click on it in the Suggestions list box, click Change to make the correction, and then continue searching the document for errors.
- Click Ignore Once to skip the current instance of the highlighted text and continue searching the document for errors.
- Click Ignore All to skip all instances of the highlighted text and continue searching the document for spelling errors. Click Ignore Rule to skip all instances of a highlighted grammatical error.
- To type your correction directly in the document, click outside the Spelling and Grammar dialog box, make the correction, and then click Resume in the Spelling and Grammar dialog box.
- To add an unrecognized word to the dictionary, click Add to dictionary.

The Spelling and Grammar Checker compares the words in your document to the default dictionary that is installed automatically with Word. If you regularly use terms that are not included in the main dictionary, you can create a custom dictionary and then select it as the new default dictionary. A custom dictionary includes all the terms in the main dictionary, plus any new terms that you add. To create a custom dictionary and select it as the new default dictionary, you would follow these steps:

1. Click **Tools** on the menu bar, click **Options**, click the **Spelling & Grammar** tab, and then click **Custom Dictionaries**. The Custom Dictionaries dialog box opens.
2. Click **New**. The Create Custom Dictionary dialog box opens.
3. Type a name for the custom dictionary in the File name text box, and click **Save**. You return to the Custom Dictionaries dialog box.
4. In the **Dictionary list** box, click the new custom dictionary to select it, click **Change Default**, and then click **OK**.

You'll see how the Spelling and Grammar checker works as you check the Tree FAQ document for mistakes.

To check the Tree FAQ document for spelling and grammatical errors:

1. Press **Ctrl+Home** to verify that the insertion point is located at the beginning of the document, to the left of the "F" in "Frequently Asked Questions."
2. Click the **Spelling and Grammar** button on the Standard toolbar. The Spelling and Grammar dialog box opens with the word "About" highlighted in green, indicating a possible grammatical error. The word "about" (with a lowercase "a") is suggested as a possible replacement. The line immediately under the dialog box title bar indicates the possible type of problem, in this case, Capitalization. See Figure 2-4. Prepositions of five or more letters are capitalized in titles so no change is required here.

   Trouble? If you see the word "plannting" selected instead of "About," your computer is not set up to check grammar. Click the Check grammar check box to insert a check, and then click Cancel to close the Spelling and Grammar dialog box. Repeat Steps 1 and 2.

Figure 2-4 Spelling and Grammar dialog box

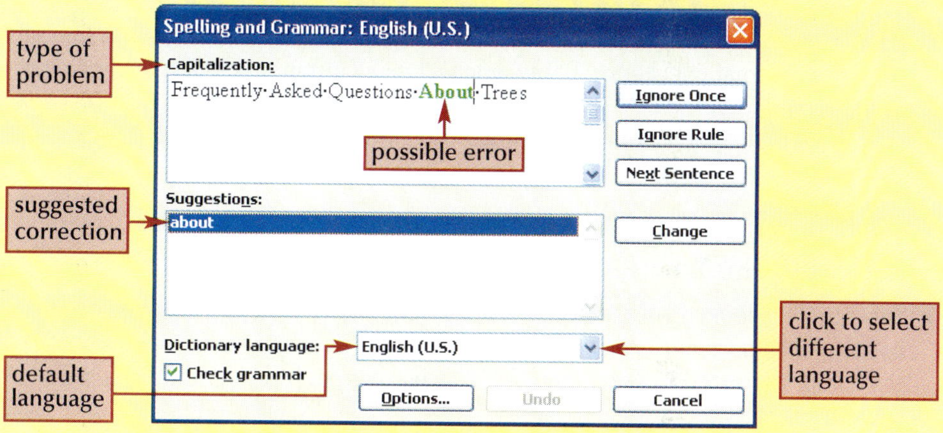

3. Click the **Ignore Rule** button. The word "plannting" is highlighted in red, with "planting," "planning," and "plantings" listed as possible corrections.
4. Verify that "planting" is highlighted in the Suggestions list box, and then click the **Change** button. "Planting" is inserted into the document, and the misspelled word "shalllow" is highlighted in the document.
5. Verify that "shallow" is selected in the Suggestions list box, and then click the **Change** button. The word "composts" is highlighted in green, with "and composts" listed as a possible correction. The type of problem "Comma Use" has to do with using a comma without "and" before the last item in a list. Marilee likes the list as it stands, so you'll ignore this suggestion.
6. Click the **Ignore Rule** button. You click Ignore Rule to ignore the rule throughout the entire document. (You can click Ignore Once to ignore a grammatical rule in the currently selected text.)

The last sentence of the document is selected. According to the type of problem listed at the top of the dialog box, the highlighted text is a sentence fragment. In this case, Word is correct. The word "call" lacks a direct object—that is, you need to indicate whom the reader should call. You can fix this problem by clicking outside the Spelling and Grammar dialog box and typing the change directly in the document.

7. Click outside the Spelling and Grammar dialog box just to the right of "call," press the **spacebar**, type **Marilee Brigham**, and then click the **Resume** button in the Spelling and Grammar dialog box. A message box opens indicating that the spelling and grammar check is complete. Notice that the last sentence is no longer a sentence fragment; that is because "Marilee Brigham" completes the sentence.

   Trouble? If you don't see the word "call," the Spelling and Grammar checker dialog box is covering it. Click the title bar of the Spelling and Grammar dialog box, and drag the dialog box out of the way.

8. Click the **OK** button. The Spelling and Grammar dialog box closes. You return to the Tree FAQ document.

Although the Spelling and Grammar checker is a useful tool, remember that there is no substitute for careful proofreading. Always take the time to read through your document to check for errors the Spelling and Grammar checker might have missed. Keep in mind that the Spelling and Grammar checker probably won't catch *all* instances of words that are spelled correctly but used improperly. And, of course, the Spelling and Grammar checker cannot pinpoint phrases that are confusing or inaccurate. To produce a professional document, you must read it carefully several times, and, if necessary, ask a co-worker to read it, too.

To proofread the Tree FAQ document:

1. Scroll to the beginning of the document and begin proofreading. When you get near the bottom of the document, notice that the word "Too" is used instead of the word "Two" in the paragraph on mulch. See Figure 2-5. You will correct this error after you learn how to select parts of a document.

Figure 2-5 **Word "Too" used incorrectly**

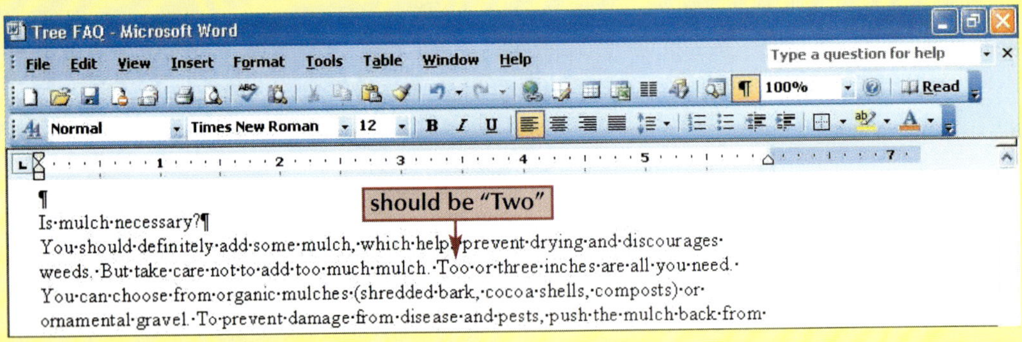

2. Finish proofreading the Tree FAQ document.

To make all of Marilee's changes, you need to learn how to select parts of a document.

Selecting Parts of a Document

Before you can do anything to text (such as deleting, moving, or formatting it), you often need to highlight, or **select** it. You can select text by using the mouse or the keyboard, although the mouse is usually easier and more efficient. With the mouse you can quickly select a line or paragraph by clicking the **selection bar** (the blank space in the left margin area of the Document window). You can also select text using various combinations of keys. Figure 2-6 summarizes methods for selecting text with the mouse and the keyboard. The notation "Ctrl+Shift" means you press and hold the two keys at the same time. Note that you will use the methods described in Figure 2-6 as you work on the Tree FAQ document.

Figure 2-6 Methods for selecting text

To Select	Mouse	Keyboard	Mouse and Keyboard
A word	Double-click the word.	Move the insertion point to the beginning of the word, hold down Ctrl+Shift, and then press →.	
A line	Click in the selection bar next to the line.	Move the insertion point to the beginning of the line, hold down Shift, and then press →.	
A sentence	Click at the beginning of the sentence, then drag the pointer until the sentence is selected.		Press and hold down the Ctrl key, and click within the sentence.
Multiple lines	Click and drag in the selection bar next to the lines.	Move the insertion point to the beginning of the first line, hold down Shift, and then press → until all the lines are selected.	
A paragraph	Double-click in the selection bar next to the paragraph, or triple-click within the paragraph.	Move the insertion point to the beginning of the paragraph, hold down Ctrl+Shift, and then press ↓.	
Multiple paragraphs	Click in the selection bar next to the first paragraph in the group, and then drag in the selection bar to select the paragraphs.	Move the insertion point to the beginning of the first paragraph, hold down Ctrl+Shift, and then press ↓ until all the paragraphs are selected.	
An entire document	Triple-click in the selection bar.	Press Ctrl+A.	Press and hold down the Ctrl key and click in the selection bar.
A block of text	Click at the beginning of the block, then drag the pointer until the entire block is selected.		Click at the beginning of the block, press and hold down the Shift key, and then click at the end of the block.
Nonadjacent blocks of text	Press and hold the Ctrl key, then drag the mouse pointer to select multiple blocks of nonadjacent text.		

Deleting Text

When editing a document, you frequently need to delete text. You already have experience using the Backspace and Delete keys to delete a few characters. To delete an entire word or multiple words, you select the text. After you select the text, you can either replace it with something else by typing over it, or delete it by pressing the Delete key. You need to delete the word "Too" and replace it with "Two," so you'll use the first method now.

To replace "Too" with "Two":

1. Press **Ctrl+End**. The insertion point moves to the end of the document.
2. Press and hold the **Ctrl** key while you press the ↑ key three times. The insertion point is now positioned at the beginning of the paragraph that begins "You should definitely add some mulch." (The status bar indicates that this is line 5 of page 2.)
3. In the second line of the paragraph, double-click the word **Too** (in the phrase "Too or three inches"). The entire word is highlighted.
4. Type **Two**. The selected word is replaced with the correction. The sentence now correctly reads: "Two or three inches are all you need."

Next, Marilee wants you to delete the phrase "or problems" and the word "any" in the paragraph before the one you've just corrected. Peter explains that you can do this quickly by selecting multiple items and then pressing Delete. As you'll see in the following steps, selecting parts of a document by clicking and dragging takes a little practice, so don't be concerned if you don't get it right the first time. You can always try again.

To select and delete multiple items:

1. Press the ↑ key five times. As shown in Figure 2-7, the insertion point is now located in the sentence that begins "To avoid any root damage or problems." The status bar indicates that this is line 1 of page 2.

Figure 2-7 Text to be deleted

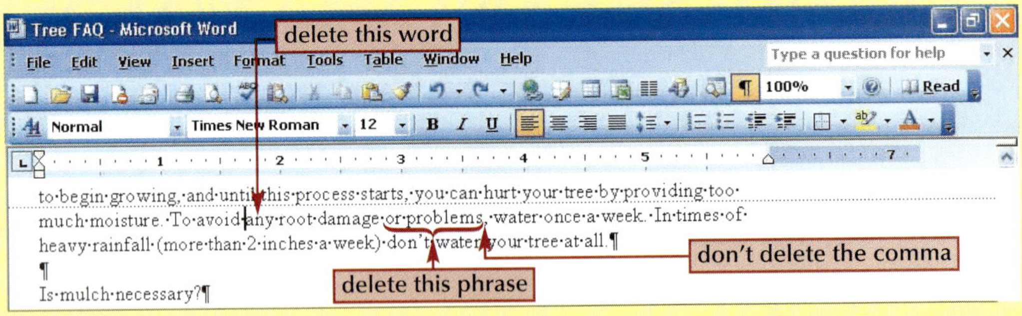

2. Double-click the word **any**. The word and the space following it are selected.
3. Press and hold the **Ctrl** key, click to the left of "or" and drag to select the phrase "or problems," and then release the **Ctrl** key. Do not select the comma after the word "problems." At this point the word "any" and the phrase "or problems" should be selected.

   Trouble? If you don't get Step 3 right the first time (for instance, if you accidentally selected the word "damage"), click anywhere in the document and then repeat Steps 2 and 3.

4. Press the **Delete** key. The selected items are deleted and the words around them move in to fill the space. As you can see in Figure 2-8, you still need to delete the extra space before the comma.

Figure 2-8 **Paragraph after deleting phrase**

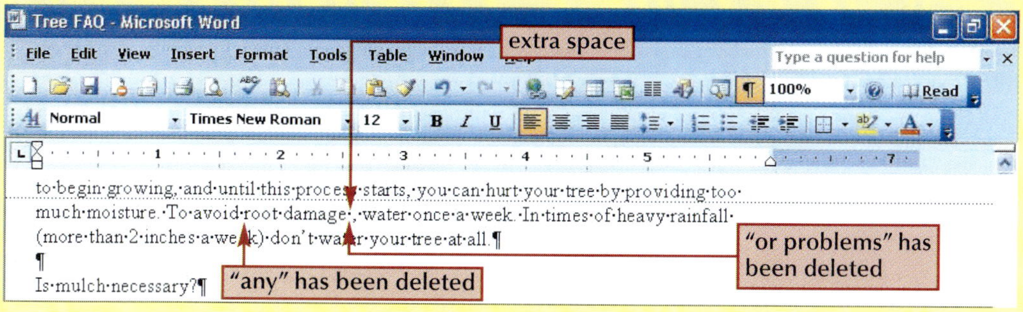

Trouble? If you deleted the wrong text, click the Undo button (not the Redo button) on the Standard toolbar to reverse your mistake, and then begin again with Step 2.

Trouble? If your screen looks slightly different from Figure 2-8, don't be concerned. The text may wrap differently on your monitor. Just make sure you deleted the correct text.

5. Click to the right of the word "damage," and then press the **Delete** key. The extra space is deleted.

6. Scroll down to display the last line of the document (if necessary), drag the mouse pointer to select "Marilee Brigham," press the **Delete** key, press the **spacebar**, and then type your first and last name. This change will make it easier for you to retrieve your document if you print it on a network printer used by other students.

You have edited the document by replacing "Too" with "Two" and by removing the text that Marilee marked for deletion. Now you are ready to make the rest of the edits she suggested.

Moving Text within a Document

One of the most useful features of a word-processing program is the ability to move text. For example, Marilee wants to reorder the four points Peter made in the section "Do I have to do anything to the tree before planting?" on page 1 of his draft. You could reorder the list by deleting an item and then retyping it at a new location, but it's easier to select and then move the text. Word provides several ways to move text: drag and drop, cut and paste, and copy and paste.

Dragging and Dropping Text

One way to move text within a document is called drag and drop. With **drag and drop**, you select the text you want to move, press and hold down the mouse button while you drag the selected text to a new location, and then release the mouse button.

Reference Window

Dragging and Dropping Text

- Select the text you want to move.
- Press and hold down the mouse button until the drag-and-drop pointer appears, and then drag the selected text to its new location.
- Use the dotted insertion point as a guide to determine exactly where the text will be inserted.
- Release the mouse button to drop the text at the insertion point.

Marilee wants you to change the order of the items in the list on page 1 of the document. You'll use the drag-and-drop method to reorder these items. At the same time, you'll practice using the selection bar to highlight a line of text.

To move text using drag and drop:

1. Scroll up until you see "Do I have to do anything to the tree before planting?" (line 29 of page 1). In the list of steps involved in planting a tree, Marilee wants you to move the third step ("Remove any tags from the trunk and branches.") to the top of the list.
2. Move the pointer to the selection bar to the left of the line "Remove any tags from the trunk and branches." The pointer changes from an I-beam to a right-facing arrow.
3. Click to the left of the line "Remove any tags from the trunk and branches." The line is selected. Notice that the paragraph mark at the end of the line is also selected. See Figure 2-9.

Figure 2-9 Selected text to drag and drop

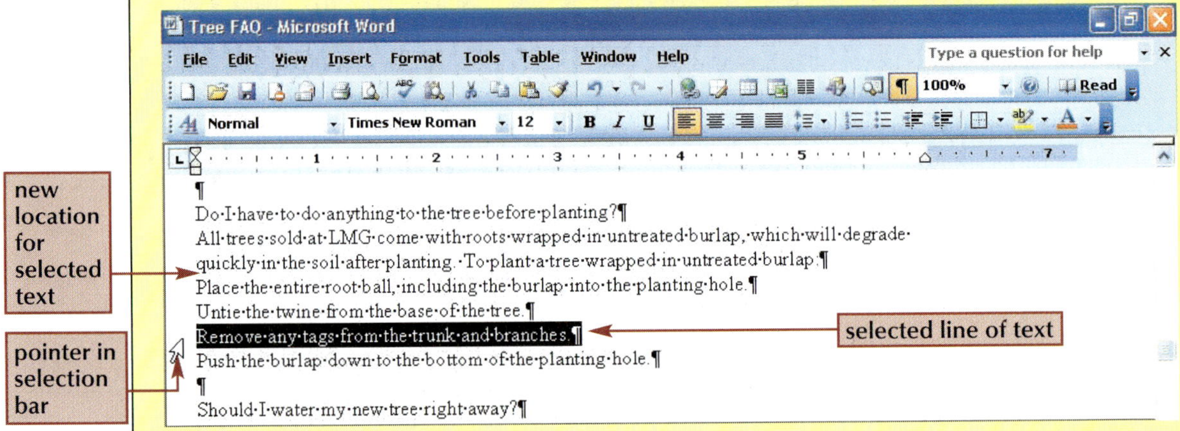

4. Position the pointer over the selected text. The pointer changes from a right-facing arrow to a left-facing arrow.
5. Press and hold down the mouse button until the drag-and-drop pointer appears. Note that a dotted insertion point appears within the selected text. (You may have to move the mouse pointer slightly left or right to see the drag-and-drop pointer or the dotted insertion point.)
6. Drag the selected text up until the dotted insertion point appears to the left of the word "Place." Make sure you use the dotted insertion point, rather than the mouse pointer, to guide the text to its new location. The dotted insertion point indicates exactly where the text will appear when you release the mouse button. See Figure 2-10.

Figure 2-10

Moving text with drag-and-drop pointer

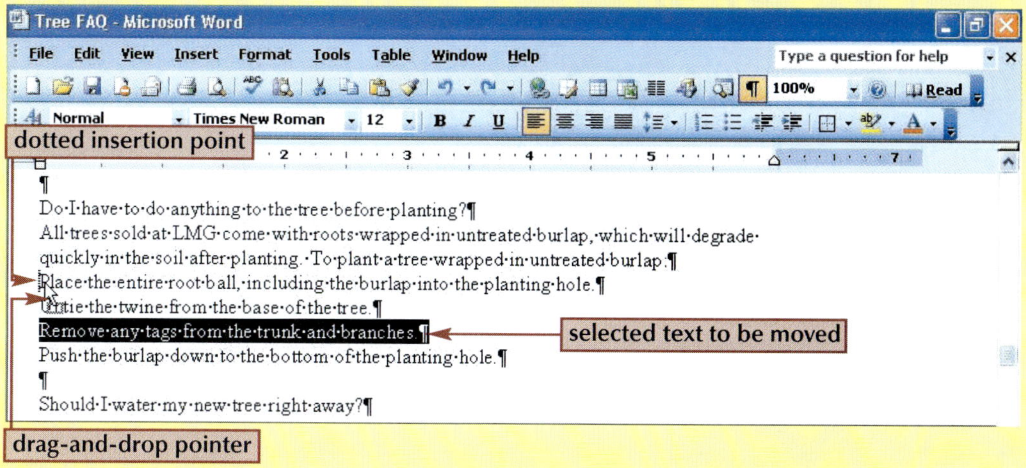

7. Release the mouse button. The selected text moves to its new location as the first step in the list. A Paste Options button appears near the newly moved text, as shown in Figure 2-11. When you move the mouse pointer over the Paste Options button, it changes to include a list arrow.

Figure 2-11

Paste Options button

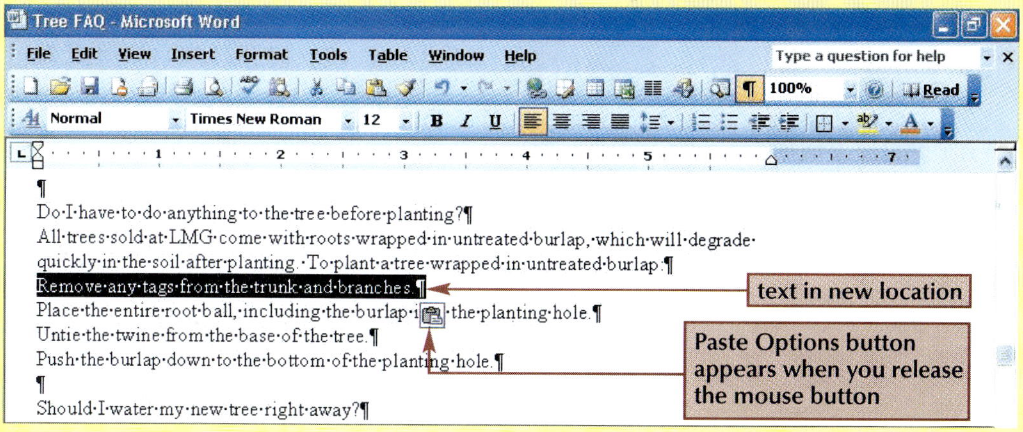

Trouble? If the selected text moves to the wrong location, click the Undo button on the Standard toolbar, and then repeat Steps 2 through 7. Remember to hold down the mouse button until the dotted insertion point appears to the left of the word "Place."

Trouble? If you don't see the Paste Options button, your computer is not set up to display it. Read Step 8, and then continue with Step 9.

8. Click the **Paste Options** button. A menu of text-moving commands appears. These commands are useful when you are inserting text that looks different from the surrounding text. For instance, suppose you selected text formatted in the Times New Roman font and then dragged it to a paragraph formatted in the Arial font. You could then use the Match Destination Formatting command to format the moved text in Arial.

9. Deselect the highlighted text by clicking anywhere in the document. The Paste Options menu closes, but the button remains visible. It will disappear as soon as you perform another task.

Dragging and dropping works well if you're moving text a short distance in a document. However, Word provides another method, called cut and paste, that works well for moving text both long and short distances.

Cutting or Copying and Pasting Text

To **cut** means to remove text from the document and place it on the **Clipboard**, a feature that temporarily stores text or graphics until you need them later. To **copy** means to copy text to the Clipboard, leaving the original material in its original location. To **paste** means to transfer a copy of the text from the Clipboard into the document at the insertion point. To **cut and paste**, you select the text you want to move, cut (or remove) it from the document, and then paste (or insert) it into the document in a new location. If you don't want to remove the text from its original location, you can copy it (rather than cutting it), and then paste the copy in a new location.

Reference Window

Cutting or Copying and Pasting Text

- Select the text you want to cut or copy.
- To remove the text, click the Cut button on the Standard toolbar.
- To make a copy of the text, click the Copy button on the Standard toolbar.
- Move the insertion point to the target location in the document.
- Click the Paste button on the Standard toolbar.

Depending on how your computer is set up, when you cut or copy more than one item, the **Clipboard task pane** may open automatically, making it easier for you to select which items you want to paste into the document. (To have the Clipboard task pane open automatically, click Options at the bottom of the Clipboard task pane, and then select Show Clipboard Automatically.) You can also choose to open the Clipboard task pane via the Office Clipboard command on the Edit menu. The Clipboard task pane contains a list of all the items currently stored on the Clipboard. The Clipboard can store a maximum of 24 items. The last item cut or copied to the Clipboard is the first item listed in the Clipboard task pane.

As indicated in Figure 2-1, Marilee suggested moving the word "thoroughly" (in the paragraph under the heading "Should I water my new tree right away?") to a new location. You'll use cut and paste to move this word.

To move text using cut and paste:

1. If necessary, scroll down until you can see the paragraph below the heading "Should I water my new tree right away?" near the bottom of page 1.
2. Double-click the word **thoroughly**. As you can see in Figure 2-12, you need to move this word to the end of the sentence.

Figure 2-12 Text to move using cut and paste

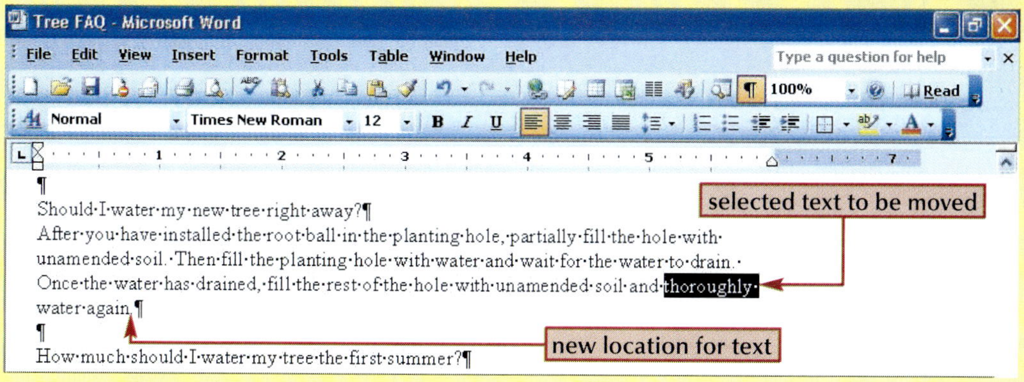

3. Click the **Cut** button on the Standard toolbar to remove the selected text from the document.
4. If the Clipboard task pane opens, click its **Close** button for now. You'll have a chance to use the Clipboard task pane shortly.
5. Click between the "n" in "again" and the period that follows it. The insertion point marks the position where you want to move the text.
6. Click the **Paste** button on the Standard toolbar. The word "thoroughly" appears in its new location, along with a Paste Options button. Note that Word also included a space before the word, so that the end of the sentence reads "and water again thoroughly." The Paste Options button that appeared in the previous set of steps (when you dragged text to a new location) disappears.

   Trouble? If the Paste Options buttons on your computer do not behave exactly as described in these steps—for instance, if they do not disappear as described—this is not a problem, just continue with the tutorial.

Peter mentions that he'll be using the paragraph on mulch and the paragraph on watering for the FAQ he plans to write on flowering shrubs. He asks you to copy that information and paste it in a new document that he can use as the basis for the new FAQ. You can do this using copy and paste. In the process you'll have a chance to use the Clipboard task pane.

To copy and paste text:

1. Click **Edit** on the menu bar, and then click **Office Clipboard**. The Clipboard task pane opens on the right side of the Document window. It contains the word "thoroughly," which you copied to the Clipboard in the last set of steps. See Figure 2-13.

Figure 2-13 Clipboard task pane

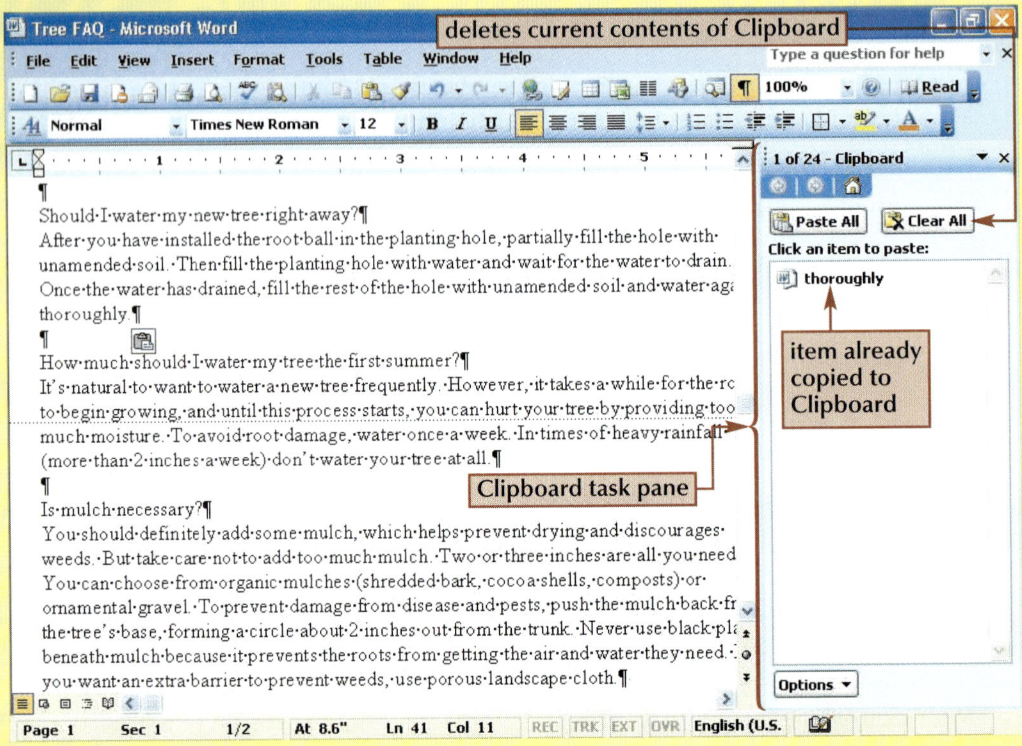

2. Click the **Clear All** button near the top of the task pane. The current contents of the Clipboard are deleted, and you see the following message on the Clipboard task pane: "Clipboard empty. Copy or cut to collect items."
3. Move the mouse pointer to the selection bar and double-click next to the paragraph that begins "After you have installed the root ball." The entire paragraph is selected.
4. Click the **Copy** button on the Standard toolbar. The first part of the paragraph appears in the Clipboard task pane.
5. If necessary, scroll down until you can see the paragraph below the heading "Is mulch necessary?"
6. Select the paragraph below the heading (the paragraph that begins "You should definitely add . . . ").
7. Click the **Copy** button on the Standard toolbar. The first part of the paragraph appears in the Clipboard task pane, as shown in Figure 2-14. Note the Clipboard icon on the Windows taskbar indicating that the Clipboard task pane is currently active.

   Trouble? If you do not see the Clipboard icon in the task pane, click the Options button at the bottom of the Clipboard task pane, and then click Show Office Clipboard Icon on Taskbar. When a check mark is next to this option, the Clipboard icon appears in the far right side of the Windows taskbar to the left of the time.

Figure 2-14

Items in the Clipboard task pane

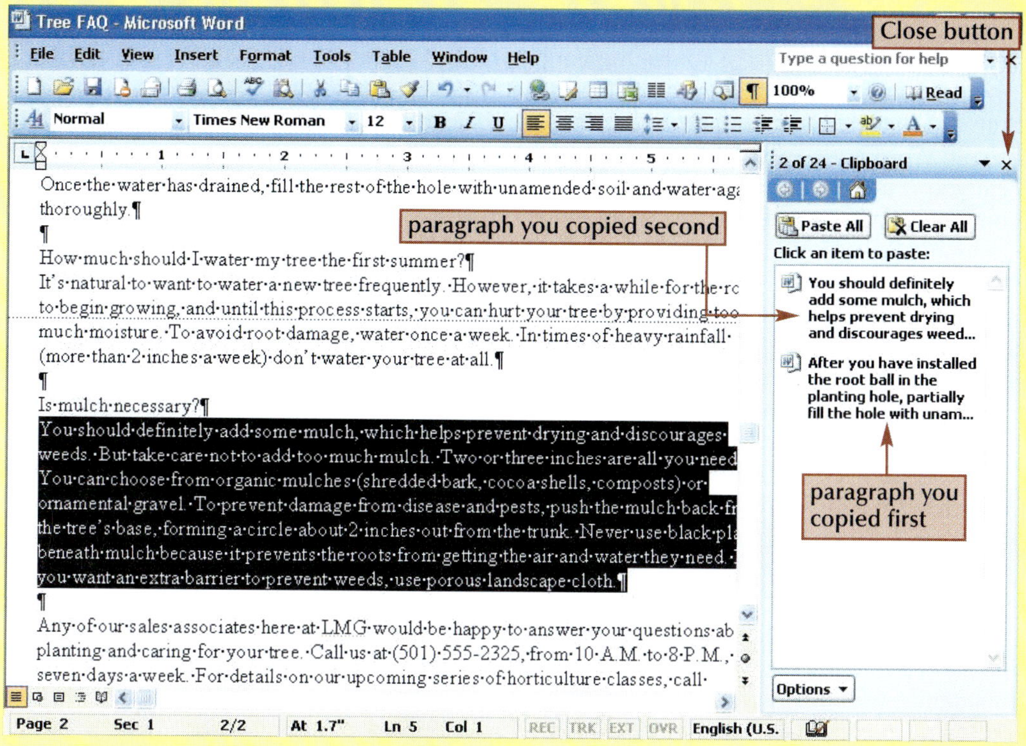

8. Click the **New Blank Document** button on the Standard toolbar. A new, blank document opens. The Clipboard icon on the Windows taskbar indicates that although the Clipboard task pane is no longer visible, it is still active.
9. Double-click the **Clipboard** icon on the right side of the Windows taskbar. The Clipboard task pane is now visible.

Now you can use the Clipboard task pane to insert the copied text into the new document.

To insert the copied text into the new document:

1. In the Clipboard task pane, click the item that begins "You should definitely add . . . " The text is inserted in the document.
2. Press the **Enter** key to insert a blank line, and then click the item that begins "After you have installed the root ball . . . " in the task pane. The text is inserted in the document.
3. Save the document as **Flowering Shrub FAQ** in the Tutorial.02\Tutorial folder, and then close the document. You return to the Tree FAQ document, where the Clipboard task pane is still open. You are finished using the Clipboard task pane, so you will delete its contents.
4. Click the **Clear All** button on the Clipboard task pane. The copied items are removed from the Clipboard task pane.
5. Click the **Close** button on the Clipboard task pane. The Clipboard task pane closes.
6. Click anywhere in the document to deselect the highlighted paragraph.
7. Save the document.

Finding and Replacing Text

When you're working with a longer document, the quickest and easiest way to locate a particular word or phrase is to use the **Find command**. To use the Find command, you type the text you want to find in the Find what text box, and then you click the Find Next button. The text in the Find what text box is the search text. After you click the Find Next button, Word finds and highlights the search text.

If you want to replace characters or a phrase with something else, you use the **Replace command**, which combines the Find command with a substitution feature. The Replace command searches through a document and substitutes the search text with the replacement text you specify. As you perform the search, Word stops and highlights each occurrence of the search text. You must determine whether or not to substitute the replacement text. If you want to substitute the highlighted occurrence, you click the Replace button. If you want to substitute every occurrence of the search text with the replacement text, you click the Replace All button.

When using the Replace All button with single words, keep in mind that the search text might be found within other words. To prevent Word from making incorrect substitutions in such cases, it's a good idea to select the Find whole words only check box along with the Replace All button. For example, suppose you want to replace the word "figure" with "illustration." Unless you select the Find whole words only check box, Word replaces "figure" in "configure" with "illustration" so the word becomes "conillustration."

As you search through a document, you can search from the current location of the insertion point down to the end of the document, from the insertion point up to the beginning of the document, or through the entire document.

Reference Window

Finding and Replacing Text

- Click Edit on the menu bar, and then click either Find or Replace.
- To find text, click the Find tab. To find and replace text, click the Replace tab.
- Click the More button to expand the dialog box to display additional options (including the Find whole words only option). If you see the Less button, the additional options are already displayed.
- In the Search list box, select Down if you want to search from the insertion point to the end of the document, select Up if you want to search from the insertion point to the beginning of the document, or select All to search the entire document.
- Type the characters you want to find in the Find what text box.
- If you are replacing text, type the replacement text in the Replace with text box.
- Click the Find whole words only check box to search for complete words. Click the Match case check box to insert the replacement text using the same case specified in the Replace with text box.
- Click the Find Next button.
- Click the Replace button to substitute the found text with the replacement text and find the next occurrence.
- Click the Replace All button to substitute all occurrences of the found text with the replacement text.

Marilee wants the company initials, LMG, to be spelled out as "Long Meadow Gardens" each time they appear in the text. You'll use the Replace command to make this change quickly and easily.

To replace "LMG" with "Long Meadow Gardens":

1. Press **Ctrl+Home** to move the insertion point to the beginning of the document.
2. Click **Edit** on the menu bar, and then click **Replace**. The Find and Replace dialog box opens.
3. If you see a **More** button, click it to display the additional search options. (If you see a Less button, the additional options are already displayed.) Also, click the **Search** list arrow, and then click **All** if it is not already selected in order to search the entire document.
4. Click the **Find what** text box, type **LMG**, press the **Tab** key, and then type **Long Meadow Gardens** in the Replace with text box.

   Trouble? If you already see the text "LMG" and "Long Meadow Gardens" in your Find and Replace dialog box, someone has recently performed these steps on your computer. Skip Step 4 and continue with Step 5.
5. Click the **Find whole words only** check box to insert a check.
6. Click the **Match case** check box to insert a check. This ensures that Word will insert the replacement text using initial capital letters, as you specified in the Replace with text box. Your Find and Replace dialog box should look like Figure 2-15.

Find and Replace dialog box **Figure 2-15**

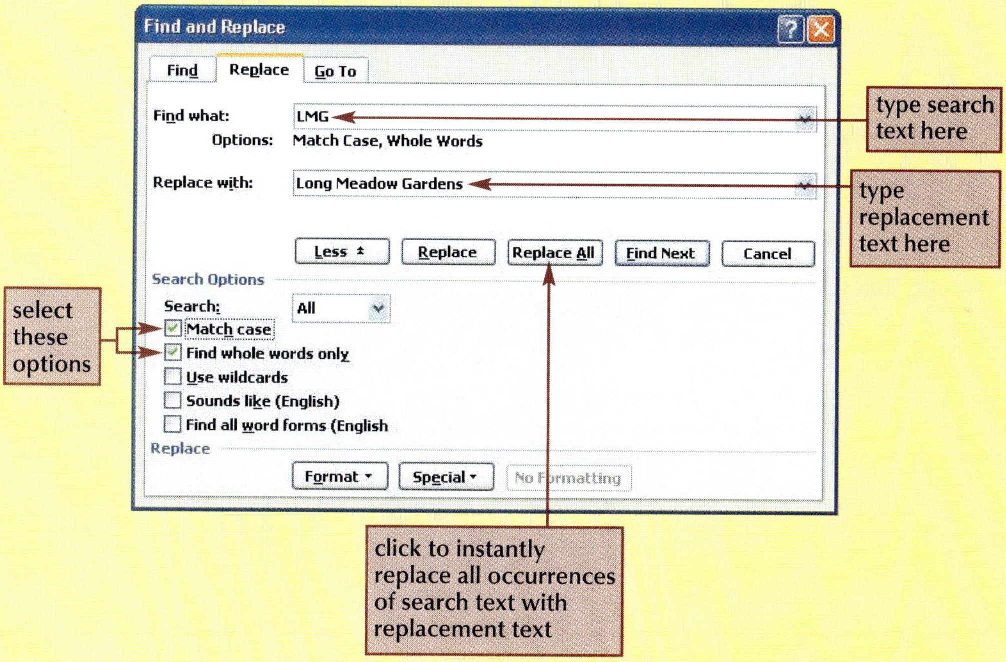

7. Click the **Replace All** button to replace all occurrences of the search text with the replacement text. When Word finishes making the replacements, you see a message box telling you that two replacements were made.
8. Click the **OK** button to close the message box, and then click the **Close** button in the Find and Replace dialog box to return to the document. The full company name has been inserted into the document, as shown in Figure 2-16. (You may have to scroll down to see this section.)

Figure 2-16 Document with "Long Meadow Gardens" inserted

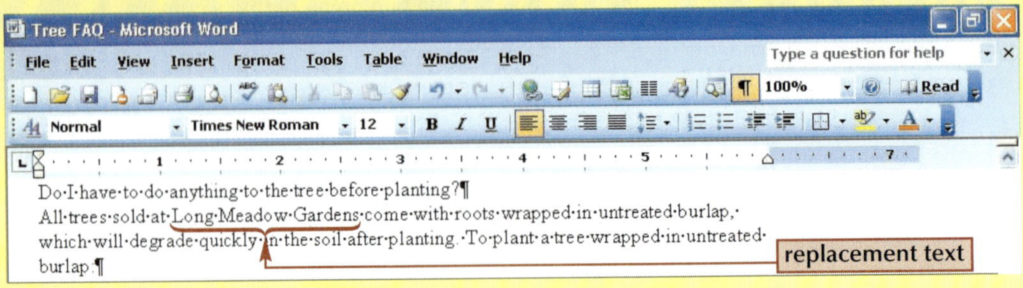

9. Save the document.

Note that you can also search for and replace formatting, such as bold and special characters, in the Find and Replace dialog box. Click in the Find what text box, enter the search text, click the Format button, click Font to open the Font dialog box, and then select the formatting for the search text. Repeat this process for the replacement text, and then complete the search or replacement operation as usual.

You have completed the content changes Marilee requested. In the next session you will make some changes that will affect the document's appearance.

Review

Session 2.1 Quick Check

1. Explain how to use the Spelling and Grammar checker.
2. True or False: You should move the insertion point to the beginning of the document before starting the Spelling and Grammar checker.
3. Explain how to select the following items using the mouse:
   a. one word
   b. a block of text
   c. one paragraph
4. Define the following terms in your own words:
   a. selection bar
   b. drag and drop
   c. Replace
5. True or False: You can display the Clipboard via a command on the Format menu.
6. What is the difference between cut and paste, and copy and paste?
7. List the steps involved in finding and replacing text in a document.

Session 2.2

Changing Margins and Page Orientation

By default, text in a Word document is formatted in **portrait orientation**, which means the page is longer than it is wide (like a typical business letter). In Portrait orientation, the default margins are 1.25 inches for the left and right margins and 1 inch for the top and bottom margins. In **landscape orientation**, the page is wider than it is long, with slightly different margins, so that text spans the widest part of the page.

When working with margins, note that the numbers on the ruler indicate the distance in inches from the left margin, not from the left edge of the paper. You can change both page margins and page orientation from within the Page Setup dialog box.

Changing Margins and Page Orientation for the Entire Document

Reference Window

- With the insertion point anywhere in your document and no text selected, click File on the menu bar, and then click Page Setup.
- If necessary, click the Margins tab to display the margin settings.
- Click the Landscape icon if you want to switch to Landscape orientation.
- Use the arrows to change the settings in the Top, Bottom, Left, or Right text boxes, or type a new margin value in each text box.
- Make sure the Apply to list box displays Whole document.
- Click the OK button.

You need to change the top margin to 1.5 inches and the left margin to 1.75 inches, per Marilee's request. The left margin needs to be wider than usual to allow space for making holes so that the document can be inserted in a three-ring binder. In the next set of steps, you'll change the margins using the Page Setup command. You can also change margins in Print Layout view by dragging an icon on the horizontal ruler. You'll have a chance to practice this technique in the Case Problems at the end of this tutorial.

To change the margins in the Tree FAQ document:

1. If you took a break after the previous session, make sure Word is running, the Tree FAQ document is open in Normal view, and nonprinting characters are displayed.
2. Press **Ctrl+Home** to move the insertion point to the top of the document.
3. Click **File** on the menu bar, and then click **Page Setup** to open the Page Setup dialog box.
4. Click the **Margins** tab, if it is not already selected, to display the margin settings. Portrait orientation is selected by default. The Top margin setting is selected. See Figure 2-17. As you complete the following steps, keep an eye on the document preview, which changes to reflect changes you make to the margins.

Page Setup dialog box **Figure 2-17**

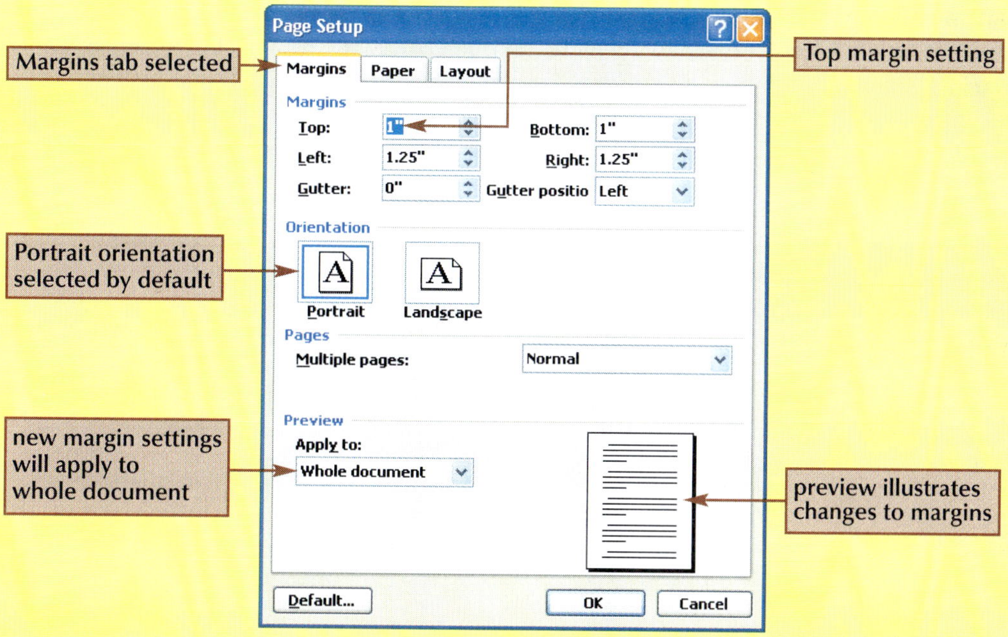

5. Type **1.5** to change the Top margin setting. (You do not have to type the inches symbol.)

6. Press the **Tab** key twice to select the Left text box and highlight the current margin setting. The text area in the Preview box moves down to reflect the larger top margin.
7. Verify that the insertion point is in the Left text box, type **1.75**, and then press the **Tab** key. The left margin in the Preview box increases.
8. Make sure the **Whole document** option is selected in the Apply to list box, and then click the **OK** button to return to your document. Notice that the right margin on the ruler has changed to reflect the larger left margin setting and the resulting reduced page area. The document text is now 5.5 inches wide. See Figure 2-18.

Figure 2-18 **Ruler after setting left margin to 1.75 inches**

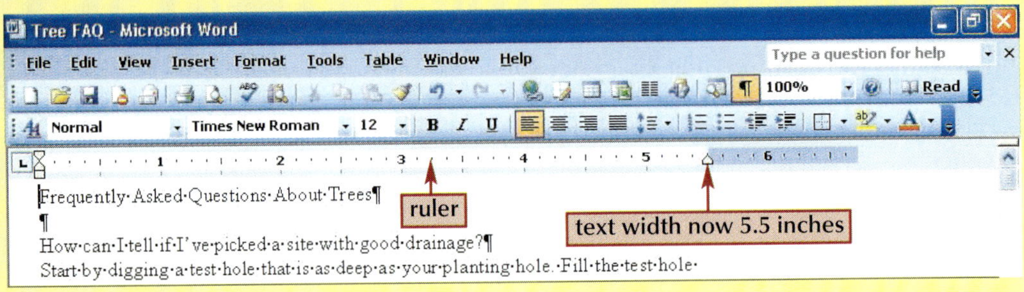

Trouble? If a double dotted line and the words "Section Break" appear in your document, Whole document wasn't specified in the Apply to list box. If this occurs, click the Undo button on the Standard toolbar and repeat Steps 2 through 8, making sure you select the Whole document option in the Apply to list box.

Next, you will change the amount of space between lines of text.

Changing Line Spacing

The **line spacing** in a document determines the amount of vertical space between lines of text. In most situations, you will want to choose from three basic types of line spacing: **single spacing** (which allows for the largest character in a particular line as well as a small amount of extra space); **1.5 line spacing** (which allows for one and one-half times the space of single spacing); and **double spacing** (which allows for twice the space of single spacing). The Tree FAQ document is currently single-spaced because Word uses single spacing by default. The easiest way to change line spacing is to use the Line Spacing button on the Formatting toolbar. You can also use the keyboard to apply single, double, and 1.5 line spacing. Before changing the line-spacing setting, you need to click in the paragraph you want to change. To change line spacing for multiple paragraphs, select all of the paragraphs you want to change. Note that changes to line spacing affect entire paragraphs; you can't change the line spacing for individual lines within a paragraph.

Changing Line Spacing in a Document

Reference Window

- Click in the paragraph you want to change, or select multiple paragraphs.
- Click the list arrow next to the Line Spacing button on the Formatting toolbar, and then click the line spacing you want.

or

- Click in the paragraph you want to change, or select multiple paragraphs.
- Press Ctrl+1 for single spacing, Ctrl+5 for 1.5 line spacing, or Ctrl+2 for double spacing.

Marilee thinks the document will be easier to read with more spacing between the lines. She has asked you to change the line spacing for the entire Tree FAQ document to 1.5 line spacing. You will begin by selecting the entire document.

To change the document's line spacing:

1. Triple-click in the selection bar to select the entire document.
2. Move the mouse pointer over the **Line Spacing** button on the Formatting toolbar to display its ScreenTip. You see the text "Line Spacing (1)," indicating that single spacing is currently selected.
3. Click the **Line Spacing** list arrow on the Formatting toolbar. A list of line spacing options appears, as shown in Figure 2-19. To double space the document, you click 2.0, while to triple space it, you click 3.0. In this case, you need to apply 1.5 line spacing.

Figure 2-19 Line Spacing list box

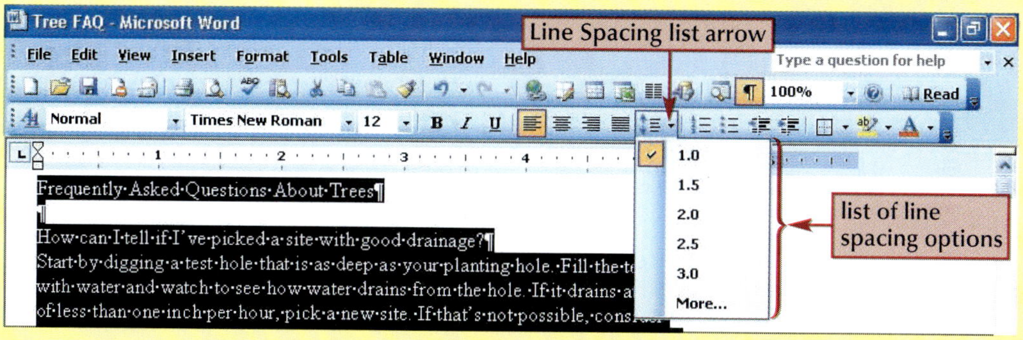

4. Click **1.5**. Notice the additional space between every line of text in the document.
5. Move the mouse pointer over the **Line Spacing** button on the Formatting toolbar to display a ScreenTip that reads "Line Spacing (1.5)." This tells you that 1.5 spacing is currently selected.
6. Click the title to deselect the text.

Now you are ready to make formatting changes that affect individual paragraphs.

Aligning Text

As you begin formatting individual paragraphs in the Tree FAQ document, keep in mind that in Word, a **paragraph** is defined as any text that ends with a paragraph mark symbol (¶). A paragraph can be a group of words that is many lines long, a single word, or even a blank line, in which case you see a paragraph mark alone on a single line. (The Tree FAQ document includes one blank paragraph before each question heading.)

The term **alignment** refers to how the text of a paragraph lines up horizontally between the margins. By default, text is aligned along the left margin but is **ragged**, or uneven, along the right margin. This is called **left alignment**. With **right alignment**, the text is aligned along the right margin and is ragged along the left margin. With **center alignment**, text is centered between the left and right margins and is ragged along both the left and right margins. With **justified alignment**, full lines of text are spaced between both the left and the right margins and the text is not ragged. Text in newspaper columns is often justified. The easiest way to apply alignment settings is by using the alignment buttons on the Formatting toolbar.

Marilee indicates that the title of the Tree FAQ should be centered and that the main paragraphs should be justified. First, you'll center the title.

To center-align the title:

1. Verify that the insertion point is located in the title "Frequently Asked Questions About Trees" at the beginning of the document.
2. Click the **Center** button on the Formatting toolbar. The text centers between the left and right margins. See Figure 2-20.

Figure 2-20 Centered title

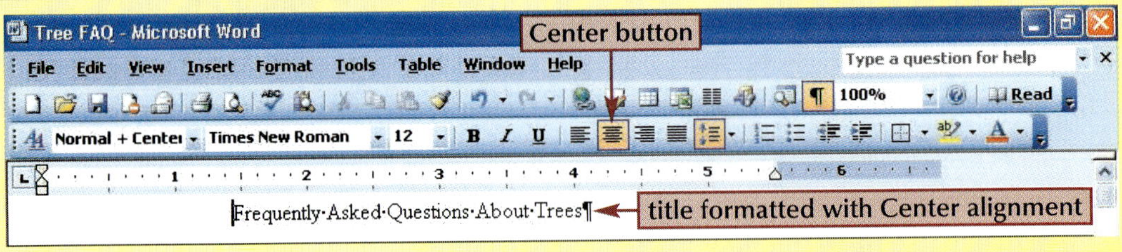

Next, you'll justify the text in the first two main paragraphs.

To justify the first two paragraphs using the Formatting toolbar:

1. Click anywhere in the paragraph that begins "Start by digging a test hole . . . "
2. Click the **Justify** button on the Formatting toolbar. The paragraph text spreads out so that it lines up evenly along the left and right margins.
3. Scroll down so you can move the insertion point to anywhere in the paragraph that begins "While you might be tempted . . . "
4. Click the **Justify** button on the Formatting toolbar again. The text is evenly spaced between the left and right margins. See Figure 2-21.

Figure 2-21 Justified paragraphs

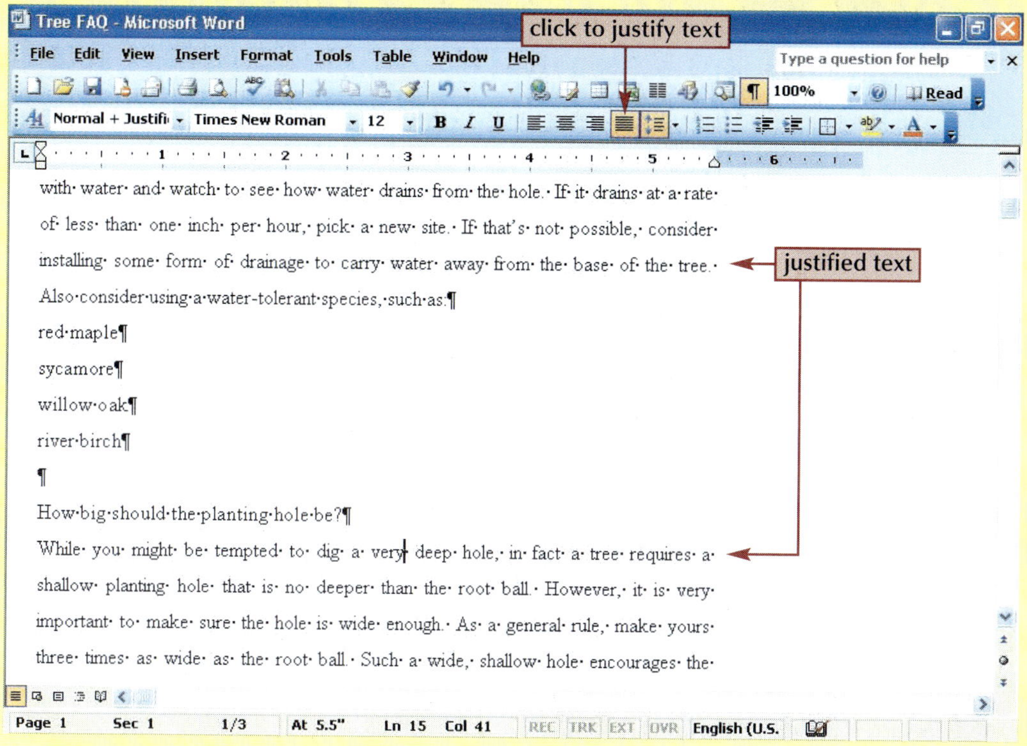

You'll justify the other paragraphs later. Now that you've learned how to change the paragraph alignment, you can turn your attention to indenting a paragraph.

Indenting a Paragraph

When you become a more experienced Word user, you might want to do some paragraph formatting, such as a **hanging indent** (where all lines except the first line of the paragraph are indented from the left margin) or a **right indent** (where all lines of the paragraph are indented from the right margin). You can select these types of indents on the Indents and Spacing tab of the Paragraph dialog box. To open this dialog box, you click Format on the menu bar and then click Paragraph.

In this document, though, you need to indent only the main paragraphs 0.5 inches from the left margin. This left indent is a simple paragraph indent. You can use the Indent buttons on the Formatting toolbar to increase or decrease paragraph indenting quickly. According to Marilee's notes, you need to indent all of the main paragraphs.

To indent a paragraph using the Increase Indent button:

1. Press **Ctrl+Home**, and then click anywhere in the paragraph that begins "Start by digging a test hole . . . "
2. Click the **Increase Indent** button on the Formatting toolbar twice. (Don't click the Decrease Indent button by mistake.) The entire paragraph moves right 0.5 inches each time you click the Increase Indent button. The paragraph is indented 1 inch, 0.5 inches more than Marilee wants.

3. Click the **Decrease Indent** button on the Formatting toolbar to move the paragraph left 0.5 inches. The paragraph is now indented 0.5 inches from the left margin. Don't be concerned about the list of tree species. You will indent the list later, when you format it as a bulleted list.
4. Move the insertion point to anywhere in the paragraph that begins "While you might be tempted . . . " You may have to scroll down to see the paragraph.
5. Click the **Increase Indent** button on the Formatting toolbar. The paragraph is indented 0.5 inches. See Figure 2-22.

Figure 2-22 **Indented paragraphs**

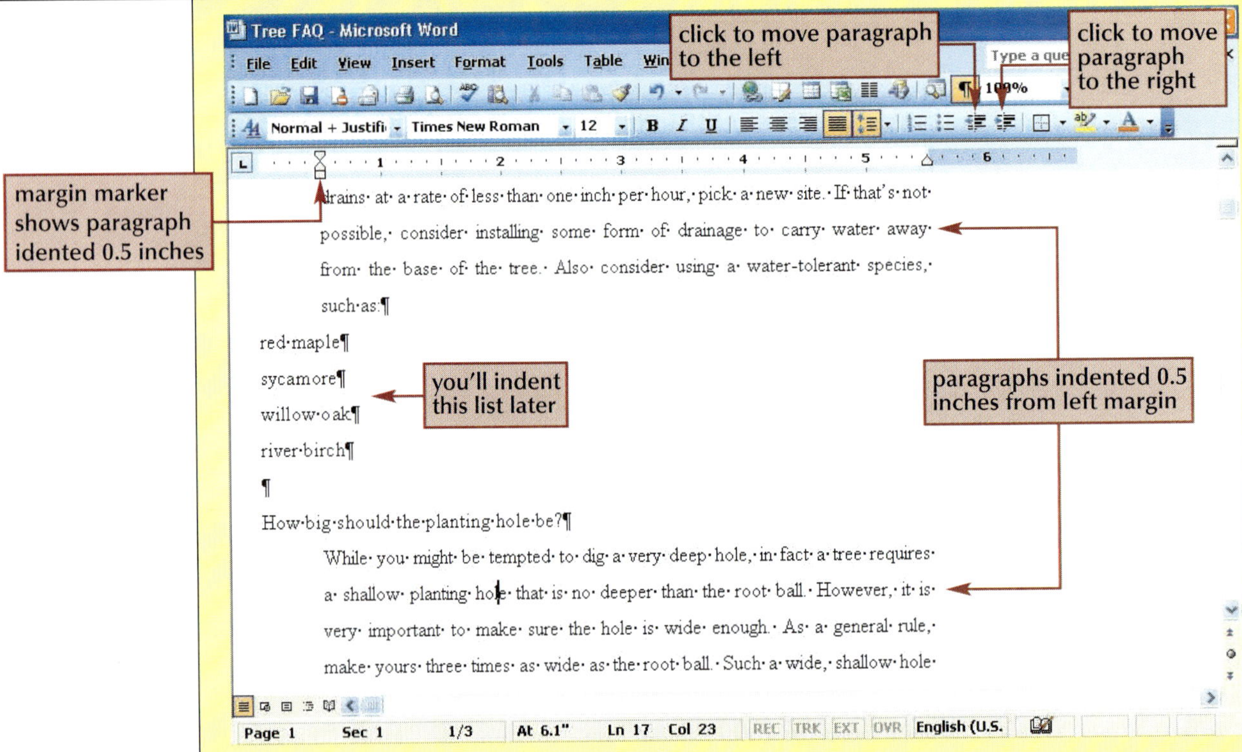

You can continue to indent and then justify each paragraph, or simply use the Format Painter command. The Format Painter allows you to copy both the indentation and alignment changes to all paragraphs in the document.

Using the Format Painter

The **Format Painter** makes it easy to copy all the formatting features of one paragraph to other paragraphs. You can use this button to copy formatting to one or multiple items.

Using the Format Painter

Reference Window

- Select the item whose formatting you want to copy.
- To copy formatting to one item, click the Format Painter button, and then use the mouse pointer to select the item you want to format.
- To copy formatting to multiple items, double-click the Format Painter button, and then use the mouse pointer to select each item you want to format. When you are finished, click the Format Painter button again to deselect it.

Use the Format Painter now to copy the formatting of the second paragraph to other main paragraphs. You'll begin by moving the insertion point to the paragraph whose format you want to copy.

To copy paragraph formatting with the Format Painter:

1. Verify that the insertion point is located in the paragraph that begins "While you might be tempted . . . "
2. Double-click the **Format Painter** button on the Standard toolbar. The Format Painter button will stay highlighted until you click the button again. When you move the pointer over text, the pointer changes to to indicate that the format of the selected paragraph can be painted (or copied) onto another paragraph.
3. Scroll down, and then click anywhere in the paragraph that begins "You may be accustomed . . . " The format of the third paragraph shifts to match the format of the first two main paragraphs. See Figure 2-23. All three paragraphs are now indented and justified. The Format Painter pointer is still visible.

Formats copied with Format Painter **Figure 2-23**

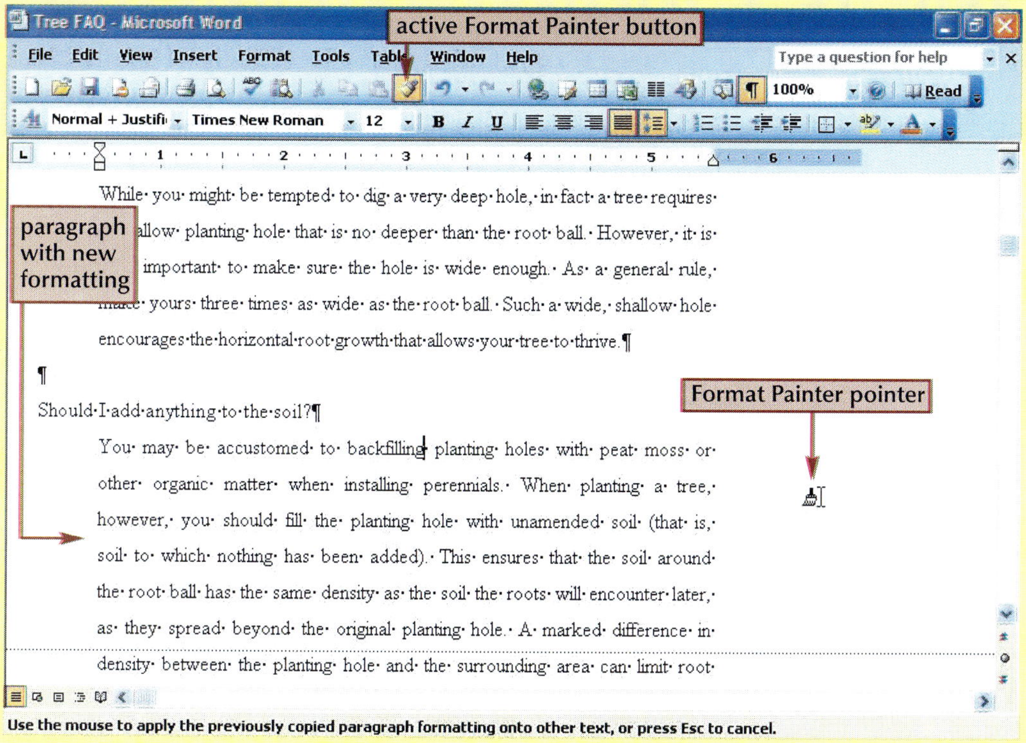

4. Scroll down to click the remaining paragraphs that are preceded by a question heading. Take care to click only the paragraphs below the question headings. Do not click the document title, the one-line questions, the lists, or the last paragraph in the document.

   Trouble? If you click a paragraph and the formatting doesn't change to match the second paragraph, you single-clicked the Format Painter button rather than double-clicked it. Move the insertion point to a paragraph that has the desired format, double-click the Format Painter button, and then repeat Step 4.

   Trouble? If you accidentally click a title or one line of a list, click the Undo button on the Standard toolbar to return the line to its original formatting. Then select a paragraph that has the desired format, double-click the Format Painter button, and finish copying the format to the desired paragraphs.

5. After you are finished formatting paragraphs with the Format Painter pointer, click the **Format Painter** button on the Standard toolbar to turn off the feature.

6. Save the document.

All the main paragraphs in the document are formatted with the correct indentation and alignment. Your next job is to make the lists easier to read by adding bullets and numbers.

Adding Bullets and Numbers

You can emphasize a list of items by adding a heavy dot, or **bullet**, before each item in the list. For consecutive items, you can use numbers instead of bullets. Marilee requests that you add bullets to the list of tree species on page 1 to make them stand out.

To apply bullets to the list of items:

1. Scroll to the top of the document until you see the list of tree species below the text "Also consider using a water-tolerant species such as:".

2. Select the four items in the list (from "red maple" to "river birch"). It doesn't matter whether or not you select the paragraph mark after "river birch."

3. Click the **Bullets** button on the Formatting toolbar. A bullet, a dark circle, appears in front of each item. Each line indents to make room for the bullet.

4. In order to make the bullets align with the first paragraph, make sure the list is still selected, and then click the **Increase Indent** button on the Formatting toolbar. The bulleted list moves to the right.

5. Click anywhere within the document window to deselect the text. Figure 2-24 shows the indented bulleted list.

Figure 2-24 Indented bulleted list

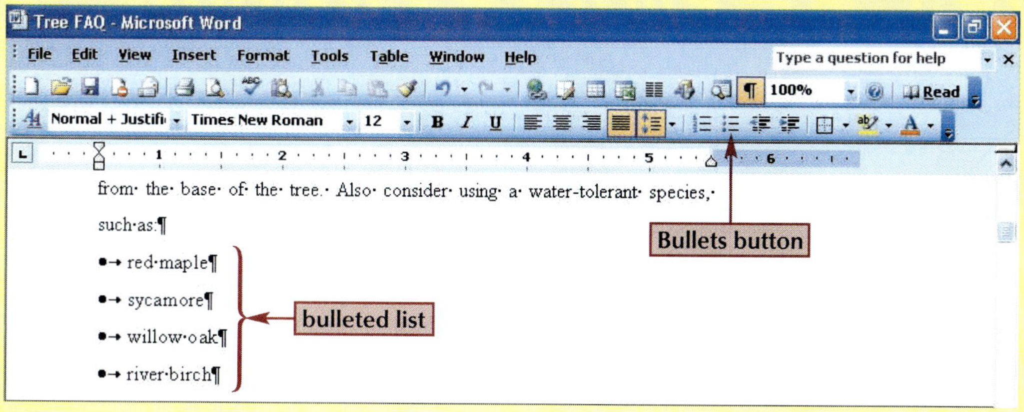

The bulleted list you just created includes the default bullet style. To select a different style of bullets (such as check marks or arrows) you can use the Bullets and Numbering command on the Format menu. You'll have a chance to try that command in the Case Problems at the end of this tutorial.

Next, you need to format the list of steps involved in planting a tree. Marilee asks you to format this information as a numbered list because this list shows sequential steps. This is an easy task thanks to the Numbering button, which automatically numbers selected paragraphs with consecutive numbers. If you insert a new paragraph, delete a paragraph, or reorder the paragraphs, Word automatically adjusts the numbers to make sure they remain consecutive.

To apply numbers to the list of steps:

1. Scroll down until you see the list that begins "Remove any tags . . . " and ends with "of the planting hole."
2. Select the entire list. It doesn't matter whether or not you select the paragraph mark at the end of the last item.
3. Click the **Numbering** button on the Formatting toolbar. Consecutive numbers appear in front of each item in the list. The list is indented, similar to the bulleted list. The list would look better if it was indented to align with the paragraph.
4. Click the **Increase Indent** button on the Formatting toolbar. The list moves to the right, so that the numbers align with the preceding paragraph.
5. Click anywhere in the document to deselect the text. Figure 2-25 shows the indented and numbered list.

Figure 2-25 Indented numbered list

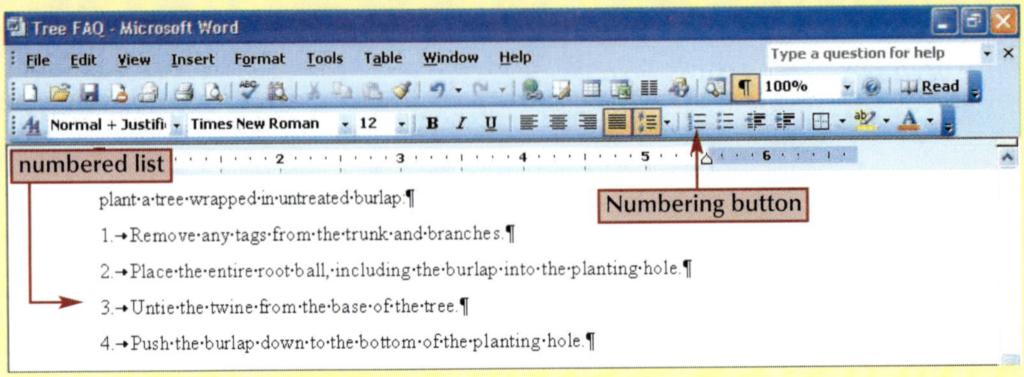

The text of the document is now properly aligned and indented. The bullets and numbers make the lists easy to read and give readers visual clues about the type of information they contain. Next, you need to adjust the formatting of individual words.

Changing the Font and Font Size

All of Marilee's remaining changes concern changing fonts, adjusting font sizes, and emphasizing text with font styles. The first step is to change the font of the title from 12-point Times New Roman to 14-point Arial. This will make the title stand out from the rest of the text.

Reference Window

Changing the Font and Font Size

- Select the text you want to change.
- Click the Font list arrow on the Formatting toolbar to display the list of fonts.
- Click the font you want to use.
- Click the Font Size list arrow, and then click the font size you want to use.

or

- Select the text that you want to change.
- Click Format on the menu bar, and then click Font.
- In the Font tab of the Font dialog box, select the font and font size you want to use.
- Click the OK button.

Marilee wants you to change the font of the title as well as its size and style. To do this, you'll use the Formatting toolbar. Marilee wants you to use a **sans serif font**, which is a font that does not have the small additional lines (called serifs) at the tops and bottoms of the letters. Sans serif fonts are often used in titles so they contrast with the body text. A **serif font** is a font that does include these small lines. Times New Roman is a serif font, and Arial is a sans serif font.

To change the font of the title:

1. Press **Ctrl+Home** to move the insertion point to the beginning of the document, and then click to the left of the title **Frequently Asked Questions About Trees** to select it.
2. Click the **Font** list arrow on the Formatting toolbar. A list of available fonts appears in alphabetical order, with the name of the current font in the Font text box. See Figure 2-26. Fonts that have been used recently might appear above a double line. Note that each name in the list is formatted with the relevant font. For example, "Arial" appears in the Arial font, and "Times New Roman" appears in the Times New Roman font.

Font list | **Figure 2-26**

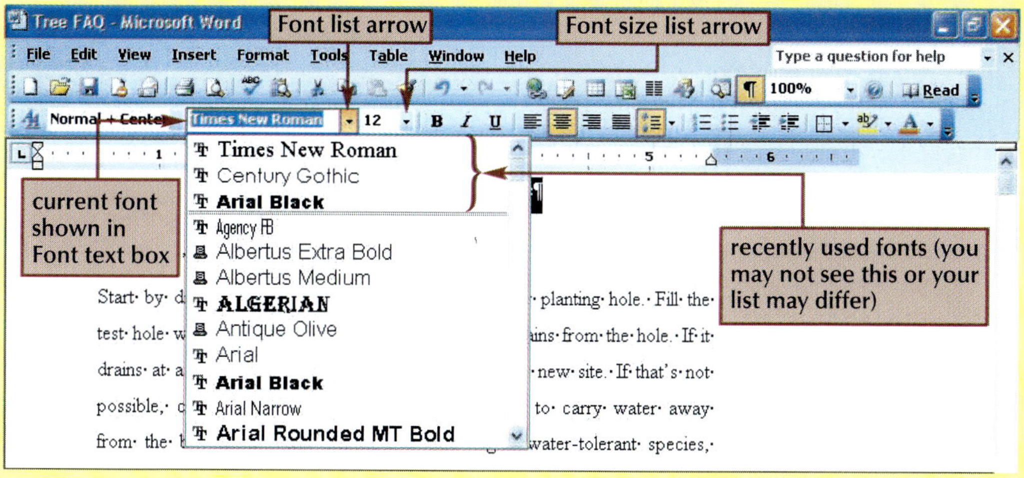

Trouble? If you don't see the fonts beginning with "A" at the top of your Font list, scroll up until you do.

3. Click **Arial** to select it as the new font. As you click, watch the font in the title change to reflect the new font.

   Trouble? If Arial doesn't appear in the font list, use another sans serif font.
4. Click the **Font Size** list arrow on the Formatting toolbar, and then click **14** in the size list. As you click, watch the title's font increase from 12 to 14 points.
5. Save your work, and then click within the title to deselect it. See Figure 2-27. Note that the font settings in the Formatting toolbar reflect the font settings of the text that is currently selected, or, if no text is selected, of the text currently containing the insertion point.

Title font and font size changed | **Figure 2-27**

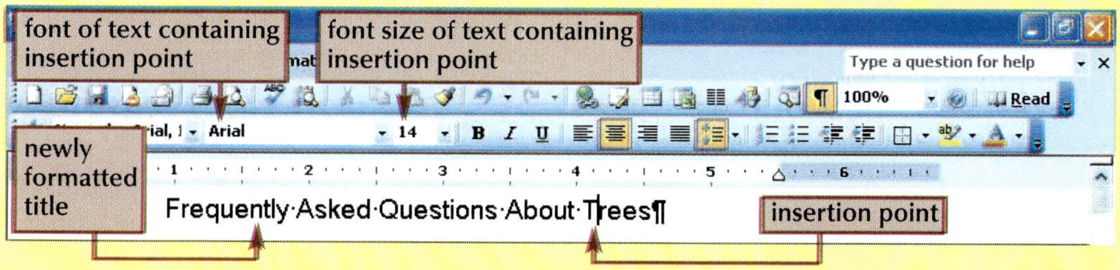

Trouble? If your font and font size settings don't match those in Figure 2-27, you might not have clicked the title. Click the title, view the font and font size settings displayed on the Formatting toolbar, and then make the necessary changes. Because of differences in fonts and monitors, the characters in your document might look different from the figure.

Emphasizing Text Using Bold, Underline, and Italic Styles

You can emphasize words in your document by formatting them with bold, underline, or italic styles. These styles help make specific thoughts, ideas, words, or phrases stand out. (You can also add special effects such as shadows to characters.) Marilee marked a few words on the document draft (shown in Figure 2-1) that need special emphasis. You add bold, underline, or italic styles by using the corresponding buttons on the Formatting toolbar. These buttons are **toggle buttons**, which means you can click them once to format the selected text, and then click again to remove the formatting from the selected text.

Bolding Text

Marilee wants to draw attention to the title and all of the question headings. You will do this by formatting them with the bold style.

To format the title and the questions in bold:

1. Select the title **Frequently Asked Questions About Trees**. It doesn't matter whether or not you select the paragraph mark following the title.
2. Press and hold the **Ctrl** key, and then select the first question in the document ("How can I tell if I've picked a site with good drainage?"). Again, whether or not you select the paragraph mark following the question is of no concern. Both the title and the first question are now selected. You can continue to select nonadjacent information by using the Ctrl key and scroll arrows.
3. Continue to hold down the **Ctrl** key, and then scroll down and select each of the remaining questions. Use the down arrow on the vertical scroll bar to view the questions. Again, whether or not you select the paragraph mark following each question is of no concern.
   Trouble? If you accidentally select something other than a question, keep the Ctrl key pressed while you click the incorrect item. This should deselect the incorrect item.
4. Release the **Ctrl** key, click the **Bold** button **B** on the Formatting toolbar, click anywhere in the document to deselect the text, and then scroll up to return to the beginning of the document. The title and the questions appear in bold, as shown in Figure 2-28.

Figure 2-28 **Text in bold**

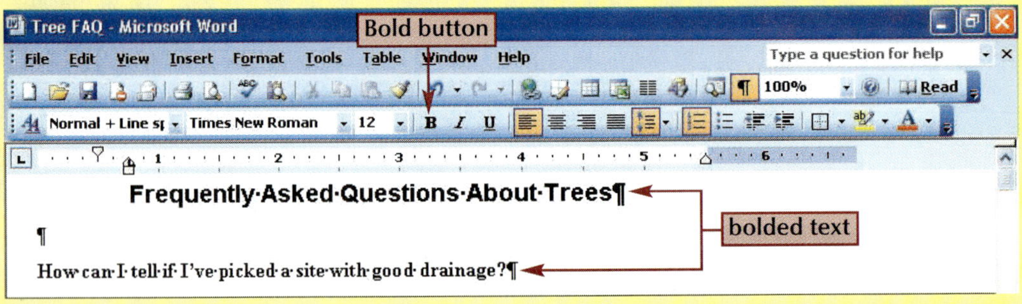

After reviewing this change, Marilee wonders if the title would look better without bold. You can easily remove bold by selecting the text and clicking the Bold button again to turn off, or toggle, bold.

5. To remove the bold, select the title, and then click the **Bold** button **B** on the Formatting toolbar. The title now appears without bold. Marilee decides she prefers to emphasize the title with bold after all.
6. Verify that the title is still selected, and then click the **Bold** button **B** on the Formatting toolbar. The title appears in bold again.

Underlining Text

The Underline button works in the same way as the Bold button. Marilee's edits indicate that the word "Note" should be inserted and underlined at the beginning of the final paragraph. Using the Underline button, you'll make both of these changes at the same time.

To underline text:

1. Press **Ctrl+End** to move the insertion point to the end of the document, then press **Ctrl+ ↑** to move the insertion point to the left of the word "Any" in the first line of the final paragraph.
2. Click the **Underline** button on the Formatting toolbar to turn on underlining. The Underline button is highlighted. Whatever text you type now will be underlined on your screen and in your printed document.
3. Type **Note:** and then click the **Underline** button on the Formatting toolbar to turn off underlining. The Underline button is no longer highlighted, and "Note:" is now underlined.
4. Press the **spacebar**. See Figure 2-29.

Word typed with underline | **Figure 2-29**

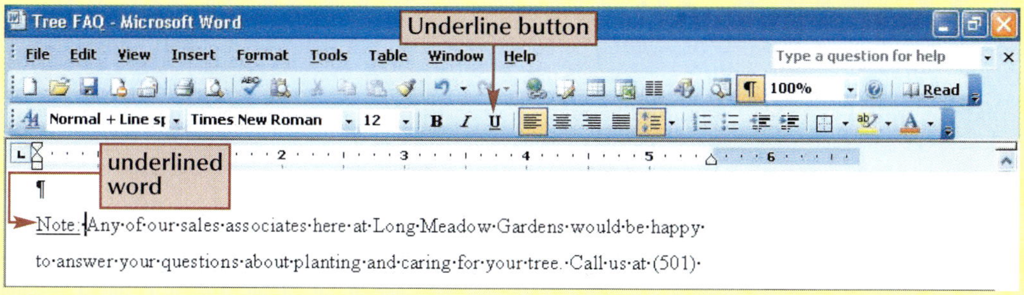

Italicizing Text

Next, you'll format each instance of "Long Meadow Gardens" in italic. This helps draw attention to the company name.

To italicize the company name:

1. Scroll up to the first question on the second page ("Do I have to do anything to the tree before planting?").
2. In the first line below the question, select **Long Meadow Gardens**.
3. Click the **Italic** button on the Formatting toolbar. The company name changes from regular to italic text. In the next step, you'll learn a useful method for repeating the task you just performed.
4. Scroll down to the last paragraph of the document, select the company name, and then press the **F4** key. The F4 key enables you to repeat your most recent action. It is especially helpful when formatting parts of a document.
5. Save the document.

Previewing Formatted Text

You have made all the editing and formatting changes that Marilee requested for the Tree FAQ document. It's helpful to preview a document after formatting it, because the Print Preview window makes it easy to spot text that is not aligned correctly.

To preview and print the document:

1. Press **Ctrl+Home**, click the **Print Preview** button on the Standard toolbar, click the **One Page** button on the Print Preview toolbar if you see more than one page, and examine the first page of the document. Use the vertical scroll bar to display the second page. (If you notice any alignment or indentation errors, click the Close button on the Print Preview toolbar, correct the errors in Normal view, save your changes, and then return to the Print Preview window.)
2. Click the **Print** button on the Print Preview toolbar. After a pause, the document prints.
3. Click the **Close** button on the Print Preview toolbar. You return to Normal view.
4. If you made any changes to the document after previewing it, save your work.

You now have a printed copy of the final Tree FAQ document, as shown in Figure 2-30.

Figure 2-30 **Final version of Tree FAQ document**

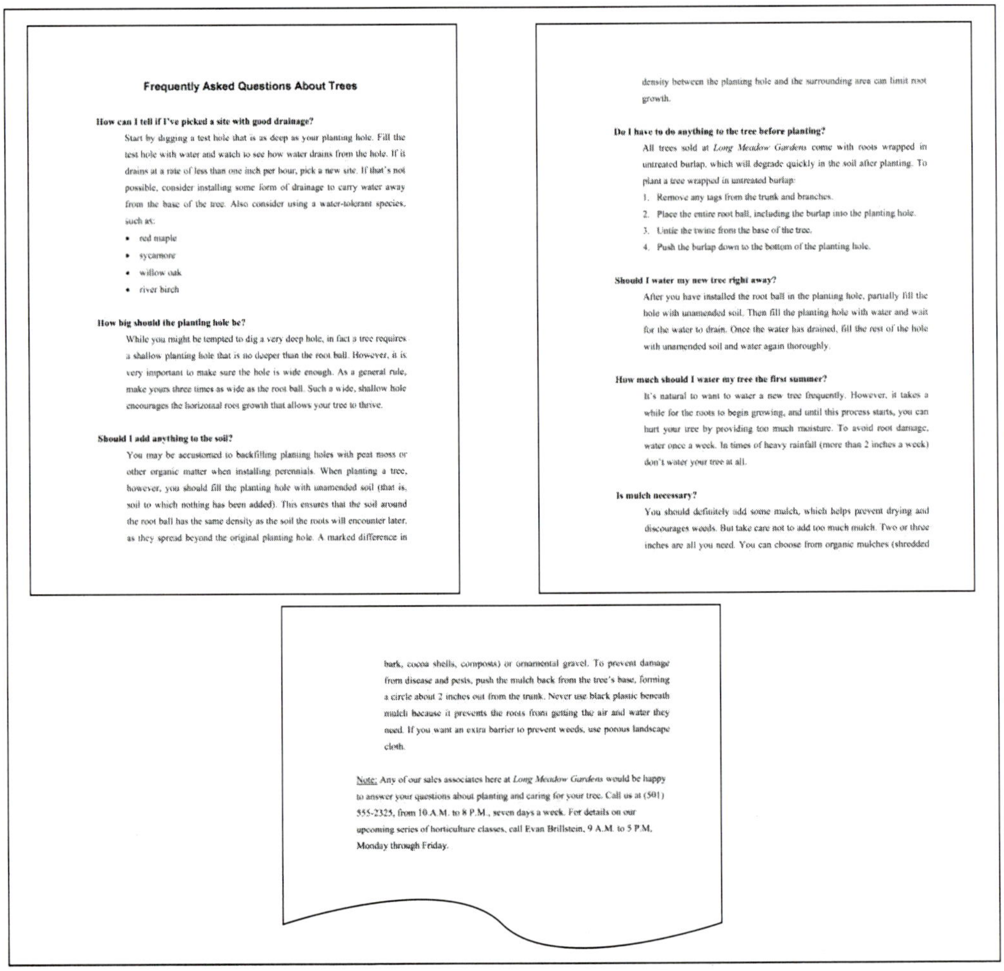

Frequently Asked Questions About Trees

How can I tell if I've picked a site with good drainage?

Start by digging a test hole that is as deep as your planting hole. Fill the test hole with water and watch to see how water drains from the hole. If it drains at a rate of less than one inch per hour, pick a new site. If that's not possible, consider installing some form of drainage to carry water away from the base of the tree. Also consider using a water-tolerant species, such as:

- red maple
- sycamore
- willow oak
- river birch

How big should the planting hole be?

While you might be tempted to dig a very deep hole, in fact a tree requires a shallow planting hole that is no deeper than the root ball. However, it is very important to make sure the hole is wide enough. As a general rule, make yours three times as wide as the root ball. Such a wide, shallow hole encourages the horizontal root growth that allows your tree to thrive.

Should I add anything to the soil?

You may be accustomed to backfilling planting holes with peat moss or other organic matter when installing perennials. When planting a tree, however, you should fill the planting hole with unamended soil (that is, soil to which nothing has been added). This ensures that the soil around the root ball has the same density as the soil the roots will encounter later, as they spread beyond the original planting hole. A marked difference in density between the planting hole and the surrounding area can limit root growth.

Do I have to do anything to the tree before planting?

All trees sold at *Long Meadow Gardens* come with roots wrapped in untreated burlap, which will degrade quickly in the soil after planting. To plant a tree wrapped in untreated burlap:

1. Remove any tags from the trunk and branches.
2. Place the entire root ball, including the burlap into the planting hole.
3. Untie the twine from the base of the tree.
4. Push the burlap down to the bottom of the planting hole.

Should I water my new tree right away?

After you have installed the root ball in the planting hole, partially fill the hole with unamended soil. Then fill the planting hole with water and wait for the water to drain. Once the water has drained, fill the rest of the hole with unamended soil and water again thoroughly.

How much should I water my tree the first summer?

It's natural to want to water a new tree frequently. However, it takes a while for the roots to begin growing, and until this process starts, you can hurt your tree by providing too much moisture. To avoid root damage, water once a week. In times of heavy rainfall (more than 2 inches a week) don't water your tree at all.

Is mulch necessary?

You should definitely add some mulch, which helps prevent drying and discourages weeds. But take care not to add too much mulch. Two or three inches are all you need. You can choose from organic mulches (shredded bark, cocoa shells, composts) or ornamental gravel. To prevent damage from disease and pests, push the mulch back from the tree's base, forming a circle about 2 inches out from the trunk. Never use black plastic beneath mulch because it prevents the roots from getting the air and water they need. If you want an extra barrier to prevent weeds, use porous landscape cloth.

Note: Any of our sales associates here at *Long Meadow Gardens* would be happy to answer your questions about planting and caring for your tree. Call us at (501) 555-2325, from 10 A.M. to 8 P.M., seven days a week. For details on our upcoming series of horticulture classes, call Evan Brillstein, 9 A.M. to 5 P.M., Monday through Friday.

Adding Comments

Peter reviews the Tree FAQ document and is happy with its appearance. He wonders if he should add some information about fertilizing new trees. He asks you to insert a note to Marilee about this using Word's Comment feature. A **comment** is an electronic version of a self-sticking note that you might attach to a piece of paper. To insert a comment in a Word document, select a block of text, click Comment on the Insert menu, and then type your comment in the comment box. To display a comment, place the mouse pointer over text where the comment has been inserted. Comments are very useful when you are exchanging Word documents with co-workers electronically, whether via e-mail, disks, or on CDs, because they allow you to make notes or queries without affecting the document itself.

You'll insert Peter's comment at the document title so that Marilee will be sure to see it as soon as she opens the document. It's easiest to work with comments in Print Layout view.

To add the comment to the document:

1. Click the **Print Layout View** button in the lower-left corner of the Word window, then click the **Zoom** list arrow and click **100%** in the list if it is not already selected. The document view changes, allowing you to see the document margins.
2. Scroll up and down through the document and notice that, in Print Layout view, a page break is represented by something more noticeable than a dotted line. You can actually see the end of one page and the beginning of another.
3. Scroll up to the beginning of the document, and then select the title **Frequently Asked Questions About Trees**. (Do not select the paragraph mark after the title.)
4. Click **Insert** on the menu bar, and then click **Comment**. A comment balloon appears in the right margin, with the insertion point ready for you to type your comment. The Reviewing toolbar opens, displaying buttons that are useful for working with comments. See Figure 2-31.

Figure 2-31 Inserting a comment

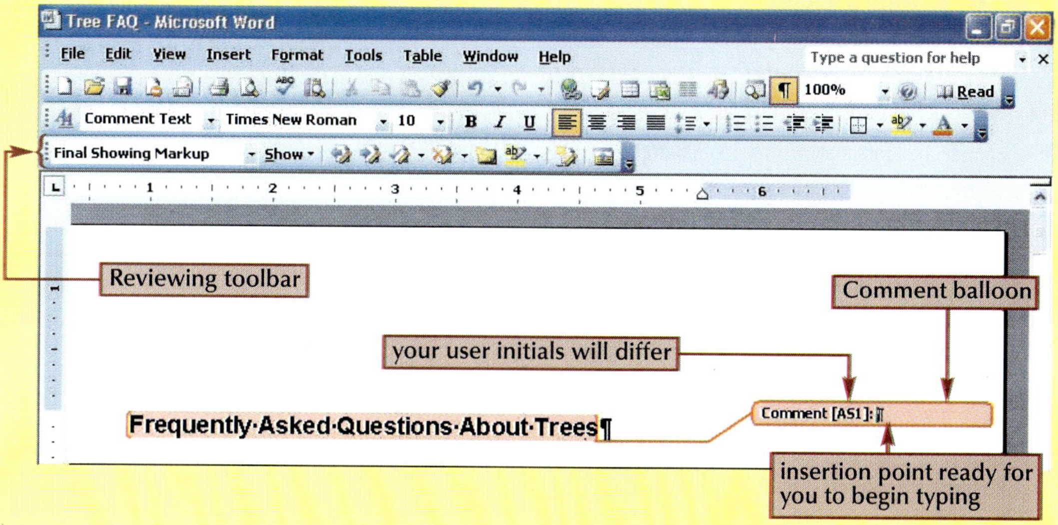

Trouble? If you can't see the entire comment balloon, scroll right to display it fully.

The comment is preceded by the user's initials and a number. Initials depend on the information entered on the Information tab in the Options dialog box. The numbers are sequential, with the first comment labeled #1, the second #2, and so on.

5. Type **Should we add a section on fertilizing new trees?** The newly typed comment is displayed in the comment balloon. Depending on the size of your monitor, you may need to scroll right to read the entire comment.
6. Click the **Normal View** button in the lower-left corner of the Word window. The title is highlighted in color with brackets around it, indicating that a comment has been inserted at this point in the document.
7. Place the mouse pointer over the title. The comment is displayed in a ScreenTip over the pointer. When you move the mouse pointer away from the title, the ScreenTip closes.
8. Save the document.

Note that to delete a comment, you can right-click the comment box in Print Layout view and click Delete Comment. To edit a comment, click in the comment box and make any deletions or additions you desire. After you insert comments in a document, you can choose to print the document with or without comments in the margin. To print the comments, select Document showing markup in the Print what list box of the Print dialog box. To print a document without comments, select Document in the Print what list box. You'll find comments useful when you need to collaborate on a document with your fellow students or co-workers.

Using the Research Task Pane

Before you finish your work for the day, Peter suggests that you use the Research task pane to look up information on plants sold at Long Meadow Gardens. The **Research task pane** provides a number of research tools, including a thesaurus, an Internet search engine, and access to the Encarta Encyclopedia and Dictionary. To take full advantage of these options, your computer must be connected to the Internet. To get started, Peter asks you to use the Research task pane to find the Latin name for "red maple."

To look up "red maple" in the Research task pane:

1. Verify that your computer is connected to the Internet. If your computer is not connected to the Internet, read, but do not attempt to perform, the following steps.
2. Use the Find command to locate and select the text "red maple". Close the Find and Replace dialog box.
3. Click the **Research** button on the Standard toolbar. The Research task pane opens. See Figure 2-32. The term you selected in the document appears in the Search for text box, ready for you to look up the definition. Next, you need to specify the reference source you want to search.

Opening the Research task pane

Figure 2-32

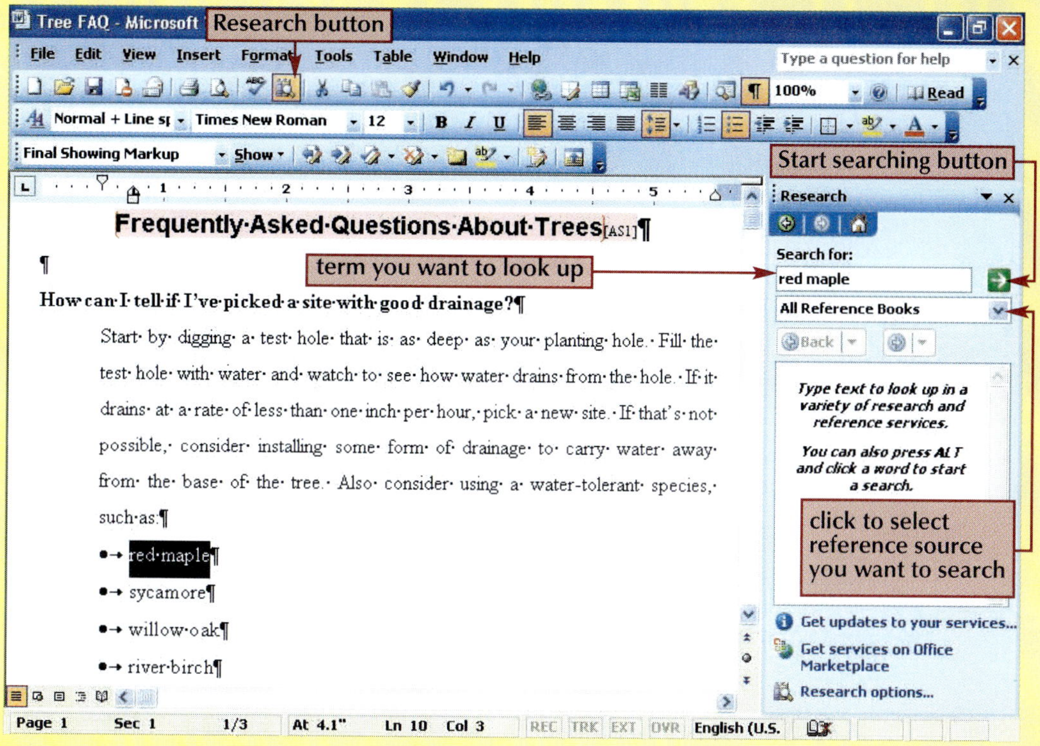

4. Verify that **All Reference Books** is selected in the list box below the Search for text box, and then click the **Start searching** button. A list of research results appears, as shown in Figure 2-33. At the top of the list is the Encarta Dictionary definition for "red maple," with the Latin name, *Acer rubrum*, at the end. If the initial search results don't provide the information you need, scroll down and click the "Can't find it?" link at the bottom of the Research task pane to display more research options. In some cases, when you click a link in the Research task pane, Internet Explorer might open a Web page with further information.

   Trouble? If All Reference Books is not selected in the list box below the Search for text box, click the list arrow and select All Reference Books. At that point the search will begin; you do not have to click the Start searching button.

Figure 2-33 **Research results**

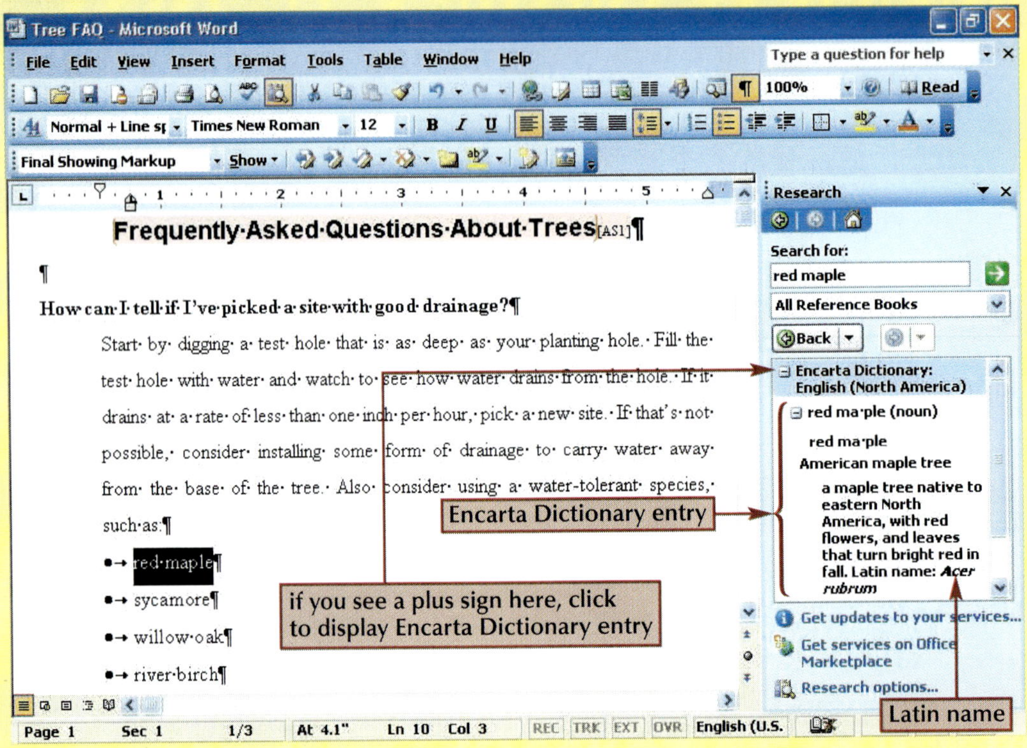

Trouble? If you see "Encarta Dictionary: English (North America)" but not the dictionary entry for "red maple," click the plus sign as indicated in Figure 2-33.

5. Click the **Close** button ☒ at the top of the Research task pane. The Research task pane closes.
6. Close the Reviewing toolbar, save, and then close the document.

In this tutorial, you have helped Peter edit and format the Tree FAQ document that will be handed out to all customers purchasing a tree at Long Meadow Gardens. Peter will e-mail the file to Marilee later so that she can review your work and read the comment you inserted.

Review

Session 2.2 Quick Check

1. What are Word's default values for the left and right margins? For the top and bottom margins?
2. Describe the steps involved in changing the line spacing in a document.
3. Describe the four types of text alignment.
4. Explain how to indent a paragraph 1 inch or more from the left margin.
5. Describe a situation in which you would use the Format Painter.
6. Explain how to transform a series of short paragraphs into a numbered list.
7. Explain how to add underlining to a word as you type it.
8. True or False: Before you can take full advantage of the Research task pane, your computer must be connected to the Internet.

Review

Tutorial Summary

In this tutorial you learned how to use the Spelling and Grammar checker, select parts of a document, delete text, and move text within a document. You also learned how to find and replace text. Next, you focused on formatting a document, including changing margins and line spacing, aligning text, indenting paragraphs, using the Format Painter, changing the font and font size, and emphasizing text with bold, underlining, and italic styles. Finally, you learned how to add a comment to a document, preview formatted text, and look up information using the Research task pane.

Key Terms

¶
1.5 line spacing
alignment
automatic page break
bullet
center alignment
Clipboard
Clipboard task pane
comment
copy
copy and paste
cut
cut and paste
double spacing
drag and drop
Find command
Format Painter
hanging indent
justified alignment
landscape orientation
left alignment
paragraph
paragraph symbol (¶)
paste
portrait orientation
ragged
Replace command
Research task pane
right alignment
right indent
sans serif font
select
selection bar
serif font
single spacing
toggle button

Practice

Apply the skills you learned in the tutorial using the same case scenario.

Review Assignments

Data File needed for the Review Assignments: Statmnt.doc

Now that you have completed the Tree FAQ document, Marilee asks you to help her create a statement summarizing customer accounts for Long Meadow Gardens' wholesale nursery. She would also like you to create a document that contains contact information for Long Meadow Gardens. Remember to use the Undo and Redo buttons as you work to correct any errors.

1. Open the file **Statmnt** located in the Tutorial.02\Review folder included with your Data Files, and then check your screen to make sure your settings match those in the tutorial.
2. Save the document as **Monthly Statement** in the same folder.
3. Change the left and right margins to 1.5 inches using the Page Setup dialog box.
4. Make all edits and formatting changes shown in Figure 2-34, and then save your work.

Figure 2-34

Long Meadow Gardens
2804 Hemlock Road
Minneapolis, MN 55401

Arial 16-point centered

Monthly Statement
June 1 – June 31, 2006
Wholesale Nursery Purchases

Times New Roman centered

Bold

Customer Name: Swenson and Sons Landscape Contractors
Customer Number: RJB-5843

Billing Address:

Type your address left align

Contact:

Type your name

Replace "report" with "statement" throughout

The enclosed report summarize your account activity for the past month. Keep in mind that we may have recieved a payment from you that arrived too late to be included in this report. Any payment received after the 25th of last month will appear on next month's report. Remember to review the billing address listed above, and notify us if any changes are necessary.

We expect payment within 15 days. After that period, an addition 3% will be added to all outstandingg charges. The items listed in this report include all invoices signed by you're authorized employees. We would be happy to fax you the signed invoices (each with an itemized list of purchases) for your inspection.

italic

Transactions ← Bold

Invoices

Total ~~Charges~~: $16,316.25

Correct Spelling and Grammar

- Trees (in burlap): $6,509.50
- Trees (container): $3,800.50
- Shrub (in burlap): $4,456.00
- Shrub (container): $680.25
- Soil Amendments: $870.00

For questions, call our Customer Service Center at 612-234-9917.

Add bullets

5. Proofread the document carefully to check for any additional errors. Look for and correct two errors that were not reported when you used the Spelling and Grammar checker.
6. Remove any Smart Tags in the document.
7. Move the last sentence of the document (which begins "For questions, call . . . ") to create a new paragraph, just above the heading "Transactions."
8. Select the Transactions portion of the document, from the heading "Transactions" down to the end of the document. Increase the indentation by 0.5 inch.
9. Open the Clipboard task pane. Select the company name and address at the top of the document and copy it to the Clipboard. Then copy the Customer Service Center phone number (above Transactions) to the Clipboard.
10. Open a new, blank document. Type your name on the first line, and then "Customer Service Center" on the next line. Move the insertion point to the third line. Open the Clipboard task pane, and then click the company address to insert this information at the insertion point. Be sure the insertion point is below the address, and then click the phone number to insert it in the document. Notice that text inserted from the Clipboard retains its original formatting, though the alignment may not carry over perfectly.
11. Left-align any centered text, clear the contents of the Clipboard task pane, close the task pane, and print the document.
12. Switch to Print Layout view. Then select the company name and insert the following comment: "Marilee, please let me know how you want this document formatted."
13. Save the document as **Customer Service Contact** in the Tutorial.02\Review folder. Close the document.
14. Save the Monthly Statement document, and then preview and print it.
15. Select the term "Amendments," which appears in the bulleted list at the end of the document. Open the Research task pane and look up the definition of "amendment." *Note*: you must have an active Internet connection to complete this step.
16. Type an asterisk (*) after "Amendments," and then on a blank line at the end of the document type an asterisk (*) followed by the definition of "amendment." After the definition include a sentence indicating that the definition is taken from the Encarta Dictionary.
17. Close the Research task pane and the Reviewing toolbar, save the Monthly Statement document, and then close it.

Apply

Apply the skills you learned to create a one-page advertising brochure.

Case Problem 1

Data File needed for this Case Problem: Tribune.doc

Blue Ridge Tribune The *Blue Ridge Tribune* is a student-run newspaper published through the Blue Ridge College Student Services Association. The newspaper is distributed around campus each Friday. The online version of the newspaper is posted on the Blue Ridge College Web site. Local businesses have a long-established tradition of advertising in the print version of the newspaper, and the paper's advertising manager, Noah McCormick, would like to ensure that this same tradition carries over to the online newspaper. When he sends out the monthly statements to his print advertisers, he would like to include a one-page brochure encouraging them to purchase an online ad. He typed the text about online advertising that is currently found on the Blue Ridge Tribune Web site and saved it as unformatted text in a Word document.

1. Open the file **Tribune** located in the Tutorial.02\Cases folder included with your Data Files, and save the file as **Tribune Brochure** in the same folder.
2. Correct any spelling or grammar errors. Make sure the right correction is selected in the Suggestions list box before you click Change.

3. Proofread for other errors, such as words that are spelled correctly but used incorrectly.
4. In the second to last sentence, replace "the BRT Advertising Office" with your name.
5. Change the right margin to 1.5 inches and the left margin to 2 inches.
6. Format the entire document in 12-point Times New Roman font.
7. Format the four paragraphs below "Did you know?" as a bulleted list.
8. Drag the third bullet (which begins "You can include . . . ") up to make it the first bullet in the bulleted list.
9. Format the first line of the document using a font, font size, and alignment of your choice. Use bold or italic for emphasis.
10. Format the entire document using 1.5 line spacing.
11. Save your work, preview the document, and then switch back to Normal view to make any changes you think necessary.
12. Print the document and then return to the Print Preview window. Open the Page Setup dialog box and switch to Landscape orientation. (Don't change any margin settings.) Observe the change in the Print Preview window.
13. Save the document as **Tribune Brochure Landscape** in the Tutorial.02\Cases folder and print it.
14. Switch to Print Layout view, and add a comment to the first line (*Blue Ridge Tribune*) asking Noah if he would like you to leave a printed copy of the brochure in his mailbox.
15. As Noah reviews the brochure, he wonders if the word "Web" should actually be capitalized. Use the Research task pane to look up "Web" in the Encarta Dictionary. In the first definition, you can see that "Web" is short for "World Wide Web." You will use this information to explain to Noah that indeed Web should be capitalized. Close the Research task pane.
16. Close the Reviewing toolbar, save, and then close the document.

Apply

Use your skills to format the summary document shown in Figure 2-35.

Case Problem 2

Data File needed for this Case Problem: Training.doc

UpTime Productivity Training UpTime, Inc. provides productivity training for large companies across the country. Matt Patterson is UpTime's marketing director for the Northeast region. He wants to provide interested clients with a one-page summary of UpTime's productivity training sessions.

1. Open the file **Training** located in the Tutorial.02\Cases folder included with your Data Files, and then check your screen to make sure your settings match those in the tutorials.
2. Save the file as **Training Summary** in the same folder.
3. Format the document as shown in Figure 2-35.

Figure 2-35

(change top margin to 1.5 inches)

UpTime Productivity Training (16-point sans serif font)
www.UpTimeTraining.com
(bold and centered)

UpTime productivity training focuses on improving productivity throughout your company. The productivity training we provide consists of four ~~general~~ components:

Improving employee morale through improved interpersonal communication.
Improving field services productivity through new technology
Improving personal productivity through improved time-management skills.
Improving company productivity through establishing management priorities.

Personal Productivity Training Seminar (bold, italic)

UpTime provides a half-day personal productivity-training seminar for all of your company's employees. This seminar has received national recognition for its effectiveness in helping employees set and attain goals. ~~This seminar improves employees' individual performances by maximizing their personal effectiveness in setting immediate and long-range goals and in prioritizing personal tasks.~~

As part of this personal productivity-training seminar, each employee in attendance ~~at the seminar~~ receives a customized personal log with planning sheets for recording events and managing daily activities. This personal log standardizes the method by which all of your employees organize and control events, improving their productivity and, at the same time, increasing your company's ability to bid contracts and bill clients.

Management Productivity Training (bold, italic)

UpTime provides management training at our Leadership Retreat facilities at Garrison Lake, New York. UpTime's management training program is designed to help managers create more effective relationships with the employees they supervise. This two-day training, focuses on helping company officials work together to identify your company's unique mission statement, guiding principles for each division, and personal role-based tasks. (move circled sentence to end of paragraph)

Field Services Technology and Training (bold, italic)

UpTime provides 30 hours of free on-site training and 6 months of free on-line consultation services. After 6 months, training and consultation are provided on a contractual basis.

UpTime's advanced technology system improves your communication field services. Our phone-fax-computer system connects your managers through e-mail, fax, and telephone to establish better communication throughout your company and to simplify procedures, streamline red tape, and eliminate bureaucracy.

(reverse order)

For more information, contact your name.

(replace with your first and last name, format in bold with underline)

Explore

4. Change the left margin using the ruler, as follows:
   a. Make sure the horizontal ruler is displayed and the document is shown in Normal view.
   b. Select the entire document.
   c. Position the pointer on the small gray square on the ruler at the left margin. A ScreenTip with the words "Left Indent" appears.
   d. Press and hold down the mouse button. A vertical dotted line appears in the document window, indicating the current left margin. Drag the margin right to the 0.5-inch mark on the ruler, and then release the mouse button. Click anywhere to deselect the document.

Explore

5. Select the list of the four training components near the top of the document, click Format on the menu bar, then use the Bullets and Numbering dialog box to create a bulleted list using check marks as the bullet symbol.
6. Italicize both occurrences of the word "free" in the second text paragraph under the "Field Services Technology and Training" heading.
7. Use the Spelling and Grammar checker to make corrections as needed, proofread for additional errors, save, and preview the document.
8. Print the document, and then close the file.

Challenge

Expand your formatting skills to create a description of new products.

Case Problem 3

Data File needed for this Case Problem: Product.doc

Ridge Top Thomas McGee is vice president of sales and marketing at Ridge Top, an outdoor and sporting-gear store in Duluth, Minnesota. Each year Thomas and his staff mail a description of new products to Ridge Top's regular customers. Thomas has asked you to edit and format the first few pages of the description of new products he plans to use for this year's mailing.

1. Open the file **Product** located in the Tutorial.02\Cases folder included with your Data Files, and then check your screen to make sure your settings match those in the tutorials.
2. Save the file as **Ridge Top Products** in the same folder.

Explore

3. Switch to Print Layout view if necessary, and then read the comment inserted at the first line of the document. Right-click the comment (point to the comment in the right margin, and press the right mouse button), and then click Delete Comment in the Shortcut menu.
4. Switch to Normal view, search for the text "your name," and replace with your first and last name.
5. Replace all occurrences of "RidgeTop" with "Ridge Top".
6. Use the Spelling and Grammar checker to correct any errors in the document. Because of the nature of this document, it contains some words that the Word dictionary on your computer may not recognize. It also contains headings that the Spelling and Grammar checker may consider sentence fragments. Use the buttons in the Spelling and Grammar dialog box to respond to each Spelling and Grammar checker query. For example, use the Ignore All button to skip over brand names.
7. Delete the phrase "a great deal" from the first sentence of the paragraph below the heading "Snuggle Up to These Prices."
8. Reverse the order of the first two paragraphs under the heading "You'll Eat Up the Prices of This Camp Cooking Gear!"

9. Find the paragraph that begins "Finding camping gear . . . " Use a toolbar button to cut the last sentence ("Prices are good through . . . ") of the paragraph from the document. Then move the insertion point to the end of the document, press the Enter key twice, and insert the cut sentence as a new paragraph. Format it in 12-point Arial font, and then italicize it.
10. Format the five Ridge Top tip items as a numbered list.

Explore

11. Reorder the items under the "Ridge Top Tips" heading by moving the fourth product idea and the following blank paragraph to the top of the list.

Explore

12. Experiment with two special paragraph alignment options: first line and hanging. First, select everything from the heading "Ridge Top Guarantees Warmth at Cool Prices" through the paragraph just before the heading "Ridge Top Tips." Next, click Format on the menu bar, click Paragraph, and then click the Indents and Spacing tab if it is not already selected. Click the Special list arrow in the Paragraph dialog box, and notice the special alignment options. Experiment with both the First line and the Hanging options. When you are finished, return the document to its original format by choosing the (none) option.
13. Justify all the paragraphs in the document.
14. Apply a 12-point, bold, sans serif font to the first heading ("Ridge Top Guarantees . . . "). Be sure to pick a font that looks professional and is easy to read. Use the Format Painter to copy the formatting and apply it to the rest of the headings.
15. Change the title's and subtitle's font to the same font you used for the headings, except set the size to 16 point.
16. Bold the title and subtitle.
17. Underline the names and prices for all of the brand name products.
18. Save and preview the document.
19. Print the document and close it.

Explore

20. The Research task pane provides access to a variety of resources. Some (such as the Encarta Dictionary) are free, while others (such as the Encarta Encyclopedia) require you to pay a subscription fee. After you find the information you need in the Research task pane, you can copy and paste it into your document. Keep in mind that you must always cite your source when you use copyrighted material, such as the definitions from the Encarta Dictionary. To practice using the Research task pane, you will look up information on the word "mountain" for use later in a Ridge Top motivational brochure on mountain climbing. Open a new, blank document, connect your computer to the Internet (if necessary), and open the Research task pane. Change the document's Zoom setting to 75% so you can see the entire document next to the Research task pane. Replace the contents of the Search for text box with the word "mountain," click the list arrow below the Search for text box, and select an option that interests you. Experiment by clicking topics in the Research task pane. To display a topic more fully, click the box that contains a hyphen (to the left of the topic). In some cases, when you click a topic, Internet Explorer will open (with the Research task pane on the left) to display more information.

Explore

21. When you are finished experimenting, close Internet Explorer, if necessary, and return to the Word window. Click the list arrow below the Search for text box and select Encarta Dictionary: English (North America). Drag the mouse pointer to select the definition that begins "a high and often rocky area...," press Ctrl+C to copy the information to the Clipboard, click in the document, and then use the Paste button to paste the definition into the document. Add some text explaining that you copied the definition from the Encarta Dictionary to demonstrate how to copy and paste information from the Research task pane.

22. Save the document as **Definition** in the Tutorial.02\Cases folder, print it, close the Research task pane, and close the document.

Challenge

Explore new ways to format an Invoice Authorization Form for a high-tech computer company.

Case Problem 4

Data File needed for this Case Problem: Form.doc

Gygs and Bytes Melissa Martinez is the purchasing manager for Gygs and Bytes, a wholesale distributor of computer parts based in Portland, Oregon. Most of the company's business is conducted via catalog or through the company's Web site, but local customers sometimes drop by to pick up small orders. In the past Melissa has had problems determining which of her customers' employees were authorized to sign credit invoices. To avoid confusion, she has asked all local customers to complete a form listing employees who are authorized to sign invoices. She plans to place the completed forms in a binder at the main desk, so the receptionist at Gygs and Bytes can find the information quickly.

1. Open the file **Form** located in Tutorial.02\Cases folder included with your Data Files, and save the file as **Invoice Authorization Form** in the same folder.
2. Correct any spelling or grammar errors. Ignore the name of the company "Gygs and Bytes."

Explore

3. When you type Web addresses or e-mail addresses in a document, Word automatically formats them as links. When you click a Web address formatted as a link, Windows automatically opens a Web browser (such as Microsoft Internet Explorer) and, if your computer is connected to the Internet, displays that Web page. If you click an e-mail address formatted as a link, Windows opens a program in which you can type an e-mail message. The address you clicked is automatically included as the recipient of the e-mail. You'll see how this works as you add a Web address and e-mail address to the statement. In the address at the top of the document, click at the end of the ZIP code, add a new line, and then type the address for the company's Web site: **www.G&B.com**. When you are finished, press Enter. Notice that as soon as you press Enter, Word formats the address in blue with an underline, marking it as a link. Move the mouse pointer over the link and read the ScreenTip. The company is fictitious and does not have a Web site.

Explore

4. In the line below the Web address, type G&B@worldlink.com and then press Enter. Word formats the e-mail address as a link. Press and hold the Ctrl key and then click the e-mail link. Your default e-mail program opens, displaying a window where you could type an e-mail message to Gygs and Bytes. (If your computer is not set up for e-mail, close any error messages that open.) Close the e-mail window without saving any changes. The link is now formatted in a color other than blue, indicating that the link has been clicked.
5. Change the top and left margins to 1.5 inches.
6. Center the first six lines of the document (containing the form title and the company addresses).
7. Format the first line of the document (the form title) in 16-point Arial, with italic.
8. Format lines 2 through 6 (the addresses, including the Web and e-mail addresses) in 12-point Arial.

Explore

9. Replace all instances of G&B, except the first two (in the Web and e-mail addresses), with the complete company name, Gygs and Bytes. In the Find and Replace dialog box, select the Match case check box to ensure that the replacement text is inserted exactly as you typed it in the Replace with text box. (Be sure to use the Find Next button to skip an instance of the search text.)

10. Format the blank ruled lines as a numbered list. Customers will use these blank lines to write in the names of authorized employees.

Explore

11. Format the entire document using 1.5 spacing. Then triple-space the numbered list (with the blank lines) and the Signature and Title lines as follows:
    a. Select the numbered list with the blank lines.
    b. Triple-space the selected text using the Line Spacing button on the Formatting toolbar.
    c. Select the "Signed:" and the "Title:" lines, and then press F4.
12. Save the document.
13. Drag "Customer Name:" up to position it before "Customer Number:".

Explore

14. Select "Customer Name:", "Customer Number:", and "Address:". Press Ctrl+B to format the selected text in bold. Note that it is sometimes easier to use this keyboard shortcut instead of the Bold button on the Formatting toolbar.
15. Delete the phrase "all employees" and replace it with "all authorized personnel".

Explore

16. Select the phrase "all authorized personnel will be required to show a photo I.D." Press Ctrl+I to format the selected text in italic. It is sometimes easier to use this keyboard shortcut instead of the Italic button on the Formatting toolbar.
17. Insert your name in the form to the right of "Customer Name:". Format your name without bold, if necessary.
18. Insert your address, left aligned, without bold, below the heading "Address:".
19. Click the Print Preview button on the Standard toolbar to check your work.

Explore

20. Click the Shrink to Fit button on the Print Preview toolbar to reduce the entire document to one page. Word reduces the font sizes slightly in order to fit the entire form on one page. Close the Print Preview window and save your work.

Explore

21. Use the Print command on the File menu to open the Print dialog box. Print two copies of the document by changing the Number of copies setting in the Print dialog box.

Explore

22. You can find out useful statistics about your documents by using the Word Count command on the Tools menu. Use this command to determine the number of words, characters (not including spaces), and paragraphs in the document, and then write these statistics in the upper-right corner of the printout.
23. Save and close the document.

Research

Go to the Web to find information you can use to create documents.

Internet Assignments

The purpose of the Internet Assignments is to challenge you to find information on the Internet that you can use to work effectively with this software. The actual assignments are updated and maintained on the Course Technology Web site. Log on to the Internet and use your Web browser to go to the Student Online Companion for New Perspectives Office 2003 at **www.course.com/np/office2003**. Click the Internet Assignments link, and then navigate to the assignments for this tutorial.

Assess

SAM Assessment and Training

If you have a SAM user profile, you may have access to hands-on instruction, practice, and assessment of the skills covered in this tutorial. Log in to your SAM account and go to your assignments page to see what your instructor has assigned.

Review

Quick Check Answers

Session 2.1

1. Click at the beginning of the document, and then click the Spelling and Grammar button on the Standard toolbar. In the Spelling and Grammar dialog box, review each error, which is displayed in color. Grammatical errors appear in green; spelling errors appear in red. Review the possible corrections in the Suggestions list box. To accept a suggested correction, click it in the Suggestions list box, and then click Change to make the correction and continue searching the document for errors.
2. True
3. a. double-click the word
   b. click at the beginning of the block, and then drag until the entire block is selected
   c. double-click in the selection bar next to the paragraph, or triple-click in the paragraph
4. a. the blank space in the left margin area of the Document window that allows you to select entire lines or large blocks of text easily
   b. the process of moving text by first selecting the text, then pressing and holding the mouse button while moving the text to its new location in the document, and finally releasing the mouse button
   c. a command on the Edit menu that is used to search for a set of characters and replace them with a different set of characters
5. False
6. Cut and paste removes the selected material from its original location and inserts it in a new location. Copy and paste makes a copy of the selected material and inserts the copy in a new location; the original material remains in its original location.
7. Click Edit on the menu bar, click Replace, type the search text in the Find what text box, type the replacement text in the Replace with text box, click Find Next, Replace, or click Replace all.

Session 2.2

1. The default top and bottom margins are 1 inch. The default left and right margins are 1.25 inches.
2. Select the text you want to change, click the Line Spacing list arrow on the Formatting toolbar, and then click the line spacing option you want. Or select the text, and then press Ctrl+1 for single spacing, Ctrl+5 for 1.5 line spacing, or Ctrl+2 for double spacing.
3. Left alignment: each line flush left, ragged right; Right alignment: each line flush right, ragged left; Center: each line centered, ragged right and left.; Justify: each line flush left and flush right.
4. To indent a paragraph, place the insertion point in the paragraph and then click the Increase Indent button on the Formatting toolbar. Each click indents the text .5 inches, so to indent 1 inch, click the button two times. Use the horizontal ruler to confirm that the text is indented to the correct position.
5. You might use the Format Painter to copy the formatting of a heading to the other headings in a document.
6. Select the paragraphs, and then click the Numbering button on the Formatting toolbar.
7. Click the Underline button on the Formatting toolbar, type the word, and then click the Underline button again to turn off underlining.
8. True

Objectives

Session 3.1
- Set tab stops
- Divide a document into sections
- Center a page between the top and bottom margins
- Create a header with page numbers
- Create a table

Session 3.2
- Sort the rows in a table
- Modify a table's structure
- Format a table
- Explore Reading Layout view

Creating a Multiple-Page Report

Writing a Recommendation

Case

Tyger Networks

Tyger Networks is a consulting company in Madison, Wisconsin, that specializes in setting up computer networks for small businesses and organizations. Susan Launspach, the program director at New Hope Social Services, recently contacted Tyger Networks about linking the computer networks at New Hope's three main offices. The offices are scattered throughout southern Wisconsin in Madison, Janesville, and Milwaukee. Each office has its own self-contained computer network. To make it easier for a social worker in one office to access data stored on a computer in another office, Susan would like to establish some kind of connection between the three networks.

Caitlyn Waller, an account manager at Tyger Networks, is responsible for the New Hope account. In a phone call, she explained to Susan that connecting the three offices will create a new type of a network known as a wide area network (WAN). Because Susan is unfamiliar with networking terminology, Caitlyn offered to write a report that summarizes the options for creating this type of a network. Working with a task force of sales and technical personnel, Caitlyn compiled the necessary information in a multi-page document. Now Caitlyn would like you to help her finish formatting the report. She also needs some help adding a table to the end of the report. Once the report is completed, Susan will present it to the board of directors at New Hope Social Services.

In this tutorial, you will format the report's title page so that it has a different layout from the rest of the report. The title page will contain only the title and subtitle and will not have page numbers like the rest of the report. You also will add a table to the report that summarizes the costs involved in creating a WAN.

Student Data Files

▼Tutorial.03

▽ Tutorial folder
- WAN.doc

▽ Review folder
- Trouble.doc

▽ Cases folder
- Budget.doc
- Contacts.doc
- SunRep.doc
- Tour.doc

Session 3.1

Planning the Document

Caitlyn divided the responsibility for the report among the members of the group. Each person gathered information about one topic and wrote the appropriate section of the report. Then Caitlyn compiled all the information into a coherent and unified report. In addition, she took care to follow the company's guidelines for content, organization, style, and format.

Because Caitlyn knows that some members of the New Hope board of directors will not have time to read the entire report, she began the report with an executive summary. The body of the report provides an in-depth explanation of the options for establishing a WAN. At the end of the report, she summarizes the costs of these options. The report's style follows established standards of business writing, and emphasizes clarity, simplicity, and directness.

In accordance with the company style guide, Caitlyn's report will begin with a title page, with the text centered between the top and bottom margins. Every page except the title page will include a line of text at the top, giving a descriptive name for the report, as well as the page number. The text and headings will be formatted to match all reports created at Tyger Networks, and will follow company guidelines for layout and text style.

Opening the Report

Caitlyn already has combined the individual sections into one document. She also has begun formatting the report by changing the font size of headings, adding formatting such as bold and italic, and by indenting paragraphs. You'll open the document and follow the steps in this section to perform the remaining formatting tasks, as indicated in Figure 3-1.

Figure 3-1

Initial Draft of Report (Page 1)

Options for Establishing a Wide Area Network

make this a vertically centered title page

Prepared for
Susan Launspach, Program Director
New Hope Social Services

set tab stop

Written by Tyger Networks:

type list of task force members and their titles

start new page

Executive Summary

This report presents options for connecting the three computer networks run by New Hope Social Services. First we describe the networks in the Madison, Janesville, and Milwaukee offices, and then we explain the options for integrating these networks into a larger structure, known as a Wide Area Network (WAN). Finally, in a table at the end of this report, we summarize the costs for implementing the various WAN connections.

insert header in this section

<u>New Hope's Existing LANs</u>

The term Local Area Network (LAN) refers to a network of computers and other devices (such as printers) that are geographically close to each other (for example, on the same floor of a building). A LAN is managed via a special computer known as a server. The majority of the computers on the three New Hope LANs are used to run Microsoft Office applications. The network operating system on the Janesville and Madison servers has been upgraded to Windows 2000 Server, while the Milwaukee server continues to run Windows NT 4. Because the three LANs are separate, a social worker in one office cannot directly access data stored on a computer in one of the other two offices.

<u>WAN Technology</u>

To allow inter-office data access, we propose connecting the three LANs, thereby creating a Wide Area Network (WAN). A WAN is a network that spans a geographical distance (between buildings, cities, or even countries). Strictly speaking, a WAN consists of one link between two points. It does not usually connect one site to several other sites in the way that a LAN connects multiple computers. Thus, to connect the three New Hope LANs, we would need to establish multiple WAN links. The following sections describe various options for creating these links. The

To open the document:

1. Start Word, and then open the file **WAN** located in the Tutorial.03\Tutorial folder included with your Data Files.
2. To avoid altering the original file, save the document as **New Hope WAN Report** in the same folder.
3. Check your settings to make sure your screen matches figures in this tutorial. In particular, be sure to display the nonprinting characters and switch to Normal view if necessary. Note that throughout this tutorial, your Zoom settings may not automatically match the Zoom settings shown in the figures. As you work through the tutorial steps, adjust your Zoom settings as necessary if you want to make your screen match the figures exactly.

Setting Tab Stops

Tabs are useful for indenting paragraphs and for vertically aligning text or numerical data in columns. A **tab** adds space between the margin and text in a column or between text in one column and text in another column. A **tab stop** is the location where text moves when you press the Tab key. When Show/Hide ¶ is selected, the nonprinting tab character → appears wherever you press the Tab key. A tab character is just like any other character you type; you can delete it by pressing the Backspace key or the Delete key.

Word provides several **tab-stop alignment styles**. The five major styles are left, center, right, decimal, and bar, as shown in Figure 3-2. The first three tab-stop styles position text in a similar way to the Align Left, Center, and Align Right buttons on the Formatting toolbar. The difference is that with a tab, you determine line by line precisely where the left, center, or right alignment should occur.

Figure 3-2 Tab stop alignment styles

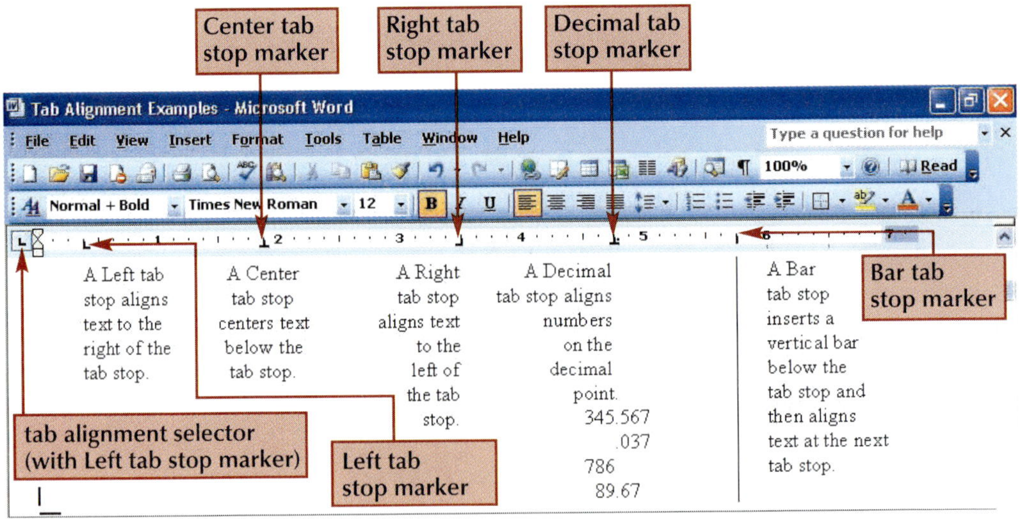

Left tabs position the left edge of text at the tab stop and extend the text to the right. **Center tabs** position text so that it's centered evenly on both sides of the tab stop. **Right tabs** position the right edge of text at the tab stop and extend the text to the left. **Decimal tabs** position numbers so that their decimal points are aligned at the tab stop.

Bar tabs insert a vertical bar at the tab stop and then align text to the right of the next tab stop. In addition, you can use a **First Line Indent tab**, which indents the first line of a paragraph, and a **Hanging Indent tab**, which indents every line of a paragraph *except* the first line.

The Word default tab-stop settings are every one-half inch, as indicated by the small gray tick marks at the bottom of the ruler shown in Figure 3-3. You set a new tab stop by selecting a tab-stop alignment style (from the tab alignment selector at the left end of the horizontal ruler) and then clicking the horizontal ruler to insert the tab stop. You can remove a tab stop from the ruler by clicking it and dragging the tab stop off the ruler.

Figure 3-3 Ruler with tab stops

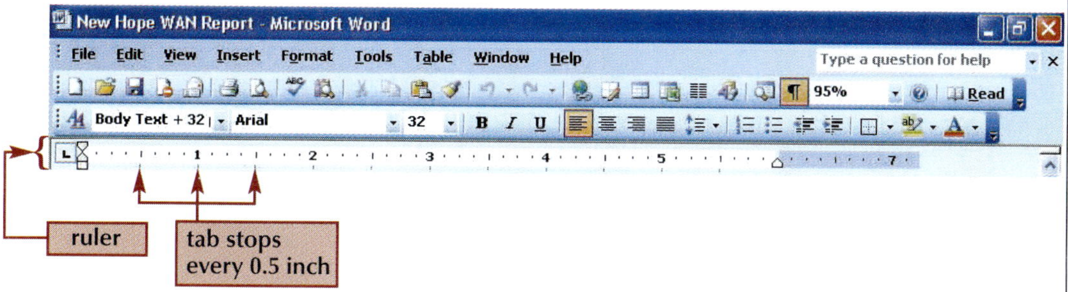

You should never try to align columns of text by adding extra spaces with the spacebar. Although the text might seem precisely aligned in the document window, it might not be aligned when you print the document. Furthermore, if you edit the text, the extra spaces might disturb the alignment. One of the main advantages of tab stops is that, if you edit text aligned with tabs, the alignment remains intact. If you want to align a lot of text in many columns, you'll find it easier to use a table, as described later in this tutorial.

To align columns using tabs, set tab stops on the horizontal ruler, type text in the first column, and then press the Tab key. The insertion point then moves to the next tab stop to the right, where you can type more text. You can continue in this way until you type the first row of each column. Then you can press the Enter key, and begin typing the next row of each column. However, sometimes you'll find that text in a column stretches beyond the next default tab stop, and as a result the columns fail to line up evenly.

Setting Tab Stops

Reference Window

- To set a tab stop, click the tab alignment selector on the far left of the horizontal ruler until the appropriate tab-stop alignment style appears, and then click the horizontal ruler where you want to position the tab stop. Press the Tab key to move the insertion point from one tab stop to another.
- To change the tab alignment or location for text that already contains tab stops, select the text and then move an existing tab stop to a new location, or click the tab alignment selector on the far left of the horizontal ruler until the appropriate tab-stop alignment style appears and then click the horizontal ruler where you want to set the tab stop.
- To remove a tab stop, click it and drag it off the horizontal ruler.

In the Tyger Networks report, you need to type the list of task force members and their titles. As you type, you'll discover whether Word's default tab stops are appropriate for this document, or whether you need to add a new tab stop.

To enter the task force list using tabs:

1. Verify that nonprinting characters are displayed, and then move the insertion point to the line below the text "Written by Tyger Networks:."
2. Type **Caitlyn Waller**, and then press the **Tab** key. A tab character appears, and the insertion point moves to the first tab stop after the "r" in "Waller." This tab stop is located at the 1.5-inch mark on the horizontal ruler. See Figure 3-4.

Figure 3-4 Tab character

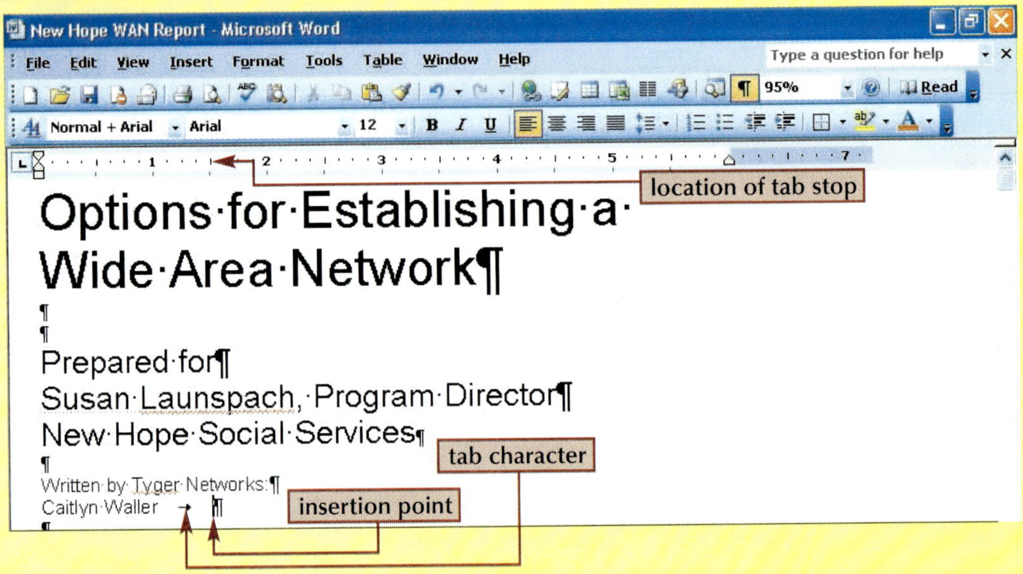

3. Type **Account Manager**, and then press the **Enter** key. The insertion point moves to a new line, ready for you to enter the next name in the list.
4. Type **Melissa J. Curlington**, and then press the **Tab** key. The insertion point moves to the first available tab stop, at the 2-inch mark on the horizontal ruler.
5. Type **Product Manager**, and then press the **Enter** key.

   As you can see, Melissa J. Curlington's title does not align with Caitlyn Waller's title on the line above. You'll fix this in a moment by inserting a new tab stop that overrides the default tab stops. But first continue typing the list of names.
6. Type **Angelo Zurlo-Cuva**, press the **Tab** key, type **Sales Engineer**, press the **Enter** key, type your first and last name, press the **Tab** key, and then type **Network Engineer**. When you are finished, your document should look like Figure 3-5.

List of task force members

Figure 3-5

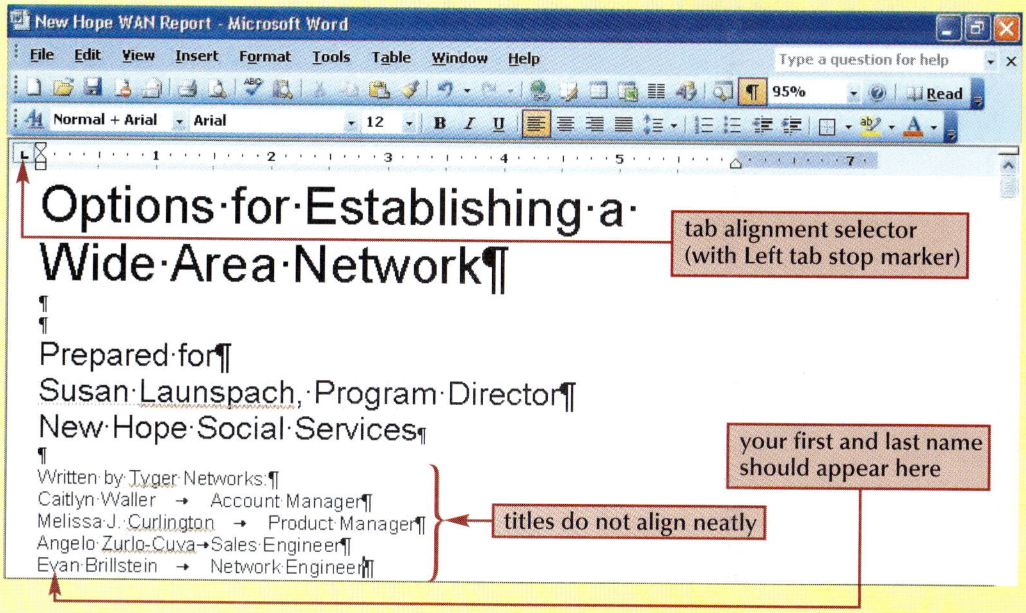

The list of names and titles is not aligned properly. You'll fix this by inserting a new tab stop.

To add a new tab stop to the horizontal ruler:

1. Click and drag the mouse pointer to select the list of task force members and titles.
2. Make sure the current tab-stop alignment style is Left tab [L], as shown in Figure 3-5. If [L] is not selected, click the **tab alignment selector** one or more times until [L] appears.
3. Click the **tick mark** on the ruler that occurs at 2.5 inches. Word automatically inserts a Left tab stop at that location and removes the tick marks to its left. The column of titles shifts to the new tab stop.
4. Deselect the highlighted text and then move the insertion point anywhere in the list of names and titles. See Figure 3-6.

Figure 3-6 **Left tab stop on ruler**

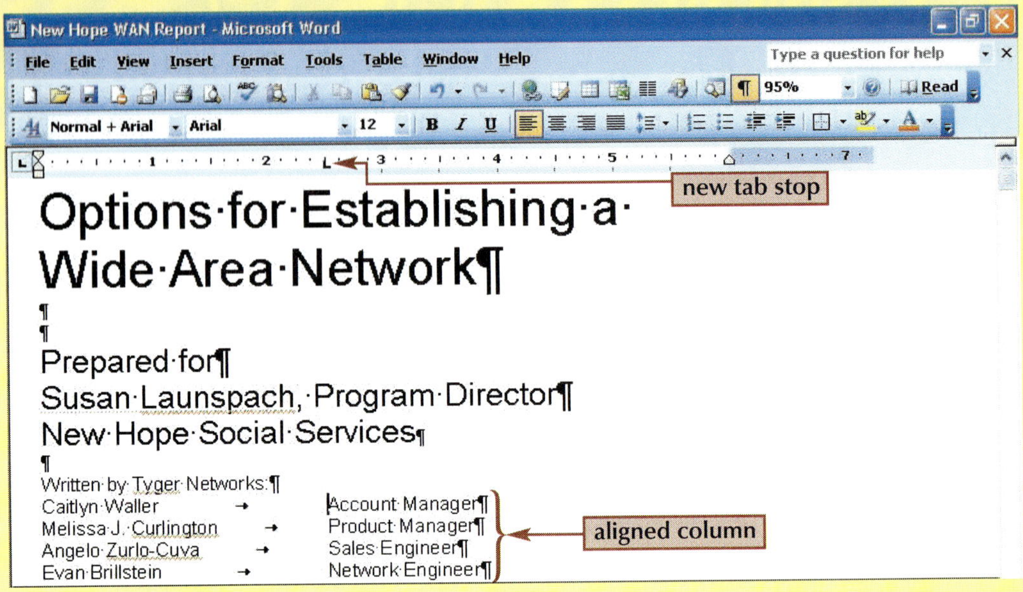

5. Click the **Save** button on the Standard toolbar to save your work.

The two columns of information are now aligned, as Caitlyn requested. Notice that Word changed the tab stops only for the selected paragraphs, not for all the paragraphs in the document. In the Case Problems at the end of this tutorial you'll have a chance to work with tab stops using the Tabs dialog box (which you can open via the Tabs command on the Format menu). Among other things, the Tabs dialog box allows you to insert a leader, which is a row of dots (or other characters) between tabbed text. A dot leader makes it easier to read a long list of tabbed material because the eye can follow the dots from one item to the next. You can also use the Tabs dialog box to clear (or remove) tab stops from a document. Next, you need to change the layout of the title page.

Formatting the Document in Sections

According to the company guidelines, the title page of the report should be centered between the top and bottom margins of the page. To format the title page differently from the rest of the report, you need to divide the document into sections. A **section** is a unit or part of a document that can have its own page orientation, margins, headers, footers, and vertical alignment. Each section, in other words, is like a mini-document within a document.

To divide a document into sections, you insert a **section break**, which appears in a document as a dotted line with the words "Section Break." A section break marks the point at which one section ends and another begins. A section can start on a new page, or a section can continue on the same page as text not included in the new section. You insert a section break with the Break command on the Insert menu. To delete a section break (or a page break), click the line representing the break and press the Delete key.

To insert a section break after the title:

1. Position the insertion point immediately to the left of the "E" in the heading "Executive Summary." You want the text above this heading to be on a separate title page and the executive summary to begin on the second page of the report.
2. Click **Insert** on the menu bar, and then click **Break** to open the Break dialog box. See Figure 3-7.

Figure 3-7 Break dialog box

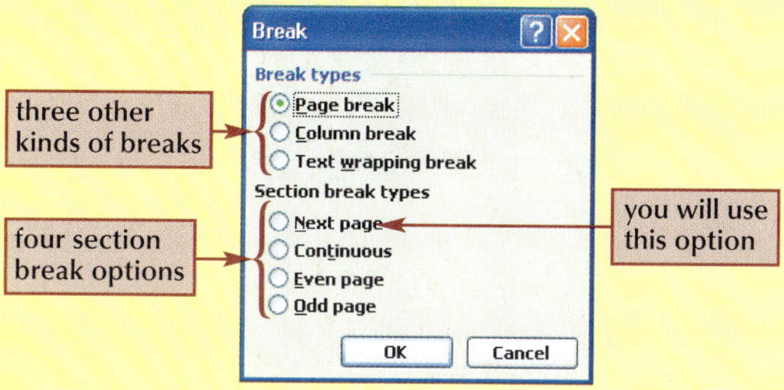

The Break dialog box can be a bit confusing, so you should study it carefully before continuing with these steps. The option buttons under "Break types" allow you to insert three different types of breaks, including a **page break**, which moves the text after it onto a new page. (You don't need to be concerned with the other options right now.) The four option buttons under "Section break types" allow you to insert four types of section breaks. Of these, the two most important types of section breaks are a Next page section break, which starts a new section on a new page, and a Continuous section break, which inserts a section break without starting a new page. If you simply want to start a new page, you can click the Page break option button in the Break dialog box. If you want to start a new page *and* insert a section break, you should click the Next page option button in the Break dialog box. Because you want the document to have a title page, and because you want to format the title page differently than the rest of the document, you will insert a section break that starts a new page. In other words, you need to click the Next page option button.

3. Under "Section break types," click the **Next page** option button, and then click the **OK** button. A double-dotted line and the words "Section Break (Next Page)" appear before the heading "Executive Summary," indicating that you have inserted a break that starts a new section on the next page. The status bar indicates that the insertion point is on page 2, section 2. See Figure 3-8.

Figure 3-8 Section break

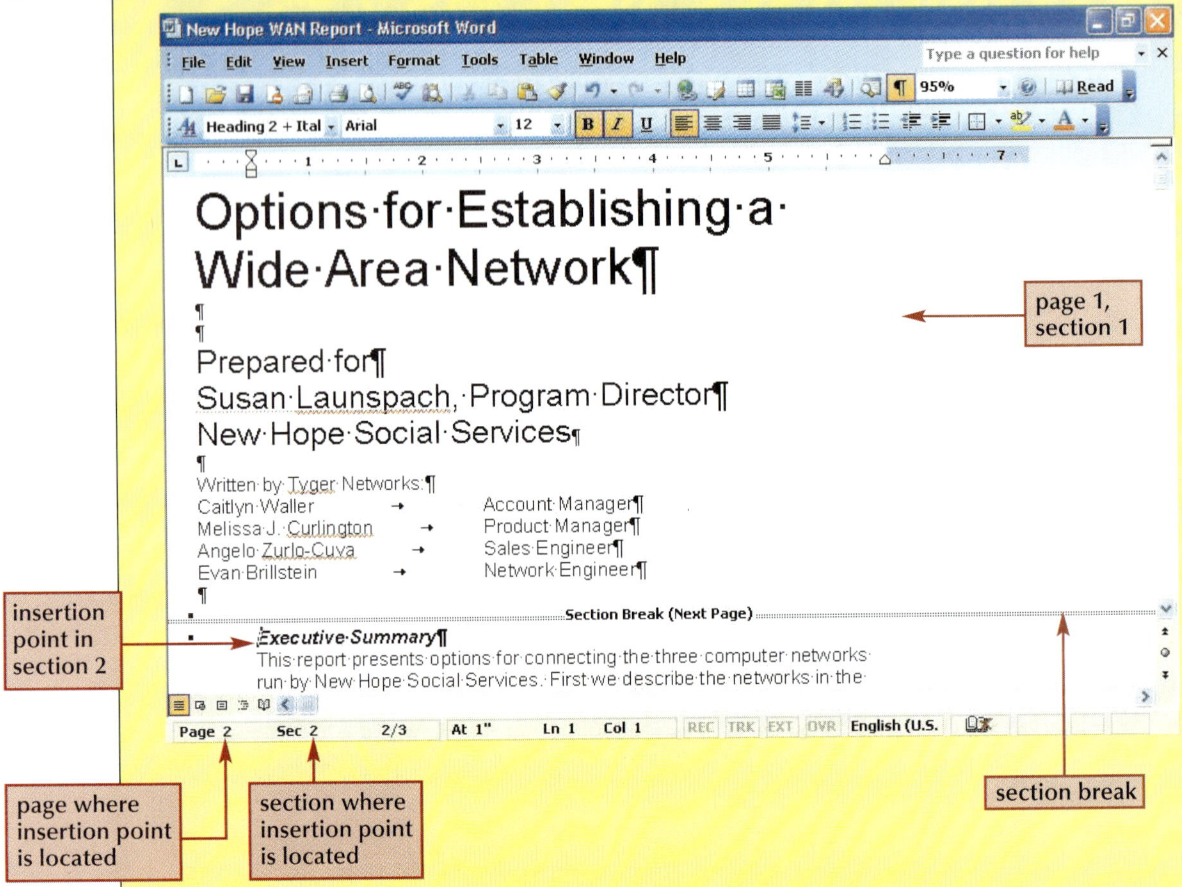

Trouble? If you see a single dotted line and the words "Page Break," you inserted a page break rather than a section break. Click the Undo button on the Standard toolbar, and then repeat Steps 1 through 3.

4. To practice deleting a section break, click the Section break line, and then press the **Delete** key. The section break line disappears and the status bar indicates that the insertion point is located in section 1, which is now the only section.
5. Click the **Undo** button on the Standard toolbar. The section break reappears.
6. Save your work.

Now that the title page is a separate section and page from the rest of the report, you can make changes affecting only that section, leaving the rest of the document unchanged.

Changing the Vertical Alignment of a Section

You're ready to center the text of page 1 vertically on the page. But first you will switch to the Print Preview window, so you can more easily observe your changes to page 1.

To see the document in Print Preview:

1. Click the **Print Preview** button on the Standard toolbar to open the Print Preview window.
2. If you don't see all three pages (as shown in Figure 3-9) click the **Multiple Pages** button on the Print Preview toolbar, and then click and drag across the top three pages in the list box to select "1 × 3 Pages." The three pages of the report are reduced in size and appear side by side. See Figure 3-9. Although you cannot read the text on the pages, you can see the general layout.

Figure 3-9 Report in Print Preview window

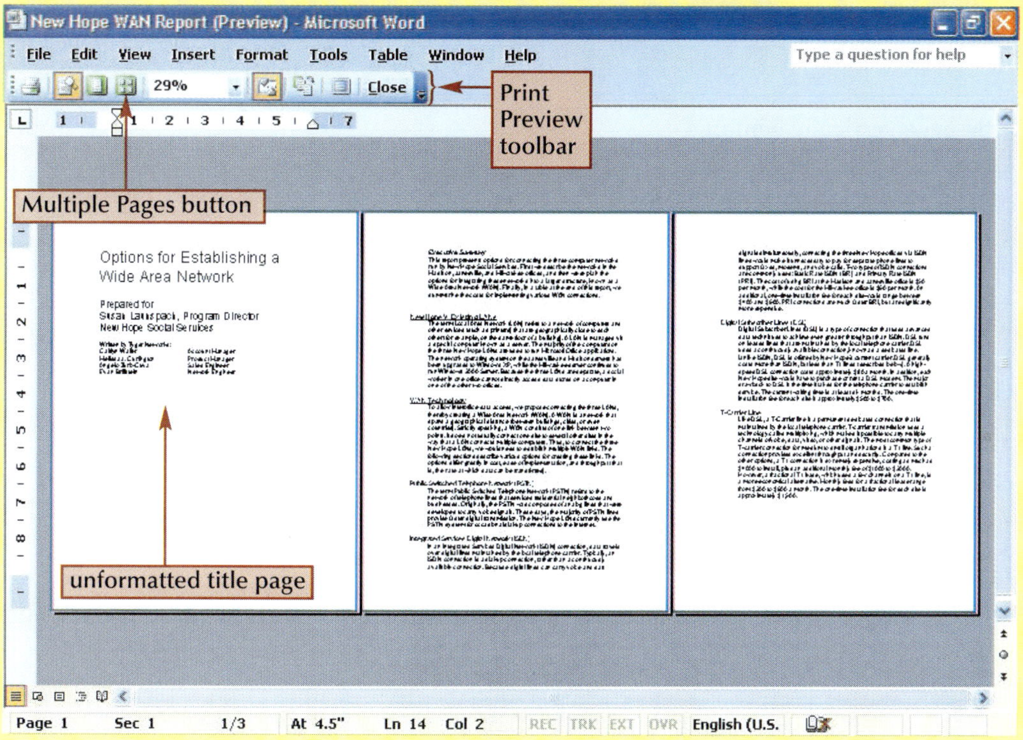

Now you can change the vertical alignment to center the lines of text between the top and bottom margins. The **vertical alignment** specifies how a page of text is positioned on the page between the top and bottom margins—flush at the top, flush at the bottom, or centered between the top and bottom margins.

You'll center the title page text from within the Print Preview window.

To change the vertical alignment of the title page:

1. Click the **Magnifier** button on the Print Preview toolbar once to deselect it. When the magnifier button is deselected, you can edit the document.
2. Click the **leftmost page** in the Print Preview window to move the insertion point to page 1 (the title page). The status bar indicates that page 1 is the current page.

   Trouble? If the size of page 1 increases when you click it, you selected the Magnifier button in Step 1 instead of deselecting it. Click the Multiple Pages button on the Print Preview toolbar, drag to select "1 × 3 Pages," and then repeat Steps 1 and 2.
3. Click **File** on the menu bar, and then click **Page Setup**. The Page Setup dialog box opens.
4. Click the **Layout** tab. In the Apply to list box, select **This section** (if it is not already selected) so that the layout change affects only the section containing the insertion point (that is, the first section) and not both sections of your document.
5. Click the **Vertical alignment** list arrow, and then click **Center** to center the pages of the current section—in this case, just page 1—vertically between the top and bottom margins.
6. Click the **OK** button to return to the Print Preview window. The text of the title page is centered vertically, as shown in Figure 3-10.

Figure 3-10 Title page vertically centered

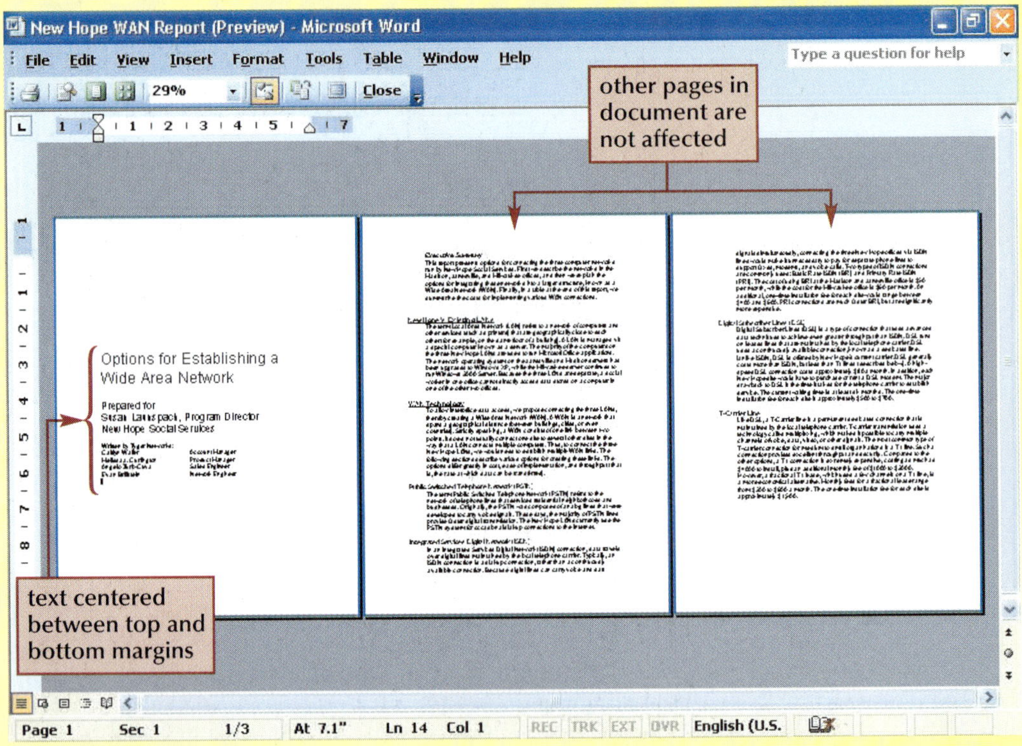

7. Click the **Close** button on the Print Preview toolbar to return to Normal view.

You have successfully centered the title page text. Next, you turn your attention to inserting a header with a descriptive name for the report and the page number at the top of every page in section 2.

Adding Headers

The report guidelines at Tyger Networks require a short report title and the page number to be printed at the top of every page except the title page. Text that is printed at the top of every page is called a **header**. For example, the information printed at the top of the page you are reading is a header. Similarly, a **footer** is text that is printed at the bottom of every page. (You'll have a chance to work with footers in the Case Problems at the end of this tutorial.)

When you insert a header or footer into a document, you switch to Header and Footer view. The Header and Footer toolbar is displayed, and the insertion point moves to the top of the document, where the header will appear. The document text is dimmed, indicating that it cannot be edited until you return to Normal or Print Layout view.

You'll create a header for the main body of the report (section 2) that prints "Options for Establishing a Wide Area Network" at the left margin and the page number at the right margin.

To insert a header for section 2:

1. Click anywhere after the section break so that the insertion point is located in section 2 and not in section 1. Refer to the status bar to verify that the insertion point is in section 2.
2. Click **View** on the menu bar, and then click **Header and Footer**. The Word window changes to Header and Footer view, and the Header and Footer toolbar appears. The header area is located in the top margin of your document, surrounded by a dashed line, and displays the words "Header -Section 2-." See Figure 3-11. (If the Header and Footer toolbar covers the header area, drag the toolbar below the header area, similar to its position in Figure 3-11.) Currently, the header is set up so that any text you type in the section 2 header will also appear in the section 1 header. In other words, the headers for sections 1 and 2 are linked. In order to create separate headers for the two sections, you need to deselect the Link to Previous button in the Header and Footer toolbar. You'll do that in the next step.

Figure 3-11 Creating a header

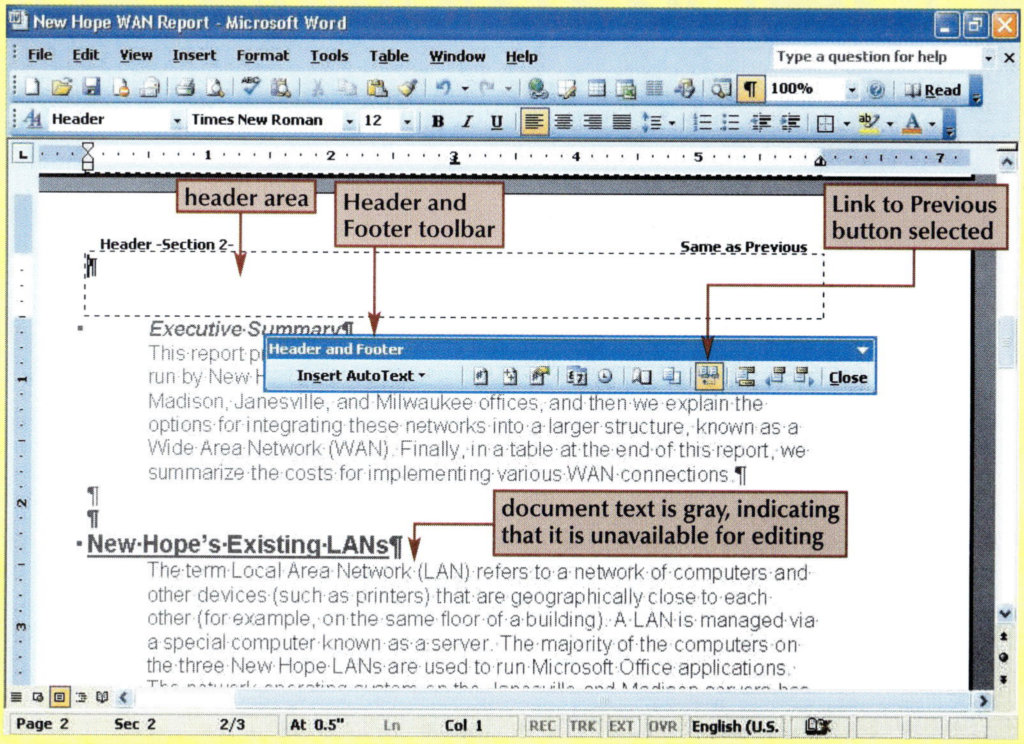

Trouble? If the header area displays "Header -Section 1-," click the Show Next button on the Header and Footer toolbar until the header area displays "Header -Section 2-."

Trouble? If the text of the document doesn't appear on the screen, click the Show/Hide Document Text button on the Header and Footer toolbar, and continue with Step 3.

3. Click the **Link to Previous** button on the Header and Footer toolbar to deselect it. When Link to Previous is selected, Word automatically inserts the header text you create in one section in the previous section. You deselected it to ensure that the header text you create in section 2 applies only to the current section (section 2), and not to the previous section (section 1).
4. Type **Options for Establishing a Wide Area Network**. The title is automatically aligned on the left. See Figure 3-12.

Figure 3-12 Header text

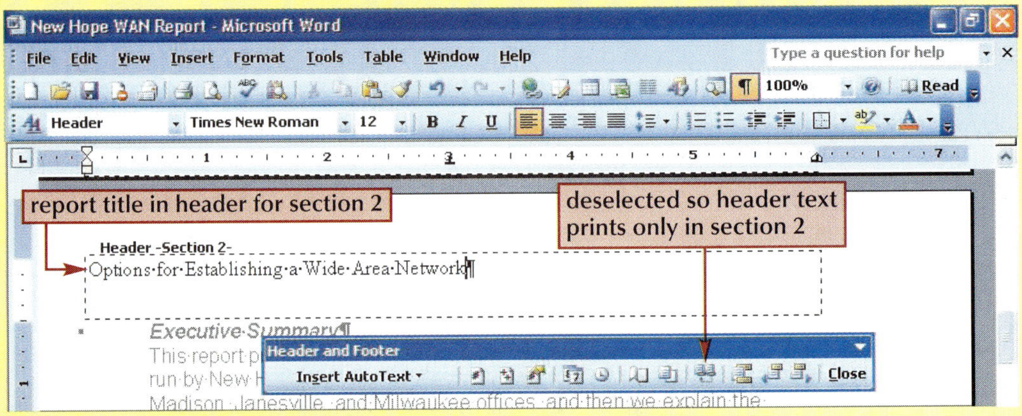

5. Press the **Tab** key to move the insertion point to the next available tab stop, on the right margin of the header area. (Notice that by default the header contains Center and Right tab stops.)
6. Type the word **Page**, and then press the **spacebar** once.
7. Click the **Insert Page Number** button on the Header and Footer toolbar. The page number "2" appears at the right-aligned tab. The page number in the header looks like you simply typed the number 2, but you actually inserted a special instruction telling Word to insert the correct page number on each page. Now consecutive page numbers will print on each page of the header within this section.
8. Click the **Close** button on the Header and Footer toolbar to return to Normal view, and then save your changes.

Trouble? If your document is not displayed in Normal view, switch to Normal view now.

Notice that you can't see the header in Normal view. To see exactly how the header will appear on the printed page, you need to switch to the Print Preview window or to Print Layout view.

To view the header and margins in Print Preview:

1. Click the **Print Preview button** on the Standard toolbar. The three pages of the document are displayed as they were earlier in the Print Preview window, although this time you can see a line of text at the top of pages 2 and 3. To read the header text, you need to increase the magnification.
2. Verify that the **Magnifier** button on the Print Preview toolbar is selected.
3. Move the pointer over the second page of the document, and then click the header text at the top of the page. The Print Preview window zooms in on the header text for page 2, as shown in Figure 3-13.

Figure 3-13 **Header text for page 2 in Print Preview**

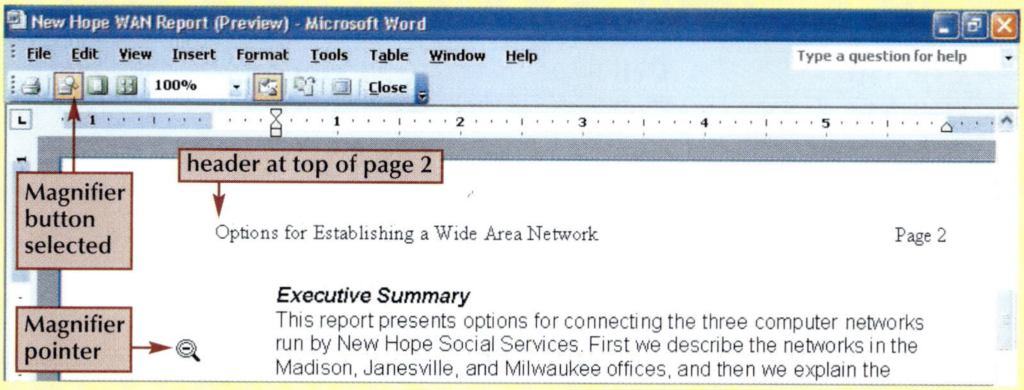

4. Use the vertical scroll bar to scroll down until you can see the header for page 3.
5. Scroll up until you can see the top of page 1. Notice that the header appears only on pages 2 and 3. The header does not appear on the title page because the title page is in a different section of the document. The correct page numbers appear on pages 2 and 3.
6. Use the **Multiple Pages** button to display all three pages of the document again.
7. Click the **Close** button on the Print Preview toolbar to return to Normal view.
8. Save your work.

The report now has the required header. You have formatted Caitlyn's report so that the results are professional-looking, presented clearly, and easy to read. Next, you will add a table that summarizes the costs of the various WAN options.

Inserting Tables

Using Word, you can quickly organize data and arrange text in an easy-to-read table format. A **table** is information arranged in horizontal rows and vertical columns. As shown in Figure 3-14, table rows are commonly referred to by number (row 1, row 2, and so forth), while columns are commonly referred to by letter (column A on the far left, then column B, and so forth). However, you do not see row and column numbers on the screen. The area where a row and column intersect is called a **cell**. Each cell is identified by a column and row label. For example, the cell in the upper-left corner of a table is cell A1 (column A, row 1), the cell to the right of that is cell B1, the cell below cell A1 is A2, and so forth. The table's structure is shown by **gridlines**, which are light gray lines that define the rows and columns. By default, gridlines do not appear on the printed page. You can emphasize specific parts of a table on the printed page by adding a **border**, which is a line that prints along the side of a table cell.

Figure 3-14 Elements of a Word table

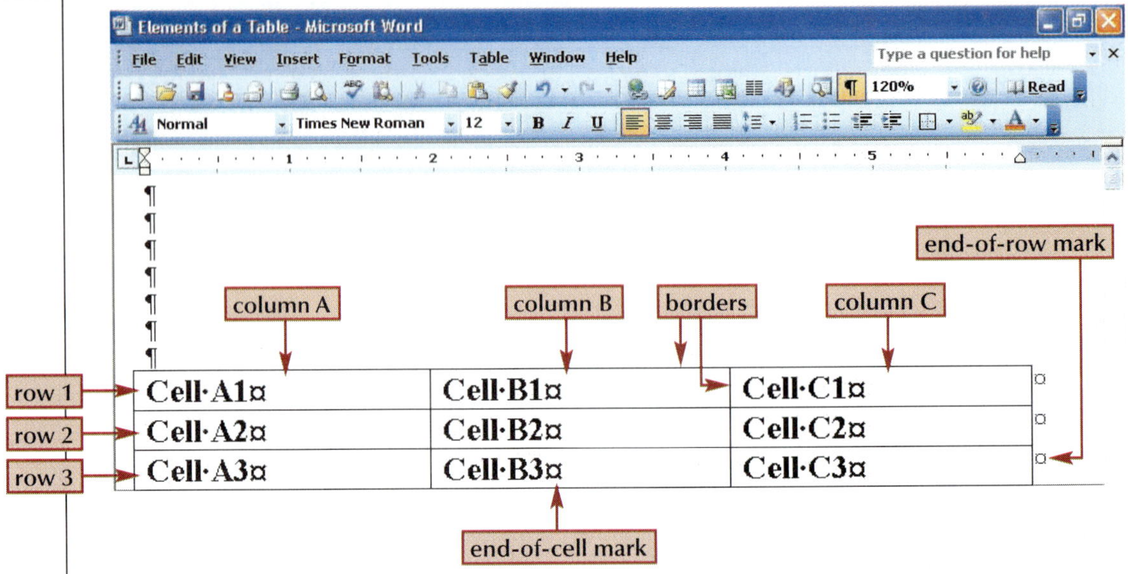

Depending on your needs, you can create a blank table and then insert information into it (as you'll do next), or you can convert existing text into a table (as you'll do in the Case Problems at the end of this tutorial).

You may be wondering why you would use a table instead of tabs to align text in columns. Tabs work well for smaller amounts of information, such as two columns with three or four rows, but tabs and columns become tedious and difficult to work with when you need to organize a larger amount of more complex information. The Word Table feature allows you to organize data quickly and to place text and graphics in a more legible format.

Creating a Table

You can create a table with equal column widths quickly by using the Insert Table button on the Standard toolbar. (You will use this technique to create the table Caitlyn requested.) You also can create a table by dragging the Draw Table pointer to draw the table structure you want. (You'll practice this method in the Case Problems.) However you create a table, you can modify it by using commands on the Table menu or the buttons on the Tables and Borders toolbar.

Caitlyn wants you to create a table that summarizes information in the Tyger Networks report. Figure 3-15 shows a sketch of what Caitlyn wants the table to look like. The table will allow the members of the New Hope board of directors to see at a glance the cost of each option. The top row of the table, called the **heading row**, identifies the type of information in each column.

Figure 3-15 Table sketch

Type of Connection	Monthly Charge
ISDN	$50 to $60
DSL	$80
T1	$1000 to $2000

Inserting a Page Break

Before you begin creating the table, you need to insert a page break because you want the table to appear on a separate page.

To insert a page break:

1. Verify that the document is displayed in Normal view.
2. Press **Ctrl+End** to position the insertion point at the end of the report.
3. Press **Ctrl+Enter**. A dotted line with the words "Page Break" appears in the document window. *Note*: You also can add a page break using the Break dialog box (the same dialog box you used earlier to insert a section break).

   Trouble? If you do not see the words "Page Break," check to make sure the document is displayed in Normal view.
4. Scroll down until the page break is positioned near the top of the document window.

The insertion point is now at the beginning of a new page, where you want to insert the table.

Inserting a Blank Table

You'll use the Insert Table button to insert a blank table structure into the new page. Then you can type the necessary information directly into the table.

To create a blank table using the Insert Table button:

1. Click the **Insert Table** button on the Standard toolbar. A drop-down grid resembling a miniature table appears below the Insert Table button. The grid opens with four rows and five columns for the table. You can drag the pointer to select as many rows and columns as you need. In this case, you need four rows and two columns.
2. Position the pointer in the upper-left cell of the grid, and then drag the pointer down and across the grid until you highlight four rows and two columns. As you drag the pointer across the grid, Word indicates the size of the table (rows by columns) at the bottom of the grid.
3. When the table size is 4 × 2, click the mouse button. An empty table, four rows by two columns, appears in your document with the insertion point blinking in the upper-left corner (cell A1). The two columns are of equal width. Each cell contains an end-of-cell mark, and each row contains an end-of-row mark. See Figure 3-16.

Figure 3-16 Empty table in Normal view

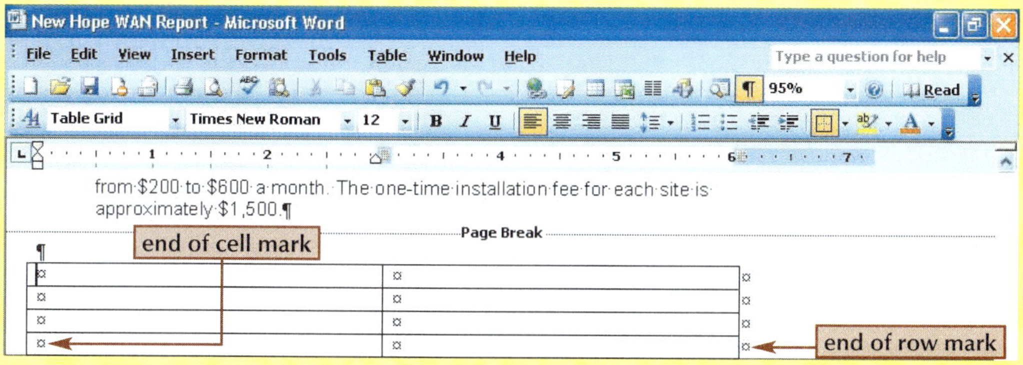

Trouble? If your table is displayed in Print Layout view, switch to Normal view and then compare your table to Figure 3-16.

Trouble? If you don't see the end-of-cell and end-of-row marks, you need to show nonprinting characters. Click the Show/Hide ¶ button ¶ on the Standard toolbar to show nonprinting characters.

Trouble? If you see the Tables and Borders toolbar displayed along with the new blank table, close it. You will learn how to use the Tables and Borders toolbar later in this tutorial.

When working with tables and graphics, it's helpful to switch to Print Layout view, which allows you to get a better sense of the overall layout of the page, including the headers. Also, some special table features are only available in Print Layout view. You'll switch to Print Layout view in the following steps.

To display the table structure in Print Layout view:

1. Click the **Print Layout View** button. Note that a Zoom setting of 100% or greater should make it easy for you to see the entire table on the screen. The table is displayed in Print Layout view, where you can see the column widths indicated on the horizontal ruler. Also, notice that the document header is visible in Print Layout view.
2. Move the mouse pointer over the empty table. The Table Move handle appears in the table's upper-left corner, and the Table Resize handle appears in the lower-right corner. See Figure 3-17. You don't need to use either of these handles now, but you should understand their function. To select the entire table quickly, you can click the Table Move handle. Then you can move the entire table by dragging the Table Move handle. To change the size of the entire table, you could drag the Table Resize handle.

Figure 3-17 Empty table in Print Layout view

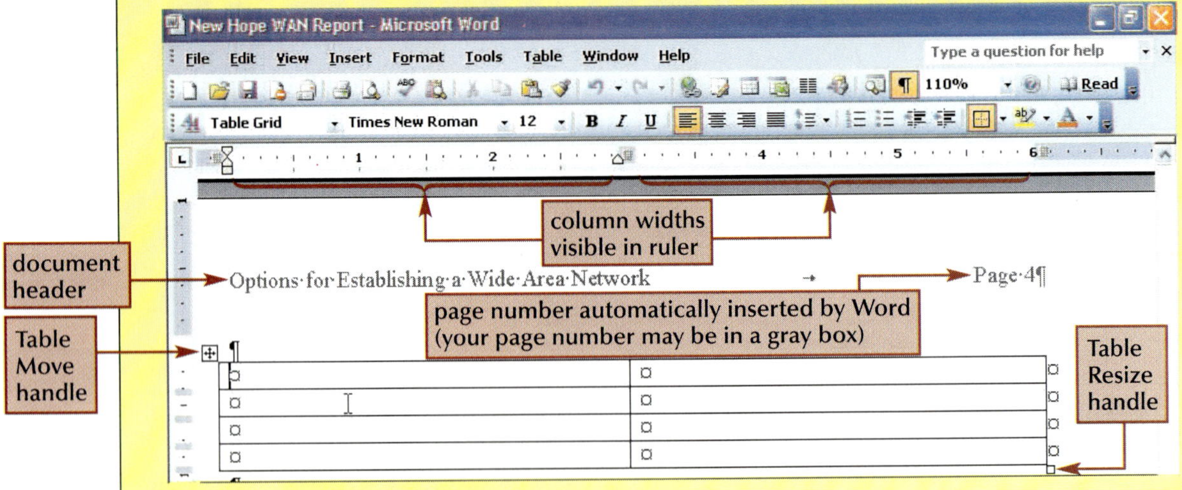

Entering Text in a Table

You can enter text in a table by moving the insertion point to a cell and typing. If the text takes up more than one line in the cell, Word automatically wraps the text to the next line and increases the height of that cell and all the cells in that row. To move the insertion point to another cell in the table, you can either click in that cell or use the Tab key. Figure 3-18 summarizes the keystrokes for moving the insertion point within a table.

Figure 3-18
Keystrokes for moving around a table

Press	To move the insertion point
Tab or →	One cell to the right, or to the first cell in the next row
Shift+Tab or ←	One cell to the left, or to the last cell in the previous row
Alt+Home	To the first cell of the current row
Alt+End	To the last cell of the current row
Alt+PageUp	To the top cell of the current column
Alt+PageDown	To the bottom cell of the current column
↑	One cell up in the current column
↓	One cell down in the current column

Now you are ready to insert information into the table.

To insert data into the table:

1. Verify that the insertion point is located in cell **A1** (in the upper-left corner).
2. Type the heading **Type of Connection**.
3. Press the **Tab** key to move to cell B1. See Figure 3-19.

Figure 3-19
Entering text in the table

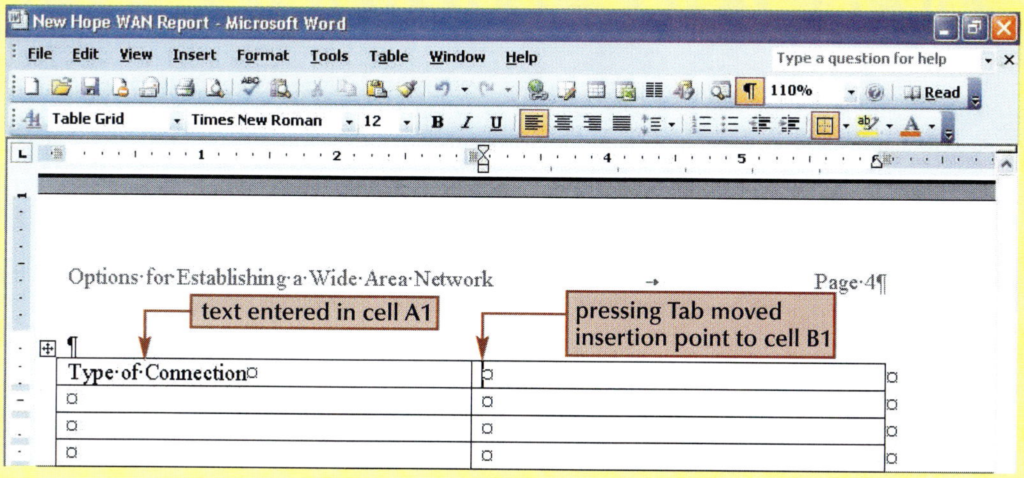

Trouble? If Word created a new paragraph in cell A1 rather than moving the insertion point to cell B1, you pressed the Enter key instead of the Tab key. Press the Backspace key to remove the paragraph mark, and then press the Tab key to move to cell B1.

4. Type **Monthly Charge**, and then press the **Tab** key to move to cell A2. Notice that when you press the Tab key in the last column of the table, the insertion point moves to the first column in the next row.

You have finished entering the heading row, the row that identifies the information in each column. Now you can enter the information about the various WAN options.

To continue entering information in the table:

1. Type **ISDN**, and then press the **Tab** key to move to cell B2.
2. Type **$50 to $60**, and then press the **Tab** key to move the insertion point to cell A3.
3. Type the remaining information for the table, as shown in Figure 3-20, pressing the **Tab** key to move from cell to cell. You'll change the column widths in the next session.

Figure 3-20 Table with completed information

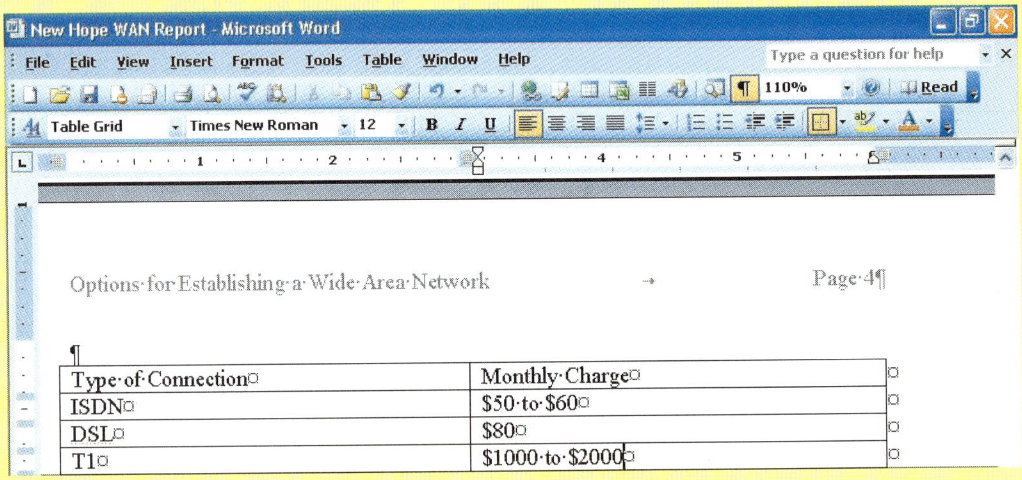

Trouble? If a new row (row 5) appeared at the bottom of your table, you pressed the Tab key when the insertion point was in cell B4, the last cell in the table. Click the Undo button on the Standard toolbar to remove row 5 from the table.

4. Save your work.

Keep in mind that many document-editing features, such as the Backspace key, the copy-and-paste feature, the Undo button, and the AutoCorrect feature, work the same way in a table as they do in the rest of the document. You will edit and format this table in the next session.

Review

Session 3.1 Quick Check

1. Define the following in your own words:
   a. section break
   b. cell
   c. table
   d. header
   e. tab stop
2. Explain how to insert a new tab stop.
3. Describe a situation in which you would want to divide a document into sections.
4. Explain how to center the title page vertically between the top and bottom margins.
5. What is the difference between a header and a footer?
6. How do you insert the page number in a header?
7. Describe how to insert a blank table consisting of three columns and two rows.
8. How do you move the insertion point from one row to the next in a table?
9. Describe a situation in which it would be better to use a table rather than tab stops.
10. Explain how to select an entire table.

Session 3.2

Displaying the Tables and Borders Toolbar

The **Tables and Borders toolbar** contains a number of useful buttons that simplify the process of working with tables. You'll display the Tables and Borders toolbar in the following steps.

To open the Tables and Borders toolbar:

1. If you took a break after the previous session, make sure Word is running and that the New Hope WAN Report document is open. Check that the nonprinting characters are displayed, that the document is displayed in Print Layout view, and that the document is scrolled so that the table is visible.
2. Click the **Tables and Borders** button on the Standard toolbar. The Tables and Borders toolbar appears.
3. Move the mouse pointer over the table. The Draw Table pointer appears. You can use this pointer to add new rows or columns in a table, and to add borders between cells. You'll have a chance to practice using this pointer in the Case Problems at the end of this tutorial. For now you'll turn it off.
4. Click the **Draw Table** button on the Tables and Borders toolbar. The pointer changes to an I-beam pointer.
5. If necessary, drag the Tables and Borders toolbar down and to the right, so that it doesn't block your view of the table, as shown in Figure 3-21.

Figure 3-21 Positioning the Tables and Borders toolbar

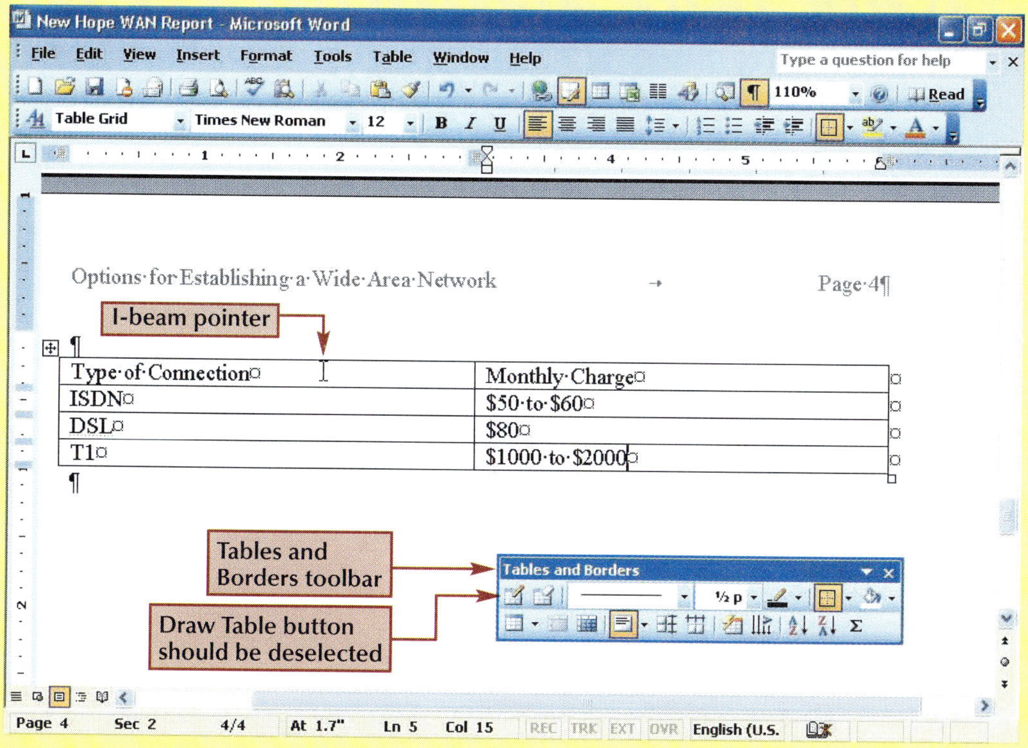

6. Move the mouse pointer over the buttons on the Tables and Borders toolbar and read the name of each button as it is displayed in a ScreenTip. In particular, notice the Merge Cells button, which you can use to combine multiple cells into one cell; the Split Cells button, which you can use to divide one cell into multiple cells; and the AutoSum button, which you can use to total a column of numbers. You'll have a chance to practice using these buttons in the Case Problems at the end of this tutorial. Notice also the two Sort buttons, which you can use to rearrange the rows in a table. You will use the Sort Ascending button in the next section.

Sorting Rows in a Table

The term **sort** refers to the process of rearranging information in alphabetical, numerical, or chronological order. When you sort a table, you arrange the rows based on the contents of one of the columns. For example, you could sort the table you just created based on the contents of the Type of Connection column—either in ascending alphabetical order (from *A* to *Z*) or in descending alphabetical order (from *Z* to *A*). Alternately, you could sort the table based on the contents of the Monthly Charge column—either in ascending numerical order (lowest to highest) or in descending numerical order (highest to lowest). When you sort table data, Word usually does not sort the heading row along with the other information; instead, the heading row remains unsorted at the top of the table.

Caitlyn would like you to sort the table in ascending alphabetical order, based on the contents of the Type of Connection column. You start by positioning the insertion point in that column.

To sort the information in the table:

1. Click cell **A2** (which contains the text "ISDN"). The insertion point is now located in the Type of Connection column.
2. Click the **Sort Ascending** button on the Tables and Borders toolbar. Rows 2 through 4 are now arranged alphabetically according to the text in the Type of Connection column. When you sort a table, all the items in a row move together as one entity. This ensures that the type of connection and the associated monthly charge don't become separated during the sort process. Also note that Word did not sort the header row along with the other rows. The header row remains in its original position at the top of the table. See Figure 3-22.

Figure 3-22

Table after being sorted

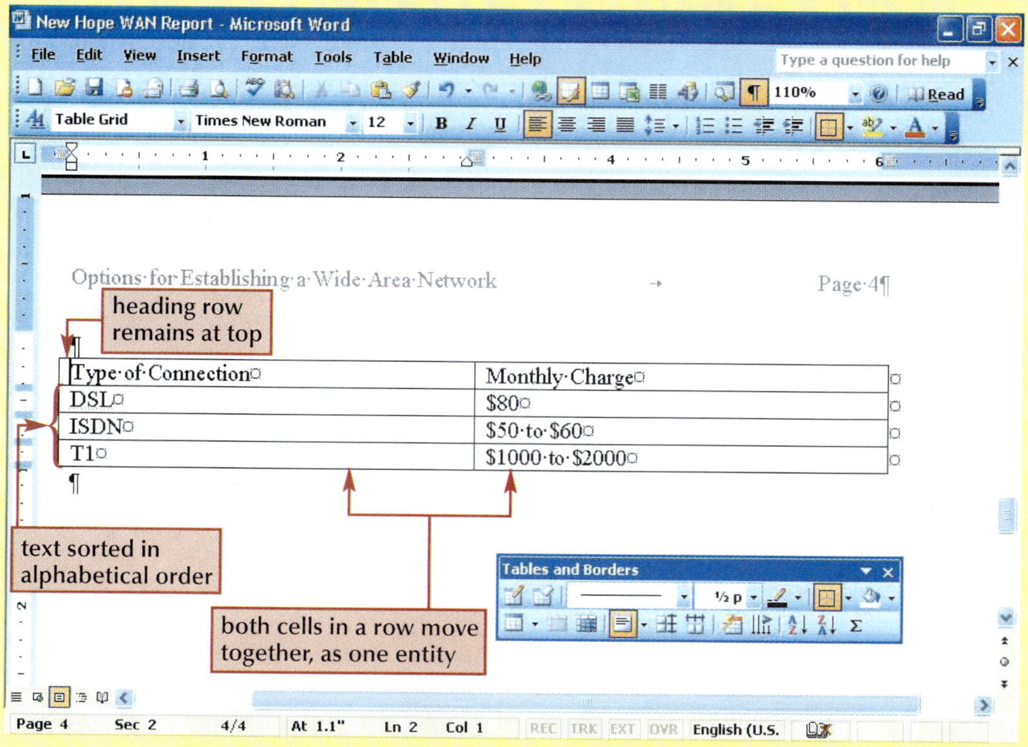

Trouble? If the sort was unsuccessful, immediately click the Undo button on the Standard toolbar, and then repeat Steps 1 and 2.

Caitlyn stops by and asks you to add an "Installation Charge" column. She also would like you to insert a new row with information about a Fractional T1 connection.

Modifying an Existing Table Structure

You will often need to modify a table structure by adding or deleting rows and columns. When you select part of a table, new buttons sometimes appear on the Standard toolbar to help you modify the table structure. For instance, when you select a column, the Insert Columns button appears to help you insert a new column in the table. In most cases, however, you'll find it easiest to use menu commands to add and delete rows and columns, because the menu commands allow you to specify exactly how you want to modify the table. For instance, by using a menu command, you can indicate whether you want to insert a column to the right or left of the selected column. By contrast, the Insert Columns button always inserts a new column to the left of the selected column.

Figure 3-23 summarizes ways to insert or delete rows and columns in a table.

Figure 3-23 Ways to insert or delete table rows and columns

To	Do this
Insert a row within a table	Select the row above or below where you want the row added, click Table on the menu bar, point to Insert, and then click Rows Above or Rows Below. Select the row below where you want the row added, and then click the Insert Rows button on the Standard toolbar.
Insert a row at the end of a table	Position the insertion point in the cell at the far right of the bottom row, then press the Tab key.
Insert a column within a table	Select the column to the right or left of where you want the column added, click Table on the menu bar, point to Insert, then click Columns to the Left or Columns to the Right. Select the column to the right of where you want the column added, then click the Insert Columns button on the Standard toolbar.
Insert a column at the end of a table	Select the rightmost column in the table, click Table on the menu bar, point to Insert, and then click Columns to the Right. Select the end-of-row markers to the right of the table, and then click the Insert Columns button on the Standard toolbar.
Delete a row	Select the row or rows to be deleted including the end-of-row marker(s), click Table on the menu bar, point to Delete, and then click Rows.
Delete a column	Select the column or columns to be deleted, click Table on the menu bar, point to Delete, and then click Columns.

Inserting Columns in a Table

Your first task is to insert a new column between the Type of Connection column and the Monthly Charge column. This column will contain information on the Installation Charge for each WAN option. You need to begin by selecting the column to the left of the location where you want to insert a column.

To insert a column in the table:

1. Click in cell **A1** (which contains the heading "Type of Connection"), and then drag the mouse pointer down until the entire Type of Connection column is selected.
2. Click **Table** on the menu bar, point to **Insert**, and then click **Columns to the Right**. A new column is inserted in the table to the right of the Type of Connection column.

   Note: Word inserts the same number of new columns as are selected. For example, if you had selected two columns in Step 1, Word would have inserted two new columns in the table.
3. Click in the new cell **B1** (the blank cell at the top of the new column), and then enter the **Installation Charge** heading and data shown in Figure 3-24.

Figure 3-24 New Installation Charge column

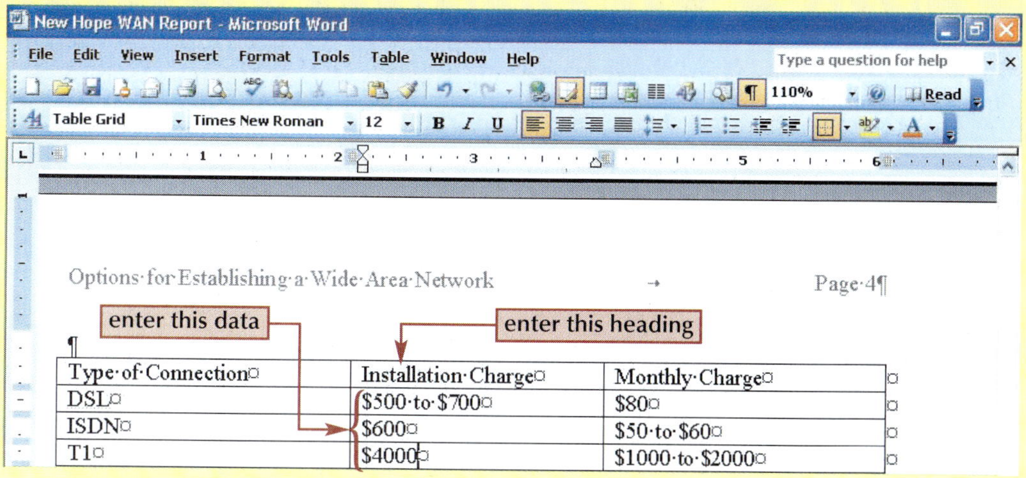

Inserting Rows in a Table

Next, you need to insert a row with information on a more economical type of T1 connection, called a fractional T1 connection. You could insert this row in its alphabetical position in the table (below the DSL row). But it's quicker to add the row to the end of the table, and then resort the table.

To insert a row at the bottom of the table:

1. Click the last cell in the Monthly Charge column (which contains "$1000 to $2000"). The insertion point is now located in the last cell in the table.
2. Press the **Tab** key. A blank row is added to the bottom of the table.

   Trouble? If a blank row is not added to the bottom of the table, click the Undo button on the Standard toolbar. Check to make sure the insertion point is in the rightmost cell of the bottom row, and then press the Tab key.
3. Enter the following information in the new row:
   Type of Connection: **Fractional T1**
   Installation Charge: **$1500**
   Monthly Charge: **$200 to $600**
4. Click anywhere in the Type of Connection column, and then click the **Sort Ascending** button on the Tables and Borders toolbar. The table rows are rearranged in alphabetical order, with the Fractional T1 row positioned below the DSL row, as shown in Figure 3-25.

Figure 3-25 Sorted table with new row

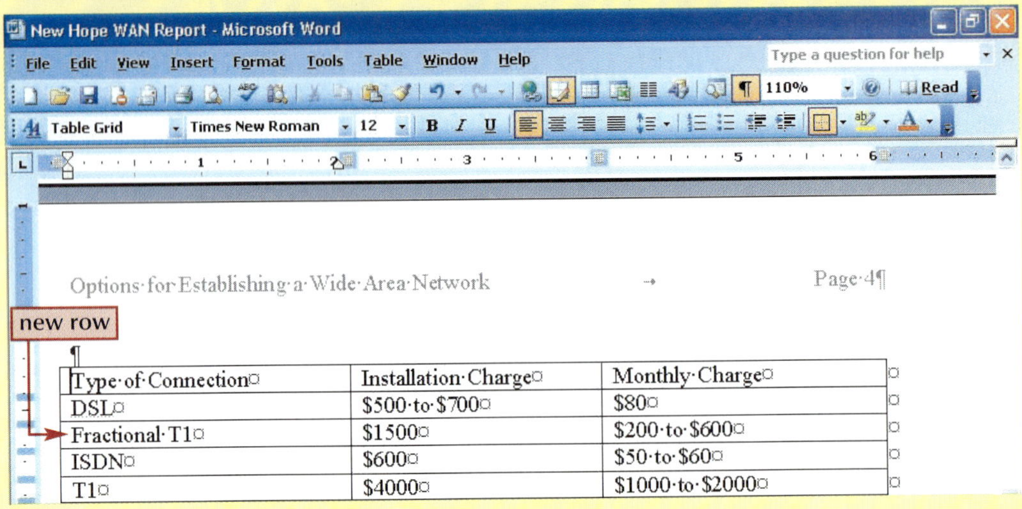

5. Save your work.

After reviewing the table, Caitlyn decides not to include the information on the full T1 connection, because it is far too expensive for New Hope's current budget. She asks you to delete the T1 row.

Deleting Rows and Columns in a Table

With Word, you can delete either the contents of table cells or the structure of the cells themselves. To delete the contents only, you select one or more cells and then press the Delete key. However, to delete both the contents and structure of a selected row or column from the table entirely, you must use one of the methods described earlier in Figure 3-23. Right now you'll use a menu command to delete the T1 row.

To delete a row using the Table menu:

1. Click the selection bar next to the T1 row, at the bottom of the table. The entire T1 row including the end-of-row marker is selected. (Take care to select the T1 row, at the bottom of the table, *not* the Fractional T1 row.)
2. Click **Table** on the menu bar, point to **Delete**, and then click **Rows**. The selected row is deleted from the table. See Figure 3-26.

Table after deleting row

Figure 3-26

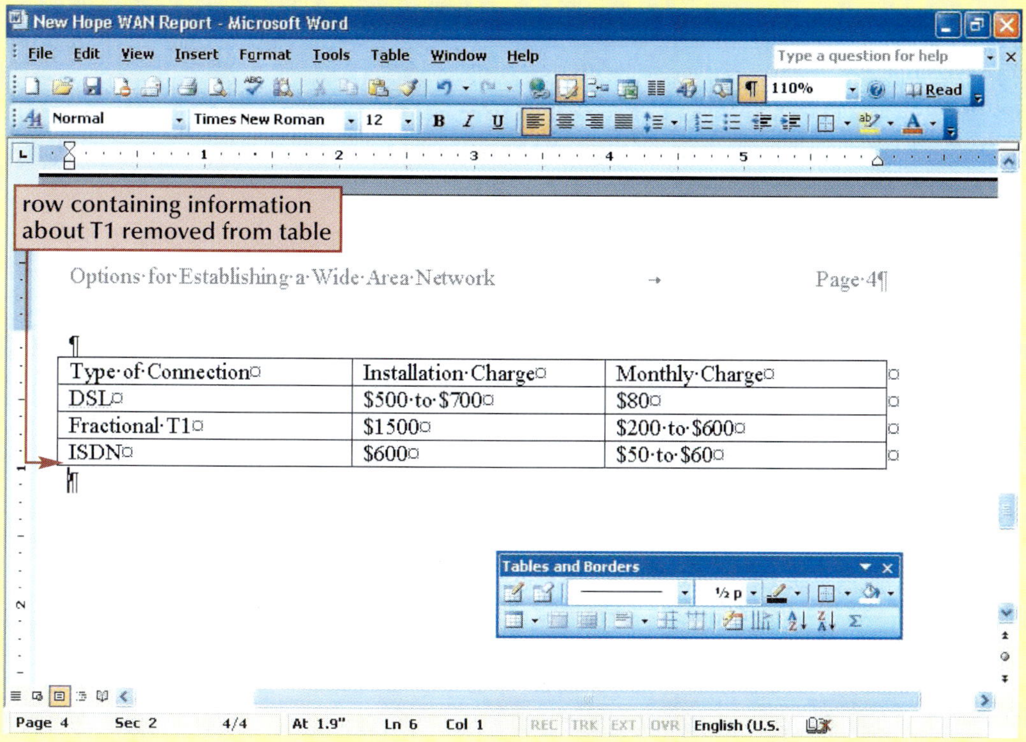

3. Save your work.

Formatting Tables

Word provides a variety of ways to enhance the appearance of the tables you create. You can alter the width of the columns and the height of the rows, or change the alignment of text within the cells or the alignment of the table between the document's left and right margins. You can change the appearance of the table borders, and add a shaded background. You can format an entire table at once using the **Table AutoFormat command** on the Table menu. (You'll have a chance to practice using this command in the Case Problems at the end of this tutorial.) In general, however, making formatting changes individually (using the mouse pointer along with various toolbar buttons and menu commands) gives you more options and more flexibility.

Changing Column Width and Row Height

Sometimes you'll want to adjust the column widths in a table to make the text easier to read. If you want to specify an exact width for a column, you should use the Table Properties command on the Table menu. However, it's usually easiest to drag the column's right border to a new position. Alternately, you can double-click a column border to make the column width adjust automatically to accommodate the widest entry in the column.

The columns in the table you have been working with are too wide for the information they contain. You'll change these widths by dragging the column borders, using the ruler as a guide. Keep in mind that to change the width of a column, you need to drag the column's right border.

To change the width of columns by dragging the borders:

1. Verify that the table is displayed in Print Layout view, and then click anywhere within the table. Verify that no part of the table is selected.
2. Move the pointer over the border between columns A and B (in other words, over the right border of column A, the "Type of Connection" column). The pointer changes to +||+.
3. Press and hold down the **Alt** key and the mouse button. The column widths are displayed in the ruler, as shown in Figure 3-27. (The widths on your computer might differ slightly.)

   Trouble? If the Research task pane opens after you perform Step 3, leave it open until you complete Step 4 and then close it.

Figure 3-27 Column widths displayed in ruler

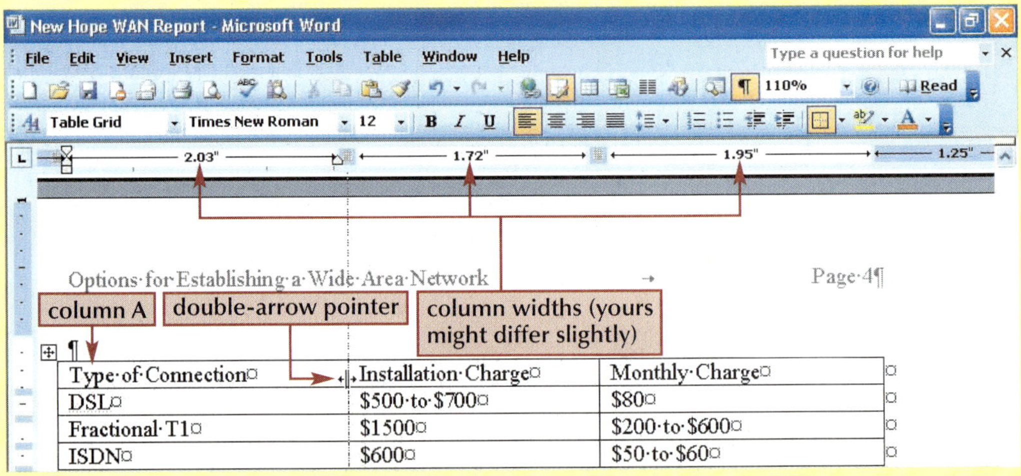

4. While holding down the **Alt** key and the mouse button, drag the pointer to the left until column A is about **1.4** inches wide, and then release the mouse button and the Alt key. As the width of column A decreases, the width of column B (the Installation Charge column) increases. The overall width of the table does not change.

   Trouble? If you can't adjust the column width to exactly 1.4 inches, make it as close to that width as possible.

Now you need to adjust the width of both columns B and C. You could do this by dragging the column border, as you did for column A. But it's much faster to double-click the right border of each column.

To change the width of columns B and C:

1. Position the mouse pointer over the right border of column B until the pointer changes to +||+, and then double-click the right border of column B (the Installation Charge column). The column shrinks, leaving just enough room for the widest entry in the column (the column heading "Installation Charge").
2. Repeat this procedure to adjust the width of column C (the Monthly Charge column). All three columns in the table are now just wide enough to accommodate the column headings.

You can change the height of rows by dragging a border. You'll make row 1 (the header row) taller so it is more prominent.

To change the height of row 1:

1. Position the pointer over the bottom border of the header row. The pointer changes to .
2. Press and hold down the **Alt** key and the mouse button. The row heights are displayed in the vertical ruler.
3. While holding down the **Alt** key, drag the pointer down until row 1 is about **0.45** inches high, then release the mouse button and the Alt key. Notice that the height of the other rows in the table is not affected by this change. See Figure 3-28.

   Trouble? If the Research task pane opens, close it.

Figure 3-28 **Table with narrower columns and a wider heading row**

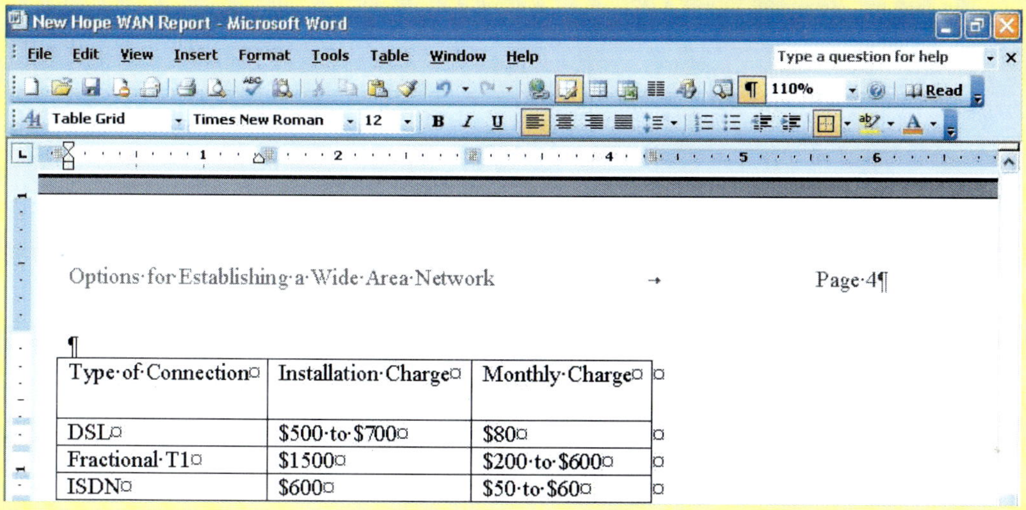

Aligning Text Within Cells

Aligning the text within the cells of a table makes the information easier to read. For example, aligning a column of numbers or percentages along the right margin helps the reader to compare the values quickly. At the same time, centering a row of headings makes a table more visually appealing. You can align text within the active cell the same way you do other text—with the alignment buttons on the Formatting toolbar. However, the Alignment buttons on the Tables and Borders toolbar provide more options.

Caitlyn would like you to align the data in the Installation Charge and Monthly Charge columns along the right side of the columns. The table also would look better with the headings centered. You'll begin by selecting and formatting all of columns B and C. For simple left and right alignment, you can use the Align buttons on the Formatting toolbar. For more sophisticated options, such as centering text horizontally and vertically in a cell, use the Align button on the Tables and Borders toolbar.

To right-align the numerical data and center the headings:

1. Move the pointer to the top of column B until the pointer changes to ⬇. Press and hold the left mouse button, and then drag right to select columns B and C.
2. Click the **Align Right** button on the Formatting toolbar. The column heads and numbers line up along the right edges of the cells.

   Notice that in the process of formatting columns B and C, you right-aligned two of the headings ("Installation Charge" and "Monthly Charge"). You will reformat those headings in the next three steps when you center the text in row 1 both horizontally and vertically in each cell.
3. Click the selection bar next to row 1. All of row 1 is selected.
4. Click the **Align** list arrow on the Tables and Borders toolbar to display a palette of nine alignment options.
5. Click the **Align Center** button in the middle of the palette. The text is centered both horizontally and vertically in the row.
6. Click anywhere in the table to deselect the row, and then save your work. See Figure 3-29.

Figure 3-29 Table with newly aligned text

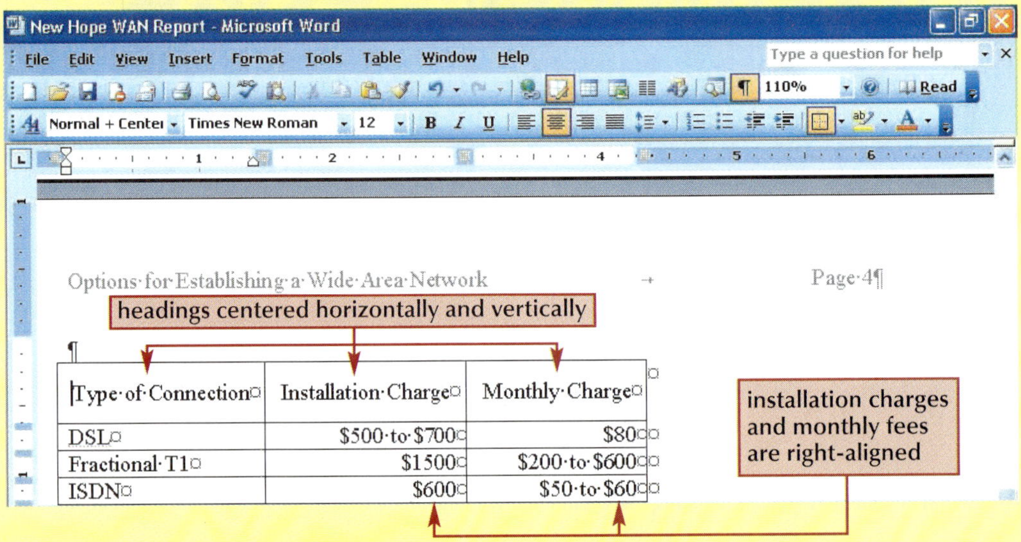

Trouble? If more than just the heading row is centered, click the Undo button on the Standard toolbar, and then repeat Steps 3 through 6.

Changing Borders

While gridlines and borders may seem to be the same things, they are different elements of a table. Gridlines are light gray lines that indicate the structure of the table on the screen but do not show on the printed page. Borders are darker lines overlaying the gridlines, which do show on the printed page. When you create a table using the Insert Table button, Word automatically applies a thin black border, so you can't actually see the underlying gridlines.

After you have created a table, you can add new borders or erase existing borders by using the buttons on the Tables and Borders toolbar. You can modify an existing border by changing its **line weight** (its thickness). You can also choose a different **line style**—for instance, you can change a single straight-line border to a triple dotted line. If you prefer, you can create a table without any borders at all. You can also turn off the underlying gridlines by using the Hide Gridlines command on the Table menu. (Depending on how your computer is set up, gridlines might be hidden by default.)

Altering Table Borders

Reference Window

- Select the cell (or cells) whose borders you want to change.
- Click the Line Weight list arrow on the Tables and Borders toolbar, and then select a line weight.
- Click the Line Style list arrow on the Tables and Borders toolbar, and then select a line style.
- Click the Borders list arrow on the Tables and Borders toolbar, and then select a position for the new border.

or

- Use the Draw Table pointer to click the parts of the table that you want formatted with the selected line weight and line style.

To modify the table's borders:

1. Click the selection bar to the left of row 1 to select the heading row.
2. Click the **Line Weight** list arrow on the Tables and Borders toolbar, and then click **2 ¼ pt**. Next, you will examine the options available in the Line Style list. Currently, a single straight-line border is selected.
3. Click the **Line Style** list arrow on the Tables and Borders toolbar, and then scroll to view the various options. Note that you can remove borders (without removing the underlying gridlines) by selecting the No Border option. Caitlyn prefers a simple border, so you decide not to change the current selection.

   Trouble? If a single, straight-line border is not selected in the Line Style list, click the first line style under "No Border" now.
4. Press the **Esc** key. The Line Style list closes. You have selected a single straight-line border, with a thickness of 2 ¼ points.
5. Click the **Outside Border** list arrow on the Tables and Borders toolbar. (The exact name shown in the ScreenTip for this list arrow will vary, depending on what option is currently selected in the list. For example, it may currently be called the All Borders list arrow instead of the Outside Border list arrow.) A palette of options appears. You want to insert a thick border at the bottom of Row 1, so you need to use the Bottom Border option.
6. Click the **Bottom Border** option (in the bottom row of the Borders palette, third from the left). The new border style is applied to the bottom border of row 1.
7. Click anywhere in the table to deselect the row. See Figure 3-30.

Figure 3-30 Row 1 with new border

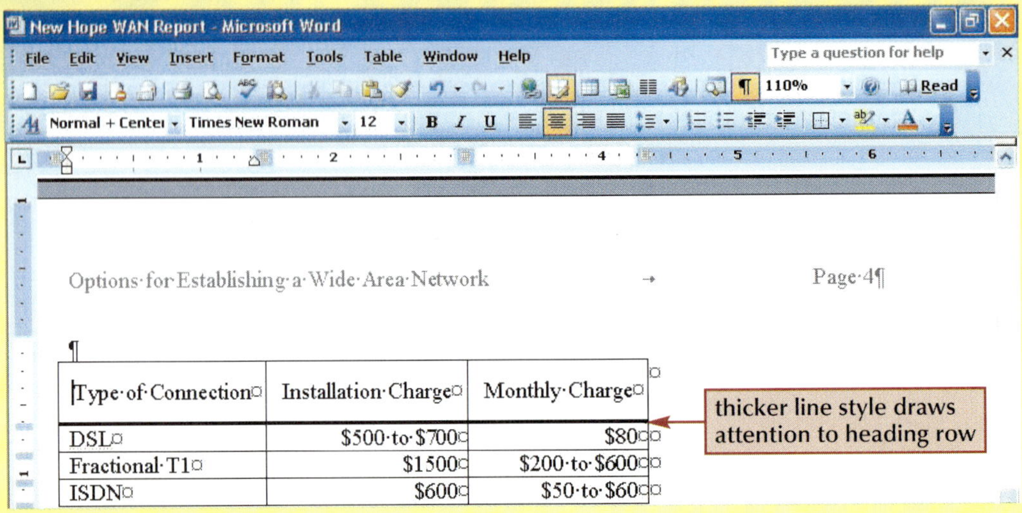

8. Save your work.

Changing the borders has made the table more attractive. You'll finish formatting the table by adding shading to the cells containing the headings.

Adding Shading

Adding **shading** (a gray or colored background) is useful in tables when you want to emphasize headings, totals, or other important items. Generally, when you add shading to a table, you also need to bold the shaded text to make it easier to read.

You will now add a light gray shading to the heading row and then format the headings in bold.

To add shading to the heading row and change the headings to bold:

1. Click the selection bar to the left of row 1 to select the heading row.
2. Click the **Shading Color** list arrow on the Tables and Borders toolbar. A palette of shading options opens.
3. Point to the fifth gray square from the left, in the top row. The ScreenTip "Gray-15%" appears.
4. Click the **Gray-15%** square. A light gray background appears in the heading row. Now you need to format the text in bold to make the headings stand out from the shading.
5. Click the **Bold** button **B** on the Formatting toolbar to make the headings bold. The wider letters take up more space, so Word breaks one or more of the headings into two lines within row 1.

   Trouble? If any of the headings break incorrectly (for example, if the last "n" in "Installation" moves to the next line), you might need to widen columns to accommodate the bold letters. Drag the column borders as necessary to adjust the column widths so no word is split incorrectly.

6. Click in the table to deselect row 1. Your table should look like Figure 3-31, although the line breaks in your heading row may differ.

Figure 3-31 Row with shading and bold headings

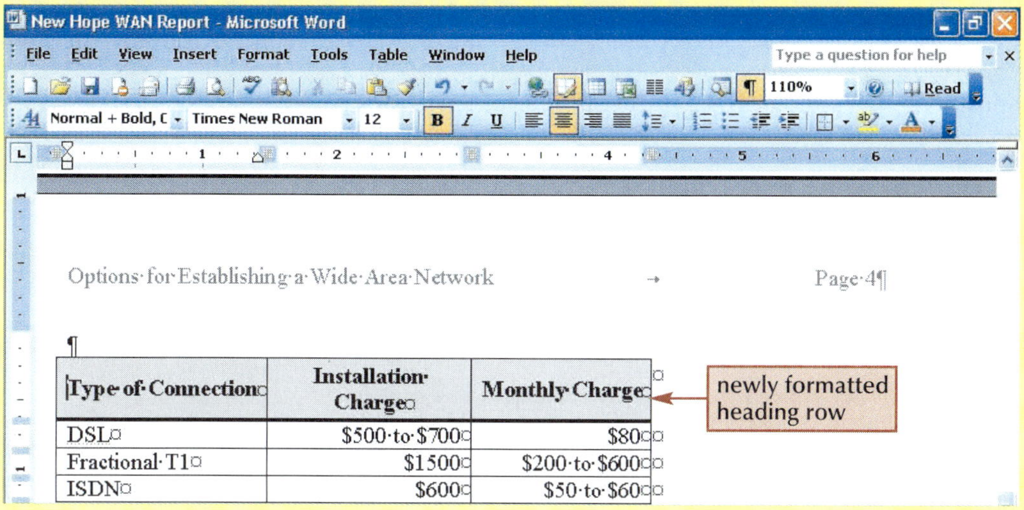

7. Save your changes.

Centering a Table

If a table doesn't fill the entire page width, you can center it between the left and right margins. The Center button on the Formatting toolbar centers only text within each selected cell. It does not center the entire table across the page. To center a table across the page (between the left and right margins), you need to use the Table Properties command.

Caitlyn thinks the table would look better if it was centered between the left and right margins.

To center the table across the page:

1. Click anywhere in the table, click **Table** on the menu bar, and then click **Table Properties**. The Table Properties dialog box opens.
2. Click the **Table** tab, if necessary.
3. In the Alignment section, click the **Center** option. See Figure 3-32.

Figure 3-32 Table Tab of the Table Properties dialog box

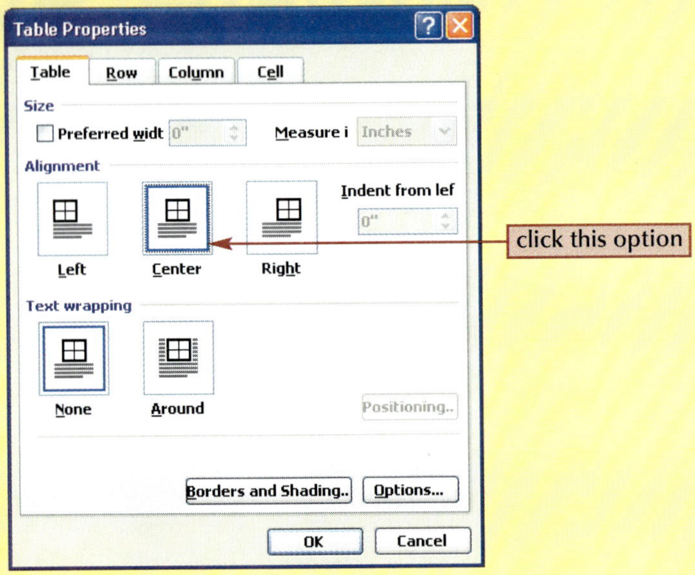

4. Click the **OK** button. The table centers between the left and right margins.
5. Save your work, and then close the Tables and Borders toolbar.

Now that you're finished with the table, you need to review the entire report quickly to make sure it requires no further work. To do that, you'll use Reading Layout view.

Reviewing a Document in Reading Layout View

As you've already seen, when you need to check the overall formatting in a document, it's useful to use the Whole Page zoom setting in Print Layout view, or the Print Preview window. But when you are only interested in the content of the document—that is, the text, tables and graphics, regardless of how they are laid out on the page—it's best to use **Reading Layout view**. This view allows you to peruse a document quickly, displaying the entire content of a page in a single screen, in a font that is large enough to read easily. Reading Layout view is designed to let you review a document online, without paying attention to margins and other page layout issues. When you're ready to concern yourself again with the document layout and formatting, you should return to Print Layout view.

Caitlyn asks you to skim the report now in Reading Layout view, to ensure that the document is completely finished.

To review the report in Reading Layout view:

1. Click the **Reading Layout** button in the lower-left corner of the document window, just to the left of the horizontal scroll bar. Exactly what you see in Reading Layout view will depend on the choices made by the last person to use Reading Layout view on your computer, though you should see the Reading Layout toolbar below the menu bar. You will probably see the Reviewing toolbar too.
2. Scroll up to display the top of the document, click the **Allow Multiple Pages** button to select it (if it is not already selected), and then verify that the **Actual Page** button is *not* selected. (If it is selected, click it to deselect it now.) Finally, verify that the **Thumbnails** button is *not* selected. (If it is selected, click it to deselect it now.) Your screen should resemble Figure 3-33. Note that instead of dividing a document into pages, Reading Layout view divides a document into screens. The content of the report fills up multiple screens. Only the first two of these screens are currently displayed.

Report Displayed in Reading Layout view **Figure 3-33**

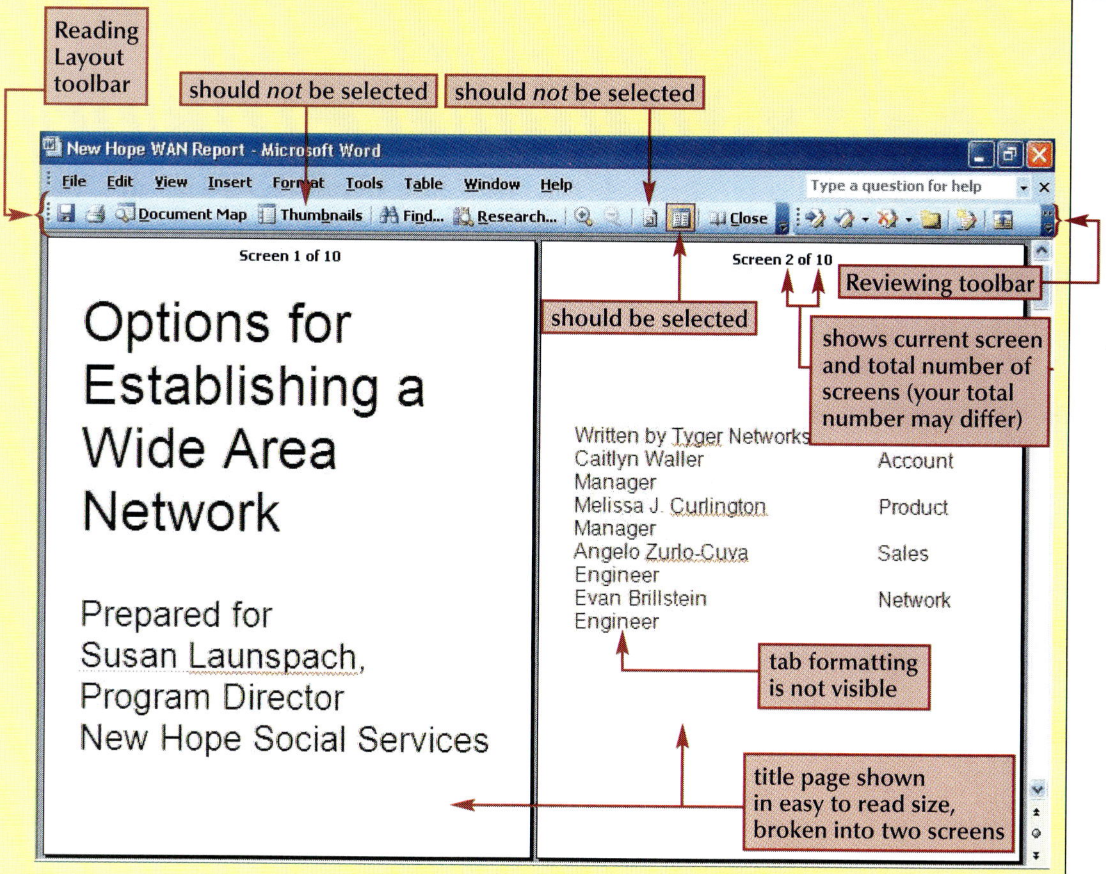

3. Click the **down arrow** button on the vertical scroll bar. Screen 2 is now displayed on the left, with screen 3 on the right.
4. Continue scrolling through the document until you have reviewed all the screens, and then return to the beginning of the document.
5. Click screen 1 to move the insertion point there.
6. Click the **Increase Text Size** button on the Reading Layout toolbar three times. Notice how the text increases in size, making it easier to read. The line breaks change to accommodate the larger sized text. These changes affect only how the text is displayed on the screen. When you return to Print Layout view later, you will see that the document has retained its original formatting.
7. Click the **Decrease Text Size** button on the Reading Layout toolbar three times to reverse the change made in Step 6. When you finish, the Decrease Text Size button should be a light shade of blue, indicating that the text cannot be made any smaller.
8. Click the **Close** button on the Reading Layout toolbar. The document returns to Print Layout view.
9. Scroll down and verify that the document's formatting has not changed.

To verify that the document's page layout settings haven't changed, you can review the document in the Print Preview window. You'll do that next, and then print a copy of the full report for Caitlyn.

To preview and print the report:

1. Click the **Print Preview** button on the Standard toolbar to open the Print Preview window.
2. Use the **Multiple Pages** button on the Print Preview toolbar to display all four pages of the report. Verify that the table is centered horizontally on the page, and that the title page is centered vertically on the page.
3. Click the **Print** button on the Print Preview toolbar to print the report, and then close the document.

You now have a hard copy of the New Hope report including the table, which summarizes the costs for creating a WAN. Your four-page report should look like Figure 3-34. You give the report to Caitlyn, so that she can add a brief introduction to the table.

Figure 3-34

New Hope WAN report

Options for Establishing a Wide Area Network

Prepared for
Susan Launspach, Program Director
New Hope Social Services

Written by Tyger Networks:

Caitilyn Waller	Account Manager
Melissa J. Curlington	Product Manager
Angelo Zurlo-Cuva	Sales Engineer
Evan Brillstein	Network Engineer

Executive Summary

This report presents options for connecting the three computer networks run by New Hope Social Services. First we describe the networks in the Madison, Janesville, and Milwaukee offices, and then we explain the options for integrating these networks into a larger structure, known as a Wide Area Network (WAN). Finally, in a table at the end of this report, we summarize the costs for implementing various WAN connections.

New Hope's Existing LANs

The term Local Area Network (LAN) refers to a network of computers and other devices (such as printers) that are geographically close to each other (for example, on the same floor of a building). A LAN is managed via a special computer known as a server. The majority of the computers on the three New Hope LANs are used to run Microsoft Office applications. The network operating system on the Janesville and Madison servers has been upgraded to Windows XP, while the Milwaukee server continues to run Windows 2000 Server. Because the three LANs are separate, a social worker in one office cannot directly access data stored on a computer in one of the other two offices.

WAN Technology

To allow interoffice data access, we propose connecting the three LANs, thereby creating a Wide Area Network (WAN). A WAN is a network that spans a geographical distance (between buildings, cities, or even countries). Strictly speaking, a WAN consists of one link between two points. It does not usually connect one site to several other sites in the way that a LAN connects multiple computers. Thus, to connect the three New Hope LANs, we would need to establish multiple WAN links. The following sections describe various options for creating these links. The options differ greatly in cost, ease of implementation, and throughput (that is, the rate at which data can be transferred).

Public Switched Telephone Network (PSTN)

The term Public Switched Telephone Network (PSTN) refers to the network of telephone lines that services residential neighborhoods and businesses. Originally, the PSTN was composed of analog lines that were developed to carry voice signals. These days, the majority of PSTN lines provide faster digital transmission. The New Hope LANs currently use the PSTN system for occasional dial-up connections to the Internet.

Integrated Services Digital Network (ISDN)

In an Integrated Services Digital Network (ISDN) connection, data travels over digital lines maintained by the local telephone carrier. Typically, an ISDN connection is a dial-up connection, rather than a continuously available connection. Because digital lines can carry voice and data

signals simultaneously, connecting the three New Hope offices via ISDN lines would make it unnecessary to pay for separate phone lines to support faxes, modems, and voice calls. Two types of ISDN connections are commonly used: Basic Rate ISDN (BRI) and Primary Rate ISDN (PRI). The cost of using BRI at the Madison and Janesville office is $50 per month, while the cost for the Milwaukee office is $60 per month. An additional, one-time installation fee for each site would range between $400 and $600. PRI connections are much faster BRI, but are significantly more expensive.

Digital Subscriber Lines (DSL)

Digital Subscriber Lines (DSL) is a type of connection that uses advanced data techniques to achieve even greater throughput than ISDN. DSL runs on leased lines that are maintained by the local telephone carrier. DSL uses a continuously available connection, known as a dedicated line. Unlike ISDN, DSL is offered by New Hope's current carrier. DSL generally costs more than ISDN, but less than T1 lines (described below). A high-speed DSL connection costs approximately $80 a month. In addition, each New Hope site would have to purchase or rent a DSL modem. The major drawback to DSL is the time it takes for the telephone carrier to establish service. The current waiting time is at least six months. The one-time installation fee for each site is approximately $500 to $700.

T-Carrier Line

Like DSL, a T-Carrier line is a permanent dedicated connection that is maintained by the local telephone carrier. T-carrier transmission uses a technology called multiplexing, which makes it possible to carry multiple channels of voice, data, video, or other signals. The most common type of T-carrier connection for medium to small organizations is a T1 line. Such a connection provides excellent throughput and security. Compared to the other options, a T1 connection is extremely expensive, costing as much as $4000 to install, plus an additional monthly fee of $1000 to $2000. However, a fractional T1 lease, which uses a few channels on a T1 line, is a more economical alternative. Monthly fees for a fractional lease range from $200 to $600 a month. The one-time installation fee for each site is approximately $1,500.

Type of Connection	Installation Charge	Monthly Charge
DSL	$500 to $700	$80
Fractional T1	$1500	$200 to $600
ISDN	$600	$50 to $60

Review

Session 3.2 Quick Check

1. Define the following terms in your own words:
   a. line weight
   b. line style
   c. gridline
   d. shading
2. In what order would the following numbers appear in a table if you sorted them in ascending numerical order: 26, 12, 65, 44?
3. Explain how to add a row to the bottom of a table.
4. What's the fastest way to modify a column to accommodate the widest entry in the column?
5. Explain how to adjust the height of a row in a table.
6. Explain how to alter the border on the bottom of a heading row.
7. How do you center a table between the left and right margins?

Review

Tutorial Summary

In this tutorial you learned how to set tab stops, divide a document into sections, center text on a page between the top and bottom margins, create a header, and create a table. You also learned how to display the Tables and Borders toolbar and how to sort the rows of a table. Finally, you learned how to add and delete rows and columns, how to format a table to improve its appearance, and how to review a document in Reading Layout view.

Key Terms

Bar tab	heading row	shading
border	Left tab	sort
cell	line style	tab
Center tab	line weight	tab stop
Decimal tab	page break	table
First Line Indent tab	Reading Layout view	Table AutoFormat command
footer	Right tab	Tables and Borders toolbar
gridlines	section	tab-stop alignment style
Hanging Indent tab	section break	vertical alignment
header		

Practice

Apply the skills you learned in the tutorial using the same case scenario.

Review Assignments

Data File needed for the Review Assignments: Trouble.doc

Susan Launspach, the program director at New Hope Social Services, has contacted Caitlyn Waller about another issue related to the agency's local area networks (LANs). Since last January, employees at the Madison office have experienced a number of problems, including malfunctioning printers and difficulty retrieving e-mail. Susan would like to hire Tyger Networks to resolve the network problems, a process known as troubleshooting. To secure the necessary funding, she needs a report outlining the basic issues, which she can then distribute to New Hope's board of directors. Working with a task force at

Tyger Networks, Caitlyn has completed a draft of this report. It's your job to format the report and add a table at the end. When you're finished, she would like you to create a separate document that lists only the new equipment recommended by Tyger Networks. Complete the following:

1. Open the file **Trouble** located in the Tutorial.03\Review folder included with your Data Files, and then save it as **Troubleshooting Report** in the same folder.
2. Check your screen to make sure your settings match those in the tutorial. Display nonprinting characters as necessary and switch to Print Layout view.
3. Select the list of task force members and their titles, and then insert a left tab stop 2.5 inches from the left margin.
4. Replace "Evan Brillstein" with your name.
5. Divide the document into two sections. Insert a section break so that the executive summary begins on a new page.
6. Vertically align the first section of the document using the Center alignment option, and view the results in Print Preview.
7. Create a header for section 2 that aligns your name at the left margin and centers the page number preceded by the word "Page." Don't forget to deselect the Link to Previous button. (*Hint*: To center the page number, use the second tab stop.) Close the Header and Footer toolbar, and then save your work.
8. Insert a page break at the end of the document.
9. Create the table shown in Figure 3-35.

Figure 3-35

Troubleshooting Option	Explanation	Cost
Cable Checker	3 devices for each office, at $225 a piece	$675
Onsite Troubleshooting	40 hours of onsite troubleshooting, at $120 an hour	$4800
Cable Tester	1 device to be shared among the three offices	$1400

10. Display the Tables and Borders toolbar.
11. Sort the table by the contents of the Troubleshooting Option column in ascending order.
12. Insert a new row just below the Cable Tester row, and then enter the following information into the new row:
    Troubleshooting option: Onsite Training
    Explanation: Informational seminar for all Madison employees
    Cost: $300
13. Modify the widths of columns A and C to accommodate only the widest entry in each, and then right-align the data in the Cost column.
14. Increase the height of the heading row and format it appropriately using shading and boldface. Center the headings vertically and horizontally in their cells.
15. Select the entire table, select the 2 ¼ pt line weight, select the single line style, and then use the Outside Border option in the Borders list box. Select the heading row and add a double ½-point border at the bottom of the heading row.
16. Center the table between the page's left and right margins and then save your work.

17. Use the Table Move handle to select the entire table. Copy the table, open a new, blank document, and paste a copy of the table into the new document. Use the Delete command on the Table menu to delete the Onsite Training and Onsite Troubleshooting rows. Adjust border formatting as needed. Save the document as **Equipment List** in the Tutorial.03\Review folder. Close the document.
18. Close the Tables and Borders toolbar.
19. Save your work, review it in Reading Layout view, preview the report, and then print it.
20. Close the document.

Apply

Apply the skills you learned to create an annual report for a small bookstore.

Case Problem 1

Data File needed for this Case Problem: SunRep.doc

Sun Porch Bookstore Annual Report As manager of Sun Porch Bookstore in San Diego, California, you must submit an annual report to the board of directors. Complete the following:

1. Open the file **SunRep** located in the Tutorial.03\Cases folder included with your Data Files, and then save it as **Sun Porch Report** in the same folder.
2. Check your screen to make sure your settings match those in the tutorials. Switch to Print Layout view.
3. Divide the document into two sections. Begin section 2 with the introduction on a new page.
4. Format the title ("Annual Report") and the subtitle ("Sun Porch Bookstore") using the font and font size of your choice. Center the first section vertically. Select the title and subtitle, and center them horizontally. Note that you can combine horizontal and vertical alignment styles. Use the Print Preview window to check your work.
5. Create a header for section 2 that aligns your name to the left margin, and "Sun Porch Annual Report" to the right margin. Click the Link to Previous button to deselect it.

Explore

6. While in Header and Footer view, click the Switch between Header and Footer button to switch to the footer area for section 2. Press the Tab key to move the insertion point to the center tab stop, and then type the word "Page" followed by a space and the page number (using the Insert Page Number button on the Header and Footer toolbar). Insert a space, type the word "of", insert another space, and then click the Insert Number of Pages button on the Header and Footer toolbar to insert the total number of pages in the document. Click the Link to Previous button to deselect it, if necessary. Close Header and Footer view when you are finished.

Explore

7. Select the list of members under the heading "Board of Directors," click Format on the menu bar, and then click Tabs. To insert a tab stop with a dot leader at the 4-inch mark, type 4 in the Tab stop position text box, verify that the Left option button is selected in the Alignment section, and then click the 2..... option button in the Leader section. Click Set. Notice the Clear button, which you can use to clear the tab stop you just set, and the Clear All button, which you can use to clear all the custom tab stops (that is, tab stops other than the default ones) from a document. Click OK to close the Tabs dialog box.
8. Insert a page break at the end of the document, and then insert a table consisting of four rows and three columns.
9. Insert the headings "Name," "Title," and "Duties." Fill in the rows with the relevant information about the store personnel who are mentioned by name in the "Store Management and Personnel" section. Add new rows as needed.
10. Adjust the table column widths so the information is presented attractively.

11. Increase the height of the heading row, use the Tables and Borders toolbar to center the column headings horizontally and vertically, and then bold them.
12. Insert a row in the middle of the table, add your name to the list as another assistant manager, and then assign yourself some duties. Adjust the column widths as needed.
13. Format the heading row with a light gray shading of your choice, and then change the outside border of the table to a single 2 ¼-point line weight.
14. Center the table on the page.
15. Save and preview the document. Close the Tables and Borders toolbar. Review the document in Reading Layout view, print it, and then close the document.

Apply

Apply skills you learned to create a report summarizing information on a European tour.

Case Problem 2

Data File needed for this Case Problem: Tour.doc

Top Flight Travel's "Masterpiece Tour" Report Each year Top Flight Travel sponsors a "Masterpiece" tour, which shepherds travelers through a two-week, whirlwind tour of the artistic masterpieces of Europe. The tour director has just completed a report summarizing the most recent tour. It's your job to format the report, which includes one table. Complete the following:

1. Open the file named **Tour** located in the Tutorial.03\Cases folder included with your Data Files, and then save it as **Masterpiece Tour Report** in the same folder.
2. Check your screen to make sure your settings match those in the tutorials. Switch to Print Layout view.
3. Replace "Your Name" in the first page with your first and last name.
4. Divide the document into two sections. Begin the second section on a new page, with the summary that starts "This report summarizes and evaluates."
5. Vertically align the first section using the Center alignment option.
6. Create a header for section 2 only that contains the centered text "Top Flight Travel." (*Hint*: To center text in the header, use the second tab stop. If necessary, deselect the Link to Previous button before you begin.) Format the header text using italic and the font size of your choice.

Explore

7. On the Header and Footer toolbar, click the Switch Between Header and Footer button to move to the footer area of the document. Using the same techniques you used to create a header in the tutorial, create a footer for section 2 only that aligns "Evaluation Report" to the left margin and the date to the right margin. (*Hint*: Deselect the Link to Previous button if necessary, and then use the Insert Date button on the Header and Footer toolbar to insert the date.) Close Header and Footer view.

Explore

8. Display the Tables and Borders toolbar, and turn off the Draw Table pointer if it is active. In the table, select the text in column A (the left column), bold the text, and then click the Change Text Direction button (on the Tables and Borders toolbar) twice so that text is formatted vertically (that is, the text reads from bottom to top). Adjust the width of column A to accommodate the newly rotated text.
9. Adjust the other column width so it is approximately 5″ wide.
10. Delete the blank row 2.
11. Format column A with a light colored shading of your choice.
12. Change the border around column A to 2 ¼-point line weight. Adjust the row heights, if necessary, to display each row heading in one line.
13. Save and preview the document. Close the Tables and Borders toolbar.
14. Review the document in Reading Layout view, print it, and then close the document.

Challenge

Go beyond what you've learned to convert text into a table and then use other advanced table commands to enhance the table.

Case Problem 3

Data Files needed for this Case Problem: Contacts.doc and Budget.doc

Contact List for Flower Box Bakery Ken Yamamoto recently opened Flower Box Bakery, a wholesale bakery catering to upscale cafes and tea shops in suburban St. Louis. He has just acquired a list of potential sales contacts from the local chamber of commerce via e-mail. The information consists of names, phone numbers, and managers for a number of new cafes and restaurants in the St. Louis area. The information is formatted as simple text, with the pieces of information separated by commas. Ken asks you to convert this text into a table and then format the table to make it easy to read. When you're finished, he needs you to sum a column of numbers in his Advertising Budget table. Complete the following:

1. Open the file named **Contacts** located in the Tutorial.03\Cases folder included with your Data Files, and then save it as **Sales Contacts** in the same folder. Check your screen to make sure your settings match those in the tutorials.
2. **Explore** Select the entire document, click Table on the menu bar, point to Convert, and then click Text to Table. In the Convert Text to Table dialog box, make sure the settings indicate that the table should have three columns. Select the AutoFit to contents option button to ensure that columns are sized appropriately, select the Commas option button, and then click the OK button. Word converts the list into a table.
3. Replace the name "Enrique Mendoza" with your first and last name.
4. Insert a new row at the top of the table, and then insert appropriate column headings.
5. **Explore** When you need to format a table quickly, you can allow Word's AutoFormat command to do the work for you. Click anywhere in the table, click Table on the menu bar, and then click Table AutoFormat to open the Table AutoFormat dialog box. Scroll down the Table styles list box to see the available options. Click options that interest you, and observe the sample tables in the Preview box. Note that you can deselect the check boxes in the "Apply special formats to" section to remove boldface or shading from columns or rows that don't require it. Select a table style that you think is appropriate for the Contacts table, deselect check boxes as you see fit, and then click the Apply button.
6. Sort the table alphabetically by column A.
7. **Explore** Place the pointer over the Table Resize handle, just outside the lower-right corner of the table. Drag the double-arrow pointer to increase the height and width of each cell to a size of your choice. Notice that all the parts of the table increase proportionally.
8. Save your work, preview the table, print it, and then close the document.
9. Open the file **Budget** located in the Tutorial.03\Cases folder included with your Data Files, and then save it as **Advertising Budget** in the same folder. If necessary, open the Tables and Borders toolbar.
10. **Explore** Select the cell containing the word "Total" and the blank cell to its right. Click the Merge Cells button on the Tables and Borders toolbar. The two cells are merged into one. Format the word "Total" so that it aligns on the right side of the new, larger cell.
11. **Explore** Click the blank cell to the right of the Total cell, and then click the AutoSum button on the Tables and Borders toolbar. Word automatically sums the costs in the third column and displays the total ($400.00) in the selected cell.
12. **Explore** Change the cost of the Missouri Monthly advertisement to $250, click the cell containing the total ($400.00), and then click the AutoSum button again. Word updates the total.
13. Save your work, preview the document, and then close it.

Create

Use your table skills to create the camp brochure shown in Figure 3-36.

Case Problem 4

There are no Data Files needed for this Case Problem.

Brochure for Camp Winnemac Angela Freedman is the publicity director for Camp Winnemac, a sleep-away camp for girls located in Northern Michigan. She asks you to create an informational brochure announcing the dates for Camp Winnemac's two summer sessions. She gives you the sketch in Figure 3-36. In the following steps, use Word table features to structure the information in the sketch:

Figure 3-36

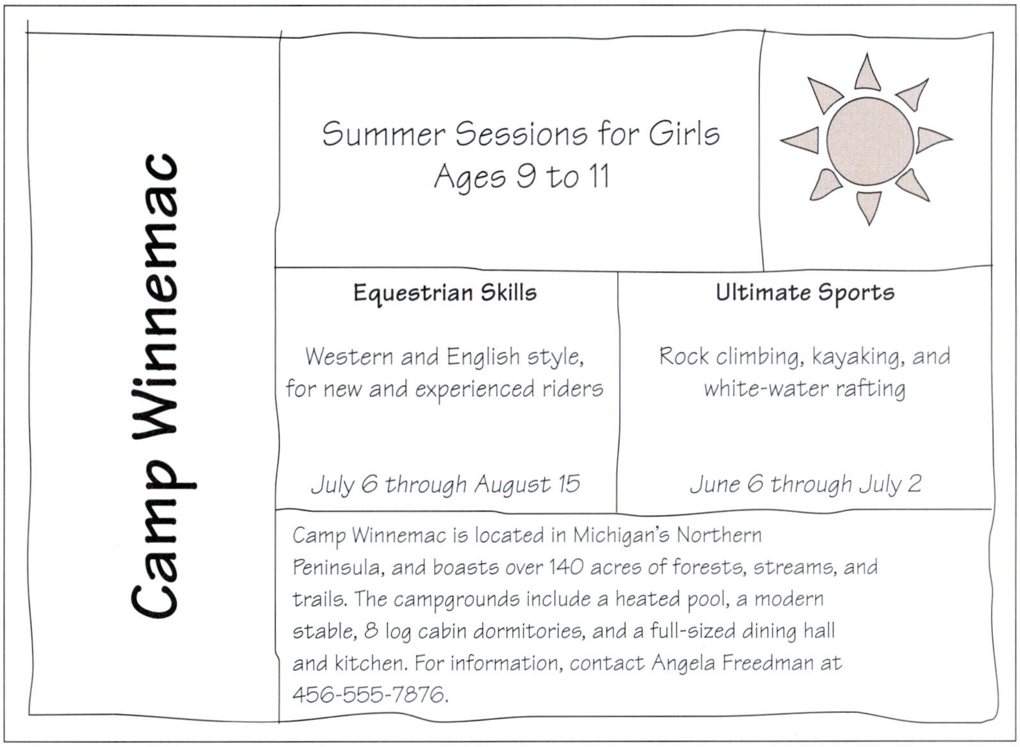

1. Open a new, blank document, and save it as **Camp Winnemac** in the Tutorial.03\Cases folder included with your Data Files.
2. If necessary, switch to Print Layout view, display rulers, and then open the Tables and Borders toolbar.

Explore

3. Click the Draw Table button on the Tables and Borders toolbar, if necessary, to select the button and change the pointer to the Draw Table pointer. Select a single-line line style, with a line weight of 1 1/2 points. Click in the upper-left corner of the document (near the paragraph mark), and then drag down and to the right to draw a rectangle about 5.5 inches wide and 3.5 inches high.

Explore

4. Continue to use the Draw Table pointer to draw the columns and rows shown in Figure 3-36. For example, to draw the column border for the "Camp Winnemac" column, click at the top of the rectangle, where you want the column to begin, and drag down to the bottom of the rectangle. Use the same technique to draw rows. If you make a mistake, use the Undo button. To delete a border, click the Eraser button on the Tables and Borders toolbar, click the border you want to erase, and then click the Eraser button again to turn it off. Don't expect to draw the table perfectly the first time. You may have to practice a while until you become comfortable with the Draw Table pointer, but once you can use it well, you will find it a helpful tool for creating complex tables. Click the Draw Table button on the toolbar again to turn off the Draw Table pointer.

Explore

5. In the left column, type the text "Camp Winnemac". With the pointer still in that cell, click the Change Text Direction button (on the Tables and Borders toolbar) twice to position the text vertically. Format the text in 26-point Times New Roman, and then center it in the cell using the Align Center option on the Tables and Borders toolbar. (*Hint*: You will probably have to adjust and readjust the row and column borders throughout this project, until all the elements of the table are positioned properly.)
6. Type the remaining text, as shown in Figure 3-36. Replace the name "Angela Freedman" with your own name. Use bold and italic as shown in Figure 3-36 to draw attention to key elements. Use the font styles, font sizes, and alignment options you think appropriate.

Explore

7. Click the Drawing button on the Standard toolbar to display the Drawing toolbar. Now you can insert the Camp Winnemac logo in the upper-right cell, using one of the tools on the Drawing toolbar. Click the upper-right cell, which at this point should be blank. Click the AutoShapes button on the Drawing toolbar, point to Basic Shapes, and then click the Sun shape. A box appears in the cell with the text "Create your drawing here." If the Drawing Canvas toolbar opens, close it. Click anywhere within the upper-right cell. The sun shape is inserted in the cell or somewhere nearby. The sun is selected, as indicated by the small circles, called selection handles, that surround it. If necessary, drag the sun to position it neatly within the cell. If the sun is not the right size, click the lower-right selection handle, and drag up or down to adjust the size of the sun so that it fits within the cell borders more precisely. With the sun still selected, click the Fill Color list arrow on the Drawing toolbar, and then click a light pink square in the color palette.
8. Adjust column widths and row heights so that the table is attractive and easy to read.

Explore

9. Now that you have organized the information using the Word table tools, you can remove the borders so that the printed flier doesn't look like a table. Click the Table Move handle to select the entire table, click Table on the menu bar, click Table Properties, click the Table tab if it is not already selected, click the Borders and Shading button, click the Borders tab if it is not already selected, click the None option, click the OK button, and then click the OK button again. The borders are removed from the flier; gridlines will not be visible on the printed page. (Depending on how your computer is set up, they may not be visible on your screen, either. If gridlines are not displayed, click Table on the menu bar, and then click Show Gridlines.)
10. Save your work, preview the flier, make any necessary adjustments, print it, and then close the document.

Research

Go to the Web to find information you can use to create documents.

Internet Assignments

The purpose of the Internet Assignments is to challenge you to find information on the Internet that you can use to work effectively with this software. The actual assignments are updated and maintained on the Course Technology Web site. Log on to the Internet and use your Web browser to go to the Student Online Companion for New Perspectives Office 2003 at **www.course.com/np/office2003.** Click the Internet Assignments link, and then navigate to the assignments for this tutorial.

Assess

SAM Assessment and Training

If you have a SAM user profile, you may have access to hands-on instruction, practice, and assessment of the skills covered in this tutorial. Log in to your SAM account and go to your assignments page to see what your instructor has assigned.

Review

Quick Check Answers

Session 3.1

1. a. in Normal view, a dotted line with the words "Section Break" that marks the point at which one section ends and another begins
   b. the intersection of a row and a column in a table
   c. information arranged in horizontal rows and vertical columns
   d. text entered one time but that is printed at the top of every page
   e. the location where text moves when you press the Tab key
2. Select the text whose tab alignment you want to change, click the tab alignment selector on the far left of the horizontal ruler until the appropriate tab stop alignment style appears, and then click in the horizontal ruler where you want to set the new tab stop.
3. You could divide a document into sections if you wanted to center only part of the document between the top and bottom margins.
4. Insert a section break, move the insertion point within the section you want to align, click File, click Page Setup, click the Layout tab, select Center in the Vertical alignment list box, make sure "This section" is selected in the Apply to list box, and then click OK.
5. A header appears at the top of a page, whereas a footer appears at the bottom of a page.
6. Click View on the menu bar, click Header and Footer, verify that the insertion point is located in the Header area, press Tab to move the insertion point to where you want the page number to appear, and then click the Insert Page Number button on the Header and Footer toolbar.
7. Move the insertion point to the location where you want the table to appear. Click the Insert Table button on the Standard toolbar. In the grid, click and drag to select three columns and two rows, and then release the mouse button.
8. If the insertion point is in the cell at the far right in a row, press the Tab key. Otherwise, press the ↓ key.

9. It's better to use a table rather than tab stops when you need to organize more than a few columns of information.
10. Click the Table Move handle.

Session 3.2

1. a. the thickness of the line used to create a border
   b. the style of the line used to create a border
   c. the outline of a row, cell, column, or table, which is hidden when the document is printed
   d. a gray or colored background used to highlight parts of a table
2. 12, 26, 44, 65
3. Click the cell at the far right in the bottom row of the table, and then press the Tab key.
4. Double-click the column's right-hand border.
5. Drag the bottom border of the row to a new position.
6. Select the row. Click the Line Style list arrow on the Tables and Borders toolbar, and select a line style. Click the Line Weight list arrow on the Tables and Borders toolbar, and select a line weight. Click the Borders list arrow on the Tables and Borders toolbar, and then click the Bottom Border option.
7. Click anywhere in the table, click Table on the menu bar, click Table Properties, click the Table tab, click Center, and then click OK.

Objectives

Session 4.1
- Identify desktop-publishing features
- Create a title with WordArt
- Work with hyperlinks
- Create newspaper-style columns

Session 4.2
- Insert and edit graphics
- Wrap text around a graphic
- Incorporate drop caps
- Use symbols and special typographic characters
- Add a page border
- Perform a mail merge

Desktop Publishing and Mail Merge

Creating a Newsletter and Cover Letter

Case

Wide World Travel, Inc.

Wide World Travel, Inc. hosts international tours for travelers of all ages. Recently, the company has expanded its business by selling clothes and shoes specifically designed for the frequent traveler. Max Stephenson, one of the Wide World tour guides, has taken on the job of managing this new retail venture. In order to generate business, he wants to create an informational newsletter. He has asked you to help him create the newsletter, as well as the form letter that will accompany each copy of the newsletter.

Max has already written the text of the newsletter, which describes some of the most popular items sold by Wide World Travel. Now Max wants you to transform this text into a publication that is neat, organized, and professional-looking. He would like the newsletter to contain headings (so the customers can scan it quickly for interesting items) as well as a headline that will give the newsletter a memorable look. He wants you to include a picture that will reinforce the newsletter content.

In this tutorial, you'll plan the layout of the newsletter and then add some information about the Wide World Travel Web site. Then you'll get acquainted with some desktop-publishing features available in Word that you'll use to create the newsletter. You'll format the title using an eye-catching design and divide the document into newspaper-style columns to make it easier to read. To add interest and focus to the text, you'll include a piece of art. You'll then fine-tune the newsletter layout, give it a more professional appearance with typographic characters, and put a border around the page to give the newsletter a finished look.

After you create the newsletter, you will use Word's mail merge feature to insert personalized information into the cover letter that will accompany the newsletter.

Student Data Files

▼**Tutorial.04**

▽ Tutorial folder
- Addresses.doc
- Clothes.doc
- Letter.doc

▽ Review folder
- Addresses.doc
- Highlights.doc
- Travel.doc

▽ Cases folder
- Convert.doc
- Grains.doc
- Knight.bmp
- Movers.doc

Session 4.1

Planning the Newsletter Document

The newsletter will provide a brief overview of some popular items sold by Wide World Travel. Like most newsletters, it will be written in an informal style that conveys information quickly. The newsletter title will help readers quickly identify the document. The newsletter text will be split into two columns to make it easier to read, and headings will help readers scan the information quickly. A picture will add interest and illustrate the newsletter's content. Drop caps and other desktop-publishing elements will help draw readers' attention to certain information and make the newsletter design attractive and professional.

Elements of Desktop Publishing

Desktop publishing is the production of commercial-quality printed material using a desktop computer system from which you can enter and edit text, create graphics, compose or lay out pages, and print documents. In addition to newsletters, you can desktop publish brochures, posters, and other documents that include text and graphics. In the Case Problems, you'll have the chance to create a brochure. The following elements are commonly associated with desktop publishing:

- High-quality printing. A laser printer or high-resolution inkjet printer produces final output.
- Multiple fonts. Two or three font types and sizes provide visual interest, guide the reader through the text, and convey the tone of the document.
- Graphics. Graphics, such as horizontal or vertical lines (called rules), boxes, electronic art, and digitized photographs help illustrate a concept or product, draw a reader's attention to the document, and make the text visually appealing.
- Typographic characters. For example, long dashes, called em dashes (—), are used in place of double hyphens (--) to separate dependent clauses; typographic medium-width dashes, called en dashes (–), are used in place of hyphens (-) as minus signs and in ranges of numbers; and typographic bullets (•) are used to draw attention to items in a list.
- Columns and other formatting features. Columns of text, pull quotes (small portions of text pulled out of the main text and enlarged), page borders, and other special formatting features that you don't frequently see in letters and other documents distinguish desktop-published documents.

Professional desktop publishers use software specially designed for desktop-publishing tasks. You can, however, use Word to create simple desktop-published documents. You'll incorporate many of the desktop-publishing elements listed above to produce the newsletter shown in Figure 4-1.

Wide World Travel newsletter **Figure 4-1**

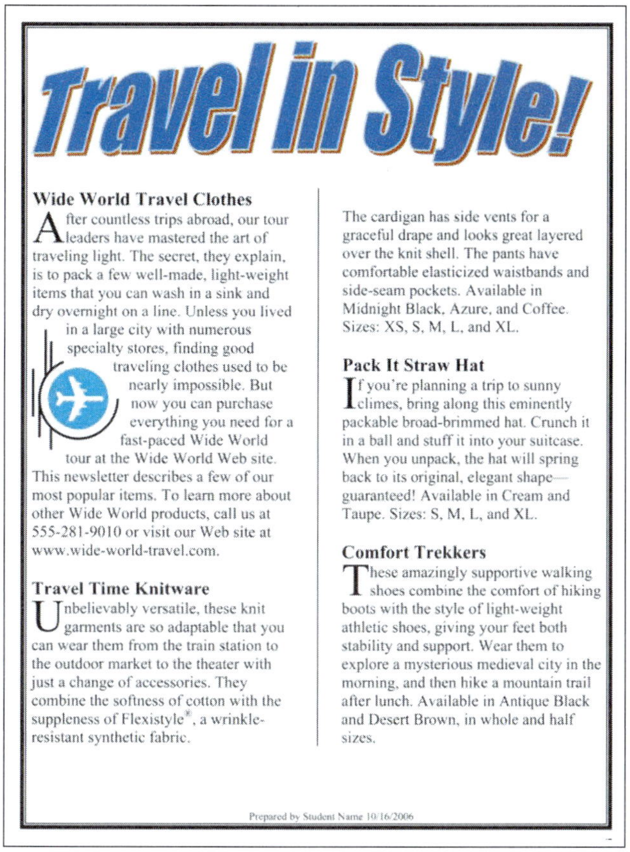

Travel in Style!

Wide World Travel Clothes

After countless trips abroad, our tour leaders have mastered the art of traveling light. The secret, they explain, is to pack a few well-made, light-weight items that you can wash in a sink and dry overnight on a line. Unless you lived in a large city with numerous specialty stores, finding good traveling clothes used to be nearly impossible. But now you can purchase everything you need for a fast-paced Wide World tour at the Wide World Web site. This newsletter describes a few of our most popular items. To learn more about other Wide World products, call us at 555-281-9010 or visit our Web site at www.wide-world-travel.com.

Travel Time Knitware

Unbelievably versatile, these knit garments are so adaptable that you can wear them from the train station to the outdoor market to the theater with just a change of accessories. They combine the softness of cotton with the suppleness of Flexistyle®, a wrinkle-resistant synthetic fabric. The cardigan has side vents for a graceful drape and looks great layered over the knit shell. The pants have comfortable elasticized waistbands and side-seam pockets. Available in Midnight Black, Azure, and Coffee. Sizes: XS, S, M, L, and XL.

Pack It Straw Hat

If you're planning a trip to sunny climes, bring along this eminently packable broad-brimmed hat. Crunch it in a ball and stuff it into your suitcase. When you unpack, the hat will spring back to its original, elegant shape—guaranteed! Available in Cream and Taupe. Sizes: S, M, L, and XL.

Comfort Trekkers

These amazingly supportive walking shoes combine the comfort of hiking boots with the style of light-weight athletic shoes, giving your feet both stability and support. Wear them to explore a mysterious medieval city in the morning, and then hike a mountain trail after lunch. Available in Antique Black and Desert Brown, in whole and half sizes.

Prepared by Student Name 10/16/2006

Working with Hyperlinks

Web pages often include special text called **hyperlinks** (or simply **links**) that you can click to display other Web pages. You can also use hyperlinks in Word documents that will be read online (that is, on a computer). For example, if you type an e-mail address and then press the Enter key, Word automatically formats the e-mail address as a hyperlink. Hyperlink text is usually formatted in blue with an underline. When you press Ctrl and click an e-mail hyperlink, an e-mail program opens automatically, ready for you to type a message. If you completed the Case Problems for Tutorial 2, you already have experience using e-mail hyperlinks.

In addition to e-mail addresses, Word also automatically formats Web page addresses, or **URLs**, as hyperlinks. (One example of a Web address is *www.microsoft.com*.) When you press Ctrl and click a Web page address that has been formatted as a hyperlink, your computer's browser opens automatically and attempts to display that Web page. The browser may not actually be able to display the Web page if your computer is not currently connected to the Internet, or if the Web page is unavailable for some other reason.

Including hyperlinks in a Word document is very useful when you plan to distribute the document via e-mail so others can read it online. For instance, if you include your e-mail address in a memo to a potential customer, the customer can click the e-mail address to begin typing an e-mail message to you in reply. However, when you know that your document will only be distributed on paper, it's a good idea to remove any hyperlinks so that the e-mail address or Web address is formatted without the underline, in the same color font as the surrounding text. To remove a hyperlink, right-click the hyperlink, and then click Remove Hyperlink in the shortcut menu. Once you remove the hyperlink, the Web address or e-mail address remains in the document, but is no longer formatted in blue with an underline.

Max would like you to complete the newsletter text by adding a reference to the Wide World Travel Web site. He does not want the company's Web address formatted as a hyperlink, so you will have to remove the hyperlink after typing the Web address. He has saved the newsletter text in a document named Clothes. You'll begin by opening the document that contains the unformatted text, often called copy, that will serve as the content for your desktop-published document.

To open the newsletter document and add the Web address:

1. Start Word, and make sure your screen matches the figures in this tutorial. In particular, be sure to display nonprinting characters.
2. Open the file **Clothes** from the Tutorial.04\Tutorial folder included with your Data Files.
3. To avoid altering the original file, save the document as **Travel Clothes** in the same folder.
4. If necessary, change the Zoom setting on the Standard toolbar to **100%** and switch to Normal view.
5. Read the document to preview its content.
6. Click to the right of the phone number (at the end of the first main paragraph), press the **spacebar**, and then type the following: **or visit our Web site at www.wide-world-travel.com**
7. Type a period at the end of the Web address, and then press the **Enter** key. The Web address is formatted as a hyperlink, in a blue font with an underline.
8. Move the mouse pointer over the hyperlink. A ScreenTip appears, with the complete URL (including some extra characters that a browser needs to display the Web page). The ScreenTip also displays instructions for displaying the Wide World Travel Web site. See Figure 4-2.

Figure 4-2 Hyperlink with ScreenTip

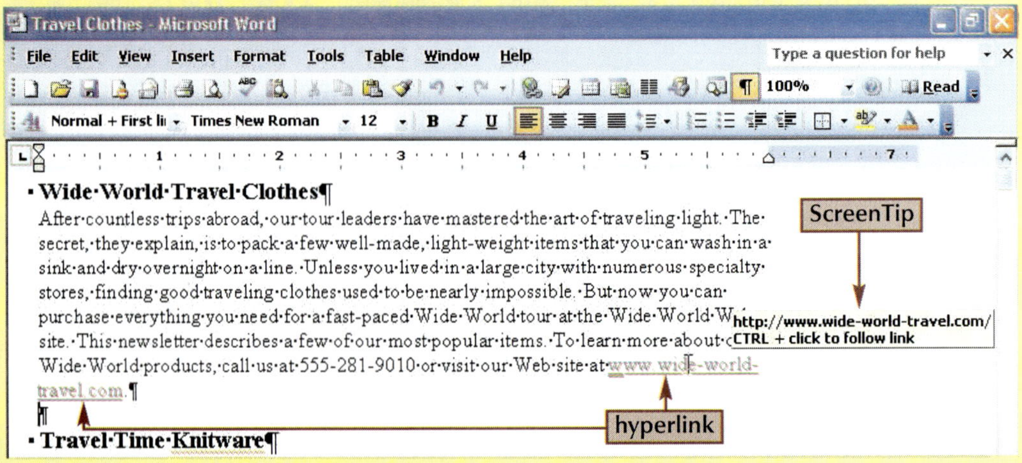

Max tells you that users will be viewing the document in printed form only. He asks you to remove the hyperlink. This will ensure that the format of the Web address matches the rest of the paragraph.

To remove the hyperlink:

1. Right-click the text **www.wide-world-travel.com**. A shortcut menu opens.
2. Click **Remove Hyperlink**. The shortcut menu closes, and the text is now formatted in black to match the rest of the paragraph.

You have finished adding the information about the company's Web site to the newsletter. Now that the newsletter contains all the necessary details, you can turn your attention to your first desktop-publishing task, adding a headline.

Using WordArt to Create a Headline

Max wants the title of the newsletter, "Travel in Style," to be eye-catching and dramatic. **WordArt** is a Word feature that allows you to insert specially formatted text into a document. WordArt provides great flexibility in designing text with special effects that express the image or mood you want to convey in your printed documents. With WordArt, you can apply color and shading, as well as alter the shape and size of the text.

You begin creating WordArt text by clicking a button on the Drawing toolbar. When you first display the Drawing toolbar, Word switches to Print Layout view. As a rule, Print Layout view is the most appropriate view to use when you are desktop publishing because it shows you exactly how the text and graphics fit on the page. The vertical ruler in Print Layout view helps you position graphical elements more precisely.

Creating Special Text Effects Using WordArt

Reference Window

- Click the Drawing button on the Standard toolbar to display the Drawing toolbar.
- Click the Insert WordArt button on the Drawing toolbar.
- Click the style of text you want to insert, and then click the OK button.
- Type the text you want in the Edit WordArt Text dialog box.
- Click the Font and Size list arrows to select the font and font size you want.
- If you want, click the Bold or Italic button, or both.
- Click the OK button.
- Click the WordArt to select it, and then drag any handle to resize and reshape it. To avoid altering the WordArt's proportions, press and hold down the Shift key while you drag a handle.

You're ready to use WordArt to create the newsletter title. First you will display the Drawing toolbar. Then you will choose a WordArt style and type the headline text.

To create the title of the newsletter using WordArt:

1. Press **Ctrl+Home** to move the insertion point to the beginning of the document.
2. Click the **Drawing** button on the Standard toolbar. The Drawing toolbar appears at the bottom of the screen. Word switches to Print Layout view.

   Trouble? If the Drawing toolbar is not positioned at the bottom of the Document window, drag it there by its title bar. If you do not see the Drawing toolbar anywhere, right-click the Standard toolbar, and then click Drawing on the shortcut menu.
3. If necessary, click **View** on the menu bar, click **Ruler** to display the vertical and horizontal rulers, type **90** in the Zoom text box, and then press the Enter key to change the Zoom setting to 90%. This Zoom setting should allow you to see the entire width of the newsletter. Throughout this tutorial, feel free to zoom in or zoom out if you prefer to see more or less of the newsletter.
4. Click the **Insert WordArt** button on the Drawing toolbar. The WordArt Gallery dialog box opens, displaying 30 different WordArt styles.
5. Click the WordArt style in the second row from the top, second column from the right, as shown in Figure 4-3.

Figure 4-3 WordArt styles

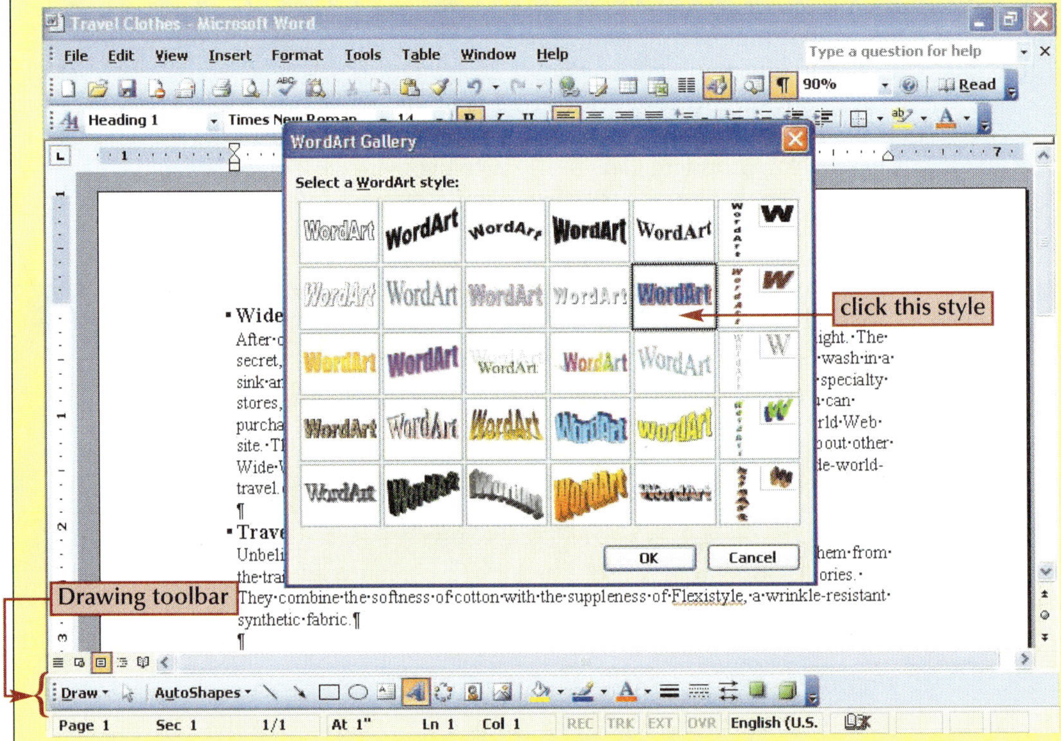

6. Click the **OK** button. The Edit WordArt Text dialog box opens, displaying the default text "Your Text Here," which you will replace with the newsletter title. Note that you can also select text in the document that you want to format as WordArt before you click the Insert WordArt button. In that case, the text you selected is displayed in the Edit WordArt Text dialog box instead of the default text "Your Text Here."

7. Type **Travel in Style** to replace the default text with the newsletter title. Notice the toolbar at the top of the Edit WordArt Text dialog box, which you can use to apply bold and italic, or to change the font or font style. You don't need to use these options now, but you might choose to when creating headlines for other documents.
8. Click the **OK** button. The Edit WordArt Text dialog box closes, and the WordArt image is inserted at the beginning of the newsletter. The "Wide World Travel Clothes" heading moves to the right to accommodate the new headline. See Figure 4-4.

WordArt headline inserted into document **Figure 4-4**

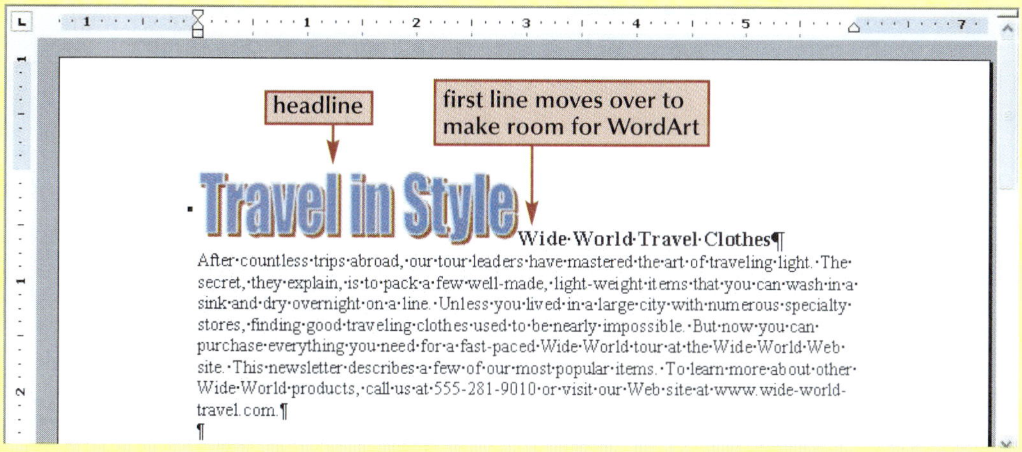

Trouble? If you see a border around the headline, the WordArt is currently selected. Click anywhere outside of the border to deselect the WordArt.

Eventually, you will position the headline so that it appears at the very top of the document, stretching from margin to margin. But for now, you can leave it in its current position.

Selecting a WordArt Object

The WordArt image you have created is not regular text. You cannot edit it as you would other text, that is, by moving the insertion point to it and typing new letters or by selecting part of it and using the buttons on the Formatting toolbar. Unlike regular text, a WordArt headline is considered an **object**—that is, something that you can manipulate independently of the text. You can think of the WordArt object as a thing that lies on top of, or next to, the text in a document. To edit a WordArt object in Word, you must first click it to select it. Then you can make changes using special toolbar buttons and dialog boxes, or by dragging it with the mouse.

Max would like you to make several changes to the newsletter headline. Before you can do this, you need to select it.

To select the WordArt headline:

1. Click the WordArt headline. The headline is surrounded by a black border with eight small black squares (called **sizing handles**). The WordArt toolbar also appears. The black sizing handles indicate that the WordArt is an **inline graphic**, that is, a graphic that is part of the line of text in which it was inserted. See Figure 4-5.

Figure 4-5 Selected headline

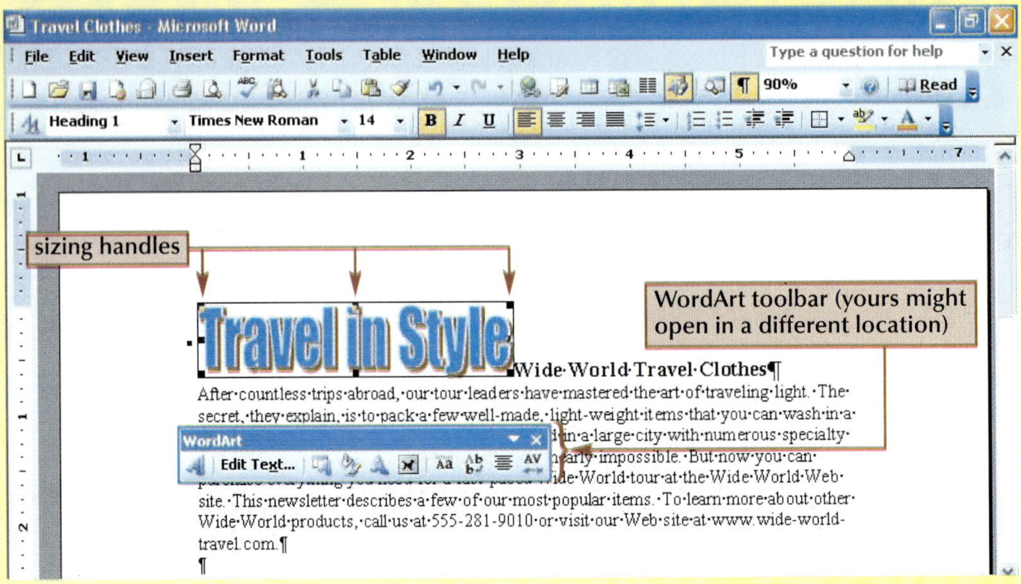

Editing a WordArt Object

Now that the WordArt object is selected, you can modify its appearance (color, shape, size, and so forth) using the buttons on the Drawing toolbar or the WordArt toolbar. First of all, Max would like you to edit the WordArt by adding an exclamation point at the end of the headline. While you're making that change, he would like you to format the headline in italic.

To change the font and formatting of the WordArt object:

1. Verify that the WordArt object is selected, as indicated by the sizing handles.
2. Click the **Edit Text** button on the WordArt toolbar. The Edit WordArt Text dialog box opens. As you recall, you used this dialog box earlier when you first created the WordArt headline.
3. Click at the end of the headline (after the "e" in Style"), and then type **!** (an exclamation point).
4. Click the **Italic** button *I* in the Edit WordArt Text dialog box. The headline in the Text box is now formatted in italic, with an exclamation point at the end.
5. Click the **OK** button. The Edit WordArt Text dialog box closes, allowing you to see the edited headline in the document.

Changing the Shape of a WordArt Object

You can quickly change the shape of a WordArt object using the **WordArt Shape** button on the WordArt toolbar. Right now, the WordArt headline has a straight shape, without any curve to it. Max wants to use an arched shape.

To change the shape of the WordArt object:

1. Verify that the WordArt headline is selected, and then click the **WordArt Shape** button on the WordArt toolbar. A palette of shape options opens.
2. Move the mouse pointer over each option in the palette to display a ScreenTip with the name of each shape. As you can see, the Plain Text shape (a straight line) is currently selected.
3. Point to the **Inflate Top** shape (fourth row down, fifth column from the left), as shown in Figure 4-6.

Figure 4-6 WordArt shapes

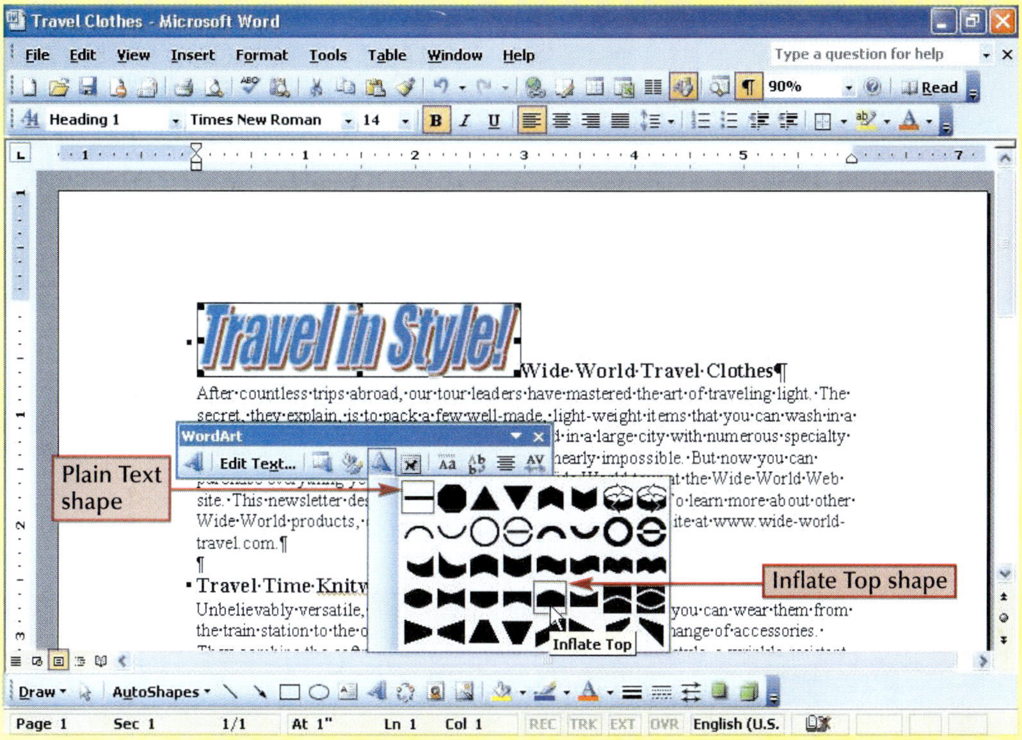

4. Click the **Inflate Top** shape. The newsletter title is formatted in the new WordArt shape.

The headline has the shape you want. Now you can take care of positioning the WordArt object above the newsletter text.

Wrapping Text Below the WordArt Object

At this point, the WordArt object is on the same line as the heading "Wide World Travel Clothes." Max would like you to set the WordArt on its own line at the top of the document. To do this, you need to change the way the text flows, or **wraps**, around the WordArt object.

You can wrap text around objects many different ways in Word. For example, you can have the text wrap above and below the object, through it, or so the text follows the shape of the object, even if it has an irregular shape. Text wrapping is often used in newsletters to prevent text and graphics from overlapping, to add interest, and to prevent excessive open areas, called **white space**, from appearing on the page. The Text Wrapping button on the WordArt or Picture toolbar provides some basic choices, whereas the Layout tab of the Format WordArt dialog box provides more advanced options. (To open the Format WordArt dialog box, click the Format WordArt button on the WordArt toolbar.) Because you want to use a relatively simple option—wrapping text so that it flows below the WordArt headline—you'll use the Text Wrapping button on the WordArt toolbar. You'll have a chance to use the Format WordArt dialog box in the Case Problems at the end of this tutorial.

To wrap the newsletter text below the WordArt headline:

1. With the WordArt object selected, click the **Text Wrapping** button on the WordArt toolbar. A menu of text wrapping options opens.
2. Click **Top and Bottom**. The text drops below the newsletter title. The WordArt is still selected, but instead of black sizing handles, you see small white circles. Like the black squares, the white circles are sizing handles. The white sizing handles indicate that the graphic object is a **floating graphic**, which means the graphic can be moved independently of the surrounding text. A number of other items appear around the WordArt object, as shown in Figure 4-7. You can use the sizing handles shown in Figure 4-7 to change the size and position of the WordArt object. You'll learn the meaning of the anchor symbol shortly. Don't be concerned if your WordArt object is not in the same position as the one in Figure 4-7.

Figure 4-7 WordArt after wrapping text

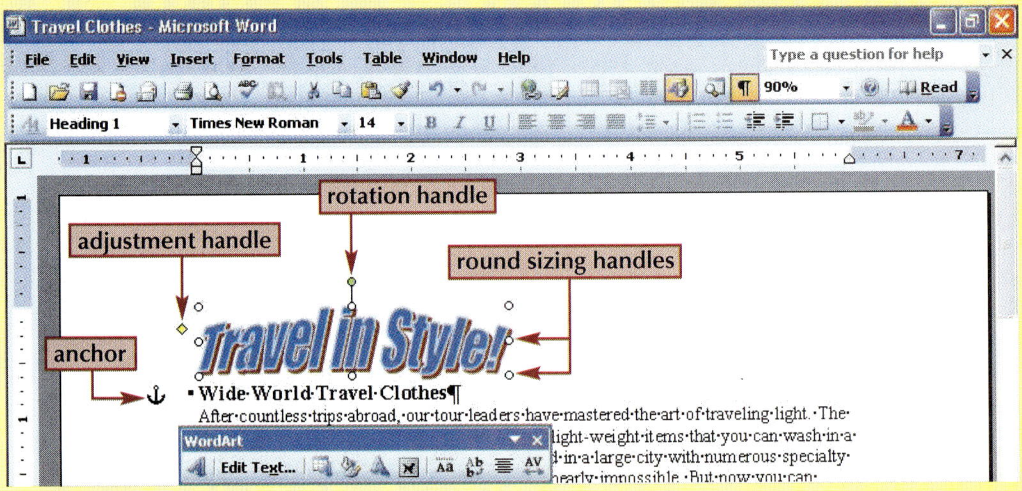

Trouble? If you can't see the anchor symbol, your Zoom setting is probably too high. Change it to 90%.

Positioning and Sizing the WordArt Object

After you choose a text wrapping style for a WordArt object, you can adjust its size and position in the document. To position a WordArt object, click it and drag it with the mouse pointer. To widen any WordArt object, drag one of its sizing handles. To keep the object the same proportion as the original, hold down the Shift key as you drag the sizing handle. This prevents "stretching" the object more in one direction than the other.

Max asks you to widen the headline so it fits neatly within the newsletter margins. As you enlarge the headline, you can practice dragging the WordArt object to a new position.

To position and enlarge the WordArt object:

1. Move the mouse pointer over the headline.
2. Use the pointer to drag the WordArt object to the right, until it is centered below the 3-inch mark in the horizontal ruler, over the top of the newsletter.
3. Click the **Undo** button on the Standard toolbar to undo the move. The headline returns to its original position, aligned along the left margin. Note that you can use this same technique to drag a WordArt object to any location in a document. (You'll learn more about dragging objects later in this tutorial, when you insert a picture into the newsletter.)
4. With the WordArt object still selected, position the pointer over the lower-right sizing handle. The pointer changes to ↘.
5. Press and hold the **Shift** key while you drag the sizing handle to the right margin, using the horizontal ruler as a guide. As you drag the handle, the pointer changes to + and a dotted outline appears to show you how big the WordArt will be when you release the mouse button. See Figure 4-8.

Figure 4-8 Resizing the WordArt Object

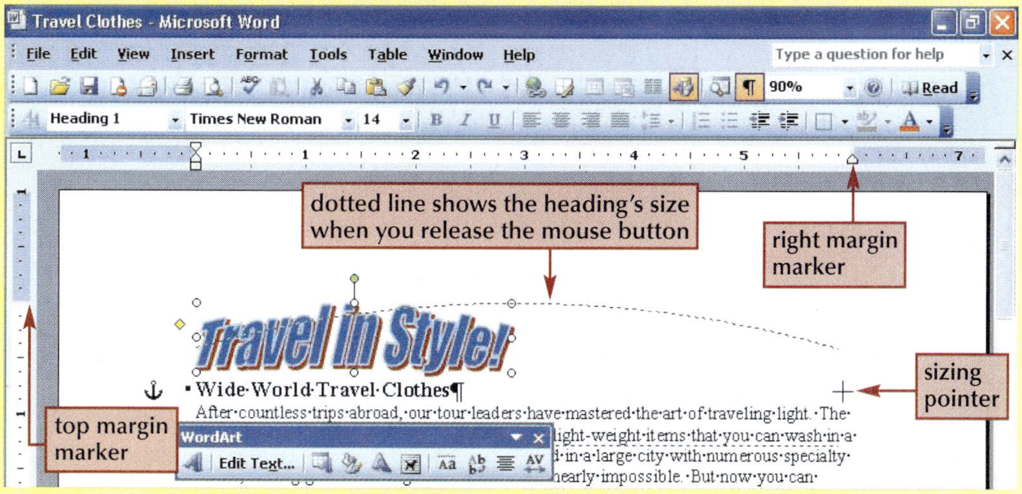

6. Release the mouse button when the dotted horizontal line stretches from the left to the right margin. The WordArt heading should be about six inches wide and a little less than 1.5 inches high at its tallest. If necessary, repeat the procedure to make the exclamation point line up with the right margin.

   Trouble? If the WordArt heading spans the margins, but is not tall enough to read easily, you probably didn't hold down the Shift key when you dragged the mouse pointer. Undo the change and begin again with Step 4.

7. If necessary, drag the headline down slightly, so that the top of the headline does not extend into the top margin, as shown in Figure 4-9. Notice that when you drag the headline down, the newsletter text also moves down to accommodate the headline.

   Trouble? If the headline jumps to the middle of the first paragraph of text, you dragged it too far. Click the Undo button, and then repeat Step 7.

In addition to moving and resizing the WordArt headline, you can drag the rotation handle to rotate the headline. You can also use the adjustment handle to increase or decrease the arch at the top of the headline. Right now you need to turn your attention to the WordArt object anchor symbol.

Anchoring the WordArt Object

After you wrap text around a WordArt object, you need to make sure the WordArt object is properly positioned within the document as a whole—a process known as anchoring. The process draws its name from the anchor symbol in the left margin, which indicates the position of the WordArt relative to the text. The anchor symbol is only visible after you wrap text around the document and when nonprinting characters are displayed. To ensure that changes to the text (such as section breaks) do not affect the WordArt, you need to anchor the WordArt to a blank paragraph before the text. At this point, the WordArt anchor symbol is probably located to the left of the first paragraph (the heading "Wide World Travel Clothes"). However, yours may be in a different position (for instance, it might be positioned above and to the left of the WordArt). In the next set of steps, you will move the anchor to a new, blank paragraph at the beginning of the document.

To anchor the WordArt object to a blank paragraph:

1. Press **Ctrl+Home**. The insertion point moves to the beginning of the newsletter text (that is, to the left of the first "W" in the heading "Wide World Travel Clothes"). The WordArt object is no longer selected; you cannot see the anchor at this point.
2. Press the **Enter** key. A new paragraph symbol is inserted either above or below the WordArt object.
3. If the new paragraph symbol is inserted above the WordArt heading, drag the WordArt heading up slightly until the paragraph mark moves below the WordArt heading.
4. Click the WordArt object. The selection handles and the anchor symbol appear. The anchor symbol is probably positioned to the left of the "Wide World Travel Clothes" heading, though it might be located to the left of the new blank paragraph instead.
5. Click the anchor and drag it up to position it to the left of the new, blank paragraph as shown in Figure 4-9, if it is not already positioned there.

Figure 4-9 Properly anchored WordArt

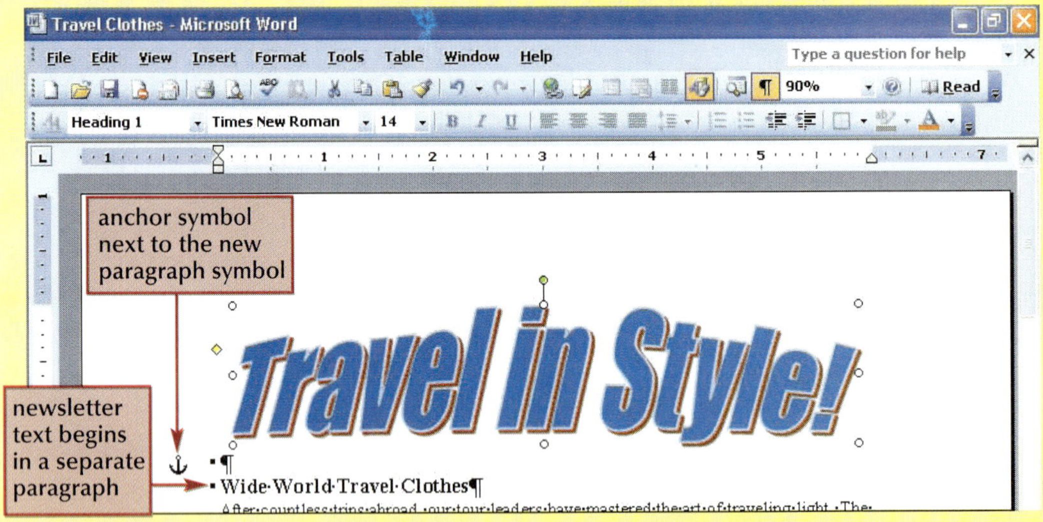

Trouble? If your WordArt headline is positioned below the new paragraph symbol, drag it up slightly to position it above the new paragraph symbol. If you notice any other differences between your headline and the one shown in Figure 4-9, edit the headline to make it match the figure. For example, you may need to drag the WordArt left or right slightly, or you may need to adjust its size by dragging one of its sizing handles.

6. Click anywhere in the newsletter to deselect the WordArt, and then save your work.

Your WordArt is now finished. Max congratulates you on your excellent work. The headline will definitely draw attention to the newsletter, encouraging potential customers to read the entire document.

Formatting Text in Newspaper-Style Columns

Because newsletters are meant for quick reading, they are usually laid out in newspaper-style columns. In **newspaper-style columns**, a page is divided into two or more vertical blocks, or columns. Text flows down one column, continues at the top of the next column, flows down that column, and so forth. The narrow columns and small type size allow the eye to take in a lot of text, thus allowing a reader to scan a newspaper quickly for interesting information.

When formatting a document in columns, you can click where you want the columns to begin and then click the Columns button on the Formatting toolbar. However, the Columns command on the Formatting menu offers more options. Using the Columns command, you can insert a vertical line between columns. The Columns command also gives you more control over exactly what part of the document will be formatted in columns.

Max wants you to divide the text below the title into two columns and add a vertical line between them.

To apply newspaper-style columns to the body of the newsletter:

1. Position the insertion point at the beginning of the second paragraph (to the left of the first "W" in "Wide World Travel Clothes").
2. Click **Format** on the menu bar, and then click **Columns**. The Columns dialog box opens.
3. In the Presets section, click the **Two** icon.
4. Click the **Line between** check box to select it. The text in the Preview box changes to a two-column format with a vertical rule between the columns.

   You want these changes to affect only the paragraphs after the WordArt headline, so you'll need to insert a section break and apply the column formatting to the text after the insertion point.
5. Click the **Apply to** list arrow, and then click **This point forward** to have Word automatically insert a section break at the insertion point. See Figure 4-10.

Figure 4-10 Completed Columns dialog box

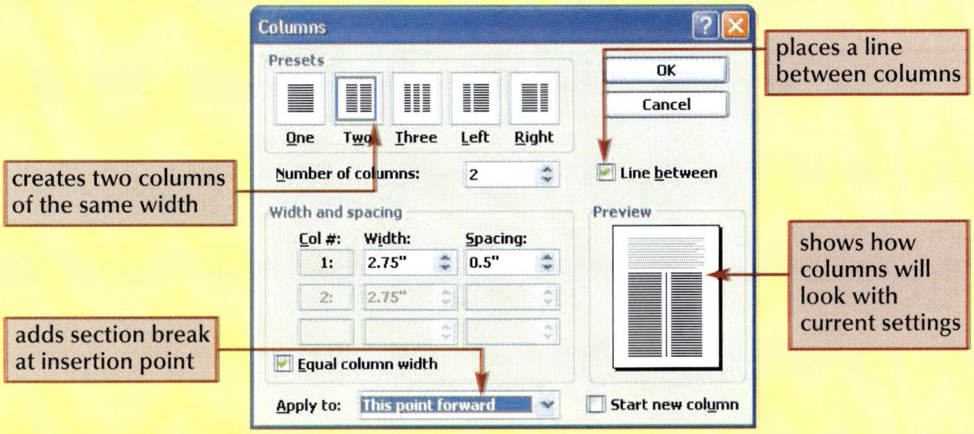

6. Click the **OK** button to return to the Document window. A continuous section break appears below the WordArt title. The word "continuous" indicates that the new section continues on the same page as the preceding text—in other words, the WordArt title and the newsletter text will print on the same page, even though they are in different sections of the newsletter. The text in Section 2 is formatted in two columns. The insertion point is in Section 2 as indicated by the information displayed in the status bar.

To get a good look at the columns, you need to change the Zoom setting so you can see the entire page at one time.

To zoom out to display the whole page:

1. Click the **Zoom** list arrow on the Standard toolbar, and then click **Whole Page**. Word displays the entire page of the newsletter so that you can see how the two-column format looks on the page. See Figure 4-11. Note that the Whole Page Zoom setting is only available in Print Layout view. You should use it whenever you want to have the entire page displayed as you edit it. Some details, such as the line between the columns, are not visible in the Whole Page Zoom setting.

Figure 4-11 Whole Page view showing two columns

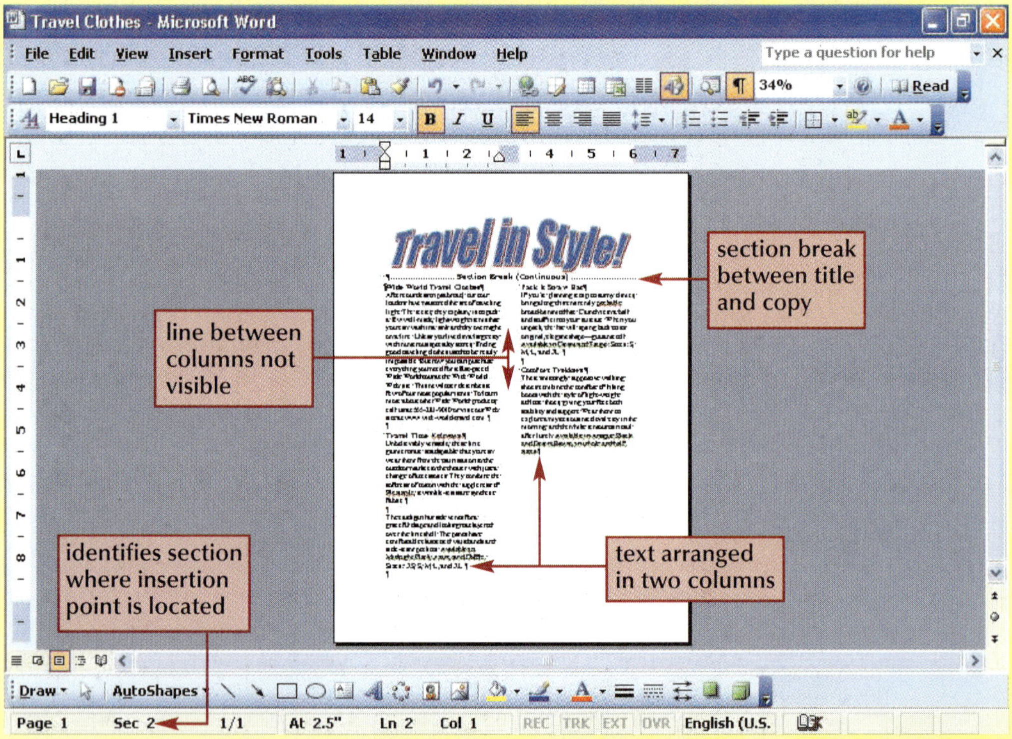

Trouble? Your columns may break at a slightly different line from those shown in the figure. This is not a problem; just continue with the tutorial.

The newsletter headline is centered on the page, and the copy is in a two-column format. The text fills the left column but not the right column. You'll fix this later, after you add a graphic and format some of the text.

2. Click the **Zoom** list arrow again, and then click **Page Width**. The Page Width option changes the Zoom setting enough to make the page span the width of the document window. Now you can read the text again.
3. Save your work.

Keep in mind that you can modify the structure of columns in a document by reformatting the document with three or more columns, or return the document to its original format by formatting it as one column. You can also insert column breaks to force text to move from one column to the next. You'll have a chance to practice modifying the columns in the Case Problems at the end of this tutorial.

Session 4.1 Quick Check

Review

1. Describe four elements commonly associated with desktop publishing.
2. True or False: When using Word's desktop-publishing features, you should display your document in Print Layout view.
3. In your own words, define the following terms:
   a. desktop publishing
   b. WordArt
   c. copy
   d. anchor
4. True or False: You can edit WordArt just as you would edit any other text in Word.
5. How do you change the text of a WordArt object after you have inserted it into a Word document?
6. What is the purpose of the WordArt Shape button on the WordArt toolbar?
7. True or False: When you first format a document into newspaper-style columns, the columns will necessarily be of equal length.

Session 4.2

Inserting Graphics

Graphics, which can include drawings, paintings, photographs, charts, tables, designs, or even designed text such as WordArt, add variety to documents and are especially appropriate for newsletters. You can use the buttons on Word's Drawing toolbar to draw pictures in your document. However, it's usually easier to create a picture in a special graphics program and then save the picture as an electronic file. (You may already be familiar with one graphics program, **Paint**, which is included as part of the Windows operating system.)

Instead of creating your own art in a graphics program, you can take a piece of art on a piece of paper (such as a photograph) and scan it—that is, run it through a special machine called a scanner. A **scanner** is similar to a copy machine except that it saves a copy of the image as an electronic file, instead of reproducing it on a piece of paper. (As you may know, many modern copy machines also function as scanners.) You can also use a digital camera to take a photograph that is then stored as an electronic file.

Electronic files come in several types, many of which were developed for use in Web pages. In desktop publishing, you will often work with **bitmaps**—a type of file that stores an image as a collection of tiny dots, which, when displayed on a computer monitor or printed on a page, make up a picture. There are several types of bitmap files, the most common of which are:

- BMP: Used by Microsoft Paint, and other graphics programs, to store graphics you create. These files, which have the .bmp file extension, tend to be very large.
- GIF: Suitable for most types of simple art. A GIF file is compressed, so it doesn't take up much room on your computer. A GIF file has the file extension .gif.
- JPEG: Suitable for photographs and drawings. Files stored using the JPEG format are even more compressed than GIF files. A JPEG file has the file extension .jpg.
- TIFF: Commonly used for photographs or scanned images. TIFF files have the file extension .tif and are usually much larger than GIF or JPEG files, but smaller than BMP files.

Once you have stored a piece of art as an electronic file, you can insert it into a document using the Picture command options on the Insert menu. You'll have a chance to explore some of these options in the Case Problems at the end of this tutorial.

If you don't have time to prepare your own art work, you can take advantage of **clip art**—a collection of ready-made images. A number of clip art selections are stored on your computer when you install Microsoft Word. You can also download additional clip art from the Web. (You'll have a chance to look for clip art on the Web in the Case Problems at the end of this tutorial.) You begin inserting clip art by opening the Clip Art task pane. From there you can search for images that are stored on your computer or on the Web. Then you copy an image to the Clipboard, and paste the image into the document.

To add visual appeal to the Travel in Style newsletter, you will insert a piece of clip art. Max wants you to use a clip art object that reflects the newsletter content.

To insert the clip art image of an airplane into the newsletter:

1. If you took a break after the previous session, make sure Word is still running, the file Travel Clothes is open, the document is in Print Layout view, and the nonprinting characters are displayed. Also verify that the Drawing toolbar is displayed.
2. Click the **Insert Clip Art** button on the Drawing toolbar. The Clip Art task pane opens, as shown in Figure 4-12. You use the top part of the Clip Art task pane to search for graphics related to a specific topic. You can click the Organize clips option (near the bottom) to open the Clip Organizer window, where you can browse among the various clip art images stored on your computer. You'll use the Clip Organizer to insert an image into the newsletter. You'll have a chance to try the Search for option in the Case Problems at the end of this tutorial. If someone recently used your Clip Art task pane to search for graphics, you may see the search topic in the Search for text box.

Figure 4-12 Clip Art task pane

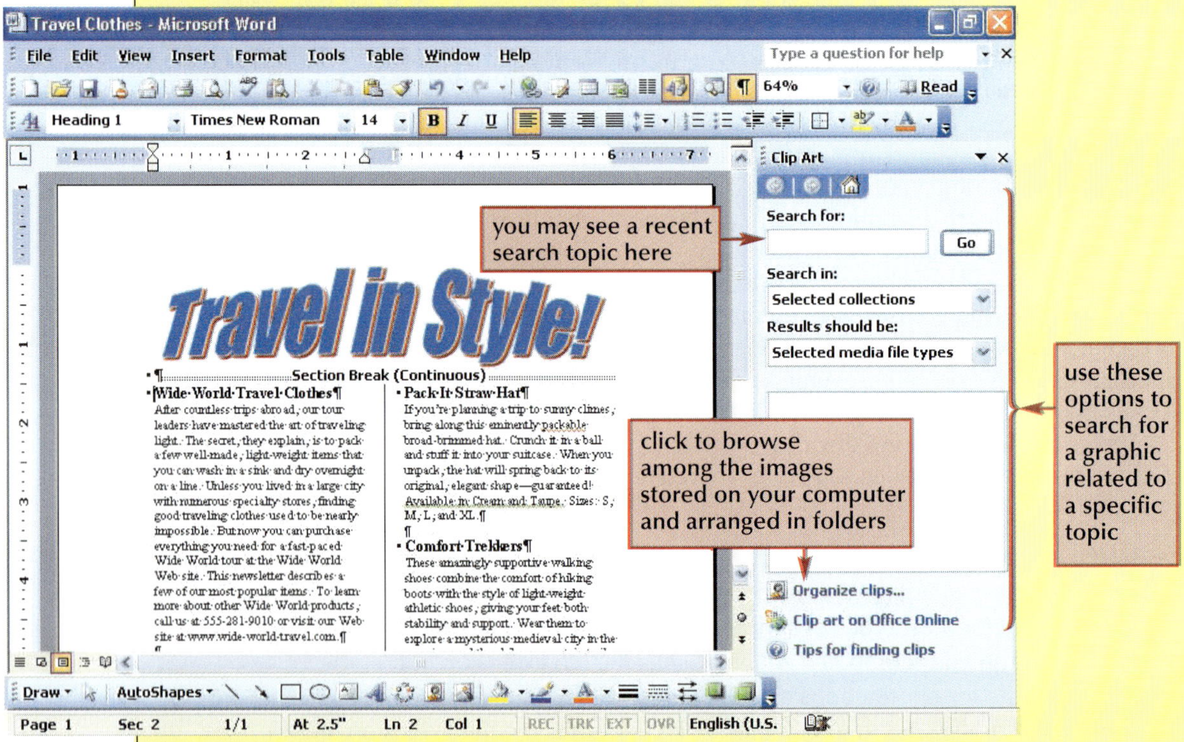

3. Click **Organize clips** near the bottom of the Clip Art task pane. The Favorites - Microsoft Clip Organizer window opens. This window is similar to Windows Explorer. For example, you click the plus sign next to a folder to display its subfolders. You select a subfolder to display its contents in the right pane. The default Microsoft Office clip art is stored in subfolders within the Office Collections folder. See Figure 4-13. You might see different folders from those shown in Figure 4-13, but you should see the Office Collections folder.

   Trouble? If you see the Add Clips to Organizer dialog box, click Now. This will organize the clip art installed on your computer into folders, so that you can then use the Clip Organizer dialog box to select a piece of clip art. The Add Clips to Organizer dialog box appears the first time you attempt to use clip art on your computer. After the clip organizing process concludes, continue with Step 4.

Figure 4-13 Microsoft Clip Organizer

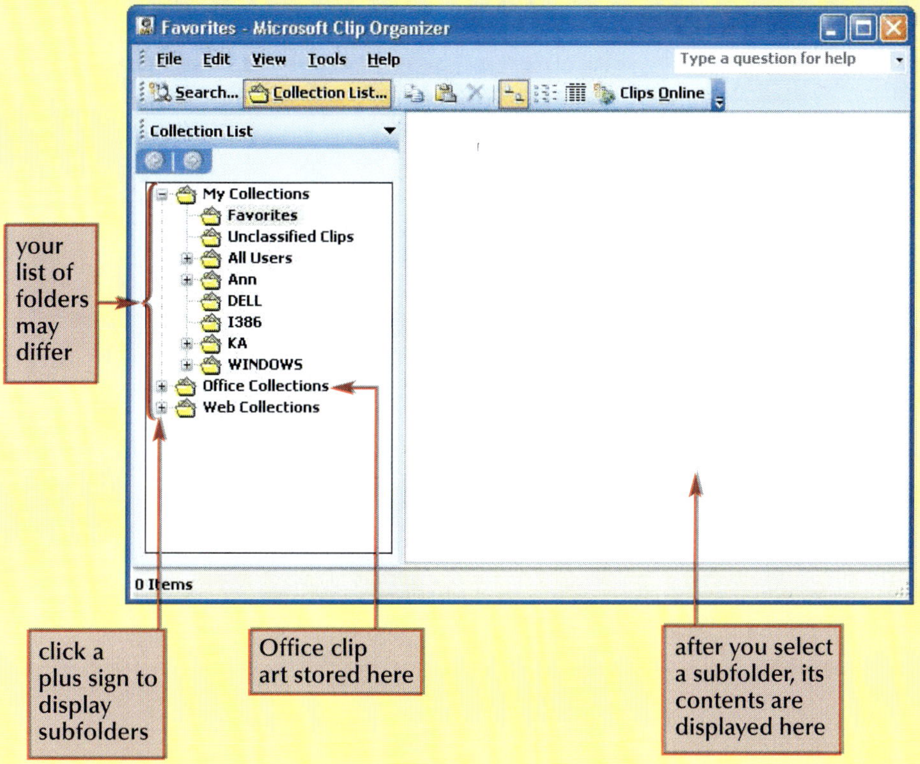

4. Scroll as needed to view the Office Collections folder, and then click the plus sign next to the **Office Collections** folder. A list of subfolders within the Office Collections folder appears. This list of folders, which is created when you install Word, organizes clip art images into related categories. The folders with plus signs next to them contain subfolders or clip art images.
5. Scroll down and examine the list of folders. Click any plus signs to open subfolders, and then click folders to display clip art images in the right pane.
6. Click the plus sign next to the **Transportation** folder to display its subfolders, and then click the **Transportation** folder to select it. Three images stored in the Transportation folder are displayed in the right pane.

   Trouble? If you don't see any images in the Transportation folder, click the Travel folder to select it and display an image of an airplane in a blue circle.

7. Move the pointer over the image of the airplane in the blue circle. An arrow button appears on the right side of the image.
8. Click the arrow button. A menu of options opens, as shown in Figure 4-14.

Figure 4-14 Image in Transportation folder selected

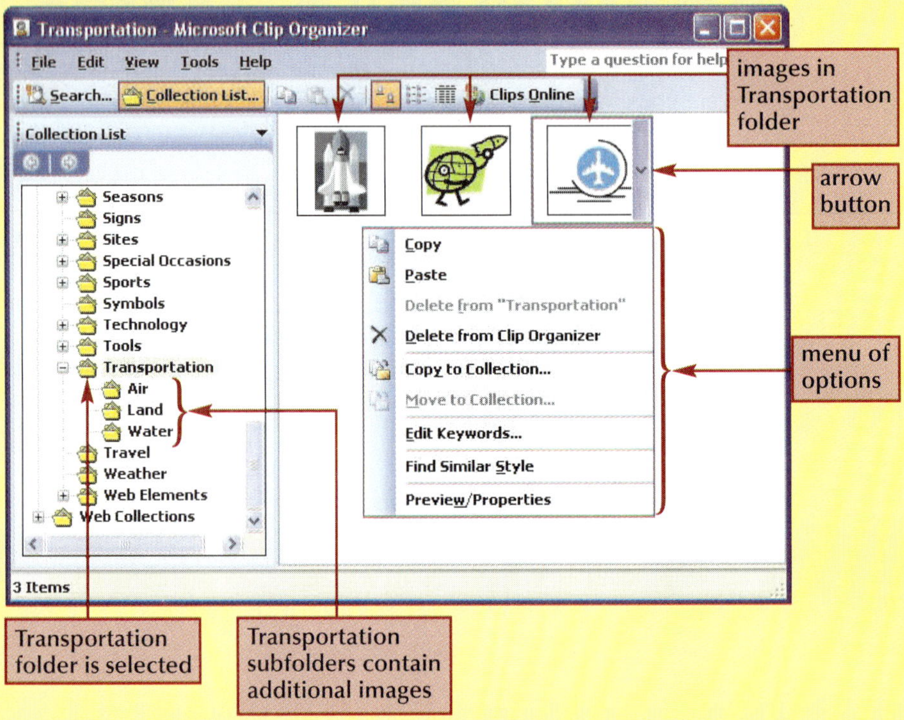

9. Click **Copy** in the menu. The image is copied to the Clipboard.

Now that you have copied the image to the Clipboard, you can paste it into the document at the insertion point. Max asks you to insert the graphic in the paragraph below the heading "Wide World Travel Clothes." Before you insert the image, you will close the Clip Art task pane.

To paste the clip art into the document:

1. Click the **Close** button in the Microsoft Clip Organizer title bar, and then click **Yes** when you see a dialog box asking if you want the item to remain on the Clipboard. You return to the Document window.
2. Click the **Close** button on the Clip Art task pane.
3. Position the insertion point to the left of the word "After" in the beginning of the first paragraph below the heading "Wide World Travel Clothes."
4. Click the **Paste** button on the Standard toolbar. The image is inserted into the document at the insertion point. The image nearly fills the left column.
5. Save the document.
6. Click the airplane image to select it. Like the WordArt object you worked with earlier, the clip art image is a graphic object with sizing handles that you can use to change its size. The Picture toolbar appears whenever a graphic object is selected. See Figure 4-15.

Newsletter with the Clip Art object inserted

Figure 4-15

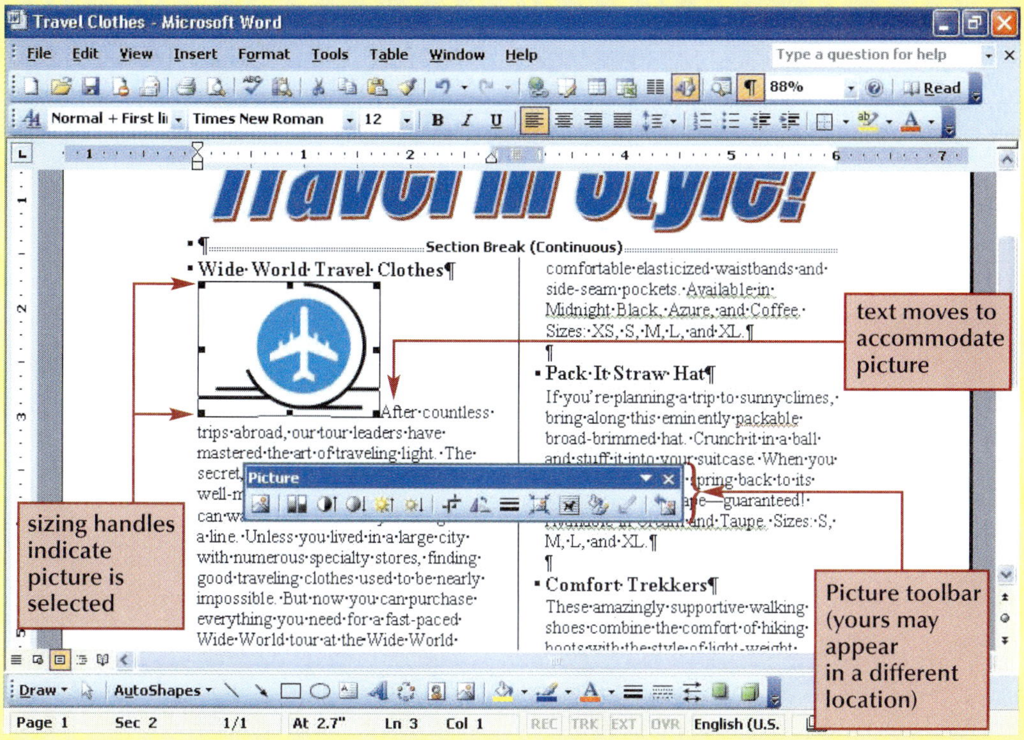

Trouble? If the Picture toolbar does not appear when you click the airplane image, right-click any toolbar, and then click Picture.

Max would like the image to be smaller so it doesn't divert attention from the text. You'll make that change in the next section.

Resizing a Graphic

It's often necessary to change the size of a graphic to make it fit into a document. This is called **scaling** the image. You can resize a graphic either by dragging its sizing handles or, for more precise control, by using the Format Picture button on the Picture toolbar.

For Max's newsletter, the dragging technique will work fine.

To resize the clip art graphic:

1. Make sure the clip art graphic is selected.
2. Drag the lower-right sizing handle up and to the left until the dotted outline forms a rectangle slightly less than 1.5 inches wide. Remember to use the horizontal ruler as a guide. See Figure 4-16. *Note*: You don't have to hold down the Shift key, as you do with WordArt, to resize the picture proportionally.

Figure 4-16 Resizing the graphic

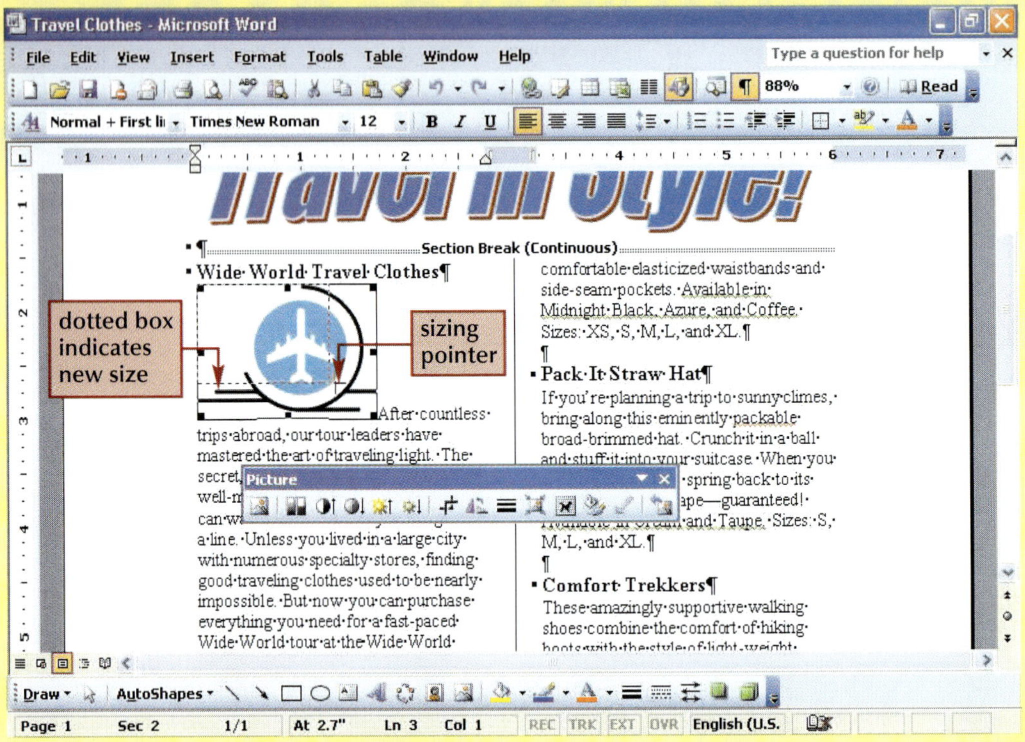

3. Release the mouse button. The airplane image is now about half as wide as the left column.

Max wonders if the graphic would look better if you deleted part of the horizontal lines on the left side of the image. You'll make that change in the next section.

Cropping a Graphic

You can **crop** the graphic—that is, cut off one or more of its edges—using either the Crop button on the Picture toolbar or the Format Picture dialog box. Once you crop a graphic, the part you cropped is hidden from view. It remains a part of the graphic image, so you can change your mind and restore a cropped graphic to its original form.

To crop the airplane graphic:

1. If necessary, click the clip art to select it. The sizing handles appear.
2. Click the **Crop** button on the Picture toolbar. The pointer changes to . To crop the graphic, you must position this pointer over a middle handle on any side of the graphic.
3. Position the pointer directly over the middle sizing handle on the left side of the picture.
4. Press and hold down the mouse button. The pointer changes to .
5. Drag the handle to the right. As you drag, a dotted outline appears to indicate the new shape of the graphic. Position the left border of the dotted outline along the left border of the blue circle. See Figure 4-17.

Cropping the graphic

Figure 4-17

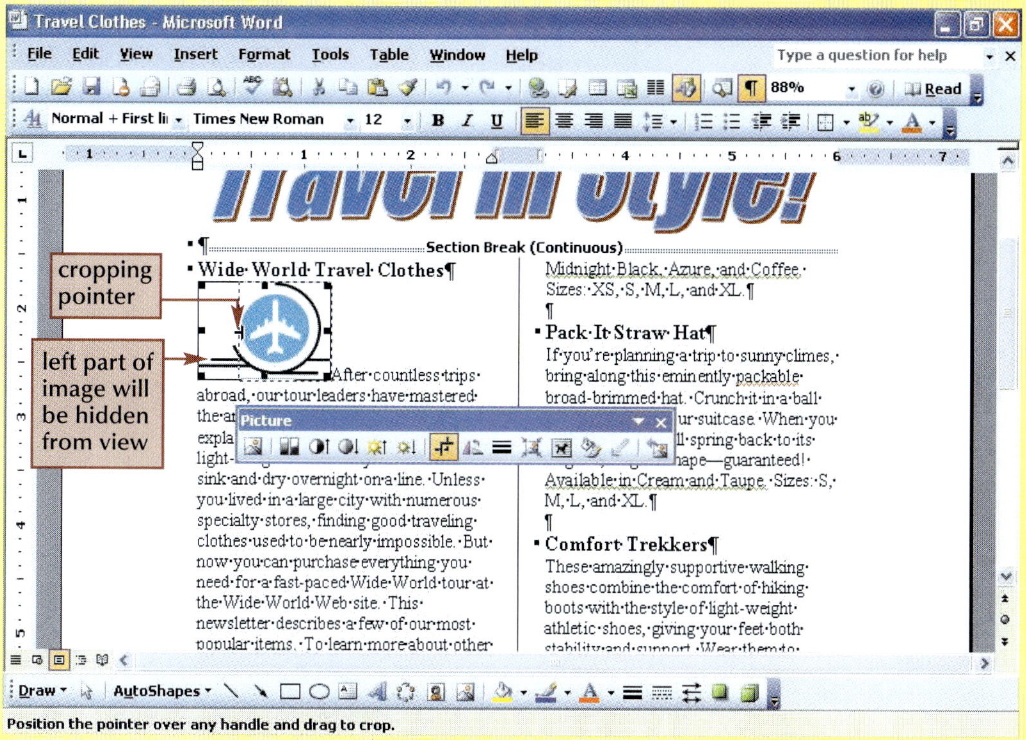

6. Release the mouse button.

   Max decides he prefers to display the whole airplane, so he asks you to return to the original image.

7. Click the **Undo** button on the Standard toolbar. The cropping action is reversed, and the full image reappears.

Rotating a Graphic

Max still isn't happy with the appearance of the graphic because of the amount of white space on the left side. He suggests rotating the image so that the airplane is positioned horizontally on the page. You can use the Rotate Left button on the Picture toolbar to rotate the image.

To rotate the airplane graphic:

1. If necessary, click the clip art to select it. The sizing handles appear.
2. Click the **Rotate Left 90°** button on the Picture toolbar. The graphic rotates 90 degrees to the left.
3. Click the **Rotate Left 90°** button again. The graphic rotates another 90 degrees, leaving the airplane upside down.
4. Click the **Rotate Left 90°** button again. The graphic rotates another 90 degrees. Now the airplane appears to be flying across the page from left to right. The selection handles become circles. See Figure 4-18. If you needed to rotate the image with the text wrapped around it, you could drag the rotation handle, which is the round green circle.

Figure 4-18 Rotated graphic

Now Max wants you to make the text wrap to the right of the graphic, making the airplane look as if it's flying into the text.

Wrapping Text Around a Graphic

For the airplane to look as though it flies into the newsletter text, you need to make the text wrap around the image. Earlier, you used Top and Bottom text wrapping to position the WordArt title above the columns of text. Now you'll apply Tight text wrapping to make the text follow the shape of the plane.

To wrap text around the airplane graphic:

1. Verify that the airplane graphic is selected.
2. Click the **Text Wrapping** button on the Picture toolbar. A menu of text wrapping options appears.
3. Click **Tight**. The text wraps to the right of the airplane, following its shape. Your screen should look similar to Figure 4-19.
4. Click anywhere in the text to deselect the graphic, and then save the newsletter. Don't be concerned if the heading "Wide World Travel Clothes" wraps around the top of the graphic. You will move the graphic away from the heading in the next section. If the heading does not wrap around the graphic, that's fine too.

Figure 4-19 Text wrapped around graphic

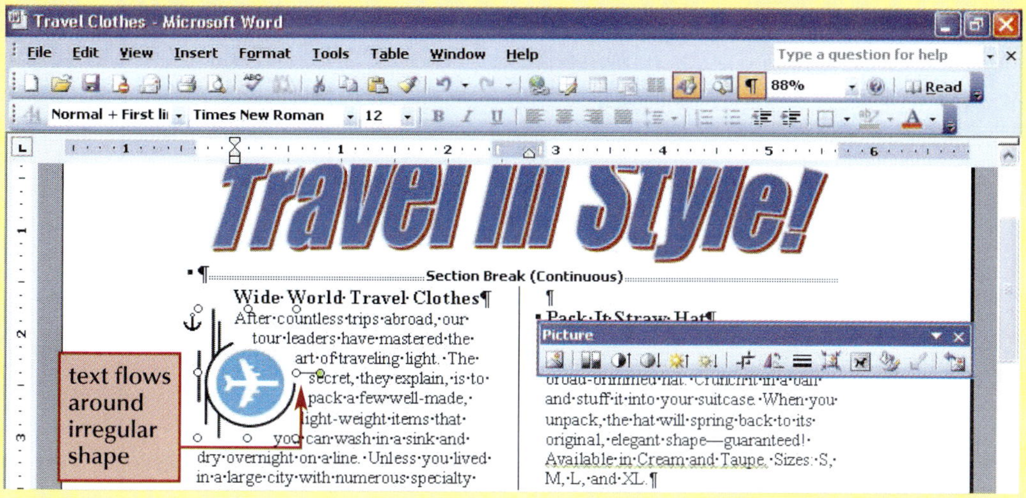

The Text Wrapping button should provide all the options you need for most situations. In some cases, however, you might want to use the more advanced options available in the Format Picture or Format WordArt dialog box. You'll have a chance to explore these options in the Case Problems at the end of this tutorial.

Moving a Graphic

Finally, Max asks you to move the graphic down to the middle of the paragraph so that it is not so close to the heading. You can do this by dragging the graphic to a new position. Like WordArt, a clip art graphic is anchored to a specific paragraph in a document. When you drag a graphic (including WordArt) to a new paragraph, the anchor symbol moves to the top of that paragraph. When you drag a graphic to a new position within the same paragraph, the anchor symbol remains in its original position and only the graphic moves. You'll see how this works when you move the airplane graphic.

To move the graphic:

1. Select the graphic. You should see an anchor symbol either within the graphic or to the left of the heading "Wide World Travel Clothes."
2. Move the mouse pointer over the graphic.
3. Click and slowly drag the pointer down. As you move the pointer, a dotted outline appears indicating the new position of the graphic.
4. Position the dotted outline so it is in the middle of the paragraph and aligned along the left margin, and then release the mouse button. The graphic moves to its new position, but the anchor remains at the top of the paragraph, to the left of the first line of the paragraph. Your newsletter should look similar to Figure 4-20.

Figure 4-20 Graphic in new position

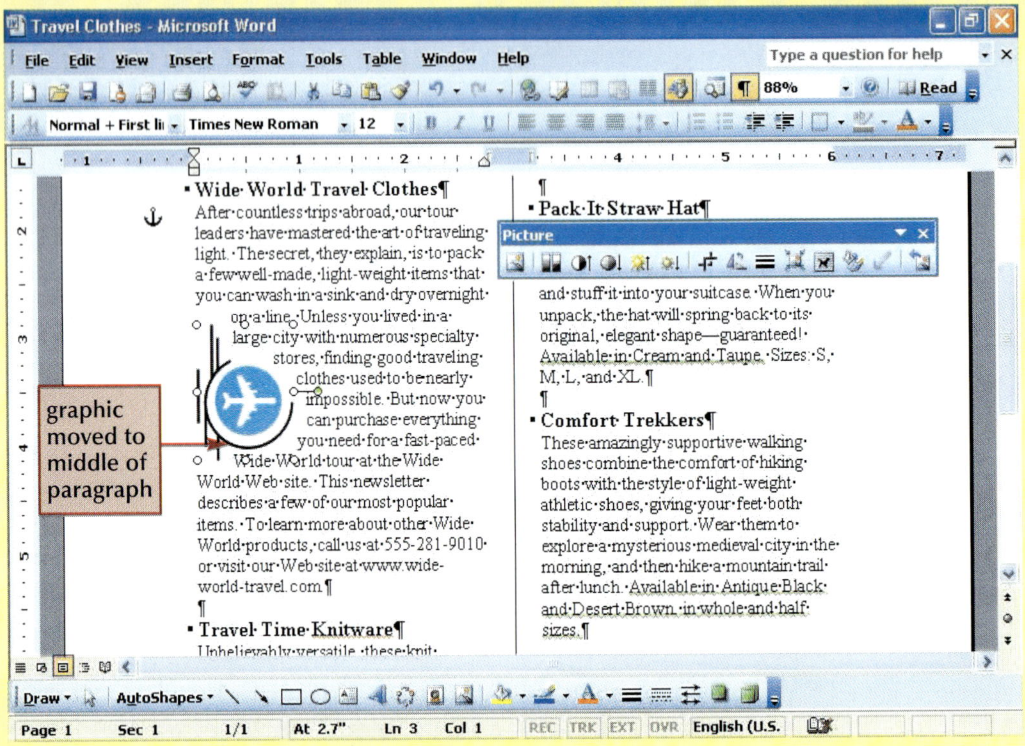

5. Click anywhere outside the graphic to deselect it.

   Trouble? If paragraph text wraps to the left of the graphic, you need to drag the graphic further to the left, so that it aligns along the left margin.

The image of the airplane draws the reader's attention to the beginning of the newsletter, but the rest of the text looks plain. Max suggests adding a drop cap at the beginning of each section.

Inserting Drop Caps

A **drop cap** is a large, capital letter that highlights the beginning of the text of a newsletter, chapter, or some other document section. The drop cap usually extends from the top of the first line of the paragraph down two or three succeeding lines of the paragraph. The text of the paragraph wraps around the drop cap. Word allows you to create a drop cap for the first letter of the first word of a paragraph.

You will create a drop cap for the first paragraph following each heading in the newsletter. The drop cap will extend two lines into the paragraph.

To insert drop caps in the newsletter:

1. If necessary, click in the paragraph below the heading "Wide World Travel Clothes" (the paragraph where you inserted the graphic).
2. Click **Format** on the menu bar, and then click **Drop Cap**. The Drop Cap dialog box opens.
3. In the Position section, click the **Dropped** icon.

4. Click the **Lines to drop** down arrow once to change the setting from 3 to 2. You don't need to change the default distance from the text. See Figure 4-21.

Figure 4-21 Drop Cap dialog box

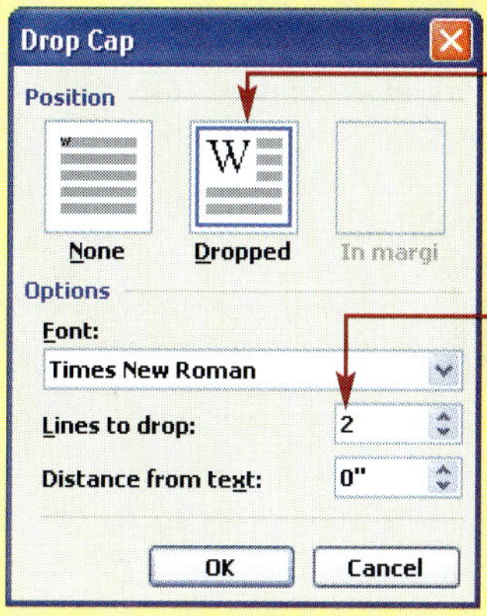

5. Click the **OK** button to close the dialog box, and then click anywhere in the newsletter to deselect the new drop cap. Word formats the first character of the paragraph as a drop cap.

Word re-wraps the text around the graphic to accommodate the drop cap above. See Figure 4-22. If the paragraph text wraps to the left of the graphic, drag the graphic closer to the left margin.

Figure 4-22 Drop Cap begins the paragraph

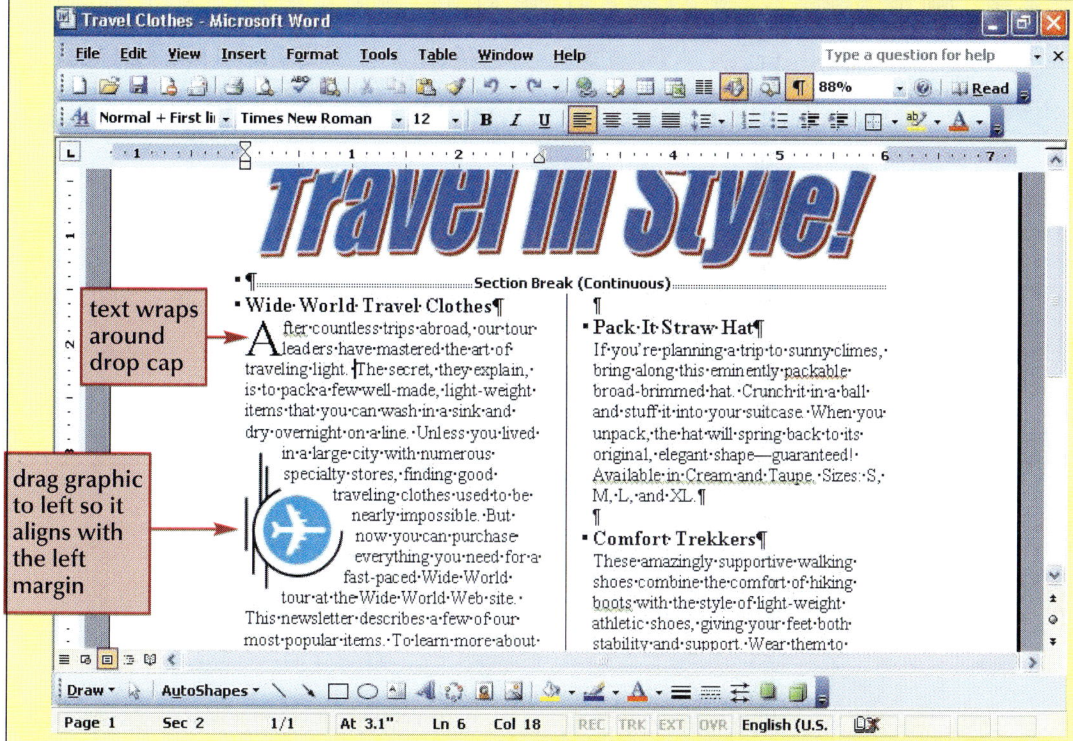

Trouble? Don't be concerned if Word now marks the "fter" of "After" as a grammatical error. Word considers drop caps to be objects, not regular text. By formatting the *A* in "After" as a drop cap, you essentially deleted the regular character *A*. Because the remaining regular characters "fter" do not appear in the Word dictionary, Word might mark it as a potential error.

6. Position the insertion point in the paragraph following the heading "Travel Time Knitware," and then repeat Steps 2-5.
7. Position the insertion point in the paragraph following the heading "Pack It Straw Hat," and then press the **F4** key. The F4 key repeats your previous action at the location of the insertion point.

   Trouble? If something else changes when you press the F4 key, you pressed another key or performed another action after Step 6. Click the Undo button on the Standard toolbar, position the insertion point in the paragraph following the heading "Pack It Straw Hat," and then repeat Steps 2 through 5.
8. Use the **F4** key to add a drop cap to the paragraph following the last heading, and then click anywhere in the text to deselect the drop cap.

The newsletter looks more lively with the drop caps. Next, you turn your attention to inserting a registered trademark symbol (®) next to a registered trademark name.

Inserting Symbols and Special Characters

In printed publications, it is customary to change some of the characters available on the standard keyboard into more polished-looking characters called **typographic symbols**. For instance, while you might type two hyphens to indicate a dash, in a professionally-produced version of that document the two hyphens would be changed to one long dash (called an em dash because it is approximately as wide as the letter "m"). In the past, desktop publishers had to rely on special software to insert and print a document containing typographic symbols, but now you can let Microsoft Word do the work for you.

Word's AutoCorrect feature automatically converts some standard characters into more polished-looking typographic symbols as you type. For instance, as Max typed the information on the Pack It Straw Hat, he typed two hyphens after the words "elegant shape." As he began to type the next word "guaranteed," Word automatically converted the two hyphens into an em dash. Figure 4-23 lists some of the other characters that AutoCorrect automatically converts to typographic symbols. In most cases you need to press the spacebar and type more characters before Word will insert the appropriate symbol. You'll have a chance to practice using AutoCorrect to insert typographic symbols in the Review Assignments at the end of this tutorial.

Figure 4-23 **Common typographic symbols**

To insert this symbol or character	Type	Word converts it to
em dash	word--word	word—word
smiley	:)	☺
copyright symbol	(c)	©
registered trademark symbol	(r)	®
trademark symbol	(tm)	™
ordinal numbers	1st, 2nd, 3rd, etc.	1st, 2nd, 3rd, etc.
fractions	1/2, 1/4	½ ¼
arrows	--> or <--	→ or ←

To insert typographic symbols into a document after you've finished typing it, you can use the Symbol command on the Insert menu.

Inserting Symbols and Special Characters

Reference Window

- Move the insertion point to the location where you want to insert a particular symbol or special character.
- Click Insert on the menu bar, and then click Symbol to open the Symbol dialog box.
- Click the appropriate symbol, or click the name from the list on the Special Characters tab.
- Click the Insert button.
- Click the Close button.

Max noticed that he forgot to insert a registered trademark symbol (®) after "Flexistyle." He asks you to insert this symbol now, using the Symbol command on the Insert menu.

To insert the registered trademark symbol:

1. Scroll down to display the paragraph below the heading "Travel Time Knitware," and then click to the right of the word "Flexistyle." (Take care to click between the final "e" and the comma.)
2. Click **Insert** on the menu bar, and then click **Symbol** to open the Symbol dialog box.
3. If necessary, click the **Special Characters** tab. See Figure 4-24.

Figure 4-24 **Inserting a typographic symbol**

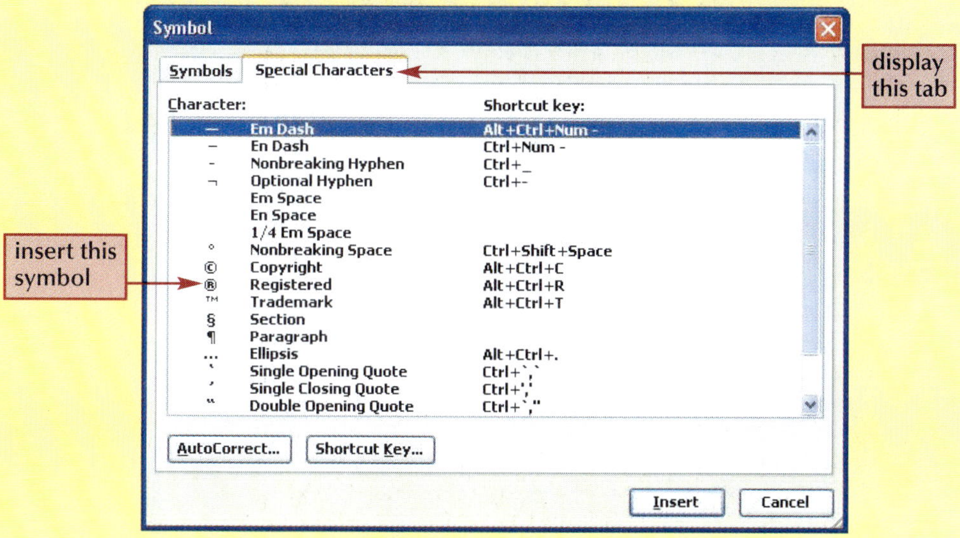

4. Click **Registered** to select it, and then click the **Insert** button.
5. Close the Symbol dialog box. Word inserts an ® immediately after the word "Flexistyle." Finally, you need to format the symbol as superscript, so that it is raised slightly above the surrounding text.
6. Select the symbol, click **Format** on the menu bar, click **Font**, verify that the Font tab is selected, click the **Superscript** check box to insert a check (in the Effects section of the Font dialog box), and then click **OK.** The registered trademark symbol is now smaller and raised slightly above the surrounding text.

Next, you need to adjust the columns of text so they are approximately the same length.

Balancing the Columns

You can shift text from one column to another by adding blank paragraphs to move the text into the next column or by deleting blank paragraphs to shorten the text so it will fit into one column. The problem with this approach is that any edits you make could throw off the balance. Instead, Word can automatically **balance** the columns, or make them of equal length. You'll balance the columns in the newsletter next.

To balance the columns:

1. Position the insertion point at the end of the text in the right column, just after the period following the word "sizes."

   Next, you need to change the zoom to Whole Page so you can see the full effect of the change.
2. Click the **Zoom** list arrow on the Standard toolbar, and then click **Whole Page**.
3. Click **Insert** on the menu bar, and then click **Break**. The Break dialog box opens.
4. Below "Section break types," click the **Continuous** option button.
5. Click the **OK** button. Word inserts a continuous section break at the end of the text. As shown in Figure 4-25, Word balances the text between the two section breaks.

Figure 4-25 Newsletter with balanced columns

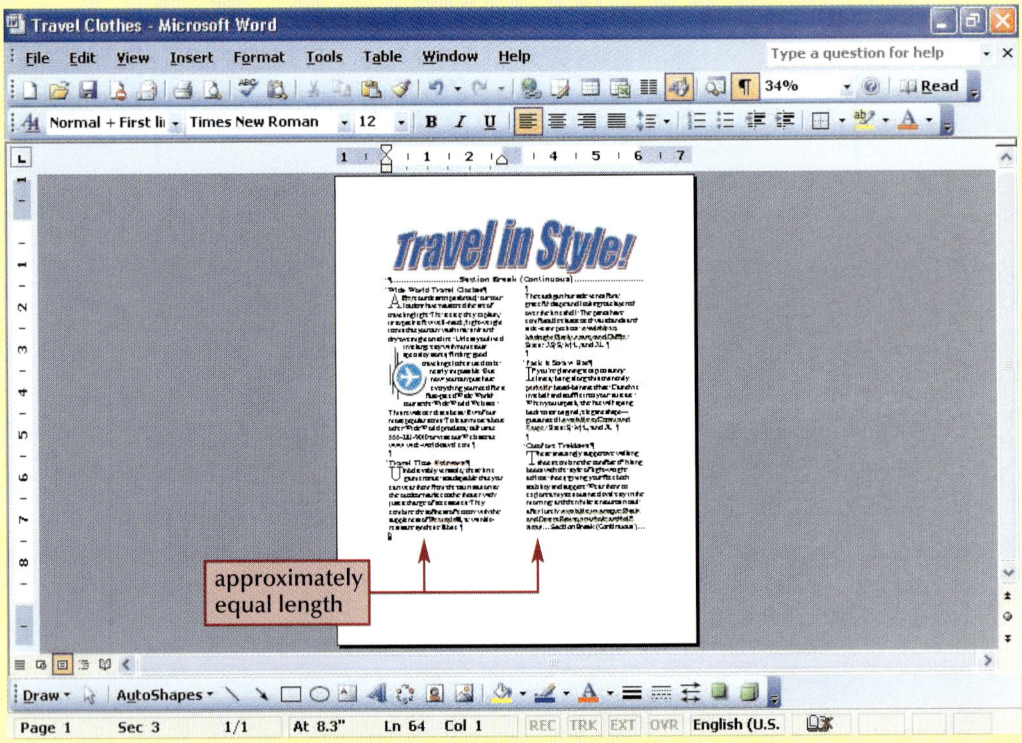

Drawing a Border Around the Page

You can add definition to a paragraph or an entire page by adding a border. You can also emphasize individual paragraphs within a document by putting a border around one or more paragraphs and by adding shading. Right now, Max wants to add a border around the entire newsletter page. (In the Case Problems at the end of this tutorial, you'll have a chance to add a border around individual paragraphs.)

To draw a border around the newsletter:

1. Make sure the document is in Print Layout view and that the Zoom setting is set to Whole Page so that you can see the entire newsletter.
2. Click **Format** on the menu bar, and then click **Borders and Shading**. The Borders and Shading dialog box opens.
3. Click the **Page Border** tab. You use the Setting options on the left side to specify the type of border you want. In this case, you want a simple box.
4. In the Setting section, click the **Box** option. Now that you have selected the type of border you want, you can choose the style of line that will be used to create the border.
5. In the Style list box, scroll down and select the ninth style down from the top (the thick line with the thin line underneath), and then verify that the Apply to option is set to **Whole document**. See Figure 4-26. (While the Borders and Shading dialog box is open, notice the Shading tab, which you can use to add a colored background to a page. You'll have a chance to use this tab in the Case Problems at the end of this tutorial.)

Adding a border to the newsletter **Figure 4-26**

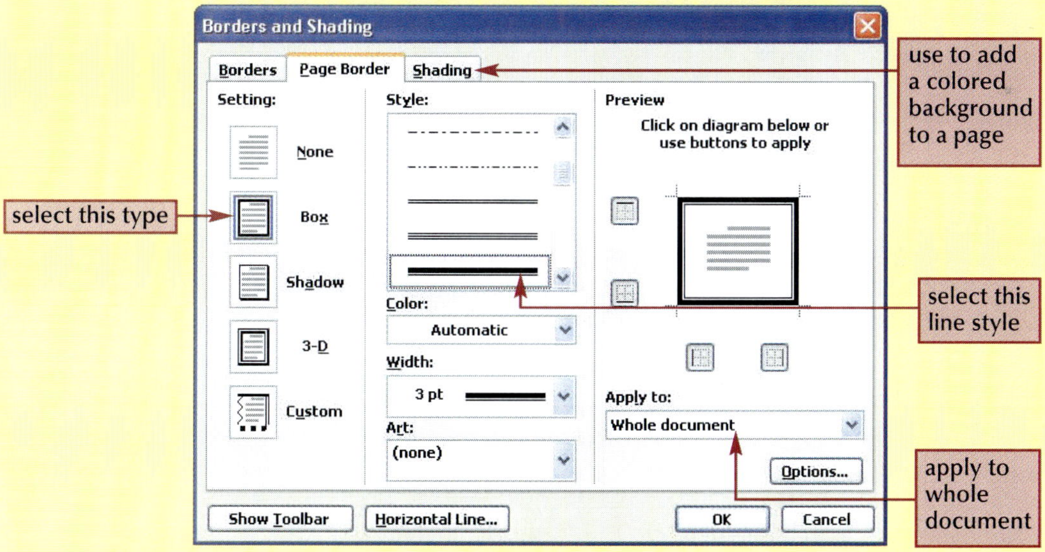

6. Click the **Options** button in the lower-right corner of the Borders and Shading dialog box. The Border and Shading Options dialog box opens. See Figure 4-27. Here you can change settings that control where the border is positioned on the page. Currently, the border is positioned 24 points from the edge of the page. To ensure that your printer will print the entire border, you need to change the Measure from setting so that it is positioned relative to the outside edge of the text rather than the edge of the page.

Figure 4-27 Border and Shading Options dialog box

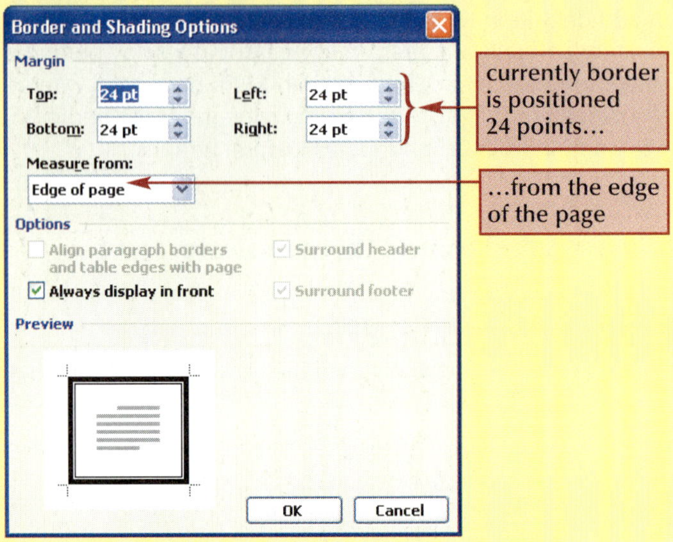

7. Click the **Measure from** list arrow, and then click **Text.** The settings in the Top and Bottom boxes change to 1 pt, and the settings in the Left and Right boxes change to 4 pts, indicating the border's position relative to the edge of the text.
8. Click the **OK** button in the Border and Shading Options dialog box, click **OK** in the Borders and Shading dialog box, and then save your work. The newsletter is now surrounded by an attractive border, as shown earlier in Figure 4-1.
9. Switch to Header and Footer view, change the Zoom setting to Page Width, create a footer that centers **Prepared by your name** and the current date at the bottom of the document. (Be sure to replace "your name" with your first and last name.) Format the footer in a small font to make it as unobtrusive as possible.
10. Close Header and Footer view to return to Print Layout view. Change the Zoom setting to Whole Page. Note that with the Whole Page Zoom setting selected in Print Layout view, there's no need to switch to the Print Preview window. (The Print Preview window provides a fast way to see how the entire document will look at one glance, but does not include the editing tools found in Print Layout or Normal view. By contrast, the Whole Page Zoom setting in Print Layout view allows you to view one page at a time while still providing access to the usual Word editing tools.)
11. Print the newsletter, close the Drawing toolbar, and then close the document but keep Word open, saving the document if prompted to do so. Unless you have a color printer, the WordArt headline and the airplane will print in black and white.

You give the printed newsletter to Max, along with a copy on disk. He thinks it looks great and thanks you for your help. He'll print it later on a high-quality color printer (to get the best resolution for printing multiple copies).

Now that the newsletter is finished, you need to create an accompanying cover letter. Max would like to use Word's mail merge feature to insert customer names and addresses into a form letter.

Understanding the Merge Process

The term **mail merge** refers to the process of combining information from two separate documents to create many final documents, each containing customized information. The two separate documents are called a main document and a data source.

A **main document** is a document (such as a letter) that contains standard text and placeholders (called **merge fields**) that tell Word where to insert variable information (such as a name or an address). You can distinguish merge fields from the other text of the main document, because each merge field name is enclosed by pairs of angled brackets—like this: << >>.

Max's main document is a letter that contains the text shown in Figure 4-28. You will replace the text in brackets with merge fields.

Figure 4-28 **Max's main document**

May 25, 2006

[insert address]

Dear [insert first name]:

Enclosed you'll find a newsletter describing Wide World Travel's exciting new Web site, where you can purchase travel clothes selected by our in-house travel experts. From now on, when you are looking for practical and elegant travel attire, think of Wide World Travel. This publication describes just a few of our most popular items. For more information, visit our Web site at www.wide-world-travel.com.

Sincerely,

Max Stephenson
Senior Travel Guide

A **data source** is a document that contains information, such as clients' names and addresses, which will be inserted into the main document. Max plans to send the newsletter to a small test group of clients for starters. His data source is a table in a Word document that contains the names and addresses of five Wide World Travel clients. This table is shown in Figure 4-29. The header row in the table contains the names of the merge fields. Each row in the table contains information about an individual client and, in mail merge terminology, is called a **record**.

Figure 4-29 **Max's data source**

a merge field name

header row includes all merge field names for this data source

First Name	Last Name	Street Address	City	State	ZIP
Deborah	Browne	3519 Olbrich Avenue	Hartford	CT	06115
Tom	Finnegan	634 Bay View Court	Hartford	CT	06114
Nikki	Nijhawan	2276 Fairlawn Avenue	Good Hope	CT	06117
Alessandra	Ramirez	1 West Main Street	Hartford	CT	06115
Melissa	Sobek	654 State Street	Newark	DE	19716

record for individual client

During a mail merge, the merge fields in the main document instruct Word to retrieve information from the data source. For example, one merge field in the main document might retrieve a first name from the data source; another merge field might retrieve a street address. For each record in the data source, Word will create a separate letter in the final document, which is called the **merged document**. Thus, if the data source contains five sets of client names and addresses, the merged document will contain five separate letters, each one containing a different client name and address in the appropriate places.

Using the Mail Merge Task Pane

Word's Mail Merge task pane walks you through the steps involved in merging documents. When you first open the Mail Merge task pane, the steps you see described there will vary, depending on what document you have open in the main Word window. To ensure that you see the same thing in the Mail Merge task pane each time, it's helpful to open a new, blank document before you open the Mail Merge task pane. Max asks you to start the mail merge process now.

To begin the mail merge process:

1. Click the **New Blank Document** button on the Standard toolbar to open a blank document. Verify that Print Layout view is selected and change the Zoom setting to 100%.
2. Click **Tools** on the menu bar, point to **Letters and Mailings**, and then click **Mail Merge**. The Mail Merge task pane opens. Depending on how your computer is set up, you might also see the Mail Merge toolbar. If you do see the Mail Merge toolbar, close it. See Figure 4-30.

Figure 4-30 Mail Merge task pane

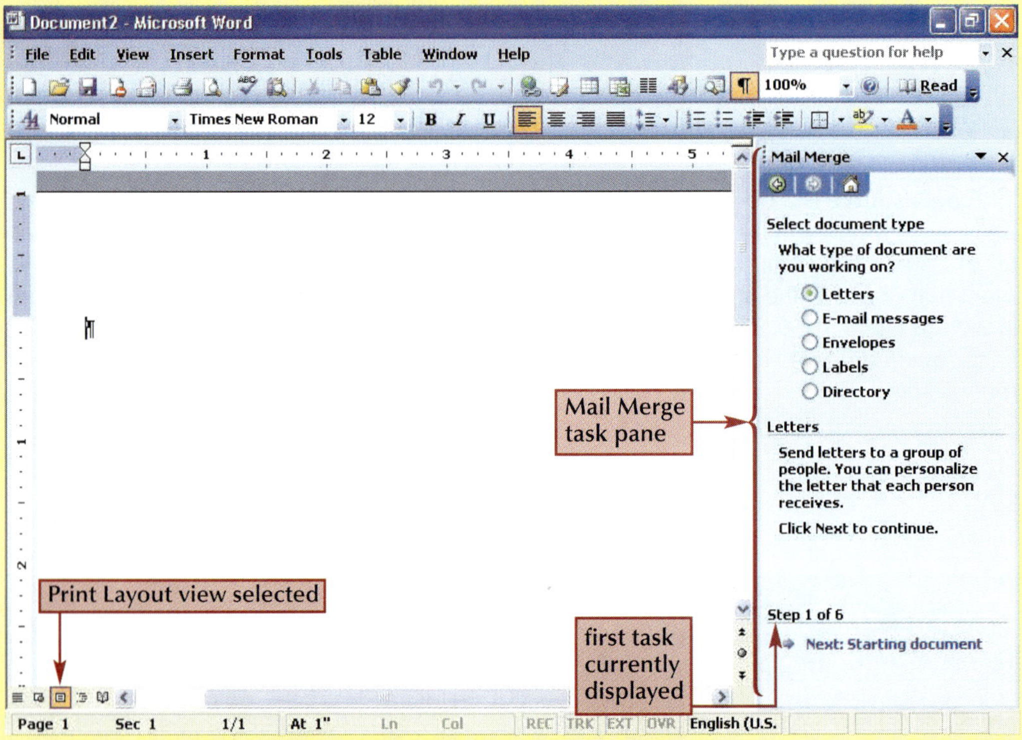

The Mail Merge task pane currently shows the first of six tasks related to completing a mail merge. Your first task is to specify the type of main document you want to use for the merge.

3. Verify that the **Letters** option button is selected in the Mail Merge task pane.

4. At the bottom of the Mail Merge task pane, click **Next: Starting document**. The Mail Merge task pane displays information and options that you can use to select a starting document—that is, to select a main document. In this case, you want to start from an existing document. Specifically, you want to use the Letter document included with your Data Files.
5. Click the **Start from existing document** option button. The task pane displays options for opening an existing document.
6. Verify that **(More files...)** is selected, click the **Open** button on the task pane, and then use the Open dialog box to select and open the file **Letter** located in the Tutorial.04\Tutorial folder. Word inserts the text of the Letter file into the new, blank document, leaving the original Letter file untouched.
7. Check your screen to make sure your document window is in Print Layout view at 100% zoom and with nonprinting characters displayed.
8. Save the document as **Cover Letter** in the Tutorial.04\Tutorial folder, and then scroll down if necessary to display the entire letter. Close the rulers if they are open.

When he first typed the letter, Max included the text in brackets as placeholder text. You will replace the bracketed text with merge fields. First, you need to tell Word where to find the list of recipients for Max's letter.

Selecting a Data Source

You can use many kinds of files as data sources for a mail merge including Word tables, Excel worksheets, Access databases, or a special file designed to store addresses for Microsoft Office applications. You can select a pre-existing file, or you can create a new data source from scratch. In this situation, you will use a pre-existing document containing a simple Word table.

To select the data source:

1. In the bottom of the Mail Merge task pane, click **Next: Select recipients**, and then verify that the **Use an existing list** option button in the task pane is selected.
2. Click **Browse** in the Mail Merge task pane. The Select Data Source dialog box opens. This dialog box is similar to Word's Open dialog box, which you've already used many times.
3. Use the Look in list arrow to open the Tutorial.04\Tutorial folder, select the **Addresses** document, and then click the **Open** button. The table from the Addresses document is displayed in the Mail Merge Recipients dialog box.
4. Click the **OK** button. The Mail Merge Recipients dialog box closes, and you return to the Cover Letter document with the Mail Merge task pane open. Under "Use an existing list," you see the name of the file selected as the data source. (Depending on where you store your Data Files, you may see only the beginning of a directory path, which identifies the location where the data source file is stored.)
5. Click **Next: Write your letter** at the bottom of the Mail Merge task pane. The task pane displays options related to inserting merge fields in the main document.

Inserting Merge Fields

Max's letter is a standard business letter, so you'll place the client's name and address below the date. You could insert individual merge fields for the client's first name, last name, address, city, and ZIP code. But it's easier to use the Address block link in the Mail Merge task pane, which inserts a merge field for the entire address at one click.

To insert an Address Block merge field:

1. Select the text **[insert address]**, and then delete it. Remember to delete the opening and closing brackets. Do not delete the paragraph mark following the text.
2. Verify that there are four blank paragraphs between the date and the salutation, and that the insertion point is positioned in the third blank paragraph below the date.
3. Click **Address block** in the Mail Merge task pane. The Insert Address Block dialog box opens. See Figure 4-31. The options in this dialog box allow you to fine-tune the way the address will be inserted in the letter.

Figure 4-31 Insert Address Block dialog box

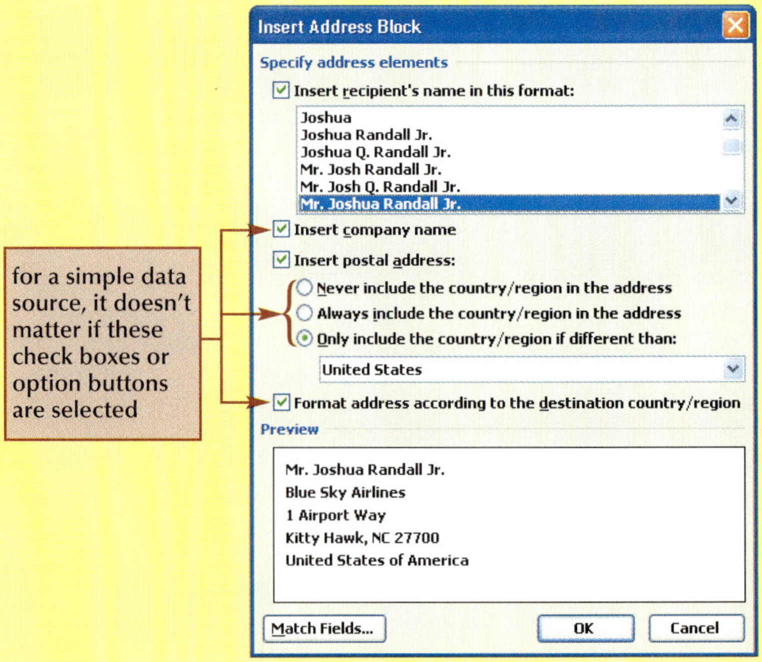

4. Verify that the **Insert recipient's name in this format** check box is selected, and then click **Joshua Randall Jr.** in the list box to ensure that Word will insert each recipient's first and last name. (The other options in this list are only useful with more complicated data sources.)
5. Verify that the **Insert postal address** check box is selected. It doesn't matter whether any of the other check boxes and option buttons are selected. (These options are only useful with more complicated data sources.)
6. Click the **OK** button. An Address Block merge field is inserted in the letter. See Figure 4-32. Depending on how your computer is set up, you might see a gray background behind the merge field. Notice the angled brackets that surround the merge field. The angled brackets are automatically inserted when you insert a merge field. It is important to note that you cannot type the angled brackets and merge field information—you must enter it via a dialog box selection.

Figure 4-32 Address Block merge field in letter

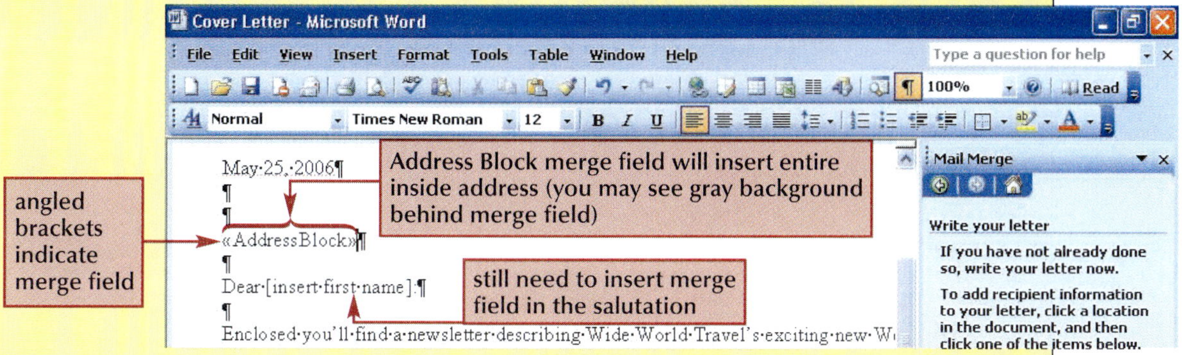

Later, when you merge the main document with the data source, Word will replace the Address Block merge field with information from the data source. Your next job is to insert a merge field that will include each client's first name in the salutation. To insert individual merge codes (rather than a code for the entire address), you need to use the More items option in the Mail Merge task pane.

To insert the merge field for the salutation:

1. Select and delete **[insert first name]** in the salutation. Remember to delete the opening and closing brackets. Do not delete the colon.
2. If necessary, insert a space to the left of the colon. When you finish, the insertion point should be positioned between the space and the colon.
3. Click **More items** in the Mail Merge task pane. The Insert Merge Field dialog box opens. The Fields list shows all the merge fields in the data source. See Figure 4-33. Note that merge fields cannot contain spaces, so Word replaces any spaces in the merge field names with underlines. You want to insert the client's first name into the main document, so you need to make sure the First_Name merge field is selected.

Figure 4-33 Insert Merge Field dialog box

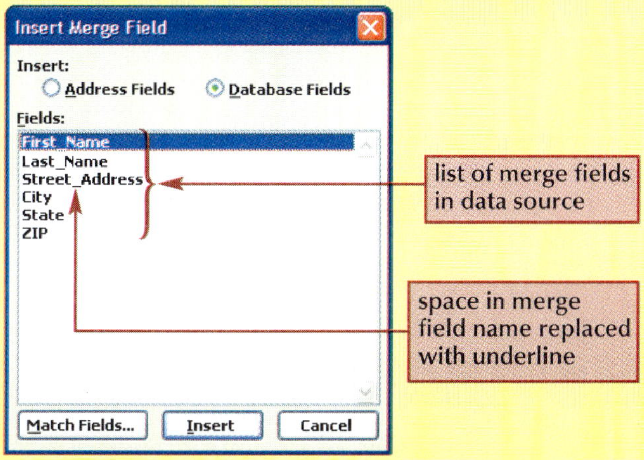

4. Verify that **First_Name** is selected, click the **Insert** button, and then close the Insert Merge Field dialog box. The First_Name merge field is inserted in the document. See Figure 4-34.

Figure 4-34 First_Name merge field inserted in document

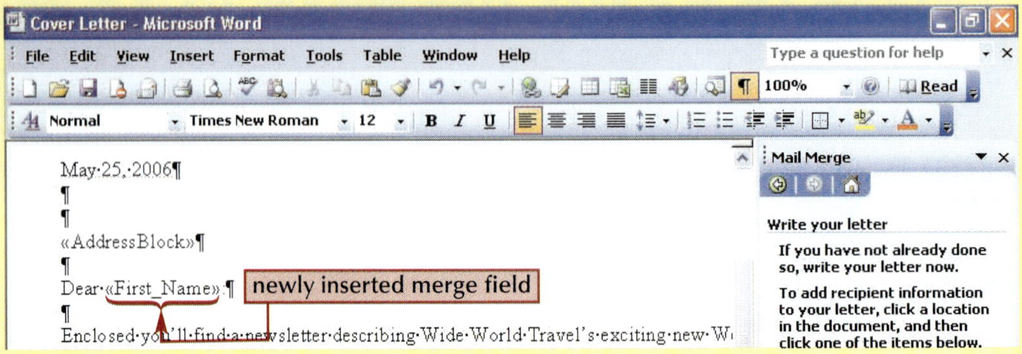

Trouble? If you make a mistake and insert the wrong merge field, click the Undo button on the Standard toolbar, and then repeat Steps 3 and 4.

5. Save your changes to the main document.

The main document now contains all the necessary merge fields, but not the data. To include data, you merge the main document and the data source. First, however, you should preview the merged document.

Previewing the Merged Document

When you preview the merged document, you can check one last time for any missing spaces between the merge codes and the surrounding text. You can also look for any other formatting problems, and, if necessary, make final changes to the main document.

To preview the merged document:

1. In the Mail Merge task pane, click **Next: Preview your letters**. The data for the first client in the data source (Deborah Browne) replaces the merge fields in the form letter. See Figure 4-35. Carefully check the letter to make sure the text and formatting are correct. In particular, check to make sure that the spacing before and after the first name in the salutation is correct because it is easy to omit spaces or add extra spaces around merge fields. Finally, notice that the task pane indicates which record is currently displayed in the document.

Previewing the merge document

Figure 4-35

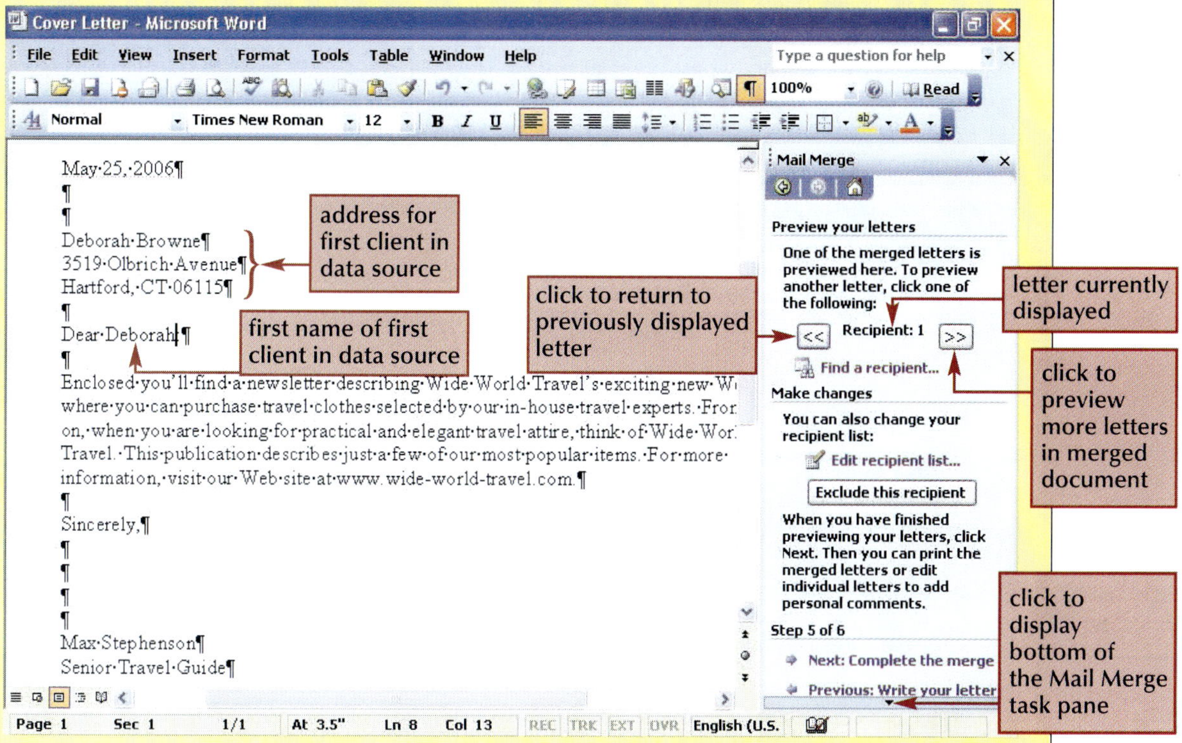

Trouble? If you need to make any changes to the form letter, click the down arrow at the bottom of the Mail Merge task pane to scroll to the bottom of the task pane, click Previous: Write your letter in the task pane, edit the document, save your changes, and then click Next: Preview your letters in the task pane. When you are finished, your screen should look like Figure 4-35.

You are ready for the final step, completing the merge.

Merging the Main Document and Data Source

Now that you've previewed the merge, you're ready to complete the merge between the main document and the data source. The result will be personalized letters to Wide World Travel clients. Because the data source consists of five records, you'll create a merged document with five pages, one letter per page.

To complete the mail merge:

1. In the Mail Merge task pane, click **Next: Complete the merge**. The task pane displays options related to merging the main document and the data source. You can use the Print option to have Word print the customized letters immediately, without displaying them on the screen. Instead, you'll use the Edit individual letters option to merge to a new document.
2. Click **Edit individual letters** in the Mail Merge task pane. The Merge to New Document dialog box opens. Here, you need to specify which records you want to include in the merge. You want to include all the records in the data source.

3. Verify that the **All** option button is selected, click the **OK** button, and then scroll as needed to display the entire first letter. Word creates a new document called Letters1, which contains five pages, one for each record in the data source. Each letter is separated from the one that follows it by a section break. See Figure 4-36. The main document with the merge fields (Cover Letter) remains open, as indicated by its button in the taskbar.

Figure 4-36 Newly merged document with customized letters

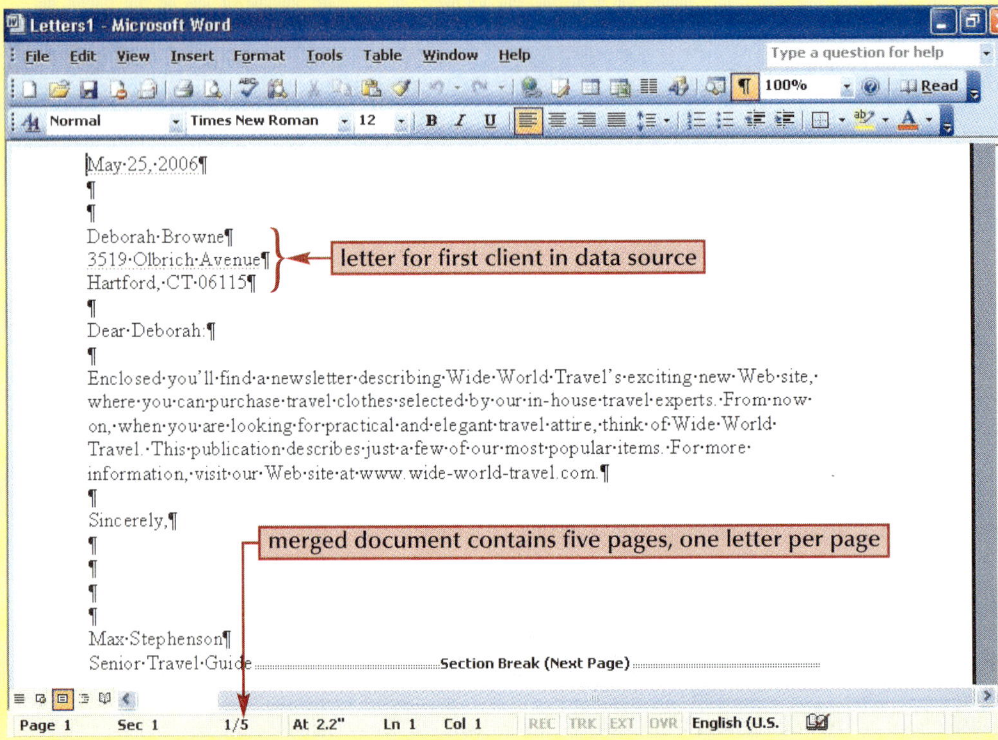

4. Save the merged document in the Tutorial.04\Tutorial folder, using the filename **Merged Cover Letters**. You saved this merged document because it is a small one. However, there's usually no need to waste disk space by saving large merged documents. Typically, you would just print the merged document and close it without saving it. If you need another copy of the merged document later, you can simply merge the data source and main document again.
5. Scroll down and review the five letters. Note the different address and salutation in each.
6. Close the Merged Cover Letters document. The document named Cover Letter reappears, along with the Mail Merge task pane.
7. Close the document and the task pane, and then click the **Yes** button if you are asked to save changes.

You have completed a mail merge and generated a merged document. Max will send the cover letters out with five sample copies of his newsletter right away.

Review

Session 4.2 Quick Check

1. Define the following in your own words:
   a. drop cap
   b. scaling
   c. clip art
   d. main document
   e. data source
2. Explain how to insert a clip art graphic in Word.
3. True or False: When inserting a drop cap, you cannot specify the number of lines you want the drop cap to extend into the document vertically.
4. Describe two different methods for inserting the registered trademark symbol in a document.
5. Describe the process for drawing a border around a page.
6. Describe the steps involved in performing a mail merge.

Review

Tutorial Summary

In this tutorial you planned a newsletter and learned about the elements of desktop publishing. You worked with hyperlinks, created a WordArt headline, anchored a WordArt object, and formatted text in newspaper-style columns. You also inserted a graphic into a document, edited the graphic, inserted drop caps, and inserted symbols and special characters. Finally, you balanced the newsletter columns, drew a border around the page, and used mail merge to create customized cover letters to accompany the newsletter.

Key Terms

balance
bitmap
clip art
crop
data source
drop cap
floating graphic
graphics
hyperlinks
inline graphic
links
mail merge
main document
merge fields
merged document
newspaper-style column
object
Paint
record
scaling
scanner
sizing handle
typographic symbols
URL
Web page
white space
WordArt
WordArt Shape button
wrap

Practice

Apply the skills you learned in the tutorial using the same case scenario.

Review Assignments

Data Files needed for the Review Assignments: Travel.doc, Highlights.doc, and Addresses.doc

Max's Wide World Travel newsletter was a success; the sales for the advertised items were brisk. Now he has been asked to create a newsletter describing the highlights of some recent Wide World Travel tours. Max has already written the text of the newsletter and asks you to transform it into a professional-looking newsletter. He asks you to create an accompanying cover letter using Word's mail merge feature. Complete the following:

1. Open the file **Travel** from the Tutorial.04\Review folder included with your Data Files, and then check your screen to make sure your Word document is displayed in Print Layout view at 100% zoom, that the nonprinting characters are displayed, and that the Drawing toolbar is open.
2. Save the document as **Travel Highlights** in the same folder.
3. In the first paragraph, replace "YOUR NAME" with your first and last name.
4. Insert "or visit our Web site at www.wide-world-travel.com" at the end of the first paragraph, immediately after the phone number (do not include the quotation marks). Add a period to complete the sentence. Then insert a blank line and remove the hyperlink from the Web address.
5. At the top of the document, create the headline "Wide World Highlights" using WordArt. In the WordArt Gallery, choose the fourth style from the left in the third row down from the top (the rainbow style with the shadow).
6. Change the shape of the WordArt object to Triangle Up, and then italicize the WordArt text.
7. Apply the Top and Bottom wrapping style to the WordArt object.
8. Insert a blank paragraph at the beginning of the document, anchor the WordArt headline to the new paragraph, and then save your work. If the WordArt moves below the new paragraph symbol, drag it up above the new paragraph. When you are finished, the anchor symbol should be positioned to the left of the new paragraph symbol, with the WordArt object positioned above the new paragraph symbol.
9. If necessary, enlarge the WordArt object to span the entire width of the page. Be sure to hold down the Shift key while you drag. When you are finished, the WordArt object should be approximately .5 inches high on the left end, and about 1 inch tall at the center.
10. Position the insertion point to the left of the first word in the paragraph (which begins "Wide World Travel, Inc."), and then format the newsletter text in two columns using the Columns dialog box. Insert a section break so that the two-column formatting is applied to the part of the newsletter after the insertion point. Do not insert a line between columns. View the new columns in Print Layout view, using the Whole Page Zoom setting.
11. Switch to Page Width zoom, and then click to the left of the paragraph that begins "We prefaced our adventure . . . "
12. Insert the clip art graphic of the Eiffel Tower from the Buildings folder in the Office Collections folder.
13. Select and resize the graphic so it is approximately 1.5 inches square.
14. Crop the image vertically about .25" on both the left and right so that, when you are finished, the image is approximately 1 inch wide.
15. Wrap text around the graphic using Tight text wrapping
16. Create a drop cap in the first paragraph under each heading, including the first paragraph below the WordArt headline, using the default settings for the Dropped position.

17. In the first paragraph below the WordArt headline, insert the trademark symbol after "Wide World Adventures." Format the symbol as superscript if it appears in the same size as the surrounding text.
18. Balance the columns. If the words in the last line of the newsletter text are spaced too far apart after you insert the section break, click at the end of the line, and then press the Enter key to move the section break to the next line.
19. Add a border around the page using a border style of your choice.
20. Preview, save, and print the newsletter. When you are finished, close the document.
21. Open the file **Highlights** located in the Tutorial.04\Review folder, and then save the document as **Highlights Cover Letter** in the same folder.
22. Merge the Highlights Cover Letter document with the Addresses file found in the Tutorial.04\Review folder. Use the Address Block merge field for the inside address. Then include a merge field that will insert the customer's first name in the salutation. Preview the merged letters and make any necessary changes before completing the merge.
23. Save the merged document as **Merged Highlights Cover Letters** and close it. Save your changes to the main document and close it. Close the task pane.

Apply

Apply the skills you learned to create a newsletter for a city agency.

Case Problem 1

Data File needed for this Case Problem: Convert.doc

City of Santa Fe, New Mexico Caroline Hestwood is the manager of information systems for the city of Santa Fe. She and her staff are planning to convert all city computers from the Windows 2000 operating system to Windows XP and to standardize application software on the latest version of Microsoft Office. Caroline writes a monthly newsletter on computer operations and training, so this month she has devoted the newsletter to the conversion. She asks you to finalize the newsletter. Complete the following:

1. Open the file **Convert** located in the Tutorial.04\Cases folder included with your Data Files, and then check your settings to be sure your document is displayed in Print Layout view at 100% zoom, that the nonprinting characters are displayed, and that the Drawing toolbar is open.
2. Save the document as **Conversion Newsletter** in the same folder.
3. If the text you want to format as WordArt has already been typed, you can begin creating your WordArt by selecting the text in the document. Select the text of the newsletter title, "Software Update." (Do not select the paragraph symbol at the end of the title.) Click the Insert WordArt button on the Drawing toolbar, and then create a Word Art title, using the style in the third row down, first column on the left.
4. Set the text wrapping style to Top and Bottom, and then verify that the WordArt is anchored to the blank paragraph at the top of the document.
5. Edit the WordArt object to set the font to 32-point Arial bold, and then apply the Arch Up (Curve) shape to the object. Resize the WordArt object so that it spans the width of the page from left margin to right margin and so that its maximum height is about 1 inch. (*Hint*: Use the sizing handles while watching the horizontal and vertical rulers in Print Layout view to adjust the object to the appropriate size.) Drag the WordArt down, if necessary, so that it is positioned below the top margin.
6. Center and italicize the subtitle of the newsletter, "Newsletter from the Santa Fe Information Management Office." Verify that the WordArt is anchored to the first paragraph in the document (which is a blank paragraph).

7. Replace "INSERT YOUR NAME HERE" with your name, then center and italicize the line containing your name.
8. Select the subtitle and the line after it (containing your name). Apply a Box style border, with Gray–15% shading. Be sure Paragraph is selected in the Apply to list box of the Borders and Shading dialog box.
9. Format all the text below the WordArt heading in two newspaper style columns. Notice that the text you italicized and centered now appears centered over the left column.
10. Undo the column formatting, click to the left of "The Big Switch," insert a continuous section break, and then format the text below the section break in two columns. The subtitle is now centered over the two columns.
11. Position the insertion point at the beginning of the first paragraph under the heading "Training on MS Office," and then open the Clip Art task pane. If any text appears in the Search for text box, delete it, type "computer," and then click Go. A group of clip art images appears in the Clip Art task pane. Click the image of a woman in a purple shirt typing on a keyboard. Close the Clip Art task pane.

Explore

12. Resize the picture so that it is 55% of its original size. Instead of dragging the sizing handles as you did in the tutorial, select the picture, and then click the Format Picture button on the Picture toolbar to open the Format Picture dialog box. Click the Size tab. Adjust the Height and Width settings to 55% in the Scale section, and make sure the Lock aspect ratio check box is selected. If you do not like the result, you can drag the sizing handles to fine-tune the adjustment.
13. Apply the Tight text wrapping option. Drag the picture down so it is positioned to the left of the second and third bullets.
14. Use the Clip Organizer to insert a second computer-related graphic in the right column, in the paragraph under the italicized heading "Why are we switching to Windows XP?" Open the Office Collections folder, open the Technology folder, and then open the Computing folder. Use the black and white image of a computer and a mouse on a blue background. Size the image to span half the column, apply the Square wrapping option, and drag the picture down so it is positioned halfway down the paragraph along the left column margin.

Explore

15. You can use the Replace command to replace standard word processing characters with typographic symbols. To replace every occurrence of two hyphens (--) with an em dash (—), position the insertion point at the beginning of the first paragraph of text (at the beginning of the paragraph under the heading "The Big Switch"). Click Edit on the menu bar, and then click Replace. Click the More button to display additional options. In the Find what text box, type two hyphens (--), and then press the Tab key to move the insertion point to the Replace with text box. Click the Special button at the bottom of the dialog box. Click Em Dash in the list. Word displays the special code for em dashes in the Replace with text box. Click the Replace All button. When the operation is complete, click the OK button, and then click the Close button.
16. Insert a drop cap in the first paragraph under each heading, using the default settings for the Dropped option.
17. Switch to Whole Page zoom and insert a border around the newsletter. Use a border style of your choice.
18. Save and print the newsletter, and then close it.

Apply

Apply the skills you learned to create an employee newsletter for a moving company.

Case Problem 2

Data Files needed for this Case Problem: Movers.doc and Knight.bmp

Morning Star Movers Martin Lott is the executive secretary to Whitney Kremer, director of personnel for Morning Star Movers (MSM), a national moving company with headquarters in Minneapolis, Minnesota. Martin assigned you the task of preparing the monthly newsletter News and Views, which provides news about MSM employees. You decide to update the layout and to use the desktop-publishing capabilities of Word to design the newsletter. You will use text assembled by other MSM employees for the body of the newsletter. Complete the following:

1. Open the file **Movers** included in the Tutorial.04\Cases folder included with your Data Files, and then save it as **Movers Newsletter** in the same folder.
2. Use the Find and Replace command to replace all instances of the name "Katrina" with your first name. Then replace all instances of "Pollei" with your last name.
3. Click at the end of the first section (to the right of the space after "contact her at"), and then type "dronzek@msm.net" (without the quotes) followed by a period. Press Enter to insert a blank line, and then remove the hyperlink.
4. Create a "News and Views" WordArt title for the newsletter. Use the WordArt style in the third row down, fourth column from the left, and set the font to 24-point Arial bold. Set the wrapping style to Top and Bottom, and then anchor the WordArt to the blank paragraph at the top of the document (if it isn't already).
5. Resize the WordArt object so that the title is centered and so that the height of the title is slightly less than .5 inch. (*Hint*: Use the sizing handles while watching the horizontal and vertical rulers in Print Layout view to adjust the object to the appropriate size.)
6. Make sure the WordArt object is positioned above the blank paragraph, click to the left of the heading "CFO Dronzek Receives Alumni Award," and then format the body of the newsletter into two newspaper-style columns. Place a vertical rule between the columns. (*Hint*: Click the Undo button and repeat the steps if the columns do not start where expected.)
7. You can change the structure of a newsletter by reformatting it with additional columns. Change the number of columns from two to three using the Columns dialog box. Make sure that the Equal column width check box is selected.

Explore

8. Position the insertion point at the beginning of the paragraph below the heading "MSM Chess Team Takes Third." Click Insert on the menu bar, point to Picture, and then click From File. Look in the Tutorial.04\Cases folder, select the file named **Knight**, and then click the Insert button.

9. Scale the height and the width of the picture to 60% of its original size. (*Hint*: To scale the size, click the Format Picture button on the Picture toolbar, and then set the Scale values on the Size tab, making sure the Lock aspect ratio check box and the Relative to original picture size check boxes are selected.) Close the Format Picture dialog box when you are finished.

Explore

10. In addition to cropping a picture with the Crop button, you can use the Format Picture dialog box. Using this dialog box allows you to be more precise, because you can specify exact cropping measurements. To try it now, verify that the graphic is selected, click the Format Picture button on the Picture toolbar, click the Picture tab if it is not already selected, and change the values in the Crop from text boxes as follows:
    Left: 0.3 Top: 0.2
    Right: 0.4 Bottom: 0.4

Explore

11. To view advanced options for wrapping text, verify that the graphic is selected, click the Format Picture button on the Picture toolbar, click the Layout tab, and then click Advanced. Click the Tight icon, and notice the additional settings at the bottom of the Advanced Layout dialog box. Among other things, you can specify to what side the text should wrap and the distance to preserve between the text and the graphic. Click the Right only option button, click OK, and then click OK again. Keep in mind that you can also access the Advanced Layout dialog box from the Format WordArt dialog box.
12. Insert a drop cap in the first paragraph after each heading except the "MSM Chess Team Takes Third" heading. Use the Dropped default settings for number of lines, but change the font of the drop cap to Arial.
13. Preview the document. If the newsletter spans two pages, click the Shrink to Fit button to reduce the newsletter to one page.
14. Add a border around the entire page of the newsletter.
15. Save the newsletter, and then preview and print it. Close the document.

Challenge

Explore new techniques as you create the two-sided brochure shown in Figure 4-37.

Case Problem 3

Data File needed for this Case Problem: Grains.doc

Wild Grains Grocery Cooperative Mary Ann Hansen is the publicity director for Wild Grains Grocery Cooperative in Athens, Georgia. Local residents pay a membership fee to join the co-op, and then receive a 10% discount on all purchases. Many members don't realize that they can take advantage of other benefits, such as free cooking classes and monthly mailings with recipe cards and coupons. To spread the word, Mary Ann would like to create a brochure describing the benefits of joining the co-op. She has already written the text of the brochure. She would like the brochure to consist of one piece of paper folded in three parts, with text on both sides of the paper, as shown in Figure 4-37.

Figure 4-37

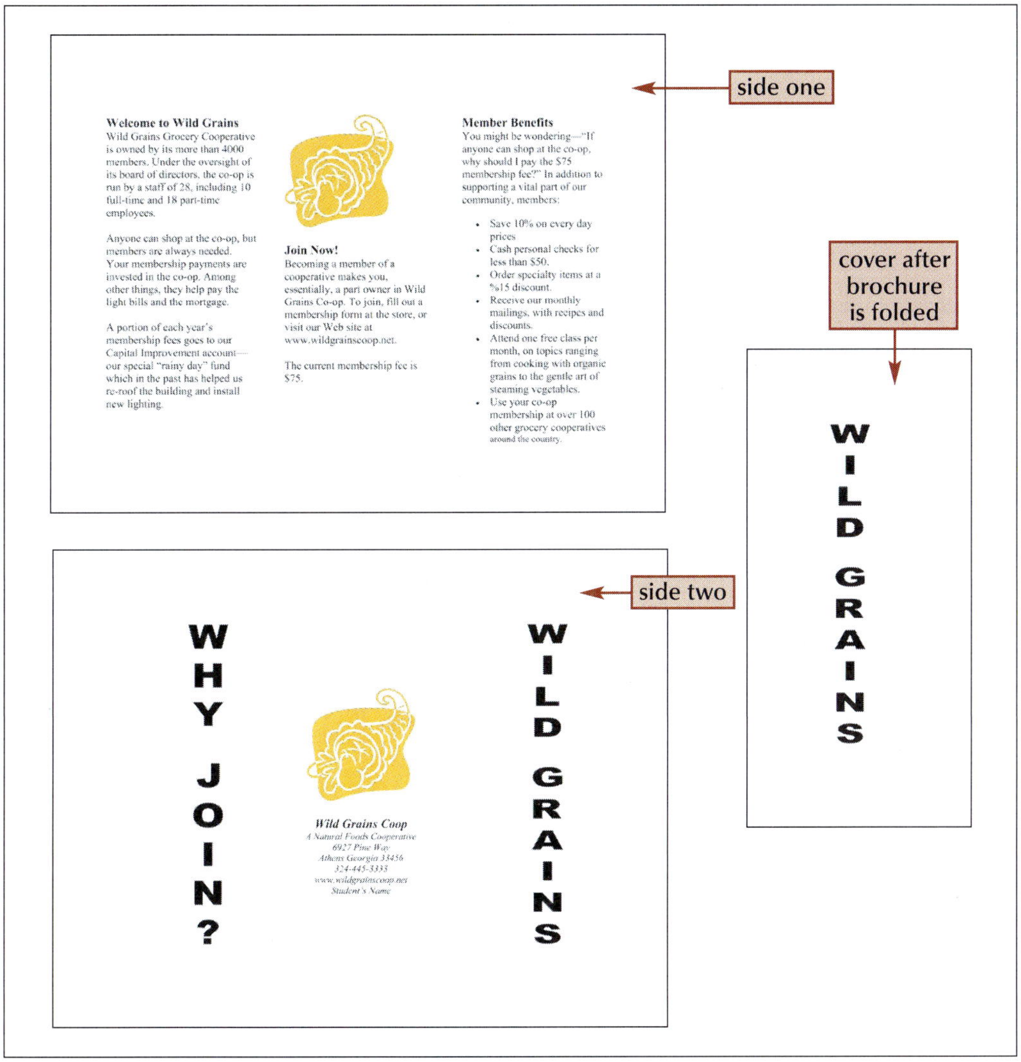

Complete the following:

1. Open the file **Grains** located in the Tutorial.04\Cases folder included with your Data Files, and then save it as **Wild Grains Brochure** in the same folder. If necessary, switch to Print Layout view.
2. On the second page, below the cornucopia graphic, click after the Web address, insert a blank line, and then type your first and last name. Remove the hyperlink from the Web address.
3. Format the entire document in three columns of equal width. Do not include a vertical line between columns. Don't be concerned that part of the text overflows onto a second page.
4. Click at the end of the list of member benefits (after "country."), and then press Ctrl+Enter to insert a page break. Remove the bullet from the new paragraph.

Explore

5. You are already familiar with adding section breaks and page breaks to a document. You can also add a column break, which forces the text after the insertion point to move to the next column. Click at the beginning of the heading "Join Now!" (just to the left of the "J"), and open the Break dialog box. Under Break types, click Column

break, and then click OK. Insert another column break before the heading "Member Benefits." On the second page, click at the top of the left column, press Enter three times to insert some blank paragraphs, and then insert another column break. This column break should move the cornucopia graphic and the text below it to the middle column. Press Ctrl+End to move the insertion point to the end of the document, and insert another column break.

6. Change the Zoom setting to Whole Page and review your work. The document should consist of two pages, with three columns each. The graphic and the co-op address should appear in the middle column on the second page.
7. Copy the cornucopia graphic in the second page, click to the left of the heading "Join Now!", and then add two blank paragraphs. Click in the first new paragraph (at the top of the column), and then paste the copied graphic at that location. The middle column of the first page now contains another cornucopia graphic, with the heading "Join Now!" below, followed by two paragraphs of text.
8. Click in the left column of page 2, and then delete all but one of the paragraph marks above the column break. With the insertion point located at the only remaining paragraph mark in the left column, insert the WordArt text "WHY JOIN?" In the WordArt Gallery, select the style in the left column, fourth row down. Be sure to type "WHY JOIN?" in all uppercase letters in the Edit WordArt Text dialog box, and format the text in bold. Save your work. Don't be concerned if part of the WordArt object is truncated. You'll fix that in Step 9, when you rotate the WordArt.

Explore

9. Select the WordArt object if it is not already selected, and then click the WordArt Vertical Text button on the WordArt toolbar. The heading is positioned vertically in the left column of page 2.
10. Adjust the size of the WordArt object (by dragging a sizing handle) so that the WordArt spans the height of the column—do *not* press Shift as you drag the handle—and the letters spread out to fill the height of the column. When you are finished, the WordArt object should be approximately 6 inches high. If you increase the size too much, the WordArt will jump to the next column. If that happens, click the Undo button and try again.

Explore

11. Click the Format WordArt button on the WordArt toolbar. In the Format WordArt dialog box, click the Colors and Lines tab, click the Color list arrow, click the black square in the upper-left corner of the palette, and then click OK. Center the WordArt in the column. The WordArt changes from a marbleized brown to all black. Save your work.
12. Copy the "WHY JOIN?" WordArt object to the Clipboard. Paste a copy of the WordArt object in the right column of page 2, double-click the WordArt object, and then change the text to "WILD GRAINS". Center the WordArt in the column. When you are finished, page 2 should consist of the "WHY JOIN?" WordArt in the left column, the graphic and address information in the middle column, and the "WILD GRAINS" WordArt in the right column. Verify that Zoom is still set to Whole Page view and examine your work.
13. Use the Page Setup command on the File menu to center both pages vertically. (*Hint*: Use the Vertical alignment setting in the Layout tab.) Save your work.

Explore

14. If you need to add a small amount of text to a document that's formatted in a complicated way, you can use a text box, which is a kind of miniature Word document. Like a graphic, a text box is an object that you can select and resize. You can edit and format the text in a text box using the usual Word tools. In Print Layout view, change the Zoom setting to 100% and scroll to display the top of the middle column on the second page. Click at the top of the middle column, insert one blank paragraph, move

the insertion point to the top of the column, and click the Text Box button on the Drawing toolbar. A gray box called a drawing canvas appears at the top of the middle column. The drawing canvas contains the text "Create your drawing here." Drag the mouse pointer inside the drawing canvas to draw a rectangle about 1.5 inches wide and one inch tall (using the rulers as a guide), and then release the mouse button. Type "Learn about the advantages of membership!" (without the quotation marks). Select the text in the text box and format it in 14-point Times New Roman, italic, bold. Use the Center Align button to center the text in the text box, and then click anywhere outside the drawing canvas to deselect the text box and the drawing canvas. Switch the Zoom setting to Whole Page and adjust the text box size and the position of the graphic as needed so that the content of the center column fits nicely on the page. Save your work.

Explore

15. To print the brochure, you need to print the first page and then print the second page on the reverse side. Click File on the menu bar, click Print, click the Pages option button, type 1, and then click OK. Retrieve the printed page, and then insert it into your printer's paper tray so that "WHY JOIN?" prints on the reverse side of the list of member benefits; likewise, "WILD GRAINS" should print on the reverse side of the "Welcome to Wild Grains" text. Whether you should place the printed page upside down or right-side up depends on your printer. You may have to print a few test pages until you get it right. When you finish, you should be able to turn page 1 (the page with the heading "Welcome to Wild Grains") face up, and then fold it inward in thirds, along the two column borders. Fold the brochure so that the "WILD GRAINS" column lies on top. *Note*: Ask your instructor if you should print the brochure before doing so.
16. Close the document.

Create

Create the table shown in Figure 4-38, and then use it as the data source for a mail merge resulting in cover letters and envelopes for your own job search.

Case Problem 4

There are no Data Files needed for this Case Problem.

Job Search Cover Letters You're ready to start looking for a job, and plan to use Word's mail merge feature to create customized cover letters to accompany your resume. You'll start by creating the table shown in Figure 4-38 and filling it with address information for potential employers. Then you'll create a cover letter to use as a main document, and customize it by inserting the appropriate mail merge fields.

Figure 4-38

First Name	Last Name	Company Name	Street Address	City	State	ZIP

Complete these steps:

1. Open a new, blank document, and then save it as **Job Search Data Source** in the Tutorial.04\Cases folder included with your Data Files.
2. Create the table shown in Figure 4-38, and then enter information for three potential employers. The information can be real or fictitious. For the First Name and Last Name columns, use the name of an appropriate contact at each company. Save your work and close the document.

3. Open a new, blank document and save it as **Job Search Cover Letter** in the Tutorial.04\Cases folder.
4. Create a cover letter that introduces yourself and describes your experience and education. Instead of an inside address, include the placeholder text "[Inside Address]". For the salutation, use "Dear Ms. [Last Name]". (You'll have a chance to change "Ms." to "Mr." where necessary when you edit the individual merged letters.) Refer the reader to your resume for more information. Use the correct business letter style for your cover letter. Include a sentence in the cover letter that mentions the company name. Use the placeholder "[Company Name]" to remind you to insert the appropriate merge field later. Save your work and close the document.
5. Open a new, blank document, open the Mail Merge task pane, and follow the steps outlined in the Mail Merge task pane. Use the Job Search Cover Letter document as the main document, and select the **Job Search Data Source** file as the data source. Use the Address block merge field for the inside address (and verify that the Insert company name check box is selected in the Insert Address Block dialog box). Add a merge field for the last name in the salutation of the letter, and add a merge field to replace the Company Name placeholder text in the body of the letter. Save your changes to the main document before completing the merge.
6. Preview your letters, and then complete the merge (choosing the Edit individual letters option). Review the letters, and edit them as necessary to use Ms. or Mr. appropriately in the salutation. Save the merged document as **Job Search Cover Letter Merged** in the Tutorial.04\Cases folder, close it, and close the Mail Merge task pane.
7. Print your main document, and then close it.
8. Open a new, blank document, and then save it as **Job Search Envelopes** in the Tutorial.04\Cases folder.

Explore

9. Open the Mail Merge task pane, click the Envelopes option button under Select document type, click Next: Starting document, click Envelope options, and then click OK in the Envelope Options dialog box to select the default settings. The document layout changes to resemble a business size envelope.
10. Continue with the steps in the Mail Merge task pane, selecting the **Job Search Data Source** file as the data source.

Explore

11. Click Next: Arrange your envelope, and then type your name and address as the return address. Notice that the insertion point is positioned in the return address, ready for you to begin typing. (Change the Zoom setting if necessary to make the text easier to read.) Click the paragraph mark in the center of the document and insert an Address block merge field. Save your work.
12. Preview the envelopes, and complete the merge (choosing the Edit individual envelopes option). Save the merged document as **Job Search Envelopes Merged** in the Tutorial.04\Cases folder, and then close it. If your computer is connected to a printer that is stocked with envelopes, print the main document. Close the main document and the Mail Merge task pane.

Research

Go to the Web to find information you can use to create documents.

Internet Assignments

The purpose of the Internet Assignments is to challenge you to find information on the Internet that you can use to work effectively with this software. The actual assignments are updated and maintained on the Course Technology Web site. Log on to the Internet and use your Web browser to go to the Student Online Companion for New Perspectives Office 2003 at **www.course.com/np/office2003**. Click the Internet Assignments link, and then navigate to the assignments for this tutorial.

Assess

SAM Assessment and Training

If you have a SAM user profile, you may have access to hands-on instruction, practice, and assessment of the skills covered in this tutorial. Log in to your SAM account and go to your assignments page to see what your instructor has assigned.

Review

Quick Check Answers

Session 4.1

1. List any four of the following: The document uses multiple fonts; the document incorporates graphics; the document uses typographic symbols; the document uses columns and other special formatting features; the printing is of high-quality.
2. True
3. a. using a desktop computer system to produce commercial-quality printed material; with desktop publishing, you can enter and edit text, create graphics, lay out pages, and print documents
   b. a Word feature that allows you to insert specially formatted text into a document.
   c. unformatted text
   d. a symbol that appears in the left margin, which shows a WordArt object's position in relation to the text
4. False
5. To change the text of a WordArt object, click the object to select it, click the Edit Text button on the WordArt toolbar, edit the text in the Edit WordArt Text dialog box, and then click OK.
6. The WordArt Shape button allows you to change the basic shape of a WordArt object.
7. False

Session 4.2

1. a. a large, uppercase letter that highlights the beginning of the text of a newsletter, chapter, or some other document section
   b. resizing an image to fit a document better
   c. premade artwork that you can insert into your document
   d. a document (such as a letter) that contains standard text and placeholders (called merge fields) that tell Word where to insert variable information (such as a name or an address)
   e. a document that contains information, such as clients' names and addresses, which will be inserted into the main document
2. Position the insertion point at the location where you want to insert the image, click the Insert Clip Art button on the Drawing toolbar, click Organize clips in the Clip Art task pane, open the folder containing the image you want, click the arrow button on the image, click Copy, and then close the Clip Organizer. Finally, paste the graphic into the document.
3. False
4. Click where you want to insert the symbol in the document, click Insert on the menu bar, click Symbol, click the Special Characters tab in the Symbol dialog box, click Registered Trademark in the list, click the Insert button, and then click the Close button. Another option is to type "(r)"and press the spacebar.
5. Click Format on the menu bar, click Borders and Shading, click the Page Border tab in the Borders and Shading dialog box, select the border type you want in the Setting section, choose a line style from the Style list box, make sure Whole document appears in the Apply to list box, and then click OK.
6. Select or create a main document. Select or create a data source. Use the Mail Merge task pane to insert merge fields into the main document. Preview the merged document. Merge the data source and the main document.

Objectives

Session 6.1
- Learn about the Mail Merge process
- Use the Mail Merge task pane
- Select a main document
- Create a data source
- Insert mail merge fields into a main document
- Edit a main document
- Preview a merged document
- Complete a mail merge

Session 6.2
- Edit an existing data source
- Sort records
- Create mailing labels and a phone directory

Creating Form Letters and Mailing Labels

Writing a Form Letter

Case

Palm Tree Athletic Club

Maria Fuentes is the facilities manager for Palm Tree Athletic Club, a chain of health and fitness clubs with branches located throughout the state of Florida. The chain has just completed major renovations at several branches, which forced club members to endure a lot of dust, noise, and inconvenience. Maria wants to show the club's gratitude by inviting each member to sign up for three free hours with a certified personal trainer. She plans to send a letter to each member announcing the free offer.

Maria doesn't have time to type personal letters to each of the club's many members. Instead, she plans to create a **form letter** that contains the information she wants to send to all members. The form letter will also contain specific details for individual members, such as name, address, and favorite type of exercise equipment. Maria has already written the letter that will be the basis for the form letter. She plans to use the mail merge process to add the personal information for each member. She asks you to create the form letter using Word's Mail Merge feature. She also asks you to create the mailing labels for the envelopes and a phone directory.

In this tutorial, you'll use Word's Mail Merge task pane to create a letter, mailing labels, and a telephone directory.

Student Data Files

▼**Tutorial.06**

▽ Tutorial folder
- Club.doc
- Phone.doc

▽ Review folder
- Assess.doc
- Insurance Data.xls
- Memo.doc

▽ Cases folder
- Auto.doc
- Creek.doc
- Gems.doc
- Promotion.doc

Session 6.1

Planning the Form Letter

Maria hopes to generate good will for the Palm Tree Athletic Club by offering each member three free hours with a personal trainer. Maria's letter is designed to inform members about the offer and mention improvements to the club that might appeal to each member. Her letter is organized to capture the reader's attention. First, she thanks club members for their patience during the renovations, and then she briefly describes the free offer. Finally, she encourages members to review the new schedules for their favorite type of exercise class.

Maria writes in a friendly, informal style. She uses a standard business-letter format and plans to print the letters on stationery preprinted with the company letterhead.

Understanding the Merge Process

Maria is satisfied with the main text of the form letter. Now she wants you to help her insert the personal information for each of the club members. To do this, you will combine, or **merge**, the form letter with a separate file containing the information about the club members. The form letter is called a **main document**, and the file containing addresses and other information is called the **data source**.

A main document can be a letter or other kind of document. It contains placeholders (called **fields**) that mark where names, addresses, and other variable information will be inserted. A field can be a data field, such as date and time fields, or merge fields, such as First_Name and Last_Name fields. As you will see in this tutorial, one of the steps before merging the main document and the data source is inserting the merge fields into the main document. Maria's main document is a letter that looks like Figure 6-1. Eventually, merge fields will replace the red text.

Figure 6-1 Maria's main document

[Date]

[First Name] [Last Name]
[Street Address]
[City], FL [ZIP Code]

Dear [First Name]:

As you've probably noticed, your branch of the Palm Tree Athletic Club has been undergoing major renovations. You'll be happy to know that we have finally cleared away the rubble. We've installed the new equipment, including a new suite of [Favorite Equipment] machines, and we will be laying the new carpet next week. We want to thank you for your patience while we knocked down walls and expanded our facilities. We realize you put up with a lot of inconvenience (not to mention noise and dust).

As a sign of our gratitude, we invite you to sign up for three free hours with one of our certified personal trainers. Just bring this letter to your branch of the Palm Tree Athletic Club and sign up for six half-hour sessions at times that are convenient for you. Our trainers are available Monday through Saturday.

While you're at the club, take a look at our new schedule for [Favorite Class] classes. We hope you'll like the additional weekend options. We've had many requests for these over the past few months.

We look forward to seeing you at Palm Tree Athletic Club.

Sincerely yours,

Maria Fuentes
Facilities Manager

Maria's data source will include the name and address of each club member, as well as information about each member's preferred exercise machine and favorite class.

Inserting information from a data source into a main document produces a final document called a **merged document**. Figure 6-2 illustrates how the data source and main document combine to form a merged document.

Figure 6-2 Merging a main document with a data source to create a merged document

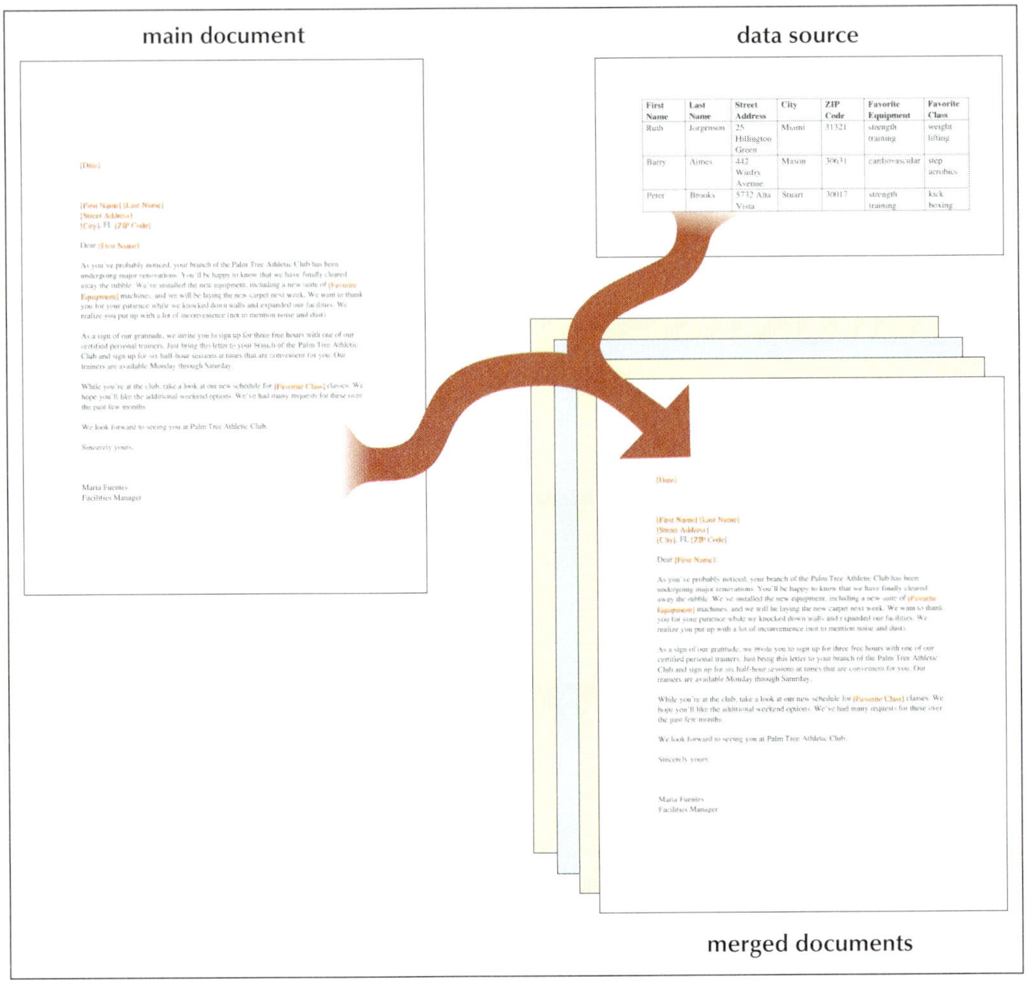

Merge Fields

During a merge, the merge fields tell Word which pieces of information to retrieve from the data source. One merge field might retrieve an address from the data source; another merge field might retrieve a telephone number. Merge fields are easy to spot in the main document because each merge field name is enclosed by pairs of angled brackets, which look like this: << >>. You can only insert merge fields into a main document by using the Mail Merge task pane or the Mail Merge toolbar. You cannot simply type merge fields into the main document. To help you quickly see fields, you can turn on field shading, which displays fields on a gray background. (You'll learn how to turn on field shading later in this tutorial.)

Merge Fields and Records

A data source is a table of information similar to the one shown in Figure 6-3. The **header row**, the first row of the table, contains the name of each merge field. The cells below the header row contain the specific information that replaces the merge fields in the main document. This information is called **data**. Each row of data in the table makes up a complete **record**, or all the information about one individual or object.

Figure 6-3 Sample data source

First Name	Last Name	Street Address	City	ZIP Code	Favorite Equipment	Favorite Class
Ruth	Jorgenson	25 Hillington Green	Miami	31321	strength training	weight lifting
Barry	Aimes	442 Winfry Avenue	Mason	30631	cardiovascular	step aerobics
Peter	Brooks	5732 Alta Vista	Stuart	30017	strength training	kick boxing

header row
record
merge field name
data stored in Favorite Class field

Data sources are commonly used to store names and addresses. However, you can also create data sources with inventory records, records of suppliers, or records of equipment. After you understand how to manage and manipulate the records in a data source, you'll be able to use them for many different types of information.

Using the Mail Merge Task Pane

The **Mail Merge task pane** walks you through the following six steps involved in merging documents:

- Select the type of document you want to use as the main document. Possible types of main documents include letters, envelopes, e-mails, labels, and directories.
- Select the document you want to use as the main document. You can type a new document or edit an existing one.
- Select the list of recipients (that is, the data source) you want to use for the merge. You can use an existing data source or create a new one.
- Complete the main document by adding merge fields.
- Preview the merged document.
- Complete the mail merge.

To ensure that you see the same thing in the Mail Merge task pane each time you open it, open a new, blank document before you open the Mail Merge task pane. Once you are familiar with merging documents, you can also use the buttons on the Mail Merge toolbar to perform the same tasks described in the Mail Merge task pane.

Maria asks you to start the mail merge process now.

To start Word and open the Mail Merge task pane:

1. Start Word, and make sure a new, blank document is displayed. Note that this new document is named "Document1."
2. Switch to Normal view if it is not selected by default. At this point, it doesn't matter whether nonprinting characters are displayed, because you won't actually be using the current document. Use any Zoom setting you want for now.
3. Click the **Other Task Panes** list arrow at the top of the task pane, and then click **Mail Merge**. (If the task pane is not displayed on your computer, click **Tools** on the menu bar, point to **Letters and Mailings**, and then click **Mail Merge**.) The Mail Merge task pane opens and the Document window switches to Print Layout view. The Mail Merge task pane displays information and options related to the first step in merging documents. Depending on how your computer is set up, you might also see the Mail Merge toolbar.

4. If you do not see the Mail Merge toolbar, click **Tools** on the menu bar, point to **Letters and Mailings**, and then click **Show Mail Merge Toolbar**.
5. Close the rulers if they are displayed. Again, the Zoom setting doesn't matter at this point. See Figure 6-4.

Figure 6-4 Starting the mail merge process

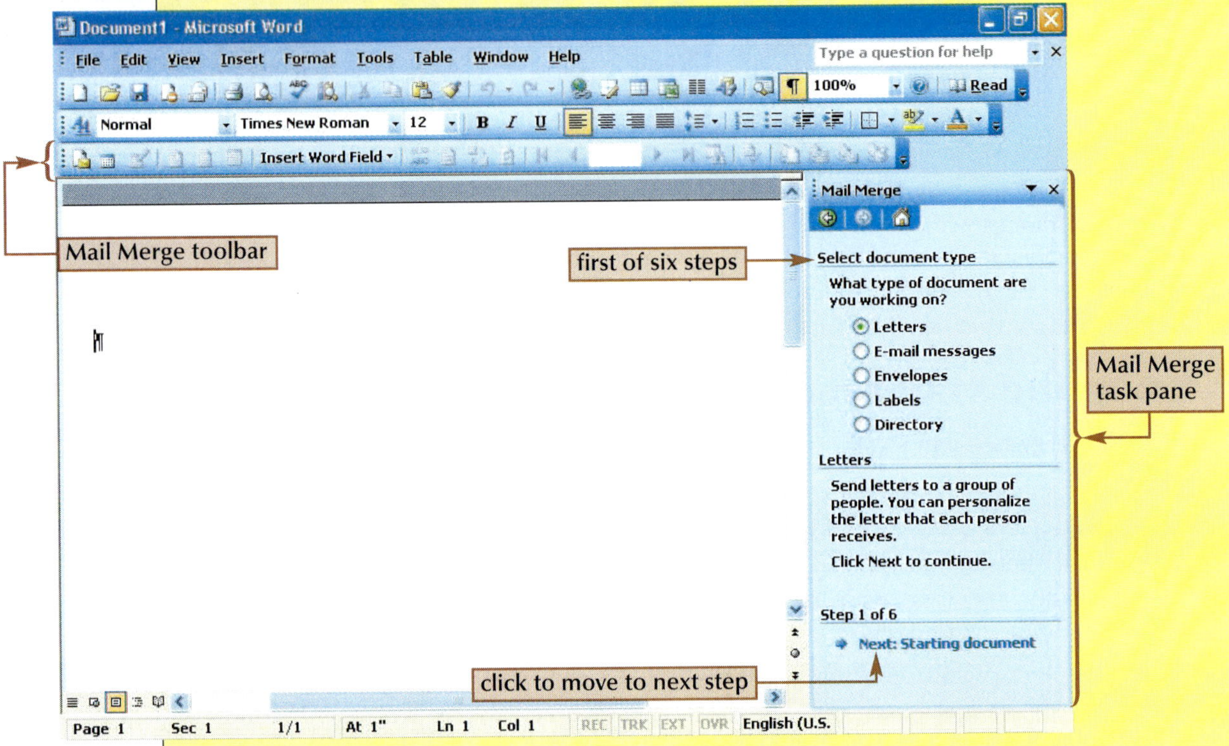

With the Mail Merge task pane open, you are ready to perform the first two steps in merging a document.

Selecting a Main Document

According to the Mail Merge task pane, your first task is to specify the type of main document you want to use for the merge. The Mail Merge task pane provides a number of options, including e-mail messages and labels. In this case, you want to create a letter.

To specify the type of merged document to create:

1. Verify that the **Letters** option button is selected in the Mail Merge task pane.
2. At the bottom of the task pane, click **Next: Starting document**. The Mail Merge task pane displays information and options that you can use to select a starting document—that is, to select a main document.

When selecting a main document, you have three choices: use the document currently displayed in the Document window; start a new document from a template; or open an existing document. Maria has already written the letter she wants to send to all Palm Tree Athletic Club members, so you don't need to create a new document. Instead, you'll use her existing document, which she saved in a file named Club. In the Case Problems at the end of this tutorial you'll have a chance to use the currently displayed document as the main document.

When you open an existing document from the Mail Merge task pane, Word actually inserts a copy of the document you select into the blank document that is currently displayed in the document window. In this case, Word will insert a copy of the file Club into the blank Document1 currently displayed in the Document window. Any changes you make to the Document1 file will not affect the Club file. You'll see how this works in the following steps.

To select a starting, or main, document:

1. In the Mail Merge task pane, click the **Start from existing document** option button (just below the "Select starting document" heading). A list box appears, with an Open button or More files link below it. The list box contains names of files that have been used for a mail merge on your computer in the past. (If this is the first time anyone has performed a mail merge on your computer, the list box will be blank except for a More Files link.) If you perform mail merges regularly with the same group of files, you can click the name of the file you want in this list box. For now, however, you will use the Open button below the list box.
2. Click **Open**. The Open dialog box appears. You'll use this dialog box to select Maria's document.
3. Select the **Tutorial.06\Tutorial** folder included with your Data Files.
4. Click **Club**, and then click **Open**. A copy of the file named Club is inserted in the Document1 file. The Use the current document option button is now selected in the task pane because you are now ready to use the current document (Document1, with the text of the Club file inserted into it) as the main document.
5. To ensure that you can see the entire letter next to the Mail Merge task pane, switch to Normal view, and then zoom to **95%**. Display nonprinting characters. At the bottom of the task pane, you see the next step in the mail merge process. See Figure 6-5.

Figure 6-5 **Main document in Normal view**

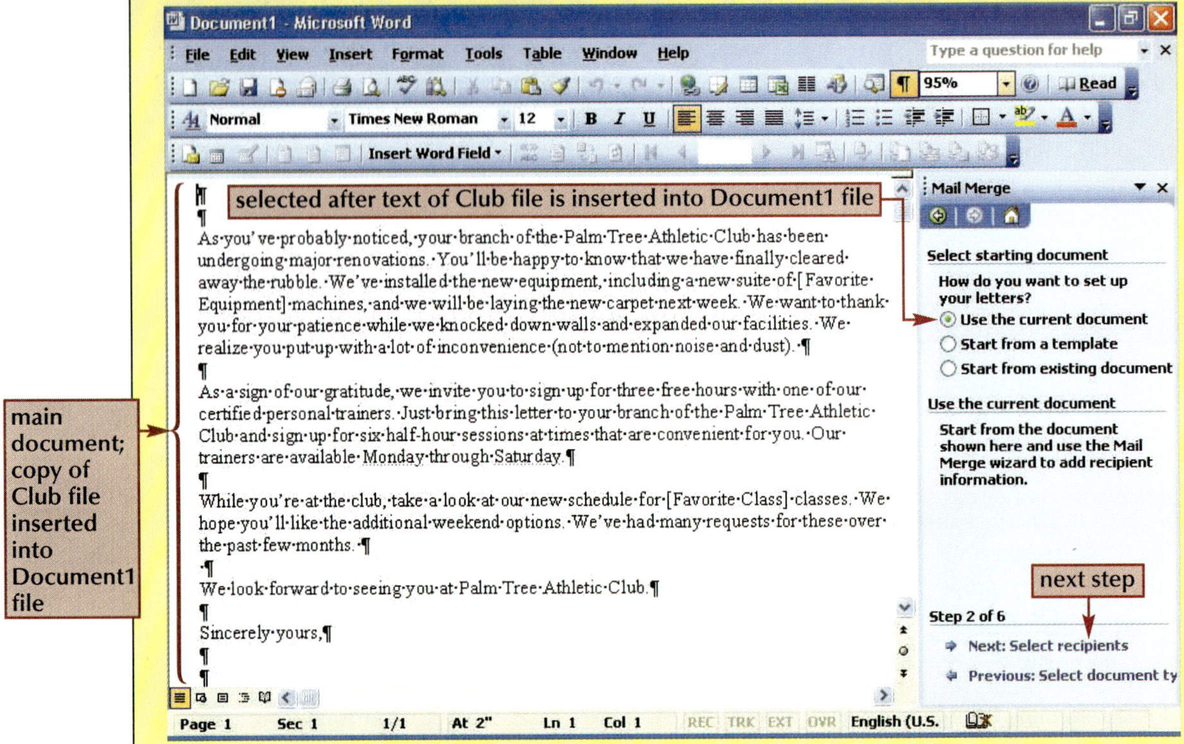

You will eventually add merge fields to this document, so you will save it now as "Club Letter with Merge Fields."

6. Save the Document1 file as **Club Letter with Merge Fields** in the Tutorial.06\Tutorial folder.

Next, you need to tell Word where to find the list of recipients for Maria's letter.

Selecting a Data Source

As you learned earlier, a data source is a table of information. Typically, the data source for a mail merge contains a list of names and addresses, but it can also contain e-mail addresses, telephone numbers, and other data. Various kinds of files can be used as the data source, including a Word table, an Excel worksheet, an Access database, or a special kind of file, called a Microsoft Office Address Lists file, which is designed to store addresses for Microsoft Outlook, as well as other Microsoft Office applications. In this tutorial, you will create an Office Address Lists file to use as your data source. Word's Mail Merge task pane walks you through the steps to create the data source.

When performing a mail merge, you can select a data source file that already contains names and addresses, or you can create a new data source, and enter names and addresses into it. When you create a new data source, the file is saved as a Microsoft Office Address Lists file. In this section, you will create a data source using the tools provided by the Mail Merge task pane. This involves two steps: deciding which fields to include in the data source and entering address information.

Selecting Fields to Include in the Data Source

You need to create a data source that contains club member information, including address, favorite exercise equipment, and preferred type of class. Maria compiled all the necessary information by asking each member to fill out a form when they first joined the club. Figure 6-6 shows one of these forms.

Member information form | **Figure 6-6**

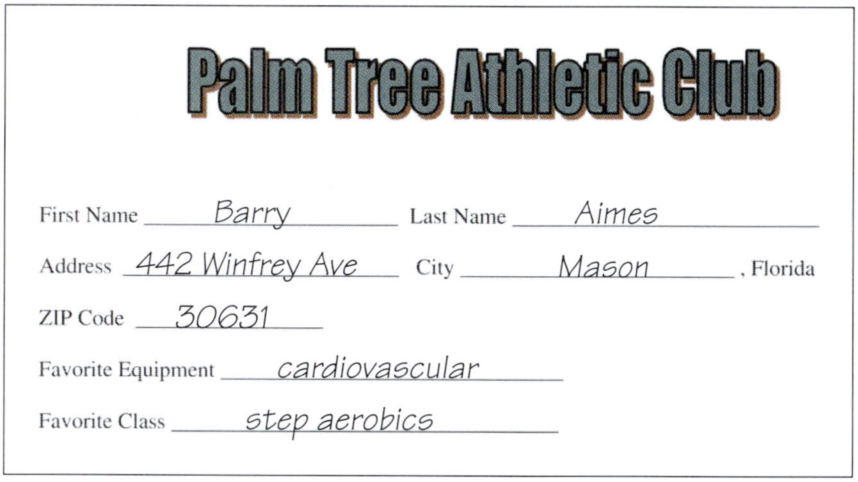

Palm Tree Athletic Club

First Name Barry Last Name Aimes

Address 442 Winfrey Ave City Mason, Florida

ZIP Code 30631

Favorite Equipment cardiovascular

Favorite Class step aerobics

Your job is to create a data source to store all the data found in the member information forms. The information on each form will make up one record in the data source. When you create your data source, you must include the field names shown in Figure 6-7.

Field names to include in Palm Tree Athletic Club data source | **Figure 6-7**

Field Names	Description
First Name	Member's first name
Last Name	Member's last name
Address	Member's street address
City	Member's city (in Florida)
ZIP Code	Member's ZIP code
Favorite Equipment	Member's favorite type of exercise equipment
Favorite Class	Member's favorite type of exercise class

When you create a new data source from within the Mail Merge task pane, Word provides a number of default fields such as First Name, Last Name, and Company. You can customize the data source by adding new fields and removing the default fields that you don't plan to use. As you create a data source, keep in mind that each field name must be unique; you can't have two fields with the same name. Although the order of field names in the data source doesn't affect their placement in the main document, it's a good idea to arrange field names logically in the data source so you can enter information quickly and efficiently. For example, you'll probably want the First Name field next to the Last Name field. Finally, note that if you include spaces in your field names, Word will replace the spaces with underscores when you insert the fields into the main document. For example, Word transforms the field name First Name into First_Name.

Reference Window

Creating a Data Source

- In Step 3 of the Mail Merge task pane, select the Type a new list option button, and then click Create.
- In the New Address List dialog box, click the Customize button.
- In the Customize Address List dialog box, click a field you want to delete, click the Delete button, and then click the Yes button. Continue to delete any unnecessary fields.
- To add a new field, click the Add button, type the name of the field in the Add Field dialog box, and then click the OK button.
- To rearrange the order of the field names, click a field name, and then click the Move Up or Move Down button.
- Click the OK button to close the Customize Address List dialog box.
- In the New Address List dialog box, enter information for the first record, click the New Entry button, and type another record. Continue until you are finished entering information into the data source, and then click the Close button.

You're ready to begin creating the data source for Maria's form letter.

To begin creating the data source:

1. In the bottom of the Mail Merge task pane, click **Next: Select recipients**, and then click the **Type a new list** option button in the task pane.
2. Below the heading "Type a new list," click **Create**. The New Address List dialog box opens, as shown in Figure 6-8. You will use this dialog box to enter a complete set of information for one person—that is, enter one record into the data source. Before you begin entering information, you need to customize the list of fields to match the list shown earlier in Figure 6-7.

Figure 6-8 Creating a data source

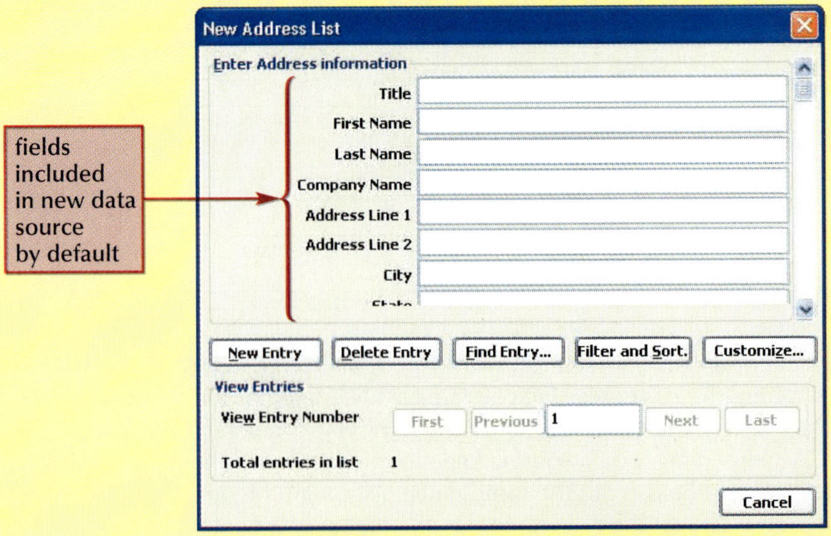

3. Click the **Customize** button. The Customize Address List dialog box opens. Here you can delete the fields you don't need, and add new ones. You'll start by deleting fields.
4. In the Field Names list box, verify that **Title** is selected, and then click the **Delete** button. A message appears asking you to confirm the deletion.
5. Click the **Yes** button. The Title field is deleted from the list of field names.
6. Continue using the Delete button to delete the following fields: **Company Name**, **Address Line 2**, **State**, **Country**, **Home Phone**, **Work Phone**, and **E-mail Address**. Next, you need to add some new fields. When you add a new field, it is inserted below the selected field, so you will start by selecting the last field in the list.
7. Verify that **ZIP Code** is selected in the Field Names list box, and then click the **Add** button. The Add Field dialog box opens, instructing you to type a name for your field.
8. Type **Favorite Equipment**, and then click the **OK** button in the Add Field dialog box. The field "Favorite Equipment" is added.
9. Use the Add button to add a **Favorite Class** field. When you are finished, your Customize Address List dialog box should look like the one shown in Figure 6-9. You could use the Move Up and Move Down buttons to rearrange the field names (for instance, to move the Favorite Class field above the Favorite Equipment field), but in this case the order is fine. You are finished customizing the list of field names.

Customized list of field names **Figure 6-9**

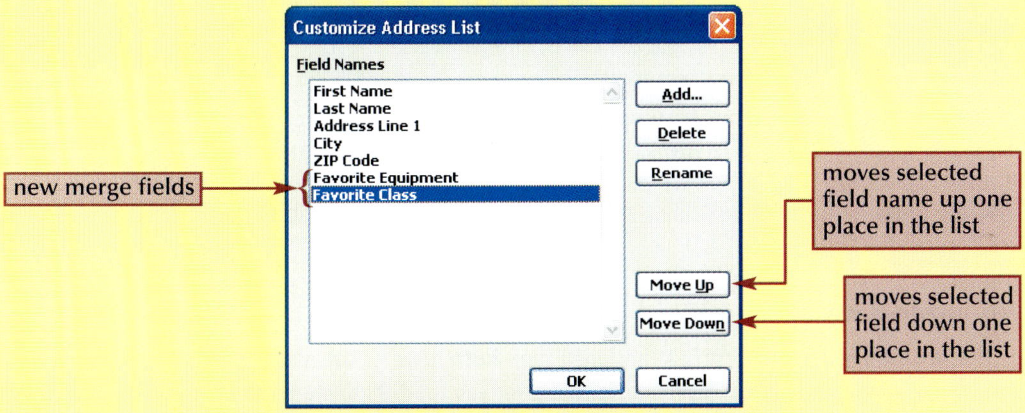

10. Click the **OK** button in the Customize Address List dialog box. The Customize Address List dialog box closes, and you return to the New Address List dialog box. As shown in Figure 6-10, this dialog box reflects the changes you just made. For instance, it no longer includes the Title field. The fields are listed in the same order they appeared in the Customize Address List dialog box.

Figure 6-10 Changes made to New Address List dialog box

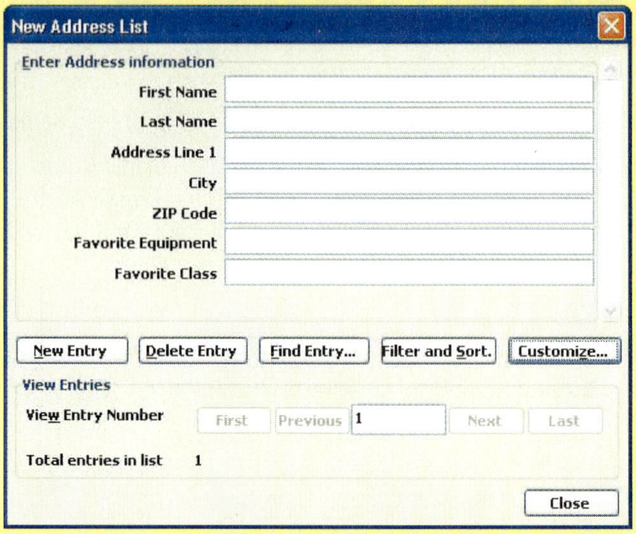

Now that you have specified the fields you want to use, you are ready to enter the member information into the data source.

Entering Data into a Data Source

You are now ready to begin entering information about each club member into the data source. Maria gives you three completed member information forms (shown earlier in Figure 6-6). She asks you to transfer the information from the paper forms into the data source. Each paper form will be used to create one new record in the data source. You'll use the New Address List dialog box to begin entering information.

To enter data into a record using the data form:

1. Click the **First Name** text box, and then type **Ruth** to enter the first name of the first member. Make sure you do not press the spacebar after you finish typing an entry in the New Address List dialog box. Add spaces only in the text of the main document, not in the data source.
2. Press the **Enter** key to move the insertion point to the Last Name field. You could also click that text box, or you could press the Tab key to move the insertion point to the next field text box. You can press Shift+Tab to move the insertion point to the previous text box.
3. Type **Jorgenson**, and then press the **Enter** key to move the insertion point to the Address Line 1 field.
4. Type **25 Hillington Green**, and then press the **Enter** key to move the insertion point to the City field.
5. Type **Miami**, and then press the **Enter** key to move the insertion point to the ZIP Code field.
6. Type **31321**, and then press the **Enter** key to move to the Favorite Equipment field.
7. Type **strength training**, and then press the **Enter** key. The insertion point is now in the Favorite Class field.
8. Type **weight lifting** but do *not* press the Enter key yet. The number at the bottom of the dialog box tells you that so far, the data source contains only one record. The "View Entry Number" in the text box indicates which record is currently displayed. See Figure 6-11.

Figure 6-11 Completed record 1

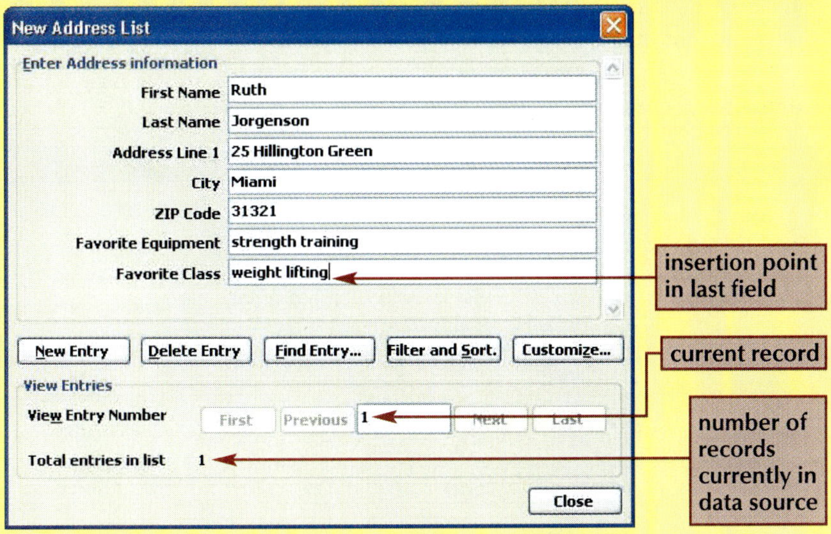

You have completed the information for the first record of the data source document. Now you're ready to enter the information for the next two records. You can create a new record by clicking the New Entry button. When the insertion point is in the bottom text box in the New Address List dialog box, you can also create a new record by pressing the Enter key twice. In the steps that follow, you use both methods.

To add additional records to the data source:

1. Click the **New Entry** button. This creates a new, blank record. The Total entries in list number at the bottom of the dialog box tells you that that the data source now contains two records.
2. Enter the information shown in Figure 6-12 into the new record.

Figure 6-12 Completed record 2

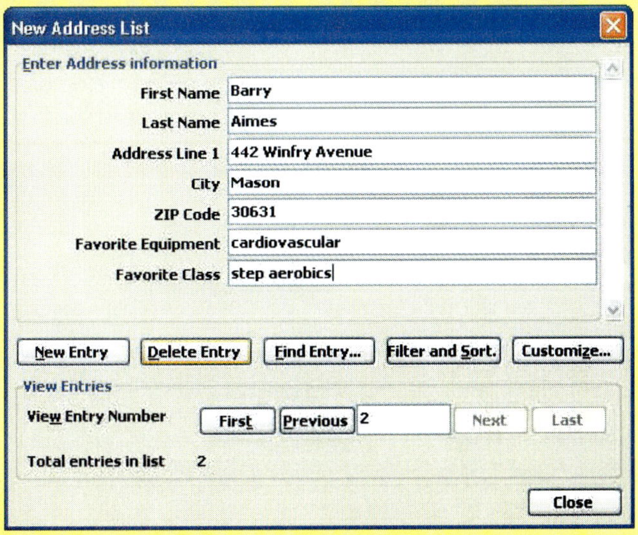

3. After entering data into the last field, press the **Enter** key twice.
4. Enter the information for the third record, as shown in Figure 6-13. After entering the information for the third record, do not create a fourth record.

Figure 6-13 Completed record 3

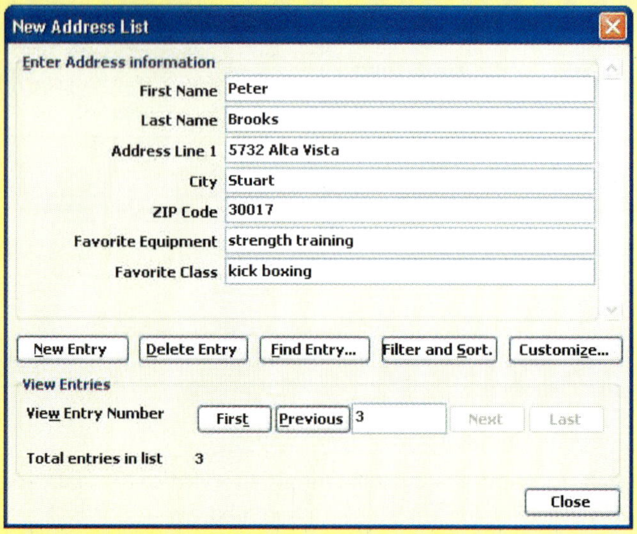

Trouble? If you create a fourth record by mistake, click the Delete Entry button to remove the unneeded fourth record.

You have entered the records for three members. Next, you need to proofread each record to make sure you typed the information correctly.

Displaying Records in a Data Source

You can display specific records in the data source by using the First, Previous, Next, and Last buttons. You'll use these buttons now to proofread each record in the data source.

To display the first record:

1. Click the **First** button at the bottom of the New Address List dialog box. The "View Entry Number" (to the right of the Previous button) changes to 1, and the first record appears with information about Ruth Jorgenson.
2. Proofread the data by comparing your information with Figure 6-11. Make any necessary corrections by selecting the text and retyping it.
3. Click the **Next** button. The "View Entry Number" changes to 2, and the information for the second record (Barry Aimes) appears. Compare your record with Figure 6-12.
4. Click the **Last** button to review the last record (Peter Brooks) in the data source. Compare your record with Figure 6-13. Make any necessary corrections.

Maria's data source eventually will contain hundreds of records for Palm Tree Athletic Club members. The current data source, however, contains only the records Maria wants to work with now.

You are finished entering records into the data source. Next, you need to save the data source.

Saving a Data Source

When you create a data source, Word saves it as a Microsoft Office Address Lists file, which is a special file designed to store address information for any Microsoft Office program.

Maria asks you to close the New Address List dialog box. When you close this dialog box, Word saves the data source as a Microsoft Office Address List.

To save the data source:

1. In the New Address List dialog box, click **Close**. The Save Address List dialog box opens, as shown in Figure 6-14. By default, Word offers to save the file to the My Data Sources folder, which is a subfolder of the My Documents folder. In this case, however, you will save the data source in the Tutorial.06\Tutorial folder. Notice that the Save as type box indicates that the data source will be saved as a Microsoft Office Address Lists file.

Figure 6-14 Saving the data source

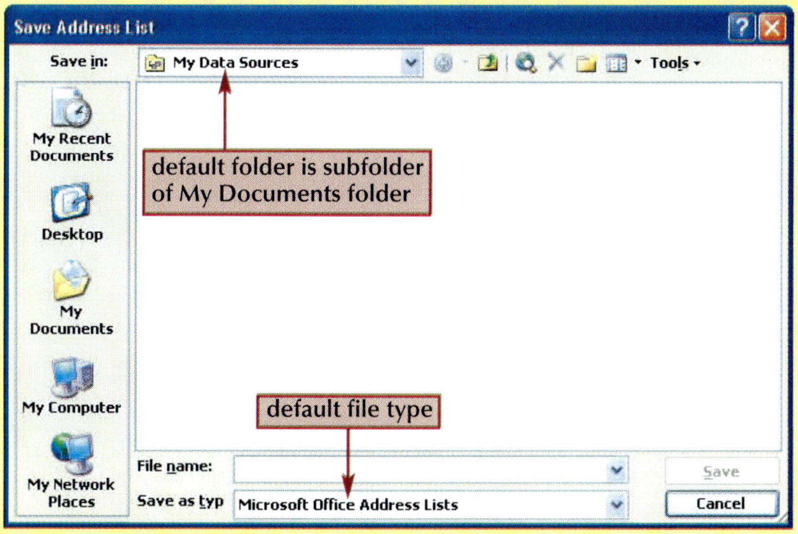

2. Select the **Tutorial.06\Tutorial** folder.
3. Click the **File name** text box, type **Club Data**, and then click the **Save** button. The Mail Merge Recipients dialog box opens, as shown in Figure 6-15. Here you can see the data source displayed as a table. The header row contains the names of the fields. The order of the field names in this dialog box does not necessarily match the order you specified earlier, when you created the data source. (You need to scroll right to see all the fields.) Each row below the header row consists of one complete record. You can use this dialog box to rearrange the records in the list and to choose which members you want to include in the mail merge. You'll use this dialog box later in this tutorial. For now, you'll close it.

Figure 6-15 Data displayed as a table

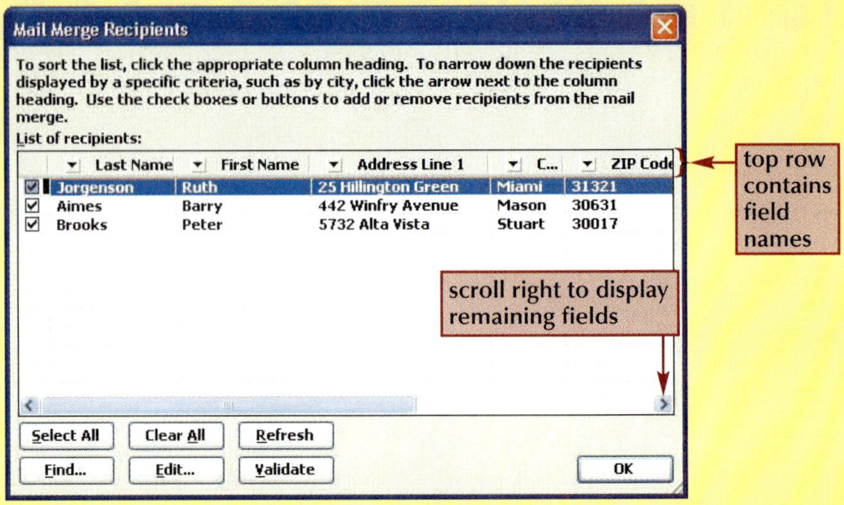

4. Click the **OK** button. The Mail Merge Recipients dialog box closes. You return to the Document window. The Mail Merge task pane indicates that you have selected an Office Address List file named "Club Data.mdb" as your data source. The task pane also indicates that the next step in the mail merge process is writing (in this case, editing) the main document. Finally, note that you could click Edit recipient list to re-open the Mail Merge Recipients dialog box. See Figure 6-16.

Figure 6-16 Selected data source

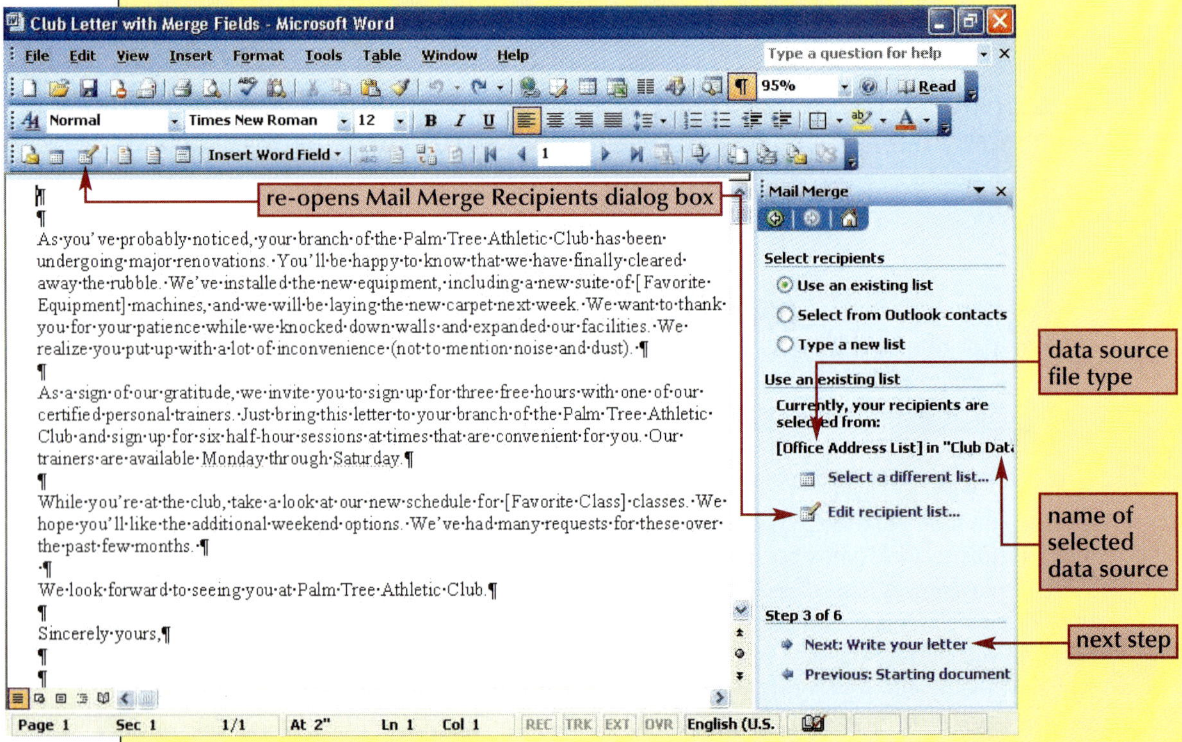

Editing a Main Document

In the first two steps of the mail merge process, you selected Maria's letter as your main document. A copy of this letter is open on your screen, next to the Mail Merge task pane. In the third step, you selected, created, and saved the data source. Now you will turn your attention back to the main document. You'll edit Maria's letter to add the current date and the merge fields.

Adding a Date Field

As you've seen, merge fields tell Word where to insert information from the data source. You can also insert other kinds of fields in a document, including a **date field**, which inserts the current date and tells Word to update the field each time the document is opened. You can also update a date field by selecting it, and then pressing the [F9] key.

You insert a date field via the Insert Date and Time dialog box. You already know how to use this dialog box to add the current date as text to a document. To insert a date field that Word updates automatically, select the Update automatically check box.

Maria wants the date to appear at the top of the document, just below where the company logo appears on the printed stationery.

To insert the date field:

1. In the Mail Merge task pane, click **Next: Write your letter**. The Mail Merge task pane displays information and options related to working with the main document. If you had originally selected a new, blank document as your main document, you would need to write the text of the form letter now. In this case, you will edit the existing letter.
2. Make sure the insertion point is at the beginning of the form letter, on the first blank line. Maria already adjusted the page's top margin to leave room for the letterhead on the company stationery. You will insert the date on the first line of the document.
3. Click **Insert** on the menu bar, and then click **Date and Time**. The Date and Time dialog box opens. You will use the Update automatically check box to have Word revise the date every time you open the document.
4. Click the third format in the Available formats list, which includes the month, the day, and the year, as in October 1, 2006.
5. If necessary, click the **Update automatically** check box to select it.
6. Click the **OK** button. The current date appears in the document. Now, whenever you or Maria print the merged document letter for Palm Tree Athletic Club's members, the current date will appear in the document.

   Trouble? If you see {DATE \@ "MMMM d, yyyy"} instead of the current date, your system is set to display field codes. To view the date instead of the field code, click Tools on the menu bar, click Options, click the View tab, click the Field codes check box to remove the check mark, and then click the OK button.

   Trouble? If the date or field code appears on a gray background, your system is set to display field shading. You will learn more about field shading in the next section.

Turning on Field Shading

To make it easier to spot fields in your document, you can turn on **field shading**. This displays fields with a gray background, which is only visible on-screen and will not appear in the printed document. Depending on how your computer is set up, field shading may already be turned on, in which case the date in your document is displayed on a gray background as shown below in Figure 6-17. Whether or not you see field shading in your document, complete the following steps.

To check the field shading setting:

1. Click **Tools** on the menu bar, then click **Options**. The Options dialog box opens.
2. Verify that the **View** tab is the active tab, and then click the **Field shading** list arrow. Note the current setting on your computer, so you can return your computer to its original state after completing this tutorial. The Always setting displays all fields with a gray background at all times. The When selected setting displays shading only on selected fields.
3. Click **Always** (if it is not already selected), and then click the **OK** button. The Options dialog box closes. The date field is displayed on a gray background. See Figure 6-17.

Figure 6-17 Shaded date field

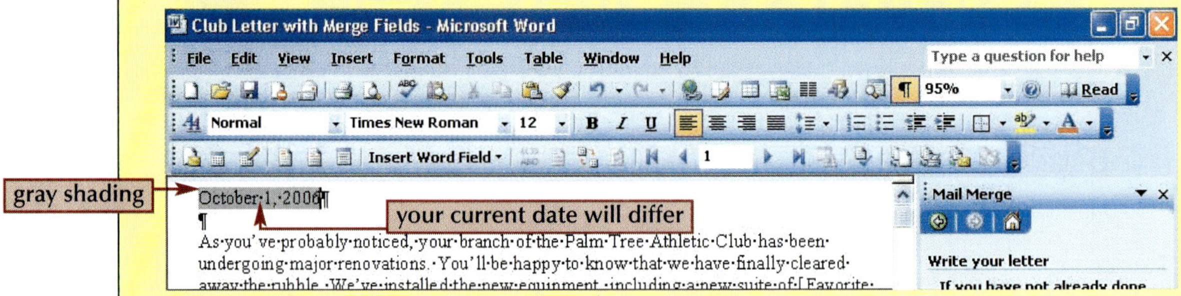

You're now ready to insert the merge fields for the letter's inside address.

Inserting Merge Fields

Maria's letter is a standard business letter, so you'll place the member's name and address below the date. You'll use merge fields for the member's first name, last name, address, city, and ZIP code. You must enter proper spacing and punctuation around the fields so that the information in the merged document will be formatted correctly. The Mail Merge task pane includes links, such as the Address block link, which you can use to insert a standard set of fields. The More items link offers more flexibility because it allows you to insert fields one at a time, rather than in predefined groups.

To insert a merge field:

1. Verify that the insertion point is positioned in the first line immediately to the right of the date field, then press the **Enter** key six times to leave space between the date and the first line of the inside address.
2. Click **More items** in the Mail Merge task pane. The Insert Merge Field dialog box opens. (You could also use the Insert Merge Fields button on the Mail Merge toolbar to open this dialog box.) As shown in Figure 6-18, the Database Fields option button is selected, indicating that the dialog box displays all the fields in the data source.

Figure 6-18

Inserting merge fields into the main document

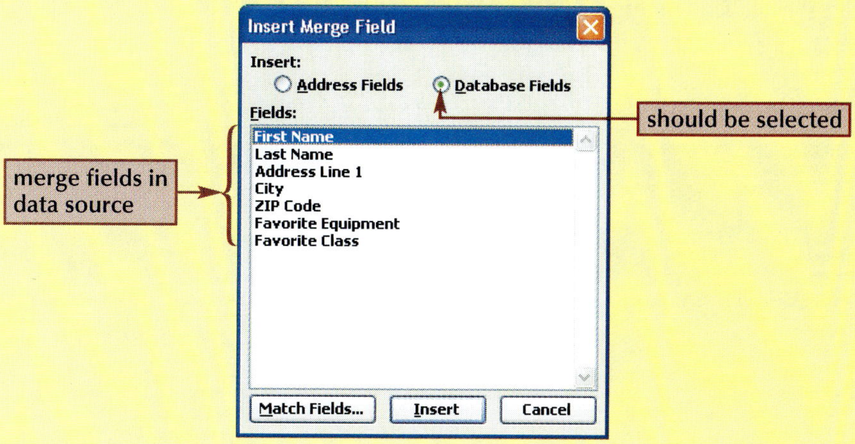

Trouble? If you see a different list, the Address Fields option button may be selected rather than the Database Fields option button. Click the Database Fields option button to select it.

3. In the Fields list, click **First Name** if necessary, click the **Insert** button, and then click the **Close** button. The Insert Merge Field dialog box closes, and the merge field is inserted into the document. The merge field consists of the field name (First_Name) surrounded by angled brackets << >> (also called chevrons). Note that Word replaces spaces in field names with underscores, so the field name "First Name" is displayed as "First_Name." Because you turned on field shading earlier, the merge field is displayed on a gray background.

Trouble? If you make a mistake and insert the wrong merge field, select the entire merge field, including the chevrons, press the Delete key, and then insert the correct merge field.

Later, when you merge the main document with the data source, Word will replace the merge field with information from the First Name field in the data source. Now, you're ready to insert the merge fields for the rest of the inside address. You'll add the necessary spacing and punctuation to the main document as well.

To insert the remaining merge fields for the inside address:

1. Press the **spacebar** to insert a space after the First Name field, click the **Insert Merge Fields** button on the Mail Merge toolbar, click **Last Name** in the Insert Merge Field dialog box, click the **Insert** button, and then click the **Close** button. Word inserts the Last Name merge field into the form letter.
2. Press the **Enter** key to move the insertion point to the next line, click the **Insert Merge Fields** button, click **Address Line 1** in the Insert Merge Field dialog box, click the **Insert** button, and then click the **Close** button. Word inserts the Address Line 1 merge field into the form letter.
3. Press the **Enter** key to move the insertion point to the next line, click the **Insert Merge Fields** button on the Mail Merge toolbar, click **City** in the Insert Merge Field dialog box, click the **Insert** button, and then click the **Close** button. Word inserts the City merge field into the form letter.
4. Type **,** (a comma), press the **spacebar** to insert a space after the comma, and then type **FL** to insert the abbreviation for the state of Florida. If Palm Tree Athletic Club had members outside Florida, you would have had to include a State field name in the data source and also in the main document form letter. Because all of the members live in Florida, you can make the state name part of the main document, where it will be the same for every letter.

5. Press the **spacebar** to insert a space after FL, use the Insert Merge Fields button to insert the **ZIP Code** merge field, and then close the Insert Merge Field dialog box. Word inserts the ZIP Code merge field into the form letter. See Figure 6-19.

Figure 6-19 **Form letter with merge fields**

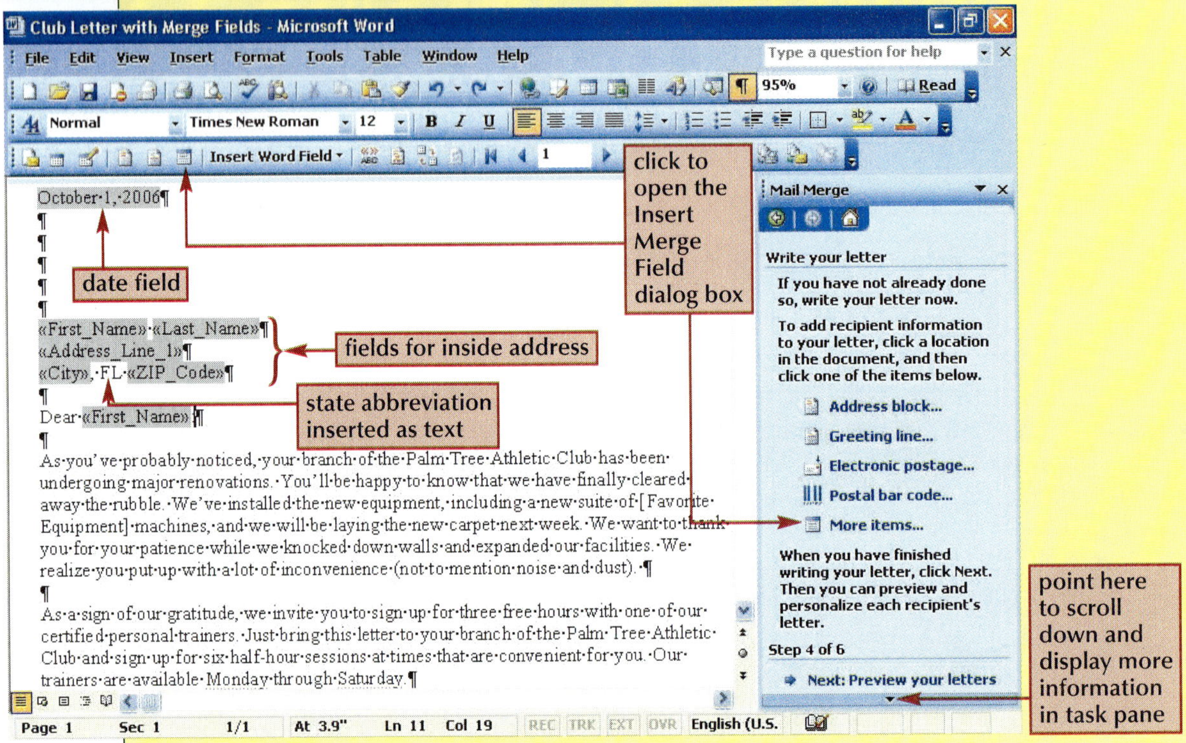

The inside address is set up to match the form for a standard business letter. You can now add the salutation of the letter, which will contain each member's first name.

To insert the merge field for the salutation:

1. Press the **Enter** key twice to leave a line between the inside address and the salutation, type **Dear**, and then press the **spacebar**.
2. Insert the **First Name** field into the document.
3. Type **:** (a colon), and then save your work. This completes the salutation.

You'll personalize the letter even more by including references to each member's favorite class and exercise equipment.

To finish personalizing the letter:

1. Select the placeholder **[Favorite Equipment]** (including the brackets) in the first paragraph of the form letter. You'll replace this phrase with a merge field. (Don't be concerned if you also select the space following the closing bracket.)
2. Use the Insert Merge Field dialog box to insert the **Favorite Equipment** merge field. Word replaces the selected text with the Favorite Equipment merge field.

3. Verify that the field has a single space before it and after it. Add a space on either side if necessary.
4. Scroll down if necessary, replace **[Favorite Class]** in the first sentence of the third main paragraph of the form letter with the **Favorite Class** field, and adjust spacing as necessary.
5. Carefully check your document to make sure the field names and spacing are correct. Your document should look like Figure 6-20.

Figure 6-20 **Form letter after inserting merge fields**

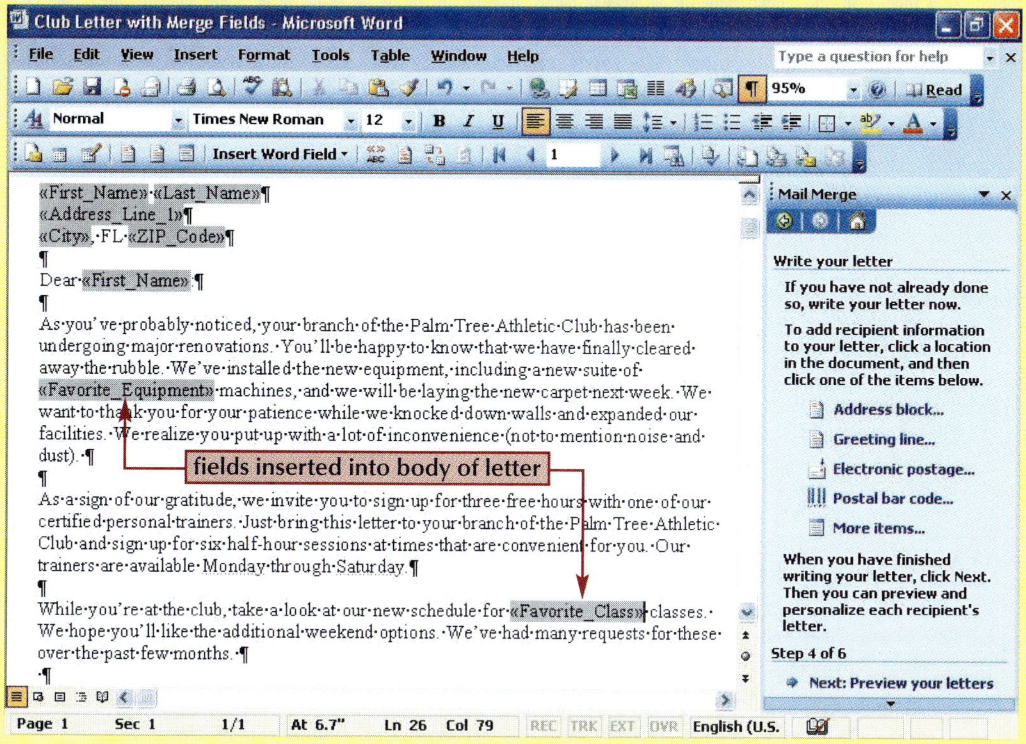

When you're finished reviewing the document, take a moment to notice the down arrow at the bottom of the Mail Merge task pane. Point to this arrow when you need to scroll the task pane and display more information. (Depending on your screen settings, you may not see this down arrow.) Be sure to use this arrow as necessary throughout the rest of this tutorial to display items that might otherwise not be visible on the task pane.

Trouble? If you see an error, edit the document as you would any other Word document. If you inserted an incorrect merge field, drag the mouse pointer to select the entire merge field, press Delete, and then insert the correct merge field.

6. Save your changes to the **Club Letter with Merge Fields** document.

The main document now contains all the necessary merge fields, but not the data. To include data, you merge the main document and the data source. First, however, you should preview the merged document.

Previewing the Merged Document

According to the Mail Merge task pane, your next step is to preview the merged document to see how the letter will look after Word inserts the information for each member. When you preview the merged document, you can check one last time for any missing spaces between the merge fields and the surrounding text. You can also look for any other formatting problems, and, if necessary, make final changes to the data source.

To preview the merged document:

1. In the Mail Merge task pane, click **Next: Preview your letters**. The Mail Merge task pane displays information and options related to previewing the merged document. The data for the first record (Ruth Jorgenson) replaces the merge fields in the form letter. See Figure 6-21. Scroll to the top of the document so you can see the inside address and salutation. Carefully check the letter to make sure the text and formatting are correct. In particular, check to make sure that the spaces before and after the merged data are correct because it is easy to omit spaces or add extra spaces around merge fields. Finally, notice that both the task pane and the Go to Record box on the Mail Merge toolbar indicate which record is currently displayed in the document.

Figure 6-21 **First letter with merged data**

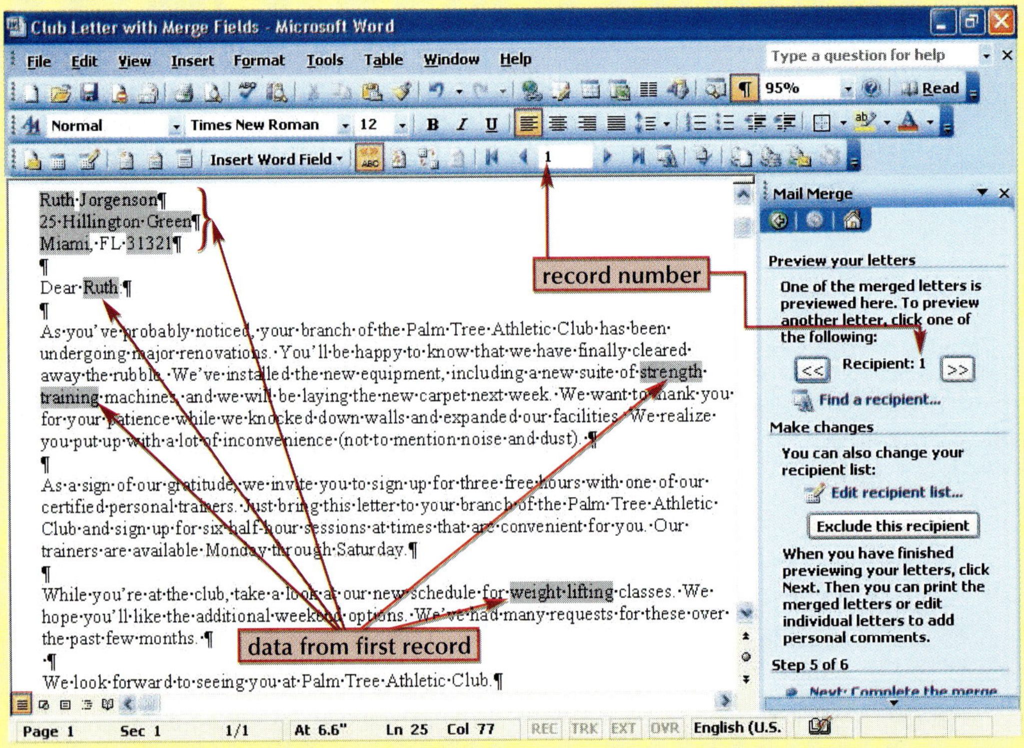

2. If you need to make any changes to the form letter, click **Previous: Write your letter** in the Mail Merge task pane, edit the document, save your changes, and then click **Next: Preview your letters** in the task pane. When you are finished, your screen should look like Figure 6-21. Before you complete the merge, you should review the data for the other two records.
3. Click the **Next Record** button on the Mail Merge toolbar to display the data for Barry Aimes in the letter. Note that you can also use the right-facing double-arrow button in the Mail Merge task pane to display the next record.
4. Click the **Next Record** button on the Mail Merge toolbar to display the data for Peter Brooks in the letter.
5. Click the **First Record** button on the Mail Merge toolbar to redisplay the first record in the letter (with data for Ruth Jorgenson).

The main document of the mail merge is completed. At this stage you could also use the Mail Merge task pane to make changes to the data source, but Maria says the data source is fine for now. You are ready for the final step, completing the merge.

Merging the Main Document and Data Source

Now that you've created the form letter (main document) and the list of member information (data source), you're ready to merge the two files and create personalized letters to send to Palm Tree Athletic Club members. Because the data source consists of three records, you'll create a merged document with three pages, one letter per page.

You could merge the data source and main document directly to the printer using the Merge to Printer button on the Mail Merge toolbar. In that case, Word immediately prints the merged document without saving it as a separate file. However, Maria wants to keep a copy of the merged document on disk for her records. So you'll merge the data source and main document to a new document.

To complete the mail merge:

1. In the Mail Merge task pane, click **Next: Complete the merge**. As shown in Figure 6-22, the task pane displays options related to merging the main document and the data source. You can use the Print option (or the Merge to Printer button on the Mail Merge toolbar) to merge directly to the printer. Alternatively, you can use the Edit individual letters option (or the Merge to New Document button on the Mail Merge toolbar) to merge to a new document.

Figure 6-22 Last step in Mail Merge task pane

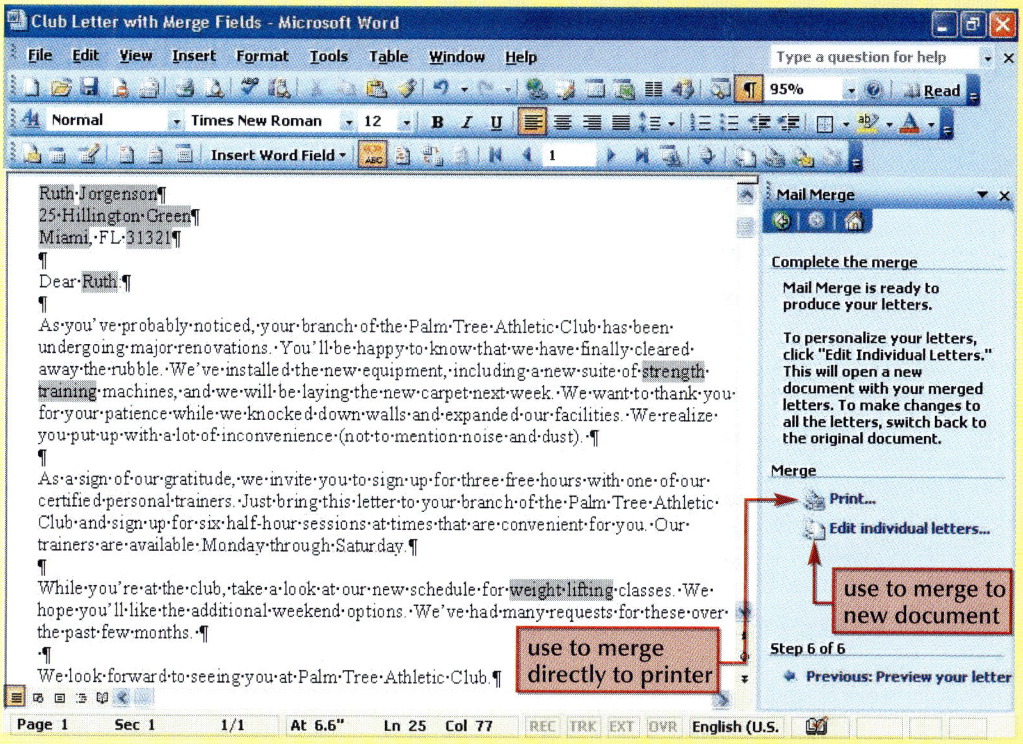

2. Click **Edit individual letters** in the Mail Merge task pane. The Merge to New Document dialog box opens. Here, you need to specify which records to include in the merge. You want to include all the records in the data source.

3. Verify that the **All** option button is selected, and then click the **OK** button. Word creates a new document called Letters1, which contains three pages, one for each record in the data source. In this new document, the merge fields have been replaced by ordinary text (the names, addresses, and so on). See Figure 6-23. Notice that the date field, which appears at the top of each letter, displays the date but still appears with the field shading. Word still recognizes the data as a field because you set the field to update automatically each time the document is opened. The field shading will not print.

   The document named Club Letter with Merge Fields remains open.

Figure 6-23 **Merged document**

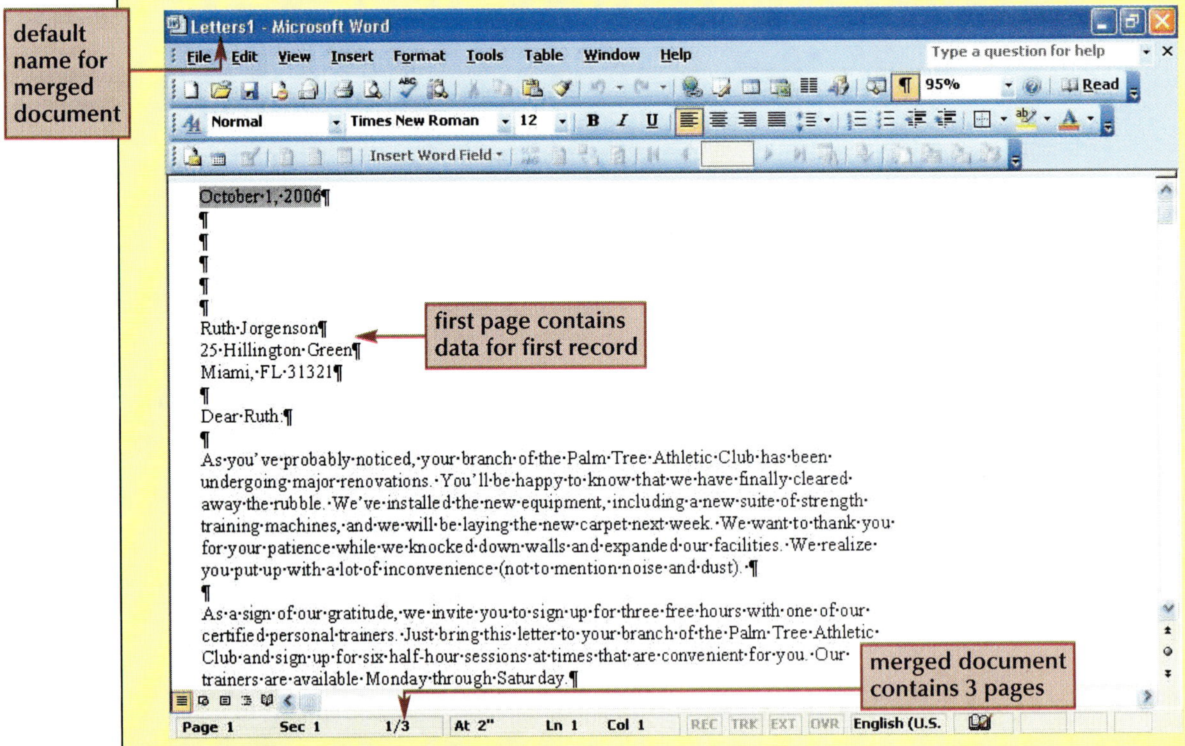

4. Save the merged document in the Tutorial.06\Tutorial folder, using the filename **Club Merged Letters 1**.

5. Click the **Print Preview** button on the Standard toolbar to switch to Print Preview.

6. Change the Zoom setting to **Page Width** so the text is large enough to read. Notice that the date field is not shaded in Print Layout view because the shading will not appear on the printed document. Scroll down to view the document. Next, you will use the Select Browse Object button (at the bottom of the vertical scroll bar) to move from one page to the next.

7. Click the **Select Browse Object** button near the bottom of the vertical scroll bar, click the **Browse by Page** button on the palette, and then click the **Previous Page** button or **Next Page** button to move among the letters. Note that each letter is addressed to a different member and that the favorite equipment and class vary from one letter to the next. You will need to scroll to read each letter.

8. Close the Print Preview window, and then save and close the **Club Merged Letters 1** document.

The document named Club Letter with Merge Fields is now the active document. You see the Mail Merge task pane again, displaying the last step of the mail merge process.

9. Save and close the **Club Letter with Merge Fields** document. When you save the main document after completing a merge, you also save any edits that you might have made to the data source. Close the **Mail Merge task pane**, if necessary. Leave the Mail Merge toolbar displayed.

You have completed the six steps of the Mail Merge task pane and generated a merged document. In the next session you will learn how to use additional mail merge features.

Session 6.1 Quick Check

Review

1. Define the following in your own words:
   a. merge field
   b. main document
   c. data source
   d. field
   e. record
2. All the information about one individual or object in a data source is called a _______________.
3. True or False: To save time, you can simply type merge fields into the main document.
4. True or False: You can use a document containing a Word table as a data source.
5. Explain how to insert a field into a main document.
6. Explain how to merge to a new document.

Session 6.2

Editing a Data Source

After you complete a mail merge, you may sometimes find that you need to make some changes to the data source and redo a merge. You can edit a data source in two ways—from within the program used to create the data source in the first place, or via the Mail Merge Recipients dialog box in Word. If you are familiar with the program used to create the data source, it's often simplest to edit the file from within that program. For example, if you were using an Excel worksheet as your data source, you could open the file in Excel, edit it (perhaps by adding new records), save it, and then reselect the file as your data source. You can use Microsoft Access to edit a Microsoft Office Address Lists file. However, it's easier to edit a Microsoft Office Address Lists file from within Word using the Mail Merge Recipients dialog box. Note that if you change the order of the data fields from within the Mail Merge Recipients dialog box, the new field order may not be apparent if you open the data source from within Access.

Reference Window

Editing a Data Source

- Open the program you used to create the data source, edit the file, save it, and then close it.
- In Word, open the Mail Merge task pane, click the Open Data Source button on the Mail Merge toolbar, navigate to the folder containing the data source, select the data source, and then click the Open button.

or

- Click the Mail Merge Recipients button on the Mail Merge toolbar, and then click the Edit button.
- To add a record, click the New Entry button, and then type a new record.
- To delete a record, display it, and then click the Delete button.
- To add or remove fields from the data source, click the Customize button, make any changes, and then click the OK button. Remember that if you remove a field, you will delete any data already entered into that field.

You'll try the second method in the following steps as you add some new records to Maria's data source. In these steps you will re-open the main document, which you closed at the end of the last session. It's important to note that, after you complete a mail merge, a connection exists between the main document file and the data source file, even after you close the main document and exit Word. That connection is maintained as long as you keep both files in their original folders.

What happens if you move one of the files to a different folder? The next time you open the main document, you will see a dialog box explaining that Word can't find the data source. In that case, click the Find Data Source button, and then use the Select Data Source dialog box to reselect the data source in its new location.

Because you did not move either Maria's main document or her data source, you don't have to be concerned about re-establishing the connection between the files. But you should keep this connection in mind as you perform mail merges in the future.

You're ready to add some club members to Maria's data source.

To add records to Maria's data source:

1. Open the document named **Club Letter with Merge Fields** in the Tutorial.06\Tutorial folder. If a warning message opens, click **Yes** to continue, close the task pane if it is open, and display the Mail Merge toolbar (if necessary). The main document still displays the data for Ruth Jorgenson, which first appeared when you previewed the merged document. You can redisplay the merge fields using a button on the Mail Merge toolbar.

   Trouble? If you see data for a member other than Ruth Jorgenson, don't be concerned. Simply proceed to Step 2.

   Trouble? If you see the merge fields instead of the data for Ruth Jorgenson, read but do not perform Step 2, and then proceed to Step 3.

2. Click the **View Merged Data** button on the Mail Merge toolbar to deselect it. The merge fields are displayed in the main document.

   Trouble? If you see the data for one of the members instead of the merge fields, click the View Merged Data button again to deselect it.

3. Click the **Mail Merge Recipients** button on the Mail Merge toolbar. The Mail Merge Recipients dialog box opens. You saw this dialog box earlier, when you first selected the data source to use for the mail merge.

4. Click the **Edit** button. The Club Data.mdb dialog box opens. (The full name of this dialog box, as shown in its title bar, includes the entire directory path for the Club Data.mdb path. Depending on where your Club Data.mdb file is stored, the path may be too long to display fully in the title bar.) Note that this dialog box looks similar to the New Address List dialog box, which you used earlier when you first entered information into the data source.
5. Use the New Entry button to enter the information shown in Figure 6-24 into the data source. When you are finished, you should have added three new records, for a total of six.

Figure 6-24 New data

First Name	Last Name	Address Line 1	City	Zip Code	Favorite Equipment	Favorite Class
Violette	Wolfgramm	3004 Falcon Parkway	Tampa	30902	cardiovascular	low-impact aerobics
Kathy	Armstrong	19284 White Sands	Tampa	30902	strength training	Pilates
Pablo	Orozco	248 North River Road	Aurora	30010	strength training	yoga

6. After you finish entering the data for Pablo Orozco, use the buttons in the View Entries section of the dialog box to review your work and make any necessary corrections.
7. Click the **Close** button. The Club Data.mdb dialog box closes, and you return to the Mail Merge Recipients dialog box, as shown in Figure 6-25. If your records look different from those in Figure 6-25, click the Edit button, edit the data source, and then click the Close button.

Figure 6-25 New Records added to data source

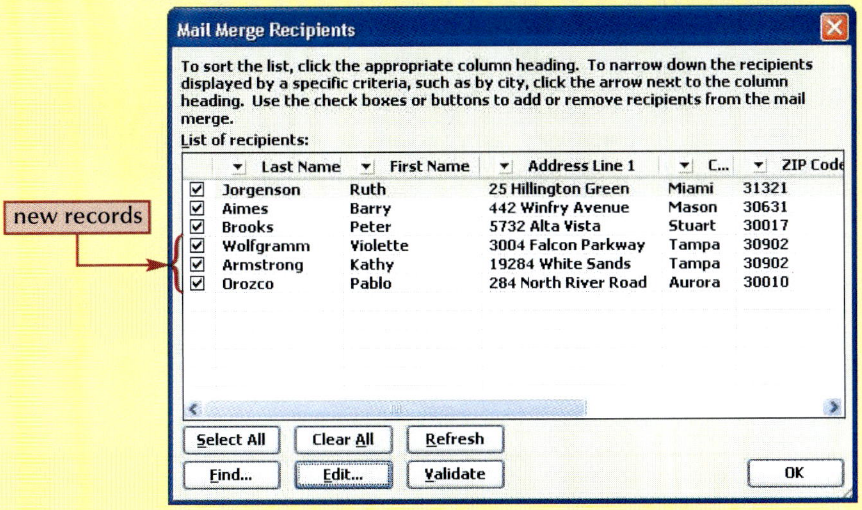

You'll leave the Mail Merge Recipients dialog box open so you can use it to make other changes to the data source.

Sorting Records

As Maria looks through the letters to Palm Tree Athletic Club members in the merged document, she notices one problem—the letters are not grouped by ZIP codes. Currently, the letters are in the order in which members were added to the data source file. She plans to use bulk mailing rates to send her letters, and the U.S. Postal Service requires bulk mailings to be separated into groups according to ZIP code. She asks you to sort the data file by ZIP code and perform another merge, this time merging the main document with the sorted data source.

You can sort information in a data source table just as you sort information in any other table. Recall that to **sort** means to rearrange a list or a document in alphabetical, numerical, or chronological order. You can sort information in ascending order (A to Z, lowest to highest, or earliest to latest) or in descending order (Z to A, highest to lowest, or latest to earliest) by clicking a column heading in the Mail Merge Recipients dialog box. The first time you click the heading, the records are sorted in ascending order. If you click it twice, the records are sorted in descending order.

Reference Window

Sorting a Data Source

- Click the Mail Merge Recipients button on the Mail Merge toolbar to display the Mail Merge Recipients dialog box.
- To sort data in ascending order, click the heading for the column you want to sort. For example, if you want to arrange the records alphabetically according to the contents of the First Name column, click the First Name column heading.
- To sort data in descending order, click the column heading a second time.

Currently, the records in the data source appear in the order you entered them, with the information for Ruth Jorgenson at the top. You'll sort the records in ascending order, based on the contents of the ZIP Code column.

To sort the data source by ZIP code:

1. Verify that the Mail Merge Recipients dialog box is still open. If it is not, click the **Mail Merge Recipients** button on the Mail Merge toolbar.
2. Click the **ZIP Code** column heading. Word sorts the rows of the data table from lowest ZIP code number to highest. The information for Pablo Orozco is now at the top of the list. See Figure 6-26. When you merge the data source with the form letter, the letters will appear in the merged document in this sort order.

Figure 6-26

Records sorted in ascending order by ZIP code

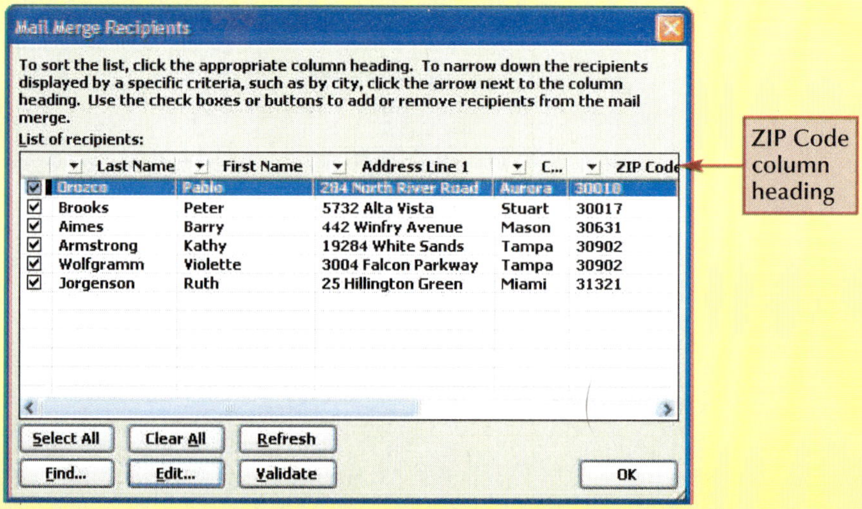

3. Click the **OK** button. The Mail Merge Recipients dialog box closes.
4. Click the **Merge to New Document** button on the Mail Merge toolbar, verify that the **All** option button is selected in the Merge to New Document dialog box, and then click the **OK** button. Word generates the new merged document with six letters, one letter per page as before, but this time the first letter is to Pablo Orozco, who has the lowest ZIP code (30010).
5. Use the Select Browse Object button to browse by page and verify that the letters in the newly merged document are arranged in ascending order by ZIP code.
6. Save the new merged document in the Tutorial.06\Tutorial folder, using the filename **Club Merged Letters 2**, and then close it. You return to the main document.

As Maria requested, you've created a merged document with the letters to Palm Tree Athletic Club members sorted by ZIP code. She then tells you that the letters to members who frequent the Tampa club need additional information.

Selecting Records to Merge

Maria plans to offer an extra hour of personal trainer time to members of the Tampa club because renovations at that branch caused the most inconvenience. Maria wants to modify the form letter slightly, and then merge it with only those records of Palm Tree Athletic Club members who live in Tampa. To select specific records in a data source, you use the Mail Merge Recipients dialog box.

To select specific records for a merge:

1. Make sure the document named Club Letter with Merge Fields is displayed in the Document window. Use the Find command on the Edit menu to find the sentence that begins "As a sign of our gratitude."
2. Change "three" to **four** in the part of the sentence that reads "...sign up for three free hours," and then save the document as **Tampa Club Letter with Merge Fields** in the Tutorial.06\Tutorial folder.
3. Click the **Mail Merge Recipients** button on the Mail Merge toolbar. The Mail Merge Recipients dialog box opens. To remove an individual record from a merge, you can deselect its check box in the leftmost column.
4. Click the check box next to the first record (for Pablo Orozco). The check mark is removed.
5. Remove the check marks for all the records *except* those for Tampa residents. See Figure 6-27. Now that you have selected only the Tampa records, you can complete the Merge.

Figure 6-27 Specific records selected in data source

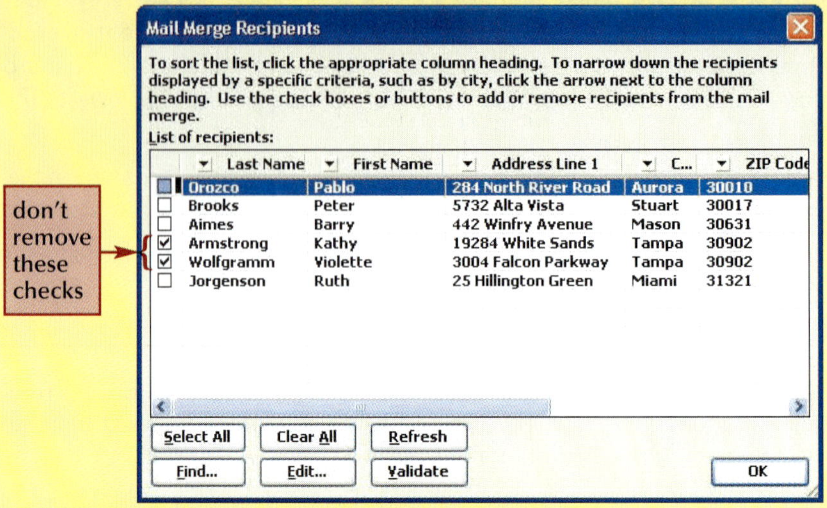

6. Click the **OK** button. The Mail Merge Recipients dialog box closes.
7. Click the **Merge to New Document** button on the Mail Merge toolbar, verify that the **All** option button is selected in the Merge to New Document dialog box, and then click the **OK** button. Word generates the new merged document with two letters, one letter per page. This time the first letter is to Kathy Armstrong.
8. Scroll through the letters in the new merged document to see that they are both addressed to members who live in Tampa.
9. Save the new merged document in the Tutorial.06\Tutorial folder, using the filename **Club Merged Letters 3**, close it, save your changes to the document named **Tampa Club Letter with Merge Fields**, and then close it.

Next, you'll create and print mailing labels for the form letter envelopes and also create a telephone list—both using the Mail Merge toolbar.

Creating Mailing Labels

Now that you've created and printed the personalized letters, Maria is ready to prepare envelopes in which to mail the letters. She could print the names and addresses directly on envelopes, or she could create mailing labels to stick on the envelopes. The latter method is easier because she can print 14 labels at one time; by comparison, printing envelopes is far too time-consuming.

Maria has purchased Avery® Laser Printer labels, which are available in most office-supply stores. Word supports most of the Avery label formats, allowing you to choose the layout that works best for you. The labels Maria has chosen come in 8 1/2 x 11-inch sheets designed to feed through a laser printer. Each label measures 4 x 1.33 inches. There are seven rows of labels per sheet, with two labels in each row, for a total of 14 labels. See Figure 6-28.

You are finished setting up the document. Next, you need to save the main document and select the data source you created earlier.

To continue the mail merge:

1. Save the main document to the Tutorial.06\Tutorial folder using the filename **Club Labels with Merge Fields.**
2. Click **Next: Select recipients**. Under "Select recipients," click the **Use an existing list** option button (if necessary), and then, under "Use an existing list," click **Browse**. The Select Data Source dialog box opens.
3. Select the file named **Club Data** in the Tutorial.06\Tutorial folder, and then click the **Open** button. The Mail Merge Recipients dialog box opens.
4. Verify that all the records are displayed with check boxes selected, and then click the **OK** button. The Mail Merge Recipients dialog box closes. A special code ("Next Record") is inserted into all the labels except the one in the upper-left corner. To see the "Next Record" code, you need to adjust the Zoom setting.
5. Change the **Zoom** setting to **100%**. The Next Record code is a special code that tells Word how to insert data into the document. You can ignore it.
6. Click **Next: Arrange your labels**. The Mail Merge task pane displays options for inserting merge fields into the document. Note that if the data source included a State field, you could use the Address block option to insert a complete set of fields for a single address. However, because the data source does not include a State field, you need to insert the fields individually, as you did when creating the form letter. (You'll have a chance to use the Address block option in the Case Problems at the end of this tutorial.)
7. Verify that the insertion point is located in the upper-left label, click **More Items** in the Mail Merge task pane, and then use the Insert Merge Field dialog box to insert the First Name field into the document. Click the **Close** button. The First Name field is inserted into the document. In the next step you continue to use the More Items link to insert merge fields.
8. Press the **spacebar** to add a space after the First Name field, insert the **Last Name** field, click **Close**, press **Enter**, insert the **Address Line 1** field, click **Close**, press **Enter**, insert the **City** field, type **,** (a comma), press the **spacebar** to insert a space, type **FL**, press the **spacebar**, insert the **ZIP Code** field, and then click **Close**. You are finished inserting the fields for the first label. Now you will update your labels so the merge fields appear on all the labels.
9. Click the **Update all labels** button, near the bottom of the Mail Merge task pane. (You may have to scroll down to see it, using the scroll button at the bottom of the task pane.) The address fields are inserted into all the labels in the document, as shown in Figure 6-31. In all except the upper-left label, the Next Record code appears to the left of the First Name merge field.

Figure 6-31 Field codes inserted into document

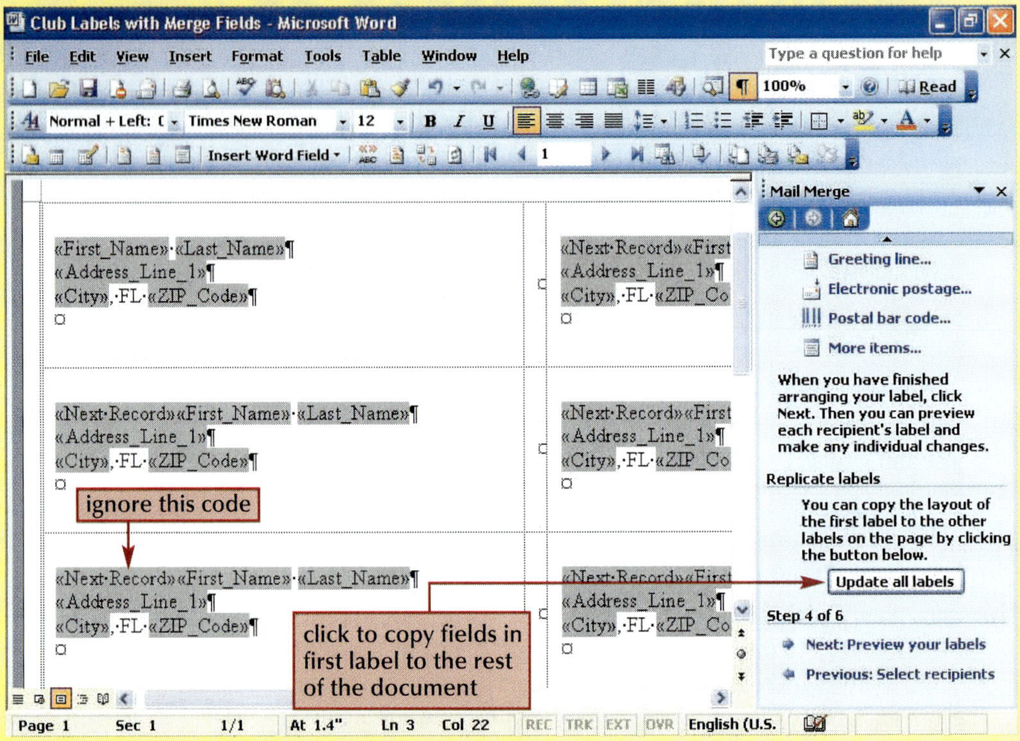

You are now ready to preview the labels and complete the merge.

To preview the labels and complete the merge:

1. Click **Next: Preview your labels** in the Mail Merge task pane. (You may have to scroll down to display this option, again using the scroll button at the bottom of the task pane.) The data for the club members is displayed in the labels. (If you see some extra text in labels that would otherwise be blank, ignore it for now.) You are ready to merge to a new document.
2. Click **Next: Complete the merge** in the task pane, click **Edit individual labels** in the task pane, verify that the **All** option button is selected in the Merge to New Document dialog box, and then click the **OK** button. The finished labels are displayed in a new document.

The labels are almost finished. All you need to do is edit the document to remove any extra text, save the document, and print the labels. For now, you'll just print the labels on an 8 1/2 x 11-inch sheet of paper so you can see what they look like. Later, Maria will print them on the sheet of labels.

To save and print the labels:

1. Scroll through the document. The document contains space for 14 labels, but the data source only contained six records. However, when you clicked the Update Labels button in the task pane earlier, the comma and the state abbreviation (FL) were copied to all the labels, including those that don't contain any address information. See Figure 6-32. You can solve this problem by deleting the extra text in the bottom four rows of labels. (As you'll see in the Case Problems at the end of this tutorial, you can avoid this issue entirely by using the Address block option for inserting fields. However, as mentioned earlier, the Address block option is only useful when your data source contains all the necessary address fields.)

Extra text in labels document **Figure 6-32**

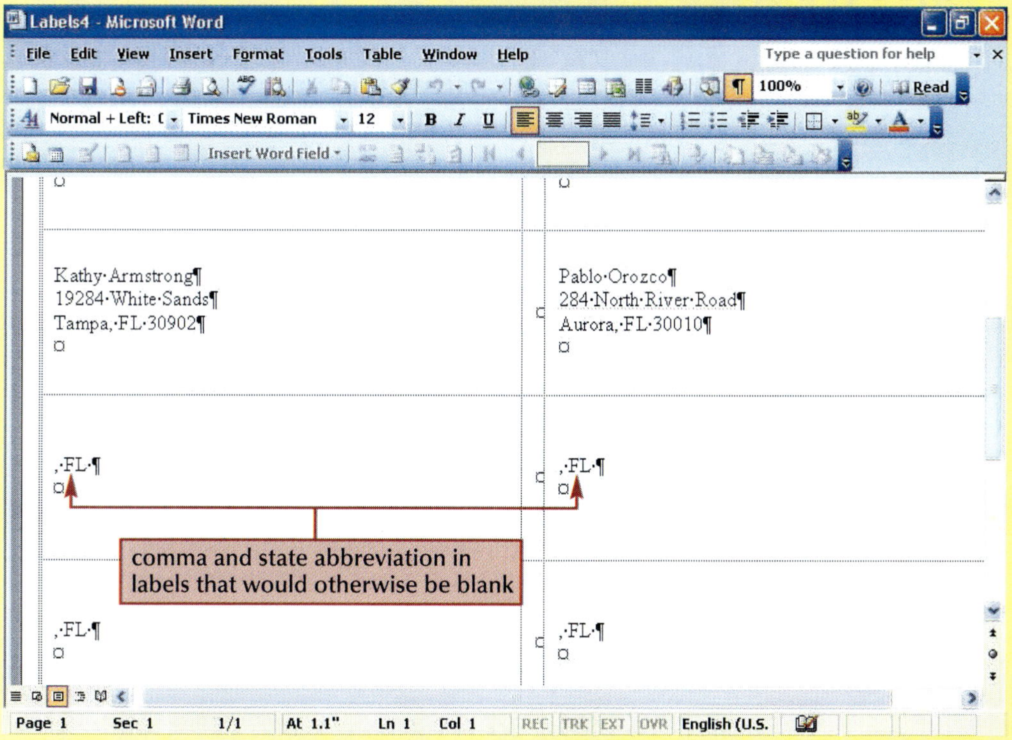

2. Change the Zoom setting to **Whole Page**, drag the mouse pointer to select the bottom four rows of labels, and then press the **Delete** key. The extra text is deleted.
3. Save the merged document in the Tutorial.06\Tutorial folder using the filename **Club Merged Labels**.
4. Print the labels on a sheet of paper, just as you would print any other document.

   Trouble? If you want to print on a sheet of labels, ask your instructor or technical support person how to feed the label sheet into the printer. If you're using a shared printer, you may need to make special arrangements so other users' documents aren't accidentally printed on your label sheet.
5. Close the merged document, and then close the task pane.
6. Click **Tools** on the menu bar, click **Options**, click the **View** tab if necessary, click the **Text boundaries** check box to deselect it, and then click the **OK** button.
7. Save changes to the main document, and then close it.

Creating a Telephone Directory

As your final task, Maria wants you to create a list of telephone numbers for all the branches of Palm Tree Athletic Club. Maria has already created a Word document containing the phone numbers for each branch. She asks you to use that document as the data source for the merge. You'll set up a mail merge as before, except this time you'll select Directory as the main document type. You'll start by examining the Word document that Maria wants you to use as the data source.

To begin creating the telephone list:

1. Open the document named **Phone** from the Tutorial.06\Tutorial folder, and review the document. Note that the information is arranged in a table, with two column headings, "Branch" and "Number." Maria wants the telephone directory in alphabetical order by branch. She asks you to sort the table before using it as the data source for the mail merge.
2. Display the Tables and Borders toolbar, use the Sort Ascending button on the Tables and Borders toolbar to sort the table alphabetically by branch, close the Tables and Borders toolbar, and then save the document as **Sorted Phone List** in the Tutorial.06\Tutorial folder.
3. Close the Sorted Phone List document, open a new, blank document, open the Mail Merge task pane, and then verify that the document is displayed in Print Layout view. If necessary, display nonprinting characters.
4. Display the rulers, and change the Zoom setting to **85%** (or a setting that will let you see the 6-inch mark on the horizontal ruler).
5. In the Mail Merge task pane, under "Select document type" click the **Directory** option button, click **Next: Starting document**, verify that the **Use the current document** option button is selected, click **Next: Select recipients**, verify that the **Use an existing list** option button is selected, and then click **Browse**. The Select Data Source dialog box opens.
6. Select the file named **Sorted Phone List** (in the Tutorial.06\Tutorial folder) as the data source, click the **Open** button, review the records in the Mail Merge Recipients dialog box, and then click the **OK** button.
7. In the task pane, click **Next: Arrange your directory**.

You're ready to insert the fields in the main document and merge the main document with the data source. Maria wants the telephone list to include the name of the club branch at the left margin of the page and the phone number at the right margin. You'll set up the main document so that the phone number is preceded by a dot leader. A **dot leader** is a dotted line that extends from the last letter of text on the left margin to the beginning of text aligned at a tab stop.

To create the main document:

1. With the insertion point at the top of the blank document, insert the **Branch** merge field, and then close the Insert Merge Field dialog box. Now you'll set a tab stop at the right margin (at the 6-inch mark on the ruler) with a dot leader.
2. Click **Format** on the menu bar, and then click **Tabs**. The Tabs dialog box opens.
3. Type **6** in the Tab stop position text box, click the **Right** option button in the Alignment section, and then click the **2 ....** option button in the Leader section to create a dot leader. See Figure 6-33.

Creating a tab with a dot leader — **Figure 6-33**

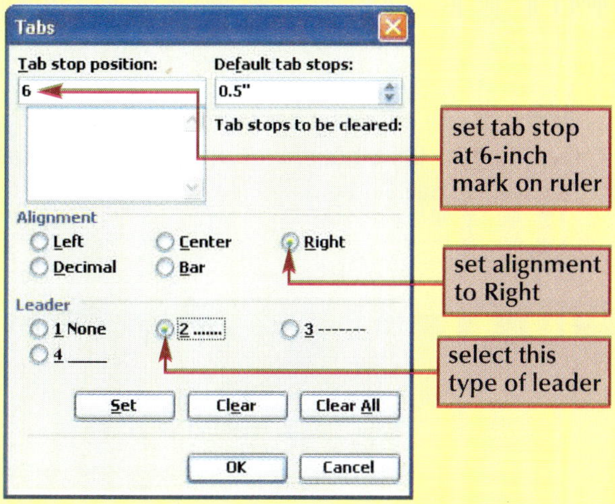

4. Click the **OK** button. Word clears the current tab stops and inserts a right-aligned tab stop at the 6-inch mark on the horizontal ruler.
5. Press the **Tab** key to move the insertion point to the new tab stop. A dotted line stretches across the page, from the Branch field to the right margin.
6. Insert the **Number** merge field at the location of the insertion point, close the Insert Merge Field dialog box, and then press the **Enter** key. You must insert a hard return here so that each name and telephone number will appear on a separate line. Notice that the dot leader shortened to accommodate the inserted field. The completed main document should look like Figure 6-34.

Completed main document for telephone directory — **Figure 6-34**

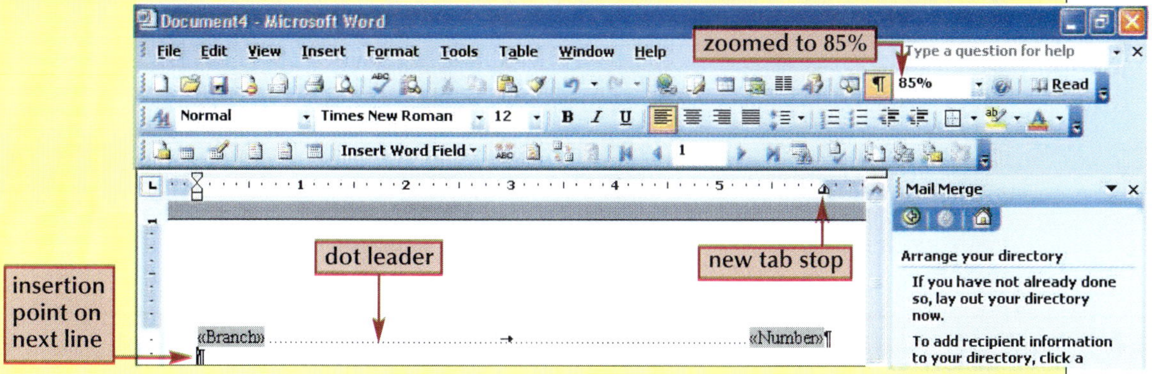

7. Save the main document in the Tutorial.06\Tutorial folder using the filename **Club Phone Directory with Merge Fields**.

You are now ready to merge this file with the data source.

To merge the files:

1. In the Mail Merge task pane, click **Next: Preview your directory**, and review the data for the first record in the document.
2. Click **Next: Complete the merge** in the task pane, click **To New Document** in the task pane, verify that the **All** option button is selected in the Merge to New Document dialog box, and then click the **OK** button. Word creates a new document that contains the completed telephone list. See Figure 6-35.

Figure 6-35 Completed telephone directory

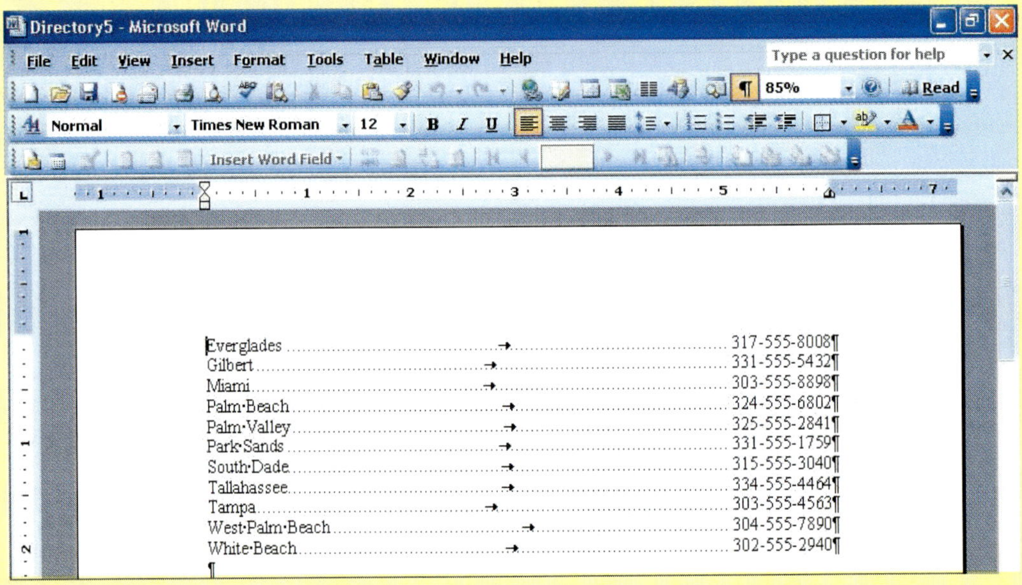

3. Save the document as **Club Phone Directory** in the Tutorial.06\Tutorial folder, and then close it.
4. If field shading was not set to Always on your computer before you started this tutorial, click **Tools** on the menu bar, click **Options**, click the **View** tab, click the **Field shading** list arrow, click **Never** or **When selected** (depending on which option was selected when you first turned on field shading), and then click the **OK** button.
5. Save and then close the main document.

You have created the telephone list. Maria will have it printed and distributed to each branch of the club. Now that you are familiar with the many types of documents you can create using Word's Mail Merge feature, you can use mail merge whenever you need to distribute customized information to a group of people. As you will learn in the Case Problems at the end of this tutorial, you can even use the Mail Merge task pane to send out mass e-mail messages.

Review

Session 6.2 Quick Check

1. True or False: After you complete a mail merge, a connection exists between the main document file and the data source file, even after you close the main document and exit Word.
2. Explain how to alphabetize a data source by last name from within the Mail Merge Recipients dialog box.
3. True or False: To create mailing labels, you cannot use the same data source file you used for a form letter.
4. Explain how to create mailing labels.
5. What is a dot leader? (The telephone directory you created in this tutorial used a dot leader.)

Review

Tutorial Summary

In this tutorial you opened the Mail Merge task pane and then completed a mail merge by selecting a main document, creating a data source, inserting merge fields into the main document, and merging the form letter with the data source. You also used the Mail Merge feature to create mailing labels and a telephone directory. In the process, you edited a data source and sorted records in a data source.

Key Terms

data source	header row	merge fields
date field	Mail Merge task pane	merged document
dot leader	main document	record
field shading	merge	sort
fields		

Practice

Apply the skills you learned in the tutorial using the same case scenario.

Review Assignments

Data Files needed for the Review Assignments: Assess.doc, Memo.doc, and Insurance Data.xls

The club's free personal training offer was a great success, and Maria was pleased with how convenient it was to send out form letters with the Word Mail Merge feature. Now Radine Robbins, the club's special events coordinator, wants to send out a letter inviting members to sign up for their annual health assessments. Members will be invited for either a cardiovascular screening or a strength screening, depending on what type of assessment they chose when they first joined the club. Radine asks you to help her with the mailing. Complete the following:

1. Open a new, blank document, and then open the Mail Merge task pane.
2. Verify that Letters is selected as the type of main document, click Next: Starting document, select the file **Assess** (in the Tutorial.06\Review folder included with your Data Files) as the main document, and then save the current document as **Health Assessment** in the Tutorial.06\Review folder.

3. In Step 3 of the Mail Merge task pane, create a new data source with the following fields: First Name, Last Name, Address Line 1, City, ZIP Code, and Type. Remove any extra fields so that the data source contains only six fields.
4. Create records using the following information:
   - Sandy Martinez, 27 Rugy Street, Tampa, 30307, cardiovascular
   - April Matthews, 200 Mesa Cortes Road, Flambeau, 31321, strength
   - Thomas Peacemaker, 372 Wilderness Avenue, Greeley, 30631, strength
   - David Menaker, 988 Heather Circle #32, Tampa, 30204, cardiovascular
5. Save the data source as **Assessment Data** in the Tutorial.06\Review folder.
6. Edit the data source to replace "David Menaker" with your first and last name. Sort the data source by ZIP code from the lowest to the highest ZIP code.
7. Check the field shading setting and set it to "Always" if that is not the current setting. Take note of your original setting so you can restore it later.
8. In Step 4 of the Mail Merge task pane, replace the field names in brackets with actual merge fields. Remember to replace [Date] with a Word date field.
9. Save your changes to the main document, and then preview the merged document. Correct any formatting or spacing problems.
10. In Step 6 of the Mail Merge task pane, click Edit individual letters to merge to a new document. Save the merged document as **Merged Health Assessment Letters**, and then close it.
11. Return to Step 5 in the Mail Merge task pane, edit the data source to select only records for members interested in cardiovascular assessments, and then complete a second merge. Save the new merged document as **Merged Cardio Assessment Letters**. Close all documents, saving all changes.
12. Open a new, blank document, open the Mail Merge task pane, and select Labels as the type of main document.
13. In Step 2 of the Mail Merge task pane, select Avery standard labels, product number 5162 - Address.
14. Click Tools on the menu bar, click Options, click the View tab, click the Text boundaries check box (in the Print and Web Layout options section) to select it, and then click the OK button. Change the Zoom setting to 75% or a setting that allows you to see all of the upper-left label and most of the upper-right label.
15. In Step 3 of the Mail Merge task pane, select the **Assessment Data** file you created earlier as the data source. Edit the data source to add a State field after the City field, and then add "FL" to the state field in each record. If a warning message opens, click OK.
16. In Step 4 of the Mail Merge task pane, click Address block, select the "Joshua Randall Jr." name format, and verify that the Insert postal address check box is selected. (It doesn't matter whether the other check boxes are selected.) Click the OK button. The AddressBlock merge field is inserted into the main document. Save the main document as **Labels with Merge Fields** in the Tutorial.06\Review folder.
17. Update all labels, preview the merged labels, merge to a new document, and save the new document as **Merged Labels** in the Tutorial.06\Review folder.
18. Click Tools on the menu bar, click Options, click the View tab, deselect the Text boundaries check box (in the Print and Web Layout Options sections), click the OK button, and then close all open documents, saving changes as necessary.

As you learned in the tutorial, you can use many types of files as your data source. For example, right now Sam Lee, the club's human resources manager, needs to send a memo to all club employees regarding their health insurance plans. The data you'll need for this mail merge is stored in a Microsoft Excel worksheet named Insurance Data. This file contains the following field names: First Name, Last Name, E-mail, Work Phone, and Number. To merge this alternate data source with a Word document, complete the following:

19. Open the document named **Memo** from the Tutorial.06\Review folder included with your Data Files, and then save it as **Insurance Memo** in the same folder. Change "Sam Lee" in the "From:" line to your first and last name.
20. With the Insurance Memo document open, open the Mail Merge task pane, and complete the first two steps. Select Letters as the document type, and use the current document (the Insurance Memo document) as the main document.
21. In Step 3 of the Mail Merge task pane, select the Excel file named **Insurance Data** in the Tutorial.06\Review folder. In the Select Table dialog box, click the OK button, and then review the records in the Mail Merge Recipients dialog box. Click the OK button.
22. In Step 4 of the Mail Merge task pane, move the insertion point after the colon (:) in To:, press the Tab key, insert the First Name field (for the employee's first name), press the spacebar, and then insert the Last Name field (for the employee's last name).
23. To the right of Date: in the memo, press the Tab key, and insert the Word date field in a format that matches "April 26, 2006."
24. Select the Word date field and the name fields, and then toggle off the Bold button. Notice that character formatting can be applied to fields just as it is applied to regular text.
25. In the body of the memo, immediately before the word individual(s), insert the Number field followed by a space.
26. Save your changes to the main document. Then preview the merged document and check each record for any mistakes.
27. Merge to a new document. Scroll through the new document to verify that the information has been correctly inserted into the memos, save the new merged document as **Merged Insurance Memos**, and then close all documents, saving any changes.
28. Create an e-mail directory using the same format as the telephone directory you created in the tutorial. Use the **Insurance Data** file as the data source. The directory should include the first name, last name, and e-mail address for each employee in the Insurance Data file. Set a right tab at six inches, and use a dot leader to separate the names from the e-mail addresses. Be sure to press the Enter key after you insert the merge field for the e-mail addresses. Save the main document as **Directory with Merge Fields**, and the merged document as **Merged Directory**.
29. Restore your field shading setting to its original state. When you are finished, close all documents, saving any changes.

Apply

Apply the skills you learned to send a letter to community leaders.

Case Problem 1

Data File needed for this Case Problem: Creek.doc

Friends of Sugar Creek Justin Chambers is chair of The Friends of Sugar Creek, an organization working to prevent a convenience store from being built on a wetlands area in northern Wisconsin. He is sending a letter to community leaders, asking for their support. He asks you to help with the mail merge. As you work on this Case Problem, turn on field shading if necessary, and restore the field shading to its original state when you are finished. Print only those documents your instructor asks you to print.

1. Open the Mail Merge task pane, and create a letter as the main document.
2. Select the existing file **Creek** from the Tutorial.06\Cases folder, and then save it in the same folder as **Sugar Creek Letter**.
3. Create a data source with the following field names: First Name, Last Name, Nickname, Title, Company, Address Line1, and E-mail Address. Arrange the field names in the order given in this step.
4. Enter the following four records into the data source (don't include the commas in the records):
   - Pierre, Joliet, Pierre, Chief Medical Officer, Peshtigo Medical Center, 1577 Cooperville Drive, joliet@pmc.org
   - David, Regenbogen, Dave, President, Regenbogen and Associates, 633 Wentworth, d_regenbogen@world.net
   - Mae, Suyemoto, Mae, Chief Engineer, Taylor and Culkins Engineering Services, 4424 Bedford, m_suyemoto@TaylorCulkins.com
   - Theodore, James, Tad, Principal, Peshtigo High School, 844 Tiger Way, tad_james@peshtigo-high-school.peshtigo.edu
5. Save the data source as **Sugar Creek Data** in the Tutorial.06\Cases folder, and then sort the records alphabetically by last name.
6. Edit the data source to replace the first name in the data source, "Theodore James," with your name. Replace "Tad" with your nickname, or a nickname you make up. Replace the e-mail address for that record with your e-mail address.
7. Change the Zoom setting to 100%. In Step 4 of the Mail Merge task pane, insert the fields into the document. Replace the field names in brackets with the actual fields, either a date field or a merge field. Remember to insert the merge field for Nickname in the body of the letter.
8. Save your changes to the main document. Preview the merged document, and then complete the merge.
9. Save the merged letters document as **Merged Sugar Creek Letters** in the Tutorial.06\Cases folder.
10. Close all open documents, saving any changes.
11. Open a new blank document, save it as **Sugar Creek Envelopes** in the Tutorial.06\Cases folder, and then open the Mail Merge task pane.

Explore

12. Use the mail merge feature to create envelopes.
    - In Step 1 of the Mail Merge task pane, select Envelopes as the type of main document.
    - In Step 2 of the Mail Merge task pane, verify that the Change document layout button is selected, and then click Envelope Options. In the Envelope Options dialog box, verify that Envelope size 10 (4 1/8 x 9 1/2 in) is selected in the Envelope size box, and then click the OK button.
    - In Step 3 of the Mail Merge task pane, select the **Sugar Creek Data** file you created earlier as the data source.
    - In Step 4 of the Mail Merge task pane, click the recipient address area of the envelope, and then insert the necessary merge fields to print a first name, last name, company name, and street address on each envelope. For the last line of the address, type "Peshtigo, WI 53734".
    - In Step 5, preview the merged envelopes.
    - In Step 6, merge to a new document, and then save the document as **Merged Sugar Creek Envelopes**.
13. Close all open documents, saving changes as necessary.

14. Create an e-mail directory of prospective contributors. Use the file named **Sugar Creek Data** (which you created earlier) as the data source. Use a dot leader to separate the name on the left from the e-mail address on the right.
15. Save the main document for the e-mail directory as **Sugar Creek E-mail Directory** in the Tutorial.06\Cases folder.
16. Save the merged document as **Merged Sugar Creek E-mail Directory** in the Tutorial.06\Cases folder.
17. Save and close all open documents.

Apply

Apply the skills you learned to create a form letter for a jewelry store.

Case Problem 2

Data File needed for this Case Problem: Gems.doc

Joseph's Gems Joseph Brennan owns a small jewelry store in Dubuque, Iowa. Frequently, he notifies regular customers (who live in nearby communities in Iowa, Wisconsin, and Illinois) of upcoming sales. He has recently decided to prepare personalized form letters to mail to all his regular customers one month before their birthdays. He'll mail the letters along with a two-page color catalog and a gift certificate. He asks you to help perform a mail merge using Word. As you work on this Case Problem, turn on field shading if necessary, and restore the field shading to its original state when you are finished. Print only those documents your instructor asks you to print.

1. Open the Mail Merge task pane and use Letters as your document type.
2. Select the file **Gems** from the Tutorial.06\Cases folder as the main document, and then save it as **Gems Letters** in the same folder.
3. Create a data source with the following field names, in the following order: First Name, Last Name, Address Line 1, City, State, ZIP Code, Birthday, Birth Month, Birthstone.
4. Enter the following five records into the data source. (Don't include the commas in the records.) Enter months by numbers (1, 2, 3), not names (January, February, March), so you can sort in ascending chronological order.
   - Kayleen, Mitchell, 882 River Way, Dubuque, IA, 52001, 23, 1, garnet
   - Tammy, Minervini, 8244 Westbrook Way, Platteville, WI, 52143, 31, 9, sapphire
   - Susan, Gardner, 804 Derby Road, Dubuque, IA, 52001, 14, 1, garnet
   - Garth, Poduska, 77 Catskill Circle, Rockford, IL, 51345, 7, 6, pearl
   - Haley, Browne, 402 Waverly Avenue, Waterloo, IA, 53400, 22, 9, sapphire
5. Save the data source as **Gems Data** in the Tutorial.06\Cases folder.
6. Edit the data source to change the first and last names in the record for Susan Gardner to your first and last names. Do not change any other information in that record.
7. At the beginning of the main document, insert a date field and merge fields for the inside address and salutation, in a proper business-letter format. Remember to include the State field in the inside address. Use the member's first name in the salutation.
8. In the body of the letter, insert the Birth Month, Birthday, and Birthstone fields at the locations indicated by the bracketed words. Put a slash (/) between the Birthday and Birth Month fields. Save your changes to the main document.
9. Open the Mail Merge Recipients dialog box and then sort records in ascending order (from 1 to 12) by birth month. Then select only the records for customers with January birthdays.
10. Preview the merged document, and then merge to a new document. Save the merged document as **Merged Gems Letters** in the Tutorial.06\Cases folder.

11. Close all open documents, saving all changes.
12. Create a main document for generating mailing labels on sheets of Avery 5162 Address labels, using the **Gems Data** file as your data source. Save the main document as **Gems Labels** in the Tutorial.06\Cases folder. (*Note:* In the tutorial, you used the Options command on the Tools menu to display the rectangular outlines of the labels, but that is not strictly necessary. If you do not see the label outlines now, do *not* display them.)
13. In Step 4 of the Mail Merge task pane, click Address block, select the "Joshua Randall Jr." name format, and verify that the Insert postal address check box is selected. (It doesn't matter whether the other check boxes are selected.) Click the OK button. The Address Block merge field is inserted into the main document. Update all labels and save your changes to the main document.
14. Preview the merged document, merge to a new document, and then save the merged document as **Merged Gems Labels** in the Tutorial.06\Cases folder. Close all open documents, saving any changes.
15. Open a new, blank document, and save it as **Gems Customer Directory** in the Tutorial.06\Cases folder.
16. Open the Mail Merge task pane, select Directory as the main document type, and then select the **Gems Data** file as your data source. Close the Mail Merge Recipients dialog box.
17. In Step 4 of the Mail Merge task pane, insert merge fields into the main document to create a directory entry that looks like the example below. Use the Address block option (as described above in Step 13) to insert the complete address, and the More items option to insert the birth month, birthday, and birthstone.
    Garth Poduska
    77 Catskill Circle
    Rockford IL 51345
    1/7
    garnet
18. Insert two blank lines after the last line of merge fields, and then save your work.

Explore

19. In the tutorial you learned how to select specific records in a data source by using the check boxes to the left of each record. You can also filter a data source to display only records that meet certain conditions. Filtering is a good option for a data source containing numerous records. To filter the Gems Data data source: Open the Mail Merge Recipients dialog box, click the list arrow at the top of the City column, and then click Dubuque. The data source displays only the records for Dubuque residents. The blue arrow next to City indicates that a filter is applied to the column. (Note that to redisplay all the records in the data source, you can click the list arrow at the top of the City column and then click All.) Click OK.
20. Preview the merged document, and then complete the merge to a new document. Save the merged document as **Merged Gems Dubuque Directory** in the Tutorial.06\Cases folder.
21. Close all open documents, saving any changes.

Create

Create the Word table shown in Figure 6-36 and use it as a data source.

Case Problem 3

Data File needed for this Case Problem: Auto.doc

Liberty Auto Sales Tom Reynolds is the customer relations manager for Liberty Auto Sales in Cadillac, Michigan. After a customer purchases a new car, Tom sends out a Sales Satisfaction Survey accompanied by a personalized form letter. He asks you to create the Word table shown in Figure 6-36 and use it as a data source for the form letters. As you work on this case problem, turn on field shading if necessary, and restore the field shading to its original state when you are finished. Print only those documents your instructor asks you to print.

Figure 6-36

First Name	Last Name	Address Line 1	City	ZIP Code	Car Make	Car Model	Sales Rep
Donald	Meyers	344 Hollister Avenue	Detroit	48235	Honda	Civic	Bruce
Arlene	Snow	46 North Alberta Road	Ecorse	48229	Toyota	Camry	Lillie
Lance	Nakagawa	4211 First Street	Kentwood	49508	Honda	Accord	Martin
Peter	Siskel	92 Waterford Place	Walker	49504	Toyota	Corolla	Bruce
Your First Name	Your Last Name	8211 University Drive	Detroit	48238	Honda	Civic	Lillie

1. In a new, blank document, create the table shown in Figure 6-36. Use your first and last name in the bottom record.
2. Display nonprinting characters (if necessary) and verify that you didn't include any extra spaces in the table.
3. Save the file as **Auto Sales Data** in the Tutorial.06\Cases folder, and then close it.
4. Open the file **Auto** from the Tutorial.06\Cases folder, and then save it as **Auto Sales Letters**.
5. Create a letter main document using the current document.
6. Select the **Auto Sales Data** document that you created earlier as the data source. Sort the records in ascending order by ZIP code.

Explore

7. Edit the main document to include the following in the letter, using a proper letter format: date, inside address, and salutation. You'll need to add the state (MI) as text. Experiment with the Greeting line link, which you can use to insert a salutation in a letter. Use the Greeting line dialog box to select settings for the salutation, then insert a salutation that includes a greeting of your choice and the customer's first name,

followed by a colon. Keep in mind that the Greeting line link offers a variety of ways to personalize form letters.
8. Edit the body of the form letter to replace words in brackets with their corresponding merge field names. Save your changes to the main document.
9. Preview the merged document and merge to a new document. Save the merged document as **Merged Auto Sales Letters** in the Tutorial.06\Cases folder.
10. Close all open documents, saving changes as necessary.
11. Create a directory that lists the make of car purchased by each customer. Save the main document as **Auto Sales Directory** in the Tutorial.06\Cases folder.
12. Select the **Auto Sales Data** file as the data source. Sort the records in the data source in ascending order by Last Name. Use a dot leader to separate the name from the make of car.
13. Preview the merged document, merge to a new document, and then save the merged document as **Merged Auto Sales Directory** in the Tutorial.06\Cases folder.
14. Close all open documents, saving any changes as needed.

Challenge

Expand on the skills you learned in the tutorial to send out mass e-mails to sales representatives.

Case Problem 4

There are no Data Files needed for this Case Problem.

E-Mail Merge for DataTech Software You are an associate product manager for DataTech, a software firm that sells a popular line of database products. Your manager has asked you to learn how to use the Mail Merge task pane to send out mass e-mails to the company's sales representatives. Before attempting to send e-mails to the sales representatives, he wants you to practice by sending e-mails to some of your friends or colleagues. As you work on this Case Problem, turn on field shading if necessary, and restore the field shading to its original state when you are finished. Print only those documents your instructor asks you to print. To complete all the steps in this Case Problem, Outlook or Outlook Express must be selected as the default e-mail program on your computer, and your computer must be connected to the Internet. If that is not the case, you can complete most of the steps, but not all.

1. Open a new, blank document, open the Mail Merge task pane, and, in Step 1, select E-mail messages as the main document type.
2. In Step 2, select the current document as the main document.
3. Save the current document as **E-mail Message** in the Tutorial.06\Cases folder.
4. In Step 3 of the Mail Merge task pane, create a new data source that contains three fields: First Name, Last Name, and E-mail Address. Add four records to the data source, using the names and e-mail addresses of your friends, fellow students, or colleagues. One of the records should include your name and e-mail address, so you can verify that the e-mail message is sent as planned.
5. Save the data source as **E-mail Data** in the Tutorial.06\Cases folder.
6. Type an informal message in the main document indicating that you are sending an e-mail in order to test Word's E-mail Merge feature. Ask the recipient to reply to your message, so you can confirm that the messages were sent to the correct address. The message should begin with a brief salutation that includes the First Name field.
7. Save your changes to the main document.
8. Preview the merged document.

Explore

9. In Step 6 of the Mail Merge task pane, click Electronic Mail.

Explore

10. In the Merge to E-mail dialog box, verify that the Email Address field is selected in the To text box. Type "Testing Word E-mail Merge" in the Subject text box, and then verify that the All option button is selected.

Explore

11. If you have Outlook Express or Outlook selected as your default e-mail program, and your computer is already connected to the Internet, Word will send your e-mail messages when you click the OK button. You can follow the progress of the merge, by reading the message that appears in the status bar telling you that each record (letter) is being merged and sent. If you do not have Outlook or Outlook Express installed on your computer, or if your computer is not connected to the Internet, the Merge to E-mail dialog box will close without any visible change to the E-mail Message main document. Click the OK button.
12. If your computer was set up to send the e-mail messages, check your e-mail account to see if you received the message. Watch for replies from the other recipients.

Explore

13. If you have Outlook installed on your computer, have established a profile in Outlook, and have selected Outlook as your default e-mail client, you can use your Outlook address book as the data source for a mail merge. To learn how: Open a new blank document, and then open the Mail Merge task pane. In Step 1 of the Mail Merge task pane, select E-mail messages as the type of document. In Step 2, use the current document. In Step 3, click the Select from Outlook contacts option button, and then click Choose Contacts Folder. (If you see the Choose Profile dialog box, select your user profile. If you don't have the option of selecting a specific user profile, accept the default setting. Click the OK button.) In the Select Contact List Folder dialog box, select your address book, and then click OK. Your Outlook contacts are displayed in the Mail Merge Recipients dialog box. Use the check boxes to deselect all of the records except the records for three friends, fellow students, or colleagues to whom you can send a test e-mail message.
14. In Step 4 of the Mail Merge task pane, type an informal e-mail message indicating that you are testing Word's e-mail merge feature. Ask the recipient to respond to the e-mail. Use the Insert Merge Fields button on the Mail Merge toolbar to insert a first name field in the document, just as you would for an ordinary mail merge. Save the main document as **Outlook E-mail** in the Tutorial.06\Cases folder. Complete the e-mail merge as described in Steps 7 through 12 of this Case Problem.
15. Close all open documents, saving any changes.

Research

Go to the Web to find information you can use to create documents.

Internet Assignments

The purpose of the Internet Assignments is to challenge you to find information on the Internet that you can use to work effectively with this software. The actual assignments are updated and maintained on the Course Technology Web site. Log on to the Internet and use your Web browser to go to the Student Online Companion for New Perspectives Office 2003 at **www.course.com/np office2003**. Click the Internet Assignments link, and then navigate to the assignments for this tutorial.

Assess

SAM Assessment and Training

If you have a SAM user profile, you may have access to hands-on instruction, practice, and assessment of the skills covered in this tutorial. Log in to your SAM account and go to your assignments page to see what your instructor has assigned.

Review

Quick Check Answers

Session 6.1

1. a. A merge field is a special instruction inserted in a main document that tells Word where to insert information from the data source.
   b. A main document is a document (such as a letter or a contract) that, in addition to text, contains merge fields to mark where variable information from the data source (such as a name or an address) will be inserted.
   c. A data source is a document (often in the form of a table) that contains information, such as names and addresses, which can be merged with the main document.
   d. A field is an instruction that tells Word where to insert variable information. You can use a variety of fields in Word, including date fields and merge fields.
   e. A record is a collection of information about one individual or object in a data source. For example, a record might include the first name, last name, address, and phone number for a member.
2. record
3. False
4. True
5. Position the insertion point in the main document where you want to insert the merge field. Click More Items in the Mail Merge task pane, or click the Insert Merge Fields button on the Mail Merge toolbar. In the Insert Merge Field dialog box, click the field you want to insert, click Insert, and then click Close. Adjust the spacing or formatting around the merge field as necessary.
6. Click Edit individual letters in the Mail Merge task pane (or click the Merge to New Document button on the Mail Merge toolbar), and then click OK.

Session 6.2

1. True
2. Open the Mail Merge Recipients dialog box, and then click the Last Name column heading.
3. False
4. In Step 1 of the Mail Merge task pane, select Labels as the main document type; in Step 2 click Label options to select a label type; in Step 3 select a data source; in Step 4 insert merge fields in the main document, and click Update Labels; in Step 5 preview the merged document; and then in Step 6 merge to a new document. Delete unnecessary text from labels that would otherwise be blank.
5. A dot leader is a dotted line extending from one tab stop to the next.

Objectives

- Learn how to share Office files online
- Create Web pages in Word
- Insert a hyperlink
- Preview a Web page in a browser
- Create Web pages in Excel
- Create Web pages in Access
- Create Web pages in PowerPoint
- Publish Web pages to the Internet

Creating Web Pages with Microsoft Office 2003

Using Word, Excel, Access, and PowerPoint to Create Web Pages

Case

Temps Abound, Inc.

Temps Abound, Inc. is an agency that provides temporary office workers to businesses. Recently, Temps Abound has been getting requests for workers who can convert Office files into Web pages to be posted on the client's Web site or intranet. The latest requests have come from the following four clients: Bayside Health, Premier Finance, Northeast Seasonal Jobs International, and Global Humanitarian.

Bayside Health provides a variety of health-related services to corporations and other social service organizations. Susan Dague, publications director, develops newsletters on a variety of topics related to health and fitness. To broaden the audience for these newsletters, she wants to transform them into Web pages and add them to Bayside Health's Web site.

David Kowlske is a financial officer at Premier Finance, a lending company that is increasing its presence on the World Wide Web. David wants customers to be able to use the company's Web site to look up the current cost of a 20-year mortgage with a fixed interest rate. He also wants customers to be able to use the company's Web site to calculate mortgage payments based on the interest rate, the size of the mortgage, and the length of the loan. David has already created the Excel workbook that contains the values and formulas he wants to include on the Web pages.

Elsa Jensen is the founder of Northeast Seasonal Jobs International (NSJI), a company that contracts with hotels and resorts to supply their seasonal help. Elsa wants to create a Web page that lists the employers and their available positions.

Labs

Web Pages & HTML

Student Data Files

▼**Web**

▽ Tutorial folder

Calculator.xls
Exercise.doc
Northeast.mdb
PeruExp.ppt

▽ Review folder

Fund.xls
MPTour.ppt
Recruits.mdb
Stir-fry.doc

She will include this Web page on NSJI's company Web site so that this information will be available to NSJI employees when they work out of the office.

Global Humanitarian is a nonprofit organization that provides a variety of services to help people in less-developed countries, including organizing service expeditions. Miriam Schwartz, the managing director, wants to share a modified version of a PowerPoint presentation describing a recent expedition to Peru with potential volunteers and contributors. She wants people to be able to view the presentation on the organization's Web site.

In this tutorial, you'll create Web pages for all four of these clients.

Sharing Office Files Online

Web Pages & HTML

Most people are familiar with sharing Office files by printing and distributing paper copies of the file to others one at a time. However, as computers with network connections become more prevalent, it's becoming common to share Office files electronically as illustrated in Figure 1. One method is to send the Office file as an e-mail message or e-mail attachment to one person or a group of people simultaneously. Another method is to post the file as a Web page on an intranet or the Internet so that people can access the file as they need it.

Figure 1 Distribution methods for files

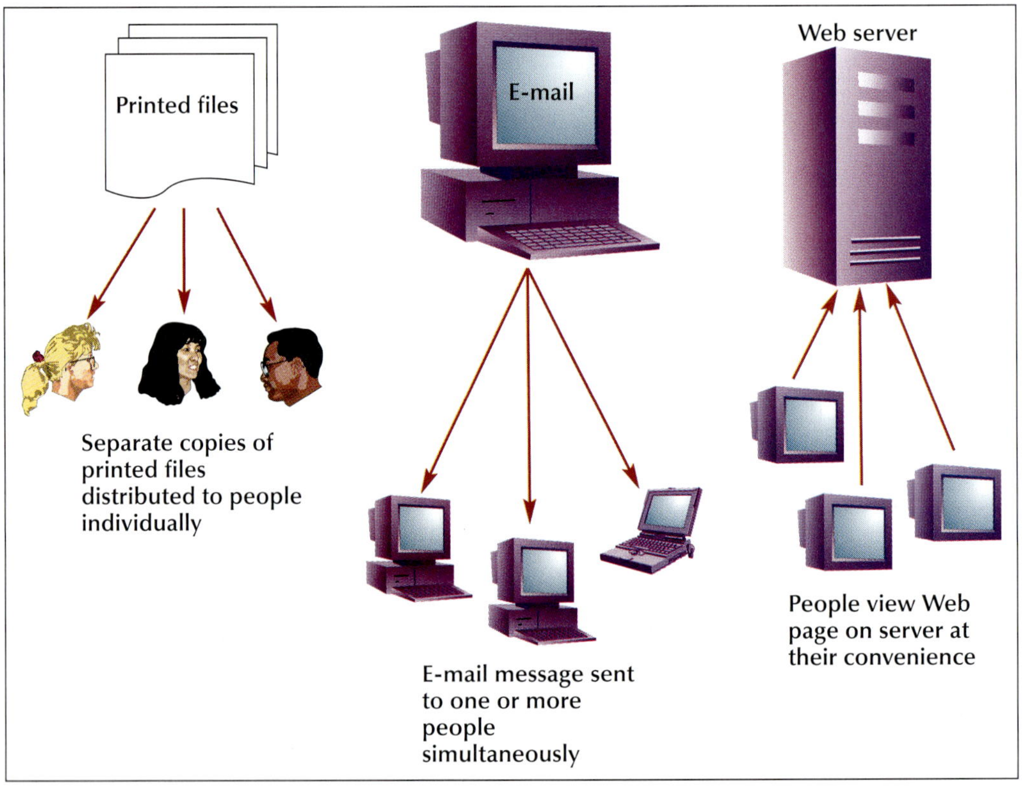

Most Web pages are created using the HTML programming language to describe the format of a Web page so that Web browsers know how to display the page. You can create a Web page by typing all of the necessary HTML code into a text document and saving the document with the .htm or .html file extension. Because a Web page contains HTML code, it is also called an **HTML document**. Professional designers create Web sites using a **Web page editor**, a software program designed specifically for that purpose, such as Macromedia Dreamweaver or Microsoft FrontPage. However, sometimes you'll want to quickly create a Web page from an existing Office file. Fortunately, you don't have to learn HTML to create Web pages; Word, Excel, Access, and PowerPoint can do the work for you.

Each Office program includes commands for saving a file as a Web page. To save a file as a Web page, you click File on the menu bar, choose the Save As or Save as Web Page command, and then change the Save as type option to Web page, Single File Web Page, or, in Word only, Web Page, Filtered.

If you save a file as a Web page, the file is saved as an HTML document and a new folder is created to contain all the supporting files (such as bullets, backgrounds, and graphics) for the Web page. For example, when you save a Web page with the filename "CompanyHomePage," a folder named "CompanyHomePage_files" is created. You use the Web page file format when you plan on creating multiple pages for a Web site.

A **single file Web page** is one file that contains the HTML document along with all the supporting files. The advantage of saving a file as a single file Web page is that you can send the single file Web page as an e-mail message or attachment and know that the recipient will have all the elements and supporting items referenced in the Web page. However, the file size of a single file Web page is larger than a Web page. Also, single file Web pages require Internet Explorer 4.0 or later.

A **filtered Web page** is an HTML document with the Office-related tags removed. Generally, you should not use filtered Web pages, which are available only in Word, unless you are experienced in creating Web pages and understand how HTML programming works.

Word creates a Web page from the entire file, and you can easily edit the content of the Web page in Word. With Excel, Access, and PowerPoint, you can choose to create a Web page from all or part of the file, but the editing ability may be more limited.

Creating Web Pages in Word

There are a few ways to create Web pages in Word. You can create a new, blank Web page document and then enter and format text and graphics as usual. You can create a Web page from a **template**, a special file that contains the design layout and tools for formatting page elements. You can also open an existing Word document and then save it as a Web page. You'll try the first and last method in this tutorial.

Creating Web Pages in Word

Reference Window

- Click Web page in the New area in the New Document task pane (*or* click the New button or the New Web Page button on the Standard toolbar *or* click the Open button and open an existing document).
- Click File on the menu bar, and then click Save as Web Page.
- Navigate to the location where you want to save the Web page.
- Type a new filename in the File name text box.
- Click the Save as type list arrow, and then click Web Page if you want to save the file as a Web page instead of a single file Web page.
- Click the Change Title button, type a page title, and then click the OK button.
- Click the Save button.

Susan (the publications director at Bayside Health) asks you to convert her current newsletter into a Web page for Bayside Health's new Web site. You'll open a blank Web page in Word, so that you can begin creating the Health News home page.

To create a new, blank Web page:

1. Start Word.
2. Click the **Show/Hide ¶** button ¶ on the Standard toolbar to display the nonprinting characters, if necessary.
3. Click **File** on the menu bar, and then click **New**. The New Document task pane opens.
4. Click the **Web page** link in the New area of the New Document task pane. A new, blank Web document opens, similar to a regular Word document. Note that the Web Layout View button is selected in the lower-left corner of the Document window, and the New button on the Standard toolbar is the New Web Page button.

As with other Word documents, you need to save the file to a storage disk. When you save the file as a Web page, you also need to specify the page title. The **page title** is the text that appears in the browser title bar each time the Web page is displayed in a browser. You should avoid using spaces in Web page filenames because some Web servers and browsers do not accept filenames with spaces.

You'll save the new document as a Web page.

To save a Web page:

1. Click **File** on the menu bar, and then click **Save as Web Page**. The Save As dialog box opens with Single File Web Page selected as the file type.
2. Click the **Save in** list arrow, and then navigate to the **Web\Tutorial** folder included with your Data Files.
3. Click the **Change Title** button. The Set Page Title dialog box opens.
4. Type **Health News Home Page** in the Page title text box, and then click the **OK** button.
5. Type **HealthHomePage** in the File name text box.
6. Click the **Save as type** list arrow, and then click **Web Page**. See Figure 2.

Figure 2 Completed Word Save As dialog box

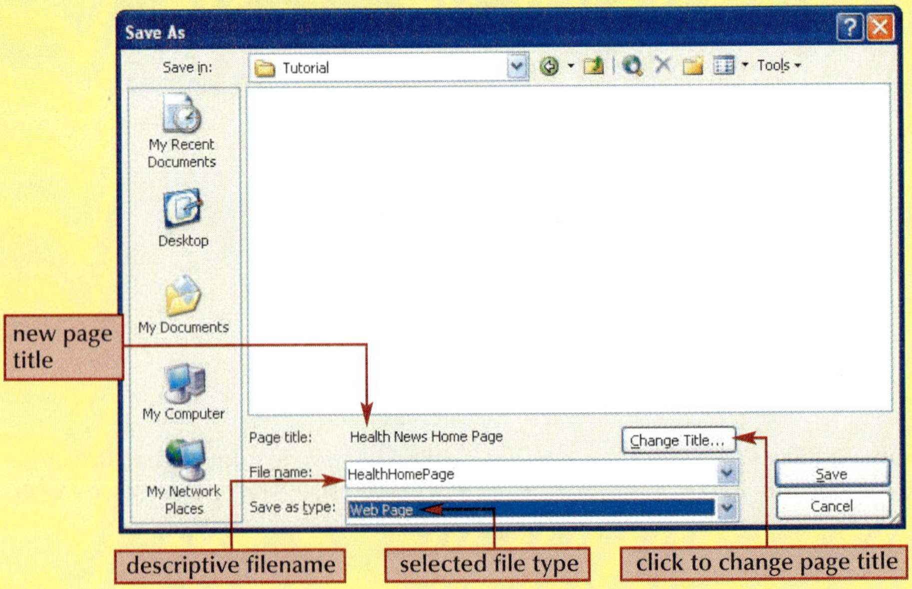

7. Click the **Save** button. The Web page is saved in the location you specified.

Word's basic editing and formatting features work the same in a Web page as they do in a regular Word document. You'll start typing the text of the home page.

To type the text of the home page:

1. Type **Bayside Health, Inc.**, and then press the **Enter** key twice.
2. Type **Welcome to our Health News Home Page**, and then press the **Enter** key twice.
3. Type **Our Health News Reports give you quick updates on these important topics:**, and then press the **Enter** key twice.
4. Click the **Bullets** button on the Formatting toolbar, and then type the following list:
   - **Exercise**
   - **Pain management**
   - **Low-fat cooking**
5. Press the **Enter** key three times, and then type your name.

You can manually transform the look of any aspect of the Web page as you would in an ordinary Word document, or you can apply a theme. A **theme** is a designed collection of formatting options that include colors, graphics, and background images.

The guidelines for formatting Web pages differ from those for documents. Although you can apply different fonts, font sizes, and colors to text, when people open your Web page in their browser, they may see something different, depending on their browser's settings. In addition, adding too many images, backgrounds, or other graphics can make the file size of the Web page large, leading to longer download times. If it takes too long, people might not wait for the page to load completely and instead jump to another page.

You'll format some of the text you typed, and then apply a theme.

To format the text of the home page:

1. Select the heading **Bayside Health, Inc.** and the subheading **Welcome to our Health News Home Page**.
2. Change the font to **Arial**, and then change the font size to **26**.
3. Click the **Font Color** button list arrow on the Formatting toolbar, and then click the red square in the third row, first column.
4. Center the heading and subheading, and then click outside the headings to deselect them. See Figure 3.

Figure 3 Formatted text of Web page

Trouble? If your document is not zoomed to 100%, click the Zoom list arrow on the Standard toolbar, and then click 100%.

Now that you have formatted the text, you'll select a theme. There are many themes available; however, some of the themes may need to be installed on first use.

To apply a theme to a Web page:

1. Click **Format** on the menu bar, and then click **Theme** to open the Theme dialog box.
2. Click **Capsules** in the Choose a Theme list box. See Figure 4.

Figure 4 Theme dialog box

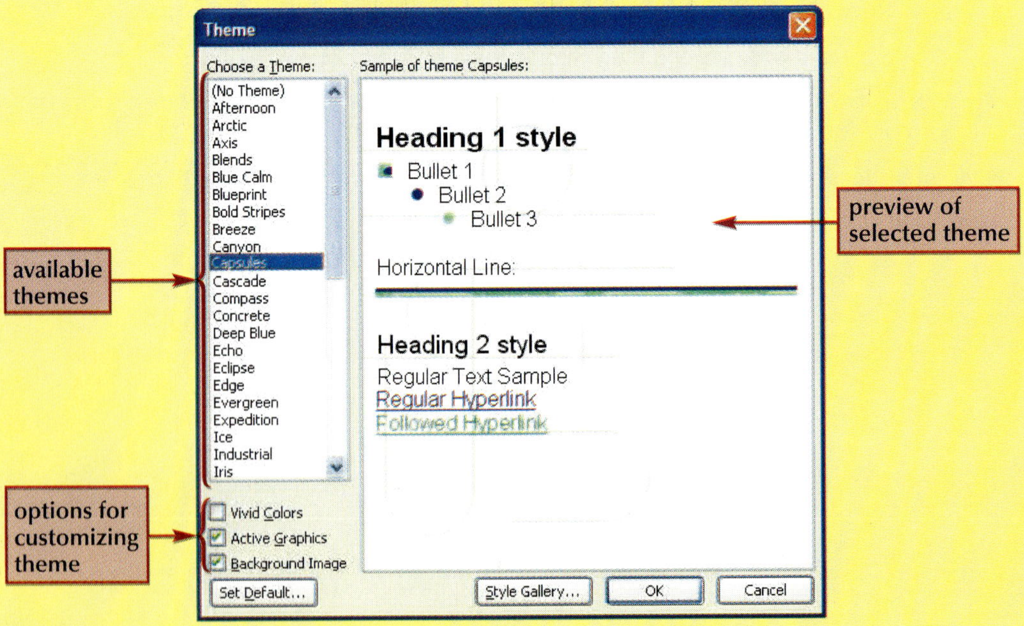

Trouble? If a dialog box opens, indicating that the Capsules theme is not installed on your computer, install the theme or select another theme.

3. Click the **OK** button. The Web page is now formatted as shown in Figure 5. The unformatted text is reformatted with the theme; however, the manual formatting you applied earlier remains intact, overriding the theme formatting.

Figure 5 **Web page with theme**

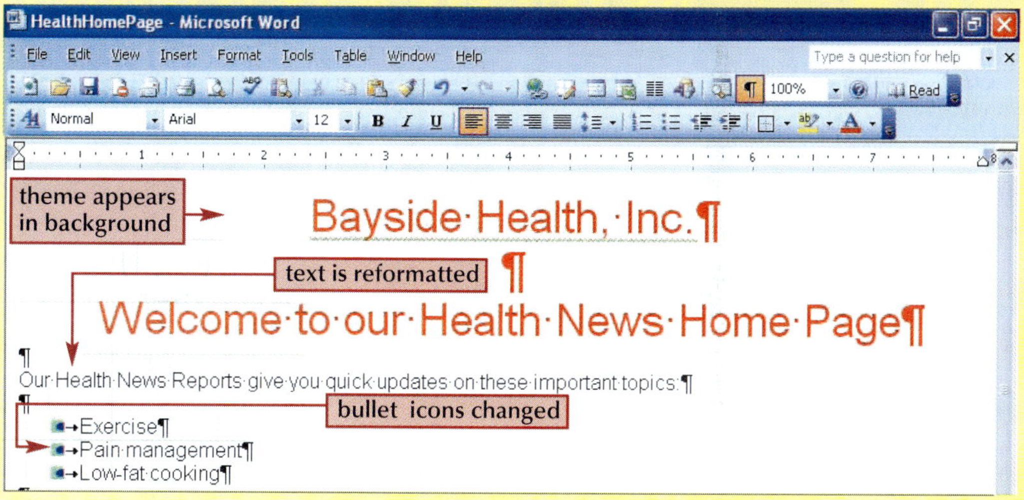

4. Click the **Save** button on the Standard toolbar to save your work.

When you have an existing document that you want share over the Web, you can save that document as a Web page rather than re-creating it in a blank Web page. Be aware, however, that not all elements you can create in a Word document convert to Web pages. One way to determine quickly which elements and features of a document will convert to a Web page and which will not is to view the page in Web Layout view.

One of the pages that Susan wants to include in the Web site will contain information about exercise. The information on exercise is currently stored as a desktop-published newsletter. You'll convert that Word document to a Web page.

To open the Exercise newsletter and view it in Web Layout view:

1. Open the **Exercise** document located in the **Web\Tutorial** folder included with your Data Files.
2. Click the **Print Layout View** button in the lower-left corner of the Document window, if necessary, to display the document in Print Layout view.
3. Click the **Zoom** button list arrow on the Standard toolbar, and then click **Whole Page**. The newsletter is resized so that you can see the entire document on your screen.
4. Press the **Ctrl+End** keys to move the insertion point to the end of the document, press the **Enter** key three times, and then type your name. As you can see in Figure 6, this newsletter is set in two columns, and it contains a WordArt headline, a border, formatted headings, and a graphic (taken from Word's clip-art collection).

Figure 6 Exercise newsletter

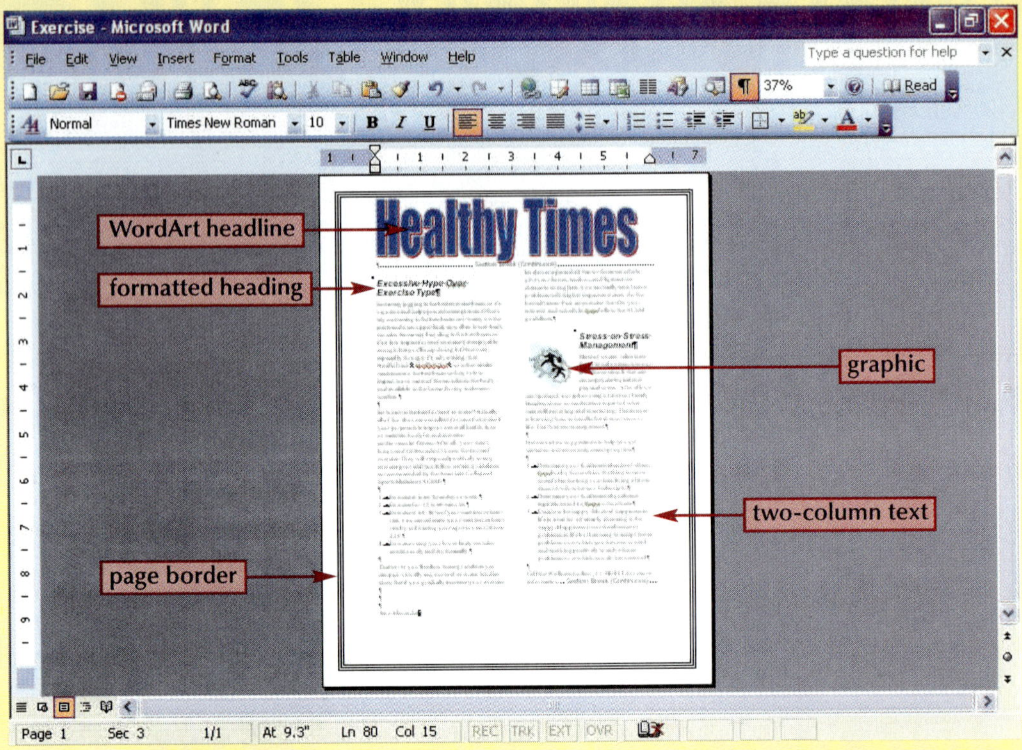

5. Click the **Web Layout View** button in the lower-left corner of the Document window.
6. Scroll through the document to see how the Web page based on this document would look. The two-column portion of the document changes to a single column, and the border is hidden. The graphic moves to the top of the second section, under the heading "Excessive Hype Over Exercise Type."

You'll update the formatting and adjust the position of graphics after you save the newsletter as a Web page.

To save an existing document as a Web page:

1. Click **File** on the menu bar, and then click **Save as Web Page**. The Save As dialog box opens.
2. If necessary, click the **Save in** list arrow, and then navigate to the **Web\Tutorial** folder included with your Data Files.
3. Type **ExerciseWebPage** in the File name text box.
4. Click the **Save as type** list arrow, and then click **Web Page**. Remember, when you save the document as a Web page instead of a single file Web page, you create not only the single HTML document but also a folder with all of the associated files in it.
5. Click the **Change Title** button, type **Exercise News Report** in the Set Page title text box, and then click the **OK** button.
6. Click the **Save** button. A message informs you that some features of the original document (the desktop-published newsletter) cannot be displayed in Internet Explorer 4.0 or Netscape Navigator 4.0.
7. Click the **Continue** button. The document is saved as a Web page.

8. Drag the graphic down to position it after the first paragraph below the heading "Stress on Stress Management." See Figure 7.

Modified Exercise Web page **Figure 7**

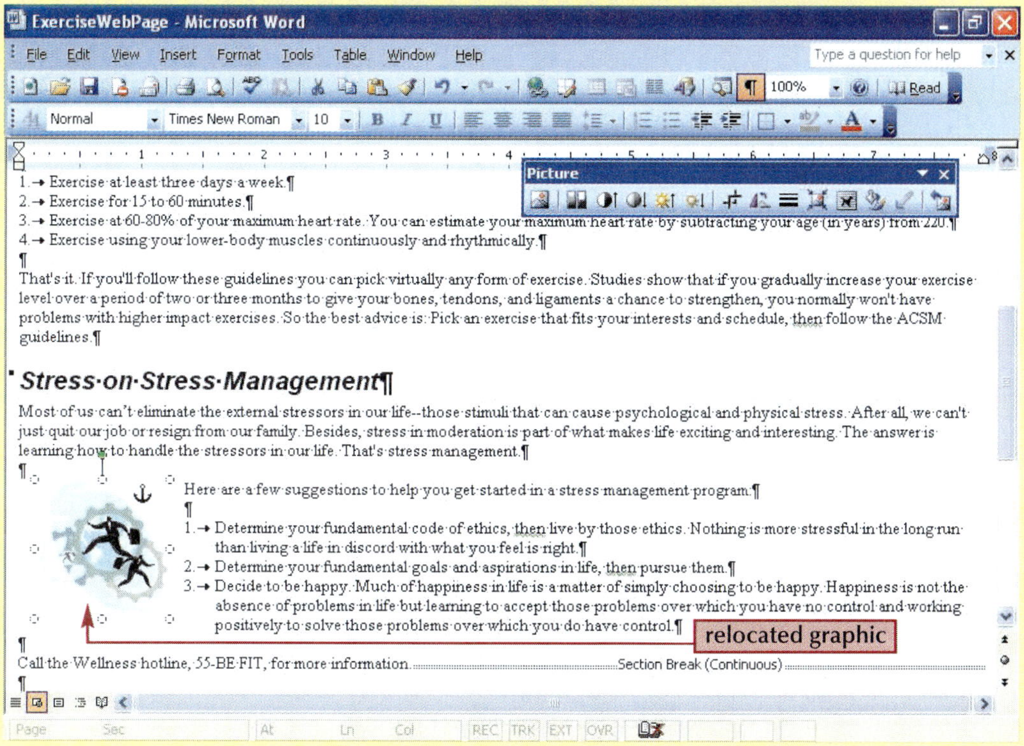

9. Save and close the Exercise Web page.

Next you'll insert hyperlinks.

Inserting Hyperlinks

Hyperlinks, or links, provide an easy way to navigate within and between Web pages. You can create a text link for each page using the appropriate text in the bulleted list. Once you change text to a link, it becomes colored and underlined, such as Exercise, and the pointer changes to 👆 when positioned over the link. You can also use a graphic for a link; the only indicator that the graphic is a link is that the pointer changes shape when positioned over the graphic.

You'll change the Exercise bullet to a hyperlink so that the Exercise Web page opens when the Exercise bullet text is clicked.

To insert a text link:

1. Select **Exercise** in the bulleted list in the HealthHomePage document.
2. Click the **Insert Hyperlink** button on the Standard toolbar. The Insert Hyperlink dialog box opens.
3. Click the **Look in** list arrow, and navigate to and click the **ExerciseWebPage** file you saved in the **Web\Tutorial** folder included with your Data Files. See Figure 8.

Figure 8 Insert Hyperlink dialog box

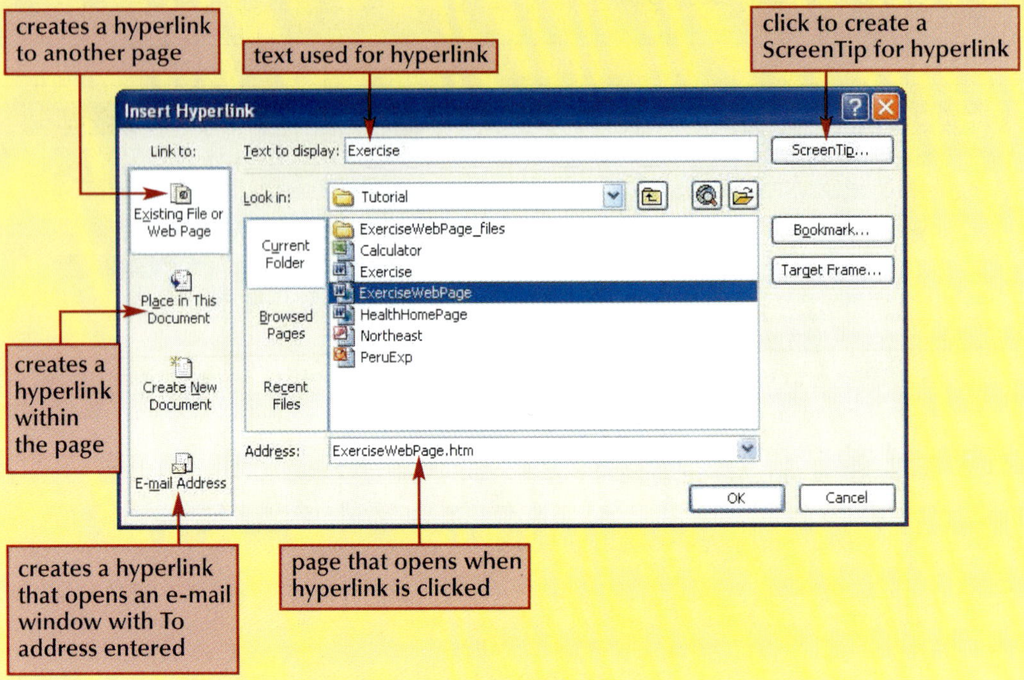

4. Click the **OK** button. The Exercise text on the home page becomes a link to open the Exercise Web page.
5. Save the HealthHomePage document.

Next you'll preview the Web pages in a browser.

Previewing Web Pages in a Browser

Before you publish Web pages for others to view, you should preview them in a Web browser to ensure that the pages look like you expect them to. Not all browsers display Web pages in the same way, so if you have access to more than one browser, you should preview your Web pages in the other browsers and, if possible, on other computers.

There are several ways to preview Web pages in a browser. You can use the Web Page Preview command on the File menu, you can display the Web toolbar and use the buttons on it to open the page in your default browser, or you can start your browser and use the Open command on the File menu. You'll preview the Web page you just created by using the Web Page Preview command. Because you will be viewing files stored on your computer, you don't have to be connected to the Internet to preview Web pages in a browser.

To preview Web pages in a browser:

1. Click **File** on the menu bar, and then click **Web Page Preview**. The home page opens in the browser window.
2. Maximize the browser window, if necessary. See Figure 9.

Figure 9

Web page previewed in Internet Explorer

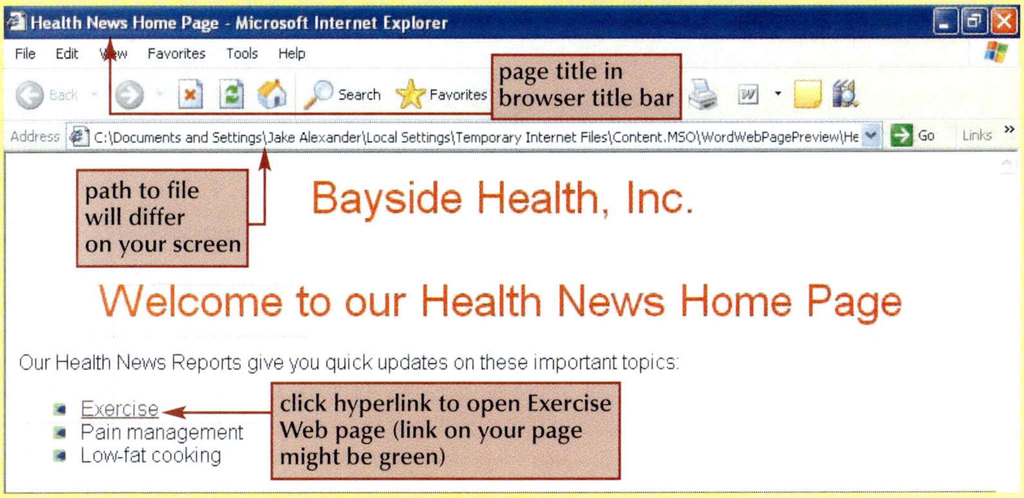

3. Click the **Exercise** link on the home page. The Exercise Web page opens in the browser window.

   Trouble? If the Exercise Web Page does not open, start your browser, open the HealthHomePage Web page, and then click the Exercise link. Close the browser when you are finished.

4. Click the **Close** button on the browser window title bar to close the Web page and exit the browser.

5. Close the HealthHomePage document, and then exit Word.

Susan will later add more text and links to the two Web pages you created. She will ultimately publish all the Web pages on a Web server so that Bayside's clients can access them through the Internet.

Creating Web Pages in Excel

You can convert Excel workbooks into two types of Web pages: noninteractive and interactive. A **noninteractive Web page** allows users to scroll through and view the contents of an Excel workbook, but does not allow users to make any changes to the values displayed in the Web page. An **interactive Web page** provides tools for users to modify and format the values displayed in the Web page from their browsers. Any changes they make in the Web page do not affect the original workbook, so only the current user sees the changes being made. Also, changes do not last from one browser session to another.

You can also choose how much of the workbook to publish. In Excel, to **publish** means to save a workbook or portions of a workbook as a Web page.

If you need to modify the content of a Web page created in Excel, where you make those changes depends on whether the page is noninteractive or interactive. You can make changes to a noninteractive Web page in either the HTML document or in the workbook, which you then resave as a Web page. You should modify an interactive Web page only in the original workbook and then resave the workbook as a Web page. When you resave a Web page, you can select previously published items in the Publish as Web Page dialog box. If you publish to an existing Web page, you can click Replace file to copy over the page or you can click Add to file to append the new data at the end of the Web page.

Reference Window

Creating Web Pages in Excel

- Click the Open button and open an existing workbook that you want to save as a Web page.
- Click File on the menu bar, and then click Save as Web Page.
- Navigate to the location where you want to save the Web page.
- Type a new filename in the File name text box.
- Click the Save as type list arrow, and then click Single File Web Page if you want to save the file as a single file Web page.
- Click the Change Title button, type a page title, and then click the OK button.
- Check the Add interactivity check box to create an interactive Web page; leave it unchecked to create a noninteractive Web page.
- Click the Publish button, click the Choose list arrow, and then click what you want to include in the Web page.
- Check the AutoRepublish every time this workbook is saved check box.
- Check the Open published web page in browser check box to preview the Web page in a browser.
- Click the Publish button.

David (a financial officer at Premier Finance) has created a workbook that calculates the cost of a 20-year mortgage with a fixed interest rate of 5.5 percent. He wants you to convert this workbook to a Web page for Premier's Web site. You'll convert David's mortgage data into a noninteractive Web page that will display the values for a $100,000 mortgage for 20 years at a fixed 5.5 percent annual interest rate.

To open the Mortgage workbook:

1. Start Excel, and then open the **Calculator** workbook located in the **Web\Tutorial** folder included with your Data Files.
2. Review the contents of the workbook, and then return to the Documentation worksheet.
3. On the Documentation worksheet, enter the current date in cell B3 and enter your name in cell B4.
4. Save the Calculator workbook as **Mortgage Values** in the **Web\Tutorial** folder.

The Loan Values worksheet displays the current mortgage cost of a $100,000 loan, along with two embedded charts that show the declining balance on the principal over 240 payments and the breakdown between total interest payments and total principal payments. The Schedule worksheet displays a sample payment schedule for a 20-year mortgage. You'll save all of the data and charts on the Loan Values worksheet as a noninteractive Web page.

To create a noninteractive Web page:

1. Click **File** on the menu bar, and then click **Save as Web Page**. The Save As dialog box opens. See Figure 10.

Excel Save As dialog box

Figure 10

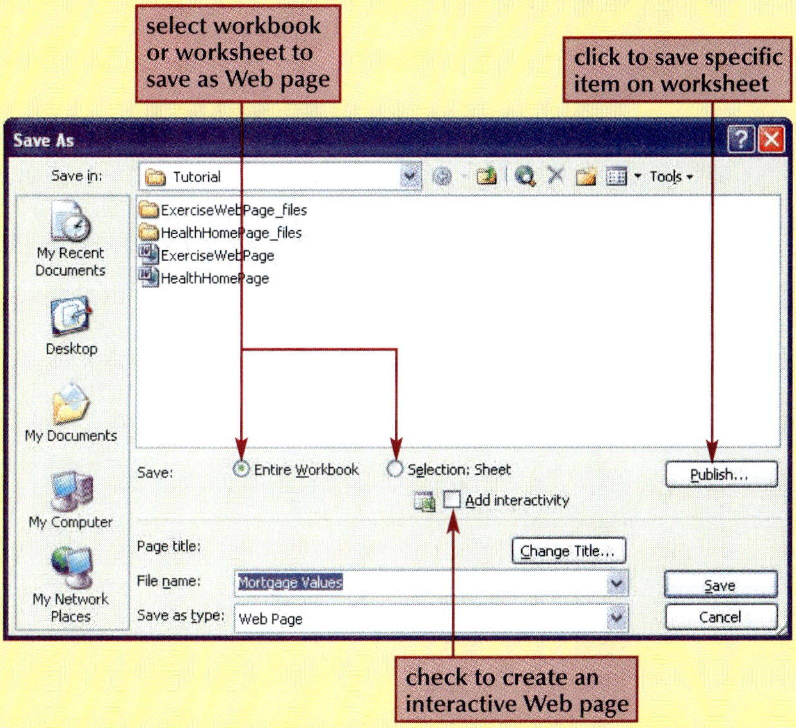

2. Verify that the **Add interactivity** check box is unchecked.
3. Click the **Change Title** button to open the Set Page Title dialog box, type **Sample Mortgage Values** in the Page title text box, and then click the **OK** button. The page title appears in the Save As dialog box above the File name text box.
4. Type **MortgageWebPage** in the File name text box.
5. Click the **Save as type** list arrow, and then click **Single File Web Page**.

The next step is to choose which components of the workbook to publish. You can choose to publish either the entire workbook or the current selection in the active worksheet (which in this case is the entire Loan Values worksheet). Or, you can click the Publish button, which opens the Publish as Web Page dialog box, to make additional choices. In the Publish as Web Page dialog box, you can choose to publish the entire workbook; a specific worksheet in the workbook; an item on the selected worksheet, such as an embedded chart or a pivot table; a contiguous range of cells in a worksheet; or a previously published selection from the workbook.

David wants only the Loan Values worksheet published as a noninteractive Web page, and he wants to include both of the embedded charts on that worksheet.

To publish all of the items on a worksheet:

1. Click the **Publish** button. The Publish as Web Page dialog box opens.
2. Click the **Choose** list arrow, and then click **Items on Loan Values**. Excel displays three more options, each of which is based on the Loan Values worksheet. You can publish all the contents of the Loan Values worksheet or either of the two embedded charts.
3. Click **Sheet All contents of Loan Values** in the list. This has the same effect as clicking the Selection: Sheet option button in the Save As dialog box. See Figure 11.

Figure 11 Publish as Web Page dialog box

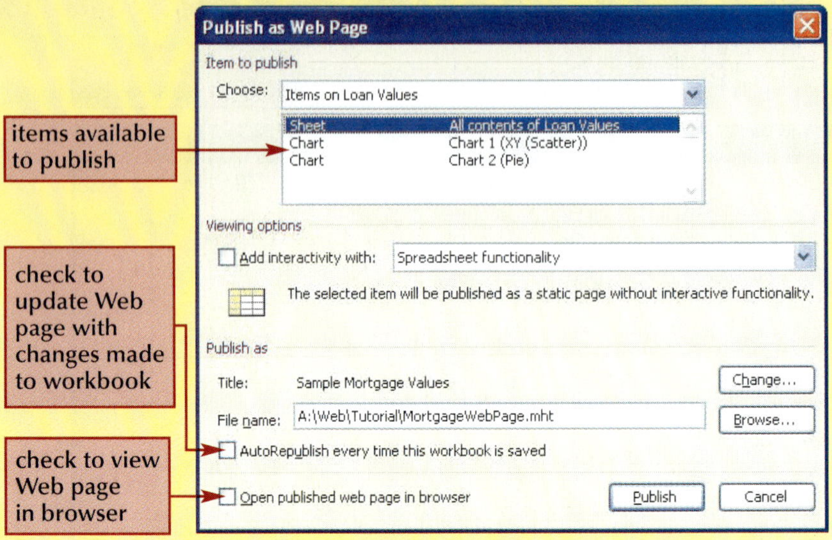

David wants the Web page to update automatically so that it always matches any changes made to the source workbook. You will turn on the AutoRepublish feature, which republishes the Web page with any changes that have been made to the source workbook whenever the workbook is saved. However, if you move either the workbook file or the Web page file, the AutoRepublish feature will not work.

To immediately view the Web page in your browser, you can check the Open published web page in browser check box. If you prefer not to immediately view the Web page, you can use the Web Page Preview command on the Web toolbar in Excel, or you can use the Open command in Internet Explorer to open the Web page file directly from the browser.

You'll turn on the AutoRepublish feature and open the Web page in the browser.

To turn on the AutoRepublish feature and open the Web page in the browser:

1. Click the **AutoRepublish every time this workbook is saved** check box to insert a check mark.
2. Click the **Open published web page in browser** check box to insert a check mark, if necessary.
3. Click the **Publish** button. The worksheet is saved as a single file Web page, and the Web page opens in a browser.
4. Click the **Maximize** button on the browser title bar to maximize the browser window, if necessary. See Figure 12.

Noninteractive Web page in Internet Explorer **Figure 12**

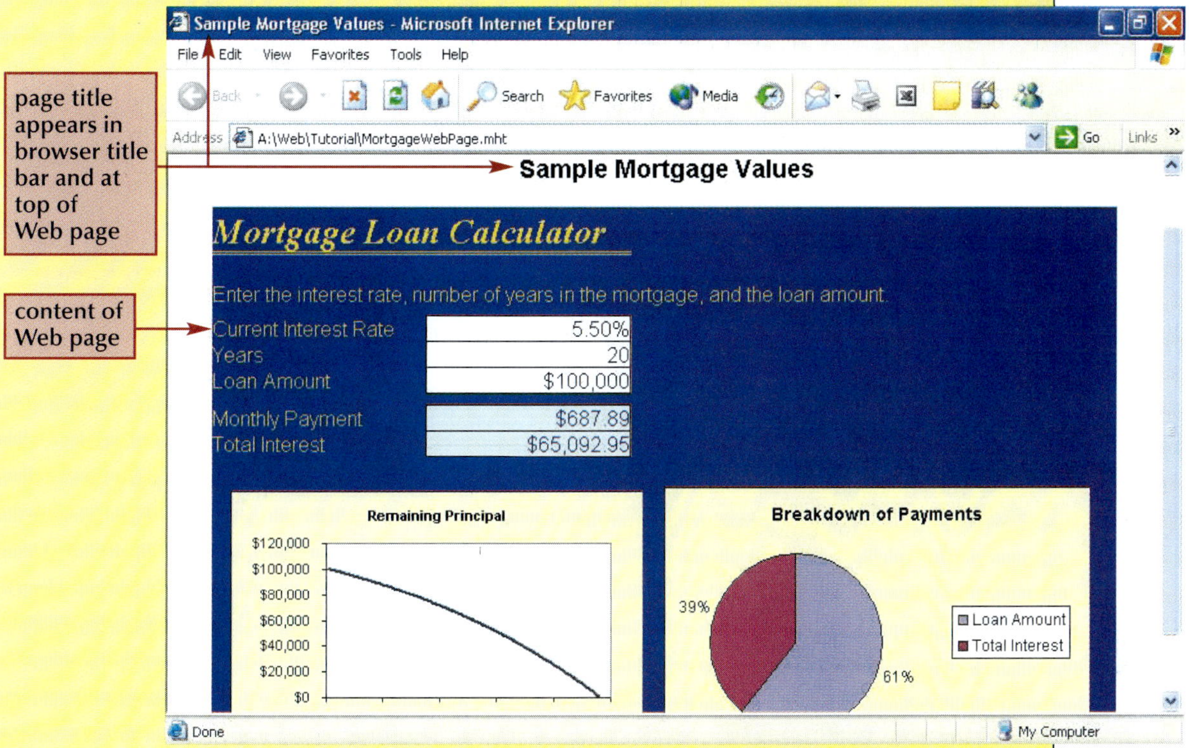

You'll close the Web browser and the workbook.

To close the browser and workbook:

1. Click the **Close** button on the browser title bar to close the Web browser and return to the Mortgage workbook.
2. Close the workbook without saving changes, but leave Excel running.

David wants to include an interactive Web page on Premier's Web site in which customers can enter different mortgage amounts to see how these values affect the overall cost of the mortgage. Users can enter data and perform calculations on an interactive Web page as long as they are using Internet Explorer 5.01 or later and have Excel on their computer. The interactivity available depends on what is in the workbook you are publishing, such as charts and pivot tables. You cannot open and modify interactive Web pages in Excel, so it's important to save a copy of the original workbook that you can modify and then republish as needed. Also, you can publish only the entire workbook with interactivity.

David already created the workbook from which he wants you to create the interactive Web page. This is the same workbook you opened when you created the noninteractive Web page.

To open the Calculator workbook:

1. Open the **Calculator** workbook located in the **Web\Tutorial** folder included with your Data Files.
2. On the Documentation worksheet, enter the current date in cell B3 and enter your name in cell B4.
3. Save the Calculator workbook as **Loan Calculator** in the **Web\Tutorial** folder.

This time, you'll publish the entire workbook as an interactive Web page. Note that Excel does not publish embedded charts or chart sheets in interactive Web pages, so the charts in the Loan Values worksheet will be removed during the conversion.

To create an interactive Web page:

1. Click **File** on the menu bar, and then click **Save as Web Page**. The Save As dialog box opens.
2. Verify that the **Entire Workbook** option button is selected.
3. Click the **Add interactivity** check box to insert a check mark.
4. Click the **Change Title** button to open the Set Title dialog box, type **Mortgage Calculator** in the Title text box, and then click the **OK** button.
5. Type **CalculatorWebPage** in the File name text box.
6. Click the **Publish** button, and then click the **AutoRepublish every time this workbook is saved** check box to insert a check mark.
7. Verify that the **Open published web page in browser** check box is checked.
8. Click the **Publish** button. The Mortgage Calculator Web page opens in your browser. It might take a minute or so to create the interactive Web page based on this workbook.

   Trouble? If Netscape is your default browser, you will not be able to view the interactive Web page. Exit Excel, and then read the next set of steps, but do not complete them.

The contents of the workbook are placed on an interactive Web page as an object called the **spreadsheet component**. The initial size of the spreadsheet component fits the current dimensions of the Web browser window. If you resize the Web browser window, you might also need to refresh the window to resize the spreadsheet component. The spreadsheet component is a fully functioning workbook. You can enter new values or formulas, resize the rows or columns, and format the appearance of the worksheet cells. You move between worksheets in the spreadsheet component by clicking the tab at the bottom of the spreadsheet component and then clicking the desired sheet name from the list.

You'll view and test the interactive workbook by placing new values on the Mortgage Calculator Web page.

To view and test an interactive Web page:

1. Click the **Maximize** button on the browser title bar. The Web browser enlarges to fit the entire screen, but the spreadsheet component does not change size.
2. Click the **Refresh** button on the Standard Buttons toolbar. If necessary, the spreadsheet component enlarges to match the new dimensions of the browser window. See Figure 13.

Mortgage Calculator Web page in Internet Explorer **Figure 13**

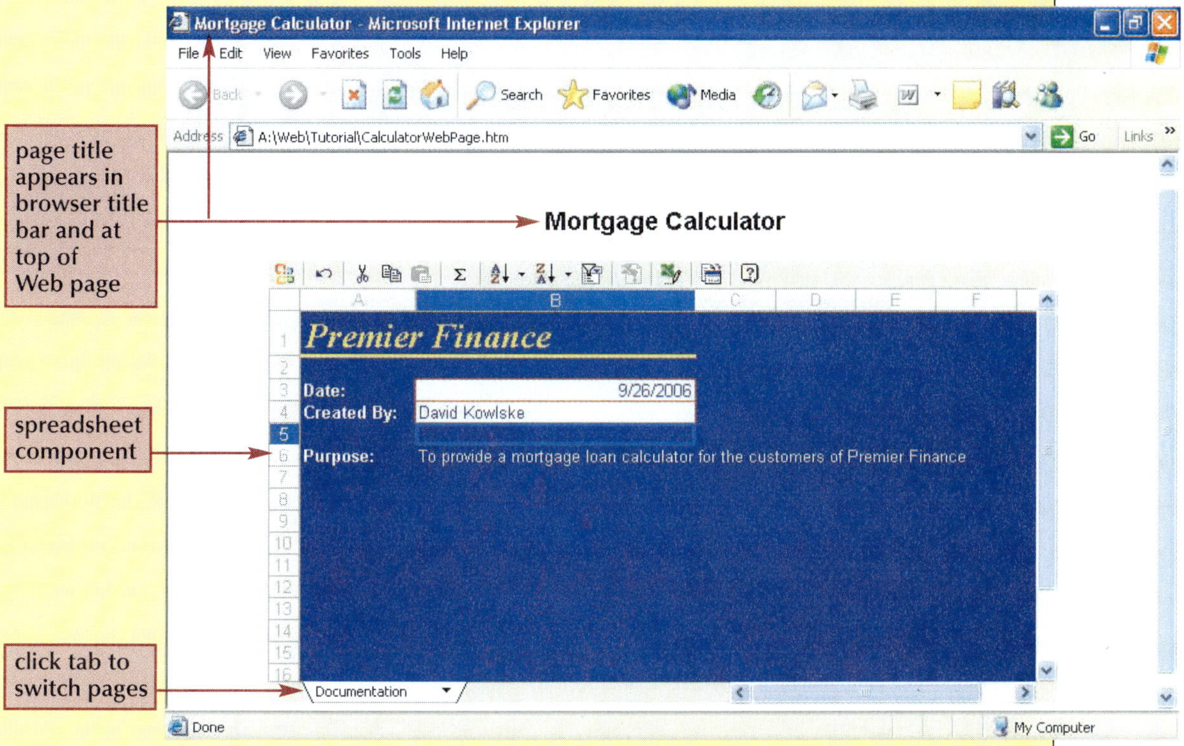

The spreadsheet component is a fully functioning object. You can enter new values or formulas, resize the rows or columns, and format the appearance of the worksheet cells. You move between worksheets in the spreadsheet component by clicking the tab at the bottom of the spreadsheet component and then clicking the desired sheet name from the list. You'll test the interactive workbook by placing new values on the Mortgage Calculator Web page.

3. Click the **Documentation** tab, and then click **Loan Values** in the list of worksheet names.
4. Click cell **B6**, type **15**, and then press the **Enter** key. The value of the monthly payment increases to $817.08, and the overall cost of the mortgage decreases to $47,075.02. See Figure 14.

Figure 14 Interactive Web page updated

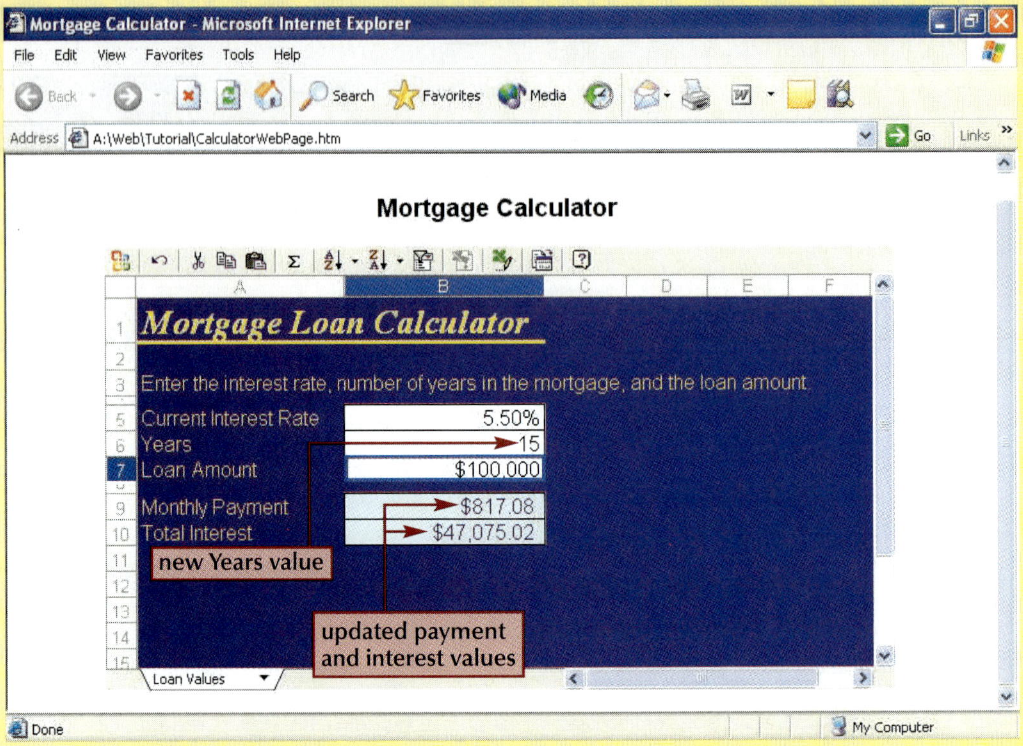

5. Click the **Close** button on the browser title bar to close the Web browser and return to the Loan Calculator workbook in Excel.
6. Close the workbook without saving changes, and then exit Excel.

Although you can make changes to both the content and the appearance of an interactive Web page, these changes are not saved in the workbook. The original content and appearance will be displayed the next time you open the Web page.

Creating Web Pages in Access

You can create three types of Web pages based on Access database objects—a static HTML page, a dynamic HTML page, or a data access page. The type of Web page you create depends on how you want the information to be shared and manipulated by other users. Note that the Web Page and Single File Web Page options do not exist in Access.

A **static HTML page** (also called a static Web page) is a Web page based on a table, query, form, or report that shows the state of the database object at the time the page was created. Static HTML pages can be displayed in any Web browser that supports HTML version 3.2 or later.

A **dynamic HTML page** (also called a dynamic Web page) is a Web page based on a table, query, or form that is created each time the page is viewed or refreshed. Dynamic HTML pages can be displayed in any browser.

Similar to a dynamic HTML page, a **data access page** is a Web page that is linked to the data in the database. You can use a data access page to view, update, manipulate, or delete data in the Access database object on which the data access page is based. You create a data access page as a database object (table, query, form, report, page, macro, or module) that contains a shortcut to the location of the page's corresponding HTML file, which is stored outside the database. Users must have access to the database from which the data access page is created to view and make changes to the database. Data access pages require Microsoft Internet Explorer 5.01 with Service Pack 2 or later.

Elsa (the founder of Northeast Seasonal Jobs International) wants you to create a Web page that lists employers and their available positions. You'll create this Web page based on the Employer Positions query, which shows selected fields from both the Employer and Position tables. Because Elsa does not want the employees to be able to make changes to this information, you'll create a static Web page.

In Access, you create a static Web page by exporting a database object to an HTML document. In the Export dialog box, you specify the filename, file type, and location for the exported object. The exported HTML document does not exist in the database as a database object; it is a separate file stored in the location you specify.

The Save formatted option in the Export dialog box enables you to display the object in a format similar to its appearance in Datasheet view, with all the column headings, shading, and so on. If you do not choose this option, the object will appear without the field names as column headings and the appropriate spacing between columns.

Creating Static Web Pages in Access

Reference Window

- Click the Open button, open an existing database, and then display the object that you want to save as a static Web page.
- Right-click the object in the Database window, and then click Export.
- Navigate to the location where you want to save the Web page.
- Click the Save as type list arrow, and then click HTML Documents.
- Click the Save formatted check box.
- Click the Export button.
- Click the Default encoding option button, and then click the OK button.

To create the Web page Elsa requested, you'll save the Employer Positions query as an HTML document.

To export the Employer Positions query as an HTML document:

1. Start Access, and then open the **Northeast** database, located in the **Web\Tutorial** folder included with your Data Files.

   Trouble? If a dialog box opens with a message about installing the Microsoft Jet Service Pack, see your instructor or technical support person for assistance. You must have the appropriate Service Pack installed in order to open and work with Access databases safely.

   Trouble? If a dialog box opens warning you that the database may not be safe, click the Open button. If a dialog box opens, warning you that Access can't open the database due to security restrictions, click the OK button, click Tools on the menu bar, point to Macro, click Security, click the Medium option button, click the OK button, restart your computer if you're requested to do so, repeat Step 1, and then click the Open button if another dialog box opens telling you that the database may not be safe. When you're finished with this tutorial, change the macro security setting back to its original level.

2. Click **Queries** in the Objects bar of the Database window, right-click **Employer Positions**, and then click **Export** on the shortcut menu. The Export dialog box opens, displaying the type and name of the object you are exporting in its title bar (in this case, the Employer Positions query).
3. Verify that the Save in list box displays the **Web\Tutorial** folder.
4. Click the **Save as type** list arrow, and then click **HTML Documents**. The query name is added to the File name text box automatically.

5. Click the **Save formatted** check box. This is because Elsa wants the Employer Positions query to appear in datasheet format. See Figure 15. There is no option to change the page title; the page title will match the object name.

Figure 15 Export dialog box

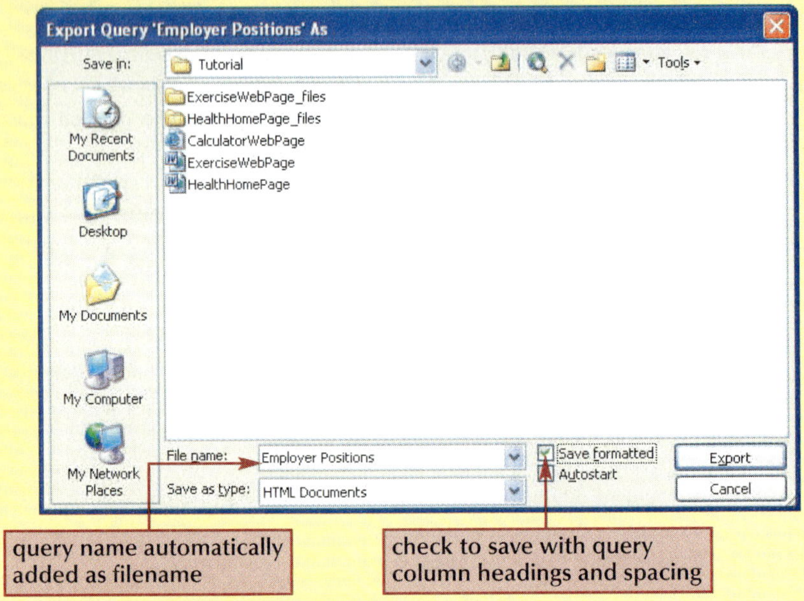

6. Click the **Export** button. The HTML Output Options dialog box opens.

   The HTML Output Options dialog box provides options for choosing an HTML template in which to display the Web page, or for using the default format. Elsa does not want to use a template for the Employer Positions query, so you can use the default settings.

7. Verify that the **Default encoding** option button is selected, and then click the **OK** button. Access exports the Employer Positions query to a new HTML document named Employer Positions in the Web\Tutorial folder, not in the Northeast database as a database object.

You will use the Web toolbar to open your browser and view the Web page you just created.

To view the Employer Positions query Web page:

1. Click **View** on the menu bar, point to **Toolbars**, and then click **Web**. The Web toolbar opens.
2. Click the **Go** button on the Web toolbar, and then click **Open Hyperlink**. The Open Internet Address dialog box opens, in which you enter the URL of the Web site or the name of the HTML document you want to view.
3. Click the **Browse** button to open the Browse dialog box, verify that the Look in list box displays the **Web\Tutorial** folder included with your Data Files, click **Employer Positions** in the list, and then click the **Open** button. The Address list box in the Open Internet Address dialog box displays the address for the Employer Positions HTML document.
4. Click the **OK** button. Internet Explorer starts and the Employer Positions Web page opens. See Figure 16.

Figure 16 Employer Positions Web page

object name becomes page title

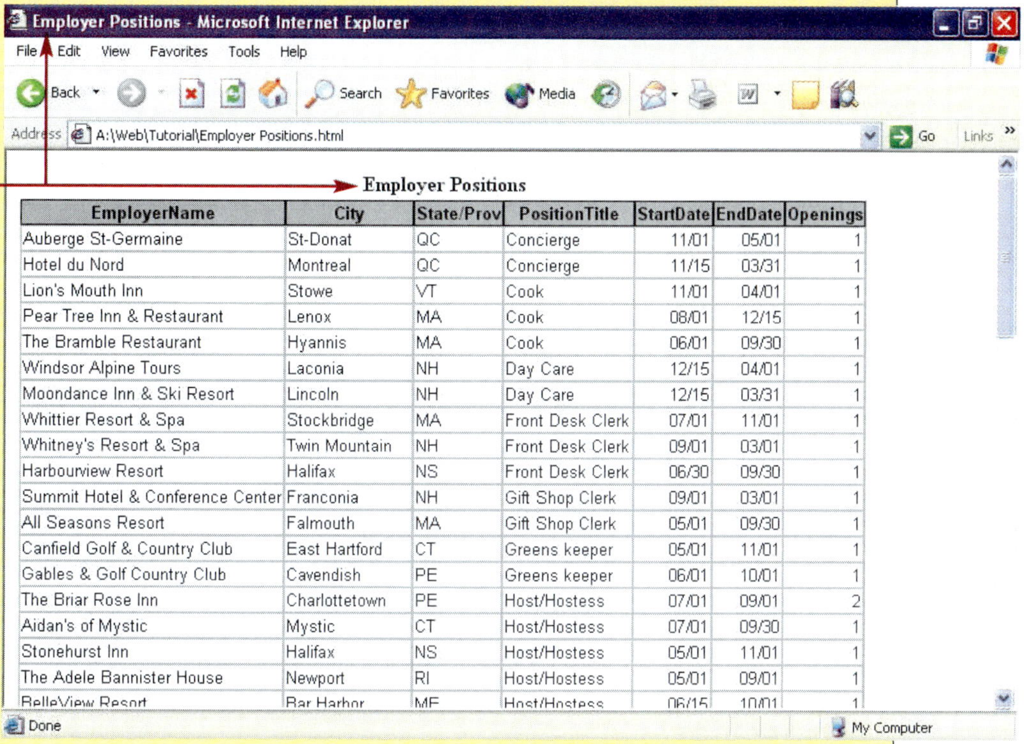

EmployerName	City	State/Prov	PositionTitle	StartDate	EndDate	Openings
Auberge St-Germaine	St-Donat	QC	Concierge	11/01	05/01	1
Hotel du Nord	Montreal	QC	Concierge	11/15	03/31	1
Lion's Mouth Inn	Stowe	VT	Cook	11/01	04/01	1
Pear Tree Inn & Restaurant	Lenox	MA	Cook	08/01	12/15	1
The Bramble Restaurant	Hyannis	MA	Cook	06/01	09/30	1
Windsor Alpine Tours	Laconia	NH	Day Care	12/15	04/01	1
Moondance Inn & Ski Resort	Lincoln	NH	Day Care	12/15	03/31	1
Whittier Resort & Spa	Stockbridge	MA	Front Desk Clerk	07/01	11/01	1
Whitney's Resort & Spa	Twin Mountain	NH	Front Desk Clerk	09/01	03/01	1
Harbourview Resort	Halifax	NS	Front Desk Clerk	06/30	09/30	1
Summit Hotel & Conference Center	Franconia	NH	Gift Shop Clerk	09/01	03/01	1
All Seasons Resort	Falmouth	MA	Gift Shop Clerk	05/01	09/30	1
Canfield Golf & Country Club	East Hartford	CT	Greens keeper	05/01	11/01	1
Gables & Golf Country Club	Cavendish	PE	Greens keeper	06/01	10/01	1
The Briar Rose Inn	Charlottetown	PE	Host/Hostess	07/01	09/01	2
Aidan's of Mystic	Mystic	CT	Host/Hostess	07/01	09/30	1
Stonehurst Inn	Halifax	NS	Host/Hostess	05/01	11/01	1
The Adele Bannister House	Newport	RI	Host/Hostess	05/01	09/01	1
BelleView Resort	Bar Harbor	ME	Host/Hostess	06/15	10/01	1

5. Scroll through the Employer Positions Web page to view its contents.
6. Click the **Close** button on the browser title bar to close the browser. You return to the database window in Access.

Because you created a static Web page, any future changes made to the underlying data in the Employer and Position tables will not appear in the Employer Positions Web page.

Next, Elsa wants you to create a Web page that shows the current information in the Employer table, and she wants changes made to the data in the Employer table to be reflected in the Web page. In addition, Elsa wants NSJI employees to be able to make changes to the Employer table from the Web page. To meet Elsa's needs, you'll create a data access page.

Creating Data Access Pages in Access

Reference Window

- Click the Open button, open an existing database, and then click Pages in the Objects bar of the Database window.
- Click the New button in the Database window.
- Click AutoPage: Columnar to select this wizard, select the table or query to use as the basis of the data access page, and then click the OK button.

You can create a data access page either in Design view or by using a wizard. To create the data access page for the Employer table, you'll use the AutoPage: Columnar Wizard.

To create a data access page for the Employer table:

1. Click **Pages** in the Objects bar of the Database window to display the Pages list. The list box does not contain any pages.
2. Click the **New** button in the Database window. The New Data Access Page dialog box opens. This dialog box is similar to ones you have used to create new forms and reports.
3. Click **AutoPage: Columnar** to select this wizard, click the list arrow for choosing the table or query as the basis for the page, click **Employer**, and then click the **OK** button. After a few moments, the AutoPage: Columnar Wizard creates the data access page and displays it in Page view. See Figure 17.

Figure 17 Employer data access page

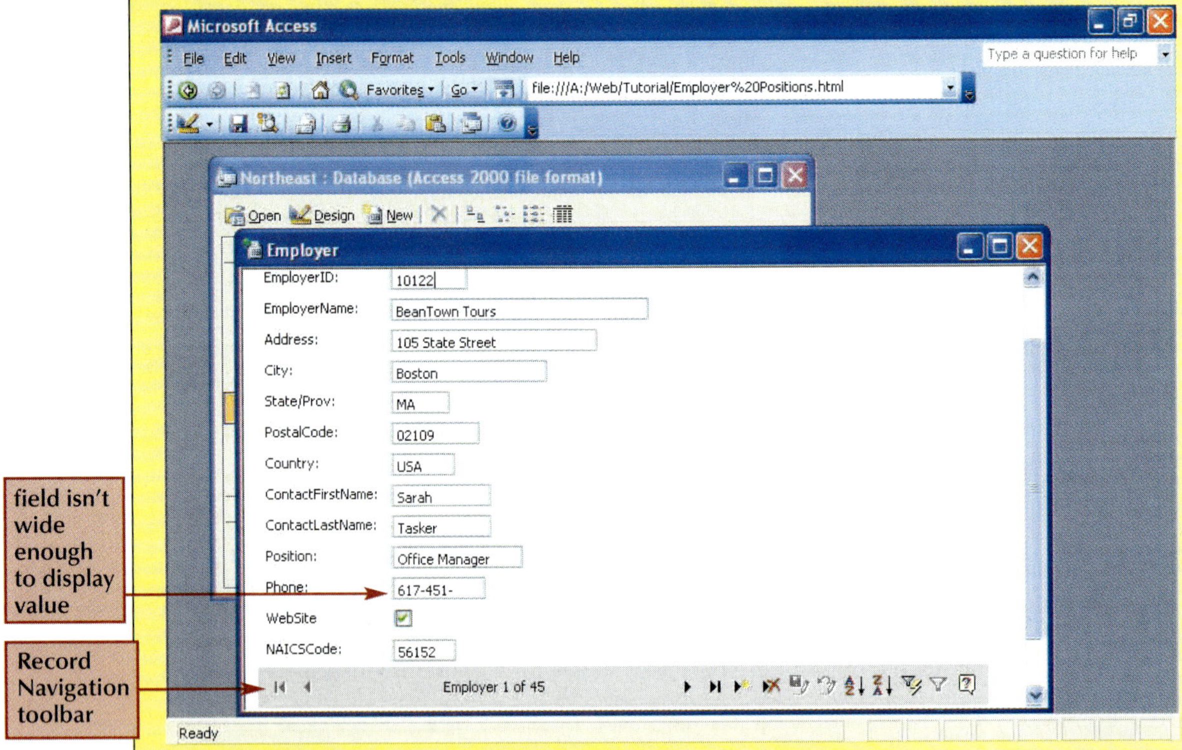

Trouble? If your data access page appears with an AutoFormat applied to it, your screen will differ slightly from the one shown in the figure. This will not affect your work with the page; continue with the tutorial.

The Phone field value is not completely visible on the data access page. You can fix this quickly in Design view.

To modify the data access page in Design view:

1. Click the **View** button for Design view on the Page View toolbar. The data access page opens in Design view.
2. Click the **Phone** field's text box to select it, and then drag the center-right sizing handle to the right until the Phone text box is approximately the same size as the Position text box above it.
3. Click the **View** button for Page view on the Page Design toolbar to switch back to Page view. The Phone field value is now completely visible.

The Record Navigation toolbar, which appears below the record, provides buttons for moving between table records, similar to the buttons you use to move between records in a form, and buttons for adding and deleting records, sorting and filtering data, and so on. Before you continue, you'll save the data access page.

To save the data access page:

1. Click the **Save** button on the Page View toolbar. The Save As Data Access Page dialog box opens.
2. Verify that the Save in list box displays the **Web\Tutorial** folder.
3. Click the **Save** button to save the data access page with the default name "Employer."

   Trouble? If a dialog box opens with a warning about the connection string, click the OK button.

Elsa has a change to make to one of the records in the Employer table. You can make the necessary changes directly in the data access page, which will simultaneously update the Employer table in the Northeast database. You can save changes you make to a record in a data access page either by moving to another record or by clicking the Save button on the Record Navigation toolbar.

To update the contact information in Page view:

1. Use the Record Navigation toolbar to move to record 3 (for the Bayside Inn & Country Club).
2. Double-click the entry **Mary** in the ContactFirstName field, type **Jeffrey**, double-click the entry **Russell** in the ContactLastName field, and then type **Hersha**.
3. Click the **Save** button on the Record Navigation toolbar.
4. Click the **Close** button on the Employer window title bar. The data access page closes, and you return to the Database window. The Employer data access page is listed in the Pages list box.

Now, you'll see how the data access page looks in Internet Explorer.

To view the Employer data access page in Internet Explorer:

1. Right-click **Employer** in the Pages list box, and then click **Web Page Preview** on the shortcut menu. Internet Explorer starts and the Employer data access page opens. See Figure 18.

Figure 18 Employer data access page in Internet Explorer

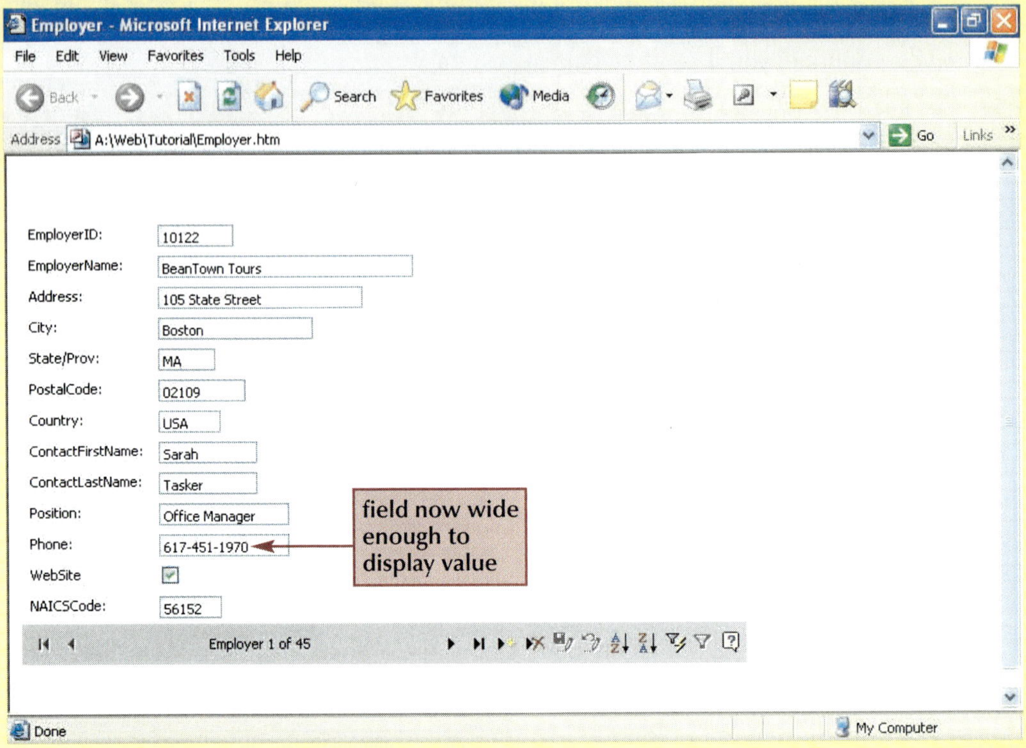

2. Click the **Close** button on the browser title bar. The browser exits and you return to the Database window.

   To confirm that the changes you made earlier to the contact information are reflected in the Employer table, you'll open the table now and view the record.

3. Click **Tables** in the Objects bar of the Database window, and then open the **Employer** table in Datasheet view.
4. Scroll to the right and notice that the contact information for the Bayside Inn & Country Club is now Jeffrey Hersha.
5. Right-click the Web toolbar, click **Web** to close the Web toolbar, and then exit Access.

Now NSJI employees can use the company's intranet to view and update employer data in Internet Explorer.

Creating Web Pages in PowerPoint

Miriam (the managing director of Global Humanitarian) asks you to convert her Peru Expedition Report presentation to a Web page. When you save a presentation as a Web page or single file Web page, each slide is saved as an HTML document and a navigation frame is added to the left of the slide frame in the presentation. The **navigation frame**, also called the outline pane, contains links to each of the HTML documents (slides). There is also a toolbar, which contains buttons for hiding the outline of the presentation, hiding the notes pane, moving to the next or previous slide, and running the presentation as a slide show. If your presentation includes graphics, PowerPoint usually converts them to separate files in GIF or JPEG format.

If you want to edit the resulting HTML documents, you need to use either a word processing program that supports HTML editing (such as Word) or a dedicated HTML editor (such as Microsoft FrontPage). You cannot edit HTML documents directly in PowerPoint.

Creating Web Pages in PowerPoint

Reference Window

- Click the Open button and open an existing presentation that you want to save as a Web page.
- Click File on the menu bar, and then click Save as Web Page.
- Navigate to the location where you want to save the Web page.
- Type a new filename in the File name text box.
- Click the Save as type list arrow, and then click Single File Web Page or Web Page.
- Click the Publish button.
- Click the Complete presentation option button or click the Slide number option button and enter the slide numbers.
- Select an option in the Browser support area.
- Click the Change button, type a page title, and then click the OK button.
- Check the Open published Web page in browser check box to preview the Web page in a browser.
- Click the Publish button.

You'll open the Peru Expedition Report presentation and save it as a Web page.

To open the presentation:

1. Start PowerPoint, and then open the **PeruExp** presentation located in the **Web\Tutorial** folder included with your Data Files.
2. Replace Miriam's name in the subtitle box with your name.
3. Review the content of the presentation, which is similar to the Peru Expedition Report presentation you created in an earlier tutorial.

Next, you'll save the presentation as a Web page. You can choose to save either the entire presentation or a consecutive group of slides. Miriam asks you to include all the slides in the Web page.

To save a presentation as a Web page and preview it in a browser:

1. Click **File** on the menu bar, and then click **Save as Web Page**. The Save As dialog box opens.
2. Verify that the Save in location is the **Web\Tutorial** folder included with your Data Files, type **PeruExpedition** in the File name text box, click the **Save as type** list arrow, and then click **Web Page**.
3. Click the **Publish** button. The Publish as Web Page dialog box opens.
4. Verify that the **Complete presentation** option button is selected.
5. Click the **Microsoft Internet Explorer 4.0 or later (high fidelity)** option button in the Browser support area, if necessary.
6. Click the **Change** button, type **Peru Expedition Report** in the Set Page Title text box, and then click the **OK** button.
7. Verify that the **Open published Web page in browser** check box is checked. See Figure 19.

Figure 19 Publish as Web Page dialog box

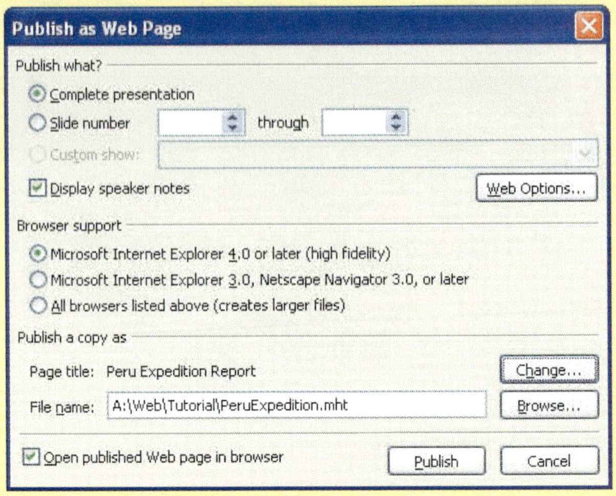

8. Click the **Publish** button. The complete presentation is saved as a Web page, and opens in your browser.
9. If necessary, maximize the browser window. See Figure 20.

Figure 20 Peru Expedition Report presentation in Internet Explorer

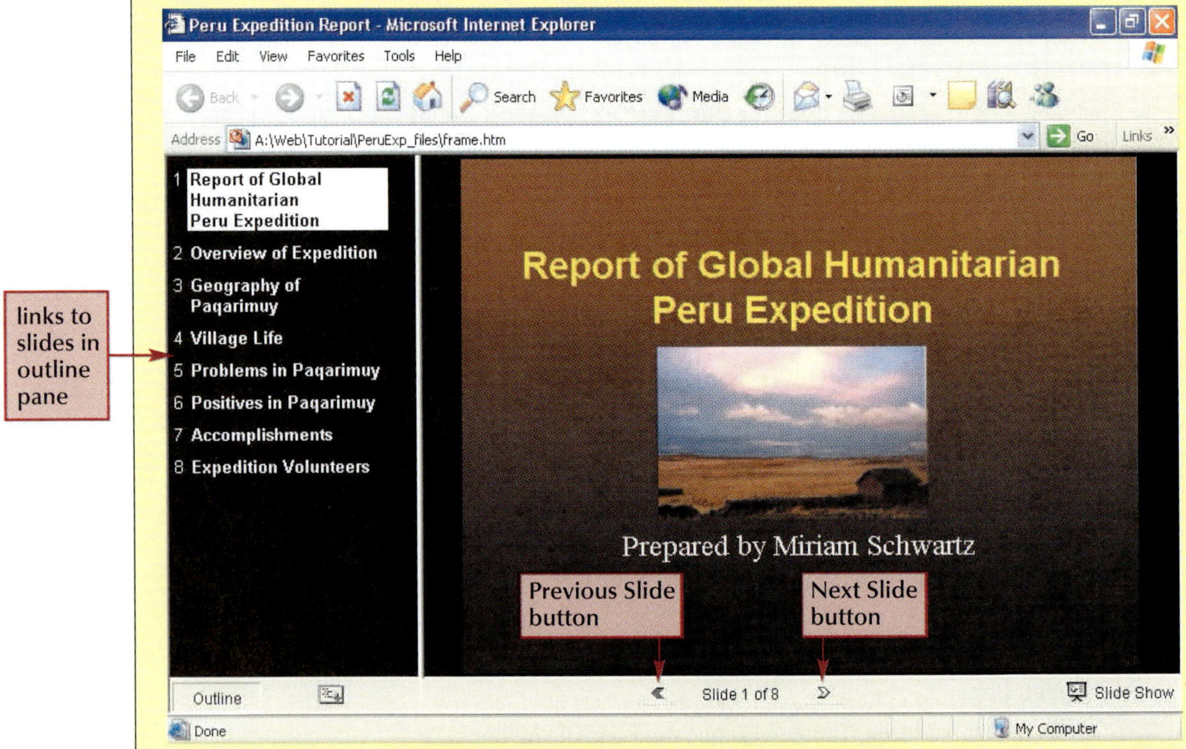

Trouble? If you don't see the outline, click the Outline button at the bottom of the screen.

The title slide of the Peru Expedition Report presentation appears in the slide pane, and an outline of the slides appears in the outline pane. Each outline item is a hyperlink to its corresponding slide. Also, a navigation bar appears at the bottom of the window. These hyperlinks and the navigation bar help you move through the presentation. The outline hyperlinks allow you to jump from one slide to any other in any order, whereas the navigation buttons help you to move one slide forward or backward.

To navigate a presentation Web page:

1. Click the **Next Slide** button on the navigation bar at the bottom of the Web page. The slide pane displays Slide 2 of the presentation. Next, you'll test the hyperlinks that enable viewers to move between slides.
2. Click the **Accomplishments** hyperlink in the outline pane. The slide pane displays the Accomplishments slide (Slide 7).
3. Click the **Previous Slide** button on the navigation bar at the bottom of the Web page. The Positives in Paqarimuy slide (Slide 6) appears in the slide pane.
4. Click the **Slide Show** button on the navigation bar to display the presentation full screen.
5. Click to display the next slide, press the **Esc** key to end the slide show, and then close the Web browser.
6. Exit PowerPoint without saving changes.

Once you create a Web page, you'll want others to be able to view it.

Publishing Web Pages

After you create a Web page, you need to copy the HTML file to a Web server or a network server so that others can view your Web pages over the World Wide Web or an intranet. If you used the Web Page option instead of the Single File Web Page option, you also need to copy the associated folder and its files. This process is called **publishing** the Web page to a server. Note that this use of the term *publish* is different from how Microsoft uses the term *publish* in Excel and PowerPoint. Publishing files to a server is also sometimes referred to as **uploading** files to a server.

You can copy the files for your Web pages to the appropriate server using a variety of methods, including FTP or Web folders. **FTP (file transfer protocol)** is a communication protocol that enables you to manipulate files and folders between remote computers. A **Web folder** is a folder from which you can transfer and manipulate files on a network server or a Web server. The actual location for the HTML files on the server, the file structure, and the filenames you use will differ depending on the server. Be sure to verify that you have permission to copy files to a server and contact your ISP or network administrator for the exact steps to follow before attempting to publish your Web pages to a server.

Also, you might need to rename the home page file to a specific filename, such as "index.htm" or "index.html," depending on the server. Ask the network administrator or ISP before publishing your Web page to a server. If you need to rename the file, be sure to test and update all links as necessary. You might need to resave the Web pages you created from Excel workbooks and any data access pages in Access, because these files contain references between the source file and the Web page.

Publishing Web Pages

Reference Window

- Contact your ISP or network administrator for the exact file structure, process, and location for publishing Web pages.
- Copy all the files and folders associated with the Web pages to the location specified by the administrator.
- View the published pages in different Web browsers and on several computer setups to test them.

After you publish Web pages to a server, you should test the pages by opening and viewing them using different Web browsers, different versions of the browsers, and several computer setups to ensure that the page content appears as you intended. Try to use the same browsers, versions, and computer setups that the people you intend to view the pages have. This final step will help to ensure that users can accurately see and use the information you published.

Review

Quick Check

1. What are three ways to share Office files?
2. What is a page title?
3. True or False: The font you apply to text on a Web page is always the same font that people see when they open that Web page in their browser.
4. What is the difference between a noninteractive Web page and an interactive Web page created from an Excel workbook?
5. If you want to link the data in a Web page to a database, what kind of Web page would you create?
6. True or False: You can create a Web page from only a complete PowerPoint presentation.
7. What should you do to test Web pages that you have published to a server?

Review

Tutorial Summary

You created Web pages from four Microsoft Office 2003 programs: Word, Excel, Access, and PowerPoint. You learned how to create a new Web page in Word, you learned how to apply a theme to that Web page, and you learned how to create a hyperlink from that page to another. You then learned how to create Web pages from existing Word documents, Excel workbooks, Access databases, and PowerPoint presentations. In addition, you learned how to create interactive Web pages from an Excel workbook, and how to create a data access page from an Access database. You also learned how to run a PowerPoint slide show from a Web page. You also learned how to preview Web pages in a browser. Finally, you learned how to publish Web pages to a server.

Key Terms

data access page
dynamic HTML page
filtered Web page
FTP (file transfer protocol)
HTML document
interactive Web page
navigation frame
noninteractive Web page
page title
publish
single file Web page
spreadsheet component
static HTML page
template
theme
upload
Web folder
Web page editor

Practice

Get hands-on practice of the skills you learned in the tutorial using the same case scenario.

Review Assignments

Data Files needed for the Review Assignments: Stir-fry.doc, Fund.xls, Recruits.mdb, and MPTour.ppt

The Temps Abound clients are pleased with the Web pages you created for them, and they've each asked you to create an additional Web page.

Bayside Health has recently been contracted to host a series of lectures on vegetarian cooking for college students. Susan asks you to begin creating a Web site that provides information on the classes. You'll need to use a desktop-published flier as the basis for one of the Web pages.

1. Start Word, and then open a new, blank Web page.
2. Add headings explaining the purpose of the Web page, and then type a paragraph of text introducing a series of vegetarian cooking classes. Add a bulleted list of class topics; include "The Fast Art of Stir-frying" as one of the topics.
3. Format the Web page using any theme. Adjust fonts and font sizes as necessary.
4. Add your name at the bottom of the document, and save the document as a Single File Web page with the filename **ClassesHomePage** in the **Web\Review** folder included with your Data Files and the page title "Cooking Classes." Leave the Web page file open.
5. Open the **Stir-fry** document located in the **Web\Review** folder.
6. Preview the document zoomed to Whole Page.
7. Preview the document in Web Layout view, and then save it as a Single File Web page named **Stir-fryClass** in the **Web\Review** folder with the page title "Fast Art of Stir-frying."
8. Format the new Web page to match the Cooking Classes page, and then save and close the Fast Art of Stir-frying page.
9. Create a hyperlink from the Stir-fry class bullet on the Cooking Classes page to the Stir-fry Class page and then save the page.
10. Preview the Cooking Classes page in your browser, click the Stir-fry class link to preview the Fast Art of Stir-frying page, exit your browser, and then exit Word.

David at Premier Finance has a workbook that displays sample values for a proposed college fund that he wants you to convert to Web pages. David wants customers to be able to view the return from monthly investments in a college savings plan. You will create both a noninteractive and an interactive version of David's workbook.

11. Start Excel, and then open the **Fund** workbook located in the **Web\Review** folder included with your Data Files.
12. Enter your name and the current date in the Documentation sheet, and then save the workbook as **College Fund** in the **Web\Review** folder.
13. Create a noninteractive Web page based on the workbook with "Sample College Fund" as the page title and **CollegeFundPage** as the filename. Publish only the contents of the Calculator worksheet, and select the options to republish the Web page every time the College Fund workbook is saved and to open the published Web page in the browser automatically.
14. Maximize the browser window, review the Web page, and then close the browser and close the College Fund workbook without saving changes.
15. Open the **Fund** workbook located in the **Web\Review** folder.
16. Enter your name and the current date in the Documentation sheet, and then save the workbook as **College Calculator** in the **Web\Review** folder.
17. Create an interactive Web page of the entire workbook with the page title "Fund Calculator" and the filename **CalculatorPage**. Make sure the Web page is republished each time the College Calculator workbook is saved, and make sure the Web page opens in the browser window automatically.
18. Maximize the browser window, refresh the screen, display the Calculator worksheet, and then enter $85,000 as the savings goal and 16 as the number of years.
19. Close the browser, and then exit Excel without saving changes.

Elsa is pleased with the Web pages you created for the Northeast database. Now she wants you to create Web pages based on objects in the Recruits database.

20. Start Access, and then open the **Recruits** database located in the **Web\Review** folder included with your Data Files.
21. Create a static Web page named **Recruiter** based on the Recruiter table, specifying the option for displaying the data in a datasheet format.
22. View the Web page in a browser, and then close the browser.

23. Use the AutoPage: Columnar Wizard to create a data access page based on the Student table.
24. Use the Record Navigation toolbar to move to the last record in the Student table (record 34), and then change the BirthDate field value for the last record to 11/16/84. Save your change using the appropriate Record Navigation toolbar button.
25. Save the data access page as **Student** in the **Web\Review** folder.
26. View the page in a browser, and then close the browser and exit Access.

Miriam has gotten positive feedback about the Peru Expedition Web page you created. Volunteers often choose to tour Cuzco and Machu Picchu following their service in a needy village, so she asks you to create a Web page giving a brief tour of Cuzco and Machu Picchu based on a modified version of an existing presentation.

27. Start PowerPoint, and then open the **MPTour** presentation located in the **Web\Review** folder included with your Data Files.
28. Replace the name in the subtitle with your name, save the presentation as a Single File Web page in the **Web\Review** folder, type **MachuPicchuTour** as the filename, enter "Tour of Machu Picchu" as the page title, include the complete presentation, optimize the browser for Microsoft Internet 4.0 or later (high fidelity), and open the published Web page in a browser automatically.
29. Review the presentation in the browser using the navigation button and links, and then view the presentation as a slide show.
30. Close the Web browser and exit PowerPoint without saving changes.

Assess

SAM Assessment and Training

If you have a SAM user profile, you may have access to hands-on instruction, practice, and assessment of the skills covered in this tutorial. Log in to your SAM account and go to your assignments page to see what your instructor has assigned.

Reinforce

Web Pages & HTML

Lab Assignments

The New Perspectives Labs are designed to help you master some of the key concepts and skills presented in this text. The steps for completing this Lab are located on the Course Technology Web site. Log on to the Internet and use your Web browser to go to the Student Online Companion for New Perspectives Office 2003 at **www.course.com/np/office2003**. Click the Lab Assignments link, and then navigate to the assignments for this tutorial.

Review

Quick Check Answers

1. printing and distributing paper copies, sending as an e-mail message or attachment, and posting the file as a Web page on an intranet or the Internet
2. the text that appears in the browser title bar each time the Web page is displayed in a browser
3. False
4. A noninteractive Web page enables people to view the content without making any changes to the content. An interactive Web page enables people to modify and format the values in the Web page from their browser.
5. data access page
6. False
7. View them from different computer setups and with different Web browsers and different versions of those browsers.

Using Excel to Manage Data

Creating a Sales Order Report

Objectives

Session 1.1
- Learn about spreadsheets and how they work
- Identify major components of the Excel window
- Navigate within and between worksheets
- Enter text, dates, data, and formulas into a worksheet
- Change the size of a column or row

Session 1.2
- Select and move cell ranges
- Calculate totals with AutoSum
- Insert and delete a column or row
- Work in edit mode
- Undo an action
- Insert, move, and rename a worksheet
- Check the spelling in a workbook
- Preview and print a workbook
- Display the formulas within a worksheet

Case

Dalton Food Co-op

Sandra Dalton and her husband, Kevin, own a farm in northern Florida. Recently, Sandra has been selling produce to local families to earn extra income. When she started, Sandra kept a paper record of customer orders, and all of the data was entered into a paper ledger with the calculations done on a tabletop calculator. Several months ago, Sandra and Kevin purchased a computer for the co-op. Bundled with the other software installed on the computer was a copy of **Microsoft Office Excel 2003** (or simply **Excel**), a computer program used to enter, analyze, and present quantitative data.

Sandra, who handles most of the financial aspects of the business, has been using Excel for several months, but as the business continues to grow and its busy season approaches, she has asked you to help. She wants you to use an Excel workbook to keep track of orders recently made at the Dalton Food Co-op.

Lab

Student Data Files

▼Tutorial.01

▽ Tutorial folder
(no starting Data Files)

▽ Review folder
(no starting Data Files)

▽ Cases folder
Balance1.xls
CFlow1.xls
Site1.xls

Session 1.1

Spreadsheets

Introducing Excel

Before you begin working with the recent orders at the co-op, you need to understand some of the key terms and concepts associated with a program such as Excel.

Understanding Spreadsheets

Excel is a computerized spreadsheet. A **spreadsheet** is an important tool used for analyzing and reporting information. Spreadsheets are often used in business for budgeting, inventory management, and decision making. For example, an accountant might use a paper-based spreadsheet like the one shown in Figure 1-1 to record a company's estimated and actual monthly cash flow.

Figure 1-1 **A sample spreadsheet**

Cash Flow Comparison
Actual versus Budget

		Jan-06
	Estimated	**Actual**
Cash balance(start of month)	$ 1,500.00	$ 1,500.00
Receipts		
Cash sales	1700.00	1852.00
Cash expenditures		
Advertising	200.00	211.00
Wages	900.00	900.00
Supplies	100.00	81.00
Total cash expenditures	1200.00	1192.00
Net cash flow	500.00	660.00
Cash balance(end of month)	$ 2,000.00	$ 2,160.00

In this spreadsheet, the accountant has recorded the estimated and actual cash flow for the month of January. Each line, or row, in this spreadsheet displays a different cash flow value. Each column contains the predicted or actual values, or text that describes those values. The accountant has also entered the total cash expenditures, net cash flow, and closing cash balance for the month, perhaps having used a calculator to do the calculations.

Figure 1-2 shows the same spreadsheet in Excel. The spreadsheet is now laid out in a grid in which the rows and columns are easily apparent. As you will see later, calculations are also part of this electronic spreadsheet, so that total cash expenditures, net cash flow, and cash balances are calculated automatically rather than entered manually. When you change an entry in the electronic spreadsheet, the spreadsheet automatically updates any calculated values based on the entry. You can also use an electronic spreadsheet to perform a **what-if analysis** in which you change one or more of the values in the worksheet and then examine the recalculated values to determine the effect of the change. (You will have a chance to explore this feature at the end of the tutorial.) So, an electronic spreadsheet provides more flexibility in entering and analyzing your data than the paper version.

Figure 1-2 The same spreadsheet in Excel

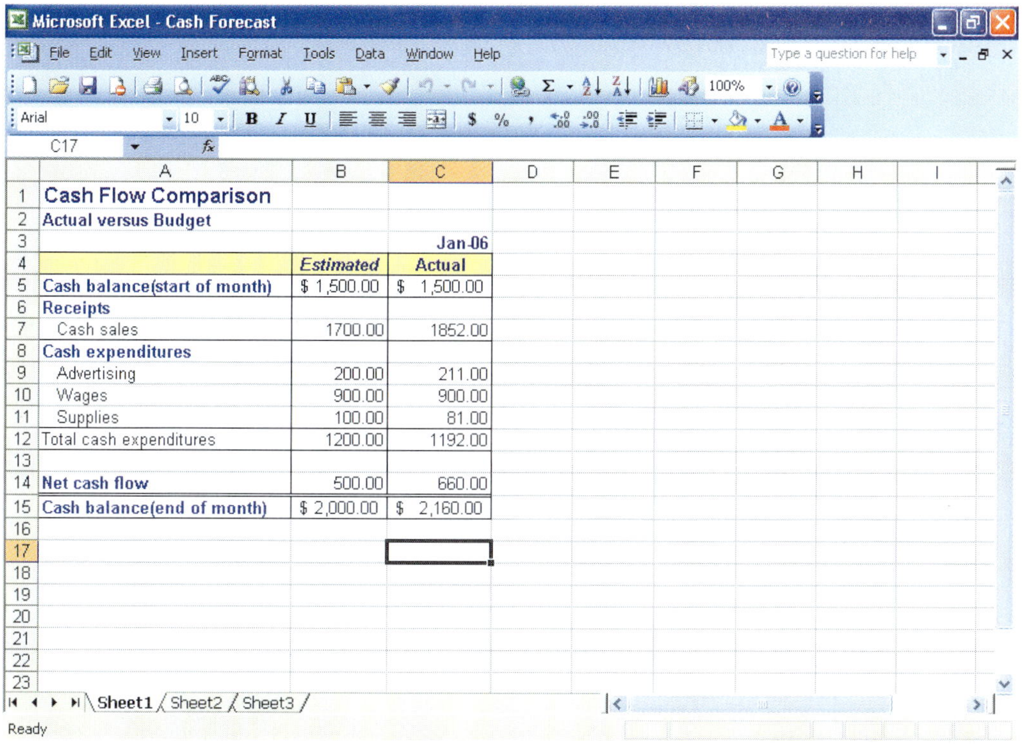

Excel stores electronic spreadsheets in files called **workbooks**. Each workbook is made up of individual **worksheets**, or **sheets**, just as a spiral-bound ledger, which an accountant would use, is made up of sheets of paper. You will learn more about multiple worksheets later in the tutorial. For now, keep in mind that the terms *worksheet* and *sheet* are often used interchangeably.

Parts of the Excel Window

Excel displays workbooks within a window that contains many tools for entering, editing, and viewing data. You will learn about some of these tools after starting Excel. By default, Excel opens with a blank workbook.

To start Excel:

1. Click the **Start** button on the taskbar, point to **All Programs**, point to **Microsoft Office**, and then click **Microsoft Office Excel 2003**. The Excel window opens. See Figure 1-3.

Figure 1-3 Parts of the Excel window

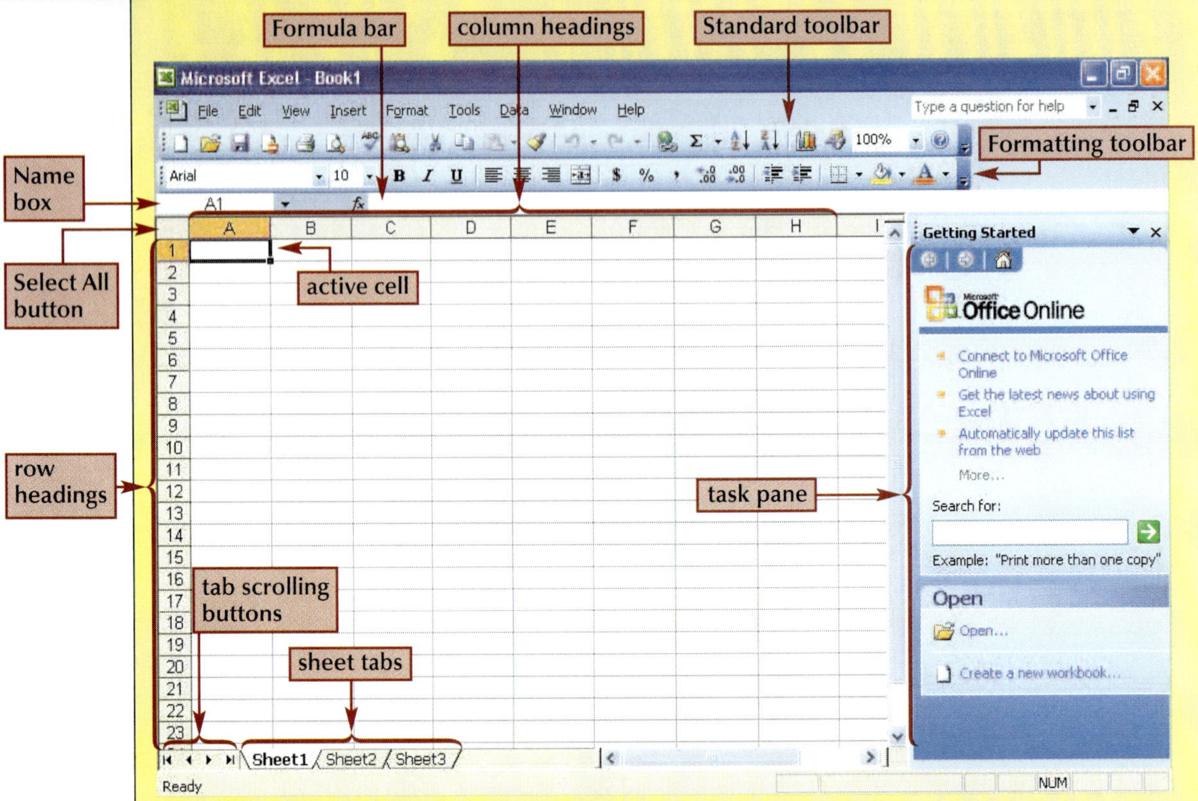

Trouble? If you don't see the Microsoft Office Excel 2003 option on the Microsoft Office submenu, look for it in a different submenu or as an option on the All Programs menu. If you still cannot find the Microsoft Office Excel 2003 option, ask your instructor or technical support person for help.

The Excel window contains many of the components that you find in other Windows programs, including a title bar, a menu bar, scroll bars, and a status bar. The Excel window also contains features that are unique to Excel. Within the Excel program window is another window, referred to as the **workbook window** or **worksheet window**. The worksheet window provides a grid of **columns** and **rows**, and the intersection of a column and row is called a **cell**. Each cell is identified by a **cell reference**, which is its column and row location. For example, the cell reference B6 indicates that the cell is located where column B and row 6 intersect. The column letter is always first in the cell reference: B6 is a correct reference; 6B is not. The cell in which you are working is called the **active cell**. Excel identifies the active cell by outlining it with a dark border. In Figure 1-3, cell A1 is the active cell. Notice that the cell reference for the active cell appears in the **Name box** next to the **Formula bar**. You can change the active cell by selecting another cell in the worksheet. As you review the layout of the Excel window shown in Figure 1-3, refer to Figure 1-4 for a description of each component.

Excel window components **Figure 1-4**

Feature	Description
Active cell	The cell in which you are currently working. A dark border outlining the cell identifies the active cell.
Column headings	The letters that appear along the top of the worksheet window. Columns are listed alphabetically from A to IV (a total of 256 possible columns).
Formula bar	The bar located immediately below the toolbars that displays the contents of the active cell. As you type or edit data, the changes appear in the Formula bar.
Name box	The box that displays the cell reference, or column and row location, of the active cell in the workbook window.
Row headings	The numbers that appear along the left side of the worksheet window. Rows are numbered consecutively from 1 to 65,536.
Select All button	Square button located at the intersection of the column and row headings that you click to select the entire contents of the worksheet.
Sheet tabs	Tabs located at the bottom of each worksheet in the workbook that display the names of the sheets. To move between worksheets, click the appropriate sheet tab.
Task pane	The pane that provides access to frequently used tasks. When you start Excel, the Getting Started task pane appears. The task pane disappears once you open a workbook. There are several task-specific panes available in Excel.
Tab scrolling buttons	Series of buttons located to the left of the sheet tabs that you can click to move between worksheets in the workbook.
Toolbars	Toolbars that provide quick access to commonly used commands. The Standard toolbar contains buttons for the most frequently used program commands, such as Save and Print. The Formatting toolbar contains buttons used to format the appearance of the workbook, such as Bold and Italics. Additional toolbars are available.

Now that you are familiar with the basic layout of an Excel window, you can try moving around within the workbook.

Navigating a Worksheet

Excel provides several ways of moving around within a worksheet. You can use your mouse to click a cell to make it the active cell, or you can use the vertical and horizontal scroll bars to display the area of the worksheet containing the cell you want to make active. You can also navigate a worksheet by using your keyboard. Figure 1-5 describes some of these keyboard shortcuts that Excel provides so you can move from cell to cell within the worksheet quickly and easily.

Shortcut keys for navigating a worksheet **Figure 1-5**

Keystroke	Action
↑, ↓, ←, →	Moves the active cell up, down, left, or right one cell
Ctrl + Home	Moves the active cell to cell A1
Ctrl + End	Moves to the last cell in the worksheet that contains data
Enter	Moves the active cell down one cell, or moves to the start of the next row in the selected range of cells
F5	Opens the Go To dialog box, in which you specify the cell you want to move to
Home	Moves the active cell to column A of the current row
Page Up, Page Down	Moves the active cell up or down one full screen
Tab, Shift + Tab	Moves the active cell to the right or left one cell

Try navigating the worksheet now.

To move around in the worksheet:

1. Click the **Close** button in the task pane to close it because you will not be using it in this session. The active cell is A1. The cell A1 is surrounded by a black border, indicating it is the active cell, and the Name box displays the cell reference A1.
2. With cell A1 the active cell, press the ↓ key on your keyboard four times to move to cell A5, and then press the → key twice to make cell C5 the active cell, as shown in Figure 1-6. Note that the column and row headings are highlighted and the cell reference appears in the Name box.

Figure 1-6 Making cell C5 the active cell

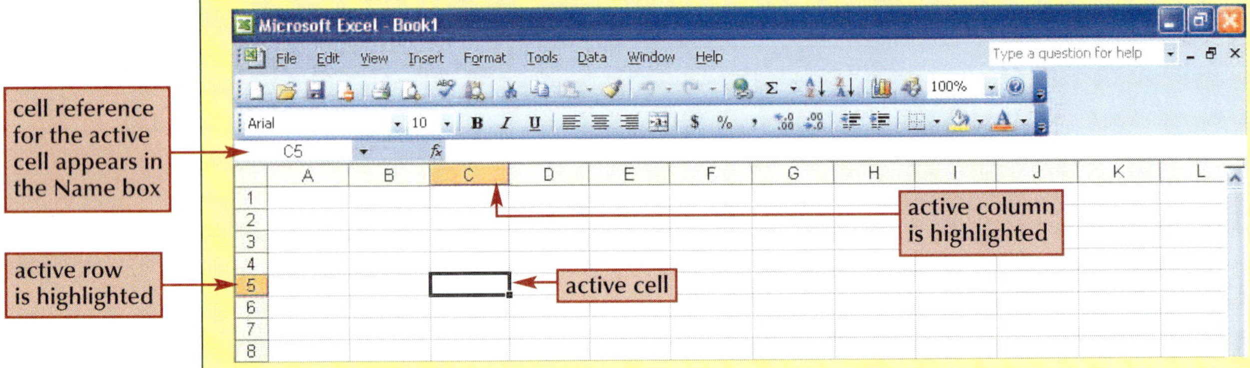

3. Press the **Enter** key to move down one cell, and the press the **Tab** key to move to the right one cell. The active cell is now D6.
4. Press the **Page Down** key to move the display down one screen. The active cell should now be cell D29. If the actual number of columns and rows displayed on your screen differs from that shown in Figure 1-2, the active cell on your screen might not be cell D29. You will learn more about working with the number of columns and rows on your screen later in this tutorial; for now the active cell on your screen should be a screen full of rows down the worksheet.
5. Press the **Page Up** key to move the display back up one screen, making cell D6 the active cell again.
6. Press the **Home** key to move to the first cell in the current row, and then press the **Ctrl + Home** keys to make cell A1 active.

You will probably use the keyboard keys to navigate a worksheet the most frequently, but there will also be situations in which you will want to go directly to a cell on your worksheet. Although you can use the Page Up and Page Down keys or use the scroll bars, you have two other options: the Name box and the Go To dialog box. You can just click in the Name box and type the cell reference you want to go to, or you can open the Go To dialog box from any location in the worksheet by pressing the F5 function key. Try using these methods to navigate the worksheet.

To use the Go To dialog box and Name box:

1. Press the **F5** key to open the Go To dialog box, type **K55** in the Reference text box, and then click the **OK** button to make cell K55 the active cell.
2. Click in the **Name** box, type **E6**, and then press the **Enter** key to make cell E6 the active cell.

Navigating Between Worksheets

By default, a new Excel workbook contains three worksheets, labeled Sheet1, Sheet2, and Sheet3. Each sheet can be used to display different information. To move from one sheet to another, click the sheet tabs at the bottom of each sheet.

To move between worksheets:

1. Click the **Sheet2** tab. Sheet2, which is blank, appears in the workbook window. Notice that the Sheet2 tab is now white with the name "Sheet2" in a bold font. This is a visual indicator that Sheet2 is the active worksheet.
2. Click the **Sheet3** tab to move to the next worksheet in the workbook.
3. Click the **Sheet1** tab to make it the active worksheet.

Now that you have some basic skills navigating through a worksheet and a workbook, you can begin work on Sandra's worksheet.

Developing a Worksheet

Before you begin to enter data in a worksheet, you should think about the purpose of the worksheet and what will be needed to meet the challenge of that purpose. Effective worksheets are well planned and carefully designed. A well-designed worksheet should clearly identify its overall goal. It should present information in a clear, well-organized format and include all the data necessary to produce results that address the goal of the application. The process of developing a good worksheet includes the following planning and execution steps:

- Determine the worksheet's purpose, what it will include, and how it will be organized.
- Enter the data and formulas into the worksheet.
- Test the worksheet, and then edit the worksheet to correct any errors or to make modifications.
- Document the worksheet and format the worksheet's appearance.
- Save and print the complete worksheet.

To develop a worksheet that records orders made at the co-op, Sandra wants to develop a planning analysis sheet that will help her answer the following questions:

1. What is the goal of the worksheet? This helps to define its purpose or, in other words, the problem to solve.
2. What are the desired results? This information describes the output—the information required to help solve the problem.
3. What data is needed to calculate the results you want to see? This information is the input—data that must be entered.
4. What calculations are needed to produce the desired output? These calculations specify the formulas used in the worksheet.

After careful consideration of these questions, Sandra has developed the planning analysis sheet shown in Figure 1-7.

Figure 1-7 **Planning analysis sheet**

Planning Analysis Sheet
Author: Sandra Dalton, Dalton Food Co-op
Date: 4/26/2006

My goal
To develop a worksheet in which I can enter food co-op orders, calculating the total quantity of the items ordered and the revenue generated.

What results do I need to see?
- A listing of each order made by customers
- The total amount of each order
- The total quantity of items ordered by all of the customers
- The total revenue generated by all of the orders

What data do I need?
- The customer's name and address
- The date of the order
- The item purchased by the customer
- The price of each item
- The quantity of items ordered by the customer

What calculations must be performed by the worksheet?
- The total amount of each order (= price of the item x the quantity ordered)
- The total quantity of items ordered (= sum of the order quantities)
- The total revenue generated by all of the orders (= sum of the total amount of each order)

Sandra also knows the information that needs to go into the worksheet, including titles, column headings, row labels, and data values. Figure 1-8 shows how Sandra wants the sales data laid out, based on a sampling of customer orders.

Figure 1-8 **Sales data for co-op worksheet**

Name	Address	Date	Item	Price	Qty	Total
Alison Wilkes	45 Lincoln Street Midtown, FL 80481	4/16/2006	Red Grapefruit	$14	2	
David Wu	315 Oak Lane Midtown, FL 80422	4/16/2006	Navel Oranges	$17	1	
Carl Ramirez	900 South Street Crawford, FL 81891	4/17/2006	Navel Oranges	$17	2	
Jerry Dawson	781 Tree Lane Midtown, FL 80313	4/18/2006	Deluxe Combo	$21	4	
TOTAL						

The first two columns contain the name and address of the person ordering items from the co-op. The Date and Item columns indicate the date that the order was placed and the item ordered. The Price column displays the price of the item. The Qty column indicates the quantity of each item ordered by the customer. The Total column will display the total amount of each order. The TOTAL row will display the total quantity of items ordered and the total revenue generated by all of the sales. With this information in hand, you are now ready to create Sandra's worksheet in Excel.

Entering Data into a Worksheet

A worksheet can contain the following types of data: text, numeric values, dates, and calculated values. A text entry is simply any combination of words, letters, and numbers, typically used to label key features of the worksheet. Numeric values are numbers on which calculations can be made. Numeric values do not contain alphabetic characters, but may contain characters such as commas, dollar signs, and percent signs. Dates are special numeric values recognized by Excel and can be used to determine date-related calculations. The power of Excel lies in the formulas that you can enter into the worksheet cells, whose calculated values are based on the text, dates, and numeric values entered into other cells in the workbook (or in more complicated cases, other workbooks). If those values are changed, the calculated values will also be changed.

Worksheet cells in Excel can also be formatted to improve or enhance the appearance of the cell contents or an entire worksheet. You'll learn about formatting later in Tutorial 3.

Entering Text

To insert text into a worksheet cell, you first make the cell active by using one of the navigation techniques discussed earlier, and then you type the text you want the cell to contain. Excel automatically aligns the text with the left edge of the cell.

First, you'll enter the column headings that Sandra wants across the top row of her worksheet.

To enter the column headings in row 1:

1. Press the **Ctrl + Home** keys to make cell A1 the active cell on the Sheet1 worksheet.
2. Type **Name** and then press the **Tab** key. Pressing the Tab key enters the text in the cell and moves the insertion point to the right to cell B1, making it the active cell.
3. Type **Address** in cell B1, and then press the **Tab** key again. Cell C1 becomes the active cell.
4. Enter the remaining column headings **Date**, **Item**, **Price**, **Qty**, and **Total** in cells C1 through G1. Press the **Enter** key after you type the text for cell G1. Figure 1-9 shows the column headings for the worksheet.

Figure 1-9 Entering text into the worksheet

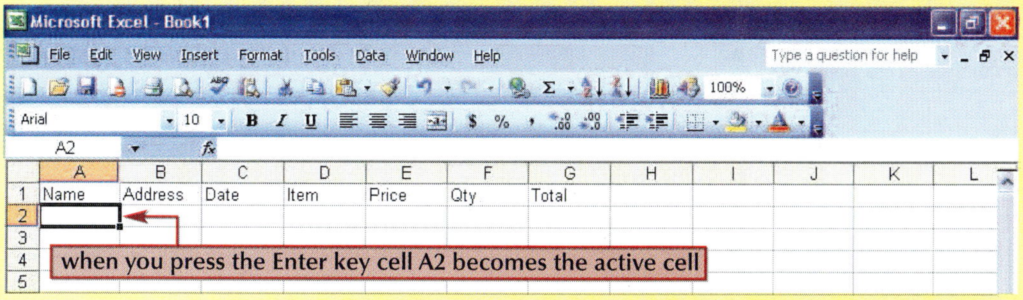

Trouble? If you make a mistake as you type, you can correct the error by clicking the cell and retyping the entry.

Note that when you press the Enter key, the active cell becomes cell A2, not cell G2. Excel recognizes that when you enter a row of data and then press the Enter key, you have completed the task of entering data in the current row, so the insertion point moves to the start of the next row. If you had started entering data in cell C1 rather than A1, pressing the Enter key would have made cell C2 the active cell.

Entering Several Lines of Text Within a Cell

In the next row, you'll enter actual sales information. One cell in this row contains the customer's address. In Sandra's records, this information is presented on two separate lines, with the street address on one line and the city, state, and ZIP code on the other. To place text on separate lines within the same cell, you press and hold the Alt key on the keyboard while pressing the Enter key.

Reference Window

Entering Multiple Lines of Text Within a Cell

- Click the cell in which you want to enter the text.
- Enter a line of text.
- Press and hold the Alt key, and then press the Enter key to move the insertion point to a new line within the cell.
- Enter the next line of text.
- Press the Alt + Enter keys for each new line of text you need to enter within the cell.

Try this technique now by entering the first customer's name and address.

To enter the address on two lines within a cell:

1. Verify that cell **A2** is the active cell, type **Alison Wilkes**, and then press the **Tab** key to move to column B, where you will enter the two-line address.
2. Type **45 Lincoln Street** in cell B2, but do *not* press the Tab or Enter key.
3. Press and hold the **Alt** key, and then press the **Enter** key to insert a line break, moving the insertion point to a new line within the cell.
4. Type **Midtown, FL 80481** on the second line of the cell, and then press the **Tab** key. Figure 1-10 shows the worksheet with the text you have entered so far.

Figure 1-10 Entering the customer name and address

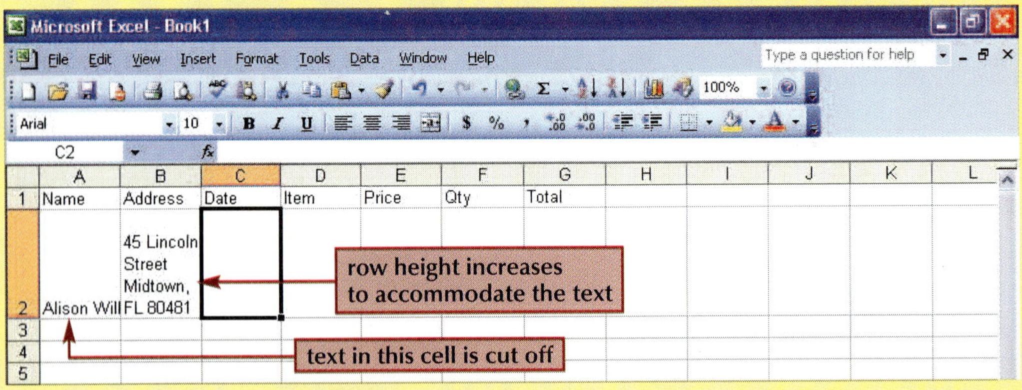

Excel has done a couple of things that you need to understand before entering more data. First, the name of the customer in cell A2 has been cut off, or truncated. When you enter more text than can be displayed within a cell, Excel will display the additional text in the cell or cells to the right as long as they are empty. If the cells to the right are not empty, Excel will truncate the display of the text when it encounters the first non-empty cell. The text itself is not affected. The complete name of the first customer is still entered in cell A2; it's just not displayed.

Second, the customer address in cell B2 does not extend into cell C2, even though that cell is empty. Instead, the height of row 2 has been increased to accommodate this text. If a cell contains multiple lines of text, Excel increases the height of the row to display all of the text entry. Note that the text in cell B2 "appears" to be on four lines, even though you entered the address on two lines. Excel wrapped the text in this way so that it would fit within the existing column width. Later in this session, you will learn how to adjust column widths and row heights to improve the worksheet's appearance.

Entering Dates

In Excel, dates are treated as numeric values, not text. This allows you to perform calculations with dates, such as determining the number of days between two dates. You'll learn how to work with date values in the next tutorial. For now, you need to know how to enter a date. You can enter a date using any of the following date formats, which are recognized by Excel:

- 4/16/2006
- 4/16/06
- 4-16-2006
- April 16, 2006
- 16-Apr-06

The appearance of a date, regardless of how you enter it in a cell, depends on the date format that has been set as the default in your version of Excel. For example, if you enter the date as the text string "April 26, 2006," Excel will automatically convert the entry to "26-Apr-2006" if the DD-MMM-YYYY format has been set as the default. You will learn about cell formats and date formats in Tutorial 3.

Sandra wants the date "4/16/2006" to appear in cell C2, so you will enter that next.

To insert the date in cell C2:

1. Verify that cell **C2** is the active cell.
2. Type **4/16/2006** and then press the **Tab** key.

   Trouble? If your computer is set up to display dates using a different date format, do not worry about their appearance at this time.
3. Type **Red Grapefruit** in cell D2, and then press the **Tab** key. Note that the text in cell D2 is completely displayed because, at this point, the cells to the right of D2 are still empty.

Entering Values

Values are numbers that represent a quantity of some type: the number of units in an inventory, stock prices, an exam score, and so on. Values can be numbers such as 378 and 25.275 or negative numbers such as –55.208. Values can also be expressed as currency such as $14.95 or as percentages such as 95%. Not all numbers are treated as values. For example, Excel treats a telephone number (1-800-555-8010) or a Social Security number (372-70-9654) as a text entry. As you type information into a cell, Excel determines whether the entry can be treated as a value, and if so, automatically right-aligns the value within the cell.

Next, you'll enter the price and quantity of the first order into cells E2 and F2.

To enter the price and quantity values:

1. Type **$14** in cell E2, and then press the **Tab** key.
2. Type **2** in cell F2, and then press the **Tab** key. Figure 1-11 shows the data for the first order. The last cell in the row is empty, but next you will enter a calculation that will give Sandra the total amount of the order.

Figure 1-11 **Entering the price and quantity values**

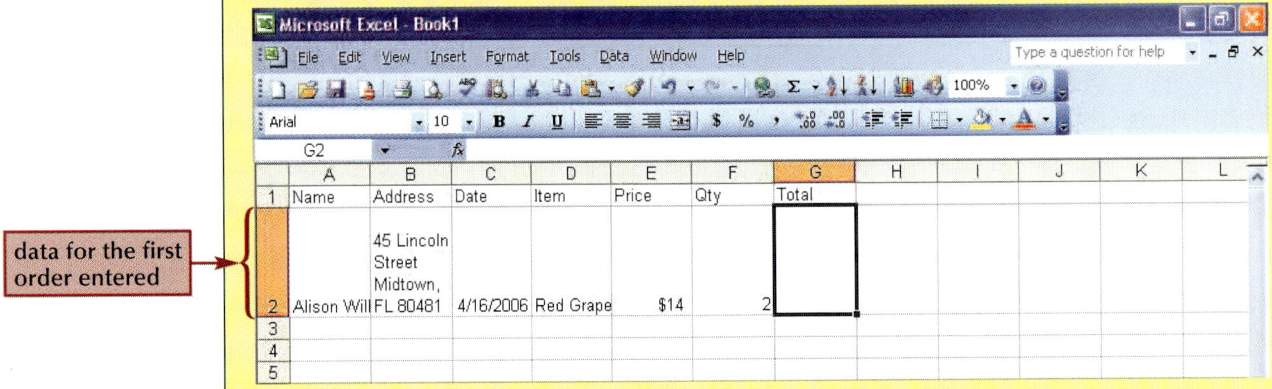

The remaining cell in this row will contain the total price of the order, which is equal to the price of the red grapefruit item multiplied by the quantity ordered. The total price of the first order is $14 multiplied by 2, or $28. Rather than entering this value into the cell, you'll let Excel calculate it for you by entering a formula.

Entering Formulas

The single most important reason for using a spreadsheet is to perform calculations on data. To accomplish that goal, you need to enter formulas. A **formula** is a mathematical expression that calculates a value. Excel formulas always begin with an equal sign (=) followed by an expression that describes the calculation to be done. A formula can contain one or more **arithmetic operators**, such as +, –, *, or /. For example, the formula *=A1+A2* calculates the sum by adding the values of cells A1 and A2. Figure 1-12 gives examples of some other Excel formulas. Note that, by convention, cell references appear in uppercase letters, but this is not a requirement for Excel formulas. You can type the formula using either upper- or lowercase letters, and Excel will automatically convert the cell references to uppercase.

Figure 1-12

Sample Excel formulas using arithmetic operators

Operation	Operator	Example	Description
Addition	+	=10+A5	Adds 10 to the value in cell A5
		=B1+B2+B3	Adds the values of cells B1, B2, and B3
Subtraction	–	=C9–B2	Subtracts the value in cell B2 from the value in cell C9
		=1–D2	Subtracts the value in cell D2 from 1
Multiplication	*	=C9*B9	Multiplies the value in cell C9 by the value in cell B9
		=E5*0.06	Multiplies the value in cell E5 by 0.06
Division	/	=C9/B9	Divides the value in cell C9 by the value in cell B9
		=D15/12	Divides the value in cell D15 by 12
Exponentiation	^	=B5^3	Raises the value in cell B5 to the third power
		=3^B5	Raises 3 to the power specified in cell B5

Reference Window

Entering a Formula

- Click the cell where you want the formula result to appear.
- Type = and then type the expression that calculates the value you want.
- For a formula that includes cell references, such as B2 or D78, type the cell reference, or use the mouse or arrow keys to select each cell.
- When the formula is complete, press the Enter key (or press the Tab key or click the Enter button on the Formula bar).

If an expression contains more than one arithmetic operator, Excel performs the calculation in the order of precedence. The **order of precedence** is a set of predefined rules that Excel follows to calculate a formula by determining which operator is applied first, which operator is applied second, and so forth. First, Excel performs exponentiation (^). Second, Excel performs multiplication (*) or division (/). Third, Excel performs addition (+) or subtraction (–).

For example, because multiplication has precedence over addition, the formula *=3+4*5* results in the value *23*. If the expression contains two or more operators with the same level of precedence, Excel applies them from left to right in the expression. In the formula *=4*10/8*, Excel first multiplies *4* by *10* and then divides the result by *8* to produce the value *5*.

When building a formula, you must add parentheses to change the order of operations. Excel will calculate any expression contained within the parentheses before any other part of the formula. The formula *=(3+4)*5* first calculates the value of *3+4* and then multiplies the total by *5*, resulting in the value *35*. (Note that without the parentheses, Excel would produce a value of *23*, as noted in the previous paragraph.) Figure 1-13 shows other examples of Excel formulas using the order of precedence rules.

Figure 1-13 Examples illustrating order of precedence rules

Formula (A1=50, B1=10, C1=5)	Order of precedence rule	Result
=A1+B1*C1	Multiplication before addition	100
=(A1+B1)*C1	Expression inside parentheses executed before expression outside	300
=A1/B1–C1	Division before subtraction	0
=A1/(B1–C1)	Expression inside parentheses executed before expression outside	10
=A1/B1*C1	Two operators at same precedence level, leftmost operator evaluated first	25
=A1/(B1*C1)	Expression inside parentheses executed before expression outside	1

Using what you know about formulas, you'll enter a formula in cell G2 to calculate the total amount of Alison Wilke's order.

To enter a formula to calculate the total amount of the first order:

1. Verify that cell **G2** is the active cell.
2. Type **=E2*F2** (the price of the item multiplied by the quantity ordered). Note that as you type the cell reference, Excel surrounds each cell with a different colored border that matches the color of the cell reference in the formula. As shown in Figure 1-14, Excel surrounds cell E2 with a blue border, matching the blue used for the cell reference. Green is used for the F2 cell border and cell reference.

Figure 1-14 Typing a formula into the active cell

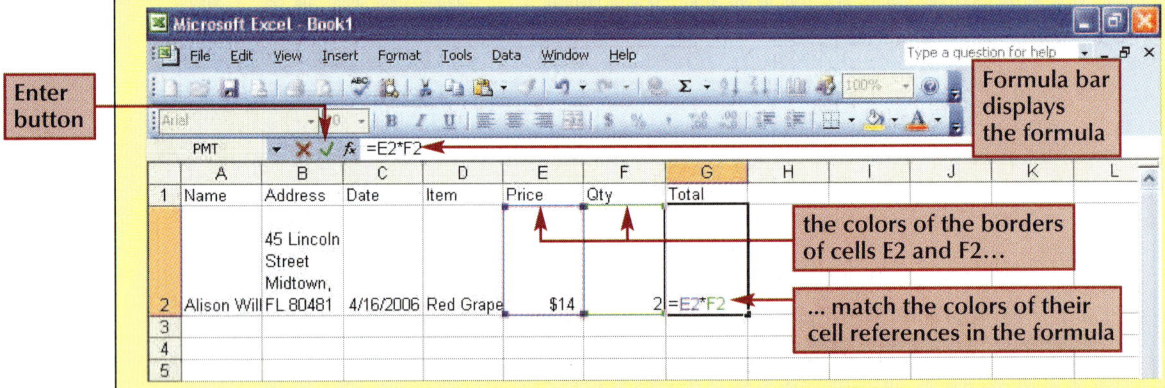

3. Press the **Enter** key. The total amount of the first order displayed in cell G2 is $28. Note that the value is displayed as currency because one of the components of the formula (cell E2) is a currency value. As you can see, the result of the formula is displayed in the worksheet. To see the formula itself, you need to select the cell and examine the formula in the Formula bar.

You can also enter formulas interactively by clicking each cell. In this technique, you type = (an equal sign) to begin the formula, and then click each cell that needs to be entered in the formula. Using this point-and-click method reduces the possibility of error caused by typing an incorrect cell reference.

Next, you'll enter the data for the second order, and then enter the formula *=E3*F3* (the price of the item multiplied by the quantity ordered) using the point-and-click method.

To enter the same formula using the point-and-click method:

1. Enter **David Wu** in cell A3, **315 Oak Lane** on one line in cell B3 and **Midtown, FL 80422** on a second line in the cell, **4/16/2006** in cell C3, **Navel Oranges** in cell D3, **$17** in cell E3, and **1** in cell F3. Be sure to press the Alt + Enter keys to enter the address information on two separate lines as you did for the address in cell B2.
2. Make sure cell **G3** is the active cell, and then type **=** (but do *not* press the Enter or Tab key). When you type the equal sign, Excel knows that you are entering a formula. Any cell that you click from now on will cause Excel to insert the reference of the selected cell into the formula until you complete the formula by pressing the Enter or Tab key or by clicking the Enter button on the Formula bar (refer to Figure 1-14).
3. Click cell **E3**. Note that the cell is highlighted in the same color as the cell reference that now appears in the formula in cell G3.
4. Type ***** to enter the multiplication operator.
5. Click cell **F3** to enter this cell reference, and then press the **Enter** key. Cell G3 now contains the formula *=E3*F3* and displays the value $17, which is the total amount of the second order.

Using AutoComplete

As you continue to work with Excel, you may find yourself entering the same text in different rows in the worksheet. To help make entering repetitive text easier, Excel provides the **AutoComplete** feature. Once you enter text in a worksheet, Excel tries to anticipate the text you are about to enter by displaying text that begins with the same letter as a previous entry. For example, two people—David Wu and Carl Ramirez—have ordered a box of navel oranges. You have already entered the data for David Wu's order. When you enter the data for Carl Ramirez's order, you will see how AutoComplete works.

To enter text using AutoComplete:

1. Enter **Carl Ramirez** in cell A4, **900 South Street Crawford, FL 81891** in cell B4 on two separate lines within the cell, and **4/17/2006** in cell C4. Do *not* enter the item for Carl's order yet.
2. Make sure cell **D4** is the active cell, and then type **N**. Note that Excel anticipates the entry by displaying "Navel Oranges," which is text you have already entered beginning with the letter N. See Figure 1-15. At this point, you can accept Excel's suggestion by pressing the Enter or Tab key to complete the text entry and to exit the cell. To override Excel's suggestion, you simply keep typing the text you want to enter into the cell.

Figure 1-15 Entering text with the AutoComplete feature

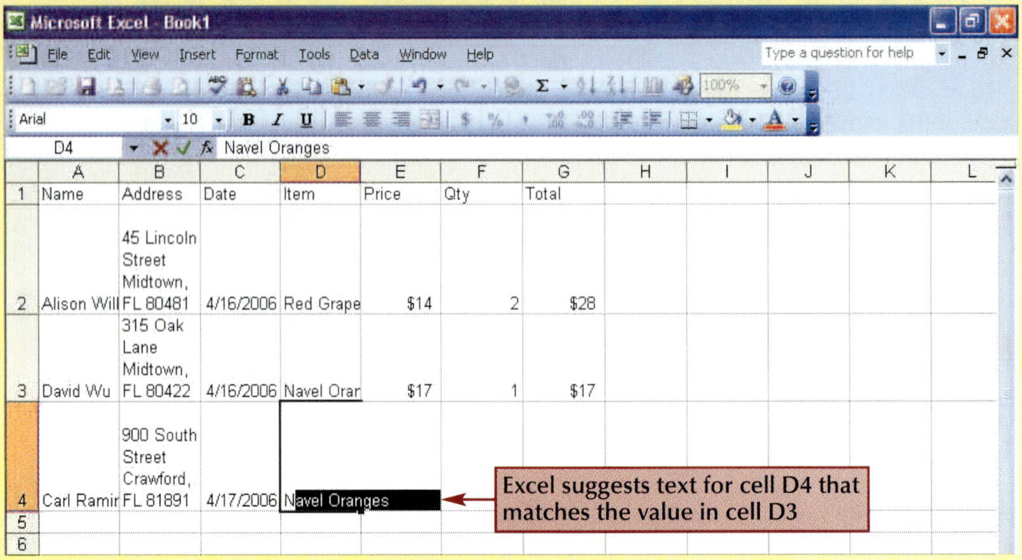

Trouble? If your version of Excel is not set up to use AutoComplete, you will not see the suggested text; therefore you must type "Navel Oranges".

3. Press the **Tab** key to accept Excel's AutoComplete suggestion and to move to cell E4.
4. Type **$17** in cell E4, press the **Tab** key, type **2** in cell F4, and then press the **Tab** key to move to cell G4.
5. Enter **=E4*F4** in cell G4 by typing the formula or by using the point-and-click method. Note that from now on in this text, when you are instructed to "enter" something versus "type" it, use the method that you most prefer; that is, press the Enter key, press the Tab key, or click the Enter button on the Formula bar. Clicking the Enter button not only enters the value in the cell, but also keeps that cell as the active cell.

Excel does not apply AutoComplete to dates or values. However, you can use another feature, AutoFill, to automatically fill in formulas. You'll learn more about AutoFill in the next tutorial.

Now you'll enter the last co-op order into the worksheet.

To enter the last order into the worksheet:

1. Enter **Jerry Dawson** in cell A5, **781 Tree Lane Midtown, FL 80313** in cell B5, **4/18/2006** in cell C5, **Deluxe Combo** in cell D5, **$21** in cell E5, and **4** in cell F5. (Remember to enter the address on two lines.)
2. In cell G5, enter the formula **=E5*F5**. Figure 1-16 shows the completed worksheet.

Figure 1-16 Four co-op orders entered

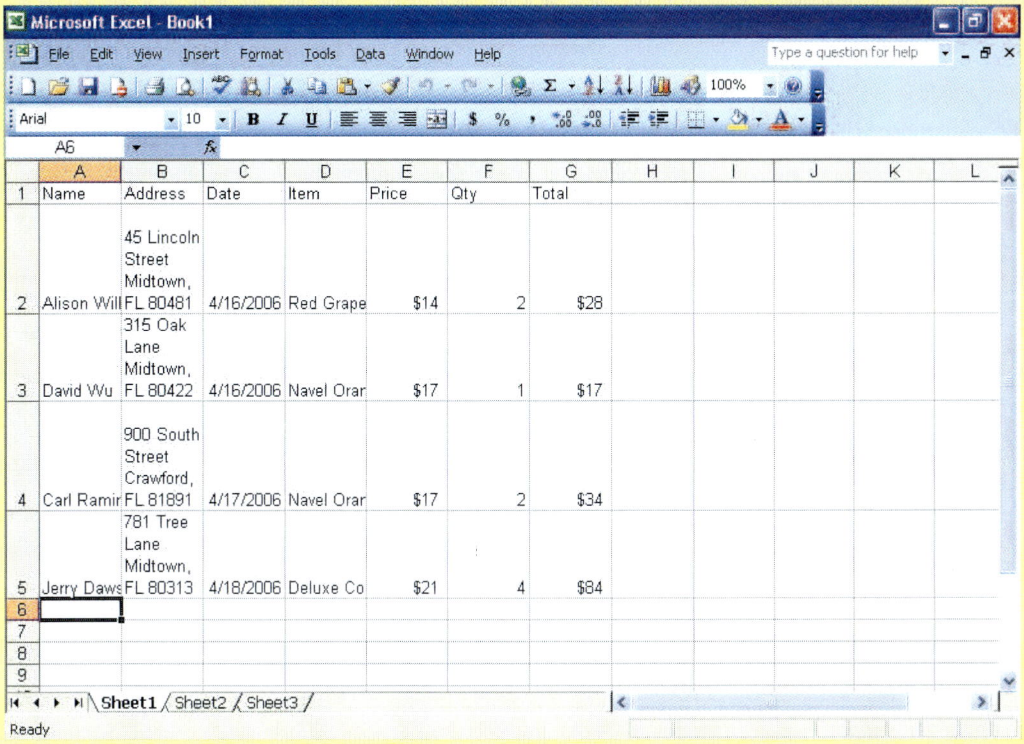

Changing the Size of a Column or Row

The default sizes of the columns and rows in an Excel worksheet may not always accommodate the information you need to enter. You can change the width of one column or multiple columns or the height of one row or multiple rows. Excel provides several methods for changing the width of a column or the height of a row. You can click the dividing line of the column or row, or you can drag the dividing line to change the width of the column or the height of the row. Heights and widths are expressed in terms of the number of characters that can be displayed in the cell, as well as the number of screen pixels, which are small units of measurement that appear as tiny dots on the screen.

Changing the Column Width or Row Height

Reference Window

- Click the column or row heading whose width or height you want to change.
- Click Format on the menu bar, point to Column or Row, and then click Width or Height (or click AutoFit or AutoFit Selection to make the column or row as large as the longest entry of the cells).
- In the Column Width or Row Height dialog box, enter the new column width or row height, and then click the OK button.

or

- Drag the column or row heading dividing line to the right or up to increase the column width or row height, or drag the dividing line to the left or down to decrease the column width or row height.

or

- Double-click the column or row heading dividing line to make the column or row as large as the longest entry of the cells in the column or row.

You'll use the drag technique to increase the width of the columns in which the data display has been truncated. As you drag the dividing line, a ScreenTip appears and displays the column width in characters and pixels.

To change the width of columns in the worksheet:

1. Move the mouse pointer to the dividing line between the column A and column B headings until the pointer changes to ↔.
2. Click and drag the pointer to the right to a length of about **20** characters (or **145 pixels**). See Figure 1-17.

Figure 1-17 Increasing the width of column A

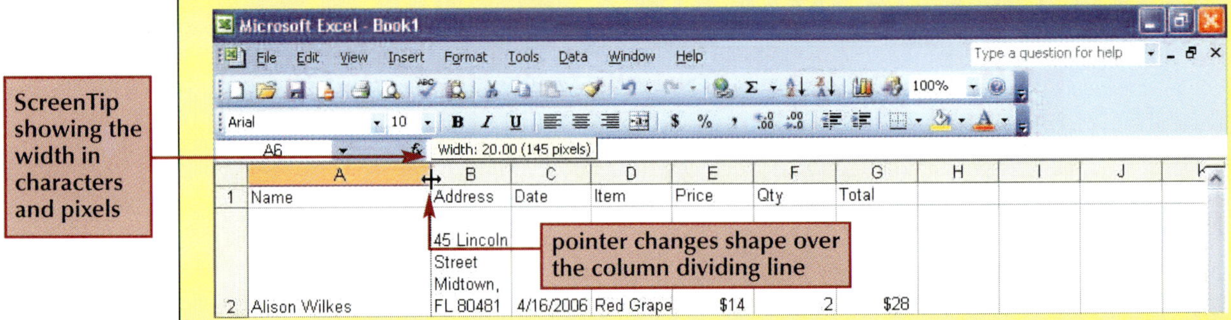

3. Release the mouse button. All the names in column A should now be visible.

   Trouble? If the text in column A is still truncated, drag the dividing line further to the right.

4. Move the mouse pointer to the dividing line between column B and column C until the pointer changes to ↔, and then increase the width of column B to **25** characters (or **180** pixels).
5. Use your mouse to increase the width of column D to **15** characters (or **110** pixels).

Changing the width of the columns does not affect the height of the rows. However, now that column A is wider and the rows are taller, there is a great deal of empty space. To remove the empty space, you'll resize the rows. Rather than choosing a size for the rows, you'll let Excel make the adjustment automatically. If you double-click the dividing line of a column or row heading, the column width or row height adjusts to match the length of the longest entry in that column or row. You'll use this technique now to modify the height of the second row in the worksheet.

To change the height of the second row:

1. Move the mouse pointer to the dividing line between the second and third rows until the pointer changes to ↕.
2. Double-click the dividing line between the second and third rows. See Figure 1-18.

Changing the height of the second row

Figure 1-18

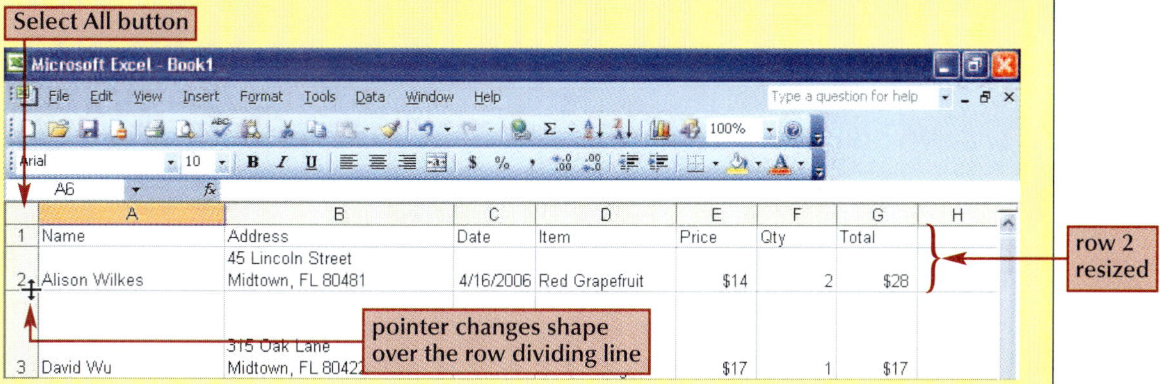

You can continue modifying the height of the remaining rows using this technique, but, for a worksheet containing a large amount of data, that would be extremely time-consuming. Another approach is to select the entire worksheet and then double-click the dividing line between any two row headings. When you do that, Excel changes the height of the rows to accommodate the data in them and reduces the amount of empty space. You can use this approach to resize columns, too.

You can select the entire worksheet by clicking the Select All button. You'll use this approach now to change the height of the remaining rows in the co-op order worksheet.

To change the height of the remaining rows:

1. Click the **Select All** button located at the junction of the row and column headings (see Figure 1-18). The row and column headings are displayed in black or dark blue, and all of the worksheet cells are displayed in light blue, indicating that the entire worksheet has been selected.
2. Move the mouse pointer to a dividing line between any two rows until the pointer changes to ┼.
3. Double-click the dividing line. Excel resizes the height of all the rows.
4. Click cell **A1** to make it the active cell and to remove the blue highlighting from the worksheet. Figure 1-19 shows the revised layout of the sheet.

Adjusting the height of the worksheet rows

Figure 1-19

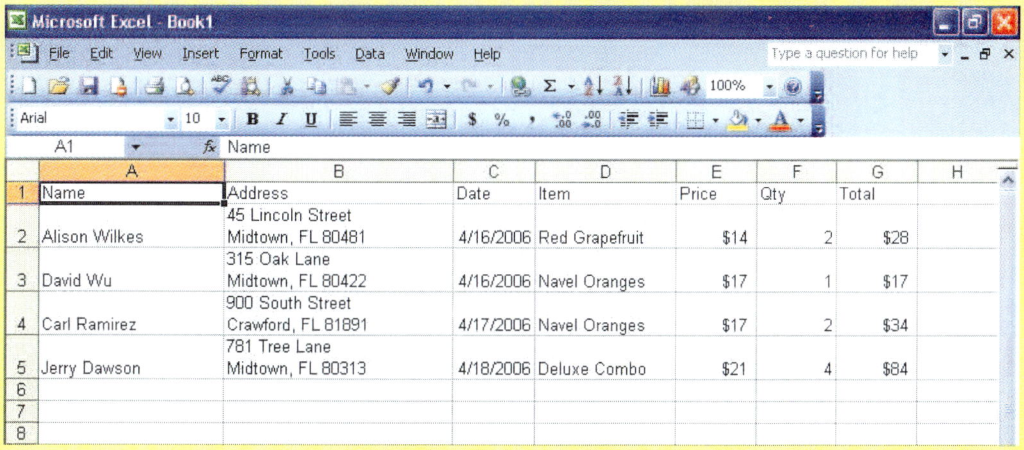

You've entered the data that Sandra wanted in the worksheet. Before proceeding further, she suggests that you save the file with the name "Dalton".

To save the workbook:

1. Click **File** on the menu bar, and then click **Save**. The Save As dialog box opens with the current workbook name, which is "Book1," in the File name text box.
2. Navigate to the Tutorial.01\Tutorial folder included with your Data Files.

   Trouble? If you don't have the Excel 2003 Data Files, you need to get them before you can proceed. Your instructor will either give you the Data Files or ask you to obtain them from a specified location (such as a network drive). In either case, be sure that you make a backup copy of your Data Files before you start using them, so that the original files will be available on your copied disk in case you need to start over because of an error or problem. If you have any questions about the Data Files, see your instructor or technical support person for assistance.
3. Replace the default filename with **Dalton**, make sure that **Microsoft Office Excel Workbook** is displayed in the Save as type list box, and then click the **Save** button. Excel saves the workbook with the name "Dalton" and closes the Save As dialog box. The new workbook name appears in the title bar of the Excel window.

   Trouble? If your computer has been set up to display file extensions, the filename "Dalton.xls" will appear in the title bar.

By default, Excel saves the workbook in Microsoft Excel Workbook format, and for most of the work you will do in this text, you will use this file format. If you are creating a workbook that will be read by applications other than Excel (or earlier versions of Excel), you can save your workbook in a different file format by following these steps:

1. Open the Save or Save As dialog box.
2. Display the location in which you want to save the file, and enter a filename, if necessary.
3. Click the Save as type list arrow, and then select the file format you want to apply.
4. Click the Save button.

Figure 1-20 describes some of the file formats in which you can save your workbooks.

Figure 1-20 Some of the formats supported by Excel

Format	Description
Microsoft Excel 4.0, 5.0, 97, 2000, 2002 Workbook	Saves the workbook in an earlier version of Excel
Single File Web Page	Saves the workbook as a single Web page file (MHTML file) that can be read by Internet Explorer 4.0 or later
Template	Saves the workbook as a template to be used for creating other Excel workbooks
Web Page	Saves the workbook in separate files that are used as the basis for a Web site, in a format that is readable by most browsers
XML Spreadsheet	Saves the workbook as an XML document

Sandra has some other changes to the workbook that she wants you to make. You'll continue working with the worksheet in the next session.

Session 1.1 Quick Check

Review

1. A(n) ______________ is the place on the worksheet where a column and row intersect.
2. Cell ______________ refers to the intersection of the fourth column and second row.
3. What combination of keys can you press to make A1 the active cell in the worksheet?
4. To make Sheet2 the active worksheet, you ______________.
5. Indicate whether Excel treats the following cell entries as text, a value, or a formula.
   a. 11/09/2006
   b. Net Income
   c. 321
   d. C11*225
   e. 201-19-1121
   f. =D1-D9
   g. 44 Evans Avenue
6. How do you enter multiple lines of text within a cell?
7. What formula would you enter to divide the value in cell E5 by the value in cell E6?

Session 1.2

Working with Ranges

Sandra has had a chance to study your work from the previous session. She likes the layout of her data, but she wants to have a title at the top of the worksheet that displays information about the sheet's contents. To make room for the title, you have to move the contents of the worksheet down a few rows. Before you attempt that, you have to first understand how Excel works with groups of cells.

A group of worksheet cells is called a **cell range**, or just **range**. Ranges can be either adjacent or nonadjacent. An **adjacent range** is a single rectangular block, such as all of the data entered in cells A1 through G5 of the Dalton workbook. A **nonadjacent range** consists of two or more separate adjacent ranges. For example, a nonadjacent range might be composed of the names of the customers in the cell range A1 through A5 and the total price of their orders in the cell range G1 through G5.

Just as a cell reference indicates the location of a cell on the worksheet, a **range reference** indicates the location and size of a cell range. For adjacent ranges, the range reference identifies the cells in the upper-left and lower-right corners of the rectangle, with the individual cell references separated by a colon. For example, the range reference for the order data you entered in the last session was A1:G5 because it included the range of cells from A1 through G5. If the range is nonadjacent, a semicolon separates the rectangular blocks A1:A5 and G1:G5, as in A1:A5;G1:G5. This nonadjacent range references the customer names in the range A1:A5 and the total amounts of their orders in the range G1:G5.

Selecting Ranges

Once you know how to select ranges of cells, you can move and copy the data anywhere in the worksheet or workbook.

Reference Window

Selecting Adjacent or Nonadjacent Ranges of Cells

To select an adjacent range of cells:
- Click a cell in the upper-left corner of the rectangle that comprises the adjacent range.
- Press and hold the left mouse button, and then drag the pointer through the cells you want selected.
- Release the mouse button.

To select a nonadjacent range of cells:
- Select an adjacent range of cells.
- Press and hold the Ctrl key, and then select another adjacent cell range.
- With the Ctrl key still pressed, continue to select other cell ranges until all of the ranges are selected.
- Release the mouse button and the Ctrl key.

To see how to select ranges, you'll start by selecting all of the cells containing order information.

To select the order data:

1. If you took a break at the end of the previous session, make sure that Excel is running and that the Dalton workbook is open.
2. Click cell **A1** on the Sheet1 worksheet, press and hold the left mouse button, and then drag the pointer to cell **G5**.
3. Release the mouse button. All the cells in the range A1:G5 are now highlighted, indicating that they are selected. See Figure 1-21.

Figure 1-21 Selecting the range A1:G5

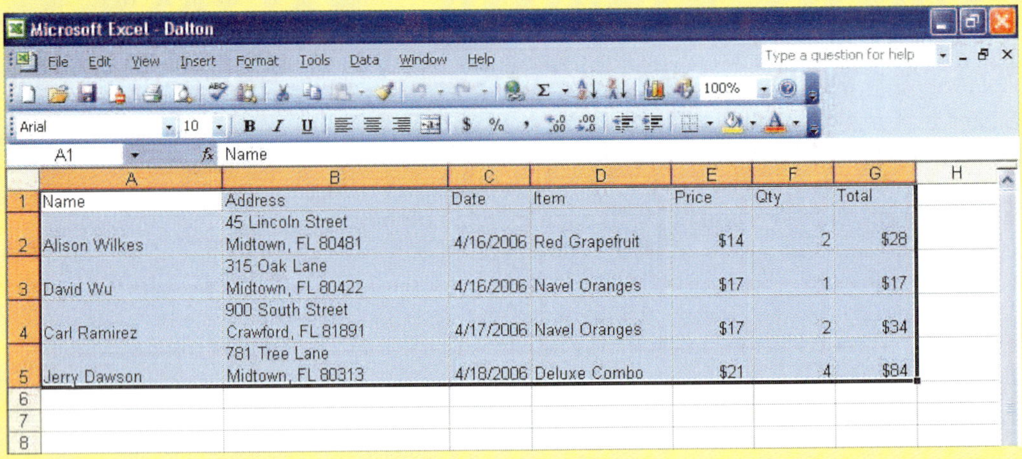

4. Click any cell in the worksheet to deselect the range.

Now try selecting the nonadjacent range A1:A5;G1:G5.

To select the nonadjacent range A1:A5;G1:G5:

1. Select the range **A1:A5**, press and hold the **Ctrl** key, select the range **G1:G5**, and then release the mouse button and the Ctrl key. See Figure 1-22 for the selected nonadjacent range.

Selecting the nonadjacent range A1:A5;G1:G5 — **Figure 1-22**

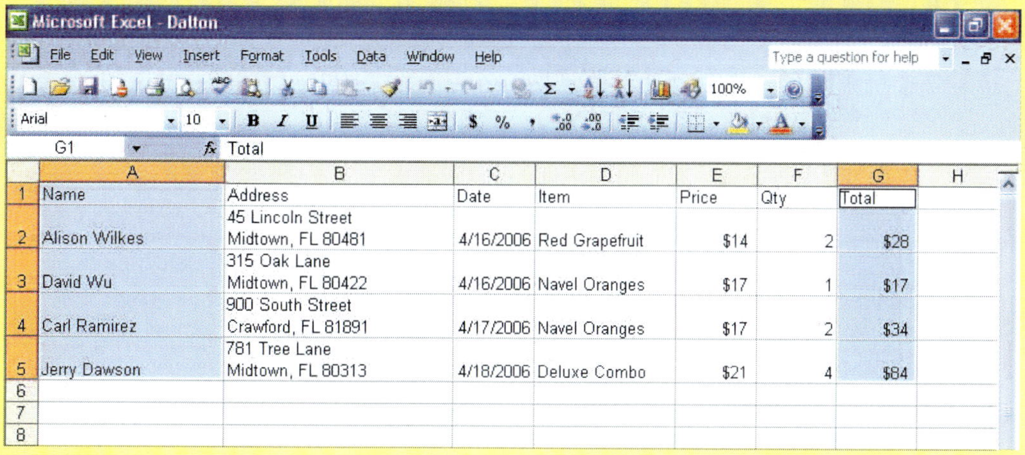

2. Click any cell in the worksheet to deselect the range.

Other Selection Techniques

You can also select large cell ranges that extend beyond the borders of the workbook window. When this situation occurs, Excel automatically scrolls the workbook window horizontally or vertically to display additional cells in the worksheet. Selecting a large cell range using the mouse drag technique can be slow and frustrating. For this reason, Excel provides keyboard shortcuts that enable you to quickly select large blocks of data without having to drag through the worksheet to select the necessary cells. Figure 1-23 describes some of these selection techniques.

Other range selection techniques — **Figure 1-23**

To Select...	Action
A large range of cells	Click the first cell in the range, press and hold down the Shift key, and then click the last cell in the range. All of the cells between the first and last cell are selected.
All cells on the worksheet	Click the Select All button, the gray rectangle in the upper-left corner of the worksheet where the row and column headings meet.
All cells in an entire row or column	Click the row or column heading.
A range of cells containing data	Click the cell where you want to begin the selection of the range, press and hold down the Shift key, and then double-click the side of the cell in the direction that you want to extend the selection. Excel selects all adjacent cells that contain data, extending the selection of the range to the first empty cell.

Try some of the techniques described to select ranges of cells in the Dalton workbook.

To select a range of cells using keyboard shortcuts:

1. Click cell **A1** to make it the active cell.
2. Press and hold the **Shift** key, click cell **A5**, and then release the Shift key. Note that all of the cells between A1 and A5 are selected.

   Trouble? If the range A1:A5 is not selected, try again, but make sure you hold the Shift key while you click cell A5.
3. Click cell **A1** to make it the active cell again. Note that you don't have to deselect one range before clicking another cell.
4. Press and hold the **Shift** key, move the pointer to the bottom edge of cell A1 until the mouse pointer changes to , and then double-click the bottom edge of cell **A1**. The selection extends to cell A5, the last cell before the empty cell A6.
5. With the Shift key still pressed, move the pointer to the right edge of the selection until, once again, the pointer changes to , double-click the right edge of the selection, and then release the Shift key. The selection extends to the last nonblank column in the worksheet, selecting the range A1:G5.
6. Click the **A** column heading. All of the cells in column A are selected. Note that you didn't have to deselect the range A1:G5.
7. Click the **1** row heading. All of the cells in the first row are selected.

Moving a Selection of Cells

Now that you know various ways to select a range of cells, you can move the co-op data down a few rows in the worksheet. To move a cell range, you first select it; then you position the pointer over the selection border, and drag the selection to a new location. Try this technique to move the order data from the cell range A1:G5 to the cell range A5:G9.

To move the order data:

1. Select the range **A1:G5**, and then move the pointer over the bottom border of the selection until the pointer changes to .
2. Press and hold the left mouse button, changing the pointer to , and then drag the selection down four rows. A ScreenTip appears indicating the new range reference of the selection. See Figure 1-24.

Figure 1-24

Moving the selection to the range A5:G9

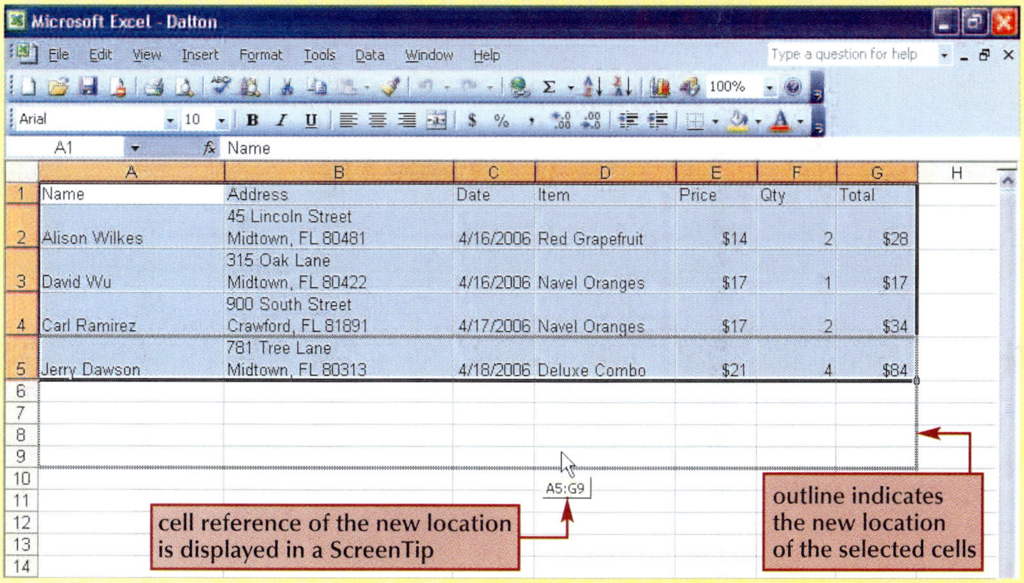

3. When the ScreenTip displays "A5:G9," release the left mouse button. The order data is now moved to range A5:G9.

   Trouble? If you selected the wrong range or moved the selection to the wrong location, click the Undo button on the Standard toolbar, and then repeat Steps 1 through 3.

4. Click cell **A1** to remove the selection and to make cell A1 the active cell so you can enter the new titles in the worksheet.

5. Type **Dalton Food Co-op** in cell A1, **List of Orders** in cell A2, **April, 2006** in cell A3, and then press the **Enter** key. Note that moving the cell range had no impact on the values in the worksheet; the values shown by the formulas in column G are also unchanged. This is because Excel automatically updated the cell references in the formulas to reflect the new location of the data. To confirm this, you'll examine the formula in cell G6.

6. Click cell **G6** and observe what is displayed in the Formula bar. The formula in cell G6 is now *=E6*F6*. Recall that when you originally entered Alison Wilke's order, the formula for this cell was *=E2*G2* because the order was originally placed in the second row of the worksheet. When you moved the data, Excel automatically updated the formula to reflect the new location of Alison Wilke's order.

The technique you used to move the cell range is called "drag and drop." You can also use the drag-and-drop technique to copy a cell range. Copying a range of cells is similar to moving a range, except that you must press the Ctrl key while you drag the selection to its new location. A copy of the original data will then appear at the location of the pointer when you release the mouse button. You'll learn more about copying and pasting in the next two tutorials.

A cell range can also be moved from one worksheet in the workbook to another. To do this, press and hold the Alt key and then drag the selection over the sheet tab of the new worksheet. Excel will automatically make that worksheet the active sheet, so you can drag the selection into its new location on the worksheet.

Calculating Sums with AutoSum

Sandra reminds you that she wants the worksheet to also display summary information about the co-op orders, including the total number of items ordered and the amount of revenue generated from those orders. You could calculate the total quantity and total revenue using the formulas *=F6+F7+F8+F9* and *=G6+G7+G8+G9*.

One problem with this approach is that as Sandra adds new orders to the worksheet, you will have to constantly update these formulas, adding cell references for the new orders. As you add more orders, the length of these two expressions will increase dramatically, increasing the possibility of making errors in the formulas.

One way to solve this problem is to use a **function**, which is a predefined formula that performs calculations using specific values. You will learn about and work with functions in more detail in the next tutorial. In this case, you'll insert one of Excel's most commonly used Financial functions, the SUM function, using the AutoSum button on the Standard toolbar. The **AutoSum** feature is a quick and convenient way to enter the SUM function. You use the **SUM function** to calculate the sum of values in a cell range. In this case, you want to calculate the sum of the values in the range F6:F9 and in the range G6:G9.

Now, you'll use AutoSum to calculate the total quantity and total revenue of the ordered items, putting these values in cells F10 and G10.

To calculate the total order quantity and revenue:

1. Click cell **A10**, type **TOTAL**, and then press the **Tab** key five times to move to cell F10.
2. With cell F10 as the active cell, click the **AutoSum** button Σ on the Standard toolbar. Excel automatically inserts the SUM function in the active cell and selects a cell range that it anticipates is the range of cells to be summed. See Figure 1-25. A ScreenTip also appears, showing the form of the SUM function. The mode indicator in the status bar changes to Point, indicating that you can point to the cell references. In this case, the range that Excel has selected for you is the correct range of cells, so all you need to do is indicate that you accept the range. You can complete the function and move to the next cell by pressing the Tab key.

Using the AutoSum button — **Figure 1-25**

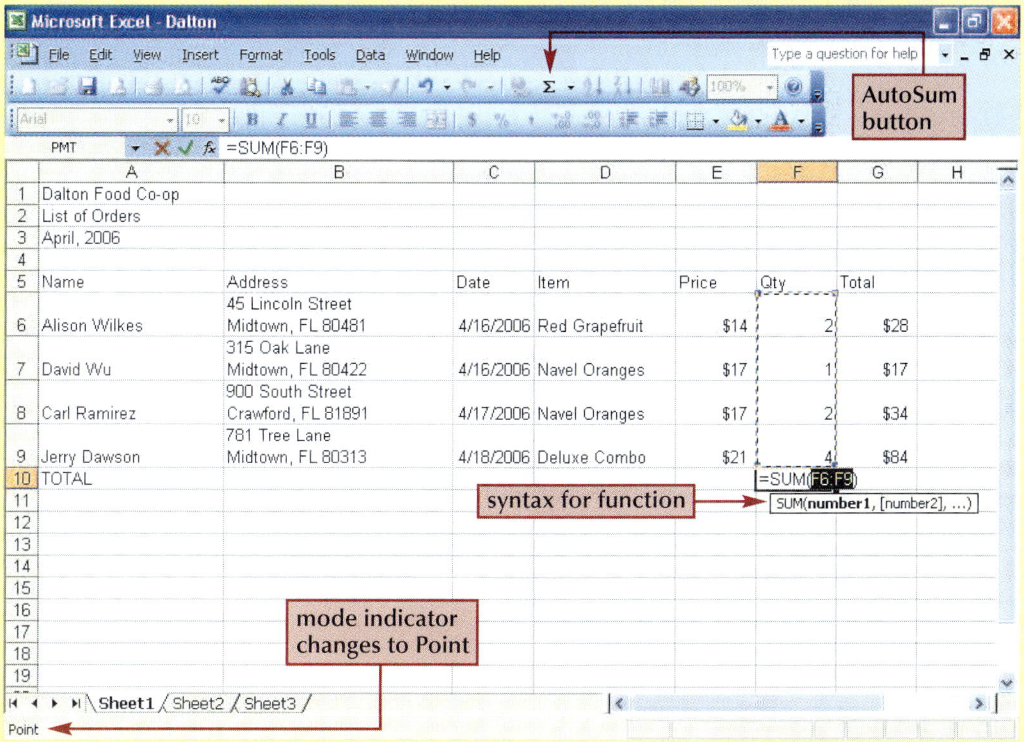

3. Press the **Tab** key to move to cell G10. The result of the formula *=SUM(F6:F9)* appears in cell F10, and you are in position to calculate the next set of values.

4. Click the **AutoSum** button Σ on the Standard toolbar to enter the SUM function in cell G10, and then press the **Enter** key to complete the formula *=SUM(G6:G9)*, accepting the range that Excel highlighted. See Figure 1-26. Nine items were sold, for a total of $163.

Calculating the total quantity and total income for the co-op — **Figure 1-26**

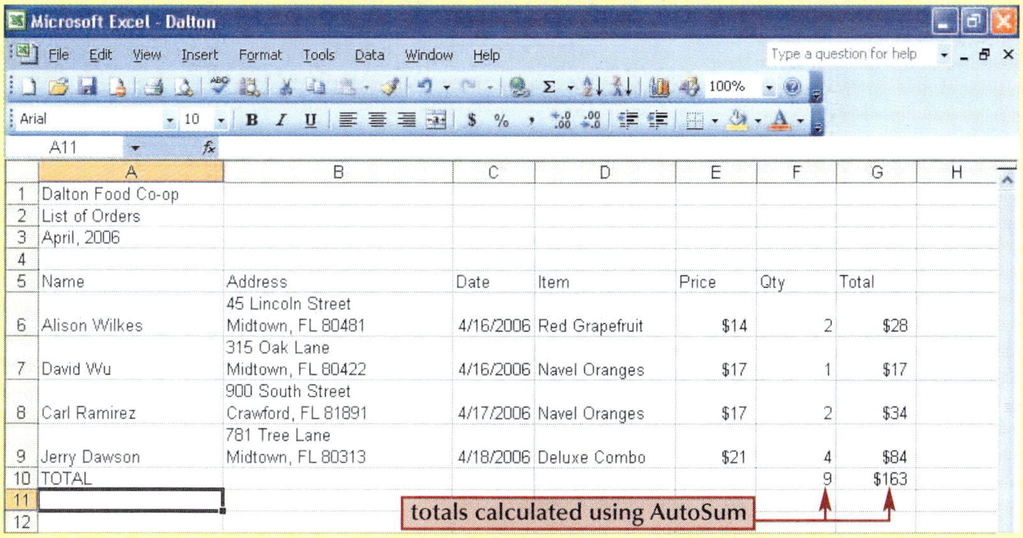

You can use AutoSum to calculate other summary values, such as the average, minimum, maximum, and total number of items in a cell range. You will learn more about using AutoSum to summarize values in Tutorial 2.

Working with Rows and Columns

Sandra has received a new order that she wants you to add to her worksheet. She wants to insert the new order right after Jerry Dawson's order, but wants to make sure the row containing the total values is still the last row. To do this, you need to insert a new row into the worksheet between row 9 and row 10.

Inserting a Row or Column

You can insert rows and columns in a worksheet, or you can insert individual cells within a row or column. When you insert rows, Excel shifts the existing rows down. When you insert columns, Excel shifts the existing columns to the right. If you insert cells within a row, Excel shifts the existing cells down; if you insert cells within a column, Excel shifts the existing cells to the right. Figure 1-27 illustrates what happens when you insert a row, a column, and cells within a row and within a column.

Figure 1-27 Inserting new rows and columns

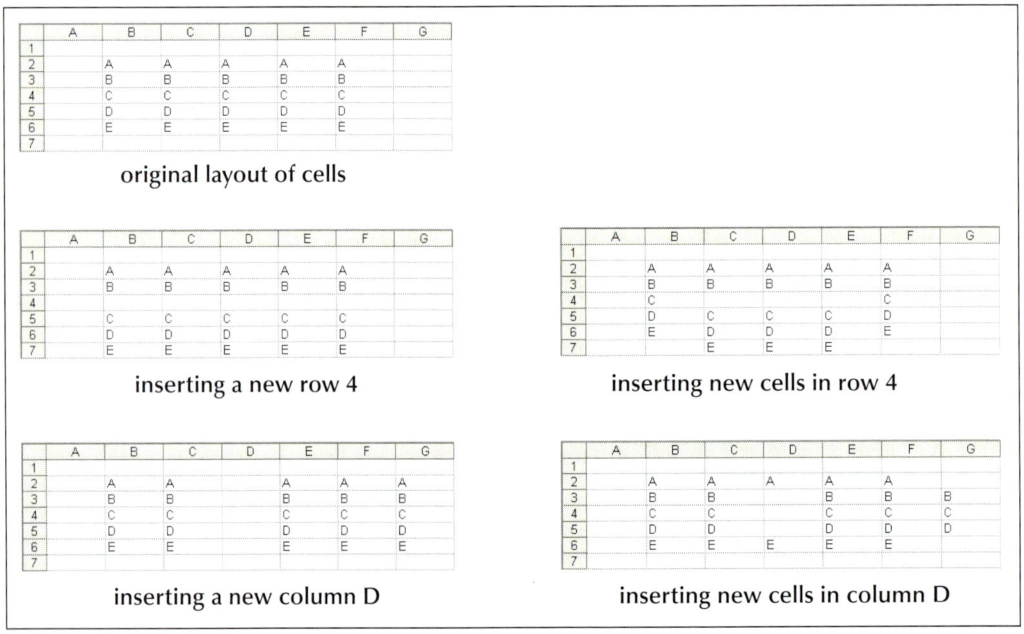

You can use the Insert menu to insert cells, rows, and columns. You can also use the right-click method to display a shortcut menu that provides the Insert command, which opens the Insert dialog box.

Inserting a Row or Column into a Worksheet

Reference Window

- Select a cell where you want to insert the new row or column.
- Click Insert on the menu bar, and then click Rows or Columns.

or

- Right-click a cell where you want to insert a new row or column, and then click Insert on the shortcut menu.
- In the Insert dialog box, click the Entire row or Entire column option button, and then click the OK button.

To insert multiple rows or columns, you select a cell range that contains multiple rows or columns before applying the Insert command. For example, to insert two new blank rows, select two rows or any portion of two rows. To insert three blank columns, select three columns or any portion of three columns.

Sometimes you might need to insert individual cells, rather than an entire row or column, into a worksheet. To insert cells into a row or column, you must select the number of cells you want to insert, and then open the Insert dialog box. In this dialog box you indicate how Excel should shift the existing cells to accommodate the cells you want to insert.

Inserting Cells into a Worksheet

Reference Window

- Select a cell range equal to the number of cells you want to insert.
- Click Insert on the menu bar, and then click Cells; or right-click the selected range, and then click Insert on the shortcut menu.
- Click the Shift cells right option button to insert the new cells into the row, or click the Shift cells down button to insert the new cells into the column.

Sandra wants the data for the new order to be entered above the TOTAL row, row 10. You'll use the right-click method to insert a new row 10, and then you'll enter the data.

To insert a new row 10:

1. Right-click cell **A10**, which is where you want to insert the new row.
2. Click **Insert** on the shortcut menu. The Insert dialog box opens. See Figure 1-28.

Figure 1-28 Insert dialog box

3. Click the **Entire row** option button, and then click the **OK** button. Excel inserts a new row 10 and shifts the calculations of the total values down one row.
4. Enter the data for Karen Paulson's order into row 10, as shown in Figure 1-29. Make sure that you press the Tab key to move from cell to cell and press the Alt + Enter keys to enter the address on two lines within cell B10.

Figure 1-29 Data entered in the new row 10

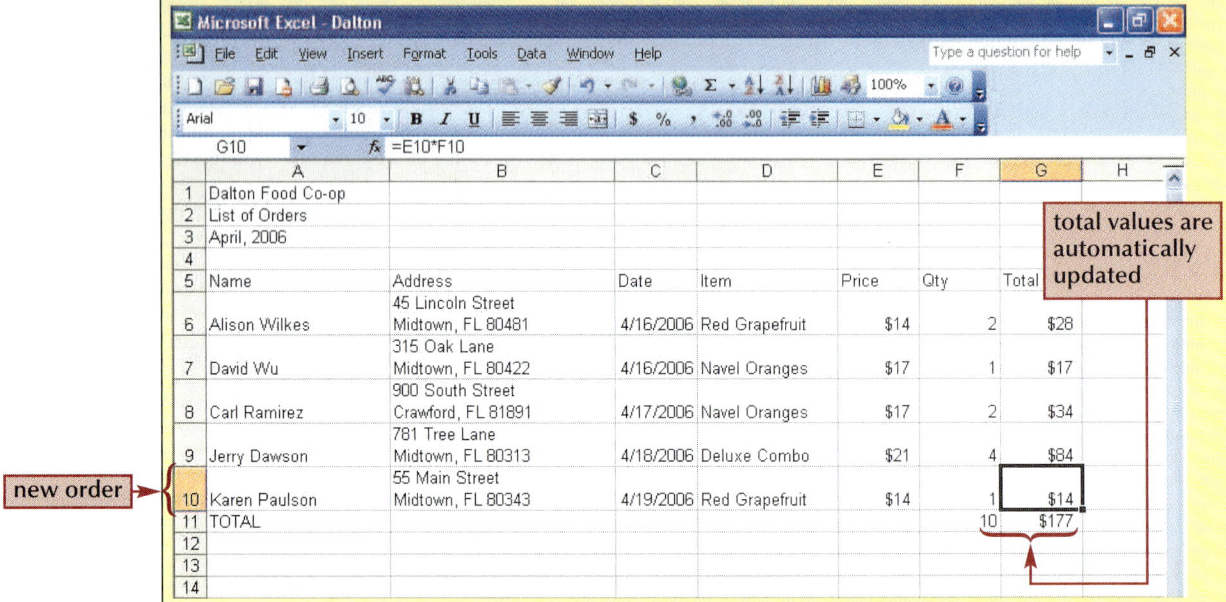

Note that Excel automatically inserts the formula *=E10*F10* into cell G10 for you. Excel recognizes that you are inserting a new set of values into a list of values and assumes that you intend to use the same formulas for the new order that you used for the previous ones. Also note that the calculations of the total quantity of items ordered and the total revenue from those orders have been updated. The functions now calculate the sums in the cell ranges F6:F10 and G6:G10. You'll learn more about how such formulas are automatically adjusted by Excel in the next tutorial.

Deleting a Row or Column

Sandra has also learned that David Wu has canceled his co-op order. You have two options for removing data from a worksheet. If you simply want to erase the contents of a cell, you can **clear** the cell, without actually removing the cell from the worksheet. If you want to remove not only the contents of the cells from the worksheet, but also the cells themselves, you can **delete** a cell range, and Excel then shifts the contents of the adjacent cells into the location of the deleted cells.

To clear the contents of a cell or range of cells, you select the range and then select the Clear command on the Edit menu or on the shortcut menu that you display by right-clicking the selection. Pressing the Delete key on the keyboard also clears the contents of the selected cells, without removing the cells themselves. To delete cells and their contents, you select the range and then choose the Delete command on the Edit menu, or right-click the selected cells, and click Delete on the shortcut menu. To adjust the adjacent cells, Excel opens the Delete Cells dialog box, which you can select to shift the remaining cells left or up, or choose to delete the entire row.

Because David Wu has canceled his order, you'll delete it from the worksheet.

To delete the row that contains David Wu's order:

1. Click the row heading for row **7**, which contains the data you want to delete.
2. Click **Edit** on the menu bar, and then click **Delete**. Excel deletes the row and shifts the next row up. See Figure 1-30. The total calculations in cells F10 and G10 are automatically updated to reflect the fact that David Wu's order has been deleted.

Deleting a row from the worksheet | **Figure 1-30**

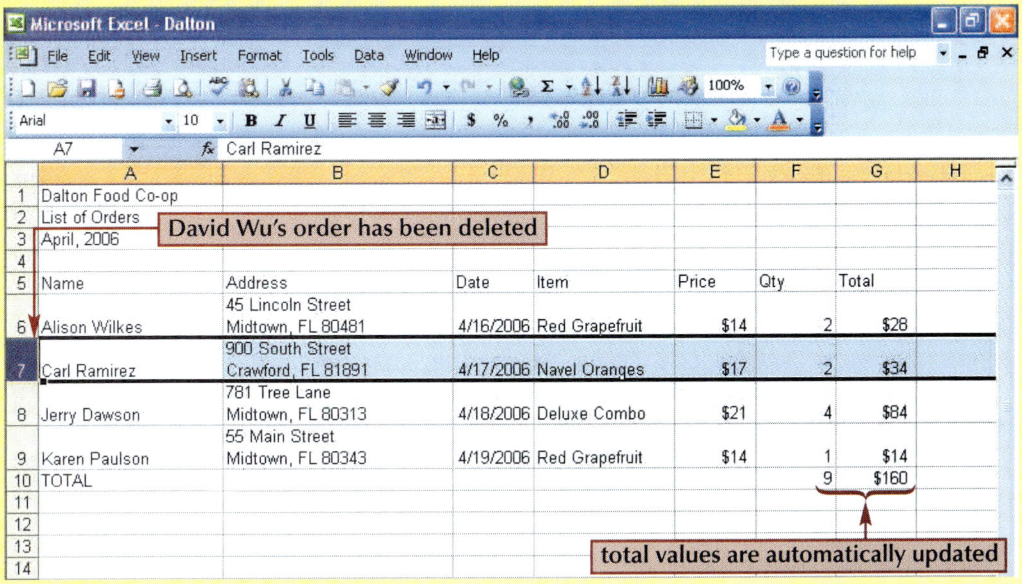

Editing Your Worksheet

When you work in Excel, you might make mistakes that you want to correct or undo. Sandra has noticed such a mistake in the Dalton workbook. The price for the Deluxe Combo box should be $23, not $21. You could simply clear the value in cell E8 and then type the correct value. However, there may be times when you will not want to change the entire contents of a cell, but merely edit a portion of the entry, especially if the cell contains a large block of text or a complicated formula. To edit the cell contents, you need to work in **edit mode**.

When you are working in edit mode, some of the keyboard shortcuts you've been using perform differently. For example, the Home, Delete, Backspace, and End keys do not move the insertion point to different cells in the worksheet; rather they move the insertion point to different locations within the cell. The Home key, for example, moves the insertion point to the beginning of whatever content has been entered into the cell. The End key moves the insertion point to the end of the cell's content. The left and right arrow keys move the insertion point backward and forward through the cell's content. The Backspace key deletes the character immediately to the left of the insertion point, and the Delete key deletes the character to the right of the insertion point.

Reference Window

Editing a Cell

- Switch to edit mode by double-clicking the cell, clicking the cell and pressing the F2 key, or clicking the cell and then clicking in the Formula bar.
- Use the Home, End, ←, or → keys to move the insertion point within the cell's content, or use the Delete and Backspace keys to erase characters.
- Press the Enter key when finished, or if you are working in the Formula bar, click the Enter button.

You'll switch to edit mode and then change the value in cell E8.

To edit the value in cell E8:

1. Double-click cell **E8**. Note that the mode indicator in the status bar switches from Ready to Edit. Also note that the value 21 appears in the cell, not $21. This is because the cell contains a numeric value, not a text string. The dollar sign ($) is used to format the value. You'll learn more about formats in Tutorial 3.
2. Press the **End** key to move the blinking insertion point to the end of the cell.
3. Press the **Backspace** key once to delete the 1 character, type **3** to update the value, and then press the **Enter** key to accept the change. The value $23 appears in cell E8, and the total amount of this order in cell G8 changes to $92. Note that the mode indicator on the status bar switches back to Ready.

If you make a mistake as you type in edit mode, you can press the Esc key or click the Cancel button on the Formula bar to cancel all changes you made while in edit mode.

Undoing an Action

As you revise your worksheet, you may find that you need to undo one of your changes. To undo an action, click the Undo button on the Standard toolbar. As you work, Excel maintains a list of your actions, so you can undo most of the actions you perform in your workbook during the current session. To reverse more than one action, click the list arrow next to the Undo button and click the action you want to undo from the list. To see how this works, you'll use the Undo button to remove the edit you just made to cell E8.

To undo your last action:

1. Click the **Undo** button on the Standard toolbar. The value $21 appears again in cell E8, indicating that your last action, editing the value in this cell, has been undone.

If you find that you have gone too far in undoing your previous actions, you can go forward in the action list and redo those actions. To redo an action, you click the Redo button on the Standard toolbar. Now you'll use the Redo button to return the value in cell E8 to $23.

To redo your last action:

1. Click the **Redo** button on the Standard toolbar. The value in cell E8 changes back to $23.

Through the use of edit mode and the Undo and Redo buttons, you should be able to correct almost any mistake you make in your Excel workbook. The Undo and Redo commands are also available on the Edit menu or by using the shortcut keys Ctrl + Z, to undo an action, and Ctrl + Y, to redo an action.

Working with Worksheets

By default, Excel workbooks contain three worksheets, labeled Sheet1, Sheet2, and Sheet3. You can add new worksheets or remove old ones. You can also give your worksheets more descriptive names. In the Dalton workbook, there is no data entered in the Sheet2 or Sheet3 worksheets. Sandra suggests that you remove these sheets from the workbook.

Adding and Removing Worksheets

To delete a worksheet, you first select its sheet tab to make the worksheet the active sheet; then right-click the sheet tab and choose Delete from the shortcut menu. Try this now by deleting the Sheet2 and Sheet3 worksheets.

To delete the Sheet2 and Sheet3 worksheets:

1. Click the **Sheet2** tab to make Sheet2 the active sheet.
2. Right-click the sheet tab, and then click **Delete** on the shortcut menu. Sheet2 is deleted and Sheet3 becomes the active sheet.
3. Right-click the **Sheet3** tab, and then click **Delete**. There is now only one worksheet in the workbook.

After you delete the two unused sheets, Sandra informs you that she wants to include a description of the workbook's content and purpose. In other words, Sandra wants to include a **documentation sheet**, a worksheet that provides information about the content and purpose of the workbook. A documentation sheet can be any information that you feel is important, for example, the name of the person who created the workbook or instructions on how to use the workbook. A documentation sheet is a valuable element if you intend to share the workbook with others. The documentation sheet is often the first worksheet in the workbook, though in this case, Sandra wants to place it at the end of the workbook.

To insert a new worksheet, you can either use the Worksheet command on the Insert menu or the right-click method. Both methods insert a new worksheet *before* the active sheet.

To insert a new worksheet in the workbook:

1. Click **Insert** on the menu bar, and then click **Worksheet**. A new worksheet with the name "Sheet4" is placed at the beginning of your workbook. Your worksheet might be named Sheet2 or another name.

Sandra wants the documentation sheet to include the following information:

- The name of the co-op
- The date that this workbook was originally created
- The person who created the workbook
- The purpose of the workbook

You'll add this information to the new sheet in the Dalton workbook.

To insert the documentation information in the new worksheet:

1. Click cell **A1**, if necessary, type **Dalton Food Co-op**, and then press the **Enter** key twice.
2. Type **Date:** in cell A3, and then press the **Tab** key.
3. Enter the *current date* in cell B3, and then press the **Enter** key.
4. Type **Created By:** in cell A4, and then press the **Tab** key.
5. Enter *your name* in cell B4, and then press the **Enter** key.
6. Type **Purpose:** in cell A5, and then press the **Tab** key.
7. Type **To enter orders for the Dalton Food Co-op** in cell B5, and then press the **Enter** key.
8. Increase the width of column A to **15** characters (**110** pixels). Figure 1-31 shows the completed documentation sheet.

Figure 1-31 Completed documentation sheet

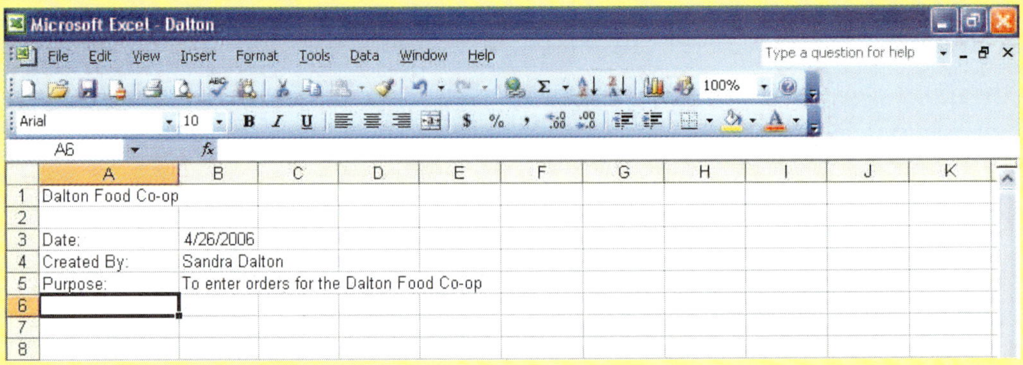

Renaming a Worksheet

The current sheet names, "Sheet4" and "Sheet1," are not very descriptive. Sandra suggests that you rename Sheet4 "Documentation" and Sheet1 "Orders." To rename a worksheet, you double-click the sheet tab to select the sheet name, and then you type a new name for the sheet. Sheet names cannot exceed 31 characters in length, including blank spaces.

To rename the worksheets:

1. Double-click the **Sheet4** tab. Note that the name of the sheet is selected.
2. Type **Documentation** and then press the **Enter** key. The width of the sheet tab adjusts to the length of the name you type.
3. Double-click the **Sheet1** tab.
4. Type **Orders** and then press the **Enter** key. Both worksheets are renamed.

Moving a Worksheet

You can change the placement of the worksheets in the workbook. To move the position of a worksheet in the workbook, click the sheet tab and then drag and drop it to a new location relative to the other worksheets. You can also make a copy of a worksheet using a similar drag-and-drop technique. To create a copy of a worksheet, press the Ctrl key as you drag and drop the sheet tab of the worksheet you want duplicated.

Moving or Copying a Worksheet

Reference Window

- Click the sheet tab of the worksheet you want to move (or copy).
- Drag the sheet tab along the row of sheet tabs until the small arrow appears in the new location. To create a copy of the worksheet, press and hold the Ctrl key as you drag the sheet tab to the new location.
- Release the mouse button. Release the Ctrl key if necessary.

Try this now by switching the location of the Documentation and Orders worksheets.

To reposition the worksheets:

1. Click the **Orders** tab, and then press and hold the left mouse button so the pointer changes to and a small arrow appears in the upper-left corner of the tab.
2. Drag the pointer to the left of the sheet tab for the Documentation sheet, and then release the mouse button. The Documentation sheet is now the second sheet in the workbook, but Sandra would prefer that the documentation sheet be the first sheet.
3. Click the **Orders** tab, and then drag the sheet tab to the right of the Documentation sheet tab to place it back in its original location.

When you create a copy of a worksheet, you move the copy of the original worksheet to a new location, while the original sheet remains at its initial position.

Using the Spell Checker

One of Excel's editing tools is the **Spell Checker**. This feature checks the words in the workbook against the program's internal dictionary. If the Spell Checker comes across a word not in its dictionary, it displays the word in a dialog box along with a list of suggested replacements. You can replace the word with one from the list, or you can choose to ignore the word and go to the next word that might be misspelled. You can also add the word to the dictionary to prevent it from being flagged in the future. There are words that are not included in the online dictionary (for example, some uncommon personal names or last names). The Spell Checker will stop at these words. You can then choose to ignore all occurrences of the word, change the word, or add the word to the dictionary. Excel checks the spelling on the current worksheet only.

To see how the Spell Checker works, you'll make an intentional spelling error in the Orders worksheet.

To check the spelling in the Orders sheet:

1. Make sure the Orders sheet is the active sheet, and then click cell **G5**. You will enter the error in this cell.
2. Type **Totale** and then click cell **A1**. The Spell Checker always starts at the active cell in the worksheet. You can start from other cells, and the Spell Checker will cycle back to the first cell in the worksheet to continue checking each cell for spelling errors. However, you will find it helpful and more efficient to begin spell checking with the first cell in the sheet, cell A1.
3. Click the **Spelling** button on the Standard toolbar. The Spelling dialog box opens, with the first word that the spell checker does not recognize, "Totale." See Figure 1-32.

Figure 1-32 Spelling dialog box

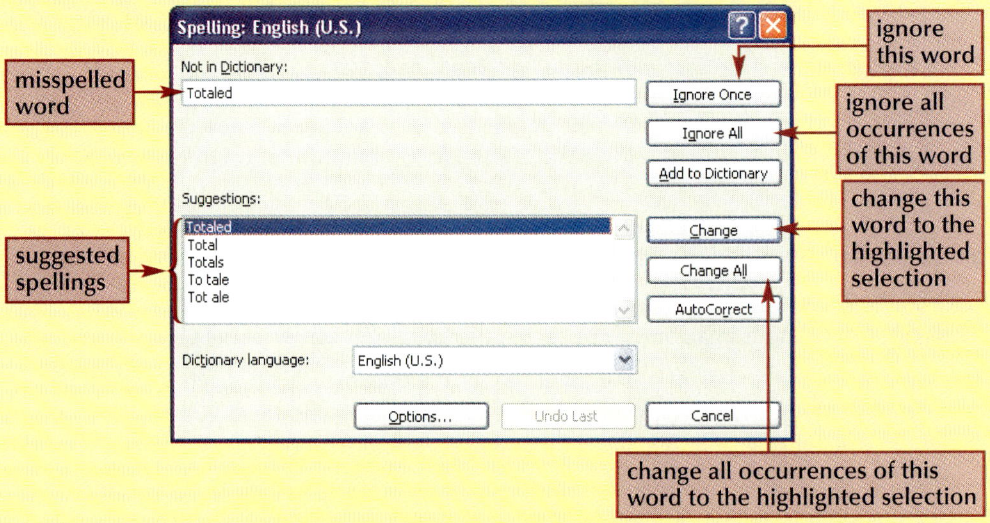

4. Click **Total** in the list of suggestions, and then click the **Change** button. The word "Totale" changes to "Total," and then Spell Checker continues to look for other potential spelling errors. There shouldn't be any other errors in this workbook.

   Trouble? If there are any other errors (you may have misspelled a name, address, or item), fix them before continuing to the next step.
5. Click the **OK** button to close the Spell Checker.

Previewing and Printing a Worksheet

Sandra would like a printed hard copy of the Dalton workbook for her records. You can print the contents of your workbook either by using the Print command on the File menu or by clicking the Print button on the Standard toolbar. If you use the Print command, Excel opens the Print dialog box in which you can specify which worksheets you want to print, the number of copies, and the print quality. If you click the Print button, your worksheet will print using the options already set in the Print dialog box. If you want to change a setting, you must open the Print dialog box using the File menu.

Before sending a worksheet to the printer, you should preview how the worksheet will appear as a printed page. You can display the worksheet in the Print Preview window either by selecting the Print Preview command on the File menu or by clicking the Print Preview button on the Standard toolbar. You can also click the Preview button in the Print dialog box. Previewing the printout is a helpful way to avoid printing errors.

If you are printing to a shared printer on a network, other people might be sending print jobs at the same time you do. To avoid confusion, you will print the contents of both the Documentation sheet and the Orders sheet. You will use the Print command on the File menu because you need to print the entire workbook and not just the active worksheet (which is the default print setting).

To open the Print dialog box:

1. Click **File** on the menu bar, and then click **Print** to open the Print dialog box.
2. Click the **Name** list box, and then select the printer to which you want to print, if it is not already selected.

   Now you need to select what to print. To print the complete workbook, select the Entire workbook option button. To print the active worksheet, select the Active sheet(s) option button. To print the selected cells on the active sheet, click the Selection option button.
3. Click the **Entire workbook** option button.
4. Make sure **1** appears in the Number of copies list box, since you only need to print one copy of the workbook. Figure 1-33 shows the Print dialog box.

Figure 1-33 **Print dialog box**

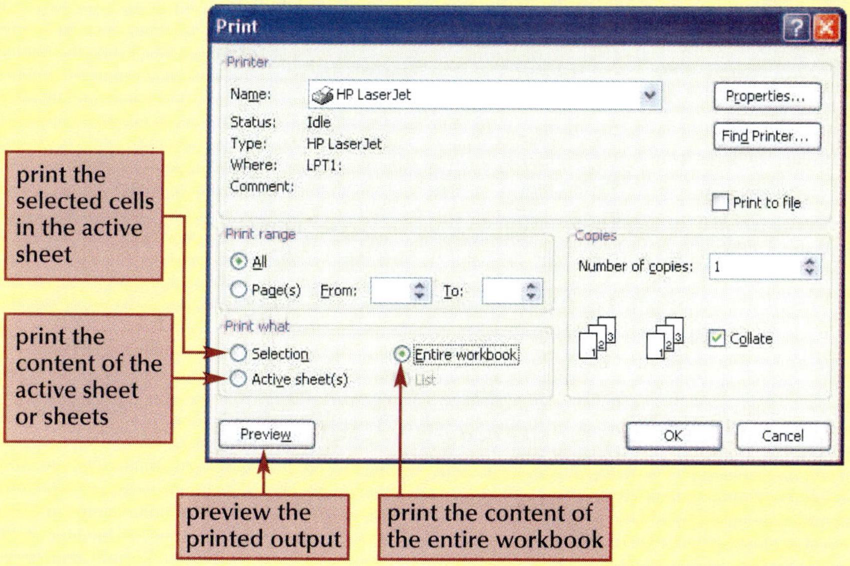

Next you will preview the worksheet to ensure that it looks correct before printing it.

To preview the workbook before printing it:

1. Click the **Preview** button in the Print dialog box. Excel displays a preview of the first full page of the worksheet, in this case the Documentation sheet, as it will appear printed. As you can see from the status bar in Figure 1-34, this is the first of three pages.

   Trouble? If the status bar on your screen indicates that there are just two pages, you can still complete the steps.

Figure 1-34 Print Preview window

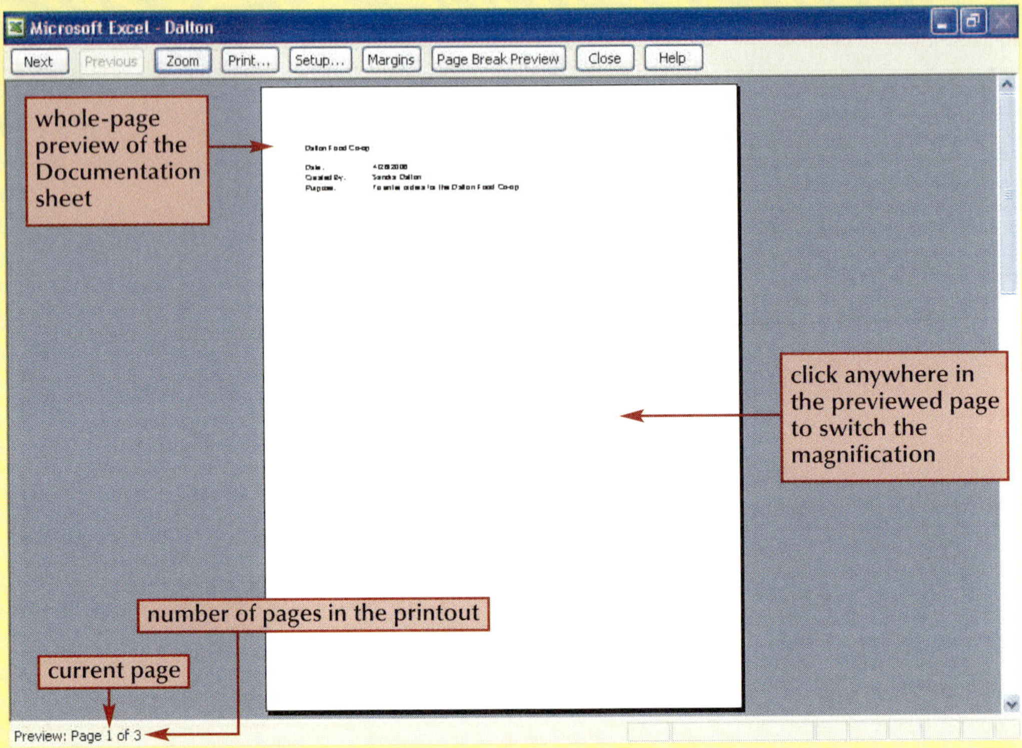

2. Click the **Next** button on the Print Preview toolbar to move to the next page in the preview. On this page you see part of the Orders worksheet, but it is difficult to read because the text is so small. To better see the content of the printed page, you can click the preview page to switch between a magnified view and a whole-page view.
3. Click anywhere within the previewed page with the pointer to increase the magnification, and click again to reduce the magnification.

Working with Portrait and Landscape Orientation

Not all of the Orders worksheet is displayed in the Print Preview window. The last column in the sheet, which displays the total amount of each order, has been cut off and is displayed on the third page of the printout. Naturally Sandra wants all of the information on a single sheet, but the problem is that the page is not wide enough to display all of this information. One way of solving this problem is to change the orientation of the page. There are two types of page orientations: portrait and landscape. In **portrait orientation** the page is taller than it is wide. In **landscape orientation** the page is wider than it is tall. In many cases, you will want to print your worksheets in landscape orientation. You'll choose this option for the Orders worksheet.

To print in landscape orientation:

1. Click the **Setup** button on the Print Preview toolbar. The Page Setup dialog box opens.
2. Verify that the Page tab is selected in the dialog box, and then click the **Landscape** option button. See Figure 1-35.

Figure 1-35 Print Setup dialog box

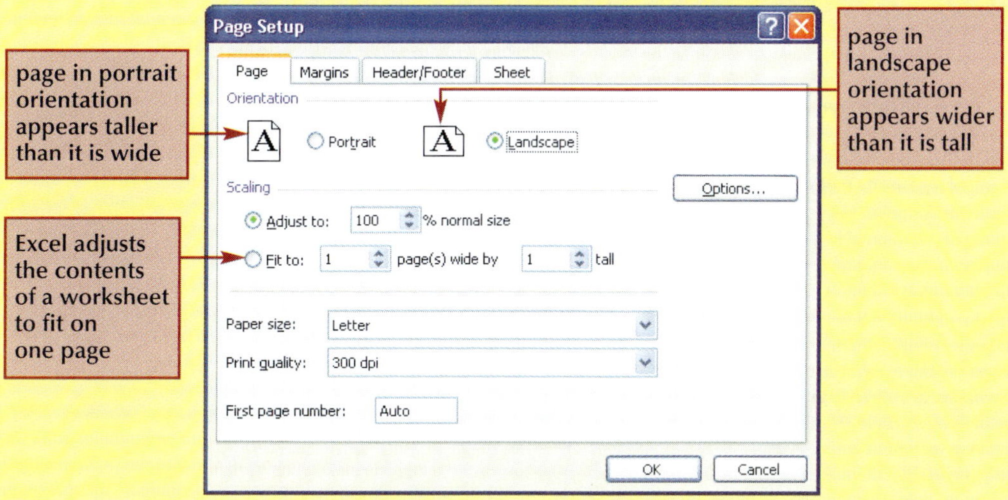

3. Click the **OK** button to close the Page Setup dialog box.
4. If necessary, click anywhere within the previewed page to switch the magnification back to a whole-page view. As shown in Figure 1-36, the entire Orders worksheet is now displayed on the second (and last) page of this printout.

Figure 1-36 Orders sheet in landscape orientation

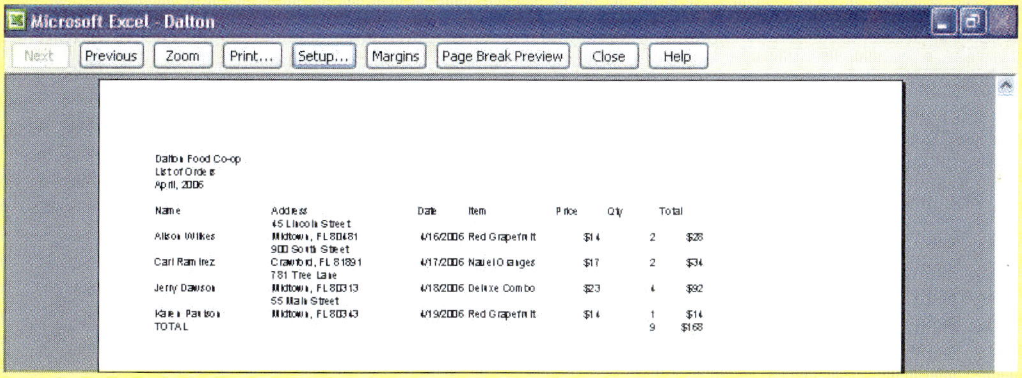

5. Click the **Print** button on the Print Preview toolbar to print the workbook and close the Print Preview window.

Note that the Documentation sheet is printed in portrait orientation, whereas the Orders worksheet is printed in landscape orientation. Changing the orientation only affects the worksheet currently displayed in the Print Preview window; it does not apply to other sheets in the workbook.

Printing the Worksheet Formulas

Sandra examines the printout and notices that none of the formulas are displayed. This is to be expected since most of the time you're only interested in the final results and not the formulas used to calculate those results. In some cases, you will want to view the formulas used in developing your workbook. This is particularly useful in situations where the results were not what you expected, and you want to examine the formulas to see if a mistake has been made. To switch to **Formula view** in your workbook, you can press the keyboard shortcut Ctrl + grave accent (`). Try this now for the Orders worksheet.

To view the worksheet formulas:

1. With the Orders worksheet active, press the **Ctrl + `** (grave accent) keys and then scroll the worksheet to the left so columns F and G are visible. (Make sure you press the grave accent key (`) and not the single quotation mark key ('). The grave accent key is usually located above the Tab key on your keyboard.) Excel displays the formulas in columns F and G. See Figure 1-37.

Figure 1-37 Viewing the worksheet formulas

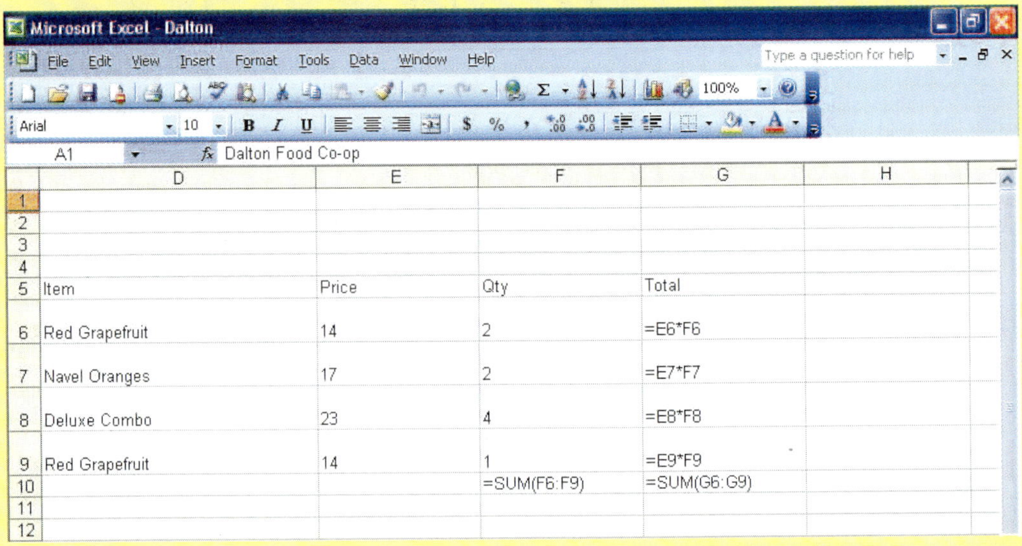

Trouble? If the Formula Auditing toolbar appears, close the toolbar.

Note that the column widths have been changed. Excel does this automatically to ensure that the entire formula can be displayed within each cell. These changed column widths will not affect the normal view of your worksheet as long as you don't change the column widths while in Formula view.

Sandra asks you to print a copy of the worksheet with the formulas displayed. First, you'll preview the worksheet.

2. Click the **Print Preview** button on the Standard toolbar. Excel displays a preview of the Orders worksheet in Formula view. Not all of the contents of the worksheet in this view are displayed on a single page. To fit the printout to a single page, you will change the setup of the page using the Page Setup dialog box.
3. Click the **Setup** button on the Print Preview toolbar. The Page Setup dialog box opens.
4. Click the **Fit to** option button to fit the Orders worksheet on one page, and then click the **OK** button. The Formula view of the Orders worksheet should now fit on a single page.
5. Click the **Print** button on the Print Preview toolbar to print the worksheet and close the Print Preview window.

   Trouble? If the Print Preview window closes and the Print dialog box opens, click the OK button to print the worksheet.

As you may have noticed while you were working in Print Preview and the Page Setup dialog box, there are a lot of options for choosing what to print and how to print. You'll examine more of these options in Tutorial 3. For now, you can switch the Orders worksheet back to Normal view and save and then close the file.

To complete your work:

1. Press the **Ctrl +`** (grave accent) keys to switch the worksheet back to Normal view. The keyboard shortcut Ctrl + ` (grave accent) works as a toggle, so you can display or hide the formulas by pressing this combination of keys.
2. Save your changes to the Dalton workbook, and then close it.

You give Sandra the hard copy of the Dalton workbook. If she needs to add new information to the workbook or if she needs you to make further changes to the structure of the workbook, she'll contact you.

Session 1.2 Quick Check

Review

1. Describe the two types of cell ranges in Excel.
2. How do you write the cell reference for the rectangular group of cells that extends from cell A5 through cell F8?
3. The ______________ button provides a quick way to enter the SUM function.
4. When you insert a new row into a worksheet, the existing rows are shifted ______________.
5. When you insert a new column into a worksheet, the existing columns are shifted ______________.
6. How do you change the name of a worksheet?
7. How does clearing a cell differ from deleting a cell?
8. What keyboard shortcut do you press to display the worksheet formulas?

Tutorial Summary

Review

In this tutorial, you learned the basics of spreadsheets and Excel. You learned about the major components of the Excel window. You also learned how to navigate within a worksheet and between worksheets in an Excel workbook. You learned how to enter text, dates, values, and formulas into a worksheet and were introduced to functions using the AutoSum button. Within the workbook, you practiced selecting and moving cell ranges. You saw how to insert new rows and columns into a workbook and how to modify the size of a column or row. You learned how to create new worksheets, rename them, and move them around the workbook. You learned how to check the spelling in a workbook, and finally, you learned how to print the contents of a workbook in different orientations and how to print the formulas in that workbook.

Key Terms

active cell
adjacent range
argument
arithmetic operator
AutoComplete
AutoSum
cell
cell range
cell reference
clear
column
delete
documentation sheet
edit mode
formula
Formula bar
Formula view
function
landscape orientation
Name box
nonadjacent range
order of precedence
portrait orientation
range
range reference
row
sheet
sheet tab
Spell Checker
spreadsheet
SUM function
tab scrolling buttons
value
what-if analysis
workbook
workbook window
worksheet
worksheet window

Practice

Practice the skills you learned in the tutorial using the same case scenario.

Review Assignments

There are no Data Files needed for the Review Assignments.

Sandra has another set of orders she wants you to enter into a new Excel workbook. The data is shown in Figure 1-38.

Figure 1-38

Name	Address	Date	Item	Price	Qty
Wendy Battle	313 Oak Street Midtown, FL 80481 (833) 555-1284	5/1/2006	Deluxe Combo	$23	2
Eugene Burch	25 Fourth Street Cabot, FL 81121 (833) 555-3331	5/1/2006	Red Grapefruit	$14	4
Nicole Sweeny	312 Olive Street Midtown, FL 81241 (833) 555-9811	5/3/2006	Deluxe Combo	$23	1
Amy Yang	315 Maple Street Midtown, FL 80440 (833) 555-3881	5/4/2006	Navel Oranges	$17	3

Note that Sandra has added the phone numbers of the customers to her data. She wants the phone numbers entered into the customer address cell, but on a different line within that cell. To complete this task:

1. Start Excel and open a blank workbook. In the range A1:F5, enter the labels and data from Figure 1-38. Make sure that the address information is inserted with the street address on the first line; the city, state, and ZIP code on the second line; and the phone number on the third line.
2. In cell G1, enter the label "Total."
3. In the cells below G1, enter formulas to calculate the total amount of each order.
4. In cell A6, enter the label "TOTAL."

5. In cell F6, use the AutoSum button to calculate the total quantity of items ordered, and in cell G6, use the AutoSum button to calculate the total revenue generated by these orders.
6. Move sales data from the range A1:G6 to the range A5:G10.
7. In cell A1, enter the text "Dalton Food Co-op." In cell A2, enter the text "List of Orders." In cell A3, enter the text "May, 2006."
8. Change the width of columns A and B to 20 characters (or 145 pixels) each. Change the width of column D to 15 characters (or 110 pixels). Change the width of column G to 10 characters (or 75 pixels).
9. Select all of the cells in the worksheet, and then reduce the amount of empty space in the rows by reducing the row height to the height of the data contained in the rows.
10. Change the name of the worksheet to "Orders".
11. Create a worksheet named "Documentation" at the beginning of the workbook and, in the Documentation sheet, enter the following:
    - Cell A1: Dalton Food Co-op
    - Cell A3: Date:
    - Cell B3: *current date*
    - Cell A4: Created By:
    - Cell B4: *your name*
    - Cell A5: Purpose:
    - Cell B5: To enter May orders for the Dalton Food Co-op
12. Increase the width of column A in the Documentation worksheet to 20 characters.
13. Check the spelling on both worksheets, correcting any errors found.
14. Delete any empty worksheets from the workbook.
15. Print the contents of the workbook with the Documentation sheet in portrait orientation and the Orders worksheet in landscape orientation.
16. Display the formulas in the Orders worksheet. Preview the worksheet before printing it, and set up the worksheet to print as a single page.
17. Save the workbook as **Dalton2** in the Tutorial.01\Review folder included with your Data Files.
18. Insert the following new order in the Orders worksheet directly below Amy Yang's order:
    - Name: Chad Reynolds
    - Address: 100 School Lane
Midtown, FL 80411
(833) 555-4425
    - Date: 5/5/2006
    - Item: Navel Oranges
    - Price: $17
    - Qty: 2
19. Remove Amy Yang's order from the worksheet, and change the quantity ordered by Eugene Burch from 4 to 3.
20. Check the spelling in the Orders worksheet again, correcting any errors found.
21. Print the contents and formulas of the Orders worksheet again.
22. Save the workbook as **Dalton3** in the Tutorial.01\Review folder, and then close the workbook.

Apply

Use the skills you have learned to create a cash flow analysis worksheet for a working couple.

Case Problem 1

Data File needed for this Case Problem: CFlow1.xls

Madison Federal Lisa Wu is a financial consultant at Madison Federal. She is working on a financial plan for Tom and Carolyn Watkins. Lisa has a cash flow analysis for the couple, and she wants you to record this information for her. Here are the relevant financial figures:

Receipts
- Employment Income: 95,000
- Other Income: 5,000

Disbursements
- Insurance: 940
- Savings/Retirement: 8,400
- Mortgage Payments: 18,000
- Children's Tuition: 10,000
- Groceries: 14,000
- Utilities: 6,000
- Other: 15,000
- Taxes: 16,300

Lisa wants you to calculate the total receipts and total disbursements and then calculate the cash surplus (receipts minus disbursements) in an Excel workbook that she has already started. To complete this task:

1. Open the **CFlow1** workbook located in the Tutorial.01\Cases folder included with your Data Files, and then save the workbook as **CFlow2** in the same folder.
2. Move the contents of the range A1:C16 to the range A5:C20.
3. Insert the text "Tom and Carolyn Watkins" in cell A1. In cell A2, insert the text "Cash Flow Analysis." In cell A3, insert the text "For the year 2006."
4. Increase the width of column A to 130 pixels, the width of column B to 160 pixels, and the width of column C to 130 pixels.
5. Insert the financial numbers listed earlier into the appropriate cells in column C.
6. Use the AutoSum button to calculate the total receipts and total disbursements, placing these values in cells C8 and C18, respectively.
7. Insert a formula to calculate the surplus in cell C20 (total receipts minus total disbursements).
8. Rename Sheet1 as "Cash Flow."
9. Insert a worksheet at the beginning of the workbook named "Documentation," and then enter the following information on the sheet:
   - Cell A1: Cash Flow Report
   - Cell A3: Date:
   - Cell B3: *current date*
   - Cell A4: Created By:
   - Cell B4: *your name*
   - Cell A5: Purpose:
   - Cell B5: Cash flow analysis for Tom and Carolyn Watkins
10. Increase the width of column A in the Documentation worksheet to 20 characters.
11. Delete any empty sheets in the workbook.
12. Use the Spell Checker to correct any spelling errors in the workbook.
13. Print the contents of the entire workbook in portrait orientation, and then save your changes to the workbook.

14. Change the couple's taxes to 18,500, and then print the Cash Flow worksheet with the recalculated values.
15. Save the workbook as **CFlow3** in the Tutorial.01\Cases folder, and then close the workbook.

Apply

Use the skills you have learned to create a balance sheet for a financial services company.

Case Problem 2

Data File needed for this Case Problem: Balance1.xls

EMS Industries Lee Evans is an agent at New Haven Financial Services. His job is to maintain financial information on investments for client companies. He has the balance sheet data for a company named EMS Industries in an Excel workbook and needs your help in finishing the workbook layout and contents. To complete this task:

1. Open the **Balance1** workbook located in the Tutorial.01\Cases folder included with your Data Files, and then save the workbook as **Balance2** in the same folder.
2. Select the range A1:C4, and then insert four new rows into the worksheet, shifting the selected cells down.
3. Enter the text "EMS Industries" in cell A1 and "Balance Sheet" in cell A2. In cell A3, enter the date "4/30/2006".
4. Increase the width of column A to 110 pixels.

Explore

5. Move the contents of the range A22:C32 to the range E5:G15, and then move the range A34:C38 to the range E20:G24.
6. Change the width of column B to 150 pixels, the width of column D to 20 pixels, and the width of column F to 240 pixels.
7. Use the AutoSum button to calculate the total current assets in cell C12; to calculate the total property, plant, and equipment assets in cell C18; to calculate the total current liabilities in cell G9; and to calculate the total long-term liabilities (only one value) in cell G13.
8. In cell C20, insert a formula to calculate the total of the current assets (cell C12) plus the noncurrent assets (cell C18). In cell G15, insert a formula to calculate the total of the current liabilities (cell G9) plus the long-term liabilities (cell G13).
9. In cell G23, enter a formula to calculate the total shareholders' equity, which is equal to the value of the common stock (cell G21) plus the value of retained earnings (cell G22). In cell G24, calculate the value of the total liabilities (cell G15) plus the shareholders' equity (cell G23).
10. Rename Sheet1 as "Balance Sheet," and then delete Sheet2 and Sheet3.
11. Insert a worksheet named "Documentation" at the front of the workbook, and then enter the following information into the sheet:
    - Cell A1: Balance Sheet
    - Cell A3: Company:
    - Cell B3: EMS Industries
    - Cell A4: Date:
    - Cell B4: *current date*
    - Cell A5: Recorded By:
    - Cell B5: *your name*
    - Cell A6: Purpose:
    - Cell B6: Balance Sheet
12. Increase the width of column A in the Documentation worksheet to 20 characters.
13. Use the Spell Checker to correct any spelling mistakes in the workbook.
14. Print the entire contents of the workbook in landscape orientation.
15. Save your changes to the workbook, and then close it.

Challenge

Challenge yourself by going beyond what you've learned to create a worksheet that calculates the weighted scores of four possible locations for a new shoe factory.

Case Problem 3

Data File needed for this Case Problem: Site1.xls

Kips Shoes Kips Shoes is planning to build a new factory. The company has narrowed the site down to four possible cities. Each city has been graded on a 1-to-10 scale for four categories: the size of the local market, the quality of the labor pool, the local tax base, and the local operating expenses. Each of these four factors is given a weight, with the most important factor given the highest weight. After the sites are analyzed, the scores for each factor will be multiplied by their weights, and then a total weighted score will be calculated.

Gwen Sanchez, the senior planning manager overseeing this project, has entered the weights and the scores for each city into an Excel workbook. She needs you to finish the workbook by inserting the formulas to calculate the weighted scores and the total overall score for each city. To complete this task:

1. Open the **Site1** workbook located in the Tutorial.01\Cases folder included with your Data Files, and then save the workbook as **Site2** in the same folder.
2. Switch to the Site Analysis sheet.
3. In cell B14, calculate the weighted Market Size score for Waukegan by inserting a formula that multiplies the value in cell B7 by the weight value in cell G7.
4. Insert formulas to calculate the weighted scores for the rest of the cells in the range B14:E17.
5. **Explore** Select the range B18:E18, and then click the AutoSum button to calculate the sum of the weighted scores for all four of the cities. Note that you can apply the AutoSum button to more than one cell at a time. Which city has the highest weighted score?
6. Switch to the Documentation sheet, and enter your name and the date in the appropriate locations on the sheet.
7. Spell check the workbook, print the entire workbook in portrait orientation, and then save your changes to the workbook.
8. **Explore** Gwen has another set of weighted scores she wants you to try. However, she doesn't want you to enter the new values in the Site Analysis worksheet, so you need to make a copy of the worksheet. To learn how to copy a worksheet, open the Excel Help task pane, and then enter "copy a worksheet" in the Search for text box. Scroll the list of topics in the Search Results task pane to locate the topic "Move or copy sheets." Open the topic, read the information about copying a sheet, and then close the Microsoft Excel Help window and the Search Results task pane.
9. **Explore** Using what you learned in Step 8, create a copy of the Site Analysis worksheet, placing the new worksheet at the end of the workbook. Rename the new sheet "Site Analysis 2".
10. In the Site Analysis 2 worksheet, change the weighted scores of Market Size to 0.2 and Labor Pool to 0.4. Which city has the highest weighted score now?
11. Print the contents of the Site Analysis 2 worksheet.
12. Save the workbook as **Site3** in the Tutorial.01\Cases folder, and then close the workbook.

Create

Use Figure 1-39, which shows the "end results," to create a workbook containing monthly budget figures over a three-month period for a college student.

Case Problem 4

There are no Data Files needed for this Case Problem.

Monthly Budget Alice Drake is a first-year student at MidWest University and has a part-time job in the admissions department. Her college-related expenses, such as tuition, books, and fees, are covered through grants and scholarships, so the money Alice makes goes towards her personal expenses. Being on her own for the first time, Alice is finding it difficult to keep within a budget. She has asked you to look at her finances and help her figure out how her money is being spent. Figure 1-39 shows the worksheet that you will create to help Alice analyze her budget.

Figure 1-39

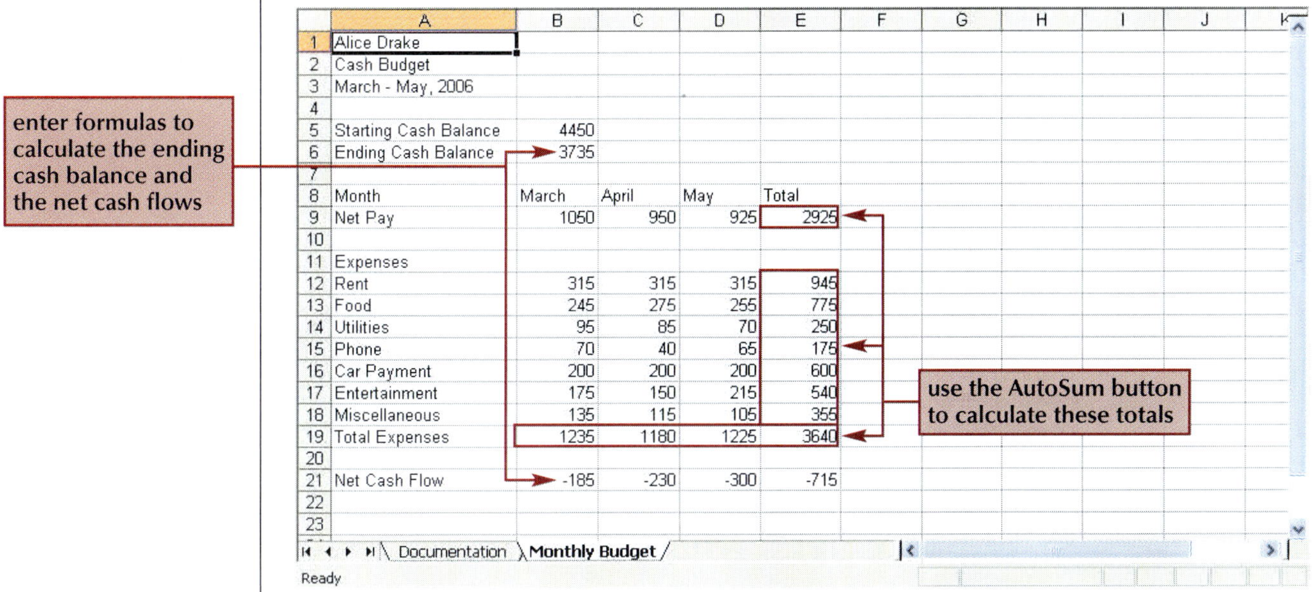

To complete this task:

1. Start Excel and save a new workbook with the name **Budget** in the Tutorial.01\Cases folder included with your Data Files.
2. On the Sheet1 worksheet, enter the labels and values as indicated in Figure 1-39. Note that the cells in which totals will be calculated have been marked. Do not enter the values shown; you will enter appropriate formulas next.
3. Using the AutoSum button, calculate the values for the total net pay, the total monthly expenses, and the total of each expense for the three months.
4. Enter formulas to calculate the net cash flow for each month and for all three months.
5. Enter a formula to calculate the ending cash balance, which is based on the value of the starting cash balance minus the total net cash flow over the three months. (*Hint:* Because two negatives make a positive, you need to *add* the total net cash flow to the starting cash balance.)
6. Rename Sheet1 as "Monthly Budget."
7. Create a worksheet named "Documentation" at the front of the workbook containing your name, the date, and the purpose of the workbook.
8. Delete any blank worksheets in the workbook.
9. Check the spelling on both worksheets, correcting any errors found.
10. Print the entire workbook in portrait orientation.
11. Save your changes to the workbook, and then close it.

Research

Use the Internet to find and work with data related to the topics presented in this tutorial.

Internet Assignments

The purpose of the Internet Assignments is to challenge you to find information on the Internet that you can use to work effectively with this software. The actual assignments are updated and maintained on the Course Technology Web site. Log on to the Internet and use your Web browser to go to the Student Online Companion for New Perspectives Office 2003 at **www.course.com/np/office2003**. Click the Internet Assignments link, and then navigate to the assignments for this tutorial.

Assess

SAM Assessment and Training

If you have a SAM user profile, you may have access to hands-on instruction, practice, and assessment of the skills covered in this tutorial. Log in to your SAM account and go to your assignments page to see what your instructor has assigned.

Reinforce

Lab Assignments

The New Perspectives Labs are designed to help you master some of the key concepts and skills presented in this text. The steps for completing this Lab are located on the Course Technology Web site. Log on to the Internet and use your Web browser to go to the Student Online Companion for New Perspectives Office 2003 at **www.course.com/np/office2003**. Click the Lab Assignments link, and then navigate to the assignments for this tutorial.

Review

Quick Check Answers

Session 1.1

1. cell
2. D2
3. Ctrl + Home
4. click the Sheet2 tab
5. a. value
   b. text
   c. value
   d. text (there is no equal sign indicating a formula)
   e. text
   f. formula
   g. text
6. Press the Alt + Enter keys to enter text on a new line within a cell.
7. =E5/E6

Session 1.2

1. An adjacent cell range is a rectangular block of cells. A non-adjacent cell range consists of two or more separate adjacent ranges.
2. A5:F8
3. AutoSum
4. down
5. to the right
6. Double-click the sheet tab and then type the new name to replace the highlighted sheet tab name.
7. Clearing a cell deletes the cell's contents but does not affect the position of other cells in the workbook. Deleting a cell removes the cell from the worksheet, and other cells are shifted in the direction of the deleted cell.
8. Ctrl + ` (grave accent)

Objectives

Session 2.1

- Learn about the syntax of an Excel function
- Use the SUM, AVERAGE, and MAX functions
- Copy and paste formulas
- Work with relative, absolute, and mixed references
- Change the magnification of the workbook window
- Insert a function using the Insert Function dialog box
- Use Auto Fill to insert formulas and complete a series
- Insert the current date using a Date function

Session 2.2 (Optional)

- Work with Financial functions
- Work with Logical functions

Working with Formulas and Functions

Developing a Family Budget

Case

Tyler Family Budget

As a newly married couple, Amanda and Joseph Tyler are trying to balance career, school, and family life. Amanda works full time as a legal assistant, and Joseph is in a graduate program at a nearby university. He recently was hired as a teaching assistant. In the summer, he is able to take on other jobs that bring additional income to the family. The couple also just moved into a new apartment. Although Joseph's and Amanda's salaries for the past year were greater than the years before, the couple seemed to have less cash on hand. This financial shortage has prompted them to take a closer look at their finances and figure out how to best manage them.

Because Amanda has agreed to take the lead role in the management of the family finances, she has set up an Excel workbook. Amanda has entered their salary amounts, which are their only income, and she has identified and entered several expenses that the family pays on a monthly basis, such as the rent and Joseph's tuition. She wants to calculate how much money they bring in and how much money they spend. She also wants to figure out their average monthly expenses and identify their greatest financial burden.

Amanda has asked for your help in completing the workbook. She wants you to insert formulas to perform the calculations she needs to get a better overall picture of the family's finances, which, in turn, should help the couple manage their money more effectively. Because the values entered cover a 12-month span, you will be able to copy and paste the formulas from one month to another and fill in series of data, such as the months of the year, rather than retyping formulas or entering each month individually. Finally, Amanda also wants the current date in her workbook, which you can enter using one of Excel's Date functions.

Student Data Files

▼Tutorial.02

▽ Tutorial folder
Budget1.xls

▽ Review folder
Family1.xls

▽ Cases folder
Sonic1.xls
Soup1.xls
Stock1.xls

Once she has a better handle on the family's finances, Amanda might want to evaluate whether buying a house would be possible in the near future, especially in light of the low interest rates that are available.

Session 2.1

Working with Excel Functions

In her budget worksheet, Amanda has already entered the couple's take-home salaries (that is, the amount of money in their paychecks minus taxes and other work-related deductions) and their expenses from the past year. You'll begin by opening her workbook so you can see what Amanda has done so far.

To open Amanda's workbook:

1. Start Excel and then open the **Budget1** workbook located in the Tutorial.02\Tutorial folder included with your Data Files.
2. On the Documentation sheet, enter *your name* in cell B3 and the *current date* in cell B4.
3. Save the workbook as **Budget2** in the Tutorial.02\Tutorial folder, and then click the **Budget** tab to make this sheet the active worksheet. See Figure 2-1. Amanda has recorded the couple's take-home salaries as income and has listed a variety of expenses in columns for each month. January's income and expenses are shown in column B, February's income and expenses are shown in column C, and so forth.

Figure 2-1 Budget worksheet

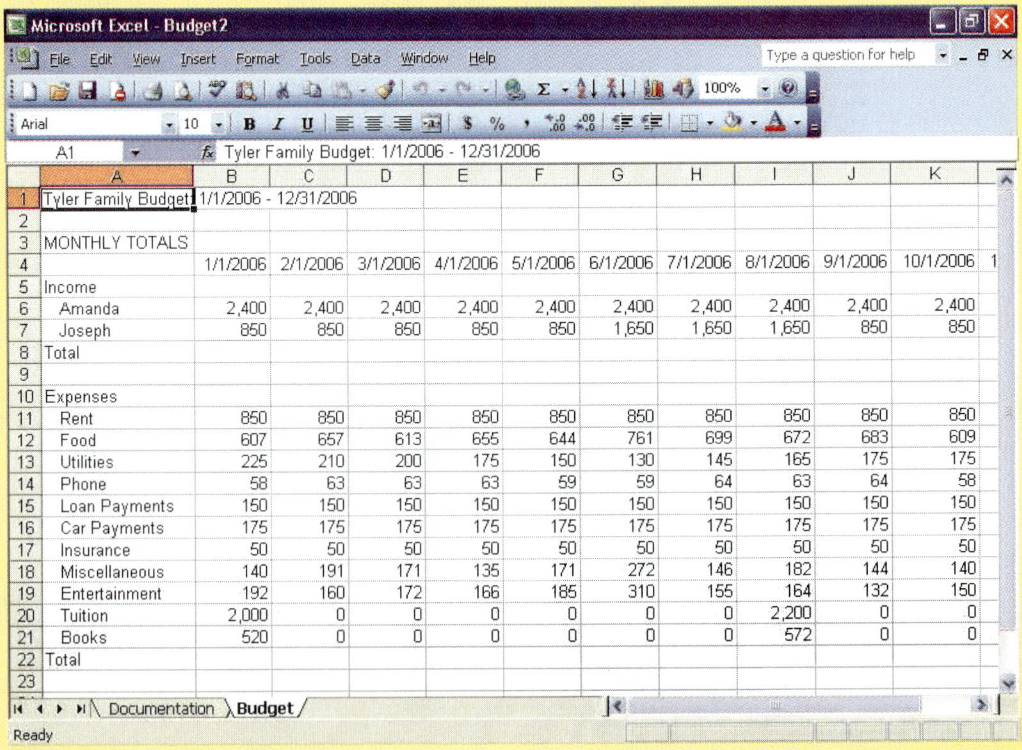

Amanda would like the worksheet to calculate the family's total income and expenses for each month. She would also like to see a year-end summary that displays the family's total income and expenses for the entire year. This summary should also display the average income and expenses so that Amanda can get a picture of what a typical month looks like for her family. Amanda realizes that some expenses increase and decrease during certain months, so she would like to calculate the minimum and maximum values for each expense category, which will give her an idea of the range of these values throughout the year. All of this information will help Amanda and Joseph budget for the upcoming year.

To perform these calculations, you'll have to add several formulas to the workbook. As discussed in the previous tutorial, formulas are one of the most useful features in Excel because they enable you to calculate values based on data entered into the workbook. For more complex calculations, you can enter formulas that contain one or more functions. Recall that a function is a predefined formula that performs calculations using specific values. Each Excel function has a name and syntax. The **syntax** is the rule specifying how the function should be written. The general syntax of all Excel functions is

FUNCTION(argument1, argument2, ...)

where *FUNCTION* is the name of the Excel function and *argument1, argument2,* and so forth are **arguments** specifying the numbers, text, or cell references used by the function to calculate a value. An argument can also be an **optional argument** that is not necessary for the function to calculate a value. If an optional argument is not included, Excel assumes a default value for it. Each argument entered in a function is separated by a comma. The convention used in this text shows optional arguments within square brackets along with the argument's default value, as follows:

FUNCTION(argument1, [argument2=value2])

where *argument2* is an optional argument and *value2* is the default value for this argument. As you learn more about individual functions, you will also learn which arguments are required and which are optional.

Another convention followed in this text is to write function names in uppercase letters, but Excel recognizes the function names entered in either uppercase or lowercase letters, converting the lowercase letters to uppercase automatically.

There are 350 different Excel functions organized into the following 10 categories:

- Database functions
- Date and Time functions
- Engineering functions
- Financial functions
- Information functions
- Logical functions
- Lookup and Reference functions
- Math and Trigonometry functions
- Statistical functions
- Text and Data functions

You can learn about each function using Excel's online Help. Figure 2-2 describes some of the more important Math and Statistical functions that you may often use in your workbooks.

Figure 2-2 Math and Statistical functions

Function	Description
AVERAGE(*number1*, [*number2*, *number3*, ...])	Calculates the average of a collection of numbers, where *number1*, *number2*, and so forth are numeric values or cell references
COUNT(*value1*, [*value2*, *value3*, ...])	Calculates the total number of values, where *value1*, *value2*, and so forth are numeric values, text entries, or cell references
MAX(*number*1, [*number2*, *number3*, ...])	Calculates the maximum of a collection of numbers, where *number1*, *number2*, and so forth are either numeric values or cell references
MEDIAN(*number1*, [*number2*, *number3*, ...])	Calculates the median, or the number in the middle, of a collection of numbers, where *number1*, *number2*, and so forth are either numeric values or cell references
MIN(*number1*, [*number2*, *number3*, ...])	Calculates the minimum of a collection of numbers, where *number1*, *number2*, and so forth are either numeric values or cell references
ROUND(*number*, *num_digits*)	Rounds a number to a specified number of digits, where *number* is the number you want to round and *num_digits* specifies the number of digits to which you want to round the number
SUM(*number1*, [*number2*, *number3*, ...])	Calculates the sum of a collection of numbers, where *number1*, *number2*, and so forth are either numeric values or cell references

For example, the **AVERAGE function** calculates the average value of a collection of numbers. The syntax of this function is AVERAGE(*number1,* [*number2,* ...]). When you enter the arguments *(number1, number2)*, you can enter these numbers directly into the function, as in AVERAGE(3, 2, 5, 8), or you can enter the references to the worksheet cells that contain those numbers, as in AVERAGE(A1:A4). You can also enter a function as part of a larger formula. For example, the formula *=MAX(A1:A100)/100* calculates the maximum value in the cell range A1:A100 and then divides that number by 100. You can include, or "nest," one function within another. For example, in the formula *=ROUND(AVERAGE(A1:A100),1)*, the first argument in the ROUND function uses the value calculated by the AVERAGE function; the second argument is a constant. The result is a formula that calculates the average value of the numbers in the range A1:A100, rounding that value to the first decimal place.

In the previous tutorial, you calculated totals using the AutoSum button on the Standard toolbar. Although using the AutoSum feature is a quick and convenient way to calculate a value, it is only one way to perform this calculation in Excel. To determine the totals Amanda wants, you can also use the **SUM function**, which calculates the sum of a collection of numbers. The syntax of the SUM function is SUM(*number1,* [*number2,* ...]), which is similar to that of the AVERAGE function.

You'll use the SUM function now to begin calculating the values Amanda needs, starting with the values for the month of January.

To calculate the total income and expenses for January using the SUM function:

1. Click cell **B8** on the Budget worksheet, type **=SUM(B6:B7)** and then press the **Enter** key. Excel displays the value 3,250 in cell B8, indicating that the total income for the month of January is $3,250.

   You can also enter the cell range for a function by selecting the cell range rather than typing it. You'll use this method to determine the total expenses for January.

2. Click cell **B22** and then type **=SUM(** to begin the function.
3. Select the range **B11:B21** using your mouse. As you drag to select the range, its cell reference is automatically entered into the SUM function, as shown in Figure 2-3.

Entering the SUM function **Figure 2-3**

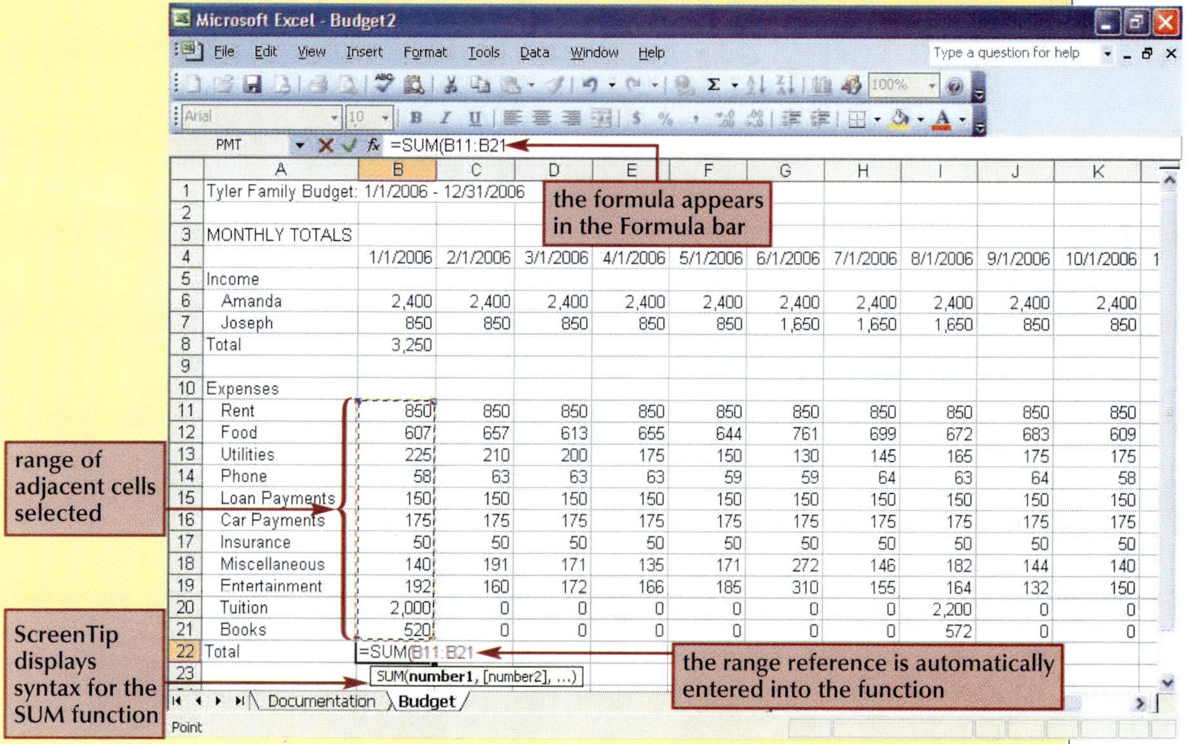

4. Press the **Enter** key to complete the formula. Note that you didn't have to type the closing parenthesis. When you press the Enter key, the closing parenthesis is inserted automatically. The value 4,967 is displayed in cell B22, indicating that the total expenses for January are $4,967.

Amanda wants to know how much money is left over at the end of each month or, in other words, the family's *net income* each month. To determine this amount, you need to enter a formula that subtracts the total monthly expenses from the total monthly income. You'll begin by calculating the net income for the month of January.

To calculate the net income for the first month:

1. Click cell **A24**, type **Net Income**, and then press the **Tab** key to move to cell B24, where you will enter the formula.
2. Type **=B8-B22** and then press the **Enter** key. Excel displays the value –1,717, which indicates that the family's net income for the month of January is a negative $1,717. Amanda and Joseph's expenses are greater than their income for that month.

Now that you've entered the formulas to calculate the total income, total expenses, and net income for January, you need to enter the same formulas for the other 11 months of the year. Entering the formulas for each of the remaining months individually would be time-consuming, but there is a quicker way.

Copying and Pasting Formulas

To use the same formula in different cells on the worksheet, you can copy the formula and paste it to a new location or locations. The cell (or range of cells) that contains the formula you copy is referred to as the **source cell** (or **source range**). The new location is the **destination cell** (or **destination range**). When you paste your selection, Excel automatically adjusts the cell references contained in the formulas. For example, if you copy cell B8, which contains the formula *=SUM(B6:B7)*, and paste the contents of the copied cell into cell C8 (the destination cell), Excel automatically changes the formula in cell C8 to *=SUM(C6:C7)*.

In effect, Excel recognizes that the intent of the function is to calculate the sum of the values in the two cells above the active cell. The new location does not even have to be in the same row as the copied cell. If you copy the formula in cell B8 to cell C10, the pasted formula would be *=SUM(C8:C9)*. You can copy the formula in one cell to a whole range of cells, and Excel will correctly adjust the cell references in the formula for each cell in the range.

Reference Window

Copying and Pasting a Cell or Range

- Select the cell or range that you want to copy, and then click the Copy button on the Standard toolbar.
- Select the cell or range into which you want to copy the selection, and then click the Paste button on the Standard toolbar.

Next, you'll copy the formula in cell B8 to the range C8:M8 to calculate the total income for the remaining months.

To copy and paste the formula from cell B8 to the range C8:M8:

1. Click cell **B8** on the Budget worksheet, and then click the **Copy** button on the Standard toolbar. Note that the copied cell has a moving border. This border is a visual reminder that the range has been copied and is ready to be pasted.
2. Select the range **C8:M8**, and then click the **Paste** button on the Standard toolbar. Excel copies the formula in cell B8 into each of the cells in the range C8:M8, changing the cell references to match the location of each cell in the range. See Figure 2-4. Note that when you paste a selection, Excel automatically displays the Paste Options button. This button provides options that give you control over the paste process. You will learn more about this button in the next tutorial.

Figure 2-4 Copying the SUM function for the monthly income

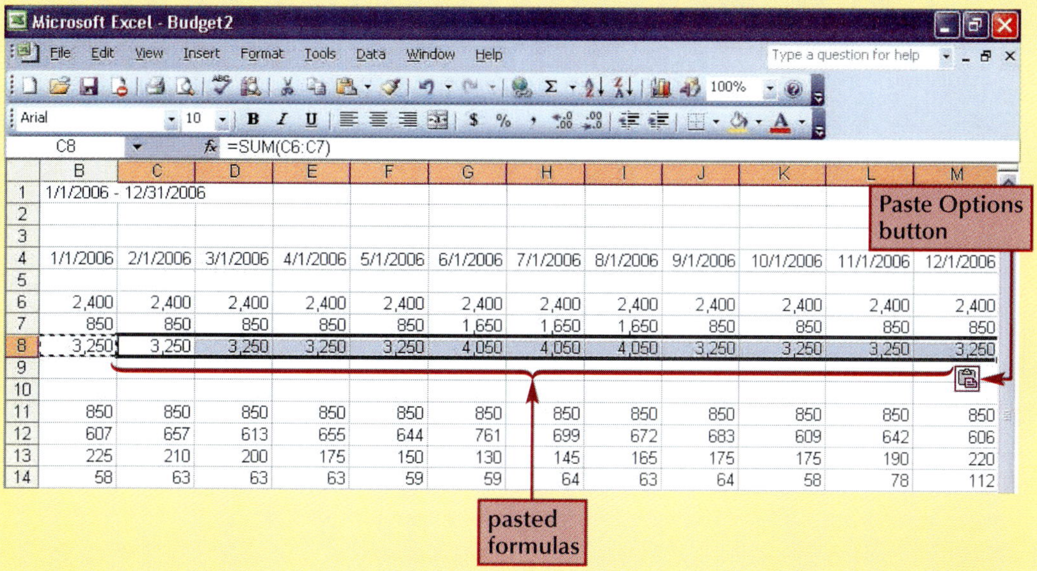

Trouble? If your screen does not match the one shown in the figure, you may have scrolled the worksheet further to the right so column B is no longer visible. You can click the left scroll button on the horizontal scroll bar to reposition the worksheet in the workbook window to better match the one in the figure.

3. Press the **Ctrl + `** (grave accent) keys to display the formulas in the range B8:M8. Notice that the cell references in each formula refer to the income values for that particular month.
4. Press the **Ctrl + `** (grave accent) keys to return to Normal view.

You are not limited to copying a single formula from one cell. You can also copy a range of formulas. When you copy a range of cells, each of which contains a formula, and then paste the selection into a new location, Excel pastes the formulas in each cell to their corresponding locations in the new cell range. You don't have to select a range that is the same size as the range being copied. You just need to select the first, or upper leftmost, cell in the destination range, and Excel will paste the selection in a range that accommodates all the cells. Any existing text or values in the destination range will be overwritten. So, be sure you paste the selection in an area of the worksheet that can accommodate the selection without deleting existing data.

Next, you need to copy the formulas for January's total expenses and net income, which are in cells B22 and B24, to the ranges C22:M22 and C24:M24. Then Amanda will be able to see each month's total expenses and net income values. Although there is no formula in cell B23, you will select the range B22:B24 and paste the selection to range C22:M24, simplifying the process. No values will appear in row 23.

To copy and paste the formulas in the range B22:B24 to the range C22:M24:

1. Scroll the worksheet to the left, if necessary, so column B is visible, select the range **B22:B24**, and then click the **Copy** button on the Standard toolbar.

   Trouble? If the Clipboard task pane opens, close it. You will not need to use it in this tutorial.

2. Select the range **C22:M24**, and then click the **Paste** button on the Standard toolbar. Figure 2-5 shows the total expenses and net income values for each month in the Budget worksheet. Note that Excel has duplicated the two formulas from the first month in each succeeding month.

Figure 2-5 **Copying and pasting a cell range**

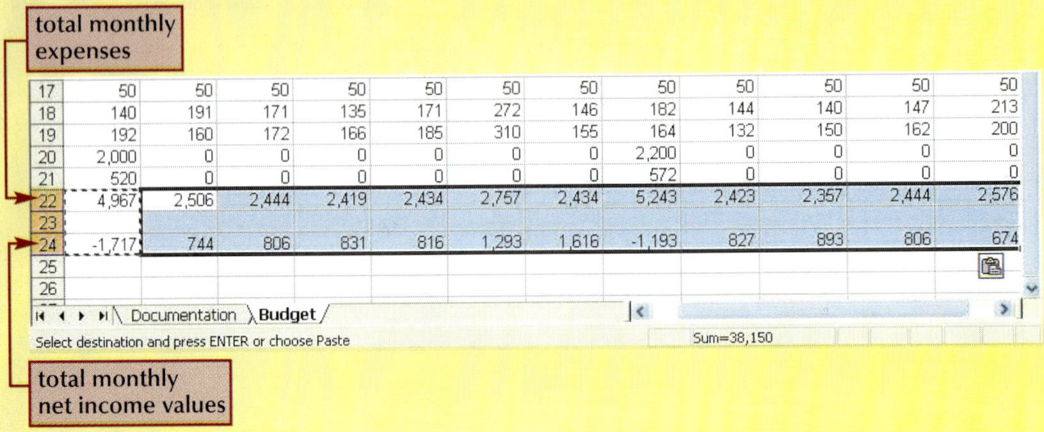

3. Press the **Esc** key to remove the moving border from the selected range.

As you can see, Excel's ability to adjust cell references when copying and pasting formulas makes it easy to create columns or rows of formulas that share a common structure.

Using Relative and Absolute References

The type of cell reference that you just worked with is called a relative reference. A **relative reference** is a cell reference that changes when it is copied and pasted in a new location. Excel interprets the reference *relative* to the position of the active cell. For example, when you copied the formula *=SUM(B6:B7)* from the source cell, B8, and pasted it in the destination range, C8:M8, Excel adjusted the cell references in each pasted formula relative to the new location of the formula itself. The formula in cell C8 became *=SUM(C6:C7)*, the formula in cell D8 became *=SUM(D6:D7)*, and so on.

A second type of cell reference is an absolute reference. An **absolute reference** is a cell reference that doesn't change when it is copied. Excel does not adjust the cell reference because the cell reference points to a fixed, or *absolute,* location in the worksheet, and it remains fixed when the copied formula is pasted. In Excel, an absolute reference appears with a dollar sign ($) before each column and row designation. For example, $B$8 is an absolute reference, and when it is used in a formula, Excel will always point to the cell located at the intersection of column B and row 8.

Figure 2-6 provides an example in which an absolute reference is necessary to a formula. In this example, a sales worksheet records the units sold for each region as well as the overall total. If you want to calculate the percent of units sold for each region, you divide the units sold for each region by the overall total. If you use only relative references, copying the formula from the first region to the second will produce an incorrect result, because Excel shifts the location of the total sales cell down one row. To correct this problem, you use an absolute cell reference, fixing the location of the total sales cell at cell B8. In the example, this means changing the formula in cell C4 from *=B4/B8* to *=B4/$B$8*.

Figure 2-6 Using relative and absolute references

Formulas Using Relative References

	A	B	C	D
1	Sales			
2				
3	Regions	Units Sold	Percent	
4	Region 1	2,238	=B4/B8	
5	Region 2	1,321		
6	Region 3	3,093		
7	Region 4	1,905		
8	Total	8,557		
9				
10				

	A	B	C	D
1	Sales			
2				
3	Regions	Units Sold	Percent	
4	Region 1	2,238	0.26154026	
5	Region 2	1,321	=B5/B9	
6	Region 3	3,093		
7	Region 4	1,905		
8	Total	8,557		
9				
10				

When the formula is copied, the relative reference to the cell (B8) is shifted down and now points to an incorrect cell (B9).

Formulas Using Absolute References

	A	B	C	D
1	Sales			
2				
3	Regions	Units Sold	Percent	
4	Region 1	2,238	=B4/$B$8	
5	Region 2	1,321		
6	Region 3	3,093		
7	Region 4	1,905		
8	Total	8,557		
9				
10				

	A	B	C	D
1	Sales			
2				
3	Regions	Units Sold	Percent	
4	Region 1	2,238	0.26154026	
5	Region 2	1,321	=B5/$B$8	
6	Region 3	3,093		
7	Region 4	1,905		
8	Total	8,557		
9				
10				

When the formula is copied, the absolute reference to the cell ($B$8) continues to point to that cell.

Another type of reference supported by Excel is the mixed reference. A **mixed reference** contains both relative and absolute cell references. A mixed reference for cell B8 is either $B8 or B$8. In the case of the mixed reference $B8, the column portion of the reference remains fixed, but the row number adjusts as the formula is copied to a new location. In the B$8 reference, the row number remains fixed, whereas the column portion adjusts to each new cell location.

As you enter a formula that requires an absolute reference or a mixed reference, you can type the dollar sign for the column and row references as needed. If you have already entered a formula and need to change the type of cell reference used, you can switch to edit mode and then press the **F4** key. As you press this function key, Excel cycles through the different references for the cell in the formula at the location of the insertion point. Pressing the F4 key changes a relative reference to an absolute reference, then to a mixed reference for the row, then to a mixed reference for the column, and then back to a relative reference.

In Amanda's family budget, monthly expenses vary greatly throughout the year. For example, tuition is a major expense, and that bill must be paid once in January and once in August. Amanda knows that the family has more entertainment and miscellaneous expenses during the month of December than at other times. The family's monthly income also fluctuates as Joseph brings in more income during the summer months than at other times. Amanda would like her budget worksheet to keep a running total of the family's net income as it progresses through the year. For example, she knows that the family will start the year with less money because of the tuition bill in January. Amanda wonders how many months pass before they recover from that major expense and begin saving money again.

One way to calculate the running total is to add the net income values of consecutive months. For example, to figure out how much money the family has saved or lost after two months, you add the net income for January to the net income for February, using the formula *=SUM(B24:C24)*. To figure out the total net income for the first three months, you use the formula *=SUM(B24:D24)*; through the first four months the formula will be *=SUM(B24:E24)*, and so on.

The starting point of the range in the formula needs to be fixed at the cell that contains the net income for January, cell B24. To be sure that the formula points to cell B24, you need to use the absolute reference $B$24. The ending cell of the range will shift as you copy the formula to the other months in the worksheet. You need to use a relative reference for the ending cell in the range so that Excel will adjust the reference as the formula is copied. The formula for the running total through the first two months will be *=SUM($B$24:C24)*. When you paste this formula to the other months of the year, Excel will adjust the cell range to calculate the total for all of the months up to that point.

To calculate the running total using an absolute reference to cell B24:

1. Click cell **A25**, type **Running Total**, and then press the **Tab** key twice to move to column C.
2. Type **=SUM(B24:C24)** in cell C25, and then press the **Enter** key. Excel displays the value –973, showing that the family's expenses exceed their income by $973 through the first two months of the year.

   Now you'll change the formula to use an absolute reference for cell B24 by selecting it in the formula and pressing the F4 key.
3. Double-click cell **C25** to switch to edit mode, and then double-click **B24** within the formula to select the cell reference.
4. Press the **F4** key to change the cell reference from B24 to $B$24. See Figure 2-7.

Figure 2-7 **Entering an absolute reference**

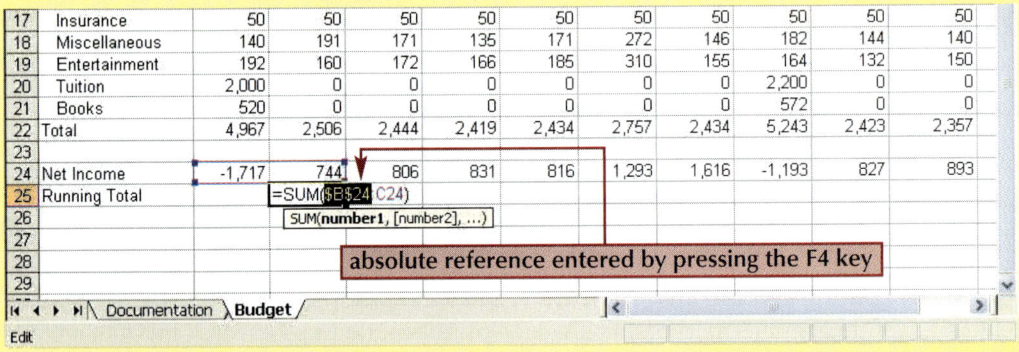

Trouble? If you pressed the F4 key too many times and passed the absolute reference, continue pressing the F4 key to cycle through the options until $B$24 is displayed in the formula.

5. Press the **Enter** key when the correct reference is displayed. Excel displays the value –973.

   Now you can copy this formula to the remaining months of the year.
6. Click cell **C25**, and then click the **Copy** button on the Standard toolbar. The moving border indicates that cell C25 has been copied.
7. Select the range **D25:M25**, and then click the **Paste** button on the Standard toolbar. Excel copies the formula to the remaining cells, as shown in Figure 2-8. The amount shown for each month represents the cash on hand that the family accumulated during the year, up to and including that month. So, for example, at the end of the year, after paying all expenses, they have a total of $6,396.

Figure 2-8 Running total of the family's net income

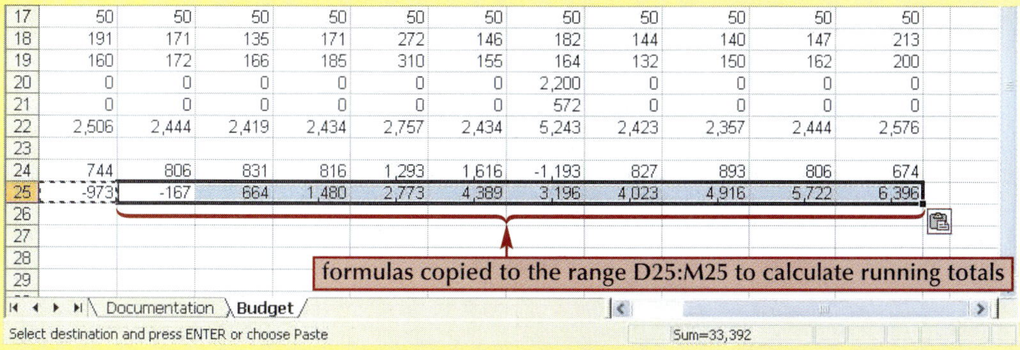

8. Press the **Ctrl + `** (grave accent) keys to examine the pasted formulas in the range D25:M25. The use of absolute and relative references ensures the integrity of the formula copied in each cell used to calculate the running net income total.

9. Press the **Ctrl + `** (grave accent) keys to return to Normal view.

Working with Other Paste Options

So far you've used the Paste button to paste formulas from a source cell or range to a destination cell or range. When Excel pastes the contents of a selected cell or range, it also pastes any formatting applied to the source cell (you'll learn about formatting in the next tutorial). If you want more control over how Excel pastes the data from the source cell, you can click the list arrow next to the Paste button and choose one of the available paste options. Figure 2-9 describes each of these options.

Figure 2-9 Paste options

Option	Description
Formulas	Pastes the formula(s), but not the formatting, of the source cell range
Values	Pastes the value(s), but not the formula(s) or formatting, of the source cell range
No Borders	Pastes the formula(s) and formatting of the source cell range, but not the format of the cell range's borders
Transpose	Pastes the formula(s) and formatting of the source cell range, except changes the orientation so that rows in the source cell range become columns, and columns become rows
Paste Link	Pastes a link to the cell(s) in the source cell range, including the formatting used
Paste Special	Opens a dialog box displaying more paste options

For example, if you want to paste the value calculated by the formula in a cell but not the formula itself, you use the Values option. This is useful in situations in which you want to "freeze" a calculated value and remove the risk of it being changed by inadvertently changing another value in the worksheet. For even more control over the paste feature, you can select the Paste Special option. When you select this option, the Paste Special dialog box opens, as shown in Figure 2-10.

Figure 2-10 Paste Special dialog box

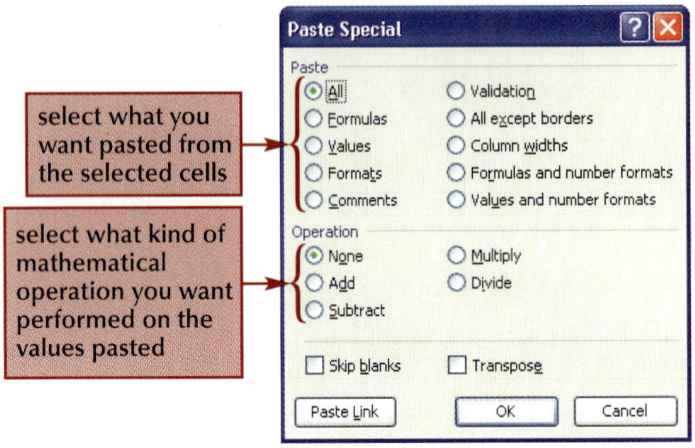

Using this dialog box, you can not only specify exactly which parts of the source cell or range—formulas, values, or formats—you want to paste, but also specify a mathematical operation you want performed as part of the paste action. For example, you can copy the value of one cell and add that value to cells in the destination range.

Another method that gives you control over the paste process is provided by the Paste Options button, which appears each time you paste a selection. By clicking this icon, you can choose from a variety of options that determine how the pasted data should be formatted. You'll explore this feature more in the next tutorial.

Changing the Magnification of a Worksheet

As you learned in Tutorial 1, an Excel worksheet can have 256 columns and more than 65,000 rows of data. You also learned that you can freeze columns and rows, so as you scroll through the data in the worksheet, the column and row headings remain visible. The number of columns and rows displayed in the workbook window depends on the zoom magnification set for the worksheet. The default zoom magnification setting is 100%. You can change this setting using the Zoom command on the View menu or the Zoom button on the Standard toolbar. Changing the zoom magnification setting allows you to see more or less of the worksheet at one time. If you decrease the magnification, you will see more of the data in the worksheet, but the data will be smaller and may be more difficult to read. If you increase the magnification, you will see less of the data in the worksheet, but the data will be larger and easier to read.

Reference Window

Changing the Zoom Magnification of the Workbook Window

- Click View on the menu bar, and then click Zoom.
- Click the option button for the percent magnification you want to apply, and then click the OK button.

or

- Click the Zoom list arrow on the Standard toolbar, and then click the percent option you want to apply.

You can change the magnification of the workbook window from 10% up to 400% or enter a percent not offered, for example, 65%, to further customize the display of your workbook window. You can also select a zoom magnification specific to the content of your worksheet. To do this, you select the worksheet's content and then choose the Selection option in the Zoom dialog box or on the Zoom list. Excel displays the content of the selection at a magnification that fills the entire workbook window.

Before continuing, Amanda wants to review the work done so far. Try changing the magnification so more of the worksheet is displayed at one time.

To change the zoom setting for the workbook window:

1. Press the **Ctrl + Home** keys to make cell A1 the active cell.
2. Click **View** on the menu bar, and then click **Zoom** to open the Zoom dialog box.
3. Click the **75%** option button in the list of options, and then click the **OK** button. At this setting, all the data in the worksheet is displayed in the workbook window, as shown in Figure 2-11.

Figure 2-11 **Budget worksheet at 75 percent magnification**

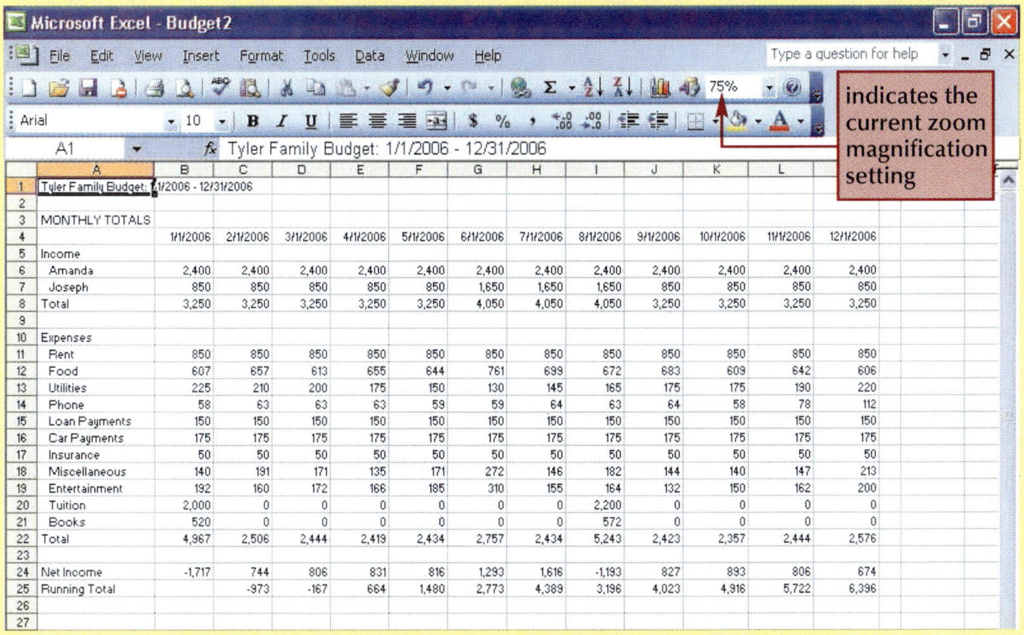

	A	B	C	D	E	F	G	H	I	J	K	L	M
1	Tyler Family Budget: 1/1/2006 - 12/31/2006												
2													
3	MONTHLY TOTALS												
4		1/1/2006	2/1/2006	3/1/2006	4/1/2006	5/1/2006	6/1/2006	7/1/2006	8/1/2006	9/1/2006	10/1/2006	11/1/2006	12/1/2006
5	Income												
6	Amanda	2,400	2,400	2,400	2,400	2,400	2,400	2,400	2,400	2,400	2,400	2,400	2,400
7	Joseph	850	850	850	850	850	1,650	1,650	1,650	850	850	850	850
8	Total	3,250	3,250	3,250	3,250	3,250	4,050	4,050	4,050	3,250	3,250	3,250	3,250
9													
10	Expenses												
11	Rent	850	850	850	850	850	850	850	850	850	850	850	850
12	Food	607	657	613	655	644	761	699	672	683	609	642	606
13	Utilities	225	210	200	175	150	130	145	165	175	175	190	220
14	Phone	58	63	63	63	59	59	64	63	64	58	78	112
15	Loan Payments	150	150	150	150	150	150	150	150	150	150	150	150
16	Car Payments	175	175	175	175	175	175	175	175	175	175	175	175
17	Insurance	50	50	50	50	50	50	50	50	50	50	50	50
18	Miscellaneous	140	191	171	135	171	272	146	182	144	140	147	213
19	Entertainment	192	160	172	166	185	310	155	164	132	150	162	200
20	Tuition	2,000	0	0	0	0	0	0	2,200	0	0	0	0
21	Books	520	0	0	0	0	0	0	572	0	0	0	0
22	Total	4,967	2,506	2,444	2,419	2,434	2,757	2,434	5,243	2,423	2,357	2,444	2,576
23													
24	Net Income	-1,717	744	806	831	816	1,293	1,616	-1,193	827	893	806	674
25	Running Total		-973	-167	664	1,480	2,773	4,389	3,196	4,023	4,916	5,722	6,396
26													
27													

More of the worksheet is visible; however, reading the individual cell values is more difficult, so you will change the magnification back to 100%.

4. Click the **Zoom** list arrow 100% on the Standard toolbar, and then click **100%** to return to this higher magnification. Although the overall appearance of your screen may differ from the figures in this text, the data is not affected.

From examining the running totals, Amanda has learned several important facts. One of the family's largest expenses is Joseph's tuition, which is paid in January and August. She has also learned that the family does not recover from this January expense and show a positive overall net income until the month of April, when the total savings amount for the year up to that point is $664. Therefore, with their current income and expenses, it takes four months to "catch up" with the tuition expenditure in January, which leaves the family short on cash during February and March. The good news is that the total net income at the end of 12 months is $6,396, which represents the amount of money the family is able to save for the entire year.

Amanda now wants to know the family's total income and its total yearly expenses. You'll place these calculations in a table below the monthly figures. First, you will copy the income and expense categories to a new cell range.

To copy the income and expense categories:

1. Click cell **A27**, type **YEAR-END SUMMARY**, and then press the **Enter** key.
2. Copy the range **A5:A24** and paste it into the range **A29:A48**. If you want to remove the selection border from the copied range, you can press the Esc key. The selection border will disappear as soon as you select another range.

   Now you will enter the formula to calculate the total income for the family over the entire year.
3. Click cell **B28**, type **Total**, and then press the **Enter** key twice. You will enter the formula to calculate Amanda's salary for the year.
4. Type **=SUM(B6:M6)** in cell B30, and then press the **Enter** key. The amount 28,800 appears in the cell.

   Now you will copy this formula to calculate Joseph's yearly income, the couple's combined income, and the yearly totals for the expense categories.
5. Click cell **B30** to select this cell again, and then click the **Copy** button on the Standard toolbar.
6. Select the range **B31:B32**, press and hold the **Ctrl** key, select the range **B35:B46**, click cell **B48**, and then release the mouse button and the Ctrl key. The nonadjacent range B31:B32;B35:B46;B48 should now be selected.
7. Click the **Paste** button on the Standard toolbar. As shown in Figure 2-12, the total values for all income and expense categories should now be pasted in the worksheet.

Figure 2-12 **Year-end totals for income and expenses**

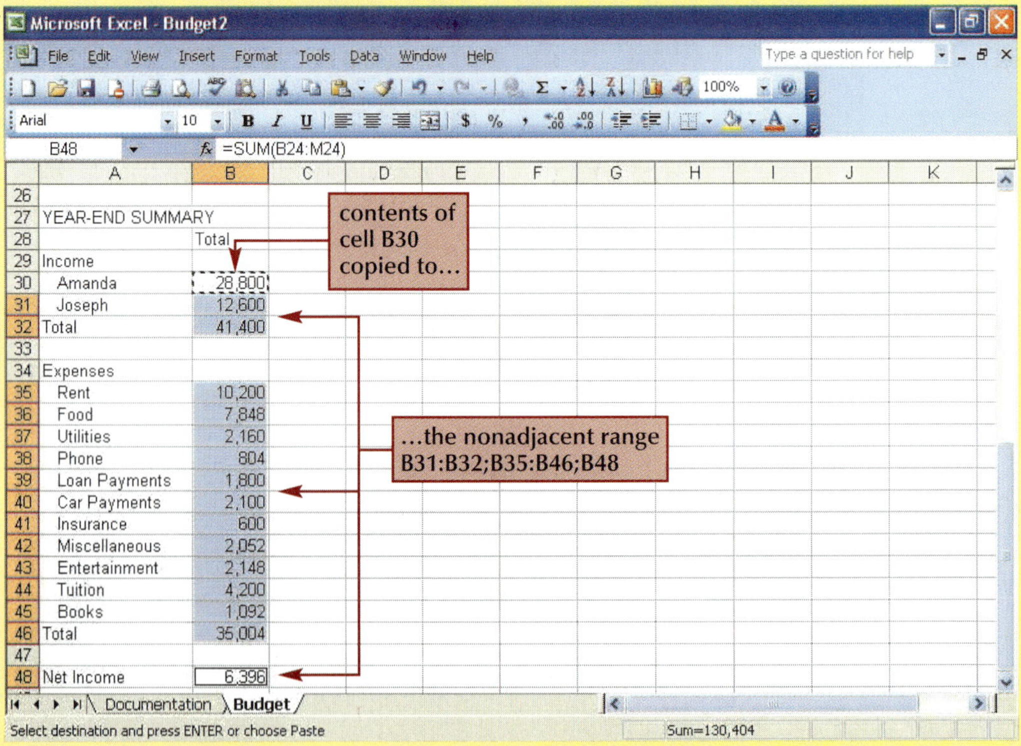

From these calculations, Amanda can quickly see that her family's yearly income is $41,400, whereas their yearly expenses total $35,004. Their largest expense is rent—a total of $10,200 per year.

Using the Insert Function Dialog Box

It's easier for Amanda to plan a budget if she knows approximately how much the family makes and spends each month. So your next task is to add a column that calculates the monthly averages for each of the income and expense categories. Rather than typing the function directly into the cell, you may find it helpful to use the Insert Function button on the Formula bar. Clicking this button displays a dialog box from which you can choose the function you want to enter. Once you choose a function, another dialog box opens, which displays the function's syntax. In this way, Excel makes it easy for you to avoid making mistakes. Try this now by entering the AVERAGE function using the Insert Function dialog box.

To insert the AVERAGE function:

1. Click cell **C28**, type **Average**, and then press the **Enter** key.
2. Click cell **C30** and then click the **Insert Function** button on the Formula bar. The Insert Function dialog box opens. See Figure 2-13.

Figure 2-13 **Insert Function dialog box**

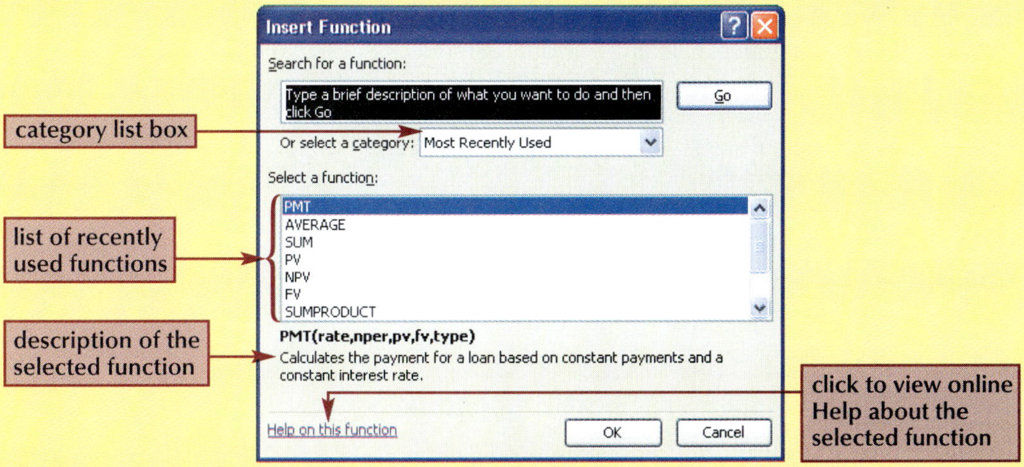

The Insert Function dialog box shows a list of the most recently used functions. As you can see from Figure 2-13, one of these is the AVERAGE function. However, your list may be different and might not include the AVERAGE function. You can display a different function list using the category list box. Try this now to display a list of the Statistical functions supported by Excel.

3. Click the **Or select a category** list arrow, and then click **Statistical**. Excel displays a list of Statistical functions. See Figure 2-14.

Figure 2-14 Excel's Statistical functions

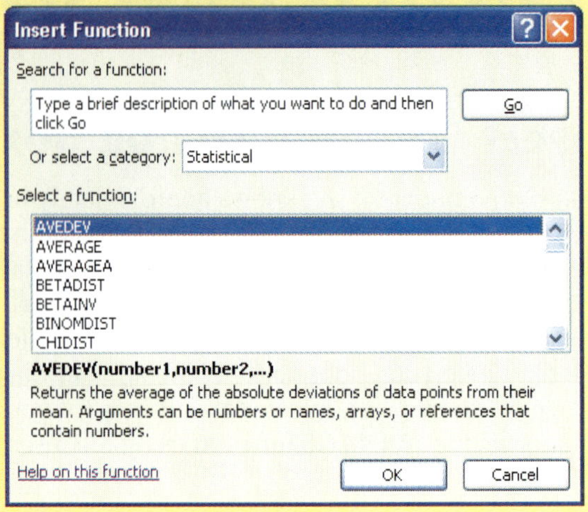

4. Click **AVERAGE** in the list, and then click the **OK** button. The Function Arguments dialog box opens.

The Function Arguments dialog box provides the syntax of the selected function in an easy-to-use form. You can enter the values needed for the arguments in the reference boxes by typing them or by selecting the cell range from the worksheet. To select a cell range in the worksheet, you can click the Collapse Dialog Box button located to the right of each argument reference. Clicking this button reduces the size of the dialog box so you can see more of the worksheet. The Collapse Dialog Box button is a toggle button and, when clicked, changes to the Expand Dialog box button, which you click to restore the dialog box to its original size.

Although Amanda's salary did not change during the past year, she wants to use this workbook as a model for the next couple of years. If her salary changes in the future, the formula to calculate the average income will be in place.

You will use the Insert Function dialog box to enter the formula to calculate the average value of the cells in the range B6:M6, which contains Amanda's monthly salary amount.

To insert values into the AVERAGE function:

1. Click the **Collapse Dialog Box** button located to the right of the Number1 argument reference box. The Function Arguments dialog box reduces in size to let you see more of the worksheet, and the Collapse Dialog Box button changes to the Expand Dialog Box button.

   Trouble? If the collapsed dialog box is still in the way of the range you need to select, drag the dialog box to another location on the worksheet.

2. Select the range **B6:M6** on the worksheet, and then click the **Expand Dialog Box** button to restore the Function Arguments dialog box to its original size, as shown in Figure 2-15.

Function Arguments dialog box

Figure 2-15

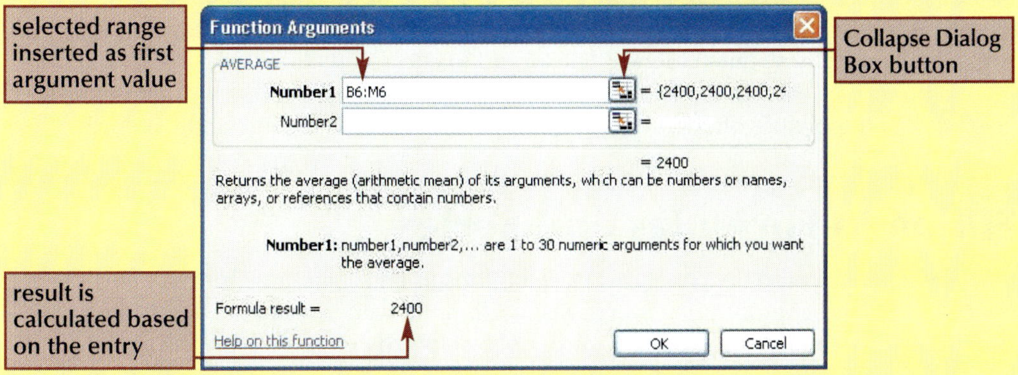

3. Click the **OK** button. The value 2,400 appears in C30.

Now you will copy the formula to calculate the average of other income and expense categories.

To copy the AVERAGE function into the remaining cells:

1. Click cell **C30**, if necessary, and then click the **Copy** button on the Standard toolbar.
2. Select the nonadjacent range **C31:C32;C35:C46;C48**, and then click the **Paste** button on the Standard toolbar. Figure 2-16 shows the monthly averages in Amanda's budget.

Year-end average values

Figure 2-16

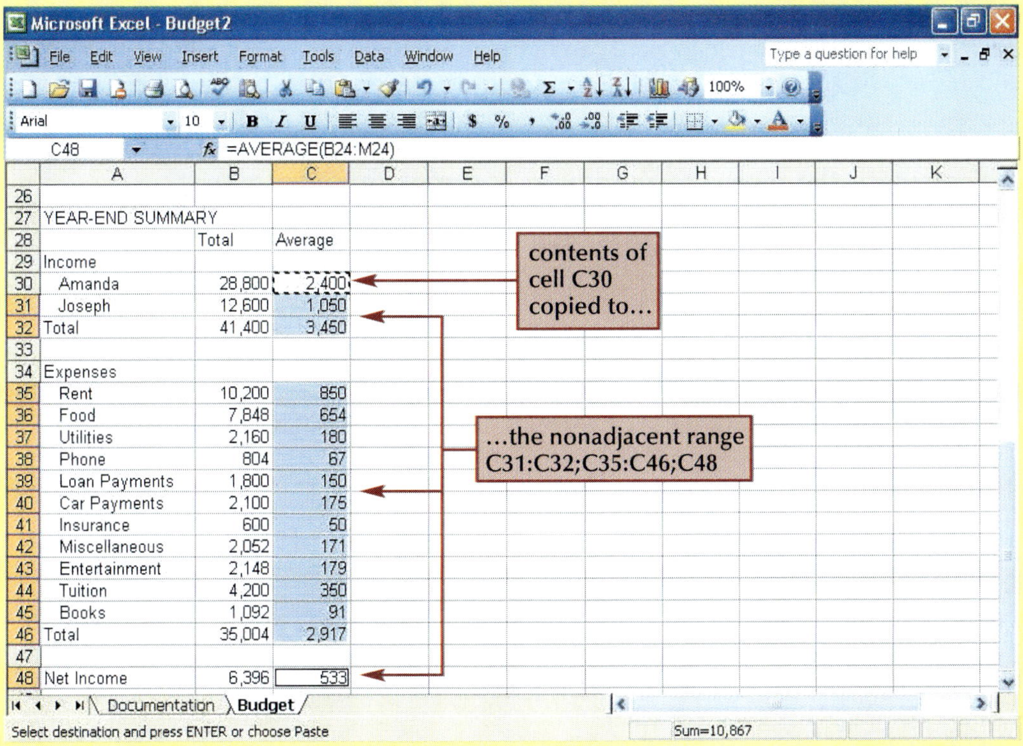

On average, the couple makes $3,450 per month and spends $2,917. Their net income is about $533 a month on average; this is the amount that Amanda can expect the family to save. It is obvious that expenses for some months will be higher than expected. Amanda wonders how much higher? She would like to calculate the maximum and minimum amounts for each of the income and expense categories. She knows that this will give her a better picture of the range of values for her family's income and expenses.

Filling in Formulas and Series

Up to now you've used the Copy and Paste buttons to enter the same formula into multiple cells. Another approach you can use is to fill in the values. You may have noticed a small black square in the lower-right corner of a selected cell or cell range. That small black square is called the **fill handle**. This Excel tool enables you to copy the contents of the selected cells simply by dragging the fill handle over another adjacent cell or range of cells rather than going through the two-step process of clicking the Copy and Paste buttons. This technique is also referred to as **Auto Fill**.

Reference Window

Copying Formulas Using the Fill Handle

- Select the cell or range that contains the formula or formulas you want to copy.
- Drag the fill handle in the direction you want to copy the formula(s), and then release the mouse button.
- To select a specific fill option, click the Auto Fill Options button, and then select the option you want to apply to the selected range.

To calculate the maximum and minimum amounts for each of the income and expense categories, you will enter the **MIN** and **MAX functions**, which have a similar syntax as the AVERAGE and SUM functions. Once you enter the formulas using the MIN and MAX functions for Amanda's income, you can use Auto Fill to fill in the formulas for Joseph's income and for the expense categories.

To calculate the year-end minimum and maximum amounts:

1. Click cell **D28**, type **Minimum**, and then press the **Tab** key.
2. Type **Maximum** in cell E28, and then press the **Enter** key twice to move back to column D where you will enter the formula to calculate minimum values.
3. Type **=MIN(B6:M6)** in cell D30, and then press the **Tab** key to move to column E where you will enter the formula to calculate maximum values.
4. Type **=MAX(B6:M6)** in cell E30, and then press the **Enter** key. Excel displays the value 2,400 in both cell D30 and cell E30 because Amanda's monthly salary is $2,400 and does not vary throughout the year.

   You will use the fill handle to copy the formulas with the MIN and MAX functions into the remaining income and expense categories.
5. Select the range **D30:E30**. The fill handle appears in the lower-right corner of the selection.
6. Position the pointer over the fill handle until the pointer changes to +, and then drag the fill handle down the worksheet until the selection border encloses the range **D30:E48**.

7. Release the mouse button. The Auto Fill Options button appears, and by default Excel copies the formulas and formats found in the source range, D30:E30, into the destination range. Note that rows 33, 34, and 47 contain zeros. This is because those rows correspond to empty cells in the monthly table. You can delete the MIN and MAX functions in those cells.

8. Select the nonadjacent range **D33:E34;D47:E47**, and then press the **Delete** key to clear the contents of the selected cells. Figure 2-17 shows the minimum and maximum values for each income and expense category.

Year-end minimum and maximum values **Figure 2-17**

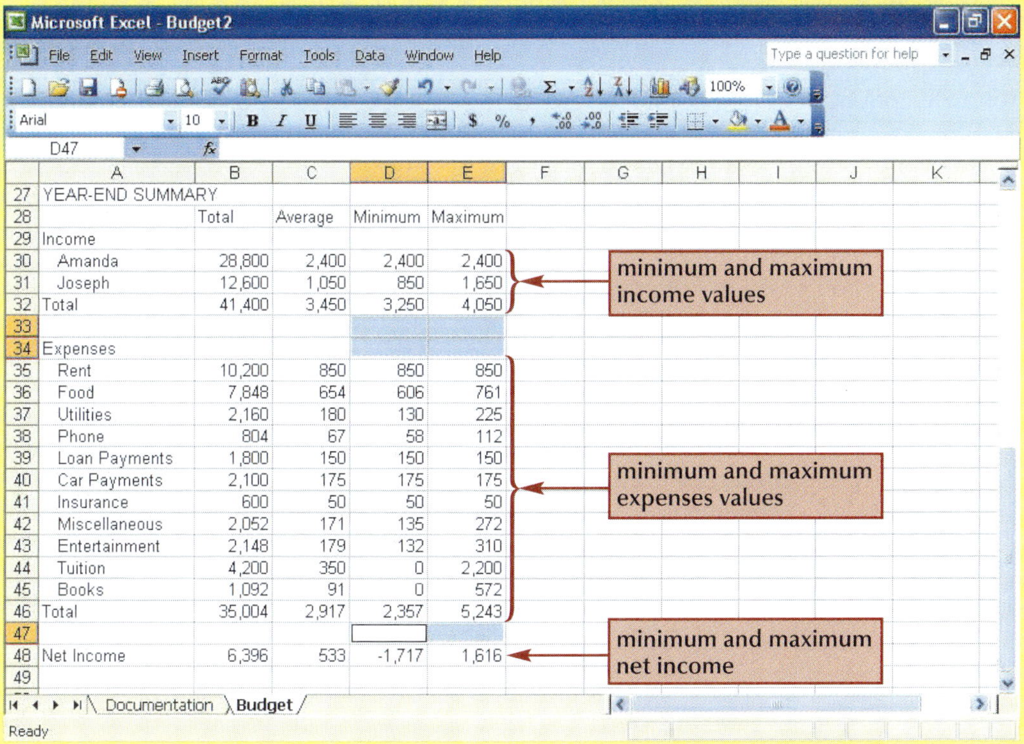

These calculations provide Amanda with an idea of the range of possible values in her budget. From these figures she can see that the maximum amount the family earned in a single month was $4,050 (cell E32), while the maximum amount the family spent in a single month was $5,243 (cell E46). How frugal can the family be? Based on her calculations, the lowest amount the family spent in a given month was $2,357 (cell D46). Amanda has also discovered that the most the family was able to save in a month was $1,616 (cell E48), while their largest deficit was $1,717—which occurred in the month of January, when a tuition payment was due. If the average values in column C give Amanda a picture of what a "typical" month looks like, the values in columns D and E give her an idea of the extremes in the family budget.

If you have a large selection to fill, you may find it difficult to use the fill handle feature of Auto Fill. If you don't want to use the fill handle, you can select the cell range that you want to fill and then use the Fill command on the Edit menu. Excel provides a list of Fill commands that you can use to fill in the selected range.

Auto Fill Options

When you use Auto Fill with formulas, Excel copies not only the formulas but also the formatting applied to the copied cell or range. However, there may be times when you only want the values in a cell copied, or maybe just the formatting. You can control what Excel does when you use the fill handle to copy formulas. When you release the mouse button, a button appears at the lower-right corner of the cell range. This is the Auto Fill Options button. Clicking this button provides a list of available options that you can choose to specify how Excel should handle the pasted selection.

The Auto Fill default option is to copy both the formulas and the formats of selected cells into the cell range. To copy only the formulas or just the formats, you can choose one of the other Auto Fill options, as shown in Figure 2-18.

Figure 2-18 **Auto Fill options**

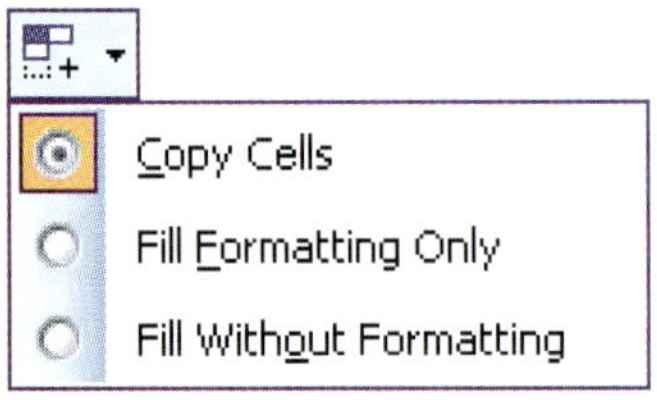

Filling a Series

The Auto Fill feature can also be used to continue a series of values, dates, or text based on an established pattern. As shown in Figure 2-19, to create a list of sequential numbers, you enter the first few numbers of the sequence and then drag the fill handle, completing the sequence. In this case, a list of numbers from 1 to 10 is quickly generated.

Figure 2-19 **Using Auto Fill to complete a series of numbers**

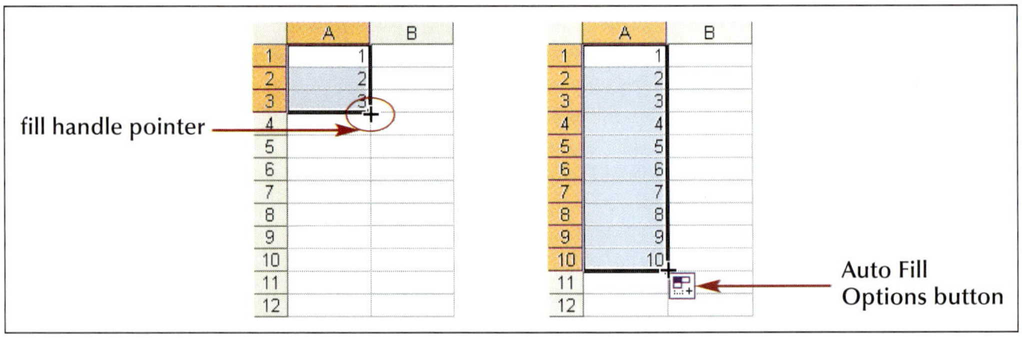

The series does not have to be numeric. It can also contain text and dates. Figure 2-20 shows a few examples of other series that can be completed using the Auto Fill feature.

Figure 2-20

Applying Auto Fill to different series

Type	Initial Selection	Extended Series
Values	1, 2, 3	4, 5, 6, ...
	2, 4, 6	8, 10, 12, ...
Dates and Times	Jan	Feb, Mar, Apr, ...
	January	February, March, April, ...
	Jan, Apr	Jul, Oct, Jan, ...
	15-Jan, 15-Feb	15-Mar, 15-Apr, 15-May, ...
	12/30/2005	12/31/2005, 1/1/2006, 1/2/2006, ...
	12/31/2005, 1/31/2006	2/28/2006, 3/31/2006, 4/30/2006, ...
	Mon	Tue, Wed, Thu, ...
	Monday	Tuesday, Wednesday, Thursday, ...
	11:00 AM	12:00 PM, 1:00 PM, 2:00 PM, ...
Patterned Text	1st period	2nd period, 3rd period, 4th period, ...
	Region 1	Region 2, Region 3, Region 4, ...
	Quarter 3	Quarter 4, Quarter 1, Quarter 2, ...
	Qtr3	Qtr4, Qtr1, Qtr2, ...

Amanda would like to replace dates in the Budget worksheet with the abbreviations of each month. Rather than directly typing this text, you will insert the abbreviations using the fill handle.

To fill in the abbreviations for the months of the year:

1. Press the **Ctrl + Home** keys to make the columns on the left and the top rows visible.
2. Click cell **B4**, type **Jan**, and then click the **Enter** button on the Formula bar. Because "Jan" is a commonly used abbreviation for January, Excel will recognize it as a month without your having to type in "Feb" for the next month in the series.
3. Position the pointer over the fill handle in the lower-right corner of cell B4 until the pointer changes to +.
4. Drag the fill handle over the range **B4:M4**, and then release the mouse button. Excel fills in the abbreviation for each month in the range of cells, as shown in Figure 2-21. As you drag the fill handle, ScreenTips for the month abbreviations appear.

Figure 2-21

Filling in the month abbreviations

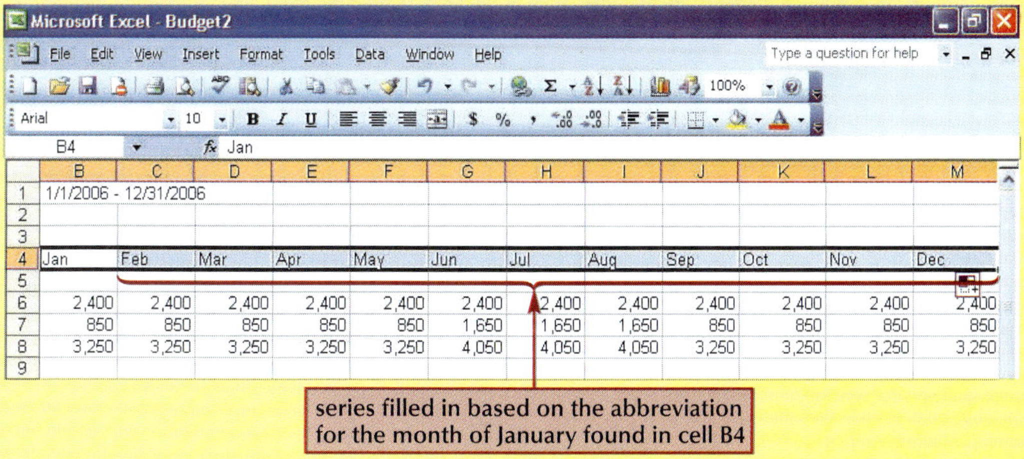

Excel provides other techniques for automatically filling in values and text. You can even create your own customized fill series. You can use Excel's online Help to explore other Auto Fill options.

Working with Date Functions

Entering the current date in a worksheet might not always address a date-related issue or need. If you want the current date to always appear in your workbook, versus the date you may have entered when you created the workbook, you can use a Date function rather than re-entering the current date each time you open the workbook. The **Date functions** provided by Excel store and calculate dates as numeric values, representing the number of days since January 1, 1900. For example, when you enter the date 1/1/2008 into a worksheet cell, you are actually entering the value 39448, because that date is 39,448 days after January 1, 1900. This method of storing dates allows you to work with dates using the same formulas you would use to work with any value. If you want to determine the number of days between two dates, you simply subtract one date from the other.

Excel automatically updates the values returned by the TODAY() and NOW() functions whenever you reopen the workbook. The **TODAY() function** displays the current date based on your computer's internal clock; the **NOW() function** displays both the date and time. If you want a permanent date (reflecting when the workbook was initially created, for example), enter the date directly into the cell without using either function.

If you have additional tasks to perform with a date or time, you can use one of the functions listed in Figure 2-22.

Figure 2-22 Date and Time functions

Function	Description
DATE(*year*, *month*, *day*)	Creates a date value for the date represented by the *year*, *month*, and *day* arguments
DAY(*date*)	Extracts the day of the month from the *date* value
MONTH(*date*)	Extracts the month number from the *date* value, where 1=January, 2=February, and so forth
YEAR(*date*)	Extracts the year number from the *date* value
WEEKDAY(*date*, [*return_type*])	Calculates the day of the week from the *date* value, where 1=Sunday, 2=Monday, and so forth. To choose a different numbering scheme, set the optional *return_type* value to "1" (1=Sunday, 2=Monday, ...), "2" (1=Monday, 2=Tuesday, ...), or "3" (0=Monday, 1=Tuesday, ...).
NOW()	Displays the current date and time
TODAY()	Displays the current date

You can use these functions to answer such questions as: On what day of the week does 1/1/2008 fall? You can calculate the day of the week with the **WEEKDAY function** as *=WEEKDAY(1/1/2008)*. This formula returns the value 7, which is Saturday—the seventh day of the week.

Because Amanda intends to use this worksheet as a model for future budgets, she wants the date on the Documentation sheet to always display the current date. You will replace the date you entered when you first opened the workbook with the TODAY() function.

To enter the TODAY() function on the Documentation sheet:

1. Switch to the Documentation sheet.
2. Click cell **B4**, type **=TODAY()**, and then click the **Enter** button on the Formula bar. Note that there are no arguments in the TODAY() function, but you still have to include the opening and closing parentheses, and there are no spaces between the parentheses. Excel displays the current date as shown in Figure 2-23.

Figure 2-23 **Inserting the current date**

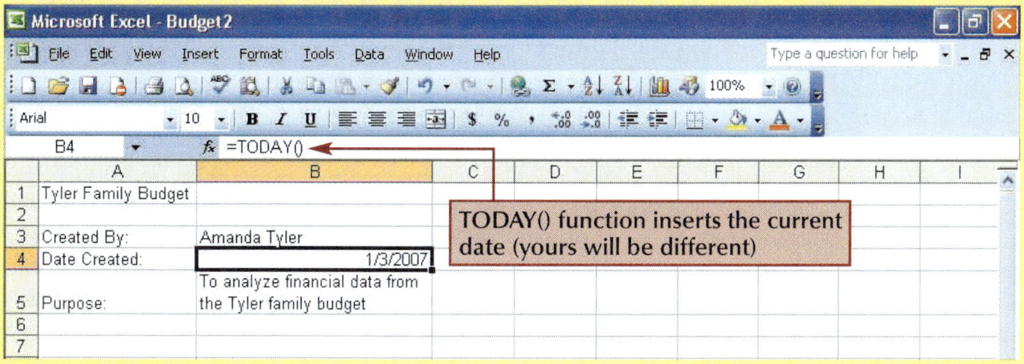

You have completed your work on the Budget2 workbook.

3. Save your changes to the workbook, and then close it.

Using Math and Statistical functions, you have been able to calculate the monthly and end-of-year values Amanda requested. With these values in place, Amanda has a better picture of the family's finances, and she is more confident about how she will manage the family budget in the year to come.

Session 2.1 Quick Check

Review

1. What is the function you enter to calculate the minimum value in the range B1:B50?
2. Cell A10 contains the formula *=A1+B1*. When you copy the content of cell A10 and paste it into cell B11, what formula is inserted into the destination cell?
3. Cell A10 contains the formula *=$A$1+B1*. When you copy the content of cell A10 and paste it into cell B11, what formula is inserted into the destination cell?
4. Express the reference to cell A1 as (a) a relative reference, (b) an absolute reference, and (c) a mixed reference (both possibilities).
5. List the steps you use in Excel to create a series of odd numbers from 1 to 99 in column A of your worksheet.
6. To display the current date in a workbook each time you reopen it, you enter the ______________ function in the cell where you want the date to appear.

Session 2.2

(**Note:** This session presents topics related to Financial functions and Logical functions. This session ***is optional and may be skipped*** without loss of continuity of the instruction.)

Working with Financial Functions

After reviewing the figures calculated in the Budget worksheet, Amanda thinks she has a better understanding of the family finances. Now she would like to determine whether the family could afford the monthly payments required to purchase a house if they were to take a loan from a bank. To do this, she wants to create a worksheet containing a "typical" month's income and expenses, and then she wants to use an Excel Financial function to calculate the monthly payments required for a loan of $175,000. Excel's **Financial functions** are the same as those widely used in the world of business and accounting to perform various financial calculations. For instance, these functions allow you to calculate the depreciation of an asset, determine the amount of interest paid on an investment, compute the present value of an investment, and so on. Although she is not a business or financial professional, Amanda's question is a financial one: Given the family budget, how great a loan payment can they afford if they want to buy a home? There are four principal factors involved in negotiating a loan:

- The size of the loan
- The length of time in which the loan must be repaid
- The interest rate charged by the lending institution
- The amount of money to be paid to the lending institution in periodic installments, called *payment periods*. (For most home loans, payments are due monthly, so the payment period is a month.)

To be sure, this is a simplified treatment of loans. Often other issues are involved, such as whether payments are due at the beginning of the payment period or at the end. For the purposes of this exercise, the above are the major factors on which Amanda will concentrate for now. Once you know any three of these factors, you can use Excel to calculate the value of the remaining fourth. Amanda is interested in a loan with the following conditions:

- The size of the loan is equal to $175,000.
- The length of time to repay the loan is equal to 30 years.
- The annual interest rate is equal to 5.5%.

She wants to calculate the fourth value—the monthly payment required by the lending institution to pay back the loan. To answer this question, you'll add a new worksheet to her workbook in which she can analyze various loan possibilities.

To create the Loan Analysis worksheet:

1. If you took a break after the last session, make sure that Excel is running and that the Budget2 workbook is open.
2. Insert a new worksheet at the end of the workbook named **Loan Analysis**, and then save the workbook as **Budget3** in the Tutorial.02\Tutorial folder included with your Data Files.
3. Click cell **A1**, type **LOAN ANALYSIS**, and then press the **Enter** key.

   Now you need to copy the labels and the average values from the Budget worksheet, which you completed in the previous session.

4. Switch to the Budget worksheet, select the nonadjacent range **A29:A48;C29:C48**, and then click the **Copy** button on the Standard toolbar.
5. Switch to the Loan Analysis worksheet, and then click cell **A3** to make it the active cell.

   Rather than pasting the formulas into this worksheet, you will simply paste the values.
6. Click the **Paste** list arrow on the Standard toolbar, and then click **Values** in the list of paste options. Excel pastes the labels from column A in the Budget worksheet into column A on the Loan Analysis worksheet and also pastes the average values from column C in the Budget worksheet into column B in the current worksheet. See Figure 2-24.

Figure 2-24 Pasting the income and expense categories and the average values

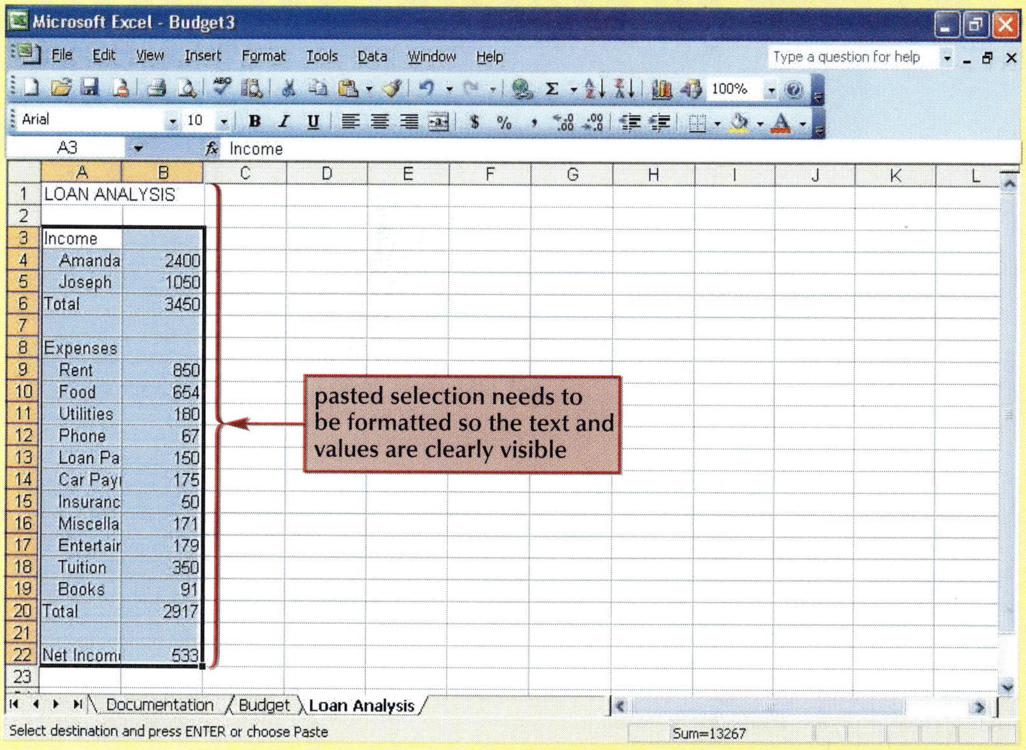

Excel pastes the cells as an adjacent range, not as a nonadjacent range. The result is that the values pasted from column C are shifted to the left into column B—right next to the labels in column A. These are the values you will need; their new location is not an issue. You will have to make some minor changes to the data, but first you need to increase the width of the columns so the values are easier to read. Then you will insert the formulas back into cells B6, B20, and B22 to calculate the total income, total expenses, and net income for a typical month.

To modify the layout of the worksheet and replace some of the values with formulas:

1. Click cell **A1** to remove the selection highlight from the pasted range.
2. Increase the width of column A to **18** characters (**131** pixels) and the width of column B to **10** characters (**75** pixels).

3. Click cell **B6**, click the **AutoSum** button Σ on the Standard toolbar, and then press the **Enter** key. Excel inserts the formula *=SUM(B4:B5)* into cell B6 to calculate the total average monthly income.
4. Click cell **B20**, click the **AutoSum** button Σ on the Standard toolbar, and then press the **Enter** key. Excel inserts the formula *=SUM(B9:B19)* into cell B20 to calculate the total average monthly expenses.
5. Click cell **B22**, type **=B6-B20** to calculate the average monthly net income, and then press the **Enter** key.

Now that you've entered the average monthly income and expense values for Amanda's budget and have widened the columns, you can enter the conditions for the loan. When you enter the amount of the loan, you will enter it as a negative value rather than as a positive value. The reason that you enter it as a negative value is because the loan is the amount owed to the lending institution; therefore, it is an expense. As you'll see later, Excel's Financial functions require loans to be entered as negative values because they represent negative cash flow. You will enter the labels and the conditions in columns D and E.

To enter the conditions of the loan in the worksheet:

1. Click cell **D3**, type **Loan Conditions**, and then press the **Enter** key to move to the next row where you will enter the Loan Amount label and the loan amount as a negative value.
2. Type **Loan Amount** in cell D4, press the **Tab** key, and then enter **-175,000** in cell E4.

   Next you will enter the length of the loan in years.
3. Type **Length of Loan** in cell D5, press the **Tab** key, and then enter **30** in cell E5.

   Now you will enter the annual interest rate, which is 5.5%.
4. Type **Annual Interest Rate** in cell D6, press the **Tab** key, and then enter **5.5%** in cell E6. Note that Excel may enter a zero, which doesn't change the value of the percentage.

   Next, you will enter the conditions under which the loan is to be repaid. In this case, you will assume that payments are due monthly.
5. Click cell **D8**, type **Payment Conditions**, and then press the **Enter** key.

   You will enter the number of payments to be made each year, which is 12.
6. Type **Payments per Year** in cell D9, press the **Tab** key, type **12** in cell E9, and then press the **Enter** key.

   Next you will enter the formula to calculate the total number of payments required to pay back the loan, which is the length of the loan (found in cell E5) multiplied by the payments per year (found in cell E9).
7. Type **Total Payments** in cell D10, press the **Tab** key, type **=E5*E9** in cell E10, and then press the **Enter** key.
8. Type **Payment Amount** in cell D11, and then press the **Tab** key.

   Before you continue, you will widen the columns so information is clearly visible.
9. Increase the width of column D to **18** characters (**131** pixels) and the width of column E to **10** characters (**75** pixels). Figure 2-25 shows the Loan Analysis worksheet with the values, loan conditions, and payment conditions entered.

Figure 2-25 Entering conditions for the loan and the monthly payments

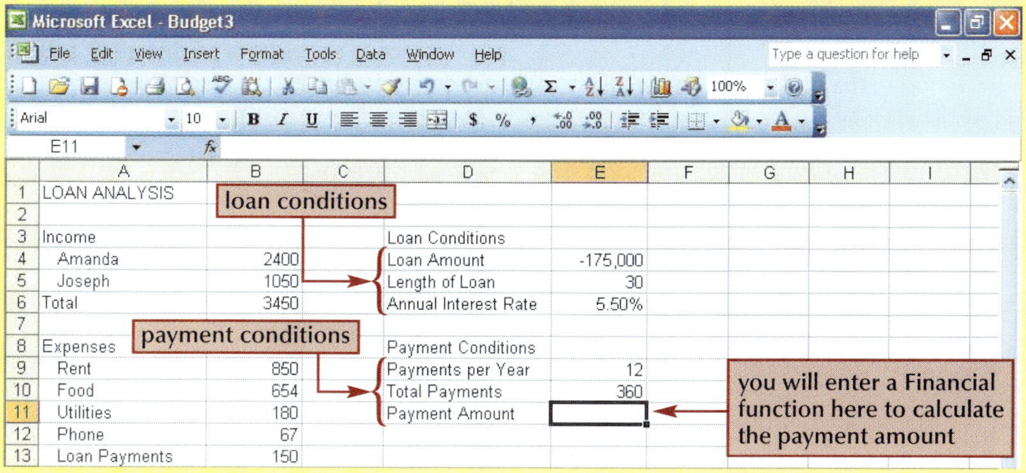

Paying off this loan will require 12 payments per year for 30 years, or 360 total payments. But how much will Amanda have to pay each month? To answer that question, you can use one of Excel's Financial functions.

Using the PMT Function

The monthly payment required to pay off a loan can be determined using the **PMT function**. The syntax of the PMT function is

=PMT(*rate*, *nper*, *pv*, [*fv*=0], [*type*=0])

where *rate* is the interest rate per payment period (determined by dividing the annual interest rate by the number of payment periods in a year), *nper* is the total number of payments, and *pv* is the present value of the future payments that will be made. In the case of a loan, the *pv* argument must be entered as a negative number. There are two optional parameters in this function: *fv* and *type*. The *fv* parameter indicates the future value of the loan and has a default value of 0. A future value of 0 means that the loan is paid off completely. The *type* parameter specifies whether payments are due at the beginning of the period (*type*=1) or at the end (*type*=0). The default value of the *type* parameter is 0.

Note that you can also use the PMT function for investments in which a specified amount of money is saved each month at a specified interest rate. In that case, the value of the *pv* argument would be positive since it represents an investment (a positive cash flow) rather than a loan (a negative cash flow).

Because the PMT function, like many Excel functions, has several required arguments, in addition to some optional arguments, you might not always remember all of the function's arguments and the order in which they should be entered. To make your task easier, you'll use the Insert Function dialog box to determine the payment amount for the loan Amanda is considering.

To select the PMT function using the Insert Function dialog box:

1. With E11 as the active cell, click the **Insert Function** button on the Formula bar. The Insert Function dialog box opens.

   To locate the PMT function, you'll enter a text description of this function in the Search for a function text box.

2. Type **loan payment** in the Search for a function text box, and then click the **Go** button. Excel displays a list of functions related to loan payments. See Figure 2-26.

Figure 2-26 Searching for functions related to loan payments

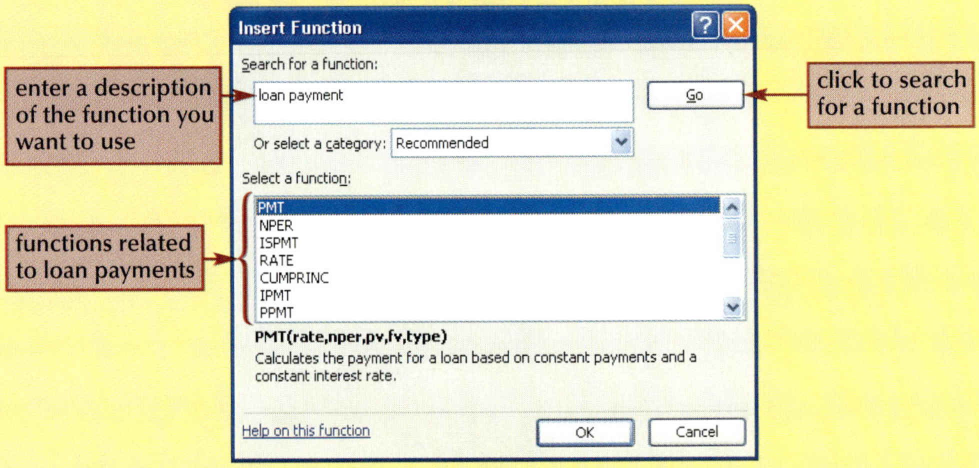

3. Verify that **PMT** is selected in the list of functions, read the description provided in the lower portion of the dialog box, and then click the **OK** button. The Function Arguments dialog box for the PMT function opens, as shown in Figure 2-27.

Figure 2-27 Function Arguments dialog box for the PMT function

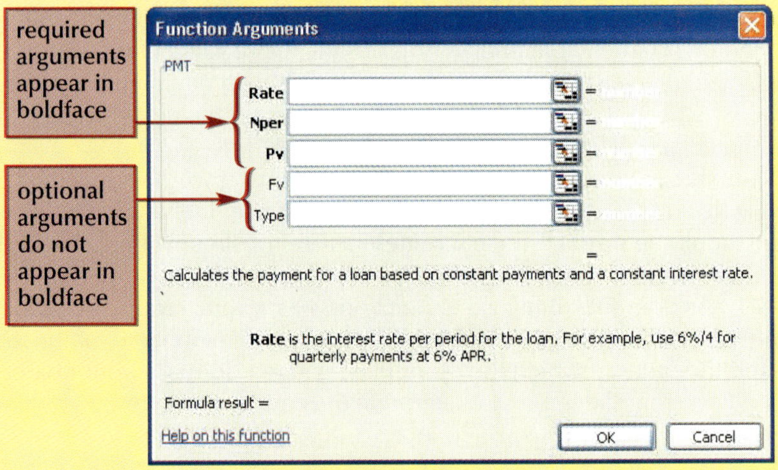

Note that, in the Function Arguments dialog box, required arguments are displayed in a boldfaced font, whereas optional arguments are not. Neither the Fv nor Type argument is displayed in a bold font. You will use this dialog box to enter values for the PMT function's arguments. The first argument that you will enter is for the rate, which is determined by dividing the annual interest rate by the number of payment periods in a year.

To enter values for the PMT function:

1. Click the **Collapse Dialog Box** button located to the right of the Rate box.
2. Click cell **E6** to enter the cell reference for the annual interest rate.

   To determine the rate, you will divide the value in cell E6 by the number of payment periods in a year (cell E9).
3. Type **/** (the division sign), and then click cell **E9** to enter the cell reference.
4. Click the **Expand Dialog Box** button to restore the Function Arguments dialog box. The expression E6/E9 should now appear in the Rate box.

   Next you will enter the value for the second argument, the *nper* argument, which is the total number of payments that need to be made for the 30-year loan. This number is displayed in cell E10.
5. Click in the **Nper** box, and then enter **E10** either by typing it directly into the reference box or by selecting the cell from the workbook.

   Finally, you will enter the *pv* (present value) argument. In the case of a loan, the present value is the amount of the loan Amanda's family is seeking. This value is stored in cell E4.
6. Click in the **Pv** box, and then enter **E4** using the method you prefer. Figure 2-28 shows the completed Function Arguments dialog box and illustrates how this dialog box relates to the function that will be inserted into cell E11.

Figure 2-28 **Entering the PMT function**

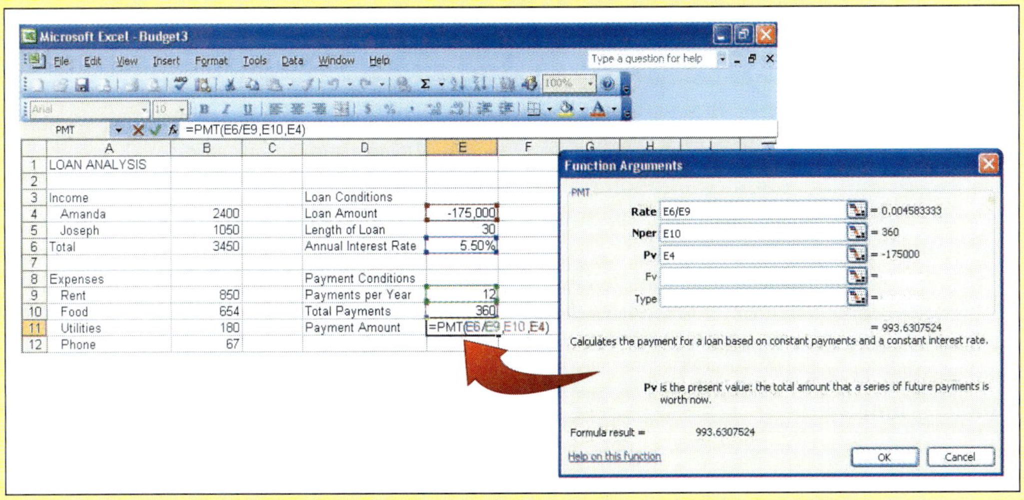

7. Click the **OK** button. Excel displays the value $993.63 in cell E11. Therefore, the required monthly payment is $993.63 for a loan of $175,000 at a 5.5% annual interest rate for 30 years.

   To see how this would affect Amanda's family budget, you will enter this information into the Expenses portion of the worksheet.
8. Click cell **A9**, type **House Payment** to replace the word "Rent," and then press the **Tab** key.

   Now you will enter a formula in cell B9 so the value House Payment is equal to the value Payment Amount.
9. Type **=E11** in cell B9, and then press the **Enter** key. The average total monthly expenses are recalculated.

If Amanda and Joseph were to buy a home with a $175,000 mortgage under the loan conditions specified in this workbook, their average monthly expenses would increase from $2,917 to $3,060.63 (cell B20), and the amount of money they could save each month would drop from $533 to about $389 (cell B22). By replacing the rent expense with the monthly home loan payment, Amanda can quickly gauge the effects of the loan on the family budget. Because the differences don't seem too unreasonable, Amanda now wants you to increase the size of the loan to $250,000, but keep all of the other factors constant.

To explore a what-if analysis for the mortgage:

1. Click cell **E4**, type **-250,000** as the new loan amount, being sure to enter this as a negative value, and then press the **Enter** key. Under this scenario, the monthly payment increases to about $1,419 and the family's monthly expenses increase to about $3,486, which is more than they make in a typical month. Obviously a loan of this size is more than they can afford.
2. Click the **Undo** button on the Standard toolbar to restore the worksheet to its previous condition.

   This time Amanda wants to know what would happen if the interest rate changed. To determine the difference between the low interest rate of 5.5% and a higher one, you will change the interest rate to 6.5%.
3. Click cell **E6**, type **6.5%**, and then press the **Enter** key. Excel calculates the monthly payment to be about $1,106. Amanda can see that if the interest rate increases by 1%, then the monthly payment increases by about $113. She wants you to change the interest rate back to 5.5%.
4. Click the **Undo** button on the Standard toolbar to change the interest rate back to its previous value.

The PMT function is just one of the many Financial functions supported by Excel. Figure 2-29 describes some of the other functions that can be used for mortgage analysis. For example, you can use the PV function to calculate the size of the loan that Amanda could afford given a specific interest rate, monthly payment, and total number of payments. If Amanda wanted to know the size of the loan she could afford by using the $850 rent payment as a loan payment, you would enter the formula *=PV(5.5%/12,360,850)*, which would return the value –$149,703.50, or a total loan of almost $150,000.

Figure 2-29 **Financial functions**

Function	Description
PMT(*rate*, *nper*, *pv*, [*fv*=0], [*type*=0])	Calculates the payments required each period on a loan or investment, where *rate* is the interest rate per period, *nper* is the total number of periods, *pv* is the present value or principal of the loan, *fv* is the future value of the loan, and *type* indicates whether payments should be made at the end of the period (0) or the beginning (1)
PV(*rate*, *nper*, *pmt*, [*fv*=0], [*type*=0])	Calculates the present value of a loan or investment based on periodic, constant payments
NPER(*rate*, *pmt*, *pv*, [*fv*=0], [*type*=0])	Calculates the number of periods required to pay off a loan or investment
RATE(*nper*, *pmt*, *pv*, [, *fv*=0], [*type*=0])	Calculates the interest rate of a loan or investment based on periodic, constant payments

You can use the other functions described in Figure 2-29 to calculate the interest rate and the total number of payment periods. Once again, if you know three of the conditions for the loan, there is an Excel function that you can use to calculate the value of the fourth.

From the calculations you have performed, Amanda now knows that a monthly mortgage payment of $993 is required to pay off a $175,000 loan in 30 years at 5.5% interest. This leaves the family with a net income of about $390 per month. The question remains whether Amanda feels that the mortgage is affordable. Amanda knows that she and Joseph will have to purchase a second car soon, that there are other expenses on the horizon, and that a new house will, no doubt, bring with it additional expenses that she may not have considered yet, such as property taxes. To prepare for those new future expenses, Amanda wants the family's net income to exceed their expenses by about $5,000 per year.

Does her current budget, with a home loan payment of $993 per month, meet that requirement? To find out, you will enter the amount of money Amanda feels that the family needs to save each year and a formula to calculate if they can achieve this goal.

To calculate the family's yearly net income:

1. Click cell **D13**, type **Is the loan affordable?** and then press the **Enter** key.

   You will enter the amount Amanda wants the family to save each year.

2. Type **Required Savings** in cell D14, press the **Tab** key, type **5,000** in cell E14, and then press the **Enter** key.

   Next, you'll enter the formula to calculate how much the family saved in one year using the average monthly net income multiplied by 12 months.

3. Type **Calculated Savings** in cell D15, press the **Tab** key, type **=B22*12** in cell E15, and then press the **Enter** key. See Figure 2-30. Note that the value in cell E15 shows five places to the right of the decimal. You'll learn how to specify the number of decimal places in Tutorial 3.

Figure 2-30 Calculating the yearly savings

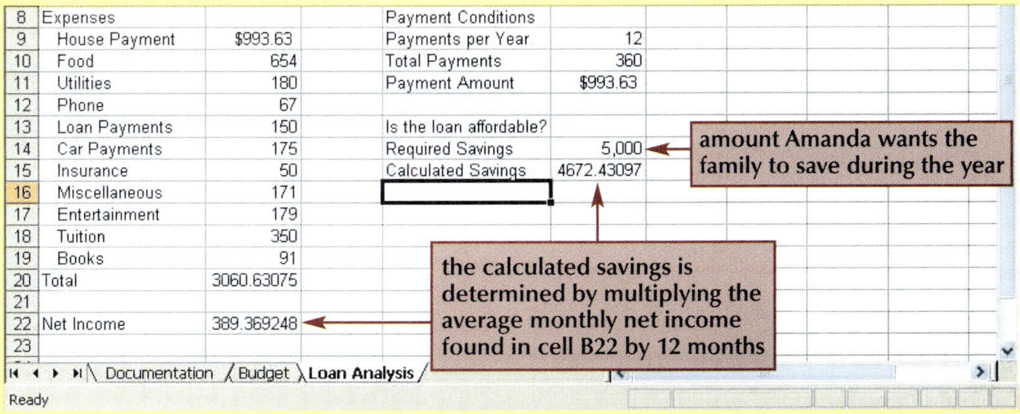

Under the proposed loan and assuming only the current expenses, the family could save about $4,672 per year, which is less than Amanda had hoped. So, Amanda would need to look at getting a smaller loan or hope that interest rates decrease in the future.

Amanda appreciates the type of information the worksheet provides, but she is concerned about getting lost in all of the numbers. She would like the worksheet to display a simple text message: "Yes" if the loan is affordable given the conditions she has set for the budget and "No" if otherwise. To add such a feature to the worksheet, you'll need to use a Logical function.

Working with Logical Functions

A **Logical function** is a function that tests, or evaluates, whether a condition in the workbook is true or false. The condition is usually entered as an expression. For example, the expression A1=10 would be true if cell A1 contains the value 10; otherwise, the expression is false.

Using the IF Function

The most commonly used Logical function is the **IF function**, which has the following syntax:

=IF(*logical_test*, *value_if_true*, [*value_if_false*])

where *logical_test* is an expression that is either true or false, *value_if_true* is the value displayed in the cell if the logical test is true, and *value_if_false* is the value displayed if the logical test is false. Note that the *value_if_false* argument is optional, though in most cases you will use it so that the function covers both possibilities.

For example, the formula *=IF(A1=10, 20, 30)* tests whether the value in cell A1 is equal to 10. If the expression A1=10 is true, the function displays the value 20 in the cell containing the function; otherwise, the cell displays the value 30. You can also construct logical tests that involve text values. The formula *=IF(A1="Retail", B1, B2)* tests whether cell A1 contains the text "Retail"; if it does, the function returns the value of cell B1; otherwise, it returns the value of cell B2.

Expressions in the logical test always include a comparison operator. A **comparison operator** indicates the relationship between two values. Figure 2-31 describes the comparison operators supported by Excel.

Figure 2-31 Comparison operators

Operator	Example	Description
=	A1 = B1	Tests whether the value in cell A1 *is equal to* the value in cell B1
>	A1 > B1	Tests whether the value in cell A1 *is greater than* the value in cell B1
<	A1 < B1	Tests whether the value in cell A1 *is less than* the value in cell B1
>=	A1 >= B1	Tests whether the value in cell A1 *is greater than or equal to* the value in cell B1
<=	A1 <= B1	Tests whether the value in cell A1 *is less than or equal to* the value in cell B1
<>	A1 <> B1	Tests whether the value in cell A1 *is not equal to* the value in cell B1

You'll use the IF function to display a text message in the worksheet indicating whether a $175,000 loan is affordable. In this case, the logical expression will test whether the value in cell E14 (the required savings) is less than the value in cell E15 (the calculated savings). The expression is E14 < E15. If this expression is true, then the loan is affordable for Amanda's family; otherwise, it is not. You will now enter the formula that includes the IF function *=IF(E14 < E15, "Yes", "No")*.

To insert the IF function to evaluate whether the loan is affordable:

1. Click cell **D16**, type **Conclusion**, and then press the **Tab** key.
2. In cell E16, type **=IF(E14<E15,"Yes","No")** and then press the **Enter** key. The text "No" appears in cell E16, indicating that the value in cell E14 is not less than the value in cell E15, and, therefore, the conditions of the mortgage are not acceptable to Amanda.

   Amanda asks you to reduce the size of the loan to $165,000 to see whether this amount changes the conclusion about the mortgage's affordability.

3. Click cell **E4**, type **-165,000** as the new loan amount, and then press the **Enter** key. As shown in Figure 2-32, the monthly payment drops to about $936 and the net yearly savings rise to about $5,354. Cell E16 displays the text string "Yes," indicating that this loan does satisfy Amanda's conditions for affordability.

Inserting a Logical function — **Figure 2-32**

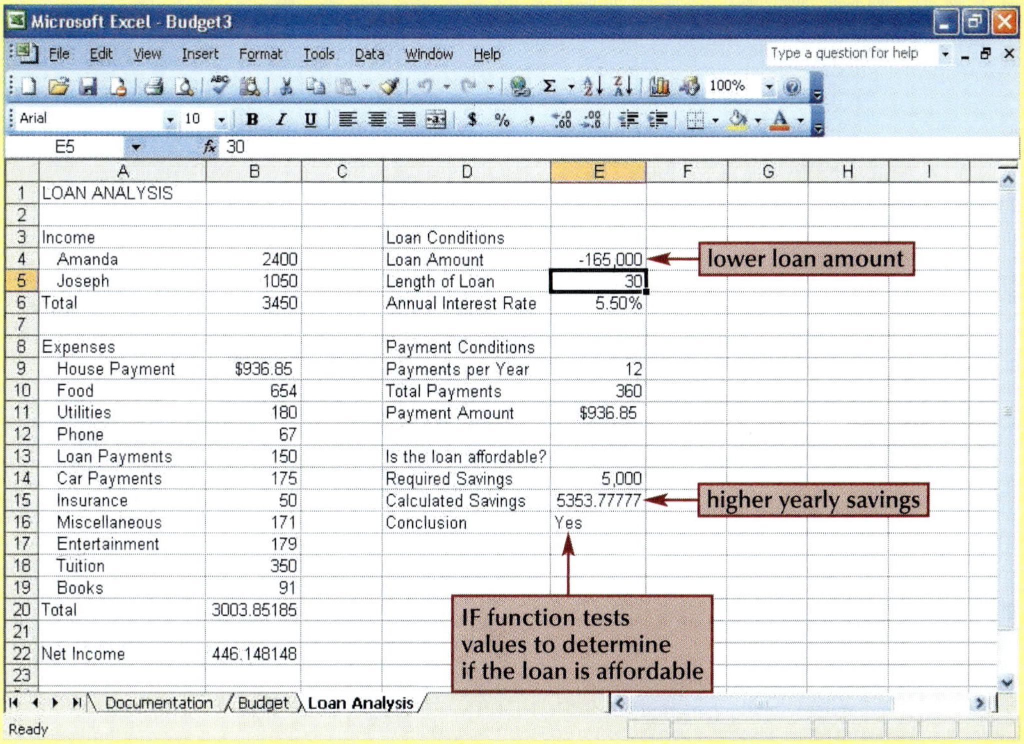

Now Amanda knows that buying a house is something that her family budget can support in the near future if she and Joseph manage their budget well. You will now save and close the Budget3 workbook.

4. Save your changes to the workbook, and then close it.

Excel has several other Logical functions that you can use to create more complicated tests. Figure 2-33 describes the syntax of each of these functions.

Figure 2-33 Logical functions

Function	Description
IF(*logical_test*, *value_if_true*, [*value_if_false*])	Returns the value *value_if_true* if the *logical_test* expression is true and *value_if_false* if otherwise
AND(*logical1*, [*logical2*, *logical3*, ...])	Returns the value TRUE if all *logical* expressions in the function are true and FALSE if otherwise
OR(*logical1*, [*logical2*, *logical3*, ...])	Returns the value TRUE if any *logical* expression in the function is true and FALSE if otherwise
FALSE()	Returns the value FALSE
TRUE()	Returns the value TRUE
NOT(*logical*)	Returns the value FALSE if the *logical* expression is true and the value TRUE if the *logical* expression is false

Amanda's budget workbook contains much of the information that she and Joseph can use to build a more stable financial picture for themselves in the future.

Review

Session 2.2 Quick Check

1. What are the four principal factors in a loan?
2. If you were to take a five-year loan for $10,000 at 7% annual interest rate, with monthly payments, what formula would you enter to calculate the monthly payment on the loan?
3. To calculate the present value of a loan based on a set, monthly payment, you could use the ______________ function.
4. What formula would you use to display the text string "Yes" if the value in cell A1 is greater than the value in cell B1 and "No" if otherwise?
5. To change a logical expression from FALSE to TRUE or from TRUE to FALSE, use the ______________ function.

Review

Tutorial Summary

In Session 2.1, you learned about the general syntax used by all Excel functions, and you learned about some of the Math and Statistical functions supported by Excel. You used the SUM function in a formula to calculate income and expenses for the month of January. You then learned how to copy and paste these formulas into other cells in the worksheet to calculate total figures for every month of the year. You learned the difference between the three types of cell references—relative, absolute, and mixed—and then you used an absolute reference to calculate a running total of the net income. You learned about the AVERAGE, MIN, and MAX functions, and then used them to summarize the entire year's budget figures. Once you entered the formulas that used these functions, you learned how to copy and paste the formulas using the Auto Fill feature. You also learned how to change the magnification of the workbook window so you can see more or less of the data in a worksheet. Finally, you used the TODAY() function to display the current date in the Documentation sheet.

In Session 2.2, you learned about the PMT function, which is a Financial function supported by Excel. You used the PMT function to calculate the monthly payment required to pay off a specified mortgage. You also learned about one of Excel's most commonly used Logical functions, the IF function. You used the IF function to display a text string indicating whether a loan was affordable.

Key Terms

Session 2.1
absolute reference
argument
Auto Fill
AVERAGE function
Date function
destination cell
destination range
F4 key
fill handle
MAX function
MIN function
mixed reference
NOW() function
optional argument
relative reference
source cell
source range
SUM function
syntax
TODAY() function
WEEKDAY function

Session 2.2
comparison operator
Financial function
IF function
Logical function
PMT function

Practice

Practice the skills you learned in Session 2.1 using the same case scenario.

Review Assignments

Data File needed for the Review Assignments: Family1.xls

Amanda appreciates the work you did on her family budget. Her friends Ken and Ava Giles have examined the workbook you created and have asked you to create a similar workbook for their budget.

Once you have completed a budget worksheet for the Giles family, they may want you to help them determine if they can afford to purchase their dream house in the country. The mortgage would be substantially higher than the family's current mortgage, but with Ava now working full time, the couple feels that they may be able to afford the higher mortgage. They would like you to create a workbook that will help them to determine if purchasing the house is possible.

To complete this task:

1. Open the **Family1** workbook located in the Tutorial.02\Review folder included with your Data Files, and then save the workbook as **Family2** in the same folder.
2. In the Documentation sheet, enter your name in cell B3, and then enter the current date in cell B4 using the TODAY() function.
3. Switch to the Budget worksheet, and then enter the formulas in the ranges C7:N7 and C14:N14 to calculate the total income and expenses, respectively, for each month. (*Hint*: Enter the formula in cells C7 and C14 first, and then copy and paste the formulas to the other cells in the ranges.)
4. In the range C16:N16, enter a formula to calculate the family's net income. (*Hint*: Enter the formula in cell C16 first, and then copy and paste the formula to the other cells in the range.)
5. In the range D17:N17, enter a formula using the SUM function to calculate the running total for net income from February through December. (*Hint*: Use an absolute reference for the appropriate cell reference.)
6. In the range C4:N4, use Auto Fill to fill in the month names January, February, March, and so forth.

7. In the range C21:F23, enter a formula to calculate the total, average, minimum, and maximum values of the two incomes.
8. In the range C25:F30, enter a formula to calculate the total, average, minimum, and maximum values of each expense category.
9. In the range C32:F32, enter a formula to calculate the total, average, minimum, and maximum values for net income.
10. Print the contents of the Budget worksheet, and save the changes you have made. If you are not continuing with the remaining steps, close the workbook.

Practice the skills you learned in Session 2.2 using the same case scenario.

(**Note:** The following steps are ***optional***. You should attempt them only if you have completed **Session 2.2** in the tutorial.)

11. Save the workbook as **Family3** to the Tutorial.02\Review folder.
12. Add a worksheet named "Loan Analysis" to the end of the workbook, and then enter the text "Loan Analysis" in cell A1 of the worksheet.
13. Switch to the Budget worksheet, copy the nonadjacent range A21:B32;D21:D32, switch to the Loan Analysis worksheet, and then paste the values, but not the formulas, into range A3:C14, using the Paste Special option. Increase the width of columns A and C to 12 characters (89 pixels) each, and column B to 15 characters (110 pixels). Edit the entries in cells C5, C12, and C14 so they contain formulas that calculate the total income, total expense, and net income.
14. Enter the following labels in the cells as indicated:
    - Cell E3: Loan Conditions
    - Cell E4: Loan Amount
    - Cell E5: Length of Loan
    - Cell E6: Annual Interest Rate
    - Cell E8: Payment Conditions
    - Cell E9: Payments per Year
    - Cell E10: Total Payments
    - Cell E11: Payment Amount
15. Widen column E to 21 characters (152 pixels).
16. In the range F4:F9, enter values for the following loan and payment conditions:
    - Loan Amount = –300,000
    - Years = 15
    - Annual Interest Rate = 6%
    - Payments per Year = 12
17. In cell F10, enter a formula to calculate the total number of payments. In cell F11, enter a formula using the PMT function to calculate the monthly loan payment.
18. In cell C8, enter the formula to make the mortgage expense equal to the result of the calculation in cell F11.
19. Enter the following labels in the cells as indicated:
    - Cell E13: Is the loan affordable?
    - Cell E14: Minimum Loan Payment
    - Cell E15: Conclusion
20. The family does not want a monthly loan payment greater than $2,500. Enter this value into cell F14, and then in cell F15 enter a formula using the IF function to display the text string "Yes" if the monthly payment is less than or equal to the value you entered in cell F14, and "No" if otherwise. Is the loan affordable under the loan conditions you have entered?
21. Print the contents of the Loan Analysis worksheet.

22. Change the loan from a 15-year loan to a 20-year loan. What effect does this have on the monthly loan payment and the conclusion about the affordability of the loan? Print the contents of the revised Loan Analysis worksheet.
23. Save your changes to the workbook, and then close it.

Apply

Apply the lessons you learned in Session 2.1 by creating a worksheet that analyzes the performance of a stock.

Case Problem 1

Data File needed for this Case Problem: Stock1.xls

Hardin Financial Carol Gilson works at Hardin Financial compiling reports on different stocks for portfolios managed by the company. Carol would like to use Excel to create a summary report for a particular stock, Point Electronics (PEC). She has entered the stock's performance for the past 50 days of trading and needs to summarize these values over the last 5 days, 10 days, and 50 days. She has asked you to help her complete the workbook. To complete this task:

1. Open the **Stock1** workbook located in the Tutorial.02\Cases folder included with your Data Files, and then save the file as **Stock2** in the same folder.
2. In the Documentation sheet, enter your name and enter the current date using the TODAY() function.
3. Switch to the Stock History worksheet, and in the range E3:E52 enter the numbers 50 through 1 in descending order using Auto Fill.
4. Column F needs to contain the opening value of the PEC stock. The opening value of the stock is equal to the closing value of the stock on the previous day. For example, the value in cell F3 should equal the value in cell I4. Enter the formula for the opening value for Day 50, and then use Auto Fill to fill in the opening values of the stock in the range F4:F51. (*Note:* The closing value for Day 1 has already been entered in cell F52 for you.)
5. In cell C4, enter a formula that calculates the highest value of the stock in the last 5 days (Day 46 through 50) using the values in column H.
6. In cell C5, enter a formula to calculate the lowest value of the stock in the same time period using the values in column G.
7. In cell C6, enter a formula to calculate the range (the difference between the maximum and minimum) of the stock's value in that time period.
8. In cell C7, enter a formula to display the stock's average closing value in the 5-day period.
9. Repeat Steps 5 through 8 for the 10-day statistics, placing the maximum, minimum, range, and average closing values in the range C9:C12.
10. Repeat Steps 5 through 8 for the 50-day statistics, placing the maximum, minimum, range, and average closing values in the range C14:C17.

Explore

11. Select range A1:C20, and then print just the selection.
12. Save your changes to the workbook, and then close it.

Create

Using what you learned in Session 2.1, create a workbook that summarizes regional sales information.

Case Problem 2

There are no Data Files needed for this Case Problem.

Maxwell Scientific Lisa Dunn manages orders for Maxwell Scientific, a mail-order company that sells science kits and education products to schools and educators. Lisa has asked you to help her with some projects. To begin, Lisa wants you to enter sales information for three different Maxwell Scientific products by region in an Excel workbook. After you enter the sales data, you need to enter formulas to calculate total, average, minimum, and maximum sales for each product and each region, and then for all the models and regions. You will also need to calculate the percentage of sales for each product.

To complete this task:

1. Open a new blank workbook and save it as **Maxwell1** in the Tutorial.02\Cases folder included with your Data Files.
2. Rename the first sheet in the workbook "Documentation," and then enter your name, the current date, and the purpose of the project in this sheet.
3. Rename the second worksheet "Sales Summary," and then enter the sales data shown in Figure 2-34.

Figure 2-34

		Units Sold	
Region	**Night Disks**	**Planet Cards**	**Solar Mobiles**
Region 1	2305	1483	824
Region 2	1281	1782	1005
Region 3	1885	2285	721
Region 4	2100	2108	1287

4. For each product, enter formulas to calculate the total sales for all regions, the average sales per region, and the maximum and minimum sales over all the regions.
5. For each product, enter a formula that uses absolute cell references to calculate the percentage of units sold per region.
6. Summarize the sales for all three of these Maxwell Scientific products by calculating the total, average, maximum, and minimum units sold for all products in all regions.
7. Calculate the percent of units sold for all products in each region.
8. Print the Sales Summary worksheet, and save your changes to the workbook. If you are not continuing with the remaining steps, close the workbook.

Using what you learned in Session 2.2, create another worksheet that determines discount prices and shipping expenses.

(**Note:** The following steps are ***optional***. You should attempt them only if you completed **Session 2.2** in the tutorial.)

9. Rename the third worksheet "Orders," and then save the workbook as **Maxwell2** in the Tutorial.02\Cases folder. Lisa has asked you to help her with another project. She wants you, using the Orders worksheet, to calculate the cost of each order and the total cost of all customer orders. Maxwell Scientific offers a 5% discount if customers order more than 50 units of a particular product. Also, customers can choose between two shipping options: standard shipping for a cost of $4.95, and express shipping for a cost of $9.95. You need to include both of these factors when calculating the cost of the order. Figure 2-35 shows a preview of the worksheet you'll create.

Figure 2-35

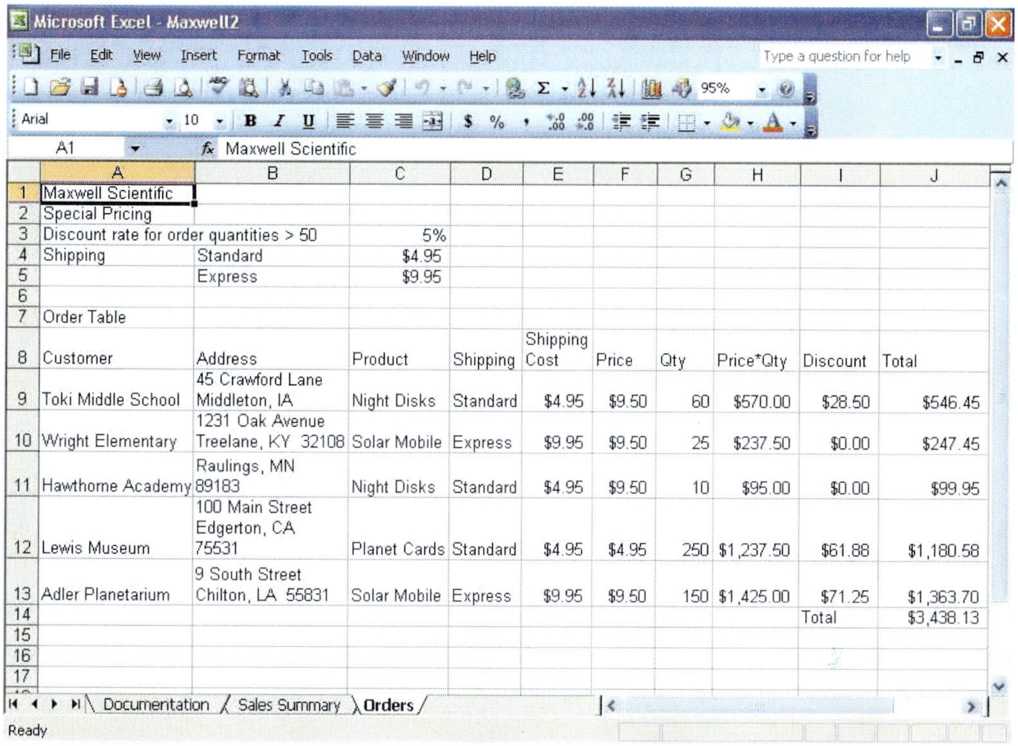

	A	B	C	D	E	F	G	H	I	J
1	Maxwell Scientific									
2	Special Pricing									
3	Discount rate for order quantities > 50		5%							
4	Shipping	Standard	$4.95							
5		Express	$9.95							
6										
7	Order Table									
8	Customer	Address	Product	Shipping	Shipping Cost	Price	Qty	Price*Qty	Discount	Total
9	Toki Middle School	45 Crawford Lane Middleton, IA	Night Disks	Standard	$4.95	$9.50	60	$570.00	$28.50	$546.45
10	Wright Elementary	1231 Oak Avenue Treelane, KY 32108	Solar Mobile	Express	$9.95	$9.50	25	$237.50	$0.00	$247.45
11	Hawthorne Academy	Raulings, MN 89183	Night Disks	Standard	$4.95	$9.50	10	$95.00	$0.00	$99.95
12	Lewis Museum	100 Main Street Edgerton, CA 75531	Planet Cards	Standard	$4.95	$4.95	250	$1,237.50	$61.88	$1,180.58
13	Adler Planetarium	9 South Street Chilton, LA 55831	Solar Mobile	Express	$9.95	$9.50	150	$1,425.00	$71.25	$1,363.70
14									Total	$3,438.13
15										
16										
17										

10. Enter formulas to calculate the total amount of each order and the total amount of all the customer orders. Use IF functions to calculate the shipping cost and discount for each order.
11. Preview the completed Orders worksheet, and then print it.
12. Save your changes to the Maxwell2 workbook.
13. Maxwell Scientific is considering changing its bulk discount rate from 5% to 8%. It is also looking at changing standard shipping charges to $5.50 and express shipping to $10.95. Lisa wants you to make these changes in the Orders worksheet. Change the discount rate and the shipping charges. What effect does the changes have on the current orders?
14. Print the revised Orders worksheet.
15. Save the workbook as **Maxwell3** in Tutorial.02\Cases folder, and then close the workbook.

Challenge

Go beyond what you learned in Session 2.2 to use the IF function as you create a payroll worksheet.

Case Problem 3

Data File needed for this Case Problem: Sonic1.xls

Sonic Sounds Jeff Gwydion manages the payroll at Sonic Sounds. He has asked you for help in setting up an Excel worksheet to store payroll information. The payroll contains three elements: each employee's salary, 401(k) contribution, and health insurance cost. The company's 401(k) contribution is 3% of an employee's salary for those who have worked for the company at least one year; otherwise, the company's contribution is zero. Sonic Sounds also supports two health insurance plans: Premier and Standard. The cost of the Premier plan is $6,500, and the cost of the Standard plan is $5,500. The workbook has already been set up for you. Your job is to enter the formulas to calculate the 401(k) contributions and health insurance costs for each employee. Figure 2-36 shows the worksheet as it will appear at the end of this exercise.

Figure 2-36

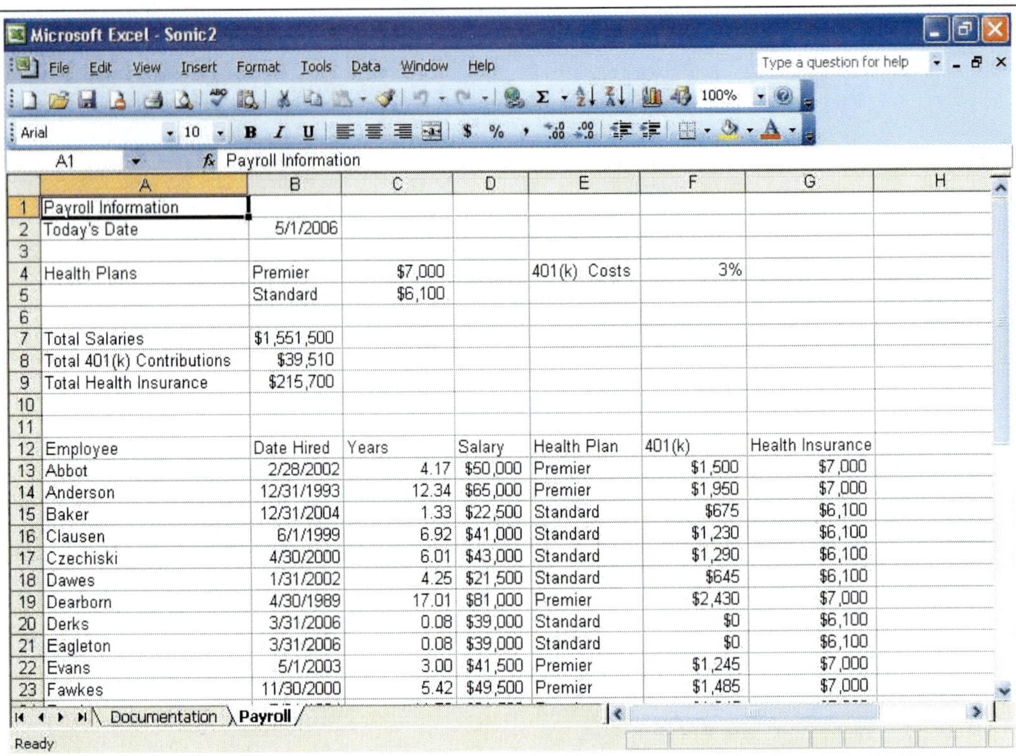

	A	B	C	D	E	F	G	H
1	Payroll Information							
2	Today's Date	5/1/2006						
3								
4	Health Plans	Premier	$7,000		401(k) Costs	3%		
5		Standard	$6,100					
6								
7	Total Salaries	$1,551,500						
8	Total 401(k) Contributions	$39,510						
9	Total Health Insurance	$215,700						
10								
11								
12	Employee	Date Hired	Years	Salary	Health Plan	401(k)	Health Insurance	
13	Abbot	2/28/2002	4.17	$50,000	Premier	$1,500	$7,000	
14	Anderson	12/31/1993	12.34	$65,000	Premier	$1,950	$7,000	
15	Baker	12/31/2004	1.33	$22,500	Standard	$675	$6,100	
16	Clausen	6/1/1999	6.92	$41,000	Standard	$1,230	$6,100	
17	Czechiski	4/30/2000	6.01	$43,000	Standard	$1,290	$6,100	
18	Dawes	1/31/2002	4.25	$21,500	Standard	$645	$6,100	
19	Dearborn	4/30/1989	17.01	$81,000	Premier	$2,430	$7,000	
20	Derks	3/31/2006	0.08	$39,000	Standard	$0	$6,100	
21	Eagleton	3/31/2006	0.08	$39,000	Standard	$0	$6,100	
22	Evans	5/1/2003	3.00	$41,500	Premier	$1,245	$7,000	
23	Fawkes	11/30/2000	5.42	$49,500	Premier	$1,485	$7,000	

To complete this task:

1. Open the **Sonic1** workbook located in the Tutorial.02\Cases folder included with your Data Files, and then save the workbook as **Sonic2** in the same folder.
2. In the Documentation sheet, enter your name and then enter the date using the TODAY() function.
3. Switch to the Payroll worksheet. In cell C13, enter a formula to calculate the number of years the first employee has worked at Sonic Sounds. Use an absolute reference for cell B2. Divide the difference by 365. (*Hint*: You need to subtract the date the employee was hired from the current date, which is in cell B2, and then divide the difference by the number of days in a year. For the purposes of this exercise, do not try to account for leap years.)
4. Use Auto Fill to calculate the number of years the remaining employees in the table have worked for the company.

Explore

5. In the range F13:F45, insert a formula to calculate the 401(k) contributions for each employee. The formula should determine that if the number of years employed is greater than or equal to 1, then the contribution is equal to the contribution percentage in cell F4 multiplied by the employee's salary; otherwise, the contribution is zero.

Explore

6. In the range G13:G45, enter a formula to calculate the health insurance cost for each employee by testing whether the name of the employee's plan is equal to the name of the health plan in cell B4. If it is, then the cost of the health plan is equal to the value of cell C4; otherwise, the cost is equal to the value of cell C5.

7. In the range B7:B9, enter the formulas to calculate the total salaries, 401(k) contributions, and health insurance costs.
8. Print the contents of the Payroll worksheet.
9. Rework the analysis, assuming that the cost of the Premier plan has risen to $7,000 and the cost of the Standard plan has risen to $6,100.
10. Print the revised Payroll worksheet.
11. Save your changes to the workbook, and then close it.

Challenge

Go beyond what you learned in Session 2.2. Use the PMT, PPMT, and IPMT functions to create a payment schedule for a small business.

Case Problem 4

Data File needed for this Case Problem: Soup1.xls

The Soup Shop Ken Novak is the owner of a diner in Upton, Ohio, named The Soup Shop. Business has been very good lately, so Ken is considering taking out a loan to cover the cost of upgrading and expanding the diner. Ken wants your help in creating an Excel workbook that provides detailed information about the loan. He would like the workbook to calculate the monthly payment needed for a five-year, $125,000 loan at 6.5% interest. Ken believes that the expansion will increase business, so he also wants to know how much he would save on interest payments by paying off the loan after one, two, three, or four years.

To do this type of calculation, you need to know what part of each monthly payment is used to reduce the size of the loan (also referred to as payments toward the principal) and what part is used for paying interest on the loan. Excel provides two functions to calculate these values, both of which are similar to the PMT function used to calculate the total monthly payment. To calculate how much of a monthly payment is used to pay off the principal, you use the PPMT function, which has the following syntax:

=PPMT(*rate*, *period*, *nper*, *pv* [,*fv*=0] [,*type*=0])

where *rate* is the interest rate period, *period* is the payment period you want to examine (such as the first period, the second period, and so forth), *nper* is the total number of payment periods, *pv* is the amount of the loan, *fv* is the future value of the loan (assumed to be zero), and *type* indicates whether the payment is due at the beginning (*type*=1) or at the end (*type*=0) of the month. The function to calculate how much of the monthly payment is used for paying the interest is the IPMT function, which has a similar syntax:

=IPMT(*rate*, *period*, *nper*, *pv* [,*fv*=0] [,*type*=0])

As with the PMT function, the value of the *pv* argument should be negative when you are working with loans—as you are in this case.

Ken wants you to use these two functions to create a payment schedule that indicates for each of the 60 months of the loan, how much of the monthly payment is being used to pay off the loan and how much is being used to pay interest on the loan. You can then use this schedule to discover how much Ken could save in interest charges by paying off the loan early. Figure 2-37 shows the worksheet as it will appear at the end of this exercise.

Figure 2-37

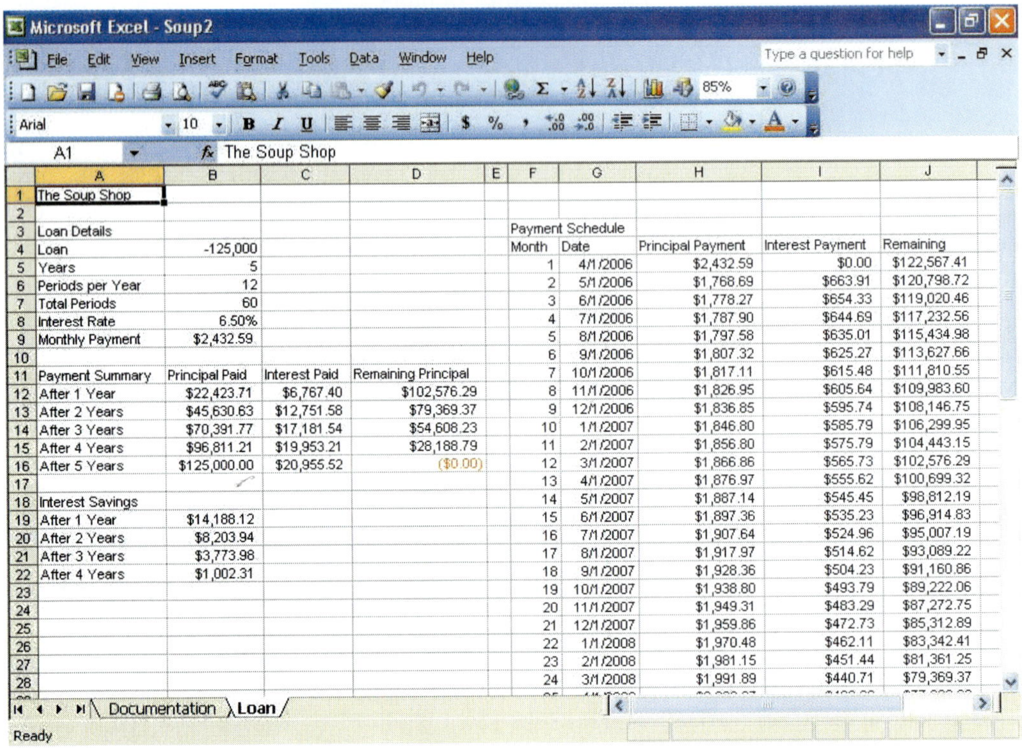

To complete this task:

1. Open the **Soup1** workbook located in the Tutorial.02\Cases folder included with your Data Files, and then save the workbook as **Soup2** in the same folder.
2. Enter your name and the current date in the Documentation sheet.
3. Switch to the Loan worksheet, and then in the range B4:B8, enter the following loan details:
   - Loan Amount = –125,000
   - Years = 5
   - Periods per Year = 12
   - Interest Rate = 6.5% (annually)

   In cell B7, enter a formula to calculate the total number of payment periods.
4. In cell B9, enter a formula using the PMT function to calculate the total monthly payment required to pay off the loan. Assume that payments are made at the beginning of each period, *not* at the end, which is the default. (*Hint*: Use the *fv* and *type* arguments.)
5. In the range F5:F64, enter the numbers 1 through 60 using Auto Fill. Each number indicates the payment period in the payment schedule.
6. Ken would like his payment schedule to include the dates on which the payments are due. In cell G5, enter the date 4/1/2006. This is the due date for the first payment. In cell G6, enter the date 5/1/2006. This is the due date for the second payment. Use the Auto Fill to enter the rest of the due dates into the range G7:G64.

Explore

7. In cell H5, enter a formula using the PPMT function to calculate the amount of the first month's payment devoted to reducing the principal of the loan. The details of the loan should reference the appropriate cells in the B4:B8 range of the worksheet using absolute references. The period number should reference the value in cell F5 using a relative reference. Be sure to indicate in the function that the payments are made at the beginning, not the end, of the month.

Explore

8. In cell I5, enter a formula using the IPMT function to calculate the amount of the first month's payment that is used for paying the interest on the loan.

Explore

9. In cell J5, enter a formula that calculates the amount of the principal remaining to be paid. Ken would like this expressed as a positive value. To calculate this value, construct a formula that is equal to the *negative* of the value in cell B4 (the amount of the loan) minus the running total of the principal payments. To calculate a running total of the principal payments, use the formula =SUM($H$5:H5). Note that this formula uses both an absolute reference and a relative reference, much like the running total example in the tutorial.
10. Using Auto Fill, copy the formulas in the range H5:J5 to the range H5:J64. (*Hint*: The value displayed in cell J64 should be $0.00, indicating that the loan is completely paid off. Also, the interest payment for the last month should be $13.11.)
11. In cell B12, enter a formula to calculate the total amount of payments made to the principal in the first 12 months of the schedule. In cell C12, enter a formula to calculate the total amount of the interest payments. In cell D12, enter a formula to calculate the amount of the remaining principal. Once again, Ken wants this expressed as a positive value, so the formula must subtract the value in cell B12 from the *negative* of the value in cell B4.
12. Repeat Step 11 for the range B13:D13, calculating the totals for the first 24 months. In the range B14:D14, calculate the totals for the first 36 months. In the range B15:D15, calculate the 48-month totals. In the range B16:D16, calculate the 60-month totals.
13. In the range B19:B22, enter a formula to calculate the amount of money Ken would save in interest payments if he paid off the loan after one year, two years, three years, and four years.

Explore

14. Preview the worksheet before printing it. Open the Page Setup dialog box, change the page orientation of the worksheet to landscape orientation, and then select the option so the worksheet will print on one page. Preview the worksheet again and then print it.
15. Save your changes to the workbook and then close it.

Research

Use the Internet to find and work with data related to the topics presented in this tutorial.

Internet Assignments

The purpose of the Internet Assignments is to challenge you to find information on the Internet that you can use to work effectively with this software. The actual assignments are updated and maintained on the Course Technology Web site. Log on to the Internet and use your Web browser to go to the Student Online Companion for New Perspectives Office 2003 at **www.course.com/np/office2003**. Click the Internet Assignments link, and then navigate to the assignments for this tutorial.

Assess

SAM Assessment and Training

If you have a SAM user profile, you may have access to hands-on instruction, practice, and assessment of the skills covered in this tutorial. Log in to your SAM account and go to your assignments page to see what your instructor has assigned.

Review

Quick Check Answers

Session 2.1

1. =MIN(B1:B50)
2. =B2+C2
3. =$A$1+C2
4. (a) A1 (b) $A$1 (c) $A1 and A$1
5. Enter the values 1 and 3 in the first two rows of column A. Select the two cells and then drag the fill handle down over the range A1:A99, completing the series.
6. TODAY()

Session 2.2

1. the loan amount, the interest rate, the number of payment periods, and the payment due each period
2. =PMT(7%/12,5*12,10000)
3. PV
4. =IF(A1>B1, "Yes", "No")
5. NOT

Objectives

Session 3.1
- Format data using the Comma, Currency, and Percent styles
- Copy and paste formats using the Format Painter
- Modify and apply number formatting styles
- Change font type, style, size, and color
- Change alignment of cell contents
- Apply borders and background colors and patterns

Session 3.2
- Merge a range of cells into a single cell
- Hide rows, columns, and worksheets
- Add a background image to a worksheet
- Format worksheet tabs
- Clear and replace formats
- Create and apply styles
- Apply an AutoFormat
- Set up a worksheet for printing
- Add headers and footers to printouts

Developing a Professional-Looking Worksheet

Formatting a Sales Report

Case

NewGeneration Monitors

NewGeneration Monitors is a computer equipment company that specializes in computer monitors. Joan Sanchez, sales manager, has been entering sales data for three of the company's monitors into an Excel workbook. She plans on including the sales data in a report to be presented later in the week. Joan has made no attempt to change or enhance the presentation of this data. She has simply entered the numbers. She needs you to transform her raw figures into a presentable report.

To create a professional-looking document, you will learn how to work with Excel's formatting tools to modify the appearance of the data in each cell, the cell itself, and the entire worksheet. You will also learn how to format printouts, create headers and footers, and control which parts of the worksheet are printed on which pages.

Student Data Files

▼Tutorial.03

▽ Tutorial folder
- Back.jpg
- Sales1.xls

▽ Review folder
- Region1.xls

▽ Cases folder
- Blades1.xls
- Running1.xls
- WBus1.xls

Session 3.1

Formatting Worksheet Data

The data for Joan's sales report has already been stored in an Excel workbook. Before going further, you will open the workbook and save it with a new filename.

To open the Sales report workbook:

1. Start Excel and then open the **Sales1** workbook located in the Tutorial.03\Tutorial folder included with your Data Files.
2. On the Documentation worksheet, enter *your name* in cell B3, and enter the *current date* in cell B4.
3. Save the workbook as **Sales2** in the Tutorial.03\Tutorial folder.
4. Click the **Sales** tab to display the unformatted worksheet, shown in Figure 3-1.

Figure 3-1 **The unformatted Sales worksheet**

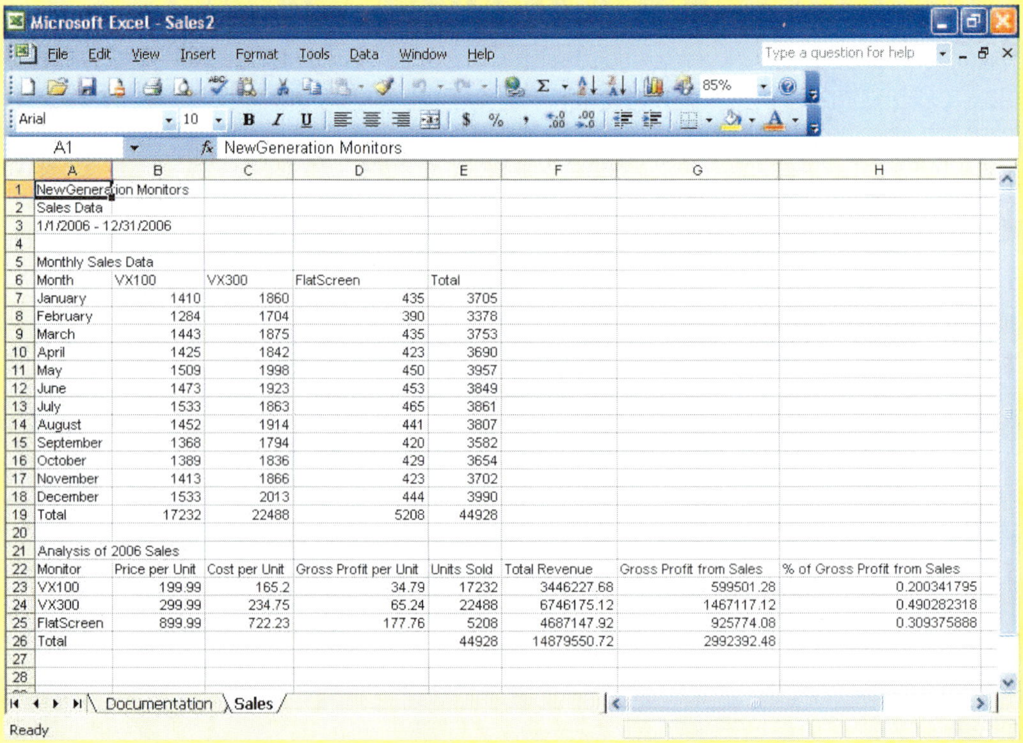

	A	B	C	D	E	F	G	H
1	NewGeneration Monitors							
2	Sales Data							
3	1/1/2006 - 12/31/2006							
4								
5	Monthly Sales Data							
6	Month	VX100	VX300	FlatScreen	Total			
7	January	1410	1860	435	3705			
8	February	1284	1704	390	3378			
9	March	1443	1875	435	3753			
10	April	1425	1842	423	3690			
11	May	1509	1998	450	3957			
12	June	1473	1923	453	3849			
13	July	1533	1863	465	3861			
14	August	1452	1914	441	3807			
15	September	1368	1794	420	3582			
16	October	1389	1836	429	3654			
17	November	1413	1866	423	3702			
18	December	1533	2013	444	3990			
19	Total	17232	22488	5208	44928			
20								
21	Analysis of 2006 Sales							
22	Monitor	Price per Unit	Cost per Unit	Gross Profit per Unit	Units Sold	Total Revenue	Gross Profit from Sales	% of Gross Profit from Sales
23	VX100	199.99	165.2	34.79	17232	3446227.68	599501.28	0.200341795
24	VX300	299.99	234.75	65.24	22488	6746175.12	1467117.12	0.490282318
25	FlatScreen	899.99	722.23	177.76	5208	4687147.92	925774.08	0.309375888
26	Total				44928	14879550.72	2992392.48	
27								
28								

The Sales worksheet contains two tables. The table in the upper portion of the worksheet displays the monthly sales figures for three of NewGeneration's monitors: the VX100, the VX300, and the FlatScreen. The other table presents an analysis of these sales figures. Although the data in the worksheet is accurate and complete, the numbers are not as easy to read as they could be, which also makes interpreting the data more difficult. To help improve the readability of the data presented in a worksheet, you can change its appearance by formatting it.

Formatting is the process of changing the appearance of your workbook. A properly formatted workbook can be easier to read, appear more professional, and help draw attention to the important points you want to make. Formatting only changes the appearance of the data; it does not affect the data itself. For example, if a cell contains the value 0.124168, and you format the cell to display only up to the thousandths digit (so the value appears as 0.124), the cell still contains the precise value, even though you cannot see it displayed in the worksheet.

Unless you specify different formatting, Excel automatically displays numbers in the worksheet cells using the **General number format**, which, for the most part, formats numbers just the way you enter them. There are some exceptions to this approach. For example, if the cell is not wide enough to show the entire number, the General number format rounds numbers that contain decimals and uses scientific notation for large numbers.

If you don't want to use the General number format, you can choose from a wide variety of number formats. Formats can be applied using either the Formatting toolbar or the Format menu. Formats can also be copied from one cell to another, giving you the ability to apply a common format to different cells in your worksheet.

Using the Formatting Toolbar

The Formatting toolbar is one of the fastest ways to format a worksheet. By clicking a single button on the Formatting toolbar, you can increase or decrease the number of decimal places displayed in a selected range of cells, and display a value as currency with a dollar sign or a percentage with a percent sign. You also can use the Formatting toolbar to change the font type (for example, Times New Roman or Arial), style (such as bold), color, or size.

When Joan entered the monthly sales figures for the three monitors, she was concerned with entering the figures as accurately and as efficiently as possible and wasn't concerned with the appearance of the numbers in the worksheet. She entered the sales figures without including a comma to separate the thousands from the hundreds and so forth. Now, to make the numbers easier to read, Joan wants all the values to appear with commas, and for the figures that are whole numbers, she doesn't want any zeros after the decimal point (also referred to as "trailing zeros"). She believes that these changes will make the worksheet easier to read.

To insert commas in the figures in Joan's worksheet, you will apply the Comma style using its button on the Formatting toolbar. By default, Excel automatically adds two decimal places to the numbers that you have formatted with the Comma style. You will then need to use the Decrease Decimal button on the Formatting toolbar to change the number of decimal places displayed in a number.

To apply the Comma style and remove the trailing zeros:

1. Select the range **B7:E19** in the Sales worksheet.
2. Click the **Comma Style** button on the Formatting toolbar. Excel adds the comma separator to each of the values in the table and displays the values with two digits to the right of the decimal point.

   Trouble? If you do not see the Comma Style button on the Formatting toolbar, click the Toolbar Options button on the Formatting toolbar, point to Add or Remove Buttons, point to Formatting, and then click on the menu of available buttons.

   Because Joan wants whole numbers displayed without trailing zeros, you will remove any that are displayed.
3. Click the **Decrease Decimal** button on the Formatting toolbar twice to remove the zeros. Figure 3-2 shows the worksheet with the formatting changes you have made so far.

Figure 3-2 Applying the Comma style

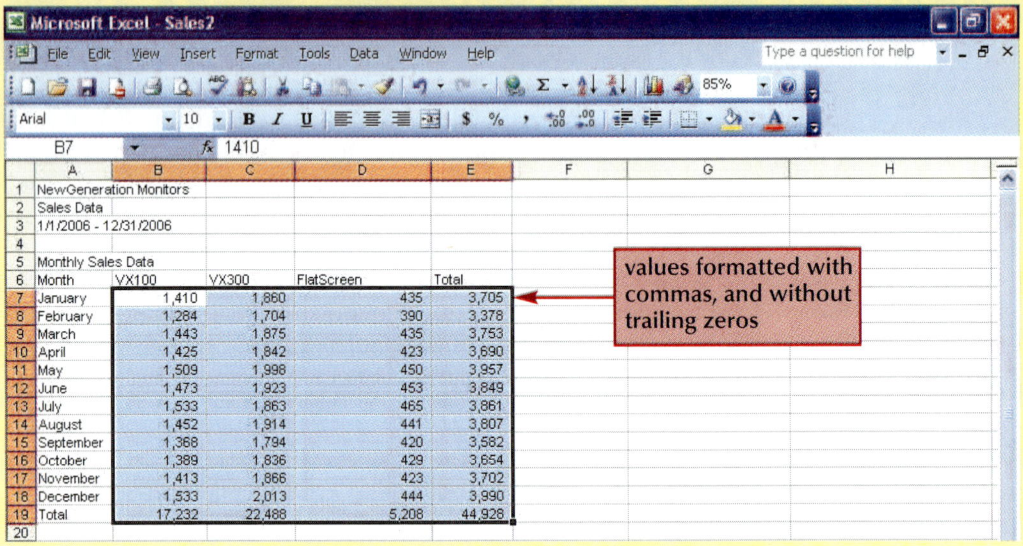

Joan wants the price and production cost of each monitor as well as last year's total sales and gross profit displayed using dollar signs, commas, and two decimal places. A quick and easy way to format the values with these attributes is to use the Currency style, which is available as a button on the Formatting toolbar. When you apply the Currency style, Excel adds a dollar sign and comma separator to the value and displays two decimal places. Try applying the Currency style to the total sales and profit values.

To apply the Currency style:

1. Select the nonadjacent range **B23:D25;F23:G26**.

   Trouble? To select a nonadjacent range, select the first range, press and hold the Ctrl key, and then select the next range.

2. Click the **Currency Style** button $ on the Formatting toolbar. As shown in Figure 3-3, Excel adds the dollar signs and commas, and keeps two decimal places to display the values as currency. Also note that the alignment of the dollar signs is along the left edge of the cell and the decimal points are aligned vertically.

Figure 3-3 Applying the Currency style

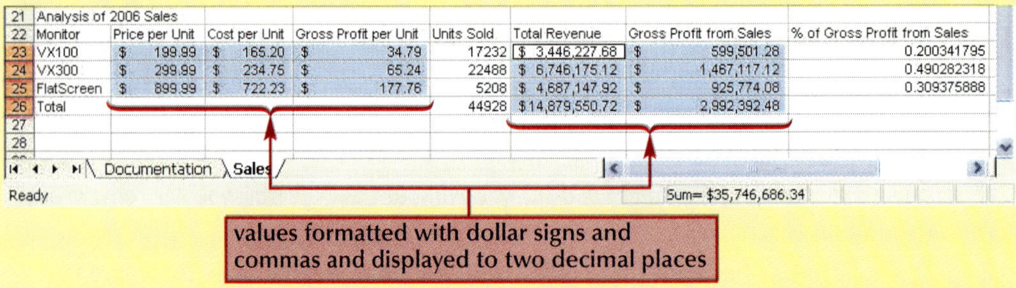

Finally, the range H23:H25 displays the percentage that each monitor contributes to the overall profit from sales. Joan wants these values displayed with a percent sign and two decimal places. To format a value as a percent, you can apply the Percent style. By default, Excel does not display any decimal places with the Percent style; therefore, you will need to increase the number of decimal places displayed.

To apply the Percent style and increase the number of decimal places:

1. Select the range **H23:H25**.
2. Click the **Percent Style** button on the Formatting toolbar. The values appear with percent signs and without zeros.
3. Click the **Increase Decimal** button on the Formatting toolbar twice to display the percentages to two decimal places. Figure 3-4 shows the values in column H formatted with percent signs and to two decimal places.

Figure 3-4 **Applying the Percent style**

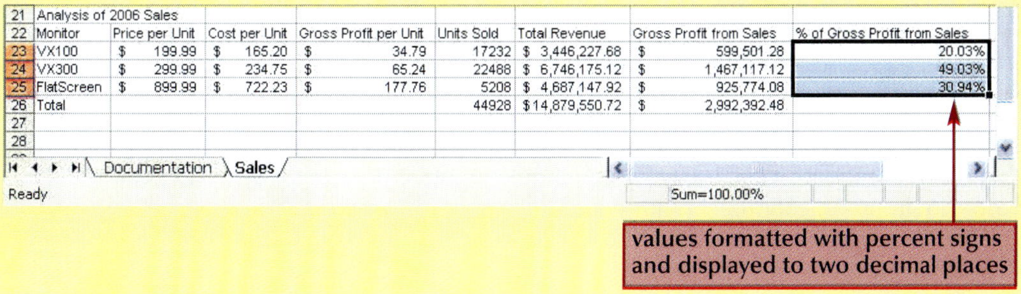

21	Analysis of 2006 Sales							
22	Monitor	Price per Unit	Cost per Unit	Gross Profit per Unit	Units Sold	Total Revenue	Gross Profit from Sales	% of Gross Profit from Sales
23	VX100	$ 199.99	$ 165.20	$ 34.79	17232	$ 3,446,227.68	$ 599,501.28	20.03%
24	VX300	$ 299.99	$ 234.75	$ 65.24	22488	$ 6,746,175.12	$ 1,467,117.12	49.03%
25	FlatScreen	$ 899.99	$ 722.23	$ 177.76	5208	$ 4,687,147.92	$ 925,774.08	30.94%
26	Total				44928	$14,879,550.72	$ 2,992,392.48	
27								
28								

By displaying the percentages, you can quickly see that one monitor, the VX300, accounts for almost half of the profit from monitor sales.

Copying Formats

As you look over the sales figures, you see that one area of the worksheet still needs to be formatted. The Units Sold column in the range E23:E26 still does not display the comma separator you used with the sales figures. To fix a formatting problem like this one, you can use the Format Painter button located on the Standard toolbar. When you use the **Format Painter** option, you "paint" a format from one cell to another cell or to a range of cells. This is a fast and efficient way of copying a format from one cell to another.

Copying Formatting Using the Format Painter

Reference Window

- Select the cell or range whose formatting you want to apply to other cells.
- To apply the formatting to one cell or an adjacent range of cells, click the Format Painter button on the Standard toolbar, and then click the destination cell or drag the Format Painter pointer over the adjacent range.
- To apply the formatting to nonadjacent ranges, double-click the Format Painter button on the Standard toolbar, and then drag the Format Painter pointer over the first range and then over the other ranges you want to format.

You will use the Format Painter button to copy the format used in the sales figures and to paste that format into the range E23:E26.

To copy the formatting to the range E23:E26 using the Format Painter button:

1. Select cell **B7**, which contains the formatting that you want to copy. You do not have to copy the entire range, because the range is formatted in the same way.
2. Click the **Format Painter** button on the Standard toolbar. As you move the pointer over the worksheet area, the pointer changes to .
3. Drag the pointer over the range **E23:E26** to apply the modified Comma style format to the sales figures.

Another approach is to use the fill handle discussed in Tutorial 2 to fill in the format (not the values) from one cell to another. To use this approach, you have click the Auto Fill Options button and select the Fill Formatting option. This technique only works when the cell or cells that you want to format are adjacent to the cell containing the format you want to copy. You can also use the Paste Special command from the Copy and Paste buttons to paste only the format of a selected group of cells into a new range of cells. This technique was also discussed in Tutorial 2. One of the advantages of the Format Painter button is that it does what these two methods do, but it does so in fewer steps. However, you should use the approach with which you feel most comfortable.

The Format Painter button and the buttons on the Formatting toolbar are fast and easy ways to copy and apply cell formats, but on occasion you will need more control over your formatting choices than is provided by these toolbar buttons. In those cases, you will need to use the Format Cells dialog box.

Using the Format Cells Dialog Box

Joan agrees that formatting the values has made the worksheet easier to read, but she has a few other suggestions. She does not like the way the currency values are displayed with the dollar signs placed at the left edge of the cell, leaving a large blank space between the dollar sign and the numbers, which is characteristic of values that use an accounting format. She would rather see the dollar sign placed directly to the left of the dollar amounts, which would eliminate the blank space.

The convenience of the Formatting toolbar's one-click access to many of the formatting tasks you will want to perform does have its limits. As you can see in the worksheet, when you use the Formatting toolbar, you cannot specify how the format is applied. To make the change that Joan suggests, you will open the Format Cells dialog box, which gives you more control over the formatting by providing categories of formats from which you can choose and modify to suit your needs.

To open the Format Cells dialog box:

1. Select the nonadjacent range **B23:D25;F23:G26**.
2. Click **Format** on the menu bar, and then click **Cells**. The Format Cells dialog box opens, as shown in Figure 3-5. In addition to the General format category, there are 11 number format categories from which to choose.

Format Cells dialog box — **Figure 3-5**

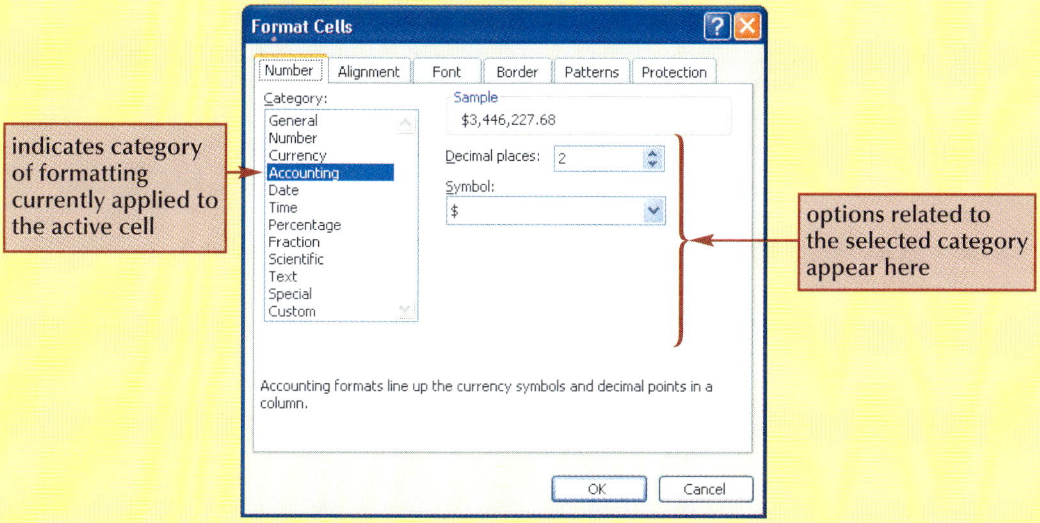

The Format Cells dialog box contains the following six tabs, each dedicated to a different set of format properties. You can apply the options available in this dialog box to any cell or range of cells that you select. The six tabs are:

- **Number:** Provides options for formatting the appearance of numbers, including dates and numbers treated as text (for example, telephone numbers)
- **Alignment:** Provides options for controlling how data is aligned within a cell
- **Font:** Provides options for selecting font types, sizes, and styles and other formatting attributes, such as underlining and colors
- **Border:** Provides options for adding borders around cells
- **Patterns:** Provides options for creating and applying background colors and patterns to cells
- **Protection:** Provides options for locking or hiding cells to prevent other users from modifying their contents

Excel supports several categories of number formats, ranging from Accounting, which you applied using the Currency Style button, to Scientific, which might be used for recording engineering data. Figure 3-6 describes the number format categories.

Figure 3-6 Number format categories

Category	Description
General	Default format that displays numbers as they are entered
Number	Used for a general display of numbers, with options for the formatting of negative numbers and the number of decimal places
Accounting	Used for displaying monetary values with dollar signs aligned at the left edge of the cell, the decimal points aligned vertically, and comma separators inserted
Currency	Used for displaying monetary values with dollar signs aligned next to leftmost digit and comma separators inserted (decimal points are not aligned)
Date, Time	Used for displaying date and time values
Percentage	Used for displaying decimal values as percentages
Fraction, Scientific	Used for displaying values as fractions or in scientific notation
Text	Used for displaying values as text strings
Special	Used for displaying ZIP codes, phone numbers, and social security numbers
Custom	Used for displaying numbers used in coding or specialized designs

As shown in the Format Cells dialog box in Figure 3-5, the Accounting format displays numbers with a dollar sign, a comma separator, and two decimal places. The Currency format is similar to the Accounting format. When you apply the Currency format to a number, the number appears with a dollar sign, a comma separator, and two decimal places. However, the difference between the two formats is how these attributes appear in the cell. The Accounting format lines up the decimal points and aligns the dollar signs at the left edge of the cell border (creating blank spaces between the dollar signs and the values, as you saw earlier). The Currency format aligns the dollar sign closer to the number, which removes the blank spaces. Joan prefers the Currency format, so you will apply this format to the nonadjacent range that you already selected.

To modify and apply the Currency format:

1. On the Number tab, click **Currency** in the Category list box. The Format Cells dialog box displays the options available for customizing the Currency category and provides a preview of the selected format. As shown in the Negative numbers list box, Excel displays negative currency values either with a minus sign (-) or with a combination of a red font and parentheses. Joan wants negative currency values to be displayed with a minus sign, which is one of the variations of the Currency format available to you.
2. Click the first entry in the Negative numbers list box, and then click the **OK** button. Excel changes the format of the currency values, removing the blank spaces between the dollar signs and the values and changing the alignment of the decimal points.

By using the Format Cells dialog box, you can control the formatting to ensure that text and values are displayed the way you want them to be.

Changing Font Type, Size, Style, and Color

A **font** is a set of characters that use the same typeface, style, and size. A **typeface** is the specific design of a set of printed characters, including letters, numbers, punctuation marks, and symbols. Some of the more commonly used fonts are Arial, Times Roman, and Courier. Each font can be displayed using one of the following **font styles**: regular, *italic*, **bold**, or ***bold italic***. Fonts can also be displayed with special effects, such as ~~strikeout~~, underline, and color.

Fonts can also be rendered in different sizes. **Font sizes** are measured using points. A **point** is a unit of measurement used in printing and is equal to approximately 1/72 of an inch. By default, Excel displays characters using a 10-point Arial font in a regular style. To change the font used in a selected cell, you either click the appropriate buttons on the Formatting toolbar or select options in the Format Cells dialog box.

In the logo that the company uses on all its correspondence and advertising materials, the name "NewGeneration Monitors" appears in a large Times New Roman font, which is a serif font. Characters that are designed as **serif fonts** have small lines stemming from and at an angle to the upper and lower ends of the character. **Sans serif fonts** do not include the small lines. A serif font is considered easier to read than a sans serif font. Joan wants the title in cell A1 to reflect this company-wide format, so you will format the title accordingly.

To change the font and font size of the title:

1. Click cell **A1** to make it the active cell.
2. Click the **Font** list arrow on the Formatting toolbar, scroll down the list of available fonts, and then click **Times New Roman**.

   Trouble? If you do not have the Times New Roman font installed on your computer, choose a different Times Roman font or choose MS Serif or another serif font in the list.
3. Click the **Font Size** list arrow on the Formatting toolbar, and then click **18**. Figure 3-7 shows the revised format for the title in cell A1.

Figure 3-7 Changing the font and font size

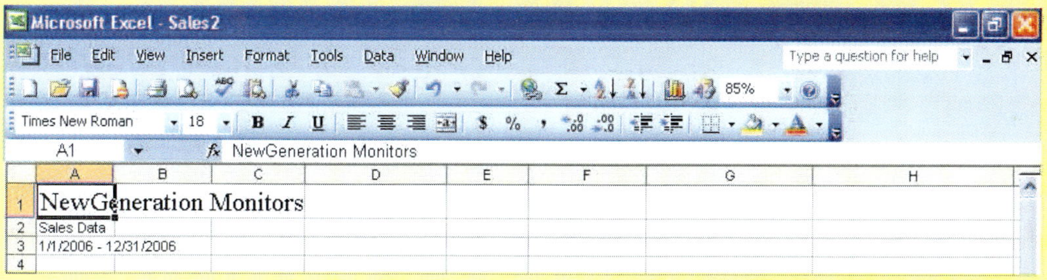

Joan wants the column titles of both tables displayed in bold font and the word "Total" in both tables displayed in italics. To make these modifications, you will again use the Formatting toolbar.

To apply the bold and italic styles:

1. Select the nonadjacent range **A6:E6;A22:H22**.
2. Click the **Bold** button on the Formatting toolbar. The titles in the two tables now appear in a boldface font.

   Trouble? Some of the title text may appear truncated within their cells. You'll fix this problem shortly.

3. Select the nonadjacent range **A19;A26**.
4. Click the **Italic** button on the Formatting toolbar. The word "Total" in cells A19 and A26 is now italicized.

Joan points out that NewGeneration's logo usually appears in a red font. Color is another one of Excel's formatting tools and can dramatically enhance the presentation of your data if you have a color printer. Excel provides a palette of 40 different colors. If the color you want is not listed, you can modify Excel's color configuration to create a different color palette. Excel's default color settings will work for most situations, so in this case you will not modify Excel's color settings. You will apply a red color to the name of the company and the two subtitles, which describe the contents of this worksheet.

To change the font color of the title to red:

1. Select the range **A1:A3**.
2. Click the **Font Color** list arrow on the Formatting toolbar to display a color palette, and then position the pointer over the Red square (third row, first column from the left) on the palette, as shown in Figure 3-8.

Figure 3-8 **Choosing a font color**

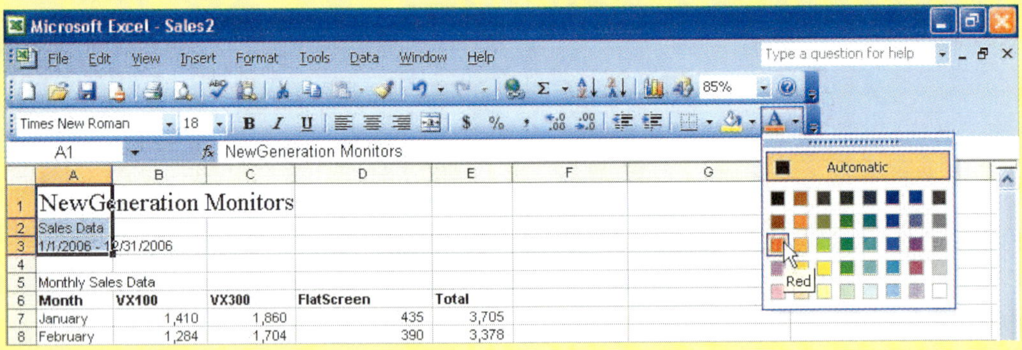

3. Click the **Red** square to change the color of the font in the selected cells to red. See Figure 3-9.

Figure 3-9 **Changing the font color of a cell**

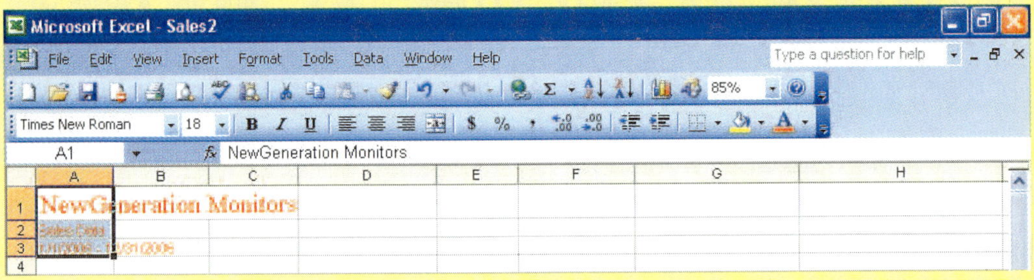

Aligning Cell Contents

When you enter numbers and formulas into a cell, Excel automatically aligns them with the cell's right edge and bottom border. Text entries are aligned with the left edge and bottom border. The default Excel alignment does not always create the most readable worksheets. As a general rule, you should center column titles, and format columns of numbers so that the decimal places are lined up within a column. You can change horizontal alignment using the alignment tools on the Formatting toolbar or the options on the Alignment tab in the Format Cells dialog box.

Next, you will center the column titles above the values in each column in the two tables.

To center the column titles:

1. Select the nonadjacent range **B6:E6;B22:H22**.
2. Click the **Center** button on the Formatting toolbar. Excel centers the text in the selected cells in each column.

The Formatting toolbar also provides the Align Left button and the Align Right button so that you can left-align and right-align cell contents. If you want to align cell contents vertically, you have to open the Format Cells dialog box and choose the vertical alignment options on the Alignment tab.

Another alignment option available in the Format Cells dialog box is to center text across a range of cells. Joan wants the text in the cell range A1:A3 to be centered at the top of the worksheet across the first eight columns of the worksheet. This time you will open the Format Cells dialog box to make this formatting change.

To center the titles and subtitles across the first eight columns of the worksheet:

1. Select the range **A1:H3**.
2. Click **Format** on the menu bar, and then click **Cells** to open the Format Cells dialog box.
3. Click the **Alignment** tab.
4. Click the **Horizontal** list arrow in the Text alignment pane, click **Center Across Selection**, and then click the **OK** button. See Figure 3-10.

Figure 3-10 Centering text within and across columns

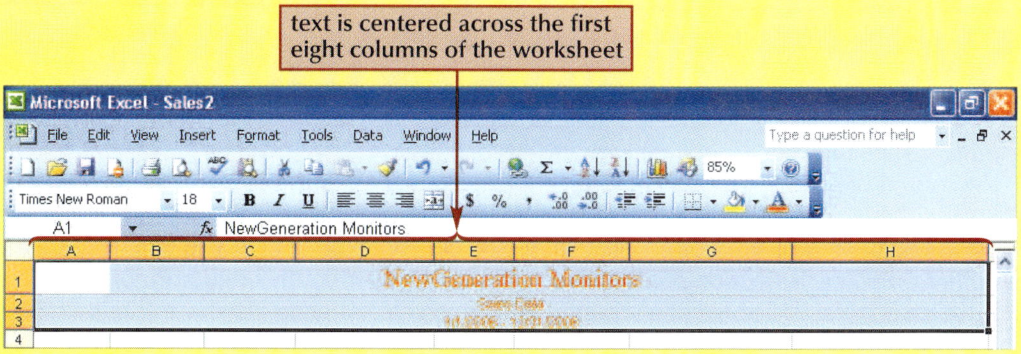

The text in these cells is centered horizontally across the selection. Note that centering the text does not affect the location. The title and subtitles are still placed in cells A1 through A3. In general, you should only use this approach for text that is in the leftmost column of the selection, and there should be no text in any other column. If you had text in column B in the previous set of steps, then that text would have been centered across columns B through H, and the text in column A would have remained where it was.

Indenting and Wrapping Text

Sometimes you will want a cell's contents offset, or indented, a few spaces from the cell's edge. This is particularly true for text entries that are aligned with the left edge of the cell. Indenting is often used for cell entries that are considered "subsections" of your worksheet. Joan wants you to indent the names of the months in the range A7:A18 and the monitor titles in the range A23:A25. You will indent the text using one of the indent buttons on the Formatting toolbar.

To indent the months and monitor titles:

1. Select the nonadjacent range **A7:A18;A23:A25**.
2. Click the **Increase Indent** button on the Formatting toolbar. Excel shifts the contents of the selected cells to the right. See Figure 3-11.

Figure 3-11 Indenting text within cells

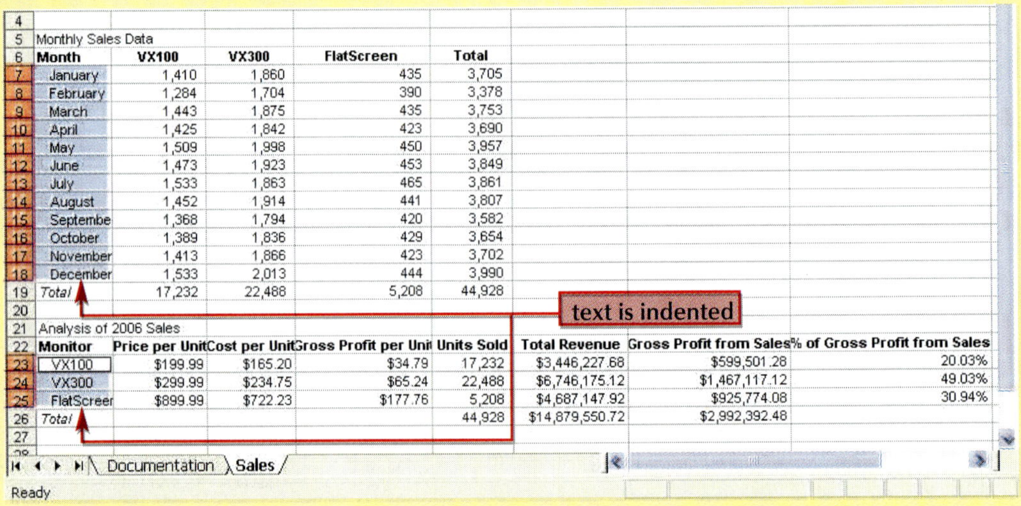

Clicking the Increase Indent button increases the amount of indentation by roughly one character. To decrease or remove an indentation, click the Decrease Indent button or modify the Indent value using the Format Cells dialog box.

If you enter text that is too wide for a cell, Excel either extends the text into the adjoining cells (if the cells are empty) or truncates the display of the text (if the adjoining cells contain text or values). To avoid cutting off the display of text in a cell, you can widen the columns, or place the text on several lines using the method you learned in Tutorial 1 (pressing the Alt key to move to a second line with a cell). You can also have Excel wrap the text within the cell for you. To wrap text within a cell, you click the Wrap text check box on the Alignment tab of the Format Cells dialog box.

Joan notes that some of the column titles in the second table are long. For example, the "Cost per Unit" label in cell C22 is much longer than the values below it. This formatting has caused some of the columns to be wider than they need to be. Another problem is that the text for some cells has been truncated because the columns are not wide enough. Joan suggests that you wrap the text within the column titles and then change the width of the columns where necessary. To make this change, you will use the Format Cells dialog box.

To have Excel automatically wrap text within a cell:

1. Select the range **A22:H22**.
2. Click **Format** on the menu bar, and then click **Cells** to open the Format Cells dialog box.
3. Make sure that the Alignment tab is selected, select the **Wrap text** check box in the Text control pane, and then click the **OK** button. The text in many of the selected cells now appears on two rows within the cells.
4. Change the width of columns **A** and **D** to about **12** characters (**89** pixels) each, columns **B** and **C** to about **10** characters (**75** pixels) each, columns **F** and **G** to about **13** characters (**96** pixels) each, and column **H** to about **17** characters (**124** pixels) each. See Figure 3-12.

Figure 3-12 Wrapping text and resizing the worksheet columns

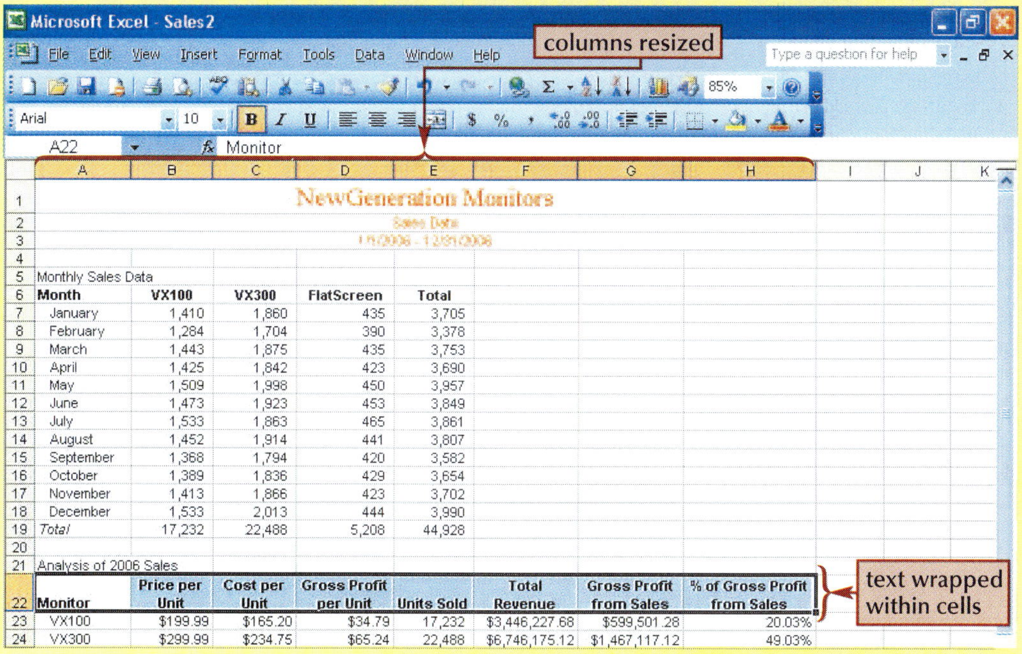

Trouble? If your screen does not match Figure 3-12, resize the columns so the values are easy to read. If some of the text is still hidden, you may need to resize the height of row 22 by dragging the bottom row border down (see Tutorial 1 for a description of resizing rows and columns).

Other Formatting Options

Excel supports even more formatting options than have been discussed so far. For example, instead of wrapping the text, you can have Excel shrink it to fit the size of the cell. If you reduce the cell later on, Excel will automatically resize the text to match. You can also rotate the contents of the cell, displaying the cell entry at almost any angle (see Figure 3-13). Joan does not need to use either of these options in her workbook, but they might be useful later for another project.

Figure 3-13 **Rotating text within a cell**

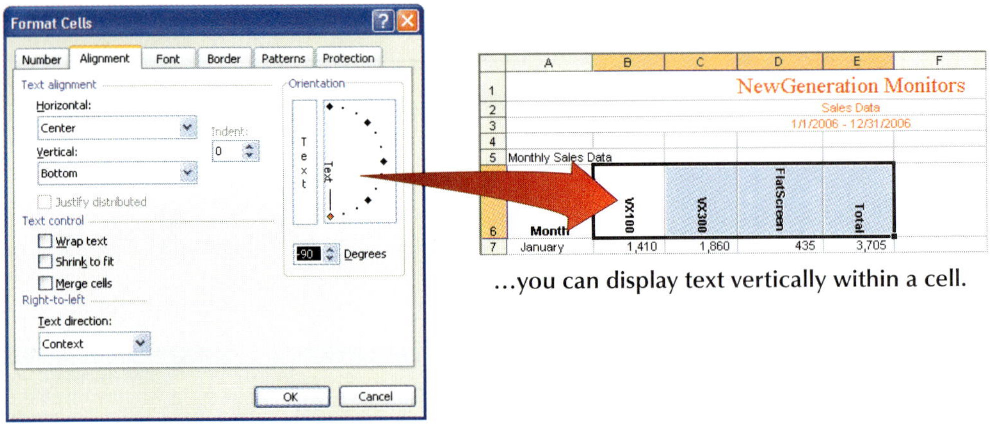

...you can display text vertically within a cell.

By rotating the orientation of the text...

Working with Cell Borders and Backgrounds

Up to now, all the formatting you have done has been applied to the contents of a cell. Excel also provides a range of tools to format the cells themselves. Specifically, you can add borders to cells and color a cell's background.

Adding a Cell Border

As you may have noticed from the printouts of other worksheets, the gridlines that appear in the worksheet window are not normally displayed on the pages that you print. **Gridlines** provide a visual cue for the layout of the cells in a worksheet. Although you can choose to print the gridlines using the Page Setup dialog box, you might want to display borders around individual cells in a worksheet. This would be particularly useful when you have different sections or tables in a worksheet, as in the Sales worksheet.

You can add a border to a cell using either the Borders button on the Formatting toolbar or the options on the Border tab in the Format Cells dialog box. The Borders button allows you to create borders quickly, whereas the Format Cells dialog box lets you further refine your choices. For example, you can specify the style, thickness, and color using the options available in the Format Cells dialog box.

Joan wants you to place a border around each cell in the two tables in the worksheet. You'll select the appropriate border style from the list of available options on the Borders palette.

To create a grid of cell borders in the two tables:

1. Select the nonadjacent range **A6:E19;A22:H26**.
2. Click the **Borders** list arrow on the Formatting toolbar, then move the pointer over the gallery of borders to highlight the All Borders option as shown in Figure 3-14.

Figure 3-14 **Border options**

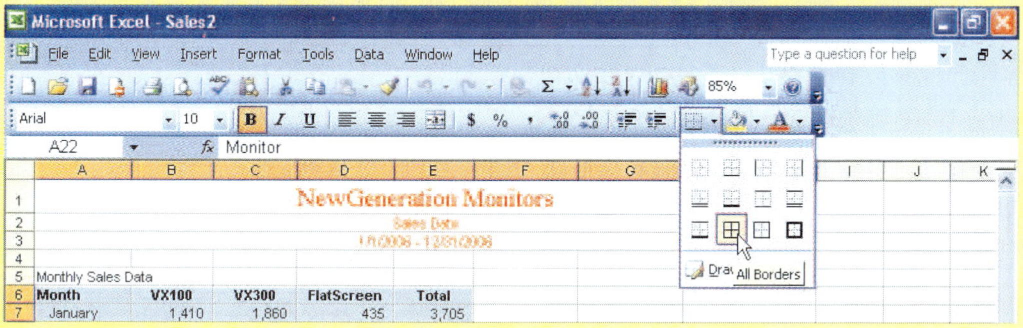

3. Click the **All Borders** option (third row, second column from the left) in the borders gallery. A thin border appears around each cell in the selected range.
4. Click any cell to deselect the range and to see the applied border.

You can also place a border around the entire range itself (and not the individual cells) by selecting a different border style. Try this by creating a thick border around the cell range.

To create a thick border around a selected range:

1. Select the nonadjacent range **A6:E19;A22:H26** again.
2. Click the **Borders** list arrow on the Formatting toolbar, and then click the **Thick Box Border** option (third row, fourth column from the left) in the borders gallery.
3. Click any cell to deselect the range so you can see the thick border applied to the tables. The interior borders should be unchanged.

If you want a more interactive way of drawing borders on your worksheet, you can use the Draw Borders button, which is another option on the borders gallery. To see how this option works, you will add a thick black line under the column titles in both of the tables.

To draw borders using the Draw Borders button:

1. Click the **Borders** list arrow on the Formatting toolbar, and then click the **Draw Borders** button at the bottom of the borders gallery. The pointer changes to , and a floating Borders toolbar opens with four tools. The Draw Border button (currently selected) on the Borders toolbar draws a border line on the worksheet; the Erase Border button erases border lines; the Line Style button specifies the style of the border line; and the Line Color button specifies the line color.
2. Click the **Line Style** list arrow to display a list of line style options, and then click the **thick line** option (the ninth from the top) in the list.

3. Click and drag the pointer over the lower border of the range **A6:E6**. The lower border thickens, matching the top border in thickness.
4. Click and drag the pointer over the lower border of the range **A22:H22**. The lower border thickens.
5. Click the **Close** button on the floating Borders toolbar to close it.

Finally, you will add a double line above the Total row in each table. You will add the line using the options in the Format Cells dialog box.

To create the double border lines:

1. Select the nonadjacent range **A18:E18;A25:H25**.
2. Click **Format** on the menu bar, and then click **Cells** to open the Format Cells dialog box.
3. Click the **Border** tab. The Border tab displays a diagram showing what borders, if any, are currently surrounding the selected cells.

   The bottom border is currently a single thin line. You want to change this to a double line.
4. Click the **double line** style in the Style list box located on the right side of the tab, and then click the **bottom border** in the border diagram to apply the double-line style. The bottom border changes to a double line. See Figure 3-15.

Figure 3-15 Border tab in the Format Cells dialog box

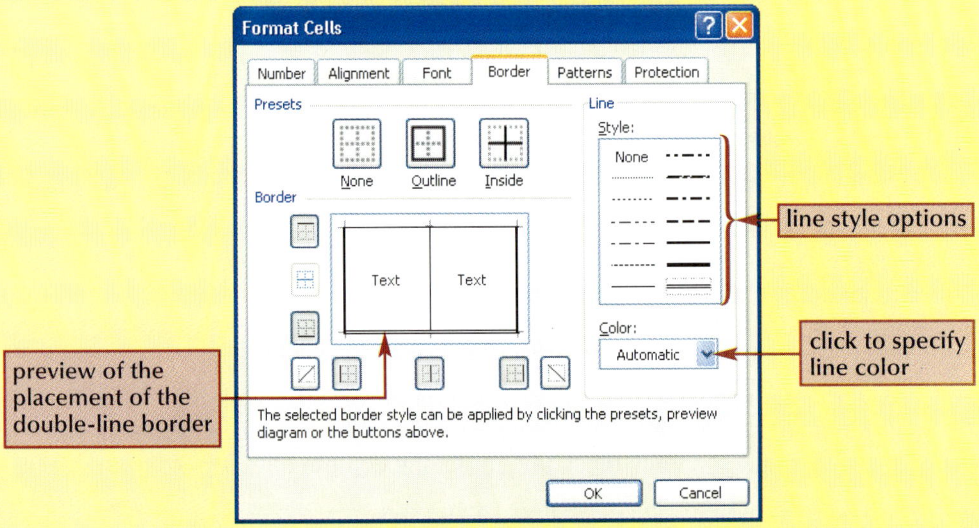

5. Click the **OK** button to close the dialog box, and then click cell **A1** to deselect the ranges. Figure 3-16 shows all of the border styles you've applied to the two tables.

Border styles applied to the worksheet **Figure 3-16**

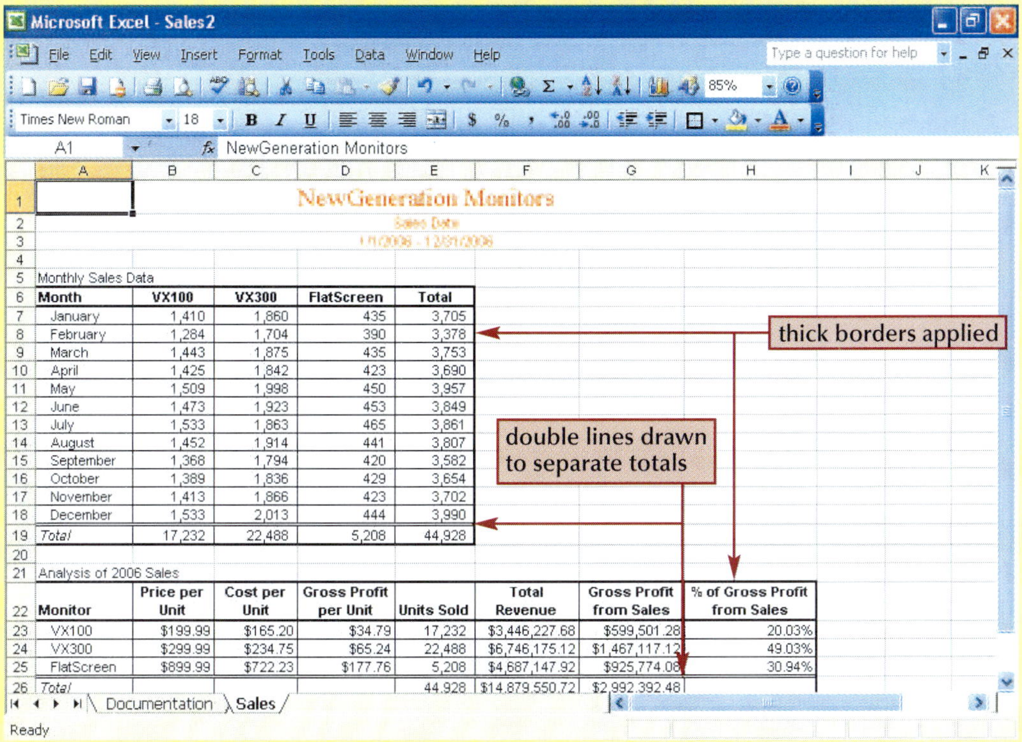

Month	VX100	VX300	FlatScreen	Total
January	1,410	1,860	435	3,705
February	1,284	1,704	390	3,378
March	1,443	1,875	435	3,753
April	1,425	1,842	423	3,690
May	1,509	1,998	450	3,957
June	1,473	1,923	453	3,849
July	1,533	1,863	465	3,861
August	1,452	1,914	441	3,807
September	1,368	1,794	420	3,582
October	1,389	1,836	429	3,654
November	1,413	1,866	423	3,702
December	1,533	2,013	444	3,990
Total	17,232	22,488	5,208	44,928

Monitor	Price per Unit	Cost per Unit	Gross Profit per Unit	Units Sold	Total Revenue	Gross Profit from Sales	% of Gross Profit from Sales
VX100	$199.99	$165.20	$34.79	17,232	$3,446,227.68	$599,501.28	20.03%
VX300	$299.99	$234.75	$65.24	22,488	$6,746,175.12	$1,467,117.12	49.03%
FlatScreen	$899.99	$722.23	$177.76	5,208	$4,687,147.92	$925,774.08	30.94%
Total				44,928	$14,879,550.72	$2,992,392.48	

You can also specify a color for the cell borders by using the Color list box located on the Border tab (see Figure 3-15). Joan does not need to change the border colors, but she would like you to change the background color for the column title cells. When you copy the formatting of a cell, any border that you have applied is also copied.

Applying Background Colors and Patterns

Patterns and color can be used to turn a plain worksheet full of numbers and labels into a powerful presentation of information that captures your attention and adds visual emphasis to the different sections of the worksheet. If you have a color printer or a color projection device, you might want to take advantage of Excel's color tools. By default, worksheet cells are not filled with any color (the white you see in your worksheet is not a fill color for the cells). To change the background color in a worksheet, you can use the Fill Color button on the Formatting toolbar, or you can use the Format Cells dialog box, which also provides patterns that you can apply to the background. When choosing to apply color to a worksheet, you must always give consideration to the availability of a color printer. Also, if you plan to print a worksheet as an overhead, black print on a clear overhead transparency is easier to read than other colors.

Joan wants to change the background color of the worksheet. When she prints her report later in the week, she will be using the company's color laser printer. Therefore, she would like you to explore using background color in the column titles for the two sales tables. She suggests that you try formatting the column titles with a light-yellow background.

To apply a fill color to the column titles:

1. Select the nonadjacent range **A6:E6;A22:H22**.
2. Click the **Fill Color** button list arrow on the Formatting toolbar. The color palette appears.
3. Position the pointer over the **Light Yellow** square (fifth row, third column from the left) on the color palette, as shown in Figure 3-17.

Figure 3-17 Selecting a fill color

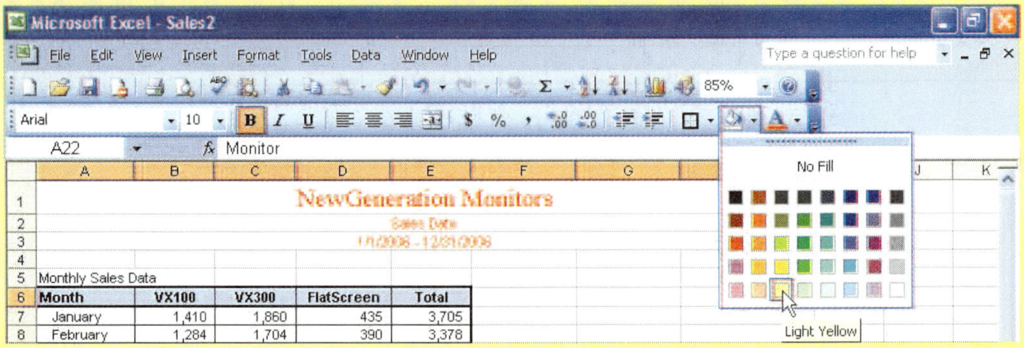

4. Click the **Light Yellow** square to apply the color to the selected range, and then click any cell to deselect the range and to see the applied color. The column titles now have light-yellow backgrounds.

Joan would also like to investigate whether you can apply a pattern to the fill background. Excel supports 18 different fill patterns. To create and apply a fill pattern, you have to open the Format Cells dialog box.

To apply a fill pattern to the column titles:

1. Select the nonadjacent range **A6:E6;A22:H22**.
2. Click **Format** on the menu bar, click **Cells** to open the Format Cells dialog box, and then click the **Patterns** tab to display the options provided.
3. Click the **Pattern** list arrow to display a gallery of patterns and a palette of colors that you can apply to the selected pattern. The default pattern color is black. First, you will choose a crosshatch pattern, which is a pattern using crossed diagonal lines.
4. Click the **50% Gray** pattern (first row, third column) in the pattern gallery, as shown in Figure 3-18.

Figure 3-18 Selecting a fill pattern

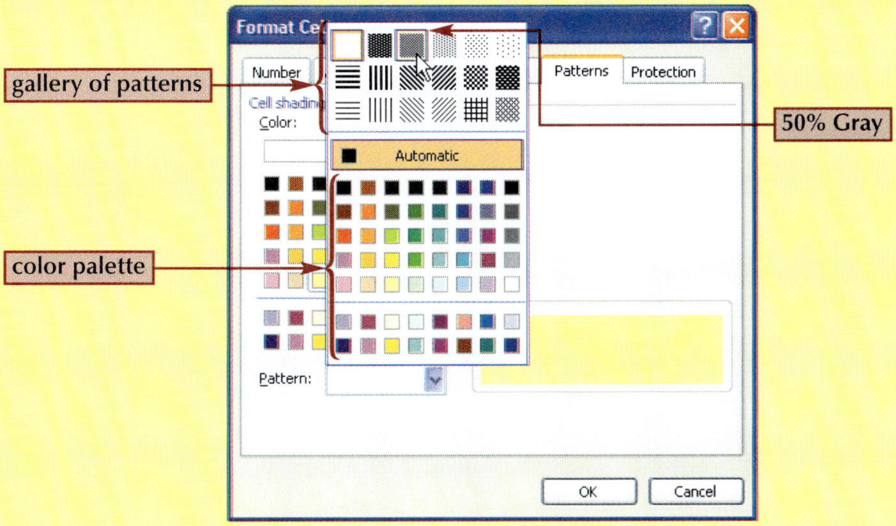

5. Click the **OK** button, and then click any cell to deselect the ranges and to see the pattern.

The background pattern you have chosen overwhelms the text in these column titles. You can improve the appearance by changing the color of the pattern itself from black to a light orange.

To change the pattern color:

1. Select the range **A6:E6;A22:H22**. The default (or automatic) color of a selected pattern is black, but you want to choose a brighter and lighter color for the pattern.
2. Click **Format** on the menu bar, and then click **Cells** to open the Format Cells dialog box again. The Patterns tab should be displayed automatically because it is the last set of options you used.
3. Click the **Pattern** list arrow to display the gallery of patterns and the color palette.
4. Click the **Light Orange** square (third row, second column) in the color palette, click the **OK** button to close the dialog box, and then click cell **A1** to deselect the range and to see the color applied to the pattern. See Figure 3-19. The column titles now appear in a light-orange patterned background. The pattern and the color do not overwhelm the column titles.

Figure 3-19 Cells with formatted backgrounds

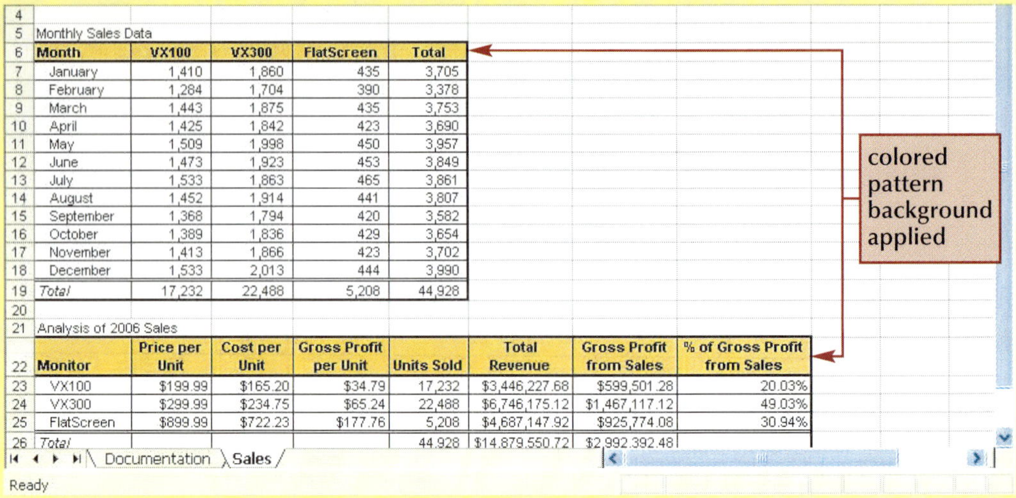

Monthly Sales Data

Month	VX100	VX300	FlatScreen	Total
January	1,410	1,860	435	3,705
February	1,284	1,704	390	3,378
March	1,443	1,875	435	3,753
April	1,425	1,842	423	3,690
May	1,509	1,998	450	3,957
June	1,473	1,923	453	3,849
July	1,533	1,863	465	3,861
August	1,452	1,914	441	3,807
September	1,368	1,794	420	3,582
October	1,389	1,836	429	3,654
November	1,413	1,866	423	3,702
December	1,533	2,013	444	3,990
Total	17,232	22,488	5,208	44,928

Analysis of 2006 Sales

Monitor	Price per Unit	Cost per Unit	Gross Profit per Unit	Units Sold	Total Revenue	Gross Profit from Sales	% of Gross Profit from Sales
VX100	$199.99	$165.20	$34.79	17,232	$3,446,227.68	$599,501.28	20.03%
VX300	$299.99	$234.75	$65.24	22,488	$6,746,175.12	$1,467,117.12	49.03%
FlatScreen	$899.99	$722.23	$177.76	5,208	$4,687,147.92	$925,774.08	30.94%
Total				44,928	$14,879,550.72	$2,992,392.48	

5. Save your changes to the workbook.

Joan is pleased with the progress you have made. In the next session, you will explore other formatting features.

Review

Session 3.1 Quick Check

1. Describe two ways of applying the Currency style to cells in your worksheet.
2. If the number 0.05765 has been entered into a cell, what will Excel display if you:
   a. format the number using the Percent style with one decimal place?
   b. format the number using the Currency style with two decimal places and a dollar sign?
3. Which two buttons can you use to copy a format from one cell range to another?
4. A long text string in one of your worksheet cells has been truncated. List three ways to correct this problem.
5. How do you center the contents of a single cell across a range of cells?
6. Describe three ways of creating a cell border.
7. How would you apply a colored background pattern to a selected cell range?

Session 3.2

Formatting the Worksheet

In the previous session, you formatted individual cells within the worksheet. Excel also provides tools for formatting the columns and rows in a worksheet. You will explore some of these tools as you continue to work on Joan's sales report.

Merging Cells into One Cell

Joan has several other formatting changes that she would like you to make to the Sales worksheet. She wants you to format the titles for the two tables in her report so that they are centered in a bold font above the tables. You could do this by centering the cell title across a cell range, as you did for the title in the last session. Another way is to merge several cells into one cell and then center the contents of that single cell. Merging a range of cells into a single cell removes all of the selected cells from the worksheet, except the cell in the upper-left corner of the range. Any content in the other cells of the range is deleted. To merge a range of cells into a single cell, you can use the Merge cells check box on the Alignment tab in the Format Cells dialog box or click the Merge and Center button on the Formatting toolbar.

To merge and center the cell ranges containing the table titles:

1. If you took a break after the previous session, make sure that Excel is running and that the Sales2 workbook is open.
2. In the Sales worksheet, select the range **A5:E5**.
3. Click the **Merge and Center** button on the Formatting toolbar. The cells in the range A5:E5 are merged into a single cell whose cell reference is A5. The text in the merged cell is centered as well.
4. Click the **Bold** button **B** on the Formatting toolbar.
5. Select the range **A21:H21**, click the **Merge and Center** button on the Formatting toolbar, and then click the **Bold** button **B** on the Formatting toolbar.
6. Click cell **A1** to deselect the range. Figure 3-20 shows the merged and centered table titles.

Figure 3-20 Merging and centering cells

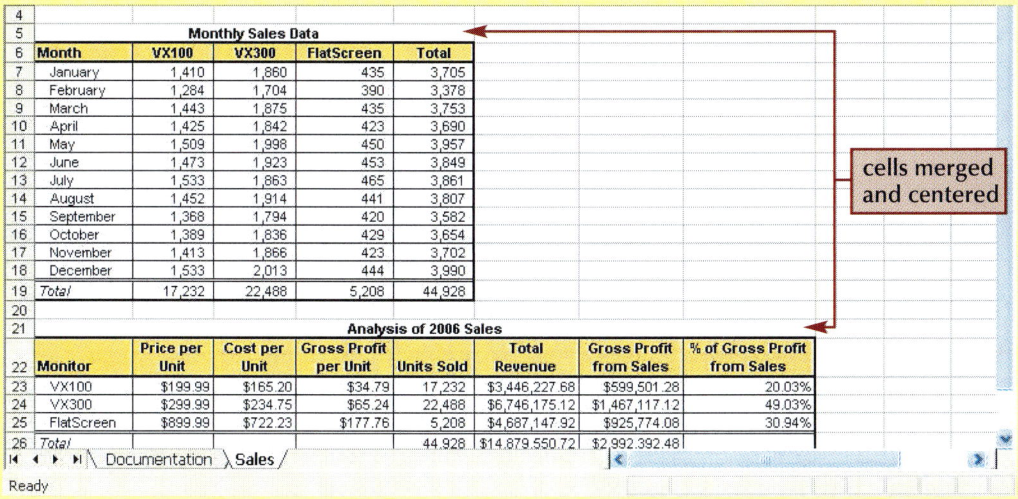

Monthly Sales Data

	Month	VX100	VX300	FlatScreen	Total
7	January	1,410	1,860	435	3,705
8	February	1,284	1,704	390	3,378
9	March	1,443	1,875	435	3,753
10	April	1,425	1,842	423	3,690
11	May	1,509	1,998	450	3,957
12	June	1,473	1,923	453	3,849
13	July	1,533	1,863	465	3,861
14	August	1,452	1,914	441	3,807
15	September	1,368	1,794	420	3,582
16	October	1,389	1,836	429	3,654
17	November	1,413	1,866	423	3,702
18	December	1,533	2,013	444	3,990
19	*Total*	17,232	22,488	5,208	44,928

Analysis of 2006 Sales

	Monitor	Price per Unit	Cost per Unit	Gross Profit per Unit	Units Sold	Total Revenue	Gross Profit from Sales	% of Gross Profit from Sales
23	VX100	$199.99	$165.20	$34.79	17,232	$3,446,227.68	$599,501.28	20.03%
24	VX300	$299.99	$234.75	$65.24	22,488	$6,746,175.12	$1,467,117.12	49.03%
25	FlatScreen	$899.99	$722.23	$177.76	5,208	$4,687,147.92	$925,774.08	30.94%
26	*Total*				44,928	$14,879,550.72	$2,992,392.48	

To split a merged cell back into individual cells, regardless of the method you used to merge the cells, you select the merged cell and then click the Merge and Center button again. You can also merge and unmerge cells using the Alignment tab in the Format Cells dialog box.

Hiding Rows, Columns and Worksheets

Sometimes Joan does not need to view the monthly sales for the three monitors. She does not want to remove this information from the worksheet, but she would like the option of temporarily hiding that information. Excel provides this capability. Hiding a row or column does not affect the data stored there, nor does it affect any other cell that might have a formula referencing a cell in the hidden row or column. Hiding part of your worksheet is a good way of temporarily concealing nonessential information, allowing you to concentrate on the more important data contained in your worksheet. To hide a row or column, first you must select the row(s) or column(s) you want to hide. You can then use the Row or Column option on the Format menu or right-click the selection to open its shortcut menu.

You will hide the monthly sales figures in the first table in the worksheet.

To hide the monthly sales figures:

1. Select the headings for rows **7** through **18**.
2. Right-click the selection, and then click **Hide** on the shortcut menu. Excel hides rows 7 through 18. Note that the total sales figures in the range B19:E19 are not affected by hiding the monthly sales figures. See Figure 3-21.

Figure 3-21 Hiding worksheet rows

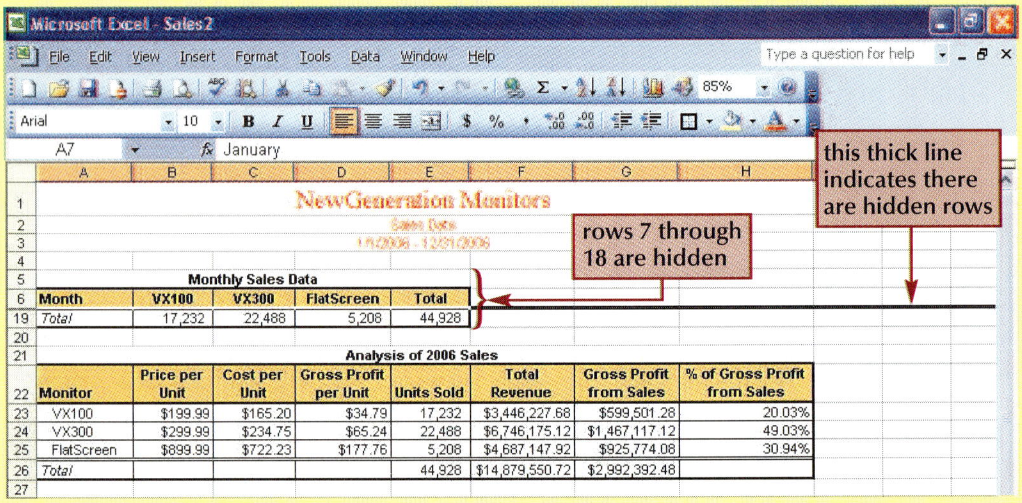

To unhide a hidden row or column, you must select the headings of the rows or columns that border the hidden area; then you can use the right-click method or the Row or Column command on the Format menu to choose the Unhide option. You will let Joan know that it is easy to hide any row or column that she does not want to view. But for now you will redisplay the hidden sales figures.

To unhide the monthly sales figures:

1. Select the row headings for rows **6** and **19**.
2. Right-click the selection, and then click **Unhide** on the shortcut menu. Excel redisplays rows 7 through 18.
3. Click cell **A1** to deselect the rows.

Hiding and unhiding a column follows the same process, except that you select the worksheet column headings rather than the row headings. For example, to hide column B, you select the column heading B. To unhide the column, you must select columns A and C.

On other occasions Joan would like to hide an entire worksheet. This could occur in situations where a worksheet contains detailed information and she only wants to display the summary figures from another sheet. To show how to hide an entire worksheet, you should suggest that she hide the documentation sheet located at the front of the workbook.

To hide the Documentation sheet:

1. Click the **Documentation** sheet tab to make it the active sheet.
2. Click **Format** on the menu bar, point to **Sheet**, and then click **Hide**.

The Documentation sheet disappears from the workbook. It is still present in the workbook, it is just hidden at this point. Excel maintains a list of the hidden worksheets in the current workbook, so you can always select one of those sheets to be redisplayed. Do this now to unhide the Documentation sheet.

To unhide the Documentation sheet:

1. Click **Format** on the menu bar, point to **Sheet**, and then click **Unhide**. Excel displays the Unhide dialog box, listing all hidden worksheets in the workbook.
2. Verify that **Documentation** is selected in the list of hidden worksheets, and click the **OK** button.

   The Documentation sheet should be redisplayed in the workbook and made the active sheet.
3. Click the **Sales** sheet tab to return to the Sales worksheet.

Adding a Background Image

In the previous session you learned how to create a background color for individual cells within the worksheet. Excel also allows you to use an image file as a background for a worksheet. The image from the file is tiled repeatedly until the images fill up the entire worksheet. Images can be used to give the background a textured appearance, like that of granite, wood, or fibered paper. The background image does not affect the format or content of any cell in the worksheet, and if you have already defined a background color for a cell, Excel displays the color on top, hiding that portion of the image.

Adding a Background Image to the Worksheet

Reference Window

- Click Format on the menu bar, point to Sheet, and then click Background.
- Locate the image file that you want tiled over the worksheet background.
- Click the Insert button.

If you add a background and then decide against it, you can remove the background image by clicking Format on the menu bar, pointing to Sheet, and then clicking Delete Background. The image will automatically be removed.

Joan wants you to experiment with using a background image for the Sales worksheet. You will add the image file that she has selected.

To add a background image to the worksheet:

1. Click **Format** on the menu bar, point to **Sheet**, and then click **Background**. The Sheet Background dialog box opens.
2. Navigate to the Tutorial.03\Tutorial folder, click the **Back** image file, and then click the **Insert** button. The Back image file is applied repeatedly to, or is "tiled over," the worksheet, creating a textured background for the Sales sheet. Notice that the tiling is hidden in the cells that already contain a background color. To make the sales figures easier to read, you'll change the background color of those cells to white.
3. Select the nonadjacent range **A7:E19;A23:H26**.
4. Click the **Fill Color** list arrow on the Formatting toolbar, click the **White** square (lower-right corner) in the color palette, and then click cell **A1** to deselect the range, making the background image easier to see. Figure 3-22 shows the Sales worksheet with the formatted background.

Figure 3-22 Inserting a background image

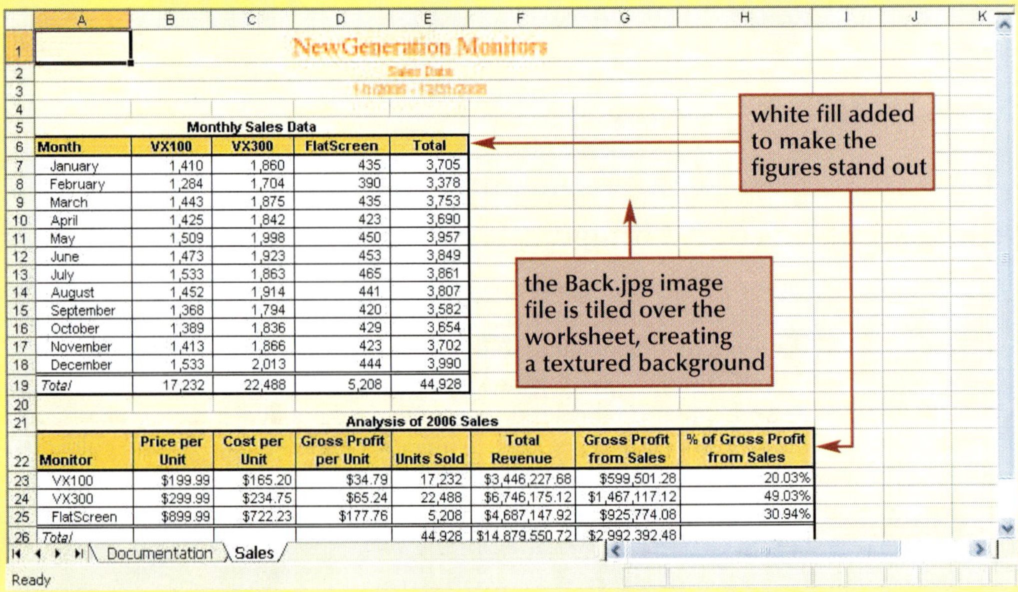

Monthly Sales Data

Month	VX100	VX300	FlatScreen	Total
January	1,410	1,860	435	3,705
February	1,284	1,704	390	3,378
March	1,443	1,875	435	3,753
April	1,425	1,842	423	3,690
May	1,509	1,998	450	3,957
June	1,473	1,923	453	3,849
July	1,533	1,863	465	3,861
August	1,452	1,914	441	3,807
September	1,368	1,794	420	3,582
October	1,389	1,836	429	3,654
November	1,413	1,866	423	3,702
December	1,533	2,013	444	3,990
Total	17,232	22,488	5,208	44,928

Analysis of 2006 Sales

Monitor	Price per Unit	Cost per Unit	Gross Profit per Unit	Units Sold	Total Revenue	Gross Profit from Sales	% of Gross Profit from Sales
VX100	$199.99	$165.20	$34.79	17,232	$3,446,227.68	$599,501.28	20.03%
VX300	$299.99	$234.75	$65.24	22,488	$6,746,175.12	$1,467,117.12	49.03%
FlatScreen	$899.99	$722.23	$177.76	5,208	$4,687,147.92	$925,774.08	30.94%
Total				44,928	$14,879,550.72	$2,992,392.48	

Note that you cannot apply a background image to all of the sheets in a workbook at the same time. If you want to apply the same background to several sheets, you must format each sheet separately.

Formatting Sheet Tabs

In addition to the sheet background, you can also format the background color of worksheet tabs. This color is only visible when the worksheet is not the active sheet in the workbook. By default, the tab of the active sheet in a workbook is white. If you change the color of a tab, the tab changes to white with a narrow colored stripe at the bottom of the tab when the sheet is active. You can use tab colors to better organize the various sheets in your workbook. For example, worksheets that contain sales information could be formatted with blue tabs, whereas sheets that describe the company's cash flow or budget could be formatted with green tabs. To explore how to color worksheet tabs, you will change the tab color of the Sales worksheet to light orange.

To change the tab color:

1. Right-click the **Sales** tab, and then click **Tab Color** on the shortcut menu. The Format Tab Color dialog box opens.
2. Click the **Light Orange** square (third row, second column from the left) in the color palette, and then click the **OK** button. Because the Sales sheet is the active worksheet, the tab is white with a light-orange horizontal stripe at the bottom of the tab.
3. Switch to the Documentation sheet so you can see the light-orange color of the Sales sheet tab, and then switch to the Sales sheet again.

Clearing and Replacing Formats

Sometimes you might want to change or remove some of the formatting from your workbooks. As you experiment with different formats, you can use the Undo button on the Standard toolbar to remove formatting choices that did not work out as well as you expected. Another choice is to clear the formatting from the selected cells, returning the cells to their previous format. To see how this option works, you will remove the formatting from the company name in cell A1 on the Sales worksheet.

To clear the formatting from cell A1:

1. Make sure cell **A1** is selected.
2. Click **Edit** on the menu bar, point to **Clear**, and then click **Formats**. Excel removes the formatting that was applied to the text and removes the formatting that merged the cells and then centered the text across the range.
3. Click the **Undo** button on the Standard toolbar to undo your action, restoring the formats you cleared.

Sometimes you will want to make a formatting change that applies to several different cells. If those cells are scattered throughout the workbook, you may find it time consuming to search for and replace the formats for each individual cell. If the cells share a common format that you want to change, you can use the Find and Replace command to locate the formats and modify them.

Reference Window

Finding and Replacing a Format

- Click Edit on the menu bar, and then click Replace.
- Click the Options >> button, if necessary, to display the format choices.
- Click the top Format list arrow, and then click Format.
- Specify the format you want to find in the Find Format dialog box, and then click the OK button.
- Click the bottom Format list arrow, and then click Format.
- Enter the new format, which will replace the old format, and then click the OK button.
- Click the Replace All button to replace all occurrences of the old format; click the Replace button to replace the currently selected cell containing the old format; or click the Find Next button to find the next occurrence of the old format before replacing it.
- Click the Close button.

In the Sales worksheet, the table titles and column titles are displayed in a bold font. After seeing how the use of color has made the worksheet come alive, Joan wants you to change the titles to a boldface blue. Rather than selecting the cells that contain the table and column titles and formatting them, you will replace all occurrences of the boldface text with blue boldface text.

To find and replace formats:

1. Click **Edit** on the menu bar, and then click **Replace**. The Find and Replace dialog box opens. You can use this dialog box to find and replace the contents of cells. In this case, you will use it only for finding and replacing formats, leaving the contents of the cells unchanged.
2. Click the **Options >>** button to display additional find and replace options. See Figure 3-23. The dialog box expands to display options that allow you to find and replace cell formats. It also includes options to determine whether to search within the active sheet or the entire workbook. Currently no format options have been set.

Figure 3-23 Find and Replace dialog box

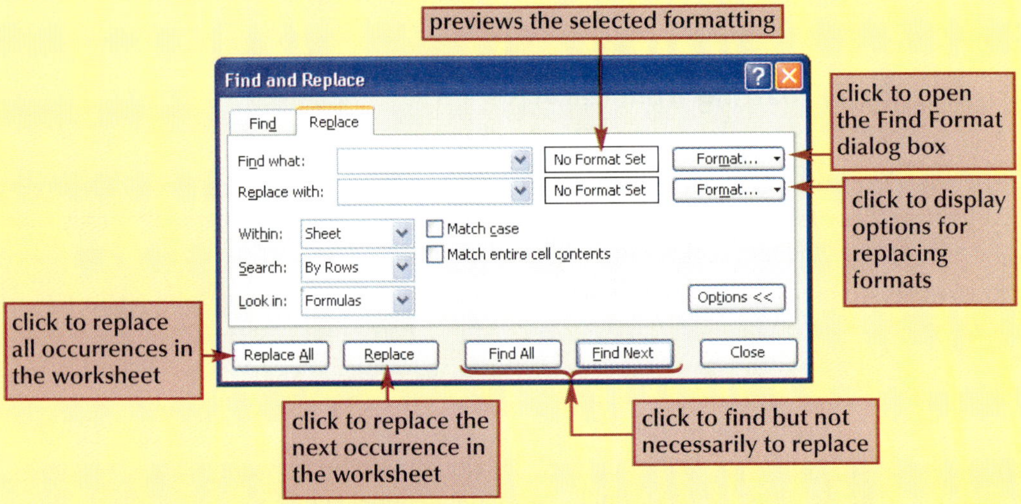

Trouble? If the button on your workbook appears as Options <<, the additional options are already displayed, and you do not need to click any buttons.

3. Click the top **Format** button to open the Find Format dialog box. Here is where you specify the format you want to search for. In this case, you are searching for cells that contain boldface text.

4. Click the **Font** tab, and then click **Bold** in the Font style list box. See Figure 3-24.

Figure 3-24 Find Format dialog box

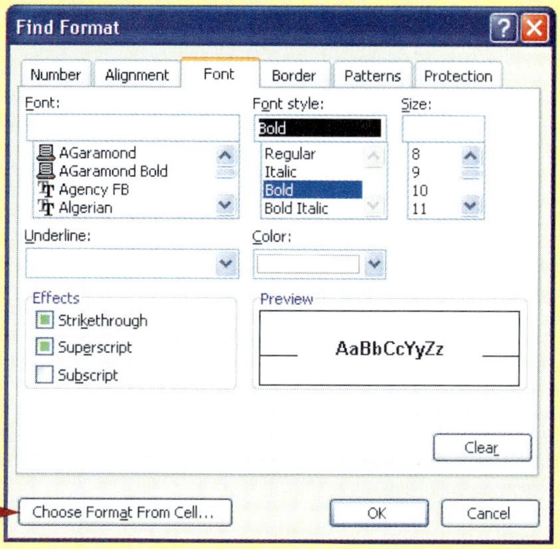

5. Click the **OK** button.

   Next, you will specify the new format that you want to use to replace the boldface text. In this case, you will specify blue boldface text.

6. Click the bottom **Format** button to open the Replace Format dialog box again, and then click **Bold** in the Font style list box.
7. Click the **Color** list box, click the **Blue** square (second row, sixth column from the left) in the color palette, and then click the **OK** button.
8. Click the **Replace All** button to replace all boldface text in the worksheet with blue boldface text. Excel indicates that it has completed its search and made 15 replacements.
9. Click the **OK** button, and then click the **Close** button to close the Find and Replace dialog box. See Figure 3-25. The boldface text has been replaced with blue boldface text.

Figure 3-25 Sales worksheet with blue boldface text

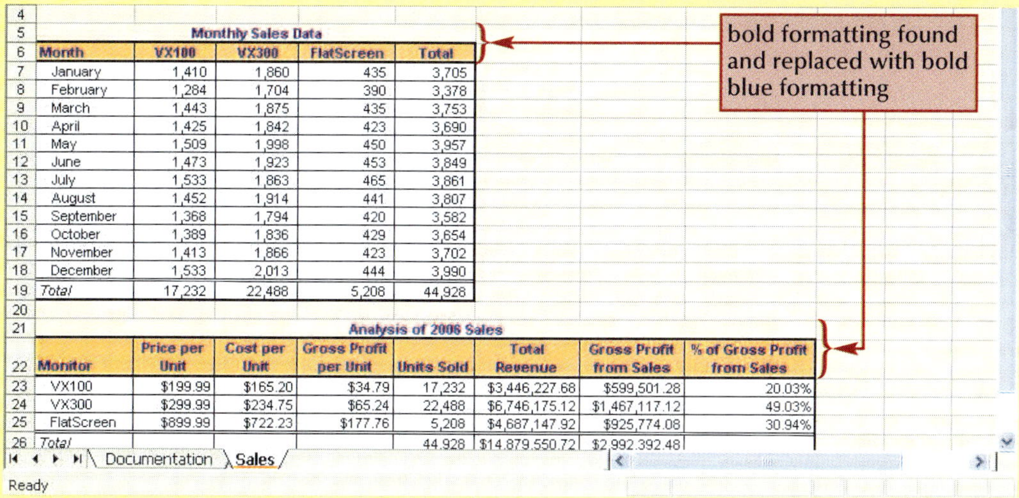

Monthly Sales Data

Month	VX100	VX300	FlatScreen	Total
January	1,410	1,860	435	3,705
February	1,284	1,704	390	3,378
March	1,443	1,875	435	3,753
April	1,425	1,842	423	3,690
May	1,509	1,998	450	3,957
June	1,473	1,923	453	3,849
July	1,533	1,863	465	3,861
August	1,452	1,914	441	3,807
September	1,368	1,794	420	3,582
October	1,389	1,836	429	3,654
November	1,413	1,866	423	3,702
December	1,533	2,013	444	3,990
Total	17,232	22,488	5,208	44,928

Analysis of 2006 Sales

Monitor	Price per Unit	Cost per Unit	Gross Profit per Unit	Units Sold	Total Revenue	Gross Profit from Sales	% of Gross Profit from Sales
VX100	$199.99	$165.20	$34.79	17,232	$3,446,227.68	$599,501.28	20.03%
VX300	$299.99	$234.75	$65.24	22,488	$6,746,175.12	$1,467,117.12	49.03%
FlatScreen	$899.99	$722.23	$177.76	5,208	$4,687,147.92	$925,774.08	30.94%
Total				44,928	$14,879,550.72	$2,992,392.48	

Using Styles

If you have several cells that employ the same format, you can create a style for those cells. This can be a faster and more efficient way of updating formats than copying and replacing formats. A **style** is a saved collection of formatting options—number formats, text alignment, font sizes and colors, borders, and background fills—that can be applied to cells in a worksheet. When you apply a style, Excel remembers which styles are associated with which cells in the workbook. If you want to change the appearance of a particular type of cell, you need only modify the specifications for the style, and the appearance of any cell associated with that style will be automatically changed to reflect the new style.

You can create a style in one of two ways: by selecting a cell from the worksheet and basing the style definition on the formatting choices already defined for that cell or by manually entering the style definitions into a dialog box. Once you create and name a style, you can apply it to cells in the workbook.

Excel has eight built-in styles: Comma, Comma [0], Currency, Currency [0], Followed Hyperlink, Hyperlink, Normal, and Percent. You have been using styles all of this time without knowing it. Most cells are formatted with the Normal style, but when you use the Percent Style button, Excel formats the selected text using the definitions contained in the Percent style. Similarly, the Currency Style button applies the format as defined in the Currency style. As you'll see, you can modify these style definitions or create some of your own.

Creating a Style

Joan wants you to further modify the appearance of the worksheet by changing the background color of the months in the first table and the monitor names in the second table to yellow. Rather than applying new formatting to the cells, you will create a new style called "Category" and then apply the new style to the category columns of the tables in the worksheet. You will create the style using the format already applied to cell A7as a basis.

To create a style using a formatted cell:

1. Click cell **A7** to select it. The format applied to this cell becomes the basis of the new style that you want to create.
2. Click **Format** on the menu bar, and then click **Style**. The Style dialog box opens. All of the formatting options associated with the style of the active cell are listed. For example, the font is 10-point Arial. The check boxes indicate whether these various formatting categories are part of the style definition. If you deselect one of the formatting categories, such as Border, then that category will not be part of the style definition.

   To create a new style for this cell, you simply type a different name into the list box.
3. Type **Category** in the Style name list box, as shown in Figure 3-26. At this point, cell A7 is no longer formatted using the Normal style; rather it is formatted using the Category style you just created.

Style dialog box **Figure 3-26**

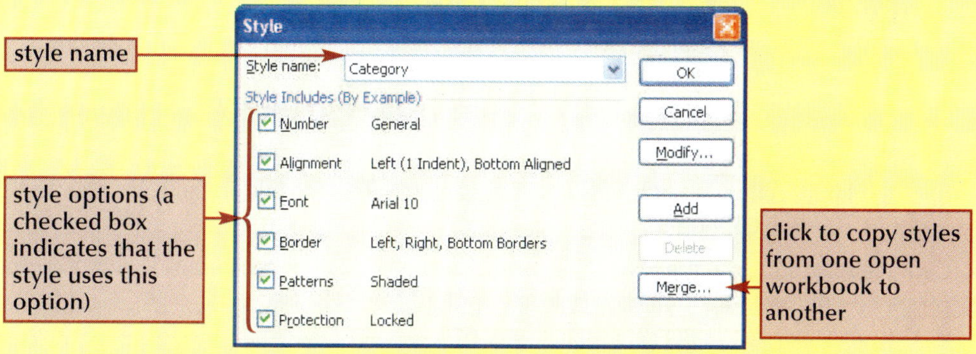

Now you will modify the properties of this style.

4. Click the **Border** check box to deselect it. Category style will not include any border format options.

   Next, you will modify the pattern of the style.

5. Click the **Modify** button to open the Format Cells dialog box, and then click the **Patterns** tab.
6. Click the **Yellow** square (fourth row, third column from the left) in the color palette, and then click the **OK** button to close the Format Cells dialog box and redisplay the Style dialog box.

   If you click the OK button in the Style dialog box, the style definition changes and is applied to the active cell and the Style dialog box closes. If you click the Add button in the dialog box, the style change is saved and applied, but the Style dialog box remains open for further style changes.

7. Click the **OK** button to save the new style and apply it to the background color of cell A7.

Now you need to apply this style to other cells in the workbook.

Applying a Style

To apply a style to cells in a worksheet, you first select the cells you want associated with the style and then open the Style dialog box.

To apply the Category style:

1. Select the nonadjacent range **A8:A18;A23:A25**.
2. Click **Format** on the menu bar, and then click **Style**. The Style dialog box opens.
3. Click the **Style name** list arrow, and then click **Category**. The formatting options change to reflect the associated options for the selected style.
4. Click the **OK** button to close the dialog box and apply the Category style to the selected range, and then click cell **A1** to deselect the cells. A yellow background color is applied to all of the month and monitor cells in the two tables.

The yellow background appears a bit too strong. You decide to change it to a light-yellow background. Since all the month and monitor cells are now associated with the Category style, you need only modify the definition of the Category style to make this change.

To modify the Category style:

1. Click **Format** on the menu bar, and then click **Style**.
2. Click the **Style name** list arrow, and then click **Category**. The options in the Style dialog box change to reflect the selected Category style.
3. Click the **Modify** button to open the Format Cells dialog box, and then click the **Patterns** tab, if necessary.
4. Click the **Light Yellow** square (fifth row, third column from the left) in the color palette, and then click the **OK** button.
5. Click the **Add** button in the Style dialog box. Excel changes the background color of all the cells associated with the Category style.

   Trouble? If you clicked the OK button instead of the Add button, the Category style would have been applied to the active cell as well as the ranges formatted with the Category style. Click the Undo on the Standard toolbar to undo the application of the Category style to cell A2, and then skip Step 6.
6. Click the **Close** button. See Figure 3-27. The updated Category style is applied to the ranges using that format.

Figure 3-27 Category style in the Sales worksheet

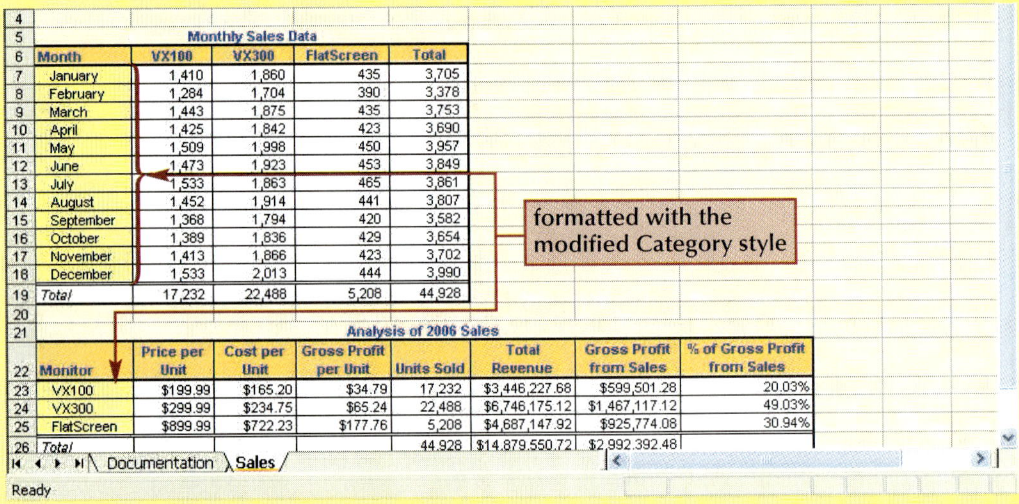

Monthly Sales Data

Month	VX100	VX300	FlatScreen	Total
January	1,410	1,860	435	3,705
February	1,284	1,704	390	3,378
March	1,443	1,875	435	3,753
April	1,425	1,842	423	3,690
May	1,509	1,998	450	3,957
June	1,473	1,923	453	3,849
July	1,533	1,863	465	3,861
August	1,452	1,914	441	3,807
September	1,368	1,794	420	3,582
October	1,389	1,836	429	3,654
November	1,413	1,866	423	3,702
December	1,533	2,013	444	3,990
Total	17,232	22,488	5,208	44,928

Analysis of 2006 Sales

Monitor	Price per Unit	Cost per Unit	Gross Profit per Unit	Units Sold	Total Revenue	Gross Profit from Sales	% of Gross Profit from Sales
VX100	$199.99	$165.20	$34.79	17,232	$3,446,227.68	$599,501.28	20.03%
VX300	$299.99	$234.75	$65.24	22,488	$6,746,175.12	$1,467,117.12	49.03%
FlatScreen	$899.99	$722.23	$177.76	5,208	$4,687,147.92	$925,774.08	30.94%
Total				44,928	$14,879,550.72	$2,992,392.48	

The Category style becomes part of the Sales2 workbook, but it is not available to other workbooks. However, you can copy styles from one workbook to another. Copying styles allows you to create a collection of workbooks that share a common look and feel.

To copy styles from one workbook to another, open the workbook containing your customized styles, and then open the workbook into which you want to copy the styles. Open the Styles dialog box, click the Merge button, and select the first workbook. All of the styles in that workbook will be copied into the second workbook for use on that workbook's contents. Note that if you make changes to the style definitions later on, you will have to copy them again. Excel will not automatically update styles across workbooks.

Using AutoFormat

Excel's **AutoFormat** feature provides a gallery of 17 predefined formats that you can select and apply to your worksheet cells. Rather than spending time testing different combinations of fonts, colors, and borders, you can apply an existing format to your worksheet.

You have done a lot of work already formatting the data in the Sales worksheet to give it a more professional and polished look, but you decide to see how the formatting you have done compares to one of Excel's AutoFormat designs.

You'll apply an AutoFormat design to the sales figures table so that you can compare a predefined format to the format you have worked on.

To apply an AutoFormat design to the table:

1. Select the range **A5:E19**.
2. Click **Format** on the menu bar, and then click **AutoFormat**. The AutoFormat dialog box opens. See Figure 3-28. The dialog box displays a preview of how each format will appear when applied to cells in a worksheet.

Figure 3-28 AutoFormat gallery

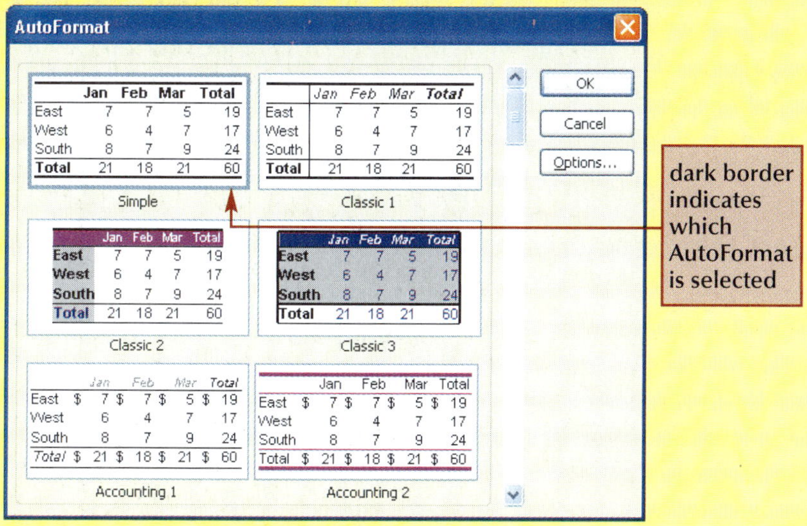

3. Click **Classic 3** in the list of available designs, click the **OK** button, and then click cell **A1** to remove the highlighting from the table. Figure 3-29 shows the appearance of the Classic 3 design to the cells containing the monthly sales data.

Figure 3-29 Applying an AutoFormat

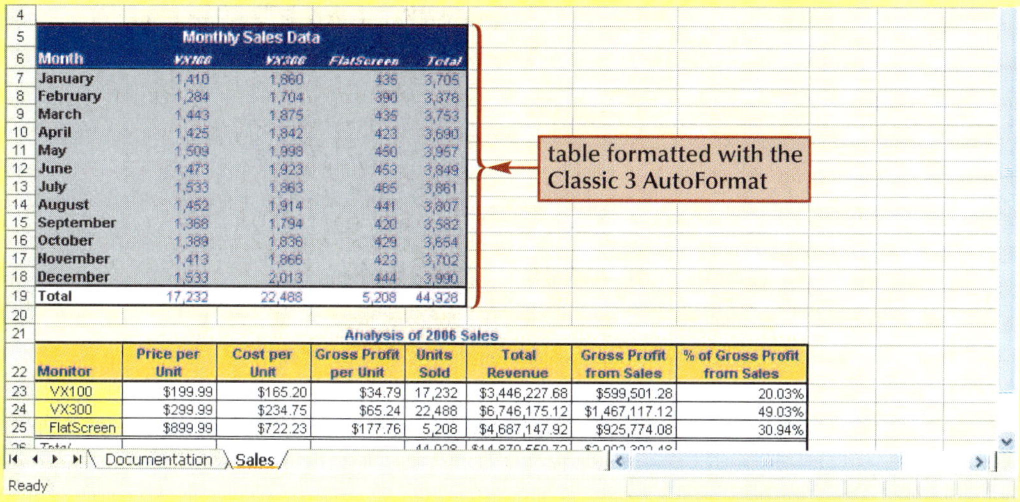

The colors and contrast of the AutoFormat design do not complement the background, so you will revert to the format you created.

4. Click the **Undo** button on the Standard toolbar to remove the AutoFormat design.

Although you will not use AutoFormat in this case, you can see how an AutoFormat design can be a starting point. You could start with an AutoFormat design and then make modifications to the worksheet to fit your own needs.

Formatting the Printed Worksheet

You have settled on an appearance for the Sales worksheet—at least the appearance that is displayed on your screen. But that is only half of your job. Joan also wants you to format the appearance of this worksheet when it is printed out. You have to decide on the position of the report on the page, the size of the page margins, the orientation of the page, and whether the page will have any headers or footers. You can make many of these choices using the Page Setup dialog box, which you can open from the File menu or from within Print Preview.

Defining the Page Setup

As you learned in Tutorial 1, you can use the Page Setup dialog box to change the page orientation, which determines if the page is wider than it is tall or taller than it is wide. You can also use the Page Setup dialog box to control how a worksheet is placed on a page. You can adjust the size of the **margins**, which are the spaces between the page content and the edges of the page. You can center the worksheet text between the top and bottom margins (horizontally) or between the right and left margins (vertically). You can also use the Page Setup dialog box to display text that will appear in the area at the top of a page or at the bottom of a page for each page of a worksheet. You can open the Page Setup dialog box using the File menu or using the Print Preview toolbar. Working from within Print Preview can be helpful. Each time you close a dialog box in which you have made a change or selected an option, you will see how that action impacts the worksheet before printing it.

By default, Excel places a one-inch margin above and below the report and a ¾-inch margin to the left and right. Excel also aligns column A in a worksheet at the left margin and row 1 at the top margin. Depending on how many columns and rows there are in the worksheet, you might want to increase or decrease the page margins or center the worksheet between the left and right margins or between the top and bottom margins.

You will increase the margin size for the Sales worksheet to one inch all around. You will also center the worksheet between the right and left margins.

To change the margins and positioning of the worksheet:

1. Click the **Print Preview** button on the Standard toolbar. The Print Preview window opens, displaying the worksheet as it will appear on the printed page.
2. Click the **Setup** button on the Print Preview toolbar, and then click the **Margins** tab. The Margins tab, as shown in Figure 3-30, provides a diagram that shows you the placement of the worksheet on the page. In addition to adjusting the sizes of the margins, you can also adjust the positioning of the worksheet on the printout.

Figure 3-30 Margins tab in the Page Setup dialog box

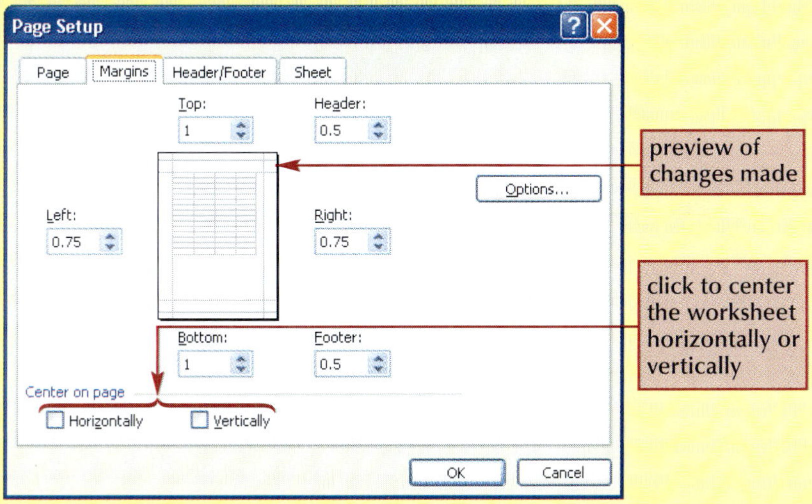

3. Click the **Left** up arrow to set the size of the left margin to **1** inch, and then click the **Right** up arrow to increase the size of the right margin to **1** inch.
4. Click the **Horizontally** check box, and then click the **OK** button to close the Page Setup dialog box and return to Print Preview.

Note that this printout does not fit on a single page. As indicated in the status line located in the lower-left corner of the Print Preview window, the worksheet covers two pages instead of one; two columns of the bottom table have been moved to the second page. You could try to reduce the left and right margins, so the worksheet fits on a single page, but as you learned in Tutorial 1, you also can change the page orientation to landscape, making the worksheet page wider than it is tall. This will accommodate all the columns of the bottom table so all the data will fit on the same page.

To change the page orientation:

1. Click the **Setup** button on the Print Preview toolbar to open the Page Setup dialog box again.
2. Click the **Page** tab and then click the **Landscape** option button, as shown in Figure 3-31.

Figure 3-31 Changing the page orientation

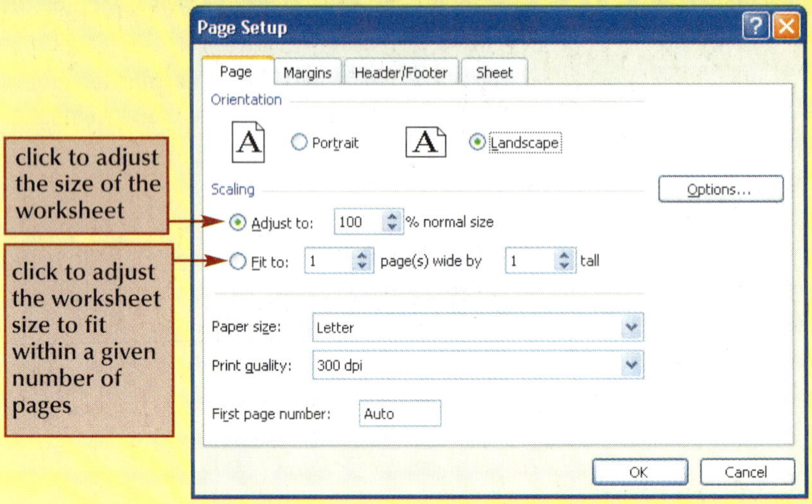

3. Click the **OK** button to close the dialog box and return to the Print Preview window. The preview of the printed worksheet in landscape orientation shows that the report will fit on a single page.

The Page tab in the Page Setup dialog box contains other useful formatting features. You can reduce or increase the size of the worksheet on the printed page. The default size is 100 percent. You can also have Excel automatically reduce the size of the report to fit within a specified number of pages.

Working with Headers and Footers

Joan wants you to add a header and footer to the report. A **header** is text printed in the top margin of every worksheet page. A **footer** is text printed at the bottom of every page. Headers and footers can add important information to your printouts. For example, you can create a header that displays your name and the date the report was created. If the report covers multiple pages, you can use a footer to display the page number and the total number of pages. You use the Page Setup dialog box to add headers and footers to a worksheet.

Excel tries to anticipate headers and footers that you might want to include in your worksheet. Clicking the Header or Footer list arrow displays a list of possible headers or footers (the list is the same for both). For example, the "Page 1" entry inserts the page number of the worksheet prefaced by the word "Page" in the header; the "Page 1 of ?" displays the page number and the total number of pages. Other entries in the list include the name of the worksheet or workbook.

If you want to use a header or footer not available in the lists, you click the Custom Header or Custom Footer button and create your own header and footer. The Header dialog box and the Footer dialog box are similar. Each dialog box is divided into three sections: left, center, and right. If you want to enter information such as the filename or the date into the header or footer, you can either type the text or click one of the format buttons located above the three section boxes. Figure 3-32 describes the format buttons and the corresponding format codes.

Figure 3-32 Header/Footer formatting buttons

Button	Name	Formatting Code	Action
	Font	None	Sets font, text style, and font size
	Page Number	&[Page]	Inserts page number
	Total Pages	&[Pages]	Inserts total number of pages
	Date	&[Date]	Inserts current date
	Time	&[Time]	Inserts current time
	File Path	&[Path]&[File]	Inserts path and filename
	Filename	&[File]	Inserts filename
	Tab Name	&[Tab]	Inserts name of active worksheet
	Insert Picture	&[Picture]	Inserts an image file
	Format Picture	None	Opens the Format Picture dialog box

Joan wants a header that displays the filename at the left margin and today's date at the right margin. She wants a footer that displays the name of the workbook author, with the text aligned at the right margin of the footer. You'll create the header and footer now.

To add a custom header and footer to the workbook:

1. Click the **Setup** button on the Print Preview toolbar, and then click the **Header/Footer** tab. The Header/Footer dialog box opens.
2. Click the **Custom Header** button. The Header dialog box opens. See Figure 3-33.

Figure 3-33 Header dialog box

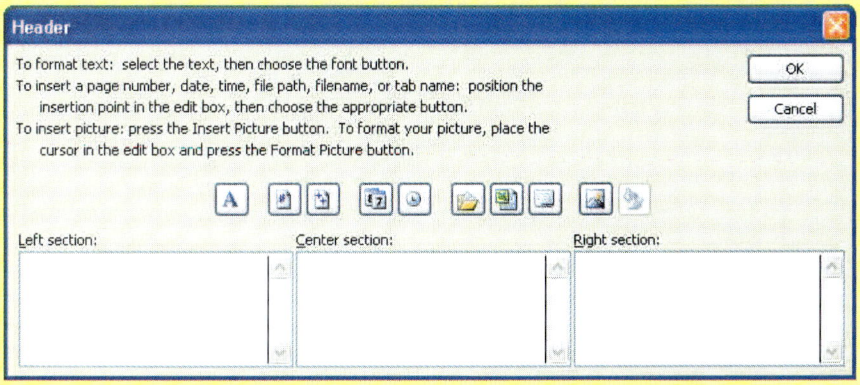

3. In the Left section box, type **Filename:** and then press the **spacebar**.
4. Click the **Filename** button to insert the format code. The formatting code for the name of the file "&[File]" appears after the text that you entered.
5. Click the **Right section** box, and then click the **Date** button. Excel inserts the &[Date] format code into the section box.
6. Click the **OK** button to close the Header dialog box, and then click the **Custom Footer** button to open the Footer dialog box, which duplicates the layout of the Header dialog box. Now you will create a footer that centers the page number and the total number of pages at the bottom of the printout.

7. Click the **Center section** box, type **Page**, press the **spacebar**, click the **Page Number** button, press the **spacebar**, type **of**, press the **spacebar**, and then click the **Total Pages** button. The text and codes in the Center section should appear as "Page &[Page] of &[Pages]"—which, if the worksheet was divided into five pages, would appear as "Page 1 of 5."

   Next, you will enter the workbook author in the right section of the footer.

8. Click the **Right section** box, type **Prepared by:**, press the **spacebar**, and then type your name.

9. Click the **OK** button to return to the Page Setup dialog box, which provides a preview of the custom header and footer that you created, and then click the **OK** button to return to Print Preview. As shown in Figure 3-34, the worksheet now is displayed with the new header and footer.

Figure 3-34 Preview of the custom header and footer

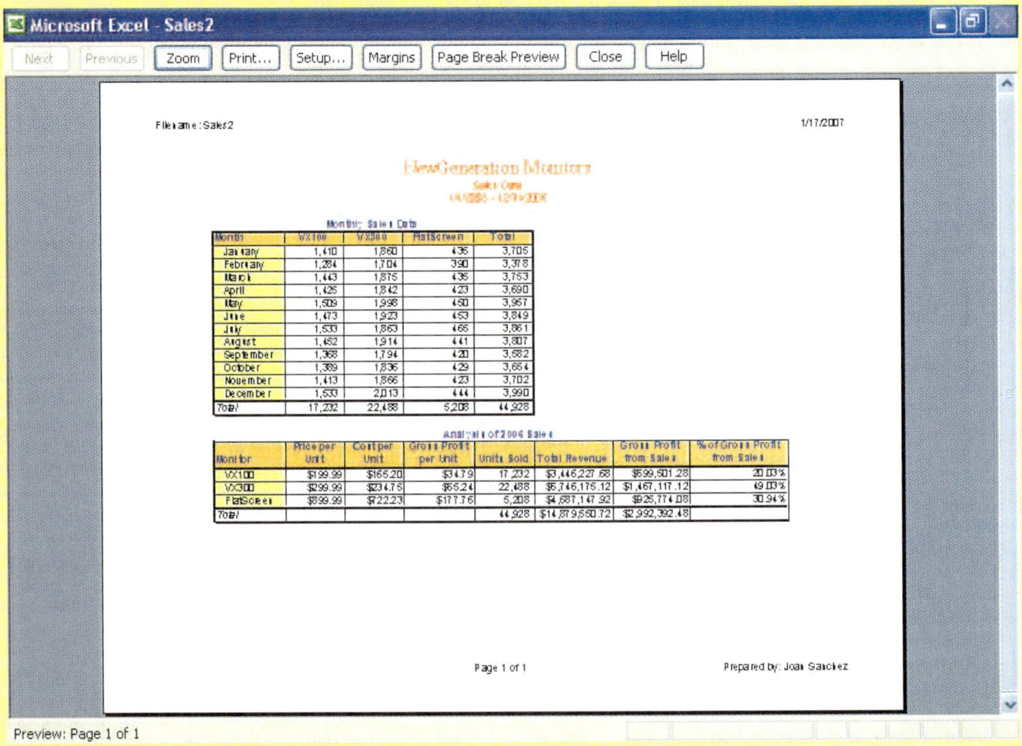

10. Click the **Close** button on the Print Preview toolbar.

Note that a header or footer is added only for the printed worksheet—not the entire workbook. You can define different headers and footers for each sheet in your workbook.

Working with the Print Area and Page Breaks

When you displayed the worksheet in the Print Preview window, how did Excel know which parts of the active worksheet you were going to print? The default action is to print all parts of the active worksheet that contain text, formulas, or values, which will not always be what you want. If you want to print only a part of the worksheet, you can define a **print area** that contains the content you want to print. To define a print area, you must first select the cells you want to print, and then select the Print Area command on the File menu.

A print area can include an adjacent range or nonadjacent ranges. You can also hide rows or columns in the worksheet in order to print nonadjacent ranges. For her report, Joan might decide against printing the sales analysis information. To remove those cells from the printout, you will define a print area that excludes the cells for the second table.

To define the print area:

1. Select the range **A1:H19**.
2. Click **File** on the menu bar, point to **Print Area**, and then click **Set Print Area**. Excel places a dotted black line around the selected cells of the print area. This is a visual indicator of what parts of the worksheet will be printed.
3. Click the **Print Preview** button on the Standard toolbar. The Print Preview window displays only the first table. The second table has been removed from the printout because it is not in the defined print area.
4. Click the **Close** button on the Print Preview toolbar.

Another way to preview the print areas in your worksheet is through **page break preview**, which displays a view of the worksheet as it is divided up into pages. Anything outside of the print area is grayed out. Try previewing the contents of the Sales worksheet using page break preview.

To switch to page break preview:

1. Click cell **A1** to remove the selection.
2. Click **View** on the menu bar, and then click **Page Break Preview**. The workbook window adjusts to display the worksheet with any page break inserted in it and the Welcome to Page Break Preview dialog box, as shown in Figure 3-35. The dialog box serves to remind you that you can adjust the page breaks. A page number appears as a watermark on each page to be printed out. Notice that the second table is grayed out because it is not part of the printed area of the worksheet.

Figure 3-35 Using Page Break Preview

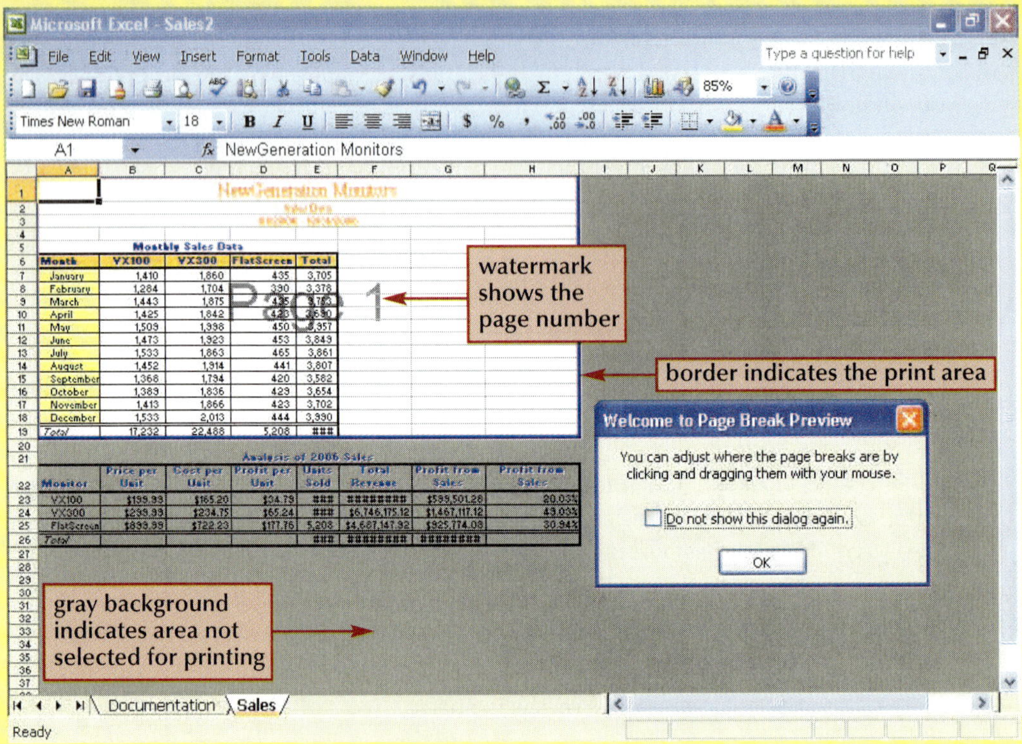

3. Click the **OK** button to close the dialog box before you change the dimensions of the printed area to include the other table.
4. Position the pointer at the bottom border of the print area (located at row 19) until the pointer changes to ↕, and then click the border and drag it down to row **26**. The print area has now been expanded to the cell range A1:H26.

   Trouble? If you are unsure of the location of the bottom border, click row 19 to make the border easier to see, and then repeat Step 3.
5. Click **View** on the menu bar, and then click **Normal** to switch back to Normal view.

Another approach that Joan might take is to place the two tables on separate pages. You can do this for her by inserting a **page break**, which forces Excel to place a portion of a worksheet on a new page. Before you insert a page break, you need to indicate where in the worksheet you want the break to occur. If you select a cell in the worksheet, the page break will be placed directly above and to the left of the cell. Selecting a row or a column places the page break directly above the row or directly to the left of the column. You will place a page break directly above row 20, which will separate the first sales table from the second.

To insert a page break:

1. Click row **20**, click **Insert** on the menu bar, and then click **Page Break**. Another black dotted line appears—this time above row 20, indicating there is a page break at this point in the print area.

2. Click cell **A1** to remove the selection, click **View** on the menu bar, click **Page Break Preview**, and then click the **OK** button to close the Welcome to Page Break Preview dialog box. As shown in Figure 3-36, the second table will now appear on page 2 of the printout.

Figure 3-36

Inserting a page break

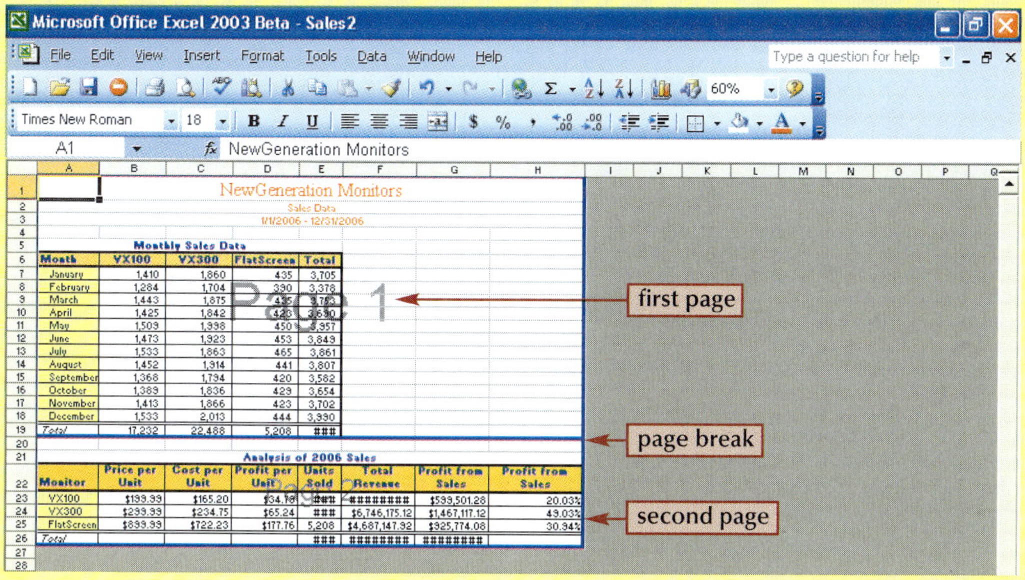

3. Click **View** on the menu bar, and then click **Normal** to return to Normal view.

As Joan reviews the preview of the worksheet, she notices that the name of the company, "NewGeneration Monitors," and the two subtitles appear on the first page, but not on the second. That is not surprising because the range that includes the titles and subtitles is limited to the first page of the printout. However, Joan would like to have this information repeated on the second page.

You can repeat information, such as the company name, by specifying which cells in the print area should be repeated on each page. This is particularly useful in long tables that extend over many pages. In such cases, you can have the column titles repeated for each page of the printout.

To set rows or columns to repeat on each page, you will open the Page Setup dialog box from the worksheet window.

To repeat the first three rows on each page:

1. Click **File** on the menu bar, click **Page Setup**, and then click the **Sheet** tab. The Sheet tab displays options you can use to control how the worksheet is printed. Note that the print area you have defined is already entered into the Print area box. Because Joan wants the first three rows of the worksheet to be repeated on each printed page, you will have to select them.

2. Click the **Rows to repeat at top** box, move your pointer over to the worksheet, and then click and drag over the range **A1:A3**. A flashing border appears around the first three rows in the worksheet. This is a visual indicator that the contents of the first three rows will be repeated on all pages of the printout. In the Rows to repeat at top box, the cell reference $1:$3 appears. See Figure 3-37.

Figure 3-37 Sheet tab of the Page Setup dialog box

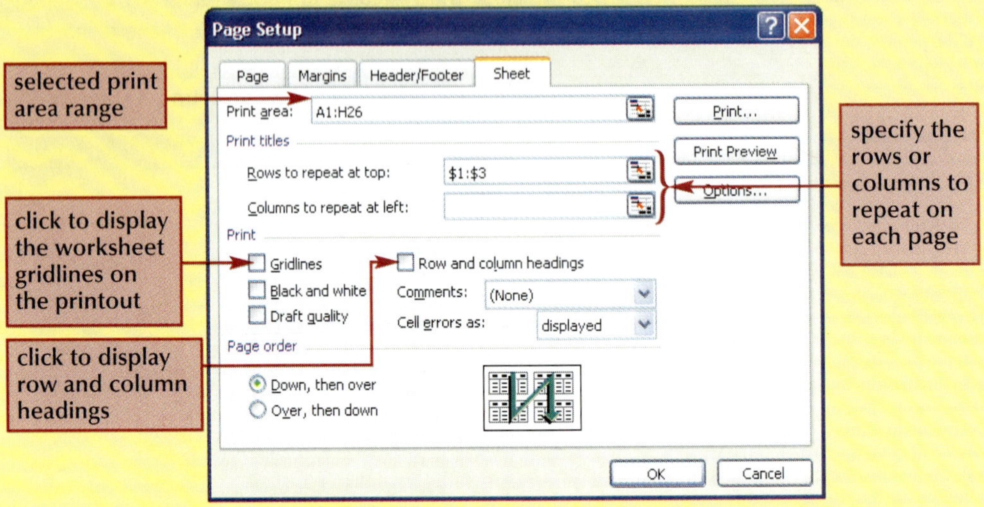

Trouble? If the Page Setup dialog box is in the way, you can move it to another location in the workbook window, or you can select the range using the Collapse Dialog Box button.

3. Click the **Print Preview** button, and then click the **Next** button on the Print Preview toolbar to display the second page of the printout. Now the title and two subtitles appear on this page as well. See Figure 3-38.

Figure 3-38 Second page of the printout

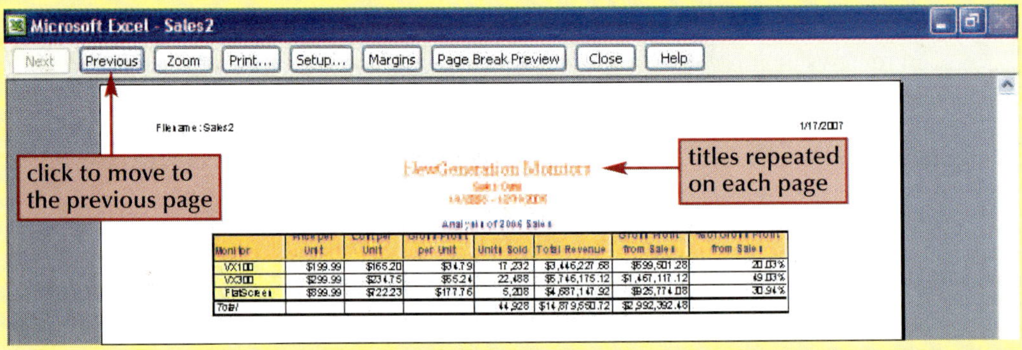

4. Click the **Print** button on the Print Preview toolbar, make sure the settings in the Print dialog box are correct, and then click the **OK** button.

   For now, your work is done. When you save the workbook, your printing options are saved along with the file, so you will not have to re-create the print format in the future.

5. Save your changes to the workbook, and then close it.

Note that the Sheet tab also provides other options, such as the ability to print the worksheet's gridlines or row and column headings. You can also have Excel print the worksheet in black and white or draft quality. If there are multiple pages in the printout, you can indicate whether the pages should be ordered going down the worksheet first and then across, or across first and then down.

You show the final version of the workbook and the printout to Joan. She is very happy with the way in which you have formatted her report. She will spend some time going over the printout and will get back to you with any further changes she wants you to make.

Review

Session 3.2 Quick Check

1. Describe two ways of merging a range of cells into one.
2. How do you clear a format from a cell without affecting the underlying data?
3. How do you add a background image to the active worksheet?
4. To control the amount of space between the content on a page and its edges, you can adjust the page's ______________.
5. By default, Excel prints what part of the active worksheet?
6. How do you define a print area? How do you remove a print area?
7. How do you insert a page break into your worksheet?

Review

Tutorial Summary

In this tutorial, you learned how to use Excel's formatting tools to design your worksheet. You saw how to quickly format cells using the buttons on the Formatting toolbar, and you learned how the Format Cells dialog box can give you even more control over the appearance of your worksheet. You saw how to create and edit cell borders using the Borders button and the Draw Borders button. You also learned how to change cell backgrounds using colors and patterns and external graphic files. The tutorial also demonstrated how to apply the formats in one cell range to another through the use of the Format and Replace dialog box and through styles. Finally, you learned how to format the appearance of your printed worksheet through the use of customized headers, footers, and print areas.

Key Terms

AutoFormat	General number format	point
font	gridline	print area
font size	header	sans serif font
font style	margin	serif font
footer	page break	style
Format Painter	page break preview	typeface
formatting		

Practice

Practice the skills you learned in the tutorial using the same case scenario.

Review Assignments

Data File needed for the Review Assignments: Region1.xls

Joan Sanchez has another report that she wants to format. The report displays regional sales for the three monitor brands you worked on earlier. As before, Joan wants to work on the overall appearance of the worksheet so the printout of the report is polished and professional looking. Figure 3-39 shows a preview of the worksheet you'll create for Joan.

Figure 3-39

NewGeneration Monitors

Regional Sales Report

1/1/2006 - 12/31/2006

Sales by Region

Region	VX100	VX300	Flatscreen	Total
Northeast	1,723	2,248	520	4,491
East	3,446	4,497	1,041	8,984
Southeast	2,067	2,698	624	5,389
Midwest	1,723	2,248	520	4,491
Southwest	1,378	1,799	416	3,593
West	4,308	5,622	1,302	11,232
Canada	1,378	1,799	416	3,593
Europe	861	1,124	260	2,245
Asia	348	453	109	910
Total	17,232	22,488	5,208	44,928

Regional Analysis

	Region	Units Sold	Total Sales	Profit from Sales	% of Profit
VX100	Domestic	14,645	$ 2,928,853	$ 509,499	17.03%
	Foreign	2,587	$ 517,374	$ 90,001	3.01%
	Total	17,232	$ 3,446,227	$ 599,500	20.03%
VX300	Domestic	19,112	$ 5,733,408	$ 1,246,866	41.67%
	Foreign	3,376	$ 1,012,766	$ 220,250	7.36%
	Total	22,488	$ 6,746,174	$ 1,467,116	49.03%
Flatscreen	Domestic	4,423	$ 3,980,655	$ 786,232	26.27%
	Foreign	785	$ 706,492	$ 139,541	4.66%
	Total	5,208	$ 4,687,147	$ 925,773	30.94%
Total	Domestic	38,180	$12,642,918	$ 2,542,598	84.97%
	Foreign	6,748	$ 2,236,632	$ 449,793	15.03%
	Total	44,928	$14,879,550	$ 2,992,391	100.00%

To format the report:

1. Open the **Region1** workbook located in the Tutorial.03\Review folder included with your Data Files.
2. Enter your name and the current date in the Documentation sheet, and then save the workbook as **Region2** in the Tutorial.03\Review folder.
3. Switch to the Regional Sales worksheet.
4. Format the text in cell A1 with a 20-point, italicized, red, Times New Roman font. Format the text in cells A2 and A3 with a red font. Select the range A1:F3, and center the text across the selection. Do not merge the cells.
5. Select the range A5:E16, and then apply the List 2 format from the AutoFormat gallery.
6. Change the format of all values in the Sales by Region table to display a comma separator, but no decimal places. Resize column E to about 14 characters.
7. Change the format of the Units Sold values in the second table to display a comma separator, but no decimal places.
8. Indent the region names in the range A7:A15 by one character.
9. Display the text in cell A18 in bold.
10. Change the format of the values in the Total Sales and Profit from Sales columns to display a dollar sign on the left edge of the cell and no decimal places.
11. Change the format of the values in the % of Profit column to display a percent sign and two decimal places.
12. Allow the text in the range B19:F19 to wrap to a second line of text. Bold and center the text within each cell.

13. Merge and center the cells in the range A20:A22, and change the vertical text alignment to center. (*Hint*: Use the correct Text alignment option in the Format Cells dialog box to vertically align the text; see Figure 3-13.) Apply this format to the cells in the following ranges: A23:A25, A26:A28, and A29:A31.
14. Change the background color of the cells in the range A19:F19;A20:A31 to Sea Green (third row, fourth column of the color palette). Change the font color to white.
15. Change the background color of the cells in the range B20:F31 to white. Change the background color of the cells in the range B22:F22;B25:F25;B28:F28;B31:F31 to Light Green (fifth row, fourth column of the color palette).
16. Apply a thin black border to each of the cells in the range A19:F31.
17. Place a double line on the bottom border of the cells in the range B22:F22;B25:F25;B28:F28.
18. Set the print area as the range A1:F31. Insert a page break above row 18. Repeat the first three rows of the worksheet on every page of any printouts you produce from this worksheet.
19. Set up the page to print in portrait orientation with one-inch margins on all sides. Center the contents of the worksheet horizontally on the page.
20. Add a footer with the following text in the Left section box of the footer (with the date on a separate line): "Filename: *the name of the file*" and "Date: *current date*," and then the following text in the Right section box of the footer: "Prepared by: *your name*." In the Center section, place the text "Page *page_number* of *total_pages*" where *page_number* is the number of the page and *total_pages* is the total number of pages in the printout.
21. Add a header with the text "Regional Sales Report" displayed in the Center section using a 14-point Times New Roman font with a double underline. (*Hint*: Select the text in the Center section, and then click the Font button in the Footer dialog box to open the Format Cells dialog box.)
22. Preview the two-page worksheet, and then print it.
23. Save your changes to the workbook and then close it.

Apply

Use the skills you learned in this tutorial to format a worksheet that presents an annual sales report.

Case Problem 1

Data File needed for this Case Problem: Running1.xls

Jenson Sportswear Quarterly Sales Carol Roberts is the national sales manager for Jenson Sportswear, Inc., a company that sells sportswear to major department stores. She has been using an Excel worksheet to track the results of her staff's sales incentive program. She has asked you to format the worksheet so that it looks professional. She also wants a printout before she presents the worksheet at the next sales meeting. To complete this task:

1. Open the **Running1** workbook located in the Tutorial.03\Cases folder included with your Data Files, and then save the file as **Running2** in the same folder.

Explore

2. In the Documentation sheet, enter your name and the current date. Format the date so that it appears as *Weekday, Month Day, Year* where *Weekday* is the day of the week, *Month Day* is the name of the month and the day, and *Year* is a four-digit year.
3. Switch to the Sales worksheet, and then enter the formulas to calculate the following results:
   a. the totals for each product
   b. the quarterly subtotals for the Shoes and Shirts departments
   c. the totals for each quarter and the grand total

4. Using Figure 3-40 as a guide, format the worksheet with the following attributes:

Figure 3-40

	A	B	C	D	E	F
1	Jenson Sportswear, Inc.					
2	Sales Report					
3	1/1/2006 - 12/31/2006					
4						
5	Quarterly Sales by Product					
6	**Shoes**	**Qtr1**	**Qtr2**	**Qtr3**	**Qtr4**	**Total**
7	Running	2,250	2,550	2,650	2,800	10,250
8	Tennis	2,800	1,500	2,300	2,450	9,050
9	Basketball	1,250	1,400	1,550	1,550	5,750
10	**Subtotal**	**6,300**	**5,450**	**6,500**	**6,800**	**25,050**
11						
12	**Shirts**	**Qtr1**	**Qtr2**	**Qtr3**	**Qtr4**	**Total**
13	Tee	1,000	1,150	1,250	1,150	4,550
14	Polo	2,100	2,200	2,300	2,400	9,000
15	Sweat	250	250	275	300	1,075
16	**Subtotal**	**3,350**	**3,600**	**3,825**	**3,850**	**14,625**
17						
18	**Grand Total**	**9,650**	**9,050**	**10,325**	**10,650**	**39,675**

5. Create a style named "Subtotal" that is based on the font, border, and pattern formats found in the cell ranges B10:F10 and B16:F16.
6. Use the Page Setup dialog box to center the table both horizontally and vertically on the printed page and to change the page orientation to landscape.
7. Add the filename, your name, and the date on separate lines in the Right section box of the footer.
8. Preview the sales report and then print it.
9. Save your changes to the workbook and then close it.

Apply

Use the skills you have learned in this tutorial to format a revenue report for women-owned businesses.

Case Problem 2

Data File needed for this Case Problem: WBus1.xls

Wisconsin Department of Revenue Ted Crawford works for the Wisconsin Department of Revenue. Recently he compiled a list of the top 50 women-owned businesses in the state. He would like your help in formatting the report, in regard to both how it appears in the worksheet window and how it appears on the printed page. A preview of the worksheet you'll create is shown in Figure 3-41.

Figure 3-41

	A	B	C	D	E	F	G
1	**Wisconsin's top 50 women-owned businesses**						
2	**Rank**	**Name**	**Sales**	**Employees**	**Year Founded**	**Line**	
3	1	Jockey International	$ 450,000,000	500	1930	Manufacturing Clothing	
4	2	Astronautics	$ 425,000,000	1,400	1959	Manufacturing Flight & Electronic Equip.	
5	3	Pleasant Company	$ 74,000,000	280	1986	Mail Order Books, Dolls & Accessories	
6	4	Dawes Transport	$ 52,000,000	163	1981	Trucking	
7	5	East Capitol Drive Foods Inc.	$ 45,800,000	285	1984	Grocery Stores	
8	6	TSR Inc.	$ 40,000,000	140	1986	Manufacturing Toys & Games	
9	7	Ricom Electronics	$ 34,000,000	52	1982	Mail Order Consumer Electronics	
10	8	Rollette Oil Co.	$ 32,300,000	46	1960	Gasoline Service Stations	
11	9	Mainline Industrial Distributors	$ 31,000,000	125	1964	Industrial Equipment	
12	10	Mueller Graphics	$ 27,100,000	48	1982	Printing Equip. & Supplies	
13	11	Nor-Lake Inc.	$ 26,000,000	208	1947	Refrigeration & Heating Equip.	
14	12	V & J Foods	$ 25,000,000	1,200	1984	Restaurant	
15	13	Fuchs Holding Corporation	$ 24,000,000	103	1955	Trucking Firm	
16	14	O'Connor Oil Corporation	$ 18,600,000	110	1961	Petroleum Bulk Stations	
17	15	A. D. Schinner Co.	$ 17,000,000	34	1910	Distributor Packaging Products	
18	16	Pro-Track Corporation	$ 15,000,000	51	1982	Distributor Footwear	
19	17	Racine Travel Service Inc.	$ 15,000,000	36	1979	Travel Agencies	
20	18	Runzheimer International, Ltd.	$ 14,000,000	165	1933	Info-Management Consultant	
21	19	Triangle Wholesale	$ 14,000,000	55	1981	Distributor Liquor & Beer	

To complete this task:

1. Open the **WBus1** workbook located in the Tutorial.03\Cases folder included with your Data Files, and then save the file as **WBus2** in the same folder.
2. Enter your name and the current date in the Documentation sheet, and then switch to the Business Data worksheet.
3. Change the font in cell A1 to a boldface font that is 14 points in size. Merge and center the title across the range A1:F1.
4. Display the text in the range A2:F2 in bold, and then center the text in the range C2:F2. Place a double line on the bottom border of the range A2:F2.
5. Display the sales information in the Accounting format with no decimal places. Increase the width of the column, if necessary.
6. Display the employees' data using a comma separator with no decimal places.
7. Change the background color of the cells in the range A3:F3 to light green, and then change the background color of the cells in A4:F4 to white.
8. Use the Format Painter to apply the format found in the cell range A3:F4 to the cell range A5:F52.
9. Set up the worksheet page so it prints in landscape orientation with a bottom margin of 1.5 inches. Also, center the contents of the worksheet horizontally on the page.
10. Set the print area as the cell range A1:F52, and then repeat the first two rows of the worksheet in the printouts.

Explore

11. Remove the existing header and footer from the printed page. (*Hint*: Choose (none) from the list of available header and footer text to remove the previous header and footer text.) Insert a customized footer that displays the following text on three separate lines in the Right section box of the footer:
    Compiled by: *your name*
    current date
    Page *page number* of *total number of pages*

Explore

12. Fit the worksheet on a printout that is one page wide and two pages tall.
13. Preview the worksheet, and then print it.
14. Save your changes to the workbook, and then close it.

Challenge

Using Figure 3-42 as your guide, challenge yourself by experimenting with more formatting techniques to enhance a worksheet presenting regional sales figures.

Case Problem 3

Data File needed for this Case Problem: Blades1.xls

Sales Report at Davis Blades Andrew Malki is a financial officer at Davis Blades, a leading manufacturer of roller blades. He has recently finished entering data for the yearly sales report. Andrew has asked you to help him with the design of the main table in the report. A preview of the format you will apply is shown in Figure 3-42.

Figure 3-42

Davis Blades

Sales Report

1/1/2006 - 12/31/2006

Units Sold

		Northeast	East	Southeast	Midwest	Southwest	West	All Regions
Black Hawk	Qtr 1	641	748	733	676	691	783	4,272
	Qtr 2	708	826	811	748	763	866	4,722
	Qtr 3	681	795	780	719	734	833	4,542
	Qtr 4	668	779	764	705	720	816	4,452
	Total	2,698	3,148	3,088	2,848	2,908	3,298	17,988
Blademaster	Qtr 1	513	598	587	541	552	627	3,418
	Qtr 2	567	661	648	598	611	693	3,778
	Qtr 3	545	636	624	575	587	666	3,633
	Qtr 4	534	623	611	564	576	653	3,561
	Total	2,159	2,518	2,470	2,278	2,326	2,639	14,390
The Professional	Qtr 1	342	399	391	361	368	418	2,279
	Qtr 2	378	441	432	399	407	462	2,519
	Qtr 3	363	424	416	383	391	444	2,421
	Qtr 4	356	415	407	376	384	435	2,373
	Total	1,439	1,679	1,646	1,519	1,550	1,759	9,592
All Models	Qtr 1	1,496	1,745	1,711	1,578	1,611	1,828	9,969
	Qtr 2	1,653	1,928	1,891	1,745	1,781	2,021	11,019
	Qtr 3	1,589	1,855	1,820	1,677	1,712	1,943	10,596
	Qtr 4	1,558	1,817	1,782	1,645	1,680	1,904	10,386
	Total	6,296	7,345	7,204	6,645	6,784	7,696	41,970

To complete this task:

1. Open the **Blades1** workbook located in the Tutorial.03\Cases folder included with your Data Files, and then save the file as **Blades2** in the same folder.
2. Enter your name and the current date in the Documentation sheet, and then switch to the Sales worksheet.
3. Change the font of the title in cell A1 to a 16–point, dark blue, boldface, Times New Roman font. Change the subtitles in cells A2 and A3 to an 8-point, blue font. Reduce the height of row 2 and row 3 to 12 characters.
4. Add a solid black bottom border to the range A1:K1.
5. Format the text in cell A5 in a 12-point, blue, Arial font. Vertically align the text in this cell with the bottom of the cell.

Explore

6. Merge the cells in the range A6:A10, and align the contents of the cell vertically at the top of the cell. Repeat this for the following ranges: A11:A15, A16:A20, and A21:A25.
7. Change the background color of the cell range A6:I10 to light yellow. Change the background color of the range A11:I15 to light green. Change the background color of the range A16:I20 to light turquoise. Change the background color of the range A21:I25 to pale blue.
8. Reverse the color scheme for the subtotal values in the range B10:I10, so that instead of black on light yellow, the font color is light yellow on a black background. Reverse the subtotal values for the other products in the table.
9. Apply the borders, as shown in Figure 3-42, to the cells in the range A6:I25.

Explore

10. Rotate the column titles in the range C5:I5 by 45 degrees. Align the contents of each cell along the bottom-right corner of the cell. Change the background color of these cells to white, and then add a border to each cell.

Explore

11. Open the Options dialog box from the Tools menu. Deselect the Row & column headings and Gridlines options to remove the row and column headings and gridlines from the Sales worksheet window.

12. Set the print area as the range A1:K25.
13. Leave the page orientation as portrait, but center the worksheet horizontally on the page.
14. Create a custom footer with the text "Filename: *the name of the file*" left-aligned and with the text "Prepared by: *your name*" and "*the current date*" right-aligned, with your name and date on separate lines.
15. Preview the worksheet and then print it.
16. Save your changes to the workbook and then close it.

Create

Using Figure 3-43 as a guide, test your knowledge of formatting by creating your own design for a payroll worksheet.

Case Problem 4

There are no Data Files needed for this Case Problem.

Oritz Marine Services Vince DiOrio is an information systems major at a local college. He works three days a week at a nearby marina, Oritz Marine Services, to help pay for his tuition. Vince works in the business office, and his responsibilities range from making coffee to keeping the company's books.

Recently, Jim Oritz, the owner of the marina, asked Vince if he could help computerize the payroll for the employees. He explained that the employees work a different number of hours each week at different rates of pay. Jim now does the payroll manually, and finds it time consuming. Moreover, whenever he makes an error, he is annoyed at having to take the additional time to correct it. Jim is hoping that Vince can help him.

Vince immediately agrees to help. He tells Jim that he knows how to use Excel and that he can build a worksheet that will save him time and reduce errors. Jim and Vince meet to review the present payroll process and discuss the desired outcome of the payroll spreadsheet. Figure 3-43 displays the type of information that Jim records in the spreadsheet.

Figure 3-43

Employee	Hours	Pay Rate	Gross Pay	Federal Withholding	State Withholding	Total Deductions	Net Pay
Bramble	16	9.50					
Cortez	30	10.50					
DiOrio	25	12.50					
Fulton	20	9.50					
Juarez	25	12.00					
Smiken	10	9.00					
Smith	30	13.50					
Total							

To complete this task:

1. Create a new workbook named **Payroll1**, and save it in the Tutorial.03\Cases folder included with your Data Files.
2. Name two worksheets "Documentation" and "Payroll," and then delete the third sheet.
3. On the Documentation sheet, include the name of the company, your name as the author of the workbook, the date the workbook is being created, and a brief description of the purpose of the workbook.
4. On the Payroll worksheet, enter the payroll table shown in Figure 3-43.

5. Enter the formulas to calculate total hours, gross pay, federal withholding tax, state withholding tax, total deductions, and net pay, using the following information:
   a. Gross pay is equal to the number of hours multiplied by the pay rate.
   b. Federal withholding tax is equal to 15% of the gross pay.
   c. State withholding tax is equal to 4% of the gross pay.
   d. Total deductions are the sum of federal and state withholdings.
   e. Net pay is equal to the difference between the gross pay and the total amount of deductions.
6. Format the appearance of the payroll table using the techniques you learned in this tutorial. The appearance of the payroll table is up to you; however, do not use an AutoFormat design to format the table.
7. Format the printed page, setting the print area and inserting an appropriate header and footer. Only a few employees are entered into the table at present. However, after Jim Oritz approves your layout, many additional employees will be added, which will cause the report to cover multiple pages. Format your printout so that the worksheet title and column titles appear on every page.
8. Preview your worksheet, and then print it. Save your changes.
9. Add the following new employees to the worksheet. The employee list should be in alphabetical order, so these new employees should be inserted at the appropriate places in the sheet:

Name	Hours	Pay Rate
Carls	20	10.50
Lopez	35	11.50
Nelson	20	9.50

10. Preview the revised worksheet, and then print it.
11. Save this revised workbook as **Payroll2** in the Tutorial.03\Cases folder, and then close the workbook.

Research

Use the Internet to find and work with data related to the topics presented in this tutorial.

Internet Assignments

The purpose of the Internet Assignments is to challenge you to find information on the Internet that you can use to work effectively with this software. The actual assignments are updated and maintained on the Course Technology Web site. Log on to the Internet and use your Web browser to go to the Student Online Companion for New Perspectives Office 2003 at **www.course.com/np/office2003**. Click the Internet Assignments link, and then navigate to the assignments for this tutorial.

Assess

SAM

SAM Assessment and Training

If you have a SAM user profile, you may have access to hands-on instruction, practice, and assessment of the skills covered in this tutorial. Log in to your SAM account and go to your assignments page to see what your instructor has assigned.

Review

Quick Check Answers

Session 3.1

1. Click the Currency Style button on the Formatting toolbar; or click Format on the menu bar, click Cells, click the Number tab, and then select Currency from the Category list box.
2. a. 5.8%
   b. $0.06
3. Format Painter button and Copy button
4. Increase the width of the column; decrease the font size of the text; or select the Shrink to fit check box or the Wrap text check box on the Alignment tab in the Format Cells dialog box.
5. Select the range, click Cells on the Format menu, click the Alignment tab, and then select Center Across Selection in the Horizontal list box.
6. Use the Borders button on the Formatting toolbar; use the Draw Borders button in the Border gallery; or click Cells on the Format menu, click the Border tab, and then choose the border options in the dialog box.
7. Click Cells on the Format menu, click the Patterns tab, click the Pattern list arrow, and then select the pattern type and color.

Session 3.2

1. Select the cells and either click the Merge and Center button on the Formatting toolbar; or click Cells on the Format menu, click the Alignment tab, and then click the Merge cells check box.
2. Select the cell, click Edit on the menu bar, point to Clear, and then click Formats.
3. Click Format on the menu bar, point to Sheet, and then click Background. Locate and select an image file to use for the background, and then click the Insert button.
4. margins
5. Excel prints all parts of the active worksheet that contain text, formulas, or values.
6. To define a print area, select a range in the worksheet, click File on the menu bar, point to Print Area, and then click Set Print Area. To remove a print area, point to Print Area on the File menu, and then click Clear Print Area.
7. Select the first cell below the row at which you want to insert the page break, and then select Page Break on the Insert menu.

Objectives

Session 4.1
- Create column and pie charts using the Chart Wizard
- Move and resize a chart
- Embed a chart in a worksheet
- Place a chart on a chart sheet
- Separate a slice from a pie chart

Session 4.2
- Edit the data source
- Change the location of a chart
- Modify chart objects
- Insert and format chart text
- Create 3-D charts
- Add and modify drawing objects using the Drawing toolbar
- Print a chart

Working with Charts and Graphics

Charting Sales Data

Case

Vega Telescopes

Alicia Kendall is a sales manager at Vega Telescopes, one of the leading manufacturers of telescopes and optics. She has been asked to present information on last year's sales for four of Vega's most popular telescopes: the 6- and 8-inch BrightStar and the 12- and 16-inch NightVision. Her presentation will be part of a sales conference that will be held next week in Charlotte, North Carolina.

As part of her presentation, Alicia would like to include a report that shows the sales figures for each model in the United States, Europe, and Asia. She knows that this kind of information is often best understood when presented visually, that is, in a graphical or pictorial form. She would like to use a column chart to show the sales data and a pie chart to show how each model contributes to Vega's overall sales of these four popular telescope models. Alicia is especially interested in making the charts visually appealing, and she wants to draw attention to the top-selling telescope model. She also will need printouts of the charts.

Alicia has asked you to help her create charts that will clearly and effectively present the sales data. Your task is to format the charts and individual chart components to enhance the presentation of the data, which will help Alicia explain and highlight the data at the sales conference. You will also add a drawing object that points out the top-selling telescope, and you will print the completed charts.

Student Data Files

▼Tutorial.04

▽ Tutorial folder
- Space.jpg
- Vega1.xls

▽ Review folder
- VegaUSA1.xls

▽ Cases folder
- CIC1.xls
- Powder1.xls
- Pixal1.xls

Session 4.1

Excel Charts

Alicia's sales data has already been entered into a workbook for you. You will begin by opening the workbook so you can examine the sales data.

To open Alicia's workbook:

1. Start Excel and then open the **Vega1** workbook located in the Tutorial.04\Tutorial folder included with your Data Files.
2. Enter *your name* and the *current date* in the Documentation sheet.
3. Save the workbook as **Vega2** to the Tutorial folder, and then switch to the Sales worksheet to view the sales data as shown in Figure 4-1.

Figure 4-1 Sales worksheet for Vega Telescopes

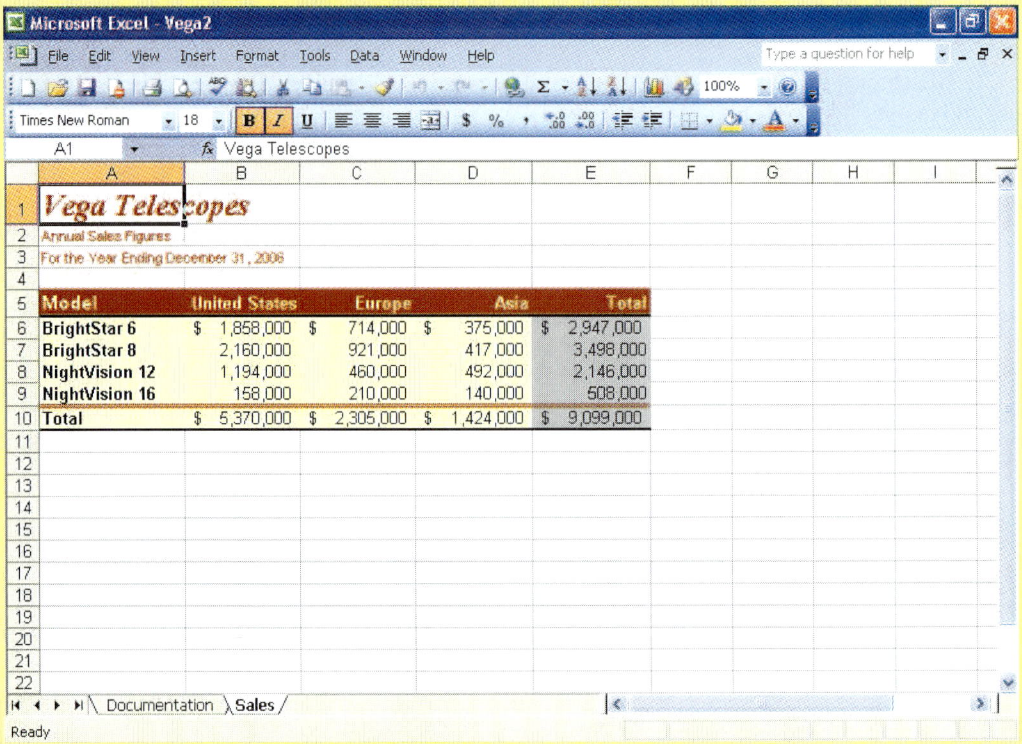

The Sales worksheet shows the annual sales, in U.S. dollars, for each of the four Vega telescope models. The sales data is broken down by world regions. As Alicia has explained, she wants two charts. The first chart should show the sales for each telescope in each region represented by columns, in which the height of the column represents the sales volume for each model. The second should be a pie chart that interprets how the total sales of each telescope model relate to overall sales. Sketches of the charts Alicia wants to create are shown in Figure 4-2.

Figure 4-2 Sketch of column and pie charts

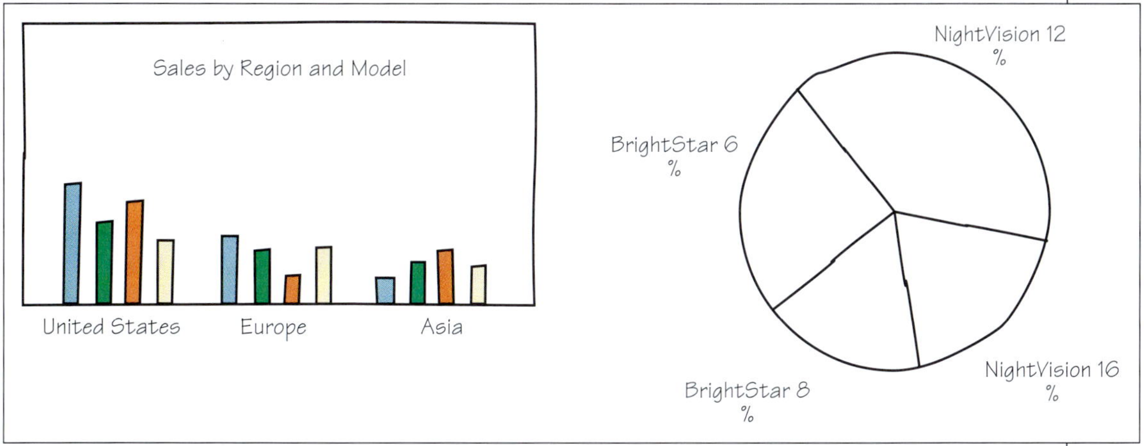

Charts, also known as graphs, provide a visual representation of the workbook data. Using charts, one can often see trends in the data that are more difficult to detect by viewing the raw numbers in a table. A chart can also be used to highlight items of interest, such as a region with low sales or an unexpectedly good sales month. Excel makes it easy to create charts through the use of the **Chart Wizard**, a series of dialog boxes that prompt you for information about the chart you want to create. This includes information such as the chart type, the cell range that the chart is based on, and features that the chart will contain. You will use the Chart Wizard to create the first chart that Alicia sketched for you—the column chart of the sales figures broken down by region and telescope model.

Creating a Chart Using the Chart Wizard

The Chart Wizard is a series of four dialog boxes, and each one is a step in the process of creating your chart. At each point in the process, you provide more detailed information about the chart you want Excel to create. Figure 4-3 describes the four steps in the Chart Wizard.

Figure 4-3 Tasks performed in each step of the Chart Wizard

Dialog Box	Task Options
Chart Type	Select from list of available chart types and corresponding sub-types, or choose to customize a chart type
Chart Source Data	Specify the cells that contain the data on which the chart will be based and the cells that contain the labels that will appear in the chart
Chart Options	Change the appearance of the chart by selecting the options that affect titles, axes, gridlines, legends, data labels, and data tables
Chart Location	Specify where the chart will be placed: embedded as an object in the worksheet containing the data or on a separate worksheet, also called a chart sheet

You can stop the Chart Wizard at any time, and Excel will complete the remaining dialog boxes for you using the default specifications for the chart you have chosen.

Reference Window

Creating a Chart Using the Chart Wizard

- Select the data you want to chart.
- Click the Chart Wizard button on the Standard toolbar.
- In the first step of the Chart Wizard, select the chart type and sub-type, and then click the Next button.
- In the second step, make any modifications or additions to the chart's data source, and then click the Next button.
- In the third step, make any modifications to the chart's appearance, and then click the Next button.
- In the fourth step, specify the location for the chart, and then click the Finish button.

Before starting the Chart Wizard, you can select the cell range that contains the data that will be used in the chart. If you don't select a cell range, the Chart Wizard will "guess" at the cell range. If the selected range isn't correct, you can select the correct cell range as you work with the Chart Wizard. To create the first chart that Alicia wants, you'll select the data in the cell range A5:D9. The range needs to include both the labels and the sales figures for each telescope model. You will not include the total sales within each region.

To start the Chart Wizard:

1. Select the range **A5:D9**.
2. Click the **Chart Wizard** button on the Standard toolbar. The first step of the Chart Wizard is shown in Figure 4-4.

Figure 4-4 Step 1 of the Chart Wizard

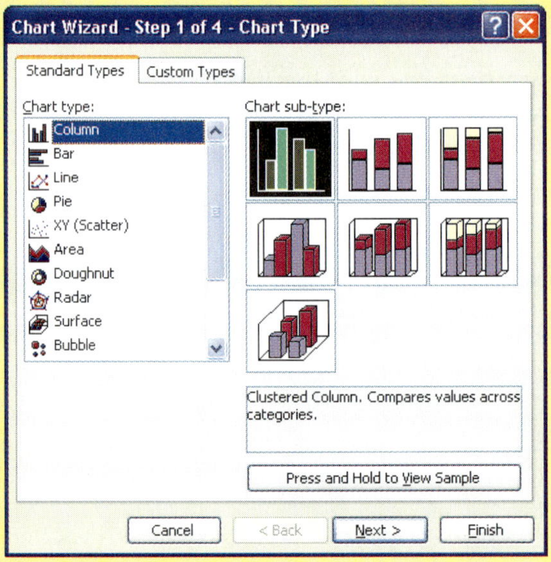

Choosing a Chart Type

The first step of the Chart Wizard provides the chart types, from which you choose the one that you feel will best display the data you want to plot. Excel supports 14 types of charts, ranging from the column chart, similar to the one shown in Alicia's first sketch, to stock market charts that can be used to record the daily behavior of stocks. Figure 4-5 provides information about some of the chart types. The charts are useful in different situations. When you want to compare the values from different categories (such as the sales of different telescope models), you will want to use a column, bar, or line chart. If you want to compare the values of individual categories to a whole collection of categories, you will want to use either a pie chart or a doughnut chart. If your data doesn't contain categories and you want to compare one set of numeric values with another, you will probably want to create an XY Scatter (scatter) chart or a bubble chart. Finally, for stock market data, you can use an Excel stock chart.

Figure 4-5 Excel chart types

Icon	Chart Type	Description
	Column	Compares values from different categories. Values are indicated by the height of the columns.
	Bar	Compares values from different categories. Values are indicated by the length of the bars.
	Line	Compares values from different categories. Values are indicated by the height of the line. Often used to show trends and changes over time.
	Pie	Compares relative values of different categories to the whole. Values are indicated by the size of the pie slices.
	XY (scatter)	Shows the patterns or relationship between two or more sets of numeric values. Often used in scientific studies and statistical analyses.
	Area	Similar to the line chart, except that areas under the lines are filled with colors indicating the different categories.
	Doughnut	Similar to the pie chart, except that it can display multiple sets of data.
	Radar	Compares a collection of values from several different data sets.
	Surface	Compares three sets of values in a three-dimensional chart.
	Bubble	Similar to the XY (scatter) chart, except the size of the data marker is determined by a third numeric value.
	Cylinder, Cone, Pyramid	Similar to the column chart, except that cylinders, cones, and pyramids are used in place of columns.

Each chart type has its own collection of sub-types that provide an alternative format for the chart's appearance. For example, the column chart type has seven different sub-types, including the clustered column and the stacked column. There are also 3-D, or three-dimensional, sub-types.

Finally, Excel also supports 20 additional "custom" chart types with additional formatting options. Some of the custom charts actually combine the properties of two or more of the main chart types. You can also create your own customized chart designs and add them to the custom chart list.

Alicia wants you to create a column chart for the sales data, in which values are arranged into separate columns. To see whether the chart you are creating is the right one, you will click the button in the first dialog box that lets you preview the chart before continuing with the Chart Wizard.

To select the chart type and preview it:

1. Verify that the **Column** chart type is selected in the Chart type list box and that the first sub-type, **Clustered Column**, is also selected.
2. Press the **Press and Hold to View Sample** button, but do not release the mouse button. A preview of the selected chart is displayed, as shown in Figure 4-6.

Figure 4-6 Preview of the clustered column chart

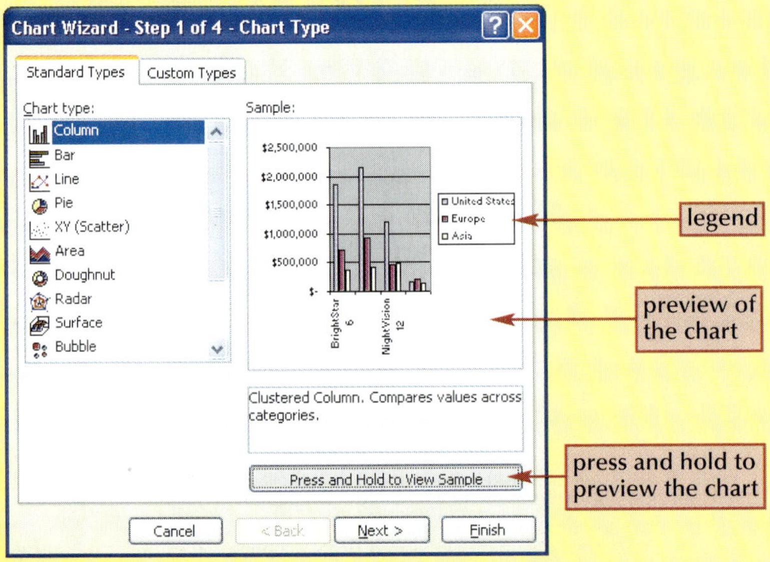

The Chart Wizard has assigned a different colored column to represent the sales values within each region. The legend on the right identifies the regions. The blue columns represent the United States, the maroon columns represent Europe, and the yellow columns represent Asia. Though the size of the Sample pane prevents you from viewing much of the chart's detail, you can see that the columns are clustered into groups; each group represents a different model. The first cluster represents sales for the BrightStar 6 telescope. The second cluster represents sales for the BrightStar 8 and so forth. Because this is the chart type that Alicia wants you to create, you can continue to the next step of the Chart Wizard.

3. Release the mouse button, and then click the **Next** button to go to step 2 of the Chart Wizard.

Choosing a Data Source

In the second step of the Chart Wizard, shown in Figure 4-7, you specify the **data source** for the chart, indicating the cell range that contains the chart's data. Excel organizes the data source into a collection of **data series**, where each data series is a range of data values that is plotted as a unit on the chart. In the case of this column chart, each data series contains the sales values of each sales region. A data series consists of **data values**, which are plotted on the chart's vertical axis, or **y-axis**. On the horizontal axis, or **x-axis**, are the data series' **category values**, or **x values**. In this chart, the data values are the sales values and the category values are the names of the different telescope models.

Figure 4-7 Specifying the data source

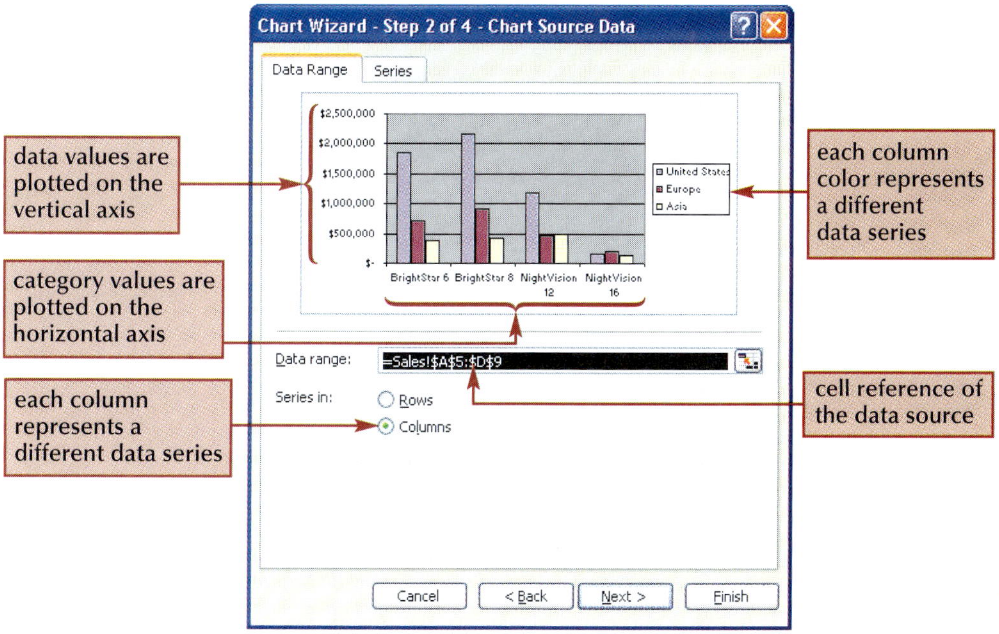

In this case, the Chart Wizard has organized the data source by columns, so that the left-most column contains the category values and the subsequent columns each contain a different data series. The first row of the data contains the labels that identify each data series. In general, if the data spans more rows than columns, then the Chart Wizard interprets the data series by columns; otherwise, the Chart Wizard interprets the data series by rows.

In Alicia's sketch, she has indicated that she wants the name of the region to be the category value, which means that each telescope model represents a different data series. Therefore, you need to ensure that the Chart Wizard organizes the data source by rows and not columns. The first row will contain the category values, and each subsequent row will contain a data series. The first column will then contain the labels of each series.

To organize the data source by rows:

1. Click the **Rows** option button. Excel changes the orientation of the data source. The category values now represent the three regions rather than the four telescope models. See Figure 4-8.

Figure 4-8 Changing the orientation of the data source

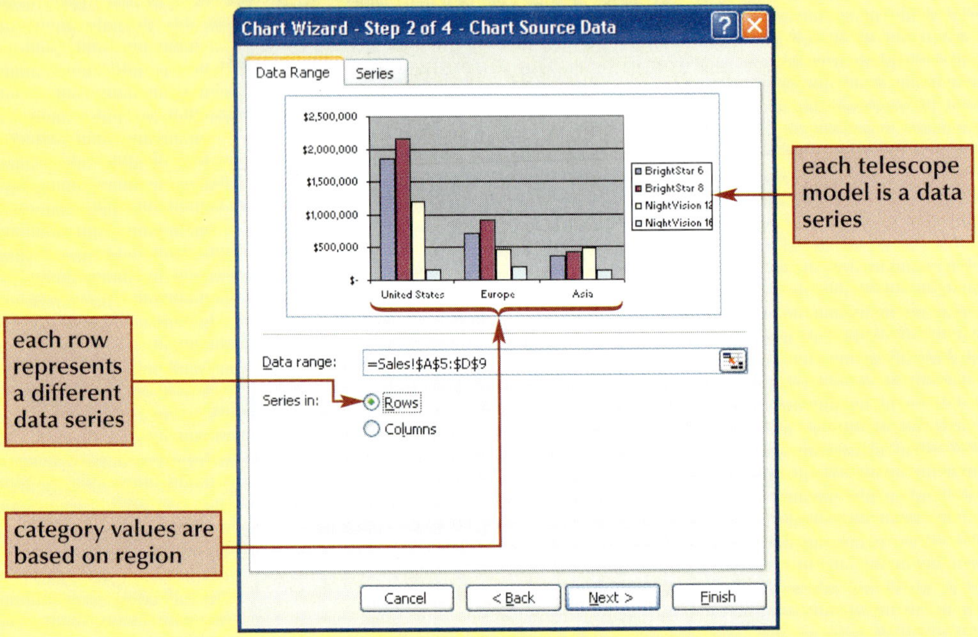

You can further define the data range using the Series tab. From this tab, you can add or remove individual data series from the chart or change the category values. Although it is recommended that you select the data series before starting the Chart Wizard, it is not necessary because you can define all of the data series and chart values using the Series tab. However, selecting the data series first does save time. You will switch to the Series tab so you can view its options.

To view the Series tab:

1. Click the **Series** tab. The Series tab lists all of the data series used in the chart and the corresponding cell references for the cell that contains the name of the data series, the cells that contain the values for the data series, and the cells the contain the category labels. Note that the cell references include the name of the sheet from which the values are selected. See Figure 4-9.

Figure 4-9 Series tab

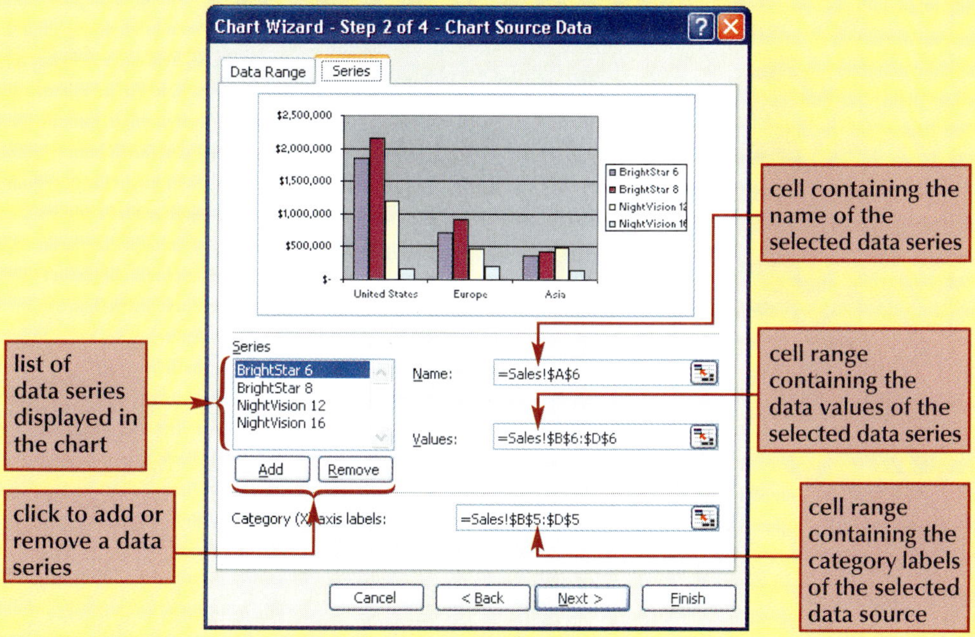

You do not have to make any changes in the data series at this point, so you will continue in the Chart Wizard.

2. Click the **Next** button to go to step 3 of the Chart Wizard.

Choosing Chart Options

The third step of the Chart Wizard provides the options that you can use to control the appearance of the chart. To better understand the options available to you, first you'll explore the terminology that Excel uses with respect to charts. Figure 4-10 shows the elements of a typical Excel chart.

Figure 4-10 Excel chart elements

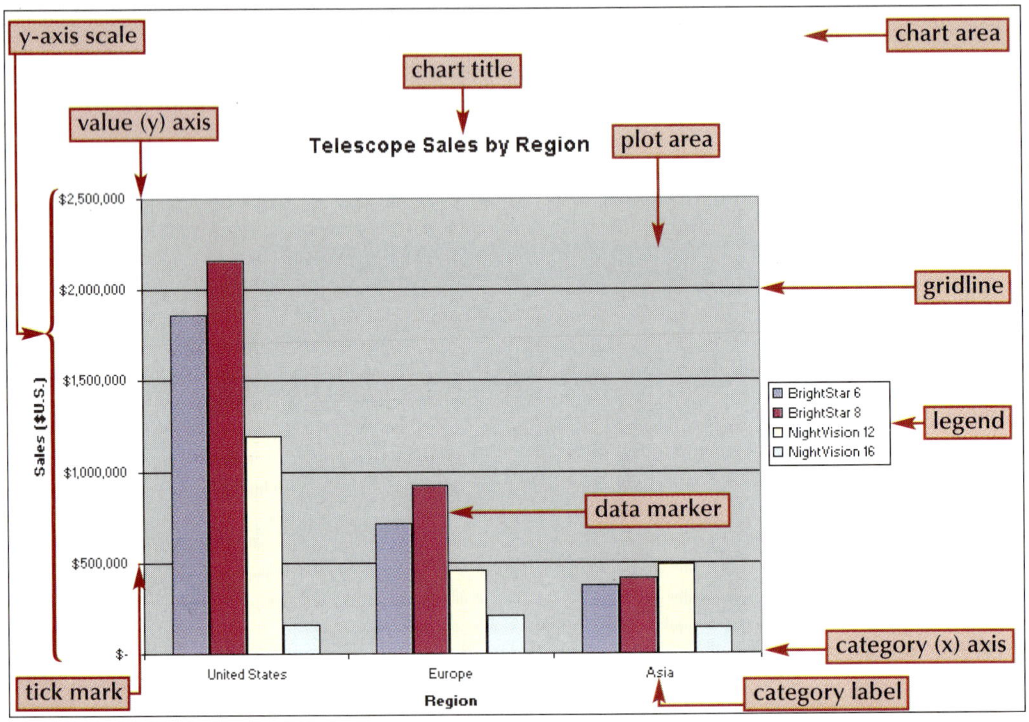

The basic element of the chart is the **plot area**, a rectangular area containing a graphical representation of the values in the data series. Each graphical representation is called a **data marker**. Each column in a column chart is an example of a data marker. Other types of data markers include the pie slices used in pie charts and the points used in XY (scatter) charts.

Most charts have two axes that border the plot area: an x-axis (or horizontal axis) and a y-axis (or vertical axis). As mentioned earlier, values from the data series are plotted along the y-axis, whereas the category labels are plotted along the x-axis. Each axis can have a title that describes the values or labels displayed on the axis. In Figure 4-10, the x-axis title is "Region" and the y-axis title is "Sales ($U.S.)."

The range of values that spans along an axis is called a **scale**. Excel automatically chooses a scale to match the range of values in the data series. In the chart shown in Figure 4-10, the scale of the y-axis ranges from $0 to $2,500,000. Next to the values on the scales are **tick marks**, which act like the division lines on a ruler, making it easier to read the scale. Your charts might also contain **gridlines**, which extend the tick marks across the plot area. Excel divides gridlines into two types. **Major gridlines** are the lines that extend the tick marks across the plot area; **minor gridlines** are the lines that divide the space between the major gridlines.

If your chart contains more than one data series, the chart will usually have a **legend** identifying the format of the data marker used for each series. Above the plot area, you can add a **chart title** to describe the contents of the plot area and the data series. The entire chart and all of the elements discussed so far are contained in the **chart area**.

You can format these various chart elements in the third step of the Chart Wizard. You can also format these features later on, after the chart has been created. As shown in Figure 4-11, step 3 of the Chart Wizard contains six tabs: Titles, Axes, Gridlines, Legend, Data Labels, and Data Table. Each tab provides tools for formatting different elements of your chart.

Step 3 of the Chart Wizard **Figure 4-11**

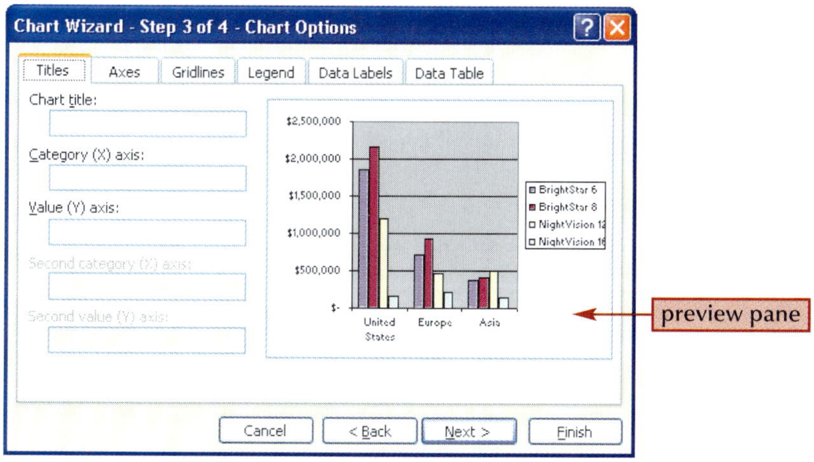

Alicia wants you to add descriptive titles to the chart and to each of the axes. She also wants you to remove the gridlines because they are not necessary in such a simple, straightforward chart. Using the Titles and Gridlines tabs, you will make these changes now.

To insert titles into the chart:

1. Make sure that the **Titles** tab is active.
2. Click the **Chart title** text box, type **Telescope Sales by Region**, and then press the **Tab** key. The preview pane updates the chart image to reflect the addition of the chart title to the chart area.
3. Type **Region** in the Category (X) axis text box, and then press the **Tab** key.
4. Type **Sales ($U.S.)** in the Value (Y) axis text box, and then press the **Tab** key. The preview pane shows all of the new titles you entered into the chart.
5. Click the **Gridlines** tab.
6. Click the **Major gridlines** check box for the Value (Y) axis to remove the major gridlines from the chart.
7. Click the **Next** button to move to the last Chart Wizard dialog box, shown in Figure 4-12.

Step 4 of the Chart Wizard **Figure 4-12**

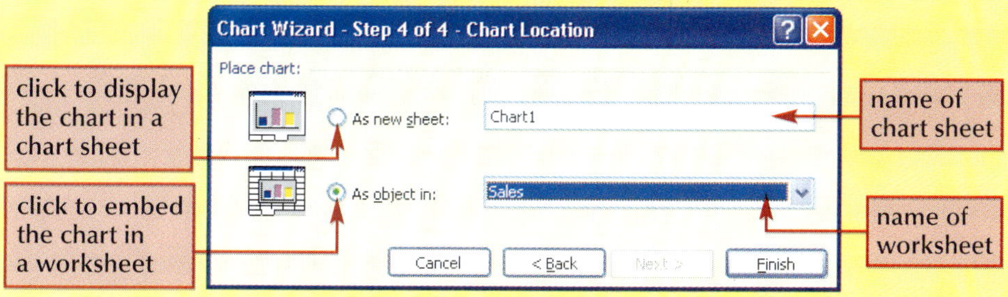

Choosing the Chart Location

In the final step of the Chart Wizard, you choose a location for the chart. You can either create an embedded chart or a chart sheet. An **embedded chart** is a chart that is displayed within a worksheet. The advantage of creating an embedded chart is that you can place the chart alongside the data source, giving context to the chart. A **chart sheet** is a new sheet that is automatically inserted into the workbook, occupying the entire workbook window and thus providing more space and details for the chart. Figure 4-13 provides examples of each type of chart.

Figure 4-13 Example of an embedded chart and a chart sheet

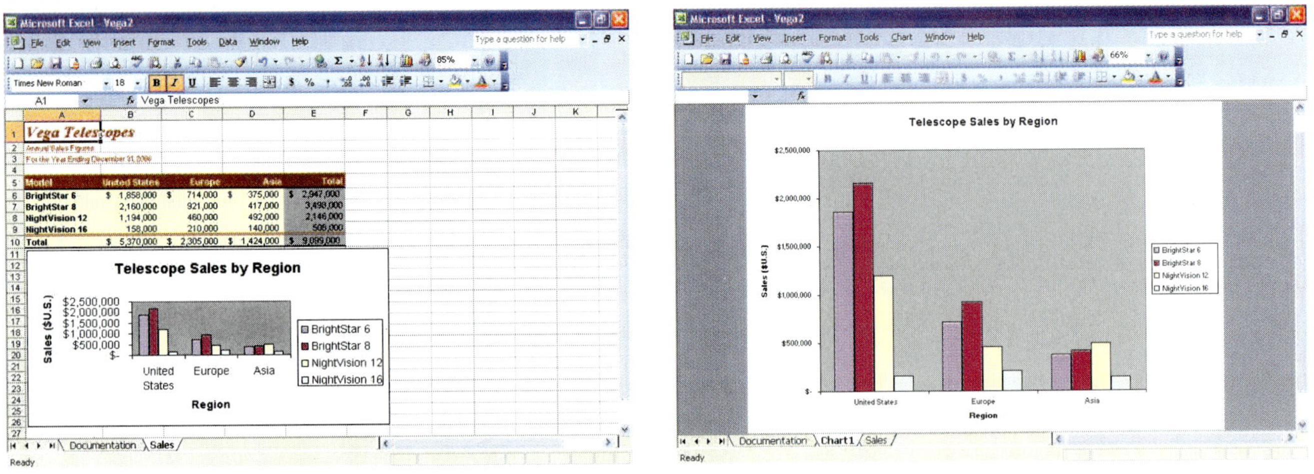

embedded chart in the Sales worksheet

chart sheet named "Chart1"

For this first chart, you'll embed the chart in the Sales worksheet.

To embed the clustered column chart in the Sales worksheet:

1. Make sure that the **As object in** option button is selected and that **Sales** is selected in the adjacent list box.
2. Click the **Finish** button. Excel creates the column chart with the specifications you selected and embeds the chart in the Sales worksheet, as shown in Figure 4-14.

Embedded column chart

Figure 4-14

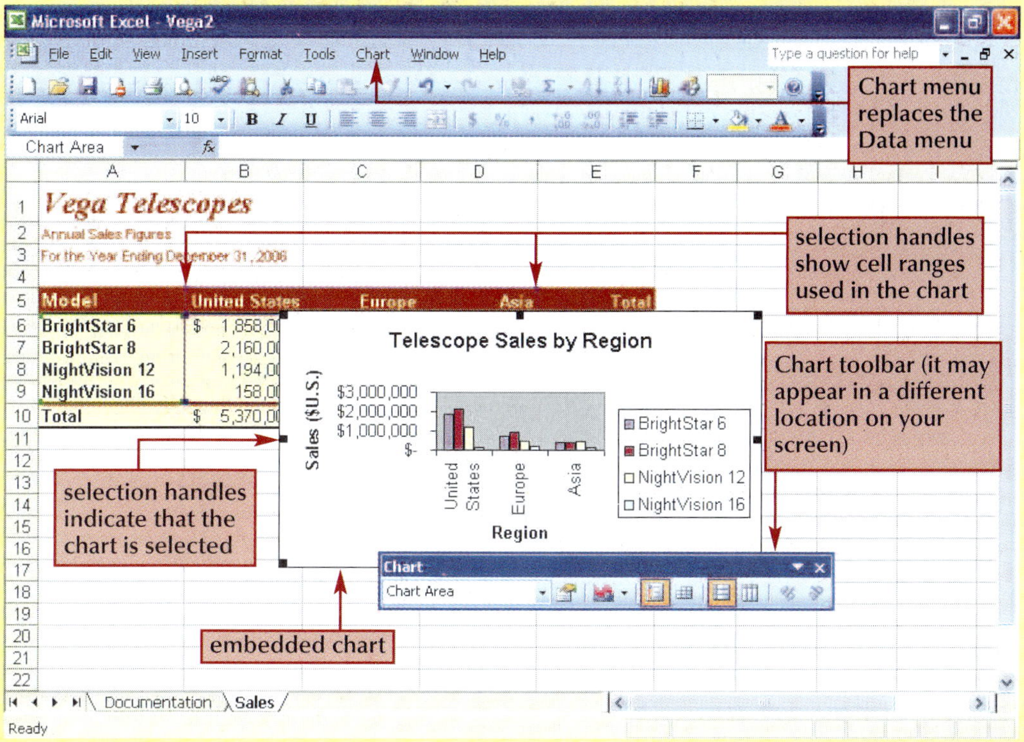

Trouble? If the Chart toolbar is not visible, it may have been closed during a previous Excel session. Click View on the menu bar, point to Toolbars, and then click Chart to redisplay the toolbar.

When the Chart Wizard creates the embedded chart, the chart appears with selection handles around it. The selection handles indicate that the chart is an **active chart** and is ready for additional formatting. The Chart toolbar also appears when the chart is selected. (Note that the Chart toolbar doesn't always appear when a chart is selected if the toolbar was closed in an earlier Excel session.) Another change that occurs is the Chart menu replaces the Data menu on Excel's menu bar. You will also find that certain Excel commands are not available to you when a chart is the active object in the workbook window. When a chart is not active, the default Excel menus return and the Chart toolbar disappears.

Try switching between the chart and the worksheet.

To switch between the embedded chart and the worksheet:

1. Click anywhere in the worksheet outside of the chart to deselect it. The Chart toolbar disappears and the Data menu replaces the Chart menu on the menu bar. There are no selection handles around the chart.
2. Move the pointer over a blank area of the chart so that the pointer changes to ⇖ and the ScreenTip "Chart Area" displays in the chart, and then click in the empty chart area. The Chart toolbar and the Chart menu reappear, and the selection handles appear around the chart.

   Trouble? If you clicked one of the chart's elements, you made that element active rather than the entire chart. Click a blank area in the chart to select the entire embedded chart.

Moving and Resizing an Embedded Chart

The Chart Wizard has a default size and location for embedded charts, which might not match what you want in your worksheet. In this case, the new chart is covering some of the data in the Sales worksheet and the chart titles seem to overwhelm the plot area. You will move the chart so you can see all of the sales data, and then you will make the chart a little larger to make it easier to read.

To move and resize the embedded chart:

1. Verify that the embedded chart is still selected, and then move the pointer over a blank area of the chart so that the pointer changes to ⇱ and the ScreenTip "Chart Area" displays.
2. Drag the embedded chart so that the upper-left corner of the chart aligns with the upper-left corner of cell A11. Note that as you drag the chart with the pointer, an outline of the chart area appears, which you can use as a guideline.
3. Release the mouse button when the chart is positioned correctly. The chart moves to a new location in the worksheet.

   To resize the chart, you drag a selection handle in the direction that you want the chart resized. To keep the proportions of the chart the same, press and hold the Shift key as you drag one of the corner selection handles.
4. Move your pointer over the lower-right selection handle until the pointer changes to ⤡.
5. Drag the lower-right corner of the embedded chart until that corner is aligned with the lower-right corner of cell F26.
6. Release the mouse button when the chart is resized, and then, if necessary, scroll the worksheet so the chart is visible. Figure 4-15 shows the chart, repositioned and resized.

Figure 4-15 Embedded chart moved and resized

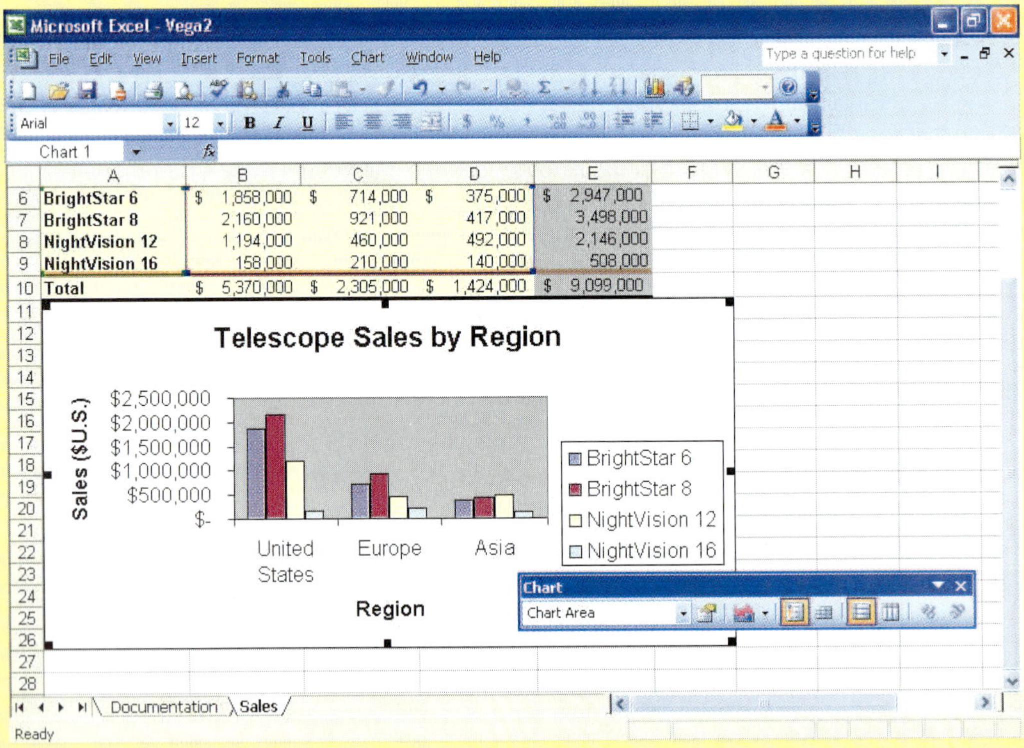

Updating a Chart

Every chart you create is connected to its data source. As a result, if you change values in the data source, Excel automatically updates the chart to reflect the change. This is true for category labels as well as for data values.

Alicia sees two changes that she would like you to make to the Sales worksheet. First, the European sales amount for the BrightStar 6 model should be $914,000, not $714,000. She also wants to change the label "United States" to "USA." You'll make these changes and observe how the embedded chart is automatically updated.

To update the column chart:

1. Scroll the worksheet so both the chart and the sales data are visible.
2. Click cell **C6**, type **914000**, and then press the **Enter** key. The data marker corresponding to European sales for the BrightStar 6 changes to reflect the new sales value.
3. Click cell **B5**, type **USA**, and then press the **Enter** key. The x-axis reflects the change to the category name.

Creating a Pie Chart

The second chart that Alicia sketched (shown in Figure 4-2) is a pie chart that shows the relative contribution of each telescope model to the total sales. In a pie chart, the size of each slice is determined by the relative value of a single data point to the sum of all values in the data series. Unlike the column chart you just created, a pie chart has only one data series, which is the total sales for each model from all regions.

To create the pie chart:

1. Select the nonadjacent range **A6:A9;E6:E9**, and then click the **Chart Wizard** button on the Standard toolbar. The first step of the Chart Wizard opens.
2. Click **Pie** in the Chart type list box, make sure that the first chart sub-type **Pie** is selected, and then click the **Next** button.

   Because you already selected the data series for the chart, which appears in columns, you do not have to make any changes, so you can bypass the second step of the Chart Wizard.
3. Click the **Next** button to move to the third step of the Chart Wizard. You will enter the chart title that Alicia wants in this dialog box.
4. Make sure that the **Titles** tab is active, click the **Chart title** text box, and then type **Total Telescope Sales**.

   Next you will add data labels to the chart that display the percentage of sales for each model.
5. Click the **Data Labels** tab, and then click the **Percentage** check box. The preview of the charts reflects the options you have chosen. See Figure 4-16.

Figure 4-16 **Displaying percentage labels in a pie chart**

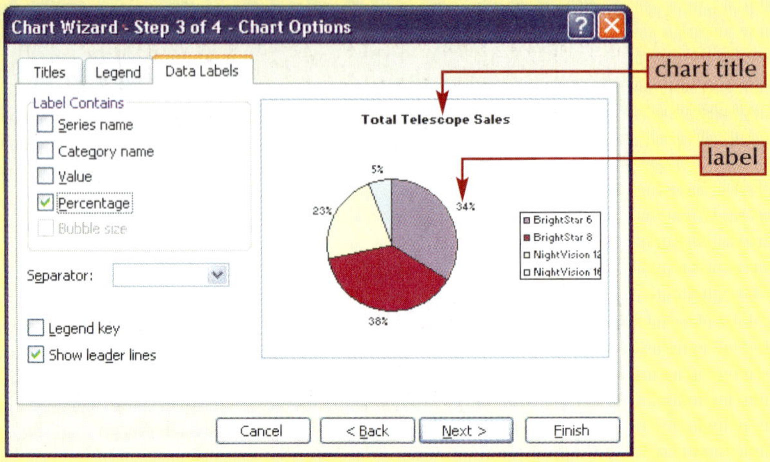

6. Click the **Next** button to display the final step of the Chart Wizard. You will place the pie chart in its own chart sheet and name the sheet "Pie Chart of Sales."
7. Click the **As new sheet** option button, and then type **Pie Chart of Sales** in the adjacent list box. The text you type in the text box will appear on the tab of the chart sheet.
8. Click the **Finish** button. Figure 4-17 shows the completed pie chart displayed on a chart sheet, which has been inserted before the Sales sheet. Note that the zoom magnification of the chart sheet on your screen might differ, depending on the settings and resolution of your monitor.

Figure 4-17 **Pie chart of total telescope sales**

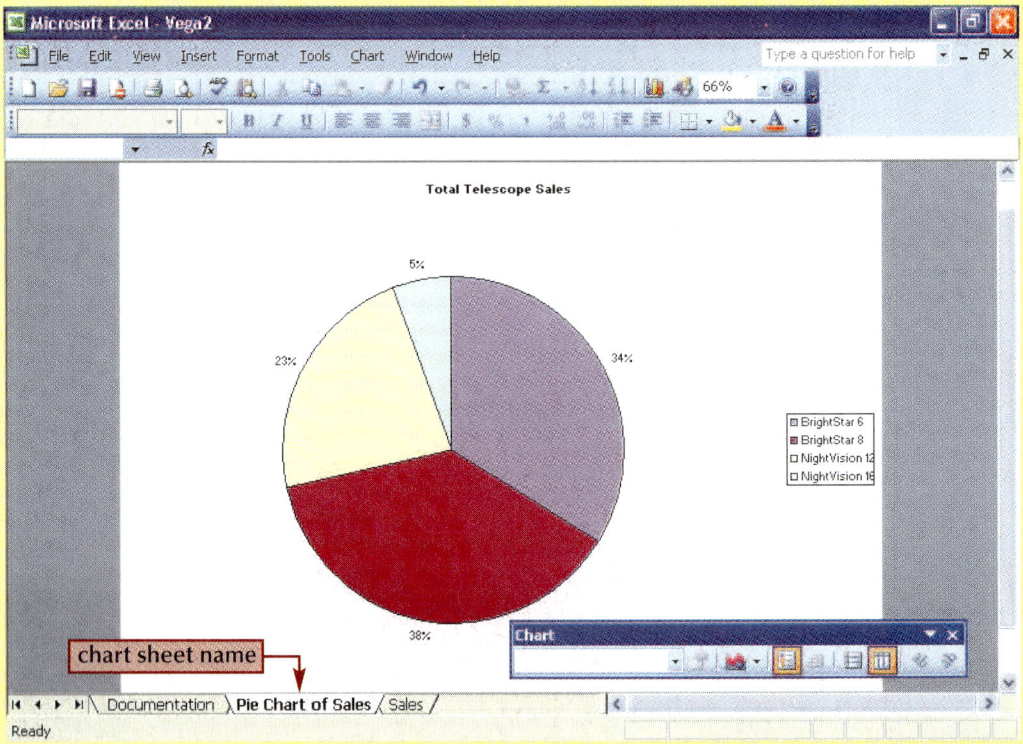

After reviewing the pie chart, Alicia has a few questions about the chart's appearance. She wonders why the slices are organized the way they are and whether the arrangement of the pie slices can be changed. The slices are arranged in a counterclockwise direction following the order that they appeared in the table. The first entry is for the BrightStar 6 telescope, the next is for the BrightStar 8, and so forth. Alicia asks whether it would be possible to move the placement of the BrightStar 6 telescope.

Rotating the Pie Chart

You cannot change the order in which the slices are arranged in the pie chart without changing their order in the data series, but you can rotate the chart. This is done by breaking the chart into 360-degree increments, starting from the top of the pie. Using this approach, the first slice starts at 0 degrees—a value that you can change. Based on Alicia's suggestion, you will change the starting point to 180 degrees, so that the first slice appears at the bottom of the pie chart.

To rotate the pie chart:

1. Double-click the pie chart to open the Format Data Series dialog box, and then click the **Options** tab.
2. Double-click the value in the Angle of first slice text box, and then click the **Degrees** up arrow to increase the angle of first slice value to **180**. As you click the up arrow, the pie chart in the preview pane rotates accordingly, as shown in Figure 4-18.

Rotating the pie chart 180 degrees **Figure 4-18**

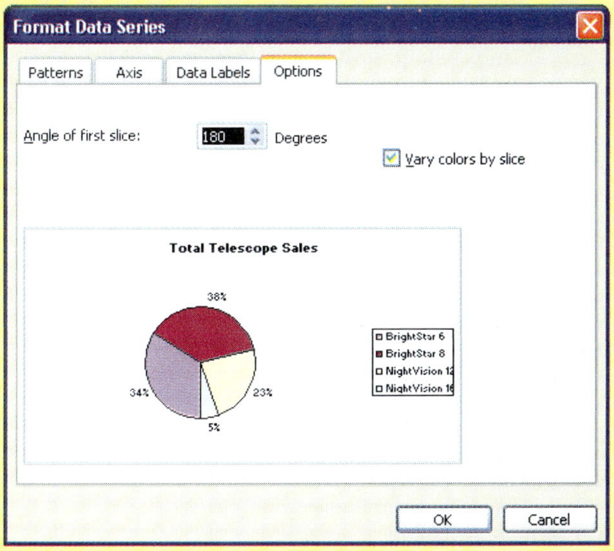

3. Click the **OK** button to close the dialog box.

Alicia tells you that the company is particularly interested in the sales performance of the BrightStar 6 telescope, because the company is considering replacing this scope with a six-inch version of the NightVision. Alicia has seen pie charts in which a single slice is removed from the others to give it greater emphasis. She wants the slice for the BrightStar 6 removed from the other slices to draw attention to this telescope.

Exploding a Slice of a Pie Chart

This method of emphasizing a particular pie slice over others is called separating or "exploding" the slice. An exploded slice is more distinctive because it is not connected to the other slices in the pie and it appears to be bigger. Excel allows you to explode any or all of the slices in the pie. A pie chart with one or more pie slices separated from the whole is referred to as an exploded pie chart.

Reference Window

Creating an Exploded Pie Chart

To explode one pie slice from a pie chart:
- Click the pie chart to select it, and then click the pie slice you want to explode.
- Drag the selected pie slice away from the rest of the pie, and then release the mouse button.

To explode all the pie slices in a pie chart:
- Click the pie chart to select it.
- Drag any pie slice to explode all the slices an equal distance apart, and then release the mouse button.

Next, you'll separate the BrightStar 6 telescope pie slice from the rest of the pie.

To explode the slice for the BrightStar 6 telescope:

1. Make sure that the pie chart is still selected, and then click the pie slice representing the total sales for the BrightStar 6. When you position the pointer over the pie slice, a ScreenTip appears with the corresponding worksheet cell information.
2. Drag the pie slice down and to the left. As you drag the pie slice, an outline marks your progress.
3. Release the mouse button, moving the slice into its new position. See Figure 4-19 for the location of the exploded pie slice.

Exploding a pie slice

Figure 4-19

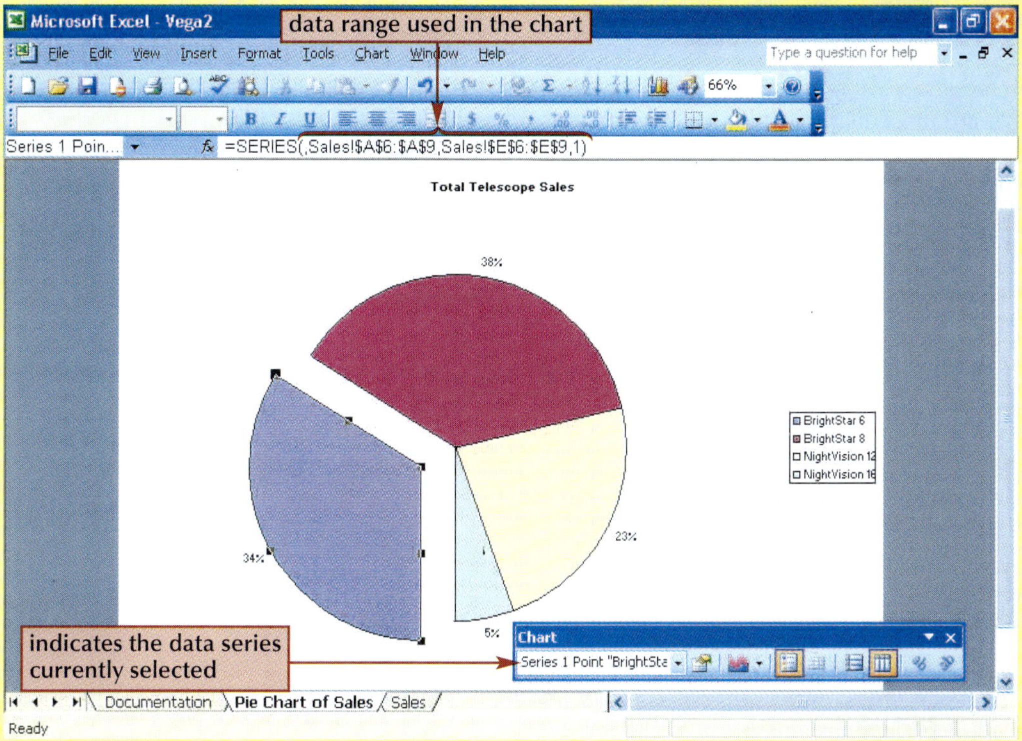

You have created the two charts that Alicia wanted, so you can save your work and then close the workbook and Excel.

4. Save your changes to the workbook, and then close it.

Rotating the pie and exploding a pie slice are both examples of formatting the appearance of an Excel chart after it has been created with the Chart Wizard. In the next session, you will learn about the other tools available that you can use to format the charts that you create.

Session 4.1 Quick Check

Review

1. What is the difference between a chart type and a chart sub-type?
2. Which chart would you most likely use to track the daily values of a stock?
3. What is a data series?
4. What is the difference between the plot area and the chart area?
5. What are gridlines?
6. Describe the two types of chart locations.
7. A chart that shows the relative contribution of each data value to the whole is called a(n) ______________ chart.
8. A pie chart in which all slices are separated from one another is called a(n) ______________ chart.

Session 4.2

Modifying a Chart

In the last session, you used the Chart Wizard to create two charts. Although the Chart Wizard presents you with a variety of choices concerning your chart's appearance, the wizard does not provide every possibility. To make further modifications to your charts, you can use the formatting tools and commands available on the Chart toolbar and the Chart menu.

Editing the Data Source

After you create a chart, you can change the data that is used in the chart. You might need to change the data if you selected the wrong data or if you decide to display a different data series.

Reference Window

Editing the Data Source of a Chart

- Select the chart whose data source you want to edit.
- Click Chart on the menu bar, click Source Data, and then click the Series tab.
- To remove a data series, select the data series in the Series list box, and click the Remove button.
- To add a data series, click the Add button, and then select the cell references for the new data series.
- To revise a data series, select the data series in the Series list box, click the reference box for the data series, and then select a new cell reference.
- Click the OK button.

Alicia can see from the charts that 16-inch telescopes comprise a small portion of Vega's sales. For this reason, she wants you to remove the NightVision 16 from the two charts you created. You will begin by removing the NightVision 16 data series from the column chart.

To remove the NightVision 16 data series from the column chart:

1. If you took a break after the previous session, make sure that Excel is running and the Vega2 workbook is open.
2. Switch to the Sales worksheet, and then click the embedded column chart to select it.
3. Click **Chart** on the menu bar, and then click **Source Data**. The Source Data dialog box opens. Note that this dialog box is identical to the second dialog box in the Chart Wizard.
4. Click the **Series** tab, click **NightVision 16** in the Series list box, and then click the **Remove** button. The preview of the chart reflects the change you have made. See Figure 4-20.

Removing the NightVision 16 from the column chart

Figure 4-20

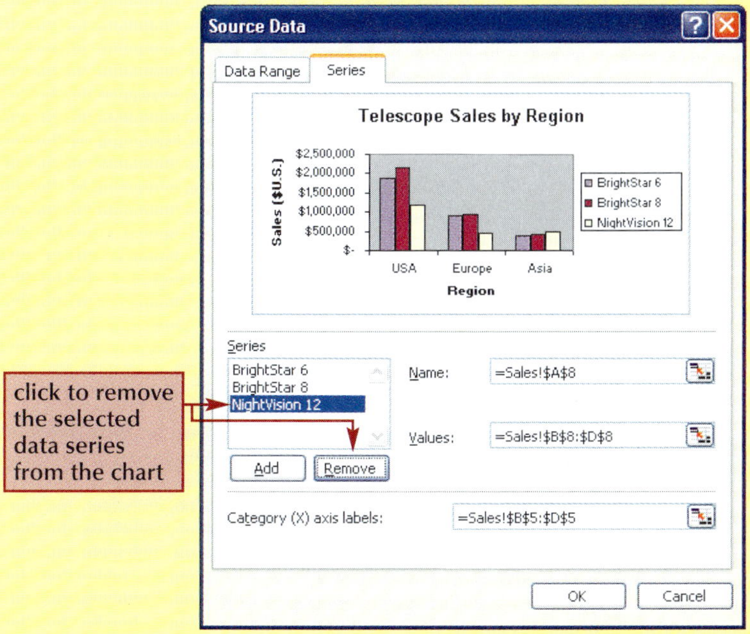

5. Click the **OK** button. The NightVision 16 sales data is no longer represented in the column chart.

Removing the NightVision 16 pie slice from the pie chart presents a slightly different challenge. Unlike the column chart (which has multiple data series), the pie chart has only one data series. To remove the NightVision 16 from the pie chart, you will have to change the cell reference of the chart's data source to exclude the NightVision 16 row.

To remove the NightVision 16 from the pie chart:

1. Switch to the Pie Chart of Sales worksheet.
2. Click **Chart** on the menu bar, click **Source Data** to open the Source Data dialog box, and then verify that the Series tab is selected. From this dialog box, you can see that the values for the data series are found in the cell range E6:E9 on the Sales worksheet and the category labels come from the range A6:A9 on the same sheet. You have to change these cell references to remove the NightVision 16 telescope from the chart.
3. Click the **Collapse Dialog Box** button for the Values reference box, select the range **E6:E8**, and then click the **Expand Dialog Box** button to redisplay the Source Data dialog box with the new value range.
4. Click the **Collapse Dialog Box** button for the Category Labels reference box, select the range **A6:A8**, and then click the **Expand Dialog Box** button to redisplay the Source Data dialog box. As shown in Figure 4-21, the preview pane displays the new pie chart with the NightVision 16 telescope excluded.

Figure 4-21 **Removing the NightVision 16 from the pie chart**

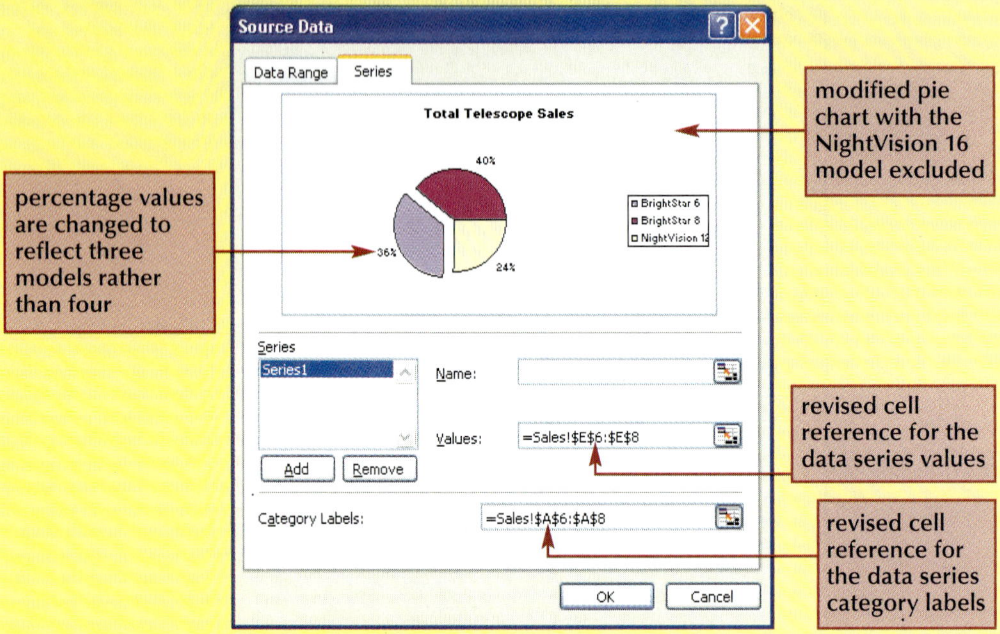

5. Click the **OK** button to save your changes to the chart.

Note that when you removed the NightVision 16 from the data series, the percentages in the pie chart changed as well to reflect a total sales figure based on only three models rather than four.

Changing the Chart Location

Alicia has decided that she prefers the chart sheet to the embedded chart. She wants you to move the embedded column chart on the Sales worksheet to a chart sheet. Rather than re-creating the chart using the Chart Wizard, you will use the Location command on the Chart menu. You will move the embedded chart to a chart sheet, which you will name "Column Chart of Sales."

To change the location of the embedded column chart:

1. Switch to the Sales worksheet, and then, if necessary, click the embedded column chart to select it.
2. Click **Chart** on the menu bar, and then click **Location**. The Chart Location dialog box opens. The dialog box is identical to the fourth dialog box in the Chart Wizard.
3. Click the **As new sheet** option button, type **Column Chart of Sales** as the name of the chart sheet, and then click the **OK** button. The column chart moves into its own chart sheet.

Changing Chart Options

As mentioned, the dialog boxes to change the chart's data source and location look identical to the dialog boxes for steps 2 and 4 of the Chart Wizard. Dialog boxes for the remaining two Chart Wizard steps are also available through commands on the Chart menu. Recall that the third step of the Chart Wizard allowed you to format the chart's appearance by adding or removing chart titles, gridlines, legends, and labels.

Alicia wants to revisit some of the chart options selected earlier. After seeing that the percent labels in the pie chart provided useful information, she wants you to add labels to the column chart displaying the actual sales values for each column. You will use the Chart Options dialog box to make this change.

To revise the chart options for the column chart:

1. Click **Chart** on the menu bar, and then click **Chart Options**. The Chart Options dialog box opens. Note that the dialog box is identical to step 3 of the Chart Wizard.
2. Click the **Data Labels** tab.
3. Click the **Value** check box, and then click the **OK** button. The sales figures for each model now appear above the corresponding column. See Figure 4-22. The values appear to be a little crowded, and you will change this next.

Figure 4-22 Adding labels to the columns

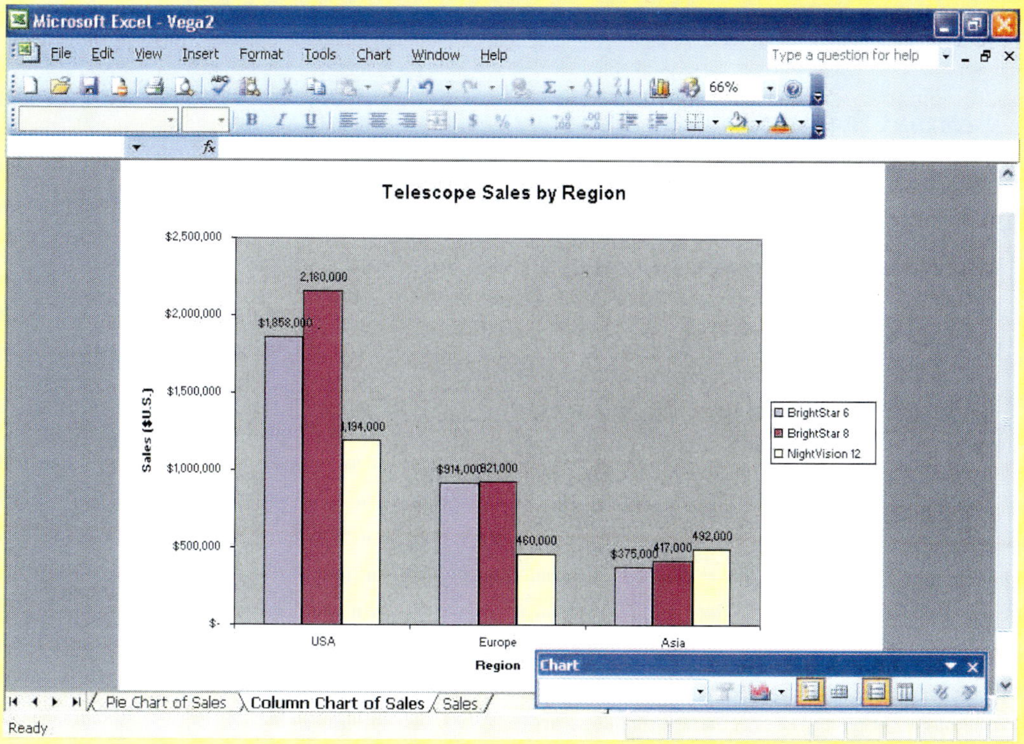

Alicia has a few changes that she wants you to make to the chart labels. You cannot make these changes by modifying the chart options. Instead, you have to format the individual elements within the chart.

Formatting Chart Elements

So far, all of the formatting that you have done has applied to the chart as a whole. You can also select and format individual chart elements, such as the chart title, legend, and axes. To select an individual chart element, you either click on the element or select the element's name from a drop-down list on the Chart toolbar. You can then use buttons on the Formatting toolbar or open a dialog box to modify the element's appearance. You can also double-click a chart element to both select it and open a dialog box or right-click the chart element and select a format from a shortcut dialog box.

In some cases, a chart element will be composed of several elements. For example, a data series will have several data markers. If you click on one data marker, you select all of the markers in the series. If you click that marker again, the selection is confined to that specific marker, removing the selection from other markers in the series. In this way, you can format all of the elements at once or confine your formatting to a specific element.

You'll have a chance to try these selection and formatting techniques in the steps that follow.

Formatting Chart Text

Alicia wants you to change the alignment of the data labels that appear above the columns. She feels that the labels would look better if you changed their alignment from horizontal to vertical. She would also like the labels to appear within and at the bottom of the columns themselves, so she suggests that you change the color of the data labels as well. You will make these changes by double-clicking the data label to open the Format Data Labels dialog box.

To format the data labels:

1. Double-click the data label **$1,858,000**, located above the first column in the chart. The Format Data Labels dialog box opens. The Format Data Labels dialog box has four tabs. You use the Font and Number tabs to change font-related options for text and values and to apply number formats to values as you did in the previous tutorial. You use the Patterns tab to change the fill color, patterns, and borders around labels. You use the Alignment tab to change the alignment of the text in the label.

   The $1,858,000 label is part of the set of labels for the BrightStar 6 data series. By double-clicking the first data label, you've selected all of the labels for this particular series. Any changes you make in this dialog box will apply to all of the labels for the BrightStar 6 sales data (but not for the labels in the other data series).

2. Click the **Font** tab, click the **Color** list box, and then click the **Yellow** square (fourth row, third column from the left) in the color palette.

   Trouble? If you are working with a black-and-white printer, select the White font color, located in the bottom-right corner of the color palette.

3. Click the **Alignment** tab.
4. In the Orientation section, change the value in the Degrees box to **90**. The text changes to a vertical orientation with an angle of 90 degrees.
5. Click the **Label Position** list arrow, and then select **Inside Base** to display the values label inside and at the base of each column in the chart. See Figure 4-23.

Figure 4-23 **Changing the orientation of the data labels**

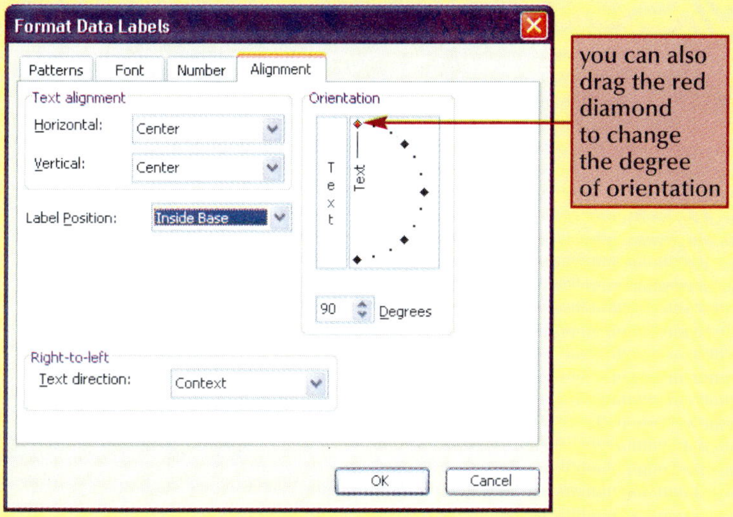

6. Click the **OK** button. The labels for the BrightStar 6 data series have been rotated 90 degrees and now appear in a yellow font at the base of the columns.

   Next you'll make a similar change to the labels for the BrightStar 8 data series. Rather than double-clicking the label, you'll use the shortcut menu.

7. Right-click the **$2,160,000** label above the second column in the chart, click **Format Data Labels** from the shortcut menu, and then repeat Steps 2 through 6 to change the label to a white font rotated 90 degrees and displayed at the inside base of each column.

   Finally, you'll select the data labels for the NightVision 12 data series using the Chart toolbar.

8. Click the **Chart Objects** list arrow on the Chart toolbar, scroll down the list of options, click **"NightVision 12" Data Labels** to select this chart element, and then click the **Format Data Labels** button on the Chart toolbar.
9. Repeat Steps 3 through 6 to rotate the label to **90** degrees and display it at the inside base of each column. You don't have to change the color of the font.
10. Click the **OK** button to save your changes. Figure 4-24 shows the revised labels for all of the data series in the chart.

Figure 4-24 Revised data labels

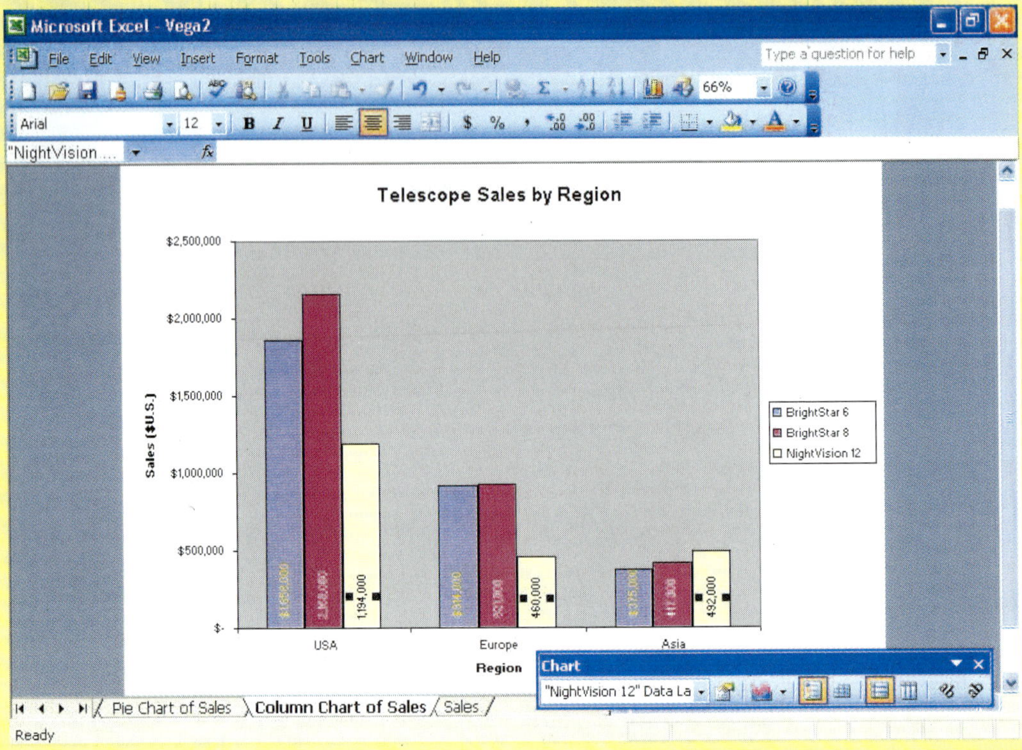

Next, Alicia wants you to add some additional text to the chart.

Inserting Unattached Text

Excel classifies chart text in three categories: label text, attached text, and unattached text. Label text includes the category names, the tick mark labels (which you've just worked with), and the legend text. Label text often is linked to cells in the worksheet. Attached text includes the chart title and the axes titles. Although the text appears in a predefined position, you can edit and move it. Unlike label text, attached text is not linked to any cells in the worksheet. Finally, unattached text is any additional text that you want to include in the chart. Unattached text can be positioned anywhere within the chart area and formatted with the same tools you use to format label and attached text.

To add unattached text to a chart, you type the text in the Formula bar. Excel automatically creates a text box for the text entry and places the text box in the chart area. You can then resize the text box and move it to another location in the chart area. You can format the text using the Format Text Box dialog box.

Inserting Unattached Text into a Chart

Reference Window

- Select the chart.
- In the Formula bar, type the text that you want to include in the chart.
- To resize the new unattached text box, click and drag one of the text box's selection handles.
- To move the unattached text box, click the border of the text box, and drag the text box to a new location in the chart area.
- To format the unattached text, select the text box and click the appropriate formatting buttons on the Formatting toolbar; or double-click the border of the text box to open the Format Text Box dialog box, use the options provided on the dialog box tabs, and then click the OK button.

Alicia wants you to add the text "Vega Sales from the Last Fiscal Year" to the upper-right corner of the plot area, and she wants the text to be ivory in color.

To add unattached text to the chart:

1. Click the column chart to select it, click in the Formula bar above the chart, type **Vega Sales from the Last Fiscal Year**, and then press the **Enter** key. Excel places a text box containing the new unattached text in the middle of the chart area. The text box is selected so you can modify its appearance.
2. Click the **Font Color** list arrow on the Formatting toolbar, and then click the **Ivory** square (sixth row, third column from the left) in the color palette.
3. Move the pointer over the edge of the unattached text box until the pointer changes to ✥, drag the text box to the upper-right corner of the plot area, and then release the mouse button. The text should now be placed in the upper-right corner of the plot.

You can double-click an unattached text box at any time to open the Format Text Box dialog box, in which you can change the font format, alignment, and color. You can also create a border around the text. Try this now by creating a yellow border.

To create a border for the text box:

1. Verify that the text box is still selected, and then double-click the border of the selected text box to open the Format Text Box dialog box.

   Trouble? If you double-clicked the text in the text box, the Format Text Box dialog box did not open. Try double-clicking the border of the text box again.
2. Click the **Colors and Lines** tab.
3. Click the **Color** list box in the Line section, click the **Ivory** square (sixth row, third column) in the color palette, and then click the **OK** button.
4. Click outside the chart to deselect it. Figure 4-25 shows the text box with the ivory border.

Figure 4-25 **Adding unattached text to a chart**

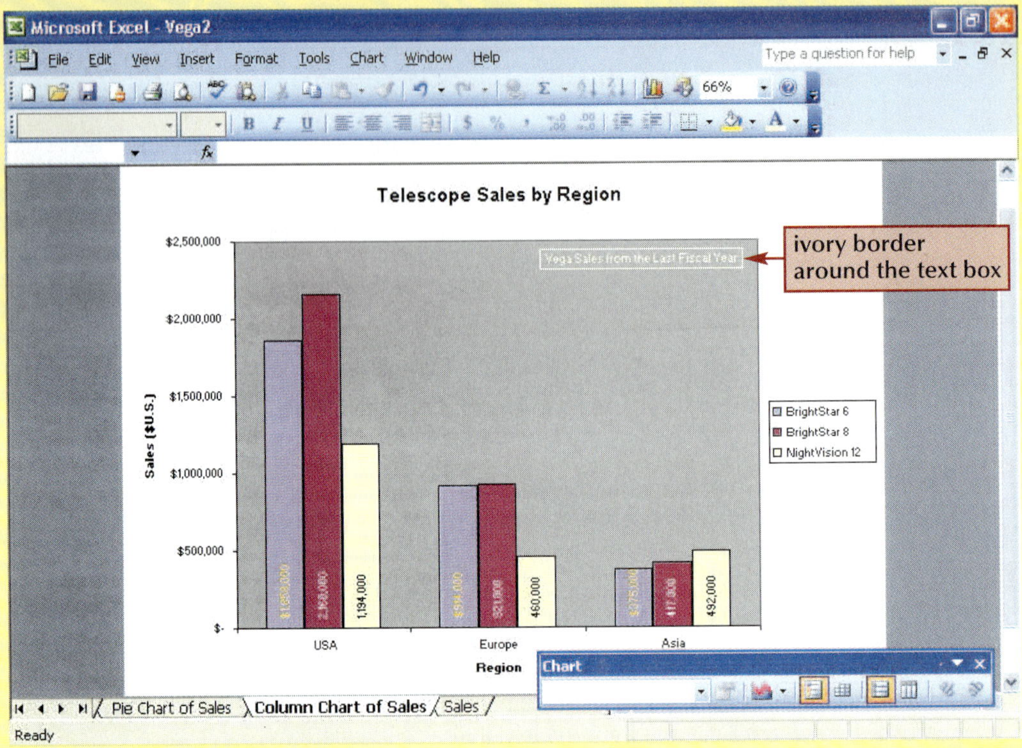

Now that you have formatted the chart labels and added unattached text, you can turn to some of the other features of Excel charts that need modifying.

Working with Colors and Fills

The formatted data labels and the unattached text help to clarify the sales data, but Alicia feels that the column chart lacks visual appeal. Alicia has seen objects filled with a variety of colors that gradually blend from one color to another. She wonders if you can do the same thing for the columns in the column chart. One idea she has is to make the columns appear more like tubes, such as telescope tubes.

When you want to fill a column (or area) in a chart with a pattern or color, you are actually modifying the appearance of the data marker in the chart. You will concentrate only on the fill color used in the data marker. Other data markers have other patterns that you can modify. For example, in an XY (scatter) chart, the data markers are points that appear in the plot. You can specify the color of those data points, their size, whether a line will connect the data points and, if so, the color, thickness, and style of that line.

You will format the data markers in the column chart beginning with the column that represents the BrightStar 6 telescope.

To format the fill color of the chart columns:

1. Double-click the first column on the left in the chart to open the Format Data Series dialog box for that data series. You can use the options available on the different dialog box tabs to control one or more aspects of the selected data marker. For example, you use the options provided on the Patterns tab to control the border style that appears around the column as well as the interior appearance of the column. Currently, the column is formatted with a black border and filled with a pale-blue color.

2. Click the **Fill Effects** button to open the Fill Effects dialog box. The tabs in this dialog box provide a full range of options that you can use to create sophisticated and lush colors and patterns.
3. Make sure the **Gradient** tab is displayed in the dialog box.

You use the options on the Gradient tab to create fill effects that blend together different and varying amounts of color. Three color options are:

- **One color:** To create a blend that uses different shades of one color
- **Two colors:** To create a blend from one color into another
- **Preset:** To apply a predefined blend style, including Early Sunset, Nightfall, Ocean, Rainbow, and Chrome

You can also specify the direction of the blending effect, choosing from horizontal, vertical, diagonal up, diagonal down, from corner, and from center. For the selected column in the current chart, you will create a blend fill effect using a single color starting from a dark shade of the pale-blue color. You will use a horizontal shading style to give the color dimension.

To create the fill effect:

1. Click the **One color** option button on the Gradient tab, and then drag the scroll box to the **Dark** end of the shading scale. Note that as you change the shading scale, the images in the Variants section reflect the degree of shading.
2. Click the **Vertical** option button in the Shading styles section. Now the images in the Variants section show the varying degrees of shading vertically.
3. Click the bottom-right Variants box, which shows the darker edges of the shading on the left and right edges of the object, as shown in Figure 4-26.

Figure 4-26 Specifying a fill effect

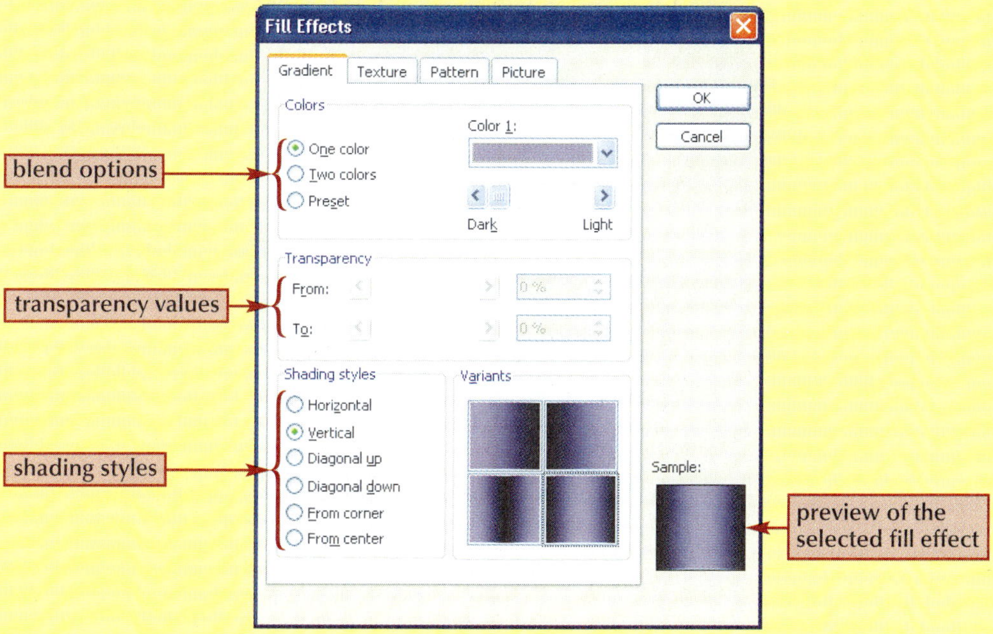

4. Click the **OK** button twice to close the dialog boxes and redisplay the chart. Excel displays the first column series with a dark-blue color on the left and right side of the column, giving it the illusion of appearing as a tube.

   Next you will create a similar blend for the other columns.

5. Double-click the second column from the left in the chart to open the Format Data Series dialog box.
6. Click the **Fill Effects** button to open the Fill Effects dialog box.
7. Click the **One color** option button, drag the scroll box to the **Dark** end of the shading scale, make sure the **Vertical** option button is selected, select the bottom-right Variants option, and then click the **OK** button twice.
8. Double-click the third column, and then repeat Steps 6 and 7 to create a one-color fill effect that goes from the dark end of the ivory scale to the light end.
9. Click outside the chart area. Figure 4-27 shows the revised column chart with blends for each of the three data series.

Figure 4-27 **Columns with the applied fill effects**

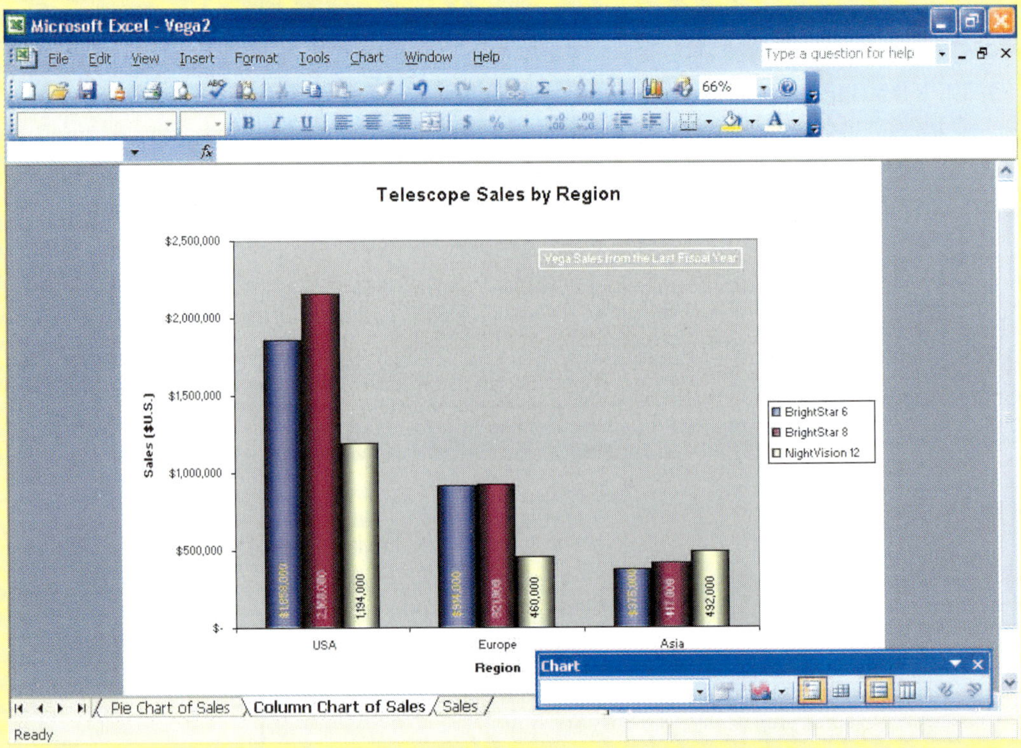

Using a Graphic Image as a Background

Next Alicia wants to replace the solid gray background with a graphic image. She has a graphic file that shows an image from the Hubble telescope, which she thinks would work well with the theme of telescope sales.

To insert this image into the chart, you will open the Format Plot Area dialog box.

To fill the plot area with an image:

1. Click the **Chart Objects** list arrow on the Chart toolbar, click **Plot Area**, and then click the **Format Plot Area** button on the Chart toolbar. The Format Plot Area dialog box opens.
2. Click the **Fill Effects** button on the Patterns tab to open the Fill Effects dialog box.
3. Click the **Picture** tab, and then click the **Select Picture** button. The Select Picture dialog box opens.
4. Navigate to the Tutorial.04\Tutorial folder, select the **Space** file, and then click the **Insert** button. The image appears in the Fill Effects dialog box.
5. Click the **OK** button twice to close the dialog boxes, and then click outside the chart area. Figure 4-28 shows the revised column chart with the new background image.

Figure 4-28 Chart with space background image

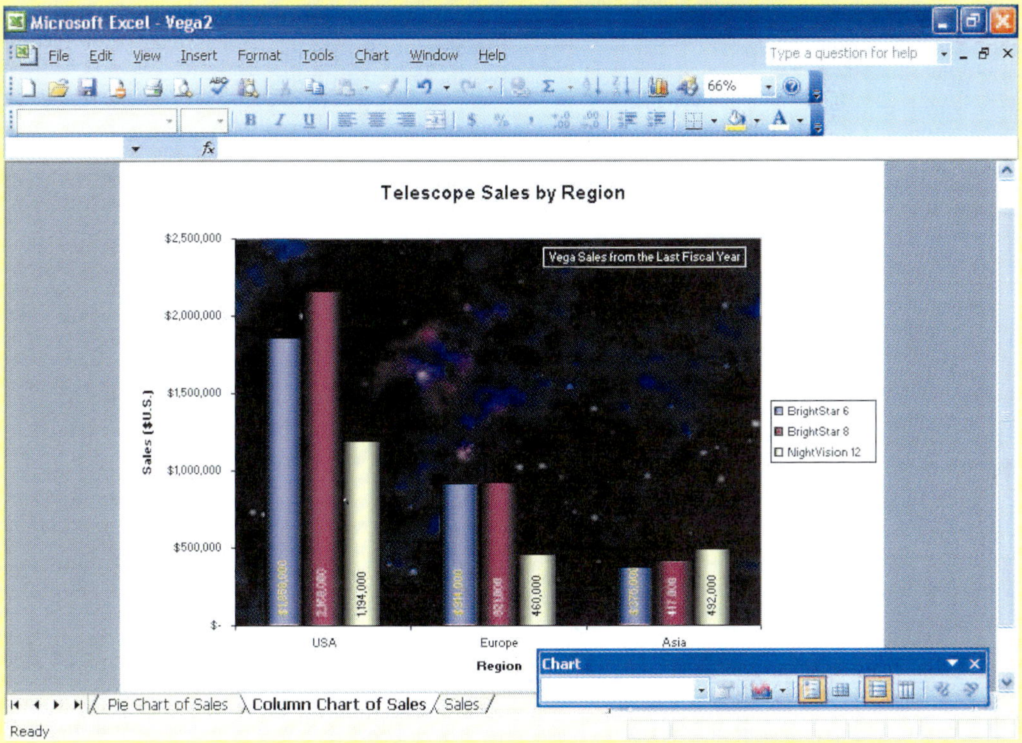

Graphic images can be applied to other elements in the chart. For example, you can replace the data markers in the chart with graphic images. To do this, select the data markers and open the Fill Effects dialog box that you used to create a background image for the chart. Select the image file that you want to use in place of the data marker. If you are working with a column chart, you can also choose to either stack or stretch the chosen image to the height of the column. Figure 4-29 shows the effect of these two options on the appearance of the column chart.

Figure 4-29 Replacing columns with graphics

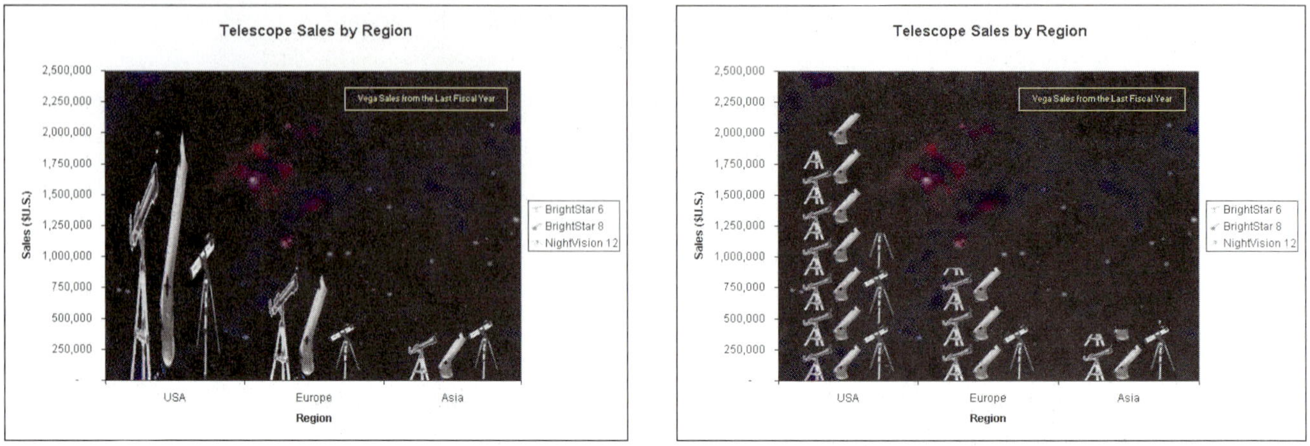

the Stretch option stretches the graphic over the height of the column

the Stack option stacks the graphic up to the height of the column

Excel provides several ways of adding special effects to your charts, and you must be careful not to overdo it. Some effects, however interesting, can actually make your charts more difficult to read and interpret. Remember also that some of your effects may look good in color, but will not transfer well to a black-and-white printout.

Changing the Axis Scale

Alicia might want you to make one other change to the column chart. She knows that the scale used by the chart is automatically set by Excel. Excel uses the data that you have plotted and determines an appropriate scale for the y-axis, usually designed to cover a range of reasonable values. Alicia wants you to examine the scale that Excel set for this chart to see if a change is warranted. She also thinks that expressing the sales in terms of dollars on the chart is a bit unwieldy for sales of this magnitude. She would rather have the sales expressed in terms of thousands of dollars.

To view the y-axis scale:

1. Click the **Chart Objects** list arrow on the Chart toolbar, click **Value Axis**, and then click the **Format Axis** button on the Chart toolbar. The Format Axis dialog box opens. You can use this dialog box to format the scale's appearance and to change the range and increments used in the scale.
2. Click the **Scale** tab. See Figure 4-30.

Scale tab in the Format Axis dialog box

Figure 4-30

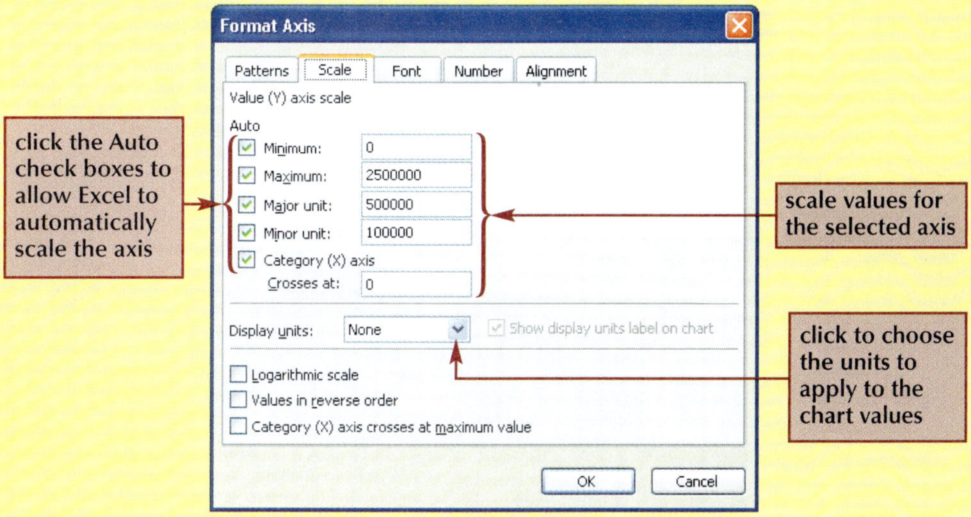

There are four values that comprise the scale: the minimum, maximum, major unit, and minor unit. The minimum and maximum values are the smallest and largest tick marks that appear on the axis. The major unit is the increment between the scale's **major tick marks**. The chart also has a second set of tick marks, called **minor tick marks**, that may or may not be displayed. The difference between major and minor tick marks is that axis values appear next to major tick marks, whereas no values appear next to minor tick marks.

In the current chart, the scale that Excel displayed ranges from 0 to 2,500,000 in increments of 500,000. The minor tick mark increment is 100,000, but these tick marks are not displayed on the axes. Alicia wants to reduce the increment value to 250,000 in order to show more detail on the chart. Then she wants to change the display units from none to thousands.

To revise the y-axis scale:

1. Double-click the current entry in the Major unit box, and then type **250000**. Note that when you manually change a scale value its Auto check box is automatically deselected.
2. Click the **Display units** list arrow, and then select **Thousands** in the list.
3. Make sure that the **Show display units label on chart** check box is selected, and then click the **OK** button. Figure 4-31 shows the revised y-axis scale.

Figure 4-31 Revised scale for the y-axis

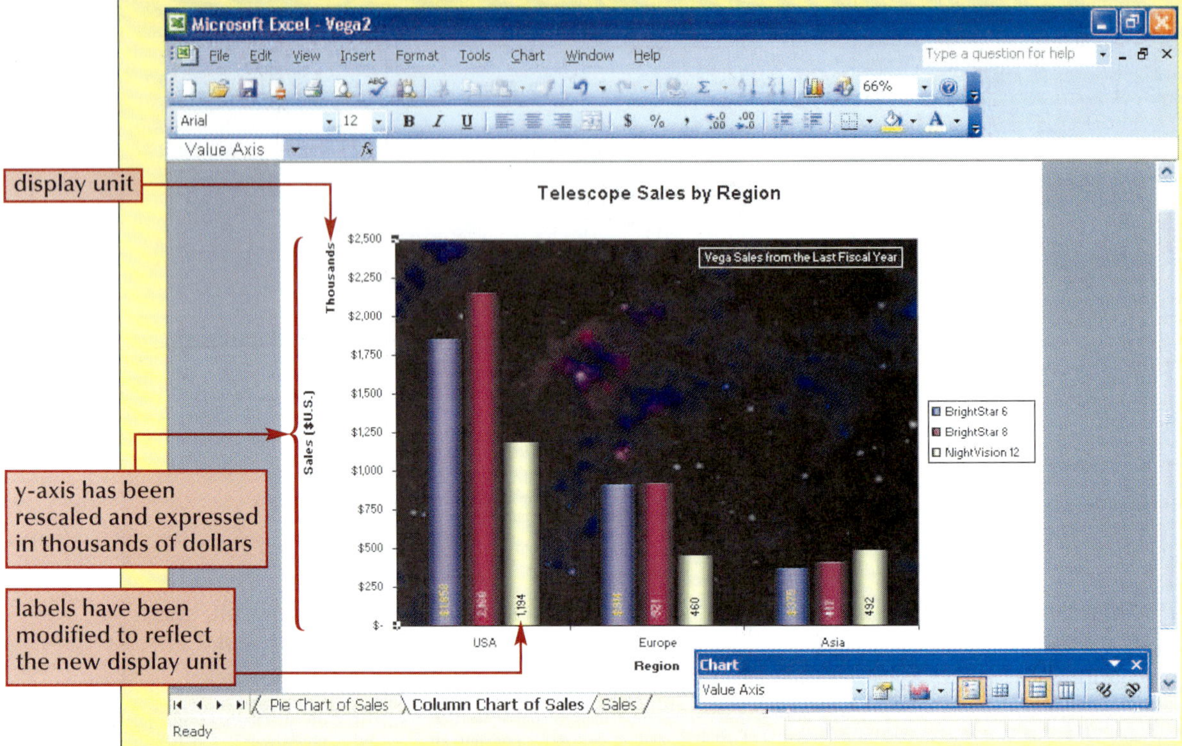

In this chart, $2,500,000 is displayed as $2,500. Because you have changed the display units in this way, you need to include information about the new value. Excel does this for you by adding the text "Thousands" to the value axis. Also note that the label values for each column now use the thousands display unit, so the Asian sales for the BrightStar 6 are displayed as $375 rather than $375,000.

Pleased with the latest version of the column chart, Alicia now wants you to go back to the pie chart and make some modifications there.

Working with Three-Dimensional Charts

Many of the Excel charts can be displayed either as two-dimensional "flat" charts or as charts that appear in three dimensions. Alicia wants you to change the pie chart to a three-dimensional pie chart. To do this, you have to change the chart type.

To change the pie chart to 3-D:

1. Switch to the Pie Chart of Sales chart sheet.
2. Click **Chart** on the menu bar, and then click **Chart Type**. The Chart Type dialog box opens.
3. Click the second chart sub-type in the top row, as shown in Figure 4-32.

Figure 4-32 Changing to a 3-D pie chart

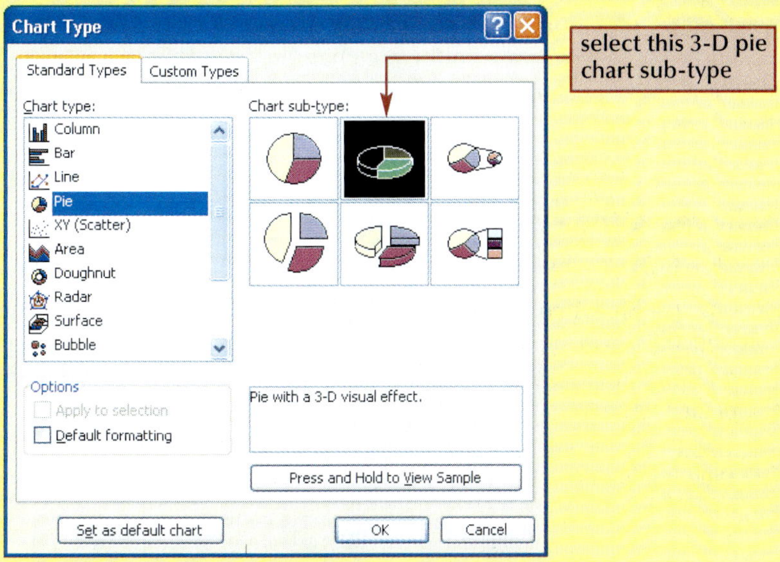

4. Click the **OK** button. Excel displays the pie chart in three dimensions. Note that Excel has retained the rotation you applied to the chart in the last session, and the BrightStar 6 slice is still exploded. See Figure 4-33.

Figure 4-33 3-D pie chart

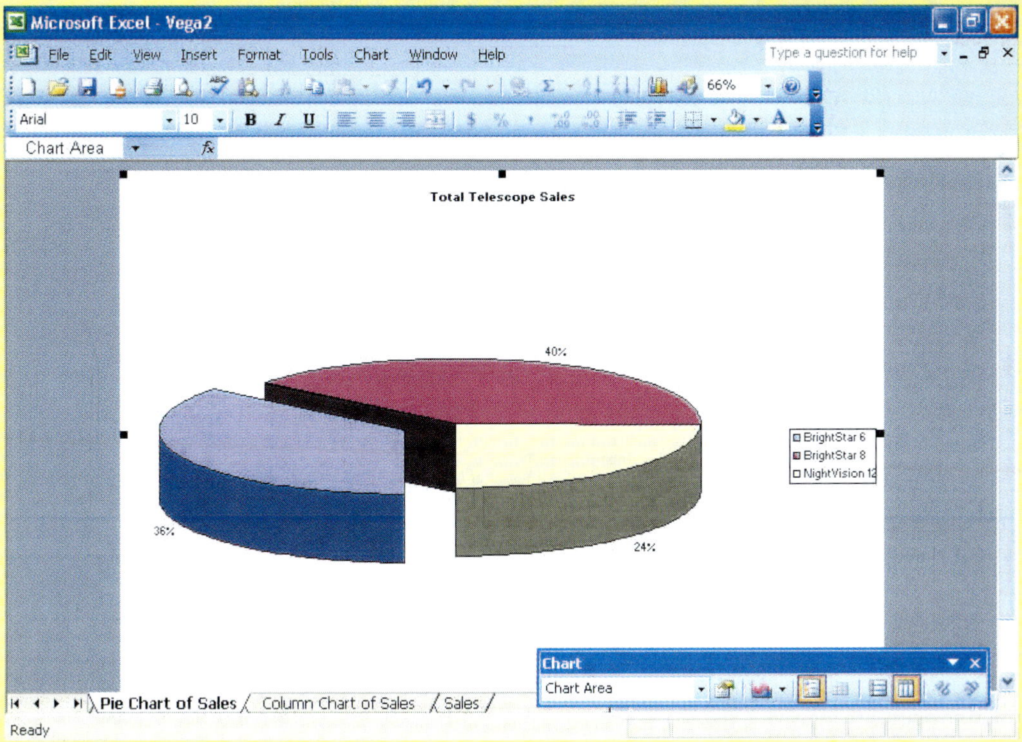

In a 3-D chart, you have several options to modify the 3-D effect. One of these is **elevation**, which is the illusion that you're looking at the 3-D chart from either above or below the chart. Another of these is **perspective**, which is the illusion that some parts of the 3-D chart are farther away from you than others. Finally, you can rotate a 3-D chart to bring different parts of the chart to the forefront. In a pie chart, you can change the elevation and rotation, but not the perspective.

Alicia likes the 3-D view of the pie chart but feels that the angle of the pie is too low. She wants you to change the angle of the pie so that the viewer is looking "down" on the chart more.

To increase the elevation above the pie chart:

1. Click **Chart** on the menu bar, and then click **3-D View**. The 3-D View dialog box opens.
2. Click the **Elevation** up button twice to increase the elevation to **25** degrees. See Figure 4-34. Note that there are also buttons that you can use to rotate the pie chart. Clicking one of the rotation buttons is similar to the rotation setting that you applied to the pie chart at the end of the first session.

Figure 4-34 3-D View dialog box

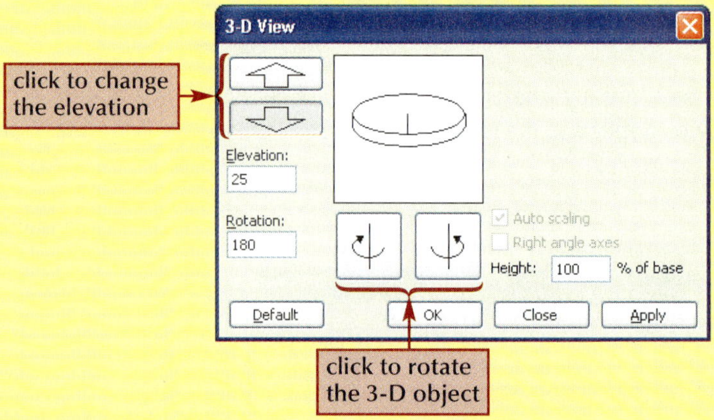

3. Click the **OK** button. Excel redraws the pie chart, giving the illusion that the observer is at an elevation above the chart.

The charts you have created present the sales data effectively, but Alicia also wants to be sure that the top-selling telescope model is clearly illustrated.

Using the Drawing Toolbar

One of the big stories from the past fiscal year was the successful introduction of the NightVision telescopes, and Alicia wants to highlight the fact that the company had in excess of $1,800,000 in sales of the NightVision 12. She has seen charts that contain shapes, like starbursts and block arrows, that give added emphasis to details and facts contained in the chart. Alicia wants to do something similar with the pie chart.

To create a graphical shape, you can use the tools provided on the Drawing toolbar. The Drawing toolbar is a common feature of all Office 2003 products. You can use the Drawing toolbar to add text boxes, lines, block arrows, and other objects to charts and worksheets. In Excel, an **object** is any entity that can be manipulated. A chart is an Excel object, as are its elements. Next, you will learn how to use the Drawing toolbar to create and format one type of object, an AutoShape.

Displaying the Drawing Toolbar

Depending on your Excel configuration, the Drawing toolbar may or may not be displayed in the Excel window when you start Excel. (The default is to not show the toolbar.) As with all toolbars, you can choose to display or hide the Drawing toolbar. Although you can display the Drawing toolbar using the View menu, you will display the toolbar by clicking the Drawing button on the Standard toolbar.

To display the Drawing toolbar:

1. Click the **Drawing** button on the Standard toolbar. The Drawing toolbar appears in the workbook window.
2. If necessary, drag the Drawing toolbar to the bottom of the worksheet window, and then release the mouse button. The Drawing toolbar should now be anchored to the bottom of the window.

Now you will use the Drawing toolbar to add a drawing object to the pie chart.

Working with AutoShapes

The Drawing toolbar contains a list of predefined shapes called **AutoShapes**. These AutoShapes can be simple squares or circles or more complicated objects such as flow chart objects and block arrows. Once you insert an AutoShape into a chart or worksheet, you can resize and move it, like any other object. You can modify the fill color of an AutoShape, change the border style, and even insert text.

Inserting an AutoShape

Reference Window

- Click the AutoShapes list arrow on the Drawing toolbar.
- Point to the AutoShape category that you want to use, and then click the AutoShape that you want to create.
- Position the crosshair pointer over the location for the AutoShape in the chart or worksheet, and then drag the pointer over the area where you want the shape to appear. To draw an AutoShape in the same proportion as the shape on the palette, press and hold the Shift key as you drag the pointer to draw the shape.
- Release the mouse button.
- To resize an AutoShape, click the shape to select it, and then drag one of the nine selection handles.
- To rotate an AutoShape, click the green rotation handle that is connected to the shape, and drag the handle to rotate the shape.
- To change the shape of the AutoShape, click the yellow diamond tool, and then drag the tool to change the shape.

You will now add a multi-pointed star to the pie chart to highlight the success of the NightVision 12 telescope.

To add a multi-pointed AutoShape star to the pie chart:

1. Click the **AutoShapes** list arrow on the Drawing toolbar, point to **Stars and Banners**, and then click the **16-Point Star** AutoShape (second row, second column from the left) on the AutoShapes palette. A ScreenTip appears when you position the pointer over an AutoShape on the palette so you will know which shape you are selecting.
2. Move the pointer to the upper-right corner of the chart area, about one inch to the right of the chart title. As you move the pointer over the worksheet, the pointer shape changes to +.

   To draw an AutoShape in the same proportion as the shape on the palette, you must press and hold the Shift key as you drag the pointer to draw the shape.
3. Press and hold the **Shift** key, and then click and drag the pointer down and to the right about one and one-half inches. Note that pressing the Shift key allows you to create a perfect 16-point star; otherwise, the shape might be lopsided.
4. Release the mouse button. A 16-point star appears in the upper-right corner of the chart area. See Figure 4-35.

Figure 4-35 Adding an AutoShape to the pie chart

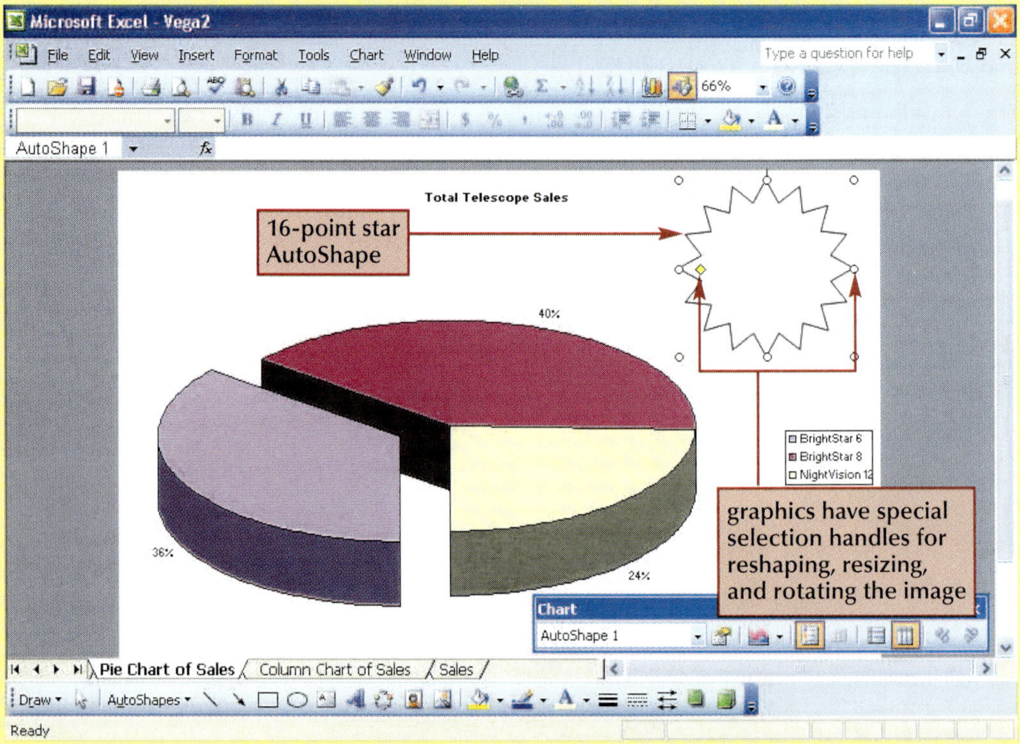

Trouble? If the AutoShape on your screen does not match the size and shape of the AutoShape shown in the figure, you can resize the object again by pressing and holding the Shift key as you drag a selection handle. Or click the Undo button on the Standard toolbar to delete the object, and then repeat Steps 1 through 4 to redraw the AutoShape, being sure to press and hold the Shift key to draw the object proportionally.

You probably noticed that the selection handles of the AutoShape appear as open circles and that there is also a diamond tool. You can use the diamond tool to change the shape of the AutoShape. For example, you can change the size of the jagged points of the star by dragging the diamond tool either toward the center of the star (to increase the size of the points) or away from the center (to decrease the size of the points). You may have also noticed a green selection handle that is attached to the AutoShape through a vertical line. This is a rotation handle. By clicking and dragging this handle, you can rotate the AutoShape.

Formatting an AutoShape

In addition to modifying the shape, size, and rotation of an AutoShape, you can add text to it. To add text to an AutoShape, you first select it and then start typing the desired text. The text will automatically be placed within the boundaries of the shape.

Inserting Text into an AutoShape

Reference Window

- Click the border of the AutoShape to select the object.
- Type the text you want to appear in the AutoShape.
- Select the text within the AutoShape.
- Format the text using the options on the Formatting toolbar.
- Click outside of the shape to deselect it.

To highlight the success of the NightVision 12, you will add the text that Alicia wants to the AutoShape star.

To insert text into the AutoShape:

1. Make sure that the 16-point star is still selected.
2. Type **NightVision 12 Sales Exceed $1.8 Million!**
3. Click **Format** on the menu bar, click **AutoShape** to open the Format AutoShape dialog box, and then click the **Alignment** tab.

   Trouble? If there is no Alignment tab in the dialog box that opens, close the dialog box. Click the AutoShape again, making sure that the object, and not just its frame, is selected. Then repeat Step 3.
4. Click the **Horizontal** list arrow, and then click **Center**.
5. Click the **Vertical** list arrow, click **Center**, and then click the **OK** button.

   Trouble? If the text does not wrap logically within the boundaries of the AutoShape, resize the star to better accommodate the text.

The star with text adds value to the overall appearance of the chart. However, the star could use some background color to make it more visually interesting. In keeping with the other colors you have been using in the charts, you will format the AutoShape by adding a yellow background.

To change the background color of the AutoShape:

1. Make sure the 16-point star is still selected.
2. Click the **Fill Color** list arrow on the Drawing toolbar, and then click the **Ivory** square (sixth row, third column) in the color palette.

   Trouble? If the background color does not change to ivory, you may have selected the text in the star rather than the star itself. Click the Undo button on the Standard toolbar, and then repeat Steps 1 and 2, being sure to select the AutoShape.

The AutoShape definitely looks better with the ivory background. You decide to try one more thing: if adding a shadow effect to the star will be too much or will add depth to the object. To add a shadow effect to an object, you can choose one of the available shadow effects provided on the Drawing toolbar.

To add a drop shadow to the AutoShape:

1. Make sure the 16-point star is still selected.
2. Click the **Shadow Style** button on the Drawing toolbar to display the gallery of shadow options.
3. Click **Shadow Style 6** (second row, second column from the left) in the shadow gallery, and then click outside the star to deselect it.

   As a final step, Alicia feels that the pie chart is a little too far to the left. You will move it down and to the right to center it better.
4. Click the **Chart Objects** list arrow on the Chart toolbar, and then click **Plot Area**.
5. Click on the gray selection border around the plot area, drag the border down and to the right, and then click outside the chart area. Figure 4-36 shows the revised pie chart with the formatted AutoShape and the relocated pie.

Figure 4-36 **Drop shadow added to the 16-point star AutoShape**

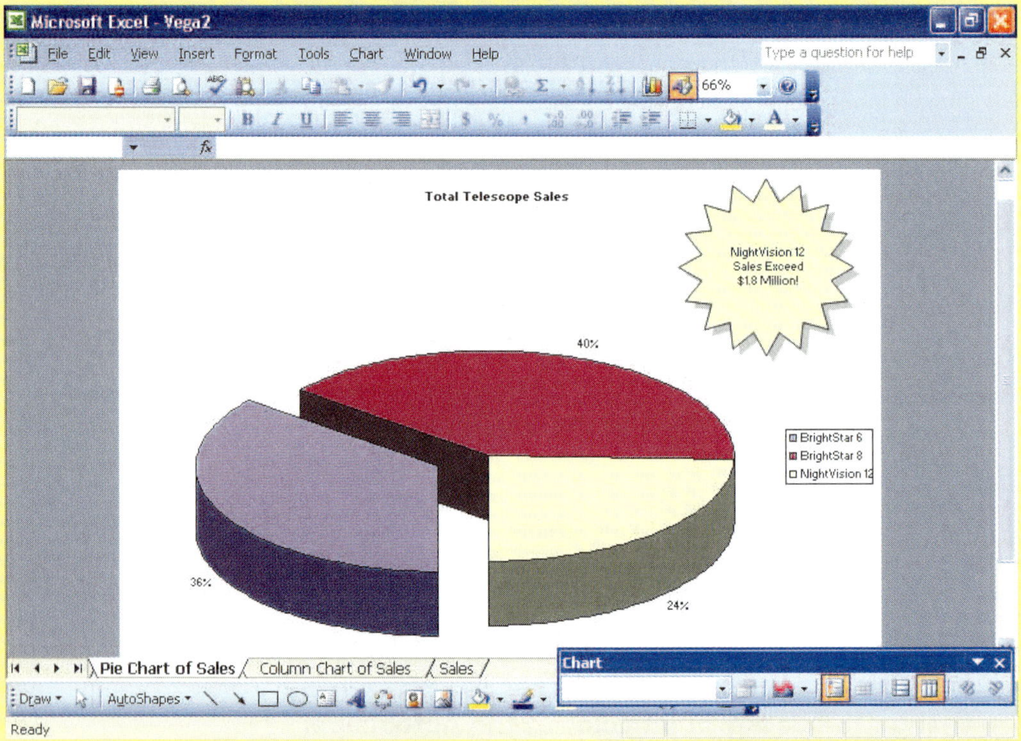

Alicia doesn't want any other changes to be made, so you will hide the Drawing toolbar, which will increase the workspace on your screen.

6. Click the **Drawing** button on the Formatting toolbar. The Drawing toolbar closes.

Printing Your Charts

Now that you have completed your work on the two charts for Alicia, you will make hard copies of them. Printing a chart sheet is similar to printing a worksheet. As when printing a worksheet, you should preview the printout before sending the worksheet to the printer. From the Print Preview window, you can add headers and footers and control the page layout, just as you do for printing the contents of your worksheets. You also have the added option of resizing the chart to fit within the confines of a single printed page.

To print both charts at the same time, you will select both chart sheets, open Print Preview, and then set up each chart to print on its own page.

To set up the two charts for printing:

1. Make sure the Pie Chart of Sales worksheet is the current sheet.
2. Press and hold the **Shift** key, and then click the **Column Chart of Sales** tab. Both chart sheets are selected.
3. Click the **Print Preview** button on the Standard toolbar. The Print Preview window opens, showing the pie chart on the first of two pages.
4. Click the **Setup** button on the Print Preview toolbar to open the Page Setup dialog box. The Page Setup options are similar to the options for printing a worksheet, except that a new dialog box tab, Chart, appears.
5. Click the **Chart** tab. See Figure 4-37.

Figure 4-37 Chart tab in the Page Setup dialog box

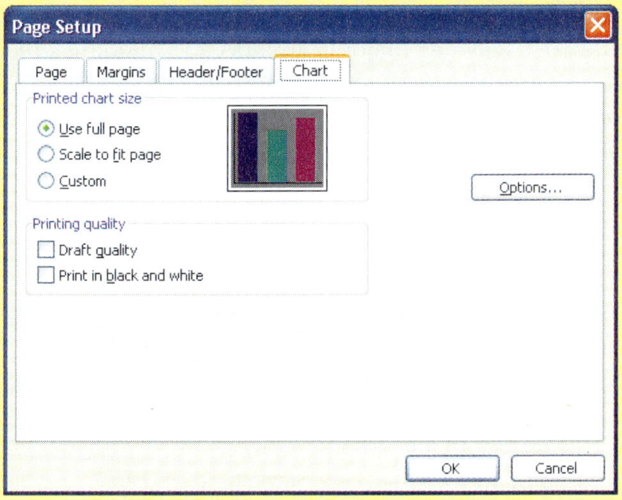

Excel provides three choices for defining the size of a chart printout. These are:

- **Use full page:** The chart is resized to fit the full page, extending to fit the full width and height of the page. The proportions of the chart may change since it is extended in all directions to fit the page. This is the default option.
- **Scale to fit page:** The chart is resized until one of the edges reaches a page margin. The chart expands in both dimensions (width and height) proportionally until one dimension fills the space between the margins.
- **Custom:** The dimensions of the printed chart are specified on the chart sheet using the Zoom tool.

You will use the Scale to fit page option because you do not want to have the charts resized disproportionately.

To set the size of the charts:

1. Click the **Scale to fit page** option button, and then click the **OK** button. The Use full page option and the Scale to fit page option will often result in charts that are close in the same size. You may not see much difference in the chart size in the Print Preview window.
2. Click the **Next** button to preview the column chart printout.
3. Click the **Setup** button, click the **Scale to fit page** option button on the Chart tab, and then click the **OK** button.
4. Click the **Print** button to open the Print dialog box, make any necessary changes, and then click the **OK** button to send both chart sheets to the printer.

   For now, there are no other changes to be made. Alicia will use the printouts of the charts at the meeting next week.
5. Save your changes to the workbook and then close it

Alicia is pleased with the results and will get back to you with any other tasks she might need you to do before the sales meeting next week.

Review

Session 4.2 Quick Check

1. How would you remove a data series from a column chart?
2. How would you change the location (either embedded or as a chart sheet) of a chart?
3. What is the difference between label text, attached text, and unattached text?
4. What is the difference between major tick marks and minor tick marks?
5. How would you change a column chart into a 3-D column chart?
6. What is an AutoShape?
7. Describe the three options for sizing a chart on the printed page.

Review

Tutorial Summary

In this tutorial, you learned how to work with charts in Excel. You saw how to use Excel's Chart Wizard to create a basic chart and learned about the different types of charts that can be created by Excel. You also learned how to embed charts within a worksheet or place them on their own chart sheet in the workbook. You used Excel's editing tools to modify the chart's appearance by inserting additional text, changing font and background colors and images, rotating the chart in three dimensions, and changing the scale of the chart. This tutorial also introduced you to the Drawing toolbar, which you used to create an AutoShape, placing that shape on a chart to provide additional emphasis on key points. Finally, you learned about the different options Excel provides for printing your completed charts.

Key Terms

active chart
attached text
AutoShape
category values
chart
chart area
chart sheet
chart title
Chart Wizard
data marker
data series
data source
data value
elevation
embedded chart
exploded pie chart
gridline
horizontal axis
label text
legend
major gridline

major tick mark	plot area	vertical axis
minor gridline	scale	x-axis
minor tick mark	tick mark	x value
object	unattached text	y-axis
perspective		

Practice

Practice the skills you learned in the tutorial using the same case scenario.

Review Assignments

Data File needed for the Review Assignments: VegaUSA1.xls

Alicia has another workbook that shows the monthly United States sales for the three major telescope models. She wants you to create a column chart showing the monthly United States sales figures and a pie chart showing the total sales figures for each telescope model. To complete this task:

1. Open the **VegaUSA1** workbook located in the Tutorial.04\Review folder included with your Data Files, and then save the workbook as **VegaUSA2** to the same folder.
2. Enter your name and the current date in the Documentation sheet, and then switch to the Monthly Sales worksheet.
3. Select the range A6:D18, and then start the Chart Wizard.
4. Use the Chart Wizard to create a column chart, using the first chart sub-type. Specify "United States Telescope Sales" as the chart title, "Month" as the x-axis title, and "Sales ($U.S.)" as the y-axis title. Place the chart on a chart sheet named "Monthly Sales Chart."
5. Format the x-axis labels, changing the alignment to 90 degrees.
6. Change the scale of the y-axis using thousands as the display unit.
7. Change the background color of the plot area to white.
8. Place the chart legend at the bottom of the chart. (*Hint*: Open the Format Legend dialog box and select the Bottom option on the Placement tab.)
9. Use the Drawing toolbar to create an 8-point star located in the upper-left corner of the chart area.
10. Insert the text "NightVision 12 sales remained high in Autumn!" into the 8-point star you just created. Center the text both horizontally and vertically.
11. Change the fill color of the 8-point star to ivory, and apply Shadow Style 1 to the shape.
12. Return to the Monthly Sales worksheet, select the nonadjacent range B6:D6;B19:D19, and use the Chart Wizard to create a pie chart of the data. Assign the chart the title "Pie Chart of Total Sales" and display the sales values next to the pie slices. Place the pie chart in a chart sheet named "Pie Chart of Total Sales."
13. Apply the Late Sunrise fill effect to the pie chart's chart area.
14. Select both charts, and then open the Print Preview window.
15. Use the Setup dialog box to scale both charts to fit their respective pages and to add a footer to the charts displaying your name and the date in the lower-right corner of the page. Print the charts.
16. Save your changes to the workbook and then close it.

Apply

Use the skills you have learned to create a worksheet displaying a 3-D column chart.

Case Problem 1

Data File needed for this Case Problem: CIC1.xls

Cast Iron Concepts Andrea Puest, the regional sales manager of Cast Iron Concepts (CIC), a distributor of cast-iron stoves, is required to present a report of the company's first-quarter sales for the states of New Hampshire, Vermont, and Maine. Her sales data covers four major models: Star Windsor, Box Windsor, West Windsor, and Circle Windsor. The Circle Windsor is CIC's latest entry in the cast-iron stove market.

Andrea will make a presentation of her sales figures next month and has asked for your help in creating a chart showing the sales results. She wants to create a 3-D column chart, with each column representing the sales for a particular model and state. To complete this task:

1. Open the **CIC1** workbook located in the Tutorial.04\Cases folder included with your Data Files, and then save the file as **CIC2** to the same folder.
2. Enter your name and the current date in the Documentation sheet, and then switch to the Sales worksheet.
3. Select the range A5:D9, and then start the Chart Wizard.
4. Use the Chart Wizard to create an embedded 3-D column chart that compares values across categories and across series. The data series in the chart should be organized by columns, not rows. Specify "Windsor Stove Sales" as the chart title. Do not specify titles for the axes. Do not include a legend.
5. Move the embedded chart so that the upper-left corner of the chart is located in cell A11, and then resize the chart so that it covers the range A11:E32.
6. Change the font of the chart title to a 14-point, bold, dark-blue Arial font.
7. Add the subtitle "1/1/2006 - 3/31/2006" as unattached text to the chart. Format the text in an 8-point, bold, dark-blue Arial font and place it under the chart's main title.
8. Change the color of the chart area to tan.
9. **Explore** Change the 3-D view of the chart so that its elevation equals 10 degrees, its rotation equals 120 degrees, and its perspective equals 15.
10. Change the font of the y-axis (also called the "series axis") labels (the names of the states) to an 8-point regular Arial font.
11. Change the font of the x-axis labels (the model names) to an 8-point regular Arial font, displayed at a –90 degree angle.
12. **Explore** Select the walls of the 3-D plot, and change the wall color to white.
13. Center the contents of the worksheet horizontally on the page, and then add a header that displays your name and the date in the upper-right corner of the worksheet.
14. Preview and then print the worksheet.
15. Save your changes to the workbook, and then close it.

Challenge

Broaden your knowledge and challenge your skills by exploring how to use Excel to create a Pareto quality control chart.

Case Problem 2

Data File needed for this Case Problem: Powder1.xls

Dantalia Baby Powder Kemp Wilson is a quality control engineer for Dantalia Baby Powder. Part of the company's manufacturing process involves a machine called a "filler," which pours a specified amount of powder into bottles. Sometimes the heads on the filler become partially clogged, causing the bottles to be under-filled. If that happens, the bottles must be rejected. On each assembly line, there are a certain number of bottles rejected during each shift.

Kemp's job is to monitor the number of defective bottles and locate the fillers that may have clogged filler heads. One of the tools he uses to do this is a Pareto chart. A Pareto chart is a column chart in which each column represents the total number of defects assigned to different parts of the production process. In this case, the columns would represent the 24 different fillers in the assembly line. The columns are sorted so that the part that caused the most defects is displayed first, the second-most is displayed second, and so forth. Superimposed on the columns is a line that displays the cumulative percentage of defects for all of the parts. Thus, by viewing the cumulative percentages, you can determine, for example, what percentages of the total defects are due to the three worst parts. In this way, Kemp can isolate the problem filler heads and report how much they contribute to the total defects.

Kemp has a worksheet listing the number of defects per filler head from a recent shift. The data is already sorted going from the filler head with the most defects to the one with the fewest. The cumulative percent values have also been calculated already. Kemp wants you to create a Pareto chart based on this data. To complete this task:

1. Open the **Powder1** workbook located in the Tutorial.04\Cases folder included with your Data Files, and then save the file as **Powder2** to the same folder.
2. Enter your name and the current date in the Documentation sheet, and then switch to the Quality Control Data worksheet.
3. Select the range A5:C29, and then start the Chart Wizard.
4. **Explore** Use the Chart Wizard to create a custom chart, selecting the Line – Column on 2 Axes option in the Custom Types list box. Specify "Filler Head Under Fills" as the chart title. Specify "Filler Head" as the x-axis title, "Count of Under Fills" as the y-axis title, and "Cumulative Percentage" as the second y-axis title. Do not include a legend. Place the chart on a chart sheet named "Pareto Chart."
5. Change the alignment of the x-axis labels to an angle of 90 degrees.
6. Change the alignment of the second y-axis title to –90 degrees.
7. **Explore** Change the scale of the second y-axis so that the values range from 0 to 1.0.
8. **Explore** Select the data series that displays the number of defects for each filler head, and add data labels that display the number of defects above each column. Do *not* display labels above the lines that represent the cumulative percentages. (*Hint*: Use the Data Labels tab in the Format Data Series dialog box.)
9. **Explore** From the Format Data Series dialog box for the chart's columns, use the Options tab to reduce the gap separating the columns to 0 pixels.
10. Change the fill color of the chart columns and the plot area to white.
11. Examine the Pareto chart, and determine approximately what percentage of the total number of defects can be attributed to the three worst filler heads.
12. Add a header to the Pareto Chart sheet that displays the name of the worksheet in the center and your name and the date on the right of the page, and then print the Pareto chart.
13. Save your changes to the workbook, and then close it.

Challenge

Go beyond what you've learned in the tutorial by exploring how to use Excel to chart stock market data.

Case Problem 3

Data File needed for this Case Problem: Pixal1.xls

Charting Stock Activity You work with Lee Whyte, a stock analyst who plans to publish a Web site on stocks. One component of the Web site will be a five-week record of the activity of various key stocks. Lee has asked for your help in setting up an Excel workbook to keep a running record of the trading volume, open, high, low, and close values of some of the stocks he's tracking.

Lee wants you to create a stock market chart of the activity of Pixal Inc. stock as a sample. The last six weeks of the stock's performance have been saved in a workbook. He wants you to create a chart sheet for the data that has been entered. To complete this task:

1. Open the **Pixal1** workbook located in the Tutorial.04\Cases folder included with your Data Files, and then save the file as **Pixal2** to the same folder.
2. Enter your name and the current date in the Documentation sheet, and then switch to the Pixal Data worksheet.
3. Select the range B6:G36, and then start the Chart Wizard.

4. Use the Chart Wizard to create a stock chart using the Volume-Open-High-Low-Close subtype. Specify "Pixal Inc." as the chart title. Specify "Date" as the x-axis title, "Volume (mil)" as the y-axis title, and "Price" as the second y-axis title. Remove the gridlines and do not include a legend. Place the chart in a chart sheet named "Pixal Chart."
5. Change the scale of the first y-axis so that the scale ranges from 0 to 5 with a major unit of 0.5.
6. Change the scale of the second y-axis so that the scale ranges from 15 to 21 with a major unit of 1.
7. Change the alignment of the second y-axis title to –90 degrees.

Explore

8. Change the scale of the x-axis so that the major unit occurs every seven days.
9. Double-click the column data series that displays the volume of shares traded and, using the Options tab, reduce the gap between adjacent columns to 0 pixels.
10. Change the fill color of the plot area to light yellow.
11. Change the font size of the chart title to 16 points.

Explore

12. In the upper-right corner of the plot area, insert the Rounded Rectangular Callout AutoShape from the Drawing toolbar. Enter the following quote into the AutoShape: "Pixal Inc. is experiencing a tough first quarter" – Stock Reviews
    Format the text in a bold, red, 14-point font. Resize the AutoShape if necessary.
13. Add the Shadow Style 6 drop shadow to the AutoShape.
14. Add your name and the date to the right section of the header. Scale the chart to fit the page in landscape orientation.
15. Save the changes, and then print the chart sheet.

Explore

16. Lee has a new week's worth of data for the Pixal worksheet. Enter the data shown in Figure 4-38 to the table of stock activity, and then modify that chart's data source to include the new data values for each data series.

Figure 4-38

Date	Volume (mil)	Open	High	Low	Close
2/17/2006	0.35	16.30	16.95	16.75	16.85
2/18/2006	0.45	16.85	17.20	17.05	17.15
2/19/2006	0.52	17.15	17.45	17.25	17.25
2/20/2006	0.40	17.25	17.35	16.95	17.25
2/21/2006	0.38	17.25	17.55	16.75	16.95

17. Save your changes to a new workbook named **Pixal3** in the Cases folder, and then reprint the chart sheet with the new data values. Close the workbook.

Create

Test your knowledge of charts by creating a workbook with an XY (scatter) chart that presents data from a cancer research study.

Case Problem 4

There are no Data Files needed for this Case Problem.

Relating Cancer Rates to Temperature A 1965 study analyzed the relationship between the mean annual temperature in 16 regions in Great Britain and the annual mortality rates in those regions for a certain type of breast cancer. Lynn Watson is working on a symposium on the history of breast cancer research and has asked you to chart the data from this historic study. Figure 4-39 shows a preview of the workbook and chart that you'll create.

Figure 4-39

	A	B	C
1	Breast Cancer Study		
2	Mortality Index vs. Temperature		
3	Great Britain, 1965		
4			
5	Region	Temperature (F)	Mortality
6	1	31.8	67.3
7	2	34.0	52.5
8	3	40.2	68.1
9	4	42.1	84.6
10	5	42.3	65.1
11	6	43.5	72.2
12	7	44.2	81.7
13	8	45.1	89.2
14	9	46.3	78.9
15	10	47.3	88.6
16	11	47.8	95.0
17	12	48.5	87.0
18	13	49.2	95.9
19	14	49.9	104.5
20	15	50.0	100.4
21	16	51.3	102.5
22			
23			

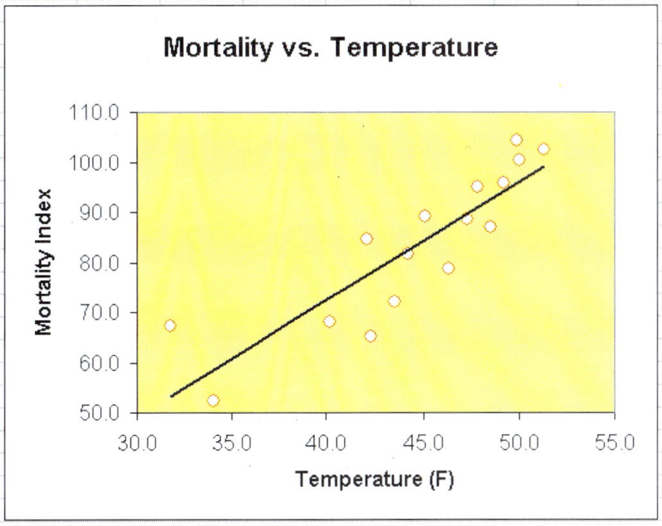

To complete this task:

1. Create a new workbook and save it as **BCancer** in the Tutorial.04\Cases folder included with your Data Files. The workbook should contain a Documentation sheet displaying your name, the date, and the purpose of the workbook. Name one of the other worksheets "Breast Cancer Data," and then add the titles and data shown in Figure 4-39.

Explore

2. Use the Chart Wizard to create an embedded XY (scatter) chart with no data points connected. Specify "Mortality vs. Temperature" as the chart title. Specify "Temperature (F)" as the title of the x-axis and "Mortality Index" as the title of the y-axis. Remove the gridlines. Do not include a legend. The scatter chart should be embedded on the Breast Cancer Data worksheet.
3. Change the scale of the x-axis to cover the temperature range 30 to 55 degrees Fahrenheit.
4. Change the scale of the y-axis to cover the mortality index range 50 to 110.

Explore

5. Double-click one of the data points in the chart to open the Format Data Series dialog box, and make the following changes to the appearance of the data points:
   - Change the marker style to a circle that is 7 points in size.
   - Change the background color of the circle to white.
   - Change the foreground color of the circle to red.

Explore

6. Open the Add Trendline dialog box from the Chart menu, and select the Linear trend line option on the Type tab. The purpose of the linear trend line is to display whether a linear relationship exists between the 16 regions' mean annual temperature and their annual mortality index. Does it appear that such a relationship exists? What does a high mean annual temperature imply about the annual mortality index?
7. Change the fill color of the plot area to light yellow.
8. Set up the worksheet to print in landscape orientation, centered horizontally and vertically on the page. Enter your name and the date in the right section of the page's header. Print the chart.
9. Save your changes to the workbook and close it.

Research

Use the Internet to find and work with data related to the topics presented in this tutorial.

Internet Assignments

The purpose of the Internet Assignments is to challenge you to find information on the Internet that you can use to work effectively with this software. The actual assignments are updated and maintained on the Course Technology Web site. Log on to the Internet and use your Web browser to go to the Student Online Companion for New Perspectives Office 2003 at **www.course.com/np/office2003**. Click the Internet Assignments link, and then navigate to the assignments for this tutorial.

Assess

SAM

SAM Assessment and Training

If you have a SAM user profile, you may have access to hands-on instruction, practice, and assessment of the skills covered in this tutorial. Log in to your SAM account and go to your assignments page to see what your instructor has assigned.

Review

Quick Check Answers

Session 4.1

1. A chart type is one of the 14 styles of charts supported by Excel. Each chart type has various alternate formats, called chart sub-types.
2. stock chart
3. A data series is a range of data values that is plotted on a chart.
4. The plot area contains the actual data values that are plotted in the chart, as well as any background colors or images for that plot. The chart area contains the plot area and any other element (such as titles and legend boxes) that may be included in the chart.
5. Gridlines are lines that extend out from the tick marks on either axis into the plot area.
6. embedded charts, which are placed within a worksheet, and chart sheets, which contain only the chart itself
7. pie
8. exploded pie

Session 4.2

1. Click Chart on the menu bar, click Source Data, click the Series tab, select the data series in the Series list box, and then click the Remove button.
2. Click Chart on the menu bar, click Location, and then select a new location.
3. Label text is text that consists of category names, tick mark labels, and legend text. Attached text is text that is attached to other elements of the chart, such as the chart title or axes titles. Unattached text is additional text that is unassociated with any particular element of the chart.
4. Major tick marks are tick marks that appear on the axis alongside the axis values. Minor tick marks do not appear alongside any axis value, but instead are used to provide a finer gradation between major tick marks.
5. Click Chart on the menu bar, click Chart Type, and then select one of the 3-D chart sub-types for the column chart.
6. An AutoShape is a predefined shape available on the Drawing toolbar. You can add an AutoShape to any worksheet or chart. You can change the size or shape of an AutoShape, and you can change its fill color.
7. Use full page, in which the chart is resized to fit the full size of the printed page (the proportions of the chart may change in the resizing); Scale to fit page, in which the chart is resized to fit the page but retains its proportions; and Custom, in which the dimensions of the printed chart are specified in the chart sheet.

Objectives

- Learn about object linking and embedding (OLE)
- Embed an Excel chart in a Word document
- Edit an embedded Excel chart in Word
- Link an Excel worksheet to a Word document
- Update a linked Excel worksheet
- Test and break a link

Integrating Word and Excel

Creating a Letter that Includes a Chart and a Table

Case

Lifestyles Home Care, Inc.

In 1989, Caitlin Sheehan founded Lifestyles Home Care, Inc., in Woburn, Massachusetts. Lifestyles Home Care provides in-home services for elderly and disabled people. Currently, when people are discharged from a hospital or when they become incapacitated by illness or a disability, they can obtain services that enable them to continue to live at home rather than move to a nursing home. The state of Massachusetts contracts with various agencies to coordinate and arrange for these services either free of charge or on a sliding fee scale for those people who meet established income guidelines. Lifestyles is one of the companies that various state-contracted agencies use to provide personal care and homemaking services, perform light chores, and provide transportation services for their clients. Each year, Lifestyles serves an increasing number of clients, and this year it has received more referrals from state-contracted agencies than any other home care company.

Over the past six months, Caitlin has worked on a new business plan to expand the services that Lifestyles offers and to make those services available to anyone who wants to pay for them, not just to those clients who meet the income guidelines for state-supported services. The new services are meal planning and preparation, shopping, scheduling medical appointments, driving, bill payment and mail organization, and companionship. In addition, Caitlin wants to hire care managers; care managers are coordinators who assess a client's needs and recommend and establish appropriate services. Care managers also can monitor the services once they are in place, and reassess the service plan as necessary. This service is especially helpful for those clients whose families live out of the area and, therefore, cannot check on their loved ones on a regular basis.

Student Data Files

▼Tutorial.01

▽ Tutorial folder
- LHCGrowth.xls
- LHCLetter.doc
- LHCServiceReferrals.xls

▽ Review folder
- LHCGrowthUpdated.xls
- LHCMemo.doc
- LHCServicesDistribution.xls

▽ Cases folder
- MusicLetter.doc
- MusicRentals.xls
- TutorFees.xls

Caitlin will begin marketing the new services offered by Lifestyles to the social work departments at local hospitals. Hospital social workers help soon-to-be discharged patients by establishing a discharge plan, which frequently includes home care services. The social workers at local hospitals are already aware of Lifestyles because of the services it currently provides. Caitlin plans to send a letter to the social work departments announcing the new, expanded service offerings. She has drafted the body of the letter, which describes the new service plans and introduces the new brochure. She wants the letter to include the information from the state indicating that Lifestyles is the most referred home care company, so she used the state's information and created a pie chart. She also wants the letter to include a table she has created outlining the company's growth over the past five years.

You'll complete the letter for Caitlin using Microsoft Office 2003. She created the letter in Word, but she created the chart and table in Excel. Fortunately, Office 2003 allows you to share information between its programs.

Object Linking and Embedding

Caitlin's letter requires the chart that she created in Excel comparing the number of referrals to Lifestyles Home Care with the number of referrals to other home care companies and the table showing the company's growth. The first page of the letter, a Word document, and the chart and table, Excel files, are shown in Figure 1-1.

Figure 1-1 Lifestyles Home Care documents to integrate

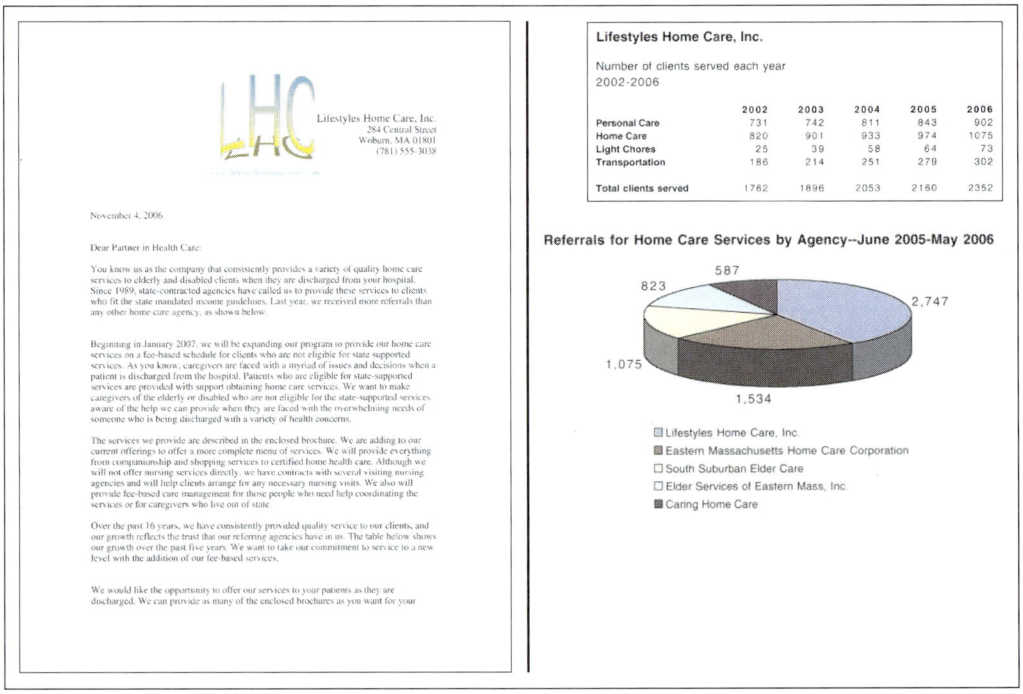

Lifestyles Home Care, Inc.
284 Central Street
Woburn, MA 01801
(781) 555-3038

November 4, 2006

Dear Partner in Health Care:

You know us as the company that consistently provides a variety of quality home care services to elderly and disabled clients when they are discharged from your hospital. Since 1989, state-contracted agencies have called us to provide these services to clients who fit the state mandated income guidelines. Last year, we received more referrals than any other home care agency, as shown below.

Beginning in January 2007, we will be expanding our program to provide our home care services on a fee-based schedule for clients who are not eligible for state supported services. As you know, caregivers are faced with a myriad of issues and decisions when a patient is discharged from the hospital. Patients who are eligible for state-supported services are provided with support obtaining home care services. We want to make caregivers of the elderly or disabled who are not eligible for the state-supported services aware of the help we can provide when they are faced with the overwhelming needs of someone who is being discharged with a variety of health concerns.

The services we provide are described in the enclosed brochure. We are adding to our current offerings to offer a more complete menu of services. We will provide everything from companionship and shopping services to certified home health care. Although we will not offer nursing services directly, we have contracts with several visiting nursing agencies and will help clients arrange for any necessary nursing visits. We also will provide fee-based care management for those people who need help coordinating the services or for caregivers who live out of state.

Over the past 16 years, we have consistently provided quality service to our clients, and our growth reflects the trust that our referring agencies have in us. The table below shows our growth over the past five years. We want to take our commitment to service to a new level with the addition of our fee-based services.

We would like the opportunity to offer our services to your patients as they are discharged. We can provide as many of the enclosed brochures as you want for your

Lifestyles Home Care, Inc.

Number of clients served each year
2002-2006

	2002	2003	2004	2005	2006
Personal Care	731	742	811	843	902
Home Care	820	901	933	974	1075
Light Chores	25	39	58	64	73
Transportation	186	214	251	279	302
Total clients served	1762	1896	2053	2160	2352

Putting all these pieces together into one Word document is possible because Office 2003 supports **object linking and embedding** (**OLE**, pronounced "oh-lay"), a way of transferring and sharing information between programs. OLE is often referred to as **integration**, which is a general term for sharing information (the terms are often used interchangeably). An **object** is anything that can be manipulated as a whole; in other words, it is the specific information that you want to share between programs and can be anything from a chart or a table (as in Caitlin's case) to a picture, video, sound clip, or almost anything else you can create on a computer. The program used to create the object is called the **source program**, and the program used to create the file where you want to insert the object is called the **destination program**. Likewise, the file that initially contains the object is called the **source file**, and the file where you want to insert the object is called the **destination file**.

Both linking and embedding involve inserting an object into a destination file; the difference lies in where their respective objects are stored. With **embedding**, a copy of the object becomes part of the destination file. You can make changes to the object in either the destination file or the source file, but the changes you make in one file do not appear in the other file. This is helpful when you do not want to change the original object. Embedding enables you to edit an object using its source program's commands, which is not possible with regular copying and pasting.

With **linking**, the object does not exist as a separate object in the destination file. Instead, OLE creates a direct connection, or **link**, between the source and destination programs, so that the object exists in only one place—the source file—but the link displays the object in the destination file as well. You edit the object in the source file, and the link ensures that the changes will appear in the destination file. Figure 1-2 summarizes embedding and linking and compares their advantages and disadvantages.

Figure 1-2 Comparing integration methods

	Embedding	Linking
Description	Displays and stores an object in the destination file.	Displays an object in the destination file along with the source file's location; stores the object in the source file.
Use if you want to	Include the object in the destination file, and edit the object using the source program without affecting the source file.	Edit the object in the source file and have the changes appear in the destination file.
Advantages	The source file and destination file can be stored separately. You can use source program commands to make changes to the object in the destination file.	The destination file size remains fairly small. The source file and the object in the destination file remain identical.
Disadvantages	The destination file size increases to reflect the addition of the object from the source file.	The source and destination files must be stored together.

Figure 1-3 illustrates the differences between embedding and linking.

Figure 1-3 Embedding contrasted with linking

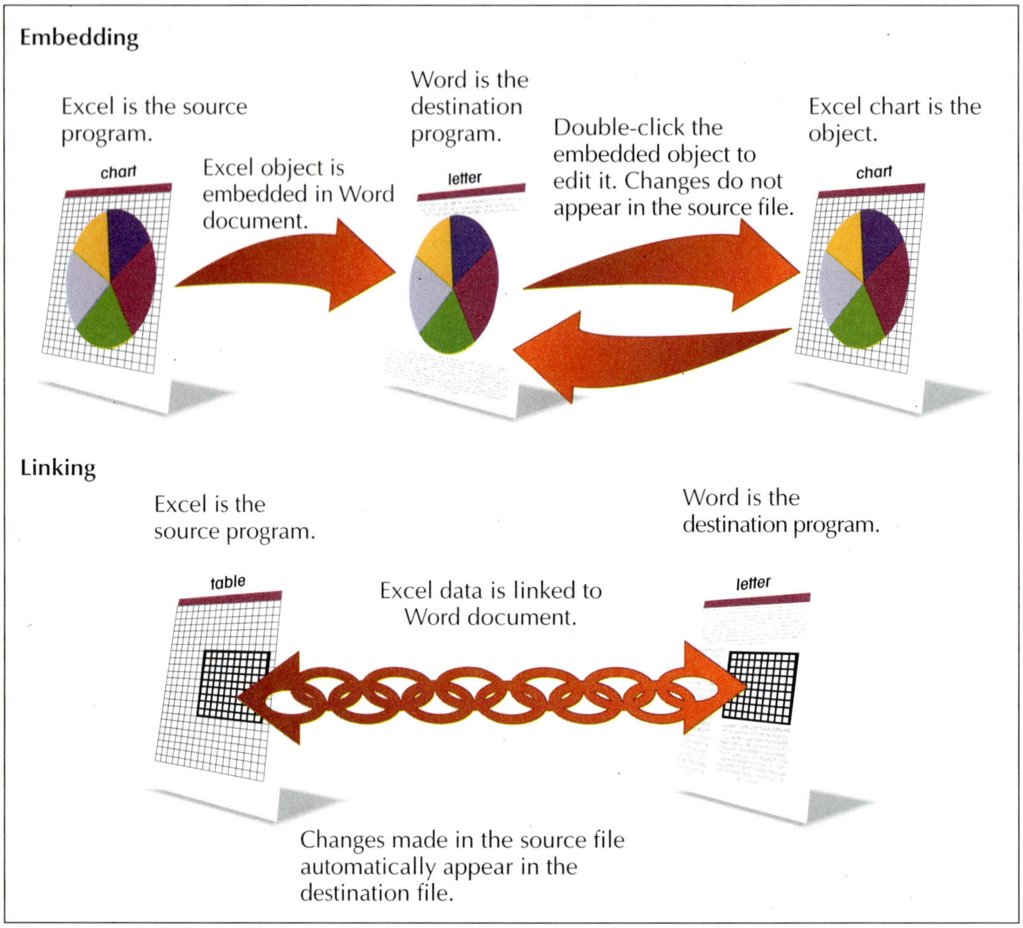

Caitlin wants to integrate the pie chart into the hospital letter. She knows that the data in the chart will not change, but she might want to modify the chart's size and appearance once it is integrated into the letter, so she asks you to embed the pie chart in the letter. Then she can use Excel commands to modify the chart from within the Word document. Caitlin wants you to link the table listing the company's growth over the past five years between the Word document and the Excel workbook, because she does not yet have the final numbers for the current year. This way, when Caitlin updates the data in the Excel table, that latest information will appear in the Word document.

Caitlin has given you the Word file containing her letter. The first thing you'll do is embed the pie chart. You need to first start Word and then open the letter.

To open the letter in Word:

1. Start Word, and then open the document **LHCLetter**, which is located in the Tutorial.01\Tutorial folder included with your Data Files. The letter opens in Print Layout view. See Figure 1-4.

Figure 1-4 Lifestyles Home Care hospital letter

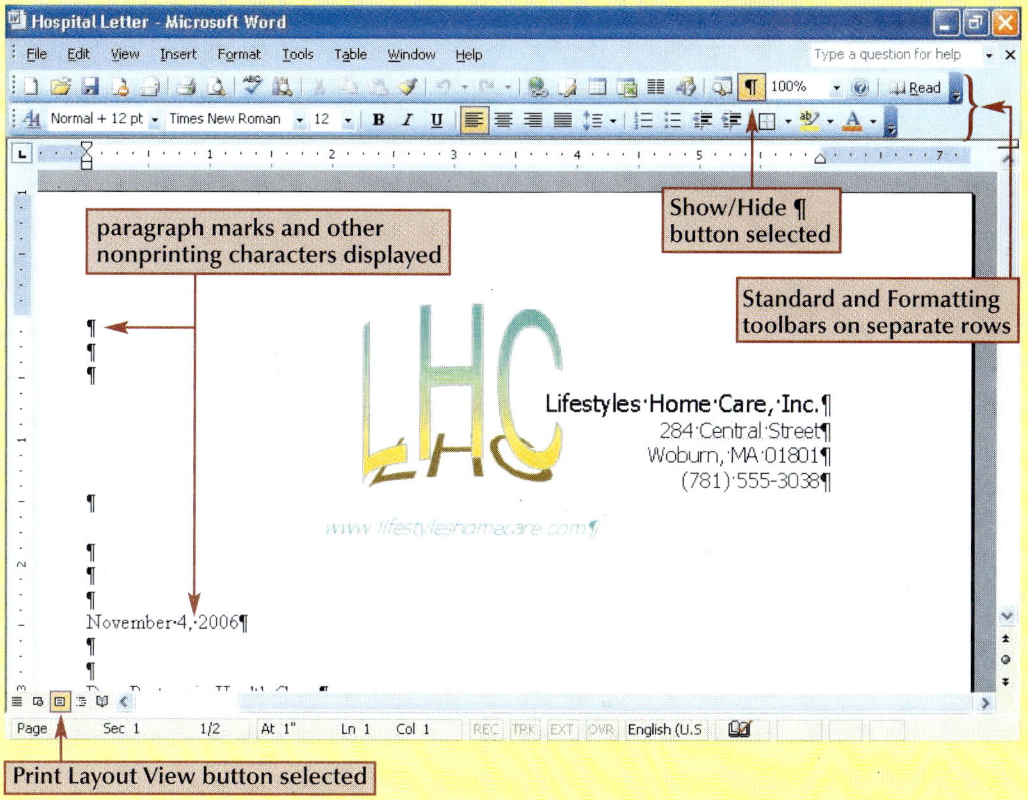

Trouble? If you don't have the Data Files for the Integration tutorials, you need to get them before you can proceed. Your instructor will either give you the Data Files or ask you to obtain them from a specific location (such as a network drive). In either case, be sure that you make a backup copy of your Data Files before you start using them, so that the original files will be available on your copied disk in case you need to start over because of an error or problem. If you have any questions about the Data Files, see your instructor or technical support person for assistance.

Trouble? If the Word toolbars appear on one row, click Tools on the menu bar, click Customize, click the Options tab in the Customize dialog box, click the Show Standard and Formatting toolbars on two rows check box to select it, and then click the Close button.

Trouble? If your document does not show the nonprinting characters, click the Show/Hide ¶ button ¶ on the Standard toolbar.

2. Click **File** on the menu bar, and then click **Save As** to display the Save As dialog box.
3. Save the file as **Hospital Letter** in the Tutorial.01\Tutorial folder.

You're ready to embed the Excel chart that shows the current distribution of services provided by Lifestyles Home Care. To do this, you need to have access to both Word and Excel. The letter is already open, so now you need to start Excel and open the file containing the pie chart.

To open the chart in Excel:

1. Start Excel as usual. You do not need to close the Word document or exit Word. Notice that a Microsoft Excel - Book 1 button appears on the taskbar next to the Hospital Letter - Microsoft Word button.
2. Open the workbook **LHCServiceReferrals**, which is located in the Tutorial.01\Tutorial folder included with your Data Files. The workbook opens with a pie chart in the active worksheet.

   Trouble? If the Excel toolbars appear on one row, click Tools on the menu bar, click Customize, click the Options tab in the Customize dialog box, click the Show Standard and Formatting toolbars on two rows check box to select it, and then click the Close button.
3. Click **File** on the menu bar, and then click **Save As** to display the Save As dialog box.
4. Save the file as **Referrals Chart** in the Tutorial.01\Tutorial folder. See Figure 1-5.

Figure 1-5 Referrals worksheet with pie chart

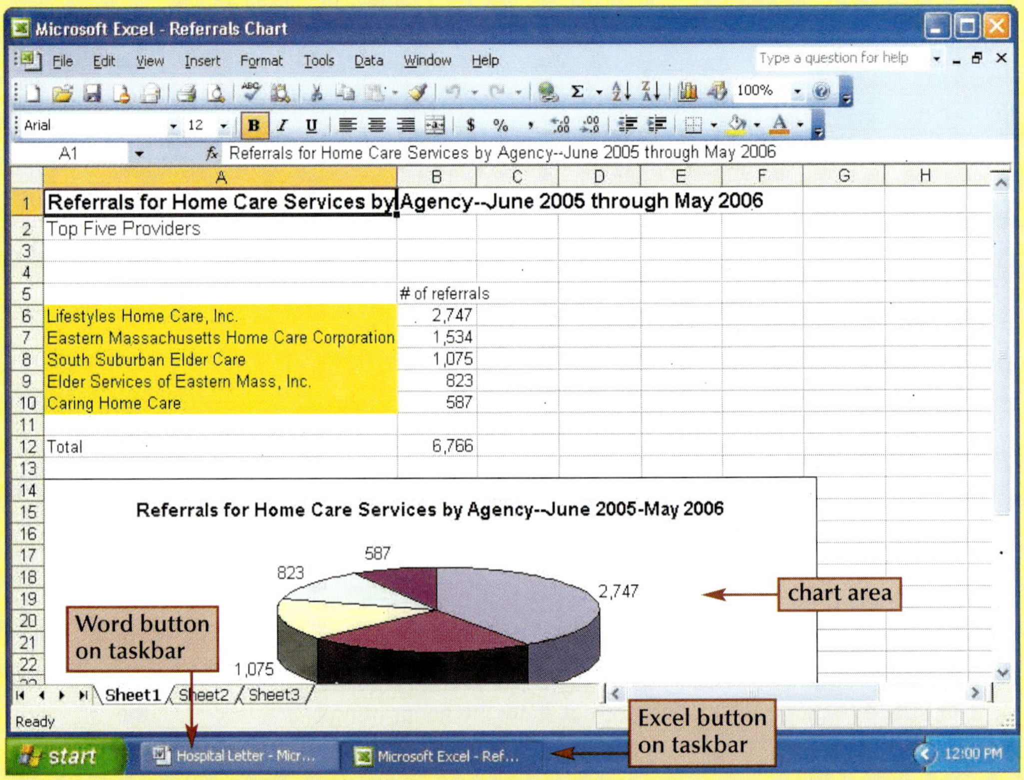

With both programs and files open, you can embed the pie chart into the letter.

Embedding an Excel Chart in a Word Document

Caitlin wants her letter to include the pie chart showing the current distribution of services provided by Lifestyles Home Care. The data for the chart will not change, so you'll embed the pie chart from the source file into the Word document. That way, if Caitlin wants to resize or modify the format of the pie chart in the letter, she can make these changes using Excel commands without affecting the source file. (Recall that when you embed an object, you automatically have access to the object's source program commands and features to manipulate the embedded object in the destination program.)

Embedding an Object

Reference Window

- Start the source program, open the file containing the object to be embedded, select the object or information you want to embed in the destination program, and then click the Copy button on the Standard toolbar.
- Start the destination program, open the file that will contain the embedded object, and then position the insertion point where you want to place the object.
- Click Edit on the menu bar, and then click Paste Special to open the Paste Special dialog box.
- In the Paste Special dialog box, click the Paste option button, click Microsoft Office Excel Chart Object in the As list box, and then click the OK button.

or

- In the source file, select the object or information you want to embed, and then click the Copy button on the Standard toolbar.
- Start the destination program, open the file that will contain the embedded object, and then position the insertion point where you want to place the object.
- Click the Paste button on the Standard toolbar in the destination program.
- Click the Paste Options button that appears in the document window, and then click Excel Chart (entire workbook).

Now you can embed the pie chart in the hospital letter using the Paste Special dialog box.

To embed the Excel chart in the Word document:

1. Scroll down until you can see all of the pie chart in the worksheet, and then click the chart area (the white area around the pie) to select the chart. When the chart is selected, sizing handles appear around the chart area. See Figure 1-6.

Figure 1-6 Pie chart selected in worksheet

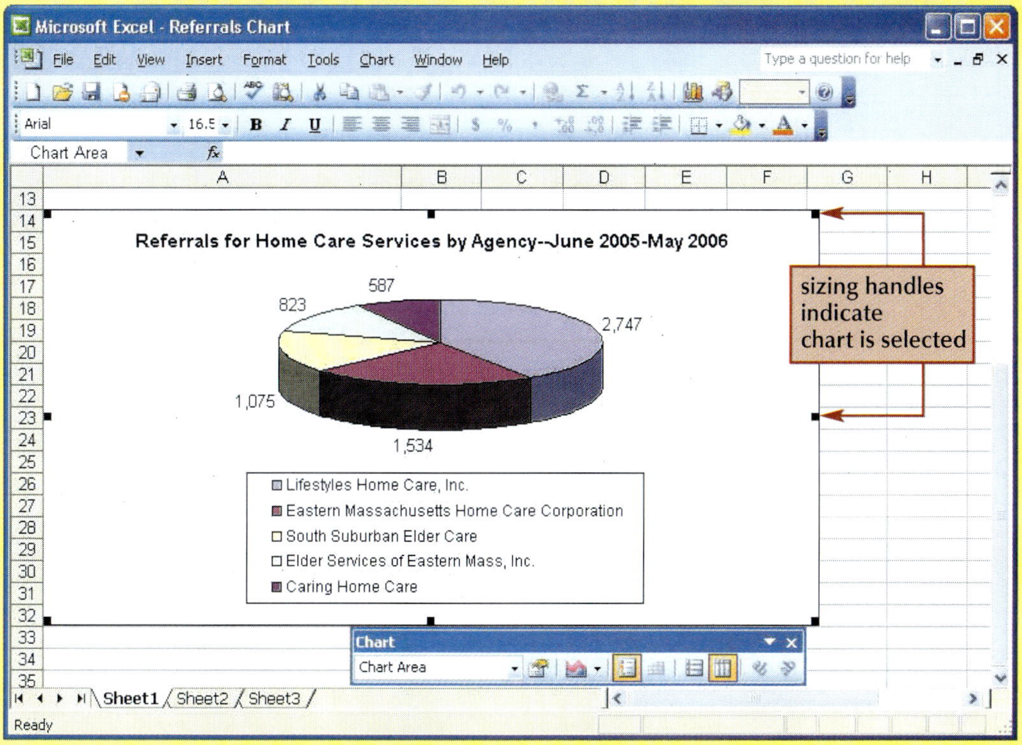

2. Click the **Copy** button on the Excel Standard toolbar to copy the chart to the Clipboard. The chart now appears with a rotating, dashed line around its frame, indicating that it has been copied.

   Trouble? If the Copy button is not available, you probably clicked the chart instead of the chart area. Click any cell in the worksheet to deselect the chart item, click the white area around the chart, and then repeat Step 2.

3. Click the **Hospital Letter - Microsoft Word** button on the taskbar to return to the Hospital Letter document.

4. Click to the left of the paragraph mark immediately above the second paragraph in the body of the letter, which begins "Beginning in January 2007", to position the insertion point where you need to embed the pie chart. See Figure 1-7.

Figure 1-7 Placement for the pie chart in the hospital letter

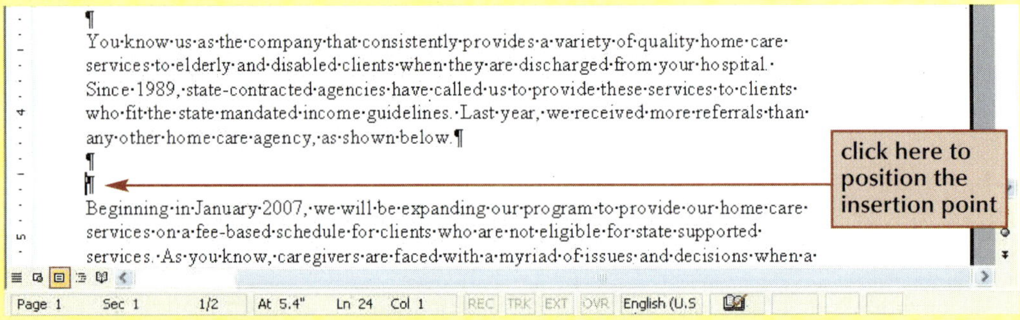

5. Click **Edit** on the menu bar, and then click **Paste Special**. The Paste Special dialog box opens. See Figure 1-8.

Figure 1-8 Paste Special dialog box

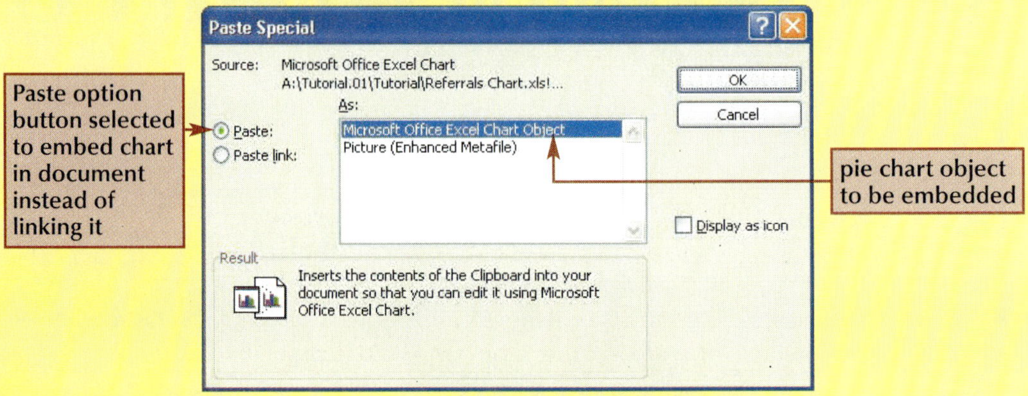

6. Make sure the **Paste** option button is selected. This option will embed the chart. If you wanted to link the chart, you would click the Paste link option button.

7. In the As list box, click **Microsoft Office Excel Chart Object**, if necessary, to select the chart as the object to embed.

   Trouble? If the Microsoft Office Excel Chart Object option does not appear in the As list box, you might not have selected and copied the chart correctly. Click the Cancel button in the Paste Special dialog box, click the Microsoft Excel - Referrals Chart button on the taskbar, and then repeat Steps 1 through 6, making sure that when you select the chart, sizing handles appear around the chart area, and that when you copy the chart, a rotating dashed line appears around the chart area.

8. Click the **OK** button. The Paste Special dialog box closes, and after a few moments, the Excel pie chart appears in the letter. The Paste Options button appears in the document next to the chart. See Figure 1-9.

Pie chart embedded in the hospital letter **Figure 1-9**

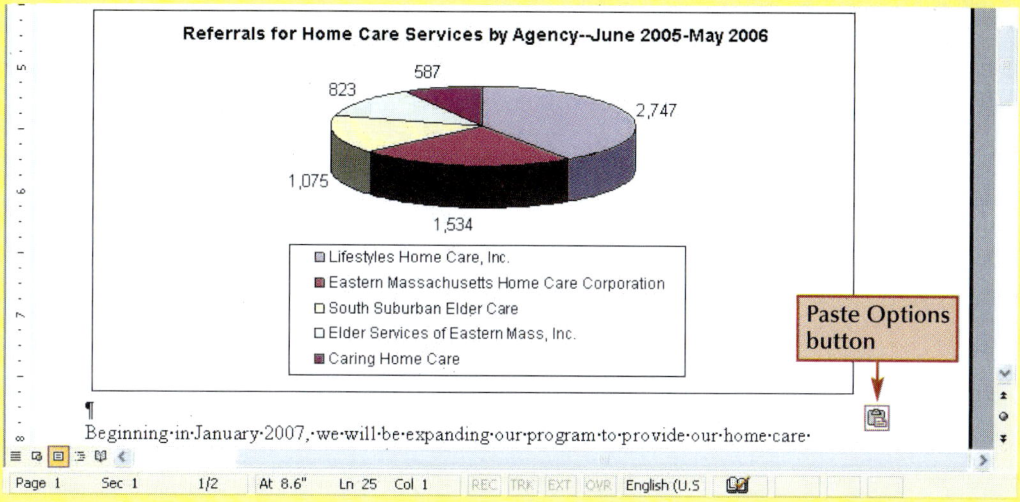

You can click the Paste Options button to select from a list of pasting options for the object (for example, you could change the object to a linked object). You'll leave the pasted object as it is.

9. Click the **Save** button on the Word Standard toolbar to save the letter with the embedded chart.

10. Click the **Microsoft Excel - Referrals Chart** button on the taskbar, click any cell in the worksheet outside of the chart area, and then close the Referrals Chart workbook without saving any changes.

11. Click the **Hospital Letter - Microsoft Word** button on the taskbar to return to the Hospital Letter document.

After reviewing the letter with the embedded pie chart, Caitlin decides that the pie chart would be more impressive if it were rotated so that the pie slice showing the percentage of total referrals to Lifestyles appeared in front. Because you embedded the chart, you can use Excel chart commands from within the Word document to modify the chart.

Modifying an Embedded Object

When you edit an embedded object within the destination program, the changes affect only the embedded object; the original object in the source program remains unchanged. When you double-click an embedded object, the destination program's menu bar and commands change to the menu bar and commands of the embedded object's source program, which you use to modify the embedded object.

Now that you have embedded the pie chart in Word, you can rotate the chart so that the Lifestyles pie wedge appears in front.

To edit the pie chart from within Word:

1. Double-click the embedded chart in the hospital letter. After a moment, a dashed border appears around the chart, and Excel commands and buttons appear in the Word menu bar and toolbars. See Figure 1-10.

Figure 1-10 Active Excel chart in the hospital letter

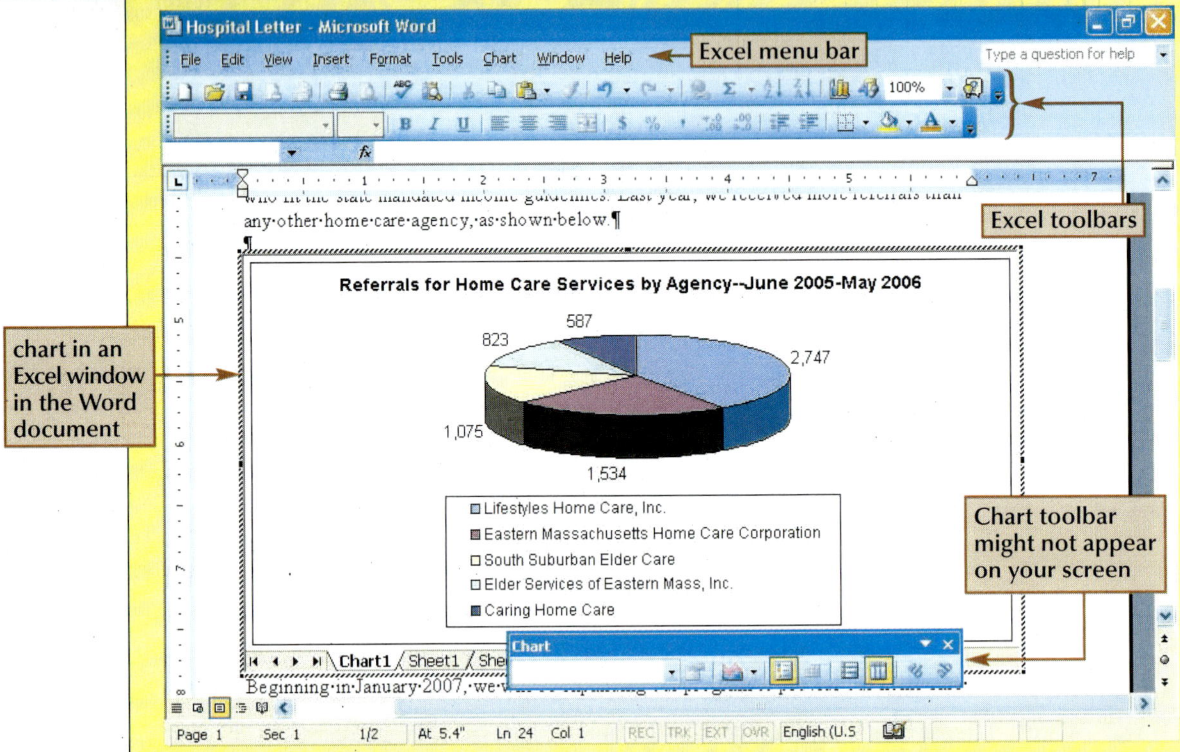

Now you can modify the chart. The chart is a 3-D pie chart, and you want to rotate it so that the Lifestyles pie wedge appears in front. You do this using the 3-D View dialog box.

2. Click **Chart** on the menu bar, and then click **3-D View**. The 3-D View dialog box opens. See Figure 1-11.

Figure 1-11 3-D View dialog box

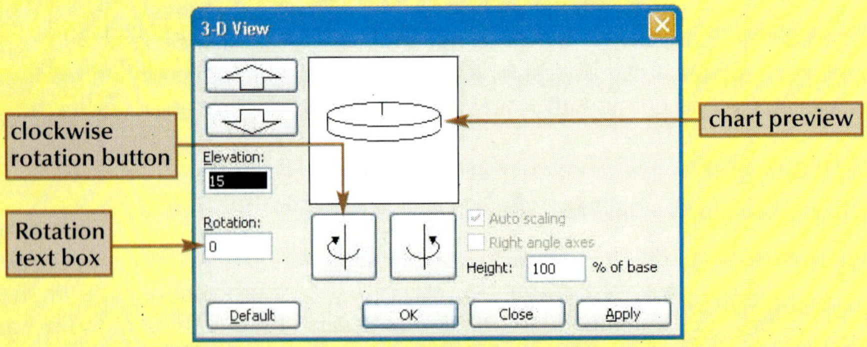

The Rotation text box shows the current value of 0, and the chart preview shows the median line pointing straight up. You want to move the Lifestyles wedge from the right side of the pie to the front of the pie, so you need to move the median line clockwise, from the right to the left.

3. Click the **clockwise rotation** button until the Rotation text box shows the value **110**. As you click the clockwise rotation button, watch the pie chart move in the preview box.
4. Click the **OK** button. The Lifestyles pie wedge appears at the front of the pie chart. See Figure 1-12.

Figure 1-12 Revised embedded pie chart

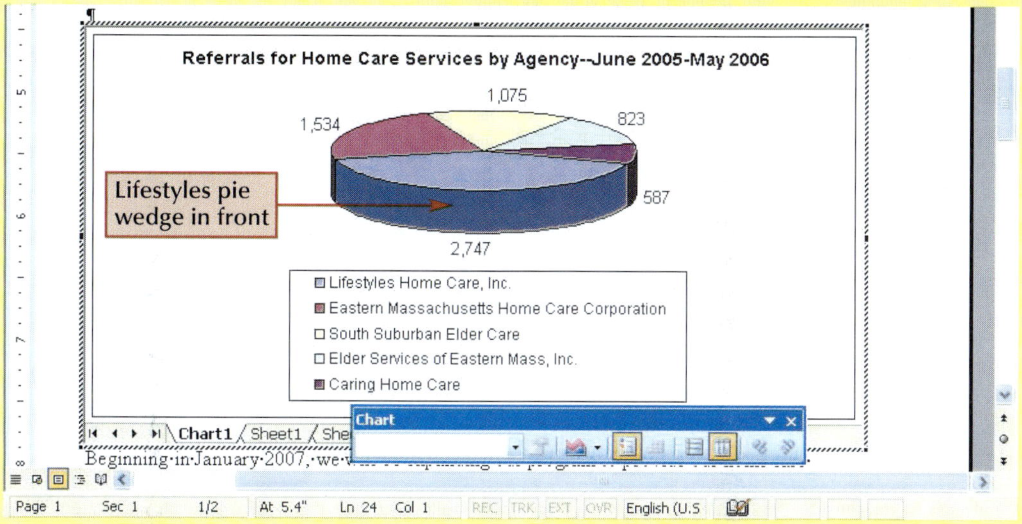

5. Click a blank area of the document outside of the selected chart to deselect the chart and return to Word's menus and toolbars.
6. Click the **Save** button on the Standard toolbar to save the document.

If you were to open the Referrals Chart workbook, you would see that the pie chart there remained unchanged.

Your final task is to include the table outlining the growth of Lifestyles Home Care over the past five years in the letter. To do this, you will link the table from Excel to Word.

Linking an Object from Excel to Word

Caitlin created an Excel workbook named LHCGrowth showing the growth of the Lifestyles Home Care agency over the past five years. She does not yet have the final numbers for the current year, so, unlike the information in the pie chart, the table is subject to change. Because Caitlin wants you to finish setting up the letter now, you'll link the table from the LHCGrowth workbook to the Hospital Letter document instead of embedding it as you did the chart. When Caitlin receives the current year's data, she can update the table in the Excel workbook, and the changes will appear in the Word document. This will keep the information up to date in both files.

Reference Window

Linking an Object

- Start the source program, open the file containing the object to be linked, select the object or information you want to link to the destination program, and then click the Copy button on the Standard toolbar.
- Start the destination program, open the file that will contain the link to the copied object, position the insertion point where you want the linked object to appear, click Edit on the menu bar, and then click Paste Special.
- Click the Paste link option button in the Paste Special dialog box, select the option you want in the As list box, and then click the OK button.

or

- In the source file, select the object or information you want to link, and then click the Copy button on the Standard toolbar.
- Start the destination program, open the file that will contain the linked object, and then position the insertion point where you want to place the object.
- Click the Paste button on the Standard toolbar in the destination program.
- Click the Paste Options button that appears in the document window, and then click a linking option on the menu.

Now you will link the growth table to the letter using the Paste Options button. This button appears when you paste text or other information from one Office document to another. You first need to open the LHCGrowth workbook, and then select the table object for linking.

To link the table to the letter:

1. Click the **Microsoft Excel** button on the taskbar to switch back to Excel, click the **Open** button on the Standard toolbar to open the Open dialog box, navigate to the **Tutorial.01\Tutorial** folder included with your Data Files, and then double-click the Excel workbook **LHCGrowth**.
2. Save the workbook as **Growth Table** in the same folder.
3. Select cells **A6** through **F12**, and then click the **Copy** button on the Excel Standard toolbar to copy the data to the Clipboard.
4. Click the **Hospital Letter - Microsoft Word** button on the taskbar to return to the hospital letter.
5. Scroll the document and position the insertion point to the left of the paragraph mark above the paragraph that begins "We would like the opportunity." This is where you want the table to appear. See Figure 1-13.

Figure 1-13 Placement for linking the Excel worksheet to the hospital letter

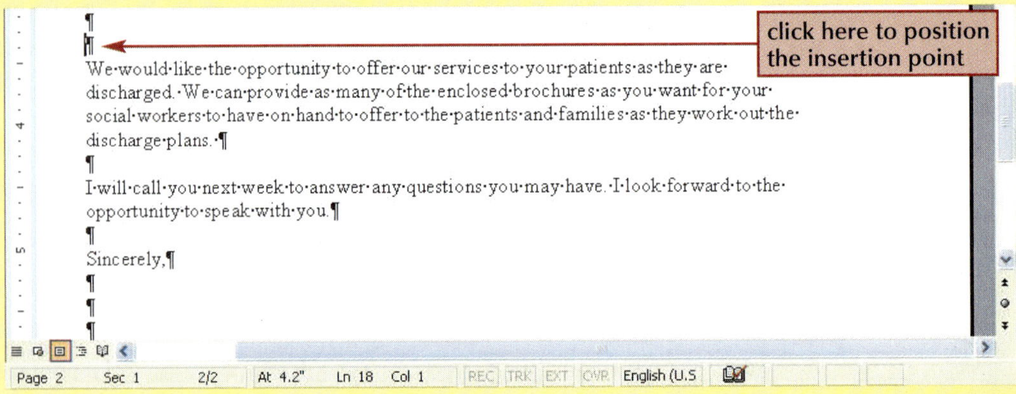

6. Click the **Paste** button on the Word Standard toolbar. The table from Excel is inserted in the letter, and the Paste Options button appears in the lower-right corner of the new table. You will use this button to link the original growth table contained in the Excel worksheet and the new growth table inserted in the letter.
7. Move the pointer over the **Paste Options** button so that it changes to , and then click it to open the Paste Options shortcut menu. See Figure 1-14.

Figure 1-14 Linked growth table

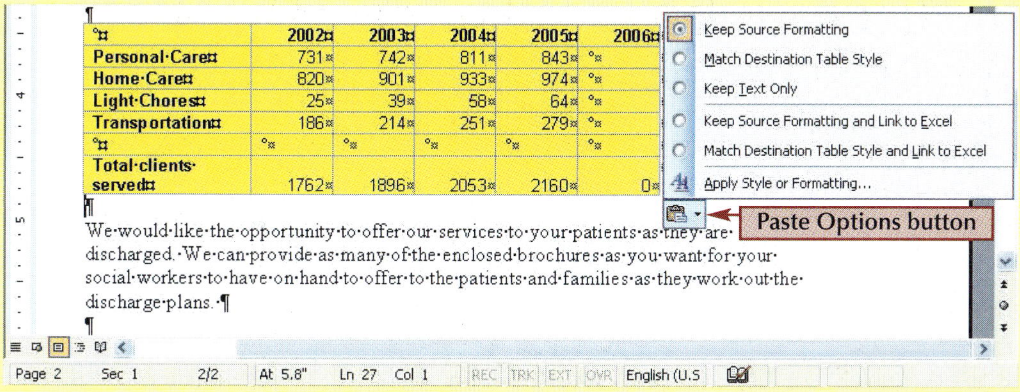

Figure 1-15 describes the commands on the Paste Options menu after you link an object.

Figure 1-15 Paste Options commands

Choose this Paste Options command:	To do the following:
Keep Source Formatting	Paste the object without linking and match the formatting in the source file
Match Destination Table Style	Paste the object without linking and format the object in the Word default table style
Keep Text Only	Paste the object as text only, not as a table or other formatted object; Word separates table columns with tab characters and table rows with paragraph symbols
Keep Source Formatting and Link to Excel	Link the pasted object to Excel and match the formatting in the Excel source file; any formatting changes you make to the pasted object remain when you change the data in the source file
Match Destination Table Style and Link to Excel	Link the pasted object to Excel and format the linked data in the Word default table style; any formatting changes you make to the pasted object remain when you change the data in the source file
Apply Style or Formatting	Open the Style and Formatting task pane to select styles to apply to the pasted object

8. Click the **Match Destination Table Style and Link to Excel** option button. This means that the table will be linked, rather than embedded, and that its format will match the default table style in Word. The growth table in Word is now formatted in 12-point Times New Roman text, the same as the rest of the letter, the yellow fill is removed, and it is linked to the Excel worksheet.
9. Click the **Save** button on the Word Standard toolbar to save the Hospital Letter.
10. Switch to Excel, and then click the **Close Window** button on the menu bar to close the workbook.

Caitlin just received the current year's figures from her assistant. She asks you to update the growth table with the new information.

Updating Linked Objects

Now that you have linked the table from the workbook to the letter, you can edit the information in the source file (the Excel workbook), and the changes will appear in the Word document. When making changes, you can have one or both files open.

To update the table in Excel:

1. Switch back to Word, right-click the Excel table in the Word document, point to **Linked Worksheet Object** on the shortcut menu, and then click **Open Link**. The source file opens in Excel.

   Trouble? If the Linked Worksheet Object command is not on the shortcut menu, click a blank area of the document, and then try right-clicking the table again.

2. Right-click a blank area of the taskbar and then click **Tile Windows Horizontally** on the shortcut menu. The source and destination files each appear in a reduced window, stacked one on top of the other.

   Trouble? If you see more than two windows on your screen, then you had more than two documents open. Close all open documents except the Hospital Letter Word document and the Growth Table Excel workbook, and then repeat Step 2.

3. Scroll the Word window so that you can see the first item of the table in the document.

4. Click in the Excel window to make it the active window, and then scroll the Excel window so that you can see the first item of the table in the worksheet.

   The first entry you need to add is Personal Care in 2006.

5. In the Excel window, click cell **F7**, type **902**, and then press the **Enter** key.

6. Click anywhere in the Word window to make it the active window, right-click anywhere in the table, click **Update Link** on the shortcut menu, and then scroll back up the document, if necessary, to see the top of the table. The number you added in the Excel worksheet for the number of clients receiving personal care in 2006, 902, now appears in the destination document because you linked the table from Excel to Word. See Figure 1-16.

Figure 1-16 Linked documents tiled horizontally

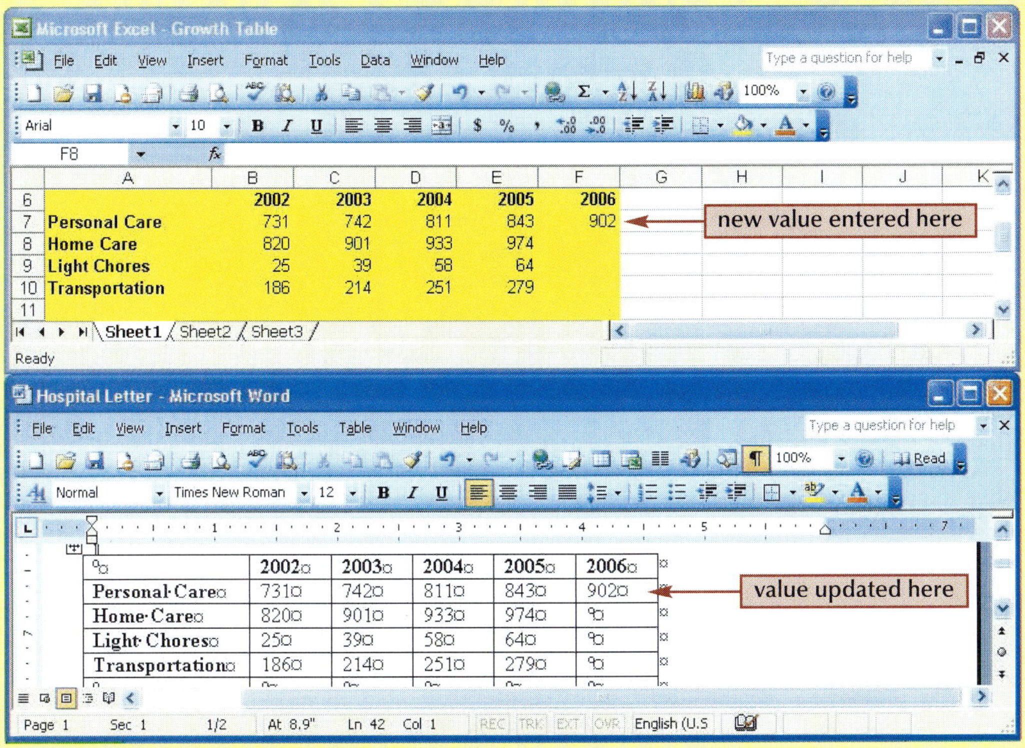

Trouble? If the Update Link command is not on the shortcut menu, click a blank area of the document, and then right-click the table again.

7. Right-click a blank area of the taskbar, and then click **Undo Tile** on the shortcut menu to view just one program window at a time.
8. Click the **Save** button on the Word Standard toolbar to save the changes to the letter.

   Trouble? If Word is not the active program window, click the Hospital Letter - Microsoft Word button on the taskbar to switch to the letter.

What would happen if you were working on the new growth table in Excel without the Word document open? Would you still be able to update the information in the letter? To find out, enter the rest of the data for 2006 in the Excel workbook with the Word document closed. You can then reopen the letter to verify that the changes appear there as well.

To edit the linked object with the Word document closed:

1. Close the letter, and then click the **Microsoft Excel - Growth Table** button on the taskbar. The Growth Table worksheet becomes the active window.
2. Enter **1075** in cell F8, enter **73** in cell F9, and then enter **302** in cell F10.
3. Click the **Save** button on the Standard toolbar.
4. Click the **Microsoft Word** button on the taskbar, click **File** on the menu bar, and then look for Hospital Letter near the bottom of the File menu. The filename will be preceded by the number 1 and by the drive and folder name in which the file is stored.

5. Click **Hospital Letter** to open the letter. A dialog box opens telling you that the document contains links and asking if you want to update the links.
6. Click the **Yes** button, and then scroll the document to view the linked table. Notice that the new data for 2006 appears in the linked table in Word. See Figure 1-17.

Figure 1-17 Values updated in linked document

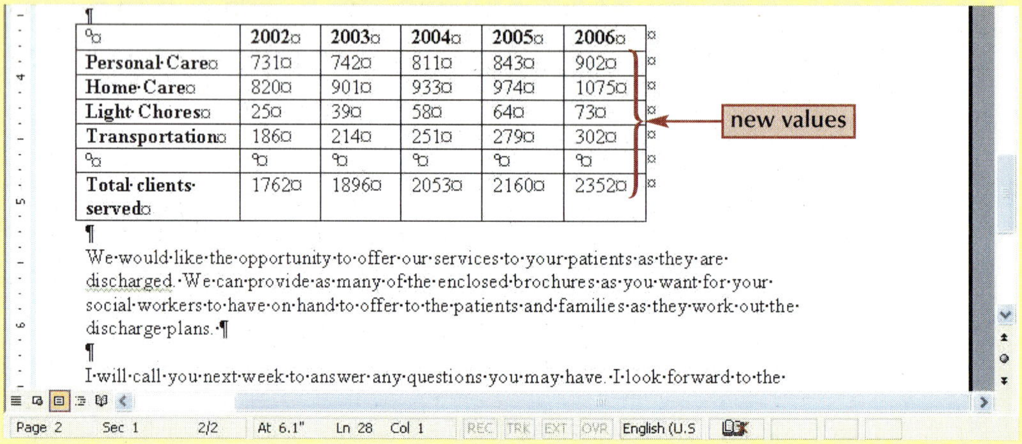

	2002	2003	2004	2005	2006
Personal Care	731	742	811	843	902
Home Care	820	901	933	974	1075
Light Chores	25	39	58	64	73
Transportation	186	214	251	279	302
Total clients served	1762	1896	2053	2160	2352

We would like the opportunity to offer our services to your patients as they are discharged. We can provide as many of the enclosed brochures as you want for your social workers to have on hand to offer to the patients and families as they work out the discharge plans.

I will call you next week to answer any questions you may have. I look forward to the

Linked documents are effective in many cases, but sometimes you'll want to break the link.

Breaking Links

Once you are finished working with linked documents, you can break the link between the two documents. You do this by using the Links command on the Edit menu in the destination file. Once you break a link, the only changes you can make to the object in the destination file are resizing, moving, and deleting. Also, any such changes you make to the object in the source file no longer appear in the destination file once the link is broken. In other words, when you break the link, the object acts as a pasted picture in the destination file.

Reference Window

Breaking the Link Between Linked Objects

- In the destination program, click Edit on the menu bar, and then click Links to open the Links dialog box.
- Select the appropriate entry in the Source file list box, click the Break Link button, and then click the Yes button.
- Save the destination file to ensure that the link will be broken.

You are finished updating the growth table with the data from the current year, and you are ready to give Caitlin the finished letter. Because the data in the table is final, Caitlin asks you to break the link between the Hospital Letter document and the Growth Table workbook, so that she can store the letter and workbook separately.

To break the link between the Hospital Letter document and the Growth Table workbook:

1. In the Word window, right-click anywhere in the linked table, point to **Linked Worksheet Object** on the shortcut menu, and then click **Links** to open the Links dialog box. There is one entry in the Source file list box. See Figure 1-18.

Figure 1-18 Links dialog box

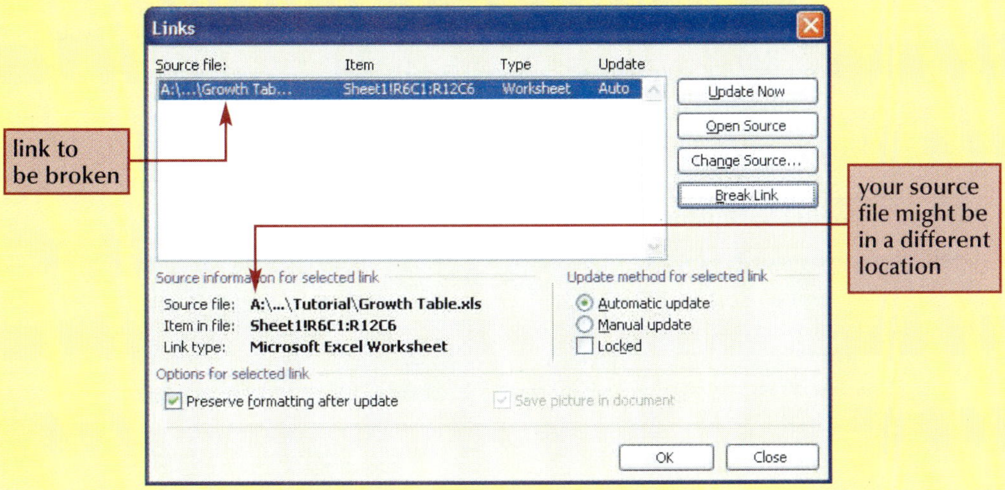

Trouble? Depending on the disk drive used for your Data Files, the filename path in the Links dialog box might be different from the one shown in Figure 1-18.

2. With the link selected in the Source file list box, click the **Break Link** button. A dialog box opens, asking you to confirm that you want to break the selected link.
3. Click the **Yes** button. The link is broken, and the dialog box closes.

   You'll confirm that the link is indeed broken by editing the growth table in Excel, and then verifying that the change is not made in the letter.

4. Switch to the Excel workbook, and then enter **500** in cell F10.
5. Switch to the Word document, and then right-click the table. Note that the various Link commands no longer appear on the shortcut menu.
6. Click a blank area in the document window to close the shortcut menu, and then click **Edit** on the Word menu bar. The Links command is grayed out on the Edit menu, which means that this command is not available because there are no links in the document. This confirms that the link between the two files is broken.
7. Click a blank area in the document window to close the Edit menu.
8. Switch to the Excel workbook, click the **Close Window** button ☒ on the Excel menu bar, and then click the **No** button when prompted to save the changes to the file. You do not want to save the change you made to the data, because this change was made simply to test the broken link. The workbook closes.
9. Switch to the Word document, and then save the **Hospital Letter** document.

   If you had closed the Hospital Letter document without saving it, the link to the Excel object would still be intact. Because you saved the letter, the link remains broken.

Caitlin asks you to print a copy of the letter so that she can review it before mailing out any letters.

To finish the letter and then preview and print it:

1. Move the pointer over the table to make the Table Move Handle appear above the upper-left corner of the table, click the **Table Move** handle to select the entire table, and then click the **Center** button on the Formatting toolbar to center the table on the page.
2. Scroll to the bottom of the letter, and then replace Caitlin Sheehan's name with your own.
3. Click the **Print Preview** button on the Standard toolbar to preview the letter.
4. If necessary, click the **Multiple Pages** button on the Print Preview toolbar, and then select **1 x 2 Pages** to view both pages of the letter. See Figure 1-19.

Figure 1-19 Preview of completed customer letter

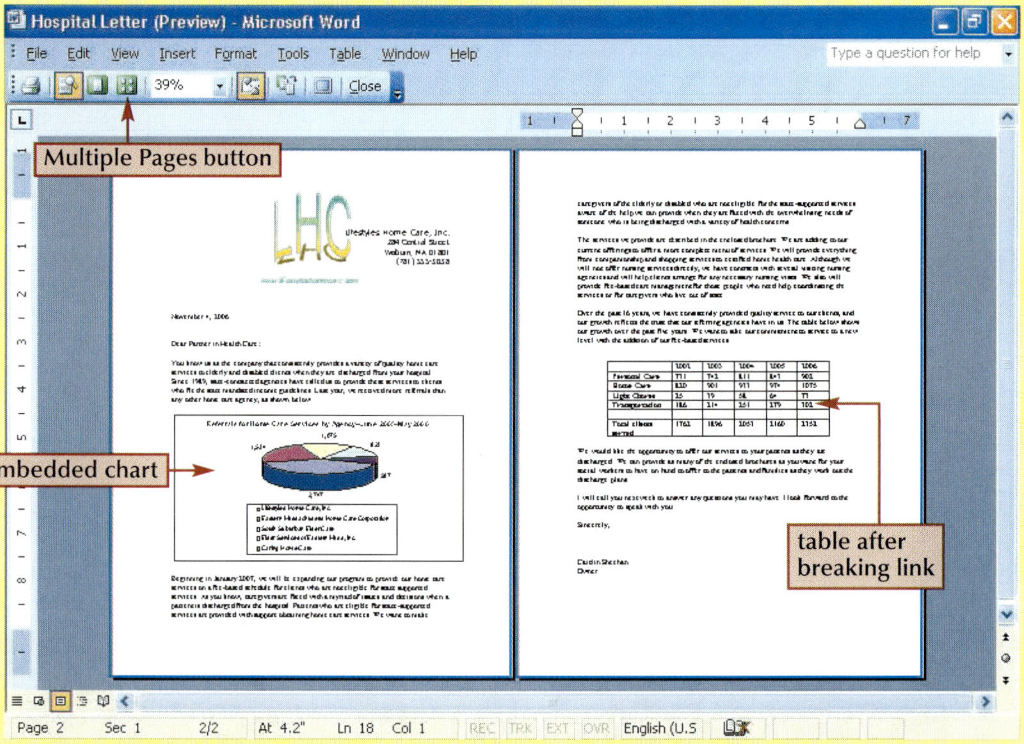

5. Print the letter, and then click the **Close** button on the Print Preview toolbar.

   Trouble? If your printed letter contains a table of data instead of the pie chart, click the **Magnifier** button on the Print Preview toolbar if it is selected, right-click the table, point to Chart Object on the shortcut menu, and then click Convert to open the Convert dialog box. Click the Activate as option button, click Microsoft Office Excel Chart, and then click the OK button. Save the document, and then print it again.
6. Save and close the letter.
7. Exit all open programs.

You have integrated the pie chart (showing the percentage of referrals to Lifestyles) and the growth table from Excel into the letter Caitlin created in Word. She is pleased with the finished letter and will send it to the local hospitals as soon as the new brochure is finished.

Review

Quick Check

1. What is an object?
2. What is the difference between embedding an object and linking an object?
3. When an object is embedded between two programs, how many copies of the object exist?
4. If an Excel chart is linked to a Word document, which program is the source program?
5. True or False: Any changes you make to a linked object in the source file appear in both the destination and source files.
6. If you no longer want an object linked between two documents, what should you do?
7. If you break the link between the source Excel file and the destination Word file, change the number of Personal Care clients in 2006 from 902 to 1000 in the Excel file, and then close the Word file without saving changes, what will the number of Personal Care clients be when you reopen the Word file? Why?

Review

Tutorial Summary

In this tutorial, you learned how to integrate Excel data in a Word document. You learned how to copy data from an Excel workbook and how to embed the copied data in a Word document. You also accessed commands in Excel (the source program) to modify the embedded object from within the document in Word (the destination program). You also integrated data by linking copied data from Excel to a Word document. You then learned how to update the links in Word (the destination program) after the data was changed in Excel (the source program). Finally, you learned how to break the links in the destination program.

Key Terms

destination file
destination program
embedding
integration
link
linking
object
object linking and embedding (OLE)
source file
source program

Practice

Get hands-on practice of the skills you learned in the tutorial using the same case scenario.

Review Assignments

Data Files needed for the Review Assignments: LHCMemo.doc, LHCServicesDistribution.xls, and LHCGrowthUpdated.xls

Caitlin wants to send a memo to all Lifestyles employees introducing the plans for the expanded offerings and the new brochure. She already wrote the memo, and she asks you to embed an Excel chart showing the current distribution of services offered by Lifestyles. She also wants you to link an Excel worksheet listing the updated growth figures for the past five years.

To create the memo:

1. Start Word, and then open the Word document **LHCMemo** in the Tutorial.01\Review folder included with your Data Files.
2. Save the document as **Employee Memo** in the same folder.
3. Start Excel, and then open the **LHCServicesDistribution** workbook in the Tutorial.01\Review folder included with your Data Files.

4. Save the workbook as **Distribution Chart** in the same folder.
5. Embed the chart from the **Distribution Chart** workbook into the **Employee Memo** document on the blank line above the paragraph that begins "LHC has grown steadily."
6. Double-click a blank area of the chart. Describe what happens. Why does this occur?
7. Explode the Home Care wedge of the pie, and then deselect the chart. (*Hint*: Single-click the Home Care wedge twice to select only that wedge, and then drag the wedge away from the rest of the pie to explode it.)
8. Switch to Excel, and then close the **Distribution Chart** workbook without saving changes.
9. Open the **LHCGrowthUpdated** workbook in the Tutorial.01\Review folder included with your Data Files, and then save it as **Growth Table 2** in the same folder.
10. Copy the growth table.
11. Switch to the employee memo, place the insertion point in the blank paragraph mark above the heading "New Services," paste the Excel table and then use the Paste Options button to link the growth table to the Employee Memo, but keep the formatting of the *source* file when you link the table.
12. Switch to Excel, press the Esc key to deselect the table, and then change the number of home care clients in 2006 to 1354, and the number of transportation clients in 2006 to 331.
13. Switch back to the employee memo and update the link.
14. Replace Caitlin Sheehan's name at the top of the memo with your own. Center the pie chart horizontally on the page. (*Hint*: Click the chart once to select it, and then center it.) Center the table and fine-tune its format. Finally, make sure that there is one blank line between the chart and the table and any text above and below them, and that the page break is in a logical place.
15. Save the memo, and then preview and print it.
16. Break the link between the employee memo and the table.
17. Test that the link is broken by changing the number of clients in 2006 who received light chores service from 89 to 100 in the table in the Excel workbook, and then try to update the link in the Word document.
18. Exit all open programs. When prompted to save files, click the Yes button.

Apply

Apply the skills you learned to link an Excel table to a letter and embed an Excel chart in a letter.

Case Problem 1

Data Files needed for this Case Problem: MusicLetter.doc and MusicRentals.xls

Making Music Caleb Jacobson is the owner of Making Music, a small music retail store in Danbury, Connecticut. Caleb sells instruments and accessories, sheet music, lesson books, and a few music collectibles, and he offers repair service for most common instruments. Caleb and some of his staff also teach piano and guitar lessons in a room upstairs from the store. In addition, Making Music rents and sells band instruments to middle and high school students at area schools. Currently, Making Music has arrangements with three area middle schools and two high schools to show up on the school grounds in September each year to rent or sell band instruments to interested students. Caleb wants to make arrangements with more schools to expand his business. He decides to write a letter of introduction to the music departments at several schools in nearby towns. He wants to include an updated list of instruments that he rents and sells, the current monthly rental fees, the total cost if a student rents until the instrument is paid off, and the cost if a student buys the instrument outright. He wants to be able to update this information if his prices change. He also wants to include a chart showing the instruments he sells and rents the most. You'll use Excel and Word to create the letter for Caleb.

1. Start Word, and then open the **MusicLetter** document in the Tutorial.01\Cases folder included with your Data Files.

2. Save the document as **School Letter** in the same folder.
3. At the top of the letter, replace the <Current Date> placeholder text with the current date. At the bottom of the letter, replace Caleb Jacobson's name with your own.
4. Start Excel, and then open the **MusicRentals** workbook in the Tutorial.01\Cases folder included with your Data Files.
5. Save the workbook as **Rental Fees** in the same folder.
6. Copy cells A9 through E17 in the Rental Prices worksheet to the Clipboard.
7. Switch to Word.
8. Link the Excel worksheet object into the Word document in the blank paragraph above the second paragraph in the body of the letter, matching the style of the Word document, and then save the document.
9. Switch to Excel.
10. Change the purchase price of a clarinet to $720, and then save the changes to the workbook.
11. Switch to Word and update the link. Note that the change you just made in the previous step is now reflected in the Word document.
12. Center the table, and then save the changes to the letter.
13. Switch to Excel, and then click the Rentals Chart 2005–2006 sheet tab in the Rental Fees workbook to make that worksheet active.
14. Copy the pie chart to the Clipboard. (*Hint*: There is no need to select the chart before you copy it because it is on its own chart sheet.)

Explore

15. Switch to Word, position the insertion point above the last paragraph in the body of the letter, and then click the Paste button to embed the pie chart in the school letter. When the Paste Options button appears, click it, and then click Excel Chart (entire workbook). (This is the same as using the Paste option in the Paste Special dialog box.)
16. Click the embedded chart once to select it, and then drag the lower-left sizing handle up and to the right approximately one inch to resize the chart so that it is small enough to fit on the page.
17. Edit the embedded chart so that the data labels show the percentage as well as the category name. (*Hint*: Right-click anywhere on the pie chart after you've activated Excel from within the letter, click Format Data Series on the shortcut menu, and then click the Data Labels tab in the Format Data Series dialog box.) Drag individual labels as necessary to make them readable on the chart. Click outside the chart to deselect it.
18. Switch to Excel. Note that the change you made in the previous step is not reflected in the Excel worksheet.
19. Close the **Rental Fees** workbook.
20. Save the **School Letter** document, and then preview it. Make any adjustments necessary so that the page break is in a logical spot, and then print the document.
21. Exit all open programs, saving changes if prompted.

Create

Expand the skills you learned in this tutorial to create a document and then link and update Excel tables to the document.

Case Problem 2

Data File needed for this Case Problem: TutorFees.xls

Learning Fulfillment Centers In 1997, Enrique Garcia founded Learning Fulfillment Centers in Phoenix, Arizona, to offer tutoring services for students who need extra help to keep up with their class work. He received so many requests for advanced course work that he quickly expanded his offerings to include advanced work for students who wanted to move ahead. In early 2001, Enrique opened two more offices in greater Phoenix. One of the reasons Learning Fulfillment Centers has been successful is the initial assessment that the staff conducts to evaluate each student and customize a plan for that student. Enrique plans to send out a letter to families in the area. He wants to include in the letter Excel tables that list his fees. You'll use Word and Excel to create the letter for Enrique.

1. Start Word, and create a new document. Write a letter to local families who have children. Briefly explain what Learning Fulfillment Centers offers. Include paragraphs that describe the initial assessment, the tutoring, and the advanced course work. Leave space after the tutoring and advanced course work paragraphs to link Excel tables listing the fees. Type your name and address in the inside address, and include the current date. Include a closing paragraph that mentions how successful the company is and how much it has grown. Remember to include a proper salutation and closing. Use your own name as the signatory in the letter.
2. Save the file as **Parent Letter** in the Tutorial.01\Cases folder included with your Data Files.
3. Start Excel, and open the **TutorFees** workbook in the Tutorial.01\Cases folder included with your Data Files.
4. Save the workbook as **Learning Expenses** in the same folder.
5. Link the appropriate data from the Learning Expenses workbook to appropriate paragraphs in the Parent Letter document.
6. In the Excel workbook, change the base hourly rate for writing to $55. Make this change in both worksheets.
7. Update the links in the Word document to reflect the new writing fee.
8. Save, preview, and then print the letter.
9. Close any open programs, saving files as needed.

Review

Quick Check Answers

1. An object is anything that can be manipulated as a whole; the specific information that you want to share between programs, such as a chart, table, picture, video or sound clip, or almost anything else you can create on a computer.
2. Embedding stores a copy of the object in the destination file, and any changes made to the source file do not appear in the destination file; linking stores the object in the source file but displays it in the destination file, and any changes to the object in the source file appear in the destination file.
3. two
4. Excel
5. True
6. break the link
7. 1000. Closing the Word document without saving keeps the link intact.

Objectives

Session 1.1
- Open and view an existing PowerPoint presentation
- Switch views and navigate a presentation
- View a presentation in Slide Show view
- Create a presentation using the AutoContent Wizard

Session 1.2
- Add, move, and delete slides
- Promote and demote text in the Outline tab
- Create speaker notes for slides
- Check the spelling and style in a presentation
- Preview and print slides
- Print outlines, handouts, and speaker notes

Creating a Presentation

Presenting Information About Humanitarian Projects

Case

Global Humanitarian, Austin Office

In 1985, a group of Austin, Texas business leaders established a nonprofit organization called Global Humanitarian. Its goal was to alleviate abject poverty in the third world through public awareness and personal involvement in sustainable self-help initiatives in third-world villages. Today, Global Humanitarian is a large umbrella organization and clearinghouse for national and international humanitarian organizations. Its five major functions are to help provide the following: entrepreneurial support, service expeditions, inventory surplus exchange, funding and grant proposals, and student internships.

The president of Global Humanitarian is Norma Flores, who sits on the board of directors and carries out its policies and procedures. The managing director of the Austin office is Miriam Schwartz, and the managing director in Latin America is Pablo Fuentes, who lives and works in Lima, Peru. Miriam wants you to use PowerPoint to develop a presentation to provide information about Global Humanitarian's current projects to potential donors, expedition participants, and student interns.

In this tutorial, you'll examine a presentation that Miriam created to become familiar with **Microsoft Office PowerPoint 2003** (or simply **PowerPoint**). You'll then create a presentation based on content that PowerPoint suggests by using the AutoContent Wizard. You'll modify the text in the presentation, and you'll add and delete slides. You'll check the spelling and style of the presentation, and then you'll view the completed slide show. Finally, you'll save the slide show and print handouts.

Student Data Files

▼**Tutorial.01**

▽ Tutorial folder
- Lorena.ppt

▽ Review folder
- VillageOP.ppt

▽ Cases folder
- LASIK.ppt
- Seafoods.ppt

Session 1.1

What Is PowerPoint?

PowerPoint is a powerful presentation graphics program that provides everything you need to produce an effective presentation in the form of on-screen slides, a slide presentation on a Web site, black-and-white or color overheads, or 35-mm photographic slides. You may have already seen your instructors use PowerPoint presentations to enhance their classroom lectures.

Using PowerPoint, you can prepare each component of a presentation: individual slides, speaker notes, an outline, and audience handouts. The presentation you'll create for Miriam will include slides, notes, and handouts.

To start PowerPoint:

1. Click the **Start** button on the taskbar, point to **All Programs**, point to **Microsoft Office**, and then click **Microsoft Office PowerPoint 2003**. PowerPoint starts and the PowerPoint window opens. See Figure 1-1.

   Trouble? If you don't see the Microsoft Office PowerPoint 2003 option on the Microsoft Office submenu, look for it on a different submenu or as an option on the All Programs menu. If you still cannot find the Microsoft Office PowerPoint 2003 option, ask your instructor or technical support person for help.

Figure 1-1 Blank PowerPoint window

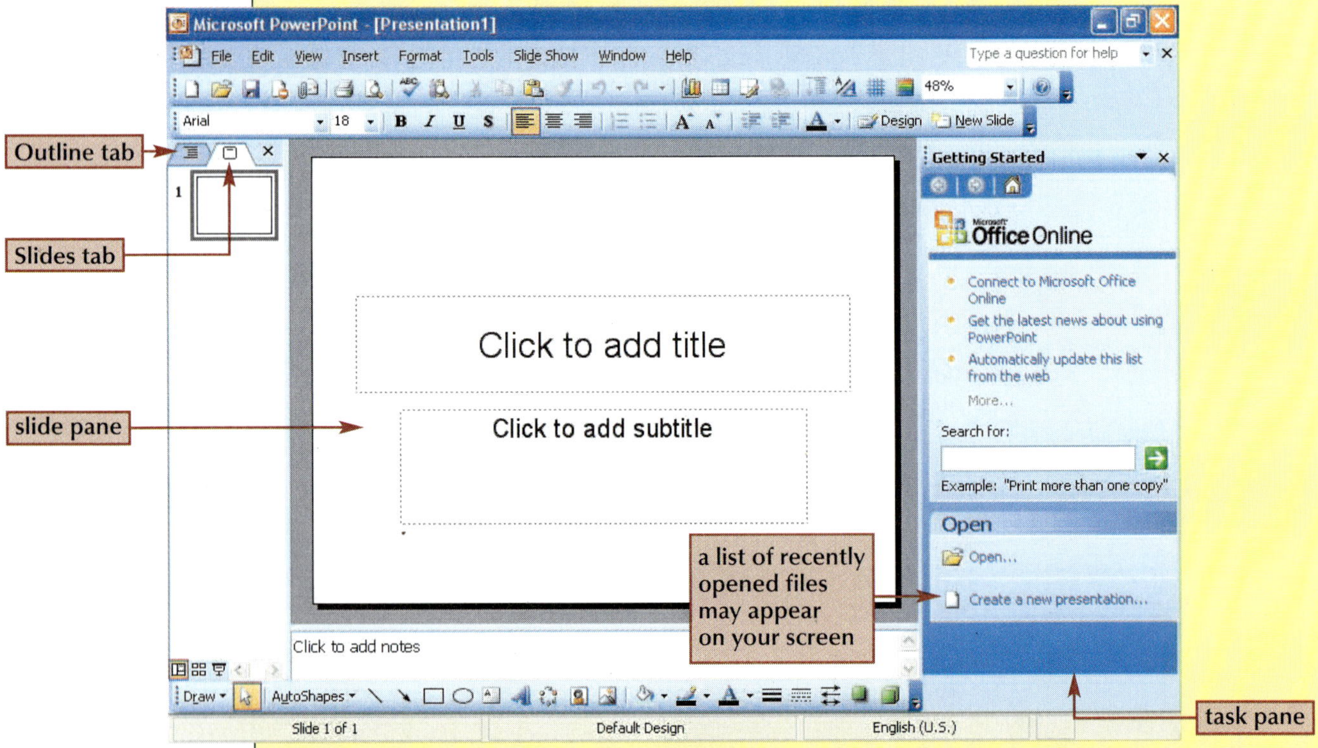

Trouble? If the PowerPoint program window is not maximized, click the Maximize button on the program window title bar.

Trouble? If the Office Assistant (an animated icon, usually a paper clip with eyes) opens when you start PowerPoint, right-click the Office Assistant, and then click Hide to close it.

Opening an Existing PowerPoint Presentation

Before you prepare the presentation on Global Humanitarian, Miriam suggests that you view an existing presentation recently prepared under Norma's and Miriam's direction as an example of PowerPoint features. When you examine the presentation, you'll learn about some PowerPoint capabilities that can help make your presentations more interesting and effective. You'll open the presentation now.

To open the existing presentation:

1. Make sure you have access to the Data Files in the Tutorial.01 folder.

   Trouble? If you don't have the PowerPoint Data Files, you need to get them before you can proceed. Your instructor will either give you the Data Files or ask you to obtain them from a specified location (such as a network drive). In either case, be sure that you make a backup copy of your Data Files before you start using them, so that the original files will be available on your copied disk in case you need to start over because of an error or problem. If you have any questions about the Data Files, see your instructor or technical support person for assistance.

2. Click the **Open** link under Open in the Getting Started task pane. The Open dialog box appears on the screen.

   Trouble? If you don't see the Open link, either click More or point to the small triangle at the bottom of the task pane to view additional links.

3. Click the **Look in** list arrow to display the list of disk drives on your computer, and then navigate to the **Tutorial.01\Tutorial** folder included with your Data Files.

4. Click **Lorena** (if necessary), and then click the **Open** button to display Miriam's presentation. The presentation opens in Normal view. See Figure 1-2.

PowerPoint window with presentation open **Figure 1-2**

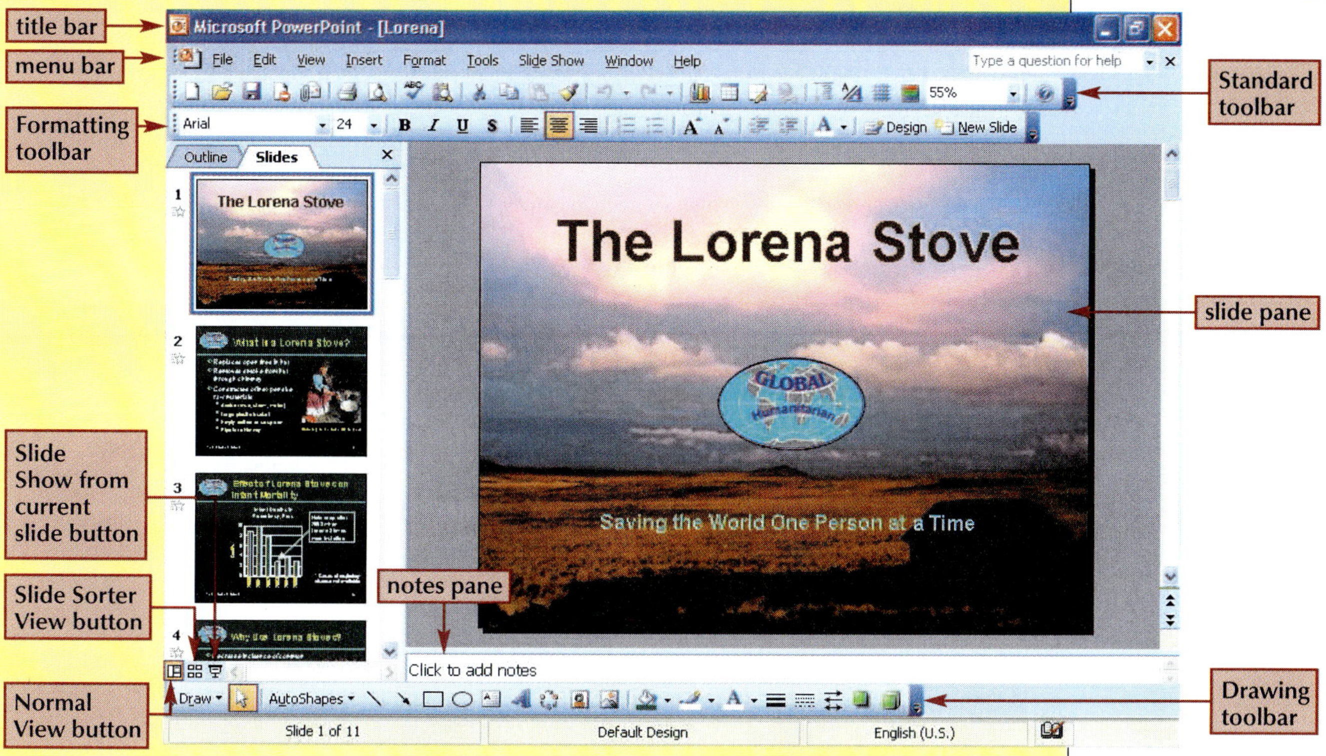

Trouble? If you see filename extensions on your screen (such as ".ppt" appended to "Lorena" in the filename), don't be concerned; they won't affect your work.

Trouble? If your screen doesn't show the Drawing toolbar, click View on the menu bar, point to Toolbars, and then click Drawing.

Trouble? If your screen shows the Standard toolbar and the Formatting toolbar on the same line, click Tools on the menu bar, click Customize, click the Options tab, click the Show Standard and Formatting toolbars on two rows check box to select it, and then click the Close button.

Switching Views and Navigating a Presentation

The PowerPoint window contains features common to all Windows programs, as well as features specific to PowerPoint. One obvious difference between the PowerPoint window and other Office programs is that the PowerPoint window is divided into sections. The section in the center of the screen, to the left of the task pane, is the slide pane. The **slide pane** shows the current slide as it will look during your slide show. Just below the slide pane is the notes pane. The **notes pane** contains notes (also called speaker notes) for the presenter; for example, the notes pane might contain specific points to cover or phrases to say during the presentation. During a slide show, the audience does not see the contents of the notes pane.

Along the left edge of the PowerPoint window, you can see two tabs, the Outline tab and the Slides tab. The **Slides tab** is on top when you first start PowerPoint. It shows a column of numbered slide **thumbnails** (miniature images) so you can see a visual representation of several slides at once. You can use the Slides tab to jump quickly to another slide in the slide pane by clicking the desired slide. The **Outline tab** shows an outline of the titles and text of each slide of your presentation.

At the bottom left of the PowerPoint window, just above the Drawing toolbar, are three view buttons: the Normal View button, the Slide Sorter View button, and the Slide Show from current slide button. These three buttons allow you to change the way you view a slide presentation. PowerPoint is currently in Normal view. Normal view is best for working with the content of the slides. You can see how the text and graphics look on each individual slide, and you can examine the outline of the entire presentation. When you switch to Slide Sorter view, the Slides and Outline tabs disappear from view and all of the slides appears as thumbnails. Slide Sorter view is an easy way to reorder the slides or set special features for your slide show. Slide Show view is the view in which you run the slide show presentation. When you click the Slide Show from current slide button, the presentation starts, beginning with the current slide (the slide currently in the slide pane in Normal view or the selected slide in Slide Sorter view).

Next you'll try switching views. PowerPoint is currently in Normal view with Slide 1 in the slide pane.

To switch views in PowerPoint:

1. Click the **Slide 2** thumbnail in the Slides tab. Slide 2 appears in the slide pane.
2. Click the **Next Slide** button at the bottom of the vertical scroll bar in the slide pane. Slide 3 appears in the slide pane.
3. Drag the scroll box in the slide pane vertical scroll bar down to the bottom of the scroll bar. Notice the ScreenTip that appears as you drag. It identifies the slide number and the title of the slide at the current position.

4. Click the **Outline** tab. The text outline of the current slide appears in the Outline tab.
5. Drag the scroll box in the vertical scroll bar of the Outline tab up to the top of the scroll bar, and then click the **slide icon** next to Slide 3. Slide 3 again appears in the slide pane.
6. Click the **Slides** tab. The Outline tab disappears behind the Slides tab.
7. Click the **Slide Sorter View** button. Slide Sorter view appears, and Slide 3 has a colored frame around it to indicate that it is the current slide.
8. Position the pointer over the **Slide 2** thumbnail. A thin, colored frame appears around Slide 2.
9. Click the **Slide 2** thumbnail to make it the current slide.
10. Double-click the **Slide 1** thumbnail. The window switches back to Normal view and Slide 1 appears in the slide pane. You could also have clicked the Normal View button to switch back to Normal view.

Now that you're familiar with the PowerPoint window, you're ready to view Miriam's presentation.

Viewing a Presentation in Slide Show View

Slide Show view is the view you use when you present an on-screen presentation to an audience. When you click the Slide Show from current slide button or click the Slide Show command on the View menu, the slide show starts. If you click the Slide Show from current slide button, the current slide fills the screen, and if you click the Slide Show command on the View menu, the first slide fills the screen. No toolbars or other Windows elements are visible on the screen.

In Slide Show view, you move from one slide to the next by pressing the spacebar, clicking the left mouse button, or pressing the → key. Additionally, PowerPoint provides a method for jumping from one slide to any other slide in the presentation during the slide show: you can right-click anywhere on the screen, point to Go to Slide on the shortcut menu, and then click one of the slide titles in the list that appears to jump to that slide.

When you prepare a slide show, you can add special effects to the show. For example, you can add **slide transitions**, the manner in which a new slide appears on the screen during a slide show. You can also add **animations** to the elements on the slide; that is, each text or graphic object on the slide can appear on the slide in a special way or have a sound effect associated with it. A special type of animation is **progressive disclosure**, a technique in which each element on a slide appears one at a time after the slide background appears. Animations draw the audience's attention to the particular item on the screen.

You can also add a footer on the slides. A **footer** is a word or phrase that appears at the bottom of each slide in the presentation.

You want to see how Miriam's presentation will appear when she shows it in Slide Show view at Global Humanitarian's executive meeting. You'll then have a better understanding of how Miriam used PowerPoint features to make her presentation informative and interesting.

To view the presentation in Slide Show view:

1. With Slide 1 in the slide pane, click the **Slide Show from current slide** button. The slide show begins by filling the entire viewing area of the screen with Slide 1 of Miriam's presentation. Watch as the slide title moves down the slide from the top and the Global Humanitarian logo and motto gradually appear on the screen.

   As you view this first slide, you can already see some of the types of elements that PowerPoint allows you to place on a slide: text in different styles, sizes, and colors; graphics; and a background picture. You also saw an example of an animation when you watched the slide title slide down the screen and the logo and motto gradually appear.

2. Press the **spacebar**. The slide show goes from Slide 1 to Slide 2. See Figure 1-3. Notice that during the transition from Slide 1 to Slide 2, the presentation displayed Slide 2 by scrolling down from the top of the screen and covering up Slide 1.

Figure 1-3 **Slide 2 in Slide Show view**

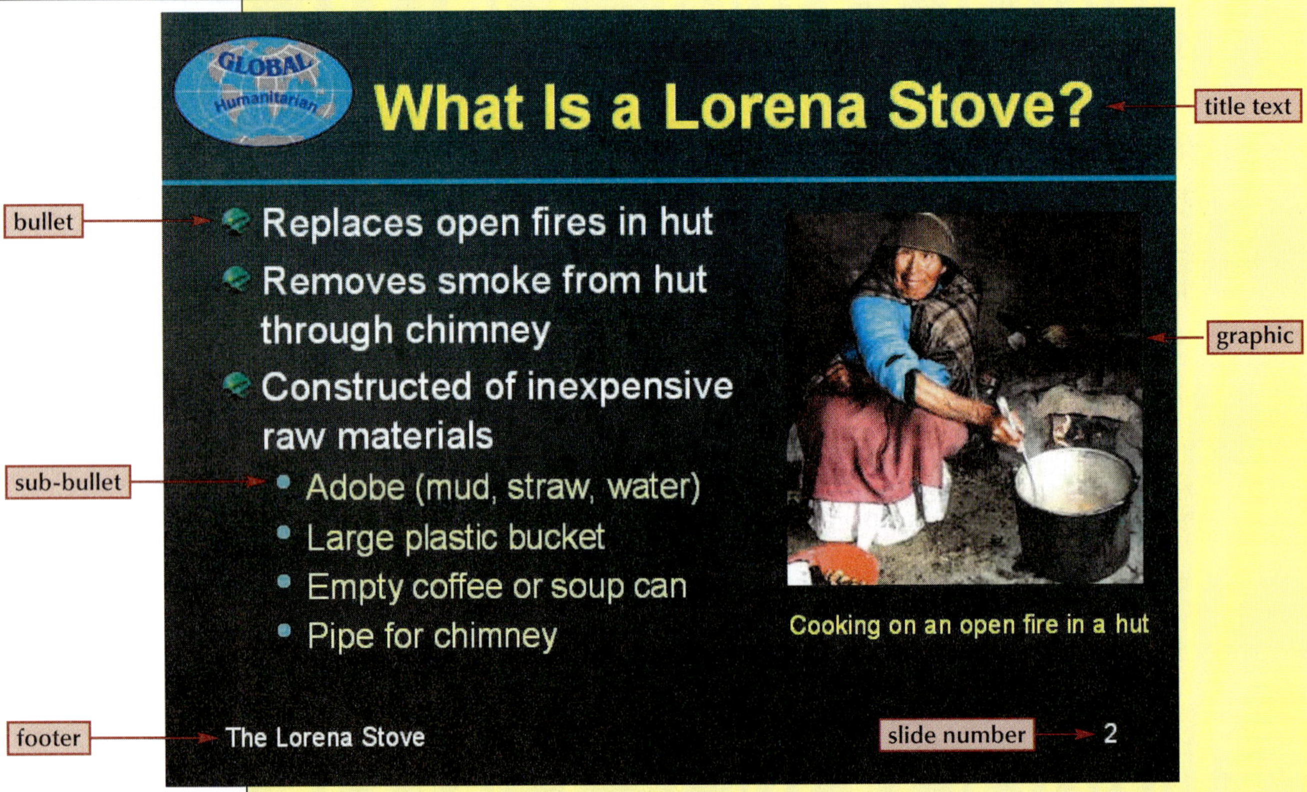

Trouble? If you missed the transition from Slide 1 to Slide 2, or if you want to see it again, press the ← key to redisplay Slide 1, and then press the spacebar to go to Slide 2 again.

Notice in Figure 1-3 that Slide 2 displays: (1) a colored background that varies in color across the slide, (2) Global Humanitarian's logo, (3) a title in large yellow text, (4) a bulleted list (with green textured bullets and white text, or solid cyan bullets with light yellow text), (5) a footer, (6) the slide number (in the lower-right corner of the slide), and (7) a photograph of a villager using an open fire.

3. Click the left mouse button to proceed to Slide 3. During the transition from Slide 2 to Slide 3, you again see the slide scroll down onto the screen from the top. Once the slide appears on the screen, you see a chart slowly appear. PowerPoint supports features for creating and customizing this type of chart, as well as graphs, diagrams, tables, and organization charts.

4. Press the **spacebar**. The title of Slide 4 appears on screen. What you don't see on the screen is a bulleted list. That's because this slide is designed for progressive disclosure. Additional slide elements will appear on screen after you press the spacebar or click on the screen.
5. Press the **spacebar** to reveal the first bulleted item on Slide 4. The item is animated to fly onto the screen from the bottom.
6. Press the **spacebar** again to reveal the next bulleted item. As this item appears, the previous item dims. Dimming the previous bulleted items helps focus the audience's attention on the current bulleted item.
7. Press the **spacebar** again to cause the last bulleted item to dim.

So far, you've seen important PowerPoint features: slide transitions, progressive disclosure, animations, and graphics (photos and drawings). Now you'll finish the presentation and see custom animations and simple drawings.

To continue viewing the slide show:

1. Press the **spacebar** to go to Slide 5, and then press the **spacebar** again. The label "Fuel chamber" and its accompanying arrow appear gradually on the screen. This is another example of an animation.
2. Press the **spacebar** three more times, pausing between each to allow the label and arrow to appear gradually on the screen.
3. Press the **spacebar** once more. A graphic labeled "smoke" comes into view, and you hear the sound of wind (or a breeze). The smoke object is an example of a user-drawn graphic.
4. Press the **spacebar** again to animate the smoke graphic and repeat the sound effect. The smoke graphic travels from the fuel chamber up the stovepipe.
5. Go to **Slide 6**. The graphic on this slide is a simple diagram drawn using drawing tools on the Drawing toolbar, which include not only shapes like circles, ovals, squares, and rectangles, but also arrows, boxes, stars, and banners.
6. Continue moving through the slide show, looking at all the slides and pausing at each one to read the bulleted items and view the graphics, until you reach Slide 11, the last slide in the slide show.
7. Press the **spacebar** to move from Slide 11. A black, nearly blank, screen appears. This signals that the slide show is over, as indicated by the line of text on the screen.
8. Press the **spacebar** one more time to return to the view from which you started the slide show, in this case, Normal view.
9. Close the current presentation by clicking the **Close Window** button ☒ on the menu bar, and then click the **No** button when asked if you want to save changes.

As you can see from this slide show, PowerPoint has many powerful features. You'll learn how to use many of these features in your own presentations as you work through these tutorials.

You're now ready to create Miriam's presentation on general information about Global Humanitarian's current projects. Before you begin, however, you need to plan the presentation.

Planning a Presentation

Planning a presentation before you create it improves the quality of your presentation, makes your presentation more effective and enjoyable, and, in the long run, saves you time and effort. As you plan your presentation, you should answer several questions: What is my purpose or objective for this presentation? What type of presentation is needed? Who is the audience? What information does that audience need? What is the physical location of my presentation? What is the best format for presenting the information contained in this presentation, given its location?

In planning your presentation, you should determine the following aspects:

- **Purpose of the presentation**: to provide general information about Global Humanitarian
- **Type of presentation**: training (how to become involved with Global Humanitarian)
- **Audience for the presentation**: potential donors, potential participants in humanitarian expeditions, and potential student interns
- **Audience needs**: to understand Global Humanitarian's mission and how to join the effort
- **Location of the presentation**: small conference rooms to large classrooms
- **Format**: oral presentation accompanied by an electronic slide show of 10 to 12 slides

You have carefully planned your presentation. Now you'll use the PowerPoint AutoContent Wizard to create it.

Using the AutoContent Wizard

PowerPoint helps you quickly create effective presentations by using a wizard, a special window that asks you a series of questions about your tasks, and then helps you perform them. The AutoContent Wizard lets you choose a presentation category, such as "Training," "Recommending a Strategy," "Brainstorming Session," or "Selling a Product or Service." After you select the type of presentation you want, the AutoContent Wizard creates a general outline for you to follow and formats the slides using a built-in design template and predesigned layouts. A **design template** is a file that contains the colors and format of the background and the font style of the titles, accents, and other text. Once you start creating a presentation with a given design template, you can change to any other PowerPoint design template or create a custom design template. A **layout** is a predetermined way of organizing the objects on a slide. You can change the layout applied to a slide or you can customize the layout of objects on a screen by moving the objects.

In this tutorial, you'll use the AutoContent Wizard to create a presentation with the goal of training employees, volunteers, and prospective donors on Global Humanitarian's mission. Because "Training" is predefined, you'll use the AutoContent Wizard, which will automatically create a title slide and standard outline that you can then edit to fit Miriam's needs.

To create the presentation with the AutoContent Wizard:

1. Click **File** on the menu bar, and then click **New**. The New Presentation task pane opens on the right side of the PowerPoint window.
2. Click the **From AutoContent wizard** link in the New Presentation task pane. The first dialog box of the AutoContent Wizard opens on top of the PowerPoint program window. The green square on the left side of the window indicates where you are in the wizard.
3. Read the information in the Start dialog box of the AutoContent Wizard, and then click the **Next** button. The next dialog box in the AutoContent Wizard appears. Note that the green square on the left side of the dialog box moved from Start to Presentation type. The Presentation type dialog box allows you to select the type of presentation you want.

4. Click the **General** button, if necessary, and then click **Training**. See Figure 1-4.

Figure 1-4 **Selecting the type of presentation in the AutoContent Wizard**

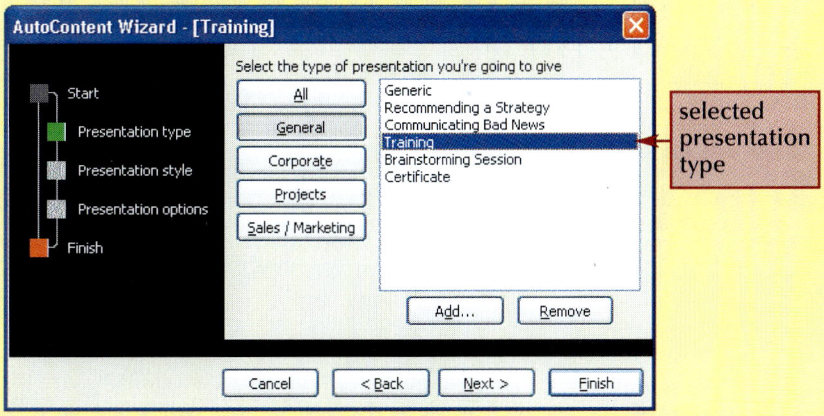

5. Click the **Next** button. The Presentation style dialog box opens with the question, "What type of output will you use?" You could also change this option after you create the presentation. As noted in your plan, you want to create an on-screen presentation.

   Trouble? If a dialog box opens telling you that PowerPoint can't display the template used in this document because the feature is not currently installed, you must install the Training template before continuing. If you are working on your own computer, click the Yes button. If you are working in a lab, ask your instructor or technical support person for help.

6. Click the **On-screen presentation** option button to select it, if necessary, and then click the **Next** button. The Presentation options dialog box opens. In this dialog box, you specify the title and footer (if any) of the presentation.

7. Click in the **Presentation title** text box, type **Global Humanitarian**, press the **Tab** key to move the insertion point to the **Footer** text box, and then type **Overview of Global Humanitarian**.

   The title will appear on the title slide (the first slide) of the presentation. The footer will appear on every slide (except the title slide) in the presentation. If the other two options are checked, they will appear on either side of the footer on the presentation slides.

8. Click the **Date last updated** check box to clear it, and leave the **Slide number** check box checked. You don't want to clutter the screen with information that is not pertinent for the audience. See Figure 1-5.

Figure 1-5 **Selecting information in the AutoContent Wizard**

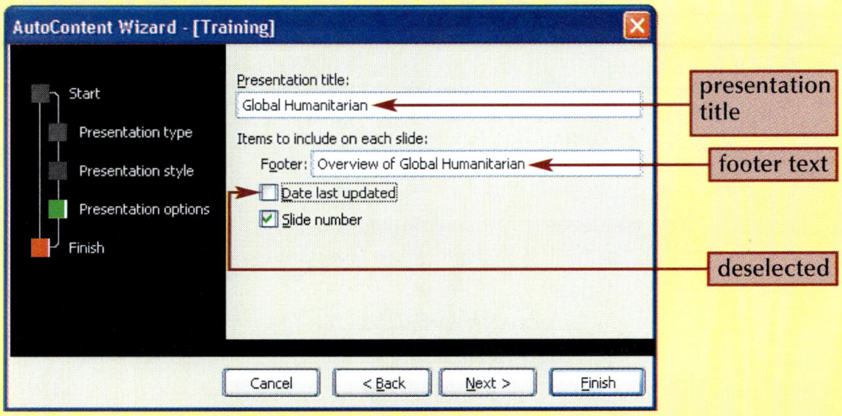

9. Click the **Next** button. The Finish dialog box opens, letting you know that you completed the questions for the AutoContent Wizard.
10. Click the **Finish** button. PowerPoint displays the AutoContent outline in the Outline tab and the title slide (Slide 1) in the slide pane. The filename in the title bar "Presentation" followed by a number is a temporary filename. See Figure 1-6.

Figure 1-6 **Outline and slide after completing the AutoContent Wizard**

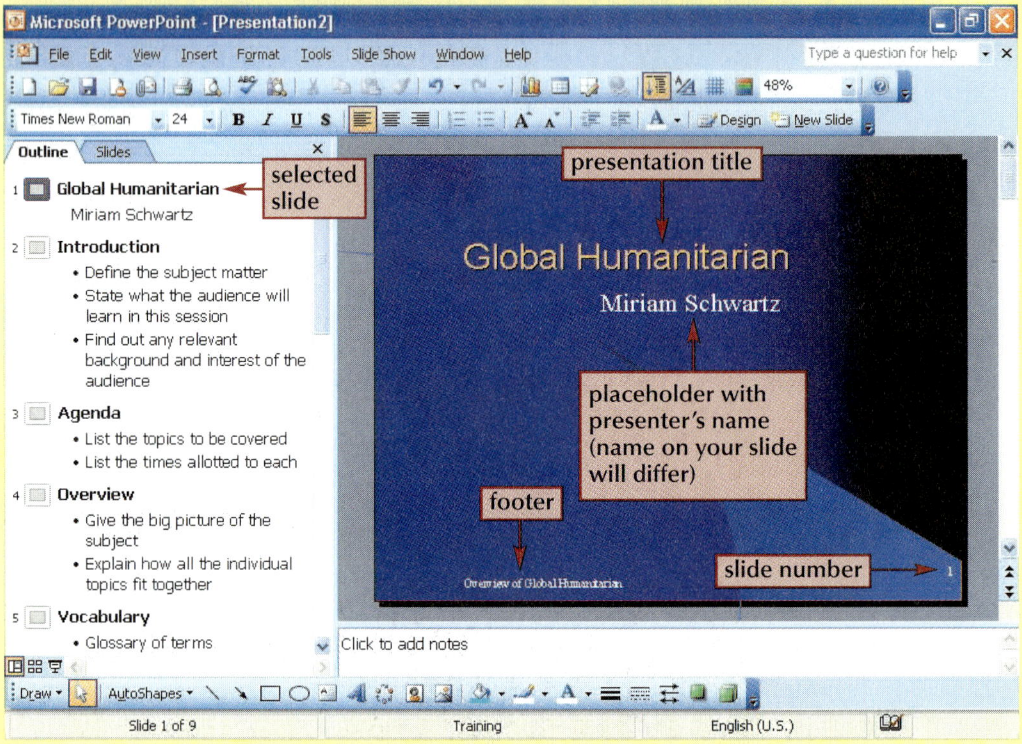

The AutoContent Wizard automatically displays the presenter's name (actually the name of the registered PowerPoint user) below the title in Slide 1. The name that appears on your screen will be different from the one shown in Figure 1-6.

Next, you'll save and name the presentation you created.

To save and name the presentation:

1. Click the **Save** button on the Standard toolbar. The Save As dialog box opens.
2. Click the **Save in** list arrow, and then navigate to the **Tutorial.01\Tutorial** folder included with your Data Files, if necessary.
3. Click immediately after Global Humanitarian, the default filename, in the **File name** text box, press the **spacebar**, type **Overview**, and then click the **Save** button. PowerPoint saves the presentation as Global Humanitarian Overview and displays that name in the title bar of the PowerPoint window.

In the next session, you'll edit the text of Miriam's presentation, as well as create notes.

Session 1.1 Quick Check

Review

1. Describe the components of a PowerPoint presentation.
2. Name and describe the two panes and two tabs in the PowerPoint window in Normal view.
3. Define or describe the following:
   a. progressive disclosure
   b. slide transition
   c. design template
   d. layout
4. What are some of the questions that you should answer when planning a presentation?
5. Describe the purpose of the AutoContent Wizard.
6. Describe Slide Show view.

Session 1.2

Modifying a Presentation

Now that you've used the AutoContent Wizard, you're ready to edit some of the words in the presentation to fit Miriam's specific needs. You'll keep the design template, which includes the blue background and the size and color of the text, used by the AutoContent Wizard.

The AutoContent Wizard automatically creates the title slide, as well as other slides, with suggested text located in placeholders. A **placeholder** is a region of a slide, or a location in an outline, reserved for inserting text or graphics. To edit the AutoContent outline to fit Miriam's needs, you must select the placeholders one at a time, and then replace them with other text. Text placeholders are a special kind of **text box**, which is a container for text. You can edit and format text in a text box, or you can manipulate the text box as a whole. When you manipulate the text box as a whole, the text box is treated as an **object**, something that can be manipulated or resized as a unit.

When text is selected, the text box is active and appears as hatched lines around the selected text with sizing handles (small circles) at each corner and on each side of the box. You drag **sizing handles** to make a text box or other object larger or smaller on the slide. When the entire text box is selected as a single object, the text box appears as a dotted outline with sizing handles.

Many of the slides that the AutoContent Wizard created in your presentation for Global Humanitarian contain bulleted lists. A **bulleted list** is a list of paragraphs with a special character (dot, circle, box, star, or other character) to the left of each paragraph. A **bulleted item** is one paragraph in a bulleted list. Bullets can appear at different outline levels. A **first-level bullet** is a main paragraph in a bulleted list; a **second-level bullet**—sometimes called a **sub-bullet**—is a bullet beneath (and indented from) a first-level bullet. Using bulleted lists reminds both the speaker and the audience of the main points of the presentation. In addition to bulleted lists, PowerPoint also supports numbered lists. A **numbered list** is a list of paragraphs that are numbered consecutively within the body text.

When you edit the text on the slides, keep in mind that the bulleted lists aren't meant to be the complete presentation; instead, they should emphasize the key points to the audience and remind the speaker of the points to emphasize. In all your presentations, you should follow the 6 × 6 rule as much as possible: Keep each bulleted item to no more than six words, and don't include more than six bulleted items on a slide.

Reference Window

Creating Effective Text Presentations

- Think of your text presentation as a visual map of your oral presentation. Show your organization by using overviews, making headings larger than subheadings, including bulleted lists to highlight key points, and numbering steps to show sequences.
- Follow the 6 × 6 rule: Use six or fewer items per screen, and use phrases of six or fewer words. Omit unnecessary articles, pronouns, and adjectives.
- Keep phrases parallel.
- Make sure your text is appropriate for your purpose and audience.

Miriam reviewed your plans for your presentation and she has several suggestions for improvement. First, she wants you to replace the text that the AutoContent Wizard inserted with information about Global Humanitarian. She also wants you to delete unnecessary slides, and change the order of the slides in the presentation. You'll start by editing the text on the slides.

Editing Slides

Most of the slides in the presentation contain two placeholder text boxes. The slide **title text** is a text box at the top of the slide that gives the title of the information on that slide; the slide **body text** (also called the **main text**) is a large text box in which you type a bulleted or numbered list. In this presentation, you'll modify or create title text and body text in all but the title slide (Slide 1).

To edit the AutoContent outline to fit Miriam's needs, you must select text in each of the placeholders, and then replace that text with other text. You'll now begin to edit and replace the text to fit Miriam's presentation. The first text you'll change is the presenter's name placeholder.

To edit and replace text in the first slide:

1. If you took a break after the previous session, make sure PowerPoint is running, and then open the presentation **Global Humanitarian Overview** located in the Tutorial.01\Tutorial folder included with your Data Files. Slide 1 appears in the slide pane and the Outline tab is on top.
2. Position the pointer over the presenter's name (currently the registered PowerPoint user's name) in the slide pane so that the pointer changes to I, and then drag it across the text of the presenter's name to select the text. The text box becomes active, as indicated by the hatched lines around the box and the sizing handles at each corner and on each side of the text box, and the text becomes highlighted.
3. Type your first and last name (so your instructor can identify you as the author of this presentation), and then click anywhere else on the slide. As soon as you start to type, the selected text disappears, and the typed text appears in its place. (The figures in this book will show the name Miriam Schwartz.)

   Trouble? If PowerPoint marks your name with a red wavy underline, this indicates that the word is not found in the PowerPoint dictionary. Ignore the wavy line for now, because spelling will be covered later.

You'll now edit Slides 2 through 9 by replacing the placeholder text and adding new text, and by deleting slides that don't apply to your presentation.

To edit the text in the slides:

1. Click the **Next Slide** button at the bottom of the vertical scroll bar in the slide pane. Slide 2 appears in the slide pane.
2. Drag across the word **Introduction** (the title text) to select it. See Figure 1-7.

Figure 1-7 **Selecting title text**

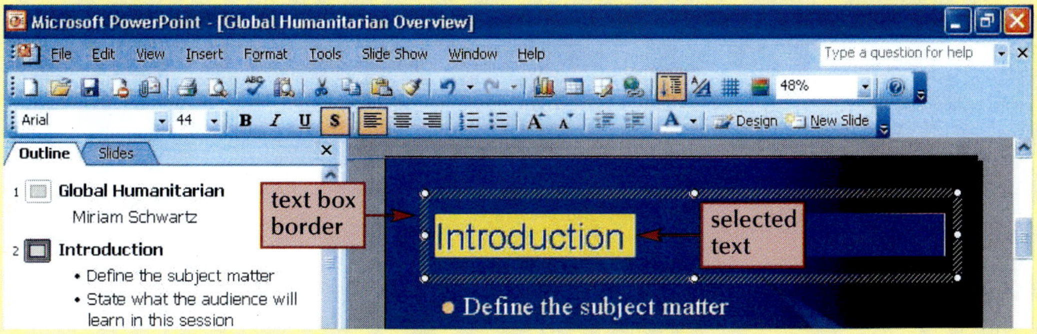

Now you're ready to type the desired title. As you perform the next step, notice not only that the words you type replace the selected text in the slide pane, but also that the slide title on the Outline tab changes.

3. Type **Are You Rich?** and then click in a blank space in the slide pane, just outside the edge of the slide, to deselect the text box. The hatched lines and sizing handles disappear. Notice that the slide title changed on the Outline tab as well.

Trouble? If you clicked somewhere on the slide and selected another item, such as the bulleted list, click another place, preferably just outside the edge of the text box, to deselect all items.

Now you're going to edit the text from the Outline tab.

4. In the Outline tab, select the text **Define the subject matter**. The text is highlighted by changing to white on black.
5. Type **Home has non-dirt floor: top 50%**. Don't include a period at the end of the phrase. This bulleted item is an incomplete sentence, short for "If you live in a home with a non-dirt floor, you're in the top 50% of the wealthiest people on earth."
6. Select the text of the second bulleted item in either the Outline tab or the slide pane, and then type **Home has more than one room: top 20%**. Again, don't include a period.
7. Select the text of the third bulleted item in the slide pane, and then type **Own more than one pair of shoes: top 5%**.

With the insertion point at the end of the third bulleted item, you're ready to create additional bulleted items.

To create additional bulleted items:

1. With the insertion point blinking at the end of the last bulleted item, press the **Enter** key. PowerPoint creates a new bullet and leaves the insertion point to the right of the indent after the bullet, waiting for you to type the text.
2. Type **Own a refrigerator: top 3%** and then press the **Enter** key.
3. Type **Own a car, computer, microwave, or VCR: top 1%**.

4. Click in a blank area of the slide pane to deselect the bulleted list text box. The completed Slide 2 should look like Figure 1-8.

Figure 1-8 **Slide 2 after adding text**

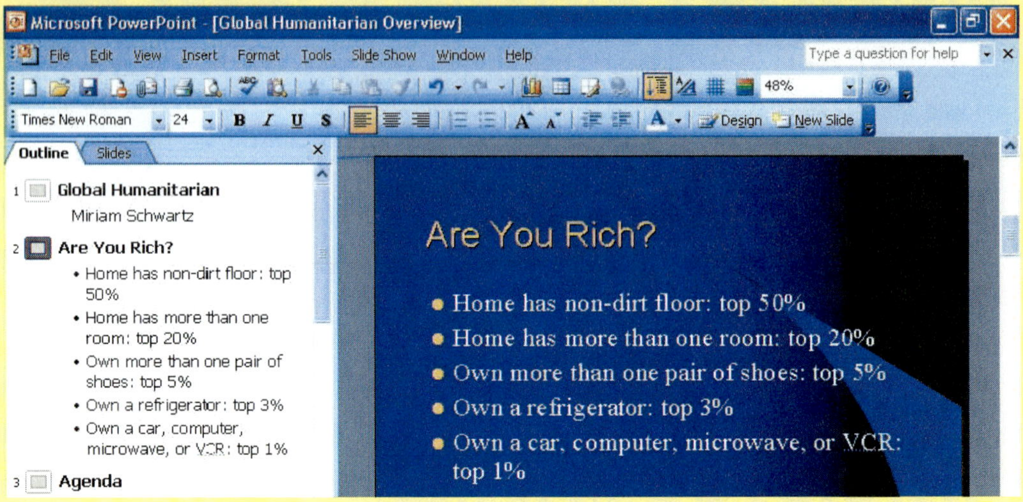

You're now ready to edit the text on another slide and create sub-bullets.

To create sub-bullets:

1. Click the **Next Slide** button at the bottom of the vertical scroll bar four times to move to Slide 6. Slide 6 appears in the slide pane and on the Outline tab.
2. Select the title text **Topic One**, and then type **How You Can Help**.
3. Select all the text in the body text placeholder, not just the text of the first bulleted item.
4. Type **Become a member of Global Humanitarian**, press the **Enter** key, and then type **Contribute to humanitarian projects**. You've added two bulleted items to the body text.

   Now you'll add some sub-bullets beneath the first-level bulleted item.
5. Press the **Enter** key to insert a new bullet, and then press the **Tab** key. The new bullet changes to a sub-bullet. In this design template, sub-bullets have a dash in front of them, which you won't be able to see until you start typing the text.
6. Type **Health and Education**, and then press the **Enter** key. The new bullet is a second-level bullet, the same level as the previous bullet.
7. Type **Water and Environment**, press the **Enter** key, type **Income Generation and Agriculture**, press the **Enter** key, and then type **Leadership and Cultural Enhancement**.

   Now you want the next bullet to return to the first level.
8. Press the **Enter** key to create a new, second-level bullet, and then click the **Decrease Indent** button on the Formatting toolbar. The bullet is converted to a first-level bullet. You can also press the Shift+Tab key combination to move a bullet up a level.
9. Type the remaining two first-level bulleted items: **Join a humanitarian expedition** and **Become a student intern**, and then click in a blank area of the slide to deselect the text box. See Figure 1-9.

Slide 6 after adding text

Figure 1-9

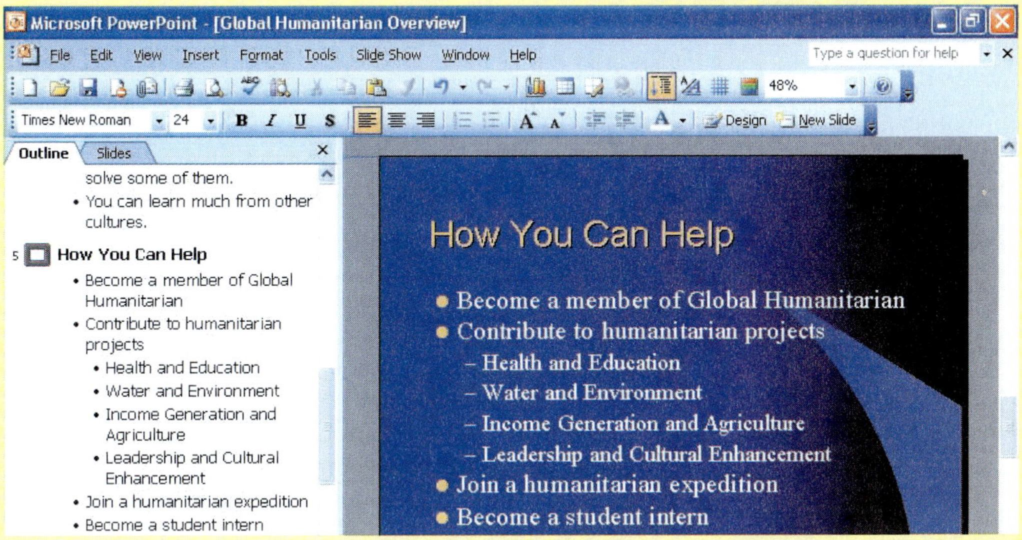

You have completed editing Slide 6. Miriam suggests that you delete the previous three slides, which are unnecessary for your presentation, before you edit the other slides.

Deleting Slides

When creating a presentation, you'll often delete slides. The AutoContent Wizard may create slides that you don't think are necessary, or you may create slides that you no longer want. You can delete slides in several ways: in Normal view, by clicking the slide thumbnail in the Slides tab or by clicking the slide icon in the Outline tab to select the slide, and then pressing the Delete key or using the Delete command on the shortcut or Edit menu; or in Slide Sorter view, by selecting the slide and then pressing the Delete key. Keep in mind that once you delete a slide, you can recover it by immediately clicking the Undo button on the Standard toolbar.

You need to delete Slide 3 ("Agenda"), Slide 4 ("Overview"), and Slide 5 ("Vocabulary").

To delete Slides 3 through 5:

1. With Slide 6 in the slide pane, click the **slide icon** next to Slide 3 ("Agenda") on the Outline tab. You might need to drag the Outline pane scroll box up to view Slide 3. This causes Slide 3 to appear in the slide pane. Now you're ready to delete the slide.
2. Right-click the Slide 3 ("Agenda") **slide icon** on the Outline tab, and then click **Delete Slide** on the shortcut menu. The entire slide is deleted from the presentation, and the rest of the slides are renumbered so that the slide that was Slide 4 becomes Slide 3, and so on. The renumbered Slide 3 ("Overview") appears in the slide pane.
3. Click the **Slides** tab. The Outline tab disappears and the Slides tab appears with thumbnails of all of the slides. With the Slides tab on top, notice that the labels identifying the Slides and Outline tabs change to icons.
4. With **Slide 3** ("Overview") selected in the Slides tab, press and hold the **Shift** key, and then click **Slide 4** on the Slides tab. Slides 3 and 4 are both selected on the Slides tab.
5. Click **Edit** on the menu bar, and then click **Delete Slide**. Both slides are deleted from the presentation. The new Slide 3, entitled "How You Can Help," now appears in the slide pane.

   Trouble? If the Delete Slide command is not on the Edit menu, click the double arrow at the bottom of the menu to display all of the commands on the menu.

Now you'll finish editing the presentation and save your work.

To edit and save the presentation:

1. Go to **Slide 4** ("Topic Two"), and then edit the title text to read **Benefits of Joining Global Humanitarian**. Notice that as you type the last word, PowerPoint automatically adjusts the size of the text to fit in the title text box.

   Trouble? If the font size of the text doesn't automatically adjust so that the text fits within the body text placeholder, click the AutoFit Options button that appears in the slide pane, and then click the AutoFit Text to Placeholder option.

2. Select all the body text, not just the text of the first bulleted item, in the body text placeholder, and then type the bulleted items shown in Figure 1-10.

Figure 1-10 Completed Slide 4

3. Go to **Slide 5**, and then modify the title and body text so that the slide looks like Figure 1-11.

Figure 1-11 Completed Slide 5

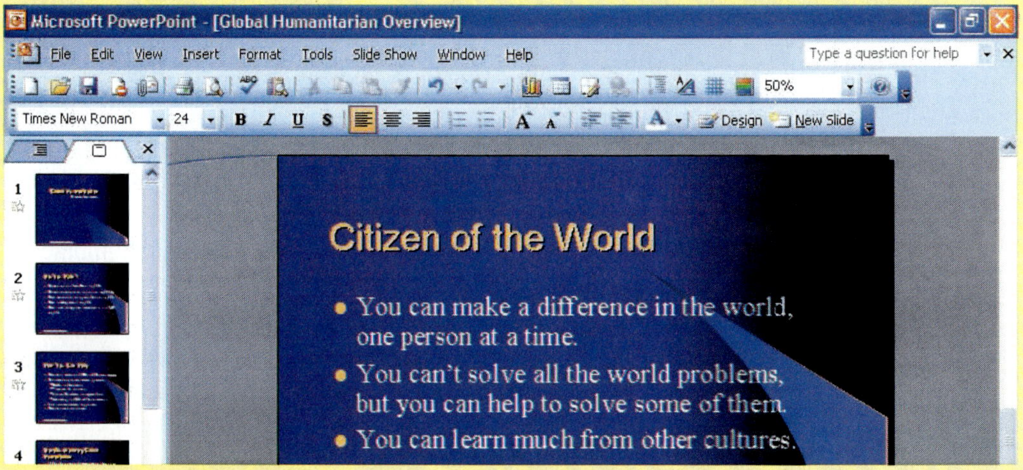

4. Delete **Slide 6** ("Where to Get More Information").
5. Click the **Save** button on the Standard toolbar to save the presentation.

Miriam reviews your presentation and wants you to add a slide at the end of the presentation stating what action you want your readers to take as a result of your presentation.

Adding a New Slide and Choosing a Layout

Miriam suggests that you add a new slide at the end of the presentation explaining how individuals and families can join Global Humanitarian. When you add a new slide, PowerPoint formats the slide using a slide layout. PowerPoint supports four **text layouts**: Title Slide (placeholders for a title and a subtitle, usually used as the first slide in a presentation); Title Only (a title placeholder but not a body text placeholder); Title and Text (the default slide layout, with a title and a body text placeholder); and Title and 2-Column Text (same as Title and Text, but with two columns for text). PowerPoint also supports several **content layouts**—slide layouts that contain from zero to four charts, diagrams, images, tables, or movie clips. In addition, PowerPoint supports combination layouts, called **text and content layouts**, and several other types of layouts.

When you insert a new slide, it appears after the current one, and the Slide Layout task pane appears with a default layout already selected. This default layout is applied to the new slide. To use a different layout, you click it in the Slide Layout task pane.

To insert the new slide at the end of the presentation:

1. Because you want to add a slide after Slide 5, make sure Slide 5 is still in the slide pane.
2. Click the **New Slide** button on the Formatting toolbar. The Slide Layout task pane opens with the first layout in the second row under Text Layouts selected as the default, and a new Slide 6 appears in the slide pane with the default layout applied. See Figure 1-12.

New slide added **Figure 1-12**

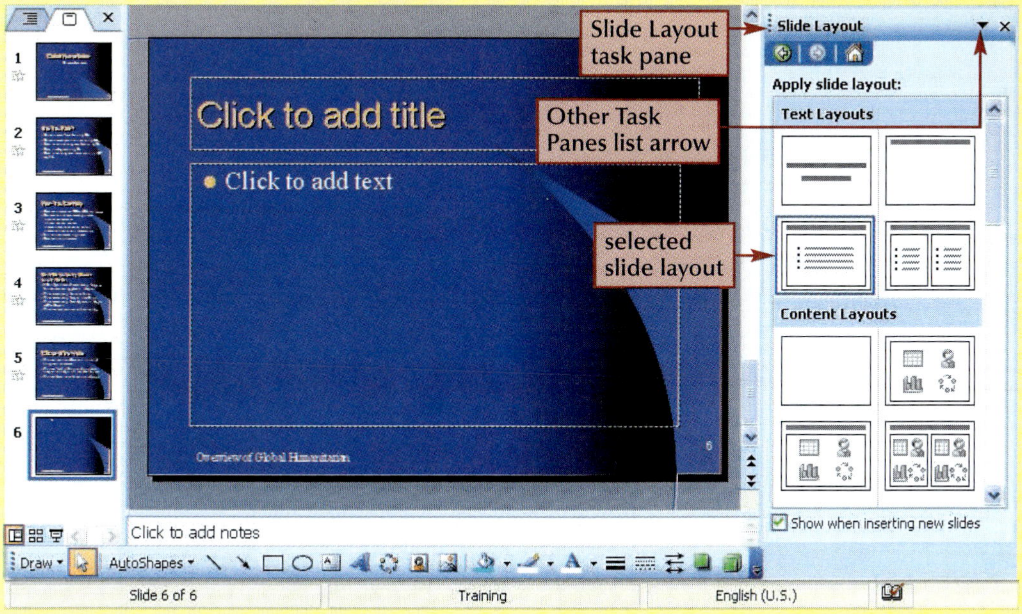

You'll accept the default layout for this slide. If you wanted a different layout, you would click the desired layout in the Slide Layout task pane.

Trouble? If the Slide Layout task pane does not appear, click View on the menu bar, click Task Pane, click the Other Task Panes list arrow at the top of the task pane, and then click Slide Layout. To make the Slide Layout task pane open automatically when you insert a new slide, click the Show when inserting new slides check box at the bottom of the task pane.

3. Position the pointer over the selected layout in the task pane. A ScreenTip appears, identifying this layout as the Title and Text layout.

   Next you'll close the Slide Layout task pane to provide a larger view of the slide pane.

4. Click the **Close** button [X] in the Slide Layout task pane title bar to close the task pane.

   Trouble? If you accidentally click the Close button of the PowerPoint window or Presentation window, PowerPoint will ask you if you want to save the changes to your presentation. Click the Cancel button so that the presentation doesn't close, and then click the correct Close button on the task pane title bar.

The new slide contains text placeholders. On a new slide, you don't need to select the text on the slide to replace it with your text. You only need to click in the placeholder text box; the placeholder text will disappear and the insertion point will be placed in the text box, ready for you to type your text. Once you type your text, the dotted line outlining the edge of the text box will disappear. You'll add text to the new slide.

To add text to the new slide:

1. Click anywhere in the title text placeholder in the slide pane, where it says "Click to add title." The title placeholder text disappears and the insertion point blinks at the left of the title text box.
2. Type **Global Humanitarian Memmbership**. Make sure you type "Memmbership" with two *m*s in the middle. You'll correct this misspelling later. Again, the font size decreases to fit the text within the title placeholder.
3. Click anywhere in the body text placeholder. The placeholder text disappears and the insertion point appears just to the right of the first bullet.
4. Type **Individual membership: $75 per year**, press the **Enter** key, type **Family membership: $150 per year**, press the **Enter** key, type **Visit our Web site at www.globalhumanitarian.org**, and then press the **Enter** key.

   When you press the Enter key after typing the Web site address, PowerPoint automatically changes the Web site address (the URL) to a link. It formats the link by changing its color and underlining it. When you run the slide show, you can click this link to jump to that Web site if you are connected to the Internet.

5. Type **Call Sam Matagi, Volunteer Coordinator, at 523-555-SERV**.

You have inserted a new slide at the end of the presentation and added text to the slide. Next you'll create a new slide by promoting text in the Outline tab.

Promoting, Demoting, and Moving Outline Text

You can modify the text of a slide in the Outline tab as well as in the slide pane. Working in the Outline tab gives you more flexibility because you can see the outline of the entire presentation, not only the single slide currently in the slide pane. Working in the Outline tab allows you to easily move text from one slide to another or to create a new slide by promoting bulleted items from a slide so that they become the title and body text on a new slide.

To **promote** an item means to increase the outline level of that item—for example, to change a bulleted item into a slide title or to change a second-level bullet into a first-level bullet. To **demote** an item means to decrease the outline level—for example, to change a slide title into a bulleted item on the previous slide or to change a first-level bullet into a second-level bullet. You'll begin by promoting a bulleted item to a slide title, thus creating a new slide.

To create a new slide by promoting outline text:

1. Click the **Outline** tab. The outline of the presentation appears.
2. Drag the scroll box in the slide pane up until the ScreenTip displays "Slide: 3 of 6" and the title "How You Can Help." Slide 3 appears in the slide pane and the text of that slide appears at the top of the Outline tab.
3. In the Outline tab, move the pointer over the bullet to the left of "Contribute to humanitarian projects" so that the pointer becomes ✥, and then click the bullet. The text for that bullet and all its sub-bullets are selected.

   Now you'll promote the selected text so that it becomes the title text and first-level bullets on a new slide.
4. Click the **Decrease Indent** button on the Formatting toolbar. PowerPoint promotes the selected text one level. Because the bullet you selected was a first-level bullet, the first-level bullet is promoted to a slide title on a new Slide 4, and the second-level bullets become first-level bullets on the new slide. See Figure 1-13.

Figure 1-13 **Promoting a bulleted item to become a new slide**

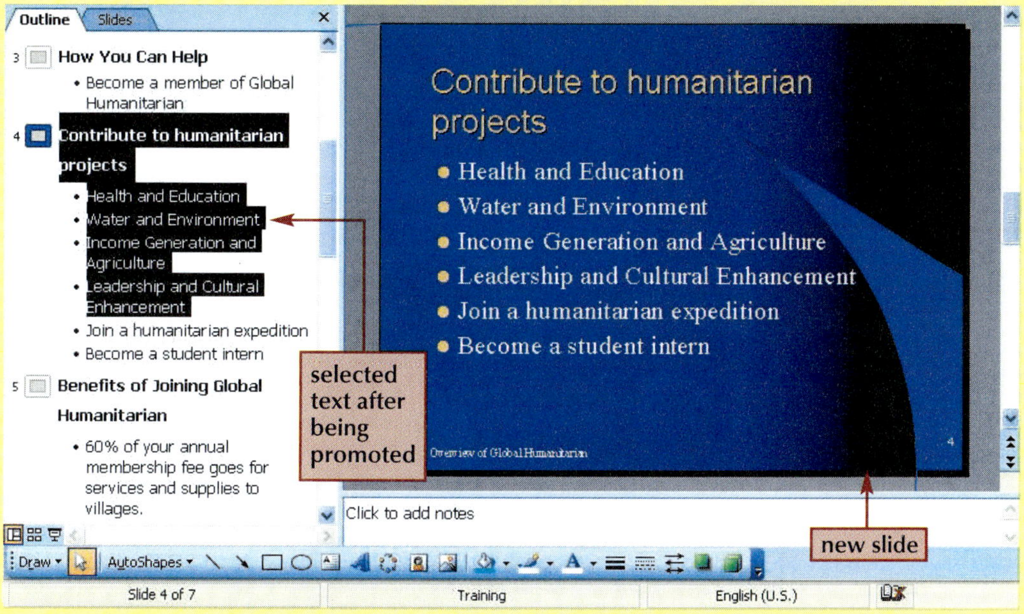

Now you'll edit this text, and then move some of the bulleted items to another slide.

5. Click anywhere to deselect the text, select the Slide 4 title text in the Outline tab, and then type **Types of Humanitarian Projects in Third-World Villages**. Notice that the title changes in the slide pane as well.

   Trouble? If all of the text on the slide becomes selected when you try to select the title text, make sure you position the pointer just to the left of the title text, and not over the slide icon, before you drag to select the text.

6. Click the bullet to the left of "Join a humanitarian expedition" (the fifth bullet in Slide 4) in the Outline tab, and then, while holding down the left mouse button, drag the bullet and its text up until the horizontal line position marker is just under the bulleted item "Become a member of Global Humanitarian" in Slide 3, as shown in Figure 1-14.

Figure 1-14 Moving text in the Outline tab

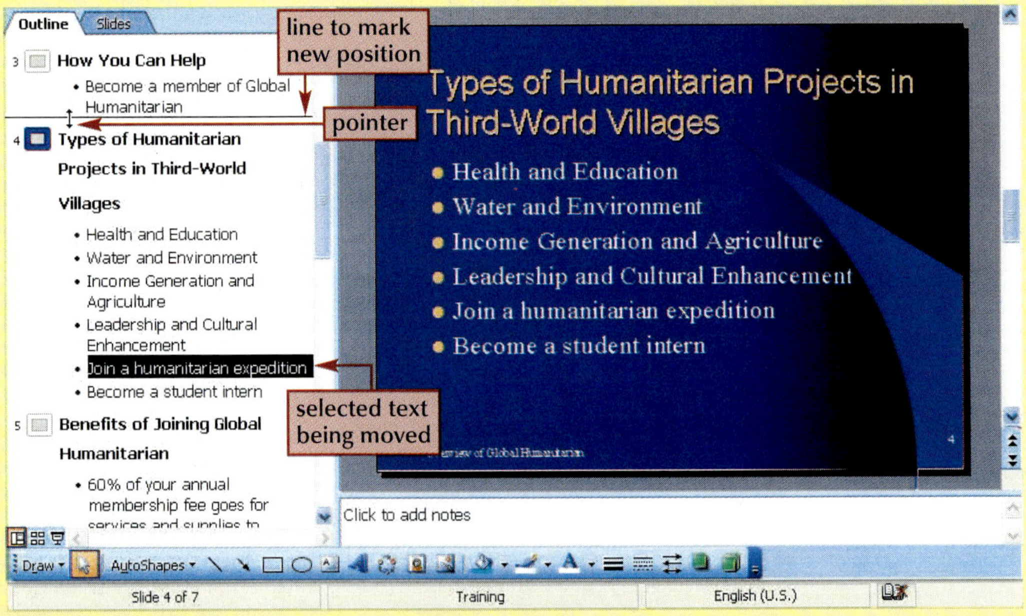

7. Release the mouse button. The bulleted item moves to the new position.
8. Using the same procedure, move the bulleted item "Become a student intern" from the end of Slide 4 to the end of Slide 3 in the Outline tab.

As you review your slides, you notice that in Slide 5, the phrase "Your membership fee" is repeated three times. You'll fix the problem by demoting some of the text.

To demote text on Slide 5:

1. Click the **slide icon** next to Slide 5 ("Benefits of Joining Global Humanitarian") in the Outline tab.
2. Click immediately to the right of "Your membership fee" in the second bulleted item in the Outline tab, and then press the **Enter** key. The item "saves lives" becomes a new bulleted item, but you want that item to appear indented at a lower outline level.
3. Press the **Tab** key to indent "saves lives," and then press the **Delete** key, if necessary, to delete any blank spaces to the left of "saves lives."

4. Click the bullet to the left of "Your membership fee prevents illness" in the Outline tab, press and hold down the **Shift** key, and then click the bullet to the left of "Your membership fee helps make villagers self-sufficient." This selects both bulleted items at the same time.
5. Click the **Increase Indent** button on the Formatting toolbar to demote the two bulleted items. Note this has the same effect as pressing the Tab key.
6. Delete the phrase "Your membership fee" and the space after it from the two items that you just demoted. Your slide should now look like Figure 1-15.

Slide 5 after demoting text to sub-bullets **Figure 1-15**

Miriam looks at your presentation and suggests that you move the current Slide 4 ahead of Slide 3. You could make this change by clicking the slide icon and dragging it above the slide icon for Slide 3 in the Outline tab. Instead, you'll move the slide in Slide Sorter view.

Moving Slides in Slide Sorter View

In Slide Sorter view, PowerPoint displays all the slides as thumbnails, so that several slides can appear on the screen at once. This view not only provides you with a good overview of your presentation, but also allows you to easily change the order of the slides and modify the slides in other ways.

To move Slide 4:

1. Click the **Slide Sorter View** button at the bottom of the Outline tab. You now see your presentation in Slide Sorter view.
2. Click **Slide 4**. A thick colored frame appears around the slide, indicating that the slide is selected.
3. Press and hold down the left mouse button, drag the slide to the left so that the vertical line position marker appears on the left side of Slide 3, as shown in Figure 1-16.

Figure 1-16 Moving a slide in Slide Sorter view

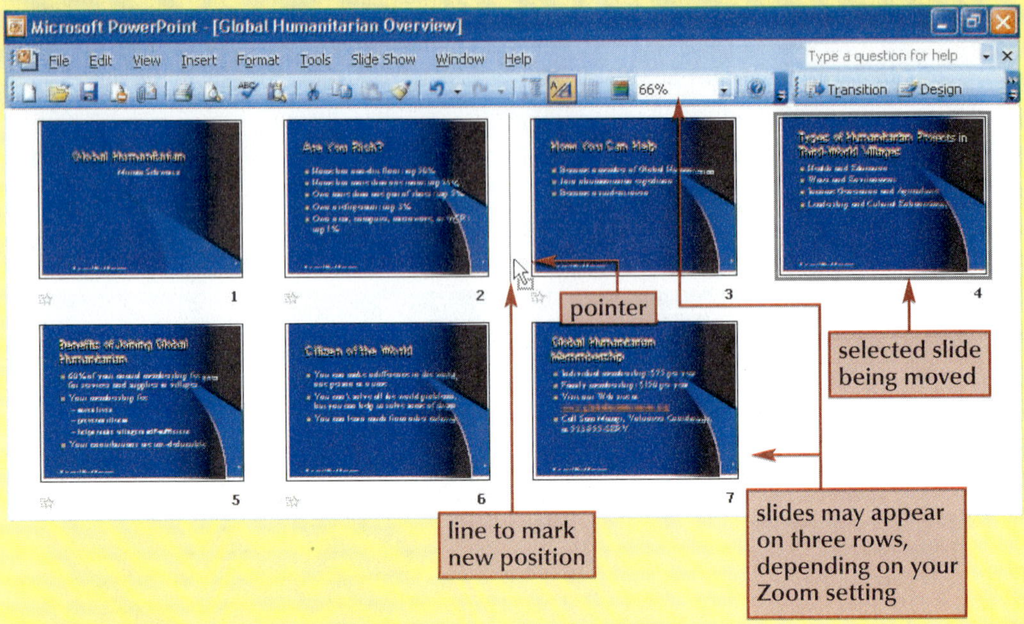

4. Release the mouse button. Slides 3 and 4 have switched places.
5. Click the **Normal View** button to return to Normal view.

Miriam is pleased with how you have edited your presentation slides. Your next task is to check the spelling and style of the text in your presentation.

Checking the Spelling and Style in a Presentation

Before you print or present a slide show, you should always perform a final check of the spelling and style of all the slides in your presentation. This will help to ensure that your presentation is accurate and professional looking.

Checking the Spelling

If PowerPoint finds a word that's not in its dictionary, the word is underlined with a red wavy line in the slide pane. When you right-click the word, suggestions for alternate spellings appear on the shortcut menu, as well as commands for ignoring the misspelled word or opening the Spelling dialog box. You can also click the Spelling button on the Standard toolbar to check the spelling in the entire presentation.

You need to check the spelling in the Global Humanitarian presentation.

To check the spelling in the presentation:

1. Go to **Slide 7**. The spelling check always starts from the current slide.
2. Click the **Spelling** button on the Standard toolbar. The Spelling dialog box opens. The word you purposely mistyped earlier, "Memmbership," is highlighted in the Outline tab and listed in the Not in Dictionary text box in the Spelling dialog box. Two suggested spellings appear in the Suggestions list box, and the selected word in the Suggestions list box appears in the Change to text box.

3. With "Membership" selected in the Suggestions list box and in the Change to text box, click the **Change** button. If you knew that you misspelled that word throughout your presentation, you could click the Change All button to change all of the instances of the misspelling in the presentation to the corrected spelling.

   The word is corrected, and the next word in the presentation that is not in the PowerPoint dictionary, Matagi, is flagged. This word is not misspelled; it is a surname.

4. Click the **Ignore** button. The word is not changed on the slide. If you wanted to ignore all the instances of that word in the presentation, you could click the Ignore All button. A dialog box opens telling you that the spelling check is complete.

   Trouble? If another word in the presentation is flagged as misspelled, select the correct spelling in the Suggestions list, and then click the Change button. If your name on Slide 1 is flagged, click the Ignore button.

5. Click the **OK** button. The dialog box closes.

Next, you need to check the style in the presentation.

Using the Style Checker

The **Style Checker** checks your presentation for consistency in punctuation, capitalization, and visual elements and marks problems on a slide with a light bulb. For this feature to be active, you need to turn on the Style Checker.

To turn on the Style Checker:

1. Click **Tools** on the menu bar, click **Options** to open the Options dialog box, and then click the **Spelling and Style** tab.

2. Click the **Check style** check box to select it, if necessary. Now you'll check to make sure the necessary Style Checker options are selected.

   Trouble? If a message appears telling you that the Style Checker needs to use the Office Assistant, click the Enable Assistant button. If another message appears telling you that PowerPoint can't display the Office Assistant because the feature is not installed, click the Yes button only if you are working on your own computer. If you are in a lab, ask your instructor or technical support person for assistance.

3. Click the **Style Options** button in the Options dialog box, click the **Slide title style** check box to select it, if necessary, click the list arrow to the right of this option, and then click **UPPERCASE**. When you run the Style Checker, it will suggest changing all of the titles to all uppercase.

4. Click the **Body text style** check box to select it, if necessary, click the list arrow to the right of this option, and then click **Sentence case**, if necessary. When you run the Style Checker, it will check to make sure that the text in each bullet in the body text has an uppercase letter as the first letter, and that the rest of the words in the body text start with a lowercase letter.

5. Click the bottom two check boxes under End punctuation to clear them, if necessary. Some of the bulleted lists in this presentation are complete sentences and some are not, so you want PowerPoint to allow variation in the end punctuation. See Figure 1-17.

Figure 1-17 Style Options dialog box

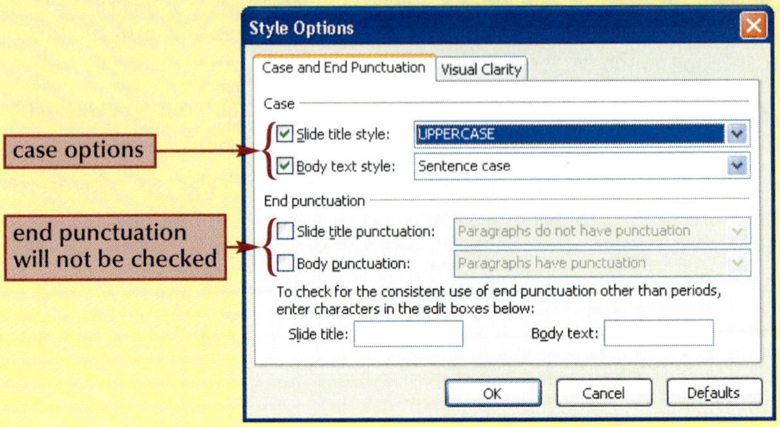

6. Click the **OK** button to close the Style Options dialog box, and then click the **OK** button to close the Options dialog box.

From now on, PowerPoint will check the style in your presentation as you display each slide in the slide pane. Now you'll go through your presentation and check for style problems.

To fix problems marked by the Style Checker:

1. Go to **Slide 1**. A light bulb appears next to the title. This indicates that the Style Checker found a problem with the slide title. Since you did not type any of the titles in all uppercase letters, a light bulb will appear on every slide marking the titles as not matching the style.
2. Click the **light bulb**. The Office Assistant appears and displays a dialog box with a description of the problem and three options from which you can choose. See Figure 1-18.

Figure 1-18 Using the Style Checker

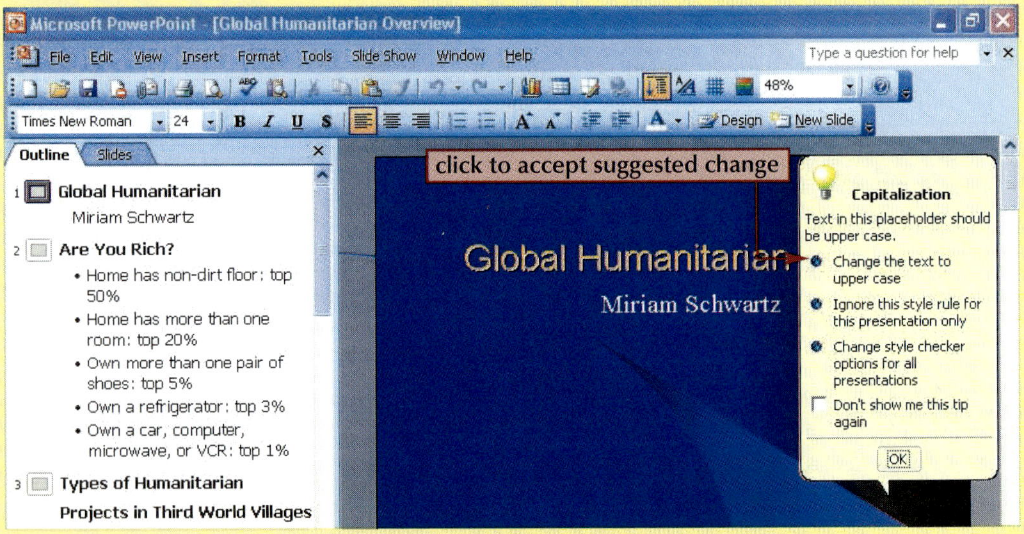

Trouble? If a message appears telling you that PowerPoint can't display the Office Assistant because the feature is not installed, click the Yes button only if you are working on your own computer. If you are in a lab, ask your instructor or technical support person for assistance.

3. Click the **Change the text to upper case** option button in the Office Assistant dialog box. All of the title text is now changed to uppercase.
4. Go to **Slide 2**.
5. Use the Style Checker to change the title text to uppercase.
6. Go to **Slide 3**, and then change the title text to uppercase. Another light bulb appears on Slide 3 next to the body text.

   Trouble? If, in this or subsequent steps, the light bulb doesn't appear by the body text, go to the next or the previous slide, and then return to the current slide as a way of telling the Style Checker to recheck the slide.
7. Click the **light bulb** to see that the error in the body text is another capitalization error, and then click the **Change the text to sentence case** option button in the Office Assistant dialog box. All the words in the bulleted items are converted to lowercase (except the first word in each bulleted item); that is, all the bulleted items are converted to sentence case.
8. Go to **Slide 4**, change the title text to uppercase, and then click the **light bulb** next to the body text. The Style Checker detects that the first bulleted item is in mixed case (the words "Global Humanitarian" are capitalized), but the organization's name should remain capitalized, so you don't need to make any changes here.
9. Click the **OK** button in the Office Assistant dialog box. PowerPoint ignores the style for that slide, and the light bulb no longer appears.
10. Correct the title and body text on Slide 5, and the title text on Slide 6, and then go to Slide 7.
11. Correct the title text on Slide 7, but do not correct the capitalization in the body text on Slide 7. The words that start with an uppercase letter in the body text on this slide are proper nouns or are part of the phone number. Now you need to turn off the Style Checker.
12. Click **Tools** on the menu bar, click **Options**, click the **Check style** check box on the Spelling and Style tab to clear it, and then click the **OK** button. The Style Checker is turned off.

As you create your own presentations, watch for the problems marked by the Style Checker. Of course, in some cases, you might want a certain capitalization that the Style Checker detects as an error. In these cases, just ignore the light bulb, or click it, and then click the OK button. The light bulb never appears on the screen during a slide show or when you print a presentation.

Using the Research Task Pane

PowerPoint enables you to use the Research task pane to search online services or Internet sites for additional help in creating a presentation. Using these resources helps you make your presentations more professional. For example, you could look up specific words in a thesaurus. A **thesaurus** contains a list of words and their synonyms, antonyms, and other related words. Using a thesaurus is a good way to add variety to the words you use or to choose more precise words. You could also look up information in online encyclopedias, news services, libraries, and business sites.

Miriam thinks the word "rich" in Slide 2 may be too informal. She asks you to find an appropriate replacement word. You'll now look for synonyms in the Office thesaurus.

To do research using the thesaurus:

1. Go to **Slide 2**, and then highlight the word **RICH** in either the Outline tab or the slide pane. Be careful not to highlight the question mark at the end of the phrase.
2. Click the **Research** button on the Standard toolbar. The Research task pane opens with the word "RICH" in the Search for text box.
3. Click the list arrow next to All Reference Books in the task pane, and then click **Thesaurus: English (U.S.)**.
4. Click the **green arrow** button next to the Search for text box to begin a search for synonyms for the word "rich," if necessary. The thesaurus provides several suggestions in a list organized so that the most relevant words are in bold, and additional synonyms are indented under the bold terms.
5. Scroll down, if necessary, to see the word "full" in boldface, and then click the **minus sign** button next to "full (adj.)." The minus sign changes to a plus sign, and the list of words under "full" collapses.

   After looking over the list, Miriam decides that "full" and "opulent" do not convey the correct meaning. She decides that "wealthy" is the most appropriate synonym.
6. Position the pointer over the word **wealthy**, indented under the bold term **wealthy (adj.)**. A box appears around the term and a list arrow appears at the right side of the box.
7. Click the list arrow on the side of the box, as shown in Figure 1-19.

Figure 1-19 Using the Thesaurus in the Research task pane

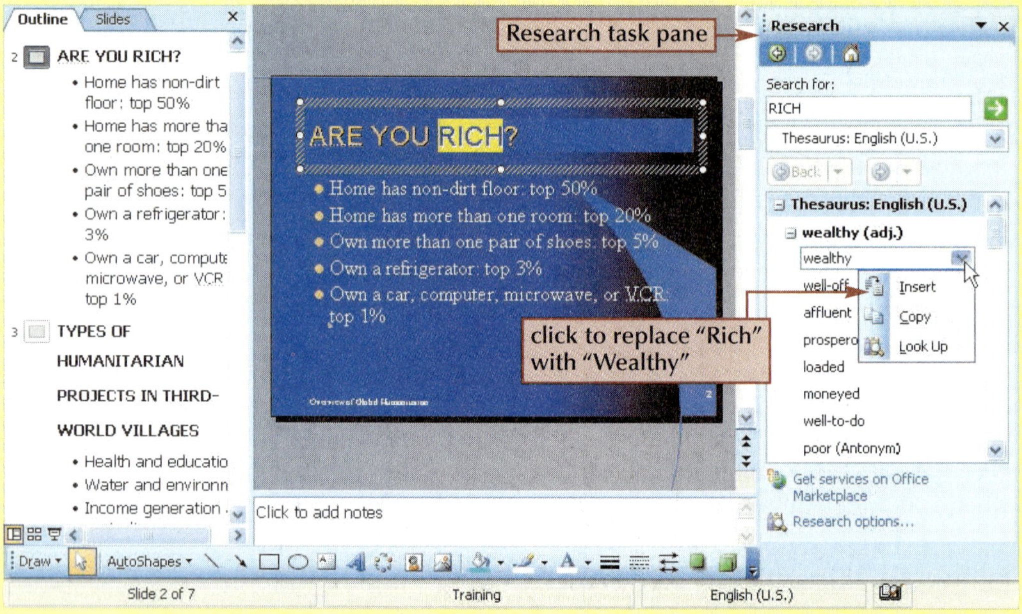

8. Click **Insert**. "WEALTHY" replaces "RICH" in the slide.
9. Close the task pane.

Creating Speaker Notes

When you show the presentation to Miriam, she is satisfied. Now you're ready to prepare the other parts of Miriam's presentation: the notes (also called speaker notes) and audience handouts (a printout of the slides). **Notes** are printed pages that contain a picture of and notes about each slide. They help the speaker remember what to say when a particular slide appears during the presentation. **Handouts** are printouts of the slides; these can be arranged with several slides printed on a page.

You'll create notes for only a few of the slides in the presentation. For example, Miriam wants to remember to acknowledge special guests or Global Humanitarian executives at any meeting where she might use this presentation. You'll create a note reminding her to do that.

To create notes:

1. Click the **Slides** tab, and then click **Slide 1** in the Slides tab. Slide 1 appears in the slide pane. The notes pane currently contains placeholder text.
2. Click in the notes pane, and then type **Acknowledge special guests and Global Humanitarian executives.** See Figure 1-20.

Figure 1-20 Notes on Slide 1

3. Click **Slide 2** in the Slides tab, click in the notes pane, and then type **Everyone in this room is in the top one percent of wealthy people who have ever lived on earth.**
4. Go to **Slide 3**, click in the notes pane, and then type **Give an example of each of these project types.** These are all the notes that Miriam wants.
5. Click the **Save** button on the Standard toolbar to save the changes to the presentation.

Before Miriam gives her presentation, she'll print the notes of the presentation so she'll have them available during her presentations. You can now view the completed presentation to make sure that it is accurate, informative, and visually pleasing.

To view the slide show:

1. Go to **Slide 1**, and then click the **Slide Show from current slide** button at the bottom of the Slides tab.
2. Proceed through the slide show as you did earlier, clicking the left mouse button or pressing the spacebar to advance from one slide to the next.
3. If you see a problem on one of your slides, press the **Esc** key to leave the slide show and display the current slide on the screen in Normal view, fix the problem on the slide, save your changes, and then click the **Slide Show from current slide** button to resume the slide show from the current slide.
4. When you reach the end of your slide show, press the **spacebar** to move to the blank screen, and then press the **spacebar** again to return to Normal view.

Now you're ready to preview and print your presentation.

Previewing and Printing a Presentation

Before you give your presentation, you may want to print it. PowerPoint provides several printing options. For example, you can print the slides in color using a color printer; print in grayscale or pure black and white using a black-and-white printer; print handouts with 2, 3, 4, 6, or 9 slides per page; or print the notes pages (the speaker notes printed below a picture of the corresponding slide). You can also format and then print the presentation onto overhead transparency film (available in most office supply stores).

Usually you'll want to open the Print dialog box by clicking File on the menu bar, and then clicking Print, rather than clicking the Print button on the Standard toolbar. If you click the Print button, the presentation prints with the options chosen last in the Print dialog box. If you're going to print your presentation on a black-and-white printer, you should first preview the presentation to make sure the text will be legible. You'll use Print Preview to see the slides as they will appear when they are printed.

To preview the presentation:

1. Go to **Slide 1**, if necessary, and then click the **Print Preview** button on the Standard toolbar. The Preview window appears, displaying Slide 1.
2. Click the **Options** button on the Preview toolbar, point to **Color/Grayscale**, and then click **Grayscale**. The slide is displayed in grayscale.
3. Click the **Next Page** button on the Preview toolbar. As you can see, part of the background graphic covers the text on Slide 2. See Figure 1-21. You'll need to remove the background from the slides so you can read them after you have printed them.

Figure 1-21 Slide 2 in Preview window

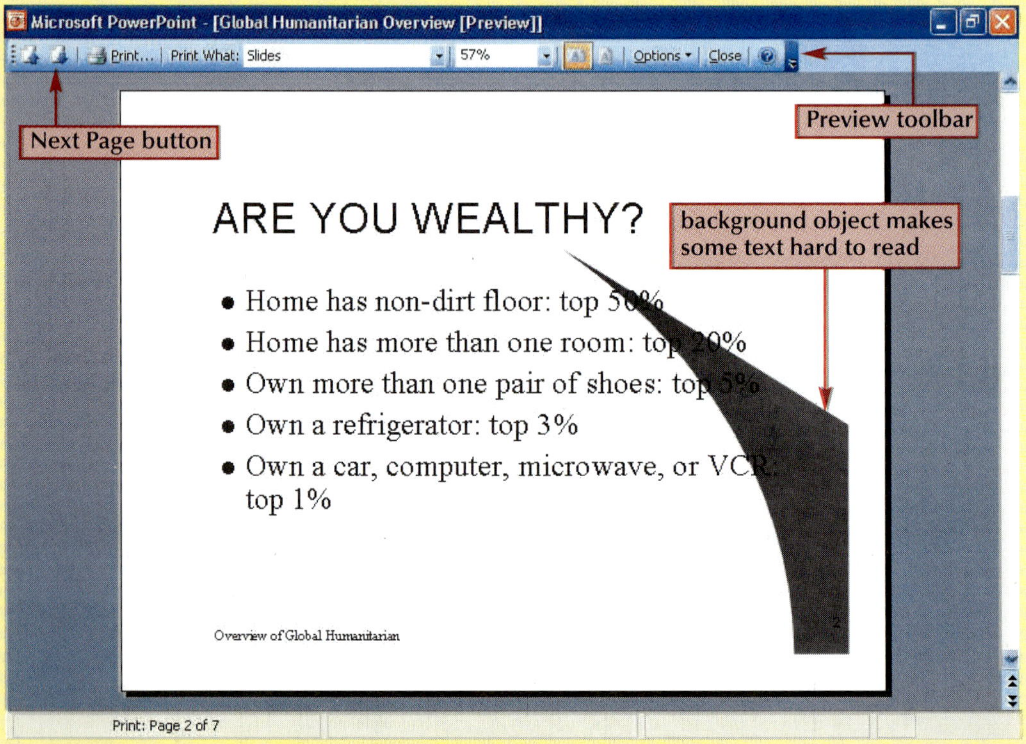

4. Click the **Close** button on the Preview toolbar to return to Normal view.
5. Click **Format** on the menu bar, click **Background** to display the Background dialog box, click the **Omit background graphics from master** check box, and then click the **Apply to All** button. The slide appears as before, but without the background graphic.
6. Click the **Print Preview** button on the Standard toolbar, and then click the **Next Page** button on the Preview toolbar. You can now easily read the text on Slide 2.
7. Click the **Print What** list arrow on the Preview toolbar, and then click **Handouts (4 slides per page)**. The preview changes to display four slides on a page.
8. Click the **Print** button on the Preview toolbar. The Print dialog box opens. See Figure 1-22.

Print dialog box **Figure 1-22**

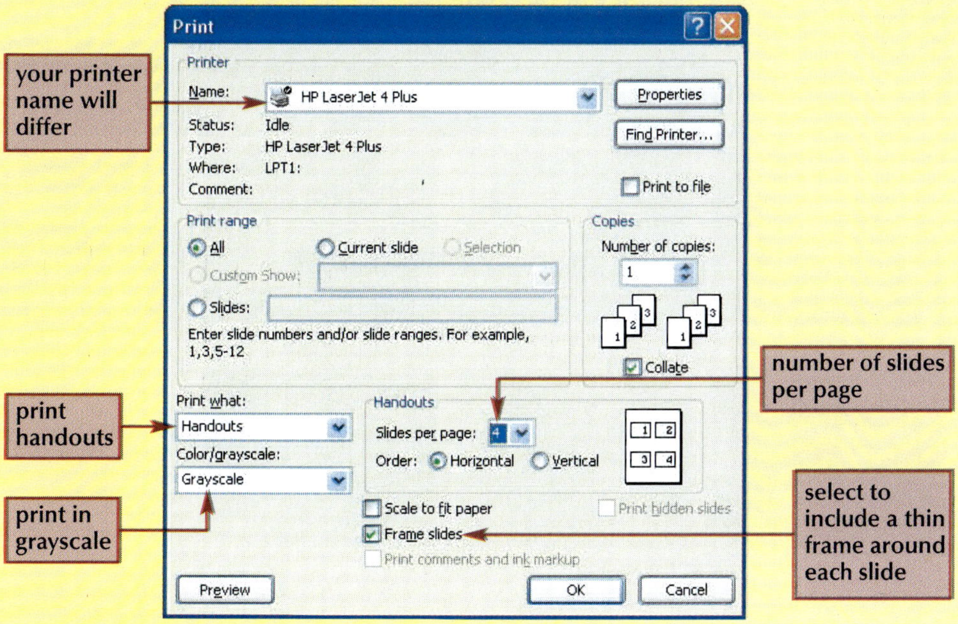

9. Compare your dialog box to the one shown in Figure 1-22, make any necessary changes, and then click the **OK** button to print the handouts on two pages. Now you're ready to print the notes.
10. Click the **Print What** list arrow on the Preview toolbar, and then click **Notes Pages**. The current slide is displayed as a notes page, with the slide on the top and the notes on the bottom.
11. Click the **Print** button on the Print Preview toolbar, click the **Slides** option button in the Print range section of the Print dialog box, and then type **1-3**. These are the only slides with notes on them, so you do not need to print all seven slides as notes pages.
12. Click the **OK** button to print the notes. Slides 1-3 print on three pieces of paper as notes pages.
13. Click the **Close** button on the Preview toolbar. The view returns to Normal view.

Your last task is to view the completed presentation in Slide Sorter view to see how all the slides look together. First, however, you'll restore the background graphics.

To restore the background graphics and view the completed presentation in Slide Sorter view:

1. Click **Format** on the menu bar, click **Background**, click the **Omit background graphics from master** check box to clear it, and then click the **Apply to All** button. The background graphics are restored to the slides.
2. Click the **Slide Sorter View** button at the bottom of the Slides tab. The slides appear on the screen in several rows, depending on the current zoom percentage shown in the Zoom box on the Standard toolbar and on the size of your monitor. You need to see the content on the slides better.
3. Click the **Zoom** list arrow on the Standard toolbar, and then click **75%**. See Figure 1-23.

Figure 1-23 Completed presentation in Slide Sorter view

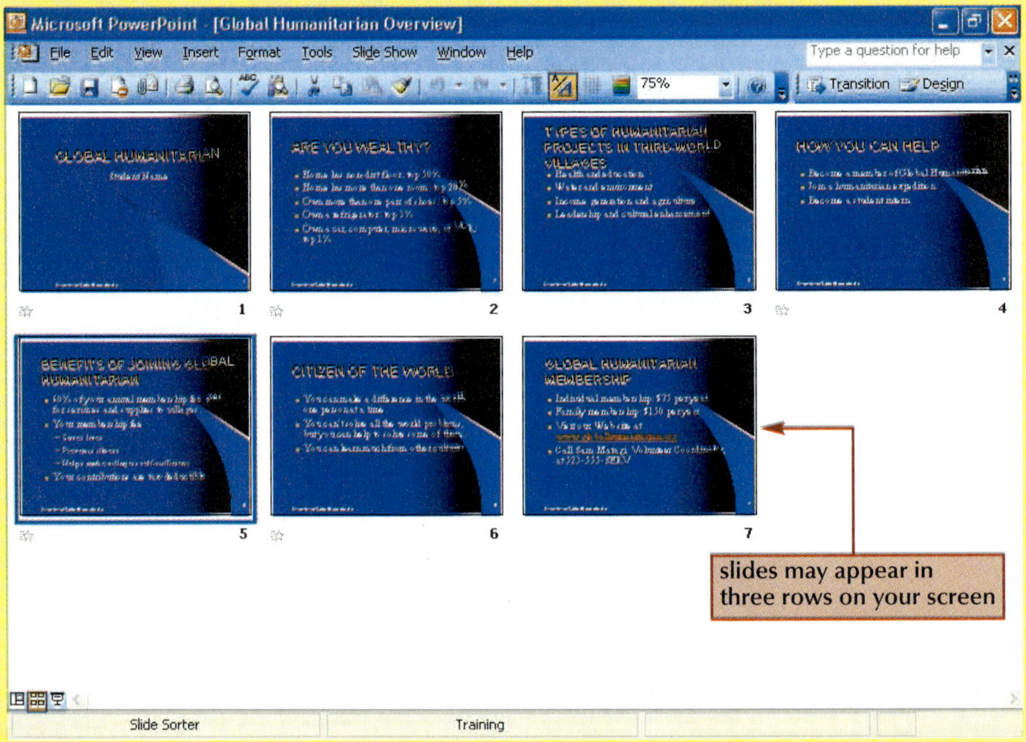

4. Compare your handouts with the slides shown in Slide Sorter view.
5. Click the **Close window** button. A dialog box appears asking if you want to save your changes.
6. Click the **Yes** button to save the changes and close the presentation.

You have created a presentation using the AutoContent Wizard, edited it according to Miriam's wishes, and created and printed notes and handouts. Miriam thanks you for your help; she believes that your work will enable her to make an effective presentation.

Review

Session 1.2 Quick Check

1. Explain how to do the following in the Outline tab:
   a. move text up
   b. delete a slide
   c. change a first-level bullet to a second-level bullet
2. What does it mean to promote a bulleted item in the Outline tab? To demote a bulleted item?
3. Explain a benefit of using the Outline tab rather than the slide pane.
4. What is the Style Checker? What is an example of a consistency or style problem that it might mark?
5. What are notes? How do you create them?
6. Why is it beneficial to preview a presentation before printing it?

Review

Tutorial Summary

In this tutorial, you learned how to plan and create a PowerPoint presentation by modifying AutoContent slides. You learned how to edit the text in both the Outline tab and the slide pane; add a new slide and choose a slide layout; delete slides; and promote, demote and move text in your outline. You also learned how to check your presentation for consistency, create speaker notes, and preview and print your presentation.

Key Terms

animation
body text
bulleted item
bulleted list
content layout
demote
design template
first-level bullet
footer
handout
layout
main text
note
notes pane
numbered list
object
Outline tab
placeholder
PowerPoint
progressive disclosure
promote
second-level bullet
sizing handle
slide pane
slide transitions
Slides tab
Style Checker
sub-bullet
text and content layout
text box
text layout
thesaurus
thumbnail
title text

Practice

Practice the skills you learned in the tutorial using the same case scenario.

Review Assignments

Data File needed for the Review Assignments: VillageOP.ppt

Miriam Schwartz, the managing director of the Austin, Texas headquarters of Global Humanitarian, asks you to prepare a PowerPoint presentation explaining the Village Outreach Program to potential donors and volunteers. She gives you a rough draft of a PowerPoint presentation. Your job is to edit the presentation. Complete the following:

1. Open the presentation **VillageOP** in the Tutorial.01\Review folder included with your Data Files.
2. Save the file as **Village Outreach Program** in the same folder.
3. In Slide 1, change the subtitle placeholder ("Global Humanitarian") to your name.

4. In Slide 2, use the Outline tab to demote the bulleted items "Health," "Education," "Clean water," and "Environment," so that they become second-level bulleted items.
5. Below the sub-bulleted item "Clean water," insert another second-level bulleted item: "Agriculture and Income-producing Projects."
6. In Slide 3, delete all occurrences of the word "the" to reduce the number of words in each bulleted item and thus approach the 6 × 6 rule.
7. Move the last bulleted item in Slide 3 ("Assist villagers in organizing health committees") in the Outline tab so it becomes the second bulleted item in the body text of Slide 3.
8. Go to Slide 5, and then promote the bulleted item "Agriculture and Income-producing Opportunities" in the Outline tab so it becomes the title of a new slide (Slide 6).
9. Return to Slide 5 and promote the last three second-level bulleted items so they become bullets on the same level as "Help villagers build."
10. In Slide 7, move the second bulleted item ("Mobilize resources") so it becomes the fourth bulleted item.
11. Add a new Slide 8 with the default Title and Text layout.
12. In Slide 8, type the slide title "Village Projects."
13. Type the following as first-level bulleted items in Slide 8: "Wells," "Water Pumps," "Greenhouses," "Lorena Stoves," "First aid supplies," and "School supplies."
14. In Slide 2, add the following speaker note: "Relate personal experiences for each topic."
15. In Slide 3, add the following speaker note: "Explain that we need volunteers, especially physicians, dentists, optometrists, and nurses."
16. Switch to Slide Sorter view, and then drag Slide 5 to the left of Slide 4.
17. Use the Research task pane to replace "Agriculture" on Slide 6 with another word, and then make this same change on Slide 2.
18. Check the spelling in the presentation and change or ignore each flagged word as appropriate.
19. Turn on the Style Checker, set the Case options so that the slide title style is uppercase and the body text style is sentence case, and then examine the slides for elements that the Style Checker flags, correcting slides as appropriate. Turn off the Style Checker when you are finished.
20. View the presentation in Slide Show view. Look carefully at each slide and check the content. If you see any errors, press the Esc key to end the slide show, fix the error, and then start the slide show again.
21. Go to Slide 6. When you viewed the presentation, did you notice the typographical error "load" in the final bulleted item? (It should be "loan.") If you did not fix this error already, fix it now.
22. Save the changes to the presentation, preview the presentation in grayscale, and then print the presentation in grayscale as handouts, four slides per page.
23. Print Slides 2 and 3 as notes pages in grayscale, and then close the file.

Apply

Apply the skills you learned to create a new presentation for an e-commerce company using the AutoContent Wizard, and then modify the content.

Case Problem 1

There are no Data Files needed for this Case Problem.

e-Commerce Consultants Kendall Koester founded e-Commerce Consultants, a consulting company that helps local businesses with their e-commerce needs, including Web page design, order fulfillment, and security. Kendall hired you to prepare a presentation to businesses to sell the services of e-Commerce Consultants. Complete the following:

1. Start PowerPoint, and then start the AutoContent Wizard.
2. In the Presentation type window, select the Sales/Marketing category, and then select Selling a Product or Service.
3. In the Presentation style window, select On-screen presentation.

4. In the Presentation options window, type "Developing Strategies for Your Future" as the presentation title, and type "e-Commerce Consultants" as the footer.
5. Omit the date last updated from the presentation, but include the slide number.
6. In Slide 1, change the subtitle placeholder to your name, if necessary.
7. In Slide 2 ("Objective"), replace the slide title with "What We Offer," and replace the body text with the following first-level bulleted items: "Overcoming barriers to e-commerce," "Surviving today's shaky market," "Setting up your Web site," and "Managing your orders."
8. In Slide 3 ("Customer Requirements"), leave the title text as is, and then replace the body text with the following bulleted items: "Web site design and development," "Order taking and fulfillment," "Security," and "Other." Don't modify or delete the radial diagram on the slide.
9. In Slide 4, change the slide title to "Meeting Your Needs," and then replace the body text with the following first-level bulleted items: "Promoting your product," "Securing startup funds," "Arranging for credit card accounts," and "Answering all your questions." Don't modify or delete the three pyramid diagrams.
10. Delete Slides 5 ("Cost Analysis") and 6 ("Our Strengths").
11. In the new Slide 5 ("Key Benefits"), leave the title text as is, and then replace the body text with the following first-level bulleted items: "You can focus on your products, your services, and your bottom line."; and "We'll help you sell your product on the Internet."
12. In Slide 6 ("Next Steps"), leave the title text as is, and then replace the body text with the following first-level bulleted items: "List what you want us to do," "Draw up an agreement," "Determine a timeline," "Establish the order-fulfillment process," and "Launch the Web-based e-commerce system."
13. Save the presentation as **e-Commerce Consultants** in the Tutorial.01\Cases folder included with your Data Files.
14. In Slide 2, indent (demote) "Managing your orders" so it is a sub-bullet under "Setting up your Web site," and then add another sub-bullet, "Handling online credit."
15. In Slide 3, add the following sub-bulleted items under "Web site design and development": "know-how," "graphic design," "software," and "programming."
16. In Slide 4, insert a new first bullet "We can help by," and then make all the other phrases the sub-bullets.
17. Move the last bulleted item "Answering all your questions" up to become the first sub-bullet.
18. In Slide 6 ("Next Steps"), delete excess words like "a," "an," and "the" to achieve the 6×6 rule as closely as possible.
19. Add a new slide after Slide 6 with the Title and Text layout, type "Your Account Representative" as the title text, and then type the following information in five bullets: Kendall Koester, e-Commerce Consultants, 1666 Winnebago St., Pecatonica, IL 61063, 555-WEB-PAGE. The city, state, and Zip code should all be part of the same bulleted item. (Note that the first letter of "e-Commerce" changes to an uppercase letter as soon as you press the spacebar. This is PowerPoint's AutoFormat.)
20. Click to the right of the first letter "E" in "E-Commerce," press the Backspace key, and then type "e."
21. Turn on the Style Checker, set the Case options so that the slide title style is title case and the body text style is sentence case, and then go through each slide of the presentation to see if the Style Checker marks any potential problems. (Don't forget to double-check each slide by moving to the next or previous slide and then back to the current slide to recheck it.) When you see the light bulb, click it, and then assess whether you want to accept or reject the suggested change. You'll want to accept

most of the suggested changes, but make sure you leave words like "Web" and "Internet" capitalized, and don't change the capitalization of the address and phone number you typed on Slide 7. Turn off the Style Checker when you are finished.

22. Check the spelling in the presentation. Correct any misspellings, and ignore any words that are spelled correctly.
23. View the presentation in Slide Show view.
24. Save the presentation, preview it in grayscale, print the presentation in grayscale as handouts with four slides per page, and then close the file.

Apply

Apply the skills you learned to modify an existing presentation for a seafood distributor.

Case Problem 2

Data File needed for this Case Problem: Seafoods.ppt

Northwest Seafoods Paul Neibaur is president of Northwest Seafoods, a seafood distribution company with headquarters in Vancouver, British Columbia. He buys fish and other seafood from suppliers and sells to restaurant and grocery store chains. Although his company has been in business and profitable for 27 years, Paul wants to sell the company and retire. He wants you to help him create a PowerPoint presentation to prospective buyers. Complete the following:

1. Open the file **Seafoods** located in the Tutorial.01\Cases folder included with your Data Files, and then save it as **Northwest Seafoods** in the same folder.
2. In Slide 1, replace the subtitle placeholder ("Paul Neibaur") with your name.
3. In Slide 2, add the speaker's note "Mention that regular customers are large grocery stores and fast-food franchises."
4. Add a sixth bulleted item to Slide 2: "Contracts with 13 distributors."
5. Move the second bulleted item ("Low debt") so that it becomes the last bulleted item.
6. In Slide 3, edit the third bulleted item so that "walk-in freezers," "cutting devices," and "other equipment" are second-level bulleted items below the main bullet.
7. Promote the bulleted item "Experienced employees" and its sub-bullets so that they become a new, separate slide.
8. Use the Slides tab to move Slide 5 ("Profitability") to become Slide 4.
9. Add a new slide after Slide 7 with the Title and Text layout, and then replace the title placeholder text with "British Columbia Business Brokers."
10. Create three new bulleted items with the address on the first line ("107-5901 Granville Street"), the city, province, and postal code on the second line ("Coquitlam, BC V6M 4J7"), and the phone number on the third line ("604.555.SELL").
11. Check the spelling in the presentation. Correct any spelling errors and ignore any words that are spelled correctly.
12. Turn on the Style Checker, change the options so that the slide title style is uppercase and the body text style is sentence case, and then go through all the slides correcting any flagged style problems. Be sure not to let the Style Checker change the case for "Small Business Administration" or modify the address you typed on Slide 8; otherwise, accept the Style Checker's suggested case changes. Turn off the Style Checker when you are finished.
13. View the presentation in Slide Show view.
14. Go to Slide 4. When you viewed the presentation, did you notice the two typographical errors on this page? If you did not fix these errors, fix them now.
15. Save the presentation, preview the presentation in grayscale, print the presentation in grayscale as handouts with four slides per page, and then print Slide 2 as a notes page, and then close the file.

Challenge

Explore more advanced features of PowerPoint by formatting text, paragraphs, and lists, and by changing slide layouts and adding a design template.

Case Problem 3

Data File needed for this Case Problem: LASIK.ppt

Camellia Gardens Eye Center Dr. Carol Wang, head ophthalmologist at the Camellia Gardens Eye Center in Charleston, South Carolina, performs over 20 surgeries per week using laser-assisted in situ keratomileusis (LASIK) to correct vision problems of myopia (nearsightedness), hyperopia (farsightedness), and astigmatism. She asks you to help prepare a PowerPoint presentation to those interested in learning more about LASIK. Complete the following:

1. Open the file **LASIK** located in the Tutorial.01\Cases folder included with your Data Files, and then save it as **Camellia LASIK** in the same folder.
2. In Slide 1, replace the subtitle placeholder ("Camellia Gardens Eye Center") with your name.
3. In Slide 2, move the first bulleted item down to become the third bulleted item.
4. Edit the sub-bullets "Myopia," "Hyperopia," and "Astigmatism" in the first item so they're part of the first-level bullet and there are no sub-bullets. Be sure to add commas after the first two words, and add the word "and" before the last word.
5. Add a fourth bulleted item with the text "Patients no longer need corrective lenses."
6. **Explore** Still in Slide 2, center the text in the title text box. (*Hint*: Click anywhere in the title text, and then position the pointer over the buttons on the Formatting toolbar to see the ScreenTips to find a button that will center the text.)
7. **Explore** In Slide 3, change the bulleted list to a numbered list. (*Hint*: Select all of the body text, and then look for a button on the Formatting toolbar that will number the list.)
8. **Explore** Have PowerPoint automatically split Slide 3 into two slides. (*Hint*: First, click the AutoFit Options button in the slide pane and click the Stop Fitting Text to This Placeholder option button. Then, with the insertion point in the body text box, click the AutoFit Options button again, and then click the appropriate option.)
9. **Explore** On the new Slide 4, change the numbering so it continues the numbering from Slide 3 rather than starting over at number 1. (*Hint*: Right-click anywhere in the first item in the numbered list, click Bullets and Numbering on the shortcut menu, click the Numbered tab, and then change the Start at value.)
10. At the end of the title in Slide 4, add a space and "(cont.)," the abbreviation for continued.
11. In Slide 5, demote the two bullets under "With low to moderate myopia," so they become sub-bullets.
12. **Explore** Still in Slide 5, tell the PowerPoint Spell Checker to ignore all occurrences of the word "hyperopia," which is not found in PowerPoint's dictionary. (*Hint*: Right-click the word to see a shortcut menu with spelling commands.)
13. **Explore** If any of the bulleted text doesn't fit on the slide, but drops below the body text box, set the text box to AutoFit. (*Hint*: Click anywhere in the text box, click the AutoFit Options button that appears, and then click the desired option.)
14. In Slide 6, join the final two bullets to become one bullet. Be sure to add a semicolon between the two bullets and change the word "Other" to lowercase.
15. In Slide 8, move the second bullet "Schedule eye exam to determine" (along with its sub-bullets) up to become the first bullet.
16. In Slide 8, edit the bulleted item ("Analysis of . . .") so that "eye pressure," "shape of cornea," and "thickness of cornea" are sub-bullets below "Analysis of."
17. **Explore** Change the layout of Slide 8 so that the body text appears in two columns. (*Hint*: Click the AutoFit Options button in the slide pane, and then click Change to Two-Column Layout.) Drag the last two bullets over to the second column in the body text. (*Hint*: After you select the bulleted item, position the pointer over the selected

text instead of over the bullet, and then drag the pointer to immediately after the new bullet in the second column, using the vertical line indicator that appears to help guide you.)

18. Add a new Slide 9, and then apply the Title Only layout in the Text Layout section of the Slide Layout task pane.

Explore

19. In Slide 9, add the title "Camellia Gardens Eye Center," create a new text box near the center of the slide, and then add the address "8184 Camellia Drive" on the first line, "Charleston, SC 29406" on the second line, and the phone number "(843) 555-EYES" on the third line. (*Hint*: Click the Text Box button on the Drawing toolbar, and then click on the slide at the desired location.)

Explore

20. Change the size of the text in the new text box on Slide 9 so that it's 32 points. (*Hint*: Click the edge of the text box to select the entire text box and all of its contents, and then click the Font Size list arrow on the Formatting toolbar.)

Explore

21. Turn on the Style Checker, and then set the style options for end punctuation so that the Style Checker checks to make sure that slide titles do not have end punctuation, and that paragraphs in the body text have punctuation. Set the slide title style to title case and the body text style to sentence case. Also, set the Visual Clarity options so that the maximum number of bullets should not exceed six, the number of lines per title should not exceed two, and the number of lines per bulleted item should not exceed two. (*Hint*: Use the End punctuation section of the Case and End Punctuation tab and the Legibility section of the Visual Clarity tab in the Style Options dialog box.)

Explore

22. Go through all the slides, correcting problems of case (capitalization) and punctuation. Be sure not to let the Style Checker change the case for proper nouns. Let the Style Checker correct end punctuation for complete sentences, but you shouldn't allow (or you should remove) punctuation for words or phrases that don't form complete sentences. Do not accept the Style Checker's suggestions to remove question marks in the slide titles.

Explore

23. Change the Style Options back so that the next time the Style Checker is run, only the Slide title style and Body text style options on the Case and End Punctuation tab and the Fonts options on the Visual Clarity tab are selected, and then turn off the Style Checker.
24. Check the spelling in the presentation.

Explore

25. Apply the design template called "Watermark," which has a white background with violet circles. (*Hint*: Click the Design button on the Formatting toolbar, and then use the ScreenTips in the Slide Design task pane to find the Watermark design template.) If you can't find the Watermark design template, choose a different design template.
26. View the presentation in Slide Show view.
27. Save the presentation, preview it in grayscale, print the presentation in grayscale as handouts with four slides per page, and then close the file.

Research

Use the Internet to research bestsellers and use PowerPoint's Help system to find out how to format text.

Case Problem 4

There are no Data Files needed for this Case Problem.

Book Review Your English teacher asks you to prepare a book review for presentation to the class. The teacher asks you to review any book from a bestseller list, past or present, such as the Barnes & Noble Top 100 Books or Amazon's Top 100 Bestsellers. To help you give your class presentation, you want to use PowerPoint slides. Your task is to prepare a presentation of at least six PowerPoint slides. Complete the following:

1. Go to **www.bn.com**, **www.amazon.com**, or any other bestseller list, and find the title of a book you have read. If you can't find a book from among these lists, get approval from your instructor to report on another book.

2. Use the AutoContent Wizard to begin developing slides based on "Generic" from the General category of presentation types.
   a. Title the presentation "Review of" followed by your book title, and then add "Review of" followed by the book subject as the footer. For example, the title might be "Review of Harry Potter and the Order of the Phoenix," along with the footer "Review of a Recent Bestseller."
   b. Include both the date and the slide number.

Explore

3. Use PowerPoint's Help system to find out how to italicize text. Close the Help window and the task pane, and then edit Slide 1 so that the book title is italicized.
4. In Slide 1, change the subtitle to your name, if necessary.
5. In Slide 2 ("Introduction"), include the following information in the bulleted list: title, author(s), publisher, publication year, and the number of pages in the book.
6. In Slide 3 ("Topics of Discussion"), include the categories used in reviewing the book, for example, "Plot," "Action," "Characterization," "Description," "Humor," and "Comparison with Other Books in the Series."
7. Delete Slides 4 through 9.
8. Create at least one slide for each of the topics you listed on Slide 3, and then include bulleted lists explaining that topic.

Explore

9. Connect to the Internet, and then use the Research task pane to find additional information about the topic of the book you've chosen or about the author. (*Hint*: In the Research task pane, type the topic or author name into the Search for text box, make sure your computer is connected to the Internet, select a research site such as Encarta Encyclopedia, and then click the green arrow button, if necessary, to start searching.) You might want to create one or more new slides, cut and paste information into the new slides, and then edit the information into one or more appropriate bulleted lists.
10. Create a slide titled "Summary and Recommendations" as the last slide in your presentation, giving your overall impression of the book and your recommendation for whether the book is worth reading.
11. View the presentation on the Outline tab. If necessary, change the order of the bulleted items on the slides, or change the order of the slides.

Explore

12. If you see any slides with more than six bulleted items, split the slide in two. (*Hint*: With the insertion point in the body text box, click the AutoFit Options button that appears near the lower-left corner of the text box, and then click the appropriate option.)
13. Turn on the Style Checker, and then go through all the slides, correcting problems of case (capitalization), punctuation, number of bulleted items per slide, and number of lines per bulleted item. Be sure not to let the Style Checker change the case for proper nouns. Let the Style Checker correct end punctuation for complete sentences, but you shouldn't allow (or you should remove) punctuation for words or phrases that don't form complete sentences.
14. Check the spelling of your presentation.
15. View the presentation in Slide Show view. If you see any typographical errors or other problems, stop the slide show, correct the problems, and then continue the slide show. If you find slides that aren't necessary, delete them.
16. Save the presentation as **Book Review** in the Tutorial.01\Cases folder included with your Data Files.
17. Preview the presentation in grayscale, and then print the presentation in grayscale as handouts with four slides per page. Print speaker notes if you created any, and then close the file.

Research

Go to the Web to find information you can use to create presentations.

Internet Assignments

The purpose of the Internet Assignments is to challenge you to find information on the Internet that you can use to work effectively with this software. The actual assignments are updated and maintained on the Course Technology Web site. Log on to the Internet and use your Web browser to go to the Student Online Companion for New Perspectives Office 2003 at **www.course.com/np/office2003**. Click the Internet Assignments link, and then navigate to the assignments for this tutorial.

Assess

SAM

SAM Assessment and Training

If you have a SAM user profile, you may have access to hands-on instruction, practice, and assessment of the skills covered in this tutorial. Log in to your SAM account and go to your assignments page to see what your instructor has assigned.

Review

Quick Check Answers

Session 1.1

1. A presentation's components can consist of individual slides, speaker notes, an outline, and audience handouts.
2. The slide pane shows the slide as it will look during your slide show. The notes pane contains speaker notes. The Outline tab shows an outline of your presentation. The Slides tab displays thumbnails of each slide.
3. a. a feature that causes each element on a slide to appear one at a time
   b. the manner in which a new slide appears on the screen during a slide show
   c. a file that contains the colors and format of the background and the font style of the titles, accents, and other text
   d. a predetermined way of organizing the objects on a slide
4. What is my purpose or objective? What type of presentation is needed? What is the physical location of my presentation? What is the best format my presentation?
5. The AutoContent Wizard lets you choose a presentation category and then creates a general outline of the presentation.
6. The view you use to present an on-screen presentation to an audience.

Session 1.2

1. a. Click a slide or bullet icon, and then drag the selected item up.
   b. Right-click the slide icon of the slide to be deleted in the Outline tab, and then click Delete Slide on the shortcut menu; or, move to the slide you want to delete in the slide pane, click Edit on the menu bar, and then click Delete Slide.
   c. Click the slide or bullet icon in the Outline tab, and then click the Decrease Indent button on the Formatting toolbar.
2. Promote means to decrease the level (for example, from level two to level one) of an outline item; demote means to increase the level of an outline item.
3. In the Outline tab, you can see the text of several slides at once, which makes it easier to work with text. In the slide pane, you can see the design and layout of the slide.
4. The Style Checker automatically checks your presentation for consistency and style. For example, it will check for consistency in punctuation.
5. Notes are notes for the presenter. They appear in the notes pane in Normal view or you can print notes pages, which contain a picture of and notes about each slide.
6. By previewing your presentation, you make sure that the slides are satisfactory, and that the presentation is legible in grayscale if you use a monochrome printer.

Objectives

Session 2.1
- Create a presentation from a template
- Apply a new template
- Insert, resize, and recolor a clip-art image
- Modify the design using the slide master
- Insert a bitmap image on a slide
- Reformat text and resize text boxes
- Apply a second design template
- Insert tab stops to align text
- Change the layouts of existing slides
- Reposition text boxes

Session 2.2
- Create and modify a table
- Create a diagram using the Diagram Gallery
- Draw a simple graphic using AutoShapes
- Modify and rotate an AutoShape graphic
- Insert and rotate text boxes
- Create a summary slide

Applying and Modifying Text and Graphic Objects

Presenting and Preparing for an Expedition to Peru

Case

Global Humanitarian, Lima Office

The objectives of Global Humanitarian's expeditions are to help villagers build homes, schools, greenhouses, wells, culinary water systems, and Lorena adobe stoves; to provide medical and dental services; and to teach basic hygiene, literacy, and gardening skills. The village council of Paqarimuy, a small village in the puna (also called the altiplano, or high-altitude plains of the Andes Mountains), requested help in accomplishing some of these objectives. Therefore, Pablo Fuentes, the managing director of Global Humanitarian in Lima, Peru, is organizing a service expedition to that village. He plans the expedition as a two-week trip. To complete everything he hopes to accomplish, he needs approximately 25 volunteers. He thinks that the best way to recruit volunteers is to present a PowerPoint slide show to interested students at local colleges and universities. During the presentation, he can give an overview to the audience members so that they will have enough information to consider the trip. He can answer questions that the audience might have during and after the presentation. He asks you to help prepare a PowerPoint presentation to prospective expedition participants.

In this tutorial, you'll create a new presentation based on a design template, modify the design template, apply a design template to an existing presentation, and then enhance the presentation by adding graphics to the slides. You will also add a slide summarizing the content of the presentation.

Student Data Files

▼**Tutorial.02**

▽ Tutorial folder
- GHLogo.jpg
- MntTop.jpg
- PeruExp2.ppt

▽ Review folder
- Boots.jpg
- Camera.jpg
- Food.jpg
- GHLogo.jpg
- PackList.ppt
- Personal.jpg
- PrMeds.jpg
- SlpBag.jpg
- Vitamins.jpg

▽ Cases folder
- Excycle.jpg
- MyBody.ppt
- Payroll.ppt
- PESLogo.jpg
- PKPBadg.jpg
- PKPKey.jpg
- SBcam.jpg
- SBfile.jpg
- SBpages.jpg
- SBpaper.jpg
- SBpens.jpg
- SBphoto.jpg
- SBsciss.jpg
- StrMach.jpg
- Treadmil.jpg
- Vitamins.jpg
- Weights.jpg

Session 2.1

Planning a Presentation

Before creating his text presentation, Pablo and his staff planned the presentation as follows:

- **Purpose of the presentation**: to convince potential volunteers to apply for a position in the Peru expedition
- **Type of presentation**: an onscreen (electronic) information presentation
- **Audience**: students, health professionals, and other people interested in serving villages in a third-world country
- **Location of the presentation**: a conference room at the offices of Global Humanitarian, as well as classrooms and business offices
- **Audience needs**: to recognize the services they can provide and the adventure they can enjoy as expedition volunteers
- **Format**: one speaker presenting an onscreen slide show consisting of seven to 10 slides

After planning the presentation, Pablo and his staff discuss how they want the slides to look.

Creating a New Presentation from a Design Template

Plain white slides with normal text (such as black Times New Roman or Arial) often fail to hold an audience's attention. In today's information age, audiences expect more interesting color schemes, fonts, graphics, and other effects.

To make it easy to add color and style to your presentations, PowerPoint comes with design templates. A **design template** is a file that contains the color scheme, text formats, background colors and objects, and graphics in the presentation. The **color scheme** is the eight colors used in a design template. A **graphic** is a picture, clip art, photograph, shape, design, graph, chart, or diagram that you can add to a slide. A graphic, like a text box, is an object. Pablo asks you to create a new presentation with the Teamwork design template so that he can see what it looks like.

Reference Window

Creating a New Presentation from a Design Template

- Click File on the menu bar, and then click New.
- Click the From design template link in the New Presentation task pane.
- Click the design template you want to use.

You'll begin enhancing Pablo's presentation by changing the design template.

To create a new presentation from a design template:

1. Start PowerPoint, and then click the **Create a new presentation** link at the bottom of the Getting Started task pane. The New Presentation task pane opens.

   Trouble? If you don't see the Create a new presentation link in the Getting Started task pane, point to the small, downward-pointing triangle at the bottom of the task pane to scroll the task pane automatically so that you can see the commands at the bottom of the task pane.

Trouble? If PowerPoint is already running and the task pane is not open, click File on the menu bar, and then click New to open the New Presentation task pane.

2. Click the **From design template** link in the New Presentation task pane. Slide 1 (the title slide) of a new blank presentation opens in Normal view and the Slide Design task pane opens. Notice that Default Design appears in the status bar below the slide pane to indicate that this is the current design template. A thumbnail showing the Default Design template also appears in the Slide Design task pane under Used in This Presentation. In the Default Design template, the slides have black text on a plain white background.
3. Move the pointer over the **Default Design template** thumbnail under Used in This Presentation in the task pane. A ScreenTip appears, identifying the template. See Figure 2-1.

Figure 2-1 Blank presentation with Default Design template applied

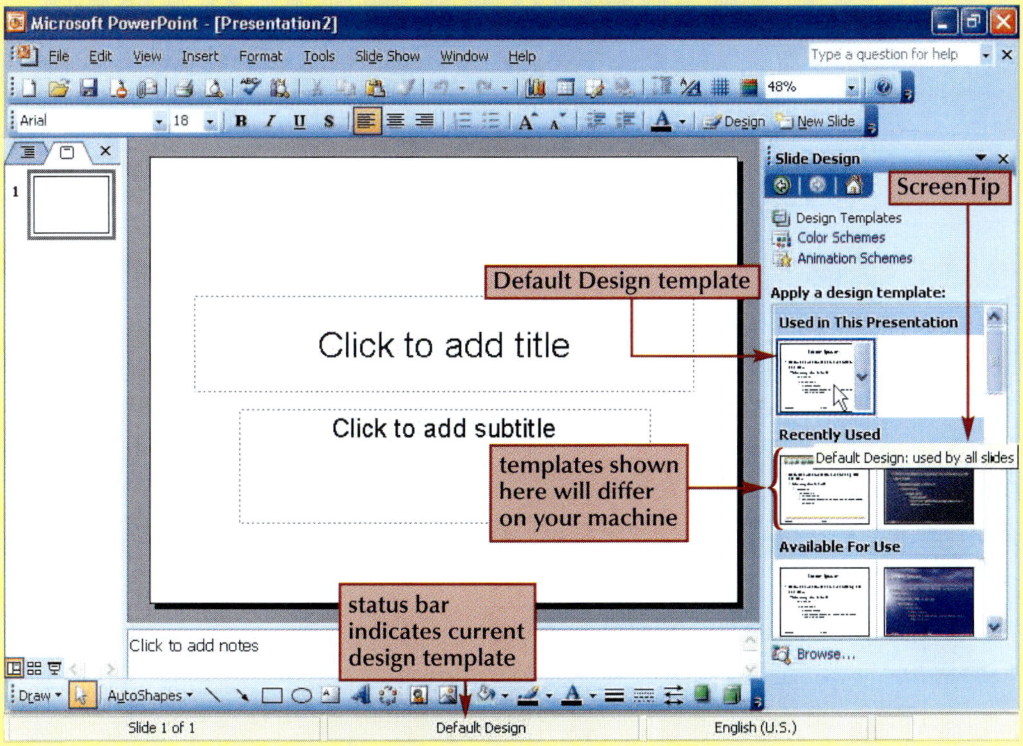

4. Scroll down through the thumbnail views of the design templates, and move the pointer over the thumbnails under **Available For Use** until you find **Teamwork**, a dark green thumbnail.

   Trouble? If the Teamwork template is not in the task pane, you must install it. If you are working in a lab, ask your instructor or technical support person for help. If you are working on your own computer, click the Additional Design Templates thumbnail to install additional templates.
5. Click the **Teamwork** design template. The design template of the new presentation changes from Default Design to Teamwork. See Figure 2-2.

Figure 2-2 Teamwork design template applied

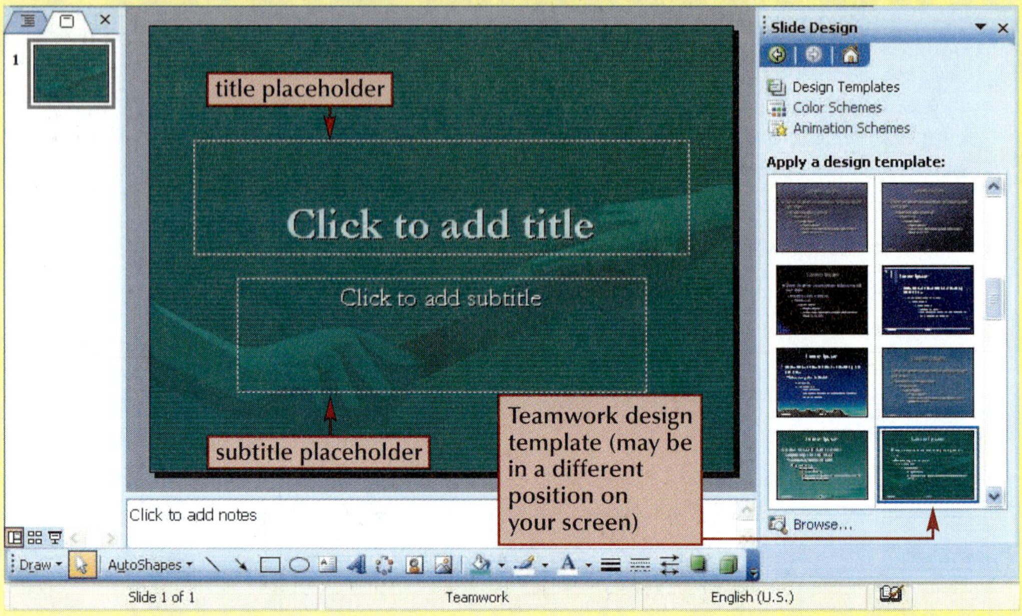

6. Click in the **title** placeholder in the slide pane, and then type **Peru Expedition 2006**.
7. Click in the **subtitle** placeholder and then type your own name.
8. Click the **Close** button in the Slide Design task pane.
9. Save the presentation as **PeruExp** in the Tutorial.02\Tutorial folder included with your Data Files.
10. Click **File** on the menu bar, and then click **Print** to open the Print dialog box.
11. Click the **Color/grayscale** list arrow, click **Grayscale**, click the **Print what** list arrow, and then click **Slides**, if necessary.
12. Click the **OK** button. The one-page presentation prints in full slide format (one slide fits the entire page).
13. Close the presentation (but leave PowerPoint running).

Pablo takes the new presentation you created, adds more slides to the presentation, and saves the file as PeruExp2. After considering the Teamwork design template, he decides that he doesn't like it because the hands in the background are hard to see. You'll change the design template now.

Applying a Design Template

The design template you choose for your presentation should reflect the content and the intended audience. For example, if you are presenting a new curriculum to a group of elementary school teachers, you might choose a template that uses bright, primary colors. Likewise, if you are presenting a new marketing plan to a mutual fund company, you might choose a plain-looking template that uses dark colors formatted in a way that appears sophisticated.

Although Pablo's presentation is serious, he wants to make the trip seem attractive to prospective participants. He decides that he wants to use a color scheme that includes a dark blue background with a color gradient and some graphics representing the Peruvian Andes Mountains. He thinks such a design would give his presentation more interest.

Applying a Different Design Template

Reference Window

- Display the Slide Design templates in the task pane by clicking the Design button on the Formatting toolbar.
- Scroll through the design template thumbnails until you see one you'd like to apply, and then click the design template thumbnail.

To change the design template:

1. Open the presentation file **PeruExp2** located in the Tutorial.02\Tutorial folder included with your Data Files.
2. Save the file in the same folder using the filename **Peru Expedition**. The presentation title slide appears in the slide pane.
3. Click the **Design** button on the Formatting toolbar to open the Slide Design task pane.
4. Scroll down through the thumbnail views of the design templates in the task pane under Available For Use, and then click the **Mountain Top** template. Don't forget to move the pointer over the templates to see their names. The design template of Peru Expedition changes from Teamwork to Mountain Top. See Figure 2-3.

Figure 2-3 Presentation with Mountain Top design template applied

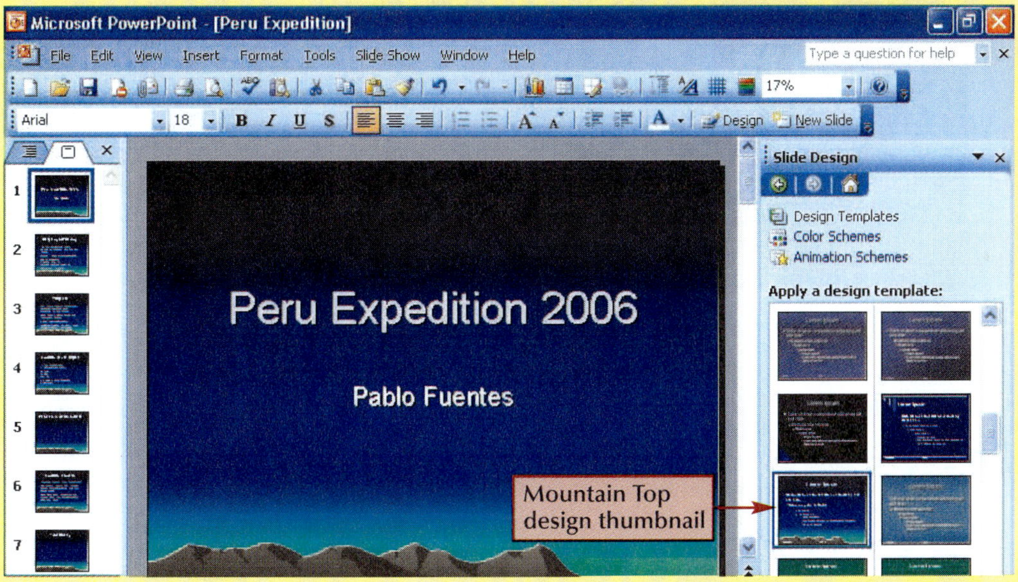

As you can see, the title slide has a dark blue background with varying color, and a background graphic of a mountain top along the bottom of the slide. Next, you'll modify this template to make it more appropriate for this presentation.

Understanding Graphics

Graphics add information, clarification, emphasis, variety, and even pizzazz to a PowerPoint presentation. PowerPoint enables you to include many types of graphics in your presentation: graphics created using another Windows program; scanned photographs, drawings, or cartoons; and other picture files or clip art located on a CD or other disk. You can also create graphics using the drawing tools in PowerPoint. In addition, you can add graphical bullets to a bulleted list.

Inserting Clip Art

Slide 6, "Expedition Information," has six bulleted items of text. Pablo wants to include some clip art to add interest to this slide. In PowerPoint, **clip art** refers specifically to images in the Media Gallery that accompanies Office 2003, or images that are available from the Clip Art and Media section of Microsoft Office Online. Pablo decides that an image of a globe would help emphasize the global aspects of the expedition.

To add clip art to a slide, you can use a slide layout that has a place for clip art, or you can insert the clip art as you would a picture. If you insert clip art using the Insert Clip Art button on the Drawing toolbar, the Clip Art task pane opens and you can search for clips that match keywords you type, and then browse the results. If you insert clip art by clicking a button on a layout that includes a placeholder for clip art, you can browse through all of the clips stored on your machine as well as search for clips that match keywords you type. You'll change the existing slide layout before adding clip art.

To change the layout of a slide and add clip art:

1. Go to **Slide 6** ("Expedition Information").
2. Click **Format** on the menu bar, and then click **Slide Layout** to display the Slide Layout task pane.
3. Scroll down the task pane until you see Text and Content Layouts, and then click the **Title, Text, and Content** layout (the first layout under Text and Content Layouts). The bulleted list moves to the left side of the slide and the content placeholder appears on the right of the slide. See Figure 2-4. Notice that PowerPoint automatically reduces the size of the text in the bulleted list so that it will fit properly within the reduced text box.

Figure 2-4 **Slide 6 after changing slide layout to Title, Text, and Content**

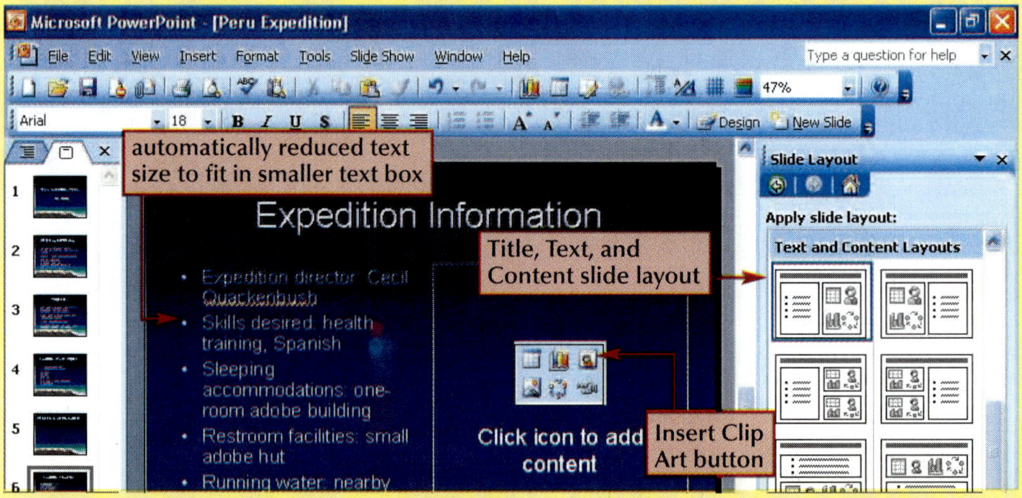

Trouble? If the text size doesn't automatically change or if it doesn't change to a small enough size, click anywhere in the body text, click the AutoFit Options button that appears near the lower-left corner of the body text, and then click the AutoFit Text to Placeholder option button.

4. Click the **Close** button in the task pane title bar to close the task pane.
5. Click the **Insert Clip Art** button in the content placeholder. The Select Picture dialog box opens. If necessary, drag the box by its title bar so you can see all of it. Now you'll search for a piece of clip art that relates to a globe.
6. Type **globe** in the Search text box at the top of the dialog box, and then click the **Go** button. Depending upon how Office was installed on your computer, PowerPoint displays from just a few to over 250 pieces of clip art that contain a representation of a globe.
7. If necessary, drag the scroll button up to the top of the scroll bar in the Select Picture dialog box, and then double-click the image of a globe in the center of a red circular background. The Select Picture dialog box closes, the content placeholder disappears from the slide, and the clip art you selected appears in its place. See Figure 2-5.

Figure 2-5 Slide 6 with clip art inserted

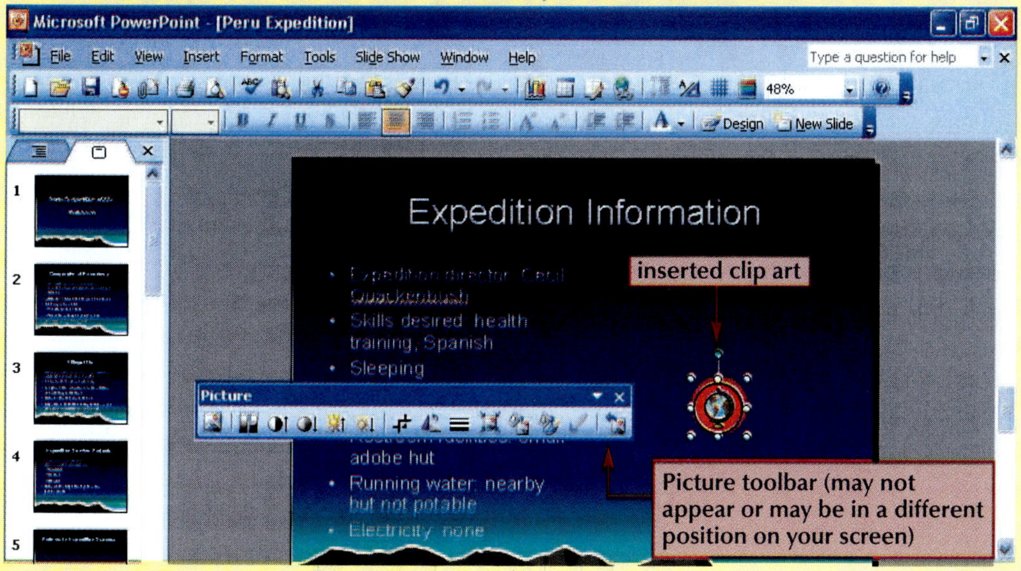

Now you'll modify this clip art image by changing its size and some of its colors.

Resizing Clip Art

The clip art is too small, and so is the body text box, making the autofit text in the bulleted list too small. You will increase the size of the clip art and the text box.

To resize the clip art image:

1. Drag the upper-right corner sizing handle of the globe clip art toward the upper-right corner of the slide until the image is approximately tripled in size.
2. Position the pointer over the selected clip art image so that it changes to , and then drag the entire clip art image so that it's centered between the top and bottom of the slide, and near the right edge of the slide. Compare your screen to Figure 2-6 and adjust the size or position of the graphic as necessary.

Figure 2-6 Slide 6 with repositioned clip art

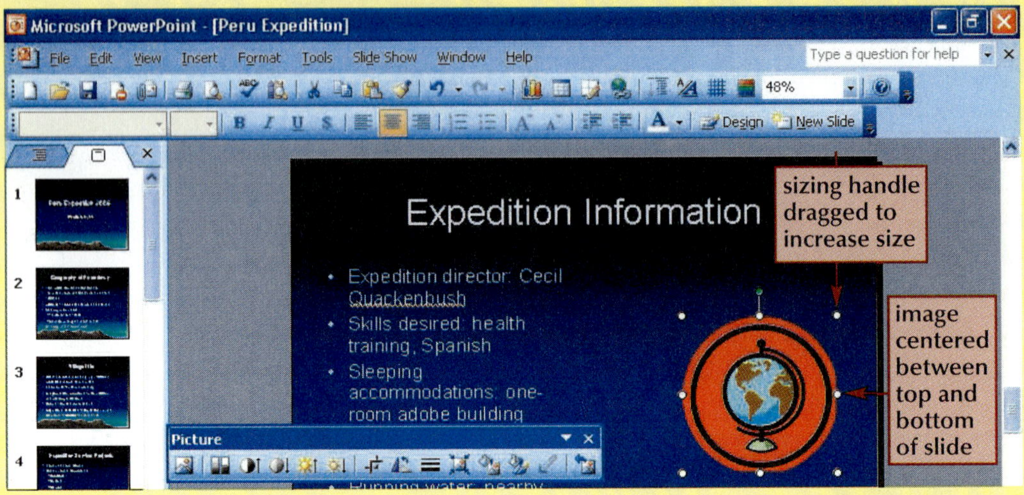

3. Click anywhere in the body text to display the text box and its sizing handles, and then drag the right-center sizing handle to the right until it just touches the left edge of the clip art.

With the clip art inserted and resized, you're ready to change some of the colors.

Recoloring Clip Art

Pablo thinks the red colors on the clip art don't match the blue hues of the design template, so he asks you to change the red to dark blue. You can recolor clip art, but you may not always be able to change the color on other types of pictures.

To recolor a clip art image:

1. Click the **clip art** in Slide 6 to select it. The sizing handles appear around the image, and the Picture toolbar appears.

   Trouble? If the Picture toolbar doesn't appear automatically, click View on the menu bar, point to Toolbars, and then click Picture.

2. Click the **Recolor Picture** button on the Picture toolbar to display the Recolor Picture dialog box. The colored rectangular tiles under Original are all of the colors used in this piece of clip art.
3. Drag the scroll box down to the bottom of the scroll bar in the dialog box so you can see the red and off-red tiles. See Figure 2-7.

Figure 2-7 Recolor Picture dialog box

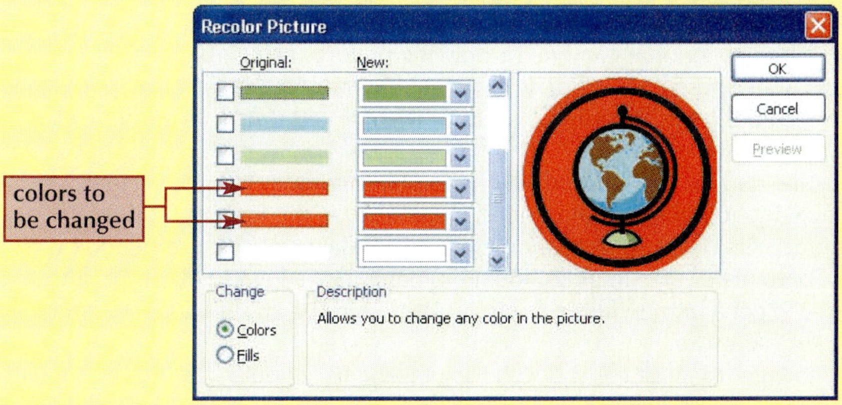

4. Click the **off-red color tile** list arrow in the New column, and then click the **light violet tile** on the palette of default colors. The **default colors** are those colors associated with the overall color scheme of the design template. The globe's shadow in the Preview box changes from off-red to light violet.
5. Change the **red tile** in the New column to the **royal blue tile** (not the dark blue tile) on the palette of default colors.
6. Click the **Preview** button in the Recolor Picture dialog box, and then drag the dialog box by its title bar so that you can see the colors applied to the clip art on the slide. The recolored clip art looks much better than the red colors did.
7. Click the **OK** button, and then click outside the selected object to deselect it. See Figure 2-8.

Figure 2-8 Recolored clip art and resized body text box

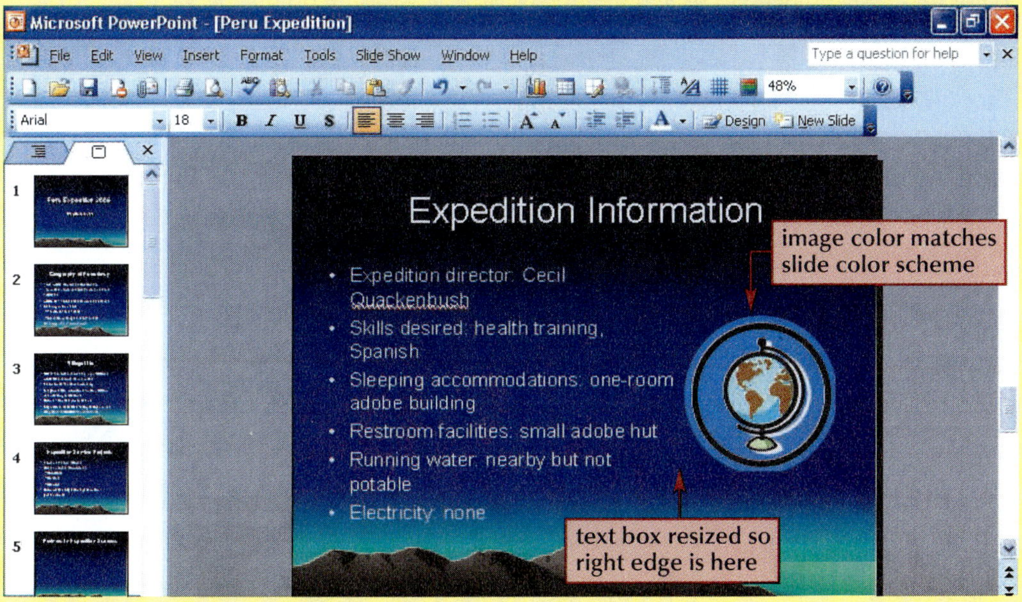

8. Click the **Save** button on the Standard toolbar to save your changes.

You'll now add a picture to one of the slides. To add a picture to a slide, the picture must be a computer file located on an electronic medium, such as a CD or hard disk. Picture files are generated by taking photographs with a digital camera, scanning photographs taken with a conventional camera, or drawing pictures using graphics software (such as Microsoft Paint). These types of picture files are bitmap images. A **bitmap image** is a grid (or "map") of colored dots that form a picture. The colored dots are called **pixels**, which stands for picture elements.

Instead of using the current background graphic of the Mountain Top design template, Pablo prefers an actual photograph of the Andes Mountains, in the form of a bitmap image. To get a bitmap file of the Andes Mountains, Pablo scanned a picture he took with a 35mm camera. Pablo also wants to add Global Humanitarian's logo to all of the slides in the presentation. To get a bitmap file of the logo, Pablo hired a graphic artist to create the file using graphics software.

To make these changes to all of the slides in the presentation, you'll need to modify the design template in Slide Master view.

Modifying the Design Template in the Slide Master

A **master** is a slide that contains the elements and styles of the design template, including the text and other objects that appear on all the slides of the same type. Masters never appear when you show or print a presentation. PowerPoint presentations have four types of masters: the **title master**, which contains the objects that appear on the title slide (most presentations have only one title slide, but some have more than one); the **slide master**, which contains the objects that appear on all the slides except the title slide; the **handout master**, which contains the objects that appear on all the printed handouts; and the **notes master**, which contains the objects that appear on the notes pages.

You use slide and title masters so that all the slides in the presentation have a similar design and appearance. This ensures that your presentation is consistent. To make changes to the masters, you need to switch to Slide Master view. You'll do this now.

To switch to Slide Master view:

1. Click **View** on the menu bar, point to **Master**, and then click **Slide Master**. The view changes to Slide Master view, and the Slide Master View toolbar appears. See Figure 2-9.

Figure 2-9 Slide Master view

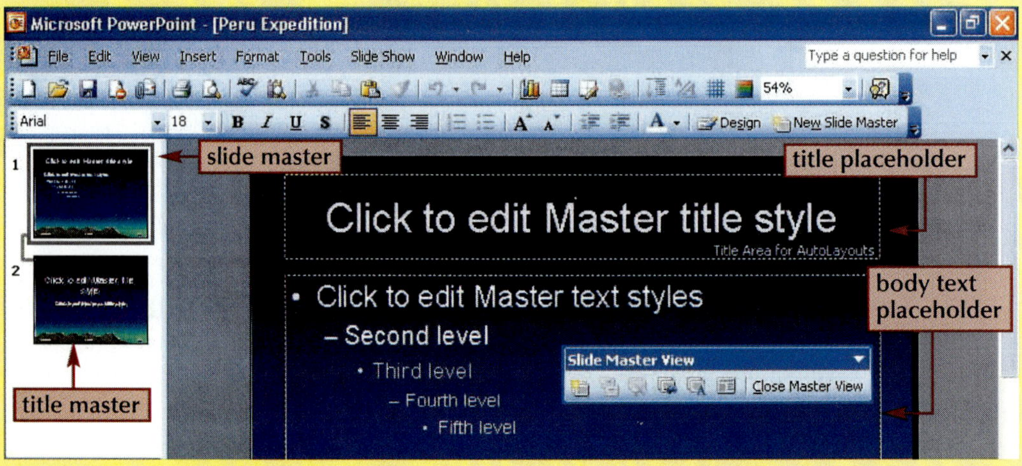

As you can see from the thumbnail slides in the Slides tab, Slide Master view includes two slides: the slide master (as Slide 1) and the title master (as Slide 2). The slide master is currently selected and appears in the slide pane. In Slide Master view, you always see both the slide master and the title master. They appear in Slide Master view as a set, and this is referred to as a **slide-title master pair**.

2. Click the **title master** (Slide 2) in the Slides tab. The slide pane now displays the master for the title slide.
3. Click **View** on the menu bar, point to **Master**, and then click **Handout Master**. The layout of handouts appears in the slide pane, and the Handout Master View toolbar appears. You can click the buttons on this toolbar to change the layout of the handout master.
4. Click **View** on the menu bar, point to **Master**, and then click **Notes Master**. The layout of the notes pages appears in the slide pane, and the Notes Master View toolbar opens.
5. Click the **Close Master View** button on the Notes Master View floating toolbar. PowerPoint returns to Normal view.

You can modify the slide and title master in Slide Master view by changing the size and design of the title and body text, adding or deleting graphics, and changing the background. You cannot delete or add objects to the background unless you are in Slide Master view.

Modifying Slide and Title Masters

Reference Window

- Click View on the menu bar, point to Master, and then click Slide Master; *or* press and hold the Shift key and then click the Normal View button at the bottom of the Slides or Outline tab to switch to Slide Master view.
- Click the thumbnail of the master slide type that you'd like to modify, either the slide master (Slide 1) or the title master (Slide 2).
- Make any changes to the slide or title master such as changing the background color; modifying the text size, color, font, or alignment; inserting clip art, bitmap images, or other graphics; and changing the size or location of text placeholders.
- Click the Normal View button or click the Close Master View button on the Slide Master View toolbar to return to Normal view.

Before you can insert Pablo's photograph of the Andes Mountains, you must delete the graphic of the mountains currently in the design template.

To modify the slide master:

1. Switch again to Slide Master view. The slide master appears.

   You're going to delete the background image containing the mountain tops. The image is made up of three bitmaps that need to be deleted individually: the sky, the brown mountains, and the dark shading on the mountains.

2. Position the pointer over the bitmap image so that it changes to ✥, and then click the teal-green area at the lower-right side of the slide as shown in Figure 2-10. Be careful not to click inside the placeholder titled Object Area for AutoLayouts or inside the placeholder for the Number Area. Sizing handles appear around the selected bitmap.

Figure 2-10 First bitmap in background image selected

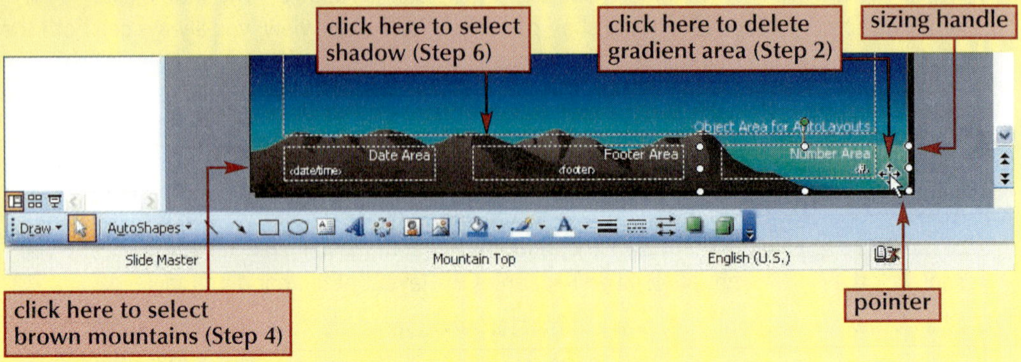

3. Press the **Delete** key. The selected bitmap is deleted.

   Trouble? If you accidentally deleted the Number Area placeholder, click the Undo button on the Standard toolbar, and then repeat Steps 2 and 3.

4. Click the brown mountain at the lower-left side of the slide as indicated in Figure 2-10. Be careful not to click inside the Date Area placeholder.
5. Press the **Delete** key. The bitmap of the mountains is deleted.

   Trouble? If you accidentally deleted the Date Area placeholder, click the Undo button on the Standard toolbar, and then repeat Steps 4 and 5.

6. Click the dark brown shadow in the area just above and to the left of the Footer Area placeholder, as indicated in Figure 2-10. Be careful not to click inside the Footer Area placeholder.
7. Press the **Delete** key. The last bitmap is deleted. The bottom of the slide no longer contains any graphics.

   Trouble? If you have difficulty selecting the shadow, click the Footer Area placeholder, press the ↓ key three times, and then repeat Steps 6 and 7. After you delete the shadow, click the Footer Area placeholder again, and then press the ↑ key three times to return the Footer Area placeholder to its original position.

8. Click the **Save** button on the Standard toolbar to save your changes.

Because you deleted the mountain graphic in Slide Master view, it will be deleted from every slide in the presentation, except the title slide. Now you'll insert the new photo of the Andes Mountains on all of the slides.

Inserting and Modifying a Bitmap Image on a Slide

To add the new bitmap image to all of the slides, you will insert it on the slide master in Slide Master view. To insert a bitmap image on just one slide, you use the same procedure in Normal view.

Inserting a Graphic on a Slide

Reference Window

- If necessary, switch to Normal view, and then open the Slide Layout task pane by clicking Format on the menu bar and clicking Slide Layout.
- Click one of the Content layouts or one of the Text and Content layouts to change the layout of the current slide.
- Click the Insert Clip Art or Insert Picture button in the content placeholder, and then find the desired clip art or navigate to the folder containing the desired picture file.
- Double-click the graphic that you want to insert into the slide.

or

- Click the Insert Picture button on the Drawing toolbar, navigate to and click the picture file you want to insert, and then click the Insert button.

To insert a graphic into a slide:

1. Click the **Insert Picture** button on the Drawing toolbar. The Insert Picture dialog box opens.
2. Navigate to the Tutorial.02\Tutorial folder included with your Data Files.
3. Click **MntTop**, the bitmap image file of the photograph, and click the **Insert** button. The picture is inserted into your slide master in the middle of the slide, and the Picture toolbar appears.

   Trouble? If the Picture toolbar doesn't appear, click View on the menu bar, point to Toolbars, and then click Picture.

You need to move and resize the image to fit along the bottom of the slide master.

To reposition and resize a picture on a slide:

1. Position the pointer over the bitmap image so that it changes to , and then drag the photo to the lower-left corner of the slide. See Figure 2-11.

Figure 2-11 Slide master with bitmap image

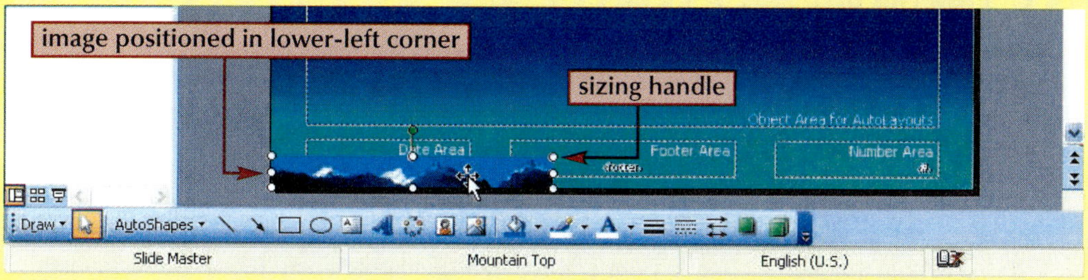

   Trouble? If the Picture or Slide Master View toolbar covers the lower-left corner, drag the toolbar by its title bar to another location on the screen.

   As you can see, the selected bitmap image has sizing handles in each corner and on each side of the picture. You'll drag a sizing handle to resize the image to the width of the slide.

2. Drag the upper-right sizing handle up and to the right until the width of the bitmap image is the same as the width of the slide, and approximately double its original height. See Figure 2-12. Because you are dragging a corner sizing handle, the height and width of the image resizes proportionally.

Figure 2-12 Resized picture of Andes Mountains

You have two tasks left to perform on the bitmap image. First, the blue sky in the background of the photo interrupts the gradient colors in the background. You'll set a transparent color, which is a color on the bitmap image that becomes transparent (invisible). Second, you'll change the order of objects so that the bitmap image is behind the placeholders at the foot of the slide.

To set a color to transparent in a bitmap image:

1. Make sure the image is still selected, and then click the **Set Transparent Color** button on the Picture toolbar. The pointer changes to .
2. Click anywhere in the blue sky above the mountain tops in the bitmap image. The sky color becomes transparent so that the slide background color appears.

Now you want to make sure the mountain top picture is behind the three text placeholders at the bottom of the slide. To do this, you will change the order of the objects on the slide. Imagine each object is on a piece of paper and you lay each piece of paper down on the slide as you add objects. Objects you add last will be on top of the other objects on the slide.

To change the order of objects on a slide:

1. Make sure the image is still selected, click the **Draw** button on the Drawing toolbar, point to **Order**, and then click **Send to Back**. The bitmap image is sent to the back of all the objects on the slide master, including the slide background, so you can no longer see the mountains. Therefore, you need to move the mountains one object forward.
2. Make sure you can still see the sizing handles of the selected image, click the **Draw** button on the Drawing toolbar, point to **Order**, and then click **Bring Forward**. The mountains now properly appear in the slide master, in front of the background but behind the text placeholders.

   Trouble? If you accidentally deselected the mountain image before you brought it forward again, click the Undo button on the Standard toolbar to bring the image to the front again, and then repeat Steps 1 and 2.

As you can see, changing the drawing of mountaintops to a digital photograph of Andean mountaintops makes the background graphic more realistic. Now you'll make the same changes on the title master that you just made on the slide master.

To change the background graphic on the title master:

1. Make sure the resized bitmap image that you just added to the slide master is still selected, and then click the **Copy** button on the Standard toolbar. The image is copied to the Clipboard.
2. Click the **title master** thumbnail (Slide 2) in the Slides tab. The title master appears in the slide pane. The original drawing of the mountain top appears at the bottom of the slide.
3. Delete all three components of the original mountain top drawing, as you did before.
4. Click the **Paste** button on the Formatting toolbar to paste the bitmap image on the slide.
5. Send the image to the back, so that it's behind all the other objects on the title master, and then bring it forward one object to place it in front of the background. Now both the title master and the slide master have the bitmap image of Andean mountaintops as a background picture in the design template.
6. Click the **Save** button on the Standard toolbar to save your changes.

Next, Pablo wants you to change the font of the body text on the slide master, and to modify the color of the title text on the slide master.

Modifying Text on a Slide

In PowerPoint, text is described in terms of the font, font size, and font style. A **font** is the design of a set of characters. Some names of fonts include Arial, Times New Roman, Helvetica, and Garamond. Font size is measured in **points**. Text in a book is typically printed in 10- or 12-point type. **Font style** refers to special attributes applied to the characters; for example, bold and italics are font styles.

Pablo wants you to replace the current subtitle and body text font (Arial) with a different font (Times New Roman), and to change the color of the title text from light violet to light blue. He also wants you to add the Global Humanitarian logo on the slides by placing it next to the title text on each slide.

Modifying the Format of Text on a Slide

To change the format of all the text in a text box, you first need to select the text box. To do this, you click the edge of it. This changes the text box border to a thick line composed of little dots. On the other hand, when you click *inside* a text box, you make the box active—that is, ready to accept text that you type or paste—but this doesn't select the text box, as indicated by the borders composed of slanted lines. When you select a text box (with a border of a thick line composed of little dots), any formatting changes you make are global formatting changes and are applied to all of the text in the text box. (This is different than if you select specific text within the text box and make a local formatting change to the selected text.)

You'll now select text boxes in the slide and title to change the font on all the slides.

To modify the fonts in text boxes on a slide:

1. Click the **slide master** thumbnail (Slide 1) in the Slides tab.
2. Click the dotted-line edge of the body text placeholder on the slide master in the slide pane. The entire placeholder text box is selected, as indicated by the border, which is now a thick line composed of little dots and sizing handles.

   Trouble? If the box surrounding the placeholder is composed of slanted lines, the text box is active, not selected. Click the edge of the text box to change it to a thick line composed of dots.
3. Click the **Font** list arrow Arial on the Formatting toolbar, scroll down, if necessary, and then click **Times New Roman** to change the body text font from Arial to Times New Roman.
4. Click the dotted-line edge of the title placeholder to select the entire text box, click the **Font Color** list arrow A on the Drawing or Formatting toolbar, click **More Colors** to open the Colors dialog box, and then click the **Standard** tab. You can now see a honeycomb of color cells from which to select a new font color. See Figure 2-13.

Figure 2-13 Standard tab in the Colors dialog box

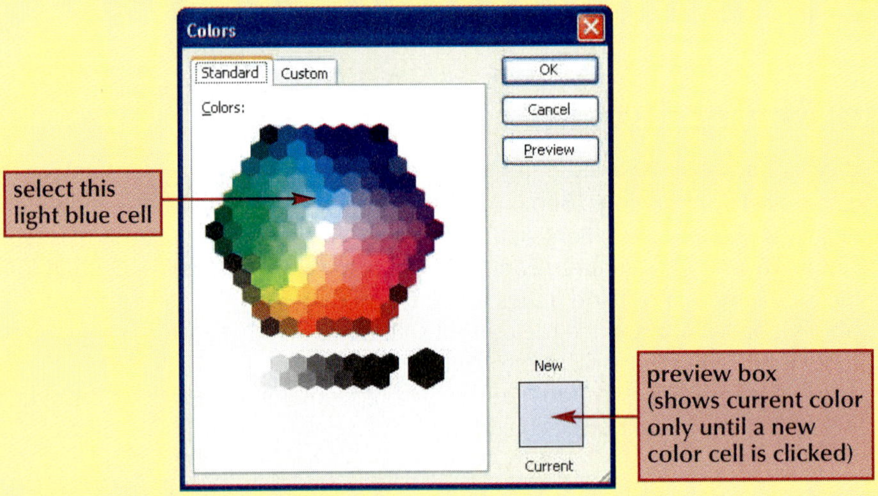

5. Click the light blue cell, as indicated in Figure 2-13. The light blue color appears under New in the preview box in the lower-right corner of the dialog box.
6. Click the **OK** button. The font color of the title on the slide master changes from light violet to light blue. Now you'll change the text alignment so that the title text on the slide master is left-aligned rather than centered.
7. With the title text box still selected, click the **Align Left** button on the Formatting toolbar. The title text is now left-aligned.
8. Click the **title master** thumbnail (Slide 2) in the Slides tab. Note that the changes you made to the text boxes on the slide master have also been applied to the text boxes on the title master. Any changes you make to the format of the text on the slide master are also applied to the text on the title master. This does not, however, work in reverse; in other words, text-formatting changes that you make to the title master do not affect the text on the slide master.

   You don't want the title text on the title master left-aligned.

9. Select the **title** text box on the title master, and then click the **Center** button on the Formatting toolbar. The text is center-aligned, while the title text on the slide master stays left-aligned.

Next, you need to resize the title text box on the slide so you can insert the Global Humanitarian logo next to the title.

Resizing a Text Box on a Slide

To resize a text box, you need to select it, and then drag a sizing handle. You'll resize the title text box on the slide master by dragging the left-center sizing handle. As with the formatting changes you made to the text, you would follow this same procedure to resize text boxes in Normal view.

To resize a text box:

1. Click the **slide master** thumbnail in the Slides tab, and then select the title text box. The sizing handles appear.
2. Drag the left-center sizing handle to the right approximately one inch, as shown in Figure 2-14, and then release the mouse button. This leaves room for the logo, which will go in the upper-left corner of the slide master, to the left of the title text box.

Resizing the title text placeholder **Figure 2-14**

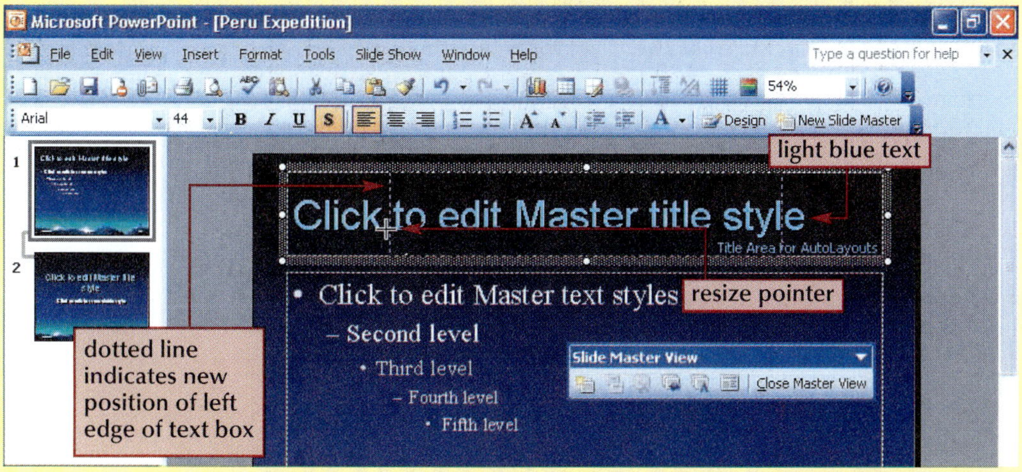

3. Insert the picture file **GHLogo**, located in the Tutorial.02\Tutorial folder included with your Data Files, into the slide master.
4. Drag the logo up near the upper-left corner of the slide, so that the top of the logo is aligned with the top of the title text box.
5. Drag the lower-right sizing handle up and to the left until the logo just fits in the space to the left of the title placeholder.
6. Set the black area surrounding the globe to transparent, and then click a blank area of the slide to deselect the logo. See Figure 2-15.

Figure 2-15 Slide master after adding and reformatting logo

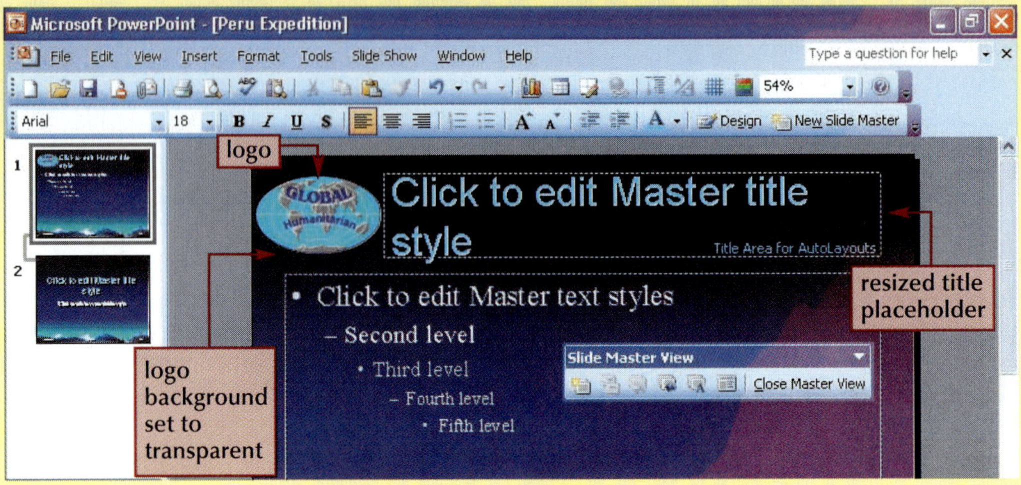

Trouble? If your slide master does not look like the one shown in Figure 2-15, make any necessary adjustments now.

7. Click the **Close Master View** button on the Slide Master View toolbar. The presentation returns to Normal view.
8. Save the presentation.

Applying a Second Design Template

Normally all your slides in one presentation will have the same design template. On occasion, however, you might want to apply a second design template to only one, or a few, of the slides in your presentation. Pablo wants you to change the design template for Slide 8, "Expedition Costs (Per Person)" from the modified Mountain Top design template to the Globe design template. All of the other slides present points about the expedition itself. He wants this slide to stand out from the others because it lists the costs of the trip for each participant.

To apply a second design template to a presentation:

1. Go to **Slide 8** ("Expedition Costs (Per Person)"). When you want to apply a design template to only one slide, you'll usually want that slide to appear in the slide pane.
2. Click the **Design** button on the Formatting toolbar to open the Slide Design task pane.
3. Scroll the task pane until you locate the Globe design template, but do not click it. If you just click the Globe design template, it will appear on all the slides rather than just the selected slide.
4. Position the pointer over the **Globe** design template, and then click the **Design Template** list arrow. See Figure 2-16.

Figure 2-16 **Applying a new design template to this slide only**

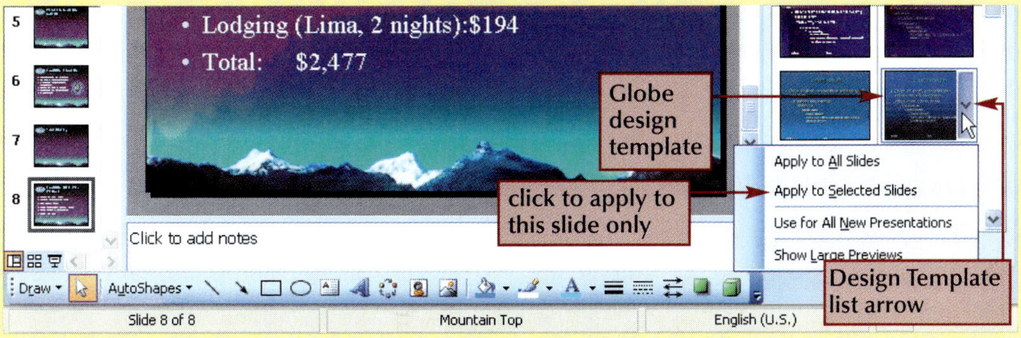

Trouble? If you clicked the design thumbnail instead of the Design Template list arrow, click the Undo button on the Standard toolbar, and then repeat Step 4.

5. Click **Apply to Selected Slides**. Because Slide 8 is the only selected slide in the Slides tab, it's the only one to which the design template is applied.
6. Click the **Close** button in the Slide Design task pane, select the title text box in the slide pane, and then adjust the size and alignment of the title text box so that it's similar to the title text box on the other slides and so that the text doesn't overlap the Global Humanitarian logo. You need to change the body text font to match the other slide.
7. Select the body text box, change the font to Times New Roman, change the font size to 36, and then click a blank area of the slide. See Figure 2-17.

Figure 2-17 **Slide 8 with Globe design template**

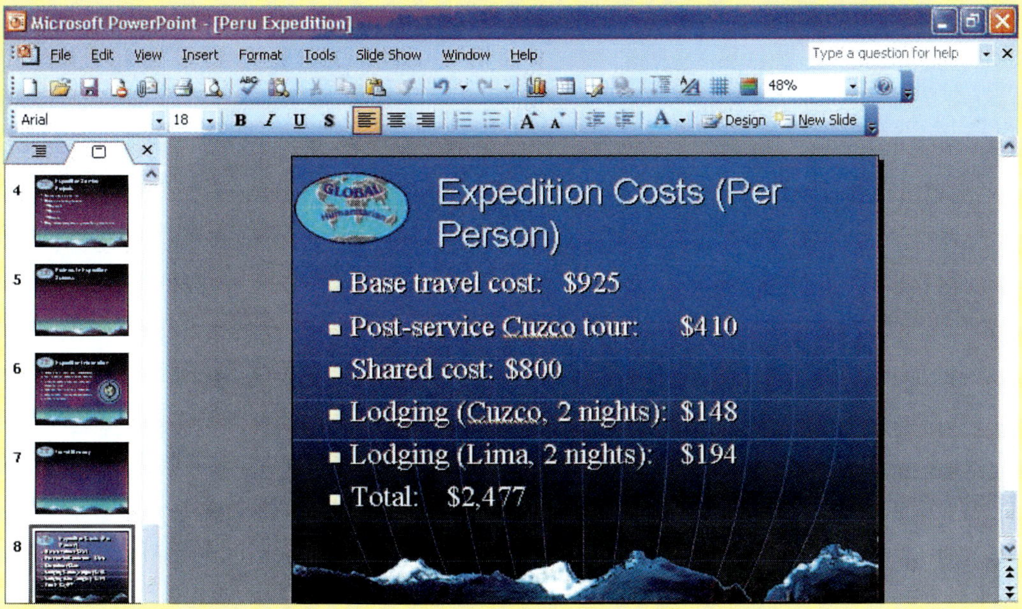

8. Save your changes.

You applied the Globe design template to only one slide in the presentation. The modified Mountain Top design remains on the other slides. The next time you switch to Slide Master view, you will see a second slide-title master pair for the Globe design template below the customized Mountain Top slide-title master pair. Now you need to modify the tab stops on Slide 8 to align the dollar amounts.

Adding and Modifying Tab Stops

A **tab** adds space between the left margin and the beginning of the text on a particular line, or between the text in one column and the text in another column. (When you create several long columns of data, however, you probably want to use a table instead of tabs.) For example, in Slide 8 ("Expedition Costs"), Pablo typed the cost description and a colon, pressed the Tab key to add space, and then typed the dollar amounts for each expense. A **tab stop** is the location where the insertion point moves (including any text to the right of it) when you press the Tab key. The default tab stops on a slide are set at one-inch intervals. You can add your own tab stops to override the default tab stops to align text on a slide. You can set tab stops so that the text left-aligns, right-aligns, center-aligns, or aligns on a decimal point.

The default tab stops on the ruler are left tabs, which position the left edge of text at the tab stop and extend the text to the right. However, you want to align the right sides of the dollar amounts in Slide 8, so you want to use a right tab stop, which positions the right edge of text at the tab stop and extends the text to the left. You'll change the tab stops on Slide 8 now.

To change the tab stops:

1. Click **View** on the menu bar, and then click **Ruler**. Horizontal and vertical rulers appear on the screen.

   Trouble? If rulers were already visible on your screen, then clicking Ruler on the View menu hid them. Click View on the menu bar, and then click Ruler again to redisplay the rulers.

2. Click anywhere in the body text box. The default tab stops for the body text appear as light gray rectangles, or hash marks, under the ruler, and the Left Tab button appears to the left of the horizontal ruler. When Pablo typed the text on this slide, he pressed the Tab key after typing the colon in each line, so the dollar amounts on each line are aligned at the next available tab stop. See Figure 2-18.

Tabs for body text box on ruler **Figure 2-18**

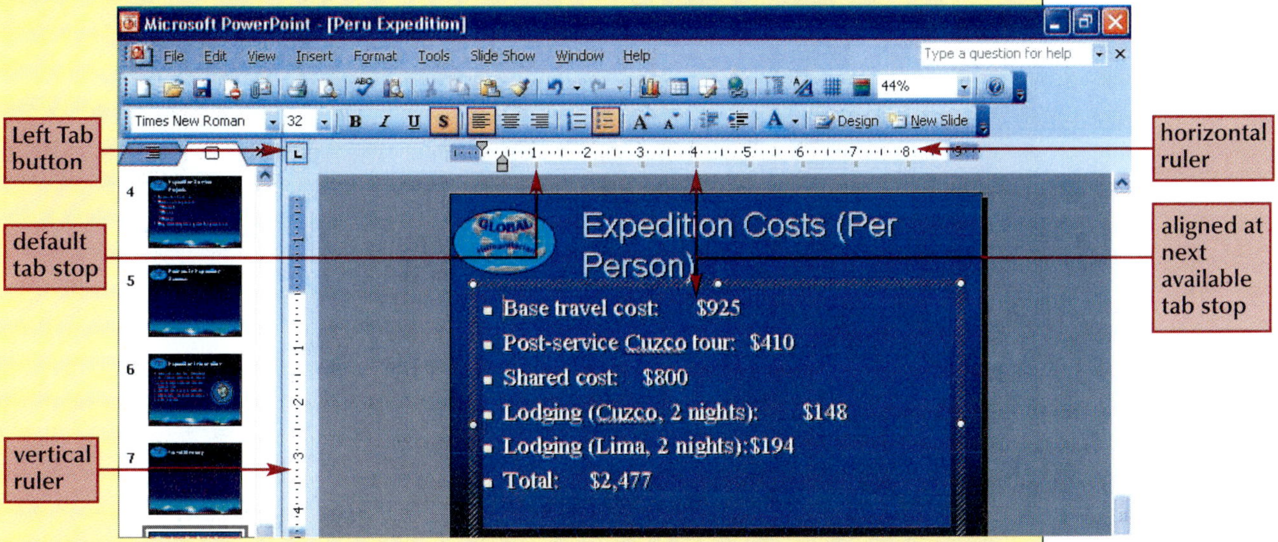

Trouble? If a button other than the Left Tab button appears to the left of the ruler, click the Tab button as many times as necessary until the Left Tab button appears.

3. Click the **Left Tab** button to the left of the horizontal ruler so that the button changes to the Center Tab button, and then click the **Center Tab** button to change it to the Right Tab button. If you were to click the Tab button again, the Decimal Tab button would appear, and if you were to click once more, the Left Tab button would appear again.
4. Position the pointer immediately before the word "Base" in the first bulleted item, and then click and drag to the bottom of the body text to select all of the bulleted items. The selected text is highlighted.
5. Click just below the 8-inch mark in the white area of the horizontal ruler, and then click anywhere within the selected text. A new, right tab stop appears at the location you clicked, the default tab stops to the left of the new tab stop disappear, and the dollar amounts in the body text box become right-aligned at the new tab stop. See Figure 2-19.

Slide 8 after inserting new tab stop in body text paragraphs **Figure 2-19**

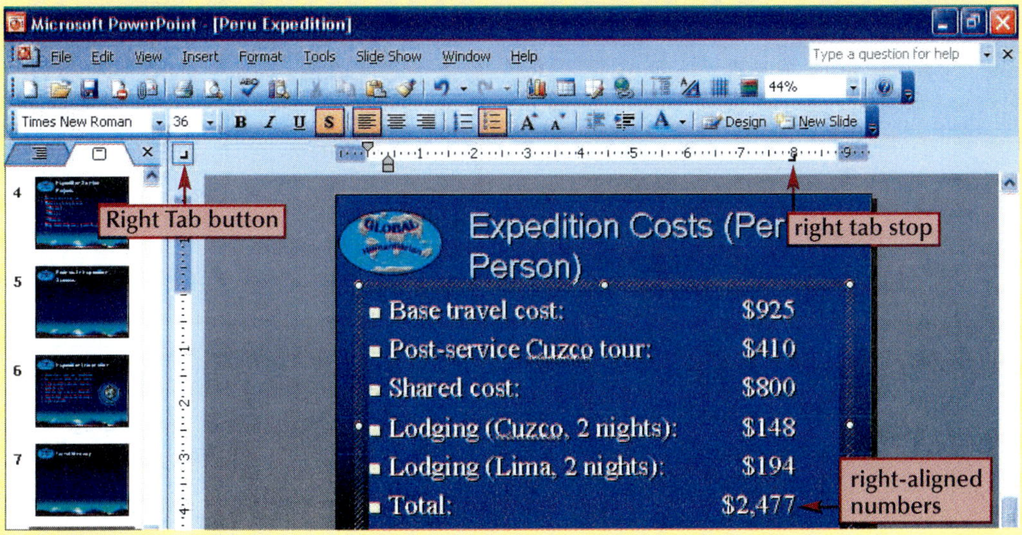

Trouble? If you used the wrong type of tab, drag the new tab stop off the ruler to delete it, click the Tab button as many times as necessary to display the Right Tab button, and then repeat Steps 4 and 5. If you clicked in the wrong place on the ruler, drag the tab stop character to the right or left until it's positioned where you want it.

6. Click **View** on the menu bar, and then click **Ruler**. The rulers disappear from the slide pane.
7. Click a blank area of the slide pane to deselect the text box, and then save your changes.

Next, you'll insert footers and slide numbers.

Inserting Footers and Slide Numbers

When you used the AutoContent wizard, you typed footer text to be displayed at the bottom of each slide. A **header** is text that appears at the top of each page. PowerPoint already provides a footer placeholder on the slide master, and both header and footer placeholders on the notes and handout masters.

As part of the overall slide design, Pablo wants you to include footers and the current slide number on each slide, except the title slide. You'll use the footer placeholders to add the footer and the slide number to each of the slides (except the title slide).

To insert a footer into your presentation:

1. Click **View** on the menu bar, click **Header and Footer** to open the Header and Footer dialog box, and then click the **Slide** tab, if necessary, to display the slide footer information. In the Preview box in the lower-right corner of the dialog box, two of the rectangles at the bottom of the preview slide are black. These black rectangles correspond to the selected check boxes on the Slides tab, in this case, the Date and time and the Footer check boxes.
2. Click the **Date and time** check box to clear it. The left rectangle in the Preview box turns white.
3. Click the **Slide number** check box to select it. The right rectangle in the Preview box turns black. Now the slide number will appear on each slide.
4. Make sure the Footer check box is selected, and then click in the **Footer** text box.
5. Type **Peru Expedition 2006**, and then click the **Don't show on title slide** check box to select it. See Figure 2-20. The slide number and the text you typed in the Footer text box will appear on every slide except the title slide.

Header and Footer dialog box

Figure 2-20

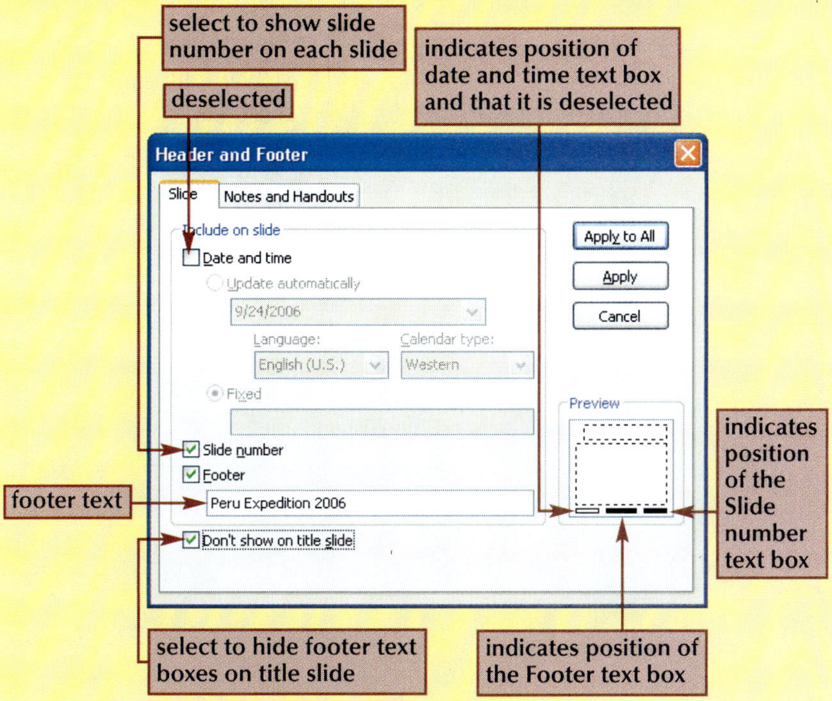

6. Click the **Apply to All** button in the Header and Footer dialog box. All the slides (except the title slide) now contain a footer.

The footer has several problems. First, after you applied the new design template to Slide 8, the mountains at the bottom of the slide appear in front of the footer. Second, the footer text isn't legible because the font is too small and its white color makes it unreadable against the white peak of an Andean mountaintop. You can solve these problems by modifying the slide master of the Globe design template, moving the footer on the slide master so that it appears on the left side of the slide, and increasing the font size of the text in the footer. Before you can reposition the footer placeholder text box, you need to delete the date and time placeholder text box.

To delete and reposition text boxes:

1. Display the slide master, make sure the slide master of the Globe design (Slide 3 in the Slides tab) is selected, and send the mountain bitmap image to the back and bring it forward in front of the background, as before.
2. On the same slide master, click the edge of the **date and time** placeholder (labeled Date Area) in the lower-left corner of the slide, and press the **Delete** key. The placeholder text box is deleted.
3. Select the **footer** placeholder (labeled Footer Area), currently located in the bottom middle of the slide, and then press the ← key until the placeholder is aligned on the left with the body text placeholder. By using the ← key rather than dragging and dropping, you ensure that you move the placeholder horizontally but not vertically.

4. With the footer placeholder still selected, click the **Align Left** button on the Formatting toolbar so the text in the footer placeholder is left-aligned rather than centered in the text box.
5. With the footer placeholder still selected, press and hold the **Shift** key, and then click the **slide number** placeholder (labeled Number Area) in the lower-right corner of the slide. Both the footer and the slide number placeholders are selected.
6. Press the ↓ key two or three times until the bottoms of the two placeholders are on the bottom of the slide, as shown in Figure 2-21. Make sure that you position the bottom of the placeholders at the bottom of the slide and not at the bottom of the drop shadow behind the slide.

Figure 2-21 **Reformatted Globe design template slide master**

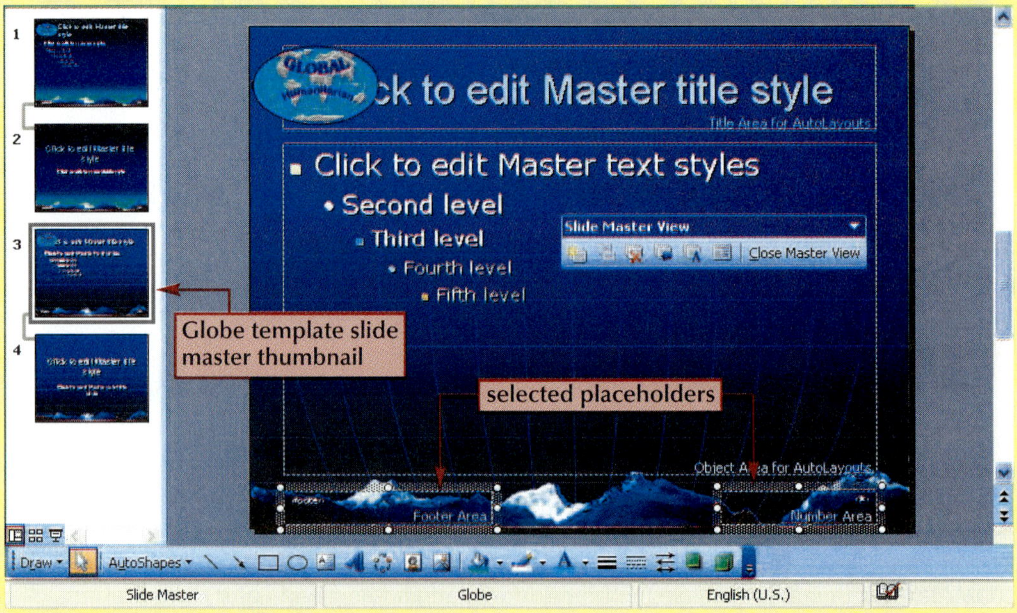

Trouble? If you can't position the text boxes where you want to, press and hold the Ctrl key while you press the ↓ key to nudge the placeholders in smaller increments than pressing the ↓ key alone.

7. With the footer and slide number placeholders still selected, click the **Font Size** list arrow on the Formatting toolbar, and then click **24** to change the font size to 24 points.
8. Click the **Mountain Top slide master** (Slide 1) in the Slides tab and then repeat Steps 2 through 7 to make the same changes on the slide master of the Mountain Top design template.
9. Click the **Close Master View** button on the Slide Master View toolbar. Now you can read the footer text and the slide number, but the footer text wraps to a second line because the footer placeholder is too small to contain all the footer text on one line.
10. Switch back to Slide Master view, select the footer placeholder, and then drag the right-center sizing handle of the footer placeholder to the right until the right edge of the text box is near the center of the slide.
11. Repeat Step 10 on the Mountain Top slide master, and then click the **Normal View** button at the bottom of the Slides tab.

12. Go to **Slide 4** to make sure that you can read the footer and the slide number on a slide with the Mountain Top design template. See Figure 2-22.

Figure 2-22 **Slide 4 with adjusted footer and slide number**

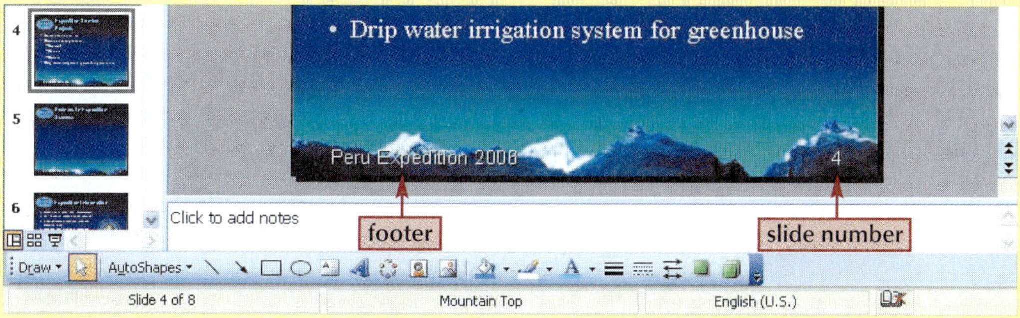

Trouble? If your footer and slide number aren't the same font size and color and in the same position as shown in Figure 2-22, return to Slide Master view and make any necessary adjustments.

13. Save the presentation.

Pablo is pleased with how the footer and page number appear at the bottom of each slide.

You've completed most of Pablo's presentation. In Session 2.2, you'll finalize the slides by creating a table, diagram, and simple drawing.

Review

Session 2.1 Quick Check

1. List at least three reasons to add graphics to your presentation.
2. Explain the meaning of the following terms:
   a. design template
   b. bitmap image
   c. graphic
   d. Default Design template
3. Describe how to do the following:
   a. make a text box active
   b. select a text box
   c. scale a graphic to change its size
   d. move an object on a slide
   e. apply a second design template to selected slides
   f. recolor clip art
4. What is the difference between the title master and the slide master?
5. What are tabs? What are tab stops? Describe how to insert a right tab stop on the ruler.
6. What are the three objects included in a footer on a slide as part of the master?

Session 2.2

Creating a Table in a Slide

Pablo wants you to create a table listing the travel itinerary for the Peru expedition in Slide 7. A **table** is information arranged in horizontal rows and vertical columns. The area where a row and column intersect is called a **cell**. Each cell contains one piece of information and is identified by a column and row label; for example, the cell in the upper-left corner of a table is cell A1 (column A, row 1), the cell to the right of that is B1, the cell below A1 is A2, and so forth. A table's structure is indicated by borders, which are lines that outline the rows and columns.

Reference Window

Inserting a Table on a Slide

- Click Format on the menu bar, and then click Slide Layout to open the Slide Layout task pane.
- Change the slide layout of the desired slide to one of the Content layouts.
- Click the Insert Table button.
- Specify the desired table size—the numbers of columns and rows—and then click the OK button.
- Add information to the cells. Use the Tab key to move from one cell to the next, and the Shift+Tab keys to move to previous cells.
- Modify the borders as desired.
- Click in a blank area of the slide to deselect the table.

The itinerary table you'll create needs to have four columns: one for the date of travel, one for the departure or arrival city, one for the time of departure or arrival, and one for the flight number. The table needs to have nine rows: one row for column labels, and eight rows for the data. Now you'll create the travel itinerary table.

To create a table:

1. If you took a break after the previous session, make sure PowerPoint is running, and then open the presentation **Peru Expedition** located in the Tutorial.02\Tutorial folder included with your Data Files.
2. Go to **Slide 7** ("Travel Itinerary"), click **Format** on the menu bar, and then click **Slide Layout** to open the Slide Layout task pane.
3. Click the **Title and Content** layout. The layout of the current slide changes.
4. Click the **Insert Table** button in the content placeholder in the slide pane. The Insert Table dialog box opens.
5. Type **4** in the Number of columns text box, press the **Tab** key to move the insertion point to the Number of rows text box, type **9**, and then click the **OK** button. A table made up of four columns and nine rows is inserted in the slide with the insertion point blinking in the first cell (cell A1), and the Tables and Borders toolbar opens.

   Trouble? If the table doesn't have four columns and nine rows, click the Undo button on the Standard toolbar to undo your creation of the table, and then repeat Steps 4 and 5.

Trouble? If the Tables and Borders toolbar doesn't appear, click View on the main menu bar, point to Toolbars, and then click Tables and Borders.

6. Close the task pane.

Now you're ready to fill the blank cells with information. To enter data in a table, you click in the cell in which you want to enter data. Once you start typing in a cell, you can use the Tab and arrow keys to move from one cell to another. If you want to add a new row at the bottom of the table, move the insertion point to the last cell in the table, and then press the Tab key. A new row will be inserted automatically.

To add information to the table:

1. With the insertion point blinking in the first cell, type **Date**, press the **Tab** key to move to cell B1, type **City**, press the **Tab** key to move to cell C1, type **Time**, press the **Tab** key to move to cell D1 (the last cell in the first row), and then type **Flight**. This completes the column labels.

   Trouble? You might have to drag the Tables and Borders toolbar by its title bar to see the table cells.

2. Press the **Tab** key. The insertion point moves to cell A2.
3. Type **Dec. 25**, and then press the **Tab** key to move to cell B2.
4. Type **Lv Dallas** (short for "Leave Dallas") in cell B2, type **4:22 PM** in cell C2, and then type **AA 982** (short for American Airlines flight 982) in cell D2. This completes the first row of data.
5. Complete the information in the rest of the cells, as shown in Figure 2-23, and then click a blank area of the slide to deselect the table.

Figure 2-23 Slide 7 with completed table

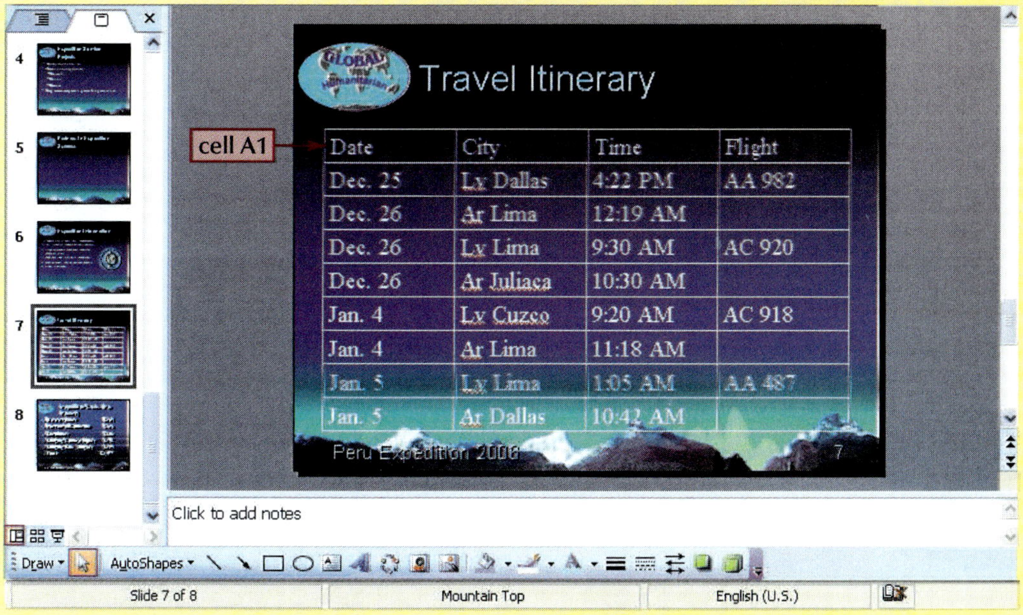

Trouble? If you pressed the Tab key after typing the last enty, you added a new row to the table. Click the Undo button on the Standard toolbar to remove the extra row.

To make the column labels appear visually separated from the data, you'll change the border below the top row so that it is more visible.

To draw a border:

1. Click anywhere in the table to make it active and display the Tables and Borders toolbar.
2. Click the **Draw Table** button on the Tables and Borders toolbar, and then move the pointer off of the toolbar. The pointer changes to .
3. Click the **Border Width** list arrow 1 pt on the Tables and Borders toolbar, and then click **3 pt** to change the border line width to three points.
4. Click the **Border Color** button on the Tables and Borders toolbar, and then click the light blue tile (the custom color *below* the main row of tiles). Now when you draw a border, it will be a 3-point, light blue line.
5. Drag along the border between the first and second rows in the table. As you draw the border, a dotted line appears to indicate the border as it is drawn. When you release the mouse button, the light blue line appears.
6. Click the **Draw Table** button on the Table and Borders toolbar to deselect it.

In addition to changing the border lines in a table, you can add and change diagonal lines within cells of a table. First, click the Table button on the Tables and Borders toolbar, click Borders and Fill, click the Borders tab, and then click one or both of the Diagonal Line buttons.

Although the colored border visually separates the column labels from the data in the table, the labels would stand out more if they were formatted differently from the data. You will format the text in the top row to be a light blue, bold, Arial font.

To modify the font in a table:

1. Drag across all the text in the top row to select it.
2. Change the font to **Arial**, as you would any other type of text.
3. Click the **Bold** button B on the Formatting toolbar to make the selected text bold.
4. Click the **Font Color** list arrow A on the Drawing or Formatting toolbar, and then click the light blue tile (the custom color *below* the main row of tiles).
5. Click a blank area of the slide pane to deselect the table. See Figure 2-24.

Figure 2-24 **Table after modifying border and column headings**

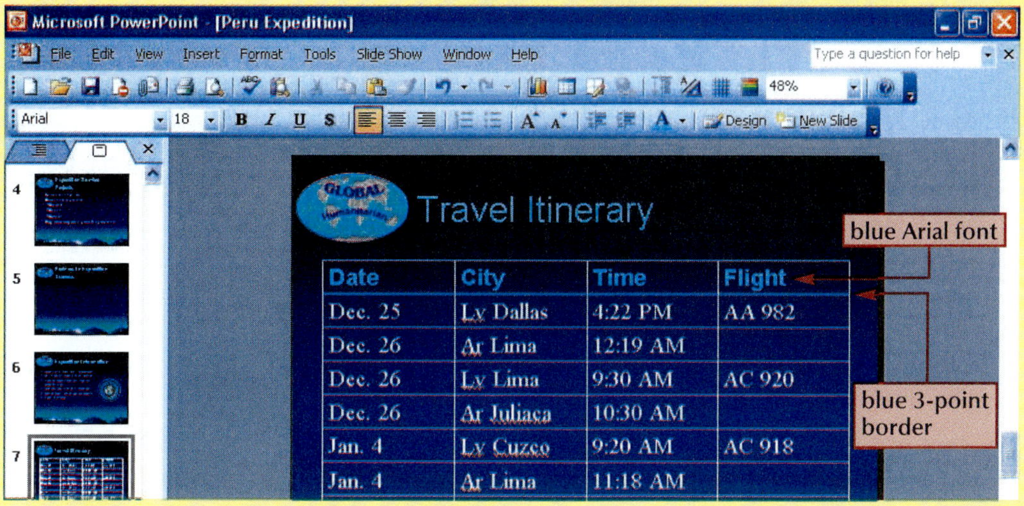

6. Save your changes.

You have completed the table that shows the flight itinerary for the Peru expedition. The Tables and Borders toolbar also lets you remove rows, add and remove columns, combine cells, split cells, and perform other modifications to the table. If you want to do any of these tasks, use PowerPoint's Help system. In addition, try right-clicking anywhere on the table to see a shortcut menu containing commands specific to working with tables.

Your next task is to create a diagram on Slide 5 to show the relationship between the four major parties involved in a humanitarian service project.

Creating a Diagram on a Slide

PowerPoint allows you to create the following types of diagrams on slides:

- **Cycle diagrams**—show a process that has a continuous cycle
- **Organizational charts**—show the relationship between individuals or units within an organization
- **Radial diagrams**—show the relationships of a core element
- **Pyramid diagrams**—show foundation-based relationships
- **Venn diagrams**—show areas of overlap between elements
- **Target diagrams**—show steps toward a goal

In the Peru Expedition presentation, Pablo wants you to add a Venn diagram on Slide 5 ("Partners in Expedition Success") to show the relationship between the four major parties involved in a humanitarian service project: the village for which the service is being performed, the volunteers who perform the service, the humanitarian organization that sponsors the service, and the donors who contribute money to support the service. You'll create the Venn diagram now.

To create a Venn diagram:

1. Go to **Slide 5**, and then change the layout to the **Title and Content** layout in the Content Layouts section.
2. Close the task pane, and then click the **Insert Diagram or Organization Chart** button in the content placeholder in the slide pane. The Diagram Gallery dialog box opens.
3. Click the **Venn Diagram** icon (the middle icon in the second row), and then click the **OK** button. A diagram with three intersecting circles and text box placeholders is added to the slide, and the Diagram toolbar opens. The text box placeholders are hard to see on the dark blue part of the background. Selection handles—gray circles with small *X*s in them—appear around the top circle in the diagram. When you see selection handles instead of sizing handles on a slide, it means that the selected object is part of a larger object, and although you can modify the selected object by changing its color or other attributes, you can't resize the individual object.

   Next, you'll edit the diagram by adding another circle, adding text, and modifying the circle colors.
4. Click the **Insert Shape** button on the Diagram toolbar. A fourth circle is added to the diagram. The new circle is the same color as the bottom circle. You'll change the color of the bottom circle.
5. Right-click the bottom circle, click **Format AutoShape** on the shortcut menu to open the Format AutoShape dialog box, and then click the **Colors and Lines** tab, if necessary.
6. Click the **Color** list arrow in the Fill section at the top of the dialog box, and then click the light blue tile (the custom color) located on its own row just above the More Colors command.
7. Click the **OK** button. The bottom circle is recolored light blue. See Figure 2-25.

Figure 2-25 Venn diagram with new shape added

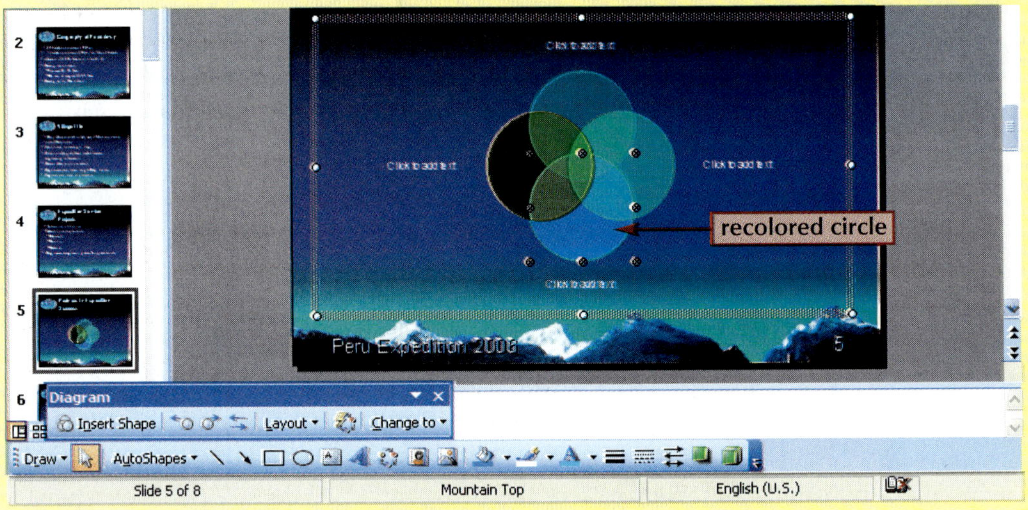

Now you'll label each circle in the Venn diagram.

To add and modify text in the Venn diagram:

1. Click in the text box placeholder (labeled "Click to add text") above the top circle, and then type **Village**.
2. Type **Volunteers** in the text box placeholder to the right of the right circle.
3. Click in the text box placeholder to the left of the left circle, type **Global**, press the **Enter** key, and then type **Humanitarian**.
4. Type **Donors** in the text box placeholder below the bottom circle.

   Because the font of the text around the Venn diagram is small, the text is hard to read. You'll increase the font size now.
5. Shift-click the four text boxes (press and hold the Shift key, and then click each of the text boxes) to select them all, and then change the font size to **24** points.
6. Click a blank area of the slide pane to deselect everything in the slide. See Figure 2-26.

Slide 5 with completed Venn diagram **Figure 2-26**

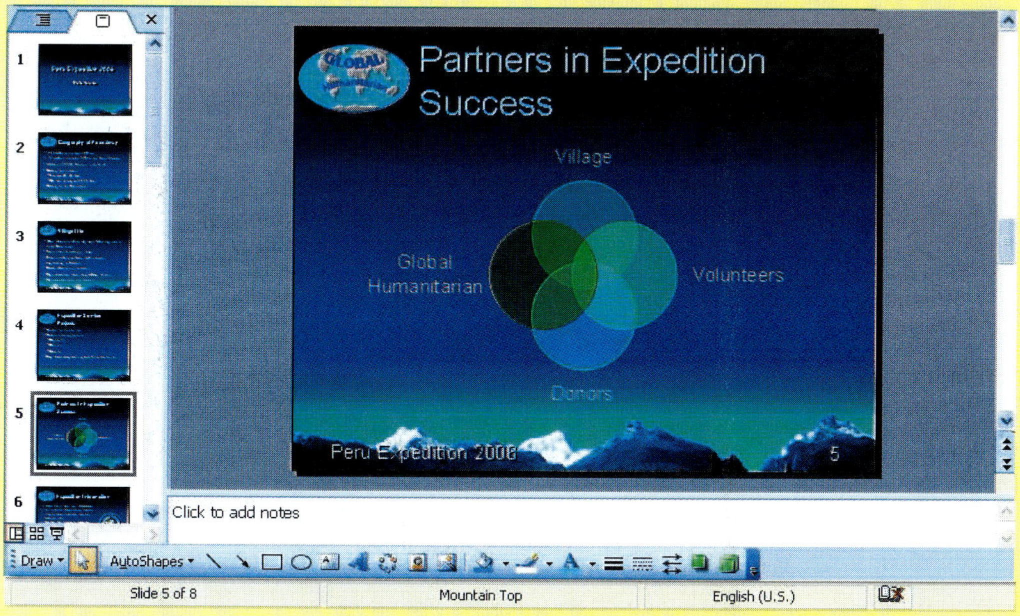

7. Save your changes.

This completes the diagram on Slide 5. When Pablo uses this slide show to give a presentation, he'll discuss how the roles of the village, volunteers, donors, and Global Humanitarian overlap to make a successful project.

Pablo now asks you to insert a new Slide 6, and create a shape in the slide.

Creating and Manipulating a Shape

For the last graphic to be included in his presentation, Pablo asks you to add an inverted triangle with labels along each side to a new Slide 6. The labels on each side of the triangle will list the three components of the Global Humanitarian strategy—village outreach projects, expeditions, and internships. Pablo wants you to use an equilateral triangle to point out that each of the three strategies is equally important. This graphic will be a strong visual reminder to potential Global Humanitarian contributors and volunteers of this threefold strategy.

To create the triangle, you'll use the triangle AutoShape. When you click the AutoShapes button on the Drawing toolbar, you are presented with the following categories of shapes from which to choose: lines, connectors, basic shapes (for example, rectangles and triangles), block arrows, flowchart shapes, stars and banners, callouts, and action buttons.

To insert a shape in a slide using AutoShapes:

1. Insert a new Slide 6, change the slide layout to **Title Only** (under Text Layouts), and then close the Slide Layout task pane.
2. Type **Global Humanitarian Strategy** in the title placeholder.
3. Click the **AutoShapes** button on the Drawing toolbar, and then point to **Basic Shapes**. The Basic Shapes palette opens.
4. Click the **Isosceles Triangle** button on the Basic Shapes palette, as indicated in Figure 2-27, and then position the pointer over the slide in the slide pane. The pointer changes to +.

Figure 2-27 Selecting an AutoShape

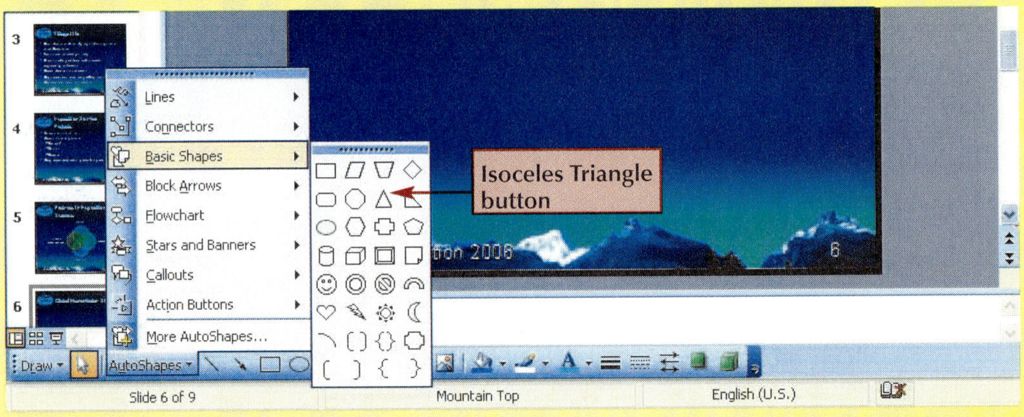

5. Position + approximately one inch below the "o" in "Global" (in the title of the slide), press and hold down the **Shift** key, and then click and and drag the pointer down and to the right. The outline of a triangle appears as you drag. Pressing the Shift key while you drag makes the triangle equilateral—the three sides are of equal length. (Similarly, if you click the Oval button, you can press and hold the Shift key while you drag to draw a circle, and if you click the Rectangle button, you can press and hold the Shift key while you drag to draw a square.)

6. Release the mouse button and the Shift key when your triangle is approximately the same size and shape as the one shown in Figure 2-28.

Figure 2-28 **Slide 6 with isosceles triangle shape**

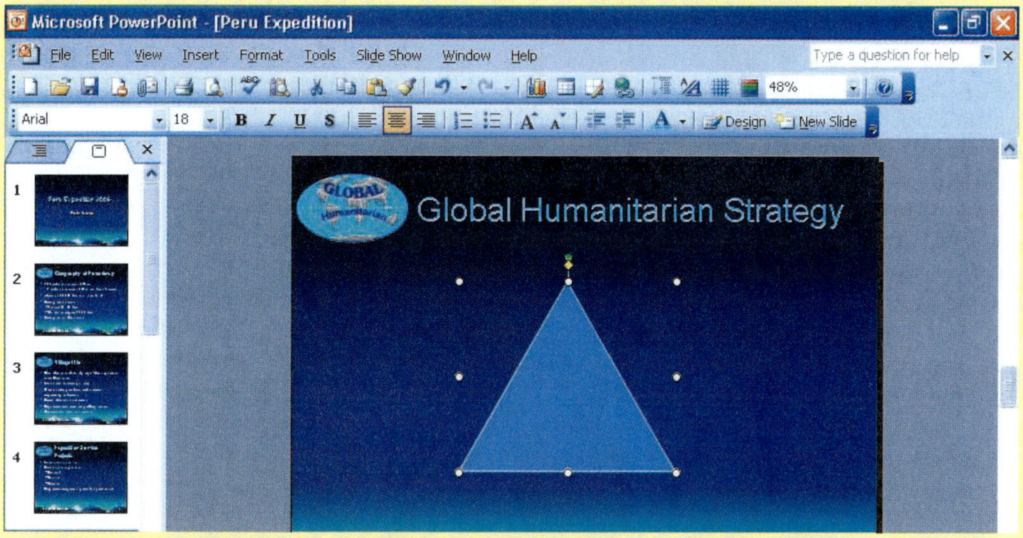

Trouble? If your triangle doesn't look like the one in Figure 2-28, you can move it by dragging it to a new location, resize or change its shape by dragging one or more of the sizing handles, or delete it by pressing the Delete key, and then repeating Steps 3 through 6 to redraw it.

In addition to the sizing handles, the selected triangle has a yellow diamond and a green circle at its top. The yellow diamond is an **adjustment handle**; if you drag it, the shape of the tip of the triangle changes without changing the overall size of the object. The green circle is the **rotate handle**, which you can drag to rotate the shape.

The default color of the drawn object is the blue color from the set of default colors, but Pablo prefers the same color of blue as the title text.

To change the fill color of an AutoShape:

1. With the triangle still selected, click the **Fill Color** list arrow on the Drawing toolbar. The color palette appears on the screen.
2. Click the light blue tile (the custom color located below the row of default tiles). The color of the triangle changes to light blue.

The triangle is the desired size and color, but Pablo wants you to flip (invert) the triangle so that it points down instead of up. You can use commands on the Draw menu on the Drawing toolbar to rotate and flip objects.

To flip an object:

1. With the triangle still selected, click the **Draw** button on the Drawing toolbar, point to **Rotate or Flip**, and then click **Flip Vertical**.
2. Click a blank region in the slide pane to deselect the triangle. Your triangle should be sized, positioned, colored, and oriented like the one shown in Figure 2-29.

Figure 2-29 Slide 6 after recoloring and flipping triangle

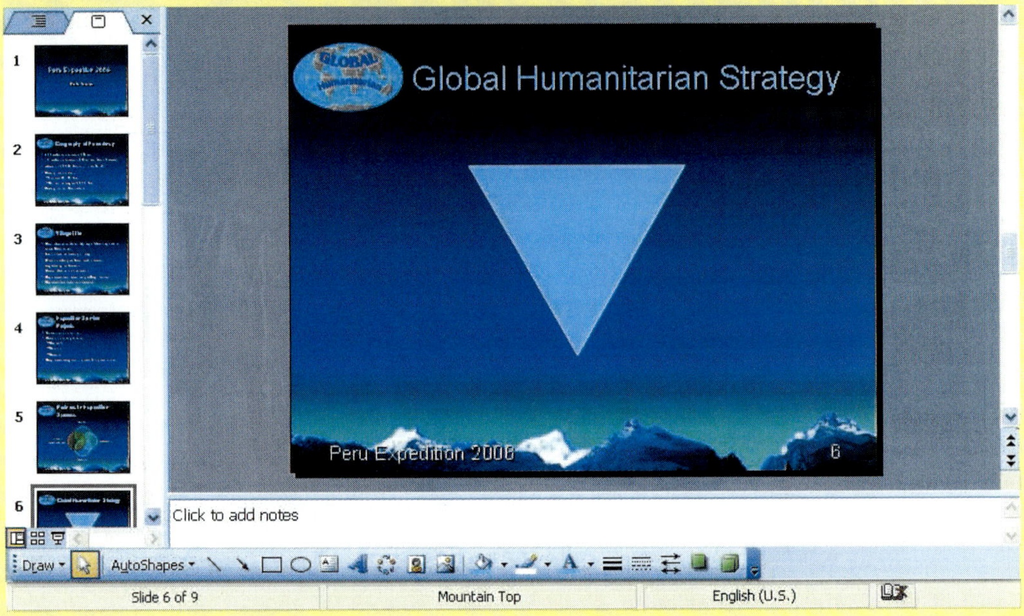

3. Save the presentation.

Now you'll add the text labels along the sides of the triangle.

Inserting Text Boxes

Sometimes you need to add a text box in a different location than any of the text box placeholders on the layouts. You need to add text boxes on each of the three sides of the triangle in Slide 6.

Adding Text to the Diagram

You're ready to add the text naming the three strategies of Global Humanitarian on each side of the triangle. You'll now add three text boxes around the AutoShape triangle you just created.

To add a text box to the slide:

1. Click the **Text Box** button on the Drawing toolbar, and then position the pointer over the slide. The pointer changes to ↓.
2. Position ↓ so it is just above and centered on the top side of the triangle, and then click. A small text box appears above the triangle with the insertion point blinking in it. The position doesn't have to be exact.

Trouble? If the insertion point is blinking in the middle of the triangle instead of in a new text box above the triangle, you clicked the edge of the triangle. Click the Undo button on the Standard toolbar, and then repeat Steps 1 and 2.

3. Click the **Center** button on the Formatting toolbar, and then type **Village Outreach Projects**.
4. Click the **Text Box** button on the Drawing toolbar, click ↓ to the right of the triangle, and then type **Expeditions**.
5. Create a third text box to the left of the triangle, click the **Align Right** button on the Formatting toolbar, and then type **Internships**.
6. Click the **Text Box** button again, and then drag to draw a text box *inside* the triangle.
7. Type **Global Humanitarian**.

   Trouble? If the text you type appears upside down, you did not drag to create the text box inside the triangle, you simply clicked. Click the Undo button on the Standard toolbar twice, and then repeat Steps 6 and 7.
8. If the text inside the triangle does not fit on one line, drag a sizing handle on the text box to increase the size of the text box.
9. Select the three text boxes that you created outside the triangle by Shift-clicking them, and then change the font size to **24** points.
10. Click in a blank area of the slide to deselect the text boxes. Your slide should now look similar to Figure 2-30.

Figure 2-30 Text boxes added in and around triangle

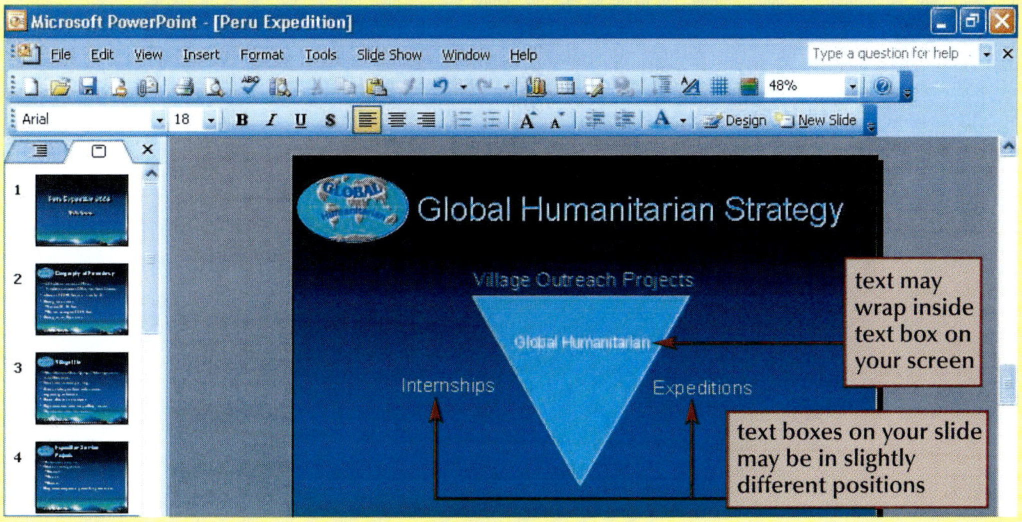

Next you'll rotate the text boxes to make them parallel to the sides of the triangle.

Rotating and Moving Text Boxes

The method for rotating text is similar to the one for rotating graphics (or rotating any other object). You use the Rotate or Flip commands on the Draw menu on the Drawing toolbar, or you drag the rotate handle on the object. You will rotate the text boxes on the left and right sides of the triangle.

To rotate and move the text boxes:

1. Click anywhere within the "Expeditions" text box. The sizing handles and the rotate handle appear around the text box.
2. Position the pointer over the rotate handle. The pointer becomes .
3. Press and hold the **Shift** key, and then drag the rotate handle counterclockwise until the top edge of the box is parallel to the lower-right edge of the triangle. Holding down the Shift key causes the rotation to occur in 15-degree increments.
4. Drag the "Expeditions" text box to position it against and centered on the lower-right edge of the triangle. See Figure 2-31.

Figure 2-31 Slide 6 with rotated and repositioned text box

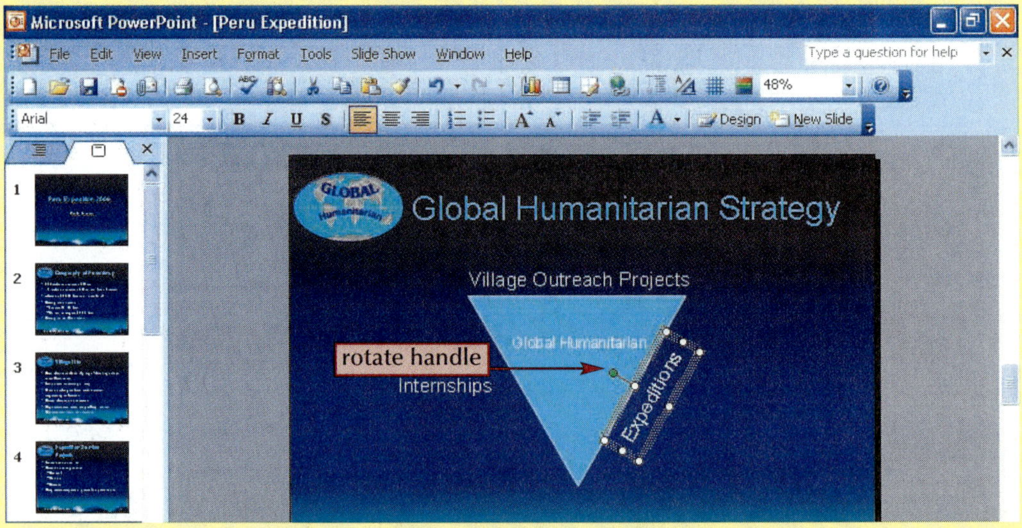

Trouble? If the edge of the text box isn't parallel to the edge of the triangle, you can repeat Steps 2 and 3 to fix the rotation. If necessary, try it without pressing the Shift key.

Trouble? If the text box jumps from one location to another as you drag it, and you can't position it exactly where you want it, hold down the Alt key as you drag the box. (The Alt key temporarily disables a feature that forces objects to snap to invisible gridlines on the slide.)

5. Rotate the "Internships" text box clockwise so that the top edge of the text is parallel to the lower-left edge of the triangle, and then position the text box so it's against and centered on the left edge of the triangle.
6. Adjust the position of (but don't rotate) the "Village Outreach Projects" text box so it's centered over the triangle.
7. Reposition the text box inside the triangle so that it is centered in the triangle.
8. Click a blank area of the slide pane to deselect the text box. Your slide should look like Figure 2-32.

Slide 6 with completed diagram **Figure 2-32**

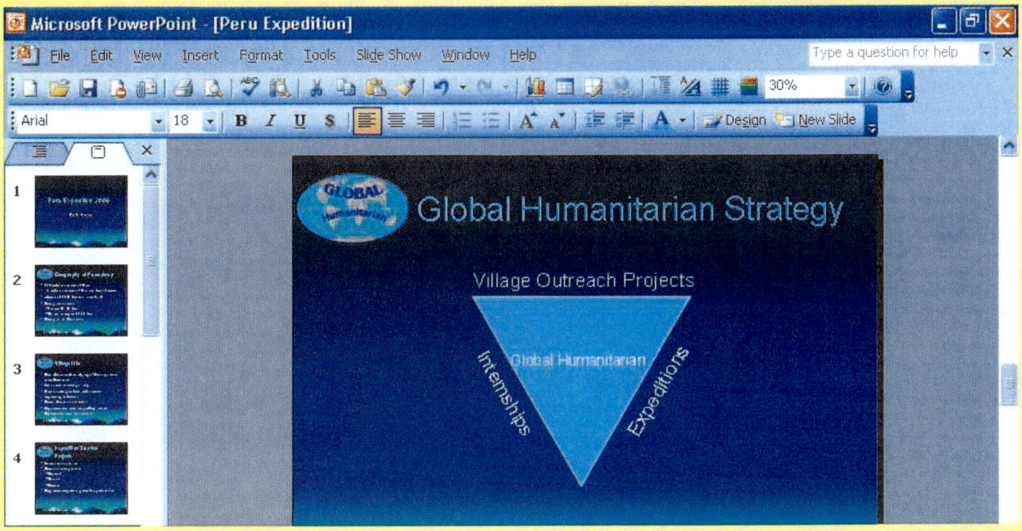

9. Save the presentation.

Pablo asks you to perform one final task before the presentation is finished. He wants you to add a summary at the end of the presentation.

Adding a Summary Slide

A **summary slide** is a slide containing the slide titles of selected slides in the presentation. PowerPoint helps you create a summary slide automatically. You'll do this now.

To create a summary slide:

1. Click the **Slide Sorter View** button at the bottom of the Slides tab. The presentation appears in Slide Sorter view.
2. Click **Slide 2**, press and hold down the **Shift** key, and then click **Slide 9**. All of the slides except Slide 1 are selected. (If you wanted to select nonsequential slides, you would press and hold the Ctrl key while you clicked the desired slides.)
3. Click the **Summary Slide** button on the Slide Sorter toolbar. PowerPoint creates a new slide in front of the first selected slide with the title "Summary Slide" and body text consisting of a list of the titles of the selected slides.

   Trouble? If you don't see the Summary Slide button on the Slide Sorter toolbar, click the Toolbar Options button on the Slide Sorter toolbar.
4. Drag **Slide 2** (the new summary slide) to the right of Slide 10. Slide 2 becomes Slide 10, and the other slides are renumbered automatically.
5. Double-click **Slide 10** to return to Normal view with Slide 10 in the slide pane.
6. Double-click **Slide** in the title text to select the entire word, press the **Delete** key, and then deselect the text box. The selected text is deleted and the title becomes "Summary." See Figure 2-33.

Figure 2-33 New summary slide

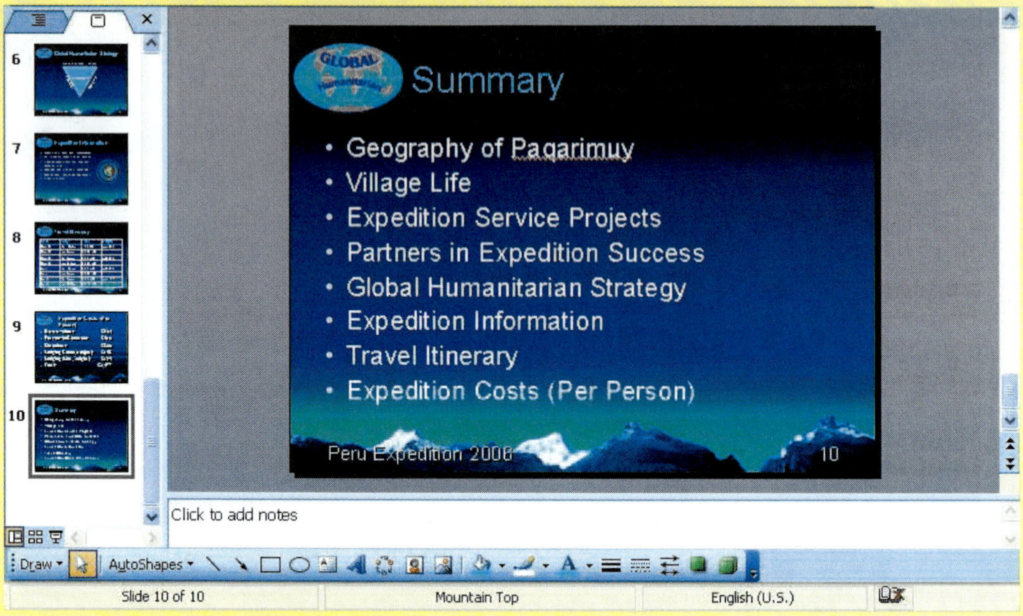

You have completed the entire presentation, so you should save the final version to the disk.

7. Save the file.

As usual, you should finish up your presentation by checking the spelling, viewing it in Slide Show view, and printing it.

To check, view, and print the presentation:

1. Click the **Spelling** button on the Standard toolbar to start checking the spelling of your presentation. Decide how to handle each word that is flagged because it was not found in the PowerPoint dictionary. (In most cases, you should click the Ignore All button because the words are proper nouns, such as "Paqarimuy" and "Cuzco.")
2. Go to **Slide 1**, and then click the **Slide Show from current slide** button at the bottom of the Slides tab. The slide show starts.
3. Press the **spacebar** or click the mouse button to advance through the slide show.
4. If you see any problems while you are watching the slide show, press the **Esc** key to exit the slide show and return to Normal view, make the necessary corrections, and then return to Slide Show view.
5. Go to **Slide 1**, and then replace Pablo's name with your own name.
6. Print the presentation in grayscale as handouts, with six slides per page. Don't worry that the footers and one of the graphics are illegible in grayscale.
7. Save the presentation, and then close the presentation.

Pablo is pleased with the additions and modifications you made to the presentation. He is anxious to use it to recruit volunteers for the next Peru expedition.

Review

Session 2.2 Quick Check

1. How do you add a table to a slide?
2. Where is cell A1 in a table?
3. What is a Venn diagram?
4. How do you add a text box to a slide?
5. How do you draw a shape, such as a rectangle or a circle, on a slide?
6. How do you rotate or flip an object using menu commands?
7. How do you rotate an object without using menu commands?
8. Describe the Summary Slide command in PowerPoint.

Review

Tutorial Summary

In this tutorial, you learned how to create a new presentation using a design template, and how to apply a new design template to selected (or all) the slides in the presentation. You learned how to insert, format, and resize graphics, including clip art and photographs. You also learned how to modify the design template in the slide master and the title master. You learned how to add tab stops to align text on a slide. You learned how to insert footer information on slides. You also learned how to insert a table, a diagram, a shape, and a text box on slides. And finally, you learned how to add a summary slide to a presentation.

Key Terms

adjustment handle	font style	rotate handle
bitmap image	graphic	slide master
cell	handout master	slide-title master pair
clip art	header	summary slide
color scheme	master	tab
default colors	notes master	tab stop
design template	pixel	table
font	point	title master

Practice

Practice the skills you learned in the tutorial using the same case scenario.

Review Assignments

Data Files needed for the Review Assignments: PackList.jpg, GHLogo.jpg, SlpBag.jpg, Boots.ppt, Camera.jpg, Food.jpg, Personal.jpg, PrMeds.jpg, Vitamins.jpg

One of the common questions from volunteers who sign up for a service expedition is, "What items will I need for the trip?" In other words, they want to see a packing list to give them an idea of what they'll have to purchase and pack if they decide to go on the trip. Pablo decides to give a presentation to all volunteers to explain what they must take on the service expedition. He asks you to create a PowerPoint presentation on the Peru expedition packing list. Complete the following:

1. Open the file **PackList** located in the Tutorial.02\Review folder included with your Data Files, and then save it as **Peru Packing List** in the same folder.
2. Apply the design template titled "Teamwork," and then replace the subtitle in Slide 1 with your name.

3. Add the footer "Packing List" and slide numbers to all the slides except Slide 1.
4. In the title master, insert the logo file **GHLogo**, also located in the Tutorial.02\Review folder, position the graphic near the lower-right corner of the slide, just above the Number Area (the slide number placeholder text box), and then make the background of the logo transparent.
5. On both the title master and the slide master, change the title font color from light blue to the light yellow-green color found among the scheme colors. Switch back to Normal view when you are finished.
6. On Slide 2, change the slide layout so you can place clip art to the right of the bulleted list, search for clip art that deals with money, and then insert the piece of clip art that shows a dollar sign in an orange circle.
7. Recolor the clip art so that it is green (the third color from the right in the color palette).
8. Resize the clip art so it fits properly on the slide, and then resize the bulleted-list text box as needed so the text is as large as possible without overlapping the clip art. If the font size does not increase automatically when you increase the size of the text box, then use the Font Size button on the Formatting toolbar.
9. In Slide 3, insert the bitmap image file **SlpBag** ("sleeping bag") located in the Tutorial.02\Review folder.
10. Resize the sleeping bag image to increase its size so it fills more of the space on the right side of the slide, and then make the background of the image transparent.
11. In Slides 4 through 9, insert appropriate bitmap images located in the Tutorial.02\Review folder, resize the images as large as possible, and make the backgrounds transparent. Modify the layouts or resize the body text boxes as needed.
12. Add a new Slide 10 using the Title Only layout (under Text Layouts), type "Areas of Personal Preparation" as the title, draw a square in the middle of the blank area of the slide below the title, and change the fill color to the light blue color in the default color palette.
13. Add text just outside of the square on each of its four sides, using the words "Physical," "Mental," "Social," and "Spiritual." It doesn't matter which word you place on which side.
14. Rotate the text on the sides of the box so the bottom edges of the text boxes face toward the square. Adjust the text boxes so that each word is centered along the edge of the square and almost resting on the box. Resize the font to a readable size.
15. Add a new Slide 11 with the Title and Content layout, type "Discount Items" as the title, insert a table with three columns and five rows, and then add the text as follows:

Item	Regular Price	Discount Price
Boots	$198	$118
Sleeping bag	$162	$98
Water filter	$51	$32
Flashlight	$26	$16

16. Select the text and numbers in columns 2 and 3, and then right-align it.
17. Draw a light yellow-green, 4½ point border below the top row, and then modify the format of the text in the top row so it is 32 points and light yellow-green.
18. Drag the bottom-center sizing handle of the table up so that the table stays the same width but decreases in height so the text fits better in the cells of the table.

19. To Slide 11 only, apply the design template titled "Glass Layers," and then change the font and alignment of the title text on the slide master for this slide so that it matches the rest of the slides.
20. Add a new Slide 12 with the Title and Content layout, type "Thank You" as the title, and then insert a Pyramid diagram. Apply the teamwork design template to this slide.
21. Click the bottom placeholder in the diagram, type "You," click the middle placeholder, type "Global Humanitarian," click the top placeholder, type "The World," and then reformat all three labels to 28-point bold Arial.
22. Create a summary slide that includes titles from all the slides except Slides 1 and 12, and change the title to "Summary." Notice that PowerPoint creates two summary slides, because all of the slide titles will not fit on a single slide.
23. Check the spelling in the presentation, view the slide show, fix any problems you see, save the presentation, print it in grayscale as handouts with six slides per page, and then close the file.

Apply

Apply the skills you learned in this tutorial to modify a presentation for a health and fitness company.

Case Problem 1

Data Files needed for this Case Problem: MyBody.ppt, Weights.jpg, StrMach.jpg, Excycle.jpg, Treadmil.jpg, Vitamins.jpg

MyBodyTrainer.com Several years ago, Jerry Wursten received an M.S. degree in exercise physiology and became a board-certified strength and conditioning specialist (CSCS). Recently, he started a new e-commerce company called MyBodyTrainer.com, which provides services and products for health, fitness, weight loss, and sports conditioning. The services include personalized training and weight-loss programs, and the products include fitness equipment and dietary supplements. Jerry's business is expanding rapidly, and he needs additional capital. He needs to hire three more CSCS employees and several other employees to process orders, and he needs to purchase additional inventory and rent additional warehouse and office space. He asks you to help him prepare a PowerPoint presentation giving an overview of his business. He will give the presentation to bankers and investors to help him raise money for his company. Complete the following:

1. Open the file **MyBody** located in the Tutorial.02\Cases folder included with your Data Files, and then save it as **MyBodyTrainer** in the same folder.
2. Apply the design template titled "Shimmer," and then replace the subtitle in Slide 1 with your name.
3. In the slide master, change the title text box so it is center-aligned, rather than left-aligned.
4. Using the AutoShapes, draw a heart in the upper-left corner of the slide master, to the left of the title text box.
5. Change the fill color of the heart to red.
6. In Slides 7 and 8, change the slide layout to Title, Text, and 2 Content, and then add two bitmap images to each slide. In Slide 7, use the **Weights** and **StrMach** (strength machines) files, and in Slide 8 use the **Excycle** (exercise cycle) and **Treadmil** (treadmill) files; these bitmap images are located in the Tutorial.02\Cases folder.
7. In Slide 8, adjust the two images so they are side-by-side and fill the area to the right of the text. Similarly, in Slide 7, adjust the size and position of the images so they are visible and attractive.

8. In Slide 9, change the layout to Title, Text, and Content, and then add the bitmap image **Vitamins**, located in the Tutorial.02\Cases folder.
9. In Slide 3, change the layout to Title, Text, and Content, insert appropriate clip art, and then, if necessary, recolor the clip art so it matches the design template color scheme. (Note that if the image you choose is a bitmap image, you will not be able to recolor it.)
10. In Slide 4, draw a large equilateral Regular Pentagon in the middle of the blank area of the slide below the title.
11. Invert the pentagon so it's pointed down.
12. Add white, 18-point Arial text just outside the pentagon on each of its five sides, using the phrases (starting at the top of the pentagon and going clockwise): "Motivation," "Strength Training," "Cardio Exercise," "Nutrition," and "Flexibility."
13. Rotate the text boxes so they are parallel to their respective sides of the pentagon. Adjust the size of the pentagon and the position of the text so that each phrase is centered along an edge, and almost resting on the shape.
14. In Slide 11, insert a table with two columns and five rows, and then add the text as follows:

Expense Item	Amount Needed
CSCS Employees	$230,000
Other Employees	$312,000
Inventory	$186,000
Rent	$21,000

Explore

15. Add a new row with "Total" in the left column and "$749,000" in the right column. (*Hint*: To add a row to an existing table, click in the last cell, in this case cell B5, and then press the Tab key.)
16. Drag the bottom-center sizing handle of the table up so that the table stays the same width but decreases in height so the text fits better in the cells of the table.
17. Right-align the text and numbers in column 2.

Explore

18. Change the fill color of the top row of the table to dark amber. (*Hint*: Use the Fill Color button on the Tables and Borders toolbar.)
19. Create a summary slide that includes titles from Slides 5 through 10, and change the slide title to "Products and Services." Leave the slide as the new Slide 5 in the presentation.
20. Check the spelling, view the slide show, fix any problems you see, and then save the presentation.
21. Print the presentation in grayscale as handouts with six slides per page, and then close the file.

Challenge

Apply the skills you learned in this tutorial, and explore some new ones, to modify a presentation for an accountancy firm.

Case Problem 2

Data File needed for this Case Problem: Payroll.ppt

Payroll Partners Payroll Partners, founded by Sara Ostergaard, is a Wichita, Kansas-based accountancy office that helps small businesses process payroll and perform other financial tasks. Recently, Sara was approached by lawyers of a national chain of payroll-processing offices who expressed interest in buying her business. Sara is interested in exploring the idea, and asks you to prepare a presentation that she can use to present to the board of directors of the national chain in hopes of getting the best deal possible. Complete the following:

1. Open the file **Payroll** located in the Tutorial.02\Cases folder included with your Data Files, and then save it as **Payroll Partners** in the same folder.
2. Apply the design template titled "Textured," and then replace the subtitle in Slide 1 with your name.
3. In the title master and slide master, change the title text so it's the same color (sky blue) as the square bullets in the main text of the slide master.
4. **Explore** In the slide master, add a yellow-gold, 3-point border around the title text box. (*Hint*: Use the Line Color and Line Style buttons on the Drawing toolbar. Note that yellow-gold is one of the default colors.)
5. Add the footer "Payroll Partners" and slide numbers to all the slides except Slide 1.
6. Change the layout of Slide 3 to Title and Content, and then insert a Venn diagram consisting of three circles.
7. Add text labels next to each of the circles (in the designated placeholders): "Software Development," "Accounting," and "Small Business Payroll."
8. Near the bottom of the slide and centered below the Venn diagram, insert a text box with the phrase "Niche Region." Change the text to 32-point, yellow-gold text.
9. **Explore** Add a yellow-gold line border around the "Niche Region" text box. (*Hint*: Select the box and then click the Line Color button on the Drawing toolbar.)
10. **Explore** Draw a black, 3-point arrow from this text box to the center of the Venn diagram where the three circles overlap. (*Hint*: Use the Arrow and Line Style buttons on the Drawing toolbar.)
11. In Slide 5, change the layout to Title, Text, and Content, and then insert clip art that deals with money. If necessary, recolor the clip art to match the slide color scheme. If necessary, use the AutoFit option to fit the text in the placeholder.
12. In Slide 6, change the font color of the asking price to yellow-gold.
13. In Slide 7, insert a table with three columns and five rows, and then add the text as follows:

Year	Gross Revenues	Earnings
2002	$180,000	$70,000
2003	$270,000	$122,000
2004	$350,000	$188,000
2005	$510,000	$238,000

14. Drag the bottom-center sizing handle of the table up so that the table stays the same width but decreases in height so the text fits better in the cells of the table.
15. **Explore** Select the top row of text, and change the vertical alignment so the text appears at the bottom of each cell in the row. (*Hint*: Use the Align Bottom button on the Tables and Borders toolbar.)

16. Right-align the text and numbers in columns 2 and 3.
17. Create a summary slide that includes titles from Slides 3 through 8, move the slide to the end of the presentation so it becomes Slide 9, and then change the title to "Summary."
18. Check the spelling, view the slide show, fix any problems you see, and then save the presentation.
19. Print the presentation in grayscale as handouts with six slides per page, and then close the file.

Create

Create a new presentation about scrapbooking by using and expanding on the skills you learned in this tutorial.

Case Problem 3

Data Files needed for this Case Problem: SBcam.jpg, SBfile.jpg, SBpages.jpg, SBpaper.jpg, SBpens.jpg, SBphoto.jpg, SBsciss.jpg

Sally's Scrapbooking Four years ago, Brian and Sally DiQuattro started a business called Sally's Scrapbooking Supplies, which distributes wholesale scrapbooking supplies to retail stores in the Atlanta area. More recently, Brian and Sally opened their own specialty retail store (called Sally's Scrapbooking) and stocked it with scrapbooking supplies, which include binders, paper and plastic sheets and protectors, colored pens and markers, stickers and die cuts, stencils, scissors and cutting boards, glues and adhesives, and other miscellaneous items. As part of their marketing, Brian and Sally give presentations to scrapbooking clubs, women's clubs, crafts clubs, church groups, genealogical societies, and others interested in preserving their family histories through picture scrapbooks. The DiQuattros asked you to prepare a presentation for members of these organizations. The seven slides in your completed presentation should look like the slides shown in Figure 2-34.

Figure 2-34

The following information will help you in creating the slide show. Read all the steps before you start creating your presentation.

1. The design template is called "Crayons."
2. The font is Comic Sans MS, the default font for the Crayons design template, but if your system doesn't support Comic Sans MS, you could use Eras Medium BT, Futura Bk BT, Kids, Microsoft Sans Serif, Technical, or some other font of your choosing.
3. In Slide 1, add your name in the subtitle placeholder.
4. Slides 2 through 7 contain one or more bitmap images. You'll find all these images in the Tutorial.02\Cases folder. You should use each image once.
5. The text at the bottom of the slides is a footer and an automatic slide number.
6. Modify the slide master so that the footer on your slides is in the same place as shown in the figure.
7. The content on Slides 2 through 7 reviews the following points:
   a. Quality supplies are critical in scrapbooking.
   b. Scrapbookers need acid-free and lignin-free paper to protect their photos from damage. (Lignin is a substance in paper that yellows over time.)
   c. Scrapbookers need archival-quality pens with ink that won't bleed through the paper.
   d. Page layout is easy with the right die cuts and stickers.
   e. Buy quality cutting tools and keep them sharpened.
   f. File photos in groups to prepare to lay out pages.
8. Remember to check the spelling in the final presentation, and to view the slide show.
9. Print the final presentation in grayscale as handouts with four slides per page.
10. Save the file as **Sally's Scrapbooking** to the Tutorial.02\Cases folder.

Research

Use the Internet to collect information about a collegiate honor society and create a new presentation based on this information.

Case Problem 4

Data Files you might use in this Case Problem: PESLogo.jpg, PKPBadge.jpg, PKPKey.jpg,

College Honor Society Honor societies recognize students who distinguish themselves in academics and leadership. Your assignment is to prepare a PowerPoint presentation on an honor society at your college or university. Complete the following:

1. Gather information on an honor society from honor society advisors, college advisement centers, or the office of the Dean of Students. For the names, locations, and phone numbers, call information at your college, or consult your student directory or catalog. You can also gather information from the Internet. For general information about members of the Association of College Honor Societies, including a list of most honor societies in the United States and Canada, consult **www.achsnatl.org**. For information on a specific national, nondiscipline-specific honor society, Phi Kappa Phi, consult **www.phikappaphi.org**. For a national freshman honor society, Phi Eta Sigma, consult **www.phietasigma.org**.
2. Create a new PowerPoint presentation based on an appropriate design template. Type the name of the society on the title slide, and type your name as the subtitle.
3. Create at least eight slides with information about the society. Information on your slides might include local and national names and addresses of advisors and officers, purposes, eligibility, activities, scholarships, recognition programs, famous members, history, meetings, local and national conventions, merchandise, and publications.
4. Modify the slide master by adding a text box or graphics object, changing the font attributes, or making some other desired change that will appear on all the slides.

5. Include the slide number and an appropriate footer on each slide, except the title slide. In the slide master, change the font style, size, and color, and change the position of the footer and slide number text.
6. Include in your presentation at least one piece of clip art.

Explore

7. Click Insert on the menu bar, point to Picture, and then click Clip Art to open the Clip Art task pane. Click the Clip Art on Office Online link in the task pane to go to Microsoft's Design Gallery Live, where you can search through hundreds of pieces of clip art. Find and insert at least one image connected specifically to the honor society you are describing. If you can't find the image on the Design Gallery Live site, look elsewhere on the Web, or request an image from the local chapter of the honor society. If you choose to describe Phi Kappa Phi or Phi Eta Sigma, bitmap images of their logos are located in the Tutorial.02\Cases folder.
8. Recolor the clip art you inserted to match the presentation color scheme or the colors of the other graphics in your presentation.
9. Include a table or an organizational chart in your presentation. (For information on organizational charts, use the PowerPoint Help system.) You might include a table with the name, description, location, and dates of chapter activities; a table listing the chapter merchandise and prices; or a table with names, addresses, phone numbers, and e-mail addresses of chapter officers. You might include an organizational chart showing the structure of officers in the honor society.
10. Include a drawing that you create from lines, arrows, AutoShapes, or text boxes. For example, you might create a diagram showing the procedure for becoming a member of the honor society, using text boxes and arrows.
11. Apply a second design template to one of the slides.
12. Create a summary slide, and change its title to "Summary of Phi Kappa Phi" (but use the name of your selected honor society).
13. Check the spelling in your presentation, view the slide show, and then save the presentation to the Tutorial.02\Cases folder using the filename **Honor Society**.
14. Print the presentation in grayscale as handouts with four slides per page, and then close the file.

Research

Go to the Web to find information you can use to create presentations.

Internet Assignments

The purpose of the Internet Assignments is to challenge you to find information on the Internet that you can use to work effectively with this software. The actual assignments are updated and maintained on the Course Technology Web site. Log on to the Internet and use your Web browser to go to the Student Online Companion for New Perspectives Office 2003 at **www.course.com/np/office2003**. Click the Internet Assignments link, and then navigate to the assignments for this tutorial.

Assess

SAM

SAM Assessment and Training

If you have a SAM user profile, you may have access to hands-on instruction, practice, and assessment of the skills covered in this tutorial. Log in to your SAM account and go to your assignments page to see what your instructor has assigned.

Review

Quick Check Answers

Session 2.1

1. Graphics add information, clarification, emphasis, variety, and pizzazz.
2. a. a file that contains the color scheme, graphics, text formats, and background colors and objects in the presentation
   b. a grid (or "map") of colored dots that form a picture
   c. a picture, clip art, photograph, shape, design, graph, chart, or diagram
   d. the design template applied to a presentation if no other template is chosen (black text on a white background)
3. a. Click anywhere in the text box.
   b. Click the edge of the text box.
   c. Drag a sizing handle.
   d. Drag the object (or in the case of a text box, the edge of the box).
   e. Display the slide in the slide pane, click the list arrow of the desired design template in the Design Template task pane, and then click Apply to Selected Slides.
   f. Select the clip-art image, click the Recolor Picture button on the Picture toolbar, and modify the original colors to new colors.
4. The title master is a slide that contains the objects that appear on the title slide of the presentation. The slide master is a slide that contains the objects that appear on all the slides except the title slide.
5. Tabs add space between the left margin and the beginning of the text on a particular line, or between the text in one column and the text in another column. Tab stops are the locations where text moves when you press the Tab key. Click the Tab button until the Right Tab button appears, and then click the desired location on the ruler.
6. date and time, footer, and slide number

Session 2.2

1. Change the slide layout to a Content layout, click the Insert Table button, set the desired number of columns and rows, insert information into the cells, and modify the table format as desired.
2. upper-left corner
3. a diagram used to show overlap between different elements
4. Click the Text Box button on the Drawing toolbar, and click or drag at the desired location in the slide.
5. Click the AutoShapes list arrow on the Drawing toolbar, point to the appropriate category (such as Basic Shapes), click the desired shape button, move the pointer into the slide pane, and then drag the pointer to draw the figure.
6. Select the triangle, click the Draw button on the Drawing toolbar, point to Rotate or Flip, and then click the appropriate command.
7. Drag the rotate handle of the object in the slide pane.
8. a method for automatically creating a slide with the titles of the slides selected in Slide Sorter view

Objectives

Session 3.1
- Insert slides from another presentation
- Create and apply a custom design template
- Apply graphics and sounds
- Add a textured background

Session 3.2
- Create a chart (graph)
- Create an organization chart
- Apply slide transitions and animations
- Use the pointer pen during a slide show
- Hide slides in a presentation
- Prepare a presentation to run on another computer

Presenting a Slide Show

Customizing and Preparing a Presentation

Case

Global Humanitarian, Peru Expedition

Pablo Fuentes, the managing director of Global Humanitarian in Lima, Peru, recently led a humanitarian expedition to Paqarimuy, a village in the Peruvian altiplano. The board of directors of Global Humanitarian asked Pablo to give a report on the expedition. He decided that he wants to present the report using a PowerPoint presentation, and he now asks you to help him prepare the presentation. He emphasizes the importance of preparing a high-quality presentation that includes a custom design template, graphics, sound effects, animations, charts, graphs, and other elements to maximize the visual effects of the presentation.

To help you get started, Pablo prepared a presentation with most of the text and some of the graphics of the expedition report. He also gave you access to other PowerPoint presentations from which you can extract slides.

In this tutorial, you'll insert slides from one presentation into another presentation; create a custom design template; add a digital image, movie, and sound clips to a presentation; create a graph and organization chart; apply special visual effects to your slides; and save the presentation ro a CD so it can be run on another computer.

Labs

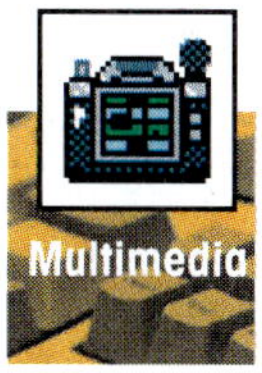

Student Data Files

▼**Tutorial.03**

▽ Tutorial folder
- MPLogo.jpg
- Paq.wav
- PaqaPic.jpg
- PaqMovie.avi
- PeruPlan.ppt
- PeruRep.ppt
- Taq.wav

▽ Review folder
- Cuzco.wav
- CuzcTour.ppt
- HuaynaP.wav
- MachPicc.wav
- PeruExp.ppt
- PeruLogo.jpg
- SacsMov.avi
- SacsSnd.wav

▽ Cases folder
- ACWBus.ppt
- Alaskan.ppt
- Applause.wav
- Atorv.jpg
- bedrm1.jpg
- bedrm2.jpg
- Bonnie.jpg
- Bowls.jpg.
- cabinfnt.jpg
- Drugs.jpg
- fireplac.jpg
- fitness.jpg
- GeNetics.ppt
- kitchen.jpg
- livingrm.jpg
- Totem.jpg

Session 3.1

Planning the Presentation

Before you begin to create Pablo's slide show, he discusses with you the purpose of, and the audience for, his presentation:

- **Purpose of the presentation**: to present details of the recent humanitarian expedition to Paqarimuy
- **Type of presentation**: report
- **Audience**: Global Humanitarian's board of directors
- **Audience needs**: an overview of the expedition with pictures and data
- **Location of the presentation**: small boardroom for the Board of Directors; office or classroom for other interested parties
- **Format**: on-screen slide show

With this general plan for the presentation, Pablo prepares the text and some of the pictures for the report.

Inserting Slides from Another Presentation

After Pablo discusses his presentation plan with you, he gives you two presentation files: PeruRep, which contains the text and some pictures to include with his report; and PeruPlan, a presentation used to show expedition plans to prospective volunteers. First, you'll open PeruRep and look through it to see what information Pablo has already included. Then, you'll add slides to it from the PeruPlan presentation.

To insert slides from another presentation, you first need to open the presentation to which you want to add the slides. Then you use the Slides from File command on the Insert menu to insert specific slides from any other presentation. If the inserted slides have a different design than the current presentation, the design of the current presentation will override the design of the inserted slides.

Reference Window

Inserting Slides from Another Presentation

- Go to the slide after which you want to insert slides from another presentation.
- Click Insert on the menu bar, and then click Slides from File to open the Slide Finder dialog box.
- Click the Browse button, and then open the presentation file in the Slide Finder dialog box from which you want to get the slides.
- Click the slides that you want inserted into your presentation to select them.
- Click the Insert button, and then click the Close button in the Slide Finder dialog box.

To open the PeruRep presentation and save it with a new name:

1. Open the file **PeruRep**, located in the Tutorial.03\Tutorial folder included with your Data Files.
2. Maximize the PowerPoint window, if necessary.
3. Save the presentation file as **Peru Expedition Report**. See Figure 3-1.

Slide 1 of Peru Expedition Report

Figure 3-1

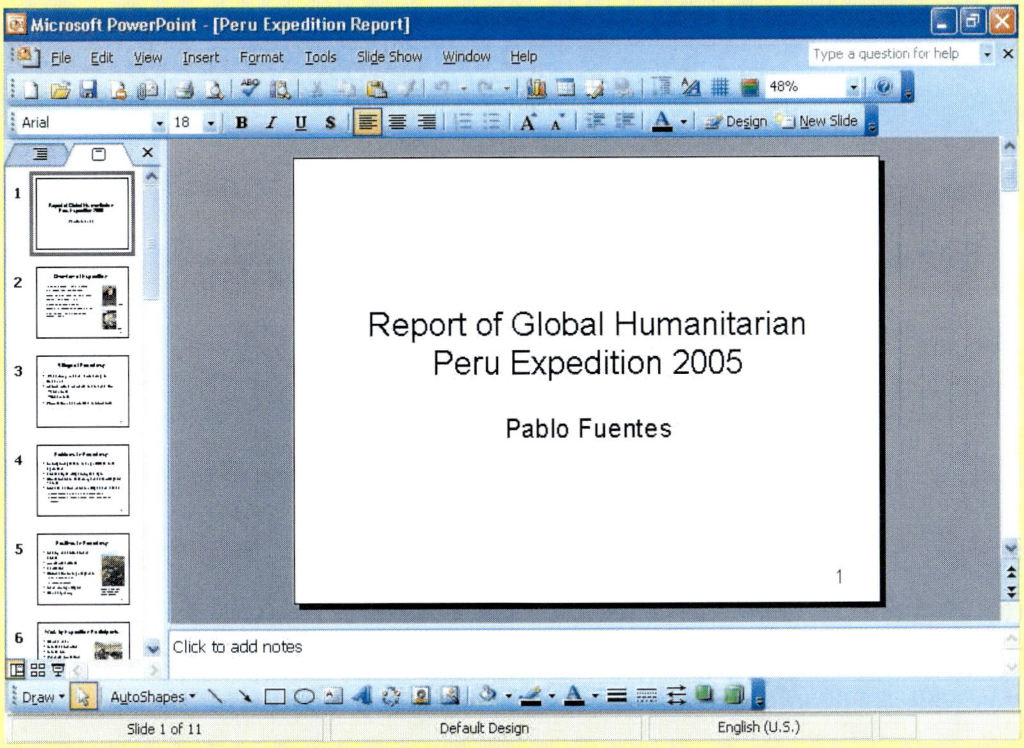

Trouble? If you're using a floppy disk for your Data Files, you won't have enough space to save the file you create in this tutorial. If you don't have access to a hard disk or some other high-capacity disk, skip those steps in which you're asked to insert a digital image or a movie into the presentation. Then you'll have enough room to save the results to a floppy disk.

4. Scroll through all 11 slides of the presentation so you have an idea of its current content. Notice that there is no design template applied to this presentation because you are going to create your own design template later in this tutorial.

Your first task is to insert slides from the presentation file PeruPlan. Pablo told you that he wants you to insert Slides 2 and 3 from PeruPlan.

To insert slides from one presentation into another:

1. Go to **Slide 2** of Peru Expedition Report. When you insert slides from another presentation, they are inserted after the current slide.
2. Click **Insert** on the menu bar, and then click **Slides from Files**. The Slide Finder dialog box opens.
3. Click the **Browse** button, navigate to the **Tutorial.03\Tutorial** folder included with your Data Files, and then double-click **PeruPlan**. The slides in PeruPlan are listed horizontally in the Slide Finder dialog box. Notice that the slides have a shaded red background and that the slide titles are yellow. See Figure 3-2.

Figure 3-2 Slide Finder dialog box

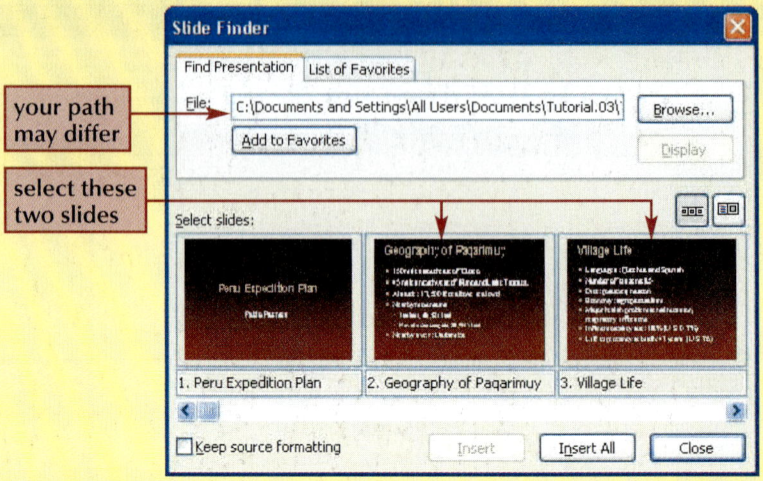

4. Click the **Slide 2** thumbnail ("Geography of Paqarimuy"), and then click the **Slide 3** thumbnail ("Village Life") to select them. The two selected slides have a dark-blue frame around them.
5. Click the **Insert** button, and then click the **Close** button in the Slide Finder dialog box. The two new slides are inserted into the current presentation after the current slide. See Figure 3-3.

Figure 3-3 New Slide 4 after inserting two slides from other presentation

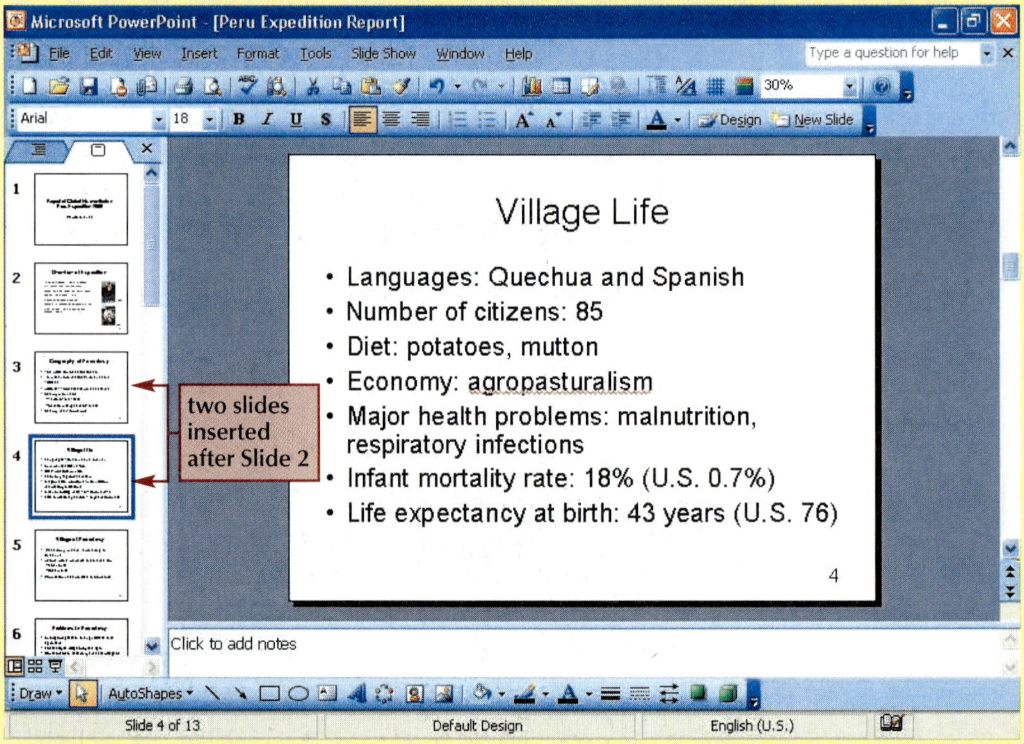

Slides 2 and 3 from PeruPlan are now Slides 3 and 4 in Peru Expedition Report. The two new slides contain detailed information about the village that was helped during the Peru expedition. The Peru Expedition Report presentation now has 13 slides.

With most of the slides now created for the presentation, you're ready to create a custom design template.

Creating a Custom Design Template

As you recall, a design template is a file that contains the color scheme, attributes, and format for the titles, main text, other text, and background for the presentation. You have used several of the design templates that come with PowerPoint. Sometimes, however, you'll want to design your own, custom template. When you create a design template, you need to make sure that the colors go well together, that the text remains clear and legible, and that the color scheme meets the needs of your presentation.

Creating a Custom Design Template

Reference Window

- Using an existing or new presentation, create the desired color scheme, bullets, fonts, background color, and background graphics.
- If you don't want any existing slides, text, or other objects in your custom design template, delete all but the first slide, and delete any text or foreground objects from the slide.
- Click File, click Save As, click the Save as type list arrow, and then click Design Template.
- Navigate to the desired location in the Save in list box, type a filename, and then click the Save button.

For the report on the Peru expedition, Pablo doesn't want you to use any of the built-in design templates; instead, he wants you to create a completely original design that better matches the subject and the colors of the pictures.

Creating a Custom Color Scheme

A **color scheme** is a set of matching colors that makes up the background, fonts, and other elements of a presentation. Each of the design templates included with PowerPoint, including the Default Design template, has several color schemes associated with it. It is easy to select colors that don't match or make text illegible; for example, red text on a blue background might seem like a good combination, but it's actually difficult to read at a distance from the screen. It's usually safer, therefore, to select one of the built-in color schemes and stick to it, or make only minor modifications.

A PowerPoint color scheme includes eight items to which you can assign a color:

- **Background**—the default color of the area on which you add text and other objects.
- **Text and lines**—the default color of the body text and of lines drawn on the slide.
- **Shadows**—the default color of the shadow applied to an object (e.g., a shape or a text box). This does not, however, specify the color of the text shadow that you apply using the Font dialog box.
- **Title text**—the default color of the title (but not the subtitle) text on the title slide and of the title text on other slide layouts.
- **Fills**—the default color that fills shapes (e.g., the color of a square or circle).
- **Accent**—a color that might appear automatically in a PowerPoint chart or graph or one that you can use, if you choose, for bullets, fills, and accented text. Accent colors appear by default only in multicolored charts, but not automatically in text, AutoShapes, lines, and other objects.

- **Accent and hyperlink**—the default color for hyperlink text and another color that might appear by default in multicolored charts.
- **Accent and followed hyperlink**—the default color for hyperlinks that have been followed; in other words, if you click a hyperlink and thereby jump to another location, when you return to the original slide, the color of the hyperlink text will be changed to indicate that you have followed that hyperlink. This color also appears by default in some multicolored charts.

Once you have specified a coordinated set of eight colors, they will appear by default in text and objects, but you can use any of the eight to change the default color of text, fills, shadows, and so forth.

As you look at the pictures of Paqarimuy, you can see that the colors are mostly earth tones—browns and yellows—so you'll create a color scheme now using those colors.

To create a custom color scheme:

1. Click the **Design** button on the Formatting toolbar to display the Slide Design task pane, and then click the **Color Schemes** link in the task pane. The task pane changes to show the color schemes associated with the current design. You can create the color scheme with any slide in the slide pane.
2. If necessary, scroll down so you can see the last color scheme in the task pane, the one with the dark-brown background. See Figure 3-4.

Figure 3-4 Slide Design task pane open

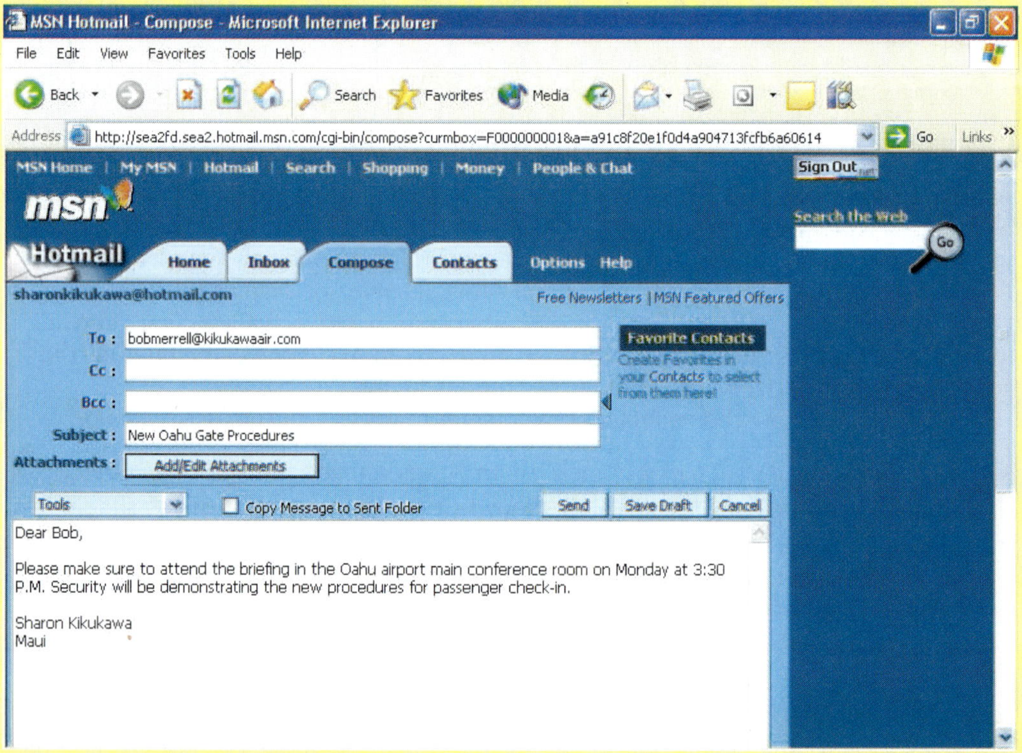

3. Click the color scheme thumbnail with the dark-brown background and tan title text, located in the bottom-right corner of the task pane. PowerPoint applies the color scheme to all the slides in your presentation.

You think the title text could stand out a little more, so next, you'll modify the color of the title text.

4. Click the **Edit Color Schemes** link at the bottom of the task pane. The Edit Color Scheme dialog box opens with the Custom tab on top. Here you can see color tiles of each of the major elements of the slide—the background, the text and lines, the shadows, and so forth.
5. Click the **Title text** tile, click the **Change Color** button to open the Title Text Color dialog box, and then click the **Standard** tab. See Figure 3-5.

Figure 3-5 Standard tab in Title Text Color dialog box

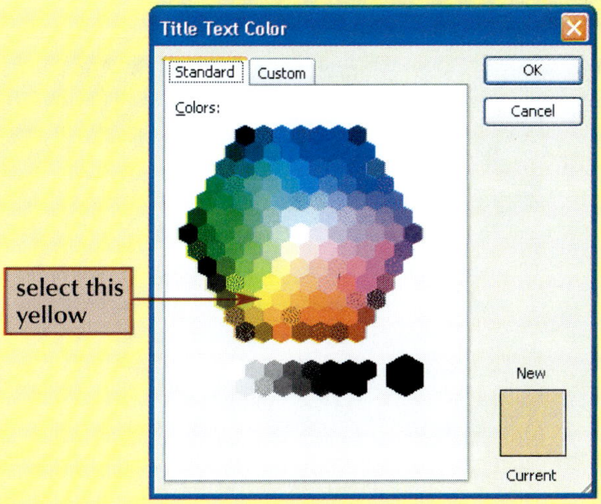

6. Click the bright-yellow tile indicated in Figure 3-5, and then click the **OK** button. The Title Text Color dialog box closes. The Title text color tile changes from tan to yellow, and the title text in the preview pane on the right side of the dialog box changes to yellow also.
7. Click the **Apply** button. The Edit Color Scheme dialog box closes and the new color scheme is applied to your presentation. As you can see in the slide pane, the title is now bright yellow. If you look at the other slides on the Slides tab on the left, you see that the titles on those slides are also bright yellow.
8. Click the **Close** button on the task pane title bar.

You'll now change the background of the slides. You could have used the Edit Color Scheme dialog box to change to a solid color for the background (by clicking the Background tile), but if you want special effects, such as shading, you must use the Background dialog box.

Creating a Custom Background

The color scheme of your presentation has a brown background, but Pablo asks you to add shading to the background to add interest and a professional touch to the presentation. You decide to use a **gradient fill**, which is a type of shading in which one color blends into another or varies from one shade to another.

When you use a gradient fill, you also choose a shading style and a variant. The **shading style** identifies the direction in which the shading will be applied—horizontally, vertically, diagonally up, diagonally down, from a corner, or from the title. A **variant** is a variation of a particular shading style; there are four variants of each shading style.

You'll change the background of your presentation to a two-color gradient fill.

To create a custom background with a two-color gradient fill:

1. Click **Format** on the menu bar, and then click **Background**. The Background dialog box opens.
2. Click the **Background fill** list arrow (underneath the preview box), and then click **Fill Effects**. The Fill Effects dialog box opens.
3. Click the **Gradient** tab, if necessary, and then click the **Two colors** option button in the Colors section. Two shades of the background color appear on the right side of the Colors section. See Figure 3-6.

Figure 3-6 **Gradient tab in Fill Effects dialog box**

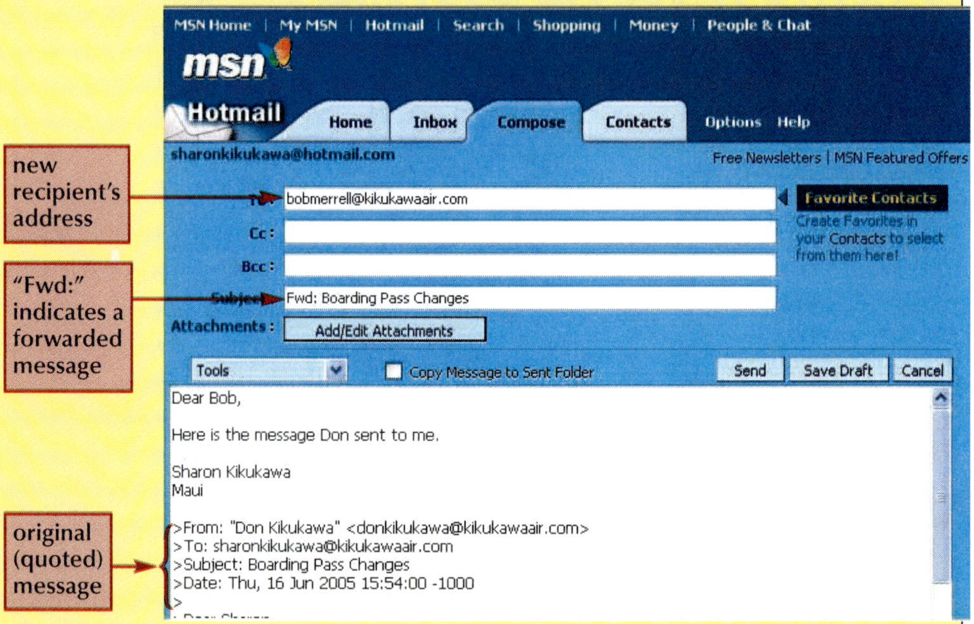

PowerPoint automatically sets the two colors to dark brown and medium brown. You can change one or both of these colors by clicking the Color 1 or Color 2 list arrows and then selecting the desired color, but a dark gradient fill works well with light text colors, so you choose to keep the two colors as they are. The horizontal shading style is selected by default, and this style works well for most presentations. The default variant is the variant in the upper-left corner of the Variants section of the dialog box in which the color varies from dark to light. You'll use the default shading style, but you'll select a different variant.

4. Click the variant in the lower-left corner of the Variants section, as indicated in Figure 3-6. This variant places the dark brown at the top and bottom of the slide, and the lighter brown in the middle.
5. Click the **OK** button. The Fill Effects dialog box closes.
6. Click the **Apply to All** button in the Background dialog box. The Background dialog box closes, and the background gradient fill and variant you selected are applied to all the slides.
7. Save the presentation.

As you can see from the slide pane and the Slides tab, all of the slides now have a background with a gradient fill. You'll now modify the fonts used on the slides.

Modifying Fonts and Bullets

All the current text in your presentation is in a sans serif font called Arial. This is a good general-purpose font, but Pablo wants something with a bit more pizzazz. In this case, he wants you to change the title font from Arial to Impact, a thicker sans serif font, and change the body text font from Arial to Book Antiqua, an attractive serif font. Rather than change the fonts on each of the individual slides, you can make these changes for all the slides at once by changing the fonts on the slide master and title master. As you might recall, the title master contains the objects that appear on the title slide, and the slide master contains the objects that appear on all the slides except the title slide. Now you'll modify the fonts on these two masters.

To modify the fonts on the slide master:

1. Shift-click the **Normal View** button. (If you position the mouse pointer over the Normal button while you hold down the Shift key, you'll see that the ScreenTip becomes Slide Master View.)
2. Click the border of the title placeholder text box to select the entire box, click the **Font** list arrow Arial on the Formatting toolbar, scroll down until you see **Impact**, and then click that font name. The title font changes from Arial to Impact.

   Trouble? If your computer doesn't have the Impact font installed, keep Arial as the font, but make it bold by clicking the Bold button **B** on the Formatting toolbar.
3. Select the placeholder text box for the bulleted list text (the body text), and change the font to **Book Antiqua**. See Figure 3-7.

   Trouble? If your computer doesn't have the Book Antiqua font installed, select Times New Roman instead.

Figure 3-7 Slide master with new fonts

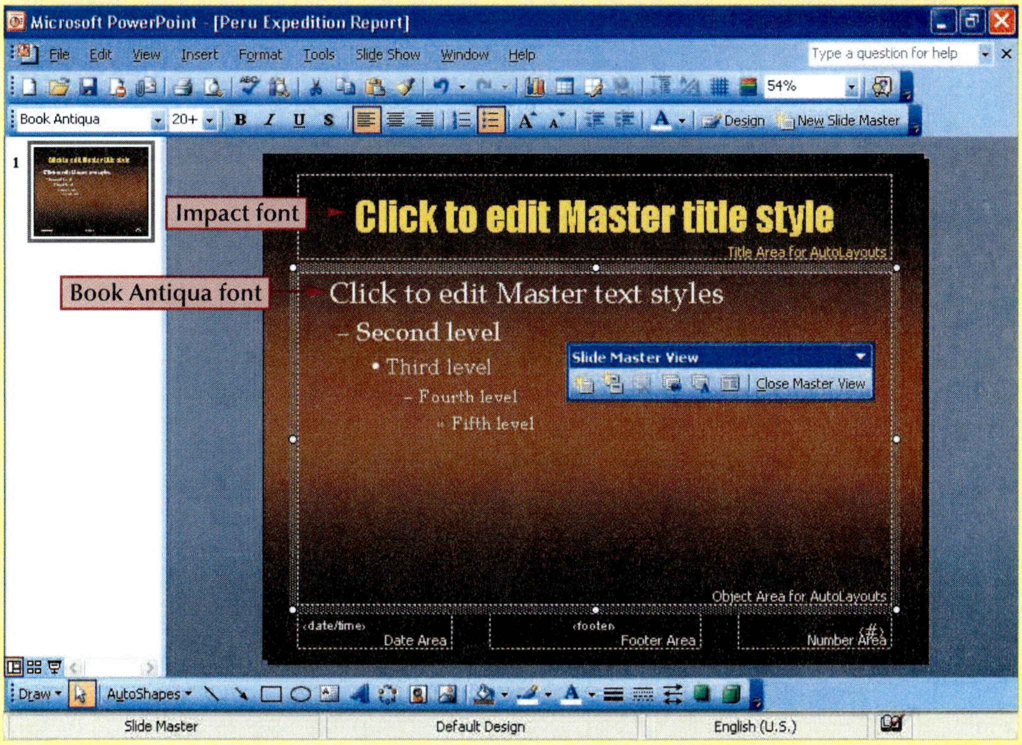

You have made the fonts more interesting. Now you're ready to change the bullets.

To change the bullets style on the slide master:

1. Right-click the line that reads "Click to edit Master text styles," and then click **Bullets and Numbering** on the shortcut menu. The Bullets and Numbering dialog box opens with the Bulleted tab on top. See Figure 3-8.

Figure 3-8 **Bullet tab in Bullets and Numbering dialog box**

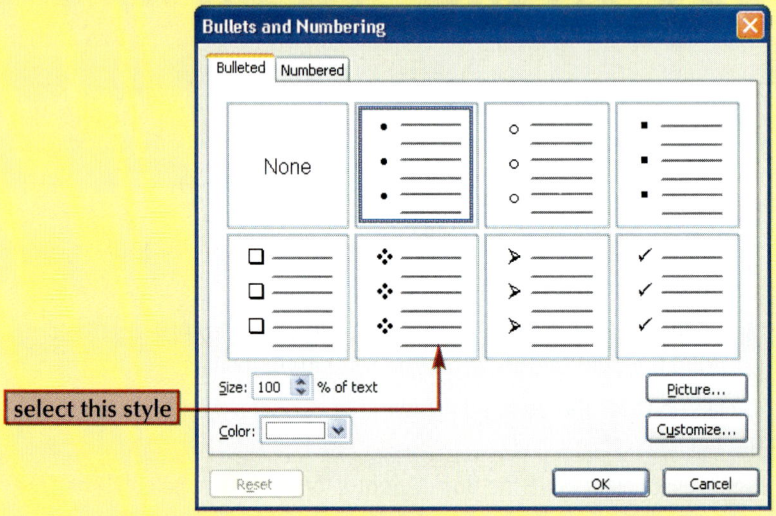

2. Click the four-diamond bullet style, as indicated in Figure 3-8.

   Trouble? If you don't see the four-diamond bullet style in your dialog box, choose another style.

3. Click the **Color** list arrow, and then click the bright-yellow tile. The new bullets will be bright yellow.
4. Click the **OK** button to accept the changes to the top-level bullets. You now see a yellow four-diamond bullet on the first-level bulleted item.
5. Using the same procedure, change the bullet in the second line ("Second level") to a solid, blue-gray, small square. (The blue-gray color is the right-most tile on the color palette.)
6. Click the **Normal View** button to return to Normal view, and then click the **Slide 3** thumbnail in the Slides tab to see the effect of the changes you made. See Figure 3-9.

Slide 3 with new fonts and bullets

Figure 3-9

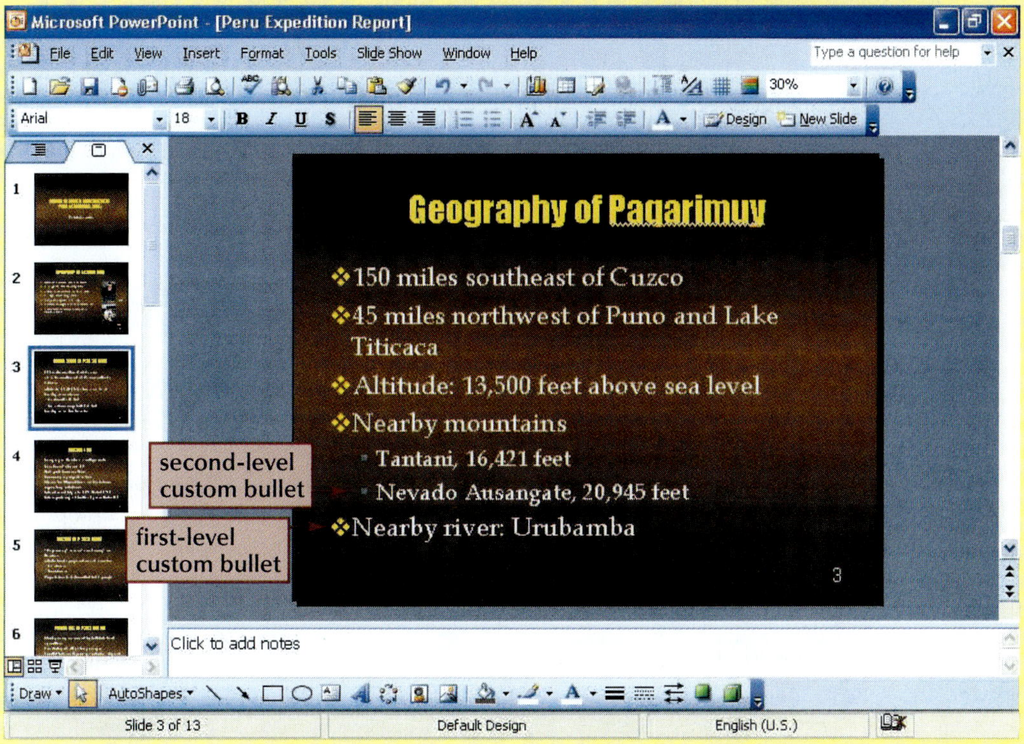

Trouble? If your bullet characters or colors are different from those shown in Figure 3-9, return to the slide master and make any necessary changes.

7. Save the presentation.

You've almost completed the custom design template. Your final task is to add a digital image to the title and slide masters.

Adding a Background Image

Pablo realizes that the best-known image of Peru is Machu Picchu, the ancient Incan ruins located on the edge of the Peruvian jungle. He wants you to add a photo of Machu Picchu to the background of all the slides in the presentation.

Because Pablo wants this image to be on all the slides in the presentation, you'll add it to the title and slide masters. (You'll recall that you added an image to the background when you worked with the title and slide masters in Tutorial 2.)

To add a background image to the slide master:

1. Shift-click the **Normal View** button to return to Slide Master view.
2. Click the **Insert Picture** button on the Drawing toolbar. The Insert Picture dialog box opens.
3. Click the **Look in** list arrow and navigate to the **Tutorial.03\Tutorial** folder included with your Data Files, click **MPLogo**, if necessary, and then click the **Insert** button. A small picture of Machu Picchu appears in the middle of the slide master.

4. Drag the picture so it's positioned with its left edge flush with the left edge of the title placeholder text box, and then adjust the size of the title text box so its left edge is to the right of the picture. See Figure 3-10.

Figure 3-10 Slide master after adding logo and adjusting title placeholder

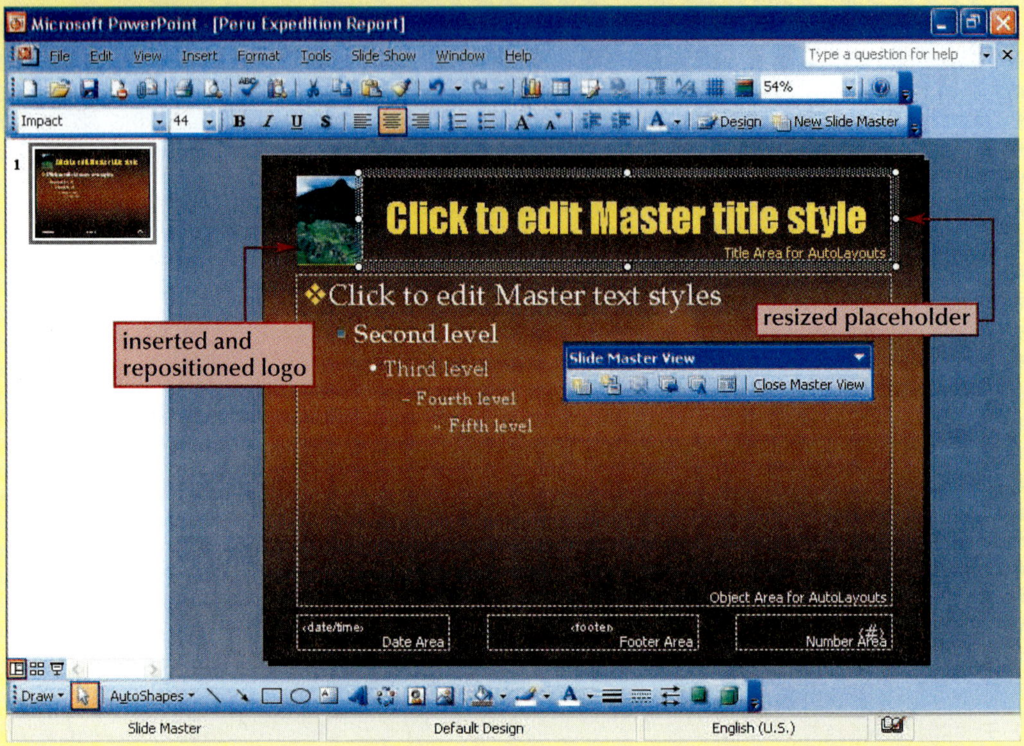

Trouble? If the Slide Master View toolbar is in the way, drag it out of the way by its title bar.

Recall that the title text on the title slide is in a different position than the title text on the rest of the slides. But notice that PowerPoint doesn't automatically include a title master with the Default Design template. You'll need to add a title master, and then modify it to reposition the background graphic to an appropriate spot.

5. Click the **Insert New Title Master** button on the Slide Master View toolbar. A title master is added and the view switches to Title Master view.

   Next, you'll change the size of the Machu Picchu picture. In the past, when you changed a picture size, you dragged the sizing handles. However, if you want to change the picture to a specific, predetermined size (in this case, two inches in height), you should use the Size tab in the Format Picture dialog box. You'll do that now.

6. Click the **Machu Picchu** image to select it, and then click the **Format Picture** button on the Picture toolbar. The Format Picture dialog box opens.

   Trouble? If the Picture toolbar does not appear on your screen, click View on the menu bar, point to Toolbars, and then click Picture.

7. Click the **Size** tab, drag to select the value in the Height text box in the Size and rotate section, type **2**, make sure that the **Lock aspect ratio** check box is checked, and then click the **OK** button. The image is resized so that the height is two inches and the width is proportional to the original width.

8. Drag the **Machu Picchu** picture into the title master so it's centered just above the title placeholder text box, as shown in Figure 3-11.

Title master after moving logo

Figure 3-11

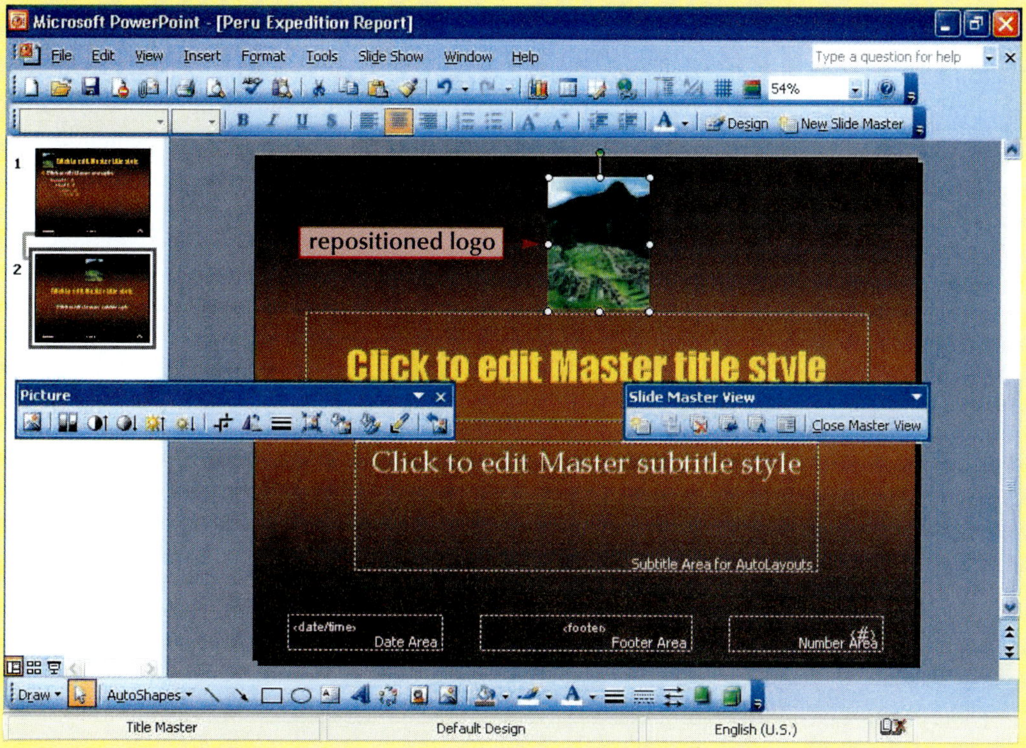

9. Resize the two title placeholders to a little larger than half their original height by selecting each one and dragging a sizing handle, and then drag the picture and the two title placeholders down so they are better centered vertically in the slide, as shown in Figure 3-12.

Title master after moving objects

Figure 3-12

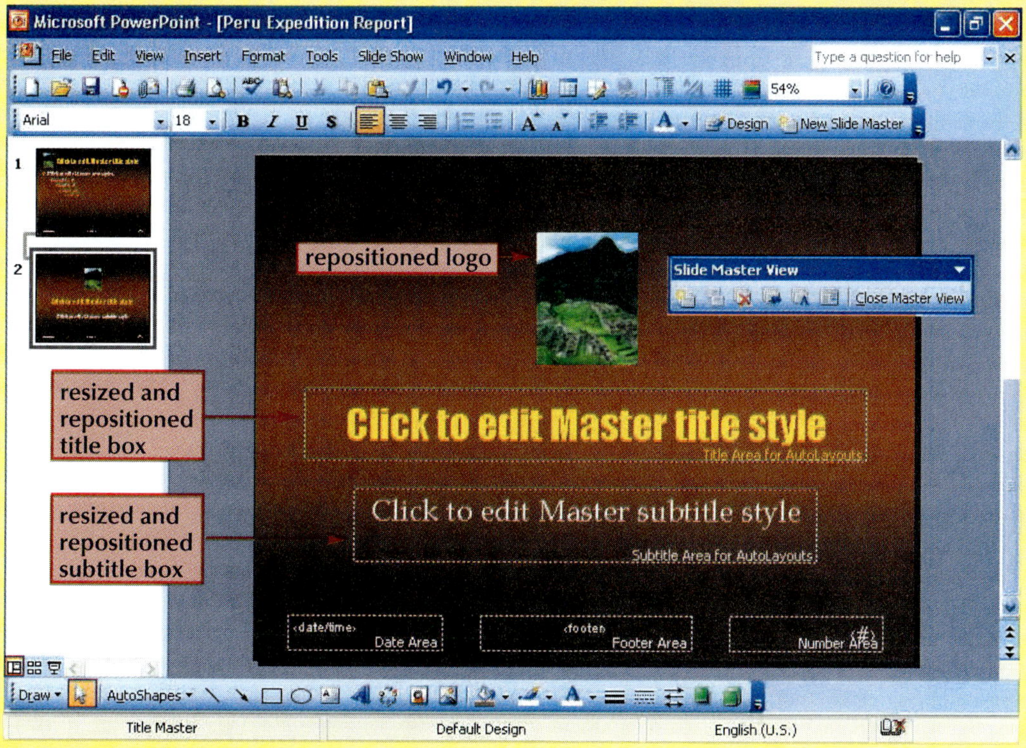

10. Click the **Normal View** button to return to Normal view, and then save the presentation.

The design template is now complete, with a customized color scheme, gradient background, new fonts, and the picture of Machu Picchu in the background of all the slides. Pablo now asks you to save the custom design template so he can apply it to other presentations.

Saving a Custom Design Template

You used several built-in design templates in earlier tutorials by clicking the Design button on the Formatting toolbar to display the Slide Design task pane, and then clicking the desired design template. What if you want to use a custom design template? That's exactly what Pablo wants. When he creates another expedition plan, report, or some other presentation that would look good using the custom design of the Peru Expedition Report presentation, he wants to be able to select that design from the task pane, just as he would any other design template. Fortunately, PowerPoint allows you to save the design from any PowerPoint presentation as a design template.

The default location for a PowerPoint presentation saved as a design template is the Templates folder. If you save a design template to that folder, then the next time you start PowerPoint, your custom template will appear as one of the templates in the Slide Design task pane. No matter where a template is stored, however, you can create a new presentation based on the template by clicking the Browse link at the bottom of the Slide Design task pane.

When you save a PowerPoint presentation as a design template, not only are all the design elements saved, but also all of the content—the slides, text, and graphics—is saved. Therefore, you usually want to delete all the slides but the title slide, and you even want to delete the text and foreground graphic (if any) from that slide, leaving only the objects on the title master and slide master. This will reduce the file size and conform to the standard of built-in templates. You'll delete the content and then save the custom design template now.

To save a presentation as a design template:

1. Click the **Slide Sorter View** button to switch to Slide Sorter view, click **Edit** on the menu bar, click **Select All** to select all the slides, press and hold the **Ctrl** key, click **Slide 1** to deselect just that slide, and then release the **Ctrl** key. All the slides except Slide 1 are now selected, as indicated by the thick border around them.
2. Press the **Delete** key to delete all the selected slides. Only Slide 1 remains.
3. Return to Normal view, and then delete all of the text (but not the placeholder text boxes) on the slide. Only the design and title master graphics and placeholders remain on the slide. See Figure 3-13.

Slide with only background colors, background object and placeholders

Figure 3-13

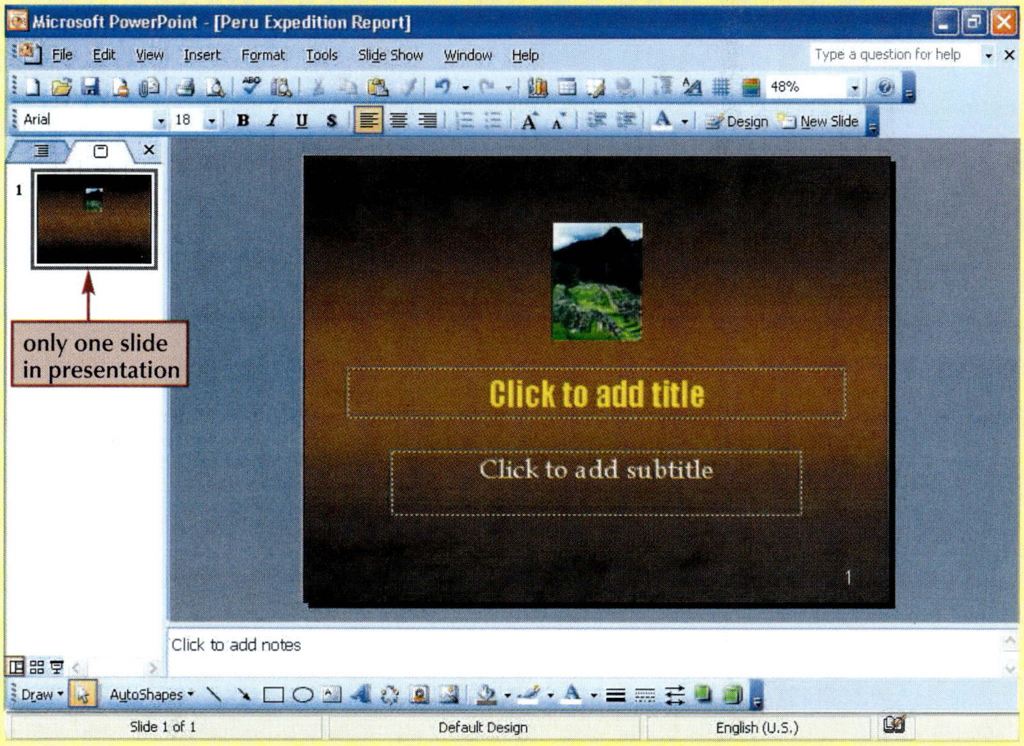

4. Click **File**, click **Save As**, click the **Save as type** list arrow, and then click **Design Template**. The Save in folder changes to Templates. Normally, you would save a design template file in this folder. For the purposes of this tutorial, however, you need to save your template file to the same location where you saved Peru Expedition Report (in the Tutorial.03\Tutorial folder).
5. Click the **Save in** list arrow, and then navigate to the **Tutorial.03\Tutorial** folder included with your Data Files (or to the location where you saved Peru Expedition Report).
6. Replace the text in the File name text box with **Peru Template**, and then click the **Save** button. PowerPoint saves the file as a design template.
7. Click the **Close Window** button ☒ on the right side of the menu bar. PowerPoint should still be running, but with no file in the presentation window.

You have now created a custom design template that Pablo and others can use with any new presentation.

Using a Custom Design Template

You decide to test your new custom design template on a new presentation.

To apply a custom design template:

1. Click the **New** button on the Standard toolbar to open a new presentation.
2. Click the **Design** button on the Formatting toolbar to open the Slide Design task pane. Because you saved your design template in the Tutorial.03\Tutorial folder rather than in the default design template folder, your new template doesn't appear in the task pane, so you need to direct PowerPoint to your folder by clicking the Browse link.

3. Click the **Browse** link at the bottom of the Slide Design task pane, and then change the Look in folder to the **Tutorial.03\Tutorial** folder included with your Data Files (or the location where you saved Peru Template).
4. Double-click **Peru Template** in the list of files in the Tutorial.03\Tutorial folder. As you can see, the new presentation has the design of your custom design template.
5. Click the **New Slide** button on the Formatting toolbar to create a Title and Text slide. Again, you can see the design of your custom design template, with the yellow title text, the picture of Machu Picchu in the upper-left corner, and the yellow diamond bullet in the main text placeholder. If you were actually creating a presentation, you would add text and other objects to the title slide and to the other slides.
6. Click the **Close Window** button on the right side of the menu bar, and then click the **No** button in the dialog box that asks if you want to save changes.

You can now report to Pablo that your custom design template works as planned.

Multimedia

Applying Graphics and Sounds to Your Presentation

PowerPoint allows you to add various types of graphics and sounds to your presentation. You're already familiar with adding clip art, drawn images, and digital photos to a slide. In fact, the original PeruPlan file came with images of Paqarimuy and other places and people of Peru. Moreover, you have already inserted the image of Machu Picchu into the slide background, and in Tutorial 2, you inserted a photo, clip art, and drawings you created using the tools on the Drawing toolbar. In addition to still photos and other graphics, you can insert movies and sounds into a presentation.

Reference Window

Adding Movies and Sounds to a Presentation

- On the slide to which you want to add a movie or sound, click Insert on the menu bar, point to Movies and Sounds, and then click the desired source (the Clip Organizer or a user-specified file) for the movie or sound.
- Select the movie or sound file from a specified folder and click the OK button, or click the desired movie or sound in the Clip Art task pane.
- When asked whether you want the movie or sound to start automatically or when clicked, click either the Automatically or When Clicked button.

For the presentation on the Peru expedition, you'll use photos, movies, and sound files that are included with your Data Files. In other presentations, you might have to acquire the graphics and sounds in other ways. For example, you can do the following:

- Use a digital camera to take digital photographs.
- Scan prints of photos or slides to create digital images.
- Create images or movies using graphics software.
- Record sound files with a microphone attached to your computer and appropriate software.
- Download images or sound clips from the Internet.
- Insert images or sounds from the PowerPoint Clip Art Organizer.
- Use built-in PowerPoint sound effects (you'll learn about these later in this tutorial).

Pablo asks you to insert a digital image of the village of Paqarimuy into Slide 3, a video clip of the Peruvian altiplano into Slide 5, and sound clips into Slides 2 and 6. All of these files were created by Pablo or other members of the humanitarian expedition.

Adding a Digital Photo to a Slide

In Tutorial 2, you added a photo to the slide master. In a similar way, you can add any photo to a slide as long as it is in, or converted to, a digital format. The procedure for adding a photo to a slide is the same as the procedure for adding a photo to the slide master. You'll begin by adding the digital image to Slide 3.

To add an image to a slide:

1. Open **Peru Expedition Report** and go to **Slide 3** ("Geography of Paqarimuy").
2. Make sure the Slide Layout task pane appears on the right side of your screen, and then click the thumbnail for the **Title, Text, and Content** layout (the top-left thumbnail under Text and Content Layouts). The slide layout now includes a title, a placeholder for bulleted text, and a content placeholder on the right side of the slide.
3. If the bulleted text extends below the bottom of the slide, click anywhere in the body text box, click the **AutoFit Options** button located in the slide pane adjacent to the selected text box, and then click the **AutoFit Text to Placeholder** option button. The font size automatically decreases so that all the text fits on the slide. See Figure 3-14.

Figure 3-14 Slide 3 after changing slide layout

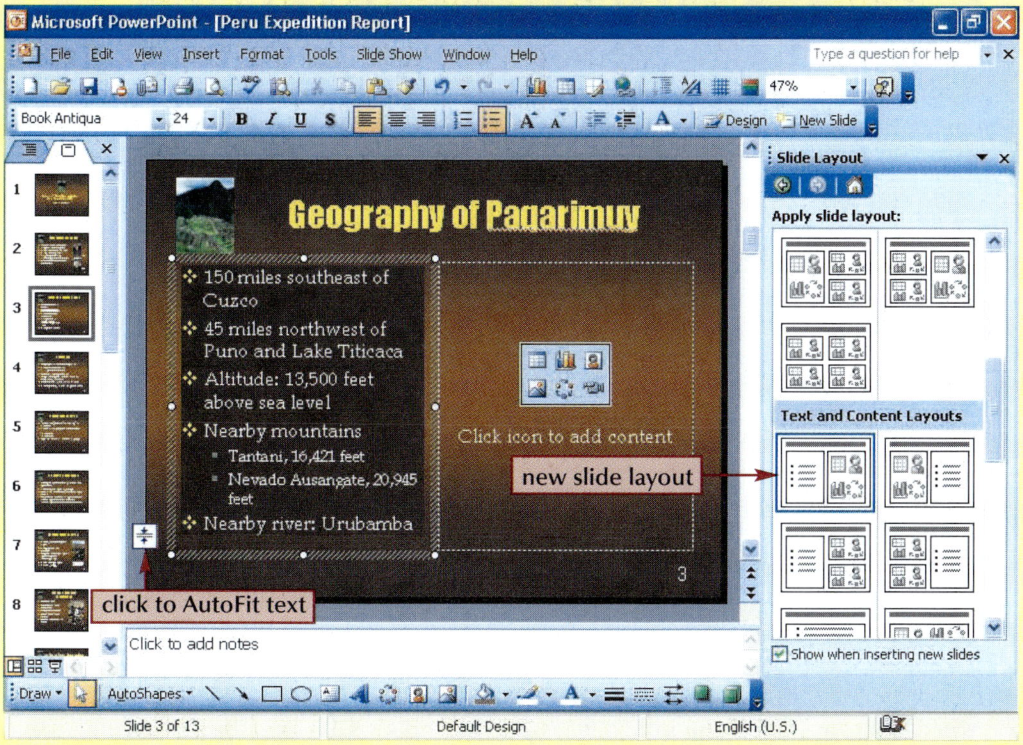

4. Click the **Insert Picture** button in the content placeholder. The Insert Picture dialog box opens.

5. If necessary, click the **Look in** list arrow and switch to the **Tutorial.03\Tutorial** folder included with your Data Files, click **PaqaPic** (a digital photograph of the village of Paqarimuy), and then click the **Insert** button. The picture of Paqarimuy is inserted into the slide. See Figure 3-15.

Figure 3-15 Slide 3 after adding picture

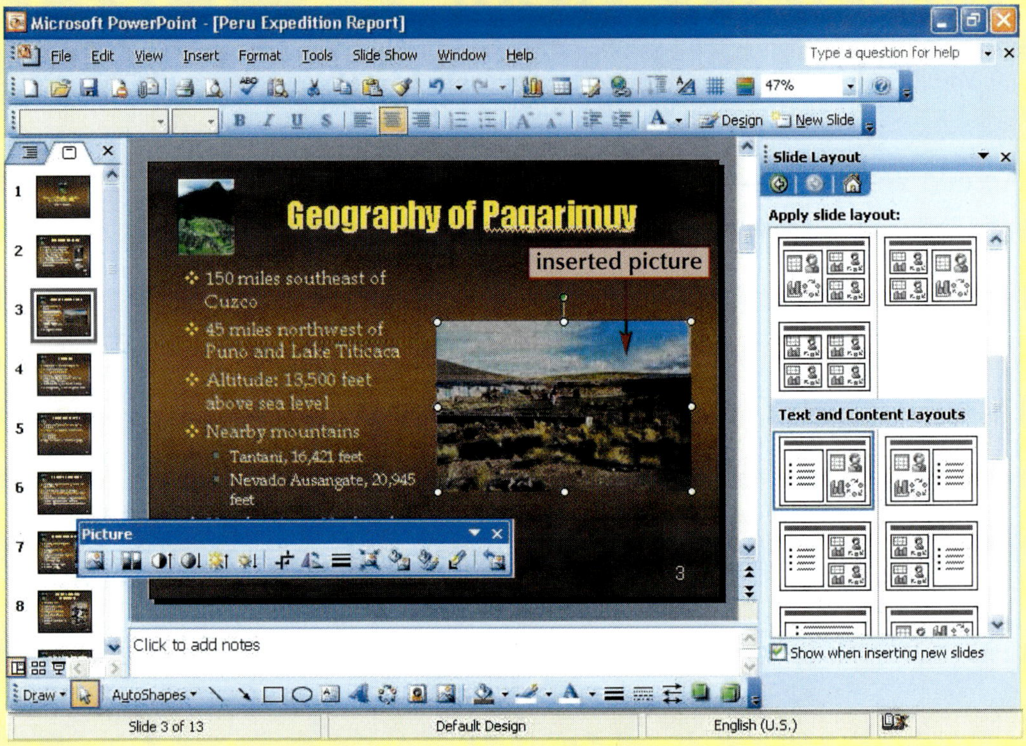

6. Click a blank area of the slide to deselect the picture.

You could have moved or resized the picture of Paqarimuy, but its position and size are adequate.

Adding a Movie

A **video clip**, or **digital movie**, is an animated picture file. Files with the filename extension .avi are video clips. Another common video format is an animated GIF. An **animated GIF** file is actually a series of images that are quickly displayed one after another. These files are identified with the file extension .gif.

Pablo wants to give his audience an idea of how barren and desolate the Peruvian altiplano can be, so he asks you to add a video clip to one of the slides. Pablo's video clip shows a 180-degree pan of the land around Paqarimuy. He prepared a simple, low-resolution video clip for this purpose. He made it low resolution to keep the file size smaller so it would load faster into the PowerPoint presentation and take up less disk space.

You can insert a video clip in two ways. You can change the layout to a Content layout, click the Insert Media Clip button, and then use the dialog box that opens, or you can use commands on the menu bar. You'll add the movie now using the Insert Media Clip button in a Content layout.

To add a movie to a slide and view it:

1. Go to **Slide 5**, click the **Title, Text and Content** layout, and then close the task pane.
2. Click the **Insert Media Clip** button in the content placeholder. The Media Clip dialog box opens, displaying thumbnails of all available media clips, both video and sound, that have been categorized in the Microsoft Clip Organizer. The Clip Organizer lets you add clips to or delete clips from the Clip Art task pane. Video clips are identified by an animation star in the lower-right corner of the thumbnail.

   You need to import the video clip that Pablo recorded into the Clip Organizer.
3. Click the **Import** button in the Media Clip dialog box, click the **Look in** list arrow, navigate to the **Tutorial.03\Tutorial** folder included with your Data Files, click **PaqMovie**, and then click the **Add** button. The clip appears as the first clip in the Media Clip dialog box.

   Trouble? If the clip is already in the Media Clip dialog box, you don't need to add it again, although doing so is not a problem.
4. Double-click the **PaqMovie** thumbnail in the Media Clip dialog box. PowerPoint displays a message asking you how you want your movie to start—automatically, or when clicked during the slide show. In other words, do you want the movie to begin automatically as soon as the slide appears during the slide show, or do you want the viewer or presenter to click the movie to play it?
5. Click the **Automatically** button to indicate that you want the movie to play automatically. The first frame of the movie appears in the right side of the slide. Now you'll increase the size of the movie picture, but you don't want to make it too big or its low resolution will become a distraction.
6. Drag the upper-right sizing handle of the picture until the height is about two inches, move the picture to the right-center of the slide, and then resize the text box so its right edge is near the left edge of the movie picture. Compare your screen to Figure 3-16 and make any necessary adjustments.

Figure 3-16 Slide 5 after inserting movie

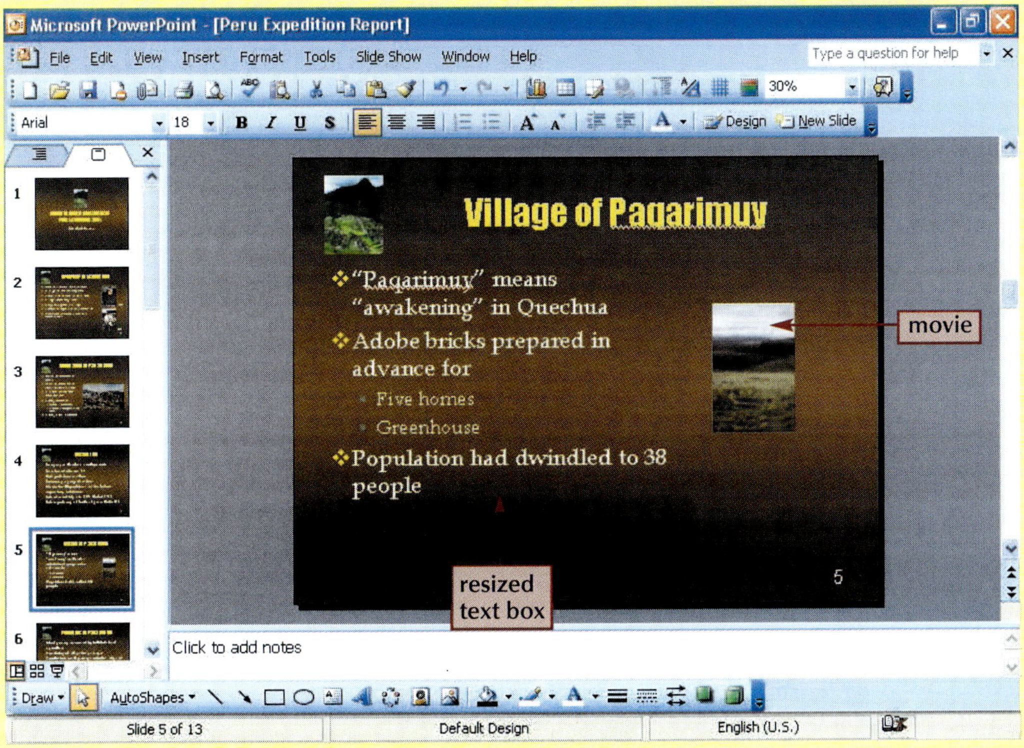

Having inserted the digital movie, you are now ready to view it.

7. Double-click the **movie** object. As you can see, the movie shows the rolling hills of the puna grassland and high Andes Mountains, along with alpaca grazing in the foreground. In fact, the video is an animated, wider-angled view of the picture shown in Slide 7.

Because you clicked the Automatically button, the movie will play when Slide 5 appears during the slide show. But Pablo wants the movie to play continuously while Slide 5 is on the screen during the slide show. You'll set the movie so that it loops continuously.

To edit the movie object:

1. Right-click the **movie** object, and then click **Edit Movie Object** on the shortcut menu. The Movie Options dialog box opens. This dialog box includes several options for playing and displaying the clip while the slide show is running. See Figure 3-17.

Figure 3-17 Movie Options dialog box

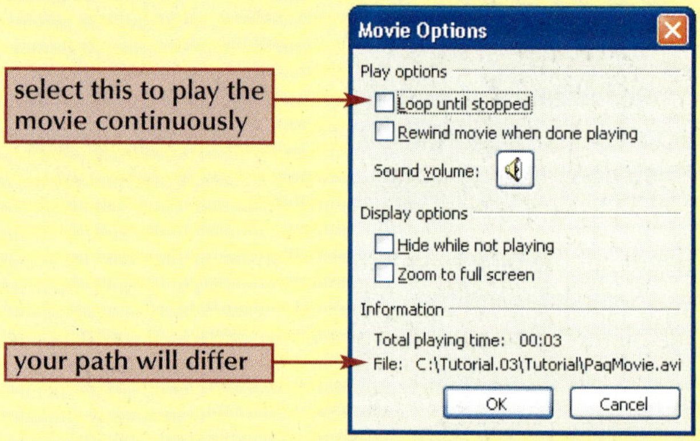

2. Click the **Loop until stopped** check box to select it, and then click the **OK** button.

   Now you'll test it to see how it works.

3. Click the **Slide Show from current slide** button to start the slide show from the current slide. Slide 5 appears in Slide Show view and the movie plays continuously.
4. Right-click anywhere on the slide, and then click **End Show** on the shortcut menu to return to Normal view.
5. Save the presentation.

Next, you'll add sound to your presentation.

Adding Sound Clips

Now that you've added the movie, Pablo wants you to add sound clips of the spoken names of the two villages mentioned in the presentation: Paqarimuy and Taquile. If someone views the presentation without his assistance, the pronunciation of these two names will be available. Pablo's recordings are in .wav files, which is the most common file format for short sound clips.

As with video clips, there are a couple of ways you can add a sound clip to a slide. You can use the Insert Media Clip button in a Content layout, as you did when you inserted the video clip, or you can use menu commands. You'll add the sound files now using menu commands.

To add sound clips to the presentation:

1. Go to **Slide 2**, where the word "Paqarimuy" first appears in the presentation.
2. Click **Insert** on the menu bar, point to **Movies and Sounds**, and then click **Sound from File**. The Insert Sound dialog box opens.
3. Click the **Paq** sound file, located in the **Tutorial.03\Tutorial** folder included with your Data Files, click the **OK** button, and then click the **When Clicked** button to indicate that you don't want the sound to play automatically. PowerPoint inserts a sound icon in the middle of the slide to indicate that a sound clip is available on that slide.
4. Drag the **sound** icon immediately to the right of "Paqarimuy, Peru," and then click a blank area of the slide to deselect the icon. See Figure 3-18.

Figure 3-18 Slide 2 after inserting sound clip

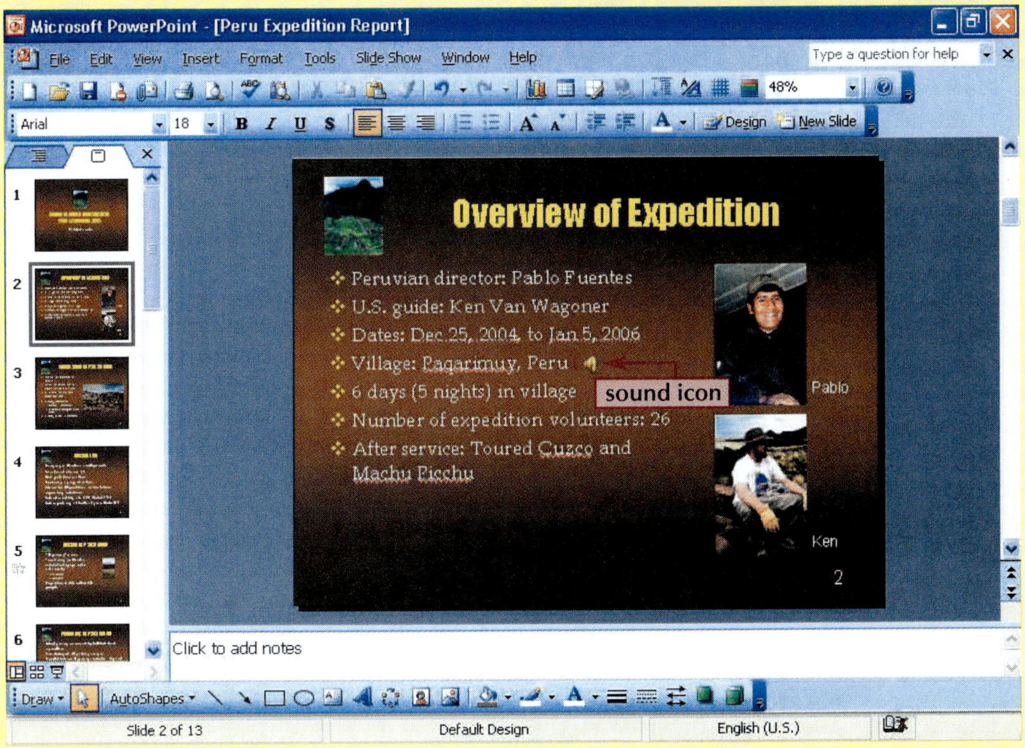

5. Double-click the **sound** icon to play the sound clip.
6. Go to **Slide 6**, where the name of another Peruvian village (Taquile) appears.
7. Using the same method as before, insert the sound clip **Taq** (located in the **Tutorial.03\Tutorial** folder included with your Data Files) into Slide 6, and then drag its **sound** icon to the right of the word "Taquile." Make sure you indicate that you want the sound clip to play when clicked.
8. Double-click the **sound** icon in Slide 6 to hear the pronunciation of "Taquile."
9. Click the **Slide Show from current slide** button. Slide 6 appears in Slide Show view.
10. Click the **sound** icon on the slide, listen to the sound being played, and then press the **Esc** key to end the slide show and return to Normal view.
11. Save the presentation.

Now, anyone who wants to know how to pronounce the names of the villages can click the sound icons during the slide show.

Adding a Textured Background

Pablo was so pleased with the work of the expedition volunteers that he wants a way to highlight Slide 12, which shows a group photograph of the volunteers. He decides that he wants you to add an appropriate textured background to the slide. You'll do that now.

Reference Window

Applying a Textured Background

- Click Format on the menu bar, and then click Background to display the Background dialog box.
- Click the Background fill list arrow, and then click Fill Effects to display the Fill Effects dialog box.
- Click the Texture tab, click the desired texture tile, click the OK button, and then click the Apply or Apply to All button.

To add a textured background:

1. Go to **Slide 12**, click **Format** on the menu bar, click **Background** to display the Background dialog box, click the **Background fill** list arrow, click **Fill Effects** to display the Fill Effects dialog box, and then click the **Texture** tab. As you can see, PowerPoint provides various textures that you can use as slide backgrounds, including green, white, and brown marble. See Figure 3-19.

Figure 3-19 Texture tab in Fill Effects dialog box

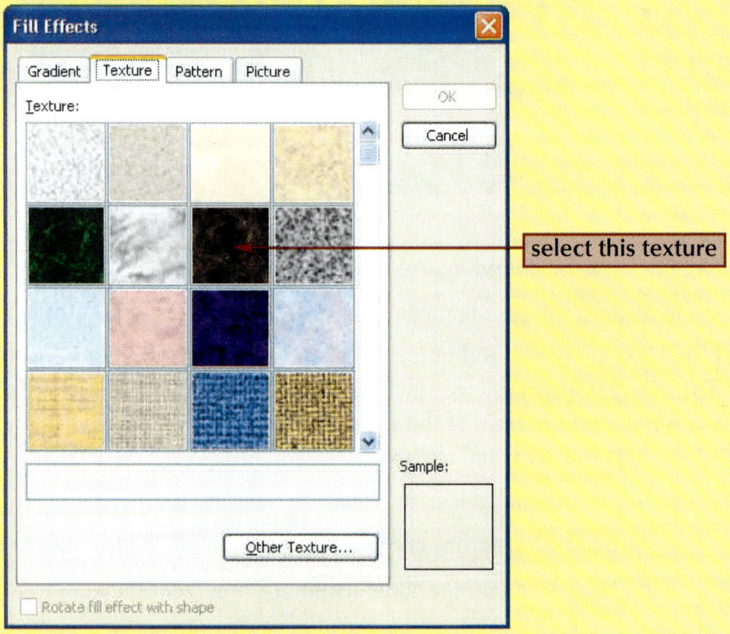

You'll select the brown marble for the background of Slide 12.

2. Click the **Brown marble** tile (as indicated in Figure 3-19), click the **OK** button to return to the Background dialog box, and then click the **Apply** button. The brown marble background appears in Slide 12. If you had clicked the Apply to All button, the textured background would have appeared on all the slides. See Figure 3-20.

Figure 3-20 Slide 12 with textured background

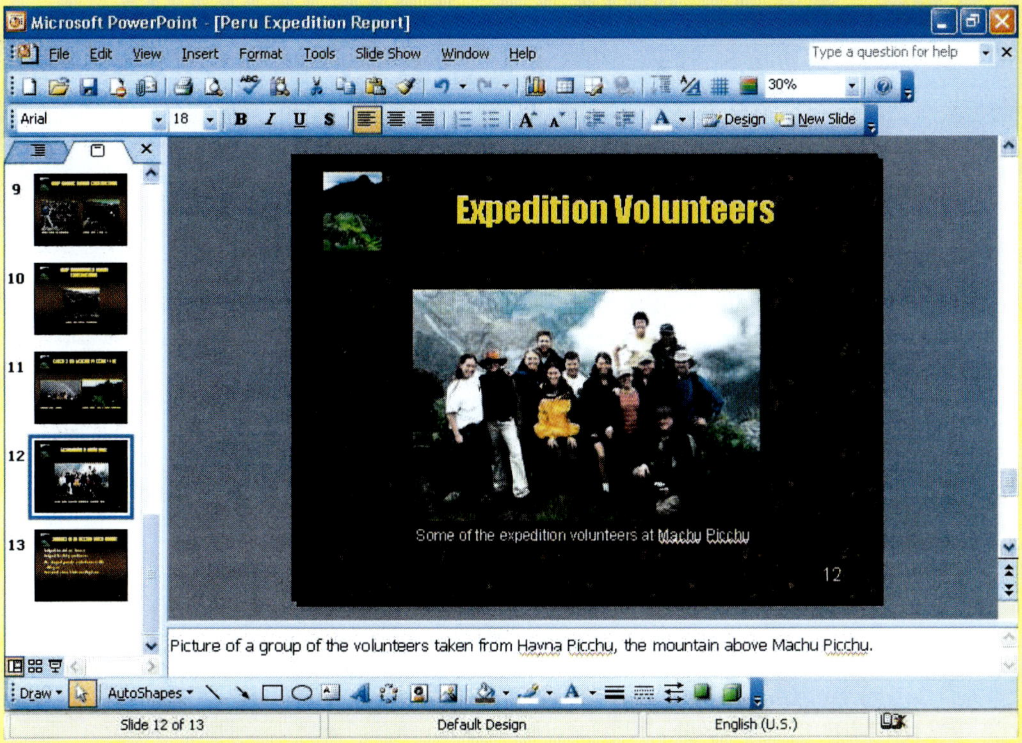

3. Save the presentation.

Pablo is pleased with how Slide 12 stands out from the others, and he is happy with the progress you're making on the presentation.

Session 3.1 Quick Check

Review

1. Describe how to insert slides from one presentation into another.
2. What is a color scheme?
3. In creating a custom design template, what are four (or more) elements in your presentation that you might want to change?
4. Define variant as it applies to a gradient fill background.
5. Describe how to save a PowerPoint presentation as a design template.
6. What is a video clip?

Session 3.2

Creating a Chart (Graph)

A **chart**, or **graph**, is a visual depiction of data in a datasheet. The **datasheet** is a grid of cells, similar to a Microsoft Excel worksheet. **Cells** are the boxes that are organized in rows and columns, in which you can add data and labels. The rows are numbered 1, 2, 3, etc., and the columns are labeled A, B, C, etc. You can use a chart to show an audience data trends or to visually compare data.

Reference Window

Creating a Chart (Graph)

- Change the slide layout to a Content layout.
- Click the Chart button in the content placeholder.
- Edit the information in the datasheet for the data that you want to plot.
- Modify the chart type, if necessary.
- Modify the chart options, adding titles, modifying the font, and so forth, as desired.
- Click outside the chart area to make the chart inactive.

Pablo feels that the presentation should stress the importance of a village greenhouse by showing the average daytime high and nighttime low temperatures during each month of the year. He asks you, therefore, to add a new slide with a chart showing this relationship. You'll create the chart now.

To insert a chart:

1. If you took a break after the previous session, open the presentation **Peru Expedition Report** located in the **Tutorial.03\Tutorial** folder included with your Data Files.
2. Go to **Slide 10**, the slide before which you want to insert the new slide with a graph.
3. Click the **New Slide** button on the Formatting toolbar to insert a new Slide 11, and then click the **Title and Content** layout in the Slide Layout task pane.
4. Click the title placeholder, and then type **Climate of Paqarimuy**.
5. Close the task pane to provide more space for the slide pane, and then click the **Insert Chart** button in the content placeholder. PowerPoint inserts a sample chart and datasheet. See Figure 3-21.

New Slide 11 for creating chart

Figure 3-21

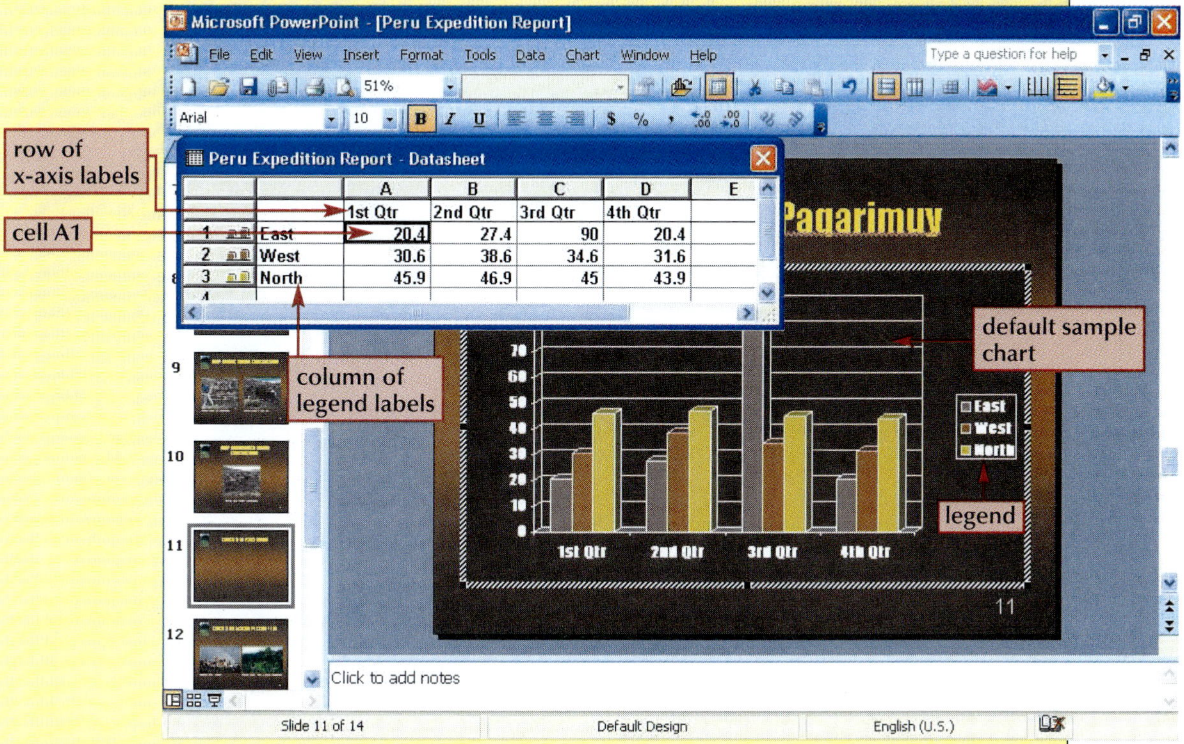

To create the chart for Pablo's presentation, you simply edit the information in the sample datasheet on the screen. When you work with a datasheet, the cell in which you are entering data is the **active cell**. The active cell has a thick border around it. In this chart, you want only two rows: one for the daytime high temperature, and the other for the daytime low temperature. You'll begin by deleting the third row of data on the datasheet.

To modify the chart:

1. Click the row **3** heading on the left side of the datasheet. The entire row is selected.
2. Press the **Delete** key to clear the entire row.
3. Click the first cell in row 1 with the label "East," just to the left of cell A1, type **High** (to indicate the high temperature), and then press the **Enter** key. The label is changed and the active cell moves down to the first cell in row 2. Notice that the legend in the chart also changed to reflect the new row label.
4. Replace the label "West" with **Low**.
5. Click the cell with the label "1st Qtr," just above cell A1 in column A, type **J** (for January), and then press the **Tab** key to move to the label for column B.
6. Type **F** (for February), press the **Tab** key to move to the label for column C, type **M** (for March), press the **Tab** key, type **A** (for April), and then press the **Tab** key. The active cell moves to the top cell in column E and the datasheet scrolls left.
7. Continue labeling the rest of the columns **M**, **J**, **J**, **A**, **S**, **O**, **N**, and **D** to label columns E through L. Notice that empty columns are added to the chart as you add column labels to the datasheet. See Figure 3-22.

Figure 3-22 Datasheet for creating a chart

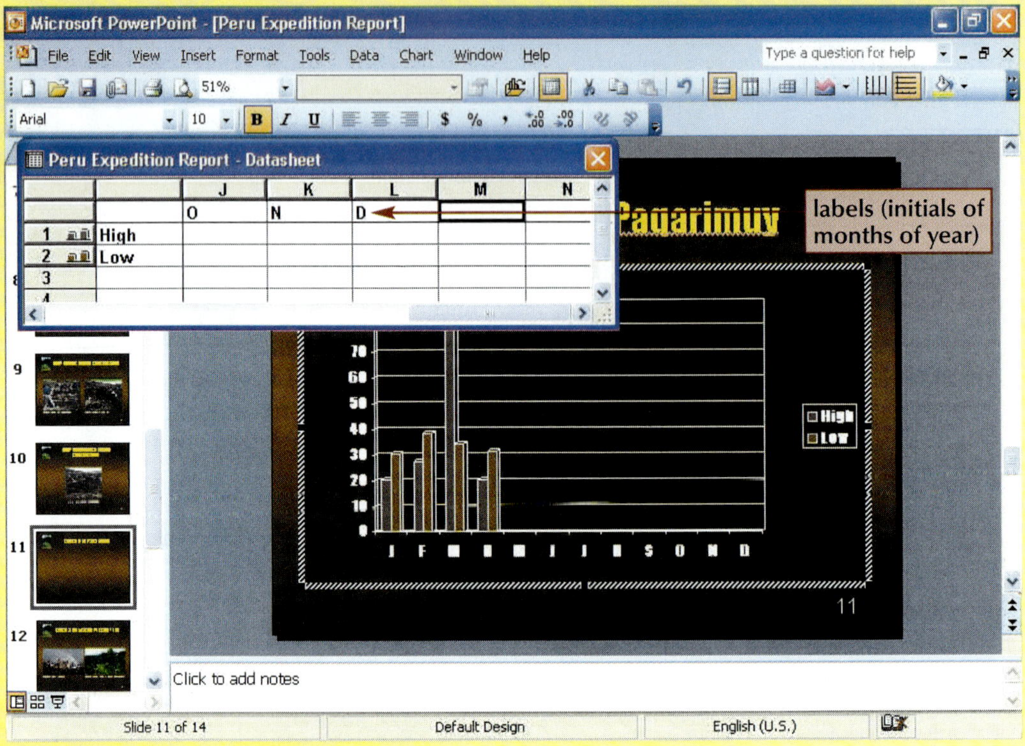

So far, you've created the labels for your chart. Now you'll type the data—the high and low average temperatures for each month in Paqarimuy.

To insert the data into the datasheet:

1. Drag the horizontal scroll button on the bottom of the datasheet all the way to the left so that you can see cell A1.
2. Click cell **A1** (which currently contains the number 20.4), type **48** (the average high temperature in degrees Fahrenheit during the month of January), press the **Tab** key to go to cell B1, type **50** (the average high during February), press the **Tab** key to go to cell C1, type **49** (the average high during March), and continue in the same way typing the temperatures **45**, **42**, **38**, **36**, **37**, **40**, **43**, **45**, and **48** in cells D1 through L1 for the months of April through December.
3. Scroll back to the left to see cell A2, click cell **A2** (which currently contains the number 30.6), and type the following 12 numbers, pressing the **Tab** key between each one, to fill cells A2 through L2 with the nighttime low temperatures for January through December: **25**, **27**, **26**, **23**, **22**, **21**, **21**, **21**, **22**, **23**, **25**, and **26**. Your datasheet is now complete and the chart contains columns to reflect all of the data you entered.

The chart now contains all of the data, but you need to modify the chart to make it more useful to your audience. The chart type is a column chart, but you want to change it to a line chart. You also want to include some additional labels on the chart, and to change the font to make the labels more legible. First, you'll change the chart type.

To change the chart type:

1. Click **Chart** on the menu bar, click **Chart Type** to open the Chart Type dialog box, click the **Standard Types** tab, if necessary, and then click **Line** in the Chart type list box. See Figure 3-23.

Figure 3-23 Chart Type dialog box

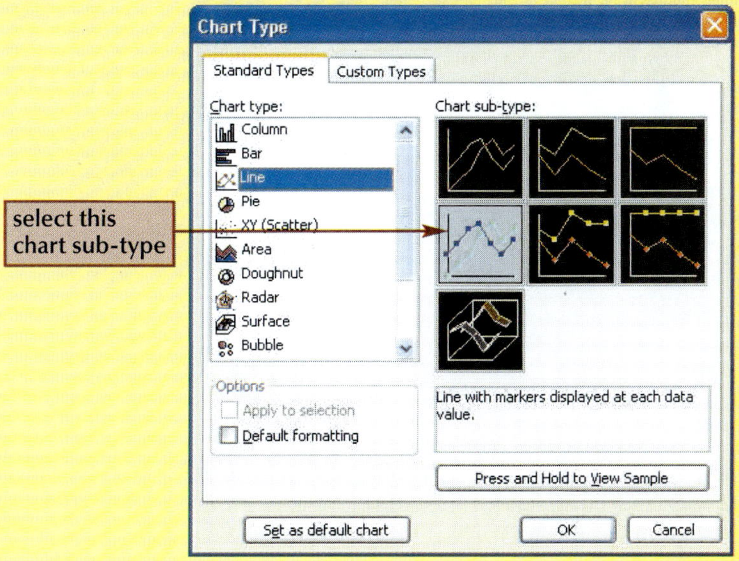

2. If necessary, click the first chart thumbnail in the second row in the Chart sub-type section, as indicated in Figure 3-23, and then click the **OK** button. The chart changes to a line chart. Now that you have entered the desired chart type, you'll add a chart title and an axis label.
3. Click **Chart** on the menu bar, click **Chart Options** to open the Chart Options dialog box, and then click the **Titles** tab, if necessary.
4. Click in the **Chart title** text box, and then type **Average Monthly Temperatures**. After a moment, the chart title you typed appears above the preview of the chart on the right.
5. Click in the **Value (Y) axis** text box, type **Temperature (degrees F)** to indicate that the temperatures are in Fahrenheit, and then click the **OK** button. Your chart should now look like the one shown in Figure 3-24.

Figure 3-24 Datasheet and chart after adding data

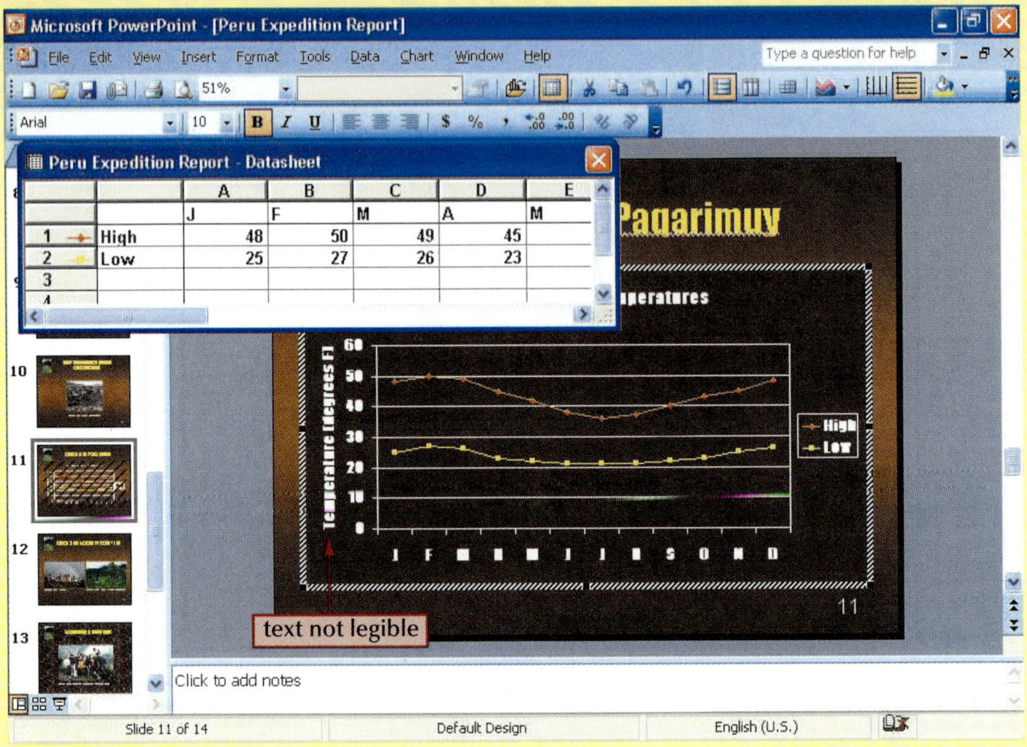

You've almost completed the chart. The only problem now is that PowerPoint automatically uses the title text font, bold Impact, for the chart labels, but this font is not legible in the chart. You'll change all the text in your chart to Arial.

To change the font of the chart labels:

1. Click in the chart area, and then click the **chart title** ("Average Monthly Temperatures") to select the chart title text box.

   Trouble? If you can't see the chart title because the datasheet is in the way, drag the datasheet out of the way by its title bar.

2. Click the **Font** list arrow on the Formatting toolbar, click **Arial**, and then click the **Bold** button **B** on the Formatting toolbarto turn off the bold formatting.
3. Double click the **legend** (which shows the line color and symbols for High and Low) to open the Format Legend dialog box, click the **Font** tab, click **Arial** in the Font list box, click **Regular** in the Font style list box, and then click the **OK** button.
4. Change the font of the **Value axis title** (the title written vertically along the y-axis) to **Arial Regular.**
5. Double-click one of the **Category axis labels** (the labels along the x-axis) to open the Format Axis dialog box. Notice that you can't select this axis as a text box because it's part of the data in the datasheet, not a separate text box.

   Trouble? If the Format Chart Area dialog box opens instead of the Format Axis dialog box, you did not double-click the Category axis. Click the Cancel button, position the pointer over one of the labels on the Category axis so that you see a ScreenTip identifying the Category axis, and then double-click.

6. Click the **Font** tab, if necessary, change the font to **Arial** and the font style to **Regular**, and then click the **OK** button.
7. Double-click one of the **Value axis labels** (the temperature values along the left edge of the graph), change the font to **Arial Regular**, and then click the **OK** button.
8. Click anywhere on the slide outside the chart area to close the datasheet and make the chart inactive, and then click outside the chart again to deselect the chart object. Your completed Slide 11 should look like Figure 3-25.

Figure 3-25 **Slide 11 with completed chart**

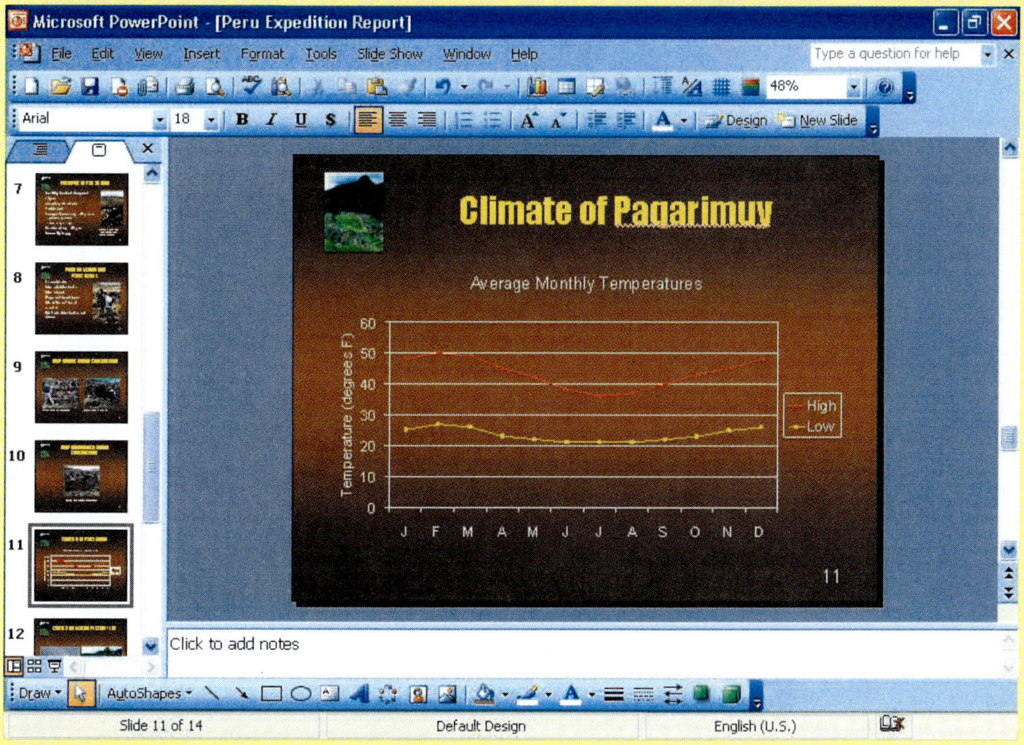

9. Save the presentation.

Pablo is pleased with your chart, which graphically shows how cold the climate is in Paqarimuy, and hence the need for a greenhouse to grow certain vegetables.

Building and Modifying an Organization Chart

Because the members of the board of directors and prospective volunteers for future projects like to know how each expedition is organized, Pablo wants you to create an organization chart showing the people involved in the Peru expedition. An **organization chart** is a diagram of boxes connected with lines, showing the hierarchy of positions within an organization. Fortunately, PowerPoint provides a feature for easily creating and modifying an organization chart.

Reference Window

Creating an Organization Chart

- Change the slide layout to one of the Content layouts, click the Insert Diagram or Organization Chart button in the content placeholder, click the Organization Chart button, and then click the OK button.
- Type the personnel names, positions, and other information, as desired, into the boxes of the organization chart.
- To add new boxes, click the Insert Shape list arrow on the Organization Chart toolbar, and then click the desired box.
- Select the organization chart boxes and modify the font and fill color if desired.
- Click anywhere outside the organization chart area.

Now you'll insert a new Slide 14 and create an organization chart.

To create an organization chart:

1. Go to **Slide 13** ("Expedition Volunteers"), insert a new Slide 14, give the slide the title **Expedition Organization**, change the slide layout to **Title and Content**, and then close the task pane.
2. Click the **Insert Diagram or Organization Chart** button in the content placeholder to open the Diagram Gallery dialog box, click the **Organization Chart** icon (the first icon in the first row), and then click the **OK** button. PowerPoint creates a skeleton of a basic organization chart and displays the Organization Chart toolbar, as shown in Figure 3-26. Now you'll add text to the boxes in the organization chart, delete some boxes, and add new boxes to create the desired chart.

Figure 3-26 New Slide 14 with organization chart

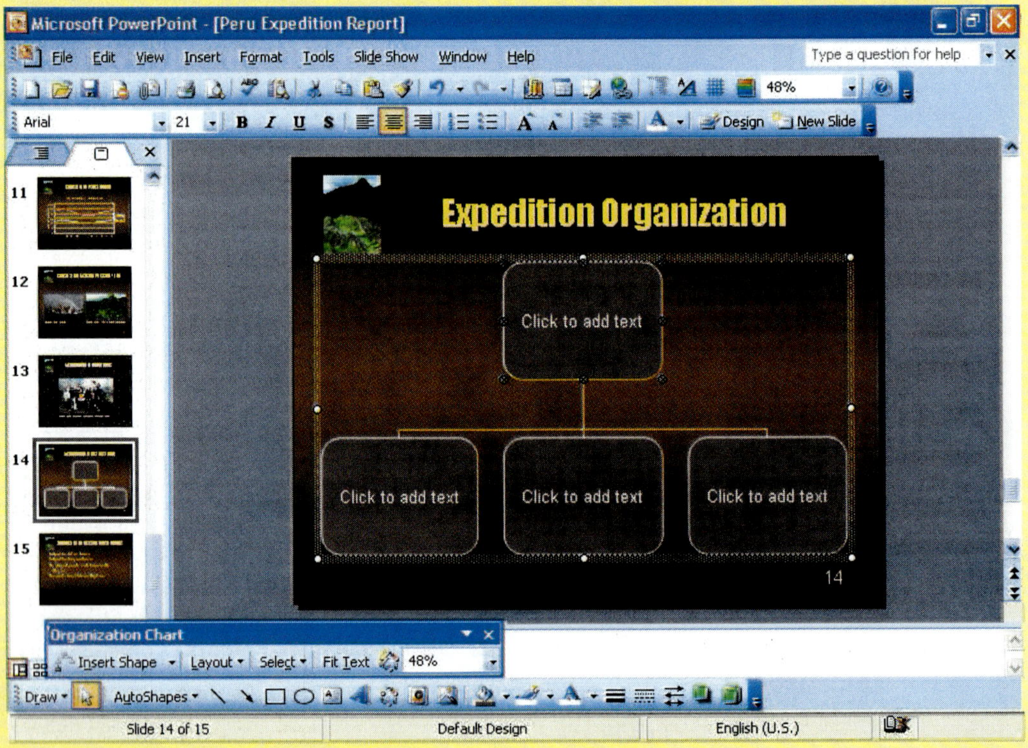

3. Click the **top (level 1)** box of the organization chart. A light-blue insertion point, which might be hard to see, blinks in the center of the box.
4. Type **Pablo Fuentes**, press the **Enter** key, and then type **Expedition Coordinator**. The text you typed replaces the placeholder text in the box. The text overlaps the edges of the box. You'll fix this later.
5. Click outside of the level 1 box, but inside the organization chart area, to deselect the level 1 box but keep the organization chart active.

Now you'll delete all but one of the three boxes on level 2 because only one person, Ken Van Wagoner, is on the level below Pablo in the organization chart.

To modify an organization chart:

1. Click the edge of the first box in level 2. The gray selection handles at the corners of the box indicate that it's been selected. See Figure 3-27.

Figure 3-27 Preparing to delete an organization chart box

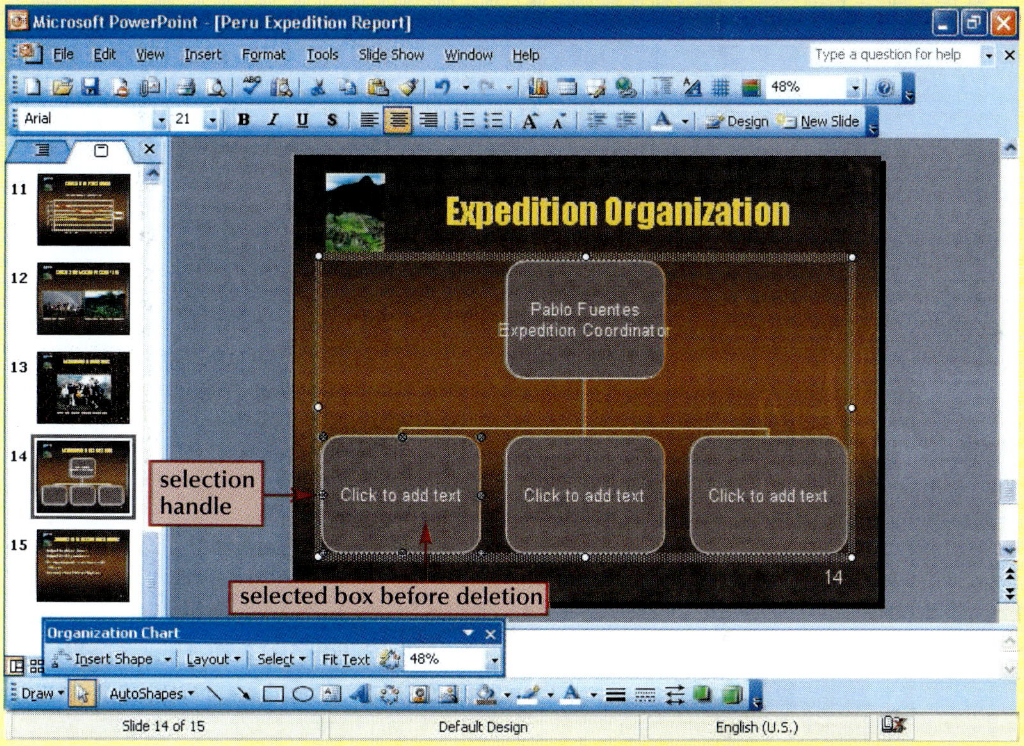

Trouble? If the box has a hatched line around it and no selection handles, click the edge of the box again.

2. Press the **Delete** key to delete the selected box, and when the next box in that row automatically becomes selected, press the **Delete** key again to delete it. Now you should have only one box in level 2.
3. Click in the **level 2** box, type **Ken Van Wagoner**, press the **Enter** key, and then type **Expedition Leader**. Now you're ready to add level 3 boxes below Ken Van Wagoner.

4. Click the **Insert Shape** list arrow on the Organization Chart toolbar, click **Subordinate**, click in the new **level 3** box, and then type **Cultural Team Leader**. You won't type a name associated with the various team leaders because Pablo's audience doesn't know the expedition volunteers, and is interested only in the organization. Now you'll insert a box for another team leader, a co-worker of the cultural team leader.
5. Click the **Insert Shape** list arrow on the Organization Chart toolbar, click **Coworker**, click in the new level 3 box, and then type **Medical Team Leader**.
6. Insert another level 3 co-worker box with the text **Educational Team Leader**, and then click anywhere on the slide outside the organization chart. Compare your Slide 14 to Figure 3-28.

Figure 3-28 **Organization chart with first three levels completed**

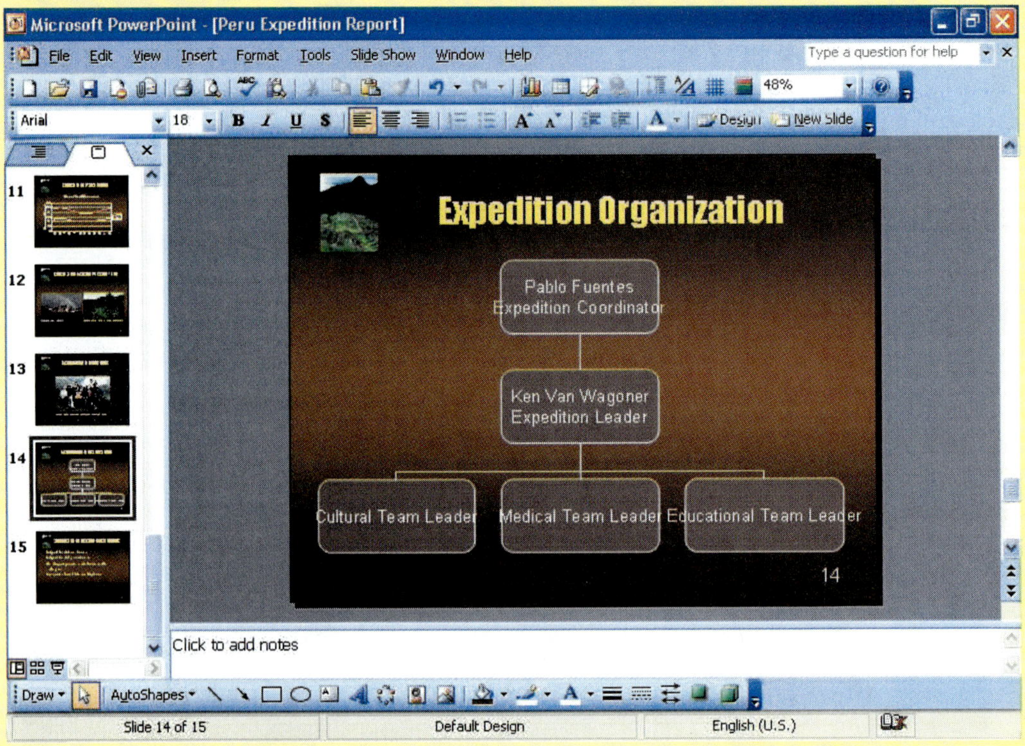

You've made good progress on the organization chart and have to add only three more boxes, subordinates to the Medical Team Leader box.

7. Click anywhere in the organization chart to activate it, and then click the edge of the **Medical Team Leader** box to select it.
8. Click the **Insert Shape** button on the Organization Chart toolbar. You don't have to use the list arrow because the default is to insert a subordinate box. Your chart now has a level 4 box. PowerPoint draws a bent line from the bottom of the Medical Team Leader box to the side of the new subordinate box, but you want a line straight down from the Medical Team Leader box.
9. With the Medical Team Leader box still selected, click **Layout** on the Organization Chart toolbar, and then click **Standard**. Now the subordinate is connected with a straight line to the Medical Team Leader box.
10. Click in the **level 4** box, and then type **Health Team**.

11. Insert two more level 4 boxes to the right of the Health Team box, one with the text **Hygiene Team** and the other with the text **Dental Team**, and then click outside the chart area to deselect the organization chart. Your chart should look like Figure 3-29.

Slide 14 with all boxes of organization chart — **Figure 3-29**

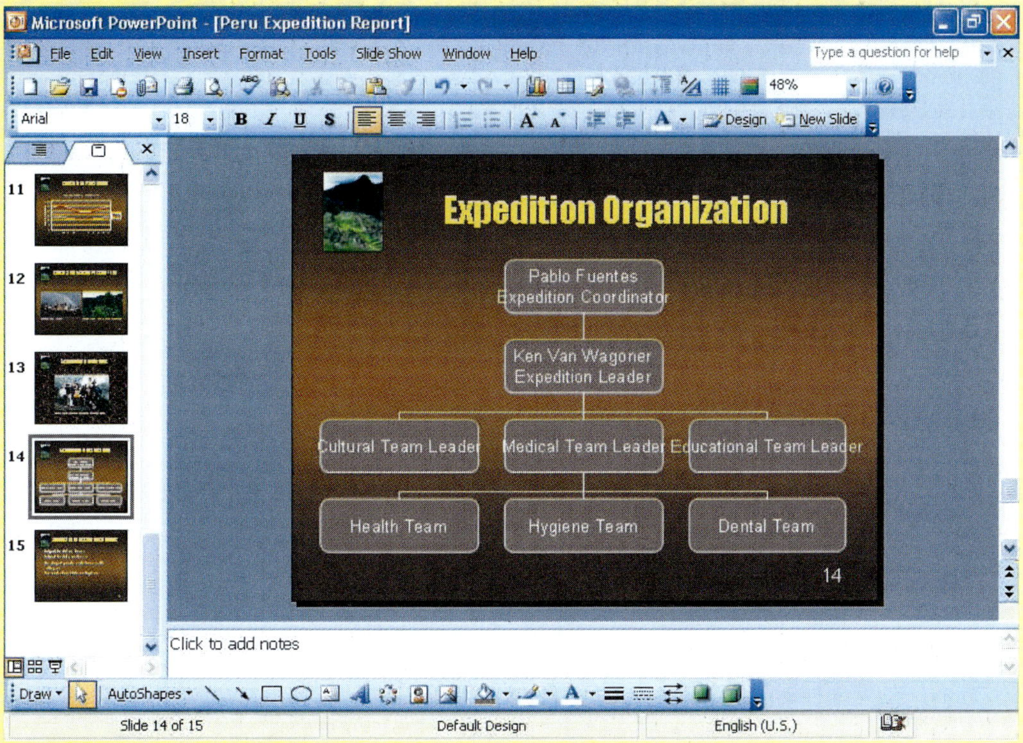

You completed all the organization chart boxes. Pablo looks over this slide and tells you that he thinks yellow text on a dark-brown background would be better for this chart than the default colors of white text on a light-brown background. He also wants you to increase the font size to make the text more legible. Now you'll modify the chart accordingly.

To change font size and color, change the fill color, and make other adjustments:

1. Click anywhere in the organization chart to make it active, press and hold the mouse button, drag from the far upper-left corner of the organization chart area to the lower-right corner to select all elements of the chart (so that a dotted-line border surrounds all of the organization chart boxes), and then release the mouse button. Selection handles appear on all the selected boxes of the chart. Make sure all of the boxes are selected.

   Trouble? If some of the boxes aren't selected, press and hold the Ctrl key, and then click them.

   You'll start by changing the font size and color.

2. Click the **Font Size** list arrow on the Formatting toolbar, and then click **16**. The font size of the selected boxes changes to 16 points.

3. Click the **Font Color** list arrow [A ▾] on the Formatting toolbar, and then click the yellow tile in the color palette. The font color of all the organization chart text changes to yellow.

4. Click the **Fill Color** list arrow on the Drawing toolbar, and then click the dark-brown tile located on the far left of the color palette. The box fill color changes to dark brown.
5. Click a blank area of the slide to deselect the chart. See Figure 3-30.

Figure 3-30 Slide 14 with completed organization chart

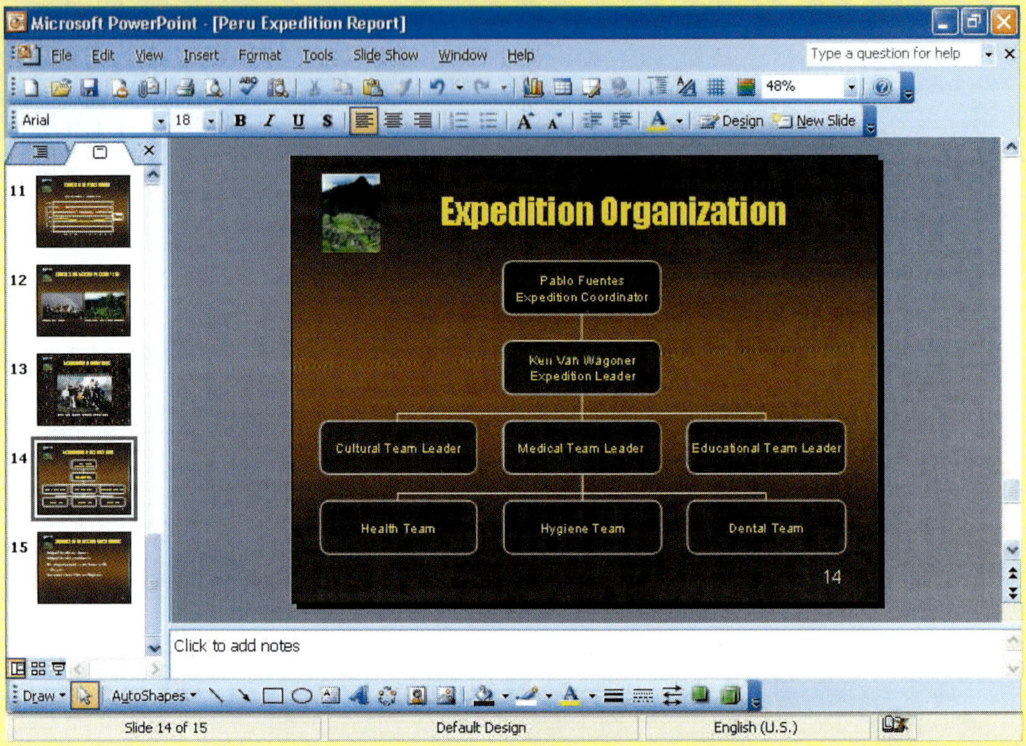

Trouble? If the text doesn't fit inside any of the boxes, click the edge of the box to display the selection handles, drag the left-center or right-center selection handle until the box is large enough to contain the text, and then drag the entire box to position it so it doesn't overlap with other boxes.

6. Save the presentation.

This completes Slide 14 with its organization chart, and completes the text and content of all the slides in the Peru Expedition Report presentation. The only thing left to do is add some special effects and animations.

Applying Special Effects

Special effects—such as causing one slide to fade out as another slide appears, animated (moving) text, and sound effects—can liven up your presentation, help hold your audience's attention, and emphasize key points. On the other hand, special effects can also distract or even annoy your audience. Your goal is to apply special effects conservatively and tastefully so that, rather than making your presentation look gawky and amateurish, they add a professional look and feel to your slide show.

Reference Window

Using Special Effects

- Don't feel that you must include special effects in your slides. Special effects can distract your audience from the message of the presentation. When in doubt, leave them out.
- If you include transitions, use only one type of transition for all the slides. This will keep your audience from trying to guess what the next transition will be and, instead, will help them stay focused on your message.
- If you include animation, use only one type of animation for all the bulleted lists in the slides. This will keep your presentation consistent and conservative.
- Use sound effects sparingly, just enough to provide emphasis, but not enough to distract the audience from your message.

Pablo wants you to add a few special effects to your presentation. The first special effect that you will add is a slide transition.

Adding Slide Transitions

A slide **transition** is a method of moving one slide off the screen and bringing another slide onto the screen during a slide show. Although applying transitions is usually easier in Slide Sorter view because you can easily select several (or all) slides at once, you can also apply a transition in Normal view.

Reference Window

Adding Slide Transitions

- Switch to Slide Sorter view, and then select the slide(s) to which you want to add a transition.
- Click the Transition button on the Slide Sorter toolbar to display the Slide Transition task pane.
- Click the desired transition effect in the Slide Transition task pane.
- Set the speed, if desired.

You'll add a transition to all the slides in the presentation.

To add a transition effect:

1. Click the **Slide Sorter View** button to switch to Slide Sorter view, click the **Zoom** list arrow on the Standard toolbar, and then click a percentage that enables you to see all 15 slides at once. On some screens, no change is needed; on others, the zoom might need to be changed to 50% to make all the slides fit in the window.
2. Click **Edit** on the menu bar, and then click **Select All** (or press the **Ctrl+A** key combination) to select all the slides. Now when you apply a slide transition, all the slides will have that transition.
3. Click the **Transition** button on the Slide Sorter toolbar. The Slide Transition task pane opens.

   Trouble? If the Transition button is not visible on the Slide Sorter toolbar, click the Toolbar Options button on the Slide Sorter toolbar to see the rest of the buttons on the Slide Sorter toolbar.
4. Scroll down the **Apply to selected slides** list box in the task pane, and then click **Dissolve**. PowerPoint demonstrates the dissolve transition in the slide thumbnails in the slide sorter pane, and a transition icon appears below the lower-left corner of each slide. See Figure 3-31.

Figure 3-31 Completed presentation with Dissolve transition applied to all slides

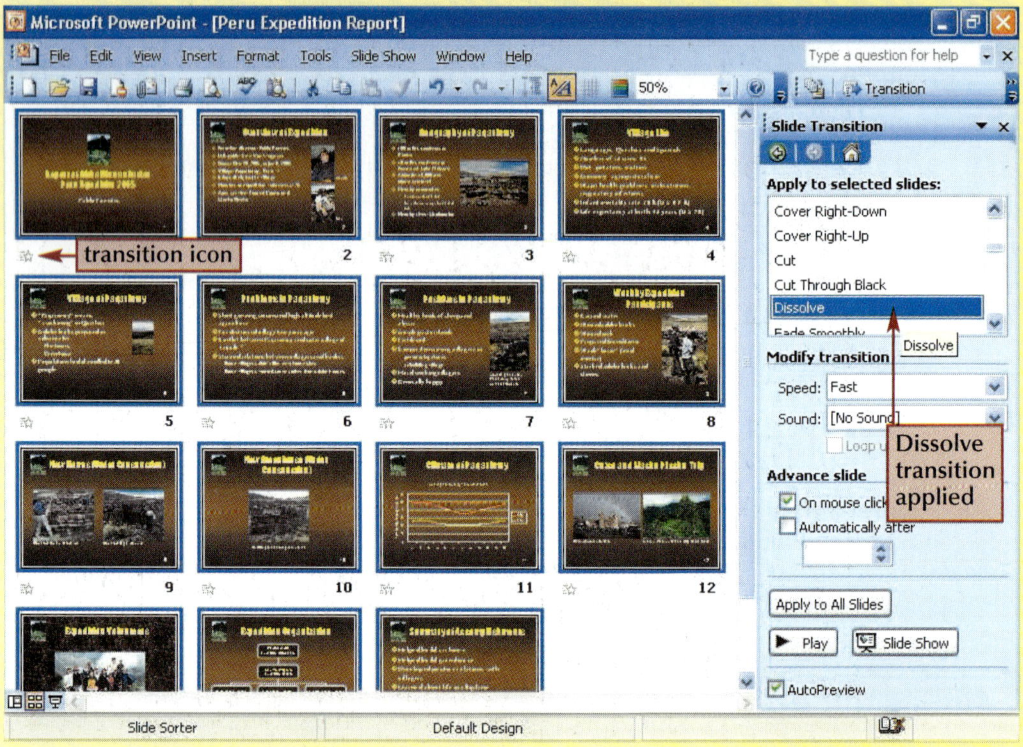

You can change the speed of the dissolve using the Modify transition section of the Slide Transition task pane.

5. Click the **Speed** list arrow in the task pane, and then click **Medium**. The transition speed is now set to medium.
6. Make sure that the **On mouse click** check box in the task pane is checked, and that the **Automatically after** check box is not.
7. Click a blank area of the slide sorter pane to deselect the slides. You'll test the transition by clicking a transition icon.
8. Click the **transition** icon below Slide 2. PowerPoint momentarily displays the Slide 1 image at that location, and then performs the dissolve transition to Slide 2. Click any of the transition icons to see how the transition looks for that slide.

When Pablo advances the slide show from one slide to another, each slide will dissolve onto the screen. Now that you've added transitions to the slides, you're ready to add animation.

Applying a Built-In Animation Scheme

An **animation scheme** is a special visual or audio effect applied to an object, such as a graphic or a bulleted list, on a slide. For example, you can add an animation effect to display bulleted items on a slide one item at a time. This process is called **progressive disclosure**. When a slide with a bulleted list has a progressive disclosure animation effect added, only the slide title appears when you first display the slide in your slide show.

Then, when you click the left mouse button (or press the spacebar), the first bulleted item appears. When you click the left mouse button again, the second bulleted item appears, and so on. The advantage of this type of animation effect is that you can focus your audience's attention on one item at a time, without the distractions of items that you haven't discussed yet.

Applying an Animation Scheme

Reference Window

- In Slide Sorter view, select the slide(s) to which you want to add an animation effect.
- Click the Design button on the Slide Sorter toolbar, and then click the Animation Schemes link in the Slide Design task pane.
- Click the desired animation effect displayed in the task pane.

PowerPoint supports three general types of animations: Subtle (the simplest and most conservative animations), Moderate (moderately simple and moderately conservative animations), and Exciting (more complex and less conservative animations). For academic or business presentations, you should generally stick with Subtle or maybe Moderate animations. If you're giving a casual or informal presentation, such as one describing a group game or explaining an exciting travel vacation, you might want to use Exciting animations. For this presentation, you will apply a Moderate animation.

Note that if you apply an animation effect after applying a slide transition, the animation effect will override the transition previously applied. On the other hand, if you apply a transition effect after applying an animation effect, both effects will be applied.

Now you'll add an animation effect to the bulleted lists in Pablo's presentation. For some presentations, you might include only one or two animation effects, but Pablo wants to try various animation effects before he completes his final presentation.

To add an animation scheme:

1. In Slide Sorter view, click **Slide 2**, press and hold the **Shift** key, and then click **Slide 8** to select the first seven slides that have bulleted lists.
2. Click the **Design** button on the Slide Sorter toolbar to display the Slide Design task pane, and then click the **Animation Schemes** link in the task pane. A list of the PowerPoint built-in animations appears in the task pane.

   Trouble? If the Design button is not visible on the Slide Sorter toolbar, click the Toolbar options button on the Slide Sorter toolbar to see the rest of the buttons on the Slide Sorter toolbar.
3. Scroll down the **Apply to selected slides** list box until you see the **Moderate** animations, and then click **Ascend**. PowerPoint demonstrates the Ascend animation on each of the selected slides.

   Trouble? If the animation doesn't show automatically, click the AutoPreview check box at the bottom of the task pane to select it.
4. Click **Slide 15**, the only other slide with a bulleted list, to select it, and then apply the **Ascend** animation to it.
5. Close the task pane.

You'll test the transitions and animation effects you applied to the presentation.

To run a slide show with transitions and animation effects:

1. Click **Slide 1**, and then click the **Slide Show from current slide** button. Slide 1 appears in Slide Show view by dissolving onto the screen.
2. Click the left mouse button. The title of Slide 2 appears on the screen.
3. Click the left mouse button again. The first bulleted item on Slide 2 appears and ascends up the screen to its final location.
4. Continue clicking the left mouse button to progress through the slide show, and then return to Slide Sorter view.
5. Save the presentation.

Next, you'll apply a custom animation effect to Slide 2.

Applying Custom Animation

The built-in animation schemes offer you many ways to display titles and bulleted items on the screen, but they don't allow you to change the color of previously viewed bulleted items, animate other types of objects (user-added text boxes, sound icons, pictures, and so forth), add sound effects to animations, or change the order of animations. To do these types of things, you have to apply custom animations.

For example, in Slide 2, Pablo wants you to modify the presentation to do the following:

- Add a sound effect to each bulleted item so that it makes a "whooshing" sound when the item appears on the screen during the slide show.
- Dim (change color) each bulleted item after the next bulleted item appears on the screen.
- Animate the sound icon to appear on screen after the bulleted item that contains the word "Paqarimuy."
- Animate the two pictures, along with their captions, so that they appear after the bulleted list.

You'll apply these custom animations to Slide 2 now.

To apply custom animations:

1. Double-click **Slide 2** to switch to Normal view with Slide 2 in the slide pane.
2. Click **Slide Show** on the menu bar, and then click **Custom Animation**. The Custom Animation task pane opens, and a number appears next to each bulleted item in the slide pane. PowerPoint automatically assigns a number to each animated item in the slide. If you animate additional objects on a slide, PowerPoint will assign them new numbers. You use the numbers to help you customize the animation. These numbers do not appear in Slide Show view. The sound icon has a pointing finger next to it. This indicates that you chose to have the sound played when the mouse is clicked instead of playing automatically when the slide appears during a slide show. See Figure 3-32.

Slide 2 with animated text **Figure 3-32**

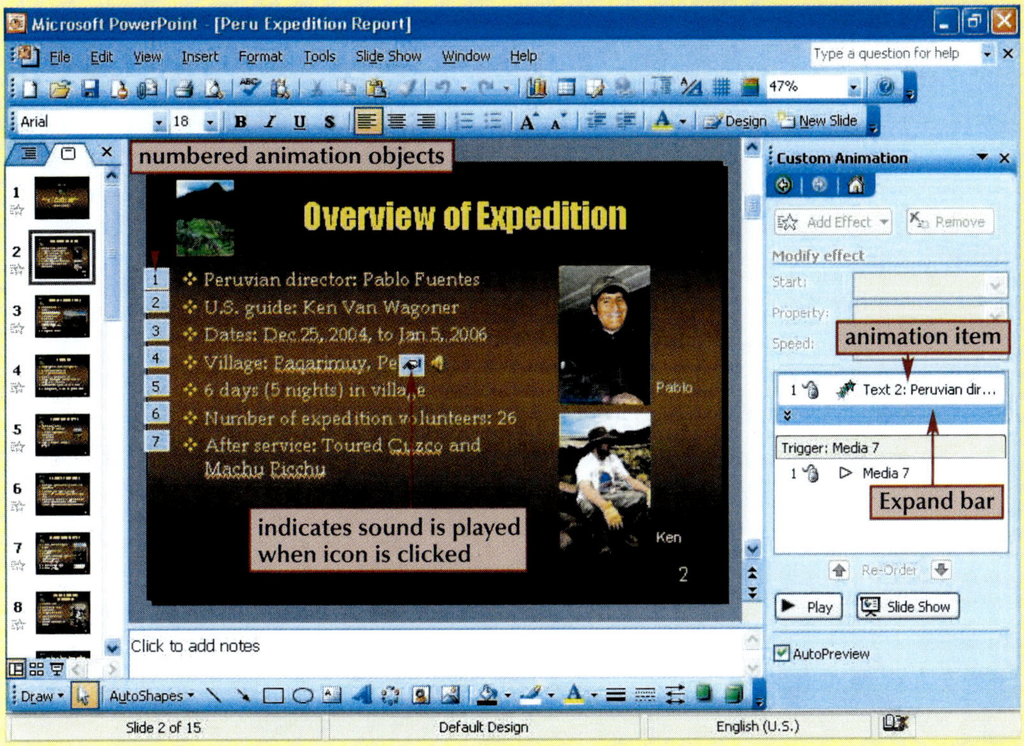

3. Click anywhere within the **bulleted list** text box to select it. This box contains animation items 1 through 7, but only item 1 (called Text 2) appears in the Custom Animation task pane. Because the other items are part of the same text box, PowerPoint doesn't usually display them.
4. In the task pane, click the animation item **1, Text 2: Peruvia...** list arrow, and then click **Effect Options** to display the Ascend dialog box.
5. Click the **Sound** list arrow, drag the scroll bar down to the bottom, and then click **Whoosh** to add this sound effect to the progressive disclosure.

   Trouble? If a message appears telling you that sound effects are not installed, check with your instructor or technical support person if you are working in a lab. If you are working on your own computer, click the Yes button to install the feature now.
6. Click the **After animation** list arrow, and then click the gray tile (the right-most tile in the color palette).
7. Click the **OK** button. The slide automatically animates the progressive disclosure.

   Trouble? If you don't hear anything, you may not have a sound card in your computer system, or you may need to turn up the volume.

You applied custom animation effects to the bulleted list in Slide 2. Next, you'll animate the sound icon so that it appears on the screen along with bulleted item number 4 ("Village: Paqarimuy, Peru") because the sound clip gives the pronunciation of "Paqarimuy."

To animate the sound icon:

1. Click a blank area of the slide to deselect the text box, and then click the **sound** icon to select it. Sizing handles appear at each corner of the object, and the animation item Media 7 is selected in the task pane.
2. Click the **Add Effect** button at the top of the task pane, point to **Entrance**, and then click **Fly In**. The sound icon animates by flying in from the bottom, and the icon that indicated the sound is played on a mouse click changes to animation number 8. You'll change the animation so that the icon flies in from the right.

   Trouble? If you don't see Fly In on the Entrance list, click More Effects to open the Add Entrance Effect dialog box, and then click Fly In.
3. With the sound icon still selected, click the **Direction** list arrow in the task pane, and then click **From Right**. You decide to leave the speed at Very Fast. Now you'll change the animation order by moving the sound icon up just below animation object.
4. Click the **Expand bar** in the task pane just below animation item 1, Text 2 Peruvian dir... to display all the bulleted items, 1 through 7.
5. Click animation item **8, Media 7** in the task pane, if necessary, and then click the **Re-Order Up Arrow** button near the bottom of the task pane three times so that animation item Media 7 is just below animation item 4, Village: Paqarim.... See Figure 3-33.

Figure 3-33 Slide 2 with sound icon set to animate after animation item 4

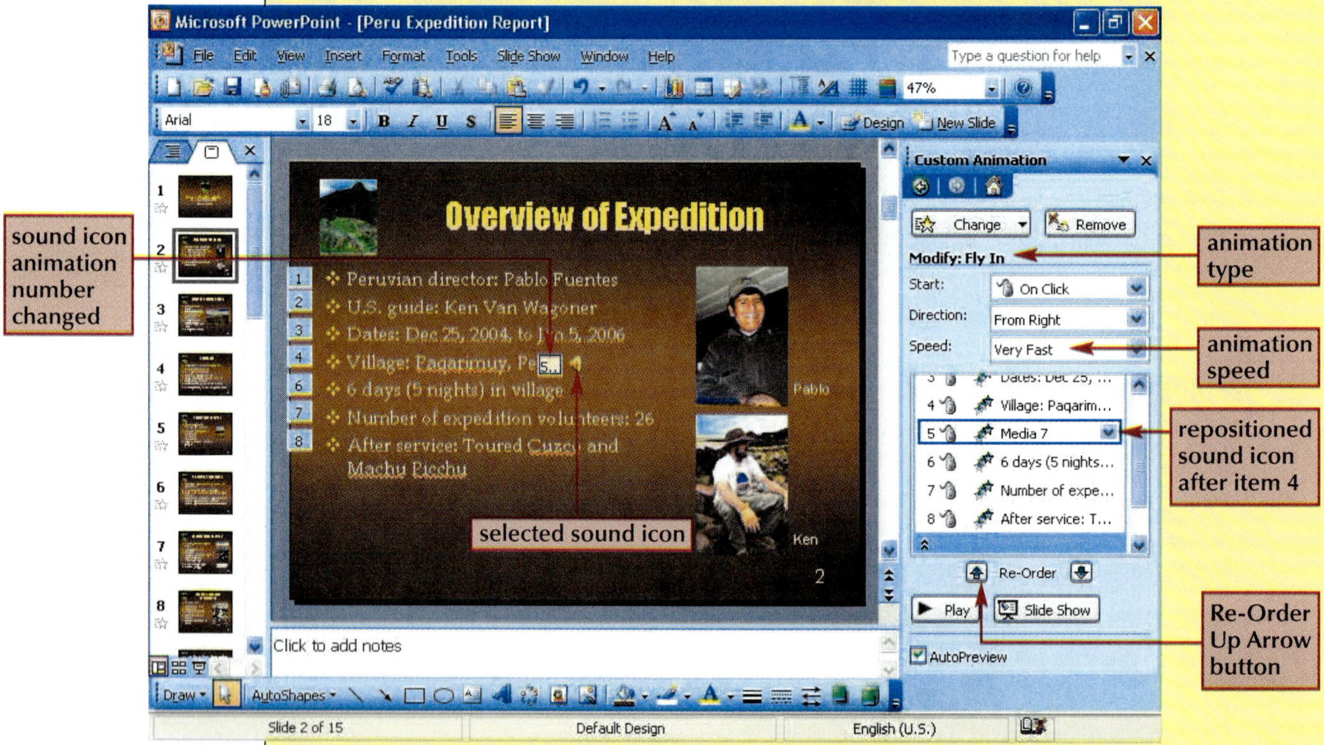

6. Click the **Play** button at the bottom of the task pane to see and hear the animations in Slide 2.

Your final task in Slide 2 is to animate the two pictures and their captions so they appear on the slide after the bulleted list.

To animate the pictures and their captions:

1. Click the picture of Pablo, animate it with the **Entrance** effect to **Fly In**, and then set the Direction to **From Right**.
2. Animate the text box "Pablo" with the same animation effect as the photo.
3. Animate the picture of Ken and the text box "Ken" so that they also fly in from the right. After you animate these objects, each one will be listed on the task pane. See Figure 3-34.

Figure 3-34 Slide 2 with picture and caption animation

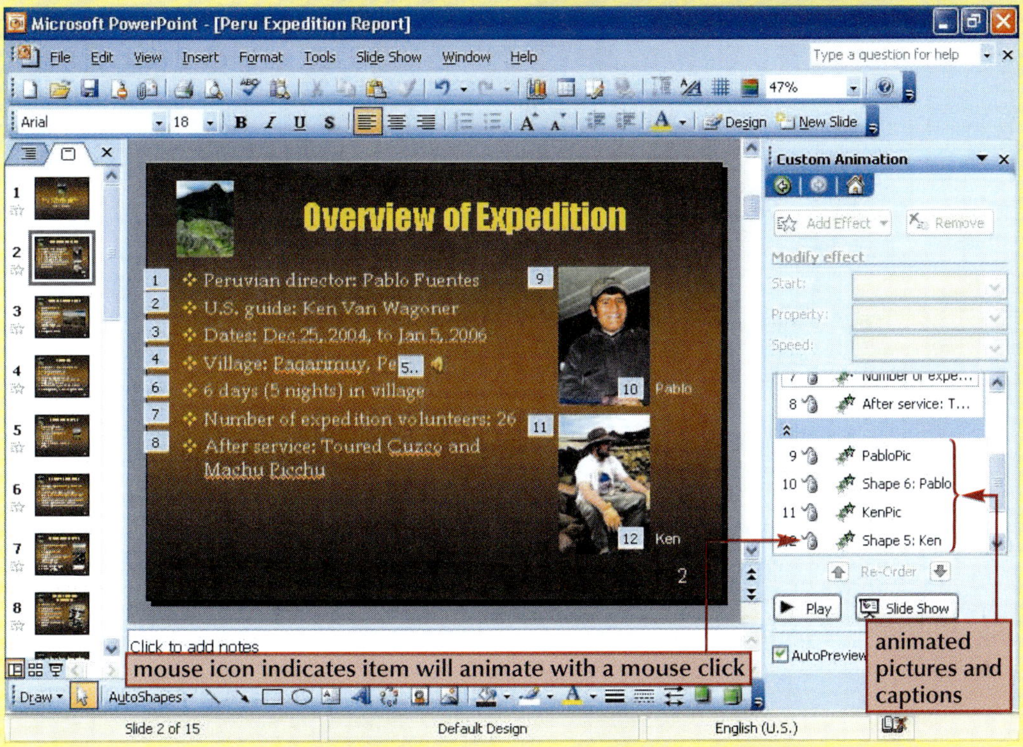

Notice that each animated object listed in the Custom Animation task pane has a mouse icon next to it, as indicated in Figure 3-34. The mouse icon indicates that during the slide show, the animation for that item occurs when someone clicks the left mouse button (or presses the spacebar). Pablo wants the sound icon, the pictures, and the captions to animate automatically, without the presenter clicking the mouse button. You'll set these objects to animate automatically now.

To change how animation occurs during a slide show:

1. In the slide pane, click the **sound** icon, press and hold the **Ctrl** key, and then click each of the two pictures and their captions so that animation items 5 and 9 through 12 are selected.
2. Click the **Start** list arrow near the top of the task pane, and then click **With Previous**. This means that during the slide show, the animation of these items will start at the same time as the animation of the previous object. In other words, it will animate automatically, without a mouse click. Now all these objects animate automatically. See Figure 3-35.

Figure 3-35 Slide 2 after completing custom animation

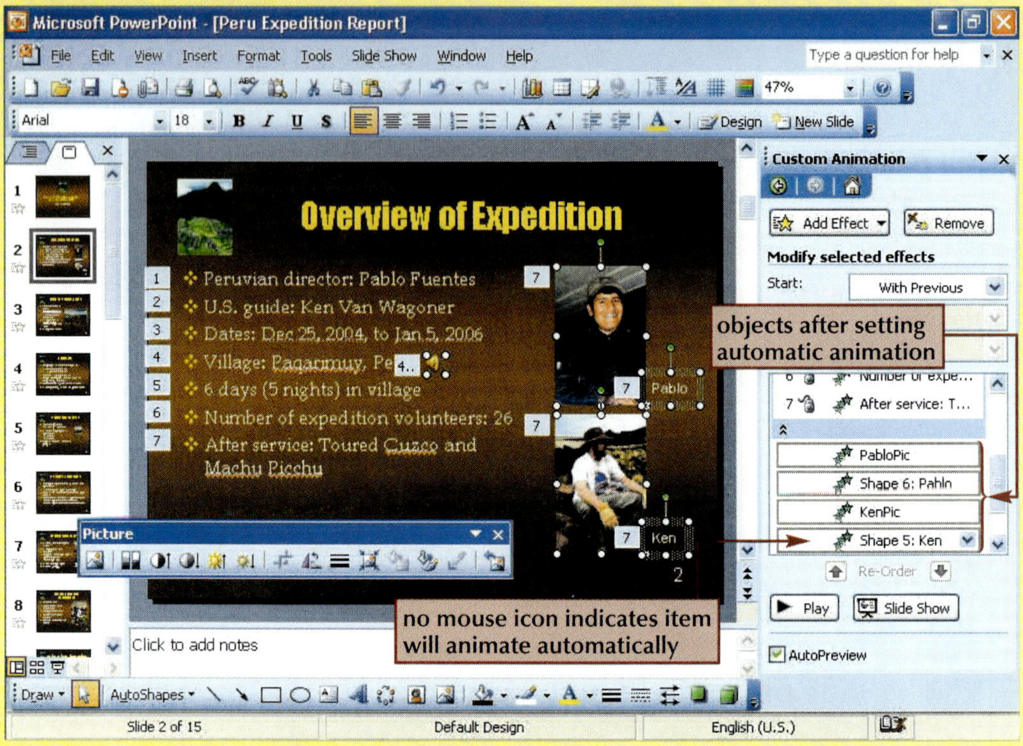

3. Click the **Slide Show from current slide** button at the bottom of the task pane to begin the slide show with Slide 2, and then press the **spacebar** seven times to display each of the seven bulleted items.
4. Press the **spacebar** once more to dim the seventh bulleted item, and then click the **sound** icon to hear the pronunciation of "Paqarimuy."
5. Press the **Esc** key to return to Normal view rather than going on to the other slides.
6. Go to **Slide 6** and animate the sound icon so that it has the same custom effect as the sound icon in Slide 2 (fly in from the right), and then set it to appear at the same time as the third bulleted item by repositioning it in the animation items list in the task pane so that it is listed immediately after the third bulleted item, and then setting its Start option to With Previous.
7. Start the slide show from Slide 6 and test the animation to make sure that the sound icon flies automatically from the right at the same time as the third bulleted item, and then end the slide show.
8. Close the task pane, and then save the presentation.

This completes the presentation. You could edit each slide, one at a time, with custom animations to focus on key information or to add interest and excitement to the slide. But Pablo feels that the presentation has enough animation.

Now you'll run through the entire slide show to see how all the animation effects, transitions, the video clip, and so on will appear.

To run through the entire slide show:

1. Go to **Slide 1**, and then click the **Slide Show from current slide** button. The slide show starts with Slide 1 dissolving onto the screen. This is the transition effect you added.
2. Click the left mouse button or press the **spacebar** to move to Slide 2, advance through the animation of the bulleted list, and then click the **sound** icon on the slide after you dim the seventh bulleted item.
3. Continue through the slide show until the title of Slide 5 ("Village of Paqarimuy") appears on the screen, click the left mouse button or press the **spacebar** three more times to display the three bulleted items. The movie starts after the last bulleted item appears on screen, and plays continuously.
4. Advance to **Slide 6** ("Problems in Paqarimuy"), click the **sound** icon on this slide at the appropriate time, and then continue advancing through the slide show.
5. When you have finished viewing the slide show, go to **Slide 1**, replace Pablo's name in the subtitle with your name, and then save the presentation.
6. Print the presentation in grayscale as handouts, with six slides per page.

Pablo now wants to practice his presentation, including marking slides with the pointer pen.

Using the Pointer Pen to Mark Slides During a Slide Show

The **pointer pen** is a PowerPoint mouse pointer icon that allows you to draw lines on the screen during a slide show. For example, you might use it to underline a word or phrase that you want to emphasize, or to circle a graphic that you want to point out. After you go through a presentation and mark it, PowerPoint gives you the choice of keeping the markings or discarding them. Now you'll show Pablo how to use the pointer pen.

To use the pointer pen during a slide show:

1. Go to **Slide 3** and start the slide show.
2. Press the **spacebar** five times to display the last bulleted item ("Nearby river: Urubamba") in Slide 3. You want to underline the phrase "13,500 feet" to emphasize that Paqarimuy is a very high-altitude village.
3. Move the mouse until you see the mouse pointer, and then click the **Pen** icon, located in the lower-left corner of the screen to open a menu. The Pen icon and others appear only when you move the mouse, and they appear as transparent until you position the pointer over them.
4. Click **Felt Tip Pen**, which changes the mouse pointer to a red-filled circle. By clicking and dragging the pen on the screen, you can draw lines.
5. Move the pointer below the "1" in "13,500," press and hold the left mouse button, and then drag the pointer from left to right to draw a line below "13,500 feet." See Figure 3-36.

Figure 3-36 Slide 3 with ink mark

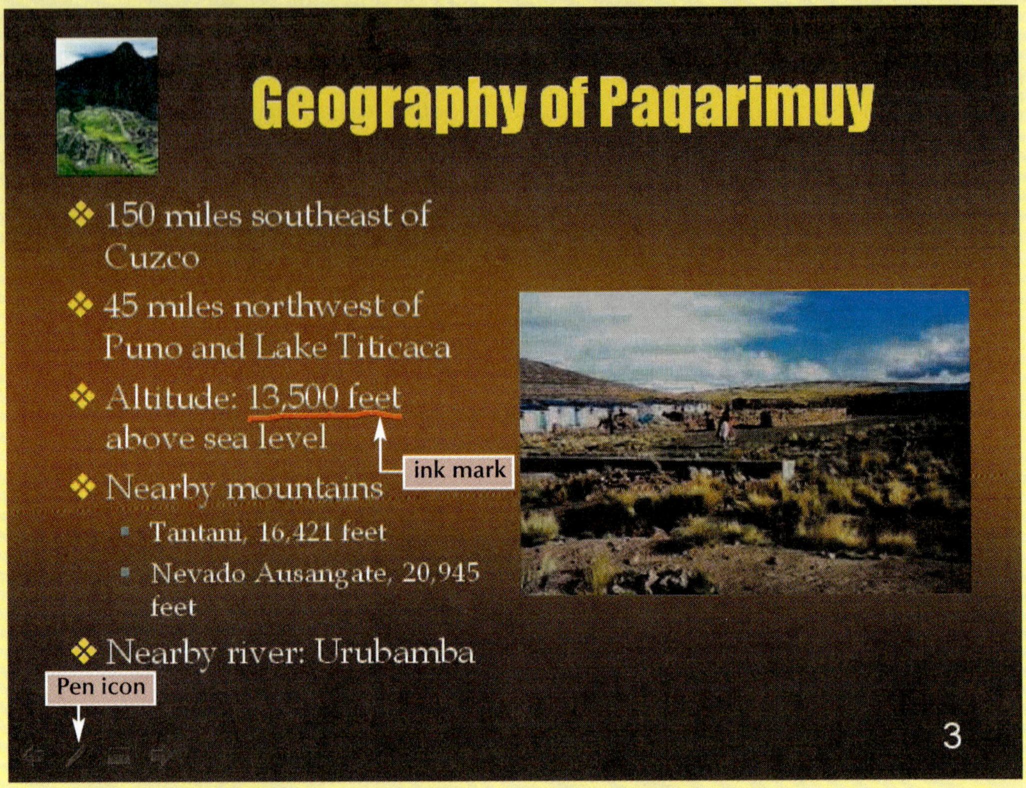

6. Press the **spacebar** to move to the next slide. Note that you cannot click the left mouse button to proceed through the slide show while a pointer pen is selected.
7. Click the **Pen** icon in the lower-left corner, and then click **Arrow**. The mouse pointer changes back to the ordinary arrow pointer.
8. Press the **Esc** key to terminate the slide show. A dialog box appears asking if you want to keep your annotations.
9. Click the **Discard** button. Slide 4 appears in the slide pane in Normal view.

As you can see, the pointer pen is a powerful tool for highlighting and pointing out information during a slide show.

Hiding Slides

Pablo decides that he can also use most of the slides in this presentation for prospective expedition volunteers; however, all of the slides are not appropriate for the volunteers. For example, he doesn't feel that Slide 11 ("Climate of Paqarimuy") with its temperature chart, will be of interest to most potential expedition volunteers. One solution is to temporarily hide that slide so it won't show up during the presentation.

You'll demonstrate how to hide and unhide a slide.

To hide and unhide a slide:

1. Go to **Slide 11**, click **Slide Show** on the menu bar, and then click **Hide Slide**. The slide remains in the slide pane in Normal view, but PowerPoint marks the slide number in the Slides tab so that you know the slide will be hidden during the slide show. See Figure 3-37. Now you'll see your slides in Slide Show view.

Figure 3-37 Slide 11 after hiding slide

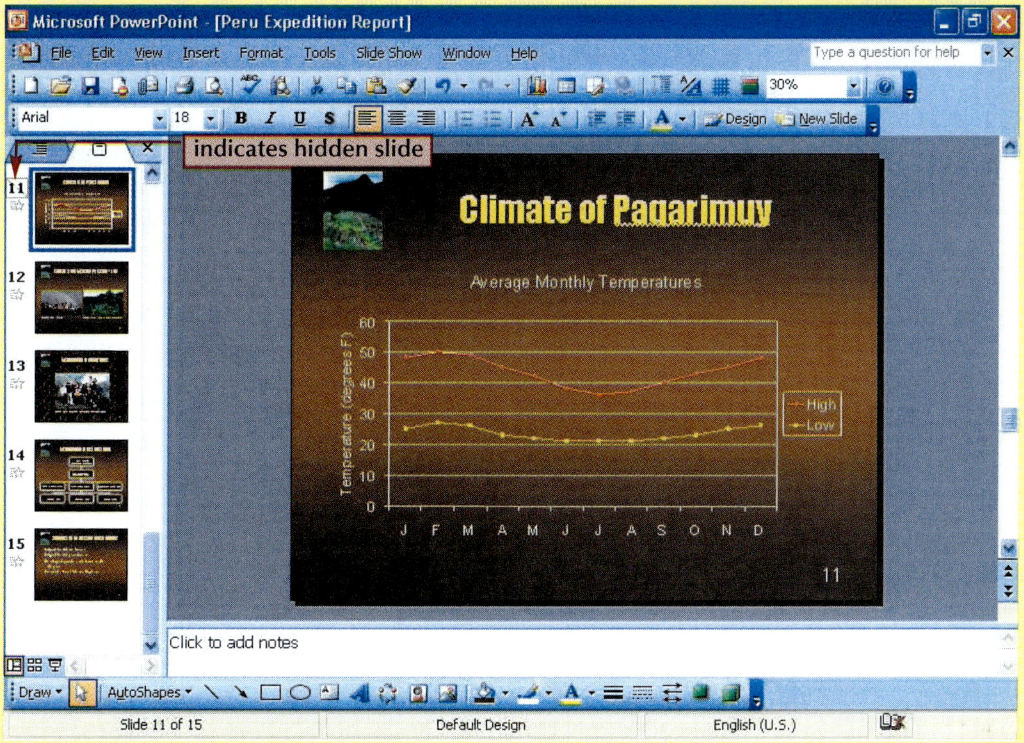

2. Go to **Slide 10**, and then click the **Slide Show from current slide** button.
3. Press the **spacebar** or click the left mouse button. Slide 12 ("Cuzco and Machu Picchu Trip") appears on the screen. The slide show skips Slide 11 ("Climate of Paqarimuy") as you intended.
4. Press the **Esc** key to end the slide show. Slide 12 appears in the slide pane in Normal view.

Now that you've seen how to hide a slide, you should go back and "unhide" it so it will be available for Pablo's presentation to the board of directors.

To unhide a slide:

1. Go to **Slide 11**, click **Slide Show** on the menu bar, and then click **Hide Slide**. This toggles the Hide Slide effect off for Slide 11. The hidden slide icon disappears from the Slides tab.
2. Go to **Slide 10**, switch to Slide Show view, and then press the **spacebar** to view Slide 11, verifying that it does indeed show up in the slide show now.
3. Return to Normal view, and then save the presentation.

Pablo is now confident that his presentation will go smoothly, providing the needed information to his audiences in an engaging manner. Your final tasks are to help him prepare the materials to run not only on his computer, but also on the computers in the rooms where he'll give his presentations.

Preparing the Presentation to Run on Another Computer

Pablo will present the electronic (on-screen) slide show to the board of directors in a suitably equipped conference room at Global Humanitarian; however, he might be using computers without PowerPoint to give presentations to potential volunteers. He knows that he doesn't need PowerPoint installed because he can use PowerPoint Viewer. **PowerPoint Viewer** is a separate program that you can use to give your slide show on any Windows 95/98/2000/NT/XP computer. The Microsoft PowerPoint license allows you to create a Viewer disk and install the Viewer program on other computers without additional charge. Pablo asks you to use the Package for CD feature to create a CD that contains the PowerPoint Viewer files and a copy of his presentation. **Package for CD** places the entire presentation on a CD so you can take the presentation and show it on any computer with the Viewer program. Pablo can then use this CD to install PowerPoint Viewer and run the presentation file on any computer. Although Pablo can't modify any of the slides using PowerPoint Viewer, he can review the entire slide show, including special effects, and he can use the pen pointer during the slide show.

Pablo wants to make sure that whatever computer he uses, the fonts (Impact and Book Antiqua) are available, so he'll save the presentation with embedded fonts. With embedded fonts, the presentation will always have the desired fonts, regardless of whether they are installed on the computer where you give the slide show. Be aware, however, that embedding fonts increases the size of the presentation file, so you want to embed fonts only if necessary.

Before completing the following steps, consult with your instructor. You'll need a computer with a CD writer (often called a "CD burner") and a blank, unused, writable CD.

To save a file with embedded fonts, and use Package for CD:

1. Click **File** on the menu bar, and then click **Save As** to display the Save As dialog box.
2. Click **Tools** on the dialog box toolbar, and then click **Save Options**. The Save Options dialog box opens.
3. Click the **Embed TrueType fonts** check box to select it, and then click the **OK** button. (In some cases, you might want to select the Embed characters in use only check box to save disk space, but the risk in this is that if you need to add text to your presentation, you might not find the needed characters.)
4. Click the **Save** button in the dialog box, and then click the **Yes** button when you're asked if you want to replace the existing file. The **Peru Expedition Report** file is now saved with the fonts embedded so it will have the same appearance on computers that might not have those fonts.
5. Click **File** on the menu bar, and then click **Package for CD**. The Package for CD dialog box opens.

   Trouble? If the Package for CD feature isn't installed, PowerPoint will ask you if you want to install it now. If you are working in a lab, ask your instructor or technical support person for assistance; if you are working on your own computer, click the Yes button.
6. Type **Peru Expedition** in the Name the CD text box. See Figure 3-38.

Package for CD dialog box **Figure 3-38**

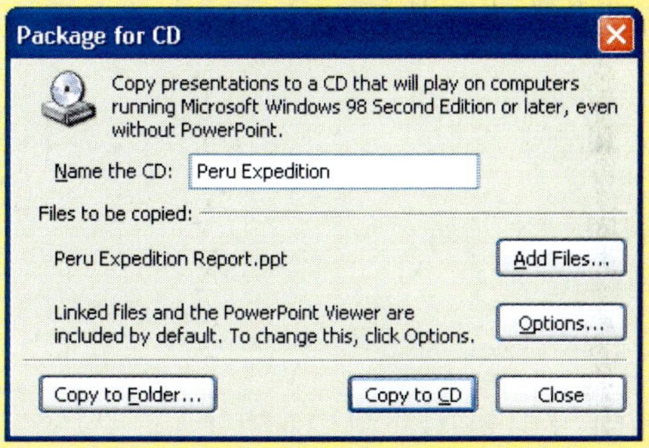

7. Click the **Copy to CD** button. The CD drive drawer on your computer automatically opens, and a message appears asking you to insert a blank CD into the drive.
8. Place a blank, writable CD in the CD drive and close the drawer, and then click the **Retry** button. PowerPoint copies the presentation files and PowerPoint Viewer to the CD. This might take a minute or so. When the copying is complete, the CD drawer opens again, and PowerPoint asks if you want to make another copy.
9. Click the **No** button in the dialog box, and then click the **Close** button in the Package for CD dialog box.
10. Close the PowerPoint program window without saving any changes to the presentation.
11. Remove the CD from the CD drive.

You can now test the CD with your PowerPoint presentation.

To run the PowerPoint presentation from a CD:

1. Insert the CD that you just created into the CD drive and close the drawer. A dialog box appears containing the PowerPoint Viewer license agreement.
2. Click the **Accept** button. The dialog box closes and the slide show starts automatically.
3. Go through the slide show.

   Trouble? If the movie does not play automatically on Slide 5, click it to play it, and then click it again to stop it. Sometimes, media clips do not play automatically when you use the Viewer.

   Trouble? If the presentation doesn't work exactly as you prepared it, don't worry. Some features don't translate to the CD exactly.
4. After the blank screen appears at the end of the presentation, click the left mouse button or press the **spacebar** to end the presentation.

You give the CD to Pablo so he can show his presentation on any computer that has a CD drive.

You've completed Pablo's presentation. He believes that the graphics, sound, and special effects for the on-screen slide show will help his audience stay focused on his presentation. He thanks you for your help.

Review

Session 3.2 Quick Check

1. Describe how to insert a chart into a slide.
2. What is an organization chart?
3. How do you insert an organization chart into a slide?
4. Define the following terms:
   a. transition effect
   b. animation effect
   c. progressive disclosure
   d. sound effect
   e. pointer pen
5. Describe how to add a transition effect to a slide.
6. What is PowerPoint Viewer?

Review

Tutorial Summary

In this tutorial, you learned how to insert slides from another presentation and create a design template by creating a custom color scheme and background and by changing the typeface and color of the font. You also learned how to add a background image, apply graphics and sound in the form of digital images, video clips, and audio clips, and add a textured background. You learned how to create a chart (graph) and an organization chart, and how to apply special effects such as slide transitions and animations. Finally, you learned how to use the pointer pen to mark slides during a slide show, hide a slide, and prepare a presentation to run on another computer.

Key Terms

active cell
animated GIF
animation scheme
cell
chart
color scheme
datasheet
digital movie
gradient fill
graph
organization chart
Package for CD
pointer pen
PowerPoint Viewer
progressive disclosure
shading style
special effect
transition
variant
video clip

Practice

Get hands-on practice of the skills you learned in the tutorial using the same case scenario.

Review Assignments

Data Files needed for the Review Assignments: CuzcTour.ppt, PeruLogo.jpg, PeruExp.ppt, Cuzco.wav, SacsSnd.avi, MachPicc.wav, HuaynaP.wav, SacsMov.wav

A key attraction to potential volunteers of the humanitarian expeditions is the tour of Peru after the service project. Pablo wants to create a PowerPoint presentation that focuses on the tourism part of the Peru expedition. He wants to provide prices, dates, pictures, and other details about the tour of the Cuzco and Machu Picchu areas of Peru. He asks you to help him create the presentation.

1. Open the presentation file **CuzcTour** from the Tutorial.03\Review folder included with your Data Files, change the name on Slide 1 from Pablo Fuentes to your name, and then save the presentation as **Cuzco Machu Picchu Tour** to your high-capacity disk (your hard disk or a Zip disk).
2. Apply the built-in color scheme for the Default Design template that has a black background and white text.

3. Change the background of all the slides to a two-color gradient fill using the default colors (Color 1 set to black and Color 2 set to green), with the Horizontal shading style and the variant with black on top and green on the bottom.
4. In the slide master, change the title text to left-aligned yellow and bold, leaving the title font at 44-point Arial. Change the main text (bulleted list text) to Times New Roman and leave it white.
5. In the slide master, change the first-level bullets to yellow squares, and the second-level bullets to medium-blue circles.
6. Also in the slide master, resize the width of the title text box about an inch smaller so that you can insert a logo to the left of the title, and then insert the graphic file **PeruLogo** (in the Tutorial.03\Review folder) and position it to the left of the title text box. Adjust the graphic size and the title text box so they look good together at the top of the slide.
7. Add a title master, and then reposition the logo on the title master so it's centered above the title text box.
8. In Normal view, change the background texture of Slide 1 (only) to Medium Wood.
9. Save the current version of the presentation as a normal presentation file, and then save it as a custom design template to the Tutorial.03\Review folder using the filename **Cuzco Machu Picchu Template**. Make sure you delete any unnecessary slides and text from the template file.
10. Close the design template file, reopen the **Cuzco Machu Picchu Tour** file, and then insert Slide 8, "Expedition Costs (Per Person)," from the presentation file **PeruExp** located in the Tutorial.03\Review folder at the end of the presentation, after Slide 8 ("Organization of Tour Company").
11. In Slide 2, insert the sound file **Cuzco**, located in the Tutorial.03\Review folder, set the sound to play automatically during the slide show, and position the sound icon to the right of the title.
12. Repeat the procedure of the previous step, except insert the sound file **SacsSnd** into Slide 4, the sound file **MachPicc** into Slide 6, and the sound file **HuaynaP** into Slide 7.
13. In Slide 4, insert the movie file **SacsMov**, located in the Tutorial.03\Review folder, and set it to play automatically during the slide show. Resize the movie object to make it easier to see, and set it to loop continuously. (*Hint*: If the sound icon moves, drag it back to its position next to the slide title. If the Title, Text, and Content layout does not apply to the slide, click Insert on the menu bar, point to Movies and Sounds, and then click Movie from File.)
14. In Slide 3, create a chart of the monthly rainfall in Cuzco. Use the following data (month, rainfall in inches): J, 6.0; F, 4.2; M, 4.0; A, 1.8; M, 0.5; J, 0.2; J, 0.1; A, 0.1; S, 0.7; O, 2.2; N, 2.8; D, 4.5. Make sure the Chart type is Column, and set the Chart sub-type to Clustered Column (the first chart sub-type in the first row). Add the Value (Y) axis label "Rainfall (inches)." Don't include a title or a label for the months.
15. Click the legend that PowerPoint automatically inserts to the right of the bar graph to select it, and then press the Delete key. (*Hint*: If the chart is no longer active, double-click it.)
16. In the graph, change the font size of the labels on the Value (Y) axis and the Category (X) axis to 24 points.
17. In Slide 8, create an organization chart. Make a single box at level 1 with the text "U.S. Expedition Head," a single box at level 2 with the text "Local Leader," and three boxes at level 3 with the text "Cuzco Tour Director," "Machu Picchu Tour Director," and "Lima Tour Director." Decrease the font size to 18 points to fit the text in the boxes.
18. Add the Push Up slide transition to all the slides, change the speed to Medium, and add the Camera sound effect to the slide transition.

19. Apply the Moderate animation scheme called Elegant to Slides 2, 4, 6, and 9 (those with bulleted lists). (*Hint*: Press and hold the Ctrl key while you click the slides to select them.)
20. In all the slides with photographs and captions (but not in the slide with the movie), set the pictures to have the Entrance animation called Zoom, set the captions to have the Entrance animation called Appear, and set the photographs to enter after the bulleted list (if any) on a mouse click, and set the caption to appear immediately, without a mouse click, after the picture is on the screen (After Previous).
21. In Slide 6, set the bulleted items to dim after animation. Set the dim color to black.
22. Hide Slide 3, and then go through the slide show. Use the pointer pen to mark words, phrases, pictures, or other objects in the slides. At the end of the show, keep the pen marks.
23. Save the presentation. (Don't unhide Slide 3.)
24. Package the presentation for a CD, and embed the fonts. Name the CD **Cuz-MP Tour**.
25. Print the presentation in grayscale as handouts with six slides per page.

Apply

Apply the skills you learned in this tutorial to modify a presentation for a pharmaceutical research lab.

Case Problem 1

Data Files needed for this Case Problem: GeNetics.ppt, Bonnie.jpg, Atorv.jpg, Drugs.jpg, Applause.wav

GeNetics Research Labs Dr. Bonnie Ornatowski, who received her Ph.D. in biochemistry from Bryn Mawr College, is a chief scientist for GeNetics Research Labs, a company based in Cambridge, Massachusetts. GeNetics takes drug formulations developed at university laboratories, tests the drugs, develops the delivery systems, gets approval for sale of the drugs from the Federal Drug Administration (FDA), sells the drugs, and then pays the university and its discoverers a royalty from the profits. Over the past six years, Bonnie has supervised the clinical testing, FDA approval, production, and marketing of a new statin drug, which lowers blood cholesterol, triglycerides (fats), and low-density lipoproteins (LDLs). Recently, Bonnie was selected as Honored Alumni from the College of Science at her alma mater, and was invited to give a presentation on some aspect of her career. She wants you to help her prepare a presentation that explains her career and her work with the new statin drug. Remember to change the slide layouts as needed when you complete the following:

1. Open the presentation file **GeNetics** from the Tutorial.03\Cases folder included with your Data Files, change the name on Slide 1 from Bonnie Ornatowski to your name, and save the presentation to a high-capacity disk using the filename **GeNetics Research Labs**.
2. Apply the design template called Digital Dots, which has a light-blue background and white text.
3. In the slide master, change the title text to light yellow, which is not one of the color scheme colors, but which you can find on the Standard tab of the Colors dialog box.
4. Change the second-level bullet to the same yellow color as you did the title text. Leave it the same character.
5. In the slide master and title master, change the slide number text box to 20-point Arial, switch to Normal view, open the Header and Footer dialog box, and display only the slide number on all of the slides (except the title slide).
6. In Slide 2, change the layout, and then add the digital image of Bonnie, which is the file **Bonnie** in the Tutorial.03\Cases folder. Position the picture to the right side of the slide, and then increase the size of the bulleted list text box so that the first two bulleted paragraphs fit on two lines each. The third one will then fit on three lines. Change the white background of the image to transparent.

7. In Slide 4, add an organization chart. In each box, include a person's name, and below the name, his or her position in the company. Don't include any punctuation in the boxes. In the top-level box, add "Karen Lamb, R&D Vice President." In the second-level boxes, add "Bonnie Ornatowski, Senior Scientist" on the left and "Alberto Thurston, Senior Scientist" on the right. Keep only two boxes on the second level. Below Bonnie, add three boxes: "James Jordan, Team 1A Leader," "Daniel Kelsch, Team 2A Leader," and "Kennedy Guisman, Team 3A Leader."
8. In Slide 7, change the slide layout to Title and Content over Text, and in the content placeholder, add the chemical structure of atorvastatin, located in the file **Atorv**. Make the size of the structure as large as possible while still fitting between the title text and the bulleted list.
9. In Slide 8, add a bar chart based on the data in the following table:

	Tot Chol	LDL-C	HDL-C	Trigly
Placebo	3	4	-2	9
Zocor	-43	-33	8	-24

10. Change the chart type to clustered column (no 3-D effect), and then add a Value (Y) axis label of "Percent Change."

Explore

11. Change the slide background of Slide 8 to only one color, bright blue (one of the color scheme colors).
12. In Slide 10, add the digital image **Drugs**, located in the Tutorial.03\Cases folder. Change the white background of the image to transparent, and then resize and reposition it to make the slide look attractive.
13. In Slide 11, add the sound clip **Applause**. Set it to play automatically in the slide show. Position the sound icon to the right of "Career" in the title.
14. Set the slide transition for all the slides to Cover Left-Down. Set its speed to Slow. Set its sound to Click.
15. In Slides 3, 9, and 10, set the text to enter by fading in one by one.
16. In Slide 9, set the bulleted items to dim to bright blue after the next item appears on the screen.
17. In Slide 10, set the image to enter using Center Revolve (under Moderate).
18. Hide Slide 4, and then go through the slide show. Use the pointer pen to make marks on some of the slides as you go through. Keep the pen marks once you're done.
19. Unhide the slide, and save the presentation.
20. Print the presentation in grayscale as handouts with six slides per page.

Challenge

Explore additional PowerPoint features that are associated with the skills you learned in this tutorial to complete a presentation for a small business.

Case Problem 2

Data Files needed for this Case Problem: Alaskan.ppt, ACWBus.ppt, Totem.jpg, Bowls.jpg

Alaskan Creative Woodworks Bobette Perkins of Anchorage, Alaska, has what she thinks is a winning business idea, but she needs money to start a company that will lead from ideas to profits. She has an appointment with the Alaska State Economic Development Agency (ASEDA), which provides small-business loans for promising new businesses and allocates grants for new businesses in economically depressed areas of Alaska. Bobette asks you to help her prepare the presentation of her business plan to the ASEDA. She has supplied information for two short presentations, but now wants you to combine the information and create an attractive, interesting slide show. Complete the following:

1. Open the presentation file **Alaskan**, located in the Tutorial.03\Cases folder included with your Data Files, change the name in Slide 1 from Bobette Perkins to your name, and save the presentation to a high-capacity disk as **Alaskan Creative Woodworks**.

2. Go to Slide 4. After Slide 4 in the current presentation, insert Slides 2, 3, and 4 from the beginning of Bobette's business plan presentation for Alaskan Creative Woodworks, located in the file **ACWBus** in the Tutorial.03\Cases folder.
3. Edit the color scheme according to the following directions: change the Background to a dark brown, Text and lines to white, Shadows to a dark green, Title text to yellow, Fills to a light brown, Accent to a light green, Accent and hyperlink to black, and Accent and followed hyperlink to medium green. Apply the new color scheme to all the slides.
4. Change the background to a two-color gradient fill, with the dark brown Background color in the upper-left corner of the slide, and the light brown Fills color in the bottom-right corner.
5. Change the title text font to 44-point bold Tahoma, if necessary. If your system doesn't have the Tahoma font, select any other TrueType sans serif font except Arial.
6. Change the body text font to Garamond, leaving other font attributes unchanged. If your computer doesn't have the Garamond font, select any other TrueType serif font except Times New Roman or any other Times font.
7. Change the first-level bullets to a yellow square.
8. Change the second-level bullets to a light green filled circle.
9. Save the presentation, and then save it as a design template with only necessary slides and content. Name the template file **Alaskan Creative Woodworks Template** and save it to the same location as your presentation. Close the template file and then reopen the presentation file.

Explore

10. In Slide 3, add an organization chart. In the top box, type "Bobette Perkins" on the first line, "President" on the second line, and "12 Years' Experience" on the third line. Add two second-level boxes, each with three lines; for the one on the left, type the text "Jianyin Shao," "V.P. Marketing," and "8 Years' Experience"; for the one on the right, type the text "Miwako Turley," "V.P. Operations," and "14 Years' Experience." Add two third-level boxes below Jianyin Shao, each with only two lines of text; for the one on the left, type "Karl Jorgensen" and "Advertising Director," and for the one on the right, type "Melissa Platt" and "Marketing Director." Add three subordinates below Miwako Turley, each box with only two lines of text; for the one on the left, type "Paulette Torre" and "Human Resources Director," for the one in the middle, type "Seymour Cleveland" and "Manufacturing Director," and for the one on the right, type "Paul Robertson" and "Executive Secretary."

Explore

11. Change the organization chart style to Bookend Fills. Click the AutoFormat button on the Organization Chart toolbar, click Bookend Fills, and then click the OK button. Insert hard returns, if necessary, in the text lines that don't fit within their boxes so that the text spans two lines.
12. In Slide 6, add a picture of a wooden totem pole, using the file **Totem**. Adjust, as desired, the slide layout, the size and position of the image, and the size of the bulleted list text box to maximize the readability and appearance of the slide. Set the picture to animate onto the screen (immediately, without a mouse click) using the Entrance effect Center Revolve.
13. In Slide 10, add a picture of wooden bowls, using the file **Bowls**. Adjust, as desired, the slide layout, the size and position of the image, and the size of the bulleted list text box to maximize the readability and appearance of the slide. Set the picture to animate in the same way as the one in Slide 6.

14. In Slide 5, add a line chart showing the trend in tourism in Alaska. Set the Chart type to Line with markers displayed at each data value (the first sub-type in the second row). In the datasheet, use the following labels in the top row: "2002," "2003," "2004," and "2005." Use the label "Tourists" in the cell to the left of cell A1. For the number of tourists in each of the above years, type (respectively) "1.25," "1.47," "1.28," and "1.42."
15. Add the Value (Y) axis label "Number of Tourists (in millions)."

Explore

16. In the chart, click the legend to select it, and then press the Delete key to delete the legend.

Explore

17. Change the thickness of the line and the size and color of the markers on the line in the chart. Click the line to select it, right-click it, click Format Data Series on the shortcut menu, and then click the Patterns tab. In the Line section, click the Weight list arrow, and then click the thickest line in the list. In the Marker section, change the size to 15 points, and then change the foreground and background colors of the marker to yellow.
18. Add the Moderate Entrance effect Zoom to the chart. Have the chart appear automatically.

Explore

19. Add the Wipe Left slide transition to Slides 4 through 9. Set the speed to Medium and the sound to Click for that transition effect.
20. Set all the slides with multiple bullets, except those with picture images, to progressive disclosure using the Moderate effect Descend with a dimming color set to a light brown-orange.
21. Go through the presentation in Slide Show view. Use the pointer pen to underline keywords. Keep the marks when you are finished.
22. Save the presentation, and then print the presentation in grayscale as handouts with six slides per page.
23. Package the presentation for a CD.

Create

Create slides for a presentation about a rental property company by using the skills you learned in this tutorial.

Case Problem 3

Data Files needed for this Case Problem: bedrm1.jpg, bedrm2.jpg, cabinfnt.jpg, fireplac.jpg, fitness.jpg, kitchen.jpg, livingrm.jpg

Recreation Rentals, Inc. Linda Halgren is a property agent for Recreation Rentals, Inc. (RRI) of Las Vegas, Nevada. RRI specializes in renting cabins and condos on behalf of their owners. She contacts owners who rent their properties, encourages them to list their properties with her, and then rents the properties to interested vacationers. Recently, Linda signed an agreement with an owner of a cabin located near one of the ski resorts at Lake Tahoe, Nevada. She wrote the text of a PowerPoint presentation and took digital photographs of the property, but she needs your help in creating an exciting presentation to show to potential renters. Create a presentation that looks like Figure 3-39. Select colors, fonts, bullets, and other elements as close to those in Figure 3-39 as you can.

Figure 3-39

Lake Tahoe Rental Cabin
Linda Halgren
Recreation Rentals, Inc
Las Vegas, Nevada
www.recreation-rentals.com
702-555-RENT (702-555-7368)
Bed and Bath
3 bedrooms
2 full bathrooms
Walkout decks
Jetted tub in master bedroom
Linens and towels provided
2
Living Room
Fireplace
All-leather furniture
Entertainment center
27" color TV
Digital cable (HBO, Showtime, ESPN, etc.)
200-watt stereo with 50 CDs
VHS and DVD player
Reading library
3
Kitchen/Dining
Farm table seats for 8
Refrigerator
Dishwasher
Microwave oven
Conventional oven
"Flat-top" range
Blender and mixer
Coffee maker
Telephone
4
Beech Mountain Club
Free guest membership
Golf
Tennis
Swimming
Fitness room
Recreation areas
5
Nearby Activities
Biking (mountain)
Bird Watching
Bowling
Canoeing
Golf
Hiking
Historic Sites
Ice Waking
Miniature golf
Movies
Museums
Rafting
Rock Climbing
Site Seeing
Skiing
Sledding
Swimming
Tennis
Theatre
Water sports
6
Average Snow Depth
Snow Depth (inches)
200
180
160
140
120
100
80
60
40
20
0
J F M A M J J A S O N D
7
Cabin Rates
Peak seasons (Winter and Summer)
$250 per night
$800 per week
Off season (Spring and Fall)
$175 per night
$650 per week
Deposit and cleaning fee required
No smoking, no pets
8

To help you complete the presentation, do the following:

1. Use a color scheme of mostly earth tones—browns, tans, black, white, and grays.
2. Change the background to a two-color gradient fill.
3. Add the digital images provided in the Tutorial.03\Cases folder included with your Data Files to the appropriate slides. Resize the images and the text boxes to maximize readability and appearance. (*Hint*: For slides with two pictures, change the slide layout to Title, Text, and 2 Content.)
4. In the slide on average snow depth, for the average depth from January through December, respectively, use these values: 182, 176, 140, 82, 56, 20, 5, 0, 0, 5, 47, 105.
5. In Slide 1 (only), add the textured background as shown.
6. Add the Newsflash slide transition to all the slides.
7. Customize the animation so that the images animate onto the screen. Once you pick an animation effect, apply the same effect to all the images.
8. Use an animation scheme to set all the slides with multiple bullets to progressive disclosure, with dimming color set to a yellowish color in the color palette.
9. Replace Linda Halgren's name on Slide 1 with your name, save the presentation with the filename **RRI Tahoe Cabin**, and then print the presentation in grayscale as handouts with four slides per page.

Research

Use the Internet to research restaurants in your area and compile the data in a presentation.

Case Problem 4

There are no Data Files needed for this Case Problem.

Comparison of Local Restaurants Students spend a lot of money on food, and new students are always interested in which local restaurants provide the best food and service at a reasonable price. Your task is to conduct a study and compare the prices of at least three restaurants in your area, and then create a PowerPoint presentation to present your results. Do the following:

1. Connect to the Internet and then go to the Web sites of at least three local restaurants of the same general type that have menus posted. Note the prices of similar menu items. Include at least three categories (appetizers, salads, entrees, desserts, breads or baked goods, drinks, and so forth), and in each category, include at least three items.
2. Open a new PowerPoint presentation titled "Comparison of . . ." and list the names of the restaurants that you studied. Add your name as the presenter. Save it using the filename **Local Restaurant Comparison**.
3. Include at least one slide explaining your methodology—how you conducted your study.
4. Include at least one table or chart comparing the relative costs of the restaurants. You'll probably want to organize the presentation with one category per slide.
5. In your presentation, include at least three pictures or clip-art images. You can acquire the pictures from the Internet, scan pictures from magazines, or take your own digital photographs.
6. Include a slide with an organization chart of a typical or representative management structure of a restaurant. Show that organization with positions (but not necessarily names). You might want to send an e-mail to one of the restaurants in your comparison asking how the store's management is set up.
7. Apply an appropriate built-in design template.
8. Apply appropriate slide transitions and custom animations to make your presentation interesting and attractive.

9. Search for sound clips on the Internet and add one or more to your presentation. Try searching for clips of money being counted or a cash register being opened.
10. Select one of the slides that you think your audience might be least interested in, and hide that slide.
11. Save the presentation using the default filename, and then print it as handouts with four or six slides per page.

Research

Go to the Web to find information you can use to create presentations.

Internet Assignments

The purpose of the Internet Assignments is to challenge you to find information on the Internet that you can use to work effectively with this software. The actual assignments are updated and maintained on the Course Technology Web site. Log on to the Internet and use your Web browser to go to the Student Online Companion for New Perspectives Office 2003 at **www.course.com/np/office2003**. Click the Internet Assignments link, and then navigate to the assignments for this tutorial.

Reinforce

Lab Assignments

The New Perspectives Labs are designed to help you master some of the key concepts and skills presented in this text. The steps for completing this Lab are located on the Course Technology Web site. Log on to the Internet and use your Web browser to go to the Student Online Companion for New Perspectives Office 2003 at **www.course.com/np/office2003**. Click the Lab Assignments link, and then navigate to the assignments for this tutorial.

Assess

SAM

SAM Assessment and Training

If you have a SAM user profile, you may have access to hands-on instruction, practice, and assessment of the skills covered in this tutorial. Log in to your SAM account and go to your assignments page to see what your instructor has assigned.

Review

Quick Check Answers

Session 3.1

1. Click Insert on the menu bar, click Slides from File to open the Slide Finder dialog box, select the desired PowerPoint file, click the desired slides, and then click the Insert button.
2. the set of matching colors that makes up the background, fonts, and other elements of the presentation
3. background, fonts, font sizes, font colors, bullets, and background graphics
4. a variation of a particular shading style
5. Delete all the slides but one, delete the text and graphics from that slide, click File, click Save As, change the file type to Design Template, and then select the desired filename and folder location.
6. an animated picture file, usually with the filename extension .avi

Session 3.2

1. Change the slide layout to one of the Content layouts, click the Chart button in the content placeholder, edit the datasheet, and then change other chart options as desired.
2. a diagram of boxes, connected with lines, showing the hierarchy of positions within an organization
3. Change the slide layout to one of the Content layouts, click the Diagram button in the content placeholder, select the organization chart, click the OK button, type text into the boxes, and then add and remove organization chart boxes as desired.
4. Definitions:
   a. transition effect: a method of moving one slide off the screen and bringing another slide onto the screen during a slide show
   b. animation effect: a special visual or audio effect applied to an object (such as graphics or bulleted text)
   c. sound effect: a sound that takes place during a slide show
   d. pointer pen: a PowerPoint mouse pointer that allows you to draw lines on the screen during a slide show
5. Select the slide in Slide Sorter view, click the Slide Transition button, and then select a slide transition.
6. PowerPoint Viewer is a separate program that you can use to present your slide show on any Windows 95/98/2000/NT computer.

Objectives

Session 4.1
- Apply a template from another presentation
- Import, modify, and export a Word outline
- Import graphics into a presentation
- Embed and modify a table from Word
- Link and modify an Excel chart

Session 4.2
- Add links to slides within a presentation and to other presentations
- Add action buttons to a presentation
- View a slide show with embedded or linked objects
- Publish a presentation as a Web page
- Learn how to collaborate with workgroups

Labs

Integrating PowerPoint with Other Programs and Collaborating with Workgroups

Presenting Information About an Annual Banquet

Case

Global Humanitarian, Fundraising

Fundraising is a major activity of Global Humanitarian. Funds are needed to help finance the following: service expeditions; village development projects (build water catchment systems, wells, irrigation systems, culinary water systems, Lorena stoves, greenhouses, schoolhouses, and clinics); student internships; and business mentoring projects. In addition, funds are needed to pay for the necessary administration costs of running this large organization.

Student Data Files

▼**Tutorial.04**

▽ Tutorial folder
- Gala.ppt
- GalaOutl.doc
- GalaTabl.doc
- Gala03.jpg
- Gala06.jpg
- Gala08.jpg
- Gala09.jpg
- Gala11.jpg
- Gala12.jpg
- GHChart.xls
- GHMission.ppt

▽ Review folder
- Chicken.jpg
- Crafts.jpg
- Dolls.jpg
- Guide.jpg
- Herd.jpg
- Loan.ppt
- LoanOtln.doc
- Loans.xls
- Mentor.jpg
- ProjTabl.doc
- Taxi.jpg
- Weave.jpg

▽ Cases folder
- GCChat.jpg
- GCDes.ppt
- GCGroup.jpg
- GCOtln.doc
- HAOHikes.doc
- HAOServ.ppt
- HAOTempl.ppt
- HeadQ.jpg
- Music.ppt
- PPCData.xls
- PPCDes.ppt
- PPCOtln.doc
- PPCTbl.doc
- Temp.jpg

Global Humanitarian raises funds in the following ways:

- **Direct appeal to individuals and companies.** Development officers meet personally with potential benefactors and follow up with mailings and telephone calls.
- **Web presence.** Global Humanitarian maintains a Web site, and they include a link on the site for people to use to make a donation.
- **Annual Global Humanitarian gala.** The gala is an annual dinner, and it is the biggest fundraising event of the year.

The Global Humanitarian administrators who oversee the annual gala are the top administrators—Norma Flores, president of Global Humanitarian; Miriam Schwartz, managing director of the Austin office; and Pablo Fuentes, managing director of the Lima office. One of their first tasks for organizing the gala is to prepare a presentation for the other administrators and volunteers who will help with the event. Norma asks you to bring together several pieces of previously prepared materials to create an effective PowerPoint presentation about the gala.

In this tutorial, you'll import, modify, and export a Microsoft Word outline to and from your presentation, and you'll import a digital photograph. You will embed and modify a Word table in your presentation and link and modify an Excel chart. You will also create and edit hyperlinks, add action buttons, create and customize a toolbar, and publish a presentation on the World Wide Web.

Session 4.1

Planning the Presentation

Before you begin to create Norma's slide show, she discusses with you her plans for the presentation.

- **Purpose of the presentation**: to present an overview of the fundraising gala and assign responsibilities
- **Type of presentation**: training
- **Audience for the presentation**: Global Humanitarian's employees and volunteers
- **Audience needs**: an overview of the gala and specific task assignments
- **Location of the presentation**: meeting rooms at Global Humanitarian headquarters
- **Format**: on-screen slide show

With the above general plan for the presentation, Norma, Miriam, and Pablo prepare the outline of the presentation, as well as some of the key information about the gala.

Applying a Template from Another Presentation

You already know how to apply a design template from a design template file. You can use a similar method to apply a design from any other presentation file.

For the gala presentation, Norma wants you to use the design template from a presentation she recently prepared about Global Humanitarian's mission and purpose. You'll apply that design template now.

To apply a design template from another presentation:

1. Open the file **Gala** from the **Tutorial.04\Tutorial** folder included with your Data Files, and then save the file with the new filename **Gala Planning** to the same folder. The title slide appears on the screen with the name of the two principal presenters, Norma Flores and Miriam Schwartz, listed. The presentation has the Curtain Call design template applied. Notice that this presentation includes only this one slide. See Figure 4-1. You'll add additional slides later.

Figure 4-1 Title page of new presentation with the Curtain Call design template applied

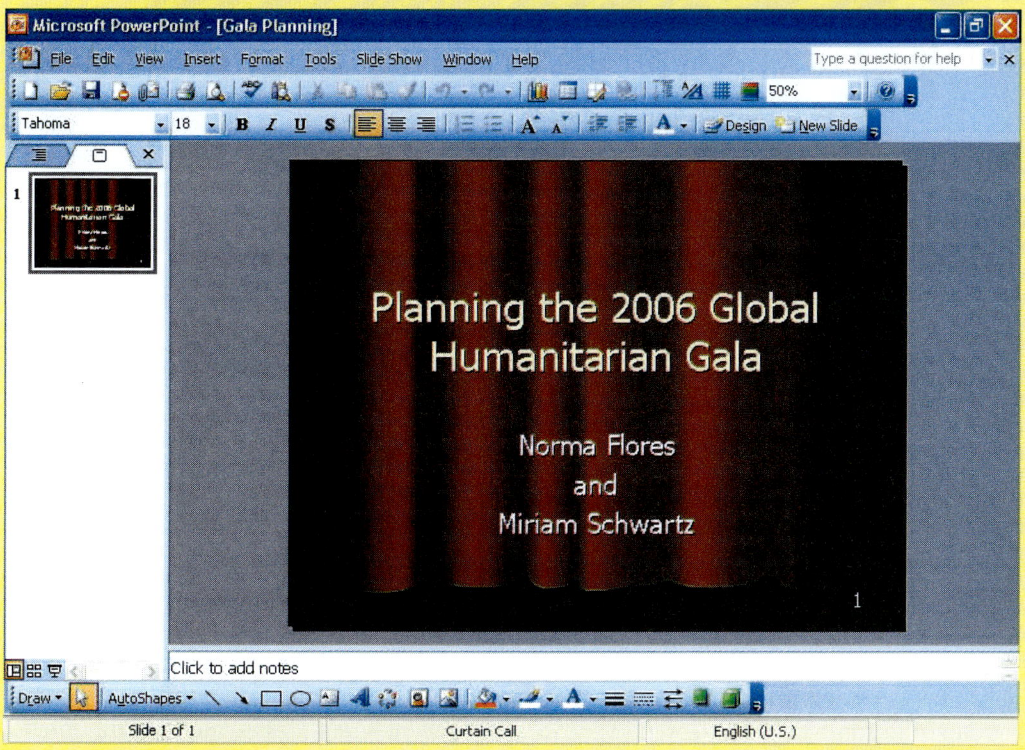

Trouble? If you're using a floppy disk for your Data Files, you won't have enough space to save all of the files you create in this tutorial. If you don't have access to a hard disk or some other high-capacity disk, skip those steps in which you're asked to create a Web page (in the "Publishing Presentations on the World Wide Web" section).

2. Click the **Design** button on the Formatting toolbar to display the Slide Design task pane. You won't use one of these built-in template files or a custom slide design, but rather a slide design already created in another presentation file.
3. Click the **Browse** link at the bottom of the task pane. The Apply Design Template dialog box opens.
4. Click the **Look in** list arrow, navigate to the **Tutorial.04\Tutorial** folder included with your Data Files, and then, if necessary, change the **Files of type** list box to **All PowerPoint Files**. The dialog box displays all the presentation files within the folder. Now you'll select the presentation Norma prepared earlier.

5. Click **GHMission**, and then click the **Apply** button. The design template from the presentation GHMission is applied to the Gala Planning presentation. See Figure 4-2.

Figure 4-2 Presentation with new design template

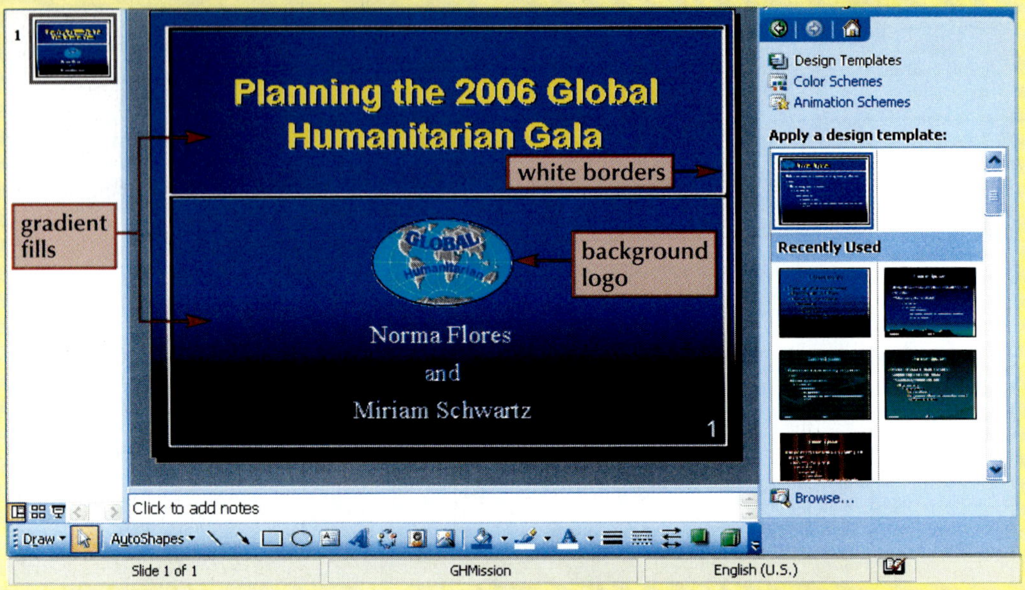

6. Close the task pane, and then save the file with its new design using the default filename.

In Figure 4-2, you can see some of the design elements that Norma created in her original presentation, including the color scheme with a blue-to-black gradient background, yellow title text, white body text, a background graphic of white borders, and the Global Humanitarian logo.

Now you're ready to add additional slides to your presentation. All the slides you will add exist in some format already; your job will be to integrate files created in other programs into the presentation. First, however, you must understand about importing, embedding, and linking objects.

Using Integration Techniques: Importing, Embedding, and Linking

As you learned in Tutorial 1, an **object** is anything in a presentation that you can manipulate as a whole. This includes clip art, photos, and text boxes, as well as other graphics, diagrams, and charts that you've already worked with. In addition, you can insert objects, such as a word-processing document or a spreadsheet chart, that were created in other Office programs. The program in which the objects are created is the **source file**; the program into which the objects are inserted is the **destination file**.

When you insert objects, you either import, embed, or link them. Refer to Figure 4-3 as you read the definitions of each of these following terms.

Figure 4-3 Integration techniques

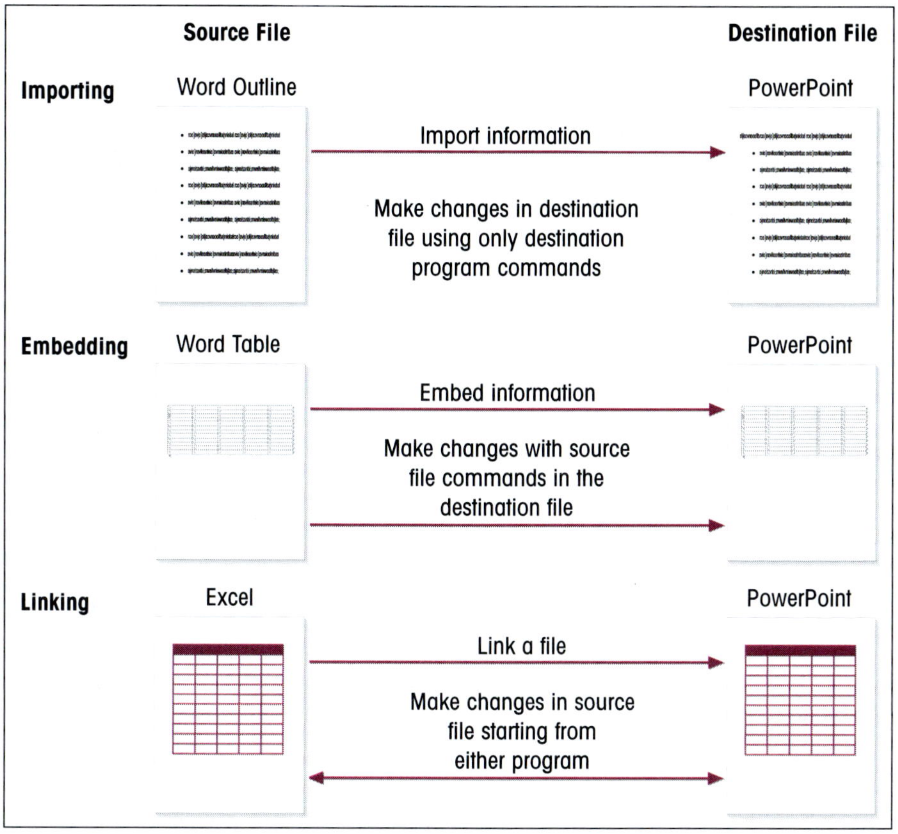

Importing an object means simply copying a file that was created using one program into another program's file. For example, when you insert graphics and sounds into a presentation, you actually import them. Imported objects become part of the PowerPoint presentation. When you import a file, the source program and the destination program don't communicate with each other in any way, as illustrated in Figure 4-3. For example, if you want to modify a graphic (such as change its size or colors) after importing it into PowerPoint, you make these changes in PowerPoint rather than in the graphics program. If you want to access the source program's commands to modify the object, you need to start the source program and then open and modify the file in the source program. To see the changes you made to the object in the destination program, you need to import the object again.

Embedding is similar to importing but allows a one-way connection to be maintained with the source program, not the source file. For example, if you embed a Word table in a PowerPoint presentation and then double-click the table, you will be able to access and use Word commands to edit the table while still in PowerPoint. When you finish editing the embedded table and return to PowerPoint, the changes you made to the table will appear in the object in PowerPoint only; the changes do not appear in the original Word file that you used to create the table. This is because the embedded object is a copy of the original Word file, not the Word file itself. Therefore, if you make subsequent changes to the original Word file using Word, the changes will not be reflected in the embedded Word table in PowerPoint. In other words, an embedded object has no relationship to the original source file, but it does maintain a connection to the source program.

When you **link** an object, you create a connection between the source file and the linked object. You do not place a copy of the source file in the destination file; instead, you place a representation of the actual source file in the destination file. When an object is linked, you can make changes to the source file, and those changes are reflected in the representation of the linked object in the destination program. When you link, for example, an Excel spreadsheet to a PowerPoint slide, the spreadsheet file must be available to the PowerPoint presentation file if you want to edit the file; otherwise, PowerPoint treats the spreadsheet as an embedded file.

You should be aware that not all software allows you to embed or link objects. Only those programs that support **object linking and embedding** (or **OLE**, pronounced oh-LAY) let you embed or link objects from one program to another. Fortunately, sophisticated programs, such as PowerPoint, Word, and Excel, are all OLE-enabled programs and fully support object linking and embedding.

Norma has created an outline in Word listing the text of many of the slides she wants to include in her presentation. Your next task is to import the Word outline into the presentation.

Importing and Exporting a Word Outline

If your presentation contains quite a bit of text, it might be easier to create the outline of your presentation in Word, so that you can take advantage of the extensive text-editing features available in that program. Fortunately, if you create an outline in a Word document, you don't need to retype it in PowerPoint. You can import it directly into your presentation.

Although you can create handouts in PowerPoint, if you want to enhance the handouts using Word's formatting commands to make it easier to read, or use the presentation of the outline as the outline for a more detailed document, you can export the outline to a Word document.

First, you'll import an outline into your presentation.

Importing the Word Outline

As you know, when you work in the Outline tab in PowerPoint, each level-one heading (also called Heading 1 or A head) automatically becomes a slide title; each level-two heading (also called Heading 2 or B head) automatically becomes a level-one bulleted paragraph; each level-three heading (also called Heading 3 or C head) automatically becomes a level-two bulleted paragraph, and so forth. Similarly, Word has an outline mode in which you can create outline text that automatically becomes level-one text, level-two text, and so forth, in the Word document. The level-one text becomes a built-in Heading 1 style; level-two text becomes a built-in Heading 2 style, and so forth. So Norma created a Word document using the outline mode (alternatively, she could have simply applied the built-in headings to the outline text). Your next task, then, is to import her outline into PowerPoint.

To import a Word outline:

1. Click **Insert** on the menu bar, and then click **Slides from Outline**. The Insert Outline dialog box opens.
2. Change the Look in folder to the **Tutorial.04\Tutorial** folder included with your Data Files, click **GalaOutl**, and then click the **Insert** button. The Word outline is inserted as new slides after the current slide in the PowerPoint presentation, with all the level-one text becoming new slide titles. See Figure 4-4. No matter what the font and font sizes of the text in the Word document were, the text is formatted with the default font and sizes of the PowerPoint presentation.

Presentation with imported Word outline

Figure 4-4

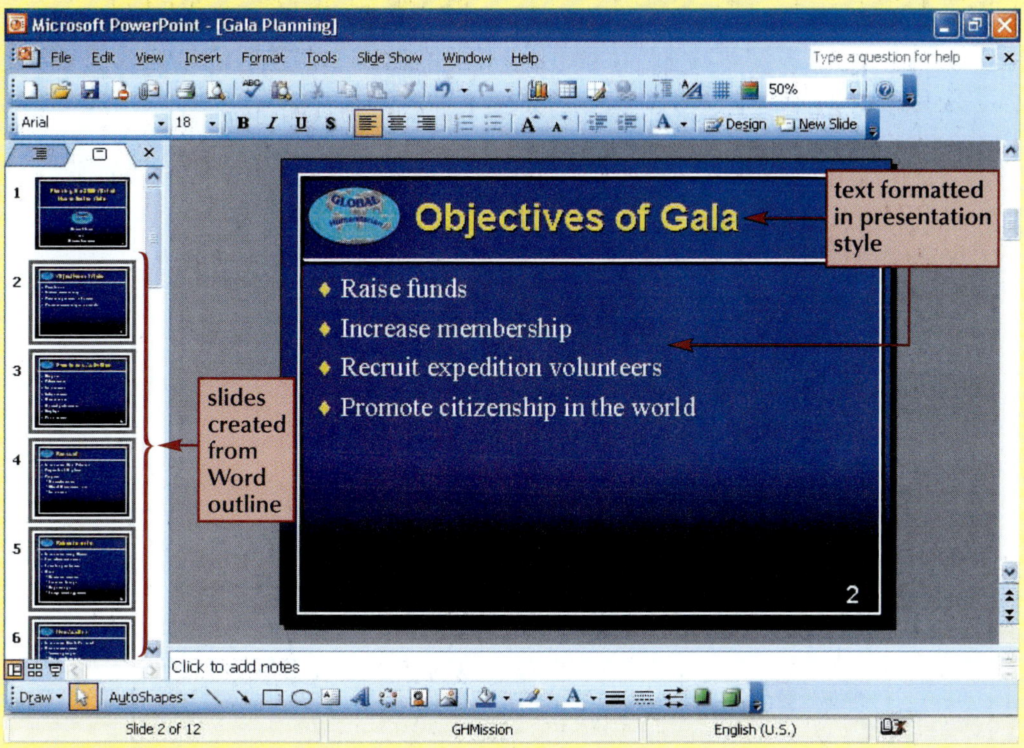

Because you imported the outline, the text is now part of PowerPoint and has no relationship with the Word file GalaOutl. Any changes you make to the PowerPoint text will have no effect on the GalaOutl file.

Exporting the Outline to Word

After looking over the presentation, Norma wants you to move the information on fundraising sources so that it appears earlier in the presentation, and then export the revised text as a Word outline so that she can create assignment sheets based on the revised outline. You'll do this now.

To modify the outline:

1. Switch to Slide Sorter view. Norma wants you to move Slide 12 ("Fundraising Sources") so that it appears earlier in the presentation.
2. Drag **Slide 12** to the left of Slide 3. The Fundraising Sources slide becomes the new Slide 3. The old Slide 3 ("Events and Activities") becomes the new Slide 4, and all the other slides similarly change their slide numbers.
3. Double-click **Slide 3** to return to Normal view, and then click the **Outline** tab so you can see the text of the outline. By changing the order of the slides, you changed the outline. See Figure 4-5.

Figure 4-5 **Presentation with modified outline**

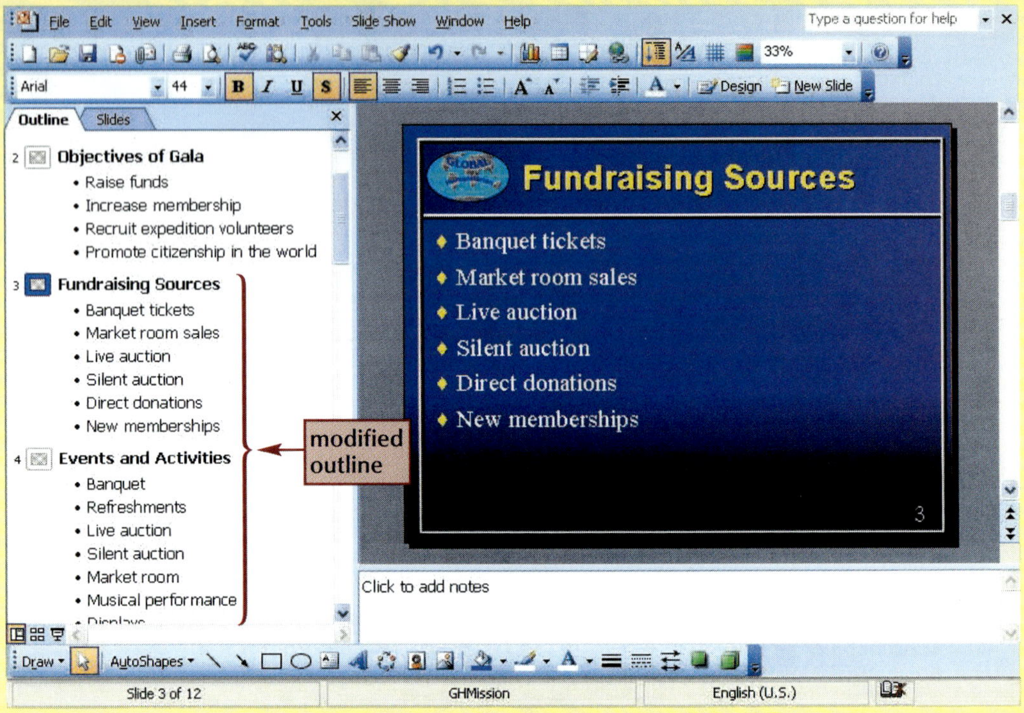

Now you'll export the revised outline to a Word file.

To export the outline to Word:

1. Click **File** on the menu bar, point to **Send to**, and then click **Microsoft Office Word**. The Send To Microsoft Office Word dialog box opens. See Figure 4-6.

Figure 4-6 **Send To Microsoft Office Word dialog box**

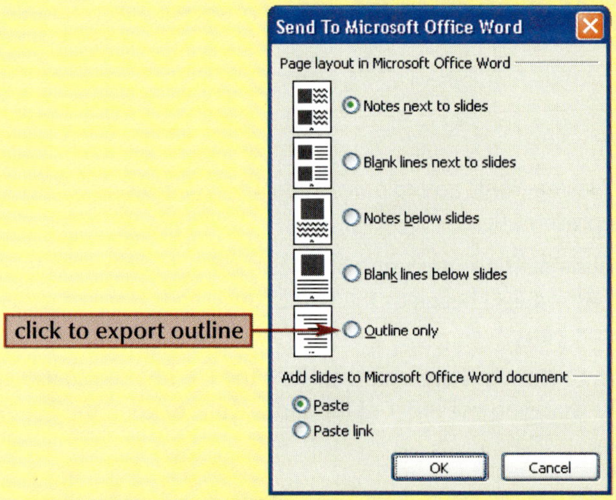

You could export the presentation in a variety of ways, but for this presentation, you'll choose to export only the outline.

2. Click the **Outline only** option button, and then click the **OK** button. Word automatically starts and opens a new Word document containing the PowerPoint text. See Figure 4-7. Notice that the process of exporting the outline preserves the font, font styles, and bullets of the PowerPoint presentation. Also notice that the text on the PowerPoint title slide becomes the title and subtitle in the Word document.

Figure 4-7 **Exported outline in Microsoft Word**

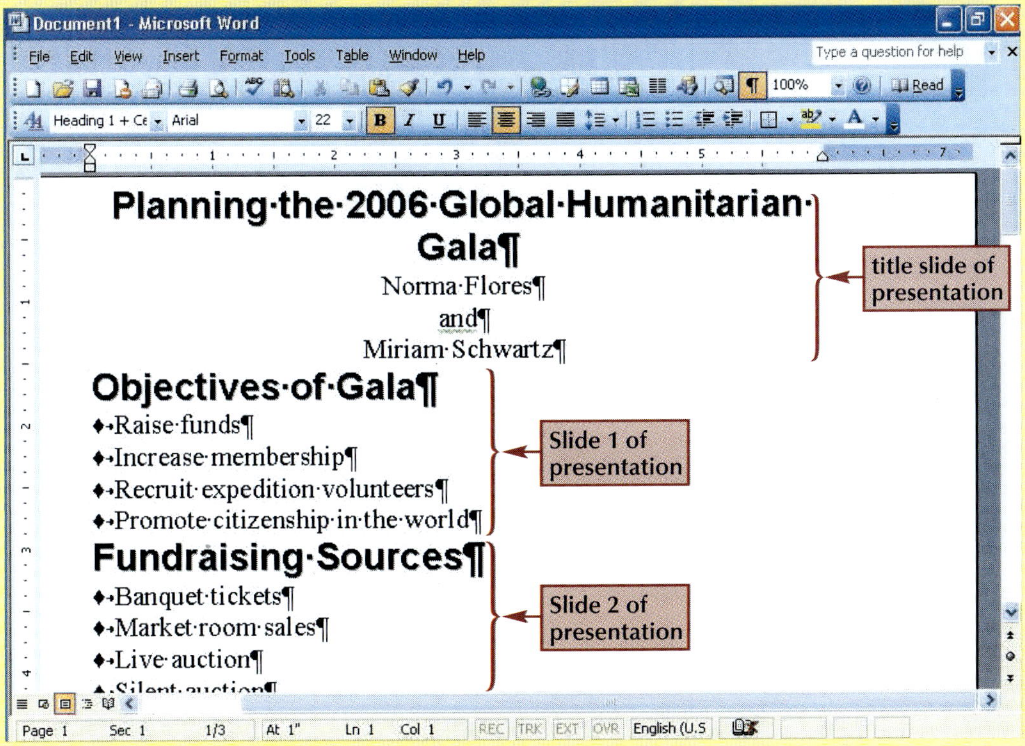

3. Save the Word document to the **Tutorial.04\Tutorial** folder using the filename **Gala Outline**, and then exit Word.

Now, Norma wants you to add digital photographs to the presentation. You'll do this next.

Importing Graphics

You already know how to import graphics, as you have inserted digital images and clip art into earlier presentations. Now, to make the Gala Planning presentation more attractive, you'll import digital photographs of last year's gala to give the Global Humanitarian personnel a better idea of some of the events.

To import (insert) graphics into the presentation:

1. Click the **Slides** tab so you don't see the outline, but rather the slide thumbnails.
2. With Slide 3 ("Fundraising Sources") in the slide pane, use the **Insert Picture** button on the Drawing toolbar to insert the file **Gala03**, located in the **Tutorial.04\Tutorial** folder. A photo of people preparing for last year's gala appears in Slide 3.

3. Reposition the picture so that it's centered between the top and bottom of the slide and aligned to the right of the bulleted text. See Figure 4-8.

Figure 4-8 **Slide 3 after importing graphic**

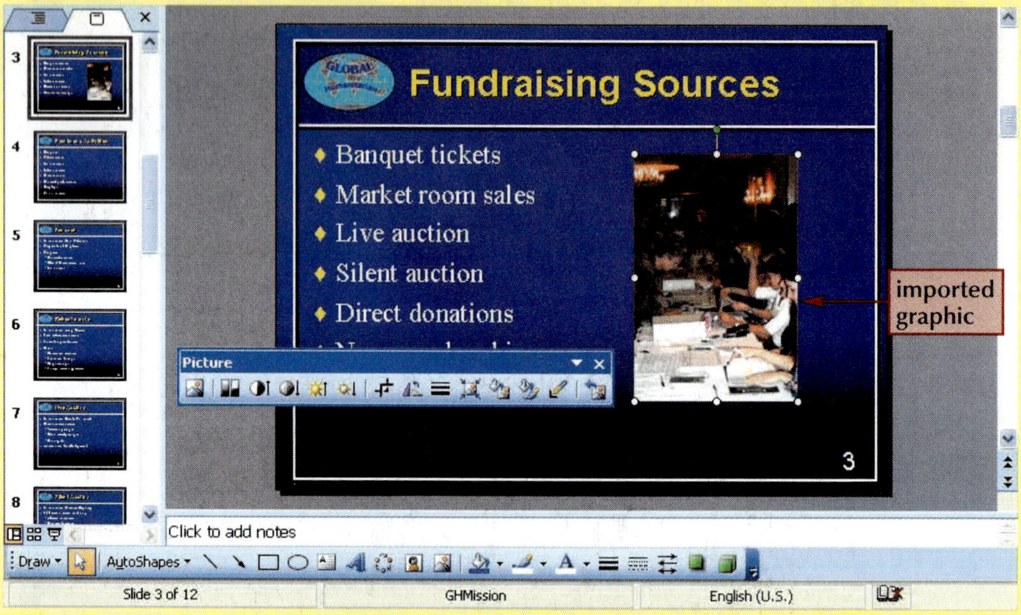

4. Repeat the above step for Slides 6, 8, 9 (put this picture below the bulleted list), 11, and 12 using the picture files **Gala06**, **Gala08**, **Gala09**, **Gala11**, and **Gala12**.
5. Save the presentation file using the default filename.

The Gala Planning presentation now has the desired design template, text slides, and graphics. Your next task will be to embed a table into one of the slides in the presentation.

Embedding and Modifying a Word Table

You know how to use PowerPoint commands to create a table in a slide, but what if you've already created a table using Word? You don't have to re-create it in PowerPoint; instead, you can copy the table and place it in a slide. If you embed the table instead of importing it, you can then edit it using Word's table commands.

Reference Window **Embedding a Word Table**

- In Normal view, click Insert on the menu bar, and then click Object to open the Insert Object dialog box.
- Click the Create from file option button to select it, click the Browse button, navigate to the location of the file you want to insert, click it, and then click the OK button.
- Make sure the Link check box is not selected.
- Click the OK button.

Now you're ready to embed the Word table. Keep in mind that Norma created the table with a black font on a white background, so it is legible in a Word document. But as you'll see, it's not legible in the PowerPoint presentation, with its dark background.

To embed a Word file in a presentation:

1. Insert a new Slide 13 into the presentation, change its slide layout to **Title Only**, close the task pane, and then type the text **Gala Personnel** in the title placeholder.
2. Click **Insert** on the menu bar, and then click **Object**. The Insert Object dialog box opens. You can now create a new embedded file or use an existing one. You'll use an existing file.
3. Click the **Create from file** option button, click the **Browse** button to open the Browse dialog box, change the Look in folder to the **Tutorial.04\Tutorial** folder included with your Data Files, click the Word filename **GalaTabl**, and then click the **OK** button. See Figure 4-9.

Figure 4-9 **Insert Object dialog box**

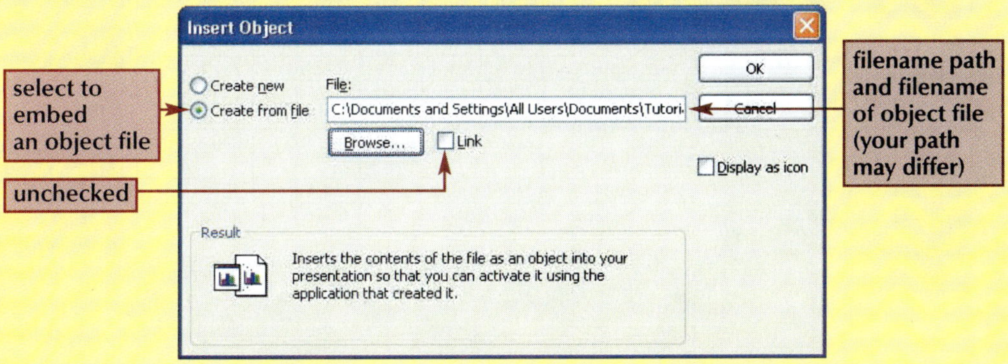

In Figure 4-9, the path and name of the file appear in the File text box. (Note that the path shown on your computer might be different.)

4. Make sure the **Link** check box is not selected, as shown in Figure 4-9, and then click the **OK** button. The embedded table appears in Slide 13.
5. Resize the table by dragging the corner sizing handles so that the table is as large as possible and still fits on the slide below the slide title, and then click a blank area of the slide, outside the table, to deselect it. You can barely read the table with its current colors, so you fix the colors next.
6. Save the presentation.

Norma asks you to modify the embedded table by changing the table color scheme. Because you embedded the table, you will use the program that created the object (in this case, Word) to make this change.

To modify an embedded object:

1. Double-click anywhere in the table in Slide 13. The embedded table object becomes active in Word; the Word ruler appears above and to the left of the table, and the Word menu bar and toolbars replace the PowerPoint menu bar and toolbars. See Figure 4-10.

Figure 4-10 **Slide 13 with embedded Word table made active**

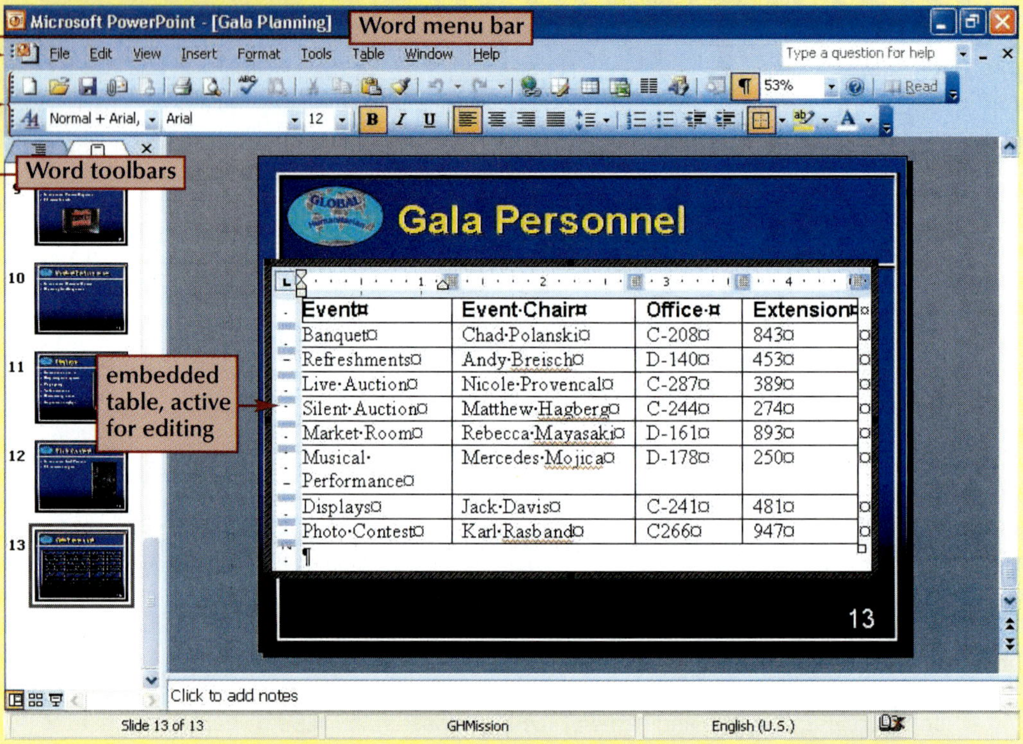

2. Click **Table** on the menu bar (which is now Word's menu bar), click **Table AutoFormat** to open the Table AutoFormat dialog box, click **Table Colorful 1** in the Table styles list, and then click the **Apply** button. The table color scheme changes so that the table text will be legible and attractive on the PowerPoint slide.
3. Click a blank area of the slide, outside the table, to return to PowerPoint with the object selected.
4. Click a blank area of the slide again to deselect the object. Now you'll see how the table looks in Slide Show view.
5. Switch to Slide Show view. As you can see, the table is attractive and legible. See Figure 4-11.

Figure 4-11 Embedded and modified table in Slide Show view

6. Press the **Esc** key to return to Normal view, and then save the presentation using the default filename.

You have now completed Slide 13, which contains the embedded object. Next, you'll link an Excel chart to the presentation.

Linking and Modifying an Excel Chart

Now you know how to insert objects into a PowerPoint slide by importing them and by embedding them. What if you needed to include in your presentation data that might change? For example, you might need to include data from an Excel worksheet, but you know that the final numbers won't be available for a while or that the numbers will change over time. In this case, you can link the data. Then, when the source file is updated, you can automatically update the linked object in the destination file so that it reflects the changes made to the source file.

Linking an Object

Reference Window

- In Normal view, click Insert on the menu bar, and then click Object to open the Insert Object dialog box.
- Click the Create from file option button, click the Browse button, navigate to the location of the file you want to insert, click it, and then click the OK button.
- Click the Link check box.
- Click the OK button.

Norma decides to include a bar graph of past and projected income and expenses from the fundraising activities at the gala. She chooses a bar graph because it emphasizes the earnings over the designated time period (the past five years), and shows trends that might help project income from this year's gala.

Miriam Schwartz already created a chart showing this data in an Excel workbook. Norma anticipates that she might have to modify Miriam's workbook after she creates the PowerPoint presentation. For example, the estimates for costs of the current gala might change as more exact values on rental fees, setup costs, celebrity appearance honoraria, auctioneer fees, and other expenses become available. Norma wants any changes made to the workbook to be reflected in the PowerPoint file, so rather than retype or import the data into a PowerPoint chart, she asks you to link Miriam's Excel workbook to the PowerPoint presentation.

You'll link Miriam's Excel graph of income and expenses to a new Slide 14 in Norma's presentation now.

To insert the chart and link the Excel worksheet:

1. With Slide 13 in the slide pane, insert a new Slide 14, set the layout to **Title Only**, and then type **Projected Income** as the slide title. (Remember to close the task pane.)
2. Click **Insert** on the menu bar, click **Object**, click the **Create from file** option button, click the **Browse** button, and then change the Look in folder to the **Tutorial.04\Tutorial** folder included with your Data Files.

   Ordinarily, you would now simply select the Excel file you want to link; however, because in this instance you'll be modifying a Data File, you'll first make a copy in case you make a mistake, or in case you or others want to go through the tutorial again.
3. Right-click the filename **GHChart**, then click **Copy** on the shortcut menu.
4. Right-click a blank area of the file list in the Browse dialog box to bring up another shortcut menu, and then click **Paste** on this shortcut menu. A copy of the income and expenses worksheet, with the filename **Copy of GHChart**, appears in the filename list.

   Because "Copy of GHChart" isn't a particularly descriptive filename, you'll change the filename to Gala Projected Income.
5. Right-click the filename **Copy of GHChart**, and then click **Rename** on the shortcut menu.
6. Type **Gala Projected Income**, and then press the **Enter** key. The copy is renamed.

   Trouble? If you get an error message that you're changing the filename extension, click the No button, repeat Step 5, type "Gala Projected Income.xls," and then press the Enter key.
7. Make sure **Gala Projected Income** is highlighted, and then click the **OK** button. The path and filename of the selected file appears in the File text box of the Insert Object dialog box. You need to select the Link check box in order to link, rather than embed, the file.
8. Click the **Link** check box to select it, and then click the **OK** button. After a few moments, the chart appears in Slide 14. You have linked the Excel workbook to the PowerPoint presentation.
9. Click anywhere in the slide outside the chart to deselect the object. See Figure 4-12. Some of the text on the chart is barely legible, but you'll soon fix that.

Slide 14 with linked Excel chart

Figure 4-12

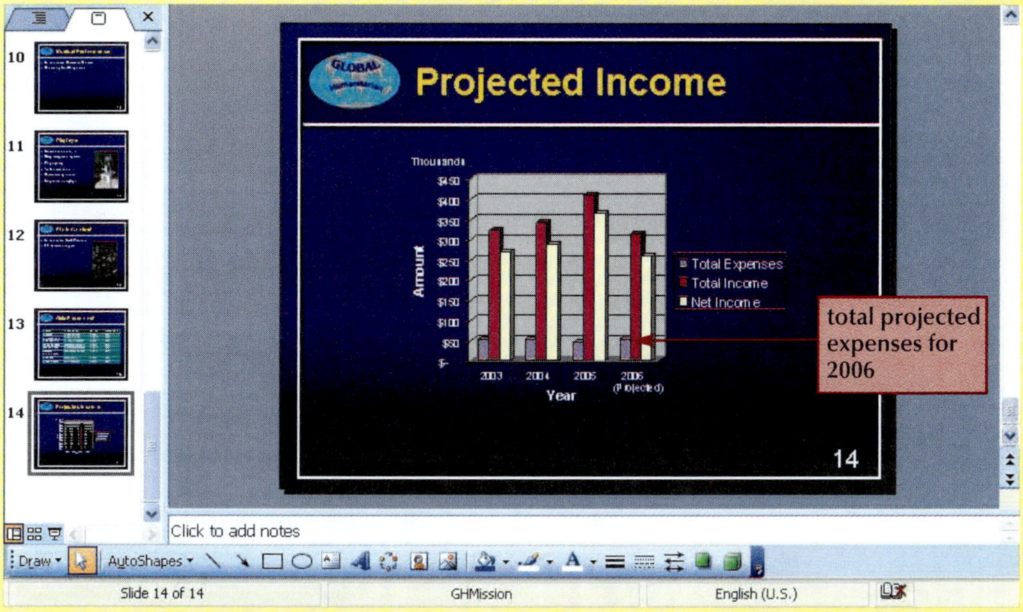

10. Save the presentation using the default filename.

Another method for linking a file to a PowerPoint presentation is to use the Paste Special command on the Edit menu in PowerPoint. You select the object in the source file that you want to link, and then click the Copy button on the Standard toolbar in the source program. Then you switch to the destination file in PowerPoint, and use the Paste Special command on the Edit menu. In the Paste Special dialog box that opens, you can choose to paste the copied object as a link. The Paste Special method is especially handy when you don't want to link an entire file to a PowerPoint presentation.

After you linked the chart, Norma received new information about the projected expenses of the gala. She asks you to make changes to the worksheet data, which will then be reflected in the chart.

To modify the linked chart:

1. Notice on the chart that the Total Expenses for 2006 (Projected) is approximately $50 thousand, and then double-click anywhere on the chart. Excel starts and opens the Gala Projected Income workbook.
2. Click the **Maximize** button on the Excel window so that Excel fills the entire screen.
3. Click the **Income Data** sheet tab near the bottom of the Excel window to display the data on the income and expenses of the gala.
4. Click cell **F4**, which currently contains the number $22,558, type **34,684**, which is the newly projected administrative salary, and press the **Enter** key. The new value is now $34,684, and the total expenses for 2006, in cell F19, changes from $54,614 to $66,740.
5. Click the **Chart** sheet tab near the bottom of the Excel window, save the worksheet using the default filename, and then exit Excel. The change you made in the chart in Excel is automatically reflected in the increased height of the Total Expenses column for the year 2006 in the PowerPoint slide.

6. Resize the chart as large as possible on the slide, and then click a blank area of the slide to deselect the chart.
7. Click the **Slide Show from current slide** button to see how the chart looks in full-screen view. See Figure 4-13.

Figure 4-13 **Linked and modified chart in Slide Show view**

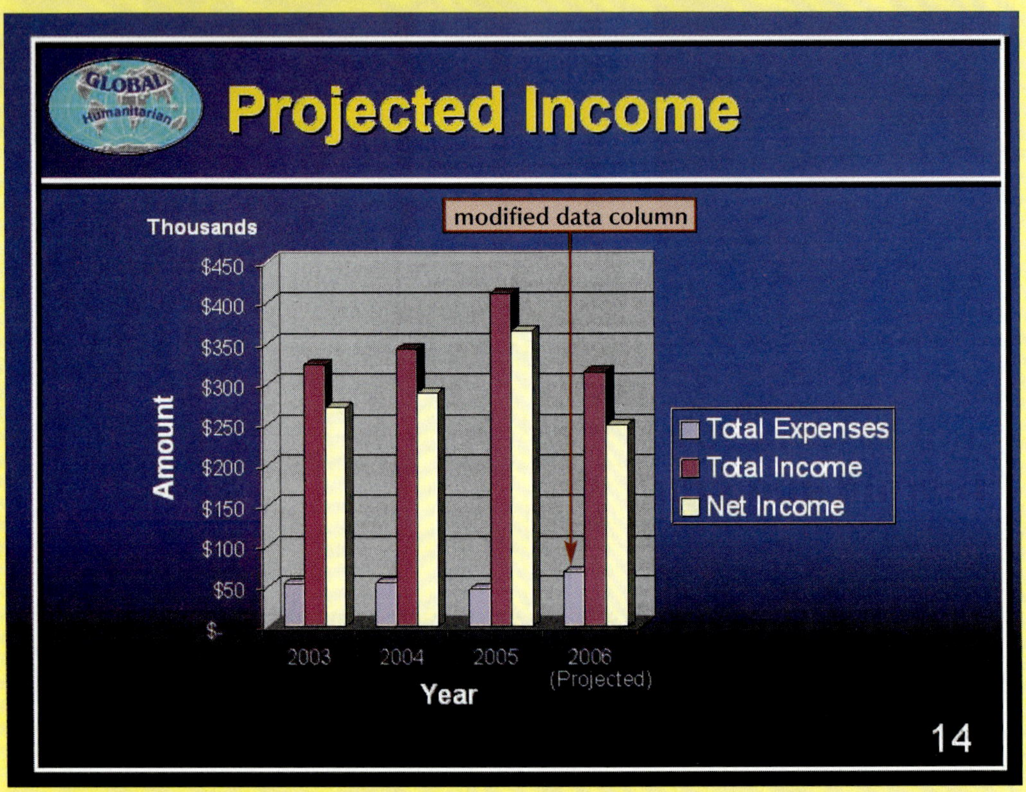

Trouble? If your chart doesn't have the approximate size and position of the chart shown in Figure 4-13, press the Esc key to return to Normal view, adjust the size or position of the chart, and then return to Slide Show view.

8. Press the **Esc** key to exit Slide Show view and return to Normal view.
9. Save the presentation using the default filename.

You have now linked and edited an Excel chart from PowerPoint. If you decide later to make further changes to the data in the workbook, you can do so either by directly starting Excel and opening Gala Projected Income or by double-clicking the chart in PowerPoint. Either way, any changes made to the workbook will be reflected in the linked object in the PowerPoint slide.

If you close and then reopen the presentation, you will see a message telling you that the presentation contains links, and asking you if you want to update them. To have PowerPoint update the links for the latest version of the source files, click the Update Links button. To have PowerPoint use the information currently in the destination file, click the Cancel button.

Session 4.1 Quick Check

Review

1. How does applying a design template from another presentation differ from applying a design template from the Templates folder?
2. Describe how you use a Word outline to create slides in PowerPoint.
3. How do you save the text of a PowerPoint presentation in the form of a Word outline?
4. Define or describe:
   a. import
   b. embed
   c. link
   d. OLE
5. If you modify the source file of a linked object, such as an Excel chart linked to a PowerPoint slide, what happens to the linked object in the PowerPoint slide?
6. If you insert a picture created with scanning software and hardware, is the picture file imported, embedded, or linked?
7. Why would you link an object rather than embed it?

Session 4.2

Creating and Editing Hyperlinks

As you know, a **hyperlink** (or **link**) is a word, phrase, or graphic image that you click to "jump to" (or display) another location, called the **target**. The target of a link can be a location within the document (presentation), a different document, or a page on the World Wide Web. Graphic hyperlinks are visually indistinguishable from graphics that are not hyperlinks. The mouse pointer changes to a hand with a pointing finger when it is positioned over a link. In a presentation, text links are underlined and are a different color than the rest of the text, unless you have made a change to the color scheme. Once you've click a text link during a slide show, the link changes to another color to reflect the fact that it has been clicked, or **followed**.

Norma wants to easily move from Slide 4, which lists the major events and activities of the Global Humanitarian gala, to any slide dealing with a particular activity. Therefore, she asks you to create hyperlinks between each item in Slide 4 and the corresponding slides in the presentation, and then to create hyperlinks from each slide back to Slide 4.

To create a hyperlink to another slide in the presentation:

1. If you took a break after the last session, open the **Gala Planning** presentation located in the **Tutorial.04\Tutorial** folder included with your Data Files, and then switch to Normal view and close the task pane, if necessary.
2. Go to **Slide 4**.

   First, you'll link the text "Banquet" with the slide that describes the banquet.
3. Double-click the word **Banquet** to select the entire word, and then click the **Insert Hyperlink** button on the Standard toolbar. The Insert Hyperlink dialog box opens. See Figure 4-14.

Figure 4-14 **Insert Hyperlink dialog box**

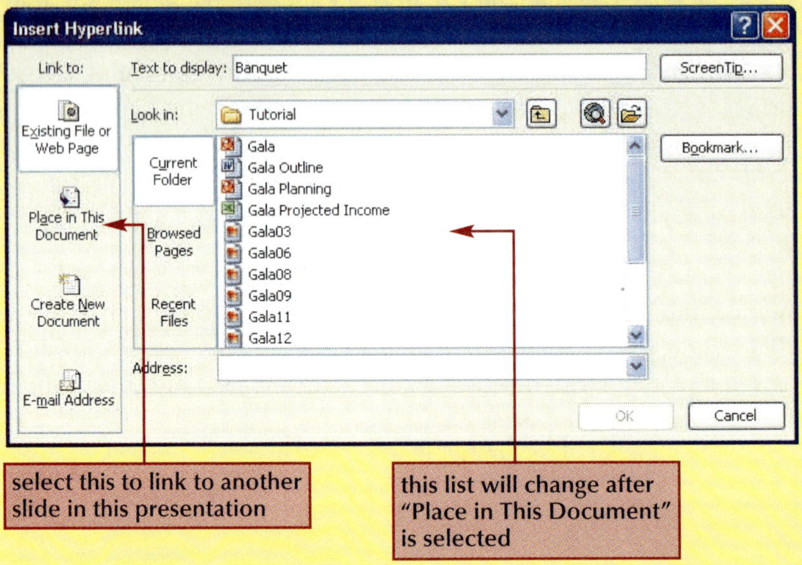

You need to identify the file or location to which you want to link. Clicking each of the buttons in the Link to panel on the left side of the dialog box changes the rest of the dialog box so that you can then specify the exact location to jump to. For example, as you can see in Figure 4-14, the current item selected in the Link to panel is Existing File or Web Page. But in this presentation, you want to link to another location within the presentation, that is, within the current document.

4. Click the **Place in This Document** button in the Link to panel on the left side of the dialog box. The dialog box changes to list all of the slides in the presentation.
5. Click **5. Banquet** in the Select a place in this document list. The Slide preview area on the right side of the dialog box shows Slide 5. See Figure 4-15.

Figure 4-15 **Insert Hyperlink dialog box after selecting a slide in current document**

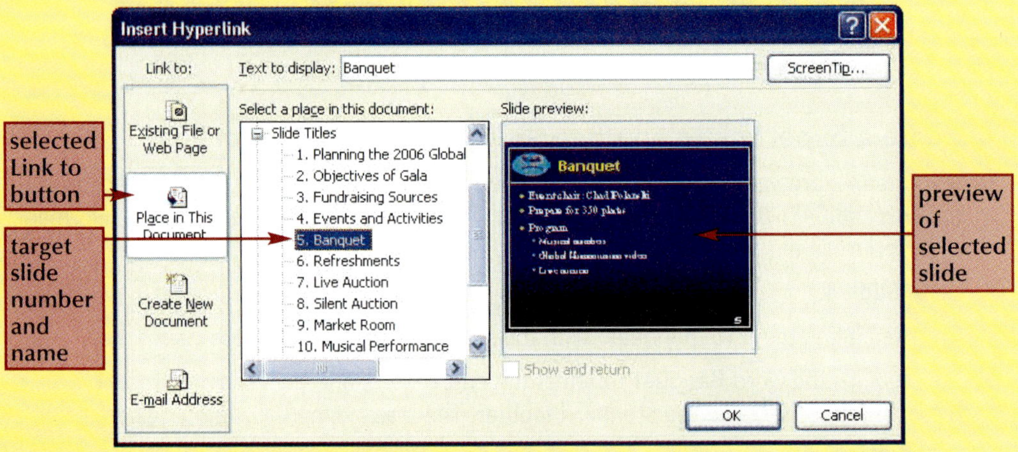

6. Click the **OK** button in the Insert Hyperlink dialog box. The word "Banquet" remains selected in the slide pane, but it is now underlined.
7. Click a blank area of the slide to deselect the text. The word "Banquet" now appears as light-blue, underlined text, indicating that the word is a hyperlink. (Recall that you can specify the hyperlink color when you set the presentation color scheme.)

8. Repeat this procedure to add hyperlinks for each of the other bulleted items in Slide 4 so that each item is a hyperlink to its corresponding slide. Slide 4 should then look like Figure 4-16.

Figure 4-16 **Slide 4 after inserting hyperlinks**

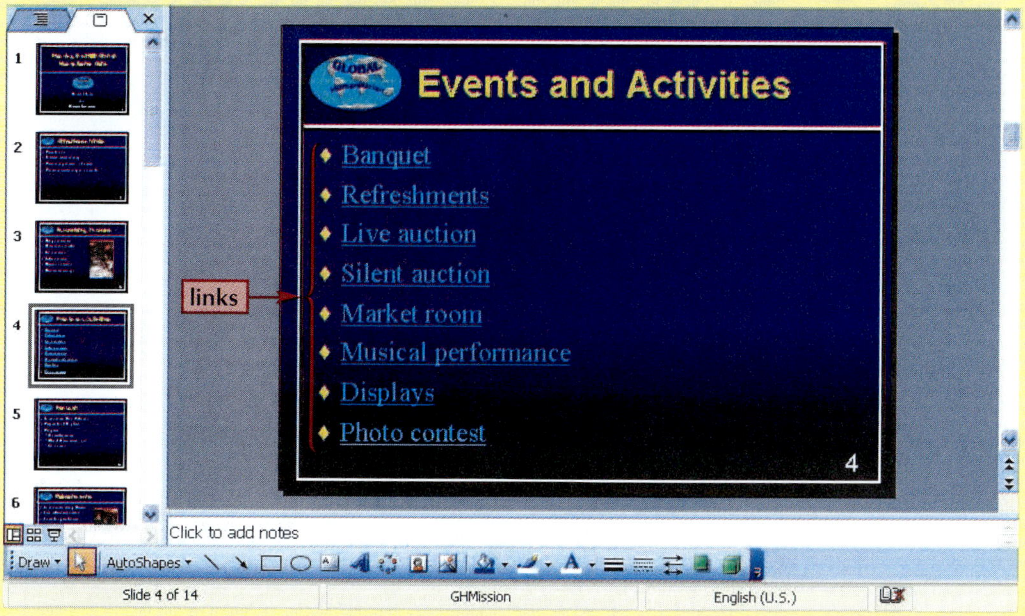

Trouble? If you make a mistake, repeat the procedure. The Edit Hyperlink dialog box will open in place of the Insert Hyperlink dialog box. You can then change the target of the hyperlink.

9. Save the presentation.

Now that you have added hyperlinks from the text in Slide 4 to the corresponding slides, you need hyperlinks from all the other slides back to Slide 4. This way, Norma can easily jump to an event slide, jump back to Slide 4, and then jump to another event slide. To create a link back to Slide 4, you will insert text on the target slide that will become the hyperlink.

To create hyperlinks from the slides back to Slide 4:

1. Go to **Slide 5**, click the **Text Box** button on the Drawing toolbar, click the text pointer near the lower-right corner of the slide (just to the left of the slide number), click the **Align Right** button on the Formatting toolbar, and then type **Return to Event List**. Clicking the Align Right button causes the text to move to the left instead of to the right, so the text won't cover the slide number.
2. Select the text **Return to Event List**, click the **Insert Hyperlink** button, set the hyperlink target to Slide 4 ("Events and Activities"), and then click the **OK** button to return to Slide 5.
3. Click the slanted-line border of the text box to select the entire text box object, drag the text box by its border to position it as shown in Figure 4-17, if necessary, and then deselect the text box.

Figure 4-17 Slide with new link text added

Now you'll add the links back to Slide 4 from the rest of the slides. Because all of the links will jump to the same slide, you can copy the text box and the link you created on Slide 5 to the other slides.

To copy a link:

1. Click the **link** text in Slide 5 to make the text box active, click the text box border to select the entire text box object, and then click the **Copy** button on the Standard toolbar.
2. Go to **Slide 6**, and then click the **Paste** button on the Standard toolbar. The link text is copied to the same position on Slide 6 as it was on Slide 5. Now you'll verify that the pasted link on Slide 6 has the same target as the original link on Slide 5.
3. Right-click the newly pasted link text, click **Edit Hyperlink** on the shortcut menu to open the Edit Hyperlink dialog box, verify that **4. Events and Activities** is selected in the Select a place in this document list, and then click the **Cancel** button.

   Trouble? If you don't see Edit Hyperlink on the shortcut menu, you clicked the text box border instead of the link text. Repeat Step 3, but make sure you right-click the link text.
4. Repeat Step 2 to paste the link text to Slides 7 through 12 (that is, all the slides that are targets of the hyperlinks on Slide 4).
5. Save the presentation.

With all the items on Slide 4 hyperlinked to the other slides and then back again, you're ready to test the results.

To use a hyperlink to jump to a specific slide:

1. Go to **Slide 4**, and then click the **Slide Show from current slide** button.
2. Click the **Refreshments** hyperlink. PowerPoint immediately displays Slide 6 ("Refreshments").
3. Click the **Return to Event List** hyperlink. PowerPoint again displays Slide 4. See Figure 4-18. The Refreshments link text is now light yellow, indicating that the hyperlink was followed.

Figure 4-18

Slide Show view of slide with followed hyperlink

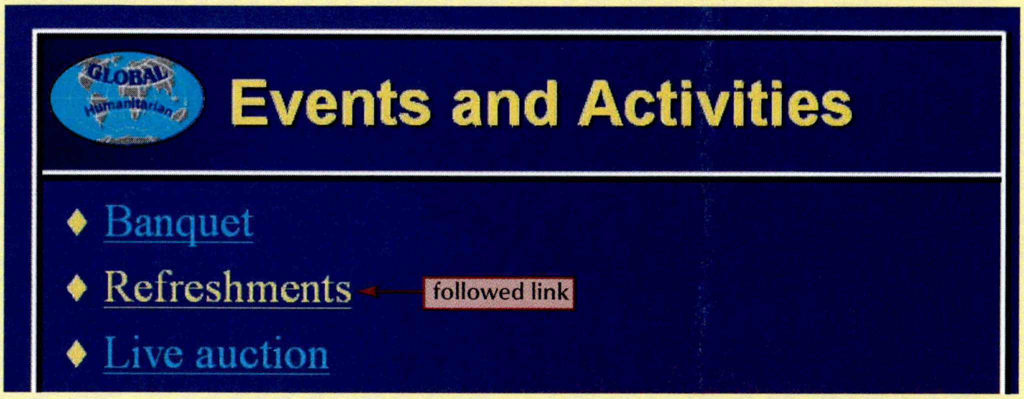

4. Try all the other hyperlinks to make sure they work, and then return to Slide 4 in Normal view.

In addition to creating hyperlinks among the slides, you can add action buttons that have essentially the same effect. For Norma's presentation, you'll insert an action button that will add a link to another presentation.

Adding Action Buttons

An **action button** is a ready-made icon for which you can easily define a hyperlink to other slides or documents, as well as several other actions. You can use one of the 12 action buttons in PowerPoint, such as Action Button: Sound.

Reference Window

Adding an Action Button as a Link to Another Presentation

- In Normal view, click Slide Show on the menu bar, point to Action Buttons, and then click the desired button.
- Click the pointer at the location on the slide where you want the action button to appear.
- In the Action Settings dialog box, click the Hyperlink to option button, click the Hyperlink to list arrow, and then click Other PowerPoint Presentation to open the Hyperlink to Other PowerPoint Presentation dialog box.
- Select the presentation to which you want to jump, and then click the OK button.
- Click the OK button in the Action Settings dialog box.
- Resize and reposition the action button icon as desired.

Norma wants you to add a link between her presentation and the **GHMission** presentation, which gives the objectives and mission of Global Humanitarian. You'll create a hyperlink to that presentation by adding an action button.

To add an action button to link to another presentation:

1. Go to **Slide 2** ("Objectives of Gala").
2. Click **Slide Show** on the menu bar, point to **Action Buttons**, and then click the **Action Button: Document** button (the second button in the third row). The pointer changes to +.

3. Click + roughly centered between the last bulleted item in Slide 2 and the bottom of the slide. A button appears on the slide and the Action Settings dialog box opens with the Mouse Click tab on top. (The dialog box covers the button.) See Figure 4-19. You can choose one of five actions to occur when you click the action button, or you can switch to the Mouse Over tab and choose an action to occur when you position the mouse pointer over the button. You will set the button so that you jump to another presentation when you click the button.

Figure 4-19 **Action Settings dialog box**

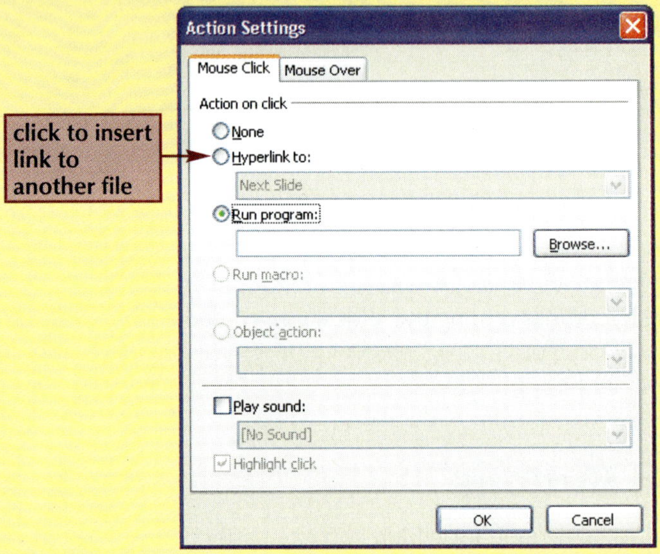

4. Click the **Hyperlink to** option button, click the **Hyperlink to** list arrow, scroll down, and then click **Other PowerPoint Presentation**. The Hyperlink to Other PowerPoint Presentation dialog box opens. It is similar to the Open dialog box.
5. Change the Look in folder, if necessary, to the **Tutorial.04\Tutorial** folder included with your Data Files, click **GHMission**, and then click the **OK** button.
6. Make sure **Global Humanitarian: Our Objectives and Mission** is selected in the Hyperlink to Slide dialog box, and then click the **OK** button. The path and filename of the file you selected appear in the Hyperlink to text box.
7. Click the **OK** button to close the Action Settings dialog box.
8. If necessary, drag the action button to the location shown in Figure 4-20, and then deselect the button.

Figure 4-20 **Slide 2 with action button**

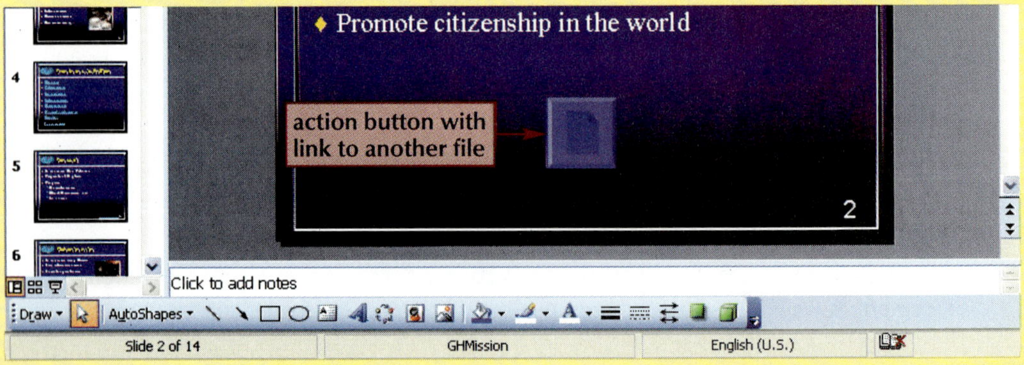

9. Switch to Slide Show view with Slide 2 ("Objectives of Gala"), on the screen, and then click the action button. Slide 1 of the GHMission presentation appears on the screen.

   Trouble? If a warning appears telling you that hyperlinks can be harmful to your computer and asking if you want to continue, click the Yes button.

10. Go through the entire GHMission presentation until you reach the blank slide at the end, and then press the **spacebar** once more. (You could also press the Esc key or right-click any slide followed by clicking End Show, and PowerPoint would return to the original presentation.) PowerPoint returns to Slide 2 of the Gala Planning presentation.

11. Return to Normal view, and then save the presentation using the default filename.

Norma looks at your work so far and is pleased with your progress. The presentation now includes an imported table from Word, an Excel chart, text links to other slides in the presentation, and an action button with a link to another presentation. In the next session, you'll help Norma ensure that her presentation will run smoothly and be available to all of her intended audience.

Viewing a Slide Show with Embedded or Linked Objects

When you present a slide show using a presentation with linked files, those files must be available on a disk so that PowerPoint can access them; and when you embed a file, the source program must be available if you want to edit the embedded object. This is because a copy of the linked file or source program for an embedded file is not included within the PowerPoint file itself; only the path and filename for accessing the linked file are there. Therefore, you should view the presentation on the system that will be used for running the slide show to make sure it has the necessary files. If embedded or linked objects don't work when you run the slide show, you'll have to edit the object path so that PowerPoint can find the objects on your disk.

To view the slide show:

1. Go to **Slide 1**, and then click the **Slide Show from current slide** button. Slide 1 appears in Slide Show view.
2. Click the **left mouse button** (or press the **spacebar**) to go to Slide 2, and then click the action button to jump to the other slide show.
3. Press the **Esc** key to return to the Gala Planning presentation.
4. Advance to **Slide 4** ("Events and Activities") and test some of the hyperlinks, using the "Return to Event List" link on each linked slide to jump back to Slide 4.
5. After viewing all the slides and testing the hyperlinks, return to Slide 1 in Normal view.

Norma is pleased with how well the embedded and linked objects work in her slide show. She now asks you to print a hard copy of the slides.

To print the presentation:

1. Switch to Print Preview and preview the slides in grayscale. The slide title is difficult to read.
2. Click the **Options** button on the Preview toolbar, point to **Color/Grayscale**, and then click **Pure Black and White**. The slide title is now legible.
3. Scroll through the slides to make sure that all the slides are legible, and stop at Slide 14. The labels on the Excel chart on Slide 14 are hidden. This is because they were formatted with white text to make them visible on the blue presentation background.
4. Click the **Close** button on the Preview toolbar, make sure Slide 14 is in the slide pane, click the **Color/Grayscale** button on the Standard toolbar, and then click **Pure Black and White**. The slide changes to black and white and the Grayscale View toolbar opens.
5. Click the **Setting** button on the Grayscale View toolbar, and then click **Light Grayscale**. The labels are now legible. See Figure 4-21.

Figure 4-21 Slide 14 in Print Preview with grayscale settings applied

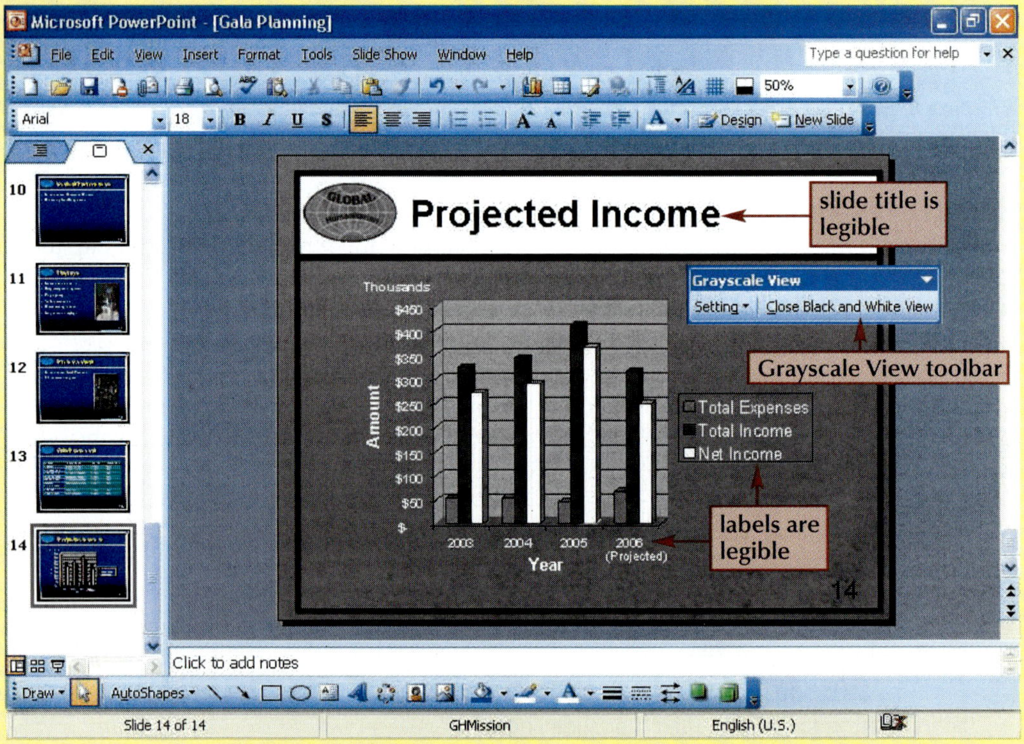

6. Click the **Close Black and White View** button on the Grayscale View toolbar, switch back to Print Preview, and then go to **Slide 14**. The grayscale settings you set in Normal view are applied in Print Preview as well.
7. Close Print Preview, go to **Slide 1**, change the subtitle to your name, and then save the presentation.
8. Print the slides as handouts, six slides per page.
9. Switch to Slide Sorter view, and then change the zoom, if necessary, to **50%** so you can see all the slides on your screen at once. See Figure 4-22.

Figure 4-22 Completed presentation in Slide Sorter view

Publishing Presentations on the World Wide Web

The Internet: World Wide Web

As you probably know, the **Internet** is the largest and most widely used computer network in the world. In fact, it's really a network of thousands of smaller networks, all joined together electronically. Part of the Internet is a global information-sharing system called the **World Wide Web** (also called the Web or WWW). The Web allows you to find and view electronic documents called **Web pages**. Organizations and individuals make their Web pages available by placing them on a **Web server**, a dedicated network computer with high-capacity hard disks. The Web, then, is a connected network of these Web servers. The location of a particular set of Web pages on a server is called a **Web site**. You can access a particular Web site by specifying its address, also called its **Uniform Resource Locator** (**URL**). To specify URLs and to view Web pages, you use a **Web browser**, a software program that sends requests for Web pages, retrieves them, and then interprets them for display on the computer screen. Two of the most popular browsers are Microsoft Internet Explorer and Netscape Navigator.

Most Web sites contain a **home page**, a Web page that contains general information about the site. Home pages are like "home base"—they are starting points for online viewers. They usually contain links to the rest of the pages in the Web site.

Publishing a Web page usually means copying HTML files to a Web server so that others can view the Web page. In PowerPoint, however, the Publish command opens a dialog box in which you can customize the Web page you are saving.

Normally, you and the organization for which you work would create Web pages using a **Web page editor**, software specifically designed for this purpose, such as Microsoft FrontPage. But sometimes you want to publish a PowerPoint presentation, for example, as a link from the organization's home page. Global Humanitarian, similar to most large organizations, has its own Web site, but Norma thinks the pictures and information in the Gala Planning presentation would make an excellent resource for all those who help organize the gala.

To prepare Norma's PowerPoint presentation (or any presentation) for viewing on the World Wide Web, first you have to convert it to a file format called HTML, with the filename extension .htm or .html. **HTML** stands for **Hypertext Markup Language**, a special language for describing the format of a Web page so that Web browsers can interpret and display the page. The HTML markings in a file tell the browser how to format the text, graphics, tables, and other objects. Fortunately, you don't have to learn Hypertext Markup Language to create HTML documents; PowerPoint does the work for you. You can easily save any PowerPoint presentation as an HTML (or related) document using PowerPoint's Publish as Web Page command. This command allows you to create a set of HTML documents (or pages)—one HTML page (with the filename extension .htm) for each slide, various graphics files, an index page, and other supporting files—or to create a single Web page file (with the filename extension .mht) that includes within it all the supporting documents and information.

If you want to edit a resulting .htm document, you'll have to use either a word processor that supports HTML editing (for example, Microsoft Word) or, better still, a dedicated HTML editor (for example, Microsoft FrontPage). PowerPoint doesn't support direct editing of HTML documents. If you want to edit a resulting .mht file, you'll have to edit the original presentation file in PowerPoint, and then save it again as a .mht file.

Publishing the Web Pages

Norma wants you to save the Gala Planning presentation as a Web page so that she can copy it to the company's Web site. You remember that you added an action button to link to the GHMission presentation, so that presentation will need to be saved as a Web page as well. You'll do this first.

To save a presentation as a Web page:

1. Open **GHMission** from the **Tutorial.04\Tutorial** folder included with your Data Files, click **File** on the menu bar, and then click **Save as Web Page**. The Save As dialog box opens, with the Save as type automatically set to Single File Web Page. See Figure 4-23.

Figure 4-23 Save As dialog box for saving a single file Web page

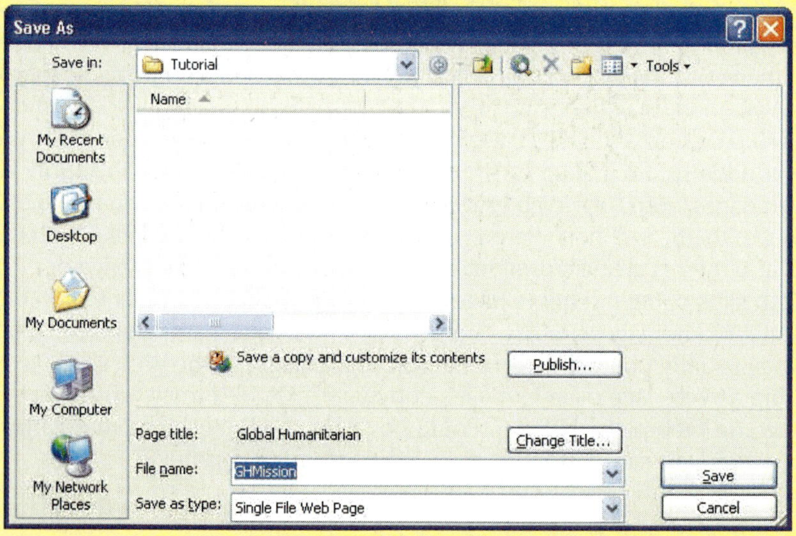

2. Change the filename in the File name text box to **GlobalHumanitarianMission** (all one word, no spaces).
3. Click the **Save** button. PowerPoint creates the Web page file GlobalHumanitarianMission in the default (Tutorial.04\Tutorial) folder.
4. Close the **GlobalHumanitarianMission** presentation without saving changes.

Having saved GlobalHumanitarianMission (from GHMission) as a Web page file, you now need to fix the hyperlinked action button in the Gala Planning presentation so that its target is the Web page file GlobalHumanitarianMission rather than the presentation file GHMission. You need to do this before you save Gala Planning as a Web page because you cannot edit Web page files within PowerPoint.

To change the hyperlink target and save the presentation as a Web page:

1. With Gala Planning in the PowerPoint window, go to **Slide 2** in Normal view.
2. Right-click the **action button**, and then click **Edit Hyperlink** on the shortcut menu. The Action Settings dialog box appears on the screen with the Mouse Click tab on top. Now you want to change the target file from GHMission to the Web page GlobalHumanitarianMission.
3. Click the **Hyperlink to** list arrow, click **Other File**, change the Look in location to the **Tutorial.04\Tutorial** folder (if necessary), click **GlobalHumanitarianMission**, and then click the **OK** button.
4. Click the **OK** button in the Action Settings dialog box. Now you're ready to save Gala Planning as a Web page.
5. Publish the Gala Planning presentation as a single file Web page, using the procedure previously described, except in the Save As dialog box, change the filename from Gala Planning (with a space) to **GalaPlanning** (without a space). This ensures that any type of browser can open the file, even browsers that don't accept spaces in the filenames.

Now that you saved the presentation as a single Web page, you're ready to see how it looks in a Web browser.

Viewing a Presentation in a Web Browser

It's always a good idea to see exactly what the presentation looks like in a browser before you actually publish it to a Web server. You can, of course, start your browser and then open the Web page, but you can also do this from within PowerPoint. You'll do this now.

To view the presentation in a Web browser from within PowerPoint:

1. With GalaPlanning still open in the PowerPoint window, click **File** on the menu bar, and then click **Web Page Preview**. PowerPoint starts your browser with the Web page open in the browser window. (In this book, we used Internet Explorer 6.0.)

   Trouble? If your computer uses a version of Internet Explorer other than 6.0, your pages will look slightly different than those shown here. If your computer uses Netscape Navigator, you will not be able to view the Web page because Navigator does not support single file Web pages at this time.
2. If necessary, maximize the browser window so it fills the screen. See Figure 4-24.

Figure 4-24 **Presentation Web page in browser**

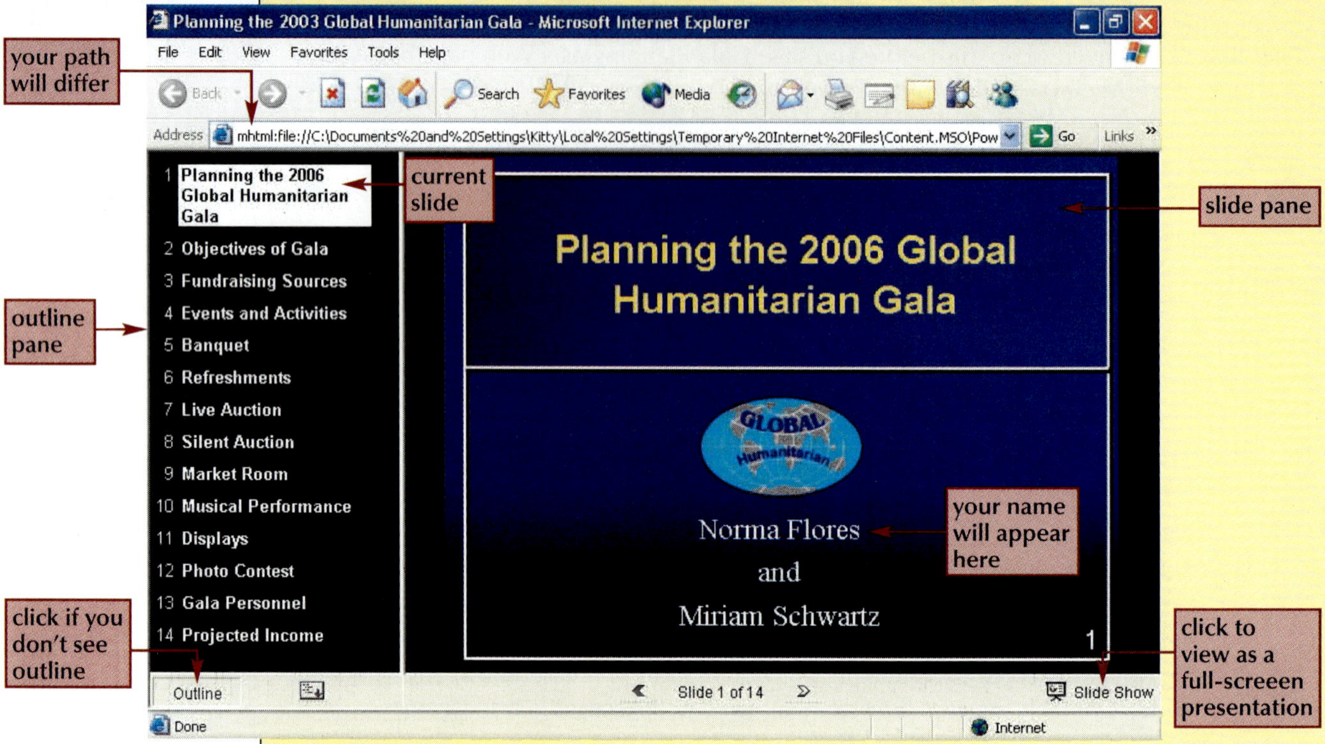

As you can see, the first slide of your presentation appears in the main frame of the browser, and an outline of the slides appears along the left edge of the outline pane. Each outline item is a hyperlink to its corresponding slide. Also, a navigation toolbar appears at the bottom of the window. These hyperlinks and the toolbar help you navigate through the presentation. Now you'll see how the navigation works.

Trouble? If you don't see the outline, click the Outline button at the bottom of the screen.

3. Click the **Next Slide** button on the navigation toolbar at the bottom of the Web page. The slide pane now displays Slide 2 of the presentation.
4. Click **4 Events and Activities** in the outline pane of the Web preview. The slide pane now displays Slide 4 ("Events and Activities").
5. Click the **Silent auction** hyperlink in Slide 4 in the contents pane. The slide pane now displays Slide 8.
6. Click the **Previous Slide** button on the browser toolbar. Slide 7 ("Live Auction") appears on the screen. As you can see, the navigation buttons help you easily move one slide forward or backward, whereas the outline hyperlinks allow you to jump from one slide to any other—in any order.
7. Click **2 Objectives of Gala** in the outline pane, and then click the **action button** on the slide. Slide 1 of the GlobalHumanitarianMission Web page appears in the browser window, or in a new window of the browser.

   Trouble? If Slide 1 of the GlobalHumanitarianMission Web page does not appear, start Internet Explorer, click File on the menu bar, click Open to open the Open dialog box, browse to the file GalaPlanning, click the OK button in the Open dialog box, and then repeat Step 7.
8. Go through the slides of GlobalHumanitarianMission as desired.

9. After going through GlobalHumanitarianMission in your browser, click the **Back** button on the browser toolbar as many times as necessary to return to Slide 2 of the GalaPlanning presentation. (You can't just press Esc to exit the GlobalHumanitarianMission Web page and return to the GalaPlanning Web page.)
10. Look through the GalaPlanning Web page as you desire, and then exit your Web browser.

    Trouble? If you had to start Internet Explorer to use the action button on Slide 2, close both Internet Explorer windows.
11. Close the presentation without saving any changes.

Norma is pleased with how the presentation looks in the browser and sends the files to the company's technical support person to publish to the Global Humanitarian Web site. Next, she wants to schedule a specific time to broadcast her presentation over the Internet to get feedback from others.

Sharing and Collaborating with Others

PowerPoint provides a wide variety of methods for delivering your presentations and collaborating with others, including sending presentations via e-mail, broadcasting a presentation over the Internet, and making a presentation available on the World Wide Web. You're probably already familiar with e-mail, and you just learned about publishing a presentation as a Web page. This section will focus on holding online meetings and broadcasting a presentation.

An **online meeting** is a method of sharing and exchanging information with people at different locations in real time (the actual time during which an event takes place) as if all the participants are together in the same room. To hold an online meeting, you can use Microsoft NetMeeting, which is installed as part of Office 2003 and is accessible within the Office 2003 programs. **NetMeeting** is a program that manages online meetings. It allows participants to write notes on an electronic "whiteboard," send and receive typed messages, and exchange files. You can also record the results of your meeting, archive the results, and put them on a Web server so that those who missed the meeting can "replay" it at a later time.

An **online broadcast** is a method for showing a PowerPoint presentation online. It may or may not include an online meeting. A broadcast in its simplest form is analogous to the broadcast of a television show: The presentation is sent electronically to all the participants at a prearranged time. To run an online broadcast in PowerPoint 2003, you need to download the presentation broadcast feature from the Microsoft Office Online Web site.

Scheduling and Hosting an Online Meeting

Reference Window

- As the presenter, click Tools, point to Online Collaboration, click Schedule Meeting, and then enter the appropriate information in the NetMeeting dialog box, including your first and last name, your e-mail address, your physical location, and the URL of the Web server you will use to host the meeting.
- Click the OK button to close the NetMeeting dialog box and open the Outlook 2003 Meeting window.
- Schedule the meeting and choose the meeting participants using the Outlook 2003 Meeting window, and then click the Send button on the Meeting window toolbar.
- Click the View This NetShow button, when, as the presenter using Outlook, an Outlook Reminder window will open a few minutes before the meeting.
- Type in the chat area or draw on the whiteboard.
- End the online meeting by clicking the End Meeting button.

Reference Window

Setting Up and Running an Online Broadcast

- If necessary, download and install the Microsoft PowerPoint 2003 broadcast feature from the Microsoft Office Online Web site.
- As presenter, schedule an online meeting with the people who you want to view the online broadcast.
- At the designated time, open the presentation you want to broadcast, click Slide Show on the menu bar, point to Online Broadcast, and then click Begin Broadcast. Your presentation is automatically saved as a Web page, and then appears in the Web browsers of the participants.
- Run the slide show as you normally would, typing notes in the chat and whiteboard areas to communicate points to the viewers.

Norma decides to arrange an online broadcast of her presentation for the people in the Peru office. Then, she and Miriam, along with the help of their staff and many volunteers, successfully plan and carry out the Global Humanitarian gala, which is a huge success.

Review

Session 4.2 Quick Check

1. What is a hyperlink?
2. What are two examples of hyperlink targets?
3. What is an action button?
4. How do you save a presentation as a single Web page?
5. Describe what a presentation looks like in your browser.
6. Describe how to broadcast a presentation over the Internet.

Review

Tutorial Summary

In this tutorial, you learned how to import, modify, and export a Microsoft Word outline to your presentation and import a digital photograph. You learned how to embed and modify a Word table in your presentation and link and modify an Excel chart. You also learned how to create and edit hyperlinks, add action buttons, create and customize a toolbar, and publish a presentation on the World Wide Web.

Key Terms

action button
destination file
embed
follow
home page
hyperlink
HTML (Hypertext Markup Language)
import
Internet
link
NetMeeting
object
object linking and embedding (OLE)
online broadcast
online meeting
publish
source file
target
Uniform Resource Locator (URL)
Web browser
Web page
Web page editor
Web server
Web site
World Wide Web

Practice

Get hands-on practice of the skills you learned in this tutorial using the same case scenario.

Review Assignments

Data Files needed for the Review Assignments: LoanOtln.doc, Loan.ppt, Mentor.jpg, ProjTabl.doc, Chicken.jpg, Crafts.jpg, Dolls.jpg, Guide.jpg, Herd.jpg, Taxi.jpg, Weave.jpg, and Loans.xls

Norma and Miriam earmarked about $50,000 of the over $400,000 raised during the Global Humanitarian gala for the Global Humanitarian Entrepreneurial Support Program. This program provides small, low-interest loans and assistance for home and family businesses in less developed countries. It also provides training and mentoring in basic business practices. Norma and Miriam want you to help prepare a presentation reporting on recent entrepreneurial projects in Peru. Complete the following:

1. Open a new, blank presentation, and then import the Word outline **LoanOtln** located in the Tutorial.04\Review folder included with your Data Files.
2. Type "Entrepreneurial Support Programs in Peru" as the title in the title slide, and type your name as the subtitle in the title slide.
3. Apply the design template from the presentation file **Loan**, located in the Tutorial.04\Review folder.
4. Turn on slide numbering in the Header and Footer dialog box.
5. Save the presentation to the Tutorial.04\Review folder using the filename **Entrepreneurial Support Programs**.
6. Switch to Slide Sorter view, select Slides 4 through 10, and then apply the Title, Text, and Content layout to the selected slides.
7. In Slide 2, change the slide layout so an object will appear below the bulleted list, and then import the digital image **Mentor**, located in the Tutorial.04\Review folder. Resize the picture so it's as large as possible without covering the slide border lines or slide number.
8. In Slide 3, embed the Word table from the file **ProjTabl**, located in the Tutorial.04\Review folder, and then resize the table so it appears as large as possible without covering the brown border lines of the slide.
9. Import the appropriate pictures from the Tutorial.04\Review folder to Slides 4 through 10.
10. In Slide 5, set the white background of the Dolls picture to be transparent.
11. In the Tutorial.04\Review folder, make a copy of the Excel file **Loans**, change the name of the copy to **Loans Chart**, and then link it to Slide 11.
12. Double-click the chart on Slide 11, edit the number of loans given in 2005 to 48, edit the number successful to 29, switch back to the worksheet containing the chart, save and close the file and exit Excel. Make sure the chart was updated on Slide 11. (Resize the chart on Slide 11 if necessary.)
13. In Slide 3, below the table, create a text box and type "[Chicken] [Dolls] [Guide] [Herd] [Crafts] [Taxi] [Weaves]," including the brackets and a space between each bracketed word. Each bracketed word corresponds to one of the entrepreneurial projects covered in the presentation. Position the text box so it's centered below the table.
14. Select "Chicken" (but not the brackets around it) and make it a link to Slide 4, select "Dolls" and make it a link to Slide 5, and so forth for the other five words in the text box so that each word is a hyperlink to the corresponding project.
15. In Slides 4 through 10, create a text hyperlink "Return to Projects List" back to Slide 3. Position the hyperlink text box in the lower-left corner of each slide, and adjust the position of the text box or the graphic so they don't overlap. (*Hint*: Remember that you can copy the hyperlink from Slide 4 to the other slides.)
16. Add a document action button to Slide 11 in the lower-left corner of the slide, and link it to Slide 3. (*Hint*: Click the Hyperlink to list arrow in the Action Settings dialog box, and then click Slides.) Add an action button to Slide 3 to jump to Slide 11.

17. After completing the slide show, save the presentation.
18. Switch to Slide Show view and test the links you added.
19. View the presentation in grayscale, make any adjustments necessary so that all the elements are legible, then print the presentation as handouts with four slides per page.
20. Save the presentation as a single Web Page named **EntrepreneurialSupportPrograms** (no spaces). Test the Web page in your browser, and then close your browser.

Apply

Apply the skills you learned in this tutorial to modify a presentation for a national programming consulting firm.

Case Problem 1

Data Files needed for this Case Problem: PPCOtln.doc, PPCDes.ppt, PPCTbl.doc, PPCData.xls, Temp.jpg, and HeadQ.jpg

Programming-Plus Corporation Donald Van Pelt of Chicago is CEO of a large national consulting firm called Programming-Plus Corporation (P+C). P+C provides freelance programming in C++, Java, and other languages; supplies temporary employees with expertise in programming; and trains corporate programmers in advanced programming techniques. Donald asks you to help prepare a PowerPoint presentation to give to sales personnel so they can present information about P+C services. Compplete the following:

1. Open a new, blank presentation, type "Programming Plus Corp." as the title in the title slide, and then type your name as the subtitle in the title slide.
2. Import the Word outline **PPCOtln**, located in the Tutorial.04\Cases folder included with your Data Files.
3. Apply the design template from the presentation file **PPCDes**, located in the Tutorial.04\Cases folder.
4. Reapply the Title and Text Slide layout to all the slides with bulleted lists. (*Hint*: Switch to Slide Sorter view, select Slides 2 through 9, open the Slide Layout task pane, click the Slide Layout list arrow for the desired layout, and then click Reapply Layout.)
5. Save the presentation to the Tutorial.04\Cases folder using the filename **PPCServices**. (You won't include any spaces in the filename in anticipation of creating a Web page because some browsers don't accept spaces in filenames.)
6. In Slide 3, embed a Word table from the file **PPCTbl**, located in the Tutorial.04\Cases folder. Resize the table so it appears as large as possible.
7. In Slide 4, change the slide layout to Title and Content, and then click the Insert Chart button to create a chart.

Explore

8. Import data from an Excel file to the chart. Click the gray square in the upper-left corner of the datasheet to select all the cells, and then press the Delete key to delete all the current data. Start Microsoft Excel, open the Excel file **PPCData**, located in the Tutorial.04\Cases folder, select all the data in the spreadsheet, click the Copy button, and then exit Excel. Return to Slide 4 in the presentation, click the cell above the unlabeled column—the cell above and to the left of cell A1—and then click the Paste button on the Standard toolbar.
9. Click Chart on the menu bar, click Chart Options, click the Titles tab, type "Amount in $Millions" as the Value (Z) axis title, click the OK button, and then deselect the chart.
10. In Slide 7, import the digital image **Temp**, located in the Tutorial.04\Cases folder. Position the image to the right of the bulleted list.
11. In Slide 2, import the digital image **HeadQ**, located in the Tutorial.04\Cases folder. Position the image below the bulleted list.
12. Still in Slide 2, insert a text box to the right of the image with the text "Contact Us" with 24-point Arial font, and then make that text a hyperlink to Slide 9.

13. In Slide 9, insert the action button titled Home and make it a hyperlink to the first slide. This will allow Donald to easily jump from the end to the beginning of the slide show.
14. After completing the slide show, save the presentation using the default filename.
15. View the slide show in Slide Show view and test the links that you inserted.
16. Omit the background graphics from the master, preview the presentation in grayscale, make any adjustments necessary, and then print the presentation as handouts with six slides per page.
17. Save the presentation as a Web page, and then view the slide show in your browser.

Apply

Use your PowerPoint skills to create a presentation for a small Internet discussion management company.

Case Problem 2

Data Files needed for this Case Problem: GCDes.ppt, GCOtln.doc, GCChat.jpg, and GCGroup.jpg

GlobalChat Crystal Bennett of Columbus, Ohio, is president of GlobalChat, a small but growing company that specializes in managing Internet discussion groups. The company sells software to individuals, families, schools, companies, and other organizations to help them set up and conduct electronic chat rooms and other types of discussion groups. Crystal asks you to help her prepare and publish a presentation on the services offered by her company. Complete the following:

1. Open a new, blank presentation, type "GlobalChat" on the first line of the title in the title placeholder, type "Bringing the World Together" on the second line in the title placeholder, and then type your name in the subtitle placeholder.
2. Apply the design template **GCDes**, located in the Tutorial.04\Cases folder included with your Data Files.
3. Select "GlobalChat" in Slide 1, increase the font size to 72 points, and change the font color to the blue color in the color scheme.
4. Import the Word outline in the file **GCOtln**, located in the Tutorial.04\Cases folder.
5. Save the presentation as **GlobalChat** in the Tutorial.04\Cases folder.
6. In Slide 2, change the slide layout to Title and Text over Content, and then import the clip art **GCChat**, located in the Tutorial.04\Cases folder.
7. Also in Slide 2, make each of the software names a hyperlink to the corresponding slide that describes the software feature.
8. On each of the three slides that describe software features, import the clip art **GCGroup**, change the slide layout to Title and Text over Content, change the size of the clip art to a height of one inch, move the clip art to the lower-right corner of the screen, and then increase the size of the bulleted list text box so it fills the remaining blank area.
9. **Explore** Select the GCGroup clip art on each of the three slides, and make it a hyperlink back to Slide 2.
10. In Slide 7, insert Action Button - Home, and then set its hyperlink target to the first slide.
11. **Explore** Change the color of the action button in Slide 7 to the bright-blue Follow Shadows Scheme Color. (*Hint*: Right-click the action button, and click Format AutoShape.)
12. Check all the hyperlinks in Slide Show view.
13. Set the slide transition for all the slides to Comb Horizontal.
14. Give Slides 2 through 7 the Exciting animation scheme called Float.
15. Start with Slide 1 and run the presentation in Slide Show view.
16. Save the presentation using the default filename, and then print the presentation as handouts with four slides per page.
17. Save the completed presentation as a single file Web page, and then view the slide show in your browser.

Create

Create a presentation using the skills you learned in this tutorial for a company selling products and services for outdoor activities.

Case Problem 3

Data Files needed for this Case Problem: HAOServ.ppt, HAOTempl.ppt, and HAOHikes.doc

High Adventure Outfitters High Adventure Outfitters (HAO) is a small business in Jackson, Wyoming, a center for many types of outdoor activities, including hiking, backpacking, camping, canoeing, hunting, and river running. The owner and president of HAO, Matthew Steinberg, provides guided tours for various types of activities in western Wyoming. Matthew asks you to set up a PowerPoint presentation on his company's supplies and services. Create the finished presentation as shown in Figure 4-25, and then create a Web page of the presentation.

Figure 4-25

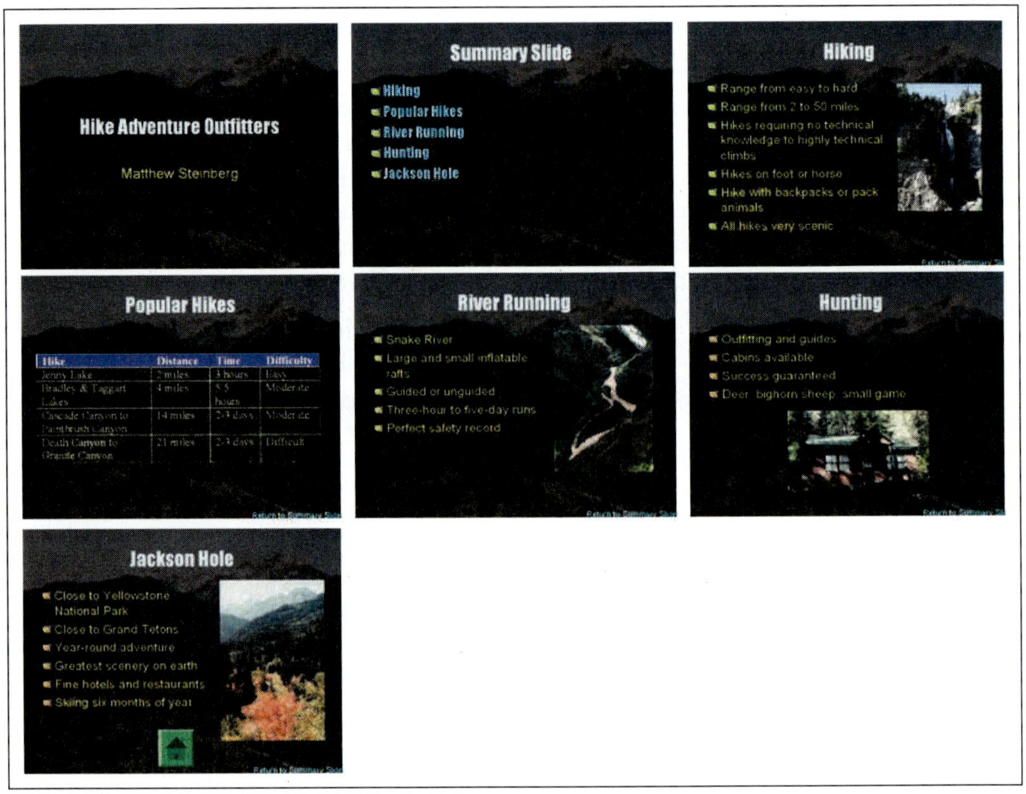

Read all the steps before you start creating your presentation.

1. The presentation is created from **HAOServ**, located in the Tutorial.04\Cases folder included with your Data Files. Change the name "Matthew Steinberg" on Slide 1 to your name, and save it as **HAOServices**.
2. The presentation uses the design template from the file **HAOTempl**, located in the Tutorial.04\Cases folder.
3. The information for the table of hikes on Slide 4 comes from the file **HAOHikes**, located in the Tutorial.04\Cases folder. You will have to modify the table later so that its size, fonts, and borders are legible and attractive. Keep this in mind and decide whether to embed or link the table.
4. Slide 2 is a summary slide featuring all the slides except the first one.
5. Slide 2 has hyperlinks from each of the bulleted items to the other slides (except Slide 1).
6. Slides 3 through 7 have a text hyperlink called "Return to Summary Slide" that links back to Slide 2.
7. Slide 7 includes an Action Button - Home, with a hyperlink to the first slide.
8. Save your final presentation, and then save it as a Web page using the filename **HAOServices**.

Research

Use the Internet to collect information about your favorite music and prepare a presentation on the topic.

Explore

Case Problem 4

Data File needed for this Case Problem: Music.ppt

My Favorite Music Prepare a presentation to your classmates on your favorite type of music, whether it's classical or popular, rhythm and blues or Broadway, jazz or rap. Do the following:

1. Using Microsoft Word, create an outline of your presentation on your favorite music. Include at least six titles, which will become slide titles. (Remember to switch to Outline view in Word to type your slide titles.) Use books and magazines from your college library, encyclopedia, the Internet, CD slipcovers and booklets, or other sources of information to get backgrounds, biographies, lyrics, reviews, and analyses on your chosen topic. If you haven't covered Microsoft Word in your courses and don't know how to create an outline with heading styles, use the Help feature of Word.
2. Save the Word file using the filename **My Music Outline** to a high-capacity disk.
3. In another Word document, create a table. Your table might list the names of musical compositions, their composers, their performers, the types of music, the years of release, or other information.
4. Save the Word file with the table using the filename **My Music Table** to the Tutorial.04\Cases folder included with your Data Files.
5. Open a new, blank presentation, and include an appropriate title of your choosing and a subtitle with your name as the presenter.
6. Import the Word outline into PowerPoint.
7. Apply the design template from the presentation file **Music**, located in the Tutorial.04\Cases folder.
8. Reapply the slide layouts to each slide, as needed, so it uses the proper font and has the proper format. (*Hint*: Switch to Slide Sorter view, select the relevant slides, open the Slide Layout task pane, click the Slide Layout list arrow for the desired layout, and then click Reapply Layout.)
9. Embed your table into a slide of your presentation. Resize and reposition it as needed to maximize its readability.
10. Insert at least two action buttons into your presentation with links to other slides within your presentation.
11. Include at least one text hyperlink in your presentation, with a link to another slide. The text of the hyperlink can be a bulleted item, the text in a table cell, or a text box.
12. Add graphics, sound effects, slide transitions, and animations to the slide show, as desired.
13. Save your presentation using the filename **MyMusic**, and print the presentation as handouts with four slides per page.
14. Save your presentation as a single file Web page and then view the slide show in your browser.

Research

Go to the Web to find information you can use to create presentations.

Internet Assignments

The purpose of the Internet Assignments is to challenge you to find information on the Internet that you can use to work effectively with this software. The actual assignments are updated and maintained on the Course Technology Web site. Log on to the Internet and use your Web browser to go to the Student Online Companion for New Perspectives Office 2003 at **www.course.com/np/office2003**. Click the Internet Assignments link, and then navigate to the assignments for this tutorial.

Assess

SAM Assessment and Training

If you have a SAM user profile, you may have access to hands-on instruction, practice, and assessment of the skills covered in this tutorial. Log in to your SAM account and go to your assignments page to see what your instructor has assigned.

Reinforce

The Internet: World Wide Web

Lab Assignments

The New Perspectives Labs are designed to help you master some of the key concepts and skills presented in this text. The steps for completing this Lab are located on the Course Technology Web site. Log on to the Internet and use your Web browser to go to the Student Online Companion for New Perspectives Office 2003 at **www.course.com/np/office2003**. Click the Lab Assignments link, and then navigate to the assignments for this tutorial.

Review

Quick Check Answers

Session 4.1

1. They are the same, except that the presentation file will usually not be found in the Templates folder, whereas the design template file will be.
2. In PowerPoint, click Insert on the menu bar, click Slides from Outline, select the Word file with the outline, and then click the Insert button.
3. Click File on the menu bar, point to Send To, click Microsoft Word, select the desired Word page layout, click the OK button, specify the filename, and then click the OK button.
4. a. Import means to insert a file that was created using one program into another program's file.
   b. Embed means to insert a file so that a connection with the source program is maintained.
   c. Link means to insert a file so that a connection between the source file and the destination file is maintained, and changes made to the source file are reflected in the linked object in the destination file.
   d. OLE means object linking and embedding.
5. The object is updated to reflect the changes made to the source file.
6. imported
7. so that modifications you make to the source file are reflected in the destination file

Session 4.2

1. A hyperlink is a word, phrase, or graphic that you click to display an object at another location.
2. Hyperlink targets can be other slides within the presentation or other presentations.
3. An action button is a ready-made icon for which you can easily define hyperlinks to other slides or documents.
4. Click File, and then click Save as Web Page.
5. A frame on the left contains an outline of the slides, the slide itself appears in a frame on the right, and navigation buttons appear at the bottom of the slide.
6. Announce to the participant the time and place of the broadcast, open the presentation that you will broadcast, click Slide Show, point to Online Broadcast, and then click Begin Broadcast.

Objectives

- Merge an Access query with a Word document
- View merged documents
- Preview and print a merged document
- Create a Word outline
- Create PowerPoint slides from a Word outline
- Copy and paste an Access query into a PowerPoint presentation
- Link an Excel chart to a PowerPoint presentation

Integrating Word, Excel, Access, and PowerPoint

Creating a Form Letter and an Integrated Presentation

Case

Lifestyles Home Care, Inc.

Caitlin Sheehan, owner of Lifestyles Home Care, has created a letter and brochure describing the new services her agency is planning to offer. She is ready to send her letter and brochure to the social work departments at all of the local hospitals. Her contacts in the social work departments are stored in an Access database.

Caitlin also needs to prepare a presentation for next month's National Home Care Conference. The demand for home care agencies that offer services for fees (rather than supplying services only to people who qualify under state income guidelines), is growing and conference organizers have asked her to discuss her business plan.

In this tutorial, you'll complete two separate tasks. First, you'll merge the letter to the hospitals with the names and addresses of the social work contacts stored in an Access database. Second, you'll create a presentation for Caitlin to use at the conference. You'll use Word to create an outline of the topics she wants to cover, and then you'll create a PowerPoint presentation from the outline. The presentation will also include an Access query and an Excel pie chart showing the most requested services. You'll use different integration methods to include these items in the presentation.

Student Data Files

▼Tutorial.03

▽ Tutorial folder
- LHCLetter2.doc
- LHCMostRequested.xls
- LHCOutline.doc
- LHCPresentation.ppt
- LHCServices.mdb
- SocialWorkContacts.mdb

▽ Review folder
- LHCEmployees.ppt
- LHCEmployeesOutline.doc
- LHCGrowth2.xls
- LHCServices.mdb
- SocialWorkContacts.mdb

▽ Cases folder
- LFCFees.xls
- LFCOutline.doc
- MusicCustomers.mdb

Planning the Form Letter

A **form letter** is a Word document that contains standard paragraphs of text and a minimum of variable text, such as the names and addresses of the letter's recipients. The **main document** of a form letter contains the text and other information (including punctuation, spaces, and graphics) that you want to keep the same in each letter. It also includes merge fields. As you remember from Access, a field contains information that varies from one record to another. A **merge field** contains instructions for replacing the field placeholder with the information that changes from one letter to another, for example, the name and address of a contact. The variable information is contained in a **data source**, which can be a Word table, an Access database, or some other source. When you merge the main document with the data source, Word replaces the merge fields with the appropriate information from the data source. The process of combining the main document with the data source is called a **merge**. The term **mail merge** is used when you are merging a main document with a list of addresses from any data source.

In this case, Caitlin's letter is the main document, and the Access database containing the contact names in the social work departments and the addresses of the local hospitals is the data source. Figure 3-1 shows Caitlin's plan for the form letter.

Figure 3-1 **Caitlin's plan for the form letter**

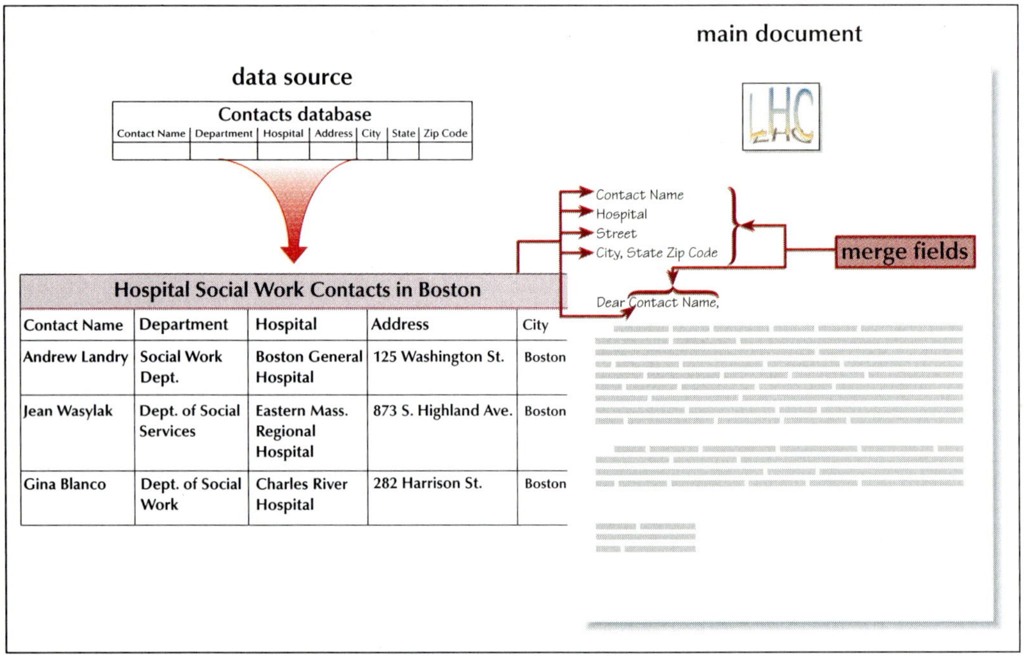

Merging Access Data with a Word Document

The first step in completing the mail merge is to specify the type of document you want to create, such as a form letter or mailing labels. Next, you select the main document, which Word also calls the **starting document**. Then you select recipients from the data source. When you specify an Access database as containing the data source for a mail merge, you select a table or query defined in the database as the actual data source.

Once you have identified the main document and the data source, you insert the merge fields into the main document. Finally, you preview the letters, make any needed changes, and merge the main document and the data source to produce customized form letters.

Selecting a Starting Document and Recipients

The main document of a mail merge can be a new or existing Word document. In this case, the starting document is Caitlin's existing letter to area hospitals. Caitlin modified the document you worked with in Integration Tutorial 1 to create a final version of the letter she wants to send. You'll begin by starting Word and opening the main document.

To open the main document:

1. Open the Word document **LHCLetter2**, which is located in the Tutorial.03\Tutorial folder included with your Data Files. The letter opens in Print Layout view.
2. Display nonprinting characters, if necessary.
3. Press the **Ctrl + End** keys to move to the end of the letter, and then replace Caitlin Sheehan's name with your own.
4. Press the **Ctrl + Home** keys to return to the beginning of the letter, and then save the file as **Main Letter** in the Tutorial.03\Tutorial folder included with your Data Files.

You need to start by selecting the type of document you want to create.

To select the main document and data source for the mail merge:

1. Click **Tools** on the menu bar, point to **Letters and Mailings**, and then click **Mail Merge**. The Mail Merge task pane opens, showing Step 1 of 6. See Figure 3-2. The Mail Merge task pane guides you through a series of six steps to create the final merged document. You navigate to the next or previous step by clicking the links at the bottom of the task pane.

Mail Merge task pane **Figure 3-2**

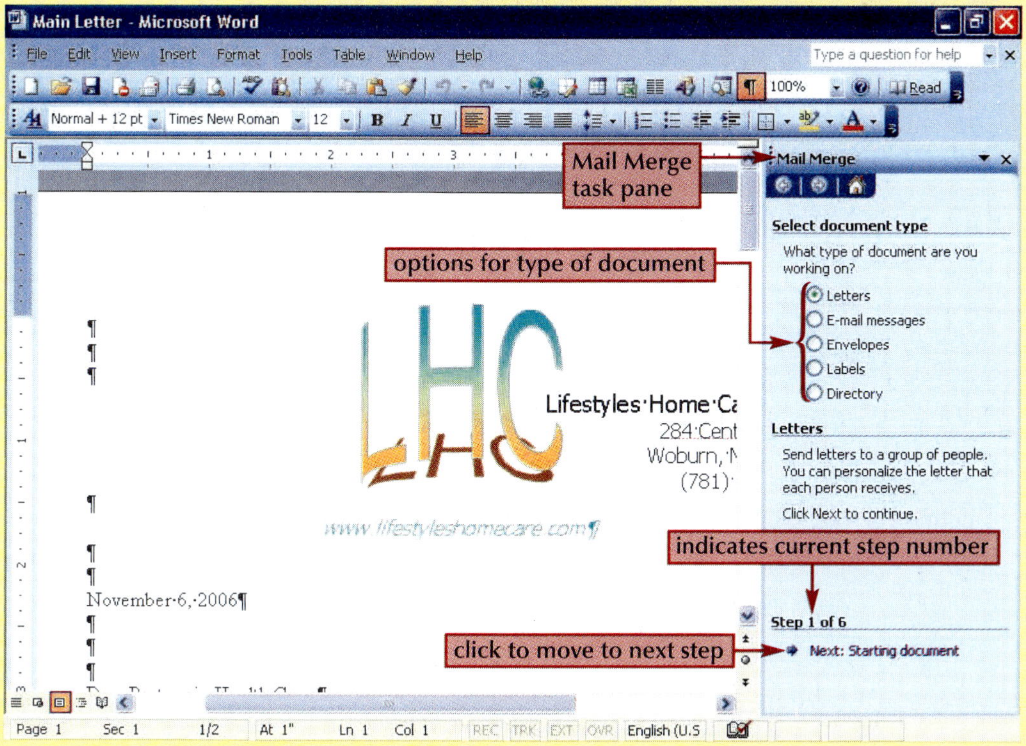

In Step 1 of the mail merge process, you select the type of document you want to create. The Letters option button is selected by default, but you can also create e-mail messages, envelopes, labels, or a directory containing the entire list.

2. Click the **Letters** option button, if necessary, and then click the **Next: Starting document** link. The Mail Merge task pane now shows the options for Step 2 of 6: Select starting document. You want to use the current document, Caitlin's letter to the hospitals, as the starting document.

3. Click the **Use the current document** option button, if necessary, and then click the **Next: Select recipients** link. The Mail Merge task pane changes to show the options for Step 3 of 6: Select recipients.

   You want to select recipients from an existing list in an Access database.

4. Click the **Use an existing list** option button, if necessary, and then click the **Browse** link. The Select Data Source dialog box opens, displaying a list of possible data sources. You need to locate the list of social worker contacts at the local hospitals, which is located in the Hospital Social Work Contacts table in the SocialWorkContacts database.

5. Click the **Look in** list arrow, navigate to the Tutorial.03\Tutorial folder included with your Data Files, click **SocialWorkContacts**, and then click the **Open** button. The Select Table dialog box opens with a list of all the tables and queries in the selected database (this database contains two tables and no queries). You need to choose a table or query in the selected database as the data source. If the database contained only one table, the Select Table dialog box would not open; instead, the Mail Merge Recipients dialog box would open immediately after you selected the database.

6. Click the **Hospital Social Work Contacts** table to select it, if necessary, and then click the **OK** button. The Mail Merge Recipients dialog box opens, as shown in Figure 3-3.

Figure 3-3 Mail Merge Recipients dialog box

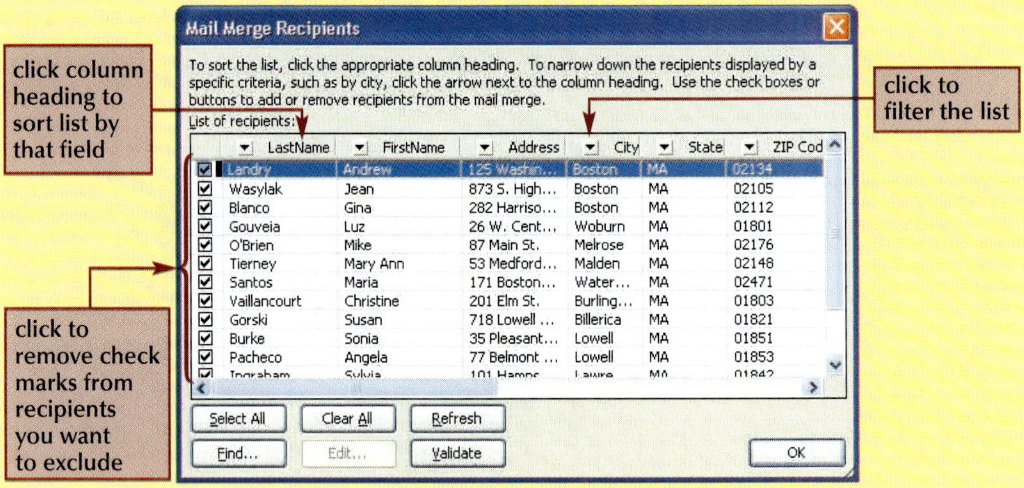

You use the Mail Merge Recipients dialog box to select the people who will receive Caitlin's letter. You can sort this list by any field by clicking a column heading. For example, if you were doing a large mass mailing, you could sort the list by ZIP code. You can also narrow the list by deselecting records individually or filtering the list to include only records that meet specific criteria. Caitlin wants to send her initial mailing only to the hospitals in Boston. You decide to filter the list to include only those hospitals.

7. Click the **City** list arrow, and then click **(Advanced...)**. The Filter and Sort dialog box opens with the Filter Records tab selected.
8. Click the **Field** list arrow, scroll down, and then click **City**. You want to merge the main document only with those hospitals in Boston.
9. Click the **Comparison** list arrow, click **Equal to**, if necessary, click the **Compare to** text box, type **Boston**, and then click the **OK** button. The Filter and Sort dialog box closes and only the addresses for the Boston hospitals are displayed in the Mail Merge Recipients dialog box.
10. Click the **OK** button to close the Mail Merge Recipients dialog box. The Use an existing list section of the Mail Merge task pane now indicates that Word will select your recipients from the Hospital Social Work Contacts table in SocialWorkContacts.mdb. Your screen should look similar to Figure 3-4.

Figure 3-4 **Recipients selected in the Mail Merge task pane**

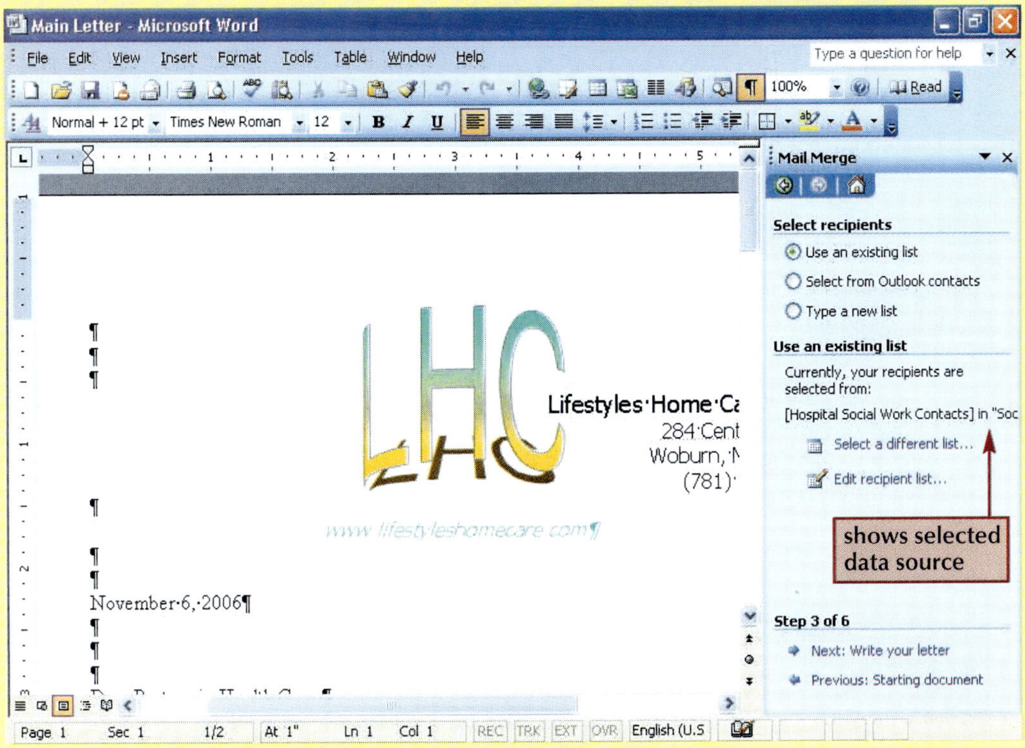

Trouble? If your screen does not show that your recipients are selected from the Hospital Social Work Contacts table in SocialWorkContacts.mdb, click the Select a different list link in the task pane, and then repeat Steps 4 through 10.

Next, you will insert the merge fields into the main document.

Inserting the Merge Fields

As noted earlier, a merge field is a special instruction that tells Word where to insert the variable information from the data source into the main document. For example, right now the letter does not have an inside address (the address for the recipient) at the top, as business letters usually do. Because this information will be different for each letter, you'll use merge fields to tell Word what information to pull from the data source.

The next step in the mail merge process is to insert the merge fields. For Caitlin's letter, you will insert the Address block and Greeting line merge fields. You then will check the merge fields to make sure they correspond with the fields in the Hospital Social Work Contacts table.

To insert the merge fields into the main document:

1. With the Mail Merge task pane showing Step 3 of 6, click the **Next: Write your letter** link. The Mail Merge task pane displays Step 4 of 6: Write your letter. Caitlin has already written the letter, but you need to add the recipient's name and address and a greeting line to personalize each copy of the letter.
2. Click in the second blank paragraph below the date in the letter. This is where the recipient's name and address will appear.
3. Click the **Address block** link in the Mail Merge task pane. The Insert Address Block dialog box opens, as shown in Figure 3-5.

Figure 3-5 Insert Address Block dialog box

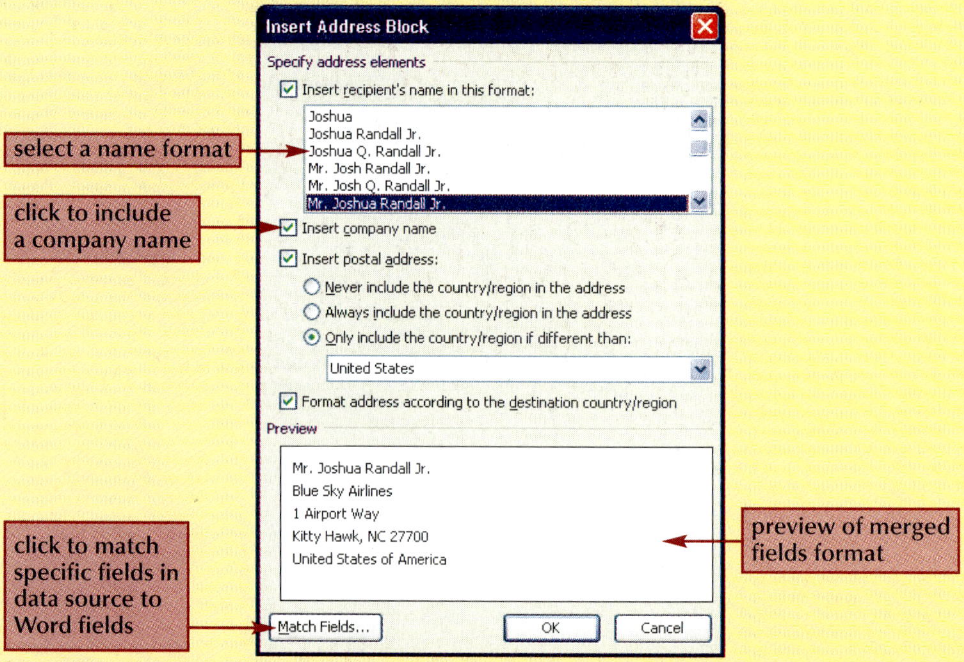

You use this dialog box to choose the format of the recipient's name and to specify whether to include the company name and country in the address. The content, tone, and style of the writing in Caitlin's customer letter is friendly and professional, so you decide to use a simple format of first and last name.

4. Click **Joshua Randall Jr.** in the Insert recipient's name in this format list box.

   After selecting address elements, you need to check to see how the fields in the Address block correspond to the fields in the Hospital Social Work Contacts table.

5. Click the **Match Fields** button. The Match Fields dialog box opens, as shown in Figure 3-6.

Figure 3-6 **Match Fields dialog box**

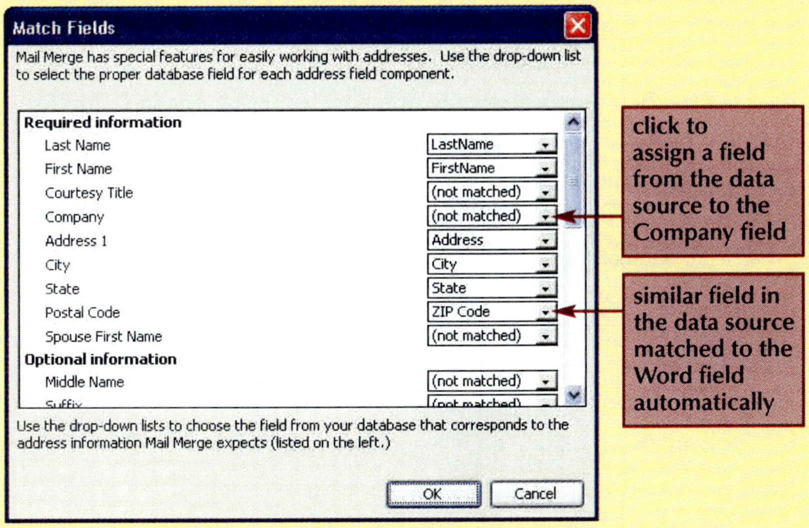

On the left are the fields Word expects in the Address block. On the right are the fields in the data source. Word automatically matches those fields that have the same or similar name; for example, it matches Postal Code with ZIP Code. Word did not find a match for the Company field. You want Word to match the Company field with the Hospital field in the Access table.

6. Click the **Company** list arrow, and then click **Hospital**.
7. Click the **OK** button to close the Match Fields dialog box, and then click the **OK** button to close the Insert Address Block dialog box. The Address block merge field appears in the main document between double chevrons (« »).

Trouble? If the Address block merge field appears between curly braces and includes additional text, such as {ADDRESSBLOCK \f}, Word is displaying field codes. Click Tools on the menu bar, click Options, click the View tab in the Options dialog box, and then click the Field codes check box to deselect it.

Now you need to insert a greeting line to personalize the salutation.

8. In the letter, click and drag to select **Partner in Health Care:** (make sure you include the colon) in the salutation line, and then press the **Delete** key. Make sure you leave a space after "Dear." You will replace the generic text with each contact's first name.
9. In the Mail Merge task pane, click the **Greeting line** link. The Greeting Line dialog box opens, as shown in Figure 3-7.

Figure 3-7 **Greeting Line dialog box**

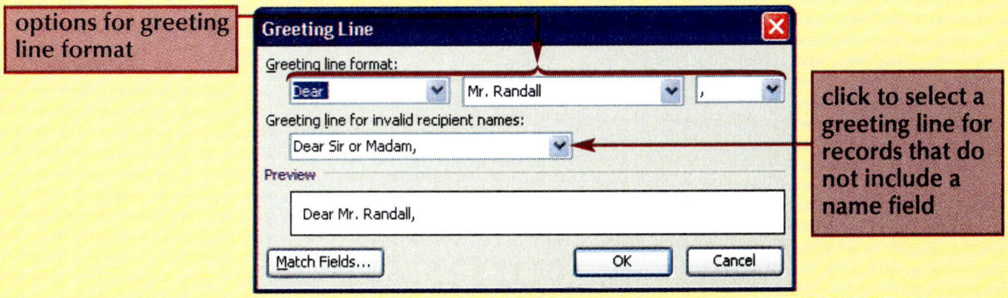

The Greeting Line dialog box shows what Word will insert as the salutation "Dear Mr. Randall" followed by a comma. Caitlin has already included "Dear" in the letter, so you need to specify that Word does not include "Dear" as well; otherwise, the salutation will read "Dear Dear Mr. Randall."

10. Click the **first list arrow** in the Greeting line format section, and then click **(none)**.

    The greeting line would now read "Dear Mr. Randall"; however, Caitlin knows all of the contacts in the social work departments personally, and she would rather start with the first name, as in "Dear Joshua" followed by a comma.

11. Click the **second list arrow** in the Greeting line format section, scroll down the list, and then click **Joshua**.

    You can accept the other options in the Greeting Line dialog box—to end the salutation with a comma and to use "Dear Sir or Madam" for records in the Hospital Social Work Contacts table that do not include a contact name.

12. Click the **OK** button. Word inserts the Greeting line merge field in the main document.
13. Click the **Save** button on the Standard toolbar to save the main document as Main Letter with the merge fields inserted.

Performing the Mail Merge

With the starting document and merge fields in place, you're ready to perform the mail merge. You can choose to merge the data to a new Word document or directly to a printer. Caitlin wants to proofread her final document before printing all of the merged documents, so you will print one copy of the merged letter, and then save the merge results in a new document. The new document you create with the merge results will contain one letter for each contact in the data source. Each letter will be identical, except for the merge fields, which will have the individual names and addresses.

To complete the mail merge:

1. With the Mail Merge task pane showing Step 4 of 6, click the **Next: Preview your letters** link, and then scroll down the document so you can see both merged fields. The first merged form letter appears with Andrew Landry at Boston General Hospital as the first recipient.
2. Click the **Next** button >> (next to Recipient: 1) in the Mail Merge task pane to preview the next recipient. The letter to Jean Wasylak at Eastern Mass. Regional Hospital appears.

   You are ready to print a copy of the letter.

3. Click the **Next: Complete the merge** link in the Mail Merge task pane. "Step 6: Complete the merge" appears in the task pane.
4. Click the **Print** link in the Mail Merge task pane. The Merge to Printer dialog box opens in which you can specify the records you want to print. Make sure you are connected to a printer and that it is loaded with paper and ready to print.

5. Click the **Current record** option button, and then click the **OK** button. The print dialog box opens.
6. Click the **OK** button. Word prints one copy of the form letter—the letter to Jean Wasylak.

   Now you can create a new document containing all of the form letters.
7. In the Mail Merge task pane, click the **Edit individual letters** link. The Merge to New Document dialog box opens.
8. Click the **All** option button, if necessary, and then click the **OK** button. Word opens a new document with the temporary name "Letters" followed by a number. This document contains one letter for each of the recipients at the Boston hospitals; each letter is separated from the next by a section break.
9. Scroll through the merged document to see the merged addresses and salutations. Word replaced each merge field with the appropriate Access data. Notice that the merged document contains six pages: Each letter is two pages long, and there are three letters in all.
10. Click the **Save** button on the Standard toolbar to open the Save As dialog box.
11. Save the document as **Merged Letters** in the Tutorial.03\Tutorial folder included with your Data Files, and then close the document. You return to the starting document.
12. Close the **Main Letter** document without saving changes.

    Because you saved the Main Letter document after you inserted the merged fields but before completing the merge, you can open it at any time, click the No button in the dialog box that opens asking if you want to run the SQL command (basically, complete the merge), open the Mail Merge task pane, and create new merged letters.

Caitlin plans to review the printed letter before she prints and mails the form letters. While she does that, Caitlin asks you to prepare her presentation for the National Home Care Conference to be held next month. In her presentation, Caitlin will explain her company's decision to add services for fees. She has already created the PowerPoint presentation file, selected a suitable template for the presentation, and created the title slide. She also quickly created a Word document in which she entered the topics for the remaining slides. She did not have time to properly organize the topics in an outline. To complete the presentation, you first need to create a Word outline from Caitlin's document.

Creating a Word Outline

You can create an outline in Word by typing text directly in Outline view in a new document. When you do, Word assigns heading styles to the text to format it as an outline. You can also format the text in an existing document by displaying it in Outline view and assigning each paragraph an appropriate heading style. You'll format Caitlin's document as an outline and then use this document to create the rest of the slides in Caitlin's PowerPoint presentation.

To open the document and display it in Outline view:

1. Open the Word document **LHCOutline**, located in the Tutorial.03\Tutorial folder included with your Data Files.
2. Save the document as **Outline for Slides** in the same folder. To format the document's text as an outline, you first need to switch to Outline view.
3. Click the **Outline View** button, located to the left of the horizontal scroll bar. The document switches to Outline view, and the Outlining toolbar is displayed. See Figure 3-8.

Figure 3-8 Document displayed in Outline view

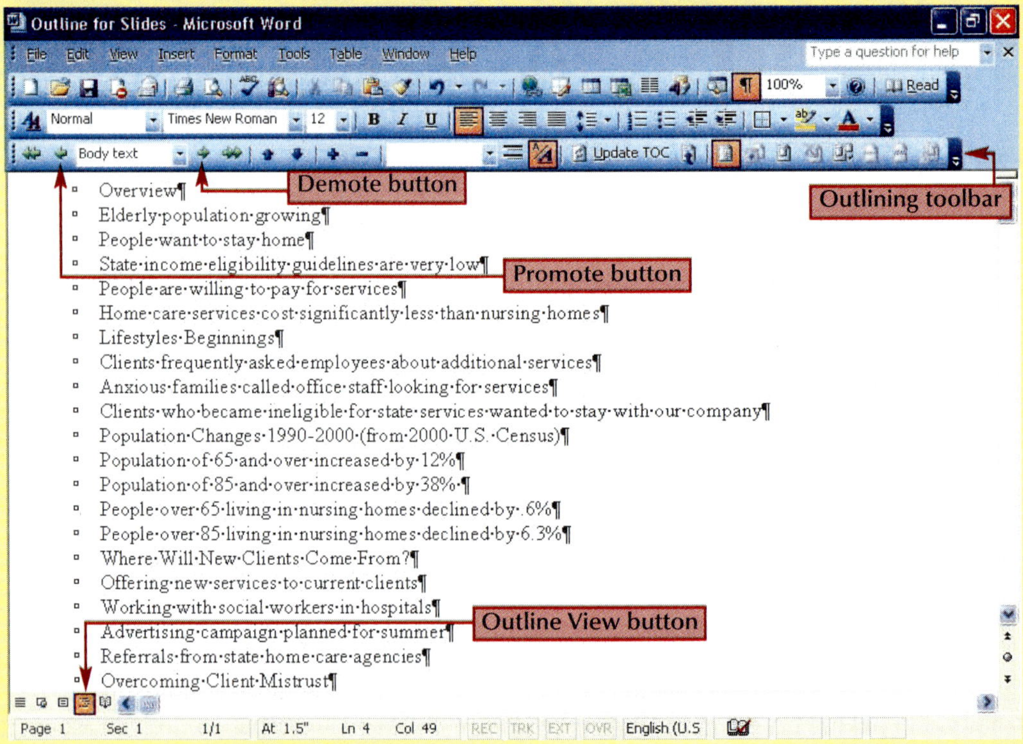

To format text as an outline, you use the Promote and Demote buttons on the Outlining toolbar. The Promote button **promotes**, or moves up, the selected paragraph to the next higher outline level. The Demote button **demotes**, or moves down, the selected paragraph to the next lower outline level. (Remember, Word refers to any text marked by a nonprinting, end-of-paragraph mark as a paragraph, even if the text consists of only one or two words, or if there is no text at all.)

The easiest way to format the text for Caitlin's outline is to select all of it and promote it to the first outline level. Then you can demote text as necessary. When you create PowerPoint slides from an outline, paragraphs at the first outline level become slide titles, paragraphs at the second outline level become first-level slide text, paragraphs at the third outline level become second-level slide text, and so on.

To format the text as a Word outline:

1. Click **Edit** on the menu bar, and then click **Select All**.
2. Click the **Promote** button on the Outlining toolbar. Word changes each paragraph to a first-level heading. Now you need to demote the necessary paragraphs to the next level.
3. Position the insertion point anywhere in the second paragraph (beginning with the word "Elderly").
4. Click the **Demote** button on the Outlining toolbar. The paragraph moves to the next lower outline level.

   Notice that the first paragraph now includes a plus sign to its left. This indicates that the first paragraph has subitems (paragraphs at a lower level) associated with it.
5. Drag to select the third through sixth paragraphs (beginning with "People" and ending with "nursing homes").
6. Press the **Tab** key. The selected paragraphs indent to the next lower outline level.
7. Refer to Figure 3-9 to format the next 14 paragraphs as indicated.

Figure 3-9 First part of formatted outline

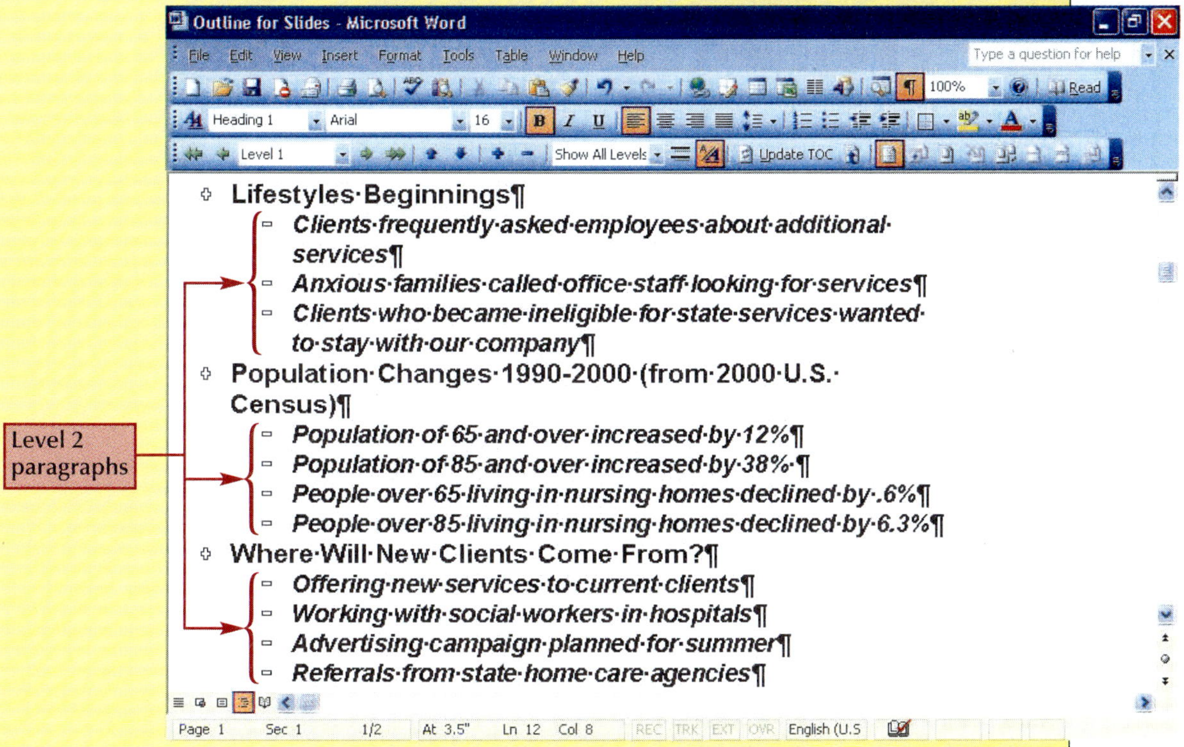

8. Scroll through the document, and then refer to Figure 3-10 to format the remaining paragraphs. Note that you must demote some paragraphs twice to move them to the appropriate level.

Figure 3-10 Remainder of formatted outline

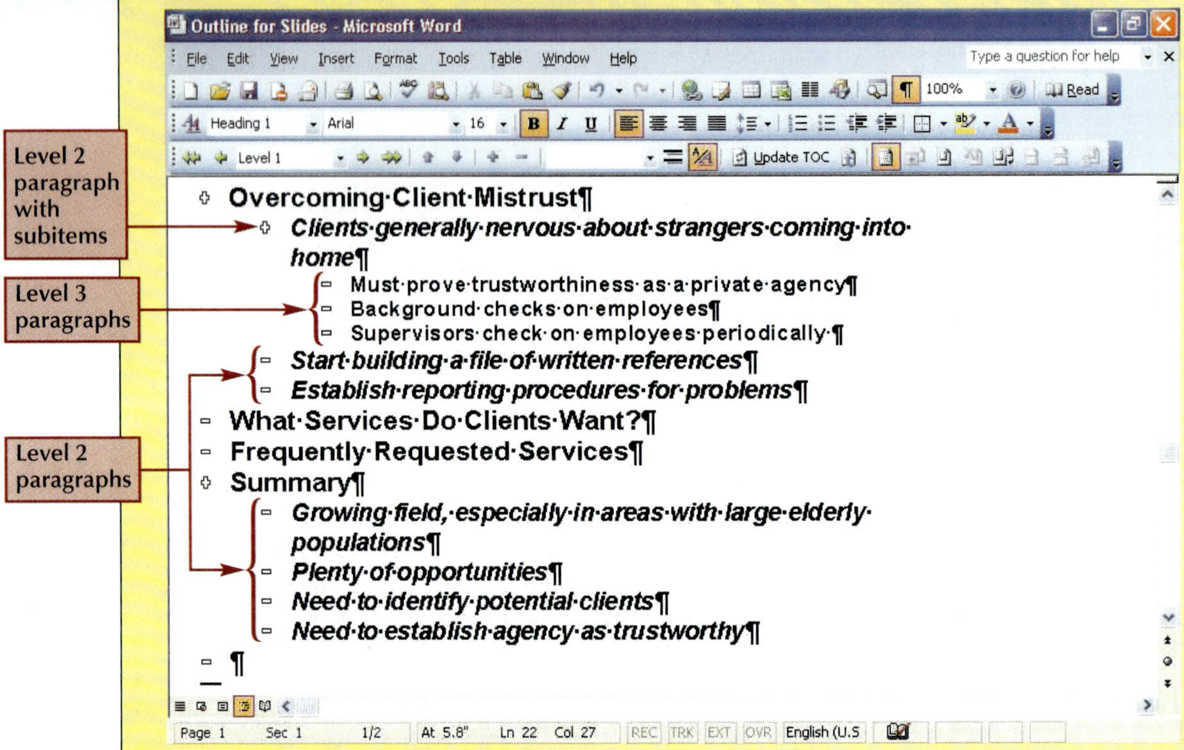

9. Save and close the document.

Creating PowerPoint Slides from a Word Outline

When you create slides from a Word outline, PowerPoint uses the heading styles in the Word document to determine how to format the text. For example, each paragraph formatted with the Heading 1 style becomes the title of a new slide, each Heading 2 becomes the first level of text on a slide, and so on. You can use an outline to create new slides in an existing presentation or to create an entirely new PowerPoint presentation. Now you can open Caitlin's PowerPoint presentation and create new slides from the outline you created.

To create new PowerPoint slides from a Word outline:

1. Open the PowerPoint file **LHCPresentation**, located in the Tutorial.03\Tutorial folder included with your Data Files. The presentation opens and displays its first and only slide, which contains the presentation title and the Lifestyles logo.
2. Save the presentation as **Home Care Conference** in the same folder.

   When you create slides from an outline (or other file), PowerPoint inserts them after the current slide. In this case, you want to insert them after the first (and only) slide in the presentation.

3. Click **Insert** on the menu bar, and then click **Slides from Outline**. The Insert Outline dialog box opens.
4. Click the **Look in** list arrow, navigate to the Tutorial.03\Tutorial folder included with your Data Files, click **Outline for Slides**, and then click the **Insert** button. PowerPoint inserts and formats the text of the Word outline to create Slides 2 through 10 and displays the first new slide (Slide 2). See Figure 3-11.

Figure 3-11 **Slides inserted from outline**

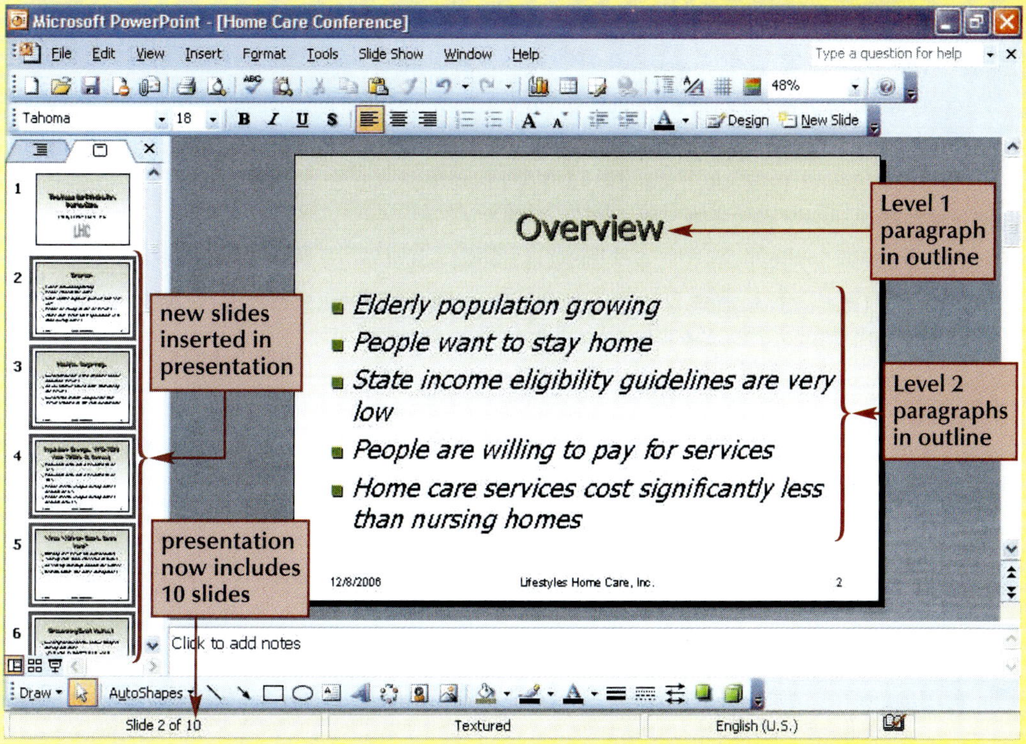

5. Click the **Next Slide** button in the slide pane scroll bar until you reach Slide 10. Notice that each Level 1 paragraph in the Word outline became a slide title, each Level 2 paragraph became a bulleted item, and each Level 3 paragraph became a subitem in a bulleted list. Also, note that PowerPoint automatically assigned the Title and Text layout to each slide.

   Slide 10 does not contain any text. There was a blank paragraph at the end of the Word outline.
6. With Slide 10 displayed in the slide pane, click **Edit** on the menu bar, and then click **Delete Slide**. Slide 10 is deleted.
7. Click the **Slide 6** thumbnail in the Slides tab. Slide 6 appears in the slide pane. The text on this slide looks a little crowded because it runs into the footer.
8. Double-click **Must** in the second bullet, press the **Delete** key twice, and then type **P**. The second bullet now is all on one line, and the rest of the text does not run into the footer.
9. Save the presentation.

With the text for all the slides in place, you can now complete the presentation by adding the Updated Services Requested Query in the LHCServices database and a chart from the LHCMostRequested workbook.

Copying and Pasting an Access Query into a PowerPoint Presentation

Caitlin wants to include the list of most requested services on Slide 7 ("What Services Do Clients Want?"). This information is stored as an Access query in the LHCServices database. To include this information, copy and paste the Access query into the PowerPoint presentation.

Caitlin knows that the data in the query will not change before the conference, so she asks you to copy and paste the query onto Slide 7.

To prepare to copy and paste the query:

1. Move to **Slide 7** in the presentation.

   This slide will include only the slide title and the pasted Access query data; therefore, the current layout of the slide, Title and Text, is inappropriate. You need to change the layout of the slide before you copy and paste the query.
2. Click **Format** on the menu bar, and then click **Slide Layout**. The Slide Layout task pane opens.
3. Click the **Title Only** layout (column 2, row 1 in the Text Layouts section in the task pane). PowerPoint applies the layout to the slide.
4. Close the Slide Layout task pane.

Now you can copy and paste the Access query on the slide.

To copy and paste the query on Slide 4:

1. Open the Access **LHCServices** database, located in the Tutorial.03\Tutorial folder included with your Data Files.

   Trouble? If a dialog box opens warning you that the database may not be safe, click the Open button. If a dialog box opens, warning you that Access can't open the database, see your instructor or technical support person.
2. Click **Queries** in the Database window, if necessary, to display the list of queries in the database, and then double-click **Updated Services Requested Query**. Access displays the results of the query in Datasheet view. See Figure 3-12.

Figure 3-12 Updated Services Requested Query results

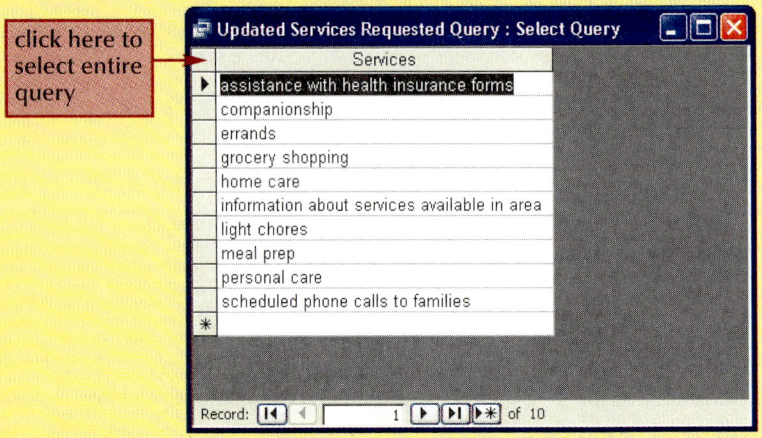

Caitlin wants all the data from the query to appear on the slide.

3. Click the **selector** to the left of the column heading (refer to Figure 3-12). Access selects all of the records in the query results window.
4. Click the **Copy** button on the Query Datasheet toolbar to copy the query results to the Clipboard.
5. Close the query and the database, and then click the **Microsoft PowerPoint - [Home Care Conference]** button on the taskbar. You return to the presentation.

   Now you can paste the query on Slide 7.
6. Click in the slide pane in the blank area below the title text box, and then click the **Paste** button on the PowerPoint Standard toolbar. PowerPoint inserts the query results as a table on the slide. You need to reposition it on the slide and reformat it to match the style of the presentation.
7. Position the pointer over the edge of the table so that it changes to ✥, and then click to select the entire table. See Figure 3-13. Make sure the selected table has a dotted outline. The dotted outline indicates that you can make changes to the entire table. A slanted line outline indicates that you can select parts of the table to change.

Figure 3-13 Access table selected on PowerPoint slide

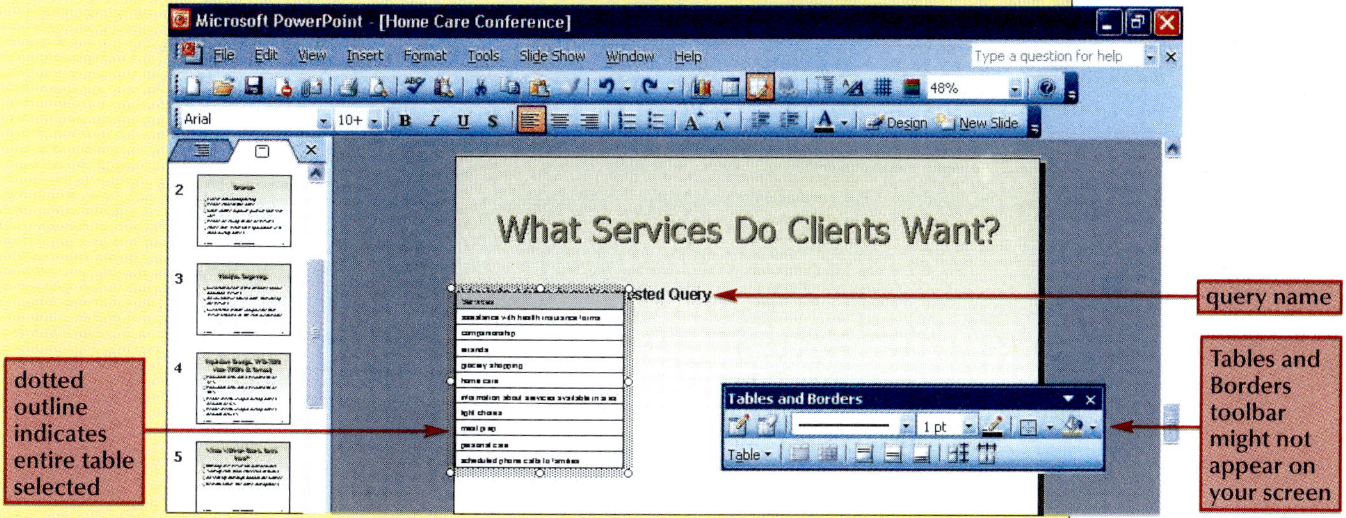

Trouble? If your table does not have a dotted outline as in Figure 3-13, click the slanted line outline.

8. Drag the table so that it is centered on the slide. Note that the query name was also pasted when you pasted the query results. You do not need this information on the slide.

   Trouble? If the Tables and Borders toolbar is in the way, drag it out of the way by its title bar.
9. Click anywhere on the text **Updated Services Requested Query** to display the border of the text box, click on the slanted line border of the text box to change it to the dotted line border, and then press the **Delete** key.

   You need to enlarge the table and the text in the table so that the table is easier to read.

10. Select the **table**, making sure the dotted line border appears, click the **Font Size** list arrow 10+ on the Formatting toolbar, and then click **20**.
11. Drag the **left** and **right sizing handles** on the table to stretch the table wide enough to accommodate the widest entry.
12. Click the word **Services** in the top row of the table, click the **Fill Color** list arrow on the Tables and Borders toolbar, click **Automatic**, and then click the **Center** button on the Formatting toolbar. The color of the first row in the table changes to a dark tan to better match the slide design, and the column header is centered.
13. Click an empty area of the slide to deselect the table. See Figure 3-14.

Figure 3-14 **Formatted Access table on PowerPoint slide**

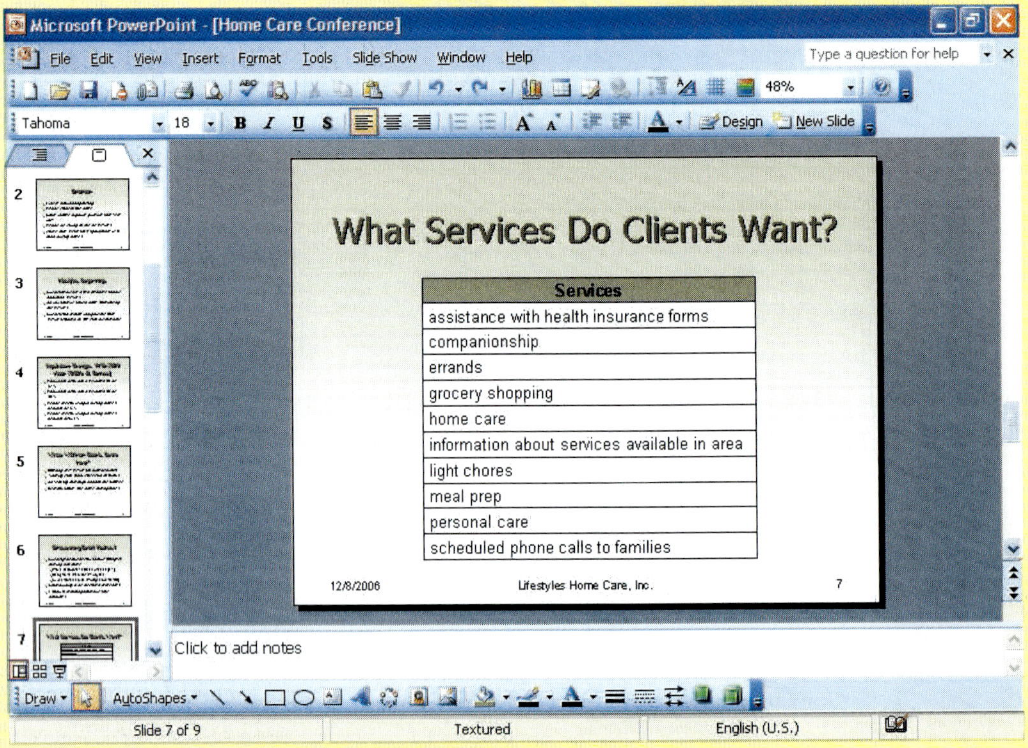

14. Save the presentation.

Now that you have inserted the Access query into Slide 7, you can complete the slide presentation by adding a chart to Slide 8.

Linking an Excel Chart to a PowerPoint Presentation

Caitlin wants to include an Excel column chart showing frequently requested services on Slide 8. She is still considering the format of the chart, so she asks you to link the chart to the presentation. This way, if she changes the chart, the revised chart will be automatically reflected in her presentation.

Linking Excel Data to a PowerPoint Presentation

Reference Window

- In Excel, select the information you want to insert into a PowerPoint presentation, and then click the Copy button on the Standard toolbar.
- In PowerPoint, click where you want to insert the Excel data, click Edit on the menu bar, and then click Paste Special.
- In the Paste Special dialog box, click Microsoft Excel Chart Object, if necessary, click the Paste link option button, and then click the OK button.

You will link the chart to the presentation now.

To link an Excel object to the presentation:

1. Move to **Slide 8** in the presentation. First, you need to change the slide layout to one appropriate for displaying the slide title and the linked chart.
2. Click **Format** on the menu bar, click **Slide Layout**, click the **Title Only** layout in the Slide Layout task pane, and then close the Slide Layout task pane.
3. Start Excel and then open the **LHCMostRequested** workbook located in the Tutorial.03\Tutorial folder included with your Data Files.
4. Scroll to the right and down so that you can see the chart, click the border of the chart area to select the entire chart (make sure the Chart toolbar displays "Chart Area" in the Chart Objects list box), and then click the **Copy** button on the Standard toolbar. Do not close the workbook.

   Trouble? If the Chart toolbar displays "Plot Area" in the Chart Objects list box, click directly on the black border around the entire chart.

   Next, you need to switch back to the presentation and link the copied chart. Do not close the Excel workbook, or you will only be allowed to paste the chart instead of linking it.
5. Click the **Microsoft PowerPoint - [Home Care Conference]** button on the taskbar to switch back to the presentation.
6. Click **Edit** on the menu bar, and then click **Paste Special**. The Paste Special dialog box opens.
7. Make sure Microsoft Office Excel Chart Object is selected, click the **Paste link** option button, and then click the **OK** button. The chart is linked to the slide.

   Trouble? If the Paste link option button is not available (grayed out), then you closed the LHCMostRequested workbook. Switch back to Excel, open the workbook, copy the chart again, and then try pasting the link again.

   You need to resize the chart so it will be readable on the slide.
8. Drag the **corner sizing handles** to resize the chart so that it looks like the one shown in Figure 3-15. When you're finished, click an empty area on the slide to deselect the chart.

Figure 3-15 Linked Excel chart on PowerPoint slide after resizing

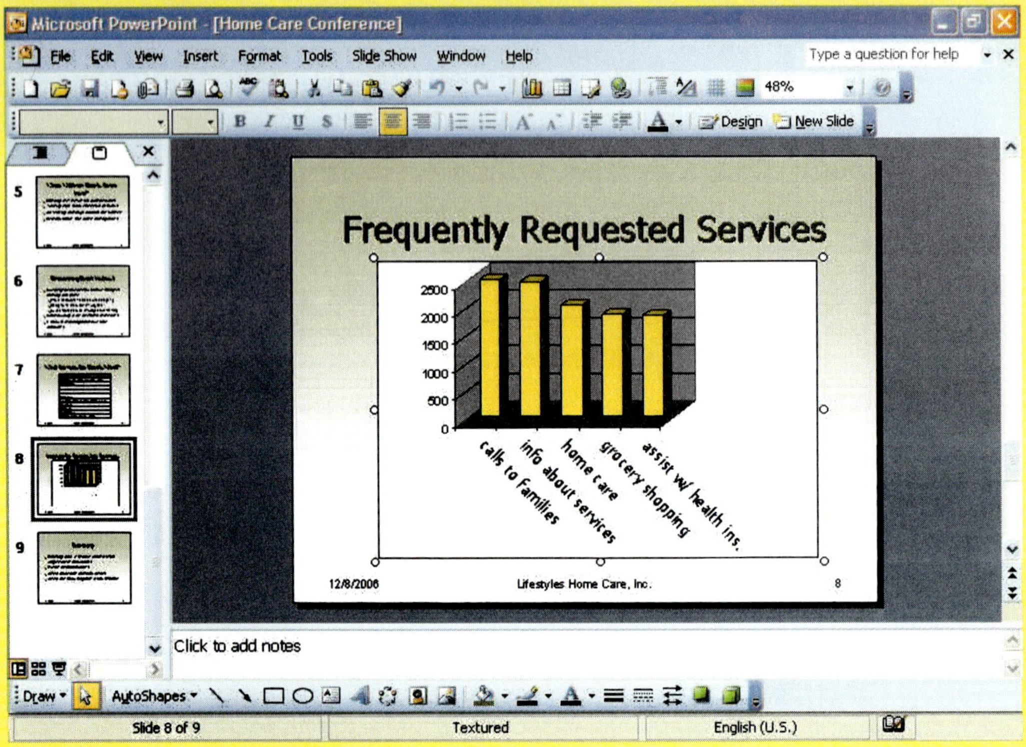

9. Save and close the presentation.
10. Click the **Microsoft Excel - LHCMostRequested** button on the taskbar, and then close the LHCMostRequested workbook.
11. Exit any open programs.

Caitlin is pleased with the finished letter and presentation. The integration features of Office make it easy for Caitlin to work with information created in different programs to produce exactly the results she wants.

Review

Quick Check

1. Describe how a mail merge works.
2. What is a merge field?
3. Why is a query a good data source for a mail merge?
4. Explain why you store the form letter with the merge fields in one document and the personalized form letter with individual names and addresses in another document.
5. How do you change heading levels in Outline view in Word?
6. What does the plus sign to the left of a paragraph in Outline view in Word indicate?
7. Describe the slide or slides that PowerPoint would create from a Word outline that has one Level 1 paragraph and three Level 2 paragraphs.

Review

Tutorial Summary

In this tutorial, you learned how to create a form letter that contains merge fields, and you learned how to merge data from a data source to the form letter. You learned how to filter only selected records from the data source into a final merged document. You also learned how to create a Word outline and then insert the outline as new slides in a PowerPoint presentation. Finally, you learned how to paste an Access query and link an Excel chart to a PowerPoint presentation.

Key Terms

data source	mail merge	merge field
demote	main document	promote
form letter	merge	starting document

Practice

Get hands-on practice of the skills you learned in the tutorial using the same case scenario.

Review Assignments

Data Files needed for the Review Assignments: SocialWorkContacts.mdb, LHCEmployeesOutline.doc, LHCEmployees.ppt, LHCGrowth2.xls, LHCServices.mdb

Now that the form letter is complete, Caitlin is ready to mail it. She needs to print the names and addresses on mailing labels that can be placed on the envelopes. Also, Caitlin wants to prepare a brief presentation to give to her employees at the next staff meeting. She wants to give the employees a thorough overview of the new services that they will be providing.

1. Open a new, blank document in Word, and then open the Mail Merge task pane so that it displays Step 1.
2. Select Labels as the document type, and then move to Step 2.
3. In Step 2, change the document layout and click the Label options link to open the Label Options dialog box. Select Avery standard in the Label products lists, and then scroll down the Product number list and choose product number 5160 - Address. Accept all other defaults in this dialog box, and then move to Step 3.
4. In Step 3, select recipients from an existing list in the Rehab Social Work Contacts table in the **SocialWorkContacts** database, which is stored in the Tutorial.03\Review folder included with your Data Files. You will print labels for all of the contacts in the list.
5. Move to Step 4. Lay out the first label by inserting the Address block item. Accept the defaults in the Insert Address Block dialog box. Match Word's Company field to the Hospital field in the table.
6. After you insert the Address block merge field in the first label, point to the small down arrow at the bottom of the task pane to scroll the task pane, if necessary, and then click the Update all labels button to copy the layout of the first label to the other labels on the page.
7. Save the main document (the one with the merge fields) as **Main Labels** in the Tutorial.03\Review folder included with your Data Files.
8. Move to Step 5 to preview the labels, and then move to Step 6 to complete the merge.
9. In Step 6, merge all of the labels to a new document. Scroll to the bottom of the page, click the first empty box on the left, and type your name. Save the document containing the merged labels as **Merged Labels** in the Tutorial.03\Review folder, print the document, and then close it. Close the Main Labels document without saving changes.

10. Open the Word document **LHCEmployeesOutline** located in the Tutorial.03\Review folder included with your Data Files, and save it as **Topics Outline** in the same folder.
11. Switch to Outline view, select all of the text, and demote all the text to Level 2.
12. Reformat the following paragraphs as Level 1 headings: Mission Statement, Overview, Why New Services?, New Services, Trust Issues, Current Employees, and Lifestyles Home Care, Inc.
13. Reformat the paragraphs in the following lists as Level 3 headings:

    Under the Level 1 heading "Why New Services?"
    - Many fewer people are eligible
    - People are willing to pay...

    Under the Level 1 heading "New Services"
    - Planning
    - Grocery Shopping
    - Meal Prep

    Under the Level 1 heading "Trust Issues"
    - Check quality...
    - Check for problems
    - Call supervisor...
    - Submit written report
    - Meet with supervisor...

    Under the Level 1 heading "Current Employees"
    - Will be offered...
    - Must attend training sessions
14. Save and close the Topics Outline document.
15. Open the PowerPoint presentation **LHCEmployees** located in the Tutorial.03\Review folder included with your Data Files, replace Caitlin's name with your own name, and then save it to the same folder as **Employee Presentation**.
16. Create new slides by inserting the Topics Outline document after Slide 1.
17. Go to Slide 3, insert a new slide as a new Slide 4 with the Title Only layout, click in the title text placeholder, and then type Current Services.
18. Open the Excel workbook **LHCGrowth2** located in the Tutorial.03\Review folder included with your Data Files, copy the range A6:F11 to the Clipboard, and then switch back to the Employee Presentation.
19. Link the contents of the Clipboard to Slide 4, and then resize the table as large as possible on the slide.
20. Insert a new slide after Slide 5 using the Title Only layout. Type **Services Requested Most Often** as the title.
21. Open the Access database **LHCServices** located in the Tutorial.03\Review folder included with your Data Files, copy the results of the Updated Services Requested Query to the Clipboard, close the query and the database, and then paste the contents of the Clipboard to the new Slide 6.
22. Center and reformat the query so that it matches the presentation design, and delete the query title.
23. Save the presentation, and then print it as handouts, six slides per page.
24. Close the presentation and the Excel workbook, and exit any open programs.

Challenge

Advance the skills you learned to merge addresses onto envelopes, and then update the merge fields for a letter to a music store's customers.

Case Problem 1

Data File needed for this Case Problem: MusicCustomers.mdb

Making Music Caleb Jacobson, the owner of Making Music, wrote a letter to his current customers providing information about the new lesson times he will be offering in the fall. He decides to send the letters in batches, using the cities as a sorting factor. Now he needs to send the letter to his customers in Ridgefield. You'll use the mail merge feature to create the envelopes for this mailing.

1. Open a new, blank document in Word, and then open the Mail Merge task pane so that it displays Step 1.
2. Select Envelopes as the document type, and then move to Step 2.
3. **Explore** In Step 2, change the document layout and click the Envelope options link to open the Envelope Options dialog box. Change the Envelope Size to 6 3/4. (The address and return address should fit on your envelope with this setting, although its position will be off if you have a different size envelope. Alternately, you may select the size from the list that matches your envelope.)
4. Click the Printing Options tab, and then make sure that the Feed method will work on your printer. For example, does your printer print face up or face down, and in which position should you place the envelope to feed it into the printer? Click the OK button, and then move to Step 3.
5. Select recipients for the envelopes by using the Ridgefield Query in the **MusicCustomers** database, which is located in the Tutorial.03\Cases folder included with your Data Files. There is only one customer who lives in Ridgefield.
6. **Explore** Move to Step 4, and arrange your envelopes by typing your name and address as the return address and then inserting the Address block in the middle of the envelope. Do not show the company name. Save the envelopes with the merge fields as **Merge Envelope** in the Tutorial.03\Cases folder included with your Data Files.
7. Preview the envelope.
8. Complete the merge by printing the envelope, and then merging the record to a new document. (If you do not have an envelope on which to print, print it on regular paper.) Save the document as **Ridgefield Envelopes** in the Tutorial.03\Cases folder included with your Data Files, and then close this document.
9. In the Merge Envelope document, go to Step 5 of 6 in the Mail Merge task pane.
10. **Explore** Double-click the word "Rd," and then type "Ave." Open the **MusicCustomers** database, and then open the Ridgefield Query. Is the change you made in Word reflected in the Access query? Close the query and open the Mailing List table. Is the change you made reflected in Jose's record (record 3) here? Why or why not?
11. **Explore** Change "Lincoln Rd." in Jose's address to "South Ave." Save and close the table and the database. Switch to the Merge Envelope document in Word, right-click anywhere on Jose's address, and then click Update Field. What happened? Why?
12. Go to Step 6, and then print the envelope. If you do not have an envelope, print it on a piece of paper.
13. Save and close the Merge Envelope document, and then exit any open program.

Create

Expand the skills you learned in this tutorial to create a new presentation for a tutoring company, based on an existing outline, with links to Excel worksheets.

Case Problem 2

Data Files needed for this Case Problem: LFCOutline.doc and LFCFees.xls

Learning Fulfillment Centers Enrique Garcia has asked his assistant, Nia Walker, to prepare a presentation to give to potential customers. You'll prepare the presentation for Nia by completing the following:

1. Open the Word document **LFCOutline** located in the Tutorial.03\Cases folder included with your Data Files. Save it as **LFC Presentation Outline** in the same folder.
2. Use Outline view to adjust the topics so that they are grouped in a way that makes sense. Save your changes and close the document.
3. Create a new PowerPoint presentation using a design template of your choice. Create a title slide for the presentation. Include your name as the subtitle. Save the presentation as **New Customer Presentation** in the Tutorial.03\Cases folder.
4. Create new slides from the LFC Presentation Outline document. Scroll through the new slides.
5. Change the layout of the last two slides to one that can accommodate linked data from Excel.
6. Open the Excel file **LFCFees**, located in the Tutorial.03\Cases folder included with your Data Files. Link the appropriate data from this workbook to the appropriate slides in the presentation, and then resize and reposition the tables as needed. Does the color in the pasted table match the design you chose for the slides? If not, change the Fill Color of the table head in the workbook, and then update the link in the presentation.
7. Create a new final slide that includes the company's motto. (You can find the motto in the LFCFees workbook.)
8. Save the presentation, and then run the slide show.
9. Print the presentation slides as handouts, four slides per page.
10. Close the presentation and the open workbook, and then exit any open programs.

Review

Quick Check Answers

1. A mail merge combines a main or starting document that contains standard text and merge fields that indicate where to print variable information with a data source that contains the variable information.
2. special instructions that tell Word where to print the variable information
3. so that the merge will use your latest query instructions to retrieve the data
4. You use the form letter with the merge fields document to print other letters with a different data source or when the list of names and addresses in the data source changes. You use the personalized form letter to print and send to each recipient.
5. Click the Promote or Demote button on the Outlining toolbar.
6. that the paragraph has subitems (paragraphs at a lower level) associated with it
7. It becomes a slide with a title and three bullets of text.